Family Law Case Library:

Children

Second Edition

Family Law Case Library:

Children

Second Edition

Editors

Charles Prest
Barrister, 6 Park Square, Leeds

His Honour Judge Stephen Wildblood QC

Family Law

Published by Family Law
a publishing imprint of
Jordan Publishing Limited
21 St Thomas Street
Bristol BS1 6JS

© Jordan Publishing Limited 2011

British Library Cataloguing-in-Publication Data

A catalogue record for this book is available from the British Library.

ISBN 978 1 84661 277 0

Typeset by Letterpart Ltd, Reigate, Surrey

Printed in Great Britain by CPI Antony Rowe, Chippenham and Eastbourne

FOREWORD TO FIRST EDITION

Most lawyers practising in Children Law and Financial Family Law have in their time experienced feelings of frustration, whether in preparation for a meeting or conference, or when drafting a position statement or skeleton argument, at not having readily to hand the crucial paragraphs of the leading authorities on particular topics, rather than having to refer to textbooks which typically state the principle and cite the authority but leave it to the practitioner to locate the key extract from the authority themselves. Now, Jordans have produced, in paper and electronic format, a Case Book to meet that need. While no doubt useful also to students, its twin volumes concentrate upon the needs of busy professionals for speedy access to the key extracts from the principal cases, presented thematically and cross-referred to the full reports in the Family Law Reports.

Careful thought has been given to each section, with clear sign-posting of topics under each head and each volume complements the other so as to cover the full range of Children and Financial Family Law. The printed page, conveniently gathered in an appropriate volume, is still the preferred way of looking up law for most lawyers; reading case reports on a screen can prove tiring. The editors are to be congratulated on producing a handy, logical and well presented Case Library, as welcome on the judicial bookshelf as in the practitioner's toolkit.

Sir Mark Potter
President of the Family Division
February 2008

PREFACE

Purpose

The Family Law Reports ('FLR') are the pre-eminent source of case reporting for family law specialists in England and Wales. They provide, authoritatively and promptly, the important decisions in the field.

In common with other law reporting series, however, the FLR have two important drawbacks. First, they grow longer every year. Nothing is removed even when it has been overtaken by a change of legislation, subsequent authority or shift in general approach. The very nature of a series of law reports is that dead wood remains standing. Secondly, they are essentially unstructured. The order in which reports appear is, more or less, the order in which the decisions were made. Even with electronic search facilities this can make it hard to find the best authorities on any given issue.

Family Law Case Library: Children ('FLCLC'), together with its companion volume, *Family Law Case Library: Finance* ('FLCLF'), aims to help the busy family law specialist find and use classic statements of the law and leading edge authorities quickly and easily. In doing so it seeks to address the drawbacks of the full reports. First, it sets out only the key extracts from the key judgments, those that are most often applied, whether explicitly or not, by the courts in England and Wales. Secondly, it presents those extracts within a thematic structure. In short, it is a digest of the FLR.

Structure

Familiarity with the structure will make it easier for readers to find what they are looking for. We have striven to make the structure clear, simple and natural, but a few minutes familiarisation with the Contents is likely to be time well spent.

The FLCLC is in nine Divisions, A–I. Most of the Divisions are themselves divided into subdivisions. As far as possible the individual extracts have been arranged in the subdivisions either in the order in which they appear in the legislation or the order in which they might typically arise.

In some instances an extract might reasonably have been included in one of two places. If so we have chosen which place to put it but have also inserted a cross-reference to it at the other place.

Headings and notes

Each extract uses the following template:

(1)   **Headings:** the reference and short title given to the extract within the FLCLC, the case name, the case reference (its neutral citation, where applicable, and the FLR reference, with FLR page references for the extract(s)), the court, and the judge (or judges) whose judgment is (are) extracted;

(2)   **Extract(s):** we have included the facts / context / argument taken from the judgment where we have thought it helpful to understanding an authority;

(3)   **Notes:** three kinds of notes have, as appropriate, been included—

- *General notes:* it is from the judgment that any authority must be derived and therefore our guiding principle has been to let each judgment speak for itself, but sometimes a note has been added to clarify or draw attention to a particular point;
- *Other significant cases on this issue:* we have tried to include the most authoritative, or the most useful, decision on each matter, but inevitably there are often other significant cases worth identifying for the reader who wants or needs to look further. However, other cases clearly identified within the extract or which are included within the same subdivision of the volume are not separately identified in this way;
- *This case is also included in relation to:* many cases are authority for more than one proposition and therefore have been included in more than one place in the volume. These notes provide a ready cross-reference to other extracts from the same case within the FLCLC.

Considered for inclusion

We have considered for inclusion all cases up to the end of [2010] 2 FLR, ie nearly 11,000 pages of reports since the first edition.

Thanks

We are very grateful to colleagues who have made suggestions about extracts for inclusion. However, responsibility for the selection, and for any errors, remains entirely ours.

Comments

We would welcome encouragement, suggestions for improving FLCLC and the identification of any errors we have made. Comments should be sent to us c/o Jordan Publishing Ltd, 21 St Thomas Street, Bristol, BS1 6JS.

Charles Prest
Stephen Wildblood

March 2011

CONTENTS

Division A
Children Act 1989, Pt I

Section 1 welfare

Parental responsibility

Section 7 reports

Division B
Children Act 1989, Pt II

ECtHR Art 8: applied to private law

Contact / making contact work / residence

Domestic violence cases

Domestic violence

Specific issue / prohibited steps

Division C
Children Act 1989, Pt III

Secure accommodation

Division D
Children Act 1989, Pts IV and V

ECtHR: Art 8 applied to public law

Parts IV and V: general

Newborn babies

Threshold criteria

Designated local authority

Interim or final order

Care or supervision order

Application to discharge section 31 order

CGs / solicitor for the child

Section 42 access to documents

Emergency protection orders / police protection

Division E
Adoption

Generally

Division F
Abduction

Hague Convention

Brussels II Revised

Non-Hague Convention

Division G
Case management

ECtHR: Art 6

ECtHR: Art 8 – inherent procedural rights

ECJ: jurisdiction

General principles

Particular case management issues arising from public law cases

Representation of child

Without notice applications

Fact-finding (split) hearings

Experts

Other witnesses

Disclosure within proceedings

Disclosure beyond proceedings / media attendance

Children Act 1989, s 91(14)

Division H
Judgment, costs and appeals
Judgment: general

Judgment: lay evidence

Judgment: expert evidence

Identifying perpetrators

Costs

Appeals

Division I
Miscellaneous

Human rights: miscellaneous domestic authorities

Inherent jurisdiction / wardship

Determining / telling of paternity

Contraceptive advice

Parental alienation

Neglect

Non-accidental head injury

Sexual abuse

TABLE OF CASES

References are to paragraph numbers.
Bold references indicate where case extracts are set out.

S and D (Children: powers of court), Re [1995] 2 FLR 456, [1995] Fam Law 602,
   (1995) 159 JPN 178, CA   **B38**, D7, D56, D58, D59, H35
S and W (Care proceedings), Re [2007] EWCA Civ 232, [2007] 2 FLR 275, [2007]
   Fam Law 488   **D7, D8**, D9, D56, D65, **G11**
S County Council v B [2000] Fam 76, [2000] 2 FLR 161, [2000] 3 WLR 53, [2000]
   Fam Law 462, FD   **G76, G79, G80, G81**
S v B and Newport City Council; Re K [2007] 1 FLR 1116, [2007] Fam Law 217,
   FD   B56
S v Knowsley Borough Council [2004] EWHC 491 (Fam), [2004] 2 FLR 716, [2004]
   Fam Law 652   **C4, C7**
S v S (Interim contact) [2009] EWHC 1575 (Fam), [2009] 2 FLR 1586   **B32**
S v S [2008] EWHC 2288 (Fam), [2009] 1 FLR 241, [2009] Fam Law 19   I4
S, Re; Newcastle City Council v Z [2005] EWHC (Fam) 1490, [2007] 1 FLR 861   A8
S, Re; WSP v Hull City Council [2006] EWCA Civ 981, [2007] 1 FLR 90, [2007]
   Fam Law 831, CA   **G55**
S-B (Children) (non-accidental injury), Re [2009] EWCA Civ 1048, [2009] 3 FCR
   663   H26
S-B (Children), Re [2009] UKSC 17, [2010] 1 FLR 1161, [2010] 1 All ER 705   G10,
        G41, H3, **H4**, H11, **H12, H24, H25, H26, H27**
S-C (Contempt) [2010] EWCA Civ 21, [2010] 1 FLR 1478, [2010] All ER (D) 186
   (Jan)   G86
Sahin v Germany; Sommerfield v Germany; Hoffmann v Germany (Application
   Nos 30943/96, 31871/96, 34045/96) (2003) 36 EHRR 33, [2002] 1 FLR 119,
   ECHR   G4, **G5**
Saunders v United Kingdom (1996) 23 EHRR 313, (1997) 2 BHRC 358, [1997]
   BCC 872, ECHR   G67
Saxton (Dec'd); Johnson and Another v Saxton and Another, Re [1962] 1 WLR
   968, [1962] 3 All ER 92, 106 SJ 668, CA   G78, G81
SC (A Minor) (Leave to Seek Residence Order), Re [1994] 1 FLR 96, [1993] Fam
   Law 618, FD   B40, B41
Schuler-Zgraggen v Switzerland (Application No 14518/89) (1995) 21 EHRR 404,
   ECHR   G1
Science Research Council v Nassé; Leyland Cars (BL Cars Ltd) v Vyas [1980] AC
   1028, [1979] ICR 921, [1979] 3 WLR 762, [1979] 3 All ER 673, HL   G75
Scott (Otherwise Morgan) and Another v Scott [1913] AC 417, (1913) FLR Rep
   657, [1911–1913] All ER Rep 1, 82 LJP 74, 29 TLR 520, HL   G86, G87, H1
Scozzari & Giunta v Italy (2002) 35 EHRR 243, ECHR   D14
Selmouni v France (Application No 25803/94) (2000) 29 EHRR 403, ECHR   I1
Serio v Serio (1983) 4 FLR 756, (1983) Fam Law 255, CA   I7
Sheffield City Council v V (Legal Services Commission Intervening) [2006] EWHC
   1861 (Fam), [2007] 1 FLR 279, [2006] Fam Law 833   D50
Singh v Entry Clearance Officer, New Delhi [2004] EWCA Civ 1075, [2005] QB 608,
   [2005] 1 FLR 308, [2005] Fam Law 9   **I1**
SK (Local authority: expert evidence) [2007] EWHC 3289 (Fam), [2008] 2 FLR
   707   G55
SL (Adoption: Home in Jurisdiction), Re [2004] EWHC 1283 (Fam), [2005] 1 FLR
   118, [2004] Fam Law 860   E17
SN v Sweden (Application No 34209/96) (2002) 39 EHRR 304, ECHR   G66
Soderback v Germany Reports of Judgments and Decisions 1998–IV (28 October
   1998)   D2
Söderbäck v Sweden [1999] 1 FLR 250, [1999] Fam Law 87, [1998] HRCD 958,
   ECHR   D5
Somerset County Council v D [2007] EWCA Civ 722, [2008] 1 FLR 399, [2007]
   Fam Law 865, [2007] All ER (D) 192 (Jul)   **D60**
Sommerfeld v Germany [2003] 2 FCR 647, ECHR   B7
Sonderup v Tondelli (2001) (1) SA 1171 (CC)   F8
Southall v General Medical Council [2010] EWCA Civ 407, [2010] 2 FLR 1550   G64
Southwark London Borough Council v B [1998] 2 FLR 1095, [1998] Fam Law 657,
   (1998) 95(35) LSG 38, FD   D15, G80
Stallinger and Kuso v Austria (1997) 26 EHRR 81, ECHR   G1
Stanton v Callaghan [1998] 4 All ER 961, [2000] 1 QB 75, [1999] 2 WLR 745, CA   G44
Stedman, Re [2009] EWHC 935 (Fam), [2009] 2 FLR 852   G86

TABLE OF STATUTES

References are to paragraph numbers.

TABLE OF STATUTORY INSTRUMENTS

References are to paragraph numbers.

LIST OF ABBREVIATIONS

ABE	Achieving Best Evidence
ACA 2002	Adoption and Children Act 2002
ADR	Alternative Dispute Resolution
AJA 1960	Administration of Justice Act 1960
AO	Adoption order
B II R	Council Regulation (EC) Number 2201/2003 Concerning Jurisdiction and the Recognition and Enforcement of Judgments in Matrimonial Matters and Matters of Parental Responsibility
BAAF	British Association for Adoption and Fostering
CA	Court of Appeal
CA 1989	Children Act 1989
CAFCASS / Cafcass	Children and Family Court Advisory and Support Service
CFR	Children and Family Reporter
CG	Children's Guardian
CJCSA 2000	Criminal Justice and Court Services Act 2000
CO	Care order
CPR	Civil Procedure Rules 1998
DV	Domestic violence
ECHR	European Convention for the Protection of Human Rights and Fundamental Freedoms 1950
ECtHR	European Court of Human Rights
EPO	Emergency protection order
FPR	Family Proceedings Rules 1991
FPC	Family Proceedings Court
GaL	Guardian ad litem
HC	Hague Convention
HL	House of Lords
HR	Human rights
HRA 1998	Human Rights Act 1998
ICO	Interim care order

IRC	Inland Revenue Commissioners
ISO	Interim supervision order
JR	Judicial review
LA	Local authority
LASSA 1970	Local Authority Social Services Act 1970
NYAS	National Youth Advocacy Service
PO	Placement order
PR	Parental responsibility
PRO	Parental responsibility order
PSO	Prohibited steps order
RCPCH	Royal College of Paediatrics and Child Health
RSC	Rules of the Supreme Court 1965
SG	Special guardianship
SGO	Special guardianship order
SO	Supervision order
UKSC	United Kingdom Supreme Court

KEY DATES

- **25 APRIL 1985**
  G v G (Minors: Custody Appeal) [1985] FLR 894

- **17 OCTOBER 1985**
  Gillick v West Norfolk and Wisbech AHA [1986] 1 FLR 224

- **1 AUGUST 1986**
  Child Abduction and Custody Act 1985 into force

- **4 APRIL 1988**
  Family Law Act 1986 into force

- **13 JUNE 1991**
  Re H; Re S (Minors) (Abduction: Custody Rights) [1991] 2 FLR 262

- **14 OCTOBER 1991**
  Children Act 1989 into force

- **21 JULY 1994**
  Re M (A Minor) (Care Order: Threshold Conditions) [1994] 2 FLR 577

- **23 SEPTEMBER 1994**
  Hokkanen v Finland [1996] 1 FLR 289

- **14 DECEMBER 1995**
  Re H and R (Child Sexual Abuse: Standard of Proof) [1996] 1 FLR 80

- **28 NOVEMBER 1996**
  Re C (Interim Care Order: Residential Assessment) [1997] 1 FLR 1

- **1 OCTOBER 1997**
  Family Law Act 1996, Pt IV into force

- **25 MARCH 1999**
  Dawson v Wearmouth [1999] 1 FLR 1167

- **19 JUNE 2000**
  Re L, Re V, Re M, Re H (Contact: Domestic Violence) [2000] 2 FLR
  334

- **2 OCTOBER 2000**
  Human Rights Act 1998 into force

- **1 APRIL 2001**
  Cafcass came into existence

- **1 DECEMBER 2003**
  Adoption and Children Act 2002, s 111 (amending Children Act 1989,
  s 4: fathers have PR if named on birth certificate) into force

- **16 AUGUST 2004**
  X Council v B (Emergency Protection Orders) [2004] EWHC
  2014 (Fam), [2005] 1 FLR 341

- **28 OCTOBER 2004**
  Re S (Identification: Restrictions on Publicity) [2004] UKHL 47, [2005]
  1 FLR 591

- **1 MARCH 2005**
  Brussels II A (Council Regulation 2201/2003) into force

- **16 JUNE 2005**
  Re J (Child Returned Abroad: Convention Rights) [2005] UKHL 40,
  [2005] 2 FLR 802

- **24 NOVEMBER 2005**
  Re G (Interim Care Order: Residential Assessment) [2005] UKHL 68,
  [2006] 1 FLR 601

- **5 DECEMBER 2005**
  Civil Partnership Act 2004 into force

- **30 DECEMBER 2005**
  Adoption and Children Act 2002, main provisions, together with the
  Family Procedure (Adoption) Rules 2005, into force

- **26 JULY 2006**
  Re G (Children) [2006] UKHL 43, [2006] 2 FLR 629

- **16 NOVEMBER 2006**
  Re D (Abduction: Rights of Custody) [2006] UKHL 51, [2007] 1 FLR
  961

- **1 OCTOBER 2007**
  Mental Capacity Act 2005 into force

- **5 DECEMBER 2007**
  Re M (Abduction: Zimbabwe) [2007] UKHL 55, [2008] 1 FLR 251

- **11 JUNE 2008**
  Re B (Care Proceedings: Standard of Proof) [2008] UKSC 35, [2008]
  2 FLR 141

- **8 DECEMBER 2008**
  Children and Adoption Act 2006, Pt 1 (inserting Children Act 1989,
  ss 11A–11P) into force

- **1 OCTOBER 2009**
  Supreme Court came into existence

- **19 NOVEMBER 2009**
  Re B (A Child) [2009] UKSC 5, [2010] 1 FLR 551

- **14 DECEMBER 2009**
  Re S-B (Children) [2009] UKSC 17, [2010] 1 FLR 1161

- **3 MARCH 2010**
  Re W (Children) (Abuse: Oral Evidence) [2010] UKSC 12, [2010]
  1 FLR 1485

- **6 APRIL 2011**
  Family Procedure Rules 2010 into force

DIVISION A

CHILDREN ACT 1989, PT I

Contents

Contents

Section 1 welfare

A1 'PARAMOUNT'

Re G (Children)

[2006] UKHL 43, [2006] 2 FLR 629 at 638

House of Lords

Baroness Hale of Richmond

[27] The 1925 Act was passed at a time when the father was sole guardian of his legitimate children and the mother the only person with parental rights over her illegitimate child. Section 1 clearly meant that, in future, such legal claims were to be ignored and the child's welfare was to prevail. In the landmark case of *J and Another v C and Others* [1970] AC 668, (1969) FLR Rep 360, this House held that this was equally applicable to disputes between parents and non-parents. In an oft-quoted passage, at 710–711 and 384 respectively, Lord MacDermott explained the meaning of the words 'shall regard the welfare of the infant as the first and paramount consideration' thus:

> '... it seems to me that they must mean more than that the child's welfare is to be treated as the top item in a list of items relevant to the matter in question. I think they connote a process whereby, when all the relevant facts, relationships, claims and wishes of parents, risks, choices and other circumstances are taken into account and weighed, the course to be followed will be that which is most in the interests of the child's welfare as that term has now to be understood. That is the first consideration because it is of first importance and *the paramount consideration because it rules upon or determines the course to be followed*.' (emphasis added)

General notes:

The Act being construed in *J v C* was the Guardianship of Infants Act 1925, the wording of which was 'first and paramount consideration'.

The same italicised words were cited by Wall LJ in relation to the Adoption and Children Act 2002, s 1: *Re P (Placement orders: parental consent)* [2008] EWCA Civ 535, [2008] 2 FLR 625: see E14 – ACA 2002, s 52: dispensing with parental consent.

A2   PLANNED AND PURPOSEFUL DELAY

C v Solihull MBC

[1993] 1 FLR 290 at 304

Family Division

Ward J

As further guidance to the justices dealing with a case of this kind where
it is envisaged that a programme of assessment is necessary and will take a
number of months to complete, I remind them of two important parts of
the Act and of the rules. The first is that delay is ordinarily inimicable to
the welfare of the child, but that planned and purposeful delay may well
be beneficial. A delay of a final decision for the purpose of ascertaining
the result of an assessment is proper delay and is to be encouraged.
Therefore, it is wholly consistent with the welfare of the child to allow a
matter of months to elapse for a proper programme of assessment to be
undertaken.

Other significant cases on this issue:

- *Hounslow LBC v A* [1993] 1 FLR 702
- *Re W (Welfare reports)* [1995] 2 FLR 142
- *Re M (Children)* [2009] EWCA Civ 1216, [2010] 1 FLR 1089 (if
  adjournment refused for reasons of delay, must establish what the
  likely delay would be)

Contrast:

- *Sylvester v Austria* [2003] 2 FLR 210: see B5 – Passage of time
- *Vigreux v Michel* [2006] EWCA Civ 630, [2006] 2 FLR 1180: see F4
  – Unacceptable delay in determining proceedings

A3 WHICH CHILD'S WELFARE

Re S (Contact: application by sibling)

[1998] 2 FLR 897 at 907 and 908

Family Division

Charles J

Whose welfare would be the court's paramount consideration on the substantive application if leave were granted?

As was agreed by all the parties before me in considering the chances of success of the substantive application if leave were granted it is necessary to consider and decide what the paramount consideration of the court would be in determining that application. Possibilities are:

(a) that the court's paramount consideration would be S's welfare, or
(b) because two children are involved the court would balance the welfare of S and Y.

Unsurprisingly the question as to the approach to be adopted by the court under the Act where an applicant for an order is a child, with the consequence that two children are involved in the proceedings, has arisen before.

Having regard to existing authority, and in particular *Re T and E (Proceedings: Conflicting Interests)* [1995] 1 FLR 581 ('*Re T and E*'), *Re F (Contact: Child in Care)* [1995] 1 FLR 510 ('*Re F*') and *Birmingham City Council v H (No 3)* [1994] 2 AC 124, [1994] 1 FLR 224 (the '*Birmingham* case'):

(1) I accept the submissions advanced on behalf of Ms R and S that if leave were to be granted the court's paramount consideration in the substantive application would be the welfare of S, and
(2) in my judgment the arguments advanced on behalf of Y that the court would balance her welfare with that of S, or that her welfare would be the court's paramount consideration, are wrong.

...

However, I agree with both Wilson J and Wall J in *Re F* and *Re T and E* respectively that the approach of the House of Lords in the *Birmingham*

case to resolve the dilemma that arose in that case when it could be said
that the upbringing or welfare of two children was involved was:

(a)   to identify the child who was the subject of the order being sought,
       and
(b)   to hold that for the purposes of s 1 'the question to be determined
       by the court' related to that child's upbringing (see in particular the
       passage from the speech of Lord Slynn cited by Wall J in *Re T and E*
       at 585D–H, and the point Wall J then makes that this approach has
       subsequently been followed by the Court of Appeal).

Also I agree with both Wilson and Wall JJ that the guidance given by the
House of Lords in the *Birmingham* case is not limited to applications
under s 34 and that in the *Birmingham* case the House of Lords has set, or
indicated, the approach to the construction and application of the Act
that is to be taken by the court when two children are involved in an
application for an order under the Act and it is arguable that the order
(and thus the decision of the court) affects the upbringing and welfare of
both children.

This case is also included in relation to:

B41   CA 1989, s 10(8): 'the child concerned'

A4   IMPORTANCE OF USING WELFARE CHECKLIST

Re G (Children)

[2006] UKHL 43, [2006] 2 FLR 629 at 642

House of Lords

Baroness Hale of Richmond

[40] My Lords, it is of course the case that any experienced family judge is well aware of the contents of the statutory checklist and can be assumed to have had regard to it whether or not this is spelled out in a judgment. However, in any difficult or finely balanced case, as this undoubtedly was, it is a great help to address each of the factors in the list, along with any others which may be relevant, so as to ensure that no particular feature of the case is given more weight than it should properly bear. This is perhaps particularly important in any case where the real concern is that the children's primary carer is reluctant or unwilling to acknowledge the importance of another parent in the children's lives.

General notes:

Cf *D MCG v Neath Port Talbot County Borough Council* [2010] EWCA Civ 821, [2010] 2 FLR 1827: see H10 – Express reference to ECHR?

This case is also included in relation to:

A6   Parenthood and welfare (1)
B23   Change of residence

A5 WISHES OF THE CHILD

Re R (Residence order)

[2009] EWCA Civ 445, [2010] 1 FLR 509 at 531 and 537

Court of Appeal

Rix and Moore-Bick LJ

RIX LJ:

[57] The importance of listening to a child once he or she has reached the age of 10 (here, the child was almost 9 ½ when he was seen by Dr Cochrane) has been stressed in the authorities. Thus in *Re L (A Child) (Contact: Domestic Violence)* [2001] Fam 260, [2001] 2 WLR 339, [2000] 2 FLR 334 at 271–272, 347 and 340 respectively, Dame Elizabeth Butler-Sloss P sitting in this court cited with approval *Contact and Domestic Violence – The Experts' Court Report* [2000] Fam Law 615 at 624 on the subject of a child's wishes:

'... while this needs to be assessed within the whole context of such wishes, the older the child the more seriously they should be viewed and the more insulting and discrediting to the child to have them ignored. As a rough rule we would see these as needing to be taken account of at any age; above 10 we see these as carrying considerable weight with 6–10 as an intermediate stage and at under 6 as often indistinguishable in many ways from the wishes of the main carer (assuming normal development). In domestic violence, where the child has memories of that violence we would see their wishes as warranting much more weight than in situations where no real reason for the child's resistance appears to exist.'

See also *Re D (Abduction: Rights of Custody)* [2006] UKHL 51, [2007] 1 AC 619, [2006] 3 WLR 989, [2007] 1 FLR 961 per Baroness Hale at para [57]:

'But there is now a growing understanding of the importance of listening to the children involved in children's cases. It is the child, more than anyone else who will have to live with what the court decides.'

[58] I respectfully conclude that the judge has erred in not giving any real effect to the child's wishes expressed in this case. He has referred to them, accepted them, but thereafter essentially ignored them. He has

attempted to reason against, and reject, the child's (partial) rationalisation of them. He has in effect wholly discounted them. And yet, the child was a mature and thoughtful child close to the age of 10, who expressed his wishes rationally and, in my judgment, with considerable emotional understanding. Moreover, those wishes, in part natural given his love for his mother and his successful upbringing to date – and therefore to be given all the more attention rather than discounted – were well supported by the still more mature understanding of Dr Cochrane and the mother that the time of the birth of his new half-sibling was not a good time at which to break up his residence with his mother. I do not understand why these well-evidenced concerns were overborne by a call for greater sophistication: in reality this was little more than a way to reinforce the judge's conclusion that he would not disturb the boy's 'settled' status.

MOORE-BICK LJ:

[75] It is quite true that in para [15] of his judgment the judge referred to L's expressed wish to return to live with his mother and to that extent it cannot be said that he overlooked entirely what, on any view, is an important element in the checklist. There is a difference, however, between acknowledging the existence of a factor and taking it properly into account. Of course it is for the judge to decide what weight to give to each of the various factors that presents itself in the case before him, but there is a distinction between simply identifying a factor and taking it properly into account, just as there is between correctly identifying a principle of law and actually applying it. In the present case I can see no indication that the judge evaluated L's expression of his wishes, that he considered to what extent his age or maturity affected the weight to be attached to them or that he considered how heavily, if at all, they weighed in favour of returning L to his mother. On the contrary, he appears, having recorded them, to have disregarded them on the grounds that they were little more than a reflection of the natural affection that L could be expected to feel for the person who was both his mother and the parent by whom he had hitherto been brought up. Of course L's wishes could not be determinative and the judge was right to say that they were not the end of the matter, but they should, in my view, have been properly taken into account. To put it another way, I see no sign that the judge really 'listened to' what L was saying: see *Re D (Abduction: Rights of Custody)* per Baroness Hale at para [57].

General notes:

The case illustrates how difficult this issue can be in practice: Ward LJ would have upheld the judge's decision.

This case is also included in relation to:

G15 Judicial treatment of litigants in person
H17 Rejecting Cafcass recommendation

A6   PARENTHOOD AND WELFARE (1)

Re G (Children)

[2006] UKHL 43, [2006] 2 FLR 629 at 631, 640 and 643

House of Lords

Lord Nicholls of Birkenhead; Baroness Hale of Richmond

LORD NICHOLLS OF BIRKENHEAD:

[2] I wish to emphasise one point. In this case the dispute is not between two biological parents. The present unhappy dispute is between the children's mother and her former partner Ms CW. In this case, as in all cases concerning the upbringing of children, the court seeks to identify the course which is in the best interests of the children. Their welfare is the court's paramount consideration. In reaching its decision the court should always have in mind that in the ordinary way the rearing of a child by his or her biological parent can be expected to be in the child's best interests, both in the short term and also, and importantly, in the longer term. I decry any tendency to diminish the significance of this factor. A child should not be removed from the primary care of his or her biological parents without compelling reason. Where such a reason exists the judge should spell this out explicitly.

BARONESS HALE OF RICHMOND:

[31] None of this means that the fact of parentage is irrelevant. The position in English law is akin to that in Australian law, as explained by Lindenmayer J in *Hodak, Newman and Hodak* (1993) FLC 92–421, and subsequently approved by the Full Court of the Family Court of Australia in *Rice v Miller* (1993) FLC 92–415 and *Re Evelyn* [1998] FamCA 55:

> 'I am of the opinion that *the fact of parenthood is to be regarded as an important and significant factor in considering which proposals better advance the welfare of the child.* Such fact does not, however, establish a presumption in favour of the natural parent, nor generate a preferential position in favour of the natural parent from which the Court commences its decision-making process ... Each case should be determined upon an examination of its own merits and of the individuals there involved.' (emphasis added)

[32] So what is the significance of the fact of parenthood? It is worthwhile picking apart what we mean by 'natural parent' in this context. There is a difference between natural and legal parents. Thus, the father of a child born to unmarried parents was not legally a 'parent' until the Family Law Reform Act 1987 but he was always a natural parent. The anonymous donor who donates his sperm or her egg under the terms of the Human Fertilisation and Embryology Act 1990 (the 1990 Act) is the natural progenitor of the child but not his legal parent: see ss 27 and 28 of the 1990 Act. The husband or unmarried partner of a mother who gives birth as a result of donor insemination in a licensed clinic in this country is for virtually all purposes a legal parent, but may not be any kind of natural parent: see s 28 of the 1990 Act. To be the legal parent of a child gives a person legal standing to bring and defend proceedings about the child and makes the child a member of that person's family, but it does not necessarily tell us much about the importance of that person to the child's welfare.

[33] There are at least three ways in which a person may be or become a natural parent of a child, each of which may be a very significant factor in the child's welfare, depending upon the circumstances of the particular case. The first is genetic parenthood: the provision of the gametes which produce the child. This can be of deep significance on many levels. For the parent, perhaps particularly for a father, the knowledge that this is 'his' child can bring a very special sense of love for and commitment to that child which will be of great benefit to the child (see, for example, the psychiatric evidence in *Re C (MA) (an infant)* [1966] 1 WLR 646). For the child, he reaps the benefit not only of that love and commitment, but also of knowing his own origins and lineage, which is an important component in finding an individual sense of self as one grows up. The knowledge of that genetic link may also be an important (although certainly not an essential) component in the love and commitment felt by the wider family, perhaps especially grandparents, from which the child has so much to gain.

[34] The second is gestational parenthood: the conceiving and bearing of the child. The mother who bears the child is legally the child's mother, whereas the mother who provided the egg is not: 1990 Act, s 27. While this may be partly for reasons of certainty and convenience, it also recognises a deeper truth: that the process of carrying a child and giving him birth (which may well be followed by breast-feeding for some months) brings with it, in the vast majority of cases, a very special relationship between mother and child, a relationship which is different from any other.

[35] The third is social and psychological parenthood: the relationship which develops through the child demanding and the parent providing for the child's needs, initially at the most basic level of feeding, nurturing, comforting and loving, and later at the more sophisticated level of guiding, socialising, educating and protecting. The phrase 'psychological parent' gained most currency from the influential work of Goldstein, Freud and Solnit, *Beyond the Best Interests of the Child* (Free Press, 1973), who defined it thus:

> 'A psychological parent is one who, on a continuous, day-to-day basis, through interaction, companionship, interplay, and mutuality, fulfils the child's psychological needs for a parent, as well as the child's physical needs. The psychological parent may be a biological, adoptive, foster or common law parent.'

[36] Of course, in the great majority of cases, the natural mother combines all three. She is the genetic, gestational and psychological parent. Her contribution to the welfare of the child is unique. The natural father combines genetic and psychological parenthood. His contribution is also unique. In these days when more parents share the tasks of child rearing and breadwinning, his contribution is often much closer to that of the mother than it used to be; but there are still families which divide their tasks on more traditional lines, in which case his contribution will be different and its importance will often increase with the age of the child.

[37] But there are also parents who are neither genetic nor gestational, but who have become the psychological parents of the child and thus have an important contribution to make to their welfare. Adoptive parents are the most obvious example, but there are many others. This is the position of CW in this case. Whatever may have been the mother's stance in the past, Mr Jackson on her behalf has not in any way sought to diminish the importance of CW's place in these children's lives or to challenge the legal arrangements put in place as a result of the first proceedings. Indeed, he asks us to restore those orders.

[38] What Mr Jackson challenges is the reversal in the parties' positions in response to the mother's removal of the children to Cornwall. He points out that, with one exception at the beginning of Bracewell J's judgment, there was no reference to the important fact that CG is these children's mother. While CW is their psychological parent, CG is, as Hallett LJ pointed out, both their biological and their psychological parent. In the overall welfare judgment, that must count for something in the vast majority of cases. Its significance must be considered and assessed. Furthermore, the evidence shows that it clearly did count for something in this case. These children were happy and doing very well in their mother's home. That should not have been changed without a very good reason.

...

[44] My Lords, I am driven to the conclusion that the courts below have allowed the unusual context of this case to distract them from principles

which are of universal application. First, the fact that CG is the natural mother of these children in every sense of that term, while raising no presumption in her favour, is undoubtedly an important and significant factor in determining what will be best for them now and in the future. Yet nowhere is that factor explored in the judgment below. Secondly, while it may well be in the best interests of children to change their living arrangements if one of their parents is frustrating their relationship with the other parent who is able to offer them a good and loving home, this is unlikely to be in their best interests while that relationship is in fact being maintained in accordance with the court's order.

Other significant cases on this issue:

• In relation to public law proceedings, note *Re L (Children) (Care proceedings: significant harm)* [2006] EWCA Civ 1282, [2007] 1 FLR 1068: see D19 – Dangers of social engineering

This case is also included in relation to:

A4   Importance of using welfare checklist
B23   Change of residence

A7   PARENTHOOD AND WELFARE (2)

Re B (A child)

[2009] UKSC 5, [2010] 1 FLR 551 at 556 and 559

Supreme Court

Lord Kerr

[20] The distraction that discussion of rights rather than welfare can occasion is well illustrated in the latter part of His Honour Judge Richards' judgment. In paras [28] and [30] he suggested that, provided the parenting that Harry's father could provide was 'good enough', it was of no consequence that that which the grandmother could provide would be better. We consider that in decisions about residence such as are involved in this case; there is no place for the question whether the proposed placement would be 'good enough'. The court's quest is to determine what is in the best interests of the child, not what might constitute a second best but supposedly adequate alternative. As the Court of Appeal pointed out at para [61], the concept of 'good enough' parenting has always been advanced in the context of public law proceedings and of care within the wider family as opposed to care by strangers.

...

Re G

[33] The Court of Appeal acknowledged that *Re G* had given the final quietus to the notion that parental rights have any part to play in the assessment of where the best interests of a child lay. Indeed, (correctly in our view) it identified this as the principal message provided by the case. It is certainly the principal message that was pertinent to the present case. It appears, however, that the urgency of that message has been blunted somewhat by reference to the speech of Lord Nicholls of Birkenhead and some misunderstanding of the opinion that he expressed. Having agreed that the appeal should be allowed for the reasons to be given by Baroness Hale of Richmond, Lord Nicholls said at para [2]:

> 'The present unhappy dispute is between the children's mother and her former partner Ms CW. In this case, as in all cases concerning the upbringing of children, the court seeks to identify the course which is in the best interests of the children.'

He then said:

'Their welfare is the court's paramount consideration. In reaching its decision the court should always have in mind that in the ordinary way the rearing of a child by his or her biological parent can be expected to be in the child's best interests, both in the short term and also, and importantly, in the longer term. I decry any tendency to diminish the significance of this factor. A child should not be removed from the primary care of his or her biological parents without compelling reason. Where such a reason exists the judge should spell this out explicitly.'

[34] As we have observed, it appears to have been in reliance on the latter passage that the justices stated that a child should not be removed from the primary care of biological parents. A careful reading of what Lord Nicholls of Birkenhead actually said reveals, of course, that he did not propound any general rule to that effect. For a proper understanding of the view that he expressed, it is important at the outset to recognise that Lord Nicholls' comment about the rearing of a child by a biological parent is set firmly in the context of the child's welfare. This he identified as 'the court's paramount consideration'. It must be the dominant and overriding factor that ultimately determines disputes about residence and contact and there can be no dilution of its importance by reference to extraneous matters.

[35] When Lord Nicholls said that courts should keep in mind that the interests of a child will normally be best served by being reared by his or her biological parent, he was doing no more than reflecting common experience that, in general, children tend to thrive when brought up by parents to whom they have been born. He was careful to qualify his statement, however, by the words '*in the ordinary way* the rearing of a child by his or her biological parent *can be expected* to be in the child's best interests' (emphasis added). In the ordinary way one can expect that children will do best with their biological parents. But many disputes about residence and contact do not follow the ordinary way. Therefore, although one should keep in mind the common experience to which Lord Nicholls was referring, one must not be slow to recognise those cases where that common experience does not provide a reliable guide.

[36] Although the factual background to the case of *Re G* was, as Baroness Hale of Richmond described it, 'novel' (a lesbian couple decided to have children together, arranged for anonymous donor insemination and brought up the children together until their relationship broke down) the issues arising and the legal principles that applied were, as Baroness Hale pointed out, just the same as would arise in the case of a heterosexual couple. After conducting what the Court of Appeal rightly described as a scholarly analysis of the statute and the authorities which pre-dated the Children Act 1989, Baroness Hale turned to consider the recommendations of the Law Commission report on private law cases relating to childcare. She said this at para [30]:

'[30] My Lords, the [Children Act 1989] brought together the Government's proposals in relation to childcare law and the Law Commission's recommendations in relation to the private law. In its Working Paper No 96, Family Law: Review of Child Law: Custody (1986), at para 6.22, having discussed whether there should be some form of presumption in favour of natural parents, the Law Commission said:

> "We conclude, therefore, that the welfare of each child in the family should continue to be the paramount consideration whenever their custody or upbringing is in question between private individuals. The welfare test itself is well able to encompass any special contribution which natural parents can make to the emotional needs of their child, in particular to his sense of identity and self-esteem, as well as the added commitment which knowledge of their parenthood may bring. We have already said that the indications are that the priority given to the welfare of the child needs to be strengthened rather than undermined. We could not contemplate making any recommendation which might have the effect of weakening the protection given to children under the present law."

Nor should we. The statutory position is plain: the welfare of the child is the paramount consideration. As Lord MacDermott explained in *J v C* [1970] AC 668, 711, this means that it "rules upon or determines the course to be followed". There is no question of a parental right. As the Law Commission explained:

> "the welfare test itself is well able to encompass any special contribution which natural parents can make to the emotional needs of their child"

or, as Lord MacDermott put it, the claims and wishes of parents "can be capable of ministering to the total welfare of the child in a special way".'

[37] This passage captures the central point of the *Re G* case and of this case. It is a message which should not require reaffirmation but, if and insofar as it does, we would wish to provide it in this judgment. All consideration of the importance of parenthood in private law disputes about residence must be firmly rooted in an examination of what is in the child's best interests. This is the paramount consideration. It is only as a contributor to the child's welfare that parenthood assumes any significance. In common with all other factors bearing on what is in the best interests of the child, it must be examined for its potential to fulfil that aim. There are various ways in which it may do so, some of which were explored by Baroness Hale in *Re G*, but the essential task for the court is always the same.

Other significant cases on this issue:

- *Re B (Role of biological father)* [2007] EWHC 1952 (Fam), [2008] 1 FLR 1015
- *Re R (Residence)* [2009] EWCA Civ 358, [2009] 2 FLR 819

A8 RELIGIOUS BELIEF AND WELFARE

Haringey London Borough Council v C, E and Another Intervening

[2006] EWCA 1620 (Fam), [2007] 1 FLR 1035 at 1045

Family Division

Ryder J

[36] I set out his position in some detail lest it be thought that this court may have misunderstood or misconstrued this devout and peaceful man and the hurt that he undoubtedly feels, which is expressed in his more emotive allegations against those who he characterises as 'the enemies of the church': the local authority and the former children's guardian, who 'are being used by Satan'. Religious, racial and cultural factors are integral elements of welfare and may on the facts of a particular case provide both the positive and negative factors and context by and within which decisions have to be made. However, whatever an individual belief system may provide for, and despite the respect that will be given to private and family life and the right to freedom of thought, conscience and religion and the freedom to manifest religion or belief in worship, teaching, practice and observance (by Arts 8 and 9 of the European Convention for the Protection of Human Rights and Fundamental Freedoms 1950 (the European Convention)) the law does not give any religious belief or birthright a pre-eminent place in the balance of factors that comprise welfare *Re P (A Minor) (Residence Order: Child's Welfare)* [2000] Fam 15, sub nom *Re P (Section 91(14) Guidelines) (Residence and Religious Heritage)* [1999] 2 FLR 573, at 586E and 597B–599E, 30 and 41–43 respectively; and *J and Another v C and Others* [1970] AC 668, at 771–711. Furthermore, the safeguarding of the welfare of vulnerable children and adults ought not to be subordinated by the court to any particular religious belief.

Other significant cases on this issue:

* *Re S; Newcastle City Council v Z* [2005] EWHC 1490 (Fam), [2007] 1 FLR 861

A9 CULTURE AND WELFARE

Re J (Child returned abroad: Convention rights)

[2005] UKHL 40, [2005] 2 FLR 802 at 813

House of Lords

Baroness Hale

[37] Like everything else, the extent to which it is relevant that the legal system of the other country is different from our own depends upon the facts of the particular case. It would be wrong to say that the future of every child who is within the jurisdiction of our courts should be decided according to a conception of child welfare which exactly corresponds to that which is current here. In a world which values difference, one culture is not inevitably to be preferred to another. Indeed, we do not have any fixed concept of what will be in the best interests of the individual child. Once upon a time it was assumed that all very young children should be cared for by their mothers, but that older boys might well be better off with their fathers. Nowadays we know that some fathers are very well able to provide everyday care for even their very young children and are quite prepared to prioritise their children's needs over the demands of their own careers. Once upon a time it was assumed that mothers who had committed the matrimonial offence of adultery were only fit to care for their children if the father agreed to this. Nowadays we recognise that a mother's misconduct is no more relevant than a father's: the question is always the impact it will have on the child's upbringing and well-being. Once upon a time it may have been assumed that there was only one way of bringing up children. Nowadays we know that there are many routes to a healthy and well-adjusted adulthood. We are not so arrogant as to think that we know best.

[38] Hence our law does not start from any a priori assumptions about what is best for any individual child. It looks at the child and weighs a number of factors in the balance, now set out in the well-known 'check-list' in s 1(3) of the Children Act 1989; these include his own wishes and feelings, his physical, emotional and educational needs and the relative capacities of the adults around him to met those needs, the effect of change, his own characteristics and background, including his ethnicity, culture and religion, and any harm he has suffered or risks suffering in the future. There is nothing in those principles which prevents a court from giving great weight to the culture in which a child has been brought up when deciding how and where he will fare best in the future. Our own society is a multi-cultural one. But looking at it from the child's

point of view, as we all try to do, it may sometimes be necessary to resolve or diffuse a clash between the differing cultures within his own family.

This case is also included in relation to:

F19   Welfare principle applies
F20   No 'strong presumption' in favour of return
F21   Other relevant factors
H39   Limits on appeal court's authority

A10   NO ORDER PRINCIPLE

G (Children)

[2005] EWCA Civ 1283, [2006] 1 FLR 771 at 773

Court of Appeal

Ward LJ

[9] I gave permission, remarking that it might be thought to be a storm
in a teacup but, nonetheless, there seemed to be some point of principle
here which it might be worth this court exploring. In the result,
Miss Bryant has placed various authorities before us where the courts
have considered s 1(5). Among them is a decision of Munby J in *Re X and
Y (Leave to Remove from Jurisdiction: No Order Principle)* [2001] 2 FLR
118 where he said at 147:

> 'So far as material for present purposes, the following principles can
> be distilled from *Dawson v Wearmouth*—
>
> (a)   The burden is on the party applying for an order to make out a
>   positive case that on the balance of probabilities it is in the
>   interests of the child that that order should be made. If he fails
>   to make out that positive case, the application will fall [perhaps
>   fail].
>
> (b)   It follows from this that if the arguments in favour of and
>   against making the order sought are no better than equal
>   balance, the order should not be made.
>
> (c)   Put in slightly different words, unless there is evidence
>   establishing that the order will lead to an improvement from
>   the point of view of the child's welfare, the order should not be
>   made.
>
> (d)   The proper application of section 1(5) is inconsistent with
>   identifying any particular factors as giving rise to a
>   presumption in favour of making an order or as being all
>   important or only to be displaced by strong countervailing
>   considerations.
>
> (e)   This is not to say that there may not, in a particular class of
>   case, have been some particular factor or factors which will
>   ordinarily be treated as relevant and which may often be
>   regarded as important or even as carrying very great weight.
>
> (f)   However, the weight or importance to be given to any relevant
>   factor will depend upon and vary according to the
>   circumstances of the individual case. Whether or not any one
>   factor tips the balance one way or the other will vary from one

case to another. This is a matter to be decided upon an evaluation of the evidence and not by applying any presumption.

(g)   The question must be examined from the point of view of the child.'

Section 1(5) of the Act reads as follows:

'Where a court is considering whether or not to make one or more orders under this Act with respect to a child, it shall not make the order, or any of the orders, unless it considers that doing so would be better for the child than making no order at all.'

[10]   There is, it seems, considerable academic learning as to the meaning to be given to s 1(5) and as to the purpose which it serves. I do not regard it necessary for the purposes of this judgment to enter those troubled waters because, in my view, this section is perfectly clear. It does not, in my judgment, create a presumption one way or another. All it demands is that before the court makes any order it must ask the question: will it be better for the child to make the order than make no order at all? The section itself gives the test to be applied and the question to be asked. If judges in each case do just that then they cannot go wrong, it being axiomatic that every case is different, and each case will depend upon its own peculiar facts.

[11]   Here, if one asks: is it better for these children to make this order than not to make it? Then the answer, to me, appears to be overwhelmingly obvious, that it is better for these children to have the order. This order was a part of a long, difficult and protracted negotiation. It was an order of clear importance to the mind of the mother. It gave her the security of knowing that if her worst fears were realised and there should be a future difficulty in returning her daughters, then that piece of paper containing the order gave everyone – be it the police or the social services or a future court – the immediate answer to the question: where should the children be living? It added to her peace of mind, and peace of mind is an integral and important factor in producing stability in the lives of the children in the care of the parent.

[12]   This order was important for another reason. It was the fruit of agreement which had dissipated so much of the unease and bitterness which had infected the litigation up to that stage. It was likely to dissipate and, as the events have shown, *has* dissipated the mistrust that each parent felt towards the other and has promoted the settlement of arrangements for contact in the future. It does not need great learning to accept that where parents can agree on future dealings with regard to the children, that is better for the children than having bitterly contested court proceedings. For that reason, this order was advantageous to the children.

[13] The third and critical factor which, in my judgment, made it a case where the order should be made, was that the court should not be astute to go behind agreements carefully negotiated in difficult questions of this sort. This negotiation covered all the matters I have indicated. It was not a case where there was no litigation and where, having come to an agreement, the parties issued proceedings simply for the sake of getting the imprimatur of the court's judgment. Here, unless there was a very good reason to go behind the agreement, the court should, in my judgment, have paid respect to the decision of the parents whose views were that an order would be beneficial to the management of their children's lives and that that management would be more beneficial with the order than without it.

Parental responsibility

A11 PR APPLICATION: PRINCIPLES TO APPLY (1)

Re S (Parental responsibility)

[1995] 2 FLR 648 at 657 and 659

Court of Appeal

Waite and Butler-Sloss LJJ

WAITE LJ:

I have engaged in this laborious review of the authorities because it is my increasing concern, both from the very fact that there are so many reported cases on this topic and from my experience when dealing with the innumerable appeals from justices to the Family Division, that applications under s 4 have become one of these little growth industries born of misunderstanding. Misunderstanding arises from a failure to appreciate that, in essence, the granting of a parental responsibility order is the granting of status. It is unfortunate that the notion of 'parental responsibility' has still to be defined by s 3 of the Children Act to mean '... all the rights, duties, powers, responsibilities and authority which by law a parent ... has in relation to the child and his property', which gives outmoded pre-eminence to the 'rights' which are conferred. That it is unfortunate is demonstrated by the very fact that, when pressed in this case to define the nature and effect of the order which was so vigorously opposed, counsel for the mother was driven to say that her rooted objection was to the rights to which it would entitle the father and the power that it would give to him. That is a most unfortunate failure to appreciate the significant change that the Act has brought about where the emphasis is to move away from rights and to concentrate on responsibilities. She did not doubt that if by unhappy chance this child fell ill whilst she was abroad, his father, if then enjoying contact, would not deal responsibly with her welfare.

It would, therefore, be helpful if the mother could think calmly about the limited circumstances when the exercise of true parental responsibility is likely to be of practical significance. It is wrong to place undue and therefore false emphasis on the rights and duties and the powers comprised in 'parental responsibility' and not to concentrate on the fact that what is at issue is conferring upon a committed father the status of parenthood for which nature has already ordained that he must bear responsibility. There seems to me to be all too frequently a failure to appreciate that the wide exercise of s 8 orders can control the abuse, if any, of the exercise of parental responsibility which is adverse to the welfare of the child. Those interferences with the day-to-day management of the child's life have nothing to do with whether or not this order should be allowed.

There is another important emphasis I would wish to make. I have heard, up and down the land, psychiatrists tell me how important it is that children grow up with good self-esteem and how much they need to have a favourable positive image of the absent parent. It seems to me important, therefore, wherever possible, to ensure that the law confers upon a committed father that stamp of approval, lest the child grow up with some belief that he is in some way disqualified from fulfilling his role and that the reason for the disqualification is something inherent which will be inherited by the child, making her struggle to find her own identity all the more fraught.

Trying, therefore, to apply those principles to this case, at the heart of it lies the finding by the judge that in terms of commitment, attachment and bone fides this father passed the test. She rightly stated that that was not the conclusive list of requirements, and she rightly had regard to the fact of his conviction. But it seems to me that however disreputable the conviction, it was not one which demonstrably and directly affected the child in her day-to-day life.

BUTLER-SLOSS LJ:

It is important for parents and it is important, indeed, for these parents to remember the emphasis placed by Parliament on the order which is applied for. It is that of duties and responsibilities as well as rights and powers. Indeed, the order itself is entitled 'parental responsibility'. A father who has shown real commitment to the child concerned and to whom there is a positive attachment, as well as a genuine bona fide reason for the application, ought, in a case such as the present, to assume the weight of those duties and cement that commitment and attachment by sharing the responsibilities for the child with the mother. This father is asking to assume that burden as well as that pleasure of looking after his child, a burden not lightly to be undertaken.

A12 PR APPLICATION: PRINCIPLES TO APPLY (2)

Re H (Parental responsibility)

[1998] 1 FLR 855 at 858 and 859

Court of Appeal

Butler-Sloss LJ

Prior to the mid-1980s the father of a putative child had no rights in respect of that child, although he might seek a custody or access order from the courts. By the Family Law Reform Act 1987, for the first time a father not married to the mother of his child had the right to apply to the court for a parental rights order, which, if granted, gave him 'all the parental rights and duties with respect to the child' (s 4(1)). Ward J in *D v Hereford and Worcester County Council* [1991] Fam 14, [1991] 1 FLR 205 and Balcombe LJ in *Re H (Minors) (Local Authority: Parental Rights) (No 3)* [1991] Fam 151, sub nom *Re H (Illegitimate Children: Father: Parental Rights) (No 2)* [1991] 1 FLR 214, approving *D v Hereford and Worcester County Council*, set out the general principles to be followed in a parental rights application. Balcombe LJ said at 158 and 218 respectively:

> 'In considering whether to make an order under s 4 of the Act of 1987, the court will have to take into account a number of factors, of which the following will undoubtedly be material (although there may well be others, as the list is not intended to be exhaustive):
>
> (1) the degree of commitment which the father has shown towards the child;
>
> (2) the degree of attachment which exists between the father and the child;
>
> (3) the reasons of the father for applying for the order.'

...

The three requirements set out by Balcombe LJ are, undoubtedly, the starting-point for the making of an order but it is clear from his judgments in *Re H* and *Re G* that he did not intend them to be the only relevant factors in considering a parental responsibility order and that his list was not exhaustive. In any event such an approach would be contrary to s 1 of the Children Act which applies to parental responsibility orders and the welfare of the child is therefore paramount. The court has the duty in each case to take into account all the relevant circumstances and to decide whether the order proposed is in the best interests of the child. Of course, it is generally in a child's interests to know and have a relationship with his father but the appropriateness of the order has to be considered on the particular facts of each individual case. If, reviewing all the circumstances, the judge considers that there are factors adverse to the father sufficient to tip the balance against the order proposed, it would not be right to make the order, even though the three requirements can be shown by the father.

Examples of this approach are to be found in *Re T (A Minor) (Parental Responsibility: Contact)* [1993] 2 FLR 450 in which this court upheld the decision of the judge where the father had behaved with callous cruelty towards the child and with no concern for the welfare of a young child. In *Re P (Parental Responsibility)* [1997] 2 FLR 722 a parental responsibility order was refused where a father was serving a long term of imprisonment although he was committed (in one sense) to his child. This court held that he had displayed a degree of criminal irresponsibility which had devalued his level of commitment to his child. Lord Woolf MR at 728H said:

> 'The situation was such that the judge had to weigh in the balance the various factors in favour and against granting parental responsibility.'

In *Re P (Terminating Parental Responsibility)* [1995] 1 FLR 1048 Singer J terminated parental responsibility, given earlier to the father, after he caused serious permanent physical injury to a child for which he was charged, convicted and sentenced to imprisonment.

In the present appeal, this father has demonstrated commitment, the child is attached to him and he has genuine reasons for fostering the relationship between himself and his child. Against that background, however, are worrying matters which are relevant and important. The appellant struck a 2-year-old child (M) twice in the face heavily and has never really accepted blame for it. He caused bruising to this child, not only in obvious places, but, more worrying, on the inner ear, along the penis and on the scrotum. These injuries were to his own son whom, one assumes, he loves and who loves him. This behaviour was not just irresponsibility or recklessness, but was found by the judge to be cruel and with an element of sadism. He has been found by the judge unfit to be trusted to see his son unsupervised, a serious reflection, on the facts of this case, upon a man wishing to promote a continuing and deepening relationship with his son. Most important of all, he poses a risk to his son for the future, not only by reason of his past behaviour, but also because he is unwilling or unable to face up to what he did. In my judgment the judge was fully justified in deciding that a man who behaved like that to his son and made no attempt to come to terms with what he had done, was not fit to have parental responsibility for the child.

General notes:

Terminating PR: see *Re P (Terminating parental responsibility)* [1995] 1 FLR 1048.

Other significant cases on this issue:

* *Re G (Parental responsibility order)* [2006] EWCA Civ 745, [2006] 2 FLR 1092 (wrong to make suspended PRO but could adjourn application)
* *Re B (Role of biological father)* [2007] EWHC 1952 (Fam), [2008] 1 FLR 1015 (biological father granted contact but not PRO)
* *R v E and F (Female parents: known father)* [2010] EWHC 417 (Fam), [2010] 2 FLR 383 (biological father granted significant contact but not PRO)

A13 EXERCISING PR: IMAGINATIVE ORDERS / AGREEMENTS

Re Z (Shared parenting plan: publicity)

[2006] 1 FLR 405 at 406

Family Division

Hedley J

[5] When the case came before me A was acting in person, E had the benefit of leading counsel and Z was separately represented by counsel through NYAS. The case was negotiated over 2 days and A paid a warm and unsolicited tribute to leading counsel for the way in which the negotiations had been facilitated. In effect, both parents consented to the discharge of all previous orders and the subsequent withdrawal of all applications for orders under the Children Act 1989. This was on the basis of agreeing the concept of a shared parenting plan and acknowledging the importance to the child of the matters set out in the second schedule. At the request of A, not opposed either by E or the guardian, I set out the two schedules that comprise the agreement albeit duly anonymised:

'First schedule

The shared parenting plan for the child

The mother and father both:

(a)   Respect the fact that they have and will continue to have a joint and equal parental responsibility for the child.

(b)   Acknowledge that the child has been looked after by them jointly under a "shared care" arrangement.

(c)   Recognise the importance of these "shared care" arrangements continuing and commit themselves accordingly to such arrangements throughout the child's childhood.

(d)   Support the principle that the child shall spend time approximately equally in both homes.

(e)   Understand the need for agreeing times, dates and dates as early in advance as possible when the child is to spend time with them during school holidays to include half term holidays.

(f)   Agree that during term time the father will collect the child from school on a Friday afternoon to spend time with him until the following Thursday morning when he will take the child back to school. This is to happen on alternate weeks during term time, the balance of the child's time being spent with the child's mother. The parents both agree to keep these arrangements under review.

(g) Agree that the school holidays, to include half term holidays, will involve the child sharing the child's time as near equally as possible between their respective homes with times, days and dates of collection and delivery being agreed as early in advance as possible.

(h) Agree to share the arrangements for the collection and delivery of the child between homes.

(i) Have decided that when the child is spending time with one parent, the other will encourage the child to telephone that parent at a reasonable frequency being some two to three days.

(j) Acknowledge that as matters stand the child should stay at her present school. If either parent wishes to consider a change of school then he/she will, for the child's benefit, enter into a constructive discussion of the matter with the other parent with a view to forming a consensual position.

(k) Agree that unless specifically required for the purposes of travel abroad the mother will retain the child's passport, the same to be delivered to her by the father following each and every holiday that he may take abroad with the child.

(l) Acknowledge the need to share as equally as possible any incidental costs/extras arising as a result of the child's school attendance and shall do so in the spirit of open and efficient exchange of information as to such costs/extras.

(m) Recognise the need for flexibility in the above arrangements for shared care such that any agreed variation in the time spent with one parent is properly compensated.

(n) Appreciate the importance of the child's Guardian making a farewell visit to the child to explain this parenting plan and the agreement reached, the Court endorsing the importance of this from the child's point of view.

Second schedule

– The knowledge that the child's parents' reason to divorce is not the child's responsibility and that the child will be parented equally.

– Treatment as an important person with unique feelings, ideas and desires and not the source of arguments between parties.

– A continuing relationship with both parents and freedom to receive love from and express love for both parents.

– The expression of love and affection for each parent without having to stifle that love because of fear of disapproval by the other parent.

– Continuing care and guidance from both the child's parents.

- Being given honest age appropriate answers about changing
  family relationships.
- The knowledge and appreciation of what is good in each
  parent without denigrating the other.
- A relaxed and secure relationship with both parents without
  being placed in a position to manipulate one against the other.
- Being able to experience regular and equal shared parenting
  and know the reason for any future cancellations or
  curtailment to the child's normal pattern of living with both
  parents.'

[6] If I may be permitted to say so, I greatly approve of the approach
adopted by the parents in this case and I very much hope that they will
prove themselves able to translate it into practice without further recourse
to litigation. It is to the great credit, not only of themselves, but of the
guardian and the parties' legal advisors that this eminently sensible, albeit
unusual, order has been agreed which meets the particular needs of Z. I
have adjourned this case into open court so that publicity could be given
to this approach in the hope that it might commend itself to others as a
basis for discussion and negotiation. Whilst in one sense invidious to
select anyone for particular tribute by the court, it is right to observe that
it is truly remarkable that a case with a history of criminal abduction and
a long history of litigation could reach this conclusion. It indicates
remarkable generosity of spirit in any wronged party.

Other significant cases on this issue:

- *A v A (Shared residence)* [2004] EWHC 142 (Fam), [2004] 1 FLR
  1195 at 1224

A14 PARENTAL AUTHORITY DWINDLES

Gillick v West Norfolk and Wisbech Area Health Authority and Another

[1986] 1 FLR 224 at 235, 236 and 237

House of Lords

Lord Fraser

2: The parents' rights and duties in respect of medical treatment of their child.

It was, I think, accepted both by Mrs Gillick and by the DHSS, and in any event I hold, that parental rights to control a child do not exist for the benefit of the parent. They exist for the benefit of the child and they are justified only in so far as they enable the parent to perform his duties towards the child, and towards other children in the family.

...

It is, in my view, contrary to the ordinary experience of mankind, at least in Western Europe in the present century, to say that a child or a young person remains in fact under the complete control of his parents until he attains the definite age of majority, now 18 in the United Kingdom, and that on attaining that age he suddenly acquires independence. In practice most wise parents relax their control gradually as the child develops and encourage him or her to become increasingly independent. Moreover, the degree of parental control actually exercised over a particular child does in practice vary considerably according to his understanding and intelligence and it would, in my opinion, be unrealistic for the courts not to recognize these facts. Social customs change, and the law ought to, and does in fact, have regard to such changes when they are of major importance.

...

In times gone by the father had almost absolute authority over his children until they attained majority. A rather remarkable example of such authority being upheld by the court was the case of *Re Agar-Ellis* (1883) 24 ChD 317 which was much relied on by the Court of Appeal. The father in that case restricted the communication which his daughter aged 17 was allowed to have with her mother, against whose moral character nothing was alleged, to an extent that would be universally condemned today as quite unreasonable. The case has been much criticized in recent years and, in my opinion, with good reason. In *Hewer v Bryant* [1970] 1 QB 357, 369 Lord Denning MR said:

> 'I would get rid of the rule in *Re Agar-Ellis* and of the suggested exceptions to it. That case was decided in the year 1883. It reflects the attitude of a Victorian parent towards his children. He expected unquestioning obedience to his commands. If a son disobeyed, his father would cut him off with a shilling. If a daughter had an illegitimate child, he would turn her out of the house. His power only ceased when the child became 21. I decline to accept a view so much out of date. The common law can, and should, keep pace with the times. It should declare, in conformity with the recent Report of the Committee on the Age of Majority [Cmnd. 3342, 1967], that the legal right of a parent to the custody of a child ends at the 18th birthday; and even up till then, it is a dwindling right which the courts will hesitate to enforce against the wishes of the child, and the more so the older he is. It starts with a right of control and ends with little more than advice.'

I respectfully agree with every word of that and especially with the description of the father's authority as a dwindling right.

Section 7 reports

A15 STATEMENTS MADE IN CONCILIATION GENERALLY NOT ADMISSIBLE

Re D (Minors) (Conciliation: privilege)

[1993] 1 FLR 932 at 933, 935 and 937

Court of Appeal

Bingham MR

To what extent, if at all, may evidence be given in proceedings under the Children Act 1989 of statements made by one or other of the parties in the course of meetings held or communications made for the purpose of reconciliation, mediation or conciliation? That is the important question raised by this appeal. The ordinary rule is, as the parties agree, that evidence of such statements may not be given. But the parties do not agree whether the rule is absolute or subject to exceptions; and if it is subject to exceptions they do not agree what those exceptions are. The question derives its importance from the steadily growing role of conciliation (an expression which we use, for convenience, to embrace reconciliation, mediation and conciliation) in resolving disputes of this kind and from the peculiar regard which the law has to the interests if children.

...

The law

A substantial and, to out knowledge, unquestioned line of authority establishes that where a third party (whether official or unofficial, professional or lay) receives information in confidence with a view to conciliation, the courts will not compel him to disclose what was said without the parties' agreement: *McTaggart v McTaggart* [1949] P94; *Mole v Mole* [1951] P 21; *Pool v Pool* [1951] P 470; *Henley v Henley* [1955] P 202; *Theodoropoulas v Theodoropoulas* [1964] P 311; *Pais v Pais* [1971] P 119; *D v National Society for the Prevention of Cruelty to Children* [1978] AC 171 at pp 191E, 226F, 236G.

...

Recent practices

...

The practice of conciliation has grown and evolved in various ways over the last 10 years, in court and out of court, voluntary or directed, and extends over many parts of the country. Resolution of disputes over children by parents locked in acrimony and controversy had gradually but perceptibly taken over from efforts to preserve the state of the marriage of the parents. Conciliation of parental or matrimonial disputes does not form part of the legal process but as a matter of practice is becoming an important and valuable tool in the procedures of many family courts. This underlines the great importance of the preservation of a cloak over all attempts at settlement of disputes over children. Non-disclosure of the contents of conciliation meetings or correspondence is a thread discernible throughout all in-court and out-of-court conciliation arrangements and proposals.

Conclusion

These practices and expressions of opinion cannot, of course, be regarded as authoritative statements of the law. But in this field as in others it is undesirable that the law should drift very far away from the best professional practice. The practice described above follows the law in recognising the general inviolability of the privilege protecting statements made in the course of conciliation. But it also recognises the special regard which the law has for the interests of children. In our judgment, the law is that evidence may not be given in proceedings under the Children Act 1989 of statements made by one or other of the parties in the course of meetings held or communications made for the purpose of conciliation save in the very unusual case where a statement is made clearly indicating that the maker has in the past caused or is likely in the future to cause serious harm to the well-being of a child.

We wish in closing to emphasise three points:

(1)   Even in the rare case which falls within the narrow exception we have defined, the trial judge will still have to exercise a discretion whether or not to admit the evidence. He will admit it only if, in his judgment, the public interest in protecting the interests of the child outweighs the public interest in preserving the confidentiality of attempted conciliation.

(2)   This judgment is concerned only with privilege properly so called, that is, with a party's right to prevent statements or documents being adduced in evidence in court. It has nothing to do with duties of

confidence and does not seek to define the circumstances in which a duty of confidence may be superseded by other public interest considerations: cf *W v Egdell* [1990] Ch 359.

(3) We have deliberately stated the law in terms appropriate to cover this case and no other. We have not thought it desirable to attempt any more general statement. If and when cases arise not covered by this ruling, they will have to be decided in the light of their own special circumstances.

A16 CFR CANNOT GUARANTEE CONFIDENTIALITY

Re G (Minors) (Welfare report: disclosure)

[1993] 2 FLR 293 at 303 and 303

Court of Appeal

Balcombe LJ and Sir Francis Purchas

BALCOMBE LJ:

Of course, the real problem here is that the court welfare officer gave assurances of confidentiality which, I have to say, she should not have given, and, indeed, the judge himself makes that very point in his judgment at p 20 of our bundle (the passage which I have read) where he says he intends to communicate with the senior court welfare officer to that effect.

There is also included in our bundle, a letter which the court welfare officer wrote to the court on 13 October 1992 which says this:

'The writer of the private letter, Miss J. Fisher, welfare officer, wishes to resist the application by the petitioner ...'

I think, in fact, that is a mistake, it was the father, but it matters not:

'... for its release to the parties. If the court is minded to grant the application, the welfare officer would wish to withdraw the letter.'

I have to say that the court welfare officer is, there, again under a mistake; she is not necessarily in a position to be able to withdraw the letter. Her evidence, if relevant, is compellable, unless she can properly claim privilege. That matter can only be decided with her present; of course, she is not present before us.

SIR FRANCIS PURCHAS:

In this case, Miss Fisher – for reasons which I understand and with which I sympathise – has apparently purported to grant immunity to certain informants. Such an act lay in the sole power of the court. In doing so, she fell into error and, in this way, placed herself into a position of embarrassment in which she was in danger of finding herself on the horns of a dilemma, namely, of being in breach of an undertaking of confidentiality given to informants or of disobeying an order of the court. This does not relate merely to the letter which has been described by my Lord.

It must be remembered that Miss Fisher was a compellable witness if summoned by the court to give evidence. On being called as a witness, it was open to her to claim privilege from disclosure of the identity of the witnesses and the circumstances of the evidence that they could give. Short of being called as a witness and then claiming privilege, there was no other way in which Miss Fisher could properly seek to protect her sources. She was acting under a serious misapprehension of the law when she said that she would withdraw the letter – it was not open to her to do this. However, upon her claiming privilege, it would then be for the court to decide, on the principles already stated, whether she should be granted the right to withhold the identity of her sources or to withdraw the letter.

General notes:

The essential issue in the case was in what circumstances and to what extent there can be a departure from the fundamental principle that all evidence upon which a judge relies must be disclosed to the parties. The Court cited *Official Solicitor v K* [1965] AC 201, that a departure from the fundamental rule is only to be made in the most exceptional circumstances, and then only where to withhold such information is necessary to prevent injury to the child or children whose welfare is in issue.

Other significant cases on this issue:

* Cf *Re C (Disclosure of information)* [1996] 1 FLR 797: see D69 – CG cannot guarantee confidentiality

A17 RELATIONSHIP BETWEEN COURT AND CFR

Re M (Disclosure: Children and Family Reporter)

[2002] EWCA Civ 1199, [2002] 2 FLR 893 at 914 and 916

Court of Appeal

Wall J

The relationship between the court and the CFR

[83] Whilst we must, of course, learn from and build upon past experience, we cannot, in my judgment import previous concepts into CAFCASS unless they fit comfortably with the new service and are in the interests of the children involved in the proceedings. Thus, in my judgment, the phrase 'officer of the court', whilst mellifluous and reassuringly resonant, is no longer apt to describe the functions of the CFR. They are officers of the service (CAFCASS), with professional duties and responsibilities defined by CJCSA 2000 and FPR 1991 as amended.

[84] This is particularly important, in my judgment, when it comes to considering the relationship between the CFR and the judiciary. Under s 7 of the 1989 Act the judge 'asks' an officer of CAFCASS to report to the court. No doubt the request is contained in an order of the court, and the CFR has a duty under s 12(1)(b) of CJCSA 2000 and FPR 1991, r 4.11 to investigate, to advise and to 'provide the court with such other assistance as it may require'. Other powers and duties are set out in FPR 1991, r 4.11B. But in my judgment, the language used is significant. The court 'asks'. The CFR investigates, advises and assists. The language is to be contrasted with s 37 of the 1989 Act, where the court directs.

[85] The relationship between the judiciary and the CFR should be, accordingly, one of collaboration and mutual co-operation. It is no more for the judge to tell CFRs how to go about their inquiries than it is for the CFR to intrude on the judicial function by making findings of fact.

...

[96] In summary, therefore, my conclusions on this important part of the case are:

(i) CFRs are not 'officers of the court'. They are officers of the Service (CAFCASS) with the duties and responsibilities laid upon them by s 12 of CJCSA 2000, s 7 of the 1989 Act and r 4.11 of the FPR 1991.

(ii) CFRs are not under the control of the judiciary. Within the scope of their employment by CAFCASS, they are independent professionals who, at the request of the court, investigate issues identified by the court as relating to the welfare of the child in question and give the court any advice and assistance it requires. During the course of those investigations, they are free to exercise their professional judgment on those issues, and in particular do not need the court's permission to disclose information to local authority child protection workers.

(iii) The relationship between CFRs and the judiciary should be collaborative and co-operative. In particular, CFRs should not hesitate to seek directions from the judge in relation to issues which arise during the course of the investigation.

(iv) CFRs should advise the court immediately if a child protection issue of sufficient gravity arises such as has required the CFR to notify the local authority. The CFR in such circumstances should seek the court's directions and any decision to terminate or continue the CFR's inquiries is for the court, not the CFR.

This case is also included in relation to:

A18 Inter-relationship with s 47 investigation

A18 INTER-RELATIONSHIP WITH S 47 INVESTIGATION

Re M (Disclosure: Children and Family Reporter)

[2002] EWCA Civ 1199, [2002] 2 FLR 893 at 918

Court of Appeal

Wall J

The inter-relationship between private law family proceedings and a local authority / police investigation under s 47 of the 1989 Act

[105]   I would therefore venture the following suggestions for CAFCASS and local authorities in cases where there are concurrent private law proceedings and s 47 investigations, or where one comes into existence during the lifetime of the other:

(i)   In all cases in which a local authority is invited to take action to protect a child under s 47 of the 1989 Act, that authority should have in place a mechanism for finding out if the child is the subject of existing private law proceedings. Both CAFCASS and the courts should be in a position to respond to an inquiry from a local authority about a particular child.

(ii)   When imparting information to the local authority for the purposes of a prospective s 47 investigation, the CFR will, of course, inform the local authority of the existence of the private law proceedings, and the stage they have reached. If, as a consequence, the local authority wishes to have access to documents on the court file, it will need the permission of the court under FPR 1991, r 4.23.

(iii)   Immediately after making the reference to the local authority, the CFR must inform the judge who commissioned the report about what he or she has done. The CFR should seek the court's directions about the next step. The advice to the judge will depend on the facts of the case and the seriousness of the allegations. In some cases the CFR may advise the judge to seek a report from the local authority under s 7: in other more serious cases a report under s 37 may be suitable. In others the CFR may suggest convening an urgent directions appointment. What is important is that from the earliest point, the judge should be fully seized with what is happening.

(iv)   Whilst the judge cannot dictate to the local authority how the s 47 investigation is conducted, there will undoubtedly be cases where it will be proper for the local authority to agree that any investigation into disputed allegations of abuse should be conducted by the judge.

Where this is a practical option, directions to achieve a speedy hearing should be given by the judge.

(v) Where a s 47 investigation has begun, judges should not hesitate to use their powers under s 7 of the 1989 Act to require the local authority to inform the court as to the state and scope of the s 47 investigation: how long it is likely to last; what is involved; whether or not there will be police involvement and if so what progress is being made in that respect.

This case is also included in relation to:

A17 Relationship between court and CFR

DIVISION B

CHILDREN ACT 1989, PT II

Contents

B35   Religious upbringing / circumcision

Sections 9–12
B36   Applying s 9(2) and 9(5): s 8 order definitions
B37   Residence order to foster parents
B38   PSO not to be used as injunction in breach of s 9(5)
B39   CA 1989, s 10(4): birth parent no longer 'parent' after adoption
B40   CA 1989, s 10(8): application for leave by child
B41   CA 1989, s 10(8): 'the child concerned'
B42   CA 1989, s 10(9): welfare not paramount
B43   CA 1989, s 10(9): applying the statutory criteria
B44   CA 1989, s 10(9): broad assessment / post-adoption contact
B45   CA 1989, s 10(9): process when birth family apply after adoption
B46   CA 1989, s 11(7) conditions (1)
B47   CA 1989, s 11(7) conditions (2)

Change of name
B48   Change of surname (1)
B49   Change of surname (2)
B50   Guidelines
B51   Use of both parents' surnames
B52   Change of first name

Leave to remove from jurisdiction / relocation within UK
B53   Payne v Payne: general principles
B54   Challenge to Payne
B55   Relocation within the UK

Special guardianship
B56   SG or adoption: basic approach
B57   SG or adoption: table of differences
B58   SG: necessary to have local authority report
B59   SG: leave and reporting restrictions
B60   Ancillary orders affecting special guardian's exercise of PR
B61   Application for leave to discharge or vary SGO

ECtHR Art 8: applied to private law

B1 ART 8: GENERAL PRINCIPLES

Hokkanen v Finland

(Case 50/1993/445/524) [1996] 1 FLR 289 at 303

European Court of Human Rights

B. Compliance with Article 8

[55] The essential object of Art 8 is to protect the individual against arbitrary interference by the public authorities. There may in addition be positive obligations inherent in an effective 'respect' for family life. Whilst the boundaries between the State's positive and negative obligations under this provision do not lend themselves to precise definition, the applicable principles are similar. In particular, in both contexts regard must be had to the fair balance that has to be struck between the competing interests of the individual and the community as a whole, and in both contexts the State is recognised as enjoying a certain margin of appreciation (see *Keegan v Ireland* (1994) 18 EHRR 342, 362, § 49).

The Court's role is not to substitute itself for the competent Finnish authorities in regulating custody and access issues in Finland, but rather to review under the Convention the decisions that those authorities have taken in the exercise of their power of appreciation (see, mutatis mutandis, *Handyside v United Kingdom* (1976) 1 EHRR 737, 755, § 50). In so doing, it must determine whether the reasons purporting to justify the actual measures adopted with regard to the applicant's enjoyment of his right to respect for family life are relevant and sufficient under Art 8.

In previous cases dealing with issues relating to the compulsory taking of children into public care and the implementation of care measures, the Court has consistently held that Art 8 includes a right for the parent to have measures taken with a view to his or her being reunited with the child and an obligation for the national authorities to take such action (see, for instance, *Eriksson v Sweden* (1989) 12 EHRR 183, 203–204, § 71; *Andersson v Sweden* (1992) 14 EHRR 615, 648, § 91; and *Olsson v Sweden (No 2)* (1994) 17 EHRR 134, 181–182, § 90). In the opinion of the Court, this principle must be taken as also applying to cases such as the present where the origin of the provisional transfer of care is a private agreement.

[56] The applicant and the Commission reasoned that a positive obligation for the Contracting State to take coercive measures was more called for where a child is in de facto care in defiance of the law and of court orders than after the termination of de jure care. The non-enforcement of the applicant's custody rights, as from 10 May 1990 until the transfer of the custody of Sini on 25 September 1991, as well as the non-enforcement of his visiting rights constituted a lack of 'respect' for his 'family life' in violation of Art 8. Notwithstanding the reasonable steps he had taken to have his parental rights enforced there was a striking lack of effective response. This fact, together with the length of the enforcement proceedings, had created a situation where his reunification with Sini had become difficult.

In addition, as regards the transfer of custody, the applicant contended that the Court of Appeal's judgment of 25 September 1991 conferred legitimacy on the illegal de facto care assumed by the grandparents. Although the grandparents had retained the child unlawfully, the length of time they had kept her was perceived by that court as an important justification for transferring custody. The measure further weakened the protection of his parental rights, notably as regards access to his daughter.

[57] In the Government's submission a distinction should be drawn between, on the one hand, a parent's custody and visiting rights in respect of a child and, on the other hand, the enforcement of such rights. Although there may be plausible reasons for a parent to have custody and access rights, it does not necessarily follow that these should be enforced, especially if it would be incompatible with the interests and welfare of the child. That was the position under Finnish law, which viewed a parent's custody of a child as a right first and foremost in the interest of the well-being and balanced development of the child and not primarily for the benefit of the parent. They referred also to Art 3 of the 1989 United Nations Convention on the Rights of the Child, Art 19(1)(b) of the 1980 European Convention on the Enforcement of Decisions Concerning Custody of Children and on Restoration of Custody of Children (European Treaty Series No 105) and Arts 1 and 12(3) of the 1980 Convention on the Civil Aspects of International Child Abduction (signed at the Hague on 25 October 1980). The Government therefore disagreed with the contention of the applicant and the Commission that forcible measures should be more readily resorted to in the situation facing the applicant. At any rate, it would not have been appropriate to use coercion to implement his parental rights.

Whilst conceding that the applicant had not been able to exercise his access rights in the way specified in the relevant court decisions, the Government emphasised that this was due to the non-compliance by the grandparents with those decisions. The latter being private persons, the State was not directly responsible under international law for their acts or omissions.

In any event, the applicant's own conduct was open to criticism: he had not availed himself of the possibility of visiting Sini in the grandparents' home; he had failed to finalise the enforcement proceedings relating to the District Court's decision on access of 14 November 1990, by not requesting imposition of the fines indicated by the County Administrative Board on 28 March 1991; and for several months he had omitted to renew his request for enforcement of the access rights granted to him by the Court of Appeal on 25 September 1991 (see paras [26] and [34] above).

The Government concluded that, in view of the difficult circumstances of the case, the national authorities had done everything that could reasonably be expected of them to facilitate reunion.

[58]   The Court recalls that the obligation of the national authorities to take measures to facilitate reunion is not absolute, since the reunion of a parent with a child who has lived for some time with other persons may not be able to take place immediately and may require preparatory measures being taken to this effect. The nature and extent of such preparation will depend on the circumstances of each case, but the understanding and co-operation of all concerned will always be an important ingredient. Whilst national authorities must do their utmost to facilitate such co-operation, any obligation to apply coercion in this area must be limited since the interests as well as the rights and freedoms of all concerned must be taken into account, and more particularly the best interests of the child and his or her rights under Art 8 of the Convention. Where contacts with the parent might appear to threaten those interests or interfere with those rights, it is for the national authorities to strike a fair balance between them (see the above-mentioned *Olsson v Sweden (No 2)* judgment, (1994) 17 EHRR 134, 181–182, § 90).

What is decisive is whether the national authorities have taken all necessary steps to facilitate reunion as can reasonably be demanded in the special circumstance of each case (ibid). The Court does not deem it necessary to deal with the applicant's and the Commission's general argument on an obligation under Art 8 to take forcible measures (see para [56] above).

[59]   Turning to the particular facts the Court will deal first with the alleged non-enforcement of the applicant's access rights and then with the alleged non-enforcement of his custody rights and the transfer of custody to the grandparents.

B2   ALL NECESSARY STEPS: COERCIVE MEASURES

Hansen v Turkey

(Case 36141/97) [2004] 1 FLR 142 at 157

European Court of Human Rights

[105]   As to the handling of the enforcement procedures by the Turkish authorities, the court notes that on each scheduled visit the applicant's former husband arranged to be absent with the children when the enforcement officers arrived. However, the authorities did not take any steps to locate the children with a view to facilitating contact with the applicant. In the face of Halil Al's consistent refusal to comply with the access arrangements, the authorities should have taken measures to allow the applicant access, including realistic coercive measures against her former husband of a type which were likely to lead to compliance.

[106]   Although measures against children obliging them to reunite with one or other parent are not desirable in this sensitive area, such action must not be ruled out in the event of non-compliance or unlawful behaviour by the parent with whom the children live (see *Ignaccolo-Zenide v Romania* (2001) 31 EHRR 7, para 106).

[107]   The court does not agree with the Government's submission that the Turkish authorities did everything that could reasonably be expected of them to enforce the applicant's right of access to her children. It finds that the fines imposed on the applicant's former husband were neither effective nor adequate. As to the Government's suggestion that the applicant could have asked the enforcement officers to enter Halil Al's home by force, the court finds that, even if this was so, it does not absolve the authorities from their obligations in the matter of enforcement, since it is they who exercise public authority (see *Ignaccolo-Zenide v Romania* (2001) 31 EHRR 7, para 111).

[108]   Having regard to the foregoing, the court concludes that the Turkish authorities failed to make adequate and effective efforts to enforce the applicant's access rights to her children and thereby violated her right to respect for her family life, as guaranteed by Art 8.

[109]   It follows that there has been a violation of Art 8 of the European Convention.

Other significant cases on this issue:

* *Damnjanovic v Serbia* (Application No 5222/07) [2009] 1 FLR 339

B3   ALL NECESSARY STEPS: OTHER INTERNATIONAL OBLIGATIONS

Maire v Portugal

(Case 48206/99) [2004] 2 FLR 653 at 665

European Court of Human Rights

[72]   Lastly, the court reiterates that the Convention must be applied in accordance with the principles of international law, in particular with those relating to the international protection of human rights (see *Streletz, Kessler and Krenz v Germany* (App Nos 34044/96, 35532/97 and 44801/98) (unreported) 22 March 2001, at para 90, and *Al-Adsani v United Kingdom (No 2)* (2002) 34 EHRR 11, at para 55). The court considers that the positive obligations that Art 8 of the Convention lays on the Contracting States in the matter of reuniting a parent with his or her children must be interpreted in the light of the Hague Convention (see *Ignaccolo-Zenide v Romania*, at para 95) and the United Nations Convention on the Rights of the Child 1989.

B4   RESPECT FOR THE RULE OF LAW

Sylvester v Austria

(Case 36812/97 and 40104/98) [2003] 2 FLR 210 at 221

European Court of Human Rights

[59] In cases concerning the enforcement of decisions in the realm of
family law, the court has repeatedly found that what is decisive is whether
the national authorities have taken all the necessary steps to facilitate
execution as can reasonably be demanded in the special circumstances of
each case (see *Hokkanen v Finland*, at para 58; *Ignaccolo-Zenide v
Romania*, at para 96; *Nuutinen v Finland*, at para 128). In examining
whether non-enforcement of a court order amounted to a lack of respect
for the applicants' family life the court must strike a fair balance between
the interests of all persons concerned and the general interest in ensuring
respect for the rule of law (see *Nuutinen v Finland*, para 129).

Other significant cases on this issue:

* *Hansen v Turkey* (Case 36141/97) [2004] 1 FLR 142 at [99]

This case is also included in relation to:

B5   Passage of time

B5   PASSAGE OF TIME

Sylvester v Austria

(Case 36812/97 and 40104/98) [2003] 2 FLR 210 at 222 and 223

European Court of Human Rights

[60]   In cases of this kind the adequacy of a measure is to be judged by the swiftness of its implementation, as the passage of time can have irremediable consequences for relations between the child and the parent who does not live with him or her. In proceedings under the Hague Convention this is all the more so, as Art 11 of the Hague Convention requires the judicial or administrative authorities concerned to act expeditiously in proceedings for the return of children and any inaction lasting more than 6 weeks may give rise to a request for a statement of reasons for the delay (see *Ignaccolo-Zenide v Romania* (2001) 31 EHRR 7, at para 102).

...

[66]   The fact remains that the decisions of 29 August and 15 October 1996 relied rather heavily on the lapse of time and the ensuing alienation between the first and second applicants. The court will therefore examine whether or not this lapse of time was caused by the authorities' failure to take adequate and effective measures for the enforcement of the return order.

[67]   The court observes that, while the main proceedings relating to the issuing of the return order were conducted with exemplary speed, as the case came before three instances in just 4 months, ending with the Supreme Court's decision of 27 February 1996, there is no explanation for the delay of more than 2 months which occurred before the file was returned from the Supreme Court to the Graz District Court on 7 May 1996. Moreover, such a delay has to be viewed as an important one, given that under Art 11 of the Hague Convention any inaction of more than 6 weeks may give rise to a request for a statement of reasons.

[68]   Admittedly, the district court immediately ordered the enforcement of the return order. But after the first unsuccessful enforcement attempt on 10 May 1996 no further steps towards enforcement were taken despite the first applicant's request of 18 June 1996. The Government argued that no further enforcement attempts could be made as long as the mother's appeal of 15 May 1996 was pending, while the applicants contested this. The court is not required to examine which was the position under domestic law, as it is for each Contracting State to equip itself with adequate and effective means to ensure compliance with its positive obligations under Art 8 of the Convention (see *Ignaccolo-Zenide v Romania* (2001) 31 EHRR 7, at para 108). At the very least, the courts were under a particular duty to give an expeditious decision on the appeal in question. Nevertheless, it took 3½ months for the Graz Regional Civil Court to decide, on 29 August 1996, to quash the enforcement order of 8 May and to refer the case back to the district court.

[69] After the Supreme Court's decision of 15 October 1996, which confirmed the setting aside of the enforcement order, it took the district court more than 5 months to obtain an opinion from the expert in child psychology, although he was already familiar with the case, as he had participated in the main proceedings. Relying on this expert's opinion, the district court found on 29 April 1997 that, given the considerable lapse of time, the removal of the second applicant from her main person of reference, namely her mother, would expose her to serious psychological harm, as her father, the first applicant, had in the meantime become a complete stranger to her. The district court's decision, which was upheld by the Graz Regional Court and, on 9 September 1997, by the Supreme Court, shows that the case was ultimately decided by the time that had elapsed. Without overlooking the difficulties created by the resistance of the second applicant's mother, the court finds, nevertheless, that the lapse of time was to a large extent caused by the authorities' own handling of the case. In this connection, the court reiterates that effective respect for family life requires that future relations between parent and child not be determined by the mere effluxion of time (see *W v United Kingdom* (1988) 10 EHRR 29, at para 65).

[70] Moreover, the court observes that the authorities did not take any measures to create the necessary conditions for executing the return order while the lengthy enforcement proceedings were pending.

[71] The court notes in particular that following the first unsuccessful enforcement attempt of 10 May 1996, the mother of the second applicant apparently changed her whereabouts with the aim of defying the execution of the return order. However, the authorities did not take any steps to locate the second applicant with a view to facilitating contact with the first applicant. On the contrary, it transpires from the correspondence exchanged from May to December 1996 between the Austrian Ministry of Justice and the US Department of State that, in the Austrian authorities' view, it fell to the first applicant's counsel to take all necessary steps to obtain the enforcement of the return order. In this connection, the court points out that it has refuted such a line of argument in *Ignaccolo-Zenide v Romania* (2001) 31 EHRR 7, finding that an applicant's omission cannot absolve the authorities from their obligations in the matter of execution, since it is they who exercise public authority (*Ignaccolo-Zenide v Romania*, at para 111).

[72] Having regard to the foregoing, the court concludes that the Austrian authorities failed to take, without delay, all the measures that could reasonably be expected to enforce the return order, and thereby breached the applicants' right to respect for their family life, as guaranteed by Art 8. Consequently, there has been a violation of Art 8.

Other significant cases on this issue:

- *Hoppe v Germany* (Case 28422/95) [2003] 1 FLR 384 at [54]
- *Hansen v Turkey* (Case 36141/97) [2004] 1 FLR 142 at [100]
- *Jevremovic v Serbia* (Application No 3150/05) [2008] 1 FLR 550 (under Art 6)
- *Adam v Germany* (Application No 44036/02) [2009] 1 FLR 560 at [58]–[66]

This case is also included in relation to:

B4   Respect for the rule of law

B6 BALANCING RIGHTS: THE INTERESTS OF THE CHILD PREVAIL

Yousef v The Netherlands

(Case 33711/96) [2003] 1 FLR 210 at 221

European Court of Human Rights

[73] The court reiterates that in judicial decisions where the rights under Art 8 of parents and those of a child are at stake, the child's rights must be the paramount consideration. If any balancing of interests is necessary, the interests of the child must prevail (see *Elsholz v Germany* (2002) 34 EHRR 58, [2000] 2 FLR 486, para 52 and *TP and KM v United Kingdom* (2002) 34 EHRR 2, [2001] 2 FLR 549, para 72). This applies also in cases such as the present.

[74] The court has not found any indication that the domestic courts in striking the balance they did between the rights of the applicant and those of the child, failed to take the applicant's rights sufficiently into account or decided in an arbitrary manner.

[75] There has therefore not been a violation of Art 8 of the Convention.

Other significant cases on this issue:

- *Maire v Portugal* (Case 48206/99) [2004] 2 FLR 653 at [77]

B7 MARGIN OF APPRECIATION WIDER FOR CUSTODY THAN ACCESS

Süss v Germany

(Application number 40324/98) [2006] 1 FLR 522 at 536

European Court of Human Rights

[87] The margin of appreciation to be accorded to the competent national authorities will vary in accordance with the nature of the issues and the importance of the interests at stake. Thus, the court has recognised that the authorities enjoy a wide margin of appreciation, in particular when deciding on custody. However, a stricter scrutiny is called for as regards any further limitations, such as restrictions placed by those authorities on parental rights of access, and as regards any legal safeguards designed to secure an effective protection of the right of parents and children to respect for their family life. Such further limitations entail the danger that the family relations between a young child and one or both parents would be effectively curtailed (see *Elsholz*, cited above, para [49]; *Sommerfeld*, cited above, para [63]; *Görgülü v Germany*, [2004] ECHR 89, [2004] 1 FLR 894, para [42]).

B8   ART 8: PRIVATE LAW SUMMARY (1)

Tavli v Turkey

(Application number 11449/02) [2007] 1 FLR 1136 at 1141

European Court of Human Rights

2.   *General principles*

[28]   The court reiterates that the essential object of Art 8 is to protect the individual against arbitrary action by public authorities. There may in addition be positive obligations inherent in ensuring effective 'respect' for private or family life. These obligations may involve the adoption of measures designed to secure respect for private life even in the sphere of the relations of individuals between themselves (see *Mikulic v Croatia* (Application No 53176/99) [2002] 1 FCR 720, at para 57).

[29]   However, the boundaries between the State's positive and negative obligations under this provision do not lend themselves to precise definition. The applicable principles are nonetheless similar. In both contexts regard must be had to the fair balance that has to be struck between the competing interests of the individual and of the community as a whole; and in both contexts the State enjoys a certain margin of appreciation (see *Keegan v Ireland* (1994) 18 EHRR 342, at para 49) and *Kroon and Others v The Netherlands* (1995) 19 EHRR 263, at para 31).

[30]   The court reiterates that its task is not to substitute itself for the competent domestic authorities in regulating paternity disputes at the national level, but rather to review under the Convention the decisions that those authorities have taken in the exercise of their power of appreciation (see *Mikulić*, cited above, at para 59, and *Hokkanen v Finland* (1995) 19 EHRR 139, [1996] 1 FLR 289, at para [55]). The court will, therefore, examine whether the Respondent State, in handling the applicant's paternity action, has complied with its positive obligations under Art 8 of the Convention.

B9   ART 8: PRIVATE LAW SUMMARY (2)

Bajrami v Albania

(Application number 35853/04) [2007] 1 FLR 1629 at 1636

European Court of Human Rights

2.   *The court's assessment*

(A)   GENERAL PRINCIPLES

[50]   The court reiterates that the essential object of Art 8 of the European Convention is to protect the individual against arbitrary action by public authorities. There are in addition positive obligations inherent in effective 'respect' for family life. In both contexts regard must be had to the fair balance that has to be struck between the competing interests of the individual and of the community as a whole; and in both contexts the state enjoys a certain margin of appreciation (see *Keegan v Ireland* (1994) 18 EHRR 342, at para 49; *Ignaccolo-Zenide v Romania* (2001) 31 EHRR 7, at para 94; *Iglesias Gil and AUI v Spain* [2005] 1 FLR 190, at para [49]; and *Sylvester v Austria* (2003) 37 EHRR 17, [2003] 2 FLR 210, at para [51]).

[51]   In relation to the state's obligation to take positive measures, the court has repeatedly held that Art 8 of the European Convention includes a parent's right to the taking of measures with a view to his being reunited with his child and an obligation on the national authorities to facilitate such reunion (see, among other authorities, *Ignaccolo-Zenide*, cited above, at para 94; *Iglesias Gil and AUI*, cited above, at para [48]; and *Nuutinen v Finland* (2002) 34 EHRR 15, at para 127).

[52]   In cases concerning the enforcement of decisions in the sphere of family law, the court has repeatedly held that what is decisive is whether the national authorities have taken all necessary steps to facilitate the execution as can reasonably be demanded in the special circumstances of each case (see *Hokkanen v Finland* (1995) 19 EHRR 139, [1996] 1 FLR 289, at para [58]; *Ignaccolo-Zenide*, cited above, at para 96; *Nuutinen*, cited above, at para 128; and *Sylvester*, cited above, at para [59]).

[53]   In cases of this kind the adequacy of a measure is to be judged by the swiftness of its implementation, as the passage of time can have irremediable consequences for relations between the child and the parent who does not live with him or her. The court notes that Art 11 of the Hague Convention on the Civil Aspects of International Child Abduction 1980 (to which Albania is not a state party) requires the judicial or

administrative authorities concerned to act expeditiously in proceedings for the return of children and any inaction lasting more than 6 weeks may give rise to a request for a statement of reasons for the delay (see *Ignaccolo-Zenide*, cited above, at para 102).

[54]   The court has also held that although coercive measures against children are not desirable in this sensitive area, the use of sanctions must not be ruled out in the event of unlawful behaviour by the parent with whom the children live (see *Ignaccolo-Zenide*, cited above, at para 106).

[55]   The court reiterates that the European Convention must be applied in accordance with the principles of international law, in particular with those relating to the international protection of human rights (see *Streletz, Kessler and Krenz v Germany* (Application Nos 34044/96, 35532/97 and 44801/98) (unreported) 22 March 2001, at para 90, and *Al-Adsani v United Kingdom* (2001) 34 EHRR 273, at para 55). Consequently, the court considers that the positive obligations that Art 8 of the European Convention lays on the Contracting States in the matter of reuniting a parent with his or her children must be interpreted in the light of the Hague Convention on the Civil Aspects of International Child Abduction 1980 (see *Ignaccolo-Zenide*, cited above, at para 95).

Other significant cases on this issue:

*   *Kaleta v Poland* (Application No 11375/02) [2009] 1 FLR 927

Contact / making contact work / residence

B10 CONTACT: FUNDAMENTAL PRINCIPLES

Re O (Contact: imposition of conditions)

[1995] 2 FLR 124 at 128

Court of Appeal

Bingham MR

It may perhaps be worth stating in a reasonably compendious way some very familiar but none the less fundamental principles. First of all, and overriding all else as provided in s 1(1) of the 1989 Act, the welfare of the child is the paramount consideration of any court concerned to make an order relating to the upbringing of a child. It cannot be emphasised too strongly that the court is concerned with the interests of the mother and the father only insofar as they bear on the welfare of the child.

Secondly, where parents of a child are separated and the child is in the day-to-day care of one of them, it is almost always in the interests of the child that he or she should have contact with the other parent. The reason for this scarcely needs spelling out. It is, of course, that the separation of parents involves a loss to the child, and it is desirable that that loss should so far as possible be made good by contact with the non-custodial parent, that is the parent in whose day-to-day care the child is not. This has been said on a very great number of occasions and I cite only two of them. In *Re H (Minors) (Access)* [1992] 1 FLR 148 at p 151A, Balcombe LJ quoted, endorsing as fully as he could, an earlier passage in a judgment of Latey J in which that judge had said:

> '... where the parents have separated and one has the care of the child, access by the other often results in some upset in the child. Those upsets are usually minor and superficial. They are heavily outweighed by the long-term advantages to the child of keeping in touch with the parent concerned so that they do not become strangers, so that the child later in life does not resent the deprivation and turn against the parent who the child thinks, rightly or wrongly, has deprived him, and so that the deprived parent loses interest in

the child and therefore does not make the material and emotional contribution to the child's development which that parent by its companionship and otherwise would make.'

My second citation is from *Re J (A Minor) (Contact)* [1994] 1 FLR 729 at p 736B–C, where Balcombe LJ said:

'But before concluding this judgment I would like to make three general points. The first is that judges should be very reluctant to allow the implacable hostility of one parent (usually the parent who has a residence order in his or her favour), to deter them from making a contact order where they believe the child's welfare requires it. The danger of allowing the implacable hostility of the residential parent (usually the mother) to frustrate the court's decision is too obvious to require repetition on my part.'

Thirdly, the court has power to enforce orders for contact, which it should not hesitate to exercise where it judges that it will overall promote the welfare of the child to do so. I refer in this context to the judgment of the President of the Family Division in *Re W (A Minor) (Contact)* [1994] 2 FLR 441 at p 447H, where the President said:

'However, I am quite clear that a court cannot allow a mother, in such circumstances, simply to defy the order of the court which was, and is, in force, that is to say that there should be reasonable contact with the father. That was indeed made by consent as I have already observed. Some constructive step must be taken to permit and encourage the boy to resume contact with his father.'

At p 449A the President added:

'I wish to make it very clear to the mother that this is an order of the court. The court cannot be put in a position where it is told, "I shall not obey an order of the court".'

Fourthly, cases do, unhappily and infrequently but occasionally, arise in which a court is compelled to conclude that in existing circumstances an order for immediate direct contact should not be ordered, because so to order would injure the welfare of the child. In *Re D (A Minor) (Contact: Mother's Hostility)* [1993] 2 FLR 1 at p 7G, Waite LJ said:

'It is now well settled that the implacable hostility of a mother towards access or contact is a factor which is capable, according to the circumstances of each particular case, of supplying a cogent reason for departing from the general principle that a child should grow up in the knowledge of both his parents. I see no reason to think that the judge fell into any error of principle in deciding, as he clearly did on the plain interpretation of his judgment, that the mother's present attitude towards contact puts D at serious risk of major emotional harm if she were to be compelled to accept a degree of contact to the natural father against her will.'

I simply draw attention to the judge's reference to a serious risk of major emotional harm. The courts should not at all readily accept that the child's welfare will be injured by direct contact. Judging that question the court should take a medium-term and long-term view of the child's development and not accord excessive weight to what appear likely to be short-term or transient problems. Neither parent should be encouraged or permitted to think that the more intransigent, the more unreasonable, the more obdurate and the more unco-operative they are, the more likely they are to get their own way. Courts should remember that in these cases they are dealing with parents who are adults, who must be treated as rational adults, who must be assumed to have the welfare of the child at heart, and who have once been close enough to each other to have produced the child. It would be as well if parents also were to bear these points in mind.

Fifthly, in cases in which, for whatever reason, direct contact cannot for the time being be ordered, it is ordinarily highly desirable that there should be indirect contact so that the child grows up knowing of the love and interest of the absent parent with whom, in due course, direct contact should be established. This calls for a measure of restraint, common sense and unselfishness on the part of both parents. If the absent parent deluges the child with presents or writes long and obsessive screeds to the child, or if he or she uses his or her right to correspond to criticise or insult the other parent, then inevitably those rights will be curtailed. The object of indirect contact is to build up a relationship between the absent parent and the child, not to enable the absent parent to pursue a feud with the caring parent in a manner not conducive to the welfare of the child.

The caring parent also has reciprocal obligations. If the caring parent puts difficulties in the way of indirect contact by withholding presents or letters or failing to read letters to a child who cannot read, then such parent must understand that the court can compel compliance with its orders; it has sanctions available and no residence order is to be regarded as irrevocable. It is entirely reasonable that the parent with the care of the child should be obliged to report on the progress of the child to the absent parent, for the obvious reason that an absent parent cannot correspond in a meaningful way if unaware of the child's concerns, or of where the child goes to school, or what it does when it gets there, or what games it plays, and so on. Of course judges must not impose duties which parents cannot realistically be expected to perform, and it would accordingly be absurd to expect, in a case where this was the case, a semi-literate parent to write monthly reports. But some means of communication, directly or indirectly, is essential if indirect contact is to be meaningful, and if the welfare of the child is not to suffer.

B11　ECHR PRINCIPLES APPLIED TO CONTACT DISPUTES

Re D (Intractable contact dispute: publicity)

[2004] EWHC 727 Fam, [2004] 1 FLR 1226 at 1236

Family Division

Munby J

[25] It is convenient at this point to remind ourselves what the European Court of Human Rights at Strasbourg has to say on these topics. I list in chronological sequence what are for present purposes the most important decisions: *Hokkanen v Finland* (1995) 19 EHRR 139; [1996] 1 FLR 289; *Ignaccolo-Zenide v Romania* (2001) 31 EHRR 7; *Nuutinen v Finland* (2000) 34 EHRR 358; *Glaser v United Kingdom* (2001) 33 EHRR 1, [2001] 1 FLR 153; *Hoppe v Germany* [2003] 1 FLR 384; *Sylvester v Austria* (2003) 37 EHRR 417, [2003] 2 FLR 210; *Hansen v Turkey* [2004] 1 FLR 142 and *Kosmopoulou v Greece* [2004] 1 FLR 800.

[26] This is not the place for any detailed exposition of the Strasbourg case-law. It suffices for present purposes if I merely extract a few of the most important points that emerge from the authorities. The first is the principle, long recognised, that, as it was put in *Kosmopoulou v Greece* [2004] 1 FLR 800 at para [47]:

'... the mutual enjoyment by parent and child of each other's company constitutes a fundamental element of family life, even if the relationship between the parents has broken down, and domestic measures hindering such enjoyment amount to an interference with the right protected by Art 8 of the Convention.'

Article 8 (of the European Convention for the Protection of Human Rights and Fundamental Freedoms 1950 (the European Convention)), of course, protects not merely the father's right to contact with his daughter but also her right to contact with her father.

[27] The second is the principle, also long recognised and most recently stated in *Hoppe v Germany* [2003] 1 FLR 384 at para [54], that:

'... in cases concerning a person's relationship with his or her child, there is a duty to exercise exceptional diligence in view of the risk that the passage of time may result in a de facto determination of the matter.'

As the court said in *Glaser v United Kingdom* (2001) 33 EHRR 1, [2001] 1 FLR 153 at para 93:

'It is ... essential that custody and contact cases be dealt with speedily.'

And as the court said in *Sylvester v Austria* (2003) 37 EHRR 417, [2003] 2 FLR 210 at para 69:

'... the court reiterates that effective respect for family life requires that future relations between parent and child not be determined by the mere effluxion of time.'

[28] The third is the principle that in private law cases, just as much as in public law cases, Art 8 includes what was described in *Hokkanen v Finland* [1996] 1 FLR 289 at para [55] as:

'... a right for the parent to have measures taken with a view to his or her being reunited with the child and an obligation for the national authorities to take such action.'

The court has repeatedly stressed that, as part of their 'obligation ... to take measures to facilitate contact by a non-custodial parent', national authorities 'must do their utmost to facilitate' co-operation between the parents: see *Hokkanen v Finland* at para 58, *Ignaccolo-Zenide v Romania* (2001) 31 EHRR 7 at para 94, *Nuutinen v Finland* (2000) 34 EHRR 358 at para 128, *Glaser v United Kingdom* (2001) 33 EHRR 1, [2001] 1 FLR 153 at para 66, *Hansen v Turkey* [2004] 1 FLR 142 at para [98] and *Kosmopoulou v Greece* [2004] 1 FLR 800 at para [45].

[29] The fourth is the general principle enunciated in *Hornsby v Greece* (1997) 24 EHRR 250, [1998] ELR 365 at para 40 and reiterated in *Immobiliare Saffi v Italy* (1999) 30 EHRR 756 at paras 63 and 66:

'... the right to a court would be illusory if a Contracting State's domestic legal system allowed a final, binding judicial decision to remain inoperative to the detriment of one party. It would be inconceivable that Art 6(1) should describe in detail procedural guarantees afforded to litigants – proceedings that are fair, public and expeditious – without protecting the implementation of judicial decisions; to construe Art 6 as being concerned exclusively with access to a court and the conduct of proceedings would be likely to lead to situations incompatible with the principle of the rule of law which the Contracting States undertook to respect when they ratified the Convention. Execution of a judgment given by any court must, therefore, be regarded as an integral part of the "trial" for the purposes of Art 6.'

...

... the right to a court as guaranteed by Art 6 also protects   the implementation of final, binding judicial decisions, which, in States that accept the rule of law, cannot remain inoperative to the detriment of one party. Accordingly, the execution of a judicial decision cannot be unduly delayed.'

[30] These positive obligations extend in principle to the taking of coercive measures not merely against the recalcitrant parent but even against the children. As the court said in *Ignaccolo-Zenide v Romania* (2001) 31 EHRR 7 at para 106:

'Although coercive measures towards children are far from desirable in such sensitive matters, sanctions should not be ruled out where the parent living with the children acts unlawfully.'

The court reiterated this in *Hansen v Turkey* [2004] 1 FLR 142 at para [106]:

'Although measures against children obliging them to reunite with one or other parent are not desirable in this sensitive area, such action must not be ruled out in the event of non-compliance or unlawful behaviour by the parent with whom the children live.'

[31] But the court has also consistently recognised that, as it was put in *Ignaccolo-Zenide v Romania* at para 94:

'... any obligation to apply coercion can only be limited since the interests, rights and freedoms of all concerned must be taken into account, and more particularly the best interests of the child and [his or her] rights under Art 8 of the Convention.'

This was elaborated in *Kosmopoulou v Greece* [2004] 1 FLR 800 at para [45]:

'the national authorities' obligation to take measures to facilitate reunion is not absolute, since the reunion of a parent with children who have lived for some time with the other parent may not be able to take place immediately and may require preparatory measures to be taken. The nature and extent of such preparation will depend on the circumstances of each case, but the understanding and co-operation of all concerned is always an important ingredient. Whilst national authorities must do their utmost to facilitate such co-operation, any obligation to apply coercion in this area must be limited since the interests as well as the rights and freedoms of all concerned must be taken into account, and more particularly the best interests of the child and his or her rights under Art 8 of the

Convention. Where contact with the parent might appear to threaten those interests or interfere with those rights, it is for the national authorities to strike a fair balance between them.'

[32] The test was set out in *Sylvester v Austria* (2003) 37 EHRR 417, [2003] 2 FLR 210 at paras 59–60:

'In cases concerning the enforcement of decisions in the realm of family law, the court has repeatedly found that what is decisive is whether the national authorities have taken all the necessary steps to facilitate execution as can reasonably be demanded in the special circumstances of each case. In examining whether non-enforcement of a court order amounted to a lack of respect for the applicants' family life the court must strike a fair balance between the interests of all persons concerned and the general interest in ensuring respect for the rule of law.

In cases of this kind the adequacy of a measure is to be judged by the swiftness of its implementation, as the passage of time can have irremediable consequences for relations between the child and the parent who does not live with him or her.'

This was repeated in *Kosmopoulou v Greece* at para [47]:

'In examining whether the non-enforcement of the access arrangements amounted to a lack of respect for the applicant's family life, the court must strike a balance between the various interests involved, namely the interests of the applicant's daughter, those of the applicant herself and the general interest in ensuring respect for the rule of law.'

It reflects what the court had earlier said in *Glaser v United Kingdom* (2001) 33 EHRR 1, [2001] 1 FLR 153 at para 66:

'The key consideration is whether [the national] authorities have taken all necessary steps to facilitate contact as can reasonably be demanded in the special circumstances of each case. Other important factors in proceedings concerning children are that time takes on a particular significance as there is always a danger that any procedural delay will result in the de facto determination of the issue before the court, and that the decision-making procedure provides requisite protection of parental interests.'

[33] Furthermore, the national authorities cannot shelter behind an applicant's lack of action: see *Ignaccolo-Zenide v Romania* (2001) 31 EHRR 7 at para 111. For, as the court put it in *Sylvester v Austria* (2003) 37 EHRR 417, [2003] 2 FLR 210 at para 71:

'... an applicant's omission cannot absolve the authorities from their obligations in the matter of execution, since it is they who exercise public authority.'

[34] This last point requires some elaboration. It is to be noted (as observed by Professor Gillian Douglas in her comment on the case in [2003] Fam Law 639) that, as defined by the court in *Sylvester v Austria*, the obligation on the State to enforce its own court orders is more onerous that had previously been suggested in *Glaser v United Kingdom* (2001) 33 EHRR 1, [2001] 1 FLR 153 at para [70]. Professor Douglas correctly pointed out that *Ignaccolo-Zenide v Romania* and *Sylvester v Austria* were both cases in which the delays complained about arose in the context of proceedings under the Hague Convention on the Civil Aspects of International Child Abduction 1980. She speculated as to whether the court had thus been 'influenced by the summary nature of abduction proceedings' or whether the court's approach was in fact 'a general one regarding delays in family matters, rather than one focused exclusively on the special nature of abduction cases'. She went on to suggest that if the latter view turned out to be correct then there might be significant implications for our domestic practice. In fact the matter has since been resolved by the court which, in *Hansen v Turkey* [2004] 1 FLR 142 at para [107], reiterated in a non-Hague Convention case the approach it had earlier adopted in both *Ignaccolo-Zenide v Romania* and *Sylvester v Austria*.

This case is also included in relation to:

B16 Nip it in the bud
B15 Grasp the nettle: making findings of fact
B18 Creative use of experts

B12 GENERAL POINTS (1)

Re O (Contact: withdrawal of application)

[2003] EWHC 3031 Fam, [2004] 1 FLR 1258 at 1261

Family Division

Wall J

[6] The particular points which this case illustrates are, in my judgment, the following:

The intractable nature of some contact disputes and the strength of the feelings they engender

(1) Disputes between separated parents over contact to their children are amongst the most difficult and sensitive cases which judges and magistrates have to hear. Nobody should pretend that they are easy, or that there is any one-size-fits-all solution.

(2) Profound emotions are often aroused in contact proceedings. The children concerned become the battleground on which are fought out the wrongs which the parents perceive each did to the other during the period they lived together. In the instant case, the father accuses the mother of child abuse, perverting the course of justice, defamation of character and perjury. A measure of O's distress at what was happening was his statement to the independent social worker appointed in the county court: 'It is like a war. You know they are fighting and they are fighting over me'.

The critical role of both parents in the lives of their children post separation

(3) The courts recognise the critical importance of the role of both parents in the lives of their children. The courts are not anti-father and pro-mother or vice versa. The court's task, imposed by Parliament in s 1 of the Children Act 1989, in every case is to treat the welfare of the child or children concerned as paramount, and to safeguard and promote the welfare of every child to the best of its ability.

Terminating non-resident parents' contact with their children is a matter of last resort

(4)   Unless there are cogent reasons against it, the children of separated parents are entitled to know and have the love and society of both their parents. In particular, the courts recognise the vital importance of the role of non-resident fathers in the lives of their children, and only make orders terminating contact when there is no alternative.

Parental alienation

(5)   The father asserts that this is a case in which the mother has deliberately alienated O from him. It is not. The principal reason that O is hostile to contact with his father is because of his father's behaviour, and not because his mother has influenced O against his father. Unfortunately, the father is quite unable to understand or accept this. The father's reliance in this case on the so-called 'parental alienation syndrome' is misplaced.

Blaming the system

(6)   The court system for dealing with contact disputes has serious faults, which were identified and addressed in Chapter 10 of the report of the Children Act Sub-Committee (CASC) of the Lord Chancellor's Advisory Board entitled *Making Contact Work*. I discuss these faults further in paras [83]–[86] below. In particular, the court process is stressful for both parents and children; it is expensive for those who are not publicly funded; it is slow and adversarial. It tends to entrench parental attitudes rather than encouraging them to change. It is ill-adapted to dealing with the difficult human dilemmas involved, notably when it comes to the enforcement of its orders.

Parental responsibility for the failure of contact

(7)   Parents must, however, take their share of responsibility for the state of affairs they have created. Blaming the system, as the father does in this case, is no answer. He must shoulder his share of the responsibility for the state of affairs he has helped to bring about. All the evidence is that he has proved incapable of doing so.

Joint residence orders

(8)   The suggestion, made by the father, that joint residence orders should be standard is not, in my judgment, an answer. There may well be more cases than we have up to now recognised in which joint

residence orders are appropriate. The philosophy behind such orders (the exercise of ongoing parental responsibility by both parents post separation) is contained within the Children Act 1989 and is sound. But joint residence orders are not a panacea, and such an order would be quite inappropriate in this case.

Alternative methods of resolving contact disputes

(9)   Fortunately, most separating parents are able to negotiate contact without the need to go to court. Contact disputes are best resolved outside the court system. *Making Contact Work* identified a number of ways in which this could be achieved.

(10)   Contact in my experience works best when parents respect each other and are able to co-operate; where the children's loyalties are not torn, and where they can move between their parents without tension, unhappiness or fear of offending one parent or the other. Such cases rarely come to court. The courts, therefore, have to deal with the cases in which there is no agreement. These are often, like the present case, the most intractable.

(11)   This is, accordingly, once of those rare cases in which an order for direct contact would be both ineffective and counter-productive. I reach that conclusion with regret. I am, however, reassured by the opinion of the child psychiatrist, Dr B, that in late adolescence or early adulthood O is likely to revisit his decision not to have contact with his father. I hope the father also takes heed of Dr B's message that if he maintains his hostile attitude to O's mother, O is likely to remain alienated from him.

Other significant cases on this issue:

•   Wall LJ reiterated these points in *Re Bradford, Re O'Connell* [2006] EWCA Civ 1199, [2007] 1 FLR 530 at [96]: see I11 – No gender bias in the family justice system

This case is also included in relation to:

I10   Parental alienation exists but it is not a syndrome

B13 GENERAL POINTS (2)

A v A (Shared residence)

[2004] EWHC 142 Fam, [2004] 1 FLR 1195 at 1201

Family Division

Wall J

The points which this case illustrates

[24] This case highlights nine particular points, which I identify below:

(1) First and foremost, yet again, it demonstrates the difficulty and complexity of cases of this nature. The dispute between these children's parents has lasted from the date of their separation in October 1997, and was amongst the most bitter and protracted of my experience. C was 3 when her parents separated. Thus throughout her short life she had never consciously experienced a time when her parents lived together in harmony.

(2) It demonstrates the distress and the damage caused to children by longstanding and continuous hostility between their parents. The pressure on B and C has been enormous. B at one point told NYAS that he could not bear it any longer. It is, of course, too early to tell if the damage caused to these two children will spill over into their adolescent and adult lives. I hope, of course, that it will not. However, there is nothing more that the court can do, and I am satisfied that the litigation must come to an end with the making of the shared residence order.

(3) It demonstrates the manner in which parents can impose their own wishes and feelings onto children and thus frustrate the formation or maintenance of a proper and loving relationship between the children and the other parent. C had been persuaded by her mother that she did not love her father and did not want to see him, when the opposite was the truth. Fortunately, the work done by NYAS, in conjunction with firm court orders, has restored the relationship between C and her father, and she now lives with him for half of her time.

(4) It demonstrates the value and importance of the children having their own separate representation in certain cases. The children in this case were separately represented in the proceedings by NYAS. The work done by NYAS was invaluable, first in restoring contact between C and her father and then in achieving a shared-care arrangement. It was a paradigm of what can be achieved by skilled

and energetic social work intervention by the children's guardian. It was also, it has to be said, exceptional in the amount of time and effort Mrs P put into the case.

(5) It demonstrates what the court can and what the court cannot achieve. On the positive side, the court was able to engage NYAS, also by conducting a formal hearing and making clear and specific findings of fact, I was able to decide categorically that allegations made by Mrs A that Mr A had been guilty of sexually inappropriate behaviour with C were untrue. On the negative side, neither NYAS nor I was able to improve the relationship between the parents or convince them of the damage which the unrelenting power struggle between them was causing to their children.

(6) It demonstrates the highly damaging and destructive nature of false allegations of sexual misconduct and abuse, and the caution which is required when such allegations are made for the first time in the middle of a bitterly contested family dispute. In this case, the allegation did not come spontaneously from C: it came from C's mother reporting something C had allegedly described. I was quite satisfied that nothing untoward had occurred between C and her father, but that because of the intensity of her feelings towards her former husband, Mrs A had distorted and misinterpreted entirely innocent activities between Mr A and C.

(7) This is a case where a shared residence order is appropriate. But it also demonstrates clearly that shared residence orders are not a panacea. Shared residence and an equal division of the children's time between their parents' houses is possible in this case because the parents live close to each other, and the children can go to school from either home. The children welcome it because, in B's words, which I have already quoted, it gives his parents nothing left to fight about. But it is a pragmatic solution which does nothing to address the underlying hostility between the parents. Whether or not is succeeds; only time will tell.

(8) The case demonstrates that intractable contact and residence disputes cut across all class barriers. In this case, the father of the children is a hospital consultant, the mother is a teacher. In their different ways, and away from each other, both are individually charming and attractive people. Their hostility towards each other, however, was tangible and frequently led to quite irrational behaviour. The Children Act Sub-Committee of the Lord Chancellor's Advisory Board on Family Law commented in its consultation on contact disputes that it was frequently the case that the more intelligent the parents, the more intransigent and bitter the dispute. This case is an example of that. Contact and residence disputes are no respecters of class barriers.

(9) Finally, the case demonstrates the benefits of judicial continuity. From the time the case unexpectedly came onto my list on 20 November 2002 to its final resolution on 16 December 2003, I heard every application in it. My familiarity with the facts and

with the parties meant that applications could be made to me at
short notice and I could make decisions swiftly. When a crisis
occurred shortly before Christmas 2002, I was able to arrange a
hearing swiftly to deal with it. It was not necessary for colleagues to
read their way into a case to which they would be coming for the
first time.

This case is also included in relation to:

B24   Shared residence

B14 HOSTILITY TO CONTACT

Re P (Contact: discretion)

[1998] 2 FLR 696 at 703 and 704

Family Division

Wilson J

... It seems to me that a mother's hostility towards contact can arise in three different situations. The first is where there are no rational grounds for it. In such a case the court will be extremely slow to decline to order contact and will do so only if satisfied that an order in the teeth of the mother's hostility would create a serious risk of emotional harm for the child. The second is where the mother advances grounds for her hostility which the court regards as sufficiently potent to displace the presumption that contact is in the child's interests. In that case the mother's hostility as such becomes largely irrelevant: what are relevant are its underlying grounds, which the court adopts. The third is where the mother advances sound arguments for the displacement of the presumption but where there are also sound arguments which run the other way. In such a situation, so it seems to me, the mother's hostility to contact can of itself be of importance, occasionally of determinative importance, provided, as always, that what is measured is its effect upon the child.

...

But to those rival sets of arguments one adds the mother's fierce embrace of the latter set, overlaid inevitably with her own sensations of anger, shame and hurt. The child-centred analysis of her attitude must then address the further problems inflicted by a direct contact order upon the children in requiring them to adopt a routine with which their principal carer so deeply disagrees, including the grave practical problems of achieving their travel to and attendance at prison in reasonably harmonious circumstances. Assuming, as I do, that this was a case which fell within the third rather than the second category, I consider that the magistrate was fully entitled to adopt the view of the welfare officer that the mother's attitude was of the greatest importance.

Other significant cases on this issue:

• *Re D (Contact: reasons for refusal)* [1997] 2 FLR 48 at 53

B15　GRASP THE NETTLE: MAKE FINDINGS OF FACT

Re D (Intractable contact dispute: publicity)

[2004] EWHC 727 Fam, [2004] 1 FLR 1226 at 1245

Family Division

Munby J

[54] False allegations of misconduct are highly damaging and destructive. I agree with Wall J when he said in *Re M*[1] at para [12]:

> 'In an intractable contact dispute, where the residential parent is putting forward an allegedly factual basis for contact not taking place, there is no substitute ... for findings by the court as to whether or not there is any substance to the allegations.'

The court should grasp the nettle. Such allegations should be speedily investigated and resolved, not left to fester unresolved and a continuing source of friction and dispute. Court time must be found – and found without delay – for fact finding hearings. Judges must resist the temptation to delay the evil day in the hope that perhaps the problem will go away. Judges must also resist the temptation to put contact 'on hold', or to direct that it is to be supervised, pending investigation of the allegations. And allegations which could have been made at an earlier stage should be viewed with appropriate scepticism. Once findings have been made, everybody must thereafter approach the case on the basis of the facts as judicially found. As Wall J said in *Re M* at para [128], 'these are not questions which can be reopened'. He went on to point out that if a parent persists in assertions contrary to such judicial findings, that is plain evidence of a refusal to recognise reality and what is in the interests of the children.

Other significant cases on this issue:

See generally within the domestic violence subdivision (B25–B29) and the fact-finding (split) hearings subdivision (G32–G43).

---

[1]　*Re M (Intractable Contact Dispute: Interim Care Order)* [2003] EWHC 1024 (Fam), [2003] 2 FLR 636 at [12].

This case is also included in relation to:

B16　Nip it in the bud
B18　Creative use of experts

B16　NIP IT IN THE BUD

Re D (Intractable contact dispute: publicity)

[2004] EWHC 727 Fam, [2004] 1 FLR 1226 at 1245

Family Division

Munby J

[56]　Too often at present, once things start going wrong, it takes too long – too often far too long – to get in front of a judge who is in a position to take potentially decisive action. Judicial case management where the case is allocated to a single judge affords real opportunities to combat this problem, particularly if the parties are able to communicate with the judge, and the judge with the parties, by fax or email. Other things being equal, swift, efficient, enforcement of existing court orders is surely called for at the first sign of trouble. A flabby judicial response sends a very damaging message to the defaulting parent, who is encouraged to believe that court orders can be ignored with impunity, and potentially also to the child. Thus, it may in some cases be appropriate for a judge who has concerns as to whether the contact ordered for Saturday will take place to include in the order a direction requiring the father's solicitor to inform the judge on Monday morning by fax or email if there have been any problems, on the basis (also spelt out in the order so that the mother can be under no illusions as to what will happen if she defaults) that the mother will thereupon be ordered to attend court personally on Tuesday morning and immediately arrested if she fails to attend. The problem can then perhaps be nipped in the bud. There is no reason why in a case of serious recalcitrance or defiance where it is possible to establish a breach of the order the court should not, then and there, make an immediate suspended committal order, so that the mother can be told in very plain terms that if she again prevents contact taking place the following Saturday she is likely to find herself in prison the following week.

This case is also included in relation to:

B15　Grasp the nettle: make findings of fact
B18　Creative use of experts

B17   COURT MUST BE RELUCTANT TO GIVE UP

Re S (Contact: promoting relationship with absent parent)

[2004] EWCA Civ 18, [2004] 1 FLR 1279 at 1288

Court of Appeal

Butler-Sloss P

[32]   No parent is perfect but 'good-enough parents' should have a relationship with their children for their own benefit and even more in the best interests of the children. It is, therefore, most important that the attempt to promote contact between a child and the non-resident parent should not be abandoned until it is clear that the child will not benefit from continuing the attempt.

General notes:

This approach is consistent with the ECtHR jurisprudence: see eg B1–B4.

Other significant cases on this issue:

*   *Re S (Unco-operative mother)* [2004] EWCA Civ 597, [2004] 2 FLR 710
*   *Re M (Contact: long-term best interests)* [2005] EWCA Civ 1090, [2006] 1 FLR 627
*   *Re C (Contact order: variation)* [2008] EWCA Civ 1389, [2009] 1 FLR 869 (s 91(14) order overturned and case remitted for rehearing)

B18   CREATIVE USE OF EXPERTS

Re D (Intractable contact dispute: publicity)

[2004] EWHC 727 Fam, [2004] 1 FLR 1226 at 1244

Family Division

Munby J

[53] We need to get away from the idea that experts are there simply to provide the court with reports. Directing reports can all too often turn into a source of further delay. 'Is your expert really necessary?' is a slogan that has its uses. In this kind of case experts and other outside agencies can often be much more use helping to facilitate contact rather than writing reports – preparing the mother and child for contact, actually being there at hand on a Saturday morning to make sure that hand-over takes place, or even acting as the go-between if the mother cannot bring herself to meet the father and there is no independent friend or relative who can help.

Other significant cases on this issue:

* *Re H (National Youth Advocacy Service)* [2006] EWCA Civ 896, [2007] 1 FLR 1028

This case is also included in relation to:

B16 Nip it in the bud
B15 Grasp the nettle: make findings of fact

B19 COMMITTAL

M v M (Breaches of orders: committal)

[2005] EWCA Civ 1722, [2006] 1 FLR 1154 at 1159

Court of Appeal

Ward LJ

[15]   The judge in this case, having found that there were these flagrant breaches which fully merited a sentence of imprisonment, richly deserved by this foolish father, nonetheless decided not to impose any penalty. The reason for that is clear. He considered the effects of such an order on the mother and the children and held he had to have regard to the welfare interests of the children.

[16]   Mr Miller does not contend that he erred in principle. I agree with that submission. As I pointed out in *A v N (Committal: Refusal of Contact)* [1997] 1 FLR 533, the welfare of the children is not the paramount consideration in committal proceedings as it is in the residence and contact proceedings by virtue of s 1(3) of the Children Act of 1989. Nonetheless, as I said at 540:

> 'It is obviously a material consideration and every judge who does any family work at all is always alive to the grievous effect the implementation of an order is likely to have on the life of the children whom the mother is unwisely seeking to protect in her own misguided way.'

[17]   In my judgment the learned deputy High Court judge was not putting the welfare of the children as paramount but was correctly having regard to their welfare interests. The question, therefore, is whether he gave improper weight to that factor. In my judgment it has to be shown that he so exceeded the generous ambit, within which there is reasonable room for disagreement, that he was plainly wrong. But he was not plainly wrong in this case. He was perfectly entitled to have regard to the deeply disturbed condition of these children, especially the elder two, whom he described as not only 'exceptionally vulnerable', but in respect of the older two, 'disturbed'. We are told that they are in fact having to seek therapeutic treatment at the P Hospital and it is perfectly obvious from any glance at this horrific case that these children are suffering grievously from the war that is being waged around them.

[18]   The judge was fully entitled to find that the consequence of the children seeing their father sent to prison would be to revolt against the

mother. It is not without significance that breach number four, on 22 January 2005, relates the following brief conversation: '[K] informed [Mrs M] that she would be to blame if Daddy went to prison'.

[19] The judge was perfectly entitled to conclude and I agree with him, that the consequence of sending father to prison would be to put these children beyond parental control and run the risk that the local authority would need to assume their care. In the longer term it would solve nothing. I agree.

[20] In the judge's conclusion, something has to be done to try and find a new way forward. I agree. That new way forward is for the High Court to do what this court requested it to do when this matter was before me on a previous occasion; that is to take a good, thorough, long look at this unhappy case and make an order which then has to be respected and obeyed. The father cannot go around believing he can flout the order of the court forever with impunity. But let the High Court consider this matter first, having full regard to the interests of the children which will then be paramount, having regard to the advice tendered by their guardian now appointed to represent their interests, having regard to the psychological evidence to be produced on both the father and the mother and to any other psychological and/or psychiatric evidence that might be admitted relating to the children themselves. But as an appeal against this order it is, in my judgment, hopeless.

[21] For my part, I thoroughly discourage applicants for committal participating in the sentencing exercise at all. That, after all, is a matter for the court, because it is the court which is, at the root of it, offended by the breaches of its order, though the court will not disregard the effect of the breach on the party for whose protection the order has been made. But it is for the court to be concerned and occasions where a disaffected applicant should move the Court of Appeal in consequence of the decision that is made, should be exceptional. This is not such an exceptional case. I refuse the application for permission to appeal.

Other significant cases on this issue:

- *Re M (Intractable contact dispute: interim care order)* [2003] EWHC 1024 Fam, [2003] 2 FLR 636 at [115]–[118]
- *Re D (Intractable contact dispute: publicity)* [2004] EWHC 727 Fam, [2004] 1 FLR 1226 at [56]–[57]
- *Re M (Contact order)* [2005] EWCA Civ 615, [2005] 2 FLR 1006
- *Re P (Committal for breach of contact order: reasons)* [2006] EWCA Civ 1792, [2007] 1 FLR 1820
- *B v S (Contempt: imprisonment of mother)* [2009] EWCA Civ 548, [2009] 2 FLR 1005

As to proper process, note:

- *G v G* [2007] EWCA Civ 680, [2007] 2 FLR 1127
- *Hammerton v Hammerton* [2007] EWCA Civ 248, [2007] 2 FLR 1133

B20 COSTS ORDERS

Re T (Order for costs)

[2005] EWCA Civ 311, [2005] 2 FLR 681 at 695

Court of Appeal

Wall LJ

[50] We recognise that irrational behaviour is commonplace in complex contact disputes, and that such behaviour may well be exacerbated by the personality of the individual parent. There is, however, in our judgment, a limit to which allowance can be made for a parent who deliberately and unreasonably obstructs contact by the other parent in circumstances where, on any objective analysis, contact is in the interests of the child and should take place. Of course there is a whole range of cases in which opposition to contact is reasonable. The classic example is the parent who has been traumatised by domestic violence, or where the parent seeking contact has been violent to the child. Equally, we accept, there are many cases in which there is a genuine dispute over the amount of contact, the suitability of holidays and overnight stays and so on.

[51] It is for this reason that the judge's findings of fact are so important. Where a judge, as here, carefully investigates the disputed areas of fact which have given rise to a parent's objections to contact, and where the judge, as here, has found in terms that the child enjoys a good relationship with the non-resident parent; that there is no reason for the resident parent to have any concerns; and that there is no reason why contact should not take place, a reasonable parent, even if still anxious, has no proper grounds for failing to implement the order. If, in these circumstances, the resident parent unreasonably fails to implement the order or an agreement as to contact, and if the matter has to return to court, it will be open to the court to find that that parent is acting unreasonably.

[52] In the instant case, the parties had reached an agreement in October 2002. There was manifestly no reason why contact should not take place in accordance with that agreement. The mother resiled from it for no good reason. She was, at the time, legally represented and plainly had access to good advice. The judge investigated the matter carefully and found that there was no good reason for her change of mind. In our judgment, she cannot in these circumstances rely on her own irrational anxieties to bring her conduct within the reasonable band. Her conduct was unreasonable, and it led to unnecessary litigation.

[53] The same, in our judgment, applies to the allegations of sexual abuse. The mother had only days before expressed her wish to move forward. Her misinterpretation of what J may or may not have said should not have led to the suspension of contact and the further intervention of the court. It is patently clear that J had not been sexually abused by his father, and the judge found that the mother was unreasonable 'in her easy acceptance of the possibility that the father had abused J'. That was a finding, in our judgment, which the judge was entitled to make. The mother and the maternal grandmother had misinterpreted innocent remarks made by J and given them a sinister interpretation that was unreasonable. The fact that the mother made and persisted in the allegations to a hearing may well in part reflect her anxious personality, but does not make it reasonable for her to have done so.

[54] In our judgment, the father was right to restrict his claim to the three hearings he identified. His approach, in our view, illustrates neatly the divide between legitimate litigation over reasonable disagreements, and irrational conduct with prolongs unnecessary litigation.

[55] Ultimately, the judge was exercising a judicial discretion. Her management of the case had been impeccable. In our judgment, she was entitled to make the orders for costs she did, and right not to assess them summarily. Quantum is ultimately a matter of assessment for the costs judge. We also do not think that, having properly set out the principles to be applied, she can be criticised for introducing in that context the concept of fairness in all the circumstances, or for stating that it would be 'an affront to justice to expect the father to pay for the costs of defending himself' against the wholly unwarranted allegations of sexual abuse which, on the judge's analysis, should never have been brought. The appeal must accordingly be dismissed.

[56] We do not think that the orders for costs which we have upheld in the instant case are either likely to or should deter a resident parent from advancing a reasonable opposition to contact which is genuinely based on a proper perception of the child's interests. But those who unreasonably frustrate contact need to be aware that the court has the power to make costs orders in appropriate cases, and that the consequences of such unreasonable behaviour may well be an order for costs made against the resident parent who has behaved unreasonably.

This case is also included in relation to:

H28 Costs: principles in private law cases

B21 SUSPENDED RESIDENCE ORDER

Re A (Suspended residence order)

[2009] EWHC 1576 (Fam), [2010] 1 FLR 1679 at 1704

Family Division

Coleridge J

[106] What is now in the best interests of the boys is the only yardstick by which I determine these applications. I have fully in mind all these factors mentioned in the welfare checklist which have been exhaustively canvassed during the hearing.

[107] I am well aware what the boys' expressed views are but they cannot be considered in isolation from the mother's vehemently held and expressed views. Any order I make has nothing to do with punishing one side for disobedience to court orders or the other for serious findings of sexual abuse. Both sides have to accept a measure of blame for the situation which has been reached.

[108] In every respect save one the children have and are doing well in their mother's care.

[109] The one respect in which she fails dismally is in her resolute opposition to children having a relationship with the whole of the paternal side of their family; father and grandparents. This is not a superficial shortcoming which can be overlooked in the overall balancing exercise. It is, as all the experts agree, a very serious failing and a very damaging deprivation from the boys' point of view. It is driven by her unshakeable conclusion, despite the clearest of findings by the court, that T, and probably N too, have been sexually abused by the father when this is simply not true. By that logic she regards him as a dangerous untreated paedophile who poses a very serious direct risk to the boys.

[110] There is no discernible basis for her opposition to contact with the grandparents save that she sees them as part of the paternal family and such a step as leading eventually to contact with the father.

[111] In furtherance of this conviction the mother has promoted and fostered in T (and gradually N, I suspect) the belief that they have been sexually abused. As her latest letter to the court demonstrates she holds these views as vehemently as ever. She will not desist in her view and the children know it full well. She is supported in this view by her partner, Sergeant W.

[112] This behaviour, left unchecked and undiluted, has already caused and will continue to cause the boys significant emotional harm to a degree which in other circumstances might well lead to their removal to foster carers by a local authority.

[113] The harm is both immediate in that it blocks their relationship with the whole paternal family and in longer term it will lead to their emotional lives into adulthood being significantly damaged. It will, in reality, mean the boys never have a relationship with the father or the paternal family and so their psychological health will be very seriously compromised.

[114] That state of affairs simply cannot continue. In some cases the court has, as an option, to accept its inability to make an effective order and so abandon further attempts to do so in the children's interest. But in this case for the court to do nothing, in the light of the expert evidence, is not, in my judgment, a responsible option. So there are only two ways ahead; either the mother must change her stance or the children must be physically removed from her daily environment and influence.

[115] To date the mother has shown no sign (apart from fleetingly last November) that she can or would change her view, sustain such a change and allow the boys a relationship with their grandparents and father, much less promote it. Or desist in the false belief that they have been abused.

[116] Such a step which requires real movement on her part, could still lead to the resolution of this case in the most satisfactory way for the boys; continued residence with her and a conventional visiting arrangement with all the paternal family.

[117] Accordingly, there remains only one option; a move to the grandparents with all that entails for their lives.

[118] The effects of such an uprooting are so blindingly obvious to everyone in the case as not to require spelling out again. All the experts and the lawyers have done so repeatedly both in writing and orally. As I say, they have caused me the greatest possible concern in my consideration of this case over many months. Without doubt a move would be very painful especially in the short term. It would also be harmful, in the longer term, to disrupt their primary attachment to their mother. But would it be as harmful, in the long term, as their being continually and unrelentingly exposed to their mother's false beliefs combined with her unremitting hostility to the paternal family undiluted by contact to them? In the end I do not think so.

[119] Both of these courses which are forced upon the court by the mother's intransigence are fraught with risk.

[120] The main consolation for the court is that I have complete confidence in the grandparents' ability to handle the situation both practically and emotionally. The plans following their removal and establishment at their grandparents are sound and properly and fully considered. They are able to support the boys through the handover and manage contact.

[121] There is a possibility that if the boys move to their grandparents the mother will distance herself from her sons and restrict her contact with them. I am not really persuaded that the evidence supports that. If, of course, she was to adopt that approach it would be further evidence of her inability to prioritise their needs above her own.

[122] In the end I find the grounds set out at B6 in support of the residence application are made out (insofar as they apply equally to the grandparents). They summarise well the situation which has been reached. As things currently stand, I shall make a residence order in favour of the grandparents.

[123] However, the question still arises as to the date from when such an order might be brought into effect given what I have said about the best solution in para [116] above. Should the order be suspended in its effect to admit of the slim possibility that the mother will see the sense in not making the children change their whole lives in support of her campaign to exclude the D's from their lives when, if she was to remain intransigent, it would in fact, achieve the opposite result?

[124] Both the father and grandparents oppose it. They both maintain that this will merely lead to further delay when the move to the grandparents is in reality inevitable. Things have gone too far and reached such a pitch that only immediate transfer is in the children's interests. They point especially to the recent letters.

[125] It seems to me (and the experts) that this 'suspended' course has one very clear advantage; the future residence of the children depends entirely on the mother's and to a lesser extent, the children's decision and action. If she (and they) abide by the court order the children stay with her (with all the obvious advantages). If she ignores it, the suspension on the order will be lifted immediately and the children move to make their home with the grandparents with all that that entails for their life. It is her choice and to a lesser extent their choice. But it is really entirely up to her.

[126] I have decided it is the best way forward. If the boys stay put but the mother's influence is mitigated by regular and proper contact it would still be the best course.

B22   CHANGE OF RESIDENCE: RARELY PEREMPTORY

Re K (Procedure: Family Proceedings Rules)

[2004] EWCA Civ 1827, [2005] 1 FLR 764 at 768 and 769

Court of Appeal

Thorpe and Wall LJJ

THORPE LJ:

[15] Of course I accept that in any case where children are at immediate risk of harm the court has a power and a responsibility to intervene to protect them. But this present case was just nowhere near that point of intervention. The judge said in his judgment – as noted by the father's solicitors and as approved by him – that in his view it was an emergency. Miss Morgan, in her able submissions, has tried to justify that categorisation, saying that there would have been an exponential increase in harm to the children had the situation then described in the professional reports been allowed to persist for a further 6 weeks. I find that submission completely unconvincing. There was nothing in this case other than concerns of chronic dysfunction. The children could have continued in that regime without any accelerated or increased risk of harm until a further investigation could be properly carried out. It seems to me – and at this stage I revert again to the procedural unfairness – that the judge did not recognise the fundamental importance of giving the mother a proper opportunity to prepare a case in response.

WALL LJ:

[19] I entirely agree with everything Thorpe LJ has said. Of course there are circumstances in which it is necessary to make peremptory orders removing the care of children from one parent to another. I myself sitting at first instance have done it on a number of occasions, one of which is reported in *A v A (Shared Residence)* [2004] 1 FLR 1195. When one does it, it has to be in the interests of the children, and either in a situation of emergency as an order necessary for their protection, or as part of a proper strategy for the overall conduct of the case.

Other significant cases on this issue:

- *M v C (Children's orders: reasons)* [1993] 2 FLR 584 at 586

B23   CHANGE OF RESIDENCE

Re G (Children)

[2006] UKHL 43, [2006] 2 FLR 629 at 642

House of Lords

Baroness Hale of Richmond

[41] Making contact happen and, even more importantly, making contact work is one of the most difficult and contentious challenges in the whole of family law. It has recently received a great deal of public attention. Courts understandably regard the conventional methods of enforcing court orders as a last resort: fining the primary carer will only mean that she has even less to spend upon the children; sending her to prison will deprive them of their primary carer and give them a reason to resent the other parent who invited this. Nor does punishment address the real sources of the problem, which may range from a simple failure to understand what the children need, to more complex fears resulting from the parents' own relationship. That is why the assistance of a professional such as Mr Martin in this case can be so valuable. It is also why more constructive measures are to be introduced under the Children and Adoption Act 2006. The court will be able to direct either parent to engage in activities which will help them to understand and work through the difficulties. The range of penalties for breach of court orders will include an order to engage in unpaid work, thus reducing the risk that punishing the parent will also punish the child.

[42] However, at least as long ago as *V-P v V-P (Access to Child)* (1980) 1 FLR 336, it was realised that a more potent encouragement to comply with court orders may be to contemplate changing the child's living arrangements. Ormrod LJ put it very directly, at 339:

> '... I do not wish to issue threats, but the mother should, I think, realise this: the father has a home with the half brother in it, he is unemployed, he is available to look after both these children full time. The mother is fully occupied, so that the grandmother is playing a very important part in this child's life ... That being so, it would be a mistake on the part of the mother, in my judgment, to assume that the order for custody in her favour is inevitable; it is not and if the situation goes on as it is at present then it may be necessary to reconsider the question of custody.'

It is, I believe, becoming more common for family judges not only to issue such warnings but also to implement them. However, the object is to ensure that the arrangements which the court has made in the best interests of the child are actually observed. Only if this is not happening will the court conclude that other arrangements will be better for the child.

Other significant cases on this issue:

*   *V v V (Contact: implacable hostility)* [2004] EWHC 1215 (Fam), [2004] 2 FLR 851
*   *Re C (Residence order)* [2007] EWCA Civ 866, [2008] 1 FLR 211
*   *Re R (Residence)* [2009] EWCA Civ 358, [2009] 2 FLR 819
*   *Re A (Residence order)* [2009] EWCA Civ 1141, [2010] 1 FLR 1083 (transfer of residence was premature)
*   *Re S (Transfer of residence)* [2010] EWHC 192 (Fam), [2010] 1 FLR 1785

This case is also included in relation to:

A4   Importance of using welfare checklist
A6   Parenthood and welfare (1)

B24　SHARED RESIDENCE

A v A (Shared residence)

[2004] EWHC 142 Fam, [2004] 1 FLR 1195 at 1201, 1202 and 1220

Family Division

Wall J

The points which this case illustrates

[24]　This case highlights nine particular points, which I identify below:

...

(7)　This is a case where a shared residence order is appropriate. But it
also demonstrates clearly that shared residence orders are not a
panacea. Shared residence and an equal division of the children's
time between their parents' houses is possible in this case because
the parents live close to each other, and the children can go to
school from either home. The children welcome it because, in B's
words, which I have already quoted, it gives his parents nothing left
to fight about. But it is a pragmatic solution which does nothing to
address the underlying hostility between the parents. Whether or not
is succeeds; only time will tell.

...

The cases on joint residence orders

[113]　There are three recent decisions of the Court of Appeal dealing
with the question of shared residence orders. They are, in chronological
order, *D v D (Shared Residence Order)* [2001] 1 FLR 495 (*D v D*); *Re A
(Children) (Shared Residence)* [2001] EWCA Civ 1795, [2002] 1 FCR 177
(*Re A*); and *Re F (Shared Residence Order)* [2003] EWCA Civ 592, [2003]
2 FLR 397 (*Re F*).

[114]　The most important of these, in my judgment, is *D v D*. In that
case there were three children who, following their parents' separation,
spent substantial amounts of time with each, despite the fact that there
was a high level of acrimony between their parents and frequent
applications to the court to sort out the detail of the arrangements. The
father argued that without a shared residence order he was treated as a

second-class parent by authorities with whom he had to deal over matters relating to the children. The judge made a shared residence order, and the mother appealed.

[115] The judgment of Hale LJ (as she then was) is valuable both for its statement as to the current law and for its historical analysis. Hale LJ cites a passage from the Law Commission's Report (Law Com No 172 published in 1988) on which the Children Act 1989 is based, and which bears repetition:

> 'Apart from the effect on the other parent, which has already been mentioned, the main difference between a residence order and a custody order is that the new order should be flexible enough to accommodate a much wider range of situations. In some cases, the child may live with both parents even though they do not share the same household. It was never our intention to suggest that children should share their time more or less equally between their parents. Such arrangements will rarely be practicable, let alone for the children's benefit. However, the evidence from the United States is that where they are practicable they can work well and we see no reason why they should be actively discouraged. None of our respondents shared the view expressed in a recent case [*Riley's* case] that such an arrangement, which had been working well for some years, should never have been made. More commonly, however, the child will live with both parents but spend more time with one than the other. Examples might be where he spends term time with one and holidays with the other, or two out of three holidays from boarding school with one and the third with the other. It is a far more realistic description of the responsibilities involved in that sort of arrangement to make a residence order covering both parents rather than a residence order for one and a contact order for the other. Hence we recommend that where the child is to live with two (or more) people who do not live together, the order may specify the periods during which the child is to live in each household. The specification may be general rather than detailed and in some cases may not be necessary at all.'

[116] It is for those reasons, Hale LJ comments, that s 8(1) of the Children Act 1989 defines a residence order as an order 'settling the arrangements to be made as to the person with whom a child is to live'.

[117] In her judgment in the case, Dame Elizabeth Butler-Sloss P helpfully cites a passage from the guidance contained in the *Children Act 1989 Guidance and Regulations*, Vol 1, *Court Orders*, published by the Stationery Office in 1991, para 2.2(8) at p 10:

> '... it is not expected that it would become a common form of order, partly because most children will still need the stability of a single

home, and partly because in the cases where shared care is
appropriate there is less likely to be a need for the court to make any
order at all. However, a shared care order has the advantage of being
more realistic in those cases where the child is to spend considerable
amount of time with both parents, brings with it certain other
benefits (including the right to remove the child from accommodation provided by a local authority under s 20), and removes any
impression that one parent is good and responsible whereas the
other parent is not.'

[118] The essence of the decision in *D v D* seems to me to be as follows.
It is a basic principle that, post separation, each parent with parental
responsibility retains an equal and independent right and responsibility to
be informed and make appropriate decisions about their children.
However, where children are being looked after by one parent, that parent
needs to be in a position to take the day-to-day decisions that have to be
taken while that parent is caring for the children. Parents should not be
seeking to interfere with one another in matters which are taking place
while they do not have the care of their children. Subject to any questions
which are regulated by court order, the object of the exercise should be to
maintain flexible and practical arrangements whenever possible.

[119] *D v D* makes it clear that a shared residence order is an order that
children live with both parents. It must, therefore, reflect the reality of the
children's lives. Where children are living with one parent and are either
not seeing the other parent or the amount of time to be spent with the
other parent is limited or undecided, there cannot be a shared residence
order. However, where children are spending a substantial amount of time
with both their parents, a shared residence order reflects the reality of the
children's lives. It is not necessarily to be considered an exceptional order
and should be made if it is in the best interests of the children concerned.

[120] These themes are reflected in two other decisions. In *Re A* there
were three children, a boy and two girls. The girls lived with their mother
and the boy lived with his father. The boy was unwilling to see his mother,
and was not doing so. A recorder made a shared residence order. The
father applied for permission to appeal. Granting permission to appeal
and allowing the appeal in part, the Court of Appeal set aside the shared
residence orders. In so doing, Hale LJ said:

> '[17] I completely appreciate why the recorder wished to make a
> shared residence order in this case. He wanted to recognise the equal
> status of each parent in relation to all three of these children. He
> may, although he does not say so, have been afraid that the father
> would not recognise this if he did not make a shared residence order
> in relation to all three children. But the law is that the parents
> already have shared parental responsibility for their children. They
> have equal and independent power to exercise that parental

responsibility. A residence order is about where a child is to live. It is very difficult to make such an order about a child who is not only not living with one of the parents but is, for the foreseeable future, unlikely even to visit with that parent. Notwithstanding, therefore, that that parent does not wish there to be any distinction between the children, because she does not wish M to feel rejected by her, the court's order has to be designed to reflect the real position on the ground. That being the case, in my view the shared residence order in relation to M was inappropriate. For that order there should be substituted an order that M is to live with his father and to have contact with his mother in the same terms as the order laid down by the learned recorder.'

[121]   In *Re F* a judge made a shared residence order in relation to two small children, notwithstanding the fact that the mother lived in Edinburgh, a considerable distance from the father's home in England. The Court of Appeal, upholding her decision, said that such a distance did not preclude the possibility that the children's year could be divided between the homes of two separated parents in such a way as to validate the making of a shared residence order. A shared residence order had to reflect the underlying reality of where the children lived their lives, and was not made to deal with parental status. Any lingering idea that a shared residence order was apt only where the children alternated between the two homes evenly was erroneous. If the home offered by each parent was of equal status and importance to the children an order for shared residence would be valuable.

Other significant cases on this issue:

- *Re P (Shared residence order)* [2005] EWCA Civ 1693, [2006] 2 FLR 347
- *Re K (Shared residence order)* [2008] EWCA Civ 526, [2008] 2 FLR 380
- *Re A (Joint residence: parental responsibility)* [2008] EWCA Civ 867, [2008] 2 FLR 1593 (legitimate to make joint residence order to confer parental responsibility on someone who could not apply for free-standing parental responsibility order)
- *Re W* [2009] EWCA Civ 370, [2009] 2 FLR 436 (review of general principles concerning shared residence, including that it is a contradiction in terms to make a contact order to someone who had a shared residence order)
- *Re AR (A child: relocation)* [2010] EWHC 1346 (Fam), [2010] 2 FLR 1577 at [52] (shared residence 'is nowadays the rule rather than the exception even where the quantum of care undertaken by each parent is decidedly unequal ...': per Mostyn J)

This case is also included in relation to:

B13 General points (2)

Domestic violence cases

B25   PROCESS AND PRINCIPLES

Re L, Re V, Re M, Re H (Contact: domestic violence)

[2000] 2 FLR 334 at 341 and 344

Court of Appeal

Butler-Sloss P

The general advice and the specific advice on contact in cases of domestic violence from the two distinguished consultant child psychiatrists which I have summarised above is informed by research and also by the responses to the consultation paper provided by the Sub-Committee. In my view it is extremely valuable information to assist in the difficult task faced by the family judge or family proceedings magistrates deciding whether to order contact in cases where domestic violence is proved.

General comments

There are however a number of general comments I wish to make on the advice given to us. The family judges and magistrates need to have a heightened awareness of the existence of and consequences (some long term), on children of exposure to domestic violence between their parents or other partners. There has, perhaps, been a tendency in the past for courts not to tackle allegations of violence and to leave them in the background on the premise that they were matters affecting the adults and not relevant to issues regarding the children. The general principle that contact with the non-resident parent is in the interests of the child may sometimes have discouraged sufficient attention being paid to the adverse effects on children living in the household where violence has occurred. It may not necessarily be widely appreciated that violence to a partner involves a significant failure in parenting – failure to protect the child's carer and failure to protect the child emotionally.

In a contact or other s 8 application, where allegations of domestic violence are made which might have an effect on the outcome, those allegations must be adjudicated upon and found proved or not proved. It will be necessary to scrutinise such allegations which may not always be true or may be grossly exaggerated. If however there is a firm basis for finding that violence has occurred, the psychiatric advice becomes very important. There is not, however, nor should there be, any presumption that, on proof of domestic violence, the offending parent has to surmount a prima facie barrier of no contact. As a matter of principle, domestic violence of itself cannot constitute a bar to contact. It is one factor in the difficult and delicate balancing exercise of discretion. The court deals with the facts of a specific case in which the degree of violence and the seriousness of the impact on the child and on the resident parent have to be taken into account. In cases of proved domestic violence, as in cases of other proved harm or risk of harm to the child, the court has the task of weighing in the balance the seriousness of the domestic violence, the risks involved and the impact on the child against the positive factors (if any), of contact between the parent found to have been violent and the child. In this context, the ability of the offending parent to recognise his past conduct, be aware of the need to change and make genuine efforts to do so, will be likely to be an important consideration. Wall J in *Re M (Contact: Violent Parent)* [1999] 2 FLR 321 suggested at 333 that often in cases where domestic violence had been found, too little weight had been given to the need for the father to change. He suggested that the father should demonstrate that he was a fit person to exercise contact and should show a track record of proper behaviour. Assertions, without evidence to back it up, may well not be sufficient.

In expressing these views I recognise the danger of the pendulum swinging too far against contact where domestic violence has been proved. It is trite but true to say that no two child cases are exactly the same. The court always has the duty to apply s 1 of the Children Act 1989 that the welfare of the child is paramount and, in considering that welfare, to take into account all the relevant circumstances, including the advice of the medical experts as far as it is relevant and proportionate to the decision in that case. It will also be relevant in due course to take into account the impact of Art 8 of the European Convention for the Protection of Human Rights and Fundamental Freedoms 1950 on a decision to refuse direct contact.

The propositions set out above are not, in my view, in any way inconsistent with earlier decisions on contact. The fostering of a relationship between the child and the non-resident parent has always been and remains of great importance. It has equally been intended to be for the benefit of the child rather than of the parent. Over the last 40 years there has been a movement away from rights towards responsibilities of the parents and best interests of the child.

[Butler-Sloss P went on to review 'earlier decisions on contact']

In conclusion, on the general issues, a court hearing a contact application in which allegations of domestic violence are raised should consider the conduct of both parties towards each other and towards the children, the effect on the children and on the residential parent and the motivation of the parent seeking contact. Is it a desire to promote the best interests of the child or a means to continue violence and/or intimidation or harassment of the other parent? In cases of serious domestic violence, the ability of the offending parent to recognise his or her past conduct, to be aware of the need for change and to make genuine efforts to do so, will be likely to be an important consideration.

General notes:

Attention is particularly drawn to:

(1)   the Practice Direction: Residence and Contact Orders: Domestic Violence and Harm issued in January 2009 [2009] 2 FLR 1400 (which is to be applied: see, for example, *Re Z (children) (unsupervised contact: allegations of domestic violence)* [2009] EWCA Civ 430, [2009] 2 FLR 877 at [27]–[28], and cf *Re R (family proceedings: no case to answer)* [2008] EWCA Civ 1619, [2009] 2 FLR 83; and

(2)   the President's Guidance in relation to Split Hearings [2010] 2 FLR 1897.

Other significant cases on this issue:

•   *Re M (Children)* [2009] EWCA Civ 1216, [2010] 1 FLR 1089 (if adjournment refused for reasons of delay, must establish what the likely delay would be)

This case is also included in relation to:

B26   Contact where allegations of DV: summary of experts' reports
B31   Interim contact (1)

B26   CONTACT WHERE ALLEGATIONS OF DV: SUMMARY OF EXPERTS' REPORTS

Re L, Re V, Re M, Re H (Contact: domestic violence)

[2000] 2 FLR 334 at 336

Court of Appeal

Butler-Sloss P

These four appeals on issues arising out of contact applications have certain features in common. In each case a father's application for direct contact has been refused by the circuit judge against a background of domestic violence between the spouses or partners. We are grateful to Wall J, the Chairman of the Children Act Sub-Committee of the Advisory Board on Family Law, for permission to look at their report on parental contact in domestic violence cases and their recommendations recently presented to the Lord Chancellor and now published (*A Report to the Lord Chancellor on the Question of Parental Contact in Cases where there is Domestic Violence* (Lord Chancellor's Department, 12 April 2000)). At our request, the Official Solicitor acted as amicus in each case and we are most grateful to him for instructing Dr J. C. Sturge, consultant child psychiatrist in consultation with Dr D. Glaser, consultant child psychiatrist to provide a joint report (*Contact and Domestic Violence – the Experts' Court Report* [2000] Fam Law 615) and to advise on the four appeals and to Mr Posnansky QC, on behalf of the Official Solicitor, for the helpful arguments addressed to us. We heard the four cases together and reserved judgment in each case. I propose to comment on the report on domestic violence (the report), and the expert psychiatric evidence (the psychiatric report) presented to us before turning to the facts of each appeal.

The report

The report by the Children Act Sub-Committee underlined the importance of the question of domestic violence in the context of parental contact to children. Domestic violence takes many forms and should be broadly defined. The perpetrator may be female as well as male. Involvement may be indirect as well as direct. There needs to be greater awareness of the effect of domestic violence on children, both short-term and long-term, as witnesses as well as victims and also the impact on the residential parent. An outstanding concern of the court should be the nature and extent of the risk to the child and to the residential parent and that proper arrangements should be put in place to safeguard the child and the residential parent from risk of further physical or emotional harm. In cases where domestic violence is raised as a reason for refusing or limiting contact, the report makes it clear that the allegations ought to be addressed by the court at the earliest opportunity and findings of fact made so as to establish the truth or otherwise of those allegations and decide upon the likely effect, if any, those findings *could* have on the court's decision on contact. The report set out suggested guidelines to which I shall refer at the end of this judgment.

The psychiatric report

Dr Sturge and Dr Glaser in their joint report to this court had the opportunity to see the responses to the Sub-Committee consultation paper and to read the report and recommendations. Their psychiatric report was read and approved by a number of other consultant child psychiatrists and incorporates the views of a distinguished group of consultants. We are extremely grateful to them for their wise advice.

They set out the psychiatric principles of contact between the child and the non-resident parent. They saw the centrality of the child as all-important and the promotion of his or her mental health the central issue amid the tensions surrounding the adults in dispute. The decisions about contact should be child-centred and related to the specific child in its present circumstances but acknowledge that the child's needs will alter over different stages of development. The purpose of the proposed contact must be overt and abundantly clear and have the potential for benefiting the child in some way. The benefits of contact to the father were set out in detail including, the importance of the father as one of the two parents, in the child's sense of identity and value, the role model provided by a father and the male contribution to parenting of children and its relevance to the child's perception of family life as an adult.

They set out many different purposes of contact, including: the maintenance or reparation of beneficial relationships, the sharing of information and knowledge and the testing of reality for the child. They set out the more limited advantages of indirect contact which included: experience of continued interest by the absent parent, knowledge and information about the absent parent, keeping open the possibility of development of the relationship and the opportunity for reparation.

They pointed out the importance of the manner in which indirect contact was managed by the resident parent.

They identified a number of risks of direct contact. The overall risk was that of failing to meet and actually undermining the child's developmental needs or even causing emotional abuses and damage directly through contact or as a consequence of the contact. Specifically that included: escalating the climate of conflict around the child which would undermine the child's general stability and sense of emotional well being. The result was a tug of loyalty and a sense of responsibility for the conflict in all children except young babies which affected the relationships of the child with both parents. There might be direct abusive experiences, including emotional abuse by denigration of the child or the child's resident carer. There might be continuation of unhealthy relationships such as dominant or bullying relationships, those created by fear, bribes or emotional blackmail, by undermining the child's sense of stability and continuity by deliberately or inadvertently setting different moral standards or standards of behaviour, by little interest in the child himself or by unstimulating or uninteresting contact. They indicated a series of situations where there were risks to contact: where there were unresolved situations, where the contact was unreliable and the child frequently let down, where the child was attending contact against his wishes so he felt undermined, where there was little prospect for change such as wholly implacable situations, where there was the stress on the child and resident carer of ongoing proceedings or frequently re-initiated proceedings.

These are all matters with which experienced family judges and magistrates in family proceedings courts are all too familiar. I have, for my part however, found the outline provided by the psychiatric report very helpful.

Domestic violence situations

The psychiatric report then moved to the central issue of domestic violence. They agreed with the Sub-Committee report that there needs to be greater awareness of the effect of domestic violence on children, both short term and long term, as witnesses as well as victims. The research was entirely consistent in showing the deleterious effects on children of exposure to domestic violence and that children were affected as much by exposure to violence as to being involved in it. All children were affected by significant and repeated inter-partner violence even if not directly involved. Research indicates that even when children did not continue in violent situations emotional trauma continued to be experienced. The context of the overall situation was highly relevant to decision making. The contribution of psychiatric disorder to situations of domestic violence and emotional abuse must be considered. In situations of contact there might be a continuing sense of fear of the violent parent by the child. The child might have post-traumatic anxieties or symptoms the proximity of the non-resident violent parent might re-arouse or perpetuate. There might be a continuing awareness of the fear the violent parent aroused in the child's main carer. The psychiatric report highlighted the possible effects of such situations on the child's own attitudes to violence, to forming parenting relationships and the role of fathers. Research shows that attitudes in boys were particularly affected.

Refusal of child to see parent

The psychiatric report addressed the problem of the child who was adamant that he did not wish to see the parent. The following factors ought to be accepted ([2000] Fam Law 615, 621):

'(i)   the child must be listened to and taken seriously;
(ii)   the age and understanding of the child are highly relevant;
(iii) the child, and the younger and the more dependent, either for developmental or emotional reasons, if in a positive relationship with the resident parent will inevitably be influenced by:
  • that parent's views;
  • their wish to maintain her or his sense of security and stability within that household.
(iv) Going against the child's wishes must involve the following.
  • Indications that there are prospects of the child changing his or her view as a result of preparation work or the contact itself, for example, there is a history of meaningful attachment and a good relationship; the non-resident parent has child-centred plans as to how to help the child to overcome his or her resistance; there are some indications of ambivalence such as an adamant statement of not wanting to see that parent accompanied by lots of positive memories and affect when talking of that parent.'

Consideration should be given to the effects on the child of making a decision that appears to disregard their feelings and wishes and when the child is forced to do something if he cannot see the sense of it.

The psychiatric report looked at the absence of a bond between child and non-resident parent and indicated the need to take into account the age and development of the child and whether there was an established history of domestic violence. In such a case it was suggested there would need to be good reason to embark on a plan of introducing direct contact and building up a relationship where the main evidence was of the non-resident parent's capacity for violence within relationships.

No direct contact

Dr Sturge and Dr Glaser considered the question in what circumstances should the court give consideration to a child having no direct contact with the non-resident parent. In their view there should be no automatic assumption that contact to a previously or currently violent parent was in the child's interests, if anything the assumption should be in the opposite direction and he should prove why he can offer something of benefit to the child and to the child's situation. They said ([2000] Fam Law 615, 623–624):

> 'Domestic violence involves a very serious and significant failure in parenting – failure to protect the child's carer and failure to protect the child emotionally (and in some cases physically – which meets any definition of child abuse).

> Without the following we would see the balance of advantage and disadvantage as tipping against contact:

> '(a) some (preferably full) acknowledgment of the violence;
> (b) some acceptance (preferably full if appropriate, ie the sole instigator of violence) of responsibility for that violence;
> (c) full acceptance of the inappropriateness of the violence particularly in respect of the domestic and parenting context and of the likely ill-effects on the child;
> (d) a genuine interest in the child's welfare and full commitment to the child, ie a wish for contact in which he is not making the conditions;
> (e) a wish to make reparation to the child and work towards the child recognising the inappropriateness of the violence and the attitude to and treatment of the mother and helping the child to develop appropriate values and attitudes;
> (f) an expression of regret and the showing of some understanding of the impact of their behaviour on their ex-partner in the past and currently;
> (g) indications that the parent seeking contact can reliably sustain contact in all senses.'

They suggested that without (a)–(f) above they could not see how the non-resident parent could fully support the child and play a part in undoing the harm caused to the child and support the child's current situation and need to move on and develop healthily. There would be a significant risk to the child's general well-being and his emotional development ([2000] Fam Law 615, 624):

> 'Without these we also see contact as potentially raising the likelihood of the most serious of the sequelae of children's exposure, directly or indirectly, to domestic violence, namely the increased risk of aggression and violence in the child generally, the increased risk of the child becoming the perpetrator of domestic violence or becoming involved in domestically violent relationships and of increased risk of having disturbed inter-personal relationships themselves.'

They added to the list (h) respecting the child's wishes ([2000] Fam Law 615, 624):

'... while this needs to be assessed within the whole context of such wishes, the older the child the more seriously they should be viewed and the more insulting and discrediting to the child to have them ignored. As a rough rule we would see these as needing to be taken account of at any age; above 10 we see these as carrying considerable weight with 6–10 as an intermediate stage and at under 6 as often indistinguishable in many ways from the wishes of the main carer (assuming normal development). In domestic violence, where the child has memories of that violence we would see their wishes as warranting much more weight than in situations where no real reason for the child's resistance appears to exist.'

In addition to the above, other evaluations of how the contact would benefit the child would need to be made. The purpose of contact needed to be answered, whether it was designed to provide information and direct knowledge of the non-resident parent or to continue or develop a meaningful father–child relationship.

Disadvantages of no direct contact

They looked at the potential detriment to the child of having no direct contact with the *non*-resident parent in the context of past domestic violence. The most relevant issues were ([2000] Fam Law 615, 625):

'(i)   deprivation of a relationship with the biological father;

(ii)   loss of the opportunity to know that parent first-hand; loss of information and knowledge that will go towards the child's identity formation. While the reality testing may give the child a negative view of the parent, that may be less worrying than the unseen, imagined villain. Where it is a positive view and the child is able to see good in the parent as well as to understand that he did things that were very wrong will help the positive image of himself or herself. While directly this may be more important for sons, daughters can be helped in their attitude to what makes a suitable partner to father her children. Children can have genetic fears – that he or she will be just like the father, sometimes fuelled by their mother's attitude, and the reality of who their father is can be helpful; if the non-resident parent has been vilified beyond the facts, then the child will have the opportunity of assessing this for themselves;

(iii)   loss of the opportunity to know grandparents and other relatives on the non-resident parent's side of the family. This can add to the loss of genealogical information (although the study by Humphrey et al indicates that clear genealogical knowledge in an adolescent is not a necessary prerequisite to healthy identity formation and good self-esteem). Occasionally successful contact with the non-resident parent's family can be achieved without contact to the parent himself or herself and without undermining the child by doing so, ie where assessment indicates that such contact can be safely achieved and is in the child's interests;

(iv) loss of that parent if the child has had a positive and meaningful relationship with him and even where it has been negative if the relationship gave the child some sense of being cared about. Continuity can also be important;

(v) if the parent is able to provide positive and supportive contact and new and different experiences, then loss of that opportunity;

(vi) absence of the opportunity for any repair to the relationships or to the harm done;

(vii) lessening of the likelihood of the child being able to get in touch and/or form a meaningful relationship at a later stage.'

They also suggested that there should be greater creativity in addressing ways of resolving contact difficulties. An example given was by seeing the parent in a safe situation where the child was in control such as, by using a one way screen with an interviewer interviewing the parent on the other side. The child could decide if he wished to enter the room to see the parent. Proxy contact was suggested with a trained go-between and supervisors to support the child at the contact sessions.

The general advice and the specific advice on contact in cases of domestic violence from the two distinguished consultant child psychiatrists which I have summarised above is informed by research and also by the responses to the consultation paper provided by the Sub-Committee. In my view it is extremely valuable information to assist in the difficult task faced by the family judge or family proceedings magistrates deciding whether to order contact in cases where domestic violence is proved.

This case is also included in relation to:

B25 Process and principles
B31 Interim contact (1)

B27 JUDICIAL DISCRETION AS TO NEED FOR FACT-FINDING HEARING

Re C (Domestic violence: fact-finding hearing)

[2009] EWCA Civ 994, [2010] 1 FLR 1728 at 1731

Court of Appeal

Thorpe LJ

[12] What the judge did not have before him is a document which I think is highly pertinent. It is a definition of the Domestic Violence Intervention Programme that is run in partnership between Cafcass and the Quorum contact service. The programme is defined in this way:

> 'DVIP's perpetrator programme takes a total of 32 sessions to complete. It is delivered mainly in small groups meeting weekly for three hours. Most sessions begin at 7 pm in the evening.
>
> There is a fortnightly, ongoing follow up group available for all those who have completed the programme'

[13] I have no hesitation at all in rejecting Ms Deignan's skilful submissions. A number of things need to be made plain. First, the obligation on the judges in the county court to conduct fact-finding hearings where there have been allegations of domestic violence arises from the judgments of this court in the conjoined appeals of *Re L (A Child) (Contact: Domestic Violence)* [2001] Fam 260, [2001] 2 WLR 339, [2000] 2 FLR 334. At that date, now 9 years ago, this court considered a situation in which it was widely said by researchers that district judges up and down the country were ignoring the investigation of past violence on the grounds that it was all history and that the focus should be on the future progress of contact. Accordingly, in our judgments we said that ordinarily speaking the history was of considerable importance and should be established before the exercise of judicial discretion as to the future.

[14] Those judgments had a wide impact and perhaps the members of this court gave insufficient attention to the burden that they were placing on judges and district judges in the county court up and down the jurisdiction. Accordingly, the President subsequently issued practice guidance, I think in 2008, and that is the guide to which Wilson LJ referred in his reasons for rejecting the first permission application.

[15] Subsequently, in an observation in the course of her speech in the case of *Re B (A Child)* [2009] UKSC 5, [2009] 1 WLR 2496, [2010] 1 FLR 551, Baroness Hale of Richmond stated that the court must:

> 'consider the nature of any allegation or admission of domestic violence and the extent to which any domestic violence which is admitted, or which may be proved, would be relevant in deciding whether to make an order about residence or contact and, if so, in what terms.'

So absolute a pronouncement risked to throw yet greater burden on an already over-stretched trial system, and accordingly the President in 2009 issued an amendment to the practice direction (Practice Direction: Residence and Contact Orders: Domestic Violence and Harm, 14 January 2009 [2009] 2 FLR 1400) making plain that it was a matter of discretion for the judge and the judge did not have to order a fact-finding preliminary hearing provided he gave reasons for declining so to do.

[16] It is well known that judges in the county court, both circuit and district judges, feel that any extension of their obligation in this area jeopardises the service that the court can give in other areas, and during the debate of the specialist judiciary at this year's President's conference it was emphasised that the obligation to order a fact-finding preliminary hearing remains always discretionary, provided that the judge refusing sufficiently explains him or herself.

[17] Now this seems to me a paradigm case in which the judge has done precisely what he ought to do and precisely what he is entitled to do, namely to exercise a broad common sense discretion and in refusing the application, to make proper explanation of his reasons. The judge quite rightly emphasised that this was a case in which prior domestic violence had been established in the criminal justice system and had been the subject of conviction and punishment. He further emphasised that there had been a bind-over in the criminal justice system and that in the family justice system there was a current undertaking by the father to refrain from any violence or harassment. This was a case in which there had been no allegation of fresh domestic violence of any significance since April 2006. This was a case in which there had never been any suggestion of violence to the child in question. This was a case in which contact had been established at a contact centre and was progressing. This was a case in which the father had successfully completed an anger management course. Given all those circumstances, the judge had to weigh them against the plea for investigation of 10 acts that predated the criminal convictions, and with due regard to all the resource consequences.

[18] It is well known that the family justice system, both in the public law and in the private law dimensions, is stretched to breaking point. Judges have an obligation to safeguard and to husband the judicial resources of the court. It is also well known that the cost to the taxpayer of funding in the family justice field is worryingly high and that the government is determined to contain it. The direction of an unnecessary hearing is wasteful both of judicial resources and of public funding in publicly-funded cases.

[19] If that were not enough, I would add that highly relevant to the exercise of the judicial discretion was the detail of what a reference to domestic violence intervention project involves. It could be said that this is not relevant to the exercise of discretion once it is conceded that referral is possible on the foundation of the criminal convictions alone, but a programme of this duration and intensity is another significant cost to the public purse. This father has successfully completed an anger management course, and I simply cannot follow and certainly not accept the assertion of the Cafcass officer to the effect that the issues tackled in an anger management programme have no relevance to the issues that would be tackled in the DVIP programme. The modules in the DVIP programme include stopping physical violence, emotional abuse, effects of domestic violence on partners and children, responsible parenting, harassment and stalking, sexual abuse, jealousy and tactics of isolation. They may indeed be said to be separate ingredients but obviously the control of passion is part and parcel of each programme.

[20] All that said, I am completely clear in my mind that the judgment of 3 June is a classic example of the exercise of a case management discretion. I support the judge's view that the management of current cases is for the judge and not for the Cafcass officer. I think that the judge was not only well within the ambit of the generous discretion that he exercised, for what it is worth, in my independent judgment, he was absolutely right to refuse to set up the fact-finding hearing that was sought.

Other significant cases on this issue:

- *AA v NA* [2010] EWHC 1282 (Fam), [2010] 2 FLR 1173

B28   NO SHORT-CUT IN FACT-FINDING PROCESS

Re Z (Unsupervised contact: allegations of domestic violence)

[2009] EWCA Civ 430, [2009] 2 FLR 877 at 885, 887 and 888

Court of Appeal

Wall LJ

[28] I make it as clear as I can that the Practice Direction is there to be obeyed. It is not designed to tell judges what to decide; it is there to tell judges how to go about deciding issues of residence and contact where there are allegations of domestic violence. Above all, it seems to me the Practice Direction places proper and firm emphasis on the importance of the fact-finding exercise and, in my judgment, that process cannot be short-circuited. Where appropriate, the judge must conduct a fact-finding hearing and it is only if, at the conclusion of that hearing, the judge finds as a fact, having heard all the evidence, that the children are in no way at risk or that, for some other reason, contact, unsupervised or unsupported, can take place that he should and could/can make an order for contact.

[29] The importance of the Practice Direction cannot be overemphasised and, however experienced the judge, its terms are simply not to be ignored. I repeat: the judge must hear *all* the evidence. It is simply not good enough for a judge to say he has heard one side, does not think much of it, therefore he is not going to permit cross-examination of the other side of the issues involved, particularly where the safety and welfare of children are concerned. There is no equivalent of the concept of 'no case to answer' in proceedings relating to children: see *Re R (Family Proceedings: No Case to Answer)* [2008] EWCA Civ 1619, [2009] 2 FLR 83.

...

[39] Mr Date has made a robust defence of the judge in his skeleton argument, for which we are extremely grateful. He not only points out in argument that the court in a contact application is exercising a very wide discretion, but he makes the point that the judge is the arbiter of the findings of fact, and if the judge takes the view that the findings of fact are not made out then it is for the judge to say so and to conduct the hearing accordingly.

[40] Speaking for myself, I do not dissent from that proposition as a generality, but it has an obvious corollary, and that corollary is that the hearing must be fair. The judge must hear all the evidence, and in this case the judge plainly did not hear all the evidence and did not hear, in particular, the evidence of the father under cross-examination. The judge must also give the parties a full and fair opportunity to make submissions and should not pre-judge issues where a Cafcass officer is involved and where the Cafcass officer has in terms said that her views are provisional pending the outcome of a proper, and properly conducted, finding of fact hearing.

...

[42] As I have already said, I accept that a judge hearing a contact application exercises a wide discretion with which, in the overwhelming majority of cases, this court will not interfere; but, as I say, the discretion must be judicially exercised, the hearing must be fair and it must follow good practice. The Practice Direction represents that good practice. In my judgment, judges at first instance are not entitled to take shortcuts, which either run the risk of compromising the welfare of children or which fail to follow accepted practice ...

Other significant cases on this issue:

- Cf *Re K (Sexual abuse: evidence)* [2008] EWCA Civ 1307, [2009] 1 FLR 921: judge premature to abort fact-finding hearing about allegations of sexual abuse

This case is also included in relation to:

G19 Everything should be done in court and on record

B29   PARTIES NO LONGER SEEKING FINDINGS OF FACT

Re F (Restrictions on applications)

[2005] EWCA Civ 499, [2005] 2 FLR 950 at 954

Court of Appeal

Thorpe LJ

[13]   When the case was before His Honour Judge Platt he knew that there was to be a criminal trial arising out of the incident of 18 March 2004. Mr Horton has informed us today – and his information is confirmed by Miss Taylor for the mother – that at the trial last month before the justices Mr RF was acquitted for the simple reason that the mother explained to the justices that she was not prepared to give evidence against him and that she did not wish to see him punished.

[14]   That leads neatly to considering the second question in the appeal, namely that on which the judge sought guidance. He felt the need for guidance because, as he said in para [6] of his judgment:

'This is the fourth out of the last five *Re L* hearings at this court in the past 4 months which have ended without an effective fact-finding exercise. The question is therefore whether the court ought simply to accede to the parties' wishes and in the context of this case simply make an order for limited contact on the terms agreed.'

He then, in para [8], recorded Mr Horton's submission that since the parties were agreed on the issue of direct and indirect contact there was no lis between them. The judge said:

'With respect that is fundamentally misconceived. Children Act proceedings are not a lis in the traditional adversarial sense. They are and should remain a simple inquiry into what solution to the particular problem which the court is facing best meets the welfare needs of the child or children concerned.'

With that passage I am in whole-hearted agreement. However, there can be no doubt that the burden imposed on the courts of trial by the decision of this court in *Re L (A Child) (Contact: Domestic Violence); In Re V (A Child); In Re M (A Child); In Re H (Children)* [2001] 2 WLR 339, [2000] 2 FLR 334 has resulted in practical difficulties. In some instances it has burdened the already stretched resources of the trial courts with difficult factual investigations into past events and past relationships. That has undoubtedly had an impact on the productivity and speed of the family justice system. Mr Horton has made a number of cogent submissions as to the ways in which procedures could be improved to reduce the burden on the courts of trial, but I do not intend to express any views in this judgment on that aspect since it is not the issue that was referred by His Honour Judge Platt for our consideration. Restricting myself to that issue alone, it seems to me that the disintegration of an intended *Re L* investigation at the last moment is likely to result from one of two possible developments. The first is the development seen in this case. The applicant withdraws the applications which have obliged the respondent to deploy the history which the court has then arranged to determine. In that event, the consequence is, it seems to me as a matter of principle, straightforward. Once the applications are withdrawn then there is no need for the defensive case, there is no need for the investigation of that case, and the court can with an easy mind accept the compromise, since the acceptance of the compromise does not at that stage risk the welfare of the children or require any proactive steps for their protection. Plainly, the regime for indirect contact agreed in this case does not expose the children to any measurable risk of harm.

[15] The other possibility is not that which confronted His Honour Judge Platt on 6 December, but it is one that is easy to posit, given the events before the justices. The resolute applicant may outface the defensive wall raised by the respondent who succumbs to the pressure of complex emotions. The respondent may in the abandonment of the defence endanger the welfare of the children and engage the court's obligation to protect. The judge may well in those circumstances determine to proceed with the investigation despite the absence of the principal defence evidence. There may be evidence from some other source; there may be material within the history; there may be a CAFCASS report, any one of which may heighten the need for investigation and form the basis for conclusions adverse to the applicant. Of course the court may always also engage child protective procedures by requesting an investigation and report from the local authority.

[16] So whilst appreciating the circumstances that led His Honour Judge Platt to grant permission and to seek guidance, it does not seem to me that it is possible to go beyond those generalisations, given the infinite variety of facts which ultimately drive the discretionary conduct and disposal of these difficult cases.

Other significant cases on this issue:

- Cf (1) *Re R (Family proceedings: no case to answer)* [2008] EWCA Civ 1619, [2009] 2 FLR 83 in which it was made plain that the judge sitting in a quasi-inquisitorial role, in pursuit of child welfare, could not entertain a submission of no case to answer, and (2) *Re Z*

(Unsupervised contact) [2009] EWCA Civ 430, [2009] 2 FLR 877 in which the judge wrongly curtailed a finding of fact hearing

B30 DANGER OF PREJUDGING WELFARE STAGE: PRIVATE LAW

Re E (Contact)

[2009] EWCA Civ 1238, [2010] 1 FLR 1738 at 1741

Court of Appeal

Ward LJ

[10] ... The judge having risen at the end of the day and reserved his judgment, there was no opportunity for further argument as to whether or not interim contact should be allowed. The father's attitude was 'I have not done any of these acts at all and therefore I should be allowed contact'. But no one addressed the possibility that the judge would find the matters proved, and no one addressed what contact should follow in the light of such findings being made by the judge. And so it seems to me that in the absence of any argument about what contact, even interim contact, should be permitted, the judge erred in expressing views about that subject. It was, it seems to me, procedurally irregular to deal with matters which had not been the subject of full or any argument, to deal with matters without giving this father the opportunity to address them. And for that procedural irregularity rather than for any suggestion of apparent bias, I would for my part find that the judge erred in his dealing with the future in the way he did following the facts which he found.

[11] His judgment ought, in my judgment, to have ended with para [34]. That made it perfectly plain that he found the facts to be proved. He expressed the view that they were of such a serious nature as to impact very substantially on the question of contact, thus fulfilling (ii) of the district judge's order. I do not for my part think for a moment that he overstepped the boundary in describing the impact as very substantial. That does not preclude him in any way or would not have precluded him in any way from going on to deal with the eventual questions of contact. But given the way he did conclude his judgment, I regret that he unwittingly fell into error with the result that the issue we have to decide is whether or not to require a complete rehearing of the facts in dispute, or simply direct that some other judge determine the questions of contact in the light of the judge's findings of fact which otherwise stand.

General notes:

The facts found stood but the welfare hearing was remitted to be heard by another judge.

Other significant cases on this issue:

- Cf *Re L (Care proceedings: risk assessment)* [2009] EWCA Civ 1008, [2010] 1 FLR 790: see G42 – Danger of prejudging welfare stage: public law

Domestic violence

B31 INTERIM CONTACT (1)

Re L, Re V, Re M, Re H (Contact: domestic violence)

[2000] 2 FLR 334 at 344

Court of Appeal

Butler-Sloss P

On an application for interim contact, when the allegations of domestic violence have not yet been adjudicated upon, the court should give particular consideration to the likely risk of harm to the child, whether physical or emotional, if contact is granted or refused. The court should ensure, as far as it can, that any risk of harm to the child is minimised and that the safety of the child and the residential parent is secured before, during and after any such contact.

This case is also included in relation to:

B25   Process and principles
B26   Contact where allegations of DV: summary of experts' reports

B32　INTERIM CONTACT (2)

S v S (Interim contact)

[2009] EWHC 1575 (Fam), [2009] 2 FLR 1586 at 1588

Family Division

Hedley J

[8]　The difficulty conceptually with an interim contact order is that it begs the very question in the proceedings namely whether there should be contact at all. On the other hand the longer the delays, if it be that contact should be ordered, the more inimical to the best interests of the child. That is quite apart from the concern (not suggested, be it said, in this case) that unscrupulous parents could effectively derail contact by the making of false or exaggerated allegations of domestic violence.

[9]　In this case the judge's order was very restrictive amounting as it did to contact for an hour once a fortnight 'completely supervised'. I was anxious that his direction for a 'contact centre' suggested that he had overlooked the distinction between 'supported' and 'supervised' contact. However, it is clear that he did not do so as the father recognised that the order requires him to obtain (and pay for) proper supervised contact and it is accepted that the facility he has obtained fulfils that requirement. It follows that the order does effectively address the issues of physical safety of the mother and children.

[10]　However, the allegations in this case are serious (and there is a past criminal conviction) and it is fairly argued on behalf of the mother that the order does not (and could not) address issues of emotional harm both to the children, one of whom is said to have witnessed violence, and to the mother. That indeed is true and is an issue unlikely to be addressed until the final hearing after a Cafcass assessment. It is the essential reason why an order for interim contact should not be made in cases involving allegations of domestic violence where such allegations (if true) would be relevant to the issue of whether, and if so what, contact order should be made. That is a matter which was well recognised by this experienced judge.

[11]　Nevertheless, he saw that even in these circumstances some balance has to be drawn. That he drew it in an unconventional manner is shown by the fact that Pauffley J stayed his order pending an appeal. On the other hand, however, he was dealing with serious and, hitherto, unusual delay and he took the view that an exceptional course was merited. This is

an appeal and thus the question for this court is whether the mother can demonstrate that the judge was plainly wrong to draw the balance as he did.

[12] As I have indicated the making of an interim contact order in these circumstances is unusual for the reasons given. Many judges indeed, no doubt with a heavy heart because of the delay, would not have done so and it is difficult to see how such a refusal as a matter of principle could be criticised. On the other hand the judge in this case was alert to all the relevant issues, recognised the difficulties of the course that he had in mind and insisted on (and has got) a proposal for fully supervised contact. To say that he was plainly wrong would in reality be to say that it could really never be right to order interim contact in a *Re L* context where the principle of contact was in issue. It may only rarely be justified, perhaps, but in the context described in this judgment I am unable to say that this decision fell outside the generous breadth of discretion afforded to a trial judge, most particularly where a limited, interim order is under consideration. For those reasons, in my judgment, this appeal fails and must be dismissed.

B33 STOPPING CONTACT A LAST RESORT

Re P (Children)

[2008] EWCA Civ 1431, [2009] 1 FLR 1056 at 1065 and 1066

Court of Appeal

Ward LJ

[36] ... I am bound to say that I came into this court believing that, having read the written submissions of counsel for the mother and counsel for the guardian, this was an exercise of discretion with which the Court of Appeal could not interfere. But as the hearing progressed I became more and more concerned that the true underlying issue has not been fully or properly dealt with in a way which enables me to be satisfied that the judge has grappled with all the alternatives that were open to him, the most obvious of which was fully to explore, with the help of the guardian and through examination and cross-examination of the parties, the extent to which they would be willing to subjugate their intense personal feelings, their passionate conviction that each of them is right, to admit the possibility that they may be wrong, to admit the possibility that change could come about and to demonstrate that by undertaking some form of counselling. I can understand that this proud, intelligent father is humiliated by the findings of domestic violence against him, is humiliated by the prospect of having to attend a domestic violence course for anger management, but Mrs Holmes also recommended Relate, the marriage guidance service, and the good Dr Stuttaford with his innumerable connections and wide experience is, I have no doubt, well able to recommend to this father some course of anger management in which he can explain his feelings of anger and bitterness at this whole horrible 6 years of unhappiness, from the day the marriage broke down, his being removed from the home, the constant difficulties over the children. It is enough to make any ordinary man just a little bit angry, but that anger has to be contained, and sadly this father at the moment shows no capacity for containing that anger; hence the need for him to subject himself to what may be the humiliation of counselling and therapy, in order that he might begin to see how the other side view his behaviour and having some understanding of what the other side think of him is vitally important, and it enables changes to be made where reasonable changes are necessary.

[37] So that was not fully explored at this hearing, nor was the mother, it seems, sufficiently challenged by her need to undergo some form of therapy and counselling, her need to participate in a programme of help which might go some little way to assuaging the father's implacable

conviction that she is a woman with severe mental problems such as spill over to the detriment of his children.

[38] In my judgment, contact should not be stopped unless it is the last resort for the judge, and I have come to the conclusion that His Honour Judge Farmer, who tried this case perfectly fairly, did not have the opportunity over a continuous space of hearing to grapple with the problems in order to be able to hear the evidence in full and rule upon it. It is, in my judgment, unsatisfactory that he should conclude by agreeing that counselling would be helpful and be willing to hear the submissions about it and amend his order if necessary. He should not have made the order until he had had those submissions and heard the case accordingly.

...

[41] I would allow the appeal and direct that this matter be reheard. As for the schooling questions, namely, whether the father is to be barred from knowing where the children are at school, and whether he is entitled to communicate with the school and visit by prior arrangement, if the father did not demur through his counsel it does not behove him well to complain to his counsel about it but since those aspects of the mother are inextricably bound up, as the Cafcass officer observed, with whether or not there should be a direct contact, that order (if there is one) should be set aside. If there is no order, the father is at liberty to apply in respect of these matters.

[42] I would set aside the whole of paras 2 and 3 of the judge's order including the order discharging Mrs Holmes, whose help in this case is going to continue. She looks aghast at the prospect, but nonetheless her help is going to be invaluable in this case and I hope that she and those who represent her will continue to play their invaluable part.

[43] Meanwhile I would order that there be no direct contact pending the rehearing, but that the indirect contact be maintained. It appears that the email communications have not been very successful. It would be preferable in my view, taking up the suggestion of my Lord, Stanley Burnton LJ, if the children were given their individual email addresses so that the father is able to communicate directly to them. As my Lord observed, there is then a record of those communications. If they are inappropriate the father will pay the price; if they are appropriate he will gain the benefit. If the children do not respond the court will draw whatever conclusions are appropriate from their failures. If gifts are not being passed on they should be, and I hope that the mother will accept this admonition from me that the order of the court that mother act as the conduit is to be obeyed, for the only other option is for the gifts to be sent directly to her home and she will not like that. She has a bit of a choice to make and a bit of encouragement to give if, about which we cannot be sure, the presents are not getting through.

General notes:

This is, in effect, an application of the fundamental principle under the ECHR that national authorities must take all necessary steps to facilitate reunion as can reasonably be demanded in the special circumstances of each case: see eg *Hokkanen v Finland* [1996] 1 FLR 289 at B1 – Art 8: general principles and cf *Re S (Contact: promoting relationship with absent parent)* [2004] EWCA Civ 18, [2004] 1 FLR 1279 at B17 – Court must be reluctant to give up.

Specific issue / prohibited steps

B34   PSO AGAINST NON-PARTY

Re H (Prohibited steps order)

[1995] 1 FLR 638 at 641 and 641

Court of Appeal

Butler-Sloss LJ

In my view a prohibited steps order which requires Mr J not to have nor to seek contact with the children does not contravene s 9(5). If a 'no contact order' had been made in this case to the mother the order would be directed at the mother as the subject of the order and the obligation would be placed upon her to prevent any contact by the children with Mr J. There could not be a 'no contact order' which would direct Mr J not to have nor to seek contact with the four children since he does not live with the children. A contact order directed at the mother would not in this case achieve the required result. In the light of the speech of Lord Brandon in *Attorney-General v Times Newspapers* [1992] 1 AC 191 at p 203, knowledge of the order against the mother brought specifically to the attention of Mr J might be sufficient to show that he had aided and abetted the mother if she was shown herself to have disobeyed the order. On the evidence before us there is nothing to show that she would voluntarily bring the children into contact with Mr J. In any event, even without the practical difficulties of proving knowledge and enforcing the order, it does not provide adequate protection for the children, particularly when they are not in the care of their mother. They are all of school age and away from their mother for much of the day. With the best will in the world this mother could not protect her children going to or from school or at school or at play, nor could the school or even the police in the absence of an injunctive order directed at Mr J.

...

Miss Haywood for Mr J sought to convince us that it was wrong in principle to make an order against him when he was neither a party nor present in court. She conceded, rightly, that a person referred to in the definition of a prohibited steps order included those who were not parties. She argued however that, other than in an emergency, a court ought not to make such an order without giving the person against whom the order was sought an opportunity to be heard. It was unfortunate perhaps with hindsight that Mr J was not allowed to take part in the family proceedings despite his application to intervene. But at the time the district judge was entitled to refuse to join him. There will be situations, as occurred here, where the need to make the prohibited steps order in the interests of the child does not become apparent until a late stage of the proceedings.

The variety of circumstances in which a judge, in his discretion, might require to make an injunctive order for the protection of children is so great that it would be wrong for this court to say anything which might reduce the necessary flexibility of this important tool. The making of an ex parte order without notice to the recipient is not limited to family proceedings. In certain cases it is a proper order to make. Where a prohibited steps order is made against a person who is not a party and served on him he might not in all cases wish to be heard and might be content to accept the prohibition. For those who wish to object to the order made, s 10 might present a procedural difficulty in that a person not within the categories set out in that section requires leave to be heard on a s 8 application (s 10(2)). I have no doubt that a person against whom a prohibited steps order was made would be given leave to make a s 8 application to vary or discharge the prohibited steps order. But in any event the judge has the power to circumvent that procedural difficulty by making an order under s 11(7)(d) which states that a s 8 order may:

'... make such incidental, supplemental or consequential provision as the court thinks fit.'

In this case we have given Mr J liberty to apply on notice to vary or discharge the order under s 11(7)(d). In my view that is sufficient to meet the justice of the case by giving Mr J an opportunity to be heard but in the meantime providing immediate protection to the children and support for the mother in her efforts to give that protection.

B35 RELIGIOUS UPBRINGING / CIRCUMCISION

Re S (Specific issue order: religion: circumcision)

[2004] EWHC 1282 (Fam), [2005] 1 FLR 236 at 237, 252 and 255

Family Division

Baron J

[1] These applications concern two children, namely R, who was born on 20 June 1994 (so she is almost 10 years old), and K, who was born on 17 September 1995 (so he is now 8½ years old). The major application is made by the mother by which, in reality, she seeks permission for both of her children to become practising members of the Islamic faith. In consequence, she wants her son K to be circumcised. Her application is opposed by the father, who is a member of the Jain sect of the Hindu faith, and who wishes his children to continue to experience both faiths; his expectation being that they will be free to prefer one religion, if any, when they are more mature.

[2] Since the parties separated finally in 2002 the children have been based with their mother, but have stayed with their father each alternate weekend from Friday after school until Sunday evening, and for one half of each school holiday and half term. In addition, they currently spend some 2½ hours with him after school each alternate Wednesday. In the light of this arrangement, the children have an excellent relationship with each of their parents and fully appreciate that they come from a mixed cultural heritage.

...

The law

[74] My starting point is that the welfare of the children is paramount. Moreover I must and do take into account all the matters which are set out in the welfare checklist at s 1(3) of the Children Act 1989. I will not set them out verbatim as they are so well known. Suffice it to say that I have each matter set out in that subsection very fully in mind.

[75] The process of deciding whether or not to make a specific issue order involves the consideration of s 1(5) of the Children Act 1989, and I must not make an order unless I consider that doing so would be better for the children than making no order at all. I have no doubt, given the

decision in *Re J (Specific Issue Orders: Muslim Upbringing and Circumcision)*, that I do have the necessary jurisdiction to deal with the question of the children's future religion and whether K should be circumcised.

[76] In *Re R (A Minor) (Residence: Religion)* [1993] 2 FLR 163, at 171, it was said:

'It is no part of the court's function to comment upon the tenets, doctrines or rules of any particular section of society provided that those are legally and socially acceptable ... The impact of the tenets, doctrines and rules of a society upon a child's future welfare must be one of the relevant circumstances to be taken into account by the court when applying the provisions of s 1 of the Children Act 1989. The provisions of that section do not alter in their impact from one case to another and they are to be applied to the tests set out in accordance with the generally accepted standards of society, bearing in mind that the paramount objective of the exercise is promoting the child's welfare, not only in the immediate, but also in the medium and long-term future during his or her minority. That is well established.'

Wall J (as he then was) in *Re J (Specific Issue Orders: Muslim Upbringing and Circumcision)* [1999] 2 FLR 678 said:

'... following *Re R (A Minor)* it is no part of the court's function to take a stance anywhere along this spectrum of opinion. English law, as I understand it to be, is as follows:

(1)   that as an exercise of joint parental responsibility, male ritual circumcision is lawful; however

(2)   where there is a disagreement between those who have parental responsibility for the child as to whether or not he should be circumcised, the issue is one within the court's jurisdiction under s 8 of the Children Act 1989; and

(3)   the court must decide the question by application of s 1 of the Children Act 1989 as to the facts of the individual case.'

[77] The case of *Re J (Specific Issue Orders: Muslim Upbringing and Circumcision)* concerned a non-practising Muslim father who sought an order requiring a non-Muslim mother to bring their child up as a Muslim and pursuant to that for there to be a circumcision.

[78] Wall J – after stating that each case would turn on its own facts – held that (as stated in the headnote):

'(1)   Only in unusual circumstances would the court require that a child be brought up in a religion which was not that of the parent with whom the child was residing. In a case such as this, where the child was unlikely to have much contact with the Muslim world even when staying with his father, it would not be appropriate to require the mother to follow Muslim practices.

(2)   While it was lawful for two parents, jointly exercising parental responsibility for a male child, to arrange for the child to be ritually circumcised in accordance with their religious beliefs, where parents, or other persons having parental responsibility for the child, including a local authority, were in dispute over whether or not to circumcise a child, that dispute should be referred to the court for resolution, if need be as a matter of urgency. The court would then decide the question by applying s 1 of the Children Act 1989 to the facts of the case. In this case circumcision was not in the child's interests, as, although circumcision would firmly identify the child with his father, and confirm him as a Muslim in the eyes of Islam, it was a painful operation, which was opposed by his mother, and which would make him an exception among his peers.'

The Court of Appeal approved that order and the headnote sets out the findings which it made.

[79] I am also reminded, per *Dawson v Wearmouth* [1999] 2 AC 308, [1999] 1 FLR 1167, that I should not make an order unless there is evidence that it is in the child's best interests for me to do so. There is no question of there being a burden of proof on one party, or in this case the party who makes the application, but I must only make the order if I believe that it is in the child's best interests and is important to improve their quality of life.

[80] The case of *Re S (Change of Names: Cultural Factors)* [2001] 2 FLR 1005 was also put forward as being important.

...

[81] In the extreme circumstances of that case, the learned judge was only able to make an order for contact twice a year at a contact centre. Whilst he ordered that the child, then some 3½ years old, be known by a Muslim name, he refused to have his name changed by deed poll so that the retention of his birth name was ensured. He permitted circumcision. The factual matrix in that case was very different from the present case.

[82] I have also taken very fully into account the analogy which Mr Turner seeks to make with the *Payne v Payne*[1] line of authorities. That case, and the long line of earlier cases, provide that the reasonable plans of the residential person should not be thwarted. However, those plans

---

[1]   [2001] EWCA Civ 166, [2001] 1 FLR 1052.

have to be reasonable and have to be scrutinised with care because the court has to be satisfied that the motivation is proper and genuine. The authorities also make the point that a contented residential parent will make a better carer because personal unhappiness is likely to reflect badly on the children. I take that fully into account.

My conclusions

[83] I have reached the following conclusions on the application of the law and in the light of the evidence in this case:

(a) The children have a mixed cultural heritage and are of an age when they know, and have experienced, life both in a Jain and Muslim household.

(b) They live with their mother but they have a close continuing relationship with their father, which is very regular and meaningful. They clearly enjoy being with him and experience a different cultural outlook each time they see him. This means they have a continuing involvement with Jainism.

(c) Their mother is a devout Muslim but she has put her religion in second place when it has suited her. Her relationship with the father lasted from 1982 until 1998 and they continued in the same household until 2002. Whilst living with the father the household style was not Muslim but predominantly Jain. Thus, for most of her adult life, the mother was not a fully practising Muslim.

(d) The current problem stems not directly from the children's needs but, as I find, from the need of the mother and her family to portray her marriage as being to a Muslim man. The court should not sanction this deception, particularly when the children know the truth about their cultural heritage.

(e) There is no convincing evidence as to how the Bohra community will react, but even if it is adverse, the mother's family will not reject her and she has other social connections which will enable her to lead a wholly satisfactory life.

(f) The children are now aged almost 10 years and 8½ years old. That is too old to seek to favour one of their religions of origin in favour of the other.

(g) Each party has the religious duty to bring the children up in their religion. Each religion regards the children as one of their own and their parents agreed during their marriage that, at the very least, they would have the best of both worlds.

(h) If the children became fully practising Muslims they would not be able or be permitted to join in the religious part of any Jain sacrament.

(i) The mother can continue to practise her religion and to teach the children about Islam at home.

(j) The children of a mixed heritage should be allowed to decide for themselves which, if any, religion they wish to follow.

(k)   Circumcision once done cannot be undone. It may have an effect on K if he wishes to practice Jainism when he grows up. He has been ambivalent about his religion and is not old enough to decide or understand the long-term implications. It is not in his best interests to be circumcised at present. The Muslim religion, whilst favouring circumcision at 10 years and below, does permit of an upper age-limit of puberty or later on conversion. By the date of puberty K would be *Gillick* competent and so he could make an informed decision.

(l)   There are genuinely held concerns that if the children become practising Muslims their relationship with their father will be affected.

(m)   It is in the children's best interests to continue their lives as heretofore, that is, enjoying the best of both worlds.

[84]   Accordingly, the mother's application is rejected.

Sections 9–12

B36 APPLYING S 9(2) AND 9(5): S 8 ORDER DEFINITIONS

Nottinghamshire County Council v P

[1993] 2 FLR 134 at 138 and 143

Court of Appeal

Sir Stephen Brown P

The judge[1] continued at p 536H:

'I am invited by the local authority to exercise my power only to make a prohibited steps order. With shame I confess it partly my failure ... that no thought was given in May 1992 as to whether or not the local authority could apply for such an order. Perhaps the lectures on the Children Act I have given and attended have so whet my appetite for the delights of the flexible range of practical remedies on the s 8 "menu", that I totally forgot to ask myself whether it was right for me even to accept this invitation to dine at the private law table.

Having given thought to this question last night, I asked counsel to address me for the first time on the local authority's power to apply for a prohibited steps order which, as drafted by counsel for the local authority, would be an order that the father do leave the household at whatever its address may be, that he do not return to it, and that he has no contact with the children except as may be approved and supervised by the local authority. On looking more closely into the application, I have observed that what was sought when the matter came before the justices was leave to apply for the prohibited steps order, that leave being granted by a single justice. The application was for the court to order that the father should not reside in the same household as the three girls, M, K and E, should not have any contact with them unless they themselves wished to have contact with him, and any such contact be supervised by the social services department, such contact to be negotiated between the parents and the children. A condition was to be that mother should not

---

[1]   Ward J. The references to his judgment are to the report at [1993] 1 FLR 514.

knowingly place the girls in a position where they came into contact with or resided with the father. The local authority's plans set out in the box provided by the forms are that the girls should reside with their mother and that the mother should receive appropriate help and resources from the social services department and other appropriate agencies regarding sexual abuse. The children should only have contact with father at their request and under supervision. That is the way the case was put.

...

Section 9(5) provides:

'No court shall exercise its powers to make a specific issue order or prohibited steps order –

(a)   with a view to achieving a result which could be achieved by making a residence or contact order; or

(b)   in any way which is denied to the High Court (by section 100(2)) in the exercise of its inherent jurisdiction with respect to children.'

In the view of this court, the application for a prohibited steps order by this local authority was in reality being made with a view to achieving a result which could be achieved by making a residence or contact order. Section 9(2) specifically provides:

'No application may be made by a local authority for a residence order or contact order and no court shall make such an order in favour of a local authority.'

The court is satisfied that the local authority was indeed seeking to enter by the 'back door' as it were. It agrees with Ward J that he had no power to make a prohibited steps order in this case.

Submissions were made to this court to the effect that a contact order in any event necessarily implied a positive order and that an order which merely provided for 'no contact' could not be constructed as a contact order. There are certain passages in editorial comment which seem to support the view. We do not share it. We agree with the judge that the sensible and appropriate construction of the term 'contact order' includes a situation where a court is required to consider whether any contact should be provided for. An order that there shall be no contact falls within the general concept of contact, and common sense requires that it should be considered to fall within the definition of 'contact order' in s 8(1). We agree with the reasoning of Ward J and would therefore dismiss the appeal of the local authority against the refusal of its application for a prohibited steps order.

This case is also included in relation to:

D41 No power to compel LA to issue public law proceedings

B37   RESIDENCE ORDER TO FOSTER PARENTS

Gloucester County Council v P

[1999] 2 FLR 61 at 69

Court of Appeal

Robert Walker LJ

I suspect that the parliamentary history of the enactment might cast some light on this puzzle, but this court was not invited to look at any material under the principle in *Pepper v Hart (Inspector of Taxes)* [1993] AC 593. The court has to take the sections as it finds them and construe them in accordance with established principles. Judge Neligan was right to treat himself as bound to follow the view of Wall J, who is very experienced in family law, but the reasoning in Wall J's judgment is very succinct.

For my part, while extremely reluctant to differ from Thorpe LJ and Wall J on a point of family law, I have come to a different conclusion from them. I see the matter in the following way:

(1)   Section 10(1) and (2) draw a clear distinction between s 8 orders made on an application by a person, and orders made by the court (in the traditional phrase) of its own motion.

(2)   The court's powers under s 10(1) and (2), and would-be applicants' rights under s 10(4) to (8), are all 'subject to the restrictions imposed by section 9'. In order to see whether there are any relevant restrictions, it is necessary to look at s 9.

(3)   The restriction in s 9(3) is (in striking contrast to all the other restrictions except that in the first part of subs (2)) procedural in character: it disqualifies a particular class of person from applying for leave under s 10(1)(a)(ii) or (2)(b).

(4)   There is no reason to read into s 9(3) a further substantive restriction which Parliament has not spelled out since to do so would (a) ignore the distinction noted at (1) above; (b) ignore the different language used in other parts of s 9, including s 9(2); and (c) curtail the court's powers in an area in which any doubt should be resolved in favour of flexibility.

For those reasons I would allow this appeal. If the appeal were allowed Judge Neligan would, in reaching a decision at the full hearing, have well in mind the policy reasons which appear to underlie s 9(3). But Parliament has not in my judgment absolutely debarred him from making a residence order in favour of Mr and Mrs B, if they remain willing to have such an order made and the judge takes the view that that exceptional course is in J's best long-term interests.

General notes:

Butler-Sloss reached the same conclusion; Thorpe LJ dissented.

B38   PSO NOT TO BE USED AS INJUNCTION IN BREACH OF S 9(5)

Re S and D (Children: powers of court)

[1995] 2 FLR 456 at 462 and 464

Court of Appeal

Balcombe LJ

Those being the facts of this case, I now turn to the relevant law. I should turn first to the Children Act 1989. I need not at this stage refer to the provisions of s 1 of that Act; I shall have to refer to them later. In any event, they are very well known.

I turn first to s 8(1) which defines a prohibited steps order as meaning:

'... an order that no step which could be taken by a parent in meeting his parental responsibility for a child, and which is of a kind specified in the order, shall be taken by any person without the consent of the court; ...'

Section 9(5) provides that:

'No court shall exercise its powers to make a ... prohibited steps order –

...

(b)   in any way which is denied to the High Court (by section 100(2)) in the exercise of its inherent jurisdiction with respect to children.'

Section 20(8) provides that:

'Any person who has parental responsibility for a child may at any time remove the child from accommodation provided by or on behalf of the local authority under this section.'

'This section' means s 20 and is the provision by a local authority of accommodation for a child in need in cases where there has not been a care order. Finally, I refer to s 100(2) which provides that:

'No court shall exercise the High Court's inherent jurisdiction with respect to children –

...

(b)   so as to require a child to be accommodated by or on behalf of a local authority; ...'

It seems to me – indeed there was not really any significant argument about this before us; both parties have accepted that this is the case – that the judge had no power to grant the injunction which he granted. Although the order is in form an injunction, in substance it is a prohibited steps order under s 8(1), since it prevents the mother from taking a step which she would be otherwise entitled to take in line with her parental responsibility, that is removing her children from accommodation provided other than under a care order by the local authority. That is, of course, what s 20(8) says she can do.

Section 9(5) taken in conjunction with s 100(2)(b) specifically prevents a judge from making a prohibited steps order so as to require a child to be accommodated by a local authority. That is the first ground which makes it clear that the judge could not make the order which he did.

However, even if the order was, in substance as well as in form, an injunction, the judge was purporting to exercise an inherent jurisdiction to protect children, which the county court does not possess. If authority be needed for that proposition, it will be found in the case of *D v D (County Court: Jurisdiction: Injunctions)* [1993] 2 FLR 802.

I do not think I need go on. Although what the judge was seeking to do was with the best of intentions because he found himself in a dilemma, nevertheless, in my judgment, it was clear that he did not have the power to make the order which he did.

Indeed, even if it had been in the High Court, a High Court judge could not have made that particular order, because that would indeed have been prohibited by s 100(2)(b) of the Children Act 1989.

...

The judge is therefore faced with the dilemma with which this judge was faced that, if he makes a care order, the local authority may implement a care plan which he or she may take the view is not in the child or children's best interests. On the other hand, if he makes no order, he may be leaving the child in the care of an irresponsible, and indeed wholly inappropriate parent.

It seems to me that, regrettable though it may seem, the only course he may take is to choose what he considers to be the lesser of two evils. If he has no other route open to him – and certainly the route chosen by the judge in this case was one which, in my judgment, was not open to him –then that is the unfortunate position he has to face.

I have to say that this is not a position to which judges who exercise jurisdiction in the family courts are unaccustomed. There is very rarely a right answer in relation to children, it is usually a case of trying to decide which is the less wrong one.

It is an unhappy position, where there is a dispute between all those whose professional duty it is to have the best interests of the children at heart, if they cannot reach agreement. But in those particular circumstances, as I see it, the judge really has no alternative. He has to choose what he believes to be the lesser of two evils. That may be making a care order with the knowledge that the care plan is one which he does not approve, or it may be making no order with the consequences to which I have already adverted.

Other significant cases on this issue:

• *Re H (Prohibited steps order)* [1995] 1 FLR 638

B39   CA 1989, S 10(4): BIRTH PARENT NO LONGER 'PARENT' AFTER ADOPTION

Re C (A minor) (adopted child: contact)

[1993] 2 FLR 431 at 432

Family Division

Thorpe J

The first point taken by Mr Hayward Smith was that the application issued by his instructing solicitor on 11 January 1993 was misconceived. Mr Hayward Smith submitted that under the provisions of s 10 of the Children Act 1989 the mother did not require preliminary leave since she was a parent within the meaning of subs (4)(a). In response Mr Spon-Smith says that she is not a parent within the terms of s 10(4)(a), since the effect of the adoption order made on 7 June 1990 was to constitute the adoptive parents the parents for the purposes of s 10(4)(a). He supports that submission by referring to s 39(2) of the Adoption Act 1976[1] which says:

'An adopted child shall ... be treated in law as if he were not the child of any person other than the adopters or adopter.'

Section 39(6)(a) provides:

'this section –

(a)   applies for the construction of enactments or instruments passed or made before the adoption or later ...'

I am quite clear that Mr Spon-Smith is correct in this submission. It would, in my judgment, be manifestly undesirable if applications of this sort could be advanced without prior screening by means of the determination of applications for prior leave.

General notes:

Contact in the context of adoption raises the following possibilities for the birth family:

---

[1]   See now s 67 of the Adoption and Children Act 2002.

- when a PO is made: see E10 – ACA 2002, ss 26 and 27: contact on making PO
- when an AO is made: see E12 – ACA 2002, s 46(6): contact on making AO
- after AO is made: see B39 – CA 1989, s 10(4): birth parent no longer a 'parent' after adoption; B44 – CA 1989, s 10(9): broad assessment / post-adoption contact; and B45 – CA 1989, s 10(9): process when birth family apply after adoption

Other significant cases on this issue:

- *Re E (Adopted child: contact: leave)* [1995] 1 FLR 57

B40 CA 1989, S 10(8): APPLICATION FOR LEAVE BY CHILD

Re N (Contact: minor seeking leave to defend and removal of guardian)

[2003] 1 FLR 652 at 653, 655 and 659

Family Division

Coleridge J

This is not a straightforward application. It concerns a boy of 11 years and 4 months old, L, born on 23 May 1991. He himself makes two applications. The first application is pursuant to r 9(2)A of the Family Proceedings Rules, that he be given leave to defend the remaining stages of the proceedings without a next friend or guardian and for the removal of his present guardian ad litem. The second application that he makes is pursuant to s 10 of the Children Act 1989, that he be given leave to apply to discharge that part of para 7 of the order of His Honour Judge Rumbelow QC made on 19 July 2002 which prohibits any person from taking any step to arrange, consent to or otherwise facilitate therapy or formal counselling for L and to substitute an order that he be permitted to continue attending for therapy and counselling at Great Ormond Street Hospital (GOSH).

...

So far as the second application is concerned, that is governed by s 10 of the Children Act 1989 and the test is in one sense similar and in another sense not so. Under subs (8) of s 10:

> 'Where the person applying for leave to make an application for a section 8 order is the child concerned, the court may only grant leave if it is satisfied that he has sufficient understanding to make the proposed application for the section 8 order.'

The similarity between that and r 9(2)A is in relation to the first part of that test, namely the decision by the court as to whether or not it is satisfied that 'he has sufficient understanding to make the proposed application'. That seems to me to be in all material senses the same test as the test required by s 9(2)A but it is a discretionary test only being triggered once the court has been satisfied in relation to the sufficiency of the child's understanding and it is now well understood that even were I to be satisfied that the first part of the s 10 test was satisfied, I would need to go on and consider whether in all the circumstances against the background that exists in this case and the nature of the application it would be appropriate to grant L the leave which he seeks.

The manner in which the court should approach the question of a child's understanding has been considered in numerous cases. The most helpful encapsulation of the case-law I find to be that of Booth J in the case of *Re H (A Minor) (Guardian ad Litem: Requirement)* [1994] Fam 11, sub nom *Re H (A Minor) (Role of Official Solicitor)* [1993] 2 FLR 552 reading from 13 and 554H respectively. She said this:

> 'The approach to be taken by a court to an application such as this was fully canvassed by the Court of Appeal in *Re S (A Minor) (Independent Representation)* [1993] 2 FLR 437, in which judgment was delivered on 26 February 1993. The test is clear. The court must be satisfied that H, in this instance, has sufficient understanding to participate as a party in the proceedings without a guardian ad litem. Participating as a party, in my judgment, means much more than instructing a solicitor as to his own views. The child enters the arena amongst other adult parties. He may give evidence and he may be cross-examined. He will hear other parties, including in this case his parents, give evidence and be cross-examined. He must be able to give instructions on many different matters as the case goes through its stages and to make decisions as need arises. Thus a child is exposed and not protected in these procedures. It has yet to be determined how far the court has power, if it has any power, in such circumstances to deny a child access to the hearing. The child also will be bound to abide by the rules which govern other parties, including rules as to confidentiality.'

I find that a very succinct and useful statement of the law, relying as it does upon the very clear statement of the law set out by the Master of the Rolls in *Re S (A Minor) (Independent Representation)* [1993] Fam 263, [1993] 2 FLR 437, relying as he did upon a passage in an unreported case of Thorpe J called *Re T (A Minor)*, 28 January 1993, where Thorpe J, as he then was, said in proceedings launched under r 9(2)A by a 13 year old without a guardian:

> 'I am bound to say that in an issue of this great complexity and with a child of only 13 years of age, I doubt whether on an application for leave I would have been persuaded that she had sufficient understanding to participate without the aid of a guardian. In a case of this sort, which was referred to the High Court with much complexity and delicacy, I would have certainly regarded the Official Solicitor as the appropriate guardian ad litem.'

I have been referred to a number of other cases. I do not think they take the matter, so far as the law is concerned, any further in relation to this particular issue. Each child and each case has to be looked at separately. Some children of 12 or 13 are more sophisticated in their understanding and grasp of the essentials of a case than others. Equally, some cases are very much more straightforward than others and would therefore be more naturally capable of being fully appreciated and analysed by a young child.

...

Having considered the evidence fully and in particular the very careful arguments advanced by counsel, I have come to the conclusion that in this particular case and against the background of this particular long and stormy application, L does not have sufficient understanding to participate in the proceedings and give instructions that are fully considered in the sense of fully considered as to their implications. His wishes and feelings are clear beyond any doubt. That those have been communicated to the court on numerous occasions by the guardian is also beyond any doubt. He feels that he has not been listened to. What that means in practice, however, of course to a child is that the adults are not doing what he wants. That is very often the state of affairs in applications similar to this. He would undoubtedly become totally embroiled in the detail of this dispute if he is allowed to participate on his own account without the protection of the guardianship structure. I do not believe that he is able to appreciate that point at his young age and at his level of understanding, and unless he is able to appreciate the extent to which he will become embroiled even further than he is now in the battle, it seems to me that he cannot make an informed decision as to whether or not he should participate as a party. It is inconceivable, in my judgment, that at his age he is able to appreciate the totality of the complex issues in this case. It is, therefore, in my judgment, not one of those cases where it would be appropriate to give leave for the child to dispense with the services of the existing guardian or bring an application on his own behalf. I can see no advantage to him and indeed I can see a whole range of disadvantages. So I shall, having considered the matter with great care and particularly bearing in mind the expert views of Dr Asen, dismiss these applications.

Other significant cases on this issue:

- *Re HG (Specific issue order: sterilisation)* [1993] 1 FLR 587
- *Re C (Leave to seek section 8 orders)* [1994] 1 FLR 26
- *Re SC (A minor) (leave to seek residence order)* [1994] 1 FLR 96
- *Re C (Residence: child's application for leave)* [1995] 1 FLR 927
- *Re S (Contact: application by sibling)* [1998] 2 FLR 897

B41   CA 1989, S 10(8): 'THE CHILD CONCERNED'

Re S (Contact: application by sibling)

[1998] 2 FLR 897 at 904

Family Division

Charles J

Who is the child concerned – does s 10(8) or (9) apply?

...

I accept that if s 10(8) is read in isolation it could be said that where the applicant for leave is a child the 'child concerned' is the child applying for leave. But in my judgment when s 10(8) is construed in its context, and in particular with regard to s 10(1) and (9) and the definitions of s 8 orders in s 8(1), it is clear that this is not the case, and using the words of s 10(1) the 'child concerned' is the child with respect to whom the court may make a s 8 order.

To find out who that child is it is necessary to consider the definition of the relevant s 8 order. When this is done it can be seen that the 'child concerned' could be the applicant for leave as was the case in *Re SC (A Minor) (Leave to Seek Residence Order)* [1994] 1 FLR 96, and in *Re C (Residence: Child's Application for Leave)* [1995] 1 FLR 927 where in each case the application was for leave to bring proceedings seeking a residence order, but that often the 'child concerned' will not be the applicant for leave.

A 'contact order' means:

> '... an order requiring the person with whom a child lives, or is to live, to allow the child to visit or stay with the person named in the order, or for that person and the child otherwise to have contact with each other.'

The introductory part of that definition has the result that two people must be identified, namely the person with whom a child lives and that child. If that definition is applied in this case, and thus to the application which Y seeks leave to make, it would read as follows:

'... an order requiring Ms R the person with whom a child S lives, or is to live, to allow the child S to visit or stay with the person named in the order Y, or for that person Y and the child S otherwise to have contact with each other.'

When this is done it can be seen that:

(1) the child referred to in the definition of a contact order is S and thus the contact order being sought would, if granted, be made with respect to the child S and not Y, or as Wall J puts it in *Re T and E (Proceedings: Conflicting Interests)* [1995] 1 FLR 581 (for example at 588C) S would be the subject of the contact order,

(2) although it is not the case here the proposed applicant for the contact order, and thus the person seeking leave, could be S, and thus the applicant for a contact order can also be the child with respect to whom the order is made or who would be the subject of the order,

(3) although it is not the case here Y, the applicant, could be an adult,

(4) S could never be an adult because the subject of the order must by definition be a child, and

(5) Y is not the subject of the proposed contact order because an order that she be allowed to visit or stay with S would not be directed to her parents and therefore she is not the child referred to in the definition of a contact order.

It follows that an analysis of the definition identifies:

(a) the child (or children) with respect to whom a contact order can be made, or who are the subject of the application for a contact order, and the order itself, and thus in my judgment,

(b) the 'child concerned' in s 10(8) and (9).

In my judgment this conclusion is supported by:

(a) the point that subss 10(8) and 10(9) are not in terms that they make alternative provisions where the applicant is or is not a child, and

(b) the point that the 'child concerned' must identify the same child in both subss 10(8) and 10(9).

These points indicate that the identification of the 'child concerned' is to be made by reference to the s 8 order that the proposed applicant seeks leave to apply for, and not by reference to the identity of the applicant for leave.

Additionally in my judgment the conclusion I have reached is supported by the lack of guidelines to the exercise of the discretion to grant leave in s 10(8) and their inclusion in s 10(9). This is because when the child concerned is the subject of the proposed s 8 order as was the case in *Re*

SC (A Minor) (Leave to Seek Residence Order) [1994] 1 FLR 96, and in *Re C (Residence: Child's Application for Leave)* [1995] 1 FLR 927 that of itself indicates that the court is to have regard to the interests of that child.

This case is also included in relation to:

A3   Which child's welfare?

B42 CA 1989, S 10(9): WELFARE NOT PARAMOUNT

Re A and W (Minors) (residence orders: leave to apply)

[1992] 2 FLR 154 at 160 and 161

Court of Appeal

Balcombe LJ

In my judgment the judge was wrong in holding that on an application for leave to apply for a s 8 order by a person other than the child concerned, the child's welfare is the paramount consideration. I reach that conclusion for the following reasons:

(1) In granting or refusing an application for leave to apply for a s 8 order, the court is not determining a question with respect to the upbringing of the child concerned. That question only arises when the court hears the substantive application. The reasoning of this court in *F v S (Adoption: Ward)* [1973] Fam 203 supports this conclusion.

(2) Some of the express provisions of s 10(9) – eg paras (e) and (d)(i) – as to the matters to which the court is to have particular regard in deciding an application for leave to apply for a s 8 order would be otiose if the whole application was subject to the overriding provisions of s 1(1).

(3) There would have been little point in Parliament providing that the court was to have particular regard to the wishes and feelings of the child's parent, if the whole decision was to be subject to the overriding (paramount) consideration of the child's welfare.

...

In the circumstances it is not strictly necessary for me to express an opinion on the other submission made by Mr Allan Levy QC for Merton as to why the judge applied the wrong test in exercising his discretion. However, as the matter was fully argued before us, and as it raises a point of some general interest, I propose to do so. Mr Levy's submission was that because of the decisions of the House of Lords in *A v Liverpool City Council* [1982] AC 363, (1981) 2 FLR 222; *Re W (A Minor) (Wardship: Jurisdiction)* [1985] AC 791, [1985] FLR 879 and *Re M and H (Minors) (Local Authority: Parental Rights)* [1990] 1 AC 686, [1988] 2 FLR 431, the court should approach the exercise of its discretion in the case where (as here) the child is in the care of a local authority on the basis that, Parliament having entrusted the care of the child to the local authority, the court should not interfere with the local authority's care of the child save in the most exceptional circumstances. In my judgment the fallacy behind this submission lies in the fact that the principle of *A v Liverpool City Council* and the other cases cited relate to the law as it was before the substantial changes introduced by the Act. Before the Act the courts would not interfere with any decision by a local authority relating to a child in its care under statutory authority unless the local authority had itself brought the matter before the court, or the facts were such as to entitle the local authority's decision to be challenged by way of judicial review. See per Lord Wilberforce in *A v Liverpool City Council* [1982] AC at p 373, (1981) FLR at p 226. However, while that principle is maintained by the Act in relation to most matters concerning a child in the care of a local authority, a residence order under s 8 is expressly excepted by s 9(1). This represents a fundamental change in the law, and the Act, by ss 9(3) and 10(9), introduces its own limitations upon the persons who, and in the circumstances in which they, may apply for leave. However, that does not mean that on the application for leave the court gives no weight to the views of the local authority. On the contrary, s 10(9)(d)(i) provides that the court is to have particular regard to the authority's plans for the child's future. And s 22(3) provides that it is the duty of a local authority to safeguard and promote the welfare of any child in its care. Accordingly, the court should approach the application for leave on the basis that the authority's plans for the child's future are designed to safeguard and promote the child's welfare and that any departure from those plans might well disrupt 'the child's life to such an extent that he would be harmed by it'.

Other significant cases on this issue:

- *Re M (Care: contact: grandmother's application for leave)* [1995] 2 FLR 86: see D27 – Application for leave

B43   CA 1989, S 10(9): APPLYING THE STATUTORY CRITERIA

Re J (Leave to issue application for residence order)

[2003] 1 FLR 114 at 117

Court of Appeal

Thorpe LJ

[13]   The statutory checklist needs to be given its proper recognition and weight. Section 10(9) of the Children Act 1989 provides:

'Where the person applying for leave to make an application for a section 8 order is not the child concerned, the court shall, in deciding whether or not to grant leave, have particular regard to—

(a)   the nature of the proposed application for the section 8 order;
(b)   the applicant's connection with the child;
(c)   any risk there might be of that proposed application disrupting the child's life to such an extent that he would be harmed by it; and
(d)   where the child is being looked after by a local authority—
    (i)   the authority's plans for the child's future; and
    (ii)   the wishes and feelings of the child's parents.'

[14]   The statutory language is transparent. Nowhere does it import any obligation on the judge to carry out independently a review of future prospects.

[15]   The decision of this court in *Re M (Care: Contact: Grandmother's Application for Leave)*[1] was centred upon a consideration in another section of the statute, s 34(3), where the court is required to determine an application in relation to contact with children in care made by a person defined by subs (1). But in the course of his judgment, Ward LJ, recognising that s 10(9) did not directly govern applications for contact for a child in care, held that, nonetheless, it would be anomalous if the court, in exercising its discretion under s 34, did not have in mind the criteria contained in s 10(9). He held that those criteria were also apposite for applications brought under s 34(3) ...

[16]   Ward LJ went on to say that, in weighing up the factors, the court should apply the following test:

---
[1]   [1995] 2 FLR 86. See D27 – Application for leave.

'(1)   If the application is frivolous or vexatious or otherwise an abuse of the process of the court, of course it will fail.

(2)   If the application for leave fails to disclose that there is any eventual real prospect of success, if those prospects of success are remote so that the application is obviously unsustainable, then it must also be dismissed: see *W v Ealing London Borough Council* [1993] 2 FLR 788, approving *Cheshire County Council v M* [1993] 1 FLR 463.

(3)   The applicant must satisfy the court that there is a serious issue to try and must present a good arguable case ...'

[17]   I would observe that all that is said directly in relation to the discharge of the judicial task under s 34(3) and not directly in relation to the discharge of the judicial task under s 10(9). In my experience, trial judges have interpreted the decision in *Re M (Care: Contact: Grandmother's Application for Leave)* as requiring them, in the determination of applications under s 10(9) to apply the three-fold test formulated by Ward LJ which has the laudable purpose of excluding from the litigation exercise applications which are plainly hopeless.

[18]   I am particularly anxious at the development of a practice that seems to substitute the test, 'has the applicant satisfied the court that he or she has a good arguable case' for the test that Parliament applied in s 10(9). That anxiety is heightened in modern times where applicants under s 10(9) manifestly enjoy Art 6 rights to a fair trial and, in the nature of things, are also likely to enjoy Art 8 rights.

[19]   Whilst the decision in *Re M (Care: Contact: Grandmother's Application for Leave)* no doubt served a valuable purpose in its day and in relation to s 34(3) applications, it is important that trial judges should recognise the greater appreciation that has developed of the value of what grandparents have to offer, particularly to children of disabled parents. Judges should be careful not to dismiss such opportunities without full inquiry. That seems to me to be the minimum essential protection of Arts 6 and 8 rights that Mrs J enjoys, given the very sad circumstances of the family.

Other significant cases on this issue:

- *Re A (Section 8 order: grandparent application)* [1995] 2 FLR 153
- *Re W (Contact: application by grandparent)* [1997] 1 FLR 793

B44   CA 1989, S 10(9): BROAD ASSESSMENT / POST-ADOPTION CONTACT

Re R (Adoption: contact)

[2005] EWCA Civ 1128, [2006] 1 FLR 373 at 383

Court of Appeal

Wall LJ

[38] In this context, Mr Bennett referred us to two decisions of this court, namely *Re J (Leave to Issue Application for Residence Order)* [2002] EWCA Civ 1364, [2003] 1 FLR 114 and *Re H* [2003] EWCA Civ 369 20 February 2003, CA, but which is not otherwise reported. Both were grandparents' applications. In the first, the maternal grandmother sought permission to intervene in care proceedings to put herself forward as the carer of her young grandchild. The local authority objected to the intervention, as I think did the guardian, and the judge refused it. The grandmother appealed and I read from the headnote:

'**Held** – allowing the appeal –

When considering a grandparent's application for leave to (1) make an application for a residence order, the statutory checklist needed to be given its proper recognition and weight. Whilst the decision in *Re M (Care: Contact: Grandmother's Application for Leave)* had served a valuable purpose in its day and in relation to s 34(3) applications, it was not appropriate to substitute the test "has the applicant satisfied the court that he or she has a good arguable case" for the test that Parliament set out in s 10(9) of the Children Act 1989 ...'

[39] Having set out the terms of the section, Thorpe LJ (who gave the leading judgment, with which Ferris J agreed) said:

'[14] The statutory language is transparent. Nowhere does itimport any obligation on the judge to carry out independently a review of future prospects.'

[40] Having then examined the decision of this court and in particular the judgment of Ward LJ in *Re M (Care: Contact: Grandmother's Application for Leave)* [1995] 2 FLR 86, he concludes with these terms:

'[17] I would observe that all that is said directly in relation to the discharge of the judicial task under s 34(3) and not directly in relation to the discharge of the judicial task under s 10(9). In my experience, trial judges have interpreted the decision in *Re M (Care: Contact: Grandmother's Application for Leave)* as requiring them, in the determination of applications under s 10(9) to apply the three-fold test formulated by Ward LJ which has the laudable purpose of excluding from the litigation exercise applications which are plainly hopeless.

[18] I am particularly anxious at the development of apractice that seems to substitute the test, "has the applicant satisfied the court that he or she has a good arguable case" for the test that Parliament applied in s 10(9). That anxiety is heightened in modern times where applicants under s 10(9) manifestly enjoy Art 6 rights to a fair trial and, in the nature of things, are also likely to enjoy Art 8 rights.'

[41] In essence, therefore, Thorpe LJ, as I understand it, was disapproving the approach of this court in *Re M*, relating to applications for permission to apply for contact to children in care, where Ward LJ had devised a test that the case would not be allowed to proceed if it was frivolous or vexatious or otherwise an abuse of the process or bound to fail, and would not be allowed to proceed if it failed to disclose that there was any eventual real prospect of success.

[42] The applicant on that basis, applying that test, had to satisfy the court that there was a serious issue to try and must present a good arguable case. By analogy, therefore, Mr Bennett argues that what the court has done in this case, is to look at the likely outcome of any prospective application for contact within the adoption proceedings, decide, applying *Re C*,[1] that it is unlikely to succeed, and has used that reasoning process to refuse the application for permission.

[43] Mr Bennett bolstered that argument by reference to the second case, *Re H*, which again was a case by a grandmother seeking permission to make an application. During the course of his judgment in that case, Thorpe LJ commented:

'[15] The whole purpose of the decision in *Re J* was to draw the attention of trial judges to the need to adopt a careful review of the s 10(9) criteria and not to replace those tests simply with a broad evaluation of the applicant's future prospects of success.'

[44] Accordingly, Mr Bennett argued, that when Her Honour Judge Judith Hughes QC applied Lord Ackner's dictum in *Re C*, she was misdirecting herself and applying the wrong test. She was, in effect, as

---

[1] *Re C (A Minor) (Adoption Order: Conditions)* [1989] AC 1, [1988] 2 WLR 474, [1988] 1 All ER 705, [1988] 2 FLR 159, HL.

I indicated a moment ago, saying that the court would be most unlikely to make a contact order contrary to the wishes of the prospective adopters, therefore the application should not proceed. That, Mr Bennett submitted, was plainly inconsistent with both *Re J* and *Re H,* and was sufficient to vitiate the judge's discretion.

[45] That is, I think, a powerful submission, but in my judgment there are two answers to it. The first lies in the language of s 10(9)(a) itself, 'the nature of the proposed application for the s 8 order'. The statute of course applies to every type of s 8 order, of which there are four. It applies to every applicant, of whom there can be an almost infinite variety. In the instant case, the application is for a contact order within adoption proceedings; and an order, moreover, designed to continue in being after the adoption order itself has been made. In these circumstances, it seems to me that the court simply cannot shut its mind to the fact that this is such an application and is, moreover, bound to have regard to the fact that, under the jurisprudence which has developed, contact orders in adoption proceedings are of themselves unusual, and that both the practice of the court and the courts in approaching them have regarded such orders as unusual.

[46] Secondly, it does not seem to me that either s 10(9) or the two cases in this court on which Mr Bennett relies prohibit a broad assessment of the merits of a particular application. What they prohibit is the determination of the application on the 'no reasonable prospects of success' criterion.

[47] It is, of course, the case that matters have moved on very substantially since *Re C.* When *Re C* was decided, the Children Act 1989 was not in force and adoption proceedings were not designated as family proceedings. Accordingly, if there was to be post-adoption contact between siblings or other members of the adopted child's family, the only way that could be enforced was by conditions being written into the adoption order under s 8 of the Children Act 1989. Equally, back in those days it was much more common, as Lord Ackner himself points out, for there to be no contact between family members and the adopted child after an adoption order had been made; although, of course, he recognises that there were exceptions to that rule.

[48] We were shown s 1 of the new Adoption and Children Act 2002, which is due in force later this year, which demonstrates the clear change of thinking there has been since 1976, when the Adoption Act was initially enacted, and which demonstrates that the court now will need to take into account and consider the relationship the child had with members of the natural family, and the likelihood of that relationship continuing and the value of the relationship to the child.

[49] So contact is more common, but nonetheless the jurisprudence I think is clear. The imposition on prospective adopters of orders for contact with which they are not in agreement is extremely, and remains extremely, unusual.

[50] So having regard to s 10(9)(a) the nature of the proposed application in this case inevitably involves, in my view, a consideration of the jurisprudence surrounding the circumstances in which such orders may or may not be made. In my view, the judge was plainly entitled in those circumstances to take into account that the court would be reluctant to make an order in the face of reasonable opposition from the prospective adopters. I use the phrase 'reasonable opposition', because it seems to me that one of the ways in which the law has shifted is demonstrated by the decision of this court in the case of in *Re T (Minors) (Adopted Children: Contact)* [1996] Fam 34. In that case, a half-sister had been assured that when her half-sister was adopted she would be given annual reports as to her progress. No report was provided. When she inquired and complained, she was told that the adopters had changed their minds and that it was not in the children's interests for the report to be provided. Furthermore, confidentiality precluded any explanation of the reasons for that refusal. She applied to the court for leave to make an application for contact. The judge refused it. She appealed to this court, and this court allowed her appeal. This court balanced carefully on the one hand the right of an adoptive family to protection of confidentiality and their right to bring up the adopted child in the way that they thought appropriate, and the inappropriateness of enforcing informal arrangements which might no longer be appropriate and which, therefore, fell to the prospective adopters to terminate. On the other hand, for the applicant it was argued that if this decision was allowed to stand it meant that adoptive parents could effectively ignore any agreement entered into in the best interests of the child in question, and that that would, in fact, result in more contests and more difficulties in prospective applications. The court came down firmly in favour of the latter proposition.

[51] Balcombe LJ (giving the leading judgment in *Re T*) said, at 41E:

> 'I am not saying that it should never be open to adopters to change their minds and resile from an informal agreement made at the time of the adoption. But if they do so they should, as Butler-Sloss LJ said in *In Re T (A Minor) (Contact After Adoption)* [1995] 2 FCR 537, 543 give their reasons clearly so that the other party to the arrangement, *and if necessary the court*, may have the opportunity to consider the adequacy of those reasons. Nor need adopters fear that their reasons, when given, will be subjected to critical legal analysis. The judges who hear family cases are well aware of the stresses and strains to which adopters in the position of Mr and Mrs H are subject and a simple explanation of their reasons in non-legal terms would usually be all that is necessary. In my judgment where

adopters in the position of Mr and Mrs H simply refuse to provide an explanation for their change of heart, particularly where, as here, the contact envisaged – the provision of a report – is of a nature which is most unlikely to be disruptive of the children's lives, it is not appropriate for the court to accept that position without more.'

The court allowed the appeal and gave permission for the application to proceed.

[52] Thus, in the instant case, had the prospective adopters resiled completely from their previous agreement in relation to contact, and had the judge in those circumstances refused permission, I think I would, speaking for myself, have allowed this appeal and allowed K's application to proceed.

[53] However, that is not the adopters' position. The principle of contact is not in dispute. Face-to-face contact indeed is offered, albeit once a year, but with the prospect of more frequent contact if the placement is secure and L is settled within it. More frequent indirect contact is also offered. It seems to me that the position of the prospective adopters, supported, as it is, by the guardian and the local authority, cannot in these circumstances be said to be unreasonable.

[54] Therefore, although the judge did not specifically refer to authority or analyse s 10(9)(a) in the way that might have been preferable, I am nonetheless quite satisfied that, speaking for myself, if one does apply s 10(9)(a) appropriately, it leads one to the proposition that the nature of this application is unlikely in the interests of the child to result in an order, and that an order might well be, in any event, inappropriate.

[55] Section 10(9)(b) was, of course, in the judge's mind. As to s 10(9)(c), this of course refers to the risk of disruption posed by the application, not by the outcome of the application. I do not think one has to be particularly far-sighted to perceive a genuine risk to L from ongoing litigation. Proceedings, unfortunately, have the effect of polarising attitudes. There would be delay. There would, undoubtedly, be tension on the part of the prospective adopters. There would be, as the judge pointed out, additional costs, none of which is in the interests of L and none of which, it seems to me, can be ignored when it comes to the question of the risk of disruption to L posed by the application.

[56] That, it seems to me, is the heart of the appeal. It is certainly the major point of law in the appeal, in what is otherwise essentially a discretionary exercise. I quite understand K's concern that there has been no evidence as to L's upset or inability to settle. Indeed, indications which have emerged have been somewhat contradictory. Equally, I understand

that we do not have statements from the prospective adopters on oath explaining why it is they are anxious about the prospects of breach of confidentiality and so on.

[57] But, speaking for myself, I do not think that formalisation of the issues in this way would advance the matter very much. I would not dream for one moment to try and go behind the obviously detailed and careful negotiations there have been. But I am reasonably confident that in this particular case both sides understand the other's position. When one comes to analyse it, helpfully with the latest report of the guardian, whose mind itself has swayed both ways on this issue, I am prepared to accept, from what the guardian tells me, that the prospective adopters are genuinely anxious, not only about the outcome of the proceedings but about the issues that they raise, that their attitude to contact is a perfectly reasonable one, and that this is now a case which has to be dealt with by the human beings on the ground and is not one dealt with by legal proceedings. All that, in my judgment, comes within s 10(9)(a).

[58] Therefore, having looked at the matter I hope carefully and I hope, as I said at the outset of this judgment, with particular sympathy for K, her half-sister and indeed the prospective adopters, I have come to the conclusion that the judge, albeit in a somewhat terse way and without perhaps ticking the boxes and going through the hoops or jumping the hurdles one would have wished her to have done, nonetheless, has reached the right conclusion.

[59] In those circumstances, I see no alternative but the dismissal of the appeal.

General notes:

Contact in the context of adoption raises the following possibilities for the birth family:

- when a PO is made: see E10 – ACA 2002, ss 26 and 27: contact on making PO;
- when an AO is made: see E12 – ACA 2002, s 46(6): contact on making AO;
- after AO is made: see B39 – CA 1989, s 10(4): birth parent no longer a 'parent' after adoption; B44 – CA 1989, s 10(9): broad assessment / post-adoption contact; and B45 – CA 1989, s 10(9): process when birth family apply after adoption.

Other significant cases on this issue:

- *Re W (Care proceedings: leave to apply)* [2004] EWHC 3342 (Fam), [2005] 2 FLR 468

• *Re R (Adoption: contact)* [2005] EWCA Civ 1128, [2006] 1 FLR 373

B45   CA 1989, S 10(9): PROCESS WHEN BIRTH FAMILY APPLY AFTER ADOPTION

Re T (Adopted children: contact)

[1995] 2 FLR 792 at 798

Court of Appeal

Balcombe LJ

It is of the highest importance that adoption proceedings should be conducted in a spirit of co-operation between the adopters and the natural family, whenever that is possible. It is equally important that if there are irreconcilable differences then those should be resolved at the time of the adoption, and not put off until some future occasion. If adopters do not feel able to cope even with indirect contact they should say so at the time. It is not acceptable, and would lead to the undesirable consequences outlined by Mr Rogers, if having agreed to some form of indirect contact, they could resile from that agreement without proffering any explanation. I am not saying that it should never be open to adopters to change their minds and resile from an informal agreement made at the time of the adoption. But if they do so they should, as Butler-Sloss LJ said in *Re T* (above), give their reasons clearly so that the other party to the arrangement, and if necessary the court, may have the opportunity to consider the adequacy of those reasons. Nor need adopters fear that their reasons, when given, will be subjected to critical legal analysis. The judges who hear family cases are well aware of the stresses and strains to which adopters in the position of Mr and Mrs H are subject and a simple explanation of their reasons in non-legal terms would usually be all that is necessary. In my judgment where adopters in the position of Mr and Mrs H simply refuse to provide an explanation for their change of heart, especially where, as here, the contact envisaged (the provision of a report) is of a nature which is most unlikely to be disruptive of the children's lives, it is not appropriate for the court to accept that position without more.

We were invited by both parties to say something about the appropriate procedures in cases involving applications for leave to apply for direct or indirect contact after adoption. In *Re C* (above) Thorpe J sought to indicate a procedure and the headnote to the report of that case in [1993] Fam 210 reads:

'Applications for such leave should be transferred to the Family Division of the High Court; in most cases it will be appropriate for the Official Solicitor to be made a respondent and for the local authority involved in the adoption proceedings to be notified of the application, but the adoptive parents should only be informed of the application if the court is satisfied that the mother has a prima facie case for leave.'

In *Re T* (above) Butler-Sloss LJ said (at p 257B) that a district judge in the local registry, to whom the application for leave would be likely to go in the first place, might think that the procedure indicated by Thorpe J in *Re C* (above) was not necessarily appropriate, and indeed in the present case the application stayed in the county court and the Official Solicitor was not joined as a respondent. In my judgment the procedure should be designed to ensure that adoptive parents are not unnecessarily disturbed by applications of this nature and also that the judge who hears the application should have as much relevant information as possible. For those reasons it will normally be appropriate for the court to direct that the adoption agency (often a local authority) should in the first instance be given notice of the application for leave. On the other hand I do not consider that the application for leave, which is intended to act as a filter to save persons who have the care of children from being vexed by applications which lack merit or prospects of success, should be treated as if it were the substantive application. Thus I do not accept Mr Karsten's suggestion that the local authority should be given the opportunity of becoming a party to the application, so that it has the same right of appeal as the applicant. Nor do I agree with Thorpe J's acceptance of Mr Spon-Smith's submission in *Re C* (above) that in most cases it will be appropriate for the Official Solicitor to be brought in as a respondent to the application for leave. I repeat that the object is to ensure that adopters in the position of Mr and Mrs H are not unnecessarily worried but that at the same time the court has before it such information as it considers necessary to determine the application for leave, bearing in mind that that is not the substantive application. In most cases it should be sufficient to notify the local authority, if that was the adoption agency; in some cases it may be necessary to transfer the application to the High Court and to bring in the Official Solicitor but I see no reason why that should be the general rule.

General notes:

Contact in the context of adoption raises the following possibilities for the birth family:

- when a PO is made: see E10 – ACA 2002, ss 26 and 27: contact on making PO;
- when an AO is made: see E12 – ACA 2002, s 46(6): contact on making AO;
- after AO is made: see B39 – CA 1989, s 10(4): birth parent no longer a 'parent' after adoption; B44 – CA 1989, s 10(9): broad

assessment / post-adoption contact; and B45 – CA 1989, s 10(9): process when birth family apply after adoption.

B46   CA 1989, S 11(7) CONDITIONS (1)

Re E (Residence: imposition of conditions)

[1997] 2 FLR 638 at 641

Court of Appeal

Butler-Sloss LJ

Section 11(7) applies to all four s 8 orders, including prohibited steps orders and specific issue orders. The wording of the subsection is wide enough to give the court the power to make an order restricting the right of residence to a specified place within the UK. But in my view a restriction upon the right of the carer of the child to choose where to live sits uneasily with the general understanding of what is meant by a residence order. In *Re D (Minors) (Residence: Imposition of Conditions)* [1996] 2 FLR 281, this court considered a similar condition placed on a residence order. In that case the mother had originally agreed that she would not bring the children into contact with the man with whom she had been living. On her subsequent application to discharge that condition this court held that a s 11(7) condition could not exclude another person from the mother's home, thereby interfering with her right to live with whom she liked. Ward LJ said:

> 'The court was not in a position to overrule her decision to live her life as she chose. What was before the court was the issue of whether she should have the children living with her.'

That decision in my judgment applies with equal force to the issue in the present appeal.

A general imposition of conditions on residence orders was clearly not contemplated by Parliament and where the parent is entirely suitable and the court intends to make a residence order in favour of that parent, a condition of residence is in my view an unwarranted imposition upon the right of the parent to choose where he/she will live within the UK or with whom. There may be exceptional cases, for instance, where the court, in the private law context, has concerns about the ability of the parent to be granted a residence order to be a satisfactory carer but there is no better solution than to place the child with that parent. The court might consider it necessary to keep some control over the parent by way of conditions which include a condition of residence. Again, in public law cases involving local authorities, where a residence order may be made by the court in preference to a care order, s 11(7) conditions might be applied in somewhat different circumstances.

The correct approach is to look at the issue of where the children will live as one of the relevant factors in the context of the cross-applications for residence and not as a separate issue divorced from the question of residence. If the case is finely balanced between the respective advantages and disadvantages of the parents, the proposals put forward by each parent will assume considerable importance. If one parent's plan is to remove the children against their wishes to a part of the country less suitable for them, it is an important factor to be taken into account by the court and might persuade the court in some cases to make a residence order in favour of the other parent. But, on the facts of the present appeal, it is clear that the welfare of the children points firmly to their living with their mother, and the advantage of remaining in London is outweighed by the other factors leading to granting a residence order to the mother.

The judge attempted to identify the present circumstances as exceptional, but even if he were justified in imposing the condition, which in my view he was not, it would give rise to the temptation to impose conditions in many cases where the proposals for the children were not, as they often are not, ideal. It is not unusual for the suggested arrangements to have the effect of depriving the children of frequent contact with the other parent and his relatives, of their present home, of their schools and their friends. There are increasing numbers of mixed marriages and the areas of concentration of mixed communities are not evenly distributed. The situation facing the judge in this case was not unique and may well become more frequent.

In my view the principles set out in a long line of authorities relating to leave to remove permanently from the jurisdiction have no application to conditions proposed under s 11(7). Miss Allen for the mother was also justified in criticising the judge for requiring the mother to live with the children in London because the father was unreliable over contact. As Miss Allen said, the mother was being penalised for the inadequacies of the father. Bearing in mind that E is 11 and A although only 6 has a close relationship with her father, the requirement for frequent rather than extended contact appears to me to be unnecessary and was not suggested to be necessary by the court welfare officer. The importance of maintaining close links with the father and with his family in London must not be under-estimated by the mother. Suitable contact arrangements can however be made for a major part of the school holidays, part of half-terms and rely less upon weekend contact which would involve the children in a 600-mile journey over 2 days. This extended contact can be made not only with the father, who may continue to put his business first but also, with the agreement of the paternal aunts, with them and the cousins in London or holidays abroad as before.

Other significant cases on this issue:

* *B v B* [2004] 2 FLR 979 (Residence: condition limiting geographic area)

B47   CA 1989, S 11(7) CONDITIONS (2)

Re H (Residence order: placement out of jurisdiction)

[2004] EWHC 3243 (Fam), [2006] 1 FLR 1140 at 1144 and 1145

Family Division

Hedley J

[18]   That brings me to the most difficult and probably most contentious aspect of the matter, which is whether there ought to be conditions attached to the residence order that, as I say, everybody accepts I ought to make. I think before dealing with the question of conditions, it would be proper for the court to express its view on the merits of the propositions which are intended to be incorporated into these conditions. They are two-fold: first, it is said there should be a condition that no steps should be taken to place these children in the care of either or both of their parents until they reach the age of 6 and the second is that contact should be restricted to twice a week until the children are at least 4 years old, which is about 15 months on from now.

...

[22]   It has been recognised over the years that s 11(7) is drawn extremely widely. It has been recognised that it would not be wise to try to define the scope of the section when it has been left deliberately vague. But it has also become apparent from a number of authorities that there are limits to the conditions and that there are matters – for example, directing that a child shall not be removed from a particular area of the jurisdiction itself – which go beyond the kind of matters that s 11(7) of the 1989 Act ought to address.

[23]   I have to say, I have some anxiety about the propriety of using s 11(7) to deal with matters as profound as change of residence and contact. My inclination is that s 11(7) is to be used for rather more limited purposes than that. However, that does not matter because I have a much more principled objection to using s 11(7) in these circumstances. It is two-fold. First, any such condition would be wholly unenforceable and I am very reluctant to make an order over which I know the court will not have any control at all. Secondly, it seems to me that the making of such conditions is in fact contrary to the principle that these children are now living in a different family, in a different culture, in a different country to which family, culture and country they forthwith must be seen to belong.

For those reasons, I do not think it would be a proper use of s 11(7) and would be contrary to the principle of the care plan in this case to make conditions of that sort.

Change of name

B48   CHANGE OF SURNAME (1)

Dawson v Wearmouth

[1999] 1 FLR 1167 at 1173

House of Lords

Lord Mackay

[The Court of Appeal] concluded as I have said that if there is a general principle underlying this appeal it is that the registration of change of a child's surname is a profound and not a merely formal issue whatever the age of the child. Any dispute on such an issue must be referred to the court for determination whether or not there is a residence order in force and whoever has or has not parental responsibility. No disputed registration or change should be made unilaterally. On the facts of this case the mother, they said, was not in breach of that principle.

From this passage in the Court of Appeal's judgment, I take it they were saying that at the stage of registration in the circumstances of this case the mother had a duty to register the child with the surname by which at that time she intended that the child should be known. It is common ground that the father had neither power nor duty to intervene in the registration process. The Court of Appeal's ultimate decision may be summarised by saying that in order to justify an order requiring a change of name, considerations relative to the child's welfare will have to be advanced for that purpose. The name chosen and registered was the mother's actual surname at the time as well as being that of Alexander's half-brother and half-sister. It was therefore a perfectly natural and logical choice to make and to justify making an order for changing that name, strong countervailing considerations would be required. The only one really suggested was that a change to the father's name would assist in maintaining Alexander's connection with him and emphasise his paternal connection. They point out that this would apply in virtually every case to an illegitimate child where the father seeks to play some role in the child's life. In the circumstances, they concluded that there was no justification for ordering an alteration in the child's name particularly as his first name was that chosen by the father.

Counsel for the father submitted that the Court of Appeal had given far too much emphasis to the registration, that while a period of usage of a name might justify making it difficult to order a change, there was no such usage in the present case and that it would be positively in the interest of the welfare of the child to have the surname which linked the child with his father and thus helped to maintain that relationship which would be beneficial for his welfare. A number of cases were cited to us in which the importance of a change of name and in which the aspect of connection with the child's father were emphasised, but in these cases the change sought by the mother was normally from a surname which was the father's established by usage, to a name which was either that of another man or her own.

The facts of this case distinguish it from these as there is no suggestion of any substantial usage and ultimately the right course, in my opinion, must be to apply the criteria in s 1 of the 1989 Act including s 1(5) and not make an order for the change of name unless there is some evidence that this would lead to an improvement from the point of view of the welfare of the child.

In this connection the welfare officer's conclusion, to which I have already referred, is relevant.[1]

The application of s 1, so long as they take account of the criteria there in question, is a matter within the discretion of the Court of Appeal and I can see no ground for suggesting that they have erred in principle. The heavy emphasis on the registration is, I think, a reflection of the fact that they considered that the judge had wrongly left that out of account and that the application must be understood as for a change from a name already registered and therefore that in the light of s 1 of the Children Act some circumstances required to be pointed to which would justify making that change in the interest of the child's welfare. In fairness to the Court of Appeal, it must be pointed out that, although they described the fact that the name sought to be changed was the duly registered name as all-important, they coupled that with the circumstances that the name Wearmouth was the mother's actual name at the time it was chosen by her, as well as being that of Alexander's half-brother and half-sister, in stating their view that their discretion should be exercised against the making of the order for change.

Counsel for the father also referred to the provisions of the European Convention on Human Rights and suggested that, in the light of the decision of the Court of Human Rights in Strasbourg in the case of *Keegan v Ireland* (1994) 18 EHRR 342, 362, if the provisions of the

---

[1]   The court welfare officer's report dated 18 December 1996 stated: 'In respect of Mr Dawson's application to have the child's surname changed to his, I would see [sic] that at this stage his surname would have no impact on the welfare of the child, and is more an issue which is in the realms of case-law.'

system for the registration of births and the emphasis of the Court of Appeal in the present case on registration were taken together, this deprived the father of his rights in terms of Art 8 of the Convention.

In my opinion, on a fair reading of the decision of the Court of Appeal they were suggesting not that the registration was conclusive of the issue in the present case but that in order to justify changing the name from that which was registered circumstances justifying the change would be required and they concluded in the exercise of their discretion that there were no such circumstances of sufficient strength to do so in the present case. In that situation, in my opinion, the argument on the Convention has no separate validity from the earlier arguments for counsel for the father to which I have referred.

This is a difficult and narrow case, but on a fair reading of the judgment of the Court of Appeal as a whole, I am satisfied that they correctly applied the provisions of the Children Act and in particular s 1 in the exercise of their discretion to refuse to make an order for change of name in the present case. For these reasons, I would dismiss this appeal.

B49   CHANGE OF SURNAME (2)

Dawson v Wearmouth

[1997] 2 FLR 629 at 633

Court of Appeal

Hirst and Thorpe LJJ (joint judgment)

Against that background[1] we turn to the Children Act 1989. In almost every case before the court exercises any jurisdiction in respect of a child the child in question will possess what might be described as his surname of origin, by which we mean the surname under which his birth has been registered. Mr Hayward-Smith's submission is that the court's jurisdiction to entertain an application to change such a surname is limited to s 13 with its side-note 'Change of child's name or removal from jurisdiction'. The relevant words of the section are then as follows:

> 'Where a residence order is in force with respect to a child, no person may —
>
> (a)   cause the child to be known by a new surname; or
> (b)   remove him from the United Kingdom;
>
> without either the written consent of every person who has parental responsibility for the child or the leave of the court.'

That specific provision he submits excludes the exercise of a general power under s 8 to make a specific issue order in relation to a child's surname. However, he accepts that there would be jurisdiction under s 8 to make a prohibited steps order in relation to a proposed change of a child's surname. The submission rests largely on the judgment of this court in the case of *Re B (Change of Surname)* [1996] 1 FLR 791. In that case the mother sought to change the surname of the three children of the family from that of her divorced husband to that of the husband whom she had subsequently married. Her application for leave was refused by the circuit judge and this court upheld his refusal. The case was transitional in that the order in relation to the children had been a custody order made in the suit prior to the commencement of the Children Act 1989. However, it was rightly treated as a deemed residence order and her application was therefore rightly treated as an application for leave under s 13. Counsel for the father sought to argue that the application was for a specific issue order under s 8. (It may be assumed that the underlying strategy was then

---

[1]   Analysis of the Births and Deaths Registration Act 1953.

to advance the argument that, since the determination of a s 8 application was subject to the s 1(3) checklist, the views of the three children aged between 17 and 12 were almost decisive.) The submission was rejected by Wilson J in these terms:

'For Miss Moulder, on behalf of the father, submits that an application relating to a child's surname under the 1989 Act is a type of application for a specific issue order within the meaning of s 8 rather than a free-standing application under s 13 of the Act. In that submission she is supported by the editors of *Rayden & Jackson Divorce and Family Matters* (Butterworths, 16th edn, 1991), vol 1, pp 1081–1082. She contends that, on a proper reading, s 13 is purely prohibitory and does not itself give jurisdiction for an order to be made.

In that s 13 specifically refers to the leave of the court I find myself in disagreement with that contention. Indeed I disagree with the general submission of Miss Moulder that an application in respect of a change of name is an application for a specific issue order. They are separate applications, as is made clear by r 4.1(2)(a) and (c) of the Family Proceedings Rules 1991 and by the different form for the order under s 13 (namely form C44 as opposed to form C43) which is required by r 4.21(5). It follows that, although pursuant to s 1(1) of the Act the welfare of the child must be the court's paramount consideration in an application under s 13, reference to the checklist of particular factors under s 1(3) is not, by statute, mandatory. That is not to deny that the checklist remains a most useful aide mémoire of the factors that may impinge on the child's welfare.'

That ruling may well be apt in any case where a residence order is in force with respect to a child whose name the application seeks to change. However the fact that the Family Proceedings Rules 1991 both in r 4.1(2) and in its forms C43 and C44 treat s 8 and s 13 as distinct sections does not in our judgment support the submission that applications in relation to children's surnames must be brought under the latter and not the former section. Further, the paragraphs in *Rayden* at pp 1081 and 1082 are directed to the general scope of the power to make specific issue orders followed by examples of specific usage including orders in relation to a change of surname. In our judgment that is an apt example of an area in which the court has power to make a specific issue order, so long as no residence order is in force. The purpose of s 13 is surely to emphasise that the rights and duties consequent upon the grant of a residence order are not so extensive as to permit a change of surname or a removal from the jurisdiction without either the written consent of every person having parental responsibility or the leave of the court. For the section re-enacts the same limitation that had been put upon custody orders by r 92(8) of the Matrimonial Causes Rules 1973. But there will be many cases in which no residence order is in force with respect to a child.

After all one of the cornerstones of the statute expressed in s 1(5) is that the court shall not make an order unless it considers that doing so would be better for the child than making no order at all. Where two parents have parental responsibility but no residence order is in force, in the event of disagreement, whether in relation to a surname or in relation to any other matter either party has the right to apply to the court for any of the four orders mentioned in s 8(1). In our judgment precisely the same right exists where one has parental responsibility and the other does not. It is only if a residence order is in force that the application falls to be brought under s 13. We accept Mr Hayward-Smith's submission that in practice it is inconceivable that such an application would ever be brought other than by the parent in whose favour the residence order had been made. For practically speaking it is only the person with whom the child resides who has the opportunity to cause a child to be known by a new surname. Mr Hayward-Smith relies on the fact that nowhere in the reported cases is there a single instance of the father of an illegitimate child applying for an order to change a child's surname, still less a decision ordering the mother of such a child to change the surname against her will. That negative consideration no doubt illustrates the reality that, absent co-operation between the parents, the mother of an illegitimate child is recognised to have the right to determine the initial surname of her child save in extreme cases involving perhaps a malicious or manifestly absurd choice. The inter-relationship between ss 13 and 8 of the statute is not particularly happy. Restrictions on making s 8 orders are specifically defined in s 9 and we would not extend the restriction perceived by Wilson J beyond the case in which the applicant for change had been granted a residence order. Even in that case the effect of this distinction seems to us to be more theoretical than real. The judge entertaining the application under s 13, rather than under s 8, will invariably have regard to the considerations identified in s 1(3) in his search for welfare as the paramount consideration even if under no specific statutory duty so to do.

Finally, as Mr Hayward-Smith accepted, the High Court in the exercise of its wardship jurisdiction prior to 1 October 1991, would have had jurisdiction to make the order sought by Mr Dawson in this case. The statutory restriction on the use of that jurisdiction contained in s 100 of the Children Act 1989 are of no application to this case.

Therefore our clear conclusion is that the jurisdiction is there. Whether it should have been exercised is another matter. If there is a general principle underlying this appeal it is that the registration or change of a child's surname is a profound and not a merely formal issue, whatever the age of the child. Any dispute on such an issue must be referred to the court for determination whether or not there is a residence order in force and whoever has or has not parental responsibility. No disputed registration or change should be made unilaterally. On the facts of this case the mother is not in breach of that principle.

Discretion

Mr Hayward-Smith submits that there was a fundamental error of principle in the judge's decision to approach the question as though the matter had been heard before the registration of Alexander's birth. Miss Duthie accepts that this was going somewhat too far, and suggests that it would have been more appropriate for the judge to say that he would put the registration on one side, or words to that effect.

As we have already observed, as a matter of principle registration is a profound matter, and consequently in our judgment a major factor to be taken into account in the exercise of the court's discretion, and one which it is wholly inappropriate for the court to put on one side as of no more than marginal significance, let alone to disregard entirely.

We thus conclude that in this respect the judge erred in principle, so that it is incumbent upon us to exercise our discretion afresh. We would add at this stage that, with respect, we do not understand the judge's suggestion in this context that in some way the father fell foul of the law's delays, seeing that the registration was obligatory not later than 4 May 1996, and his application followed a week or so later.

Mr Hayward-Smith criticises the judge's rationale in favour of the father, and submits that if these reasons are sufficient, it would follow in virtually every case that the mother of an illegitimate child could be compelled against her wishes to give the child the father's surname when the father seeks to play some role in the child's life.

He stresses, as is common ground, that in the authorities the courts have emphasised the significance of changing a child's name and have shown themselves slow to accede to such an application. He also submits that the judge gave insufficient weight to the mother's objections, and above all, to the registration, and contends that the mother's choice was a perfectly reasonable and logical one, seeing that Wearmouth was her own name at the date of registration, and also the name of her two legitimate children.

Our attention was also drawn to the mother's evidence, showing that the child's first name (Alexander) was that chosen by the father.

Miss Duthie supports the judge's reasoning and submits that he correctly identified the rights of the child.

She characterises the mother's objections which the judge rejected as no better than routine, and submits that they should carry little weight. She also points out that the mother had not chosen her own family name, but rather a name which had only been acquired through marriage, and which (she argues) signified a factually incorrect nexus between the child and the mother's ex-husband.

In summing up her arguments she submits that the mother was seeking to use the name of a former partner which she had only acquired by convention on marriage, and that when thinking of the name of a child, common sense dictated that one should look at the connection between the adults and the child, thus favouring the name of the father who had such a connection rather than that of the mother's ex-husband who had none.

In our judgment there is a major flaw in Miss Duthie's concluding submissions, seeing that the name Wearmouth was the mother's actual name at the time it was chosen by her, as well as being that of Alexander's half-brother and half-sister. It was therefore a perfectly natural and logical choice for her to make, and cannot in our view be justly criticised as alien merely because it is also the name of the mother's ex-husband.

These circumstances, coupled with the all-important fact already stressed that this was the child's duly registered name, seem to us to be very powerful factors in the mother's favour, which can only be displaced by strong countervailing considerations.

The considerations cited by the judge, and re-asserted by Miss Duthie, do not in our judgment qualify as such, seeing that, as Mr Hayward-Smith rightly submits, they would apply in virtually every case to an illegitimate child where the father seeks to play some role in the child's life. Indeed they, unlike the mother's objections, are properly to be regarded as routine in the circumstances.

We also think that it is not without relevance that the mother did not have things all her own way, since she gave the child the first name chosen by the father.

In all these circumstances we are quite satisfied that our discretion should be exercised in the mother's favour, and would allow this appeal.

B50 GUIDELINES

Re W, Re A, Re B (Change of name)

[1999] 2 FLR 930 at 931 and 933

Court of Appeal

Butler-Sloss LJ

[1] These three appeals have one issue in common, the circumstances in which a child registered at birth in one surname may have that name changed by deed poll by one parent against the wishes of the other parent. Before turning to the individual facts and issues which arise on each appeal, following the decision of the House of Lords in *Dawson v Wearmouth* [1999] 1 FLR 1167, it may be helpful to set out what appears to be the present position on change of name applications.

...

[9] The present position, in summary, would appear to be as follows:

(a) If parents are married, they both have the power and the duty to register their child's names.

(b) If they are not married the mother has the sole duty and power to do so.

(c) After registration of the child's names, the grant of a residence order obliges any person wishing to change the surname to obtain the leave of the court or the written consent of all those who have parental responsibility.

(d) In the absence of a residence order, the person wishing to change the surname from the registered name ought to obtain the relevant written consent or the leave of the court by making an application for a specific issue order.

(e) On any application, the welfare of the child is paramount and the judge must have regard to the s 1(3) criteria.

(f) Among the factors to which the court should have regard is the registered surname of the child and the reasons for the registration, for instance recognition of the biological link with the child's father. Registration is always a relevant and an important consideration but it is not in itself decisive. The weight to be given to it by the court will depend upon the other relevant factors or valid countervailing reasons which may tip the balance the other way.

(g) The relevant considerations should include factors which may arise in the future as well as the present situation.

(h)   Reasons given for changing or seeking to change a child's name based on the fact that the child's name is or is not the same as the parent making the application do not generally carry much weight.

(i)   The reasons for an earlier unilateral decision to change a child's name may be relevant.

(j)   Any changes of circumstances of the child since the original registration may be relevant.

(k)   In the case of a child whose parents were married to each other, the fact of the marriage is important and I would suggest that there would have to be strong reasons to change the name from the father's surname if the child was so registered.

(l)   Where the child's parents were not married to each other, the mother has control over registration. Consequently, on an application to change the surname of the child, the degree of commitment of the father to the child, the quality of contact, if it occurs, between father and child, the existence or absence of parental responsibility are all relevant factors to take into account.

[10]   I cannot stress too strongly that these are only guidelines which do not purport to be exhaustive. Each case has to be decided on its own facts with the welfare of the child the paramount consideration and all the relevant factors weighed in the balance by the court at the time of the hearing.

I turn now to the three appeals. The issue in the first appeal concerns the amendment of the register in relation to a child legitimated by the subsequent marriage of the parents. The issue in the second and third cases does not encompass an amendment to the register since the power to correct the register is, by s 29 of the 1953 Act, limited to clerical errors and errors of fact and substance. The main question in all three cases is by what surname the child shall be known.

B51 USE OF BOTH PARENTS' SURNAMES

Re R (Surname: using both parents')

[2001] EWCA Civ 1344, [2001] 2 FLR 1358 at 1359 and 1360

Court of Appeal

Thorpe and Hale LJJ

THORPE LJ:

[5] The court proceedings developed into an application by the mother to remove G permanently to Spain, where she intended to live in accommodation immediately adjoining accommodation acquired by Mr and Mrs R. There was therefore to be decided that primary application, together with the issues of contact and the issue as to G's surname. The parties came to a very sensible agreement at the listing on 8 May 2001 before His Honour Judge Kemp. The father accepted the mother's proposals for G's future. The mother accepted that there should be full continuing contact: visiting contact during a minimum of two visits a year in this jurisdiction, each of one week's duration, with an open invitation to the father to have visiting contact to G in Spain. The mother also conceded that the father should have parental responsibility. So the only issue for the judge to decide was the relatively minor issue of by which name G should be known.

[6] It is important to emphasise that the judge heard no oral evidence: he simply decided the issue on the statements that had been filed and on the submissions of Mr Turner, for the father, and Mr Valks, for the mother. We do not have a transcript of his judgment, but we do have a brief note which has been agreed between counsel. That shows the judge reciting the rival submissions advanced by counsel and referring to the authorities that had been cited to him, namely the decision of the House of Lords in *Dawson v Wearmouth* [1999] 2 AC 308, [1999] 1 FLR 1167 and the decision of this Court in *In re W (A Child) (Illegitimate Child: Change of Surname)* [2000] 2 WLR 258.

...

[8] There are a number of factors which seem to me to militate against the judge's conclusion. The first and most obvious is that the surname of R has a relatively insecure foundation. It is a name that the mother has adopted out of choice since G's birth. It is a name that her mother uses out of preference, but not for all purposes. Further, it is a name that the

mother has adopted for G without any consultation with the father, and during a period when he has been having regular contact. Whether it is a name that she herself will bear in the long term is obviously an open question. I also regard the proposed move to Spain as being a neutral factor in the debate. It is strongly relied upon by Mr Valks in the sense that he contends that the move to Spain will require considerable adjustment, and that to ask G to adapt to a general and social use of the name L is only to aggravate the task. Against that, it can obviously be said that the removal of G from the community in which his father lives requires every sensible counter-balancing in order to ensure that, throughout the years of development in Spain, G maintains the consciousness that he has an English father who is attached to him in every way.

[9] The judge had no evidence as to Spanish custom and made the assumption that it must accord with English custom. But in Spain there is, of course, a very different custom in relation to the naming of a child, and that custom gives the child the advantage of one of the maternal surnames and one of the paternal surnames. So combining his parents' surnames might have seemed a very sensible solution in this case, bearing in mind that G was going to be living in Spain and going to a Spanish school. That is a solution which the parties should hereafter consider as a means of bridging the divide which presumably still subsists between them following the judge's ruling.

[10] But I think it is important to recognise in this and in all cases that there must be some burden on the parent who seeks to obtain the judge's approval of change. The child here was very young and there was certainly nothing set in stone by the date of the hearing.

[11] With some hesitation, and with every respect to the judgment of His Honour Judge Kemp, I think on this occasion that he probably reached the wrong conclusion. I think that the order should not have gone as it went. In the order as drawn, in paragraph 3, he simply says:

'There be permission to change the name of the child to [GAR].'

[12] I would propose the deletion of that paragraph. I would urge the parents to consider the good sense of imitating Spanish custom in order to ease G's adjustment to a life in that culture.

HALE LJ:

[13] I have not found this an easy case. It has to be borne in mind that, in the case of *Dawson v Wearmouth* [1999] 2 AC 308, [1999] 1 FLR 1167 Lord Jauncey of Tullichettle was in effect dissenting from the other four members of the court. None of the other members agreed with his observations: they all specifically agreed with Lord Mackay of Clashfern.

They were not, therefore, associated with his remarks at 323B–C as to the importance of a blood tie or of the child bearing his father's name. In that regard, I would respectfully say that the majority view was more consistent with the modern law.

[14] The choice of surname is a matter of parental responsibility. The court may allow a change or prohibit it under s 8 of the Children Act 1989. Therefore, if the parents share parental responsibility, each has an equal voice in the name to be chosen at the outset. However, if they do not share it, the other parent nevertheless has the right to challenge any change or, indeed, any initial choice under s 8, and this father did make such a challenge as soon as he learnt that the mother had changed the registered surname of the child. If there is a change and it is opposed, then the change has to be justified under s 1 of the Children Act 1989: that is, as being in the best interests of the child. As Lord Mackay of Clashfern said in *Dawson v Wearmouth* [1999] 2 AC 308, [1999] 1 FLR 1167 at 321A and 1173H respectively, there has to be some evidence that it would lead to an improvement in the child's life.

[15] Generally, therefore, what the court is doing is balancing the long-term interests of a child in retaining an outward link with the parent with whom that child is not living against what are often shorter-term benefits of lack of confusion, convenience, lack of embarrassment and the like. I recognise that the latter set of considerations may well not be sufficient to outweigh the former. However, Butler-Sloss LJ (as she then was) referred, in *In re W (A Child) (Illegitimate Child: Change of Surname)* [2000] 2 WLR 258, to factor (h):

> 'Reasons given for changing or seeking to change a child's name based on the fact that the child's name is or is not the same as the parent making the application do not generally carry much weight.'

[16] I do not think she meant that considerations of confusion, anxiety and embarrassment for the child were of little account: it is more that the problem for the parent is of little account. It all depends upon the facts and circumstances of the particular case; and one notices that the cases listed together with *In re W (A Child) (Illegitimate Child: Change of Surname)* [2000] 2 WLR 258 were cases in which a change of name was permitted.

[17] I would like to add an aside. It for me is a matter of huge regret that the Incorporated Council of Law Reporting chose to entitle that case *In re W (A Child) (Illegitimate Child: Change of Surname)*. It is now more than 14 years since the Family Law Reform Act 1987 sought to remove such language from our law, and in particular to emphasise that no opprobrious adjectives should be attached to the child. If there is to be any opprobrium stemming from the birth of a child to parents who are not married to one another (and for my part I would not necessarily say that there was to be any such opprobrium), it should be attached to the parents, whose choice it was, and not to the child, whose choice it most definitely was not. I very much hope the Incorporated Council will pay attention to those observations should the problem arise in the future.

[18] That having been said, I return to the issue of names. It is also a matter of great sadness to me that it is so often assumed, and even sometimes argued, that fathers need that outward and visible link in order to retain their relationship with, and commitment to, their child. That should not be the case. It is a poor sort of parent whose interest in and commitment to his child depends upon that child bearing his name. After all, that is a privilege which is not enjoyed by many mothers, even if they are not living with the child. They have to depend upon other more substantial things.

[19] The crucial point, however, is that it is important for a child for there to be transparency about his parentage and for it to be acknowledged that a child always has two parents; and if it turns out (as it often does) that children have both social parents and birth parents, it is important that that fact too is acknowledged. It can be even more important in cases where there is a risk of links fading or becoming less strong as the years go on, because in the future it can prompt a child to wish to re-establish links which have become weaker or have even disappeared. We all know of cases where it has prompted a search and a reunion later in life, with great benefit for the child. That factor may be of particular importance in cases where increased distance is coming into the equation. As I say, the reason for that is the importance of recognising that children have two parents.

[20] In my judgment, parents and courts should be much more prepared to contemplate the use of both surnames in an appropriate case, because that is to recognise the importance of both parents. As it happens, it is the common practice in Spain so to do. It is not unknown, for that matter, in the USA, where women in particular will often use both names. I therefore echo what has fallen from my Lord, Thorpe LJ, in urging both parents to contemplate that course in this case.

B52 CHANGE OF FIRST NAME

Re H (Child's name: first name)

[2002] EWCA Civ 190, [2002] 1 FLR 973 at 976

Court of Appeal

Thorpe LJ

[13] There are a number of points which should be made. The first is that none of the authorities that guide the court in determining disputes as to the surname by which a child should be known seems to be of any application to a dispute of this sort. The surname by which a child is registered and known is of particular significance insofar as it denotes the family to which the child belongs.

[14] Given names have a much less concrete character. It is commonplace for a child to receive statutory registration with one or more given names and, subsequently, to receive different given names, maybe at baptism or, maybe, by custom and adoption. During the course of family life, as a child develops personality and individuality, parents or other members of the family, may be attracted to some nickname or some alternative given name which will then adhere, possibly for the rest of the child's life, or possibly only until the child's individuality and maturity allow it to make a choice for itself as to the name by which he or she wishes to be known.

[15] The second point I would mention is that the judge was perfectly right to recognise that no order of the court could prevent the mother from using the name of her choice internally. Where I depart from the judge in this observation is in his attempt to inhibit the mother from using that chosen name in external dealings within the community of the primary home. It seems to me, as a matter of ordinary course, that when a child is registered for the purposes of national health services, local educational services or community activities, there is no formal need for the production of a birth certificate to establish given names. If the parents are separated, the primary carer simply establishes with the entry of the child, either for school, for general practice medicine or for hospital treatment, the given name that is customary in the primary home.

[16] I find difficulty in accepting the judge's reason for his conclusion which, in any event, is extremely brief. He said that:

'Having found as a fact that father was, as he saw it, carrying out his duties, and that there were no sinister motives in the registration of

13 May 1999, and having regard to the fact that registration is valid in law, I have, in the best interests of the little boy, decided that his official name must remain as [MIH]. I find as a fact that it is not in his welfare to be known by a name other than his registered name for all official purposes. The mother's application for a section 8 specific issue order is therefore refused.'

[17] In my opinion that places altogether too much weight on the fortuitous fact that the father's registration was first in time. It also ignores all the realities which I have sought to discern.

[18] If issues such as this arise, it seems to me that judges must look in a worldly, common-sense way at what is likely to be best for the child and must not place too much emphasis upon the statutory process of registration. In this case the judge was concerned with a 2½-year-old boy, born to a mother in difficult circumstances. She is a single parent who has had to make shifts from the outset on her own. She has had to face an initial denial of paternity. She has had to cope with a lot of stress and anxiety. Any search for the welfare of the child must in the end lead to the question what order was likely to promote a sense of security and well-being in the mother. The mother, as a single parent and primary carer, requires a good deal of support, both in the outcome of legal proceedings and in the recognition of her liberty, matching her responsibility, to make decisions in the daily life of the child.

[19] It seems to me that the mother's initial complaint in her application of 30 November 1999 was justified. To impose upon her the father's chosen name of M simply because he happened to be 6 days prior in time, would indeed be grossly unfair. I have no doubt that the judge was plainly wrong to seek to inhibit the mother's use of the name H in her dealings with external authority, providing that she always recognised the fact that he had an immutable series of names by statutory registration.

Leave to remove from jurisdiction / relocation within UK

B53 PAYNE V PAYNE: GENERAL PRINCIPLES

Payne v Payne

[2001] EWCA Civ 166, [2001] 1 FLR 1052 at 1060, 1065 and 1077

Court of Appeal

Thorpe LJ and Butler-Sloss P

THORPE LJ:

[25] In more recent times both at first instance and in this court I have sought to apply this line of authority to a series of cases giving rise to differing facts and circumstances. We have been referred to *MH v GP (Child: Emigration)* [1995] 2 FLR 106, *Re H (Application to Remove from Jurisdiction)* [1998] 1 FLR 848 and *Re C (Leave to Remove from Jurisdiction)* [2000] 2 FLR 457. However in the first case I referred to the ratio in *Chamberlain v de la Mare* (1983) 4 FLR 434 as creating 'a presumption in favour of the reasonable application of the custodial parent'. Equally in the last case I said at 459 that:

> '... a balance then had to be struck to determine whether or not the resulting risk of harm to S was such as to outweigh the presumption that reasonable proposals from the custodial parent should receive the endorsement of the court.'

In both passages I was using the word presumption in the non-legal sense. But with the advantage of hindsight I regret the use of that word. Generally in the language of litigation a presumption either casts a burden of proof upon the party challenging it or can be said to be decisive of outcome unless displaced. I do not think that such concepts of presumption and burden of proof have any place in Children Act 1989 litigation where the judge exercises a function that is partly inquisitorial. In the context of applications for contact orders I expressed my misgivings in the use of the language of presumptions: see in *Re L*

(Contact: Domestic Violence); Re V (Contact: Domestic Violence); Re M (Contact: Domestic Violence); Re H (Contact: Domestic Violence) [2000] 2 FLR 334.

[26] In summary a review of the decisions of this court over the course of the last 30 years demonstrates that relocation cases have been consistently decided upon the application of the following two propositions:

(a)   the welfare of the child is the paramount consideration; and
(b)   refusing the primary carer's reasonable proposals for the relocation of her family life is likely to impact detrimentally on the welfare of her dependent children. Therefore her application to relocate will be granted unless the court concludes that it is incompatible with the welfare of the children.

The value of the guidance

[27] Few guidelines for the determination of individual cases, the facts of which are never replicated, have stood so long in our family law. Where guidelines can be formulated there are obvious benefits. The opportunity for practitioners to give clear and confident advice as to outcome helps to limit the volume of contested litigation. Of the cases that do proceed to a hearing clear guidance from this court simplifies the task of the trial judge and helps to limit the volume of appeals. The opportunity for this court to give guidance capable of general application is plainly circumscribed by the obvious consideration that any exercise of discretion is fact dependent and no two cases are identical. But in relocation cases there are a number of factors that are sufficiently commonplace to enhance the utility of guidelines. I instance:

(a)   the applicant is invariably the mother and the primary carer;
(b)   generally the motivation for the move arises out of her remarriage or her urge to return home; and
(c)   the father's opposition is commonly founded on a resultant reduction in contact and influence.

[28] Furthermore, guidance of this sort is significant in the wider field of international family law. There is a clear interaction between the approach of courts in abduction cases and in relocation cases. If individual jurisdictions adopt a chauvinistic approach to applications to relocate then there is a risk that the parent affected will resort to flight. Conversely, recognition of the respect due to the primary carer's reasonable proposals for relocation encourages applications in place of unilateral removal. Equally as this case demonstrates, a return following a wrongful retention allows a careful appraisal of welfare considerations on a subsequent application to relocate. Accordingly it is very desirable that there should be conformity within the international community ...

The foundation of the guidance

[29]   A review of the Court of Appeal authorities over the last 30 years demonstrates that although not the originator of the guidance, Ormrod LJ was its principal exponent. He rationalises it and its strongest statement comes in his judgment in *Moodey v Field* ((unreported) 13 February 1981) as well perhaps in the judgment of Purchas LJ in *Belton v Belton* [1987] 2 FLR 343. Since the direction has stood for 30 years and since its amplification by Ormrod LJ, first in *A v A (Child: Removal from Jurisdiction)* (1980) 1 FLR 380 over 20 years ago, it is perhaps necessary to question whether changing perceptions of child development and welfare in the interim undermine or erode his exposition. That exposition, as he himself said, was very much based on common sense. But even generally accepted perceptions can shift within a generation. The shift upon which Mr Cayford relies is in the sphere of contact. He asserts that over the last 30 years the comparative importance of contact between the child and the absent parent has greatly increased. No authority for the proposition is demonstrated. Without some proof of the proposition I would be doubtful of accepting it. Throughout my professional life in this specialist field contact between child and absent parent has always been seen as an important ingredient in any welfare appraisal. The language may have shifted but the proposition seems to have remained constant. I believe that conviction is demonstrated by the review of the contact cases over much the same period to be found in my judgment in *Re L (Contact Domestic Violence), Re V (Contact Domestic Violence), Re M (Contact Domestic Violence), Re H (Contact Domestic Violence)* [2000] 2 FLR 334, cited above, at (25). Furthermore practicalities are all against this submission. International travel is comparatively cheaper and more competitive than ever before. Equally communication is cheaper and the options more varied.

[30]   Quite apart from Mr Cayford's submission, I do not believe that the evaluation of welfare within the mental health professions over this period calls into any question the rationalisation advanced by Ormrod LJ in his judgments. In a broad sense the health and well-being of a child depends upon emotional and psychological stability and security. Both security and stability come from the child's emotional and psychological dependency upon the primary carer. The extent of that dependency will depend upon many factors including its duration and the extent to which it is tempered by or shared with other dependencies. For instance is the absent parent an important figure in the child's life? What is the child's relationship with siblings and/or grandparents and/or a step-parent? In most relocation cases the judge will need to make some evaluation of these factors.

[31]   Logically and as a matter of experience the child cannot draw emotional and psychological security and stability from the dependency unless the primary carer herself is emotionally and psychologically stable and secure. The parent cannot give what she herself lacks. Although fathers as well as mothers provide primary care I have never myself encountered a relocation application brought by a father and for the purposes of this judgment I assume that relocation applications are only brought by maternal primary carers. The disintegration of a family unit is invariably emotionally and psychologically turbulent. The mother who emerges with the responsibility of making the home for the children may recover her sense of well-being simply by coping over a passage of time. But often the mother may be in need of external support, whether financial, emotional or social. Such support may be provided by a new partner who becomes stepfather to the child. The creation of a new family obviously draws the child into its quest for material and other fulfilment. Such cases have given rise to the strongest statements of the guidelines. Alternatively the disintegration of the family unit may leave the mother in a society to which she was carried by the impetus of family life before its failure. Commonly in that event she may feel isolated and driven to seek the support she lacks by returning to her homeland, her family and her friends. In the remarriage cases the motivation for relocation may well be to meet the stepfather's career needs or opportunities. In those cases refusal is likely to destabilise the new family emotionally as well as to penalise it financially. In the case of the isolated mother, to deny her the support of her family and a return to her roots may have an even greater psychological detriment and she may have no one who might share her distress or alleviate her depression. This factor is well illustrated by the mother's evidence in this case. As recorded in Miss Hall's note she said:

> 'Things happen and I think I can't stand it. I've got to go home. But then I see Sophie and I calm down and I think I can't leave her ... I would give it a really good try to be a mother to Sophie here but in my heart of hearts I think I would not be able to do it.'

[32] Thus in most relocation cases the most crucial assessment and finding for the judge is likely to be the effect of the refusal of the application on the mother's future psychological and emotional stability.

...

[40] However there is a danger that if the regard which the court pays to the reasonable proposals of the primary carer were elevated into a legal presumption then there would be an obvious risk of the breach of the respondent's rights not only under Art 8 but also his rights under Art 6 to a fair trial. To guard against the risk of too perfunctory an investigation resulting from too ready an assumption that the mother's proposals are necessarily compatible with the child's welfare I would suggest the following discipline as a prelude to conclusion:

(a)   Pose the question: is the mother's application genuine in the sense that it is not motivated by some selfish desire to exclude the father from the child's life? Then ask is the mother's application realistic, by which I mean founded on practical proposals both well researched and investigated? If the application fails either of these tests refusal will inevitably follow.

(b) If however the application passes these tests then there must be a careful appraisal of the father's opposition: is it motivated by genuine concern for the future of the child's welfare or is it driven by some ulterior motive? What would be the extent of the detriment to him and his future relationship with the child were the application granted? To what extent would that be offset by extension of the child's relationships with the maternal family and homeland?

(c) What would be the impact on the mother, either as the single parent or as a new wife, of a refusal of her realistic proposal?

(d) The outcome of the second and third appraisals must then be brought into an overriding review of the child's welfare as the paramount consideration, directed by the statutory checklist insofar as appropriate.

[41] In suggesting such a discipline I would not wish to be thought to have diminished the importance that this court has consistently attached to the emotional and psychological well-being of the primary carer. In any evaluation of the welfare of the child as the paramount consideration great weight must be given to this factor.

Cross-applications

[42] In very many cases the mother's application to relocate provokes a cross-application by the father for a variation of the residence order in his favour. Such cross-applications may be largely tactical to enable the strategist to cross-examine along the lines of: what will you do if your application is refused? If the mother responds by saying that she will remain with the child then the cross-examiner feels that he has demonstrated that the impact of refusal upon the mother would not be that significant. If on the other hand she says that she herself will go nevertheless then the cross-examiner feels that he has demonstrated that the mother is shallow, or uncaring or self-centred. But experienced family judges are well used to tactics and will readily distinguish between the cross-application that has some pre-existing foundation and one that is purely tactical. There are probably dangers in compartmentalising the two applications. As far as possible they should be tried and decided together. The judge in the end must evaluate comparatively each option for the child, one against another. Often that will mean evaluating a home with mother in this jurisdiction, against a home with mother wherever she seeks to go, against a home in this jurisdiction with father. Then in explaining his first choice the judge will inevitably be delivering judgment on both applications.

...

BUTLER-SLOSS P:

[82]   All those immediately affected by the proceedings, that is to say the mother, the father and the child have rights under Art 8(1). Those rights inevitably in a case such as the present appeal are in conflict and, under Art 8(2), have to be balanced against the rights of the others. In addition and of the greatest significance is the welfare of the child which, according to European jurisprudence, is of crucial importance, and where in conflict with a parent is overriding (see *Johansen v Norway* (1996) 23 EHRR 33 at 67 and 72). Article 8(2) recognises that a public authority, in this case the court, may interfere with the right to family life where it does so in accordance with the law, and where it is necessary in a democratic society for, inter alia, the protection of the rights and freedoms of others and the decision is proportionate to the need demonstrated. That position appears to me to be similar to that which arises in all child-based family disputes and the European case-law on children is in line with the principles set out in the Children Act 1989. I do not, for my part, consider that the Convention has affected the principles the courts should apply in dealing with these difficult issues. Its implementation into English law does however give us the opportunity to take another look at the way the principles have been expressed in the past and whether there should now be a reformulation of those principles. I think it would be helpful to do so, since they may have been expressed from time to time in too rigid terms. The judgment of Thorpe J in *MH v GP (Child: Emigration)* [1995] 2 FLR 106 was the first time to my knowledge that the word 'presumption' had been used in the reported cases, and I would respectfully suggest that it over-emphasised one element of the approach in the earlier cases. I can understand why the word was used, since in *Tyler v Tyler* [1989] 2 FLR 158 the reformulation by Purchas LJ of the principles in *Poel v Poel* [1970] 1 WLR 1469 and *Chamberlain v de la Mare* (1983) 4 FLR 434 may itself have been expressed unduly firmly.

[83]   Section 13(1)(b) of the Children Act 1989 does not create any presumption and the criteria in s 1 clearly govern the application. The underlying principles in *Poel* (above), as explained in *Chamberlain* (above), have stood the test of time and give valuable guidance as to the approach the court should adopt in these most difficult cases. It is, in my view, helpful to go back to look again at the reasons given in both those decisions. They were based upon the welfare of the child which was the first and paramount consideration by virtue of s 1 of the Guardianship of Minors Act 1971. The view of both courts was well-summarised by Griffiths LJ in *Chamberlain* (above), that the welfare of young children was best met by bringing them up in a happy, secure family atmosphere. Their happiness and security, after the creation of a new family unit, will depend on becoming members of the new family. Reasonable arrangements made by the mother or stepfather to relocate should not in principle be frustrated, since it would be likely to have an adverse effect

upon the new family. It might reflect upon the stability of the new relationship. The stress upon the second family would inevitably have a serious adverse effect upon the children whose welfare is paramount. Even if there is not a new relationship, the effect upon the parent with the residence order of the frustration of plans for the future might have an equally bad effect upon the children. If the arrangements are sensible and the proposals are genuinely important to the applicant parent and the effect of refusal of the application would be seriously adverse to the new family, e g mother and child, or the mother, stepfather and child, then this would be, as Griffiths LJ said, a factor that had to be given great weight when weighing up the various factors in the balancing exercise.

[84] The strength of the relationship with the other parent, usually the father, and the paternal family will be a highly relevant factor, see *MH v GP (Child: Emigration)* [1995] 2 FLR 106. The ability of the other parent to continue contact with the child and the financial implications need to be explored. There may well be other relevant factors to weigh in the balance, such as, with the elder child, his/her views, the importance of schooling or other ties to the current home area. The state of health of the child and availability of specialist medical expertise or other special needs may be another factor. There are, of course, many other factors which may arise in an individual case. I stress that there is no presumption in favour of the applicant, but reasonable proposals made by the applicant parent, the refusal of which would have adverse consequences upon the stability of the new family and therefore an adverse effect upon the welfare of the child, continue to be a factor of great weight. As in every case in which the court has to exercise its discretion, the reasonableness of the proposals, the effect upon the applicant and upon the child of refusal of the application, the effect of a reduction or cessation of contact with the other parent upon the child, the effect of removal of the child from his/her current environment are all factors, among others which I have not enumerated, which have to be given appropriate weight in each individual case and weighed in the balance. The decision is always a difficult one and has not become less so over the last 30 years.

Summary

[85] In summary I would suggest that the following considerations should be in the forefront of the mind of a judge trying one of these difficult cases. They are not and could not be exclusive of the other important matters which arise in the individual case to be decided. All the relevant factors need to be considered, including the points I make below, so far as they are relevant, and weighed in the balance. The points I make are obvious but in view of the arguments presented to us in this case, it may be worthwhile to repeat them:

(a)   The welfare of the child is always paramount.

(b)   There is no presumption created by s 13(1)(b) in favour of the applicant parent.

(c)   The reasonable proposals of the parent with a residence order wishing to live abroad carry great weight.

(d)   Consequently the proposals have to be scrutinised with care and the court needs to be satisfied that there is a genuine motivation for the move and not the intention to bring contact between the child and the other parent to an end.

(e)   The effect upon the applicant parent and the new family of the child of a refusal of leave is very important.

(f)   The effect upon the child of the denial of contact with the other parent and in some cases his family is very important.

(g)   The opportunity for continuing contact between the child and the parent left behind may be very significant.

[86]   All the above observations have been made on the premise that the question of residence is not a live issue. If, however, there is a real dispute as to which parent should be granted a residence order, and the decision as to which parent is the more suitable is finely balanced, the future plans of each parent for the child are clearly relevant. If one parent intends to set up home in another country and remove the child from school, surroundings and the other parent and his family, it may in some cases be an important factor to weigh in the balance. But in a case where the decision as to residence is clear as the judge in this case clearly thought it was, the plans for removal from the jurisdiction would not be likely to be significant in the decision over residence. The mother in this case already had a residence order and the judge's decision on residence was not an issue before this court.

Other significant cases on this issue:

A long series of cases followed *Payne v Payne* including:

*   *Re B (Leave to remove: impact of refusal)* [2004] EWCA Civ 956, [2005] 2 FLR 239
*   *Re A (Temporary removal from jurisdiction)* [2004] EWCA Civ 1587, [2005] 1 FLR 639
*   *Re N (Leave to remove: holiday)* [2006] EWCA Civ 357, [2006] 2 FLR 1124
*   *Re MK (Relocation outside jurisdiction)* [2006] EWCA Civ 1013, [2007] 1 FLR 432
*   *Re J (Leave to remove: urgent case)* [2006] EWCA Civ 1897, [2007] 1 FLR 2033

For temporary leave to remove, see:

*   *Re S (leave to remove from the jurisdiction: securing return from holiday)* [2001] 2 FLR 507

- *Re A (Temporary removal from jurisdiction)* [2004] EWCA Civ 1587, [2005] 1 FLR 639
- *DS v RS* [2009] EWHC 1594 (Fam), [2010] 1 FLR 576

B54   CHALLENGE TO PAYNE

Re H (Leave to remove)

[2010] EWCA Civ 915, [2010] 2 FLR 1875 at 1882

Court of Appeal

Wilson LJ

[21]   But, says Mr Ward in making his major point in this appeal today, Mrs Perryman and indeed the judge were surveying the mother's application through the prism constructed by the decision of this court in the case of *Payne*, cited above. In this court we are well aware of the criticisms made, both domestically and internationally, of its decision in *Payne*. Nevertheless one must beware of endorsing a parody of the decision. Both Thorpe LJ, at [26(a)], and the President, Dame Elizabeth Butler-Sloss, at [85(a)], stressed that, in the determination of applications for permission to relocate, the welfare of the child was the paramount consideration. It is only against the subsidiary guidance to be collected from *Payne* that criticisms can perhaps more easily be levelled. I therefore acknowledge the controversy that surrounds the proposition expressed by Thorpe LJ, at [26(b)], that:

> 'refusing the primary carer's reasonable proposals for the relocation of her family life is likely to impact detrimentally on the welfare of her dependent children. Therefore her application to relocate will be granted unless the court concludes that it is incompatible with the welfare of the children.'

Equally, I acknowledge the controversy which surrounds his conclusion, at [32], that:

> 'Thus in most relocation cases the most crucial assessment and finding for the judge is likely to be the effect of the refusal of the application on the mother's future psychological and emotional stability.'

[22]   There is also, as most family lawyers know, an attack on the series of questions which, at [40], Thorpe LJ suggested as apt for a judge to put to himself in determining such an application. The charge is that they represent an impermissible gloss on the inquiry into welfare, by reference in particular to the checklist of specified considerations, mandated by s 1(1) and (3) of the Children Act 1989. There is also a significant argument to the effect that, although the case of *Payne* was determined only nine years ago, it represents the culmination of domestic

jurisprudence which had evolved since 1970, ie over a time when (so it is said) the value to the child of a relationship with the non-residential parent was far less well recognised.

[23]   Mr Ward brings to our attention that the controversy surrounding *Payne v Payne* has already been recognised even within this court. He refers to the decision of Wall LJ in *Re D (Leave to Remove: Appeal)* [2010] EWCA Civ 50, [2010] 2 FLR 1605. It was a decision in which the judge refused a father permission to appeal but I assume he gave leave for his decision to be cited. Wall LJ said, at [33]:

> 'There has been considerable criticism of *Payne v Payne* in certain quarters and there is a perfectly respectable argument for the proposition that it places too great an emphasis on the wishes and feelings of the relocating parent and ignores or relegates the harm done [to] children by a permanent breach of the relationship which children have with the left-behind parent.'

With respect, I wonder whether there *is* any respectable argument for the proposition that the decision in *Payne* 'ignores' the harm of which Wall LJ there spoke. I would agree, however, that there is at any rate a respectable argument for the proposition that it inappropriately 'relegates' such harm to a level below that of the harm likely to be sustained by a child through the negative impact upon the applicant of refusal of the application.

[24]   In *Re D (Leave to Remove: Appeal)* Wall LJ had observed, at [11], that the decision in *Payne* was binding upon this court and that its effect could be displaced only by a decision of the Supreme Court or by legislation. In refusing permission Wall LJ proceeded to observe that the facts of the case before him did not make that case apt for any reconsideration of *Payne*, whether in the Supreme Court or otherwise.

[25]   Mr Ward also brings to our attention a very recent development in international thinking about the proper despatch of applications for permission to relocate. I refer to the Washington Declaration on International Family Relocation made in Washington DC on 23–25 March 2010, at the conclusion of an 'International Judicial Conference on Cross-Border Family Relocation' co-organised by the Hague Conference on Private International Law and The International Centre for Missing and Exploited Children. There were more than 50 judges and other experts at the conference; and Thorpe LJ, as the Head of International Family Justice in England and Wales, was our judicial delegate at it. The substance of the declaration is to be found in paras [3] and [4], under the heading 'Factors Relevant to Decisions on International Relocation'. They state:

'3. In all applications concerning international relocation the best interests of the child should be the paramount (primary) consideration. Therefore, determinations should be made without any presumptions for or against relocation.

4. In order to identify more clearly cases in which relocation should be granted or refused, and to promote a more uniform approach internationally, the exercise of judicial discretion should be guided in particular, but not exclusively, by the following factors listed in no order of priority. The weight to be given to any one factor will vary from case to case:

(i)   the right of the child separated from one parent to maintain personal relations and direct contact with both parents on a regular basis in a manner consistent with the child's development, except if the contact is contrary to the child's best interest;

(ii) the views of the child having regard to the child's age and maturity;

(iii) the parties' proposals for the practical arrangements for relocation, including accommodation, schooling and employment;

(iv) where relevant to the determination of the outcome, the reasons for seeking or opposing the relocation;

(v)   any history of family violence or abuse, whether physical or psychological;

(vi) the history of the family and particularly the continuity and quality of past and current care and contact arrangements;

(vii) pre-existing custody and access determinations;

(viii) the impact of grant or refusal on the child, in the context of his or her extended family, education and social life, and on the parties;

(ix) the nature of the inter-parental relationship and the commitment of the applicant to support and facilitate the relationship between the child and the respondent after the relocation;

(x)   whether the parties' proposals for contact after relocation are realistic, having particular regard to the cost to the family and the burden to the child;

(xi) the enforceability of contact provisions ordered as a condition of relocation in the State of destination;

(xii) issues of mobility for family members; and

(xiii) any other circumstances deemed to be relevant by the judge.'

[26] The Washington Declaration is, in my view, extremely interesting and, subject to an aside which I articulate at [27] below, it may prove not only to be a valuable means of harmonising the approaches of different jurisdictions to the determination of applications for permission to

relocate but ultimately also to become the foundation of some reform of our domestic law. But it clearly has no such effect at the moment; and Mr Ward will not mind my saying that his final submission, namely that today we should replace the guidance given in Payne with that contained in [3] and [4] of the declaration, lacked elementary legal discipline. The document is indeed no more than a declaration, to which our jurisdiction, through Thorpe LJ, has subscribed. Paragraph 13 of the declaration provides that:

> 'the Hague Conference on Private International Law ... is encouraged to pursue the further development of the principles set out in this declaration and to consider the feasibility of embodying all or some of these principles in an international instrument.'

It is thus possible that, no doubt following amendment in various respects, the factors contained in [4] of the declaration will find their way into a protocol attached to the Hague Convention 1980, which, if ratified by the UK, would later find its way into the domestic law of England and Wales and would then impact upon the guidance set out in *Payne*. But that is all for the future.

[27] With some hesitation I make the following aside. In that the principal charge against our guidance, as it stands, is that it ascribes too great a significance to the effect on the child of the negative impact upon the applicant of refusal of the application, one is interested to discern the way in which, in para [4] of the declaration, that factor is addressed. One finds (does one not?) that it is not squarely addressed at all. The closest to any address of it is to be found in (viii), namely 'the impact of grant or refusal on the child, in the context of his or her extended family, education and social life, and on the parties'. Some may share my initial perplexity even at the terminology of (viii) in that it appears to train the consideration of the court upon impact not only 'on the child' but also, and by way of contradistinction, 'on the parties' apparently irrespective of impact on the child. It is axiomatic that our notion of paramountcy excludes from consideration all factors which have no bearing on the child. But, that possible curiosity apart, there is no square address in (viii) of the impact upon the child likely to flow from negative impact upon the applicant of refusal of the application. Indeed the reference to the child's extended family, education and social life, seems almost to draw attention away from such a factor. I wonder whether consideration might need to be given as to whether, if the present law of England and Wales does indeed place excessive weight upon that factor, para [4] of the declaration, as presently drawn, by contrast places insufficient weight upon it.

Other significant cases on this issue:

- *Re AR (A child: relocation)* [2010] EWHC 1346 (Fam), [2010] 2 FLR 1577

B55 RELOCATION WITHIN THE UK

Re L (Shared residence order)

[2009] EWCA Civ 20, [2009] 1 FLR 1157 at 1160, 1162 and 1168

Court of Appeal

Wall LJ

[11] ... so far as I am aware, the first case to reach this court in which the question of a parent's proposed relocation with a child within England and Wales has arisen where there is already in existence a shared residence order in favour of the parents in relation to the same child. Several questions therefore arise. In particular: (1) what effect, if any, does such an order have? And; (2) what weight should a judge give to the existence of such an order?

[12] Both Miss Frances Judd QC for the father and Mr David Boyd, for the mother submitted that it would be a powerful disincentive to parties entering into shared residence orders if either felt that the consequence of so doing was to place a fetter on any subsequent application to relocate. I agree. However, this provides only a partial answer to the questions posed in the previous paragraph, and it is, therefore, necessary to look at the authorities on internal relocation. They are, I think, the following (I list them in chronological order):

(1) *Re E (Residence: Imposition of Conditions)* [1997] 2 FLR 638 (*Re E*).
(2) *Re H (Children) (Residence Order: Condition)* [2001] EWCA Civ 1338, [2001] 2 FLR 1277 (*Re H*).
(3) *Re S (A Child) (Residence Order: Condition)* [2001] EWCA Civ 847, [2001] 3 FCR 154 and [2002] EWCA Civ 1795, [2003] 1 FCR 138 (*Re S (No 1)* and *Re S (No 2)*).
(4) *B v B (Residence: Condition Limiting Geographic Area)* [2004] 2 FLR 979 (*B v B*).
(5) *Re H (Agreed Joint Residence: Mediation)* [2004] EWHC 2064 (Fam), [2005] 1 FLR 8 (which, for present purposes I propose to call *Re H (No 2)*).
(6) *Re G (Contact)* [2006] EWCA Civ 1507, [2007] 1 FLR 1663.
(7) *Re B (Prohibited Steps Order)* [2007] EWCA Civ 1055, [2008] 1 FLR 613 (*Re B*).

...

[17] Giving the leading judgment in *Re E*, Butler-Sloss LJ said at 641–642:

'Section 11(7) applies to all four s 8 orders, including prohibited steps orders and specific issue orders. The wording of the subsection is wide enough to give the court the power to make an order restricting the right of residence to a specified place within the UK. But in my view a restriction upon the right of the carer of the child to choose where to live sits uneasily with the general understanding of what is meant by a residence order. In *Re D (Minors) (Residence: Imposition of Conditions)* [1996] 2 FLR 281, this court considered a similar condition placed on a residence order. In that case the mother had originally agreed that she would not bring the children into contact with the man with whom she had been living. On her subsequent application to discharge that condition this court held that a section 11(7) condition could not exclude another person from the mother's home, thereby interfering with her right to live with whom she liked. Ward LJ said:

"The court was not in a position to overrule her decision to live her life as she chose. What was before the court was the issue of whether she should have the children living with her."

That decision in my judgment applies with equal force to the issue in the present appeal.

A general imposition of conditions on residence orders was clearly not contemplated by Parliament and where the parent is entirely suitable and the court intends to make a residence order in favour of that parent, a condition of residence is in my view an unwarranted imposition upon the right of the parent to choose where he/she will live within the UK or with whom. There may be exceptional cases, for instance, where the court, in the private law context, has concerns about the ability of the parent to be granted a residence order to be a satisfactory carer but there is no better solution than to place the child with that parent. The court might consider it necessary to keep some control over the parent by way of conditions which include a condition of residence. Again, in public law cases involving local authorities, where a residence order may be made by the court in preference to a care order, section 11(7) conditions might be applied in somewhat different circumstances.

The correct approach is to look at the issue of where the children will live as one of the relevant factors in the context of the cross-applications for residence and not as a separate issue divorced from the question of residence. If the case is finely balanced between the respective advantages and disadvantages of the parents, the proposals put forward by each parent will assume considerable importance. If one parent's plan is to remove the children against their wishes to a part of the country less suitable for them, it is an important factor to be taken into account by the court and might persuade the court in some cases to make a residence order in favour of the other parent. But, on the facts of the present appeal, it is clear that the welfare of the children points firmly to their living with their mother, and the advantage of remaining in London is outweighed by the other factors leading to granting a residence order to the mother.'

...

[33] Thorpe LJ, giving the leading judgment, reviewed his previous decision in *Re H*:

'[7] The judgment that I gave in the case of *Re H* does not, on reconsideration, sufficiently reflect the fact that the imposition of a condition to a residence order restricting the primary carer's right to choose his or her place of residence is a truly exceptional order. The case of *Re H* included an endeavour on my part to rationalise the interface between the true relocation cases governed by the decision of this court in *Payne v Payne* and the internal relocation cases governed by the decision of this court in *Re E*. At the conclusion of the passage, I questioned the rationalisation for a different test to be applied to an application to relocate to Belfast as opposed to, say, an application to relocate to Dublin, and having posed the question I continued:

"All that the court can do is to remember that in each and every case the decision must rest on the paramount principle of child welfare."

[8] I see that the Recorder, reading that passage, did not have his attention sufficiently directed to the earlier case of *Re E*. In my reasoning for upholding the imposition of a condition preventing the relocation in the case of *Re H*, I did not perhaps sufficiently clearly state that the circumstances (particularly the impact upon the mother of a refusal of the condition, fully established by mental health evidence) clearly took the case into the exceptional category identified Butler-Sloss LJ in *Re E*.

[9] By way of conclusion I would only endorse the treatment of this topic by Professor Lowe and his co-authors in *International Movement of Children* (Jordan Publishing Ltd, 2004). He, at page 90, considers movement of children within the UK, and reviewing the cases, concludes that a primary carer faced with an application for a prohibited steps order or the imposition of conditions on a residence order, will not, save in an exceptional case, be restrained by the

court, because for the court so to do would be an unsustainable restriction on adult liberties and would be likely to have an adverse effect on the welfare of the child by denying the primary carer reasonable freedom of choice. Professor Lowe takes that proposition from the decision in *Re E* and in para 6.4 he states:

> "The correct approach, therefore, is to look at the issue of where the children will live as one of the relevant factors in the context of the cross-applications for residence, and not as a separate issue divorced from the question of residence. If the case is finely balanced between the respective advantages and disadvantages of the parents, the proposals put forward by each parent will assume considerable importance. If one parent's plan is to remove the children against their wishes to a part of the country less suitable for them, it is an important factor to be taken into account by the court and might persuade the court in some cases to make a residence order in favour of the other parent.'"

He then considers what might constitute an exceptional case and in particular refers to the decision of this court in *Re S (No 2)*.

What principles can be gathered from the authorities, and should there be a different approach in cases where there is a shared residence order?

[34] In my judgment, the propositions which emerge from the authorities are well summarised in the citations from the judgment of Butler-Sloss LJ in *Re E* and from Thorpe LJ's judgment in *Re B* which I have set out in paras [17] and [33] above. Should there be any difference in approach where there is a shared residence order?

[35] In my judgment, a shared residence order is, self-evidently, a species of residence order under s 8 of the 1989 Act. It settles the arrangements to be made as to the persons with whom a child is to live. In some, albeit rare cases, such as *A v A (Shared Residence)* [2004] EWHC 142 (Fam), [2004] 1 FLR 1195 an equal division of the children's time between their parents is appropriate, but there is no doubt that a shared residence order can properly be made where there is a substantial geographical distance between the parties: – see, for example, the decision of this court *Re F (Shared Residence Order)* [2003] EWCA Civ 592, [2003] 2 FLR 397, in which the mother was planning to relocate to Edinburgh, a considerable distance from where the father lived.

[36] In my judgment, therefore, it is wrong in principle to apply different criteria to the question of internal relocation simply because there is a shared residence order. Plainly, the fact of such an order is an important factor in the welfare equation, but I respectfully agree with counsel that it is not, in effect, a trump card preventing relocation. In each case what the

court has to do is to examine the underlying factual matrix, and to decide in all the circumstances of the case whether or not it is in the child's interest to relocate with the parent who wishes to move.

Special guardianship

B56 SG OR ADOPTION: BASIC APPROACH

Re S (Adoption order or special guardianship order)

[2007] EWCA Civ 54, [2007] 1 FLR 819 at 833, 837, 837 and 840

Court of Appeal

Wall LJ

Commentary on the statutory provisions

[40] We first make some general comments on the statutory regime, and its purposes. We then comment on four specific issues which have been discussed in the cases before us:

(i) Special guardianship orders within pre-existing family relationships; in this context we shall discuss the two first-instance cases to which we have been referred;
(ii) The need, under a special guardianship order, for leave for a parent to apply for a s 8 order;
(iii) Dispensing with parental consent to adoption;
(iv) In what circumstances (if any) should the court impose a special guardianship order on unwilling parties?

General comments

[41] The White Paper (para [11], above) contains a helpful summary of the main features of the special guardianship regime, as being to:

- give the carer clear responsibility for all aspects of caring for the child or young person, and for making the decisions to do with their upbringing;
- provide a firm foundation on which to build a lifelong permanent relationship between the carer and the child or young person;
- preserve the legal link between the child or young person and their birth family;
- allow proper access to a full range of support services including, where appropriate, financial support.

[42] It also gives some helpful illustrations of some circumstances in which guardianship may be appropriate:

(i)   older children who do not wish to be legally separated from their birth families;
(ii)   children being cared for on a permanent basis by members of their wider birth family;
(iii)   children in some minority ethnic communities, who have religious and cultural difficulties with adoption as it is set out in law;
(iv)   unaccompanied asylum-seeking children who need secure, permanent homes, but have strong attachments to their families abroad.

[43] It is important to emphasise that these are only illustrations. There can be no routine solutions. We repeat what this court said at para [78] in *Birmingham City Council v R* [2006] EWCA Civ 1748, [2007] 1 FLR 564 (cited at para [18], above) as to the importance of the issues raised by special guardianship:

> '... special guardianship is an issue of very great importance to everyone concerned with it, not least, of course, the child who is its subject. It is plainly not something to be embarked upon lightly or capriciously, not least because the status it gives the special guardian effectively prevents the exercise of parental responsibility on the part of the child's natural parents, and terminates the parental authority given to a local authority under a care order (whether interim or final). In this respect, it is substantially different from a residence order which, whilst it also brings a previously subsisting care order in relation to the same child to an end, does not confer on any person who holds the order the exclusivity in the exercise of parental responsibility which accompanies a special guardianship order.'

[44] It is important to note also that the statutory provisions draw strong and clear distinctions between the status of children who are adopted, and those who are subject to lesser orders, including special guardianship. As we have already pointed out, the considerations in relation to adoption in the expanded checklist contained in s 1 of the 2002 Act require the court to address the question of the child's welfare throughout his life. We do not think this point needs any further explanation or emphasis. Its consequences are, however, significant.

[45] Thus, although s 14C(1) of the 1989 Act gives special guardians exclusive parental authority, this entitlement is subject to a number of limitations. Attached to the skeleton argument prepared in the case of *Re AJ (Adoption Order or Special Guardianship Order)* [2007] EWCA Civ 55, [2007] 1 FLR 507 by Miss Lorna Meyer QC, Mr David Crowley, (the solicitor advocate for the child) and Mr Graham Jones (the solicitor advocate for the prospective adopters) was a helpful document entitled

Schedule of Main Differences between Special Guardianship Orders and Adoption which set out those differences in tabular form.

[46] For ease of reference we have attached that document to the judgment of the court in that case. It is not necessary, for the purposes of any of the appeals under consideration, for us to consider, for example, whether parental consent would be required were there to be a dispute over immunisations or sterilisation. We reproduce the document because, in our judgment, it demonstrates that, in addition to the fundamental difference in status between adopted children and those subject to special guardianship orders, there are equally fundamental differences between the status and powers of adopters and special guardians. These, we think, need to be borne in mind when the court is applying the welfare checklist under both s 1(3) of the 1989 Act and s 1 of the 2002 Act.

[47] Certain other points arise from the statutory scheme:

(i) The carefully constructed statutory regime (notice to the local authority, leave requirements in certain cases, the role of the court, and the report from the local authority – even where the order is made by the court of its own motion) demonstrates the care which is required before making a special guardianship order, and that it is only appropriate if, in the particular circumstances of the particular case, it is best fitted to meet the needs of the child or children concerned.

(ii) There is nothing in the statutory provisions themselves which limits the making of a special guardianship order or an adoption order to any given set of circumstances. The statute itself is silent on the circumstances in which a special guardianship order is likely to be appropriate, and there is no presumption contained within the statute that a special guardianship order is preferable to an adoption order in any particular category of case. Each case must be decided on its particular facts; and each case will involve the careful application of a judicial discretion to those facts.

(iii) The key question which the court will be obliged to ask itself in every case in which the question of adoption as opposed to special guardianship arises will be: which order will better serve the welfare of this particular child?

[48] The special nature of the jurisdiction also has implications for the approach of the courts:

(i) In view of the importance of such cases to the parties and the children concerned, it is incumbent on judges to give full reasons and to explain their decisions with care. Short cuts are to be avoided. It is not of course necessary to go through the welfare checklist line by line, but the parties must be able to follow the judge's reasoning and to satisfy themselves that he or she has duly considered it and has taken every aspect of it relevant to the particular case properly into account.

(ii) Provided the judge has carefully examined the facts, made appropriate findings in relation to them and applied the welfare checklists contained in s 1(3) of the 1989 Act and s 1 of the 2002 Act, it is unlikely that this court will be able properly to interfere with the exercise of judicial discretion, particularly in a finely balanced case. (We think it no co-incidence that all three of the appeals with which these judgments are concerned fall to be dismissed, although each reaches a different result.)

(iii) In most cases (as in these three appeals) the issue will be not the actual placement of the child but the form of order which should govern the future welfare of the child: in other words, the status of the child within the particular household. It is unlikely that the court need be concerned with the alternative of making 'no order' under s 1(5) of the 1989 Act and 1(6) of the 2002 Act.

(iv) For the same reason, the risk of prejudice caused by delay (to which s 1(2) of the 1989 Act rightly draws attention) may be of less pivotal importance. Indeed, in many cases, it may be appropriate to pause and give time for reflection, particularly in those cases where the order in being made of the court's own motion. This is a point to which we will return specifically when considering the first appeal.

[49] We would add, however, that, although the 'no order' principle as such is unlikely to be relevant, it is a material feature of the special guardianship regime that it is 'less intrusive' than adoption. In other words, it involves a less fundamental interference with existing legal relationships. The court will need to bear Art 8 of the European Convention for the Protection of Human Rights and Fundamental Freedoms 1950 in mind, and to be satisfied that its order is a proportionate response to the problem, having regard to the interference with family life which is involved. In choosing between adoption and special guardianship, in most cases Art 8 is unlikely to add anything to the considerations contained in the respective welfare checklists. Under both statutes the welfare of the child is the court's paramount consideration, and the balancing exercise required by the statutes will be no different to that required by Art 8. However, in some cases, the fact that the welfare objective can be achieved with less disruption of existing family relationships can properly be regarded as helping to tip the balance.

Special guardianship orders within pre-existing family relationships

[50] It is clear from the White Paper that special guardianship was introduced at least in part to deal with the potential problems arising from the use of adoption in the case of placements within the wider family. We have referred to the *Houghton Report* concerns in this respect (see para [6], above).

[51] A particular concern is that an adoption order has, as a matter of law, the effect of making the adopted child the child of the adopters for all purposes. Accordingly, where a child is adopted by a member of his wider family, the familial relationships are inevitably changed. This is frequently referred to as the 'skewing' or 'distorting' effect of adoption, and is a factor which the court must take into account when considering whether or not to make an adoption order in such a case. This is not least because the checklist under s 1 of the 2002 Act requires it to do so: see s 1(4)(f) ('the relationship which the child has with relatives.'). However, the weight to be given to this factor will inevitably depend on the facts of the particular case, and it will be only one factor in the overall welfare equation.

[52] As will be seen, the three appeals before this court illustrate the different weight to be placed on this factor in different circumstances, and that in some it may be of only marginal importance. In particular, as the case of *Re AJ (Adoption Order or Special Guardianship Order)* [2007] EWCA Civ 55, [2007] 1 FLR 507 demonstrates, both children and adults are capable of penetrating legal forms and retaining hold of the reality.

...

[55] The other case, *S v B and Newport City Council; Re K* [2007] 1 FLR (forthcoming)[1] was a decision of Hedley J given in Cardiff on 27 July 2006. The child (K) was a boy aged 6. He was living with his maternal grandparents, Mr and Mrs S, who sought an adoption order in relation to him, but, in the alternative, were prepared to accept a special guardianship order. It is, we think, an important feature of the case that in the household of Mr and Mrs S were also living their two natural children, aged 19 and 13, as well as K's cousin (described as a 'little boy'). The cousin was the son of another of Mr and Mrs S's daughters who was, of course, K's aunt, and his mother's sister.

...

[58] The judge decided that Mr and Mrs S should be appointed K's special guardians.

The judge's principal reason seems to have been that adoption would, as he put it, 'significantly skew otherwise perfectly comprehensible and not unusual family relationships and structures'. A special guardianship order was therefore to be preferred, unless it could not meet the welfare needs of the child.

[59] The judge also made both a prohibited steps order preventing K having any direct contact with his parents without an order of the courts, and an order under s 91(14) of the 1989 Act, without limitation of time,

---

[1]   [2007] 1 FLR 1116.

in respect of any application for contact by either parent in respect of the child. In addition, he made an order under s 14B(2)(a) giving leave for K to be known for all purposes by his grandparents' surname.

[60]   The case is useful for a helpful historical analysis by the judge of the law relating to adoption, which we will not repeat. The judge also set out in some detail the manner in which K's relationships with various family members would be skewed by an adoption order. We see no reason to question that analysis, or to doubt that the judge was right to make a special guardianship order on the particular facts as they presented themselves to him. However, we draw attention to the caveat which the judge himself entered in para [22] of his judgment:

> 'One purpose of adoption is of course to give lifelong status to carers where otherwise it would not exist. In a familial placement, that is not necessary because family status exists for life in any event. That is not to say that a familial placement may never be secured by adoption. One can imagine cases where the need for security against aggressive parents, including forensic aggression, may be overwhelming, or where a child has such disabilities that the need for a carer to have parental status may last long into majority, where adoption may still be right and necessary. No doubt there will be other cases too.'

[61]   The case is thus a good example of the application of the special guardianship provisions to the facts of a particular case. Whilst it contains a number of general propositions with which we do not disagree, it should not, in our judgment, be viewed as a template. Each case needs to be decided on the application of the statutory provisions to the best interests of the particular child or children concerned.

The need, under a special guardianship order, for leave for a parent to apply for a s 8 order

[62]   Under s 10(4) of the 1989 Act, a parent does not require the leave of the court to make an application for a s 8 order. However, s 91(14) enables the court to imposes specific restrictions:

> '(14) On disposing of any application for an order under this Act, the court may (whether or not it makes any other order in response to the application) order that no application for an order under this Act of any specified kind may be made with respect to the child concerned by any person named in the order without leave of the court.'

[63]   What is the position under a special guardianship order? We have seen that, under s 14D(1) and (3) of the 1989 Act, for an application to vary or discharge a special guardianship order, a parent not only needs

the court's leave, but must show a 'significant change of circumstances'. In addition, by s 10(7A) (inserted into the 1989 Act by the 2002 Act):

'If a special guardianship order is in force with respect to a child, an application for a residence order may only be made with respect to him, if apart from this subsection the leave of the court is not required, with such leave.'

[64] The effect of this (which did not appear to be in issue at the bar) was that, under a special guardianship order, the only s 8 application for which a parent requires the leave of the court is one for a residence order. This seems to be implicit in s 10(7A). There is a specific requirement for leave for an application for a residence order. It seems to follow that leave is not required to make an application for any other s 8 order.

[65] The absence of a general requirement for leave may seem surprising. Special guardianship orders are designed to produce finality, and there is, accordingly, logic in the proposition that a parent requires the leave of the court to reopen the issue of the order itself or of the child's residence. But, if so, one might expect similar considerations to apply to other forms of order under s 8. An essential component of the advantages produced by an adoption order for both adopters and children is that they are in most cases then free from the threat of future litigation. If the same protection is not available in respect of special guardianship orders, this may be a substantial derogation from the security provided.

[66] It is true that the court may invoke s 91(14) to place a filter on further applications by parents for other s 8 orders (including contact, and specific issue orders such as schooling). Furthermore, there is, we think, no doubt that the court has jurisdiction to make indefinite orders under s 91(14) of the 1989 Act. However, the test for overcoming the leave restriction has historically been seen as relatively low. The classic statement of principle is that by Butler-Sloss LJ (as she then was) in the leading case of *Re P (A Minor) (Residence Order: Child's Welfare)* [2000] Fam 15, sub nom *Re P (Section 91(14) Guidelines) (Residence and Religious Heritage)* [1999] 2 FLR 573, at 38 and 593 respectively:

'The applicant is not denied access to the court. It is a partial restriction in that it does not allow him the right to an immediate inter partes hearing. It thereby protects the other parties and the child from being drawn into the proposed proceedings unless or until a court has ruled that the application should be allowed to proceed. On an application for leave, the applicant must persuade the judge that he has *an arguable case with some chance of success. That is not a formidable hurdle to surmount.* If the application is hopeless and refused the other parties and the child will have been protected from unnecessary involvement in the proposed proceedings.' (emphasis added)

[67] In a statutory structure designed to achieve permanence and security for children and their carers outside adoption, it may seem an anomaly that the natural parent, whose parental responsibility is effectively and largely neutered, should nonetheless have an automatic right to apply to the court for s 8 relief (other than a change of residence). The very nature of such an application may be to interfere with the exercise of parental responsibility by the special guardian which is meant to be exclusive. The need to invoke s 91(14) to protect special guardians and children from the anxiety imposed by the prospect of future litigation is a possible weakness in the scheme.

[68] In any event, anomalous or not, it is plain to us that the statutory scheme for making special guardianship orders was designed generally to allow unfettered access to the court thereafter by parents in relation to all s 8 orders apart from residence. In this respect it must be accepted that special guardianship does not always provide the same permanency of protection as adoption. In our judgment, this is a factor, which, in a finely balanced case, could well tip the scales in favour of adoption.

Dispensing with parental consent for adoption

...

[This part of the judgment, which does not deal directly with special guardianship, is found at G3 – ss 47(2) and 52(1) ACA 2002: must consent be dispensed with if welfare best promoted by adoption]

In what circumstances (if any) should the court impose a special guardianship order on unwilling parties?

[73] There is no doubt, as s 14A(6)(b) of the 1989 Act makes clear, that the court has power to make a special guardianship order of its own motion, where the welfare of the child is in issue in any family proceedings, although as already noted (under s 14A(11)) it must first receive a report dealing with the matters referred to in s 14A(8). If no application for a special guardianship order has been made by any of the parties to family proceedings, a common reason will be that no party wants such an order. The statute, therefore, implicitly envisages an order being made against the wishes of the parties, and in a case in which the party seeking a different order (for example adoption) does not want to be appointed the child's special guardian. Indeed, this is the case in all three of the current appeals.

[74] In this connection, we were referred to the decision of this court in *Re M (Adoption or Residence Order)* [1998] 1 FLR 570. In *Re M* it was common ground that the court had the power to impose a residence order on unwilling parties. It is to be noted that the statutory language in

s 10(1)(b) of the 1989 Act is identical to that in s 14A(6)(b). This reinforces our view that the court has jurisdiction to impose a special guardianship order on an unwilling party. The real question, however, is whether or not it should do so.

[75] In that case (which was, of course, decided under the 1976 Act) the judge had made an adoption order in relation to a girl of 12 and dispensed with her mother's agreement to the order. This court, by a majority (Ward and Judge LJJ, Simon Brown LJ dissenting) set aside the adoption order and replaced it with a residence order in the prospective adopters' favour, combined with an order under s 91(14) of the 1989 Act designed to prevent the child's mother making an application for a residence order in her favour without the permission of the court.

[76] The facts in *Re M* were particularly stark, because the proposed adopters' case was that, if they did not obtain an adoption order in relation to the child, they would cease to care for her and return her to her mother's care, something which was plainly not in her best interests. The judge at first instance had treated the case as allowing him only two options: adoption or return to the mother. Inadequate consideration was given at first instance to what the majority thought to be in the child's best interests, assuming she could not be adopted, namely continuing to reside with the prospective adopters under a residence order with a s 91(14) prohibition on the mother making any further applications under s 8 of the 1989 Act (particularly for residence) without the court's permission. The majority felt unable to dispense with the mother's agreement to adoption on the ground that it was being unreasonably withheld, although Ward LJ was of the view that the test in s 6 of the 1976 Act was satisfied. Simon Brown LJ, on the other hand, was of the opinion that although an adoption order was 'clearly unideal' the reasonable parent in the mother's position would recognise both the near certainty of the prospective adopters relinquishing the care of the child if an adoption order was not made, and that the consequences of such a course of action would be disastrous to the child. Such a parent, accordingly, would have given her consent to the adoption.

[77] Whilst *Re M* highlights the intense difficulties of factual situations thrown up by the provisions of ss 6 and 16 of the 1976 Act, we do not find it of any particular assistance in addressing the two questions we have posed. The jurisdictional position is very clear: the court has the power to impose a special guardianship order on an unwilling party to the proceedings. Whether or not it should do so will depend upon the facts of the individual case, including the nature of the refuser's case and its interrelationship with the welfare of the particular child. What seems to us clear is that if the court comes to the view on all the facts and applying the welfare checklist under the 1989 Act (including the potential consequences to the child of the refuser implementing the threat to refuse

to be appointed a special guardian) that a special guardianship order will best serve the welfare interests of the child in question, that is the order which the court should make.

General notes:

Re S is one of three judgments handed down by the Court of Appeal on 6 February 2007 each concerned with whether an adoption or a special guardianship order should be made, the other two cases being *Re AJ (Adoption order or special guardianship order)* [2007] EWCA Civ 55, [2007] 1 FLR 507 and *Re M-J (Adoption order or special guardianship order)* [2007] EWCA Civ 56, [2007] 1 FLR 691. In both these cases the judgment was delivered by Wall LJ and in both he, and the other judges in the particular case, explicitly incorporated the extract quoted here from *Re S*. Formally therefore the approach has the combined authority of Wall, Thorpe, Tuckey, Scott Baker and Carnwath LJJ, and that of Potter P (see *Re S* at [4]).

As to the use of orders under s 91(14) of the CA 1989 to support arguments in favour of eg residence instead of special guardianship or special guardianship instead of adoption (*Re S* at [65]–[68] above) see also *Re AJ (Adoption order or special guardianship order)* [2007] EWCA Civ 55, [2007] 1 FLR 507 particularly at [47] and *S v B and Newport City Council* [2007] 1 FLR 1116 particularly at [25]–[26].

B57 SG OR ADOPTION: TABLE OF DIFFERENCES

Re AJ (Adoption order or special guardianship order)

[2007] EWCA Civ 55, [2007] 1 FLR 507 at 509 and 524

Court of Appeal

Wall LJ

[7] … We have attached to this judgment a helpful schedule, to which reference is made in para [45] of the judgment in *Re S*[1] entitled '*Schedule of Main Differences between Special Guardianship Orders and Adoption*' which set out those differences in tabular form.

---

[1]   *Re S (Adoption order or special guardianship order)* [2007] EWCA Civ 54, [2007] 1 FLR 819 at 834. See B56 – SG or adoption: basic approach.

SCHEDULE OF MAIN DIFFERENCES BETWEEN SPECIAL GUARDIANSHIP ORDERS & ADOPTION

	SPECIAL GUARDIANSHIP	ADOPTION
1 STATUS OF CARER	**Special Guardian:** *If related to child retains existing relative status.*	**Parent for all purposes:** *If related to child existing relative status changes.*
2 STATUS OF CHILD	**A child living with relatives/carers who remains the child of birth parent.**	**The child of the adoptive parent as if born as a child of the marriage and not the child of any other person** *therefore adoption includes a vesting of 'parenthood'. Section 39(1), (2) of the Adoption Act 1976 (the 1976 Act)/s 67 of the Adoption and Children Act 2002 (the 2002 Act).*
3 DURATION OF ORDER	**Ceases automatically on reaching 18 if not revoked by court earlier whether also ceases on death?** *The legal relationship created is therefore time limited and not lifelong. Section 91(13) of the Children Act 1989 (the 1989 Act).*	**Permanent** *The legal relationship is lifelong. Section 39(1) of the 1976 Act/s 67 of the 2002 Act.*
4 EFFECT ON BIRTH PARENT PR	**PR retained by birth parent** *SG can impose limitations in use (see 6 below). Section 14C(1), (2) of the 1989 Act.*	**Birth Parent PR extinguished** *Section 39(2) of the 1976 Act/s 46 of the 2002 Act.*
5 CARER'S PR	**PR vests in special guardian/s** *Section 14C(1), (2) of the 1989 Act Subject to limitations (see 6 below).*	**PR vested in adopter/s** *Section 39(1) of the 1976 Act/s 49of the 2002 Act/s 2 of the 1989 Act No limitations (but see joint operation* below).*

	SPECIAL GUARDIANSHIP	ADOPTION
6 <u>LIMITATION/RESTRICTION OF PR</u>		
(a) removal from jurisdiction	(a) up to 3 months without leave, thereafter only with written consent of all PR holders or leave of court unless court gave general leave on making SG order. *Section 14C(3)(b) and 14C(4)/14B(2)(b) of the 1989 Act.*	(a) No restriction
(b) change of name	(b) can not change surname without written consent of all PR holders or order of the court. *Section 14C(3)(a)/14B(2)(a) of the 1989 Act.*	(b) No restriction *name change may take place at time of making adoption order or thereafter*
(c) consent to adoption	(c) consent required from birth parents <u>and</u> special guardians or court must dispense with consent of birth parents <u>and</u> special guardians. *Sections 19,20,52 and 144 of the 2002 Act/s 14C(2)(b) of the 1989 Act.*	(c) consent required from adopters only or court must dispense with consent of adopters only.
(d) medical treatment	(d) may be difficulties where each special guardian agrees but birth parents do not in the following circumstances: **Sterilisation of a child** *This is the example given in the government guidance to SGO in 'Every Child Matters'; in Relation to effect of s 14C(2)(a) – no authority is cited.* **Ritual Circumcision** *See Re J (Specific Issue Orders: Child's Religious Upbringing and Circumcision) [2000] 1 FLR 571 Suggests that like sterilisation the consent of all PR holders would be required for this procedure.*	(d) no restrictions where each adoptive parent agrees (subject to age/Gillick competence of child) on giving consent for medical treatment. **However where adoptive parents themselves disagree in these scenarios a court order may be required (see below).*

	SPECIAL GUARDIANSHIP	ADOPTION
(d) medical treatment contd.	**Immunisation** See *Re C (Welfare of Child: Immunisation)* [2003] EWCA Civ 1148, [2003] 2 FLR 1095 *This added contested immunisations to the small group of important decisions where the consent of both parents was required.* **Life prolonging/Life shortening** *If the above scenarios require consent of all with PR surely it must then extend to issues of whether treatment should be given or withheld in terminal cases.* **Section 14C(1)(b) with (2)(a)** *Section 14(C)(1)(b) does not effect the operation of any enactment or rule of law which requires the consent of more than one person with PR in a matter effecting the child.* *If consent of all PR holders is required for these type of decisions does this then impose a duty upon SG to consult with birth parents in advance and to bring the matter back to court for determination if birth parents indicate an objection?*	***Section 2(7) of the 1989 Act** *Where more than one person has PR for a child each may act alone and without the other but nothing in this part shall be taken to affect the operation of any enactment which requires the consent of more than one person in a matter affecting the child.*
(e) voluntary accommodation	(e) If SG objects LA cannot accommodate child unless court order. If all SGs consent but birth parents object would appear that LA cannot accommodate child unless court order if birth parent willing and able to provide accommodation or arrange for accommodation to be provided.	(e) where adoptive parents agree they can accommodate voluntarily.

	SPECIAL GUARDIANSHIP	**ADOPTION**
(e) voluntary accommodation contd.	*This is not the case if there is in force a residence order and the residence order holder consents nor if there is a care and control order pursuant to wardship or inherent jurisdiction and the person in whose favour the order is made consents.*	
(f) removal from voluntary accommodation	(f) Any person may remove from voluntary accommodation at any time. *This is not the case if residence order holder of carer under wardship/inherent jurisdiction agrees to the voluntary accommodation.* *How is the 'exclusive' nature of the SG's PR intended to operate in these circumstances? It appears that the statute requires the consent of all PR holders therefore if SGs consent to accommodation but parents do not the parents can simply remove the child.* ***Section 20 (7),(8) and (9) of the 1989 Act***	(f) adoptive parents can remove from voluntary accommodation.
(g) consent to marriage under 18	(g) if all SG agree no restriction *the Marriage Act 1949 has been amended to enable SGs to give valid consent where SGO in force (unless also care order in force) s 3(1), (1A)(a) and (b)*	(g) if all agree no restriction

	SPECIAL GUARDIANSHIP	ADOPTION
7 DEATH OF CHILD	Special guardian must notify parents with PR *Section 14C(5) of the 1989 Act.* *Special guardians may not be able to arrange for burial/cremation in circumstances where parents wish to undertake such a task if the SGO ends on death. See by way of analogy R v Gwynedd County Council ex parte B* [1991] 2 FLR 365	No requirements for notification. *The rights and duties of legal parents do not end on death therefore would be no such conflict.*
8 REVOCATION OF ORDER	Specific statutory provision for birth parents to apply for discharge of SGO with leave of the court, leave not to be granted unless there has been a significant change of circumstances. Specific statutory provision four court to discharge of its own motion even where no application in any 'family proceedings'. *Section 14D of the 1989 Act.*	No statutory provision for revocation. *In wholly exceptional circumstances court may set aside adoption order, normally limited to where has been a fundamental breach of natural justice. See for example Re K (Adoption and Wardship)* [1997] 2 FLR 221.
9 FUTURE APPLICATIONS BY PARENTS	(a) Leave required	(a) Leave required
(a) Residence	(b) no automatic restriction	(b) Leave required
(b) Contact	(c) no automatic restriction	(c) Leave required
(c) Prohibited Steps	(d) no automatic restriction *Section 10(4)(7A) and (9) of the 1989 Act A parent is entitled to apply for any section 8 order except residence where is SGO.*	(d) Leave required *Section 10(2)(b), (4) and (9) of the 1989 Act.*
(d) Specific Issue		

	SPECIAL GUARDIANSHIP	ADOPTION
10 RESPONDENTS TO FUTURE LEGAL PROCEEDINGS RE CHILD	Birth parents would be respondents in addition to the SGs to any applications in relation to the child for s 8 orders, EPOs, Care/Supervision Orders, Secure accommodation etc.	Only adopters would be automatic respondents.
11 MAINTENANCE	Does not operate to extinguish any duty on birth parents to maintain the child.	Operates to extinguish any duty on birth parents to maintain the child *Section 12(3)(b) of the 1976 Act/s 46(2)(d) of the 2002 Act.*
12 INTESTACY	Child placed under SGO will not benefit from the rules relating to intestacy if the SGs die intestate.	Adopted Child will have rights of intestate succession.

Lorna Meyer QC
David Crowley
Graham Jones

B58　SG: NECESSARY TO HAVE LOCAL AUTHORITY REPORT

Re S (Adoption order or special guardianship order) (No 2)

[2007] EWCA Civ 90, [2007] 1 FLR 855 at 858

Court of Appeal

Wall LJ

[10]　... s 14A(11) is, in our judgment, unequivocal:

> 'The court may not make a special guardianship order unless it has received a report dealing with the matters referred to in subs (8)'.

[11]　It follows that the need for a report dealing with the matters identified in s 14A(8) as a pre-requisite for a special guardianship order being made is not limited to the receipt by the local authority of written notice under s 14A(7) by an individual who intends to make an application for such an order. It also plainly applies in relation to an order made under s 14A(6)(b) where the court (as in the instant case) considers that an order should be made, even though no application for such an order has in fact been made by any of the parties.

[12]　In practice, therefore, what in our judgment should happen in a case to which s 14A(6)(b) applies, and where there is no report under s 14A(8), is that the judge should exercise his or her powers under s 14A(9) and request the local authority to conduct the investigation and to produce a report dealing with the matters contained in s 14A(8)(a)–(c) of the 1989 Act. Until that report has been received by the judge, the court cannot make a special guardianship order.

[13]　It further follows, in our judgment, that in the instant case, the judge did not have the power to make a special guardianship order on 13 July 2006, and should not have done so.

[14]　That said, however, we agree with Miss Shelley that on the facts of this case, the court can properly adopt a pragmatic approach to the report. In para [46] of its decision in *Birmingham City Council v R* [2006] EWCA Civ 1748, [2007] 1 FLR 564, this court accepted the submission made by the local authority in that case that it was not possible for the court to define (and thereby limit) the requirements of a local authority to investigate and report under s 14A(8) where the court acts under s 14A(9).

We agree with that proposition. However, in a case to which s 14A(6)(b) applies, and in which the bulk of the information required for the report under s 14A(8) is already before the court in a different form, it would seem to us to be unduly burdensome for the local authority to be required, as it were, to start again from scratch, and produce a fresh report, much of which would simply reproduce and duplicate the information already before the court. Such an approach is not, we think, required by the statute.

[15] We therefore accept Miss Shelley's submission that the local authority should not be required to complete an entirely new report. What we think should happen is that the local authority should be asked by the court to file a report, which will fulfil the terms of s 14A(8); (i) by providing the missing information; and (ii) by setting out the remaining information in the form of cross-references to the information already before the court in other reports.

[16] None of this is in any way to diminish the importance of the report under s 14A(8) as explained in *Birmingham City Council v R*. Furthermore, we are clearly of the view that in every case in which the court is minded to invoke s 14A(6)(b), the court should carefully consider the manner in which its powers under s 14A(9) will fall to be exercised. In some cases, the information required by the report will already be before it in a different form. In such cases (for example, applications under the 2002 Act) we agree with Miss Shelley that it would be unduly burdensome on a local authority to have to start again from scratch, and to produce an entirely fresh report, much of which would be duplication.

Other significant cases on this issue:

- *O v Orkney Island Council* [2009] EWHC 3173 (Fam), [2010] 1 FLR 1449 (which authority responsible for preparing the report)

B59 SG: LEAVE AND REPORTING RESTRICTIONS

Birmingham City Council v R

[2006] EWCA Civ 1748, [2007] 1 FLR 564 at 566 and 589

Court of Appeal

Wall LJ

[2] The appeal ... raises three questions of law which, the local authority argues, have important practical implications for this local authority and for local authorities generally in cases in which the question of special guardianship arises. They are as follows:

(1) Is it open to an individual who needs the leave of the court to make an application for a special guardianship order to give notice to the local authority of his intention to apply for such an order under s 14A(7) of the 1989 Act prior to leave being obtained, thereby triggering a mandatory duty on the local authority to investigate the matter and prepare a report for the court under s 14A(8)?

(2) Is it a proper exercise of judicial discretion under s 14A(9) of the 1989 Act for the court to ask a local authority to conduct an investigation and prepare a report pursuant to s 14A(8) (a request which the local authority must obey): (a) when leave to make an application for a special guardianship order has not been obtained; and/or (b) without considering whether or not a prospective application for a special guardianship order has any realistic prospect of success?

(3) Where the court makes a request under s 14A(9) is it at the same time open to the court to define (and thereby limit) the scope of the local authority's obligation to investigate and report under s 14A(8) and the Regulations?

...

[103] We rule, accordingly, that:

(1) A person who requires the permission of the court to make an application for a special guardianship order cannot either make an application for such an order or give notice of his intention to do so unless and until he has obtained the court's permission to make the application.

(2)   Section 14(A)8 is not triggered where a person who requires the court's permission to make an application but has not obtained it, purports to give notice of his intention to make an application for a special guardianship order.

(3)   A judge should not invoke s 14A(9) to compel a local authority to perform its obligations under s 14A(8) at the instance of a person who needs but has not obtained permission to apply for a special guardianship order unless s 14A(6)(b) applies.

(4)   There is nothing in the Childrens[1] Act 1989 or the Special Guardianship Regulations 2005 which permits the court to restrict the nature and scope of a report under s 14A(8).

---

[1]   [Sic]

B60   ANCILLARY ORDERS AFFECTING SPECIAL GUARDIAN'S EXERCISE OF PR

Re L (Special guardianship: surname)

[2007] EWCA Civ 196, [2007] 2 FLR 50 at 63, 66, 66 and 68

Court of Appeal

Ward LJ

Change of name

...

[39] Sympathetic though I am to their predicament and their hurt, their concerns overlook the value of the lesson we are all taught at our mother's knee: honesty is the best policy. This family must honestly face up to its fractured constitution. E must learn to live with the fact that she is being brought up by her grandparents not her parents. It should not be difficult to say to E, 'Darling, your surname is L, not S, because L is the name you were born with, it is your parents' surname'. That is a fact she will soon absorb and with which she will soon be comfortable. It avoids the much more difficult questions that will be asked when she wishes to know 'why am I S if my parents are L?'.

[40] Although I would allow permission to appeal this issue, I would dismiss the appeal because I am satisfied that the judge's order was rightly made in the best interests of E. I wish to add, as emphatically as I can, that the rejection of this appeal should *not* be seen as any denigration at all of the stupendous effort the GP have made to bring order and normality into their granddaughter's life. I commend them for that. I urge them, however, not to exaggerate the importance they attach to this issue. In the scale of things in this child's life, her surname is a fact of little real significance. Far more important is the knowledge E will have that she has been much loved by her grandparents who have brought her up.

[41] I have deliberately refrained from addressing the argument that because the court is given the reminder to consider a change of name when making a SGO, there is some bias in favour of such an order being made. It could be argued that the degree of permanence inherent in this arrangement has a change of name as a concomitant, just as in adoption. This argument has not been fully addressed in this appeal. Miss Boyd's answer on F's behalf is that if adoption is not appropriate and if maintenance of some link with the parents is to be achieved, then the natural corollary is to preserve the parents' name. This is not the case where that dispute needs to be resolved. Ultimately the welfare of the child concerned is the litmus test and here the welfare of the child so overwhelmingly justifies the judge's decision that no presumption or starting point one way or the other makes any material difference.

...

Mother's contact

...

[47] ... Paragraph 4 of the order permitting contact between E and M, as agreed between M and the GP, only if approved in advance by the allocated social worker in writing was ignored and M and GM operated as they always had. The GM put in fresh evidence, which no one disputed, that M had called at the GP's house on nine occasions since the judgment and on those occasions enjoyed contact. What is important is that all of those visits passed uneventfully and without incident.

[48] I confess to having had grave doubts about the feasibility of operation of para 4 of the order. The nature of the relationship between M and the GM is such that both wanted and welcomed visits, especially now that M is no longer arriving under the influence of drugs. To control this by a social worker's approval in writing in advance seemed to me to be fraught with difficulty. As it transpired all parties agreed and all were content for this court to discharge this proviso, namely the words 'only if approved in advance ...', 12 months from the date of this order' of the order and for my part I also agree and would grant permission to appeal and allow the appeal to that extent.

...

[51] The GM's case rests essentially upon three foundations:

(1) her complaint about the exaggeration of the difficulties encountered with M (the unnecessary adult dispute point);

(2) the fundamental argument that, they having assumed and been awarded residence of E with contact at their discretion, it is anomalous and unfair that whilst upgrading their parental responsibility with the superior SGO, nevertheless, at the same time, diminish their autonomy of decision-making by imposing the LA's control (the inconsistency argument); and

(3) the factual argument that interposing a social worker with little prospect truly to get to know E, will confuse her and destabilise the placement because it highlights the sense of division in the family

and removes E from the core security of a family unit in which she has grown up and in which she will for the foreseeable long-term future live her life (the destabilising argument).

[52]   For reasons which I hope are already clear, I cannot accept the first two arguments. I have sympathy with the third. Supervised contact is always artificial contact. How much better it would be if M could demonstrate that she is responsible, build up the GM's trust and win her consent to relax the GM's supervisory reign and to persuade her it is safe for her to take E out on her own. How much better if the legal costs of this case had been expended from the very beginning on family therapy only now belatedly and, it seems, uncertainly put in place. In a therapeutic setting all the necessary work to reconcile M and the GM and, as vitally, all the necessary life story work could have been done and no one would have been as bruised as these parties are by this litigation. It is not the advantage of hindsight which informs my lament. If proper consideration had been given to s 14F of the Children Act 1989 and reg 3 of the Special Guardianship Regulations 2005, set out in para [32], above, some form of mediation and therapy would have been offered as the first response to this delicate problem, not as the last resort.

[53]   Forced to face matters as they are, I must have regard to the fact that E is already at nursery school, is used to being left alone, is having to get used to strange faces and so will cope well enough with a social worker entering her life for the purpose of arranging six contact visits. The judge was entitled to find E would not be sufficiently upset and the advantages of supervised contact outweighed the disadvantages.

[54]   It became increasingly apparent during the course of the hearing before us that there was considerable confusion as to how long the judge envisaged that M's contact should be supervised. On the face of the order the LA's involvement continues for year to year until the order is varied but the implication of para 4 of the order, and in particular of the terms of para 7 of the written package of family support, is that at the end of 12 months of its operation, the old regime of contact at the GM's discretion should revert. Although the judgment is not entirely clear, it seemed to be agreed after discussion that the judge intended supervision to last for one year only and that the order should be clarified to make that clear.

[55]   Accordingly, I am satisfied the GP have demonstrated an arguable case. I would give permission to appeal but allow the appeal only to the extent as set out in para [48], above. The proviso to para 4 of the order is discharged and that it is made clear that supervision of M's contact under para 3 is to continue for one year only. The GP have not persuaded me that the judge was plainly wrong to order this supervised contact and I would not allow their appeal against that part of the order.

Father's contact

[56] In essence the GP's case is that F has not demonstrated sufficient evidence of significant improvement in his powers of engagement with E and his responsibility to prove steadfast in his commitment to her. They consider that the involvement of the social workers is destabilising and 'creates a sense of 'divide' which is not conducive to E's sense of completeness'. They believe that F's ability to give presents will be manipulatively exploited. Above all, they fear that indirect contact is a prelude to direct contact and they cannot cope with that.

...

[58] Thus the judge is accepting that there is a degree of uncertainty about F's consistently maintaining the desire for contact he professes. It is, however, also clear that the judge was particularly concerned about the level of his commitment and the degree of his abstinence from drugs as matters having impact upon ordering *direct* contact at this stage. She was right not to go that far and, much as I understand and sympathise with the GP's concerns about this father, any failure by him to send cards regularly will not have the same serious impact as would his failure to attend face to face contact. In my judgment the judge was correct to order *some* indirect 'letter box' contact. Every child is entitled to know its parents and to have contact with them unless there are cogent reasons to refuse it. There are good reasons to refuse direct contact here but that is not a justification for preventing very limited indirect contact.

[59] That said, there are, nonetheless, unsatisfactory aspects of the order for F's indirect contact. No indication is given as to the number of cards or letters that may be sent or as to the time when they should be sent. Cards are appropriate in January when E has her birthday and at Christmas. That leaves a long gap for the rest of the year, too long for memory of the father to be sustained by a young child. The proper order would be to allow two more cards or letters to be sent and it would seem to me to be appropriate that one occasion might be about the time of F's birthday on 16 April and on M's birthday on 20 September. That gives a sufficient spread of time and a suitable anniversary for the communications to be meaningfully explained to a young child.

[60] There is one other unsatisfactory feature of the order. The contact 'may include suitable presents if [F] so wishes'. The GP's concern that this permission might be subject to inappropriate manipulation has some force. Presents should be limited to Christmas and E's birthday. Moreover there has to be some control over those presents and the right way to achieve that is by directing that presents may be included not only if F so wishes but also if the local authority in consultation with the GP consider the presents to be suitable.

[61]   Accordingly I would grant permission to appeal and vary para 5 of the order to the extent I have indicated.

B61 APPLICATION FOR LEAVE TO DISCHARGE OR VARY SGO

Re G (Special guardianship order)

[2010] EWCA Civ 300, [2010] 2 FLR 696 at 699

Court of Appeal

Wilson LJ

[11] More widely, however, I do not, at first sight, in any way accept that counsel were right to lead the judge to turn to s 10(9) of the Act in determining whether the mother's application for leave should succeed. That subsection applies to persons (other than the child concerned) who need to apply for leave to apply for an order under s 8 of the Act and I see no ground, upon this prima facie analysis, for considering that the matters there specified are *formally* required to be weighed upon an application for leave to apply for the discharge of a special guardianship order; one or more of them may, however, happen to be relevant to the exercise of the discretion in an individual case.

[12] I consider that, where we are required to apply statutory tests expressed in much the same language, we should, if possible, approach them in the same way. What I have in mind in particular are s 24(2) and (3) of the Adoption and Children Act 2002. Subsection (2) requires specified persons to obtain leave to apply for revocation of a placement order; and subs (3) disables the court from granting leave 'unless satisfied that there has been a change in circumstances since the order was made'. In the absence of full argument I am perplexed as to why, in relation to an application for leave to apply for revocation of a placement order, Parliament should there have required that the court should be satisfied of 'a change' in circumstances, whereas, in relation to an application for leave to apply for discharge of a special guardianship order, Parliament, by s 14D(5) of the Act of 1989, has required the court to be satisfied that there has been 'a significant change' in circumstances. Important though it is to ascribe a value to every word favoured by Parliament, I cannot think that, by s 24(3) of the Act of 2002, it was requiring proof only of an insignificant change in circumstances, whereas, in its insertion, by s 115 of the same Act, of s 14D(5) into the Act of 1989, it was requiring something different. On a more appropriate occasion we may have to consider whether there is indeed any significance in the absence of the word 'significant' in s 24(3) or whether the difference in the language is immaterial and possibly even the product of poor drafting under pressure. For the time being I proceed upon the basis that there is no relevant

difference between the reference in s 24(3) to 'a change' in circumstances and the reference in s 14D(5) to 'a significant change' in circumstances. If, then, we have for practical purposes identical language, my view is that we should adopt an identical approach; and thus that, to the extent that in *M v Warwickshire County Council* [2007] EWCA Civ 1084, [2008] 1 WLR 991, [2008] 1 FLR 1093, this court gave guidance as to the approach to an application for leave to apply for revocation of a placement order, it should apply similarly to an application for leave to apply for the discharge of a special guardianship order. Indeed in *Re A; Coventry County Council v CC and A* [2007] EWCA Civ 1383, [2008] 1 FLR 959, this court – again in an attempt to keep things as simple as possible – suggested, at [10], that the factors relevant to the exercise of the discretion under s 24(3) of the Act of 2002, as identified in the *Warwickshire* case, were identical to those relevant to the exercise of the discretion whether to grant leave to apply for an adoption order under s 42(6) of the Act of 2002.

[13] In the *Warwickshire* case, cited above, this court interpreted s 24(3) of the Act of 2002 as meaning that a change in circumstances since the order was made was a necessary, but not a sufficient, condition of leave to apply for revocation of a placement order; that, as explained at [29], the establishment of a change in circumstances gave rise to a discretion whether to grant leave, in the exercise of which the welfare of the child and the prospect of success of the proposed substantive application should both be weighed; and that, while the two considerations were linked and would often be consonant, it might be dangerous to subsume the one into the other.

[14] I suggest that, until the emergence of more robust jurisprudence in relation to the proper approach to the determination of applications for leave to apply for the discharge (or variation) of special guardianship orders, the approach should be that commended in the *Warwickshire* case. I confess that, even in the absence of the material, not presented on behalf of the mother to the judge, which now leads the grandmother to concede this appeal, I would have been persuaded, had I been in the shoes of the judge, not only that there had been a significant change in circumstances since the special guardianship order was made but that, by reference to the approach commended in the *Warwickshire* case, the resultant discretion should be exercised in favour of the grant of leave.

General notes:

Compare with:

- *M v Warwickshire County Council* [2007] EWCA Civ 1084, [2008] 1 FLR 1093: see E7 – ACA 2002, s 24 leave to apply to revoke PO;

- *Re A; Coventry County Council v CC and A* [2007] EWCA Civ 1383, [2008] 1 FLR 959: see E11 – ACA 2002, s 42(6) leave to apply for AO.

DIVISION C

CHILDREN ACT 1989, PT III

Contents

Contents

Secure accommodation

C1   PROCEDURAL ISSUES (1)

Re AS (Secure accommodation order)

[1999] 1 FLR 103 at 104

Family Division

Bracewell J

It has been made plain in various cases that the making of a secure accommodation order is a deprivation of liberty for the child, and it is by reason of that consequence that there is a specific provision in s 25(6) of the Children Act 1989 whereby no court shall exercise the powers conferred by this section in respect of a child who is not legally represented in that court unless, having been informed of his right to apply for legal aid and having had the opportunity to do so, he refused or failed to apply. It is implicit in that provision that legal representation in order to be effective must involve the taking of instructions. In the case of *J v Merthyr Tydfil County Borough Council* [1997] Fam Law 522, an appeal from an order of the family proceedings court, Wilson J determined that it was wrong for the justices to have refused to allow the appellant's solicitor an opportunity of seeing their client prior to the hearing despite the court having of its own volition contacted the local authority and made arrangements that the appellant should not be brought to the court.

In a decision of Ewbank J, *Re W (Secure Accommodation Order: Attendance at Court)* [1994] 2 FLR 1092, the judge, in exercising his discretion to refuse to allow the child concerned to attend court, explicitly dealt with the need for counsel and solicitors to be able to take instructions from the child so as to present the child's case before the court.

The deficit was compounded in the present appeal in that no guardian ad litem had been appointed, and the guardian who had knowledge of the case and who had previously represented A in the care proceedings was not even aware that the application for a secure accommodation order was being made.

I have concluded that the procedure adopted by the metropolitan stipendiary magistrate was fundamentally flawed. If the local authority were concerned about the child absconding again in the event of being informed that an application was to be made, the remedy was in their hands. They had the right to keep the child in secure accommodation for up to 72 hours without a court order. They did not avail themselves of that provision, which is plainly designed to deal with cases of gravity where there are serious concerns about the immediate conduct of the child on being informed of the pending proceedings. If they do not take that course, in my judgment they must, out of natural justice and the requirements of s 25, inform the child of the application which is to be made; the child must have the opportunity to be legally represented and for appropriate instructions to be given in order to comply with s 25(6), and, further, it is appropriate in all save the most exceptional circumstances for a guardian ad litem to be appointed. That was the first matter whereby there was a fundamental error.

The second, in my judgment, was that no sworn evidence was heard by the stipendiary magistrate, and therefore this court is not in a position to know which precise facts were agreed, which were in dispute and which were found to be proved. It is essential that in a case such as a secure accommodation application there should be clear recordings of facts as found by the court, and in order to reach those conclusions it is necessary for there to be sworn evidence unless the matters proceed by agreement between all parties, in which case the statements which have been filed will constitute the agreed evidence.

C2   PROCEDURAL ISSUES (2)

Birmingham City Council v M

[2008] EWHC 1085 (Fam), [2008] 2 FLR 542 at 547

Family Division

McFarlane J

[23]   ... Drawing matters together I conclude that the following matters
of principle should apply when a court is faced with deciding whether or
not to adjourn a secure accommodation application:

(i)   A free-standing application cannot be made for an interim secure
       accommodation order. The power to make an interim order only
       arises under s 25(5) of the Children Act 1989 if the court adjourns
       the hearing of the local authority's application.
(ii)   Accordingly, the preliminary procedural question for the court on
       any application for a secure accommodation order is whether to
       proceed to determine the application or whether to adjourn it. In
       addressing that question, the court is likely to consider:
       (a)   Whether the court has all the information that it needs to
             determine the issues raised by the application, namely (1)
             whether the criteria for making the order sought are met,
             and (2) the duration of the order (if made), and;
       (b)   Whether it would be procedurally fair to all parties to
             determine the application at that hearing.
(iii) If the court is satisfied it has all the information that it needs to
       determine the issues raised by the application and that it would be
       procedurally fair to proceed, then it is likely that there will be no
       grounds upon which the court can properly adjourn the substantive
       application. In those circumstances the court must proceed to
       determine the application for the secure accommodation order.
(iv)   As a matter of principle, if the court decides to adjourn the
       application, then the period of adjournment should be the
       minimum necessary to ensure the factors justifying an adjournment
       are addressed and the court has either the necessary information
       and/or procedural fairness is ensured.
(v)   The function and role of the children's guardian within secure
       accommodation proceedings is to provide assistance to the court
       with the issues raised by the application. It is not to oversee the
       exercise by the local authority of its statutory duties, nor to perform
       some free-standing welfare role for the benefit of the child. It is not
       accordingly a proper use of the court's power to prolong secure
       accommodation proceedings simply in order to keep a children's

guardian involved for the purposes of assisting the child, or overseeing the performance of the local authority's statutory duties.

C3 ATTENDANCE OF THE CHILD

Re W (Secure accommodation order: attendance at court)

[1994] 2 FLR 1092 at 1095, 1096 and 1097

Family Division

Ewbank J

In *Re C (A Minor) (Care: Child's Wishes)* [1993] 1 FLR 832 Waite J, as he then was, was faced with a case where a child of 13 had been in court before the magistrates and was also in court before him. He said this at p 840G:

'There has been one feature of this hearing to which I feel I should draw attention, in case it may have implications for other appeals. C was present in court throughout the hearing before the magistrates, save for brief intervals ...'

Then he went on to say:

'... I think it would be a pity if the presence of children as young as this at the hearing of High Court appeals from magistrates in family proceedings were to be allowed to develop unquestioningly into a settled practice. Most of the children concerned in care proceedings have only become involved in the first place because of some past or anticipated experience which threatens the stability and lightness of heart which could be called the national birthright of every child. I would have thought that to sit for hours, or it may be even days, listening to lawyers debating one's future is not an experience that should in normal circumstances be wished upon any child as young as this.'

On behalf of the Official Solicitor it is said that in general terms the presence of children in court is harmful to children, that children in care proceedings, and more particularly in secure accommodation proceedings, are amongst the most damaged and disadvantaged children in our community, and that it will be of no benefit to them to sit through to the end. Moreover, it is likely to increase their sense of responsibility for what is being decided, and to cause anxiety and distress. It is said that the court should be satisfied that the interests of the child indicate that the child should be in court if there is a suggestion that the child wishes to come.

...

In addition to the considerations of the interests of the child, which override any other considerations, there is also the inherent power of the court to control its own proceedings, and that is relevant in this particular case at the particular time that the district judge heard the case. It was his view on the evidence he heard or the reports he had read that the child would have to be physically 'shackled', as he put it, in court in order to control him. This in itself would be sufficient ground in the inherent jurisdiction of the court to refuse to allow the child to be in court. One can see that the prospect of disturbance or unruliness in court, or the possibility of the child being educationally subnormal, or the child being much younger than this child, would be examples of cases where the court would not allow the child to be in court for the hearing.

...

In my judgment the court in dealing with an application for secure accommodation, and probably in dealing with an application for a care order, can allow the child to be in court, but the court must always bear in mind that attendance in court is likely to be harmful to the child, and the court should only allow the child to attend if it is satisfied that attendance is in the interests of the child. Certainly where the court is of the view on the material before it that the child is likely to be unruly, the court in its inherent jurisdiction can refuse to allow the child into the court.

C4 WHO IS THE DECISION-MAKER?

S v Knowsley Borough Council

[2004] EWHC 491 (Fam), [2004] 2 FLR 716 at 727 and 730

Family Division

Charles J

Who is the decision-maker?

[42] This question arises in two contexts: first, when a secure accommodation is applied for and made; secondly, as here, when a challenge is made to the continuing lawfulness of the restriction of a child's liberty under the authorisation provided by a secure accommodation order. As to the second point, the view of Holman J in *LM v Essex County Council* [1999] 1 FLR 988 that if and when the statutory criteria cease to apply a secure accommodation order can no longer be enforced is endorsed by the judgments in *Re K (Secure Accommodation Order: Right to Liberty)* [2001] Fam 377, [2001] 1 FLR 526: see paras [30] and [97]. I respectfully agree with that view. I add that it seems to me that the endorsement by the Court of Appeal is subject to what was described as issue (ii) in the judgment of Holman J in *LM v Essex County Council* as to whether the release had to be at once, which Holman J declined to decide and thus, in my view, the effect of reg 10 of the 1991 Regulations.

...

[47] The issue of who the decision-maker should be when the lawfulness of enforcing a secure accommodation order is challenged during the maximum period stated therein was not addressed in the skeleton arguments. It was, however, argued before me. I indicated that my preliminary view was that on a challenge during the currency of a secure accommodation order that by analogy with the approach adopted by the House of Lords in *R v Secretary of State for the Home Department ex parte Khera; R v Secretary of State for the Home Department ex parte Khawaja* [1984] AC 74 (see, for example, at 97D–G and 105B–F) the court should be the decision-maker as to whether the criteria in s 25(1) are satisfied and should treat these criteria as precedent facts. It seemed to me that this fitted with the section and avoided the somewhat odd consequence that different approaches would apply when the order was made and if and when the legality of its enforcement or implementation was challenged during the currency of an order.

[48] However, I acknowledge the force of the arguments advanced on behalf of the local authority that the scheme of the Children Act 1989, when read with the Regulations – and I should add the passage I have already quoted from the judgment of Judge LJ in *Re K (Secure Accommodation Order: Right to Liberty)* [2001] Fam 377, [2001] 1 FLR 526, para [97] – show that a duty is placed on the local authority to review the continued application of the criteria set out in s 25(1), and that, therefore, when a challenge arises during the currency of an order, what is in issue is whether or not the decision of the local authority as to that aspect of its duties upon which its continued placement of the child in secure accommodation is founded is a lawful decision. Therefore I acknowledge that there is force in the proposition that during the currency of the order the relevant decision-maker is the local authority. However, the same point can be said to arise in cases where the local authority has placed a child in secure accommodation and has then sought an order from the court for the first time.

[49] As appears later in this judgment, in my view, it is not necessary for me to decide this point of law and I acknowledge that further argument on it would be useful. I, therefore, do not propose to decide the point at this stage. I, however, add that if the s 25(1) criteria are not to be treated as precedent facts that have to be established to the satisfaction of the court, this is a case where, in my view, the court would give anxious scrutiny to a decision of the local authority because that decision relates to the liberty of the child. Thus, in my view, it is a case in which the full amplitude of modern judicial review would be brought to bear: see, for example, *R (Q and Others) v Secretary of State for the Home Department* [2003] EWCA Civ 364, [2003] 3 WLR 365, at paras [112]–[115].

This case is also included in relation to:

C7 'likely to abscond'

C5 INTERIM ORDERS AND MAXIMUM PERIOD OF ORDER

C v Humberside County Council

[1994] 2 FLR 759 at 760 and 761

Family Divison

Bracewell J

Such an application may be adjourned, and an interim secure accommodation order made pending further investigation by the guardian ad litem.

Section 25(5) provides:

> '... on any adjournment of the hearing of an application under this section, a court may make an interim order permitting the child to be kept during the period of the adjournment in secure accommodation.'

This provision was considered in *Hereford and Worcester County Council v S* [1993] 2 FLR 360.

Regulation 11 of the Children (Secure Accommodation) Regulations 1991, which is headed 'Maximum initial period of authorisation by a court', provides that, subject to regs 12 and 13 (which have no relevance to this appeal), the maximum period for which a court many authorise a child to whom s 25 of the Act applies to be kept in secure accommodation is 3 months.

I am satisfied that if Parliament intended to allow a court to adjourn for one month, and then ignore that period when imposing the maximum term allowed, the regulations would have so stated unequivocally.

...

I am satisfied that a secure accommodation order affects liberty and must be strictly construed. The justices, at the adjourned hearing, were still seised of the original application, which had not then been determined, and which in my judgment was subject to a limit whereby no more than a total of 3 months' restriction of liberty could be imposed. The justices exceeded their jurisdiction, the term imposed was unlawful, and therefore this appeal is allowed.

C6   CA 1989, S 1 DOES NOT APPLY BUT WELFARE RELEVANT

Re M (Secure accommodation order)

[1995] 1 FLR 418 at 423 and 424

Court of Appeal

Butler-Sloss LJ

I have come to the conclusion on two separate lines of reasoning that welfare is relevant to a s 25 application but is not a paramount consideration and that the s 1 requirements do not apply to it.

1.   The framework of Part III of the Act is structured to cast upon the local authority duties and responsibilities for children in its area and being looked after. The general duty of a local authority to safeguard and promote the child's welfare is not the same as that imposed upon the court in s 1(1) placing welfare as the paramount consideration.

...

The jurisdiction of the court is to be found in the same section and the court applies the same criteria in s 25(1) as the local authority. To require the court to have regard to other criteria than those imposed upon the local authority within the same section would, in my view, be inconsistent with the purpose of the section which gives the court the power to authorise the local authority to keep the child in secure accommodation. It is the same power as that exercisable by the local authority in the same way albeit for a much shorter period. By s 25(3) the court has the specific duty to determine whether any relevant criteria are satisfied for keeping a child who may or may not already have been placed by the local authority, in secure accommodation for a period longer than 72 hours. In considering 'any relevant criteria' the court has a similar duty to the local authority to include the welfare of the child concerned. Whether it is a reviewing power, as Ward J suggested, or a general duty to consider the welfare of the child, is a matter of words. No one can doubt that the restriction upon the liberty of a child, generally for his own good (subject to s 25(1)(b)) is a serious step which must be taken only when there is no genuine alternative which would be appropriate and, as *The Children Act 1989 Guidance and Regulations, vol 1, Court Orders,* para 5.1 sets out, as a last resort. Clearly the welfare of the child is of great importance and must take its place in the relevant criteria. But if at the end of the day the relevant criteria are satisfied there is a mandatory requirement that the court shall make an order authorising the child to be kept in secure accommodation.

2.   The relevance of s 1. It might reasonably be argued that a s 25 application comes within the definition of 'a question with respect to the upbringing of a child'. But as one looks at the wording of s 1 its provisions are either irrelevant to or inconsistent with s 25. The paramountcy principle is inconsistent with the duties of the local authority and with s 25(1)(b). Subsection (2) is unnecessary since the application is one which requires to come to court with expedition. Subsection (3) criteria are not by subs (4) expressed to apply to Part III and in my view it is not necessary to look at them. I would only pick out the ascertainable wishes and feelings of the child. At 14, with a history of being beyond control, absconding, drug abuse and offending, it is probable that the wishes and feelings of M are inconsistent with the need for his sake to restrict his liberty. In any event he was separately represented by his own lawyers and his views were plainly before the court. A more important provision is s 1(5) which is clearly incompatible with the mandatory requirement of s 25(4). Looking at the purpose of s 25 to restrict the liberty of a child who falls within the relevant criteria, s 25(4) must prevail over s 1(5).

In my judgment s 1 was not designed to be applied to Part III of the Act. To that extent I would disagree with the vols 1 and 4 of *The Children Act 1989 Guidance and Regulations* (above), although I do agree that the welfare of the child is an important consideration. The magistrates in this case were in error in applying the s 1 criteria, but that was an error in favour of M.

C7 'LIKELY TO ABSCOND'

S v Knowsley Borough Council

[2004] EWHC 491 (Fam), [2004] 2 FLR 716 at 727

Family Division

Charles J

The meaning of 'likely'

[37] The notes to s 25 in *Family Court Practice* (Family Law, 2003) indicate that a county court judge has decided in a case called *Re D (Secure Accommodation Order)* [1999] Fam Law 311 that in the phrase 'likely to abscond' the word 'likely' should be construed in the same way as in the threshold criteria in s 31; namely, in the sense of a real possibility or a possibility that cannot sensibly be ignored. I agree.

This case is also included in relation to:

C4　Who is the decision-maker?

DIVISION D

CHILDREN ACT 1989, PTS IV AND V

Contents

ECtHR: Art 8 applied to public law
D1   Consider alternatives to removal / inherent procedural rights
D2   Removal of child (at birth) and permanent separation
D3   Art 8: public law summary

Parts IV and V: general
D4   Intervention must be proportionate
D5   Reunification not an overriding factor
D6   Removal of child placed with parents under CO
D7   Relationship between court and LA
D8   Relationship between LA and CG
D9   No court intervention once final CO made

Newborn babies
D10   Removal at birth, without notice, in exceptional circumstances
D11   Removal at birth requires court order
D12   Contact to newborn baby (1)
D13   Contact to newborn baby (2)

Threshold criteria
D14   'Significant'
D15   'Is suffering': relevant time is when protective arrangements initiated
D16   Information found / events occurring after initial intervention
D17   'Likely to suffer significant harm'
D18   'Care given … not … reasonable': objective test
D19   Dangers of social engineering
D20   The reasonable parent and cultural realities
D21   Threshold should always be recorded

Designated local authority
D22   A simple approach
D23   Further guidance
D24   Involvement of second LA

Change of name of child in care
D25   General principles
D26   Change of forename

Contact to child in care

Supervision

Section 37 direction

Section 38(6): examination or other assessment

Interim orders / authorising removal of child from parental care

Interim or final order

ECtHR: Art 8 applied to public law

D1 CONSIDER ALTERNATIVES TO REMOVAL / INHERENT PROCEDURAL RIGHTS

Moser v Austria

(Application number 12643/02) [2007] 1 FLR 702 at 712

European Court of Human Rights

[62] It is not in dispute that the transfer of custody constitutes an interference with the applicants' right to respect for their family life. This interference will only be justified if it complies with the requirements set out in Art 8(2) of the Convention.

[63] The interference had a basis in domestic law, namely Arts 176 and 176a of the Austrian Civil Code, and served a legitimate aim in that it was intended to protect the 'heath and morals' (sic) and 'the rights and freedoms' of the second applicant.

[64] The parties' argument concentrated on the necessity of the interference. The court reiterates that in order to determine whether the impugned measures were 'necessary in a democratic society', it has to consider whether, in the light of the case as a whole, the reasons adduced to justify them were relevant and sufficient for the purposes of Art 8(2) (see, among many other authorities, *K and T v Finland* (2001) 36 EHRR 255, [2001] 2 FLR 707; *Kutzner v Germany* (2002) 35 EHRR 25, para 65; *P, C and S v United Kingdom* (2002) 35 EHRR 31, [2002] 2 FLR 631, para [114]; all with a reference to *Olsson v Sweden* (1989) 11 EHRR 259, para 68). It will also have regard to the obligation which the State has in principle to enable the ties between parents and their children to be preserved (see *Kutzner*, cited above.).

[65] In doing so, it is not the court's task to substitute itself for the domestic authorities in the exercise of their responsibilities for the regulation of the public care of children and the rights of parents whose children have been taken into care, but rather to review under the Convention the decisions that those authorities have taken in their exercise of their power of appreciation (see the above-cited cases, *K and T v Finland*, para [154]; *Kutzner*, para 66, and *P, C and S v United Kingdom*,

para [115], and *Hokkanen v Finland* (Application No 19823/92) (1995) 19 EHRR 139, [1996] 1 FLR 289, para [55]).

[66] The margin of appreciation to be accorded to the competent national authorities will vary in the light of the nature of the issues and the seriousness of the interests at stake. Thus, the court recognises that while the authorities enjoy a wide margin of appreciation in assessing the necessity of taking a child into care, the court must still be satisfied in the particular case that there existed circumstances justifying the removal of the child, and it is for the respondent state to establish that a careful assessment of the impact of the proposed care measure on the parents and the child, as well as of the possible alternatives to taking the child into public care was carried out prior to the implementation of such a measure (see, in particular, *P, C and S v United Kingdom*, cited above, para [116], and *K and T v Finland*, cited above, para [166]). Following any removal into care, a stricter scrutiny is called for in respect of any further limitations by the authorities, for example on parental rights of access, as such further restrictions entail the danger that the family relations between the parents and the child are effectively curtailed (*P, C and S v United Kingdom*, para [117], and *Kutzner*, para 67, both cited above).

[67] Moreover, it is the court's well established case-law that Art 8 contains implicit procedural requirements. What is to be determined is whether, having regard to the particular circumstances of the case and notably the serious nature of the decisions to be taken, the parents have been involved in the decision-making process, seen as a whole, to a degree sufficient to provide them with the requisite protection of their interests (*Elsholz v Germany* (2002) 34 EHRR 58, [2000] 2 FLR 486, at para [52], *P, C and S v United Kingdom*, cited above, para [119], and *Venema v the Netherlands* [2003] 1 FLR 552, with references to *W v United Kingdom*, (1988) 10 EHRR 29, at para 64).

[68] The court observes that, unlike in most childcare cases, the reason for the transfer of custody of the second applicant did not lie in the first applicant's incapacity to care for him on account of any physical or mental illness or on account of any violent or abusive conduct (see, in contrast, the above cited-cases, *Scozzari and Giunta*, paras [149]–[150], *K and T v Finland*, at para [173], and *P, C and S v United Kingdom*, para [134]). It was based solely on her lack of appropriate accommodation and financial means and her unclear residence status, ie her precarious situation which would have made it difficult for her to care for a very young child.

[69] In the court's view, a case like the present one called for a particularly careful examination of possible alternatives to taking the second applicant into public care. The Government argued in essence that the courts examined alternative measures and dismissed them as not being practicable. Moreover, they alleged that the first applicant herself failed to co-operate. The applicants, for their part, maintained that no alternatives whatsoever were proposed or assessed by the authorities.

[70] The court does not share the applicants' view that the authorities made no assessment of alternatives at all. In fact, the courts noted that there was no possibility of placing the second applicant with any relatives and they examined and dismissed the alternative proposed by the first applicant to lodge her and the second applicant with a friend of hers. However, no positive action was taken to explore possibilities which would have allowed the applicants to remain together, for instance by placing them in a mother-child centre. In this connection, the court notes that according to the Government the fact that the applicants were foreigners did not exclude them from admission to a mother child centre under the Vienna Youth Welfare Act. However, this possibility was apparently not contemplated and no other measures, such as clarifying the applicant's residence status, were taken. In this connection, the court notes that the residence prohibition against the applicant was subsequently quashed by the Constitutional Court as being at variance with her rights under Art 8.

[71] This failure to make a full assessment of all possible alternatives is aggravated by the fact that no measures were taken to establish and maintain the contact between the applicants while the proceedings were pending. This is particularly serious, given that they did not have a chance to bond in the first place, since the second applicant had been removed immediately after his birth. It follows from the Juvenile Court's decision of 3 December 2000 that in the 6 months between the second applicant's birth and the decision transferring custody to the Youth Welfare Office, the first applicant had only twice been given an opportunity to see her son. Referring to reports of the Youth Welfare Office and the Juvenile Court Assistance Office, the court found that she had not properly exercised her access rights and had generally failed to co-operate with the authorities. However, the applicant alleges that she had not been able to comment on these reports.

[72] At this juncture the court will turn to the question whether the procedural requirements inherent in Art 8 were complied with. The court notes, firstly, that the first applicant was only heard once by the Juvenile Court, namely on 2 August 2000 when she had appeared in court of her own motion to give information on her situation. Second, the court notes that, in its decision of 3 December 2000, the Juvenile Court relied on a report of the Youth Welfare Office of 1 September 2000 and a report of the Juvenile Court Assistance Office of 2 November 2000 which had not been served on the applicant and on which she had had no possibility of commenting (see, as a similar case, *Buchberger v Austria* (Application No 32899/96) (unreported) 20 December 2001). Third, the court observes that the first applicant was not assisted by counsel in the proceedings before the Juvenile Court. The appeal proceedings, in which she was

represented, were conducted without any hearing and it cannot be said that the deficiency of the first instance proceedings was remedied by the opportunity to comment on the reports at issue in the appeal, since the appellate court did not examine the first applicant's complaint that no alternatives to the transfer of custody had been explored but repeated the assessment contained in the reports that she had failed to co-operate. As regards the alleged failure to exercise her access rights, the appellate court did not reply to her submissions at all. In sum, the court considers that the first applicant was not involved in the decision-making process to a degree required for the protection of her interests.

[73] Having regard to the authorities' failure to examine all possible alternatives to transferring custody of the second applicant to the Youth Welfare Office, their failure to ensure regular contacts between the applicants following their separation and the first applicant's insufficient involvement in the decision making process, the court considers that although the reasons relied on by the domestic courts were relevant, they were not sufficient to justify such a serious interference with the applicants' family life. Notwithstanding the domestic authorities' margin of appreciation, the interference was therefore not proportionate to the legitimate aims pursued.

[74] Consequently, there has been a violation of Art 8 of the Convention as regards the transfer of custody of the second applicant to the Youth Welfare Office.

This case is also included in relation to:

G1   Opportunity to comment / public hearing / public pronouncement

D2 REMOVAL OF CHILD (AT BIRTH) AND PERMANENT SEPARATION

P, C and S v United Kingdom

[2002] 2 FLR 631 at 655 and 659

European Court of Human Rights

B. The court's assessment

1. GENERAL PRINCIPLES

[113] The mutual enjoyment by parent and child of each other's company constitutes a fundamental element of family life, and domestic measures hindering such enjoyment amount to an interference with the right protected by Art 8 of the Convention (see, amongst others, *Johansen v Norway* (1996) 23 EHRR 33, at para 52). Any such interference constitutes a violation of this Article unless it is 'in accordance with the law', pursues an aim or aims that are legitimate under para 2 of Art 8 and can be regarded as 'necessary in a democratic society'.

[114] In determining whether the impugned measures were 'necessary in a democratic society', the court will consider whether, in the light of the case as a whole, the reasons adduced to justify these measures were relevant and sufficient for the purpose of para 2 of Art 8 of the Convention (see, inter alia, *Olsson v Sweden* (1988) 10 EHRR 259, at para 68).

[115] It must be borne in mind that the national authorities have the benefit of direct contact with all the persons concerned (see *Olsson v Sweden (No 2)* (1992) 17 EHRR 134, at para 90). It follows from these considerations that the court's task is not to substitute itself for the domestic authorities in the exercise of their responsibilities for the regulation of the public care of children and the rights of parents whose children have been taken into care, but rather to review under the Convention the decisions taken by those authorities in the exercise of their power of appreciation (see, for instance, *Hokkanen v Finland* (1995) 19 EHRR 139, [1996] 1 FLR 289, at para 55 and the above-mentioned *Johansen* judgment, at para 64).

[116] The margin of appreciation so to be accorded to the competent national authorities will vary in the light of the nature of the issues and the seriousness of the interests at stake. While the authorities enjoy a wide margin of appreciation in assessing the necessity of taking a child into

care, in particular where an emergency situation arises, the court must still be satisfied in the circumstances of the case that there existed circumstances justifying the removal of the child, and it is for the respondent State to establish that a careful assessment of the impact of the proposed care measure on the parents and the child, as well as of the possible alternatives to taking the child into public care, was carried out prior to implementation of a care measure (see *K and T v Finland* (2000) 31 EHRR 484, [2000] 2 FLR 79, at para 166 and *Kutzner v Germany* (unreported) 26 February 2002, at para 67). Furthermore, the taking of a new-born baby into public care at the moment of its birth is an extremely harsh measure. There must be extraordinarily compelling reasons before a baby can be physically removed from its mother, against her will, immediately after birth as a consequence of a procedure in which neither she nor her partner has been involved (*K and T* judgment cited above, at para 168).

[117] Following any removal into care, a stricter scrutiny is called for in respect of any further limitations by the authorities, for example on parental rights of access, as such further restrictions entail the danger that the family relations between the parents and a young child are effectively curtailed (the above-mentioned judgments, *Johansen*, at para 64, and *Kutzner,* at para 67). The taking into care of a child should normally be regarded as a temporary measure to be discontinued as soon as the circumstances permit, and any measures of implementation of temporary care should be consistent with the ultimate aim of reuniting the natural parent and child (*Olsson v Sweden* (1988) 10 EHRR 259, at para 81; *Johansen v Norway* (1996) 23 EHRR 33, at para 78 and *EP v Italy* (unreported) 16 September 1999, at para 69). In this regard a fair balance has to be struck between the interests of the child remaining in care and those of the parent in being reunited with the child (see *Olsson v Sweden (No 2)* (1992) 17 EHRR 134, at para 90 and *Hokkanen v Finland* (1995) 19 EHRR 139, [1996] 1 FLR 289, at para 55). In carrying out this balancing exercise, the court will attach particular importance to the best interests of the child which, depending on their nature and seriousness, may override those of the parent (*Johansen*, at para 78).

[118] As regards the extreme step of severing all parental links with a child, the court has taken the view that such a measure would cut a child from its roots and could only be justified in exceptional circumstances or by the overriding requirement of the child's best interests (*Johansen*, at para 84 and *Gnahoré v France* (2002) 34 EHRR 38, at para 59). That approach however may not apply in all contexts, depending on the nature of the parent–child relationship (see the *Soderback v Germany* judgment of 28 October 1998, *Reports of Judgments and Decisions* 1998–IV, at paras 31–34, where the severance of links between a child and father, who had never had care and custody of the child, was found to fall within the margin of the appreciation of the courts which had made the assessment of the child's best interests).

[119] The court further recalls that whilst Art 8 contains no explicit procedural requirements, the decision-making process involved in measures of interference must be fair and such as to afford due respect to the interests safeguarded by Art 8:

> '[W]hat has to be determined is whether, having regard to the particular circumstances of the case and notably the serious nature of the decisions to be taken, the parents have been involved in the decision-making process, seen as a whole, to a degree sufficient to provide them with the requisite protection of their interests. If they have not, there will have been a failure to respect their family life and the interference resulting from the decision will not be capable of being regarded as "necessary" within the meaning of Art 8.' (See *W v United Kingdom* (1988) 10 EHRR 29, at paras 62 and 64.)

[120] It is essential that a parent be placed in a position where he or she may obtain access to information which is relied on by the authorities in taking measures of protective care or in taking decisions relevant to the care and custody of a child. Otherwise the parent will be unable to participate effectively in the decision-making process or put forward in a fair or adequate manner those matters militating in favour of his or her ability to provide the child with proper care and protection (see *McMichael v United Kingdom* (1995) 20 EHRR 205, at para 92, where the authorities did not disclose to the applicant parents reports relating to their child, and *TP and KM v United Kingdom* [2001] 2 FLR 549, where the applicant mother was not afforded an early opportunity to view a video of an interview of her daughter, crucial to the assessment of abuse in the case; also *Buchberger v Austria* (unreported) 20 December 2001).

...

3. THE REMOVAL OF S AT BIRTH

...

[130] In the circumstances, the court considers that the decision to obtain the emergency protection order after S's birth may be regarded as having been necessary in a democratic society to safeguard the health and rights of the child. The local authority had to be able to take appropriate steps to ensure that no harm came to the baby and, at the very least, to take the legal power to prevent C or any other relative removing the baby with a view to foiling the local authority's actions, and thereby placing the baby at risk.

[131] It has nonetheless given consideration as to the manner of implementation of the order, namely, the steps taken under the authority of the order. As stated above (para [116]), the removal of a baby from its mother at birth requires exceptional justification. It is a step which is traumatic for the mother and places her own physical and mental health under a strain, and it deprives the new-born baby of close contact with its birth mother and, as pointed out by the applicants, of the advantages of breast-feeding. The removal also deprived the father, C, of being close to his daughter after the birth.

[132] The reasons put forward by the Government for removing the baby from the hospital, rather than leaving her with her mother or father under supervision, are that the hospital staff stated that they could not assure the child's safety and alleged tensions with the family. No details or documentary substantiation of this assertion are provided. P, who had undergone a caesarean section and was suffering the after-effects of blood loss and high blood pressure, was, at least in the first days after the birth, confined to bed. Once she had left the hospital, she was permitted to have supervised contact visits with S. It is not apparent to the court why it was not at all possible for S to remain in the hospital and to spend at least some time with her mother under supervision. Even on the assumption that P might be a risk to the baby, her capacity and opportunity for causing harm immediately after the birth must be regarded as limited, considerably more limited than once she was discharged. Furthermore, on the information available to the authorities at that stage, P's manifestation of the syndrome, sometimes known as MSBP, indicated a prevalence for exaggerating symptoms of ill-health in her children and that she had gone so far as to use laxatives to induce diarrhoea. Though the harm which such conduct poses to a child, particularly if continued over a long period of time cannot be underestimated, there was in the present case no suspicion of life-threatening conduct. This made the risk to be guarded against more manageable and it has not been shown that supervision could not have provided adequate protection against this risk, as was the case in the many contact visits over the months leading up to the care proceedings when both parents were allowed to feed the baby (see Dr Bentovim's report, para 54(vii)).

[133] The court concludes that the draconian step of removing S from her mother shortly after birth was not supported by relevant and sufficient reasons and that it cannot be regarded as having been necessary in a democratic society for the purpose of safeguarding S. There has therefore been, in that respect, a breach of the applicant parents' rights under Art 8 of the Convention.

4. THE CARE AND FREEING FOR ADOPTION PROCEEDINGS

[134] The court recalls that on 8 March 1999, after a hearing lasting about 20 days involving numerous witnesses, the judge issued a care order placing S in the care of the local authority, finding that her moral and physical health would be endangered by leaving her with her parents. On 15 March 1999, the judge freed S for adoption, thereby severing the links between the parents and S, who was adopted on 27 March 2000. No

provision for future direct contact was made, reference only being made to indirect contact at the discretion of the future adoptive parents, who as events turned out reduced contact to one letterbox contact per year. It is also not in dispute that these measures interfered with the applicants' rights under the first paragraph of Art 8 of the Convention and that they were in accordance with the law and pursued the legitimate aim of protecting S. Issues arise however as to whether they were justified as necessary within the meaning of the second paragraph (see paras [114]–[119] above).

[135] The applicants have made numerous criticisms about the procedures, which emphasise their conviction that the local authority made no effort to explore the rehabilitation of S with themselves, but rather were determined to place S for adoption from the beginning, and that insufficient consideration was given to providing for some form of continued contact with S after the care order, whether by placing her in long-term foster care or by arranging an open adoption. The Government have relied inter alia on the findings of the trial judge as to the absence of any possibility of rehabilitation with S due to the parents' lack of acceptance of any risk (the precondition for any hope of progress). They contended that adoption, which would give S a secure place in a family, was in S's best interests and that an open adoption was not possible where the birth parents opposed the adoption (as their opposition would inevitably undermine the security of the child's placement).

[136] The court does not propose to attempt to untangle these opposed considerations, which raise difficult and sensitive issues concerning S's welfare. It considers rather that the complexity of the case, and the fine balance which had to be struck between the interests of S and her parents, required that particular importance be attached to the procedural obligations inherent in Art 8 of the Convention. It was crucial for the parents in this case to be able to put forward their case as favourably as possible, emphasising for example whatever factors militated in favour of a further assessment of a possible rehabilitation, and for their viewpoints on the possible alternatives to adoption and the continuation of contact even after adoption to be put forward at the appropriate time for consideration by the court.

[137] The lack of legal representation of P during the care proceedings and of P and C during the freeing for adoption proceedings, together with the lack of any real lapse of time between the two procedures, has been found above to have deprived the applicants of a fair and effective hearing in court. Having regard to the seriousness of what was at stake, the court finds that it also prevented them from being involved in the decision-making process, seen as a whole, to a degree sufficient to provide them with the requisite protection of their interests under Art 8 of the Convention. Emotionally involved in the case as they were, the applicant parents were placed at a serious disadvantage by these elements, and it

cannot be excluded that this might have had an effect on the decisions reached and eventual outcome for the family as a whole.

[138]   In the circumstances of this case, the court concludes that there has been in this regard a breach of P, C and S's rights under Art 8 of the Convention.

General notes:

See also the subdivision on newborn babies at D10–D13.

This case is also included in relation to:

G2   Legal assistance

D3   ART 8: PUBLIC LAW SUMMARY

R v Finland

(Application number 34141/96) [2006] 2 FLR 923 and 942

European Court of Human Rights

B.   The court's assessment

...

[89] The court reiterates the guiding principle whereby a care order should be regarded as a temporary measure, to be discontinued as soon as circumstances permit, and that any measures implementing temporary care should be consistent with the ultimate aim of reuniting the natural parent and the child (see, in particular, *Olsson v Sweden (No 1)* (1989) 11 EHRR 259, para 81). The positive duty to take measures to facilitate family reunification as soon as reasonably feasible will begin to weigh on the competent authorities with progressively increasing force as from the commencement of the period of care, subject always to its being balanced against the duty to consider the best interests of the child (see *K and T v Finland* (above), para [178]). After a considerable period of time has passed since the child was originally taken into public care, the interest of a child not to have his or her de facto family situation changed again may override the interests of the parents to have their family reunited (see *KA v Finland* [2003] ECHR 27, [2003] 1 FLR 696, para [138]).

[90] Whereas the authorities enjoy a wide margin of appreciation in assessing the necessity of taking a child into public care, a stricter scrutiny is called for in respect of any further limitations, such as restrictions placed by those authorities on parental rights of access. Such further limitations entail the danger that the family relations between the parents and a young child are effectively curtailed. The minimum to be expected of the authorities is to examine the situation anew from time to time to see whether there has been any improvement in the family's situation. The possibilities of reunification will be progressively diminished and eventually destroyed if the biological parent and the child are not allowed to meet each other at all, or only so rarely that no natural bonding between them is likely to occur (see *K and T v Finland*, cited above, paras [155] and [179]).

Other significant cases on this issue:

- *Dolhamre v Sweden* (Application No 67/04) [2010] 2 FLR 912

Parts IV and V: general

D4 INTERVENTION MUST BE PROPORTIONATE

X Council v B (Emergency protection orders)

[2004] EWHC 2014 (Fam), [2005] 1 FLR 341 at 357

Family Division

Munby J

[42] I turn, therefore, to the European Convention. Pointing to the long line of Strasbourg jurisprudence on the topic, the Court of Appeal has repeatedly emphasised that any intervention under Part IV or Part V of the Children Act 1989 must be proportionate to the legitimate aim of protecting the welfare and interests of the child. As Hale LJ (as she then was) said in *Re O (Supervision Order)* [2001] EWCA Civ 16, [2001] 1 FLR 923, at [28], 'proportionality ... is the key'. The interference with family life which the exercise of such powers necessarily entails can only be justified by what she referred to in *Re C and B (Care Order: Future Harm)* [2001] 1 FLR 611, at [34], as 'the overriding necessity of the interests of the child'. More recently, in *Re B (Care: Interference with Family Life)* [2003] EWCA Civ 786, [2003] 2 FLR 813, Thorpe LJ at [34] said that:

> 'where the application is for a care order empowering the local authority to remove a child or children from the family, the judge in modern times may not make such an order without considering the European Convention for the Protection of Human Rights and Fundamental Freedoms 1950 Art 8 rights of the adult members of the family and of the children of the family. Accordingly he must not sanction such an interference with family life unless he is satisfied that that is both necessary and proportionate and that no other less radical form of order would achieve the essential end of promoting the welfare of the children.'

General notes:

Munby J continued by reviewing the ECtHR case law beginning with the summary in *Haase v Germany* [2004] 2 FLR 39, at [90]–[95].

This case is also included in relation to:

D71 EPO: general considerations (1)

D73 Contact to a child removed under an EPO

D5 REUNIFICATION NOT AN OVERRIDING FACTOR

Re R (Care: disclosure: nature of proceedings)

[2002] 1 FLR 755 at 769

Family Division

Charles J

Additional points at the welfare or disposal stage

Additionally, in my approach at the welfare or disposal stage I have had regard to decisions of the European Court of Human Rights (eg *Söderbäck v Sweden* [1999] 1 FLR 250, in particular at para 30 of the judgment; *Hokkanen v Finland* [1996] 1 FLR 289, in particular at para 58 of the judgment; and *Kroon and Others v The Netherlands* (1995) 19 EHRR 2663 and in particular paras 31 and 32 of the judgment) and English decisions which have had regard to the European Convention for the Protection of Human Rights and Fundamental Freedoms 1950 (the Convention), in particular Art 8, eg *Re F (Care: Termination of Contact)* [2000] 2 FCR 481, in particular 488G–491H, where Wall J helpfully summarises existing English authority and at 495D–498D, where he deals with arguments relating to Art 8; *Re W and B; Re W (Care Plan)* [2001] EWCA Civ 757, [2001] 2 FLR 582, paras [52]–[58], where Hale J gives an overview of Art 8 and demonstrates the overlap between its purposes and those that underlie the Children Act 1989 and makes the point that sometimes not to interfere where interference is called for may also violate a child's Convention rights and the positive obligation to secure a new family for a child who has been deprived of life with his family of birth; and *Re C and B (Care Order: Future Harm)* [2001] 1 FLR 611 and in particular paras [33] and [34], where Hale J says this:

> '[33] I would have reached that conclusion without reference to the European Convention for the Protection of Human Rights and Fundamental Freedoms 1950, but I do note that under Art 8 of the Convention both the children and the parents have the right to respect for their family and private life. If the state is to interfere with that there are three requirements: first, that it be in accordance with the law; secondly, that it be for a legitimate aim (in this case the protection of the welfare and interests of the children); and thirdly, that it be "necessary in a democratic society".

[34] There is a long line of European Court of Human Rights jurisprudence on that third requirement, which emphasises that the intervention has to be proportionate to the legitimate aim. Intervention in the family may be appropriate, but the aim should be to reunite the family when the circumstances enable that, and the effort should be devoted towards that end. Cutting off all contact and the relationship between the child or children and their family is only justified by the overriding necessity of the interests of the child.'

I therefore have recognised and taken into account:

(a)   the aim identified by Hale J in that passage; and
(b)   the advantages and benefits which flow from a child being brought up by a member of his or her birth family and having contact with other members of that family and thus his or her siblings and the non-custodial parent.

However, in my view, it is wrong to interpret and apply statements in the above cases before the European Court of Human Rights, or similar statements in the English cases, concerning the underlying aims of the Children Act 1989 (and thus, for example, statements) to the effect that the taking of a child into care should normally be regarded as a temporary measure to be discontinued as soon as circumstances permit and that any measures of implementation of temporary care should be consistent with the ultimate aim of re-uniting the natural parent and child – see, for example, para 30 of the judgment in *Söderbäck v Sweden* [1999] 1 FLR 250 – as giving a right, or as an over-riding factor, for consideration.

In my judgment, such an approach would fail to take account of:

(1)   the qualifications contained in such statements by the use of words such as 'normally' or 'generally';
(2)   references in those statements to 'temporary care' when sometimes this will not be in the best interests of the child concerned;
(3)   the references to the need for the court to strike a fair balance having regard to the rights and freedoms of all concerned and, more particularly, the best interests of the child;
(4)   the references therein to the point that Art 8 requires respect for family life and does not create a right in parent or child, and to its principal purpose of Art 8, at least where children are concerned, being the protection and welfare of the child;
(5)   the provisions of para 2(2) of Art 8 of the Convention; and
(6)   the point that in deciding what order should be made and care given, the medium- to long-term welfare needs of the child are to be considered and the fact that under s 1 of the Children Act 1989 the court's paramount consideration is the welfare of the child.

In my judgment, it is axiomatic that having carried out the appropriate consideration of the competing interests, rights and freedoms from the starting point that the aim or purpose is to keep birth families together and to promote contact with non-custodial parents and siblings while living elsewhere, the medium- to long-term welfare of a child may be best served by that child not living with and being brought up by one or more of his or her natural parents and, further, in some cases by that child not having contact with his birth family or some members of it.

However, before any decision to the effect that a child should not be brought up by one or more of his or her natural parents, or to the effect that a child should not have contact with members of his or her birth family is reached, the practicalities, advantages and risks attendant upon that child living with and being brought up by a natural parent and contact should be considered, as should the relevant competing rights, freedoms and interests of the persons concerned, having regard to (i) the underlying aims of s 8 of the Children Act 1989, and (ii) the point that the more serious the interference with the family life of the birth family the more compelling must be the justification.

This case is also included in relation to:

G22 Preparation and disclosure: duties of LA
G23 Preparation and disclosure: mirror duties of respondents
G24 Disclosure of relevant notes
G41 Court / parties / experts bound by findings made / not made
G45 Use of experts: general guidance
G51 Responsibilities on receipt of report
G75 Statement of general principles (2)
G82 Public interest immunity
H29 Costs: illustration in public law

D6 REMOVAL OF CHILD PLACED WITH PARENTS UNDER CO

G v N County Council

[2009] 1 FLR 774 at 779, 781, 782, 782, 783 and 787

Family Division

McFarlane J

[19]   The law in relation to decisions of this sort and the approach of the court fortunately has been examined by other courts on earlier occasions. The Court of Appeal in the case of *Re W (Children) (Care: Interference With Family Life)* [2005] EWCA Civ 642, sub nom *Re W (Removal Into Care)* [2005] 2 FLR 1022 considered a case involving 5-year-old twins who were the subject of a care order, and the decision had been made to remove the twins from the parents' care. Thorpe and Ward LJJ considered the legality of the various processes that were open to a parent to challenge such a decision. It was concluded that issuing an application to discharge the care order was not the appropriate mode of challenge. Thorpe LJ, in particular, said this at para [17]:

> 'Clearly any step that the local authority took, particularly a step as Draconian as the removal of the children, had to have due regard to the parents' European Convention rights and the convention rights of the children. At first sight, it was manifestly a breach of those rights and accordingly was only lawful if it could be justified on both the heads of legality and proportionality.'

Later, in the course of para [25], he said this:

> 'If there is a lesson to be learned from this litigation history, it is that parents in similar circumstances must issue the Human Rights Act challenge at the earliest possible opportunity. It should be issued prior to the removal of the children and not as a reaction to removal. The obligation on the local authority to involve and consult with the parents and the obligation on the local authority to give due notice to the parents of an intention to remove gives the parents just that opportunity. If it is not taken in advance of removal as a protective measure, it is simply that much harder to mount and succeed, given that the children will have suffered the experience of removal and will have been placed into some neutral environment.'

[20] Thus, on the basis of that authority, it seems that the mother's legal advisers were entirely right to issue a Human Rights Act challenge to the removal decision. The words that I have just read underline the importance of the local authority giving notice to the mother of the plan to remove the children before that plan is put into action so that the mother can come to this court, should she wish, to seek to challenge a decision. The fact that that did not happen in this case goes to underline the degree of failure of the local authority, if failure there has been, and the importance of giving notice unless there is a true emergency that requires the children to be removed from a parent's care.

[21] The next decision that is of relevance is, in fact, an earlier case, a decision of Munby J in *Re G (Care: Challenge to Local Authority's Decision)* [2003] EWHC 551 (Fam), [2003] 2 FLR 42. Again, that was a case following the making of a full care order where the local authority sought to remove children from a parent's care. In that judgment at para [45] Munby J spells out in plain terms what a local authority should do if it is considering taking such a step:

'In a case such as this the local authority, before it can properly arrive at a decision to remove children from their parents, must tell the parents (preferably in writing) precisely what it is proposing to do. It must spell out (again in writing) the reasons why it is proposing to do so. It must spell out precisely (in writing) the factual matters it is relying on. It must give the parents a proper opportunity to answer (either orally and/or in writing as the parents wish) the allegations being made against them and it must give the parents a proper opportunity (orally and/or in writing as they wish) to make representations as to why the local authority should not take the threatened steps. In short, the local authority must involve the parents properly in the decision-making process. In particular, the parents (together with their representatives if they wish to be assisted) should normally be given the opportunity to attend at and address any critical meeting at which crucial decisions are to be made.'

...

[26] In short, the actions of the local authority, notwithstanding the existence of a care order in a case such as this, must be in accordance with the law, must be proportionate to the level of concern and the issues in the case, must be procedurally fair, and must involve the parent in the decision-making process. Plainly, because the local authority had a care order, it was not necessary for it to seek the authority of a court by obtaining an emergency protection order to justify legally the removal of the child. However, the case-law in relation to emergency protection orders is, in my view, not wholly irrelevant to the process that should be adopted in these cases.

[27] In particular, again it is a decision of Munby J, in the case (which is well known in the context of emergency protection orders) of *X Council v B (Emergency Protection Orders)* [2004] EWHC 2015 (Fam), [2005] 1 FLR 341, there is a list of matters considered to be important in relation to the removal of a child in an emergency protection context. I propose to quote only four of the short subparagraphs in para [57] of the judgment:[1]

...

[28] Obviously those words, if they do apply at all, do not apply word for word in relation to a decision taken under a care order to remove a child, but the spirit and legal force of the principles behind them certainly should do. The local authority, through counsel, sought to distinguish the emergency protection order provisions from the current situation.

...

[29] Of those various submissions, in my view, the only one that has some weight and relevance in this context is the fact that the starting point is that there is a care order, and a court has already accepted that there is a demonstrated high level of concern about a child justifying intervention at care order level. But that is not the issue in the case, in my view. The issue is the approach a local authority should take to changing the care plan under the care order and, whilst the established level of concern and background established by the care order is there, the previously proportionate plan of having a child at home, if it is to be changed, has to be changed after a proper consideration and assessment of all of the available evidence and in a way that meets the child and the mother's human rights as described in the earlier decisions.

[30] In my view, the quality of decision-making and the consequences of it in the context of a case such as this are just as important and have consequences which are just as likely to be long term as is the case under an EPO. In fact, given the existence of the EPO procedure and, in contrast, the limited options available to a parent in a case such as this, the human rights considerations require that the quality of the process should be at least as high, if not higher, than in an EPO case. It is not the function of this court to lay down strictures as to the sort of assessment work that should be put in place before a radical change of care plan such as this, but it does seem that some form of formal assessment, whether it is called a core assessment or otherwise which draws together all of the evidence in a considered way rather than simply at LAC meetings or other professional gatherings, and gives the parent a chance to contribute to that process, and then takes stock of all of that material in the way that a core assessment would do, is the level of intervention and planning that should be brought to bear before a change of care plan as Draconian as this takes place.

---

[1] The paragraphs cited by McFarlane J were 1, 2, 3 and 7.

....

[34] The failures, as this court would see them, of the local authority process are as follows, and not necessarily in any great order of priority.

(1) It was not spelled out to the mother that the local authority had the power to remove A from her care without the need to return to court.

(2) In fact on at least one, and probably two, occasions, the local authority is recorded as expressly telling the mother that it would be returning to court in relation to A, and advice, as I have indicated, was erroneously given.

(3) The mother was told that the local authority would explain its concerns and its proposed plan in detail on 25 March. That, as I have said, was the right way forward, but the local authority changed its plan and failed to afford that important meeting time to take place.

(4) This was not an emergency situation requiring the clandestine urgent removal of the child from his school. The concerns of the local authority, taken either individually or together, are matters that would worry any professional involved in childcare work. But they were not crisis or emergency factors; they were slow-burning developing concerns which were raised over the course of time. There was nothing so pressing on that afternoon that required his emergency protection from significant harm in a way that meant that the mother could not be given notice of the process and be drawn into the decision-making itself.

(5) There was no 'letter before action' of the type that is now required under the public law outline.

(6) The decision to remove A was made without any involvement of the mother in the decision-making process.

(7) The decision to make a peremptory removal on the day was taken without recourse to those who had been party to the more measured decision to remove the boys together following discussion with the mother. It seems to have been made by the social work team leader and the social worker following discussion with the independent reviewing officer over the telephone.

(8) The situation at the family home had changed following the departure of the claimant's husband. The new social worker took over the case in the autumn of 2007, and it is accepted by the local authority that the level of monitoring of the family over the preceding years under the care order had not been at a good enough or appropriate level. However, there was no formal assessment process undertaken concerning the new family set-up with the mother and her new partner after the father had left, or any attempt to conduct a thorough assessment in the light of lack of knowledge that the local authority had of the mother's functioning over the intervening years.

(9)   In the documents there is no recorded attempt to consider any positives that there may be in the home situation, such as the level of attachment that there may or may not be between the mother and A and A and B, and no attempt to balance the negative implications of any removal, namely the shock to the child of being removed from the school and being placed in a stranger setting in a foster home.

(10) The local authority purported to have made the final decision in relation to the mother's potential to care for A prior to removing him. This decision was made without, as I have said, any discussion with the mother on the topic or any warning to her that that was the likely plan. All she was told was that they may remove him from her care. The word 'permanently' or any similar word was never used.

[35]   It follows that the local authority's concessions are well made, and this court finds that the local authority's actions on 20 March and in the short time leading up to it were unlawful, in the sense that they breached the mother's and the child's substantive and procedural rights under Art 8 of the European Convention for the Protection of Human Rights and Fundamental Freedoms 1950. The local authority's actions were legitimate in the sense that it sought to meet the legitimate aim of protecting the child, and the observation of the local authority that it took the course it did in order to protect A from harm is one that I accept and understand. There was no malevolent or sinister motive here. But that being said, the action taken was neither proportionate nor procedurally fair and failed to involve the mother in the process at all.

[36]   So the mother is entitled to a declaration in appropriately worded terms as to the unlawful nature of that action. The court then has to turn to the interim issue of A's placement in the meantime. It was accepted in submissions and it is plain from the reported decisions, including those to which I have already referred, that the court has jurisdiction under s 8 of the Human Rights Act to grant an injunction requiring A to be returned to the mother's care.

...

[47]   Having canvassed the issue with counsel, I am of one mind with them, to the extent that A's welfare is not my paramount consideration in determining whether or not an interim injunction should be granted. A's circumstances and his welfare are undoubtedly an important part of the considerations that the court has, but they are not the only consideration or the overriding or paramount consideration. A question which it seems to me is helpful to ask is to consider what the situation would be if the local authority had acted properly and had given the mother due notice of what it was proposing and she had applied to the court under the Human Rights Act to prevent the removal taking place before the local authority took action. What would the result have been on the basis of the

information that the local authority put forward to this court which mother's counsel accepts is the basis upon which the matter has to be determined at this stage?

General notes:

McFarlane J concluded that an interim injunction requiring the return of the child to his mother's care should not be made. However the local authority's course in moving headlong toward alternative planning had been halted and there was to be an assessment by an independent social worker.

Other significant cases on this issue:

- Cf *Re S (Authorising children's immediate removal)* [2010] EWCA Civ 421, [2010] 2 FLR 873

D7 RELATIONSHIP BETWEEN COURT AND LA

Re S and W (Care proceedings)

[2007] EWCA Civ 232, [2007] 2 FLR 275 at 282, 284 and 285

Court of Appeal

Wall LJ

Some basic propositions

[25] Before turning to examine the local authority's decision-making processes in these proceedings, we regret to say that we think it necessary to set out what we had previously thought to be some elementary principles of family law and practice as they affect the relationship between a judge hearing proceedings under Part IV of the 1989 Act, and the local authority which brings them.

[26] We fully endorse the statement of the law set out in para [2] of Wall LJ's reasons for listing the applications for oral hearing. The division of responsibility between the local authority and the court in care proceedings is, we think, well known, although we acknowledge that it is sometimes difficult to implement it in practice. It plainly needs, however, to be restated.

[27] Parliament has placed the responsibility for making care orders on the court, not on the local authority which brings the proceedings. Before a care order can be made, the local authority has to satisfy the court that the threshold criteria under s 31 of the 1989 Act are satisfied, and the court also has to be satisfied that a care order is in the best interests of the child concerned. To the latter end, the court is under a duty rigorously to scrutinise the care plan advanced by the local authority, and if the court does not think that it meets the needs of the child concerned, the court can refuse to make a care order. So much is elementary.

[28] The significance of local authority care plans was, we think, both recognised and reinforced by Parliament in the enactment of s 31A of the 1989 Act through the medium of s 121(2) of the 2002 Act. There is now a mandatory duty on local authorities to prepare a care plan for each child who is the subject of care proceedings, to keep that care plan under review and if some change is required, to revise the care plan or to make a new plan accordingly – see s 31A(1) and (2) of the 1989 Act. This case, it seems to us, is about both the merits of the local authority's late changes of plan on the facts, and the methodology of its decision-making processes.

[29] What, however, is equally elementary is that once the court has made a final care order, responsibility for its implementation passes to the local authority, and save for the powers identified by the House of Lords in the case of *Re S (Minors) (Care Order: Implementation of Care Plan); Re W (Minors) (Care Order: Adequacy of Care Plan)* [2002] UKHL 10, [2002] 2 AC 291, [2002] 1 FLR 815 (hereinafter *Re S; Re W*), neither the court nor the children's guardian has any further role in the children's lives.

[30] What appears not to be understood, however, and thus needs to be clearly repeated, is that not only does the court have the duty rigorously to scrutinise the care plan and to refuse to make a care order if it does not think the plan in the child's best interests; the court also has the right to invite the local authority to reconsider the care plan if the court comes to the conclusion that the plan – or any change in the plan – involves a course of action which the court believes is contrary to the interests of the child, and which would be likely to lead the court to refuse to make a care order if the local authority were to adhere to the care plan it has proposed.

[31] In the instant case, the local authority's second ground of appeal begins with the following sentence:

> 'It is submitted that the judge when faced with a cohate (sic) care plan *cannot* [emphasis supplied] adjourn the matter in order that the Director of Social Services shall reconsider the plan.'

[32] In our judgment, that submission is simply and plainly wrong. We express surprise that it was advanced. To be fair to counsel instructed on behalf of the local authority, she acknowledged in oral argument that the judge did have the power to invite the local authority to reconsider the care plan: her complaint was that he should not have exercised it on the facts of this case, or exercised it differently. That, of course, is a quite separate argument.

[33] However, the grounds of appeal advanced by the local authority contain a second, equally fallacious submission. This was:

> 'It is submitted that in asking the appellant authority to reconsider its position the judge did not adopt the "lesser of two evils" test. It is submitted that the options available to the judge in this case were the making of no order or approving the care plan.'

[34] Once again, in oral argument, counsel agreed that the second sentence of this ground of appeal should be struck through as erroneous. However, in our judgment, the first sentence is also plainly wrong. The 'lesser of two evils' test arises from the well-known judgment of Balcombe LJ given in this court in *Re S and D (Children: Powers of Court)* [1995] 2 FLR 456, at 634G–635C, citations from which we set out below. In the instant case, however, the local authority's reliance on *Re S and D* is manifestly misconceived for the simple reason that the judge had not reached the point identified by Balcombe LJ. Had the local authority (as it should have done) accepted his invitation to reconsider after reading his judgment and then restored the case to the judge's list, it might well *then* have been the case that the judge was faced with either making the care order sought by the local authority with its unacceptable care plan or making no order. But the judge had not reached that point, and was – in our view wholly properly – striving to avoid it.

[35] It is, we think, worthwhile pausing for a moment to reflect on why a court is entitled to exercise a discretionary jurisdiction to adjourn in order to invite a local authority to reconsider. The answer, we think, is, like much of what we have already said, self-evident. Care proceedings are only quasi-adversarial. There is a powerful inquisitorial element. But above all, they are proceedings in which the court and the local authority should both be striving to achieve an order which is in the best interests of the child. There needs to be mutual respect and understanding for the different role and perspective which each has in the process. We repeat: the shared objective should be to achieve a result which is in the best interests of the child.

...

[38] ... In the overwhelming majority of cases in which there is a disagreement between the local authority and the court over a child's care plan, that disagreement is resolved by careful reconsideration on both sides. In our experience, as a consequence, such disagreements are extremely rare. That is as it should be. It is patently not in the interests of the already disadvantaged children involved in care proceedings for there to be a stand-off between the court and the local authority, the result of which, as here, is still further delay in resolving the children's future placements.

...

[44] Equally misplaced, in our judgment, is the local authority's reliance on the decision of Wall J at first instance in *Re J (Minors) (Care: Care Plan)* [1994] 1 FLR 253. This was, self-evidently, another case in which the relationship between the court and the local authority was seen as one of mutual respect for the respective roles of each in the proceedings.

[45] In that case, the court made care orders even though the local authority's plans were inchoate. In the course of his judgment, Wall J said ([1994] 1 FLR 253, at 265B):

'... there are cases (of which this is one) in which the action which requires to be taken in the interests of children necessarily involves steps into the unknown provided the court is satisfied that the local authority is alert to the difficulties which may arise in the execution of the care plan, the function of the court is not to seek to oversee the plan but to entrust its execution to the local authority.'

[46] That statement, even though it was approved in the speech of Lord Nicholls of Birkenhead in *Re S; Re W*, has no application to the actions of the judge in the present case. Nor does the further statement on which the local authority sought to rely (at [1994] 1 FLR 253, at 262B), namely:

'Since in each case the evidence which requires to be called to satisfy the court as to the efficacy of the care plan will vary in substance and in degree, it is a matter for the good sense of the tribunal and the advocates appearing before it to see that a proper balance is struck between the need to satisfy the court about the appropriateness of the care plan on the one hand and the avoidance, on the other, of overzealous investigation into matters which are properly within the administrative discretion of the local authority.'

[47] In our judgment, nothing done by the judge in the instant case comes anywhere near the 'overzealous investigation' referred to: nor were the matters about which the judge was concerned 'properly within the administrative discretion of the local authority'. They went to the heart of the case, and the critical decision about CO's welfare which it was the function of the judge to make.

[48] The judge is also criticised for making an interim care order in relation to CO pending the return of the case to his list after reconsideration of the care plan by the local authority. This is a criticism we simply do not understand. What other order was the judge to make? If he had made a care order he would have abnegated his responsibility for CO's welfare and the local authority would have placed him with Mr and Mrs W. If he had made no order, the outcome would have been in the manifestly inappropriate hands of CO's parents. A further interim order was the only order the judge could make in these circumstances.

General notes:

The judgment continues with an analysis of how, having created the difficulty in the case by its late change of position before the trial judge, the local authority demonstrated its failure to understand its relationship with the court first by its failure properly to respond to the trial judge's order and secondly by its failure properly to respond to the reasons the Court of Appeal gave for granting leave to appeal.

This case is also included in relation to:

D8   Relationship between LA and CG
G11   Separate JR / HR proceedings generally to be avoided

D8   RELATIONSHIP BETWEEN LA AND CG

Re S and W (Care proceedings)

[2007] EWCA Civ 232, [2007] 2 FLR 275 at 298

Court of Appeal

Wall LJ

[97] We would also wish to associate ourselves with the views of Munby J in para [104] of the same case,[1] when he criticises the local authority for taking an important decision in pending care proceedings without any warning to the guardian and without involving her in any way. We have already expressed our agreement with a similar sentiment expressed by the judge in the instant case. Plainly, issues as to the independence of the guardian will arise if the local authority seeks to involve the guardian in pending care proceedings in its decision-making process for the child or children in question. That, however, is an entirely separate issue from the need to keep the guardian in the picture, to seek the guardian's views on a proposed course or action and to inform the guardian about what is happening or what is proposed, all of which are tasks which, as a matter of good practice, the local authority should perform as a matter or routine.

[98] In the instant case, the local authority's misunderstanding of the guardian's role is disturbing. One of the clearest manifestations of this misunderstanding is the local authority's failure to respond to an entirely proper letter written on the guardian's behalf seeking to know the outcome of the local authority's reconsideration of its position following the judgment, and asking to see a minute of the meeting in question. This local authority needs, we think, to be reminded that the guardian is appointed by the court as the children's representative, and that one of the guardian's functions is fearlessly to protect the children concerned against local authority incompetence and maladministration, as well as poor social work practice. These are duties which a local authority should respect and facilitate.

This case is also included in relation to:

D7   Relationship between court and LA
G11 Separate JR / HR proceedings generally to be avoided

---

[1]   *Re X; Barnet London Borough Council v Y and X* [2006] 2 FLR 998.

D9 NO COURT INTERVENTION ONCE FINAL CO MADE

Re S (Minors) (Care order: implementation of care plan); Re W (Minors) (Care order: adequacy of care plan)

[2002] UKHL 10, [2002] 1 FLR 815 at 822, 827, 828 and 832

House of Lords

Lord Nicholls

[23] Two preliminary points can be made at the outset. First, a cardinal principle of the Children Act 1989 is that when the court makes a care order it becomes the duty of the local authority designated by the order to receive the child into its care while the order remains in force. So long as the care order is in force the authority has parental responsibility for the child. The authority also has power to decide the extent to which a parent of the child may meet his responsibility for him: s 33. An authority might, for instance, not permit parents to change the school of a child living at home. While a care order is in force the court's powers, under its inherent jurisdiction, are expressly excluded: s 100(2)(c) and (d). Further, the court may not make a contact order, a prohibited steps order or a specific issue order: s 9(1).

[24] There are limited exceptions to this principle of non-intervention by the court in the authority's discharge of its parental responsibility for a child in its care under a care order. The court retains jurisdiction to decide disputes about contact with children in care: s 34 of the Children Act 1989. The court may discharge a care order, either on an application made for the purpose under s 39 or as a consequence of making a residence order (ss 9(1) and 91(1)). The High Court's judicial review jurisdiction also remains available.

[25] These exceptions do not detract significantly from the basic principle. The Children Act 1989 delineated the boundary of responsibility with complete clarity. Where a care order is made the responsibility for the child's care is with the authority rather than the court. The court retains no supervisory role, monitoring the authority's discharge of its responsibilities. That was the intention of Parliament.

[26] Consistently with this, in *Kent County Council v C* [1993] Fam 57, [1993] 1 FLR 308 Ewbank J decided that the court has no power to add to a care order a direction to the authority that the child's guardian ad litem should be allowed to have a continuing involvement, with a view to his applying to the court in due course if thought appropriate. In *Re T (A Minor) (Care Order: Conditions)* [1994] 2 FLR 423 the Court of Appeal rightly approved this decision and held that the court has no power to impose conditions in a care order. There the condition sought by the child's guardian was that the child should reside at home.

[27] This cardinal principle of the Children Act 1989 represented a change in the law. Before the Children Act 1989 came into operation the court, in exercise of its wardship jurisdiction, retained power in limited circumstances to give directions to a local authority regarding children in its care. The limits of this jurisdiction were considered by your Lordships' House in *A v Liverpool City Council* [1982] AC 363, (1981) 2 FLR 222 and *Re W (A Minor) (Wardship: Jurisdiction)* [1985] AC 791, sub nom *Re W (A Minor) (Care Proceedings: Wardship)* [1985] FLR 879. The change brought about by the Children Act 1989 gave effect to a policy decision on the appropriate division of responsibilities between the courts and local authorities. This was one of the matters widely discussed at the time. A report made to ministers by an inter-departmental working party *Review of Child Care Law* (September 1985) drew attention to some of the policy considerations. The particular strength of the courts lies in the resolution of disputes: its ability to hear all sides of a case, to decide issues of fact and law, and to make a firm decision on a particular issue at a particular time. But a court cannot have day-to-day responsibility for a child. The court cannot deliver the services which may best serve a child's needs. Unlike a local authority, a court does not have close, personal and continuing knowledge of the child. The court cannot respond with immediacy and informality to practical problems and changed circumstances as they arise. Supervision by the court would encourage 'drift' in decision making, a perennial problem in children cases. Nor does a court have the task of managing the financial and human resources available to a local authority for dealing with all children in need in its area. The authority must manage these resources in the best interests of all the children for whom it is responsible.

[28] The Children Act 1989, embodying what I have described as a cardinal principle, represents the assessment made by Parliament of the division of responsibility which would best promote the interests of children within the overall care system. The court operates as the gateway into care, and makes the necessary care order when the threshold conditions are satisfied and the court considers a care order would be in the best interests of the child. That is the responsibility of the court. Thereafter the court has no continuing role in relation to the care order. Then it is the responsibility of the local authority to decide how the child should be cared for.

...

[42] I return to the Children Act 1989. I have already noted, as a cardinal principle of the Act, that the courts are not empowered to intervene in the way local authorities discharge their parental responsibilities under final care orders. Parliament entrusted to local authorities, not the courts, the responsibility for looking after children who are the subject of care orders. To my mind the new starring system would depart substantially from this principle. Under the new system the court, when making a care order, is empowered to impose an obligation on an authority concerning the future care of the child. In future, the authority must submit a progress report, in circumstances identified by the court, either to the court or to the Children and Family Court Advisory and Support Service (CAFCASS). This is only the first step. The next step is that the court, when seised of what has happened after the care order was made, may then call for action. If it considers this necessary in the best interests of the child, the court may intervene and correct matters which are going wrong. In short, under the starring system the court will exercise a newly created supervisory function.

[43] In his judgment Thorpe LJ noted that the starring system 'seems to breach the fundamental boundary between the functions and responsibilities of the court and the local authority': see *Re W and B; Re W (Care Plan)* [2001] EWCA Civ 757, [2001] 2 FLR 582, para [31]. I agree. I consider this judicial innovation passes well beyond the boundary of interpretation. I can see no provision in the Children Act 1989 which lends itself to the interpretation that Parliament was thereby conferring this supervisory function on the court. No such provision was identified by the Court of Appeal. On the contrary, the starring system is inconsistent in an important respect with the scheme of the Children Act 1989. It would constitute amendment of the Children Act 1989, not its interpretation. It would have far-reaching practical ramifications for local authorities and their care of children. The starring system would not come free from additional administrative work and expense. It would be likely to have a material effect on authorities' allocation of scarce financial and other resources. This in turn would affect authorities' discharge of their responsibilities to other children. Moreover, the need to produce a formal report whenever a care plan is significantly departed from, and then await the outcome of any subsequent court proceedings, would affect the whole manner in which authorities discharge, and are able to discharge, their parental responsibilities.

[44] These are matters for decision by Parliament, not the courts ...

...

Sections 7 and 8 of the Human Rights Act

[45] Sections 7 and 8 of the Human Rights Act 1998 have conferred extended powers on the courts. Section 6 makes it unlawful for a public authority to act in a way which is incompatible with a Convention right. Section 7 enables victims of conduct made unlawful by s 6 to bring court proceedings against the public authority in question. Section 8 spells out, in wide terms, the relief a court may grant in those proceedings. The court may grant such relief or remedy, or make such order, within its powers as it considers just and appropriate. Thus, if a local authority conducts itself in a manner which infringes the Art 8 rights of a parent or child, the court may grant appropriate relief on the application of a victim of the unlawful act.

[46] This new statutory power has already been exercised. In *Re M (Care: Challenging Decisions by Local Authority)* [2001] 2 FLR 1300 a local authority reviewed its care plan for a child in its care. The authority finally ruled out any further prospect of the child returning to live with her mother or of ever going to live with her father. In proceedings brought by the parents Holman J set aside the decision. The decision-making process was unfair by not involving the parents to a degree sufficient to provide their interests with the requisite protection. In so ordering Holman J was proceeding squarely within the extended jurisdiction conferred by ss 7 and 8. The court applied the provisions of the Human Rights Act 1998 in the manner Parliament intended, there in respect of a breach of Art 8 of the Convention.

...

[62] Thus, if a local authority fails to discharge its parental responsibilities properly, and in consequence the rights of the parents under Art 8 are violated, the parents may, as a longstop, bring proceedings against the authority under s 7. I have already drawn attention to a case where this has happened. I say 'as a longstop', because other remedies, both of an administrative nature and by way of court proceedings, may also be available in the particular case. For instance, Bedfordshire Council has an independent visitor, a children's complaints officer and a children's rights officer. Sometimes court proceedings by way of judicial review of a decision of a local authority may be the appropriate way to proceed. In a suitable case an application for discharge of the care order is available. One would not expect proceedings to be launched under s 7 of the Human Rights Act 1998 until any other appropriate remedial routes have first been explored.

[63] In the ordinary course a parent ought to be able to obtain effective relief, by one or other of these means, against an authority whose mishandling of a child in its care has violated a parent's Art 8 rights. More difficult is the case, to which Thorpe LJ drew attention in *Re W and B; Re W (Care Plan)* [2001] EWCA Civ 757, [2001] 2 FLR 582, para [34], where there is no parent able and willing to become involved. In this type of case the Art 8 rights of a young child may be violated by a local authority without anyone outside the local authority becoming aware of the violation. In practice, such a child may not always have an effective remedy.

Other significant cases on this issue:

- *Re T (A minor) (care order: conditions)* [1994] 2 FLR 423
- *Re G (Care: challenge to local authority's decision)* [2003] 2 FLR 42: see G20 – Procedural unfairness in care proceedings (1)
- *X Council v B (Emergency protection orders)* [2004] EWHC 2014 (Fam), [2005] 1 FLR 341 at 356
- *Re S and W (Care proceedings)* [2007] EWCA Civ 232, [2007] 2 FLR 275: see G11 – Separate JR / HR proceedings generally to be avoided

This case is also included in relation to:

D56　Interim or final order (1)

Newborn babies

D10 REMOVAL AT BIRTH, WITHOUT NOTICE, IN EXCEPTIONAL CIRCUMSTANCES

Re D (Unborn baby)

[2009] EWHC 446 (Fam), [2009] 2 FLR 313 at 315 and 321

Family Division

Munby J

[3] The local authority's plan in relation to the unborn child is that the child should be removed from the mother immediately at birth in circumstances where, as I understand it, its plan is almost bound to be ultimately, as in the case of L, for the making of a full care order and adoption. Be that as it may, the local authority takes the view that it is imperative in the unborn child's interest that it be removed at birth. Conscious no doubt of the strictures to be found in my judgments in the Nottingham cases: *R (G) v Nottingham City Council* [2008] EWHC 152 (Admin), [2008] 1 FLR 1660, and *R (G) v Nottingham City Council and Nottingham University Hospital* [2008] EWHC 400 (Admin), [2008] 1 FLR 1668, the local authority appreciates that it does not have the power to remove the child itself at birth. Its plan envisages that, assuming the co-operation of the prison authorities (which, if I may be permitted to say so, they would probably be well advised for their own purposes to extend to the police), the police, operating in conjunction with the local authority, will exercise their powers under s 46 of the Children Act 1989 at the moment of birth, following which, depending upon the time of day, but no doubt within a matter of hours, the local authority will seek and, I anticipate, will obtain from the justices in the Family Proceedings Court, an emergency protection order, which from that point on will clothe it with parental responsibility and the power to look after the child.

[4] The immediate problem is that in circumstances which I will come to in a moment the local authority is very concerned indeed, and it seems to me with every justification, that any communication of the birth plan to the mother is likely to lead to an adverse reaction, in circumstances where there is a distinct possibility that the mother may, immediately after birth, harm both herself and the child. It goes without saying that a newborn

baby in the first seconds or moments of life is exceptionally vulnerable and that a distraught mother, who, as I will have to describe shortly, has already demonstrated her capacity to threaten violence to her children, would be capable of causing catastrophic injury to the child within a matter of moments.

[5]   The question is whether it is lawful for the local authority to conceal from the mother and her partner the nature of its birth plan. Putting the point in slightly different form, the question is whether, despite the requirements of Art 8 of the European Convention for the Protection of Human Rights and Fundamental Freedoms 1950 (the European Convention), it is lawful for the local authority not to involve the mother and her partner fully in the birth planning for her future child as would normally be required.

...

[23]   It seems to me in light of all this material that the very stringent test which the decisions both of the Strasbourg court and of the domestic courts of this country have laid down as required to be satisfied if this very drastic and highly unusual step is to be taken is more than adequately met.

[24]   I emphasise that just as it will be a rare and exceptional case where a local authority is justified in applying for an emergency protection order without prior warning to the parents, if the justification for this is that alerting the parents to what is proposed may produce the very harm against which the process is designed to protect the child, so it will be a very unusual and exceptional case where a local authority is justified in departing from the obligation laid upon it by Art 8 fully to engage the family in the planning process *before* the care proceedings start. But that there will, on rare occasions, be such exceptional cases, and cases where such an exceptional step is lawful and compatible with the European Convention, is clear as a matter of law and recognised by both the Strasbourg jurisprudence and the domestic jurisprudence of our courts.

[25]   Stressing the point again, because it must not be thought that the course which I am sanctioning in this case is a course to be adopted save in highly exceptional and rare cases, I am, however, entirely satisfied that the course proposed by the local authority in this particular case is not merely appropriate, it is imperatively demanded in the interests of the safety – the physical safety – in the period immediately following birth of the as yet unborn child. To share the local authority's planning either with the mother or with the child's father – for he could not of course be prevented from passing the information on to the mother – would, I am satisfied, be to expose the child to an utterly unacceptable degree of risk of potentially really serious physical harm.

General notes:

Without notice applications: see G30 and G31.

D11 REMOVAL AT BIRTH REQUIRES COURT ORDER

R(G) v Nottingham City Council

[2008] EWHC 152 (Admin), [2008] 1 FLR 1660 at 1663

Queen's Bench Division

Munby J

[15] The law is perfectly clear but perhaps requires re-emphasis. Whatever the impression a casual reader might gain from reading some newspaper reports, no local authority and no social worker has any power to remove a child from its parent or, without the agreement of the parent, to take a child into care, unless they have first obtained an order from a family court authorising that step: either an emergency protection order in accordance with s 44 of the Children Act 1989 or an interim care order in accordance with s 38 of the Act or perhaps, in an exceptional case (and subject to s 100 of the Act), a wardship order made by a judge of the Family Division of the High Court.

[16] Section 46 of the Children Act 1989 permits a police constable to remove a child where he has reasonable cause to believe that the child would otherwise be likely to suffer significant harm, and that power can be exercised without prior judicial authority. But the powers conferred on the police by s 46 are *not* given to either local authorities or social workers.

[17] Local authorities and social workers have no power to remove children from their parents unless they have first obtained judicial sanction for what they are proposing to do. Only a court can make a care order. Only if a court has authorised that step, whether by making an emergency protection order or by making a care order or an interim care order or in some other way, can a local authority or a social worker remove a child from a parent. And the same goes, of course, for a hospital and its medical staff.

[18] As I said during the course of the hearing, no baby, no child, can be removed simply 'as the result of a decision taken by officials in some room'.

[19] This is all elementary. It is well known to all family lawyers. And it is, or ought to be, well known to all social workers. That is why, as the media accurately reported, I made the comment during the course of the

hearing that 'The professionals involved in this case should have known better'. I went on to point out, however, that the midwives and doctors in a delivery room in the small hours could not have been expected to understand this. No doubt they acted as they did in accordance with the 'Birth Plan' that had been given to them by their superiors.

[20] Lest this judgment be misunderstood, I should make clear that what I have said is subject to two qualifications.

[21] In the first place, a social worker or a nurse is, of course, entitled to intervene if that is necessary to protect a baby from immediate violence at the hands of a parent. That is not, however, because they have any special power or privilege entitling them to intervene. It is merely an application of the wider principle that anyone who happens to be present is entitled, whether by restraining the assailant or by removing the defenceless victim from his assailant's reach, to intervene in order to prevent an actual or threatened criminal assault taking place before his very eyes. Hence the observation I made that 'You cannot remove children, short of immediate murderous intent, except by lawful means, which means either by a police officer or court order'. There is, of course, no need to show murderous intent. Any threat of immediate significant violence is enough, particularly if it involves a young child.

[22] But in the present case, as I observed, and I was not gainsaid by Mr McGuire, there was no suggestion that any risk the mother was posing to her son was a risk of exposing him to immediate physical attack or physical harm.

[23] The other qualification arises out of s 3(5) of the Children Act 1989, which provides that:

'A person who—

(a)   does not have parental responsibility for a particular child; but
(b)   has care of the child,

may (subject to the provisions of this Act) do what is reasonable in all the circumstances of the case for the purpose of safeguarding or promoting the child's welfare.'

[24] Now s 3(5) could not avail the local authority, because it did not have the 'care' of G's son. But there might be circumstances in which a hospital could rely upon s 3(5) as justifying action taken in relation to a child in its medical care, despite the absence of parental consent and the absence of any court order.

[25] For instance, medical intervention might be required in order to preserve the child's life or to protect a child from irreversible harm in

circumstances of such urgency that there is not even time to make an urgent telephone application to a judge. In such a situation of emergency, a doctor can act without parental or judicial consent and, if parents are acting unreasonably or contrary to the child's best interests, even despite a parental refusal of consent: see Grubb, *Principles of Medical Law*, (Oxford University Press, 2nd edn, 2004) para 4.21.

[26] Doctors, midwives and nurses do not have to stand idly by waiting for a court order if, for example, a premature baby desperately needs to be put in a special unit or placed on a ventilator. They are, of course, entitled to separate the child from the mother if medical necessity dictates, and even if she objects. Law, medical ethics and common sense march hand in hand.

Other significant cases on this issue:

- *P, C and S v United Kingdom* [2002] 2 FLR 631: see D2 – Removal of child (at birth) and permanent separation
- *Re F (Care proceedings: interim care order)* [2010] EWCA Civ 826, [2010] 2 FLR 1455

D12   CONTACT TO NEWBORN BABY (1)

Kirklees Metropolitan District Council v S (Contact to newborn babies)

[2006] 1 FLR 333 at 337, 338 and 340

Family Division

Bodey J

[22]   In cogent written and oral submissions, Mr Hayes for the local authority criticises the approach taken by the family proceedings court in its Reasons, for a number of reasons. He says that contact on a daily basis is unheard of, even in respect of a baby when the mother is breast-feeding (which this mother is not doing, as L is being fed formula milk). He submits that it is an imposition on foster carers to be expected to rearrange their lives around a foster child, not only during the week but also on Saturdays and Sundays. He says that there are serious resource implications for local authorities in having to finance supervision on Saturdays and Sundays, as to which he tells me that Kirklees is presently having to 'buy in' supervising workers at the weekend to comply with the family proceedings court order. He argues that there is nothing exceptional in this case to justify such extensive contact, and comments that if the mother's and the children's guardian's arguments prevail in this case, then logically they should prevail in every case of a young baby removed from his or her mother at or shortly after birth.

[23]   Accordingly, Mr Hayes expresses the local authority's considerable concerns at the 'floodgates' (his word) opening, in view particularly of the very generalised way in which the family proceedings court expressed its reasons in respect of babies removed from their mothers at or shortly after birth. He submits that the words 'reasonable contact', to be found in s 34(1) of the Children Act 1989, and the word 'appropriate' in s 31(3) of the Act, connote the need to carry out a balance, which he says the family proceedings court here failed properly to do. Since, as he maintains, the local authority's contact proposals in its interim care plan were manifestly reasonable, he submits that the court should not have 'trespassed' into the territory of considering whether even more generous contact would have been more beneficial to the child.

[24]   Lastly, Mr Hayes maintains that the family proceedings court was wrong in adopting the observations of Munby J in *Re M (Care Proceedings: Judicial Review)* [2003] EWHC 850 (Admin), [2003] 2 FLR 171 which he submits were 'obiter', ie not necessary for the decision

before him (Munby J) in that case. Accordingly, he says, the family proceedings court was wrong to characterise Munby J's observations in that case (to which I will shortly come) as 'principles'.

...

[27] Before setting out my conclusions, I will repeat the words of Munby J in *Re M*, because they were referred to the family proceedings court by the advocates, and clearly influenced the family proceedings court's approach in this case. Under the heading 'Concluding thoughts', Munby J said:

'If a baby is to be removed from his mother, one would normally expect arrangements to be made by the local authority to facilitate contact on a regular and generous basis. It is a dreadful thing to take a baby away from his mother: dreadful for the mother, dreadful for the father and dreadful for the baby. If the state, in the guise of a local authority, seeks to intervene so drastically in a family's life – and at a time when *ex hypothesi* its case against the parents has not yet even been established – then the very least the state can do is to make generous arrangements for contact. And those arrangements must be driven by the needs of the family, not stunted by lack of resources. Typically, if this is what the parents want, one will be looking to contact most days of the week and for lengthy periods. And local authorities must be sensitive to the wishes of a mother who wants to breast-feed, and must make suitable arrangements to enable her to do so – and when I say "breast-feed", I mean just that, I do not mean merely bottle-feeding expressed breast milk. Nothing less will meet the imperative demands of the European Convention. Contact two or three times a week for a couple of hours a time is simply not enough if parents reasonably want more.'

[28] It is important to note that *Re M* was an application for leave to apply for judicial review of a decision by a local authority to commence care or other protective proceedings under the Children Act 1989. The aim of such intended judicial review was to secure an injunction restraining the local authority from going ahead with its intended Children Act proceedings. Munby J, who of course has very great experience of sitting both in the Administrative Court and in the Family Division, unsurprisingly rejected that application for leave to bring such judicial review proceedings. It was in those circumstances that he added his 'Concluding thoughts'. In my judgment, therefore, Mr Hayes was correct in characterising such thoughts as 'obiter'.

[29] I would not, however, wish to dissent from Munby J's observations in *Re M (Care Proceedings: Judicial Review)* [2003] EWHC 850 (Admin), [2003] 2 FLR 171, *provided* they are not elevated into principles and *provided* it is not understood from them that the words 'most days of the

week' imply daily contact including at weekends. The judge was clearly comparing the sort of level of contact which he thought appropriate for babies removed from their mothers where supervision by or on behalf of the local authority is required (viz 'most days of the week and for lengthy periods') with contact 'two or three times a week for a couple of hours at a time', which he said would clearly not constitute reasonable contact.

[30] Nor do I consider that Munby J's comment that such contact arrangements 'must be driven by the needs of the family, not stunted by lack of resources' was intended to mean that resources are a wholly irrelevant consideration. It is clear that the practicalities of arranging contact by a mother to a baby have to be borne in mind as part of deciding what quantum of contact would constitute 'reasonable' or 'appropriate' contact under s 34, within which decision-making process at least some regard must generally be had to the extent to which the quantum of contact would be likely to impose unreasonable burdens either on the foster carer's abilities to sustain it, and/or on the resources of the local authority to facilitate it.

[31] An order for daily contact to a child in foster care, where supervision by or on behalf of the local authority is required, is, on any view, (to put it at its lowest) exceptionally unusual, a fact which was inferentially recognised in the submissions made to me on behalf of the mother and the children's guardian.

[32] Had the existing order been expressed to run for a medium or long-term period of time, then, in my judgment, it would not have constituted 'reasonable' or 'appropriate' contact, and could not have been sustained at this appeal hearing. There was no evidence to support the proposition relied on by the family proceedings court that it is *vital that contact between a parent and a child of L's age should be daily to establish maternal bonds*', a proposition which is not, in my experience, borne out by the way in which this type of case is generally dealt with by the courts, and which goes far wider in its ambit (*'a child of L's age'*) than was necessary to determine this particular case.

[33] I do not regard Munby J's observations in *Re M* as supporting any such proposition, still less as laying down any 'principles', to use the word of the family proceedings court; nor do I consider that he would have expected his observations to be so understood.

[34] I mention this because this is the second appeal from family proceedings courts which I have had before me within the last fortnight where the issue has centred around the mother of a baby removed at birth seeking to achieve 7-day-a-week contact, in reliance on the above passage in *Re M*.

[35] At the risk of repeating myself (and I realise I am doing so), Munby J did not refer to 'daily' contact, but to 'contact most days of the week'. Nor was anything which he said, in my judgment, intended to detract from the fact that each such case has to be looked at on its own particular merits, with the welfare of the child paramount, so as to determine what quantum of contact would be 'reasonable' or 'appropriate' under the relevant subsections of s 34.

[36] Bearing in mind all the relevant considerations here, and with some hesitation, I have reached the conclusion that this order was ultimately not outside the broad ambit of discretion vested in the family proceedings court, given the context (which I stress) that it was only intended to run for a number of weeks before being reviewed, with a view either to some form of rehabilitation, or else to a likely reduction in quantum. Under *G v G (Minors: Custody Appeal)* [1985] 1 WLR 647, [1985] FLR 894, this court can only interfere if the decision of the family proceedings court under appeal was plainly wrong, or if the family proceedings court erred in principle.

...

[38] In those circumstances, the local authority's appeal is dismissed.

[39] I add three points. *First*, I was told by Mr Hayes that the present foster carers are now in fact finding weekend contact onerous. He told me this on the strength of information given by the foster carers to their link worker, who in turn passed it to the key social worker, who in turn passed it to Mr Hayes, who in turn told me. There was no application for this court to receive any fresh evidence, nor any statement obtained from the foster carers or the link manager. In the light, therefore, of objection justifiably taken on behalf of the mother, it would not in my view be appropriate to take account of this information by 'deeming' it to be fresh evidence. Attention should be given to supplying the family proceedings court with proper up-to-date evidence in this respect, when the matter is before that court again on 20 July 2005.

[40] *Second*, I observe that there was no information before the family proceedings court as to the actual cost of 'buying in' agency staff to supervise weekend (or other) contact. Such information would (or might) assist the court in future where a local authority wishes to pray in aid the expense of providing the sort of contact which a parent seeks. Wholly unsubstantiated submissions about 'resources' and 'floodgates' without basic information as to how much one is actually talking about are not particularly helpful to the court.

[41] *Third*, I invite the family proceedings court to look critically at the quantum of contact as presently ordered when the case comes back before it on 20 July 2005. As I have already said, contact 7 days per week is, in my judgment and experience, (and to put it at its lowest) a quite exceptionally high level of quantum for the sort of contact which requires local authority supervision. Unless rehabilitation can be seen as being likely in the near future, I would respectfully suggest that an order involving all or most weekdays, but not weekends (or at least not every Saturday and every Sunday) might be regarded as the appropriate way forward. It is very much to be hoped, however, that the various permutations and possibilities can and will be discussed at ground level, and an accommodation as to contact reached between all parties, with the help of the children's guardian which he has expressed himself more than willing to offer.

D13   CONTACT TO NEWBORN BABY (2)

Re K (Contact)

[2008] EWHC 540 (Fam), [2008] 2 FLR 581 at 586 and 586

Family Division

Munby J

[24]   The local authority does not seek, at this stage, to terminate C's contact with K, but it does seek an order under s 34(4) authorising it to refuse to allow contact between G and K. This is not merely because contact has, in Ms SJ's (untested) opinion been 'very poor' and, in Ms AJ's opinion, undergone a 'recent deterioration.' It is essentially because of what happened on 12 March 2008, though that is only the culmination of what appears to have been a steadily deteriorating situation.

[25]   It is a very drastic thing indeed to interfere with a young mother's contact with her newborn baby, and his contact with her, particularly at a time when 'threshold' (see s 31(2) of the Act) is yet to be established. It is an even more drastic thing to deny contact altogether, and something which lies at the very extremities of the court's powers. Extraordinarily compelling reasons must be shown to justify an order under s 34(4) at this early stage in the proceedings.

...

[28]   I confess that I have not found this an altogether easy question to resolve. I am quite satisfied that, at least in the short-term, there must be an order under s 34(4). In the light of what happened on 12 March 2008, K's safety imperatively demands that I make such an order. The more difficult question is whether I should make that order so that it lasts only until the next hearing or whether I should make it so that it lasts until the final hearing.

[29]   Ms Rowley, contending for the latter, submits that it is idle to imagine that things will have changed sufficiently over the next 2 or 3 weeks to allow contact then to be resumed – and in any event, she says, whatever order I make there will be nothing to prevent G applying to vary or discharge it. Furthermore, an order under s 34(4) only 'authorises' the local authority to refuse to allow contact. It does not forbid such contact and a local authority, even if clothed with authority under s 34(4), is, of course, under a continuing duty to keep matters under review and to allow contact to resume as soon as it is safe and appropriate to do so.

[30] I can see the force of Ms Rowley's submissions, but having reflected on the matter over the weekend I think that an order in the terms she seeks would be too drastic and that it might very well send out quite the wrong 'message' to all concerned. Accordingly, I will make a s 34(4) order, but limited to expire on the date of the case management conference before Judge Inglis.

[31] This will allow the dust to settle and give G another opportunity to show that she can put K's needs before her own problems. But I do not want there to be any misunderstanding. The onus will very much be on G to demonstrate to Judge Inglis that contact, no doubt carefully supervised and, it may well be, subject to stringent conditions, is something that should be allowed to resume. The next 2 or 3 weeks will give G a breathing space to show, if she can, that she is willing and able to work together with the local authority, to take on board the local authority's concerns about her behaviour during contact, and to demonstrate as best she can that she is going to behave herself if contact resumes. *If* she is able to do this, then it *may* be that Judge Inglis will be persuaded that contact between G and K can safely and appropriately resume. If, however, she is not able to do this, then in all probability the order I have made will be extended and continued by Judge Inglis.

General notes:

This was the sequel to *R (G) v Nottingham City Council (No 2)* [2008] EWHC 400 (Admin), [2008] 1 FLR 1668.

Threshold criteria

D14 'SIGNIFICANT'

Re MA (Care threshold)

[2009] EWCA Civ 853, [2010] 1 FLR 431 at 446 and 451

Court of Appeal

Ward LJ

[47] The issue in this appeal is whether or not Roderic Wood J was plainly wrong in concluding that although M, the eldest three-year-old child of these parents, had suffered *some* harm attributable to the care given to her not being what it was reasonable to expect a parent to give her, she had not suffered *significant* harm nor was she likely so to suffer. This is the difficult question to decide. Much less difficult to my mind are the questions whether the judge was also plainly wrong to find that although S had been 'exposed to the ill-treatment and neglect suffered by A' (see para [141]) this did not amount to significant harm and there was again no real possibility that she would suffer significant harm. Finally, in the case of H, where it is not suggested he ever suffered any harm, significant or otherwise, was the judge correct to find the likelihood of harm not to be established in his case either?

[48] This is, as I understand it, the first time this court has had to consider when the dividing line between harm and significant harm is established. The Guidance issued under s 7 of the Local Authority Social Services Act 1970, designed to bring to managers and practitioners an understanding of the principles of the Children Act 1989, informed us at 3.19 that:

'It is additionally necessary to show that the ill-treatment is significant, which given its dictionary definition means considerable, noteworthy or important.'

That seems to have been seised upon and repeated by Miss Jill Black, as she then was, in her submissions to Booth J in *Humberside County Council v B* [1993] 1 FLR 257 which were accepted by the judge as apt and helpful.

[49] That case was decided six months after the Act came into operation. We had to wait for 15 years after the commencement of the Act to find

the first really considered attempt to explore the concept of significant harm. That was undertaken by Hedley J in *Re L (Care: Threshold Criteria)* [2007] 1 FLR 2050. Two paragraphs of his judgment are worthy of citation:

'[50]   What about the court's approach, in the light of all that, to the issue of significant harm? In order to understand this concept and the range of harm that it's intended to encompass, it is right to begin with issues of policy. Basically it is the tradition of the UK, recognised in law, that children are best brought up within natural families. Lord Templeman, in *Re KD (A Minor: Ward) (Termination of Access)* [1988] 1 AC 806, [1988] 2 FLR 139, at 812 and 141 respectively, said this:

"The best person to bring up a child is the natural parent. It matters not whether the parent is wise or foolish, rich or poor, educated or illiterate, provided the child's moral and physical health are not in danger. Public authorities cannot improve on nature."

There are those who may regard that last sentence as controversial but undoubtedly it represents the present state of the law in determining the starting point. It follows inexorably from that, that society must be willing to tolerate very diverse standards of parenting, including the eccentric, the barely adequate and the inconsistent. It follows too that children will inevitably have both very different experiences of parenting and very unequal consequences flowing from it. It means that some children will experience disadvantage and harm, while others flourish in atmospheres of loving security and emotional stability. These are the consequences of our fallible humanity and it is not the provenance of the state to spare children all the consequences of defective parenting. In any event, it simply could not be done.

[51]   That is not, however, to say that the state has no role, as the 1989 Act fully demonstrates. Nevertheless, the 1989 Act, wide ranging though the court's and social services' powers may be, is to be operated in the context of the policy I have sought to describe. Its essence, in Part III of the 1989 Act, is the concept of working in partnership with families who have children in need. Only exceptionally should the state intervene with compulsive powers and then only when a court is satisfied that the significant harm criteria in s 31(2) is made out. Such an approach is clearly consistent with Art 8 of the European Convention for the Protection of Human Rights and Fundamental Freedoms 1950. Article 8(1) declares a right of privacy of family life but it is not an unqualified right. Article 8(2) specifies circumstances in which the state may lawfully infringe that right. In my judgment, Art 8(2) and s 31(2) contemplate

the exceptional rather than the commonplace. It would be unwise to a degree to attempt an all embracing definition of significant harm. One never ceases to be surprised at the extent of complication and difficulty that human beings manage to introduce into family life. Significant harm is fact specific and must retain the breadth of meaning that human fallibility may require of it. Moreover, the court recognises, as Lord Nicholls of Birkenhead pointed out in *Re H and others* that the threshold may be comparatively low. However, it is clear that it must be something unusual; at least something more than the commonplace human failure or inadequacy.'

[50] In part that case echoes observations made by Munby J in *Re K; A Local Authority v N and Others* [2005] EWHC 2956 (Fam), [2007] 1 FLR 399 to the effect that:

'[26] The task of the court considering threshold for the purposes of s 31 of the 1989 Act may be to evaluate parental performance by reference to the objective standard of the hypothetical 'reasonable' parent, but this does not mean that the court can simply ignore the underlying cultural, social or religious realities. On the contrary, the court must always be sensitive to the cultural, social and religious circumstances of the particular child and family. And the court should, I think, be slow to find that parents only recently or comparatively recently arrived from a foreign country – particularly a country where standards and expectations may be more or less different, sometimes very different indeed, from those with which are familiar – have fallen short of an acceptable standard of parenting if in truth they have done nothing wrong by the standards of their own community.'

[51] I see the force and good sense in both judgments and I endorse them but with one reservation. Having more carefully considered Lord Nicholls of Birkenhead's speech in *Re H (Minors) (Sexual Abuse: Standard of Proof)* [1996] AC 563, [1996] 2 WLR 8, [1996] 1 FLR 80, at 592, 29 and 101 respectively, I have come to the conclusion that Hedley J was wrong to suggest that the threshold of significant harm may be comparatively low. To make good this criticism, I must put Lord Nicholls of Birkenhead's speech in its context ...

...

[54] The case before us is narrower: it is simply about the meaning of the word 'significant' in the phrase 'significant harm'. Given the underlying philosophy of the Act, the harm must, in my judgment, be significant enough to justify the intervention of the State and disturb the autonomy of the parents to bring up their children by themselves in the way they choose. It must be significant enough to enable the court to make a care

order or a supervision order if the welfare of the child demands it. At all times the spectre of Art 8 of the European Convention for the Protection of Human Rights and Fundamental Freedoms 1950 hangs over us all and Baroness Hale of Richmond[1] reminded us of its import:

> '[78] Children also have the right to respect for their family lives under Article 8 of the Convention. This is, of course, a qualified right. Interference by the authorities is justified if it is "necessary in a democratic society" in order to protect the child's own rights, which in this context include the right to be protected from harm. But there has to be a "pressing social need" for the interference, the reasons for it have to be "relevant and sufficient", and the interference itself has to be proportionate to the need: see, for example, *K & T v Finland* (2001) 31 EHRR 484; *Scozzari & Giunta v Italy* (2002) 35 EHRR 243; *Kutzner v Germany* (2002) 35 EHRR 653.'

Although Art 8 has, of course, more relevance to the disposal stage when the care or supervision orders can be made, it does, nonetheless, inform the meaning of 'significant' and serves to emphasise that there must be a 'relevant and sufficient' reason for crossing the threshold.

[55] If Roderic Wood J erred at all in reminding himself of the approach he should adopt, he erred only in that he put the bar too low by assuming, if he did, that the threshold for significant harm is low: see my analysis of Lord Nicholls of Birkenhead's speech. If he erred, he erred in favour of the local authority and the local authority and the guardian cannot now really be heard to complain too much about that. So I return to the essential questions. Was he plainly wrong in his conclusions?

General notes:

The case illustrates how difficult the issue can be. The judges were divided two (Hallett and Ward LJJ) to one (Wilson J) in upholding Wood J's decision.

---

[1]   *Re B (Care proceedings: standard of proof)* [2008] UKHL 35, [2008] 2 FLR 141.

D15 'IS SUFFERING': RELEVANT TIME IS WHEN PROTECTIVE ARRANGEMENTS INITIATED

Re M (A minor) (Care order: threshold conditions)

[1994] 2 FLR 577 at 583

House of Lords

Lord Mackay of Clashfern

In my opinion the opening words of s 31 link the making of an order by the court very closely with the application to the court by a local authority or authorised person ... There is nothing in s 31(2) which in my opinion requires that the conditions to be satisfied are disassociated from the time of the making of the application by the local authority. I would conclude that the natural construction of the conditions in s 31(2) is that where, at the time the application is to be disposed of, there are in place arrangements for the protection of the child by the local authority on an interim basis which protection has been continuously in place for some time, the relevant date with respect to which the court must be satisfied is the date at which the local authority initiated the procedure for protection under the Act from which these arrangements followed. If after a local authority had initiated protective arrangements the need for these had terminated, because the child's welfare had been satisfactorily provided for otherwise, in any subsequent proceedings, it would not be possible to found jurisdiction on the situation at the time of initiation of these arrangements. It is permissible only to look back from the date of disposal to the date of initiation of protection as a result of which local authority arrangements had been continuously in place thereafter to the date of disposal.

It has to be borne in mind that this in no way precludes the court from taking account at the date of the hearing of all relevant circumstances. The conditions in subs (2) are in the nature of conditions conferring jurisdiction upon the court to consider whether or not a care order or supervision order should be made. Conditions of that kind would in my view normally have to be satisfied at the date on which the order was first applied for. It would in my opinion be odd if the jurisdiction of the court to make an order depended on how long the court took before it finally disposed of the case.

Other significant cases on this issue:

* *Southwark LBC v B* [1998] 2 FLR 1095

D16 INFORMATION FOUND / EVENTS OCCURRING AFTER INITIAL INTERVENTION

Re G (Care proceedings: threshold conditions)

[2001] 2 FLR 1111 at 1112, 1114 and 1117

Court of Appeal

Hale LJ

[1] This appeal raises an issue of some practical importance in proceedings for care and supervision orders under the Children Act 1989: what have the local authority to be in a position to prove at the time when they make the application? To what extent can they rely upon evidence, which emerges, or events, which take place between the date of the application and the final hearing?

...

The threshold

...

[9] Once the threshold is crossed, the court has to decide what order, if any, to make. In doing so, s 1 of the 1989 Act applies: the child's welfare is the paramount consideration (s 1(1)), a checklist of factors is to be considered in determining his welfare, including the options available to the court (s 1(3)), and the court is not to make any order unless to do so will be better for the child than making none (s 1(5)). It is common ground that the court can take into account all the information available at the date of the hearing in deciding what order to make if the threshold has been crossed: the order is clearly looking to the future, and it would be contrary to the child's best interests to turn a blind eye to relevant matters occurring after the proceedings began.

[10] Equally, however, it is common ground that the date at which the threshold has to be crossed is when the local authority first intervened to protect the child: that is, either the date of the application or, if child protection measures (police protection or an emergency protection order) have been continuously in place since before then, the date when those began: see *Re M (A Minor) (Care Order: Threshold Conditions)* [1994] 2 AC 424, [1994] 2 FLR 577.

...

[11] *Re M* was concerned with both the actual and likely harm limbs of s 31(2)(a). Although much of the discussion was directed at when the condition that the child 'is suffering' significant harm must be met, the case also raised the problem of likely harm: by the time of the hearing his father was serving his sentence but alternative loving homes were available with the foster mother or with his mother's cousin. It would be odd indeed if actual and likely harm had to be judged at different dates. Further, the policy considerations are equally strong in each case. Just as it would be odd if the local authority were precluded from obtaining a care order on the ground of actual harm because their own intervention had cured the problem, it would be odd if a court could make an order based on the likelihood of harm from an immediate return home even though the factual basis for the interim removal had not been proved and the proceedings had taken so long to be heard that a return home would be unsettling for the child. Obviously, if the initial likelihood of harm has been removed or reduced by later events (such as the separation of the mother from an abusive partner) the court may decline to make a care order because it will not be best for the child. By contrast, a local authority may launch proceedings on the basis that a child in local authority accommodation is likely to suffer harm if returned home, because that would be so at the date when the application was made.

[12] However, real life is not quite as simple as this. Care cases, like all children cases, look to the future and not the past. Things are changing all the time while the case progresses. The local authority is not required to plead their case at the outset or indeed at all. It is now the practice in many courts to require the local authority before the final hearing to make a clear statement of the facts they wish the court to find and the basis upon which they allege that the threshold is crossed. In my view this should be routine, so that the parents can know the case they have to meet and have a fair opportunity to meet it. The judge lamented the lack of such a statement in this case.

[13] But it is often the case that measures are taken to protect a child, often in something of an emergency, before anything approaching a full picture has emerged. The question then is the extent to which the local authority can rely upon matters, which have come to light or taken place since the proceedings began. At one end of the spectrum, there will often be *information* discovered after the relevant date, which throws light on what the facts were at the relevant date. The most obvious examples are further medical evidence about the injuries which promoted removal, new complaints by the child about other forms of abuse within the home or admissions made by the parents. Often these will emerge in the course of expert assessments conducted partly for the purpose of establishing the threshold and partly for the purpose of considering the way forward.

[14] At other end of spectrum, there may be entirely new *events* which introduce a completely different risk which did not exist at the relevant date. Examples of this are not so easy to devise: it could be that proceedings are begun because a baby has suffered injuries which turn out to be completely accidental; unfortunately, the stress and strain of the proceedings has led to one parent leaving home and the complete collapse of the other. More commonly, the removal of the child on the basis of suspicions, which turn out to be unwarranted, may make it harder for the child to return home.

[15] In the middle are new *events*, which may, or may not, be capable of proving that there was a risk of significant harm at the relevant time. Acts of violence occurring while the proceedings are pending might be capable of showing that a risk of such violence existed when the proceedings began. Subsequent neglect or abuse might be capable of showing that such neglect or abuse was likely when the proceedings were brought. This raises more difficult questions because there are obvious dangers of retrospectively validating a concern which was not in fact justified at the time: there may, after all, be other reasons for things to go badly wrong after proceedings are started.

...

Conclusion on the threshold

[21] Ms Davis on behalf of the local authority argues that the judge was confusing the date upon which the threshold must have been crossed with the evidence needed to prove that it was. He also confused later-acquired evidence with later-occurring events. He was quite entitled to take the later assessments into account in considering whether the authority had proved that there was in June 1999 a real risk of D suffering significant harm at some later date. Indeed, Mr McCormick on behalf of the mother now concedes (as he did not below) that the local authority does not have to be in possession of all the information upon which it wishes to rely at the date of the application. He accepts that later-acquired information as to the state of affairs at the relevant date can be taken into account.

[22] In my view he is right to make that concession. It is a commonplace in legal proceedings that evidence gathering continues after the proceedings are begun and there is usually nothing to prevent its being used in accordance with the rules. It would be absurd if evidence coming to light during the proceedings, such as further medical evidence on the interpretation of X-rays and scans, further complaints by the children, or confessions by the parents, could not be taken into account to show what the situation was at the relevant time.

[23] Mr McCormick does not accept, however, that the local authority can rely upon later events even if these are relevant to proving the state of affairs when the proceedings began. I would agree with him that later events cannot be relied upon unless they are capable of showing what the position was at the relevant time. But if they are capable of proving this, then in my view they should be admitted for that purpose. It will then be a matter for the judge to consider how much weight they should be given. This will not always be an easy task. I can, however, give a concrete example from my own judicial experience: a baby boy was found to be suffering from several fractures of different dates. The question was whether these were attributable to a lack of care from his mother or her present partner or from elsewhere, in particular his father. The assessments of the mother and her partner were generally favourable and the boy was returned to live with them. Shortly afterwards he suffered two new fractures. That fact was clearly relevant in proving that the threshold was made out when the proceedings were begun some considerable time earlier.

D17 'LIKELY TO SUFFER SIGNIFICANT HARM'

Re H and R (Child sexual abuse: standard of proof)

[1996] 1 FLR 80 at 94

House of Lords

Lord Nicholls of Birkenhead

'Likely' to suffer harm

I shall consider first the meaning of 'likely' in the expression 'likely to suffer significant harm' in s 31. In your Lordships' House Mr Levy QC advanced an argument not open in the courts below. He submitted that likely means probable, and that the decision of the Court of Appeal to the contrary in *Newham London Borough Council v AG* [1993] 1 FLR 281 was wrong. I cannot accept this contention.

In everyday usage one meaning of the word likely, perhaps its primary meaning, is probable, in the sense of more likely than not. This is not its only meaning. If I am going walking on Kinder Scout and ask whether it is likely to rain, I am using likely in a different sense. I am inquiring whether there is a real risk of rain, a risk that ought not to be ignored. In which sense is likely being used in this subsection?

In s 31(2) Parliament has stated the prerequisites which must exist before the court has power to make a care order. These prerequisites mark the boundary line drawn by Parliament between the differing interests. On one side are the interests of parents in caring for their own child, a course which prima facie is also in the interests of the child. On the other side there will be circumstances in which the interests of the child may dictate a need for his care to be entrusted to others. In s 31(2) Parliament has stated the minimum conditions which must be present before the court can look more widely at all the circumstances and decide whether the child's welfare requires that a local authority shall receive the child into their care and have parental responsibility for him. The court must be satisfied that the child is already suffering significant harm. Or the court must be satisfied that, looking ahead, although the child may not yet be suffering such harm, he or she is likely to do so in the future. The court may make a care order if, but only if, it is satisfied in one or other of these respects.

In this context Parliament cannot have been using likely in the sense of more likely than not. If the word likely were given this meaning, it would have the effect of leaving outside the scope of care and supervision orders cases where the court is satisfied there is a real possibility of significant harm to the child in the future but that possibility falls short of being more likely than not. Strictly, if this were the correct reading of the Act, a care or supervision order would not be available even in a case where the risk of significant harm is as likely as not. Nothing would suffice short of proof that the child will probably suffer significant harm.

The difficulty with this interpretation of s 31(2)(a) is that it would draw the boundary line at an altogether inapposite point. What is in issue is the prospect, or risk, of the child suffering *significant* harm. When exposed to this risk a child may need protection just as much when the risk is considered to be less than fifty-fifty as when the risk is of a higher order. Conversely, so far as the parents are concerned, there is no particular magic in a threshold test based on a probability of significant harm as distinct from a real possibility. It is otherwise if there is no real possibility. It is eminently understandable that Parliament should provide that where there is no real possibility of significant harm, parental responsibility should remain solely with the parents. That makes sense as a threshold in the interests of the parents and the child in a way that a higher threshold, based on probability, would not.

In my view, therefore, the context shows that in s 31(2)(a) likely is being used in the sense of a real possibility, a possibility that cannot sensibly be ignored having regard to the nature and gravity of the feared harm in the particular case. By parity of reasoning, the expression likely to suffer significant harm bears the same meaning elsewhere in the Act; for instance, in ss 43, 44 and 46. Likely also bears a similar meaning, for a similar reason, in the requirement in s 31(2)(b) that the harm or likelihood of harm must be attributable to the care given to the child or 'likely' to be given to him if the order were not made.

Other significant cases on this issue

- *Re R (Care order: threshold criteria)* [2009] EWCA Civ 942, [2010] 1 FLR 673

This case is also included in relation to:

H2   Burden of proof

D18 'CARE GIVEN ... NOT ... REASONABLE': OBJECTIVE TEST

Re D (Care order: evidence)

[2010] EWCA Civ 1000, [2011] 1 FLR 447 at 460

Court of Appeal

Hughes LJ

[35] I will accept that this does demonstrate that the judge has not made what would have been a fundamental and most elementary error; indeed it would have been astonishing if he had, not least because he had been helpfully presented by counsel on all sides with an impeccable statement of law which made the objective nature of the test under s 31(2) entirely clear. For the avoidance of doubt, the test under s 31(2) is and has to be an objective one. If it were otherwise, and the 'care which it is reasonable to expect a parent to give' were to be judged by the standards of the parent with the characteristics of the particular parent in question, the protection afforded to children would be very limited indeed, if not entirely illusory. It would in effect then be limited to protection against the parent who was fully able to provide proper care but either chose not to do so or neglected through fault to do so. That is not the meaning of s 31(2). It is abundantly clear that a parent may unhappily fail to provide reasonable care even though he is doing his incompetent best.

D19   DANGERS OF SOCIAL ENGINEERING

Re L (Children) (Care proceedings: significant harm)

[2006] EWCA Civ 1282, [2007] 1 FLR 1068 at 1084

Court of Appeal

Wall LJ

[51]   There are, of course, many statements in the law reports warning of the dangers of social engineering. One of the most powerful, in my view, remains the statement of Butler-Sloss LJ (as she then was) in *Re O (A Minor) (Custody: Adoption)* [1992] 1 FLR 77 ...

> 'If it were a choice of balancing the known defects of every parent with some added problems that this father has against idealised perfect adopters, in a very large number of cases children would immediately move out of the family circle and towards adopters. That would be social engineering and it is important to bear that in mind in looking at the problems which arise in this case. It was put far better than I could hope to put it by Lord Templeman in *Re KD (A Minor) (Ward: Termination of Access)* [1988] 1 AC 806 at 812; [1988] 2 FLR 139 at 141D:
>
> > "The best person to bring up a child is the natural parent. It matters not whether the parent is wise or foolish, rich or poor, educated or illiterate, provided the child's moral and physical health are not in danger. Public authorities cannot improve on nature."'

[52]   I have taken some time on this particular point because I wish the parents fully to understand and for their lawyers to explain to them that if, at the very end of this case, the court does find the threshold criteria established and makes a care order, it will not be because, to different extents, they both suffer from learning difficulties. It will be because the court will have found the threshold criteria under s 31 satisfied ... and because the court has come to the view that a care order is in the best interests of the children.

General notes:

The rehearing of the matter also addressed this issue: *Re L (Care: threshold criteria)* [2007] 1 FLR 2050, an extract from which is cited within D14 – 'Significant'.

Other significant cases on this issue:

• *Re W (Care: threshold criteria)* [2007] EWCA Civ 102, [2007] 2 FLR 98

This case is also included in relation to:

G53 Disclosure of documents on which reliance placed

D20 THE REASONABLE PARENT AND CULTURAL REALITIES

Re K; A Local Authority v N and Others

[2005] EWHC 2956 (Fam), [2007] 1 FLR 399 at 406

Family Division

Munby J

[26] The task of the court considering threshold for the purposes of s 31 of the 1989 Act may be to evaluate parental performance by reference to the objective standard of the hypothetical 'reasonable' parent, but this does not mean that the court can simply ignore the underlying cultural, social or religious realities. On the contrary, the court must always be sensitive to the cultural, social and religious circumstances of the particular child and family. And the court should, I think, be slow to find that parents only recently or comparatively recently arrived from a foreign country – particularly a country where standards and expectations may be more or less different, sometimes very different indeed, from those with which are familiar – have fallen short of an acceptable standard of parenting if in truth they have done nothing wrong by the standards of their own community.

[27] Ms Russell, for whose sensitive and illuminating submissions I am particularly grateful, submits on behalf of the father that I must assess the facts in the context of the cultural and religious beliefs and practice of this family, including K, and in the context of the father's beliefs and cultural mores. I agree.

...

This case is also included in relation to:

D36 Application of no order principle

D21 THRESHOLD SHOULD ALWAYS BE RECORDED

Oxfordshire County Council v L

[1998] 1 FLR 70

Family Division

Hale J

By way of preliminary observation, although the threshold criteria had been conceded, it is the court's duty to be satisfied that the circumstances are as set out in s 31(2). It is, therefore, generally appropriate for the court to record the basis upon which it is so satisfied. Sometimes it may do so by making its own findings of fact on the agreed evidence. Sometimes it may do so by reference to an agreed statement of those facts. Without such a statement it is, of course, difficult to know what the basis was for the making of any order let alone a care order.

Designated local authority

D22   A SIMPLE APPROACH

Northamptonshire CC v Islington LBC

[1999] 2 FLR 881 at 887

Court of Appeal

Thorpe LJ

Although I have every sympathy with the judge's determination to do his best for a child who had been ill served within the care system and although I fully appreciate the practical advantages of the Northampton designation I am in no doubt that that conclusion is wrong in law. I have considered whether that conclusion can be reasoned without due consideration of any of the difficult issues that have divided the Family Division. However, I conclude that this case does require a decision on the following difficult issues:

(a)   What is the proper construction of s 31(8)(a) and (b) in conjunction? Is it legitimate to construe the opening phrase of s 31(8)(b) as though it read 'where the child does not ordinarily reside ...'?

(b)   What is the proper construction of the disregard section?[1] Is the judgment of Wilson J to be preferred to that of Bracewell J?

(c)   Where the case falls for decision under s 31(8)(b), what is the ambit of the judicial task? Has the judge the wide discretion which emerges from the decisions in the reported cases?

For I am first of the opinion that at the date of trial N was not ordinarily resident within either Islington or Northampton. In order to make good that conclusion I must necessarily express my view on the proper construction of s 31(8)(a) and (b) in conjunction as well as my view on the proper construction of the disregard provision. Secondly, I conclude that in determining designation under s 31(8)(b) the judge was constrained to designate Islington and not Northampton. That conclusion rests on the proper construction of what s 31(8)(b) requires of the court.

---

[1]   Section 105(6) of the Children Act 1989.

Let me begin with the proper construction of s 38(6). Wilson J demonstrated why he concluded that Parliament did not mean what it appeared to have said. Unless the court inserted the word 'ordinarily' into the first phrase of s 31(8)(b) there would be cases in which the child in question fell into neither para (a) nor para (b). As he put it:

'Take B himself. He is ordinarily resident nowhere. But is he resident in the area of a local authority? The disregard provided in s 105(6) has no bearing upon this question because it relates only to ordinary residence. Incarceration does not preclude simple "residence" – indeed it secures it – and counsel do not seek to dissuade me from the view that B must be taken for the time being to be resident in the area of Birmingham City Council, where he has lived in a secure unit for almost 4 months.'

I agree this logic and sympathise with the attempt to find a legitimate construction to avoid that result. But is the solution adopted by Wilson J legitimate? He first acknowledged the contrary view of Singer J expressed in *Re R (Care Orders: Jurisdiction)* [1995] 1 FLR 711. He then gave three reasons for his conclusion that the omission of the word 'ordinarily' from para (b) was a parliamentary slip. His first was drawn from the genesis of the subsection. Its legislative predecessor was s 20(2) of the Children and Young Persons Act 1969 which, in very similar language, expressed the test for designation but the residence in both para (a) and para (b) was expressed to be habitual. Then cl 12(10) of the draft 'Children Bill' annexed to the Law Commission Report No 172 had 'reside' without adjectival qualification in both para (a) and para (b). In relation to this genesis he said (at 184H):

'The draft Bill did not define or qualify the references to residence. It seems clear to me that, when Parliament resolved to bring the provision into line with the previous law, it inserted "ordinarily" into (a) but forgot to do so into (b).'

He then turned to s 37(5) of the Act where, as in s 31(8), in para (a) the draftsman wrote 'ordinarily resident' but in para (b) wrote 'reside'. However, s 116 of the Courts and Legal Services Act 1990 amended s 37(5) to write 'ordinarily' equally into para (b). Of that Wilson J said (at 185C):

'[Counsel] contends that it is inconceivable that, in correcting a perceived error in s 37(5), Parliament would have accidentally failed to make any necessary correction of the analogous s 31(8). I disagree ...'

Having considered authorities warning judges against reading words into an Act of Parliament he concluded (at 185F–G):

'Nevertheless for the reasons already given, I am of the firm opinion that Parliament's omission of the word "ordinarily" in s 38(8)(b) is not only accidental but inflicts a heavy defeat upon the intention of the Act by removing children resident but not ordinarily resident in the area of an authority from what purport to be and are intended to be comprehensive provisions for the making and designation of care orders.'

This court has carried out some research into the genesis of s 31(8) and also into the subsequent amendment of s 37(5) without unearthing anything of relevance to the dilemma.

So in the end it seems to me that the principal justification for the judicial rewriting of s 31(8)(b) is to ensure that it provides a mechanism for designation in all and not just the vast majority of cases. That is a powerful consideration. Although I am doubtful of the reasoning of Wilson J I agree with him that s 31(8) must be construed to provide a test for all cases and I cannot at the moment see a better solution than that which he devised.

Turning to the second question, the attraction of the construction favoured by Bracewell J is its simplicity. The ordinary residence immediately preceding the commencement of the period of disregard is deemed to continue uninterrupted. The court is relieved from what may be a contentious and disputed investigation of what other circumstances have changed within the period of disregard. Any construction of s 105(6) can be said to produce anomalous results. We should not be over-impressed by anomaly arguments where the court's function is simply to determine which authority is to be designated in the care order. I am convinced that s 31(8) was never intended to be a gateway to extensive judicial investigation of a number of relevant facts and circumstances as the prelude to the exercise of some discretionary choice. It was surely intended to be a simple test to enable the court to make a rapid designation of the authority upon which is to fall the administrative, professional and financial responsibility for implementing the care order and the care plan. Where the child has connections with more than one area ordinary residence determines on the basis that almost every child will have an ordinary residence, if not a presence, in some local authority area. In the rare case where a child lacks an ordinary residence in a local authority area the court designates the area in which occurred the events that carried the application over the s 31 threshold.

On that approach I lean towards Bracewell J's inclination to hold that the area of ordinary residence immediately prior to the commencement of the stay to be disregarded should be notionally extended throughout that stay. I would not say that developments affecting the family during the period to be disregarded cannot in any case be considered. But I would say that such cases should be exceptional.

I turn now to the third question. The Family Division judges have construed s 31(8)(b) to vest in them a broad discretion to designate any local authority area that might loosely be said to be in the frame. Wilson J in *Gateshead*[2] put it thus (at 185H–186A):

> 'B does not ordinarily reside in the area of an authority and so I must designate the authority "within whose area any circumstances arose in consequence of which the order is being made". The words "any circumstances arose ..." are very wide. Parliament might have chosen narrower words, such as "the circumstances substantially arose ...", which would often have given rise to a difficult inquiry. As they stand, the words seem to me to recognise that the circumstances which cause a care order to be made in respect of a child of B's age will often be multifarious and will have arisen at numerous different stages of his life. I consider that, in principle, where (b) applies, more than one local authority may well qualify for designation and that in that event the court can choose which to designate.'

Mr Munby QC in *Re P*[3] accepted the approach of Wilson J and indeed extended the field of choice when he said (at 101C–E):

> 'The "circumstances ... in consequence of which" a care order is made, as those words are used in s 31(8)(b), are not confined to, though they will always include, the circumstances of that period of the child's own life which is relevant to the "threshold" inquiry under s 31(2) and circumstances in the child's life which "arose" in the places where he lived during that period. In an appropriate case, the "circumstances ... in consequence of which" a care order is made will include any circumstances, whenever and wherever they arose, whether before or after the child was born and whether or not arising in any place at which the child has ever lived, which go to the inability of the child's parent to give him that quality of care which is referred to in s 31(2)(b)(i). Furthermore, the "circumstances ... in consequence of which" a care order is made will embrace the actions of any local authority, not otherwise brought within the ambit of s 31(8)(b), which itself institutes or carries on care proceedings or which becomes in some other way sufficiently involved in care proceedings for it properly to be said that a care order has been made, wholly or in part, "in consequence of" the actions of that authority.'

I have reached the conclusion that this liberality only invites unnecessarily extensive issues. The more multifarious the circumstances, the more local authorities there will be in the frame with the opportunity for, and likelihood of, unnecessary contests. The circumstances to which the judge should have regard are the primary circumstances that carry the case over

---

[2] *Gateshead Metropolitan Borough Council v L* [1996] 2 FLR 179.
[3] *Re P (Care Proceedings: Designated Authority)* [1998] 1 FLR 80.

the s 31 threshold. That may be a positive act or series of acts, such as sexual or physical abuse. If there has been extensive abuse there will usually be an ultimate or an outstanding episode that triggered local authority intervention. The judge will have no difficulty in locating that event. In other cases the foundation for the care order may be negative conduct such as neglect, consistently poor parenting or a failure to provide emotional support. Even in chronic cases without any acute episode it will usually be simple enough for the judge to discern the place or, if more than one, the principal place at which the failure occurred. In my opinion the judge's function is to carry out a rapid and not over-sophisticated review of the history to make a purely factual determination. It is a question of fact and not of discretion.

In summary, my view of these two interacting subsections is that they should be given that construction that achieves the result for which I conclude they were designed: that is a simple mechanism to determine the question of administration. If that involves a degree of artificiality and the import of legal fiction any misgivings can be met by recognising the limited purpose and effect of the court's function. After all, it must be assumed that all local authorities are equally competent, professional and committed in the discharge of responsibilities cast upon them by the making of a care order. Over the course of years the swings and roundabouts principle is likely to even out any seeming disadvantage to an individual authority by designation in a particular case. These subsections are not about child protection or the promotion of child welfare. They are to be read as a simple test, to be operated by the court in what should be the unlikely event of dispute, to determine which local authority is to be responsible for the care plan and its implementation.

I turn to apply that approach to the present case ...

D23 FURTHER GUIDANCE

London Borough of Redbridge v Newport City Council

[2003] EWHC 2967 (Fam), [2004] 2 FLR 226 at 231 and 235

Family Division

David Hershman QC sitting as a deputy High Court judge

[24] I extract the principles that I must apply to the instant case:

(1) the first question the court must consider in determining an issue of designated authority under the Children Act 1989, s 31(8) is 'ordinary residence' of the child concerned. This is to be determined at the time of the hearing (per Thorpe LJ in *Northamptonshire County Council v Islington London Borough Council* [2001] Fam 364, [1999] 2 FLR 881 at 370 and 887 respectively);

(2) when determining ordinary residence at the date of the hearing the court *shall*, by virtue of the Children Act 1989, s 105(6), disregard any period of time during which the child was provided with accommodation by the local authority (per Bracewell J in *Re BC (A Minor) (Care Order: Appropriate Local Authority)* [1995] 3 FCR 598 and per Thorpe LJ in *Northamptonshire County Council v Islington London Borough Council* at 372 and 889 respectively) described as the 'stop-the-clock approach' or extending the period of ordinary residence in the authority from where the child has moved (Area A) and delaying the notional period of residence to the area where the child moved to (Area B);

(3) the 'stop-the-clock approach' does not apply when the child is with a parent (per Wall J in *Re C (Care Order: Appropriate Local Authority)* [1997] 1 FLR 544 and per Thorpe LJ in *Re H (Care Order: Appropriate Local Authority)* [2003] EWCA Civ 1629, [2004] 1 FLR 534), relative, friend or other person connected with him (per Thorpe LJ in *Re H (Care Order: Appropriate Local Authority)*) because the child is not being provided with accommodation by or on behalf of a local authority under the Children Act 1989, s 105(6)(c);

(4) another exception to the 'stop-the-clock approach' is if there are 'exceptional circumstances' to justify looking at the history during this period of time (per Thorpe LJ in *Northamptonshire County Council v Islington London Borough Council* [2001] Fam 364, [1999] 2 FLR 881 and in *Re C (A Child) v Plymouth City Council* [2000] 1 FLR 875 at 879). The Court of Appeal has made it clear that

exceptional means more than a child having acquired a new ordinary residence (in Area B) and severing all links (in Area A) (see Swinton Thomas LJ in *Re C (A Child) v Plymouth City Council* at 880 and Thorpe LJ in *Re H (Care Order: Appropriate Local Authority)* at paras [9]–[14]);

(5)   if after having carried out this analysis the conclusion of the court is that the child is not ordinarily resident in any local authority area the court must determine the designated authority in accordance with the Children Act 1989, s 31(8)(b) (per Thorpe LJ in *Northamptonshire County Council v Islington London Borough Council* at 371 and 888 respectively);

(6)   the test to be applied in determining the 'circumstances arose in consequence of which the order is being made' under the Children Act 1989, s 31(8)(b) means the primary circumstances that carry the case over the s 31 threshold (per Thorpe LJ in *Northamptonshire County Council v Islington London Borough Council* at 373 and 890 respectively). At this point there is no consideration of 'exceptional circumstances' or of intervening events.

[25]   It follows, therefore, that the test applied of Bracewell J in *Re BC (A Minor) (Care Order: Appropriate Local Authority)* [1995] 3 FCR 598 cannot be imported into this case to stop the clock for the whole period of the proceedings. At the time of the commencement of the proceedings the children were in care and placed with foster carers. At that point, in accordance with *Re BC (A Minor) (Care Order: Appropriate Local Authority)*, s 105(6) applies and so the 'ordinary residence' remains their residence at the time of the commencement of the proceedings. From May 2002 the children were placed in local authority accommodation with their mother and so s 105(6) still applies. After February 2003 the children were placed at home with their mother and so, in accordance with *Re C (Care Order: Appropriate Local Authority)* [1997] 1 FLR 544 and *Re H (Care Order: Appropriate Local Authority)*, s 105(6) does not apply. The children at this point are no longer being provided with accommodation. Therefore, the time after February 2003 can and should be considered when determining 'ordinary residence' and of course, therefore, can the time from August 2003 when they moved to Newport. In Newport they were with their mother and so this period of time is also to be considered.

[26]   The intention of the Court of Appeal in *Northamptonshire County Council v Islington London Borough Council* [2001] Fam 364, [1999] 2 FLR 881 and *Re C (A Child) v Plymouth City Council* [2000] 1 FLR 875 was to establish a simple mechanism to determine the designated authority without the need or ability to review that decision. It seems to me that this could only be achieved if the disregard provisions apply whether or not a child is placed at home under the terms of an interim care order. Given that *Re H (Care Order: Appropriate Local Authority)* [2003] EWCA Civ 1629, [2004] 1 FLR 534 makes it plain that this is not the case, there can only be one solution, namely that the clock starts again once a child is placed at home during pending proceedings.

[27] Further, implicit in the analysis adopted in *Re H (Care Order: Appropriate Local Authority)* was an acceptance that the time to consider 'ordinary residence' was the time that the matter was being considered by the court and not, for example, at the time of the commencement of the proceedings.

[28] The consequence of this analysis is that there must be consideration of 'ordinary residence' at the time of the application subject to disregarding some periods of time to which the Children Act 1989, s 105(6) applies. The time at which this matter is determined may, therefore, be important. It follows that after a passage of time a child may have acquired 'ordinary residence' in another local authority area. If the matter was considered earlier it is possible that there would not have been a sufficient passage of time to be satisfied that the child had acquired ordinary residence. The difficulty is that on my analysis a different result might be achieved depending on the timing of the determination. There are two possible solutions:

(i)   the issue of designation should only be dealt with at the final hearing; or
(ii) the disregard provisions should apply irrespective of whether a child is placed with a 'relative, friend or other person connected with him'.

The latter is inconsistent with the Court of Appeal's decision in *Re H (Care Order: Appropriate Local Authority)*. The former is feasible but perpetuates the uncertainty in the proceedings until the very last minute. A decision made within the proceedings to designate one authority (Authority A) which is capable of variation (possibly to later designate Authority B), whilst helpful and necessary for the management of the interim orders and proceedings, leaves an uncertainty.

[29] Accordingly, on the facts the children were ordinarily resident in Redbridge at the time of the commencement of the proceedings in October 2001 and placement in foster care and a residential placement are to be disregarded. The period of time in Barking with their mother from February 2003 to August 2003 and from August 2003 to the present day are to be included. In effect the clock started again.

[30] Thus I set myself the test of determining 'ordinary residence' in those circumstances. There can be no doubt that the children have ceased ordinary residence in Redbridge. Have they acquired ordinary residence in Newport in 3 months?

[40] Having already excluded exceptional circumstances in this case, I conclude that the designated authority in these proceedings is and should be the London Borough of Redbridge.

[41] As I have already stated, on my interpretation of the law a different result might be achieved at a later date. This I am afraid is the consequence of my decision, but it is consistent with the decision of Wall J in *Re C (Care Order: Appropriate Local Authority)* [1997] 1 FLR 544.

[42] There is no bar to Redbridge making the same application later (namely that Newport be the designated authority). Assuming it is justified on the facts and the mother and children have properly settled in Newport, there is every reason to believe that a later decision might produce a different result. I appreciate that this allows the uncertainty to continue. It means that Redbridge must remain involved in the case and hold the interim orders but Newport must be aware of the real possibility that ultimately the final order may be made in its favour.

D24   INVOLVEMENT OF SECOND LA

L v London Borough of Bexley

[1996] 2 FLR 595 at 597 and 598

Family Division

Holman J

Social workers from the London Borough of Bexley have attended court and given evidence, principally in relation to an issue as to how frequent the father's contact should be and whether it should be supervised. But before and during the principal part of the hearing no one was present from or on behalf of the London Borough of Greenwich, which is, in fact, the local authority in whose care the children must be placed by virtue of s 31(8)(a). The London Borough of Bexley had, in fact, notified Greenwich of this case and hearing. There was a meeting between the key Bexley social worker and the team manager, Miss O'Reilly, of the district within Greenwich in which the mother and children actually reside. But apart from this, the London Borough of Greenwich did not propose to play any part in the proceedings.

In my judgment, this was an extremely unsatisfactory state of affairs ... In the present case, the care plan was proposed to be supplemented by the 'statement of intent' to which I have referred. But a care plan, signed and prepared by the applicant local authority alone, is almost meaningless if the child is in fact to be placed in the care of another local authority. It is essential for the court and, of course, the parents and the guardian ad litem to be confident that the actual local authority in whose care the child is to be placed is committed to, and has the financial and practical resources to implement, the proposals in the care plan.

Further, s 34(11) of the Children Act 1989 provides that:

'Before making a care order with respect to any child the court shall –

(a)   consider the arrangements which the authority have made, or propose to make, for affording any person contact with a child to whom this section applies; and

(b)   invite the parties to the proceedings to comment on those arrangements.'

In my judgment, the reference in that section to 'the authority' must be a reference to the local authority in whose care the child is to be placed, since the applicant local authority, if it is to drop out of the picture, cannot itself 'propose to make' any arrangements at all.

The importance of these considerations could scarcely be more vividly illustrated than in this case. It would have been intolerable to make a care order based on a 'statement of intent' that the children would (subject to the provisos to which I have referred) remain with their mother without being sure that the London Borough of Greenwich itself had that intention; or to make orders as to supervised contact by the father without being sure that Greenwich has the resources to provide the proposed supervision.

...

When, during the pendency of care proceedings, the child concerned becomes ordinarily resident in the area of another local authority, consideration should always be given to that local authority becoming a party to, or taking over the conduct of, the proceedings. I do not suggest that that local authority necessarily should become a party or take over the conduct of the proceedings, but consideration should always be given to it. In my experience, it is sometimes appropriate and sometimes not. Whether it is appropriate will depend on many factors in the particular case. But where it is clear that a care order, if made, will designate, or under s 31(8)(b) realistically may designate, a local authority other than the applicant local authority, then in my judgment much fuller and earlier liaison between the two local authorities is essential than occurred in this case. The care plan needs to be specifically prepared in co-operation between the two local authorities. It is essential that it be put forward as a joint document, and if there are points on which the two authorities disagree, those points should be clearly identified in the plan.

Further, even if the new local authority is not present or represented throughout the hearing, proper arrangements should be made in advance for a properly informed and appropriately authorised representative of that authority to attend court to deal with any issues which may have arisen as to the future plans for the children and personally to assure the court and the parents of that authority's commitment to what is proposed and of its capacity to implement it.

Other significant cases on this issue:

- *Re C (Care order: appropriate local authority)* [1997] 1 FLR 544

Change of name of child in care

D25   GENERAL PRINCIPLES

Re M, T, P, K and B (Care: change of name)

[2000] 2 FLR 645 at 649

Family Division

HHJ Wilkinson (sitting as a judge of the High Court)

Before I deal with the competing submissions, I want to turn to the law. The starting-point is s 33(7) of the Children Act 1989. That reads:

'While a care order is in force with respect to a child, no person may—

(a)   cause the child to be known by a new surname; or
(b)   remove him from the United Kingdom,

without either the written consent of every person who has parental responsibility for the child or the leave of the court.'

In the case of *Re S (Change of Surname)* [1999] 1 FLR 672 the Court of Appeal considered an appeal in respect of an application by two teenage girls who were in local authority care to be allowed to change their surname after their father had been charged with sexually abusing one of them. The Court of Appeal concluded that the trial judge ought not to have relied upon authorities dealing with changing the surname of a child who was not in care when considering a change of surname under s 33(7). Thorpe LJ said this at 674B:

'First the judge misdirected himself as to the authorities. At p 8 of his judgment he aptly recorded that the research that he and counsel had conducted had unearthed no authority that considered an application under s 33(7). However, he then over the following six pages reviewed authorities in relation to change of surname over the last 35 years, although it seems that he was not referred to one of the latest decisions in this court. From those authorities he drew guidance which in my opinion simply did not stand transplanting into the ground that he surveyed. It may be that those authorities distracted him from the analysis which he would have carried out had he continued from his starting-point, namely that there was no authority directly in point.'

That passage seems to have led to the view in argument before me that none of the principles relating to applications under ss 8 or 13 has any relevance on an application under s 33(7). I find that interpretation difficult to understand. It seems to me, with respect, that Thorpe LJ was merely stating that the factual issues which arise in a private law change of name dispute, are very likely to be of a completely different character from those which are likely to arise in a public law change of name dispute. In the former, the issue will, generally speaking, though not always, involve a balancing exercise between two competing surnames, in which one parent is seeking an order for a change which is considered more compatible with a change in the adult relationships. Public law cases necessarily involve the State against one or both of the parents, and the usual reason for seeking change essentially revolves around issues of child protection. For that reason many of the private law authorities will have no relevance to public law applications, and accordingly, will afford little or no guidance to the court in seeking to resolve a public law application. They are legal square pegs in factual round holes, but insofar as a public law case presented itself as a factual square hole, I see no reason for not applying the legal square pegs to the public law square holes. As I see it, the basic approach in law to private and public law applications, is not fundamentally different. In my judgment, it would be absurd to say that because this is a s 33(7) application, all the private law commonsense principles established by the authorities should be ignored and in my respectful judgment, that is not what Thorpe LJ meant. Insofar as those cases establish welfare principles which are relevant to the application before me, with its different perspective under s 33(7), they must be taken into account. My reasons for this view are as follows: s 1(1) of the Children Act 1989 states this:

'When a court determines any question with respect to—

(a)   the upbringing of a child; or
(b)   *[irrelevant]*,

the child's welfare shall be the court's paramount consideration.'

Any application to change a child's surname is a matter concerning the upbringing of a child, and accordingly, on such an application, the child's welfare is the court's paramount consideration: *Re W* (1999) *The Times*, August 5; *Dawson v Wearmouth* [1999] 1 FLR 1167.

Furthermore, as in the case of s 8 applications, there is a mandatory obligation on the court to apply the welfare checklist in s 1(3) when dealing with an application under s 33(7): see s 1(4)(b). It is true that there is no mandatory requirement to apply the welfare checklist to a private law application for a name change brought under s 13, but the difference is more theoretical than real because the checklist factors will be considered in relation to s 13 applications, as in applications under ss 8 and 33(7): *Re C (Change of Surname)* [1998] 1 FLR 549.

Ultimately, said Lord McKay of Clashfern, LC in the case of *Dawson v Wearmouth* [1999] 1 FLR 1167, 1173H:

'... the right course, in my opinion, must be to apply the criteria in s 1 of the 1989 Act including s 1(5) and not make an order for the change of name unless there is some evidence that this would lead to an improvement from the point of view of the welfare of the child.'

I respectfully suggest that that principle must apply with equal force to an application under s 33(7), as it does to an application under s 8 or 13.

In my judgment, the importance of *Re S* is this: that in addition to the application of the welfare checklist factors, Thorpe LJ states that the court should give very careful consideration to a number of other factors, first, the wishes, feelings, needs and objectives of the applicant. In *Re S* the applicants were the children themselves. In the case before me, the applicant is the local authority, but I see no reason why this should make any difference. Secondly, the court should conduct a searching scrutiny of the motives and stated objections of the respondents. Thirdly, the court needs to pay particular heed to the guardian ad litem, who has had the opportunity to make a thorough investigation of the family dynamics. Finally, it is clear from what Thorpe LJ says that it is neither necessary nor appropriate to await the outcome of the father's criminal proceedings, at any rate, once final care orders have already been made. Those, then, are the principles which, in my judgment, should be applied in determining this public law application under s 33(7).

I turn now to the welfare checklist ...

D26   CHANGE OF FORENAME

Re D, L and LA (Care: change of forename)

[2003] 1 FLR 339 at 342, 342 and 346

Family Division

Butler-Sloss P

As it has turned out, subject to any appeal that the father may be able to mount, the children were adopted at the end of last year. Upon adoption, the new adopters had the right, which I assume they exercised, to put completely different names on the adoption register, and, as I understand it, LA is now LI on the adoption register. The court has no power to deal with a change of forename because the prospective adopters, now the adopters, had the right to change it.

...

But while, as it is at the moment, the adoption order is in force, then there is nothing the court can do about the child being called LI and his adoptive parents have the rights so to address him. Because of the adoption, there is nothing that can be done at this stage to put right the change of name prior to the adoption.

So far as L is concerned, she is not to be adopted, but she is to remain long term with these foster parents. There are factors in favour of letting the changed name remain the name of the child – that is to say, R – and factors in favour of changing the name back. In favour of changing it back, is that the foster parents should not have done it in the first place. They did not consult the local authority, they just did it. And the local authority was, as with the other family, placed in a difficult position as to how to respond to the change.

...

The local authority must make sure that they advise foster parents that, if for some reason, they do want to change the name, they must never take the initiative, however good the case is, because they do not have parental responsibility. The responsibility they have, as I understand it, is under s 3(5) of the Children Act 1989, that:

> 'A person who does not have the parental responsibility for a particular child but has care of the child, may, subject to the

provisions of this Act, do what is reasonable in all the circumstances of the case, for the purpose of safeguarding or promoting the child's welfare.'

To change a child's name is to take a significant step in a child's life. Forename or surname, it seems to me, the principles are the same, in general. A child has roots. A child has names given to him or her by parents. The child has a right to those names and retains that right, as indeed, the parents have rights to retention of the name of the child which they chose. Those rights should not be set to one side, other than for good reasons. It may be that foster parents do not appreciate the underlying importance for the child of a name, and it is significant. You would not, for instance, be likely to change the forename of a child of 7, 8 or 9, I suggest even, 5, 6 or 7, because by that time the child has made that name part of his or her identity and very young children know what their names are. You ask a very young child 'what's your name?', and they will certainly be able to give you the name he or she is called by. To change that is to affect the child's identity. The right of the child and both parents to respect for that part of family life still exists, even though the child has gone into a foster placement. It may be that foster carers have not yet been sufficiently made aware that this is not a technical point. There is an underlying importance to the principle that the name should not be changed.

Having said that, one has to recognise, in reality, that names do change. Children acquire nicknames and even nicknames sometimes take over from the name that they were given as their chosen name. Children do have diminutives and they may themselves, as they get older, prefer their third name to their first name and choose to be called by it. I do think the father has become somewhat too dogmatic, if he will permit me to say so, in not seeing the distinction in the case of L, where another of her names has been used, which is not an unusual situation in modern times, rather than in the case of his son, LA, where the prospective adopters there chose a name that the parents had never thought of, and, I think the case of LRC, called L by her own parents and the first set of foster parents, and called R by the second set of foster carers, is not perhaps as serious a matter as the case of LA. There will be cases where it is appropriate to allow a change of name and the issue may need to be dealt with a degree of flexibility.

So, the first rule, in my judgment, is that no foster parent or carer, under whatever regulations, should unilaterally change the name of a child. If, for any reason, the foster parents or other such carers think the name should be changed, they should go straight away to the social worker in charge of the case or the adoption placement officer, whoever it may be, and ask for the change and explain why. That should then be a matter of careful consideration by the local authority, who does, of course, have shared parental responsibility. The parents, who remain with parental responsibility in all foster placements, though not, of course, in placements after freeing for adoption, should be consulted in foster placements, to be allowed to express their views, if they are capable of being found or able to express a view, and if it is a matter that cannot be achieved by consent, it may be necessary, and one would hope it would be rare that such a situation would arise, but it may be necessary to invoke the inherent jurisdiction of the court and ask the High Court to rule on whether the name should be changed. That has happened in a number of cases in surnames and I see no reason why it should not happen in, what I hope will be the rare case, for forenames.

If the Department of Health will issue guidance to all local authorities, and social services departments will issue guidance to their foster parents and prospective adoptive people on their lists, such a problem ought not to arise in the future. If it does, after foster parents or prospective adopters have been warned in clear terms that they should not change the name, then I think the local authority will have to deal with it, or the adoption agency will have to deal with it quite firmly, unless there are exceptional reasons why they should not do so.

Contact to child in care

D27 APPLICATION FOR LEAVE

Re M (Care: contact: grandmother's application for leave)

[1995] 2 FLR 86 at 94, 95 and 97

Court of Appeal

Ward LJ

We have been urged to rule on that part of the appeal which deals with the judge's approach to this application as there is apparent divergence of approach to applications for leave to apply for contact orders under s 34 of the Children Act and application for leave to apply for s 8 orders under s 10(9) of the Act.

...

It is quite clear that s 10(9) does not govern applications for contact to a child in care because s 9(1) provides that:

> 'No court shall make any section 8 order, other than a residence order, with respect to a child who is in the care of a local authority.'

It is equally clear, however, from s 10(9)(d) that children in care may be the object of s 10(9) applications and that must include an application for a residence order. If the court were faced with an application by a grandparent for leave to apply for a residence order, alternatively a contact order, it would be anomalous, in my judgment, were the court not to take into account for the exercise of the s 34(3) discretion the criteria specifically laid out for consideration in s 10(9). Those particular factors seem to me to be also apposite for s 34(3). The court must, of course, have regard to all the circumstances of the case, for each case is different, but in my judgment the court should always have particular regard at least to the following:

(a) *The nature of the contact which is being sought.* Contact to children in care varies infinitely from that which is frequent, to that which takes place two, three or four times a year to keep memory alive. It

varies from contact which is face-to-face, to contact which is
indirectly maintained through the exchange of letters, cards,
photographs and gifts.

(b)   *The connection of the applicant to the child.* The more meaningful
and important the connection is to the child, the greater is the
weight to be given to this factor. Grandparents ought to have a
special place in any child's affection worthy of being maintained by
contact but it is easy to envisage family circumstances, very much
like those before us in this case where, however loving the
grandparent may be, life's wheel of misfortune has diminished the
importance to the child of that blood tie and may, for example, have
strengthened the claims for contact by former foster-parents who
have forged close attachment to the child. The fact is that
Parliament has refused to place grandparents in a special category
or to accord them special treatment. Nevertheless, by virtue of
Sch 2, para 15, contact between a child and his or her family will be
assumed to be beneficial and the local authority will need to file
evidence to justify why they have considered that it is not reasonably
practicable or consistent with the child's welfare to promote that
contact.

(c)   *Disruption.* This seems to me to be the factor of crucial significance,
a fortiori when the child is in care. The child will only have come
into care if life had already been so thoroughly disrupted that such
intervention was judged to be necessary. The need then for stability
and security is usually vital. The breakdown of the foster placement
may be so harmful that it should not be placed at risk. All that is
obvious. It is, none the less, significant and appropriate that the risk
of disruption which is primarily contemplated in s 10(9)(c) is the
risk 'there might be of that *proposed application* [for a s 8 order]
disrupting the child's life to such an extent that he would be *harmed*
by it'. I add the emphasis to make two points. The harm envisaged is
harm which, through s 105(1), is defined by s 31(9) to mean
impairment of health or development as those words are there
defined. A child's upset, unhappiness, confusion or anxiety, needs to
be sufficiently severe before it can amount to an impairment of
emotional, social or behavioural development. Secondly, the risk
must arise from the proposed application. The very knowledge that
litigation is pending can be sufficiently unsettling to be harmful; if
leave is given, the process of investigating the merits of the
application can be sufficiently disruptive if it involves the children in
more interviews, psychiatric investigations and so forth. The
stressfulness of litigation may impair the ability of those who have
care of the child properly to discharge their responsibility to the
child's detriment. Questions of that sort are the narrow focus of the
court's attention in weighing this factor. That is not to say that the
court shuts its eyes to what prospects of eventual success the
application has, and if the making of a contact order would be so
manifestly disruptive as to be totally inimical to the child's welfare,

then such an obviously unsustainable claim will not be permitted to get off the starting-blocks. Except in the most obvious case, it is incumbent on the respondent to the application to produce some evidence to establish disruption.

(d) *The wishes of the parents and the local authority.* They are very material, though not determinative. That the parents' wishes are relevant is consistent with the whole underlying philosophy of the Act, a cornerstone of which is the protection of the integrity and independence of the family. When a care order is made, the local authority acquires parental responsibility. Their exercise of that responsibility commands equal protection from unwarranted interference. Their duty imposed by s 22(3) is to 'safeguard and promote [the child's] welfare'. Accordingly, per Balcombe LJ in *Re A and Others (Minors) (Residence Order: Leave to Apply)* [1992] Fam 182, sub nom *Re A and W (Minors) (Residence Order: Leave to Apply)* [1992] 2 FLR 154, at pp 193D and 161G respectively:

> '... the court should approach the application for leave on the basis that the authority's plans for the child's future are designed to safeguard and promote the child's welfare and that any departure from those plans might well disrupt "the child's life to such an extent that he would be harmed by it".'

I would adopt Butler-Sloss LJ's words in *Re B (Minors) (Care: Contact: Local Authority's Plans)* [1993] 1 FLR 543 at p 551D:

> 'Contact applications generally fall into two main categories, those which ask for contact as such, and those which are attempts to set aside the care order itself. In the first category, there is no suggestion that the applicant wishes to take over the care of the child and the issue of contact often depends on whether contact would frustrate long-term plans for the child in a substitute home, such as adoption where continuing contact may not be for the long-term welfare of the child. The presumption of contact, which has to be for the benefit of the child, has always to be balanced against the long-term welfare of the child and particularly where he will live in the future. Contact must not be allowed to destabilise or endanger the arrangements for the child and in many cases the plans for the child will be decisive of the contact application. There may also be cases where the parent is having satisfactory contact with the child and there are no long-term plans or those plans do not appear to the court to preclude some future contact. The proposals of the local authority, based on their appreciation of the best interests of the child, must command the greatest respect and consideration from the court, but Parliament has given to the court, and not to the local authority, the duty to decide on contact between the child and those named in s 34(1). Consequently the court may have the task of

requiring the local authority to justify their long-term plans to the extent only that those plans exclude contact between parent and child.'

Mutatis mutandis, those words seem to me equally apt to applications for leave under s 34(3).

I have attempted to identify the main factors which will be material for the court considering any application for leave. The list is not, however, intended to be exhaustive. I turn next to the question of what test the court must apply to decide whether or not to grant leave.

...

In my judgment the approach should be this:

(1) If the application is frivolous or vexatious or otherwise an abuse of the process of the court, of course it will fail.

(2) If the application for leave fails to disclose that there is any eventual real prospect of success, if those prospects of success are remote so that the application is obviously unsustainable, then it must also be dismissed: see *W v Ealing London Borough Council* (above),[1] approving *Cheshire County Council v M* (above).[2]

(3) The applicant must satisfy the court that there is a serious issue to try and must present a good arguable case. 'A good arguable case' has acquired a distinct meaning: see the long line of authorities setting out this as the convenient approach for the grant of leave to commence proceedings and serve out of the jurisdiction under RSC Ord 11. One should avoid unprofitable inquiry into what precisely these turns of phrase mean. Their sense is well enough known – is there a real issue which the applicant may reasonably ask the court to try and has he a case which is better than merely arguable yet not necessarily one which is shown to have a better-than-even chance, a fair chance, of success?[3] One should avoid over-analysis of these 'tests' and one should approach the matter in the loosest way possible, looking at the matter in the round because only by such imprecision can one reinforce the importance of leaving the exercise of discretion unfettered. Because the discretion is unfettered:

---

[1] [1993] 2 FLR 788.
[2] [1993] 1 FLR 463.
[3] '[I]t should be noted that paragraph (3) should, in fact, end after "... fair chance of success?", and the following passage concerning over-analysis of the tests should be of general application, not only qualifying the test set out in paragraph (3)': *Family Court Practice 2007* at p 644.

'… it would be unwise in this jurisdiction to seek to restrict the discretion of the court by imposing a rigid formula upon the conduct of proceedings.' (*W v Ealing London Borough Council* at p 794H.)

It would be equally unwise to circumscribe rigidly the manner of the exercise of discretion. Each case is different and the weight to be given to the various factors will accordingly vary from case to case.

The weight to be given to those factors is the very essence of the exercise of discretion.

General notes:

For later comment on this decision, albeit in different circumstances, see B43 – CA 1989, s 10(9): applying the statutory criteria.

D28   APPLICATION FOR LEAVE: SEPARATE POINT OF VIEW

Re W (Care proceedings: leave to apply)

[2004] EWHC 3342 (Fam), [2005] 2 FLR 468 at 475

Family Division

Sumner J

[32]   There are other considerations to which the reported cases refer. One of those is whether any application which the applicant has in mind has any independent or separate point of view to be put forward. In other words, is it an application where the interests identified are identical to those of another person who is a party to the proceedings?

[33]   One can envisage that in some cases this may amount to a positive disadvantage to join someone as a party. It could come under s 10(9)(c):

'any risk that might be of that proposed application disrupting the child's life to such an extent that he would be harmed by it;'

I am satisfied that where a person has no independent or separate point of view or is putting forward an interest identical to another person who is a party to proceedings, then it is unlikely that the court would permit them to become a party in their own right.

[34]   Authority for that is to be found in two cases which have been referred to me. The first is a decision of the Court of Appeal in *Re M (Minors) (Sexual Abuse: Evidence)* [1993] 1 FLR 822. These were public law proceedings where the local authority had obtained an interim care order in part for the purpose of facilitating an assessment by a child psychiatrist. The father, mother, and maternal grandparents had all applied for residence orders regarding the children and the local authority had applied for care orders which had been supported by the guardian ad litem.

[35]   Butler-Sloss LJ (as she then was), at 825F, said this:

'However, the maternal grandparents sought and were granted leave to intervene and appear by counsel and solicitors throughout the 20 days of the hearing. Part of the philosophy of the Children Act 1989 is to bring before the court all parties relevant to the welfare of the children. These grandparents have offered an alternative home for their grandchildren in the event that their daughter was not considered suitable by the court to have their care – what might be called "a fallback position" to keep the children within the maternal family. This was a generous offer of the grandparents, arising from their perception of the best interests of the children. The grandparents, however, unlike many cases which come before the courts, were not at odds with their daughter. Their interests are identical, and I cannot see the purpose of their being separately represented for the very lengthy hearing, when they could have been called as witnesses for the mother, and their offer could not have been presented to the court both by the court and at least communicated, even if not endorsed, by the guardian ad litem. Their intervention has lengthened the proceedings and thereby increased the costs of all the parties.'

[36] That is a most helpful observation, if I may say so. It is relevant to the appeal before me.

[37] The next case is a decision of Douglas Brown J, *North Yorkshire County Council v G* [1993] 2 FLR 732. It was a public law case and there were three children of 19 and 17 and D – the subject of the particular application – who was 14. There was an application for a care order. The 17-year-old child applied for contact. He was permitted to do so in the family proceedings court against the advice of the guardian, and the guardian appealed. The appeal was allowed.

[38] In the course of his judgment, Douglas Brown J said that the most trenchant point was that there was no practical advantage in the 17 year old being a party to the proceedings. It was argued by the local authority in these terms:

'But, says the appellant, supported by the local authority, if there is no independent separate point of view which is being put forward by the prospective party, then they should not be allowed to join the proceedings.'

[39] He then quoted the Court of Appeal decision in *Re M* to which I have just referred. He concluded:

'With great respect to Mr Sellers, who has argued the case for the respondent with economy and skill, I see no value whatever to the mother, to S, to the court, or to D, in having S separately legally represented. He can carry out the supportive role by being there, by being a witness, and by generally comforting his mother if she needs it.'

[40] In my judgment, that aspect of this case is conclusive in relation to the appeal. As between the appellant and the maternal grandmother, there

is no difference. Both wish to go together to contact with the same degree of frequency. If there is a difference, it is only that the appellant would seek to substitute for the maternal grandmother if, because of ill health, the maternal grandmother were unable to go. In my judgment, it does not require the appellant to be a party to the proceedings for that to be considered.

Other significant cases on this issue:

- *Merton London Borough Council v K; Re K (Care: representation: public funding)* [2005] EWHC 167 (Fam), [2005] 2 FLR 422

D29 DOMESTIC VIOLENCE

Re G (Domestic violence: direct contact)

[2000] 2 FLR 865 at 873 and 876

Family Division

Butler-Sloss P

But this father will not accept the extent or significance of the violence. He does not even admit that he killed the mother. He does not recognise or understand the effect of the violence on the child, not an academic exercise, but, as I have already said, the child is suffering from nightmares, reluctant to see him, diagnosed as suffering from post-traumatic stress syndrome, and currently in prolonged therapy in order to help her cope with her future life.

Recently, the Court of Appeal handed down judgments in the case of *Re L (Contact: Domestic Violence)*; *Re V (Contact: Domestic Violence)*; *Re M (Contact: Domestic Violence)*; *Re H (Contact: Domestic Violence)* [2000] 2 FLR 334. In that case the Court of Appeal requested and obtained from the Official Solicitor a report from two distinguished child psychiatrists on this question of how does one deal with domestic violence and its effect, in those appeals, on contact (Dr J. C. Sturge in consultation with Dr D. Glaser, 'Contact and Domestic Violence – The Experts' Court Report' [2000] Fam Law 615). That case is highly relevant to the present case both in respect of a potential residence order to the father and in the question of contact. The evidence of the child psychiatrist and of the psychotherapist, already set out in this judgment, confirm the concerns of both mental health experts who gave the report to the Court of Appeal.

I read one or two passages, first from my judgment in the case of *Re L (Contact: Domestic Violence)*; *Re V (Contact: Domestic Violence)*; *Re M (Contact: Domestic Violence)*; *Re H (Contact: Domestic Violence)* [2000] 2 FLR 334 when I first dealt with a report by the Children Act Sub-Committee chaired by Wall J (A Report to the Lord Chancellor on the Question of Parental Contact in Cases where there is Domestic Violence (Lord Chancellor's Department, 12 April 2000)), which underlined the importance of domestic violence in the context of parental contact to children, and I said (at 336):

'There needs to be a greater awareness of the effect of domestic violence on children, both short-term and long-term, as witnesses as well as victims ...'

I also said (at 338):

> 'The research was entirely consistent in showing the deleterious effects on children of exposure to domestic violence and that children were affected as much by exposure to violence as being involved in it. All children were affected by significant and repeated inter-partner violence even if not directly involved. Research indicates that even when children did not continue in violent situations emotional trauma continued to be experienced ... The child might have post-traumatic anxieties or symptoms the proximity of the non-resident violent parent might re-arouse or perpetuate.'

Under a heading 'The refusal of a child to see a parent' the psychiatric report indicated a number of factors of which one was that the child must be listened to and taken seriously, and consideration should be given to the effects on the child of making a decision that appears to disregard their feelings and wishes, and when the child is forced to do something if he cannot see the sense of it.

I also said in that group of factors that of course the age and understanding of the child are highly relevant and the younger child living with a resident parent who has adverse view of the non-resident parent may have a significant effect upon the view of the child. That situation does not arise in this case.

Dr Sturge and Dr Glaser said in their report, which I quoted at 339 of my judgment:

> 'Domestic violence involves a very serious and significant failure in parenting – failure to protect the child's carer and failure to protect the child emotionally ...'

Without a number of factors present, the consultants would see the balance of advantage and disadvantage as tipping against contact. Some (preferably full) acknowledgment of the violence, some acceptance (preferably full) of responsibility for that violence, full acceptance of the inappropriateness of the violence, particularly in respect of the domestic and parenting context, and of the likely ill-effects on the child.

I finally said, for the purposes of this judgment, at 342:

> 'The court deals with the facts of a specific case in which the degree of violence and the seriousness of the impact on the child have to be taken into account. In cases of proved domestic violence, as in cases of other proved harm or risk of harm to the child, the court has the task of weighing in the balance the seriousness of the domestic violence, the risks involved and the impact on the child against the positive factors (if any), of contact between the parent found to have

been violent and the child. In this context, the ability of the offending parent to recognise his past conduct, be aware of the need to change, and make genuine efforts to do so, will be likely to be an important consideration. Wall J in *Re M (Contact: Violent Parent)* [1999] 2 FLR 321 suggested at 333 that often in cases where domestic violence had been found, too little weight had been given to the need for the father to change. He suggested that the father should demonstrate that he was a fit person to exercise contact and should show a track record of proper behaviour. Assertions, without evidence to back it up, may well not be sufficient.'

All of those comments, in my judgment, apply to this case both in residence and in contact. I am extremely concerned about the failure of the father to recognise his past behaviour, which is a prerequisite of trying to do something about it.

...

I turn now to contact. The father's case is that the wishes of a 3 year old not to see him should be disregarded. I would not myself place much weight on the reluctance of a young child to attend contact if the circumstances are right, if there is no real criticism of the father, and it may well be the reluctance of the mother is coming through rather than the reluctance of the child. But, in a case of serious domestic violence, it is a different matter. The reluctance of the child, and the reoccurrence of nightmares and bedwetting, must be looked at with some care.

There have been differences in the first and last contacts, which were tense, compared with the intervening contacts when Dr W was not present. But that contact for three occasions, which may have been superficially satisfactory and successful, is only one facet of looking at the whole question of contact. The reasons which make the father an unsuitable carer are also relevant to direct contact. The failure of the father to accept the situation, the absence of remorse or of any effort to deal with his violence, or recognition that anything is amiss in the context of this case, make direct contact problematical. He now has taken against and objects to the foster-parents.

Both Dr W and Miss M advise strongly against direct contact, supported by the social workers and the guardian ad litem. The case of *Re L (Contact: Domestic Violence); Re V (Contact: Domestic Violence); Re M (Contact: Domestic Violence); Re H (Contact: Domestic Violence)* [2000] 2 FLR 334 is equally apposite to the contact applications. Although Mr Ageros has argued with vigour the discrepancies over the contacts which were good and the contacts which were less good, and that the presence of Dr W on the last occasion may have had some adverse effect on contact, and that the foster-mother was undermining contact, it does not seem to me that any of those arguments that he puts forward can stand against the undoubted fact, as I have found, that the foster-mother did not make contact difficult – on the contrary, she tried to make it work – and the very strong evidence that direct contact is actually disadvantageous to this child, seriously disadvantageous to this child.

The case against direct contact is overwhelming. I give leave under s 34(4) to terminate direct contact, save for a farewell visit if that is considered by everybody to be appropriate. I leave that entirely to the local authority. The door should, however, be left slightly open, and indirect contact by cards and presents should be provided at Christmas and birthday, and exchange of suitable information. The foster-mother has said the child should reply, if a card and/or present is sent. That would be appropriate, and it is an indication of the sensitivity with which the foster-mother is dealing with this case. She is in touch with the paternal grandmother and will continue to give her information about V.

General notes:

As to *Re L, Re V, Re M, Re H (Contact: domestic violence)* [2000] 2 FLR 334 see the subdivision *Domestic violence* at B25 – Process and principles, B26 – Contact where allegations of DV: summary of experts' reports and B31 – Interim contact (1).

D30 COURT HAS NO PROHIBITORY JURISDICTION

Re W (Contact: s 34(2) orders)

[2000] 1 FLR 502 at 506 and 507

Court of Appeal

Thorpe LJ

In broad outline it will be seen that subs (1)[1] imposes on the local authority with a child in care a duty to allow contact. Subsection (2) empowers the court on an application made by the authority or the child to make such order as it thinks appropriate with respect to the contact which is to be allowed. Subsection (3) gives the court a similar power in relation to an application made by persons other than the local authority or the child. Subsection (4) empowers the court to authorise the local authority to refuse contact thus disapplying the duty set out in subs (1). Subsection (5) permits the court to make an order for contact on the making of a care order even in the absence of an application. Subsection (6) permits the local authority to refuse contact but only in stringent circumstances. This power can override not only the duty set out in subs (1) but also a court order. Subsection (7) enables the court to write conditions into a contact order. Subsection (8) enables regulations to be made as to any departure from a court order agreed between the local authority and the person having contact. Subsection (9) provides for variation or discharge. Subsection (10) enables the order to be made at the same time as the care order or later. Subsection (11) obliges the court to investigate the proposals for contact before making a care order.

That summary is intended to set the scene. Against that background Miss Hyde repeatedly submitted that since the court is under a duty to promote the welfare of the child therefore the court must have jurisdiction to prohibit contact to a child in care. That seems to us a non sequitur. Of course insofar as the court has jurisdiction, in the exercise of that jurisdiction it must put welfare paramount. But the paramount principle does not help to determine the jurisdictional boundaries. In our judgment the strongest point for Miss Hyde is the width of the statutory language: see subs (2), 'the court may make such order as it considers appropriate' and subs (5), 'the court may make an order under this section' and subs (7), 'an order under this section may impose such conditions as the court considers appropriate'.

---

[1]   The references here and throughout are to s 34 of the CA 1989 which Thorpe LJ set out in full immediately before this extract begins.

On the other hand it is in our judgment important to construe s 34 in the context of the statute as a whole and in recognition of the statutory objectives. Perhaps the most striking reform introduced by Part IV of the statute was to shift the power from the court to the local authority on and after the making of the care order. As Butler-Sloss LJ lucidly expressed it in *Re L (Sexual Abuse: Standard of Proof)* [1996] 1 FLR 116, 124:

> 'The effect of the Children Act is to set aside the former powers of the court in wardship and to remove from the court any continuing control over children after the making of a care order unless or until a further application was made to the court ...'

...

Another legislative objective was to impose upon local authorities a clearer and a higher duty to promote contact between children in care and parents and others having a significant place in their lives. Taking these two cornerstones of the Part IV provisions in conjunction we are of the opinion that the primary purpose of s 34 is to impose obligations and restraints on local authorities with children in care. The obligation is the duty to promote contact. The restraint is upon their discretion to refuse contact unless they have first persuaded a judge that such a refusal is necessary. The power of the judge to supervise and control is the power to require the local authority to go further in the promotion of contact than the authority itself considers appropriate. The other power is to monitor the local authority's proposal to refuse contact in order to ensure that its proposal is not excessive. We do not believe that the legislation ever intended the jurisdiction of the judge under s 34 to be deployed so as to inhibit the local authority in the performance of its statutory duty by preventing contact which the local authority considers advantageous to welfare. Although we recognise the width of the statutory language we are of the opinion that the construction for which Miss Hyde contends invades unduly and unnecessarily what my Lady described as a difficult and sensitive area.

D31 CONTACT AT THE DISCRETION OF THE LA

L v London Borough of Bromley

[1998] 1 FLR 709 at 712, 713 and 716

Family Division

Wilson J

Let me, with that preamble, notice the order that was made in respect of contact:

'(1) Between each child and the mother, to be at the discretion of the local authority.

(2) Between each child and the father, to be at the rate of three sessions p a.

(3) Between each child and the paternal grandmother, to be at the rate of three sessions p a.

(4) Between each child and Mr S, to be at the discretion of the local authority.

(5) Between each child and [M], to be at the discretion of the local authority.'

So it is to be noted that the order for contact made no distinction at all between the contact provided for A and that for the two older children.

....

I now propose to analyse each of the five paragraphs of the order made by the magistrates, first of all to see what the orders mean and then to see whether they can be impugned under the principles enunciated in *G v G (Minors: Custody Appeal)* [1985] FLR 894, brought in to appeals of this character by *Re M (Section 94 Appeals)* [1995] 1 FLR 546.

At first sight, the orders seem fairly anodyne. After all, in respect of three named people, the local authority is given a discretion in relation to contact. One might ask at first blush: what problem does the local authority have with that? Then, in relation to two other named people, namely the father and the paternal grandmother, the provision, of course, is a defined provision of three occasions per annum. The guardian ad litem had been contending for no more than two occasions per annum

and the local authority somewhat less; but again at first blush one asks oneself: what is the problem, sufficient for the matter to be brought to this court, arising out of that?

I look then at the first paragraph of the order that the magistrates made. It was that the contact between each child and the mother should be at the discretion of the local authority. What does that paragraph mean? Under s 34(1) of the Children Act 1989 it is provided that:

> 'Where a child is in the care of a local authority, the authority shall ... allow the child reasonable contact with—
>
> (a)   his parents ...'

So here is cast, subject to a limited exception which it is unnecessary to address, an obligation on the local authority, quite apart from any order, to allow these children reasonable contact with the mother.

I cannot read the order for contact with the mother to be at the discretion of the local authority as in any way eroding the obligation cast upon the local authority under s 34(1)(a) to allow these children reasonable contact with the mother. The only way in which a court can erode that obligation is when it makes an order under s 34(4) of the Act, authorising the authority to refuse to allow contact between the child and any person mentioned in s 34(1). No such order, of course, was made. So I read the order for contact in favour of the mother at the discretion of the local authority to mean first that there is no inroad into the obligation of s 34(1); secondly that there is to be no definition by the court of contact between the mother and the children under s 34(2) or (3); and thirdly that the quantum of contact, together with the other arrangements for reasonable contact that must take place under s 34(1), is specifically placed to be determined by the local authority in the exercise of their discretion.

It seems to me that the magistrates did not have to make any such order. Had they made no such order, the obligation under s 34(1)(a) would have remained; there would have been no definition under s 34(3) and the local authority would have had to make the concrete arrangements for the contact to take place. But, for my part, I could not say that it was plainly wrong for the court specifically to provide that the arrangements for contact should be within the discretion of the local authority, and, notwithstanding the 'no order' principle enshrined in s 1(5) of the Act, I think that in many cases it is beneficial that the court order should spell out that the arrangements for contact between a child and his or her parent are within the discretion of the local authority. I see no impugnable feature in relation to para (1) of the order.

Let me then marry that part of the order with the sentence in the reasons where the magistrates said:

'We would expect [such contact] to be at the rate of one session per month.'

The local authority object to that sentence. They say that either they are to be conferred with a discretion as to the regularity of contact or there is to be a defined order under s 34(2) or (3); and that it is an unsatisfactory half-way house for the court, having placed the matter into the discretion of the local authority, then to go on to express the expectation that contact with the mother would take place monthly.

My conclusion on the matter is, first of all, that the reference to an expectation of monthly contact is no part of the order that was made; and that, if the local authority, having weighed the matter appropriately, decided that contact should be less than monthly, or indeed more than monthly, they could not be criticised for so doing. My own experience of hearing at first instance applications for contact under s 34 is that it is often helpful for a court to express some sort of indication as to the amount of contact which, even if it is leaving the matter in the discretion of the authority, it envisages that the authority may favour. Bearing in mind that contact is the one area of the arrangements for children in care which under the 1989 Act is expressly placed into the ultimate hands of the court, it seems to me that it is not inapt for such an indication to be given. Nevertheless I have to say that, had I been judging the matter myself, I doubt that I would have used the word 'expect'. It seems to me that that word is rather too strong. To use the word 'expect' is indeed to raise expectations such that, if the mother was to get less than monthly contact, she might harbour an inapt sense of grievance that the local authority had departed from tramlines laid by the court. So one might have said not that one 'expects' monthly contact but that 'it is possible that the local authority would favour' monthly contact, or something of that sort. But this appeal is against an order; it is not against one word in the magistrates' long reasons. And, having offered the view that that verb is slightly too strong, I propose to leave that matter there.

...

I turn to the fourth paragraph of the order, which was for contact between each child and Mr S at the discretion of the local authority. Again a technicality arises. Mr S is not within the category of people able to apply without leave for contact under s 34 of the Act; and, although he was made a party to the proceedings in the court below, it is not even clear that he applied for leave, still less that he got it. So I think one must assume that this part of the order was made of the court's own motion under s 34(5) of the Act, which provides that:

'When making a care order with respect to a child ... the court may make an order under this section, even though no application for such an order has been made with respect to the child, if it considers that the order should be made.'

What does the order in favour of contact between the children and Mr S to be at the discretion of the local authority mean? I have come tentatively to the view that it means something slightly different from the order at para (1) for contact between the children and the mother to be at the discretion of the local authority. That order in favour of the mother I have analysed, by reference to s 34(1)(a) which provides that a local authority shall allow reasonable contact between a child in care and his parents. But Mr S does not fall within s 34(1), not being a parent of any of these three children or in any of the other categories specified in the subsection. So, as it seems to me, his position has to be analysed by reference to a different provision in the 1989 Act, namely Sch 2, para 15 to the Act.

Paragraph 15(1) provides that:

'Where a child is being looked after by a local authority, the authority shall, unless it is not reasonably practicable or consistent with his welfare, endeavour to promote contact between the child and ...

(c)   any relative, friend or other person connected with him.'

Mr S was for a period of time in the status of a stepfather to the children and he is, in my judgment, a person connected with the children; and so he falls within para 15(1)(c). So, quite apart from any order which might be made in favour of Mr S, there is a statutory obligation on the local authority, although in diluted terms in comparison with those to be collected under s 34(1): here, under para 15, the authority shall, unless it is not reasonably practicable or consistent with their welfare, endeavour to promote contact between the children and Mr S.

My view is, as it was when I analysed the order for contact with the mother, that one cannot construe the order referable to Mr S as eroding the statutory obligation, albeit in this case of a qualified nature, cast on the local authority. On the other hand, my view is that the order, while not subtracting from the obligation, adds nothing to it and that, unlike in the case of the provision for the mother, the local authority retains in respect of Mr S the discretion cast upon it by para 15, namely to weigh the benefit of contact between the children and Mr S; and that, if they determine that it is inconsistent with their welfare to have contact with him, they are under no obligation even to endeavour to promote it. In my view, therefore, the paragraph of the order referable to Mr S does no more than to flag up the limited duty cast upon the local authority under para 15 of the Schedule.

In other words, in respect of Mr S, the local authority are to decide whether there should be contact, and, if so, how much contact and in what circumstances. That analysis seems to equate with what the magistrates intended; for the last sentence in their reasons is:

'The children may benefit from contact with Mr S but this will be left to the discretion of the local authority.'

This case is also included in relation to:

D35 Orders / comments affecting contact after prospective adoption
H11 Judgment often as important as the order

D32　AUTHORISATION TO REFUSE CONTACT (1)

Re T (Termination of contact: discharge of order)

[1997] 1 FLR 517 at 523, 524 and 524

Court of Appeal

Simon Brown LJ

How, then, should the judge have approached the application to discharge that order? That is the novel question raised by this appeal, a question not apparently the subject of earlier authority.

Clearly the correct starting-point for the determination of this question must be a consideration of the circumstances in which it is appropriate to make a s 34(4) order in the first place.

As to this, Mr Wood invited us to give general guidance and more particularly an endorsement of his submission that a s 34(4) order will only ever be appropriate in three particular situations:

'(i)　where not to make such an order would thwart the local authority plans for the care and upbringing of the child made pursuant to the provisions of the care plan before the court on the making of the care order, and where those plans are imminently to be put into effect;

(ii)　where the nature and quality of the contact is such that it is not in the interests of the child for it to continue;

— (iii)　where the relevant named person in the order cannot be found.'

For my part I would resolutely decline both limbs of this invitation. As to general guidance, one must note this passage from the judgment of Sir Stephen Brown P in *Re E (A Minor) (Care Order: Contact)* [1994] 1 FLR 146, 153:

'The court has been very strongly pressed by Mr Harris in particular to give what he termed "guidance" on s 34 of the Children Act 1989. I do not consider it appropriate to say more than that this case endorses the approach indicated by Butler-Sloss LJ in the case of *Re B* (above) emphasising that contact must not be allowed to destabilise or endanger the arrangements for the child.'

Where the President himself has feared to tread it would be foolish indeed for us to rush in.

As for Mr Wood's tripartite proposition, that too I would reject as unhelpfully rigid and restrictive. What is meant by 'imminently' in (i)? The form of (ii) suggests that the requirement for a final termination of contact there is even more immediate than 'imminent'. As for (iii) it would be necessary to read into that the further postulate that if such person were suddenly to appear it would be necessary to prevent contact with the child.

Perhaps the greatest help on this part of the case is to be found in Butler-Sloss LJ's judgment in *Re L (Sexual Abuse: Standard of Proof)* [1996] 1 FLR 116. Not, however, from the first of the two passages on which Mr Wood sought to rely, namely (at 124E–125A):

…

Rather the helpful passage in *Re L* is the following, under the heading 'Contact' (at 126F):

…

> 'The order giving leave to terminate contact was contrary to the local authority's present intentions and to the indications made by the judge as to the possibility of rehabilitation. Section 34(1) requires a local authority to allow the child in care reasonable contact with his parents unless by s 34(4) the court authorises termination of such contact. A s 34(4) order in our view is appropriate where there is no likelihood of rehabilitation and the child is, for instance, to be placed for adoption or with foster-parents without continuing contact with the natural family. In the context of this case it was surprising that a s 34(4) order should be made and to do so to save a further application to the court if the circumstances should change had the effect of handing over to the local authority the residual responsibility still vested in the court. It was premature to make an order which was not to be implemented in the foreseeable future.'

With the aid of that passage one reaches this position: a s 34(4) order should not be made:

(a) whilst there remains a realistic possibility of rehabilitation of the child with the person in question, or
(b) merely against the possibility that circumstances may change in such a way as to make termination of contact desirable. For an order to be justified, a probable need to terminate contact must be foreseeable and not too remote.

Beyond that it seems to me impossible to go.

This case is also included in relation to:

D34 Application to discharge authorisation to refuse contact

D33   AUTHORISATION TO REFUSE CONTACT (2)

Re H (Termination of contact)

[2005] EWCA Civ 318, [2005] 2 FLR 408 at 409, 411 and 411

Court of Appeal

Thorpe and Sedley LJJ

THORPE LJ:

[3]   At the outset [the judge] identified the basis of the local authority's application. It was not a case in which they were saying that contact should terminate forthwith, or indeed within the foreseeable future. It was not a case in which it was said that parental contact should cease absolutely once an adoptive family had been identified and the process of introduction and placement commenced. The judge was quite plain that this was a case in which there should be post-adoption contact to the parents; so he identified the local authority's intended use of the s 34(4) order in these terms:

'Why do they want it? They say that as these children approach adoption it is necessary to enable them to move to the new placement to prevent them effectively seeing their parents.'

So the local authority sought this powerful order for the relatively restricted purpose of inserting a suspension into what was foreseen to be a long-term continuing relationship between parents and children.

[4]   The judge refused them their order for a number of clearly stated reasons. The first was that there had been no adopters identified. He said:

'It seems to me that we are some way off adoption, if indeed we ever get there.'

His second consideration was that, as I have already stated, this was a case where the expert evidence supported contact to the parents as not detrimental to the interests of the children in the long term. This, therefore, was not a case for closed adoption. The third consideration was that these were parents who were not predictably disruptive, either deliberately or even subconsciously, of a future adoptive placement. Fourthly, the judge made the point that, whilst the local authority's responsible use of the power was not in doubt so long as the current social work team were in charge, he could not have the same confidence once the responsibility moved to the permanence team, who would be responsible for implementing the introduction and placement. Finally, the judge made the attractive point that, were he to make a s 34(4) order, it would be sending out the wrong signals to all presently engaged with the case and also to prospective future adopters and that was something that would be contrary to the interests of the children.

[5] In passing, the judge referred to *Re G (Adoption: Contact)* [2002] EWCA Civ 761, [2003] 1 FLR 270, which Miss Earley in the course of her submissions has said provided no foundation at all for the decision ultimately taken by the judge.

[6] We have this morning heard from Mr Horrocks, for the guardian, who has drawn attention to the line of authority that seems to be nearest to determining any principle for the present appeal. The case of *Re L (Sexual Abuse: Standard of Proof)* [1996] 1 FLR 116 was primarily concerned with standard of proof in sex abuse cases, but towards the end of her judgment Butler Sloss LJ (as she then was), having cited a passage in the judgment below, said:

> 'The order giving leave to terminate contact was contrary to the local authority's present intentions and to the indications made by the judge as to the possibility of rehabilitation. Section 34(1) requires a local authority to allow the child in care reasonable contact with his parents unless by s 34(4) the court authorises termination of such contact. A s 34(4) order in our view is appropriate where there is no likelihood of rehabilitation and the child is, for instance, to be placed for adoption or with foster parents without continuing contact with the natural family. In the context of this case it was surprising that a s 34(4) order should be made and to do so to save a further application to the court if the circumstances should change had the effect of handing over to the local authority the residual responsibility still vested in the court. It was premature to make an order which was not to be implemented in the foreseeable future.'

That principle was reiterated in the later case of *Re T (Termination of Contact: Discharge of Order)* [1997] 1 WLR 393, [1997] 1 FLR 517 and more recently in *Re S (Care: Parental Contact)* [2004] EWCA Civ 1397, [2005] 1 FLR 469.

...

[11] In the end, it seems to me that this was an impeccable judgment, clearly explaining the exercise of a judicial discretion. The function of the judge in upholding the Parliamentary intention of s 34 and in granting s 34(4) orders restrictively and stringently is an important one. This case is not directly covered by the three authorities that I have cited, for the local

authority was able to go beyond simply saying that it might need the order one day in order to achieve placement. It was saying specifically that it would certainly need it in order to ensure the safe passage from foster care to adoption.

[12] However, in my judgment, that fine variation on the theme does not carry this case outside the principles to be extracted from the three cases cited. The judge was effectively applying those principles impeccably in questioning the appropriateness of such a powerful order for such an uncertain and limited future use. Miss Earley has said that, rather than dismissing the application, he might have adjourned it. Alternatively she says, ingeniously, that he might have granted the order but written in protection for the parents by applying conditions under s 34(7). That seems to me no criticism of the judge, nor any basis for this court to interfere, given that he was not invited to take either of those courses below.

SEDLEY LJ:

[15] Lord Atkin once remarked that justice and convenience are frequently not on speaking terms. Judge Shawcross was plainly alive to this. He was rightly concerned that leaving contact in the hands of the local authority might allow the best interests of the children to take second place to the practicalities of finding adopters with the minimum of impediment.

[16] The grounds on which Miss Earley persuaded Ward LJ, contrary to his initial view, and Rix LJ to grant permission to appeal candidly placed the local authority's practical difficulties in the foreground.

[17] In my view, although arguable, this is not an acceptable approach. As this court made clear in *Re B (Minors) (Termination of Contact: Paramount Consideration)* [1993] Fam 301, sub nom *Re B (Minors) (Care: Contact: Local Authority's Plans)* [1993] 1 FLR 543, at 311 and 551 respectively, the practical convenience of the local authority matters, but only to the extent that to impede it would be contrary to the best interests of the children. On Judge Shawcross's findings this was not such a case. It was a case in which the children needed as much continued contact with their natural parents as was compatible with the long-term plan for them. The s 34(4) order would not have prevented this, but it would have transferred the discretion to the local authority. It is not surprising that the judge preferred to ensure that the lifeline of parental contact should not for the time being be placed at risk of severance.

D34 APPLICATION TO DISCHARGE AUTHORISATION TO REFUSE CONTACT

Re T (Termination of contact: discharge of order)

[1997] 1 FLR 517 at 525, 527 and 528

Court of Appeal

Simon Brown LJ and Holman J

SIMON BROWN LJ:

Given that the above is the correct approach to the making of a s 34(4) order in the first place, in what circumstances should it be discharged? More particularly, what, if any, inhibitions are there upon a person's entitlement to seek such discharge?

In answering this question it is necessary first to note the following features of the s 34 scheme:

(i) All applications under s 34 must be decided by reference to s 1(1) and the welfare checklist in s 1(3) – see s 1(4)(b) (s 34 being in Part IV of the Act).

(ii) Prima facie a child in local authority care should be allowed reasonable contact with, amongst others, his parents – see s 34(1). The local authority's obligations, indeed, go further: Sch 2, para 15(1) to the Act provides:

'Where a person is being looked after by a local authority, the authority shall, unless it is not reasonably practicable or consistent with his welfare, endeavour to promote contact between the child and—

(a) his parents; ...' [A child in local authority care is by definition 'being looked after' by them – see ss 105(4) and 22(1).]

(iii) How much or little contact is 'reasonable' must be for the local authority to decide subject to any order of the court – and the local authority's duty under Sch 2 to 'promote' (ie encourage and facilitate) contact arises only if and insofar as they perceive this to be consistent with the child's welfare. Bearing in mind, however, that even in cases of urgent necessity s 34(6) permits only refusal of contact for up to 7 days, it may be thought that reasonable contact should not ordinarily be unduly restricted unless by agreement or pursuant to court order – for which, of course, the local authority itself may apply under s 34(2).

(iv) Under s 34(3) a 'named person', including a parent, can apply for contact, or increased contact, at any time. Logically, however, if a s 34(4) order is in place – whether or not the local authority has then actually made use of it to refuse contact – any such application would need to be coupled with an application under s 34(9) for the discharge of the s 34(4) order.

(v) The only express statutory restriction upon the making of any kind of s 34 application is that provided by s 91(17) of the Act:

'Where—

(a) a person has made an application for an order under section 34;

(b) the application has been refused; and

(c) a period of less than six months has elapsed since the refusal,

that person may not make a further application for such an order with respect to the same child, unless he has obtained the leave of the court.'

With those considerations in mind, I turn now to consider what should be the court's general approach to a s 34(9) application for the discharge of a s 34(4) order.

Clearly such an application must be considered by the court, and considered indeed with the child's welfare in mind as the paramount consideration – save only in the very limited circumstances provided for by s 91(17) when the court's leave is required.

That said, it is plain that there must be demonstrable some material change of circumstance between the making of the s 34(4) order and the application to discharge it: the courts are obviously entitled to screen out what are essentially no more than disguised appeals against the original orders.

...

Applying these considerations to an application to discharge a s 34(4) order, I conclude that the court should initially have two main interlocking considerations in mind: first, the extent to which circumstances have changed from when the order was originally made; and secondly, bearing those changes in mind, the extent to which it now seems appropriate to reinvestigate the central question. The court should ask itself: where on the 'spectrum of procedure' should this particular application be placed? Clearly the greater the apparent change in circumstances, the more intensively will the court be prepared to reconsider the desirability of leaving the s 34(4) order in place.

I would not myself speak in terms of the onus being on the applicant. But it should certainly be borne in mind that there are clear implications in all this not merely for the best use of court time but more importantly for the welfare of the children themselves. Children are often aware of the court's processes and troubled by the uncertainty and disruption engendered. Nor should the courts be expected to welcome applications which essentially seek to reopen already decided questions.

Let me now return to consider the present appeal on its own facts.

HOLMAN J:

I agree with all that my Lord has said as to the proper approach of the court on an application under s 34(9) to discharge an earlier order under s 34(4), and summarise my views as follows:

(1)   It is not appropriate on such an application to reinvestigate whether the original order was appropriately made in the circumstances prevailing when it was made. Indeed the court must be astute to see that the application made under s 34(9) is a bona fide application to discharge, and not a disguised attempt to appeal, the earlier order. To this extent, but only to this extent, there is an onus on the applicant to show, as a threshold test, that there has been some change of circumstances such that the application is a genuine application made in the light of those changed circumstances. There is no greater threshold test since the discretion in s 34(9) is unqualified and there is no statutory restriction on the right to apply unless s 91(17) applies. The inquiry at this stage should not be elaborate and, indeed, one would often expect the point to be conceded.

(2)   Once that threshold is passed, the duty of the court is to apply the tests in s 1(1), (2), (3) and (5) of the Children Act. I agree with my Lord that we should not attempt to lay down any guidance save to say that it could not be right to make an order under s 34(4), nor subsequently to leave one in place, unless at the time the court is considering, or reconsidering the matter: (a) there is no realistic possibility of rehabilitation of the child with the person in question; and (b) a probable need to terminate contact is foreseeable and not too remote.

(3)   A judge hearing an application to discharge is entitled to, and indeed must, consider where on the 'spectrum of procedure' described by Butler-Sloss LJ in *Re B (Minors) (Contact)* [1994]

2 FLR 1, 5G the particular application should be placed. If that question arises at an interlocutory hearing, then the sort of considerations referred to by Butler-Sloss LJ at 6A–D are likely to be relevant.

(4) Like my Lord, I doubt whether it is helpful to speak in terms of onus once the threshold to which I have referred in para (1) above is passed. If, exceptionally, the court considers at the conclusion of the inquiry that the factors are so evenly balanced as not to come down on one side or the other on the question of discharge, then I, for my part, would consider that the order should be discharged. If an order under s 34(4) cannot be justified, it should not remain in force.

(5) Clearly, orders under s 34(3) and (4) cannot logically co-exist (unless, unusually, there is an order for contact for a limited period under s 34(3) coupled with an order under s 34(4) to take effect at the end of that period). But I see no reason why an application under s 34(3) cannot be considered together with an application under s 34(9) for the discharge of an order under s 34(4), at any rate once the threshold referred to in para (1) above is passed. Once the threshold is passed, the issues under s 34(3) and (4) need to be considered together and in the round. If the court concludes that there should be a positive order for contact under s 34(3), then, save in the unusual situation mentioned above, it will logically discharge the s 34(4) order. But the s 34(4) order does not have to be got out of the way before the court can consider s 34(3).

This case is also included in relation to:

D32 Authorisation to refuse contact (1)

D35   ORDERS / COMMENTS AFFECTING CONTACT AFTER PROSPECTIVE ADOPTION

L v London Borough of Bromley

[1998] 1 FLR 709 at 718 and 720

Family Division

Wilson J

The magistrates endorsed the care plans referable to the children; and for A the care plan was that she should be adopted. She is the least damaged of the three; she is the youngest of the three and she is appraised to be ready to move into her permanent home straightaway ...

The plan for A was, of course, for open adoption. The local authority were proposing that, even after adoption, she should see the mother once a year and the two older children twice a year; and that she should have indirect contact with the father and paternal grandmother. Such a plan for A rules out all those prospective adopters who feel that they could not tolerate any degree of openness about the adoption. So that plan, limited though it is, limits the pool of possible families for A. But it limits the pool necessarily in her interests.

But, going on from there, the orders of the magistrates and the reasons which they expressed create very grave problems in terms of A's placement. The orders themselves I have already noticed. For the mother, contact with A is to be in the discretion of the local authority; but when you marry that up with the reference in the reasons to an expectation of 12 times a year and when, to those 12 occasions, you add the three occasions of defined contact for A with her father and paternal grandmother, you get 15 occasions of contact a year.

I ask rhetorically: how many adopters are going to be able to tolerate that degree of contact with the biological family? ...

What can the local authority tell proposed adopters about this little girl in their bid to find her an early permanent home? Were these orders and reasons to remain without the addition which I am about to offer, they would have to tell the proposed adopters that in effect the regime blessed by the court for contact between A and the biological family was 15 visits a year. That is an enormous inroad into the family life into which A, as an adopted child, is intended, as a full legal member, to move.

...

So my conclusion is that, if I focus on the short term, I find all these orders for contact unimpeachable on appeal. But I also find that the reasons of the magistrates failed to address the likely need for a substantial reduction in A's contact after her adoption and indeed introduction to her adopters. That, as I have suggested, creates grave practical problems now.

The bringing of this appeal, although it has failed, enables me to say what the magistrates did not say; and it enables me to clear the way for the early implementation by the local authority of the care plan for the little girl. The care plan is that she should be adopted and for a degree of openness in the adoption but not for so much contact as to destabilise it. And if you destabilise the adopters, you destabilise the adoption. The search must be for adopters who will tolerate limited face-to-face contact with the mother; for adopters who will tolerate limited face-to-face contact with the two older children; for adopters who will tolerate some contact, perhaps indirect, with the father and the paternal grandmother. I cannot be more specific than that. Were I to do so, I would be prejudging matters. What I can say is that reasonable adopters can reasonably expect the courts, both the Bromley Family Proceedings Court (and this court, if A's case ever came up here again on appeal) to reduce contact to a level which they find acceptable, provided that it maintains some links, which at A's age can never be eradicated, between her and her biological family.

General notes:

Contact in the context of adoption raises the following possibilities for the birth family:

- when a PO is made: see E10 – ACA 2002, ss 26 and 27: contact on making PO;
- when an AO is made: see E12 – ACA 2002, s 46(6): contact on making AO;
- after AO is made: see B39 – CA 1989, s 10(4): birth parent no longer a 'parent' after adoption; B44 – CA 1989, s 10(9): broad assessment / post-adoption contact; and B45 – CA 1989, s 10(9): process when birth family apply after adoption.

This case is also included in relation to:

D31 Contact at the discretion of the LA
H11 Judgment often as important as the order

Supervision

D36 APPLICATION OF NO ORDER PRINCIPLE

Re K; A Local Authority v N and Others

[2005] EWHC 2956 (Fam), [2007] 1 FLR 399 at 414

Family Division

Munby J

[54] At K's request I saw her in private, though in the presence of her solicitor. She reiterated her views, very much as I have already set them out. She told me that she intends to go to college – the same college her older sister is already attending. She struck me as more grown up – more mature – than when she had spoken to me in similar circumstances a little under a year earlier. And I also gained the distinct impression – not merely from our conversation, but also from what went on in court during the hearing – that her understanding of and ability to speak English has improved significantly over the last year.

[55] The guardian agrees that the threshold criteria are met but, on the basis of the 'no order' principle, opposes the making of a supervision order. She considers that for the following reasons it would be better for there to be no order than a supervision order:

(i) K has indicated a clear opposition to the making of an order. The guardian does not consider that it will assist the local authority in supporting K if an order is made against her expressed wishes. The guardian believes that if such an order were to be made it would undermine the limited but positive support the social worker has been able to provide to K over the last nine months.

(ii) On the assumption that the parents are also in opposition to the orders sought by the local authority, the guardian is concerned that the making of a supervision order will be counter productive to the family working with social services in the future. While the family has not welcomed the involvement of social services the family has, over the last 9 months when there has been no order, co-operated to enable the social worker to meet with K at the family home. They have also attended, to a limited extent, the CAMHS services offered, and facilitated K's attendance for counselling. The guardian is concerned that the making of an order against the parents' wishes will make them less likely to seek and utilise the support of social services in the future.

(iii) Without some co-operation from K and her parents the local authority will be in difficulties fulfilling its responsibilities to K under the supervision order. The guardian is mindful that the local authority has worked with the family without an order since 17 January 2005.

(iv) The guardian has detailed in her report the future support she recommends the social worker provides to K and her family. The guardian considers that these limited services could be provided by the local authority under Part III of the 1989 Act rather than under Part IV. The guardian notes in this context that the local authority will continue to try to have K's case allocated to the existing social worker and that there is in any event no guarantee that the social worker will continue to be allocated even if there is a supervision order.

[56] I agree with the guardian, and essentially for the reasons she gives, that there should not be a supervision order.

[57] I have to face the realities. They are that I have a girl aged almost 17, and her parents, who are unwilling to co-operate with public authorities if required by order to do so. Compulsion was recognised as long ago as January 2005 to be no longer appropriate. K has been living at home for some time now, without the local authority having the benefit of any kind of public law order at all. It is clear that, whatever may remain to be done, things are much better for K now than they have been for quite some time. Relations between K and her parents seem much improved. There has been no recent repetition of the florid episodes of a year ago. To an extent, K and her family have been able to co-operate with the local authority despite the absence of any formal order. That co-operation is much less than might be thought desirable, but I do not think that a supervision order is going to improve matters, or increase the chances of co-operation; if anything the reverse.

[58] The local authority has rightly disavowed compulsion by means of secure accommodation; it has rightly concluded that it is not appropriate for it to share parental responsibility. I do not in any way criticise it for seeking a supervision order, but on balance I agree with the guardian that a supervision order is unlikely to achieve anything and that it may even be counter-productive.

This case is also included in relation to:

D20 The reasonable parent and cultural realities

D37 CANNOT ATTACH CONDITIONS TO SO

Re V (Care or supervision order)

[1996] 1 FLR 776 at 781, 785 and 787

Court of Appeal

Waite LJ

The findings made by the judge at the hearing can be stated shortly because they are not challenged by the parents in this appeal. They were favourable to the local authority, whose care application was fully supported by the guardian ad litem, to this extent. The judge found that, left to herself, the mother would not allow S to continue to attend Hollybank but would keep him at home. The opportunities for mobility, proper posture control, companionship, stimulation and learning at Hollybank contrasted strongly with the isolation and passivity involved in the mother's care. This meant, so the judge found, that home care for him would involve putting him at risk of significant harm. The threshold requirements for a public law order were accordingly established.

In his discretion, however, the judge declined to make a care order on the ground that he thought it would run too grave a risk of causing a breakdown in the parents' marriage and thus the collapse of the home that S undoubtedly loves and on which he is likely to be partly, at least, dependent when he comes of age and becomes a severely disabled adult in just over a year's time. The course favoured by the judge was to grant, instead, a supervision order subject to conditions ...

...

After naming the child the order continues at para 2:

'The court orders that this child shall:

(1) Attend Hollybank School as a weekly boarder and take part in all school activities as arranged.
(2) S should only not attend school if he is certified unfit by a medical practitioner.
(3) Each Monday S should take £20 from his State allowances for use in activities arranged by the school.
(4) S should attend meetings at PHAB at Dewsbury when they have been arranged.'

Miss Hamilton has argued on behalf of the guardian ad litem, with the support of the local authority (which in the interests of saving costs has not been represented on this appeal), that the judge's approach to the making of a supervision order was misconceived. In the first place, he spoke of conditions attached to his proposed supervision order. That is something, Miss Hamilton points out, for which the Act makes no provision at all. Schedule 3 is confined to dealing with directions to be given by the supervisor and requirements to be imposed with consent by the court. Those requirements, moreover, are dependent upon the consent of any 'responsible person'. Such an individual is defined in Sch 3, para 1 as meaning in relation to a supervised child:

'... any person who has parental responsibility for the child ...'

Accordingly, if the conditions imposed by the judge are to be viewed as Sch 3 requirements, they needed the consent of the mother and the father. In fact, at the stage of the hearing before the judge, no such consent had been forthcoming from either of them.

Miss Hamilton further points out, and this is accepted by counsel for the mother and the father, that the so-called conditions 2 and 3 are provisions which the judge would in any event have had no jurisdiction to introduce into a supervision order under any guise whatsoever.

Despite the brave efforts made by Mrs Pope, for the mother, and Miss Trimmer, for the father, to defend the form of order chosen by the judge, the criticisms made of it by Miss Hamilton are, in my view, well founded. The concept of a supervision order subject to conditions simply cannot be fitted into the framework of the Children Act legislation. The judge may have been misled by the suggestions in the statement of the social worker that such an option was available. The fact that Sch 3 to the Act was not cited to him may have added to his difficulties. Nevertheless, there is no escaping from the inference that the judge had misconceived the nature and the purpose of a supervision order.

...

What of a care order? The judge was clearly right to give weight to the risk of a rift in the marriage of the mother and the father. Their separation would, of course, have serious consequences for S. For myself I would, however, measure that risk, grave though its implications are, as of a great deal less account than the risk of the serious injury which S stands to suffer if he were to be deprived of the opportunities of all that Hollybank can give him during the crucial last 12 months of his minority.

For those reasons I would, for my part, grant a care order in favour of the local authority. I would envisage that in principle there should be an order for contact to the parents. We do not, however, have the local authority represented in court today. I would hope that it is sufficient to give a general indication that contact should be at the discretion of the local authority with liberty to any party to apply, if need be, to the Leeds County Court for further directions as to contact.

D38   EXTENSION OF SO

Re A (Supervision order: extension)

[1995] 1 FLR 335 at 337

Court of Appeal

Butler-Sloss and Hoffmann LJJ and Sir Tasker Watkins

There is no direct guidance in the Act on the criteria to be applied on the hearing of an extension application. One has to stand back and look at the purpose of the extension of the supervision order ...

If s 31 was to be imported into an application to extend an existing supervision order there would be no purpose to the specific provision in Sch 3, Part II, para 6. At the expiry of the one-year period the local authority or other supervisor would be required to make a fresh application under s 31. Looking at the framework of the Act, the s 31 application was clearly not intended to be invoked on extension applications, and bearing in mind the earlier provision for a 3-year period, the purpose of the alteration is in my view clear. It allows the local authority to keep in place a supervision order for 3 years as before but under the greater control of the courts, part of the philosophy of the Act at the application stage. After one year the local authority has to justify to the court that the welfare of the child requires the supervision order to continue and there is an opportunity for the application to extend to be opposed.

... If the application to extend the supervision order is within time and opposed but the hearing date is after the original supervision order has expired, the court can make one or more short extension orders pending the determination of the opposed application ...

A technical but important consequence of not importing the provisions of s 31 into an application to extend a supervision order is lack of jurisdiction in the court to make a care order on an extension application, whereas by s 31(5) the court may:

'(b)   on an application for a supervision order, make a care order.'

I am satisfied that the view of the judge that this was a s 31 application and that he had jurisdiction to make a care order was wrong. In the absence of a specific application by the local authority under s 31 there was no jurisdiction to make an interim care order.

Other significant cases on this issue:

- Cf *Wakefield MDC v T* [2008] EWCA Civ 199, [2008] 1 FLR 1569 (a supervision order cannot be made for 3 years in the first instance)

Section 37 direction

D39 GENERAL GUIDANCE

Re M (Intractable contact dispute: interim care order)

[2003] EWHC 1024 (Fam), [2003] 2 FLR 636 at 638

Family Division

Wall J

Introduction

[6] I have decided to publish my two principal judgments in this case in order to demonstrate one method of addressing an intractable contact dispute. I am immediately conscious, of course, that the case turns on its particular facts, although the phenomenon it represents is by no means uncommon. This was the second time I had used the s 37 procedure to remove children who were being denied all contact with their non-residential parent, and were suffering significant harm because of the residential parent's false and distorted belief system about the non-residential parent, which the children had imbibed.

[7] I am also conscious of the fact that there is a tendency in family law to see an outcome such as this as a panacea – a one-size-fits-all solution. I emphasise that this is not the case, indeed, this judgment comes with a series of strong health warnings.

[8] First, of course, s 37, which I set out at para [121] of this judgment, can only be used if the facts of the case meet its criteria. It must appear to the court that 'it may be appropriate for a care or supervision order to be made' with respect to the children in question. In other words, at the very lowest, the court must be satisfied that there are reasonable grounds for believing that the circumstances with respect to the children meet the threshold criteria under s 31(2) – that is to say that the children are suffering or are likely to suffer significant harm. Section 37 is, accordingly, a well-focused tool, to be used only when the case fits its criteria.

[9] It is sometimes forgotten that the court has the power to make an interim care order when it gives a direction under s 37 (see s 38(1)(b) of

the Children Act 1989). The definition of 'specified proceedings' (ibid s 41(6)(b)) includes private law proceedings for contact or residence orders in which the court has given a direction under s 37(1) and has made or is considering whether to make an interim care order. In these circumstances a children's guardian must be appointed under s 41(1) unless the court is satisfied that it is not necessary to do so in order to safeguard the children's interests.

[10] In the instant case, the children were already represented by CAFCASS Legal when I made the s 37 direction. Had they not been, I am in no doubt that I would have appointed a guardian to represent them.

[11] Although this case is but an example, it does seem to me that it is possible to extract some general considerations of wider application from it. I put these forward tentatively, as each case is different, and what fits one may not fit another. Some points are self-evident, but need stating nonetheless. I will state them in short form and then expand on them where necessary:

(1) The court must be satisfied that the criteria for ordering a s 37 report are satisfied (see para [8] above).

(2) The action contemplated (removal of the children from the residential parent's care either for an assessment or with a view to a change of residence) must be in the children's best interests. The consequences of the removal must be thought through. There must, in short, be a coherent care plan of which temporary or permanent removal from the residential parent's care is an integral part.

(3) Where, as here, the allegation is that the children have been sexually or physically abused by the absent parent, the court must have held a hearing in which those issues were addressed, and findings made about them (see para [12] below).

(4) The court must spell out its reasons for making the s 37 order very carefully, and a transcript (or a very full note) of the judgment should be made available to the local authority at the earliest opportunity (see paras [13]–[14] below).

(5) The children should be separately represented (see paras [15]–[16] below).

(6) Preferably, the s 37 report should be supported by professional or expert advice (see para [17] below).

(7) Judicial continuity is essential. Apart from saving time and resources, this means that applications can be made to the judge at short notice, and she or he can keep tight control over it.

(8) Undue delay must be avoided (see paras [18] and [19] below).

(9) The case may need to be kept under review if (as in the instant case) the decision of the court is to move the children from one parent to another (see paras [20] and [21] below).

Findings of fact

[12] In the instant case, the residential parent asserted that the children
had been sexually and physically abused by the non-residential and the
latter's parents. This was not true. I was, however, only able to proceed on
the basis that it was not true because there had been clear and compelling
findings by an experienced circuit judge, and I was able to confirm those
findings by the evidence I heard. It is, in my judgment, very important
that the local authority should know the court's findings and prepare its
report on the basis of those findings. In an intractable contact dispute,
where the residential parent is putting forward an allegedly factual basis
for contact not taking place, there is no substitute, in my judgment, for
findings by the court as to whether or not there is any substance to the
allegations.

Letting the local authority know the reasons for making the order

[13] In my judgment, it is vital for the local authority to know the
judge's thinking in making the order. Even if such an order is made
urgently, a note of the reasons for it should, in my judgment, be prepared
and made available to the local authority. Apart from anything else, clear
reasons for the order save a great deal of time, and enable the local
authority to focus on the salient points. In the instant case, I reserved
judgment and shortly afterwards handed down the first of the two
judgments set out below in a form designed to be read by both the parties
and the local authority. In its original form, the first judgment was
cross-referenced to the court bundles which were also disclosed to the
local authority. Such a course may not be practical in other cases,
particularly where the report is urgently required. However, it is not
enough, in my judgment, for the local authority simply to be told the
judge has ordered a s 37 report. The local authority needs to know why
the judge has done so.

[14] It is prosaic thought, but when making a s 37 order the court should
be clear about how the order is going to be communicated to the local
authority and by whom. There is nothing more likely to cause delay than
the absence of a speedy mechanism for conveying the order to the local
authority. I have on at least one occasion written short reasons, told the
bar what they were, and then sent them by facsimile to an identified
officer of the local authority.

Separate representation

[15] It is my view that one of the prime categories for the tandem model
of separate representation in private law proceedings is where all contact
has ceased and the issue of contact has become intractable. Children in

this situation frequently have an interest in the proceedings and in the outcome which is independent from the viewpoint being advanced by each of their parents.

[16]　As I have stated in para [10], in the instant case the children were already represented by the time the case reached me. Generally, however, if an intractable contact dispute has reached the stage where it is ripe for a s 37 report, then in my judgment it is at a stage where separate representation is necessary. If the report recommends care proceedings, the guardian already in place can act as guardian in those proceedings. If it does not, the court is going to have to try an alternative approach. This is an area where the independent tandem model, in my experience, has proved extremely helpful in providing advice and, where necessary, obtaining expert evidence.

Expert advice

[17]　In the instant case, as the first judgment shows, a complication was that removal was supported by the children's guardian and opposed by the psychiatrist she had instructed to advise on the children's behalf. It is, however, of material assistance to a court if there has been an investigation by an expert who has come to the view that the children are suffering significant harm and that local authority intervention is necessary. This advice does not, however, in my judgment necessarily have to come from a psychiatrist or psychologist. A competent Children and Family Court Advisory and Support Service (CAFCASS) report by a court reporter should identify the problem.

Delay

[18]　Where a report is ordered, the date for its receipt and for the giving of further directions must be specified. If a guardian is required, and CAFCASS Legal cannot allocate a guardian immediately, a guardian from another source should be appointed. This can either be a specialist solicitor who can then instruct an independent social worker to undertake the guardian role, or an organisation such as the National Youth Advocacy Service (NYAS).

[19]　In this case, there was inexcusable delay between 8 February 2001 when the order inviting the Official Solicitor to represent the children was made, and 27 September 2001, when the children were joined as parties to the proceedings. The very fact of ordering a s 37 report involves an element of delay. It is very important that this should be minimised. This requires strict judicial control: hence one of the needs for judicial continuity.

Keeping the case under review

[20] The object of care proceedings following the s 37 report in this case was to relieve the children from the significant harm they were suffering with their residential parent, and to restore their relationship with their non-residential parent. In the longer term, the aim was to enable the children to retain a good relationship with both parents. That objective is defeated if, having regained their relationship with the non-residential parent they then lose it with the parent from whose care they have been removed.

[21] In my judgment, therefore, it may well be desirable for the case to be kept under review – alternatively, as here, the court should satisfy itself that mechanisms were in place to address the issue of ongoing contact.

Generally

[22] It has to be acknowledged that the s 37 process is heavy on resources and takes time. At the same time, the stakes for the children are very high. Decisions to remove children from the homes they know and in which they feel secure are difficult. The consequences can be traumatic.

Other significant cases on this issue:

* *Re F (Family proceedings: section 37 investigation)* [2005] EWHC 2935 (Fam), [2006] 1 FLR 1122 (s 37 direction not yet appropriate)

D40 NOT TO FETTER LA INVESTIGATION / USE OF OFFICIAL SOLICITOR

Re M (Official Solicitor's role)

[1998] 2 FLR 815 at 818, 818 and 819

Court of Appeal

Thorpe and Butler-Sloss LJJ

THORPE LJ:

If a judge wishes to bring in the local authority under s 37 then it is, in my opinion, unnecessary and indeed undesirable that the judge should seek to fetter the local authority in the execution of its statutory function. Equally, in my opinion, if a judge seeks to bring in the Official Solicitor to the case it must be upon the basis that the Official Solicitor will have his customary unlimited discretion as to how he fulfils his function. As is pointed out by Miss McGregor in her skeleton, if the proceedings are specified then the role of the Official Solicitor is as directed by the Lord Chancellor under s 90(3) of the Supreme Court Act 1981. The direction which the Lord Chancellor has given is reported at [1991] 2 FLR 471. Equally, as Miss McGregor points out, if the proceedings are private law proceedings the role of the Official Solicitor is historic, unprescribed by statute and recognised by numerous authorities in this court to be of the widest discretionary character.

It also seems to me that it was quite wrong for the judge to have sought to use the Official Solicitor as the extension of his judicial power by which he would impose regulation on the local authority.

...

Where a judge has the opportunity of independent investigation by the Official Solicitor and where the judge has set the case over for 3 months to enable the Official Solicitor to carry out his independent investigation, it seems to me as a matter of general approach that it is undesirable to make any radical innovation in advance of the Official Solicitor's report.

BUTLER-SLOSS LJ:

I would only underline three points in particular: first, if you are going to ask the Official Solicitor to come in, it is appropriate to give the Official Solicitor the opportunity to have some space and time to work out what is the best way to deal with the case which is inevitably a difficult one if the Official Solicitor is asked to take part. Consequently, to involve both the Official Solicitor and the local authority in a s 37 inquiry under the Children Act is in my view inappropriate at the stage at which the judge did it.

D41   APPOINTMENT / LIMITED ROLE OF CG

Re CE (Section 37 direction)

[1995] 1 FLR 26 at 36, 37, 38, 41, 42, 43 and 45

Family Division

Wall J

I draw three important strands from my recitation of s 37. The first is that a precondition of the making of an order under s 37 is the fact that it has to appear to the court that it may in due course be appropriate for a care or supervision order to be made in relation to the child. The second is that the section lays down a specific timescale for the provision of the s 37 report. The third is that the s 37 report is an essentially interim measure: it is a means of assisting the court in its assessment of the options available for dealing with the child.

...

In my judgment, s 41(6)(b) is plainly complementary to s 37(1). A court makes an order under s 37 if it appears to the court that a care or supervision order may be appropriate; it appoints a guardian ad litem (unless satisfied that it is not necessary to do so in order to safeguard the child's interests) if, having made a direction under s 37 it either makes an interim care order or is considering whether to make an interim care order. The reference in s 41(6)(b) to interim orders underlines, in my judgment, the preliminary nature of the s 37 investigation.

...

Should a guardian ad litem be appointed under s 41(6)(b) where an investigation under s 37 is directed?

It is quite plain from the provisions which I have recited, and from the very wide powers given to the guardian ad litem under s 42 of the Act, that the guardian ad litem is a person of critical importance in specified (public law) proceedings. He (or as often she) is the independent voice of the child. Furthermore, he or she is the independent investigator/ watchdog endowed by the statute with the widest possible powers of investigation and charged with the duty of bringing to the attention of the court all matters relevant to the welfare of the child.

The corollary of the very wide powers given to the guardian ad litem in my judgment is the very great responsibility which the office bears. It follows that the guardian ad litem is a very valuable resource. It also follows in my judgment, that when exercising the power to appoint a guardian ad litem under s 41(6)(b) of the Act the court should exercise great caution and should give careful consideration both to the guardian's likely role and the information which the court requires the guardian to provide. In my judgment, the appointment of a guardian ad litem should in no sense be automatic in cases where a report under s 37 is directed.

It follows, in my judgment, that when making a direction under s 37(1) the court should always direct its mind to the specific purpose of the s 37 investigation and consider whether or not the interests of the child can be safeguarded without a guardian being appointed at that stage. If the court decides that at that stage it is not necessary to appoint a guardian in order to safeguard the interests of the child, no guardian should be appointed.

Plainly, where the court requires a preliminary investigation under s 37 it is not difficult to imagine circumstances in which either the guardian will have no role to play in the investigation or, to put the matter at its lowest, the need for and likely role of a guardian ad litem will not be clear until such time as the s 37 investigation is completed.

...

I therefore draw a distinction in the first category of case identified by the guardian ad litem between those cases in which the court actually makes an interim care order when directing the s 37 investigation (which I anticipate will be rare) and those cases where the court is considering making an order. In the former, I anticipate that it would be more likely that the court would take the view that the immediate appointment of a guardian ad litem would be required to protect the child's interests. In the latter, it may well be more appropriate to await the outcome of the s 37 investigation before appointing a guardian.

It is both undesirable and impossible for the court to attempt to lay down definitive criteria for the circumstances in which it is appropriate for a guardian ad litem to be appointed under s 41(6)(b) in the context of a s 37 investigation. The facts will plainly vary from case to case. However, in my judgment the following considerations are clearly relevant:

(1) Is it a case in which the court is actually making an interim order as opposed to giving consideration to making an interim order? In the former category the circumstances of the case are likely to be serious and unusual and it may well be appropriate for the appointment of a guardian ad litem to be made immediately.

(2)   If the court is only considering making an interim order, what factors are there in the circumstances of the case which require the appointment of a guardian ad litem to represent the interests of the child?

(3)   Given the timescale which the court will set for the investigation, will there in practice be time for the guardian and litem to be informed of the issues in the case and play a useful role?

(4)   Is there in any case a specific role for the guardian ad litem to play in the investigation itself, particularly where a very short timescale is fixed for the s 37 investigation?

(5)   Will the child's interests be properly safeguarded in the interim and during the course of the investigation without the appointment of a guardian ad litem?

(6)   Does the child have his or her own solicitor?

As submitted by the guardian ad litem in the instant case, the court must in my judgment be aware of the practical constraints on panels. It must also ensure that its order reaches both the local authority and the guardian ad litem (where one is appointed) promptly.

...

The meaning of s 41(6)

In the context of the duration of an order for the appointment of a guardian ad litem under s 41(6)(b) what does the phrase, ' ... and has made, or is considering whether to make, an interim care order' mean? Two interpretations were argued before me:

(1)   The whole phrase relates only to the moment when the court makes its order under s 37. At that moment the proceedings are specified proceedings because the court when it makes the s 37 order, has either made or is considering making an interim care order. For the purposes of the guardian ad litem's involvement therefore, this fixes the proceedings as specified proceedings, and the appointment stands irrespective of any subsequent change in the status of the proceedings. Thus even if the s 37 order results in a report from the local authority which states that the local authority does not intend to apply for a care or supervision order, this does not affect the validity of the guardian ad litem's appointment. On this analysis, the guardian ad litem remains in place until discharged by the court under FPR 1991, r 4.11.

(2)   The proceedings only remain specified proceedings for as long as the court has in contemplation making an interim care order. As soon as the prospect of an interim care order disappears (for example, because the local authority indicates in the s 37 report that it does not propose to apply for such an order) the proceedings cease to be 'specified proceedings'. Since the guardian ad litem is appointed

under s 41(1) 'for the purposes of any specified proceedings' the role of the guardian ad litem, if one has been appointed under s 41(6)(b), comes to an end when the proceedings cease to be specified proceedings.

I would have liked to have been able to accept the argument set out in the first of the two interpretations, but find myself, with regret, unable to do so. In my judgment, where an order has been made under s 37(1) and the proceedings have become 'specified proceedings' by virtue of s 41(6)(b) the proceedings cease to be 'specified proceedings' if the local authority, as a result of its investigation, decides not to apply for a care order or a supervision order and so informs the court.

...

The status of the guardian ad litem

What is the status of a guardian ad litem appointed under s 41(6)(b) where the local authority files its report stating that it does not intend to apply for care or supervision orders? Does his or her appointment thereby come to an end? In my judgment, the logic which I have applied hitherto requires an affirmative answer to the second question. My answer is, however, subject to two important provisos.

In my judgment it must follow, that if the proceedings cease to be 'specified proceedings' on the making of a s 37 report in which the local authority resolves not to take proceedings for a care or supervision order, any appointment of a guardian ad litem under s 41(6)(b) must cease to be 'for the purpose of any specified proceedings' (s 41(1)).

However, FPR 1991, r 4.10(9) provides that the appointment of the guardian ad litem 'shall continue for such time as is specified in the appointment or until terminated by the court'. Where no time is specified in the order (as in the instant case), the appointment of the guardian ad litem subsists until it is terminated by the court. This is my first proviso. Where an appointment of a guardian ad litem has been made under s 41(6)(b) and the proceedings thereafter cease to be 'specified proceedings', the termination of the guardian ad litem's appointment should always be by judicial rather than administrative act.

A distinction can, I think, be properly drawn between the termination of the guardian ad litem's appointment on the making of a full care order (which requires no specific judicial act) and the termination of the guardian ad litem's appointment where the proceedings cease to be 'specified proceedings'. In the former case the proceedings have, in effect, come to an end. The court has made a care order and has handed responsibility for the child over to the local authority. It is thereafter functus officio. In the case of an appointment under s 41(6)(b) where the proceedings subsequently cease to be specified, it is highly unlikely that the proceedings themselves will have come to an end. The court remains seized of the child's welfare. In these circumstances, it seems to me that the court should only dispense with the services of the guardian ad litem after giving the matter due consideration and after hearing representations from the guardian ad litem and the other parties.

It follows, in my judgment, that when a guardian ad litem is appointed under s 41(6)(b) the practice ought to be that the order making the appointment should contain a direction for the question of the guardian ad litem's continuing involvement to be reviewed on completion of the s 37 report, and to this end a directions appointment should be fixed for a date shortly after the date upon which the s 37 report is due to be received by the court. At that directions appointment, the future conduct of the case can be considered and the discharge or continuing involvement of the guardian ad litem decided upon.

It will always be open to a guardian ad litem appointed under s 41(6)(b) to apply to the court for directions as to his or her future involvement or to inform the court by letter that he or she has no representations to make. I am, however, quite clear that no appointment of a guardian ad litem under s 41(6)(b) should be terminated without an order of the court.

...

It therefore follows that although the appointment of a guardian ad litem under s 41(6)(b) cannot continue when the proceedings cease to be specified proceedings, there remains a discretion in the High Court or the county court to appoint a guardian ad litem under FPR 1991, r 9.5.

It will, I think, be an unusual case in which the court will either wish or be able to appoint the person who was the panel guardian appointed under s 41(6)(b) to act as guardian ad litem under FPR 1991, r 9.5. Important and sensitive questions of status, work loads and funding arise. Furthermore, the guardian ad litem will always be able to refuse to act. I am, however, quite satisfied that the jurisdiction exists although it should only be used with the guardian ad litem's consent, where funding is available and in those unusual cases where the guardian ad litem, in the court's view, has an important continuing role to play notwithstanding the change in the status of the proceedings.

D42 NO POWER TO COMPEL LA TO ISSUE PUBLIC LAW PROCEEDINGS

Nottinghamshire County Council v P

[1993] 2 FLR 134 at 144 and 148

Court of Appeal

Sir Stephen Brown P

It is a most regrettable feature of this case that the local authority having initially intervened under Part V of the 1989 Act in order to obtain an emergency protection order did not then proceed to seek orders under s 31 in Part IV of the Act. This is even more regrettable after Judge Heald had directed the local authority to consider the position pursuant to a direction under s 37 of the Act. In the trial bundle there appears what is headed:

'The Report of Nottinghamshire County Council

Re: Section 37 Direction Nottingham County Council and P and P.'

It then states:

'At a hearing before his Honour Judge Heald on 2 March 1992 a s 37 direction was issued to the local authority. The local authority has since reconsidered the case and the merits of making an application under s 31. The local authority does not feel it appropriate to make an application for a care or supervision order as it does not believe those orders would be effective in the protection of these children. The local authority has decided to continue with the application for a prohibited steps order in relation to the father of K and E and would intend to offer appropriate support, services, and assistance, in the light of that order being made or any other such order being made. The local authority will review this case following the court proceedings on 9 and 10 April 1992.

Signed Peter McEntee Area Director North Area

Social Services Director.'

That clearly is not a satisfactory answer to a s 37 direction and we agree with the judge that he was left in an intolerable situation. This local authority persistently and obstinately refused to undertake what was the appropriate course of action and it thereby deprived the judge of the ability to make a constructive order.

...

Since the fact of the risk of significant harm to the children has been established and not contradicted there remains upon the local authority the clear duty to take steps to safeguard the welfare of these children. It should not shrink from taking steps under Part IV of the Act. It appears from submissions made by all counsel in this court that the mother, the father and the children by their guardian ad litem would not resist the making of a supervision order in favour of the local authority pursuant to s 31 of the Act. That at least would afford a basis for the local authority to take some constructive steps in order to protect these children.

This court is deeply concerned at the absence of any power to direct this authority to take steps to protect the children. In the former wardship jurisdiction it might well have been able to do so. The operation of the Children Act 1989 is entirely dependent upon the full co-operation of all those involved. This includes the courts, the local authorities and the social workers and all who have to deal with children. Unfortunately, as appears from this case, if a local authority doggedly resists taking the steps which are appropriate to the case of children at risk of suffering significant harm it appears that the court is powerless. The authority may perhaps lay itself open to an application for judicial review, but in a case such as this the question arises, 'at whose instance?' The position is one which it is to be hoped will not recur and that lessons will be learnt from this unhappy catalogue of errors.

Other significant cases on this issue:

- *Re R (Residence)* [2009] EWCA Civ 358, [2009] 2 FLR 819

This case is also included in relation to:

B36 Applying s 9(2) and 9(5): s 8 order definitions

Section 38(6): examination or other assessment

D43 ENABLING COURT TO OBTAIN INFORMATION NECESSARY FOR ITS DECISION

Re C (Interim care order: residential assessment)

[1997] 1 FLR 1 at 4 and 5

House of Lords

Lord Browne-Wilkinson

Despite the recommendation made by their own social workers that residential assessment would be desirable, the local authority did not agree. It was initially indicated that the refusal of the local authority to countenance a residential assessment was based on financial grounds: the proposed residential assessment would cost some £18,000–£24,000. However, the reasons put forward by the assistant director of social services to the court were not linked to money. She considered in detail what she called the crucial areas: the lack of explanation of the injuries, the lack of frankness by the parents as to the cause of the injuries, the unstable relationship between the parents, the lack of the parenting skills necessary to deal with T's special needs and the fact that the demands of those special needs would produce the stress on the parents which may have led to them injuring T. In the light of those factors, she expressed the view that any consideration of rehabilitation with his parents would expose T to an unacceptable level of risk. She further said that, at the final hearing for a care order, the local authority would press for a care order with a view to T being placed in a permanent alternative placement, presumably with a view to adoption. In short, the local authority was not prepared to agree to, or pay for, the residential assessment which was proposed.

…

Before considering the exact point at issue, it is important to put s 38(6) in context. Before the passing of the Children Act 1989, the court, in the exercise of its wardship jurisdiction, retained a degree of control over its wards, even if the child was in the care of the local authority. Due to the decision of your Lordships' House in *A v Liverpool City Council* [1982] AC 363, (1981) 2 FLR 222 those powers were, as a matter of practice, limited so as to be exercised only when there were gaps in the statutory regime or in support of the powers of the local authority. Apart from such cases, it was the local authority who had the power and the duty to make decisions as to the welfare of the child in its care. This approach was strengthened by the 1989 Act, which by s 100 expressly excludes the wardship jurisdiction in certain cases.

Part IV of the Act contains a code regulating care and supervision orders (public law cases). Section 31 provides that the court may make a care or supervision order on the application of a local authority or of a very limited class of other applicants. The order, if made, places the child in the care of the local authority. But a final order can only be made if the threshold laid down by s 31(2) is crossed, ie the court is satisfied that the child is suffering or is likely to suffer significant harm and that such harm is attributable either to the care being given to the child not being what it would be reasonable to expect a parent to give to him or to the fact that the child is beyond parental control.

There are three points to note about a final care order under s 31. First, it is the court which has to decide whether or not to make a care order. Secondly, before the court can make an order it has to be satisfied that the harm being suffered or anticipated is attributable to the actual or anticipated care being received by the child, an issue likely to be dominated by the evidence as to the abilities and conduct of the parents and the relationship between the child and those parents. Thirdly, the threshold can be crossed where the harm is due to the child being beyond parental control, an issue on which the relationship between the child and his parents is central.

In many cases, including the present, the determination of the question whether the court should make a final care order under s 31 requires information to be gathered as to the child's circumstances and for that information to be placed before the court to enable it to make its decision. But there are many cases where the child will be at risk in the period pending final determination of the application for a care order. To meet this need, s 38 provides for the making of an interim care order where proceedings for a care order under s 31 are adjourned. The threshold applicable to interim care orders is lower than that laid down by s 31(2) for final orders: the court only has to be satisfied that 'there are reasonable grounds for believing' that the requirements of s 31(2) are satisfied. If so satisfied, the court may make an interim care order of limited duration, initially for not more than 8 weeks and on any renewal for not more than a further 4 weeks.

The effect of a care order is laid down by s 33. In general, this section applies as much to interim care orders as to final orders since the words 'a care order' are defined to include both: s 31(11). When a care order is made, s 33 requires the local authority to receive and keep the child in its care: s 33(1). The local authority is given parental responsibility for the child and (with certain exceptions) the power to determine the extent to which parents and others having parental responsibility for the child are allowed to meet such responsibilities: s 33(3).

Therefore the context in which s 38(6) has to be considered is this. The child is in the care of the local authority under an interim care order pending the decision by the court whether or not to make a final care order. Under the interim care order the decision-making power as to the care, residence and general welfare of the child is vested in the local authority, not in the court. However, for the purpose of making its ultimate decision whether to grant a full care order, the court will need the help of social workers, doctors and others as to the child and his circumstances. Information and assessments from these sources are necessary not only to determine whether the s 31 threshold has been crossed (including the cause of the existing or anticipated harm to the child from its existing circumstances) but also in exercising its discretion whether or not to make a final care order. It is the practice of the courts to require the local authority seeking a final care order to put forward a care plan for the court to consider in exercising such discretion. Section 38(6) deals with the interaction between the powers of the local authority entitled to make decisions as to the child's welfare in the interim and the needs of the court to have access to the relevant information and assessments so as to be able to make the ultimate decision. It must always be borne in mind that in exercising its jurisdiction under the Act, the court's function is investigative and non-adversarial: *Re L (Police Investigation: Privilege)* [1996] 1 FLR 731.

Against that background, I turn to consider the construction of s 38(6) which I have already quoted. It is important also to refer to s 38(7) which provides as follows:

'A direction under subsection (6) may be to the effect that there is to be –

(a) no such examination or assessment; or
(b) no such examination or assessment unless the court directs otherwise.'

There are two possible constructions of s 38(6) and (7), one narrow, the other purposive and broader. The Court of Appeal in *Re M*[1] adopted the narrow view. They held that the words 'other assessment of the child' had to be construed as ejusdem generis with the words 'medical or psychiatric

---

[1] *Re M (Interim Care Order: Assessment)* [1996] 2 FLR 464.

examination'. They attached decisive importance to the fact that the subsection only refers to the examination or assessment 'of the child' and makes no reference to the examination or assessment of any other person in relation to the child. They further held that for the court to order a residential assessment of the parents and child together at a specified place would involve the court in an unwarranted usurpation by the court of the local authority's power (as the authority having parental responsibility under the interim care order) to regulate where the child is to reside. In addition to supporting the arguments of the Court of Appeal in *Re M*, Mr Harris, for the local authority in the present appeal, submitted that Parliament cannot have intended the court to have power to require the local authority against its own judgment to expend scarce resources: he submitted that the local authority is the only body which can properly assess how such resources are to be allocated as between the social services and the other services it has to provide and as between the various calls on its social services budget.

My Lords, I cannot accept this narrow construction of the subsection. The Act should be construed purposively so as to give effect to the underlying intentions of Parliament. As I have sought to demonstrate, the dividing-line between the functions of the court on the one hand and the local authority on the other is that a child in interim care is subject to control of the local authority, the court having no power to interfere with the local authority's decisions save in specified cases. The cases where, despite that overall control, the court is to have power to intervene are set out, inter alia, in s 38(6) and (7). The purpose of s 38(6) is to enable the court to obtain the information necessary for its own decision, notwithstanding the control over the child which in all other respects rests with the local authority. I therefore approach the subsection on the basis that the court is to have such powers to override the views of the local authority as are necessary to enable the court to discharge properly its function of deciding whether or not to accede to the local authority's application to take the child away from its parents by obtaining a care order. To allow the local authority to decide what evidence is to go before the court at the final hearing would be in many cases, including the present, to allow the local authority by administrative decision to pre-empt the court's judicial decision.

This broad approach is supported by consideration of s 38(7) which does not appear to have been drawn to the attention of the Court of Appeal either in *Re M* or in the present case. Subsection (7) confers on the court the power to prohibit an examination or assessment which the local authority is proposing to make. It is manifestly directed to the type of conduct by social services revealed by the Cleveland Inquiry, ie repeated interviews and assessments of the child and his parents which are detrimental to the child. This negative control by the court cannot have been intended to be limited to cases where the child, and only the child, is to be assessed. If it is to be fully effective to prevent damage to the child, the power under s 38(7) must also extend to cases where it is proposed to assess the relationship between the parents and the child.

I am not convinced by the reasons which persuaded the Court of Appeal in *Re M* to adopt the narrow construction limiting the ambit of the section to assessments of the child alone, such assessments to be of the same type as medical or psychiatric examinations. First, I can see no reason for the application of the ejusdem generis principle. What is the genus? Subsection (6) refers not to the 'medical psychiatric or other examination' of the child but to 'other assessment' of the child. Some assessments, even if confined to the child itself, may not involve any examination of that child, yet plainly such an assessment is authorised by the subsection. I can find no genus to which the principle can apply.

Next, it is true that s 38(6) and (7) only refer to the assessment 'of the child' and not, as is proposed in the present case, a joint assessment of the child and the parents, including the parents' attitude and behaviour towards the child. But it is impossible to assess a young child divorced from his environment. The interaction between the child and his parents or other persons looking after him is an essential element in making any assessment of the child. This is shown particularly clearly by cases in which the courts have to decide whether the threshold requirements of s 31 are satisfied because of the harm to the child that is likely to be suffered because the child is beyond parental control. How can the court determine that issue without considering the relationship between the child and the parents? The court has no power to order the parents to take part in any assessment against their wishes, any more than, as the final words of s 38(6) show, the court can order the child to do so if the child is capable of making an informed decision. But what the interests of justice require is not a power to compel the parent to take part in such assessment but a power in the court to override the powers over the child which the local authority would otherwise enjoy under the interim care order. If the narrower construction were to be adopted the local authority could simply refuse to allow the child to take part in any assessment with his parents.

The Court of Appeal in *Re M* were much influenced by the consideration that by making an order for residential assessment at a defined place the court would be interfering with the local authority's power under s 23 to fix the child's place of residence. It has been decided by the Court of Appeal in *Re L (Interim Care Order: Power of Court)* [1996] 2 FLR 742 that the court, in making an interim care order, has no power to impose conditions on the care order as to where the child should reside. *Re L* raised no question on the powers of the court to order residential assessments under s 38(6) but Ward LJ expressed concluded views on this question which the Court of Appeal in *Re M* followed. Ward LJ said that the court had no power to order a residential assessment at a specified place. Millett LJ, whilst agreeing with Ward LJ on the only issue before the court, expressed the view that a judge could impose 'a condition which is consequential upon the giving of directions for a residential assessment under s 38(6) ...'. I can attach no weight, one way or the other, to these obiter dicta. Ward LJ does not seem to have appreciated that the whole purpose of s 38(6) is to override the powers which, apart from it, the local authority would have under an interim care order to refuse to permit any examination or assessment. He makes no reference to s 38(7).

Mr Harris sought to develop the argument by saying that, if the court could order residential assessment at a specified place, that would override the duties of the local authority as to the placement of children within their care imposed under s 23(2). The conditions under which such placement can be made are further regulated by regulations made by the Secretary of State. I do not accept this submission. Section 23 and the regulations made thereunder are concerned with placements made by local authority with foster-parents and others: s 38 is not dealing with that issue at all. It is providing for the assessment of the child for the purpose of assisting the court in its assessment of the child's best interests. An order specifying where and with whom that assessment is to take place is not 'a placement' within s 23 at all.

Much the most powerful of Mr Harris's submissions is that based on the expenditure of scarce resources by the local authority in the carrying out of an expensive assessment. In the overwhelming majority of care cases, the parties are in straitened circumstances and there is no one to pay for any examination or assessment under s 38(6) other than the local authority. In the present case, the proposed residential assessment is going to cost some £24,000 and the local authority, taking as it does a gloomy view of the result of the assessment, considers that expenditure on that scale is not a sensible allocation of its limited resources, a decision which it is far better qualified to take than the court. I accept the force of this submission but it proves too much. Mr Harris was not able to argue that if the court directed a medical examination of the child himself, which examination would be very expensive, the local authority could refuse to carry it out simply on the grounds of the expense involved and the unwise allocation of limited resources. In such a case, it will be for the court to take into account in deciding whether or not to make an order for the medical examination the expense that it involves. If that is so, the issue of resources cannot affect the proper construction of s 38(6). The consideration of the resource consequences of making the order must be the same whether the court is making an order for medical examination of the child or an order for the other assessment of the child. Therefore it is impossible to construe s 38(6) in the narrow sense simply because the court is less suitable than the local authority to assess the financial considerations.

In my judgment, therefore, s 38(6) and (7) of the Act are to be broadly construed. They confer jurisdiction on the court to order or prohibit any assessment which involves the participation of the child and is directed to providing the court with the material which, in the view of the court, is required to enable it to reach a proper decision at the final hearing of the application for a full care order. In exercising its discretion whether to order any particular examination or assessment, the court will take into account the cost of the proposed assessment and the fact that local authorities' resources are notoriously limited.

Since the point does not directly arise for decision in the present case, I express no final view on whether, on an application under s 38(6), it is appropriate for the court to enter into a detailed consideration of the resources of the local authority and the allocation of such resources. As at present advised, the course adopted by Hogg J in the present case seems to me entirely satisfactory. In exercising her discretion she took into account the substantial cost of the proposed residential assessment and the fact that the local authority had limited resources to allocate. Having weighed that factor in the balance, she exercised her discretion to make the order sought. Mr Harris argued that this exercise of her discretion was erroneous in that the judge ought to have insisted on having fuller evidence as to the resources available to the local authority to meet the cost of the residential assessment. This submission is plainly ill-founded. Whether or not it is appropriate for the judge to consider in such cases the allocation of resources by the local authority, it was for the local authority to put before the judge any evidence they wished her to consider. They cannot be heard to complain if she exercised her discretion on the basis of the only evidence put before her.

Other significant cases on this issue:

* *Re K (Care order)* [2007] EWCA Civ 697, [2007] 2 FLR 1066

D44 MAIN FOCUS OF ASSESSMENT MUST BE ON THE CHILD

Re G (Interim care order: residential assessment)

[2005] UKHL 68, [2006] 1 FLR 601 at 604, 612 and 624

House of Lords

Lord Scott, Lord Clyde and Baroness Hale

LORD SCOTT:

[6] It was not, I think, in dispute that the main purpose of the assessment in a residential unit at the Cassel Hospital, directed by the Court of Appeal for Ellie, her mother and her father, thereby reversing Johnson J's decision of 24 October 2003, was to ascertain whether by a continuing course of psychotherapy, Ellie's mother could be sufficiently changed so as to be brought to a state in which it would be safe for her to have the care of Ellie. The local authority objected, as they had successfully done before Johnson J, to the making of this order. They said that the court had not power to give such a direction. The giving of directions for therapeutic treatment of a parent could not, they said, be brought within s 38(6). The Court of Appeal disagreed: *Re G (Interim Care Order: Residential Assessment)* [2004] EWCA Civ 24, [2004] 1 FLR 876. Thorpe LJ said, at para [48], that:

> 'The essential question should always be, can what is sought be broadly classified as an assessment to enable the court to obtain the information necessary for its own decision?'

[7] My Lords, I am unable to accept that Thorpe LJ's question represented a correct formulation of the question, an affirmative answer to which would open the door to an exercise of the s 38(6) power. I do not doubt that the proposed therapeutic treatment that the mother was to receive, and an assessment of its effect on her and of her ability to benefit from it, was likely to constitute very valuable evidence informing the court's decision as to whether or not a final care order in respect of Ellie needed to be made. Nor do I doubt that a continuing assessment of the relationship between Ellie and her mother, in the light of the continuing therapeutic treatment the mother was to receive, would be similarly valuable. But that is not enough, in my opinion, to open the door to an exercise of the s 38(6) power. Section 38(6) is contemplating an assessment of the child. True it is that any meaningful assessment of a child may need to be, or include, an assessment of the child with his or her parents, or otherwise in a family context. As Lord Browne-Wilkinson said in *Re C (A Minor) (Interim Care Order: Residential Assessment)* [1997] AC 489, [1997] 1 FLR 1 at 502 and 8 respectively:

'... it is impossible to assess a young child divorced from his environment. The interaction between the child and his parents or other persons looking after him is an essential element in making any assessment of the child.'

But, to come within s 38(6), the proposed assessment must, in my opinion, be an assessment of the child. The main focus must be on the child. In the present case, the main focus of the proposed residential assessment was not on Ellie. It was on her mother. The assessment was not, for example, for the purpose of seeing whether or not Ellie and her mother had become satisfactorily bonded with one another. It was common ground by the time the case came before Johnson J that they had. Nor was it for the purpose of assessing her parents' behaviour towards her (cf *Re C (A Minor) (Interim Care Order: Residential Assessment)*). Nor was there any question about Ellie's health that needed to be assessed. What was to be assessed was her mother's capacity for beneficial response to the psychotherapeutic treatment that she was to receive. Such an assessment, no matter how valuable the information might be for the purposes of the eventual final care order decision, could not, in my opinion, be brought within s 38(6).

LORD CLYDE:

[27] Plainly, a broad and purposive construction is appropriate for s 38(6) of the Children Act 1989. Thus the phrase 'of the child' is to be understood as meaning the child in the context of his or her family, so that the investigation may extend to considering the capacity of a parent to care for the child. But, whatever the range of the investigation, it must still qualify as a 'medical or psychiatric examination or other assessment' of the child.

BARONESS HALE:

[69] In short, what is directed under s 38(6) must clearly be an examination or assessment of the child, including where appropriate her relationship with her parents, the risk that her parents may present to her, and the ways in which those risks may be avoided or managed, all with a view to enabling the court to make the decisions which it has to make under the 1989 Act with the minimum of delay. Any services which are provided for the child and his family must be ancillary to that end. They must not be an end in themselves. In this case, the judge was clearly entitled to reach the conclusion that any further inpatient treatment in the Cassel had gone beyond what fell within his power to order under s 38(6).

This case is also included in relation to:

D45 Therapeutic services must be incidental to gathering necessary information
D49 House of Lords' dicta
D57 Interim or final order (2)

D45   THERAPEUTIC SERVICES MUST BE INCIDENTAL TO GATHERING NECESSARY INFORMATION

Re G (Interim care order: residential assessment)

[2005] UKHL 68, [2006] 1 FLR 601 at 613, 616 and 622

House of Lords

Lord Clyde and Baroness Hale

LORD CLYDE:

[31]   Plainly, a distinction can be made as matter of language between what constitutes an assessment, and what constitutes treatment. Moreover, the two may co-exist. An institution directed to make an assessment may incidentally commence some form of treatment, if only to assess whether the case is susceptible to treatment. Treatment will often be accompanied by some form of assessment of the degree of success or failure as the treatment progresses. But, without engaging in the terminological distinction, it should be enough to recognise that the jurisdiction of the court is confined to obtaining information about the current state of affairs, including perhaps a forecast of what future progress might be possible, and does not extend to a continuing survey of the effects of treatment. Such a continuing oversight might, if the treatment is successful, lead to the termination of a care order, but it does not form part of the court's responsibility in deciding whether or not to impose such an order.

BARONESS HALE:

Re C (A Minor) (Interim Care Order: Residential Assessment)

[43]   The correct construction of the phrase 'medical or psychiatric examination or other assessment of the child' has already been considered by this House in *Re C (A Minor) (Interim Care Order: Residential Assessment)* [1997] AC 489, [1997] 1 FLR 1. This House unanimously decided that it should be given a broad construction, enabling the court to order 'a joint assessment of the child and the parents, including the parents' attitude and behaviour towards the child' (per Lord Browne-Wilkinson at 502 and 8 respectively) or 'any assessment which involves the participation of the child and is directed to providing the court with the material which, in the view of the court, is required to enable it to reach a

proper decision at the final hearing of the application for a full care order' (at 504 and 9 respectively). In that case, the House was not concerned with any distinction between 'assessment' and 'treatment'. But, that has since become a controversial issue: see *Re M (Residential Assessment Directions)* [1998] 2 FLR 371 per Holman J; *Re B (Psychiatric Therapy for Parents)* [1999] 1 FLR 701; *Re D (Jurisdiction: Programme of Assessment or Therapy)* [1999] 2 FLR 632; *Re C (Children) (Residential Assessment)* [2001] EWCA Civ 1305, [2001] 3 FCR 164; *Re B (Interim Care Order: Directions)* [2002] EWCA Civ 25, [2002] 1 FLR 545; and *BCC v L* [2002] EWHC 2327 (Fam) (unreported) 7 November 2002 per Charles J.

...

Section 38(6)

[61] It is against that background that s 38(6) has to be construed. It is set out at para 2 above. But it should not be construed in isolation from s 38(7):

'A direction under subsection (6) may be to the effect that there is to be—

(a) no such examination or assessment; or
(b) no such examination or assessment unless the court directs otherwise.'

As Lord Browne-Wilkinson said in Re C (A Minor) (Interim Care Order: Residential Assessment) at 501 and 7 respectively:

'The Act should be construed purposively so as to give effect to the underlying intentions of Parliament ... The purpose of subsection (6) is to enable the court to obtain the information necessary for its own decision, notwithstanding the control over the child which in all other respects rests with the local authority.'

[62] As Lord Browne-Wilkinson pointed out, the power in 38 (6) and 38(7) to decide what 'medical or psychiatric examination or other assessment' the child should undergo was a power to limit or control the parental responsibility which otherwise the local authority have for the child even under an interim care order (see ss 31(11) and 33(3)(a)). On the one hand, the court might insist that the child have such an examination or assessment even if the local authority did not want this. Otherwise, the local authority would be in control of what evidence about the child might be obtained and put before the court. This could well be unfair to the parents, whose power to meet their own responsibilities for the child can be determined by the local authority (see s 33(3)(b) and (4)). On the other hand, the court might put limits on the number and type of examinations or assessments which the child had to undergo, for example by insisting on a single report by a jointly instructed independent expert in cases of suspected non-accidental injury or sexual abuse.

[63] The legislative history makes it clear that the latter was a principal, if not the principal, purpose of s 38(6) and (7). There was no reference to such a power in either the *Review of Child Care Law: report to ministers of an interdepartmental working party* or the White Paper on *The Law on Child Care and Family Services* (Cm 62 (1987)). Nor did it feature in the draft Children Bill annexed to the *Law Commission's Report on Guardianship and Custody* (Law Com No 172 (HMSO 1988)), which reflected the proposals both of the childcare law review and of the Commission's review of the private law relating to children. But also important in the genesis of the 1989 Act was the *Report of the Inquiry into Child Abuse in Cleveland 1987* (Cm 412 (HMSO 1988)), led by Dame Elizabeth Butler-Sloss. The inquiry was very concerned about the number of examinations by different doctors of the same child, more for the purpose of providing information for the adults, than for the advantage of the child (para 11.45). It recommended that children should not be subjected to repeated medical examinations or repeated interviews solely for evidential purposes (p 245). It also recommended that the court should have to determine disputes over medical examination during the currency of an emergency protection order and to determine further medical examinations for evidential purposes after care proceedings were initiated (pp 252–253). It is fair to conclude that s 38(6) and (7) were inserted into the 1989 Act in response to these recommendations. The same is true of s 44(6), (7) and (8), which make virtually identical provision where an emergency protection order is in force.

[64] The purpose of these provisions is, therefore, not only to enable the court to obtain the information it needs, but also to enable the court to control the information-gathering activities of others. But the emphasis is always on obtaining information. This is clear from the use of the words 'examination' and 'other assessment'. If the framers of the 1989 Act had meant the court to be in charge, not only of the examination and assessment of the child, but also of the medical or psychiatric treatment to be provided for her, let alone for her parents, it would have said so. Instead, it deliberately left that in the hands of the local authority.

[65] A fortiori, the purpose of s 38(6) cannot be to ensure the provision of services either for the child or his family. There is nothing in the 1989 Act which empowers the court hearing care proceedings to order the provision of specific services for anyone. To imply such a power into s 38(6) would be quite contrary to the division of responsibility which was the 'cardinal principle' of the 1989 Act. (This is reinforced by the position in judicial review proceedings, recently considered by the House in (*G*) *v*

Barnet London Borough Council; R (W) v Lambeth London Borough Council; R (A) v Lambeth London Borough Council [2003] UKHL 57, [2004] 2 AC 208, [2004] 1 FLR 454).

[66] I appreciate, of course, that it is not always possible to draw a hard and fast line between information-gathering and service-providing. Some information can only be gathered through the provision of services. It may be necessary to observe the parents looking after the child at close quarters for a short period in order to assess the quality of the child's attachment to the parents, the degree to which the parents have bonded with the child, the current parenting skills of the parents, and their capacity to learn and develop. That is the sort of assessment which was involved in *Re C (A Minor) (Interim Care Order: Residential Assessment)*.

[67] But the court only has power to insist where this is relevant to the questions which the court has to answer. Where the threshold criteria are in issue, it must be recalled that these are phrased (in s 31(2)) in the present tense: that the child 'is suffering or is likely to suffer significant harm'; and 'that the harm or likelihood of harm is attributable to' the quality of actual or likely parental care or to the child's being beyond parental control. Where the threshold is found or conceded but the proper order is in issue, the welfare checklist is likewise focussed on the present, for example, in s 1(3)(f): 'how capable each of his parents ... is of meeting his needs'. The capacity to change, to learn and to develop may well be part of that. But it is still the present capacity with which the court is concerned. It cannot be a proper use of the court's powers under s 38(6) to seek to bring about change.

[68] These conclusions are reinforced by the Act's emphasis on reaching decisions without delay. It cannot have been contemplated that the examination or assessment ordered under s 38(6) would take many months to complete. It would be surprising if it were to last more than 2 or 3 months at most. The important decision for the court is whether or not to make a care order, with all that that entails. But the care order is not the end of the story. The court retains jurisdiction over the contact between the child and his family (see s 34). The local authority has a duty to place the child with parents or other members of the family, unless this is impracticable or inconsistent with the child's welfare (see s 23(6)). The court may sometimes have to accept that it is not possible to know all that is to be known before a final choice is made, because that choice will depend upon how the family and the child respond and develop in the future.

Conclusion

[69] In short, what is directed under s 38(6) must clearly be an examination or assessment of the child, including where appropriate her

relationship with her parents, the risk that her parents may present to her, and the ways in which those risks may be avoided or managed, all with a view to enabling the court to make the decisions which it has to make under the 1989 Act with the minimum of delay. Any services which are provided for the child and his family must be ancillary to that end. They must not be an end in themselves. In this case, the judge was clearly entitled to reach the conclusion that any further inpatient treatment in the Cassel had gone beyond what fell within his power to order under s 38(6). I would allow this appeal.

[70]   I would like to add two footnotes. First, I entirely accept that from a clinical point of view, these legalistic niceties are both unhelpful and unfair in the real world of trying to work with seriously disturbed families (see the discussion by Dr Roger Kennedy, Consultant Psychotherapist in charge of the Families Service at the Cassel, in 'Assessment and Treatment in Family Law – A Valid Distinction?' [2001] Fam Law 676). In an ideal world, the child's need for services such as the Cassel would be identified and the service provided. The only question for the court would be whether it should be provided voluntarily or under the auspices of some sort of court order. The problem is that the service needs funding and the local health trust and social services authority which have responsibility for the particular family involved may be unable or unwilling to fund it. That problem clearly requires a solution if the uniquely valuable service provided by the Cassel is to continue. But it is not permissible for the courts to try to solve the problem through a provision which was never designed for that purpose. It is sticking plaster at best, and costly sticking plaster at that. We have not heard detailed argument upon whether or not the court has power to direct the local authority or any of the parties to fund the assessment. I would, therefore, prefer to express no concluded view on the issues raised in paras [20]–[23] of the opinion of my noble and learned friend, Lord Scott of Foscote. But on the assumption that the court does have such power, the cost of any proposed assessment must be relevant to the court's decision whether or not to require the parties to provide it. However, it is inappropriate for the court to require detailed evidence from senior officers of such reluctant local authorities and insist that they prove a so-called 'money defence' (cf *Re C (Children) (Residential Assessments)* [2001] EWCA Civ 1305, [2001] 3 FCR 164 at 172, para 31). Nor should we be tolerating a situation in which an hour's directions hearing, followed by a full day's hearing, are devoted to deciding whether or not to make a direction under s 38(6), as happened in this case.

[71]   Secondly, this case is about a course of action which everyone eventually agreed was in the child's best interests and so it has happily proved to be. But, if the aims of the protocol are to be realised, it will always be necessary to think early and clearly about what assessments are indeed necessary to decide the case. In many cases, the local authority should be able to make its own core assessment and the child's guardian

to make an independent assessment in the interests of the child. Further or other assessments should only be commissioned if they can bring something important to the case which neither the local authority nor the guardian is able to bring. No one denies that this was a particularly complex and difficult case in which expert psychological assessment of the risks was essential. But that is not always so.

This case is also included in relation to:

D44 Main focus of assessment must be on the child
D49 House of Lords' dicta
D57 Interim or final order (2)

D46 ENSURE CASE FULLY INVESTIGATED AND ALL RELEVANT EVIDENCE NECESSARY IS IN PLACE

Re L and H (Residential assessment)

[2007] EWCA Civ 213, [2007] 1 FLR 1370 at 1372 and 1388

Court of Appeal

Wall LJ

[3] We heard argument in the case on 1 March 2007. At the outset, we gave permission to appeal, and at its conclusion announced that the appeal would be allowed. However, it is apparent that the case: (1) raises important questions relating to both the purpose and the proper use of s 38(6) of the 1989 Act; and (2) requires this court to re-visit the two key decisions of the House of Lords in the field, namely *Re C (A Minor) (Interim Care Order: Residential Assessment)* [1997] AC 489, [1997] 1 FLR 1 and *Re G (A Minor) (Interim Care Order: Residential Assessment)* [2005] UKHL 68, [2006] 1 AC 576, [2006] 1 FLR 601. Accordingly, we reserved the reasons for our decision, which we now give.

...

The authorities

[64] The two leading cases on s 38(6) are, undoubtedly, the two decisions of the House of Lords in *Re C (A Minor) (Interim Care Order: Residential Assessment)* [1997] AC 489, [1997] 1 FLR 1, and *Re G (A Minor) (Interim Care Order: Residential Assessment),* [2005] UKHL 68, [2006] 1 AC 576, [2006] 1 FLR 601. I will, henceforth, revert to calling them *Re C* and *Re G* respectively. It will, I think, be necessary to examine these two cases in some detail.

[65] In *Re C*, the child in question suffered severe injuries at the age of 4 months, and was the subject of an interim care order in favour of the local authority. There was a dispute within the local authority itself. The social workers dealing with the case took the view that there should be an in-depth assessment of the child and his parents at a residential unit. The question for the court was whether or not a direction should be made under s 38(6) of the 1989 Act to enable that assessment to take place. The judge made the order: this court reversed her: the House of Lords restored the judge's decision.

[66] The House of Lords had to choose between two possible constructions of s 38(6). The first, adopted by this court in *Re M (Interim Care Order: Assessment)* [1996] 2 FLR 464 (and followed by this court when *Re C* was before it) was identified as the 'narrow' construction. On this construction, as Lord Browne-Wilkinson described it (*Re C* at 501B and 7 respectively), the phrase, 'other assessment of the child' in s 38(6) had to be construed as ejusdem generis with the words 'medical or psychiatric examination'. In other words, the subsection empowered the court only to give directions in relation to examinations or assessments of the child: it did not empower the court to give directions in relation to examinations or assessments of the mother or the family as a whole.

[67] The House of Lords emphatically rejected the narrow construction. As Lord Browne-Wilkinson (who gave the leading speech) put it, at 501 and 7 respectively:

'My Lords, I cannot accept this narrow construction of the subsection. The Act should be construed purposively so as to give effect to the underlying intentions of Parliament. As I have sought to demonstrate, the dividing line between the functions of the court on the one hand and the local authority on the other is that a child in interim care is subject to control of the local authority, the court having no power to interfere with the local authority's decisions save in specified cases. The cases where, despite that overall control, the court is to have power to intervene are set out, *inter alia*, in subs (6) and (7). The purpose of subs (6) is to enable the court to obtain the information necessary for its own decision, notwithstanding the control over the child which in all other respects rests with the local authority. I therefore approach the subsection on the basis that the court is to have such powers to override the views of the local authority as are necessary to enable the court to discharge properly its function of deciding whether or not to accede to the local authority's application to take the child away from its parents by obtaining a care order. To allow the local authority to decide what evidence is to go before the court at the final hearing would be in many cases, including the present, to allow the local authority by administrative decision to preempt the court's judicial decision.

This broad approach is supported by consideration of subs (7) which does not appear to have been drawn to the attention of the Court of Appeal either in *Re M (Interim Care Order: Assessment)* [1996] 2 FLR 464 or in the present case. Subsection (7) confers on the court the power to prohibit an examination or assessment which the local authority is proposing to make. It is manifestly directed to the type of conduct by social services revealed by the Cleveland Inquiry (Report of the Inquiry into Child Abuse in Cleveland in 1987 (1988) Cm 412), ie repeated interviews and assessments of the child and his parents which are detrimental to the child. This negative control by the court cannot have been intended to be limited to cases where the child, and only the child, is to be assessed. If it is to be fully effective to prevent damage to the child, the power under subs (7) must also extend to cases where it is proposed to assess the relationship between the parents and the child.'

[68] Having stated that he saw no reason for the application of the ejusdem generis rule, Lord Browne-Wilkinson continued:

'Next, it is true that subs (6) and (7) only refer to the assessment "of the child" and not, as is proposed in the present case, a joint assessment of the child and the parents, including the parents' attitude and behaviour towards the child. But it is impossible to assess a young child divorced from his environment. The interaction between the child and his parents or other persons looking after him is an essential element in making any assessment of the child. This is shown particularly clearly by cases in which the courts have to decide whether the threshold requirements of s 31 are satisfied because of the harm to the child that is likely to be suffered because the child is beyond parental control. How can the court determine that issue without considering the relationship between the child and the parents? The court has no power to order the parents to take part in any assessment against their wishes, any more than, as the final words of subs (6) show, the court can order the child to do so if the child is capable of making an informed decision. But what the interests of justice require is not a power to compel the parent to take part in such assessment but a power in the court to override the powers over the child which the local authority would otherwise enjoy under the interim care order. If the narrow construction were to be adopted the local authority could simply refuse to allow the child to take part in any assessment with his parents.'

[69] Lord Browne-Wilkinson thus concluded:

'In my judgment, therefore, subss (6) and (7) of s 38 of the [1989] Act are to be broadly construed. They confer jurisdiction on the court to order or prohibit any assessment which involves the participation of the child and is directed to providing the court with the material which, in the view of the court, is required to enable it to reach a proper decision at the final hearing of the application for a full care order. In exercising its discretion whether to order any particular examination or assessment, the court will take into account the cost of the proposed assessment and the fact that local authorities' resources are notoriously limited.'

[70] It is, I think, important to recall that nothing in *Re G* detracts from the construction of s 38(6) enunciated by the House of Lords in *Re C*. To the contrary, several passages in the speeches of Lord Scott of Foscote and Baroness Hale of Richmond, in my judgment, reinforce the construction given to s 38(6) of the 1989 Act in the earlier case. Most striking, I think, is Lord Scott of Foscote's citation of, and agreement with, in *Re G* at 583 and 606 respectively, a passage from the judgment of Holman J in *Re M (Residential Assessment Directions)* [1998] 2 FLR 371 at 381:

'[10] In *Re M*, at 381, Holman J, after referring to Lord Browne-Wilkinson's conclusions in *Re C*, said this:

"it does seem to me that both the words of the section and the language of Lord Browne-Wilkinson nevertheless impose some limits on the extent of the court's powers. They are limited to a process that can properly be characterised as assessment rather than treatment, although no doubt all treatment is accompanied by a continuing process of assessment. And they are limited to a process which bona fide involves the participation of the child as an integral part of what is being assessed."

I agree with the learned judge's analysis.'

[71] Other passages in the speeches are to like effect. I will give only three further examples. The first is from para [8]of Lord Scott of Foscote's speech in *Re C*, at 582H and 605 respectively, and in which he is, once again, discussing Lord Browne-Wilkinson's speech in *Re C*:

'It is important, however, to bear in mind that *Re C* was a case in which a very young child had sustained serious injuries while in the care of his parents, injuries that the parents were unable satisfactorily to explain. The issue was whether an assessment of the child and his parents at a residential unit could be directed under s 38(6). The manner in which the respective parents behaved toward the child, particularly in stressful situations, was to be the subject of the proposed in-depth assessment. The focus of the assessment was the parents' behaviour towards the child and Lord Browne-Wilkinson's dicta should be read with that in mind. He cannot be taken to have intended that a direction for an examination or assessment could be made under s 38(6) whenever any information about a parent useful to the court in deciding whether or not to make a final care order could or might thereby be obtained.'

[72] My final citations are from the speech of Baroness Hale of Richmond. At 600 and 623 respectively, para [66], she says:

'I appreciate, of course, that it is not always possible to draw a hard and fast line between information-gathering and service-providing. Some information can only be gathered through the provision of services. It may be necessary to observe the parents looking after the child at close quarters for a short period in order to assess the quality of the child's attachment to the parents, the degree to which the parents have bonded with the child, the current parenting skills of the parents, and their capacity to learn and develop. That is the sort of assessment which was involved in *Re C*.'

[73] Finally, in her conclusion in para [69] of her speech, Baroness Hale of Richmond says:

'CONCLUSION

[69] In short, what is directed under s 38(6) must clearly be an examination or assessment of the child, including where appropriate her relationship with her parents, the risk that her parents may present to her, and the ways in which those risks may be avoided or managed, all with a view to enabling the court to make the decisions which it has to make under the Act with the minimum of delay. Any services which are provided for the child and his family must be ancillary to that end. They must not be an end in themselves. In this case, the judge was clearly entitled to reach the conclusion that any further in-patient treatment in the Cassel had gone beyond what fell within his power to order under s 38(6). I would allow this appeal.'

[74] Speaking for myself, I am in no doubt at all that the instant case falls within the ambiance of *Re C*, and is readily distinguishable from *Re G*. As Thorpe LJ pointed out during the course of argument, the question for the House of Lords in the latter case was aptly stated by Baroness Hale of Richmond at para [36] of her speech:

'[36] The legal issue before us is at first sight a comparatively simple one. In what circumstances may a court direct a local social services authority to pay for a family's admission to the Cassel Hospital under s 38(6) of the Children Act 1989?'

[75] *Re G* clearly decides that since the main purpose of the admission of the family in question to the Cassel Hospital was to provide therapy or treatment, it could not be brought within s 38(6) of the 1989 Act. In my judgment, whilst *Re G* plainly identifies an admission which is outwith s 38(6) it does not affect the construction of the statute laid down by the House in *Re C*, nor does it affect the use of s 38(6) for an assessment which, in the helpful and apposite words of Holman J, 'bona fide involves the participation of the child as an integral part of what is being assessed'.

[76] In my judgment, therefore, the present case is on all fours with *Re C*.

The judge's approach to the law

[77] I have already set out the judge's analysis of the law in para 46 of his judgment. The judge correctly identifies *Re C* and *Re G* as the two critical cases. However, in the passages which follow, in my judgment, the judge falls into error in a number of respects.

[78] First, the judge is plainly wrong in para 58 to characterise the assessment at the FRU as 'an assessment of the parent/s, and therapy or a programme or work to improve the skills of the parents'. I have set out the terms of the FRU's assessment in para [35], above. There is nothing about 'therapy' in its conclusions. In my judgment, the judge has misread Dr Drayton's report. The therapy to which Dr Drayton refers, and which I have set out in para [31], above is, as Thorpe LJ aptly observed during argument a 'bolt-on' to be provided, as Dr Drayton states, firstly in the form of cognitive behaviour therapy (CBT) for PH by means of a reference through his general practitioner to; and, secondly – for the couple – through Relate.

[79] This, in my view, is a serious error since it leads the judge directly to the conclusion in the same paragraph that the FRU assessment is 'as a consequence of the decision in *Re G* outside the scope of that which it is permissible to order under section 38(6)'. In my judgment, this is simply wrong. The judge has misunderstood and thus misrepresented the nature of the assessment, and has wrongly concluded that he does not have jurisdiction to order it. This alone, in my judgment, is sufficient to vitiate his conclusion.

[80] The same misunderstanding permeates the rest of his reasoning. His citation of para [71] of Baroness Hale of Richmond's speech is, in my judgment, inapt. The court had instructed Dr Drayton to make psychological assessments of the parents, and specifically to advise on whether or not a residential assessment would be appropriate – see Dr Drayton's instructions as recorded in para [16], above. Dr Drayton's clear opinion was that a residential assessment of the parents was necessary for two principal reasons. The first was 'to give professionals involved in the case important information on how well (the mother) manages the practicalities of parenting'. That, plainly, is fair and square within *Re C*. The second, which Dr Drayton regarded as more important, was that it would give the same professionals and the court 'important, if not vital information on how (the parents') relationship bears up under stress'. What was the stress? Manifestly, it was having to care full time for a child in a very structured and overseen environment.

[81] In my judgment, such an assessment is not only fair and square within *Re C*, but goes to the heart of the critical question in the case, which is whether or not M can be safely parented by his mother and father. No question, it seems to me, is more central than this to the issue of M's welfare. To characterise its 'essential nature', as the judge does, as being 'to test and assess the future strength of the relationship between (the parents)' is seriously to miss the point.

The principles underlying the 1989 Act

[82] There is, however, a further, and, in my judgment, equally important point, which goes to the root of family justice. In *Re KD (A Minor) (Ward: Termination of Access)* [1988] AC 806, [1988] 2 FLR 139 (a case decided more than a decade before the importation into English law of ECHR) Lord Templeman famously compared Art 8 of the European Convention for the Protection of Human Rights and Fundamental Freedoms 1950 with the position in England and Wales under the common law and statute. His words have resonated throughout the family justice system ever since, and, in my judgment, underlie the philosophy of the Children Act 1989. I propose to recite the whole passage, highlighting the particular sentences which, as it seems to me, are directly applicable to these proceedings. Lord Templeman said, at 812 and 140 respectively:

> 'The English rule was evolved against an historical background of conflict between parents over the upbringing of their children. The Convention rule was evolved against an historical background of claims by the state to control the private lives of individuals. Since the last war interference by public authorities with families for the protection of children has greatly increased in this country. In my opinion there is no inconsistency of principle or application between the English rule and the Convention rule. *The best person to bring up a child is the natural parent. It matters not whether the parent is wise or foolish, rich or poor, educated or illiterate, provided the child's moral and physical health are not endangered. Public authorities cannot improve on nature. Public authorities exercise a supervisory role and interfere to rescue a child when the parental tie is broken by abuse or separation. In terms of the English rule the court decides whether and to what extent the welfare of the child requires that the child shall be protected against harm caused by the parent, including harm which could be caused by the resumption of parental care after separation has broken the parental tie.* In terms of the Convention rule the court decides whether and to what extent the child's health or morals require protection from the parent and whether and to what extent the family life of parent and child has been supplanted by some other relationship which has become the essential family life for the child.' (emphasis added)

[83] Miss Budden readily agreed in argument that the underlying philosophy of the 1989 Act was, wherever possible, to enable children to be brought up by their parents or within their natural families. That is the right of every child. But children also have, of course, the right not be caused (or subjected to the likelihood of) significant harm. This inevitably means that in some cases, local authorities will have to move swiftly to protect children from significant harm which their parents have inflicted or are likely to inflict on them. In some cases, that may mean seeking judicial approval to remove children from their mothers immediately after birth.

[84] The relevance of these observations to the point under discussion in the instant case seems to me to be that before taking the step to remove children permanently from their natural families and placing them for adoption with strangers, the court has to be satisfied (applying the criteria set out in Part IV of the 1989 Act) that the threshold criteria for a care order are met, and that care orders with care plans for adoption are in the best interests of the children concerned. That, of course, requires the court anxiously to scrutinise the local authority's care plan. So much is elementary and well established. But what is equally important, in my judgment, is that the court should be astute to ensure that the case has been fully investigated, and that all the relevant evidence necessary for the decision is in place.

[85] I am not for one moment seeking to lay down any general guidelines for the circumstances in which the court should or should not order assessments under s 38(6). The courts must give the subsection a purposive construction and apply the principles set out in *Re C* and *Re G* to the facts of the cases before them. But what is equally important is that the hearing of the proceedings should be fair (or, to put the matter in the language of the European Convention, Art 6 compliant) and that the court should have before it all the relevant evidence necessary for the decision.

[86] I am left with the clear feeling, having listened to the argument in the instant case, that any final hearing which followed a denial to the parents of M the opportunity to take part in a residential assessment of the child would be unfair. I say that for a number of reasons. First, the parents have plainly been written off by the local authority as carers for either child. I have cited the relevant passage from the core assessment in para [37], above. Although the guardian is at pains to say that her evidence on the s 38(6) issue is not determinative of her final investigation, the clear impression left by her evidence is that the parents are unlikely to be able to care for either M or SA. Both the local authority and the guardian say that the judge does not need the evidence from a s 38(6) assessment. Both say – in effect – that although this mother has done everything expected of her in contact, her history is such that there is no point in any further assessment. The plain inference is that she is incapable of caring for M and SA: that is the end of the matter, and the court should therefore not permit any further expenditure of public funds on a further assessment.

[87]   There will, in my judgment, of course, be cases in which to order an assessment under s 38(6) of the 1989 Act will be a waste of time and of public funds. Sadly, it is not difficult to provide examples. Parents who have been found grievously to have injured one or more of their children and have another whilst continuing to deny causing the injuries or without any acknowledgement of their responsibility for the injuries can hardly expect to obtain an assessment of their new child under s 38(6). A woman who has a child or children by a convicted paedophile whom she does not acknowledge to be a danger of her children is in the same position. Child protection is a vital ingredient in any proceedings under the 1989 Act.

[88]   Accordingly, if the professional evidence in the instant case was unanimous that a s 38(6) assessment would serve no purpose, it would be unlikely that the judge could have been criticised for refusing to order one. But that is patently not the case. The consultant clinical psychologist brought in to advise the court (inter alia) on this very issue advises, in strong terms, that a residential assessment of M, the mother and the father is not merely desirable: he strongly recommends it. In my judgment, that is a powerful pointer to the propriety of such an order.

[89]   That pointer is, in my judgment, however, immeasurably strengthened when viewed against the fact that, if it is not ordered, the parents will be forced to go into the final hearing without an important piece of evidence, and without having been given the opportunity to demonstrate that, despite their respective histories, they have the capacity to parent M. Indeed, it seems to me that without positive evidence from such an assessment, the outcome of the July hearing is a foregone conclusion.

[90]   None of this, of course, is intended as a criticism of either the local authority or the guardian for forming a clear view. Indeed, they may prove in due course to be correct. It may be that the parents will prove unable to sustain their relationship for the period of the assessment, or otherwise demonstrate during it that they do not have the capacity to parent M, let alone M and SA together. As I stated in argument, if the parents fail in the assessment, that is likely to be the end of the case as far as they are concerned.

[91]   In my judgment, however, none of these considerations provides a good reason, on the facts of this case, for the assessment of the child under s 38(6) not to take place. As I see the case, it is manifestly in the interests of M to see if his parents are able to care for him, and it is the responsibility of the court to ensure that it has the best evidence on which to reach a conclusion about his welfare. It is also procedurally fair for his parents to be given the opportunity to demonstrate that they can overcome their manifest difficulties and care for him, and it would, in my judgment, be unfair were they to be denied that opportunity. There was

powerful, well reasoned, objective and balanced evidence from Dr Drayton that such an assessment was worthwhile. The judge's misreading of the authorities deprived him of the ability to give Dr Drayton's evidence the weight it warranted.

Other significant cases on this issue:

- *Re CH (Care or interim care order)* [1998] 1 FLR 402: see D58 – Ensuring necessary evidence available before making final order
- *Re M (Care proceedings: best evidence)* [2007] EWCA Civ 589, [2007] 2 FLR 1006: see G56 – No stone must be left unturned?
- *Re S (Residential assessment)* [2008] EWCA Civ 1078, [2009] 2 FLR 397 (refusing residential assessment a proper exercise of discretion)
- *Re F (Care proceedings: interim care order)* [2010] EWCA Civ 826, [2010] 2 FLR 1455

D47 SECTION 38(6) ASSESSMENTS CAN BE IN A FAMILY SETTING

Re A (Residential assessment)

[2009] EWHC 865 (Fam), [2009] 2 FLR 443 at 446, 447, 458 and 459

Family Division

Munby J

[7] Thus the state of affairs when the justices sat on 16 December 2008. The mother and the father had effectively been ruled out as carers for A. And the guardian was firmly of the view that the local authority's plan for special guardianship was appropriate. The paternal great-grandmother and aunt had been having contact with A for 4 hours a week. By 16 December 2008 it was common ground between the local authority and the guardian that A should be placed with them. And, as Mr Jonathan-Jones put it, the family wanted A moved to a family placement – to the paternal great-grandmother and aunt – as soon as humanly possible and before Christmas if at all possible.

...

[14] At the conclusion of the hearing the justices made two orders. The first, in standard form, ordered that A be placed in the care of the local authority until 13 January 2009. The other, so far as material for present purposes, provided as follows:

'1. That A shall reside with [the paternal great-grandmother and aunt] for the purposes of assessment until 25 February 2009 and that the Local Authority shall file a report thereon on 20 February 2009.
2. During this assessment period, A shall have contact with her mother and her father as set out in the Care Plan of 5 December 2008, namely two sessions per week for one hour, each supervised by [the paternal great-grandmother and aunt].'

...

[59] Before addressing Ms Henke's submissions directly, there are two preliminary points about s 38(6) that need to be made. In the first place, although, perhaps because they are the most protracted and expensive and most likely to cut across a local authority's planning, and thus most likely to be controversial, we tend to think of s 38(6) assessments in terms

of residential assessments in the kind of institutional settings of which the Cassel is a well-known example, s 38(6) is much wider and more general in its scope. It applies to any 'examination' (medical or psychiatric) or any 'assessment', whether short or long, and in whatever setting. Secondly, subject only to the requirement that the assessment be 'of the child', s 38(6) is not expressed as imposing any restrictions at all on what can be directed by the court. The court can direct *any* 'assessment of the child'. The only further restriction is that suggested by Lord Browne-Wilkinson's reference in *Re C*[1] to the purpose of s 38(6) as being 'to enable the court to obtain the information necessary for its own decision ... to enable it to reach a proper decision at the final hearing of the application for a full care order'. But those words, far from narrowing the scope of s 38(6) merely serve, as it seems to me, to bring out and emphasise the potential breadth of its ambit.

[60] The other preliminary observation is this: It is quite plain that, given the reasons why the guardian was arguing for it and, indeed, the reasons the justices gave for directing it, the assessment directed by the justices in the present case fell comfortably within the parameters of the permissible as described in *Re G*[2] in the various passages anthologised in paras [35]–[37] above. Moreover, in carefully directing themselves that 'The court requires evidence of how A settled in with aunt and grandmother before it will make a Special Guardianship Order', the justices were, in my judgment, acting properly in accordance with the approach set out in *Re C*.

...

[65] Where, one asks, is the vice in what the justices did here, always bearing in mind the purpose of s 38(6) as explained in *Re C* and *Re G*? I can see none. On the contrary, given the scope and purpose of s 38(6), it would, if anything, be most unfortunate if what the justices did was unlawful, because it would, to repeat, make it legally impossible for any court, without the agreement of the local authority, ever to direct an assessment in a family setting under the umbrella of an interim care order. And what is the vice in that?

---

[1]   *Re C (A minor) (interim care order: residential assessment)* [1997] 1 FLR 1: see D43.
[2]   *Re G (A minor) (interim care order: residential assessment)* [2005] UKHL 68, [2006] 1 FLR 601: see D44.

D48 POWER TO DIRECT ASSESSMENT BY NAMED LA EMPLOYEE

Re W (Assessment of child)

[1998] 2 FLR 130 at 131, 133 and 134

Court of Appeal

Ward LJ

But now a new guardian ad litem has been appointed on that child's behalf. The guardian ad litem in P's case, which is the matter before us, made an application in terms that:

> '(1) there be an assessment of the parenting skills of [the mother and father], to include an assessment of the child with her parents under s 38(6) of the Children Act 1989;
> (2) the aforesaid assessment to be carried out by an independent social worker to be appointed to this case, namely Mrs Margaret Bersey, Dr G. Redding, consultant child psychiatrist, and Dr Galway, psychiatrist.'

In fact, Mrs Bersey is not an independent social worker. She is employed by the local authority and is, therefore, at all times subject to their control. Under the terms of her employment, she has no power to act independently of the authority.

The judge, dealing with that application on 5 February 1997, came to the conclusion, and so ordered in para 12 of his order, that the court has jurisdiction, in respect of the application for that assessment order by the guardian, to appoint the named social worker, Margaret Bersey. The local authority have, with the leave of the judge, sought to appeal that part of his order.

...

It seems to me that s 38 is wide enough to give the court jurisdiction to name the person or persons by whom an assessment under s 38 is to be made. However, the court's jurisdiction is limited by this practical consideration: that a court cannot direct an individual to carry out an assessment under s 38 if that individual is unwilling or unable to do so. It would not be in the child's interests that an assessment should be performed by someone who did not wish to do so, or to risk delay prejudicial to the child whilst conducting some inquiry as to the reasons which led to that unwillingness. As I understand current practice, the court normally ascertains in advance, where an individual or individuals are to be identified in the court's direction, that those persons are willing and able to act as assessors. If the court does not take this sensible precaution, further delay inimical to a child's interests, and leading to the incurring of unnecessary and wasteful costs, will be caused.

...

It is not necessary for the purpose of this judgment to consider whether or not the court has coercive powers and particularly whether or not the court has a coercive power to direct either the local authority itself or its employee to conduct the inquiry which it is unwilling to undertake. I say nothing about that question, but I do observe that if an individual does not wish to take part in the assessment, it seems to me unthinkable that the court would coerce him to do so on pain of committal.

The passage from the opinion of Lord Browne-Wilkinson at 8F which I have cited indicates that the views and resources of local authorities are to be taken into account by a court exercising its powers under s 38. If the court has in mind to include a particular social worker in such a direction, then the court ought, and no doubt will, take into account the resources of the local authority who employs that social worker and any difficulties with regard to the authority's responsibility for and duty to supervise such a social worker which may arise as a result of the direction made. It may well be that the better direction would be that given by Johnson J in the *Berkshire County Council v C and Others* [1993] Fam 203, [1993] 1 FLR 569 decision, that the assessment should be carried out by a 'suitably qualified social worker'.

Local authority resources, both financial and human, and legal aid funds are factors to be borne in mind by the courts, who should not, in my judgment, encourage applications of this kind. The spirit of co-operation between all those who are concerned to arrive at the best result for the welfare of the child, be it the parents, the local authority, the guardian or the experts, all depend upon that spirit of partnership which has been the philosophy underpinning the day-to-day implementation of the Act.

In making these observations, I am not seeking to limit the jurisdiction which s 38 confers on the court, but merely, and I hope helpfully, pointing out the practical considerations which inevitably arise when this jurisdiction is to be exercised.

D49   SECTION 38(6) FUNDING: HOUSE OF LORDS' DICTA

Re G (Interim care order: residential assessment)

[2005] UKHL 68, [2006] 1 FLR 601 at 610, 613 and 624

House of Lords

Lord Scott, Lord Clyde and Baroness Hale

LORD SCOTT:

[20]   I want to add a word or two about the funding implications of
s 38(6) directions. The statute does not identify on whom the cost of
compliance with the directions is to fall. The effect of an interim care
order is that for the time being, the local authority becomes in loco
parentis to the child. It is natural, therefore, to suppose that a direction by
the court under s 38(6) for an examination or assessment of the child
would have to be funded by the local authority or, to the extent that the
costs can be treated as costs of the litigation, the costs could be
apportioned between the parties by a costs order. But, where there is a
direction not simply for an examination or assessment of the child, but for
an assessment at a residential unit of the whole family, both parents and
the child, or, perhaps in some cases, other very young children of the
family as well, the responsibility of the local authority seems to me much
less clear. Was s 38(6) really intended to enable the court to place the local
authority under an obligation to fund a residential programme for the
parents and child extending for many months? The problem becomes, to
my mind, the more stark where the main purpose of the programme is to
provide treatment to one or other, or both, of the parents so as to improve
their parenting skills. From where does the court derive its power to oblige
the local authority to fund treatment for the parents? One would
ordinarily expect that if medical or psychiatric treatment of a parent had
to be funded, it would be funded by the local NHS Trust. This, I am sure,
was what was in Johnson J's mind when he issued the invitation in his
order of 25 October, to which I have referred. It was an invitation that he
issued. It would be impossible to suggest that the court had had power
under s 38(6) to direct the NHS Trust to fund the programme of therapy
for Ellie's mother.

[21]   Reference was made by Lord Browne-Wilkinson in *Re C (A Minor)
(Interim Care Order: Residential Assessment)* [1997] AC 489, [1997]
1 FLR 1 to the investigative nature of the court's jurisdiction under the
1989 Act. A court discharging an investigative function can, I would

suppose, direct one or other of the parties to supply particular information that is available to that party and would assist the court in reaching its decision. But, whether the court's investigative function can enable it to require a local authority applicant in care proceedings to fund a course of treatment of the child's parent, in order to obtain information useful to the court in reaching its final decision, is another question. The cost of obtaining information or evidence likely to be useful for that purpose can, perhaps, be regarded as part of the costs of the litigation. So it might, perhaps, be possible for the burden of the funding, or some part of that burden, to be cast upon the Legal Services Commission (the LSC) supporting the parent or parents in question (see the discussion of this matter by Ryder J in *Lambeth London Borough Council v S, C, V and J (by his Guardian); Legal Services Commission Intervening* [2005] EWHC 776 (Fam), [2005] 2 FLR 1171. These funding difficulties were raised with counsel in the course of the hearing before your Lordships, but none had any clear answer to the problems. There probably is no clear answer that can be given.

[22] However, following the conclusion of oral argument on this appeal, counsel for the respondents made some further written submissions to your Lordships regarding the funding of residential assessments by the LSC from the Community Legal Fund. It appears that on 8 November 2005, the Children and Families Team at the LSC prepared a position statement regarding the extent to which the LSC would be prepared to contribute to such funding. The statement makes clear, first, that the LSC will not fund any element of treatment, therapy or training within a programme of assessment but, secondly, subject to that, will fund the costs of an assessment, or a proportion thereof, either agreed between the parties or determined by the court. So, if the assessment involves no element of treatment etc, the LSC will fund the whole cost of the programme, including accommodation and subsistence expenses.

[23] It seems to me, that the funding problems which the LSC's position statement is addressing, provide some indication that the use made of s 38(6) in some of the cases to which I have referred, and in particular by the Court of Appeal in the present case, went beyond the purpose for which s 38(6) was intended, and was not a legitimate use of the subsection. The funding of the Cassel Hospital programme might have been voluntarily undertaken by the council or by the NHS Trust or by the LSC. In the case of each of them, a refusal could, subject to the essential control that the need to obtain the court's permission constitutes, have been challenged by an application for judicial review. And, if the application were successful, the proposed funder would have to think again. But, if a programme of therapy for a parent with a view to improving his or her parenting skills, with or without continuous assessment of his or her progress, falls outside the scope of s 38(6), my present opinion, necessarily provisional as we have not had the advantage of full argument on the issue, is that the court would have no power to

direct the local authority, or any other potential funder, to undertake the funding of the programme, and that the LSC's statement of 8 November 2005 correctly reflects the legal position.

LORD CLYDE:

[33] The granting of directions under s 38(6) is a matter of discretion for the judge, and in exercising that discretion, financial considerations may be relevant. But, the costs involved should be nothing near the kind of expenditure which was in issue in the present case, where the work involved the ongoing treatment and assessment of the mother, over a period of months.

BARONESS HALE:

[70] I would like to add two footnotes. First, I entirely accept that from a clinical point of view, these legalistic niceties are both unhelpful and unfair in the real world of trying to work with seriously disturbed families (see the discussion by Dr Roger Kennedy, Consultant Psychotherapist in charge of the Families Service at the Cassel, in 'Assessment and Treatment in Family Law – A Valid Distinction?' [2001] Fam Law 676). In an ideal world, the child's need for services such as the Cassel would be identified and the service provided. The only question for the court would be whether it should be provided voluntarily or under the auspices of some sort of court order. The problem is that the service needs funding and the local health trust and social services authority which have responsibility for the particular family involved may be unable or unwilling to fund it. That problem clearly requires a solution if the uniquely valuable service provided by the Cassel is to continue. But it is not permissible for the courts to try to solve the problem through a provision which was never designed for that purpose. It is sticking plaster at best, and costly sticking plaster at that. We have not heard detailed argument upon whether or not the court has power to direct the local authority or any of the parties to fund the assessment. I would, therefore, prefer to express no concluded view on the issues raised in paras [20]–[23] of the opinion of my noble and learned friend, Lord Scott of Foscote. But on the assumption that the court does have such power, the cost of any proposed assessment must be relevant to the court's decision whether or not to require the parties to provide it. However, it is inappropriate for the court to require detailed evidence from senior officers of such reluctant local authorities and insist that they prove a so-called 'money defence' (cf *Re C (Children) (Residential Assessments)* [2001] EWCA Civ 1305, [2001] 3 FCR 164 at 172, para 31). Nor should we be tolerating a situation in which an hour's directions hearing, followed by a full day's hearing, are devoted to deciding whether or not to make a direction under s 38(6), as happened in this case.

This case is also included in relation to:

D44   Main focus of assessment must be on the child

D45   Therapeutic services must be incidental to gathering necessary information

D57   Interim or final order (2)

D50 SECTION 38(6) FUNDING AND PROPER PROCESS

A Local Authority v M

[2008] EWHC 162 (Fam), [2008] 1 FLR 1579 at 1582

Family Division

Bodey J

[15] The local authority does not consent to an order for a residential assessment at its sole expense. It says that it cannot do so, given its straitened financial position as set out below. But pragmatically (since it supports this way forward in principle) it has not proactively opposed the s 38(6) order sought by M and the children's guardian.

[16] Section 38(6) reads: 'Where the court makes an interim care order ... it may give such directions ... as it considers appropriate with regard to the medical or psychiatric examination or other assessment of the child ...'. The Act does not however address the question of how such an examination or assessment is to be funded.

[17] By 2007, case-law had established that the court could direct that the costs of a residential or other assessment were to be divided between the parties, *provided that* it fell properly within the broad definition of an assessment and was not primarily intended to provide therapeutic, educative or other such services: see *Calderdale MBC v S and the Legal Services Commission* [2004] EWHC 2529 (Fam), [2005] 1 FLR 751; *Lambeth London Borough Council v S* [2005] EWHC 776 (Fam), [2005] 2 FLR 1171; *Re G (Interim Care Order: Residential Assessment)*, [2005] UKHL 68, [2005] 3 WLR 1166, [2006] 1 FLR 601, [2006] 1 All ER 706 and *Sheffield City Council v V (Legal Services Commission Intervening)* [2006] EWHC 1861 (Fam), [2007] 1 FLR 279, FD.

[18] However, following a governmental consultation in 2007, the Funding Code under ss 8 and 9 of the Access to Justice Act 1999 was amended as from 1 October 2007 to provide that:

'The following may not be charged under any level of service unless authorised by a specific order or direction from the Lord Chancellor—

(i)   all costs or expenses of or relating to the residential assessment of a child;

(ii) all costs or expenses of or relating to treatment, therapy, training or other interventions of an educative or rehabilitative nature.'

A 'residential assessment' is defined as:

'... any assessment of a child, whether under Section 38(6) of the Children Act 1989 or otherwise, in which the child, alone or with others, is assessed on a residential basis at any location other than his or her normal residence. It also includes an assessment or viability assessment, whether residential or not, preparatory to or with a view to the possibility of a residential assessment.'

Only residential assessments are excluded in this way. The cost of non-residential assessments (which have the same objective of providing the court with the necessary information to carry out its duties) can still be shared out under the case-law referred to at para [17] above.

[19] The Legal Services Commission was served with notice of M's application for a residential assessment order and was given leave to intervene to respond to it. This was because the local authority's original contention was that the costs of the assessment should be shared equally between the parties, which would have meant the Legal Services Commission being responsible for 75% of it. The Commission thereafter wrote to the local authority explaining why it says the court no longer has power to direct that the costs of a residential assessment be shared such that the Legal Services Commission has to pay for any part. The letter sets out the legislative background and describes the Funding Code as being binding upon the court, having been laid before both Houses of Parliament in July 2007 pursuant to the Access to Justice Act 1999.

[20] After careful considered of this information, the local authority replied on 23 January 2008 accepting that the Legal Services Commission cannot now be ordered to contribute to the costs of the intended residential assessment. So the Legal Services Commission has taken no part in these proceedings. No party before me has taken issue with this stance adopted by the Legal Services Commission. It has been accepted as a given at this hearing that the court can no longer direct a sharing of the costs of a residential assessment such as to achieve a contribution from the Legal Services Commission. Since neither M nor C has any money, this leaves realistically only one party to pay: the local authority.

[21] It says however that it cannot afford to do so. The social care budget, which would pay for such an assessment, is already overspent and needs moneys transferred into it from elsewhere within the council's budget. No additional resources, I am told, have been provided to local authorities to offset their greater exposure to the expense of funding of residential assessments. In a letter dated 24 January 2008, the Director of

Resources points out that, although the local authority is only a small unitary authority, it has a high level of deprivation within its area. With an increase in government grant for 2008/2009 of approximately £3.4m, plus a proposed council tax increase for the year of a further £2.2m, and if the council can make targeted savings of a further £1m over the year, there is a predicted budget deficit for the year of approximately £2.9m. Put another way, I am told there are an average of 4.25 residential assessments ordered per annum in cases where this local authority is applicant. The local authority has averagely been required to contribute £12,500 per assessment, ie 25% of the total cost of approximately £50,000 for each assessment (the other 75% having presumably been borne by the Legal Services Commission as disbursements on the public funding certificates of the other parties). If the local authority now has to pay the full £50,000 of all ordered residential assessments, this would increase its liability by £37,500 per assessment, ie (at 4.25 assessments pa) an increased burden of £160,000 per annum. The local authority says this is unaffordable, except through serious sacrifices of other public services.

[22] The court must obviously pay careful regard to these budgeting matters and it seems there may be deserving cases nowadays where a residential assessment is simply unaffordable. Here, however, the local authority itself positively regards the intended residential assessment as the way forward. It would not presently countenance E being cared for by M and C at home during the course of an ordinary community assessment, because (based on the sort of familial problems outlined above) it considers there would be a risk of significant harm to E. It is difficult to dissent from this view. It is equally difficult to dissent from the submission of counsel for M that, unless a residential assessment is directed here to enable safe examination of (a) M and C's care of E, (b) the degree of attachment which E has to M and C, and (c) the dynamics of M and C's relationship together, then it is almost impossible to see any realistic outcome of these proceedings other than a care order on a plan for E's adoption.

[23] Weighing up all these various and competing considerations, I conclude that the local authority should pay for the revised residential assessment in question ie the 7-week period at a price of £25,000, with a report and prognosis at the end of that time. I will today fix a further hearing before myself in 7-weeks' time so that, if there is any dispute about what should happen thereafter, it will be capable of determination without delay. If things have gone reasonably well, and a further 5 weeks of assessment is recommended (ie making up the total of 12 weeks originally envisaged) it is reasonable to anticipate that the local authority may have to be required to meet that cost, making its total potential exposure up to £50,000.

[24] I observe that this case amply justifies the opposition of the Family Justice Council to the amendments which have recently been made to the

Funding Guidance. The Family Justice Council, amongst other trenchant criticisms of those amendments, said:

> '... community based assessments in such high risk cases are far less reliable [than residential assessments] and are more likely to generate delay. A parent who can manage a couple of hours observed contact at a family centre may not be a safe parent when required to provide 24 hour care. A residential assessment is a far more meaningful test of capability to meet the child's needs and provides more effective risk assessment. It therefore provides the best basis for safeguarding the interests of the child ... The Council suggests that simply because the Legal Services Commission refuses to finance residential assessments, the need for them in appropriate cases will not go away. The financial burden will of necessity shift back to local authorities ...
>
> In the Council's view the proposed timescale is inadequate as it will not allow local authorities and other agencies sufficient time to address the issue of how residential assessments are to be funded when they are ordered by the court. This risks a funding gap which could seriously prejudice the interests of the children and parents involved. The Council considers that in the current proposal the Commission is exposing itself to the risk of judicial review and challenges under the Human Rights Act. In care and adoption proceedings the issues at stake for parents and children are of the greatest possible significance. As has recently been observed, to deprive a parent of her child is indeed "a life sentence" ...'

[25] Those comments were prescient. The court is in a difficult position in cases like this, unable to spread the financial load of necessary residential assessments, yet faced with local authorities which are already struggling to make ends meet. Although consideration has to be given to councils' budgets, it is not easy for a court to appear to have to compare the relative importance of a particular residential assessment (a) with other residential assessments which have been or might be applied for in other cases involving the same local authority, and/or (b) with other council duties and aspirations, perhaps help for an elderly person or the upkeep of a park. (I do not say that these will literally be direct competing choices, but it is not far off the mark where councils are in the red).

[26] I am told by counsel on behalf of this local authority that it regards this issue as being of wide-reaching public importance, as it is aware of other similar cases in the pipeline being dealt with by other local authorities which are going to cause the parties and the court serious difficulties. This local authority itself has two other pending cases where the same question is shortly going to arise and it expresses considerable concern about the financial implications, given the budgetary problems summarised above. The only reason for its decision not to argue actively

against being ordered to pay all the costs here is that pragmatically it has little alternative, given the professional view of its own staff and of the children's guardian that a residential assessment is the only way forward in E's interests.

[27] This case demonstrates an urgent need for further consideration of the funding of necessary residential assessments. Some arrangements need to be put in place to avoid the need for routine hearings like this on a case-by-case basis, hearings which are costly and which divert judicial resources. It is unsatisfactory if not invidious that courts charged with taking serious and sensitive decisions about children, where an under-informed decision could on occasion spell disaster, should have to choose between (a) over-burdening an already over-stretched local authority or (b) denying a residential assessment to a parent for whom it represents the only hope of avoiding the loss of his or her child to adoption.

Interim orders / authorising removal of child from parental care

D51   GUIDANCE ABOUT INTERIM ORDERS

Hampshire County Council v S

[1993] 1 FLR 559 at 566

Family Division

Cazalet J

I have been told that in the light of the procedural problems which have arisen in the present case, it would help if I was to give some guidance as to the way in which justices should deal with interim applications of the nature raised in these proceedings. Accordingly, with the President' approval, I make the following observations:

(1)   Justices should bear in mind that they are not, at an interim hearing, required to make a final conclusion; indeed it is because they are unable to reach a final conclusion that they are empowered to make an interim order. An interim order or decision will usually be required so as to establish a holding position, after weighing all the relevant risks, pending the final hearing. Nevertheless, justices must always ensure that the substantial issue is tried and determined at the earliest possible date. Any delay in determining the question before the court is likely to prejudice the welfare of the child (see s 1(2) of the Act).

(2)   If justices find that they are unable to provide the appropriate hearing time, be it through pressures of work or for some other reason, they must, when an urgent interim order may have to be made, consider taking steps pursuant to r 14(2)(h) by transferring the proceedings laterally to an adjacent family proceedings court.

(3)   At the start of a hearing which is concerned with interim relief, justices will usually be called upon to exercise their discretion under r 21(2) as to the order of speeches and evidence. Circumstances prevailing will almost certainly not permit full evidence to be heard. Accordingly, in such proceedings, justices should rarely make findings as to disputed facts. These will have to be left over for the final hearing.

(4)   Justices must bear in mind that the greater the extent to which an interim order deviates from a previous order or the status quo, the more acute the need is likely to be for an early final hearing date. any disruption in a child's life almost invariably requires early resolution. Justices should be cautious about changing a child's residence under an interim order. The preferred course should be to leave the child where it is, with a direction for safeguards and the earliest possible hearing date.

(5)   When an interim order may be made which will lead to a substantial change in a child's position, justices should consider permitting limited oral evidence to be led and challenged by way of cross-examination. However, it will necessarily follow that, in cross-examination, the evidence will have to be restricted to the issues which are essential at the interim stage. To this end the court may well have to intervene to ensure that this course is followed and that there is not a 'dress rehearsal' of the full hearing.

(6)   Justices should, if possible, ensure that they have before them the written advice from the guardian ad litem. When there are substantial issues between the parties the guardian should, if possible, be at court to give oral advice. A party who is opposed to a recommendation made by the guardian should normally be given an opportunity to put questions to him or her in regard to advice given to the court.

(7)   Justices must always comply with the mandatory requirements of the rules. These include compliance with: (a) r 21(1), which requires the justices to read, before the hearing, any documents which have been filed under r 17; (b) r 21(5), which requires the justices' clerk to make an appropriate written record of the hearing and in consultation with the justices to record the reasons for the court's decision on any findings of fact; and (c) r 21(6), which requires the court, when making its order or giving its decision, to state the findings of fact and reasons for the court decision.

(8)   If shortage of time or some other circumstance delays the court in the preparation of its written finding of fact and reasons, justices should adjourn the making of their order or the giving of their decision until the following court day or the earliest possible date. At that further hearing it is permissible for one of their number to return to court and state the decision, findings of fact and reasons (see r 21(6). When the length of a hearing lasts beyond normal hours, it will often be sensible for the court to take this course so that it is not formulating its reasons and making perhaps a difficult decision under the sort of pressure which can arise when a sitting runs late into the day.

(9)   When justices grant interim relief, they should state their findings and reasons concisely. Although it will not normally be open to them to make findings on disputed facts (because the court will not have heard the full evidence), it may assist if the justices summarise briefly the essential factual issues between the parties.

D52 HOLDING ORDER / NO POWER TO IMPOSE CONDITIONS WITH ICO

Re L (Interim care order: power of court)

[1996] 2 FLR 742 at 745 and 747

Court of Appeal

Ward and Millett LJJ

WARD LJ:

As to final care orders, Nourse LJ and Wall J[1] confirmed what had earlier been stated in *Re B (Minors) (Termination of Contact: Paramount Consideration)* [1993] Fam 301, sub nom *Re B (Minors) (Care: Contact: Local Authority's Plans)* [1993] 1 FLR 543 that:

'... the court does not have the power to make a care order containing either a direction or a condition that the child in question shall reside at home, and accordingly that the position for which the guardian ad litem now contends is not one which this court can impose on the local authority, assuming of course, that such a course of action is perceived to be in the best interests of the child.'

As to interim care orders, Waite LJ was at pains to make clear in *Re G (Minors) (Interim Care Order)* [1993] 2 FLR 839:

'... it was important in the children's interests to demonstrate at this early interlocutory stage that the mind of the court was entirely open to all possibilities and to avoid taking any step which might appear to pre-judge the issues.'

An interim care order should not be regarded as a step which involved any advance judgment on the part of the court. An interim order was a neutral and effective way of preserving the status quo:

'The regime of interim care orders laid down by s 38 ... is designed to leave the court with the ability to maintain strict control of any steps taken or proposed by a local authority in the exercise of powers that are by their nature temporary and subject to continuous review. The making of an interim care order is an essentially impartial step, favouring neither one side nor the other, and

---

[1]   *Re T (A Minor) (Care Order: Conditions)* [1994] 2 FLR 423.

affording to no one, least of all the local authority in whose favour it is made, an opportunity for tactical or adventitious advantage.'

In my judgment the position is this: first, an interim care order is a holding order which should not be treated as an indication of how the matter will be finally disposed of. No irreversible decision has yet been made as this mother fears. Secondly, an interim care order is none the less a form of care order. Section 31(11) says so because a care order is there defined to include an interim care order made under s 38. Accordingly, once made, the care of the child passes to the local authority and the manner in which the child is cared for passes out of the control of the court. It must follow that the court has no more power to impose conditions on an interim order than it has to give directions under a full order.

All of that, however, is subject to s 38(6) ...

MILLETT LJ:

The court has no jurisdiction to impose a residential condition on the local authority when making an interim care order other than a condition which is consequential upon the giving of directions for a residential assessment under s 38(6) of the Children Act 1989. The submission to the contrary by counsel for the mother is, in my opinion, based on a misunderstanding of a passage in *Re T (A Minor) (Care Order: Conditions)* [1994] 2 FLR 423, 435–436. As the previous paragraph of that judgment makes clear, the court was not stating that the court had power to impose conditions on the making of an interim care order which it did not have when making a final order. The court was saying no more than that, in the particular circumstances of that case, the local authority were wise not to challenge the judge's decision in this respect because he could properly have achieved a similar result by other means.

I desire to state first, that the interim care order made in the present case is not irreversible either in law or in fact; and secondly, that since the judge was not asked to give directions under s 38(6), the choice which he had to make was between the making of an interim care order and the making of an interim supervision and residential orders. He decided in favour of an interim care order.

D53   ICO: REMOVAL FROM PARENTS (1)

Re LA (Care: chronic neglect)

[2009] EWCA Civ 822, [2010] 1 FLR 80 at 82

Court of Appeal

Thorpe LJ

[6] The judge did not consider those provisions or recite them independently, but having set out the statutory provisions in s 31 and 38 went on to consider what he described as the 'significant judicial gloss over the years since 1989'. He considered specifically the case of *Re M (Interim Care Order: Removal)* [2005] EWCA Civ 1594 [2006] 1 FLR 1043, decided by this court in 2005, and the case of *Re H (A Child) (Interim Care Order)* [2002] EWCA Civ 1932, [2003] 1 FCR 350, again decided in this court. However, he then continued to consider a decision at first instance, the decision of Ryder J in the case of *Re L (Care Proceedings: Removal of Child)* [2008] 1 FLR 575. The paragraphs in the judgment of Ryder J that require particular consideration are paras [10] and [16], and they are thus:

'[10]   Even more stark is the failure to acknowledge the need to consider on the alleged facts of this case whether:

(a)   there is an imminent risk of really serious harm ie whether the risk to ML's safety demands immediate separation (per Thorpe LJ in *Re H (a child) (Interim Care Order)* [2003] 1 FCR 350); and

(b)   if not, the question whether mother is able to provide good enough long term care should be a matter for the Court to decide at a final hearing not to be litigated at an interim hearing which effectively pre judges the full and profound trial of the Local Authority's case and the parents' response to the same thereby usurping or substituting for the function of the final hearing or issues resolution processes: *Re G (minors) (Interim Care Order)* [1993] 2 FLR 839 at 845 CA and *Re H* (Above) at paragraph 38.

[16]   The second is the nature and extent of the risk. The fact that the Local Authority and/or the children's guardian do not have knowledge of matters either generally or even because of an alleged course of conduct including the deception of a parent does not change the actual risk that a child faces it merely changes their perception or assessment of that risk. If in fact the perception of

risk could have been greater had the Local Authority or the children's guardian known of the parents alleged covert meetings, then the question still arises as to whether the consequences of that risk have been adequately protected against or can be so as to ameliorate the same. If so, there will not be an imminent risk of really serious harm because of the new information but rather a risk of harm that may be really serious but which has not yet occurred and may not do so within the proceedings if adequate arrangements can be put into place.'

[7] It is common ground at the Bar that Ryder J did not intend by those paragraphs to restate or to alter the approach that appears from the two Court of Appeal cases that I have already cited, augmented by a third case in this court, namely *Re K and H* [2006] EWCA Civ 1898, [2007] 1 FLR 2043. That is transparent from para [10](a) of the report where Ryder J identifies the source of the summary as being my judgment in the case of *Re H (A Child) (Interim Care Order)* [2002] EWCA Civ 1932, [2003] 1 FCR 350. What is it then that the three authorities in this court seem to establish? In the first, the case of *Re H*, the crucial paragraphs are [38] and [39], from which can be extracted two propositions, the first that the decision taken by the court on an interim care order application must necessarily be limited to issues that cannot await the fixture and must not extend to issues that are being prepared for determination at that fixture. The second proposition which appears from the final sentence of para [39] is that separation is only to be ordered if the child's safety demands immediate separation. In the subsequent case of *Re N* in para [27] I stated that a local authority in seeking to justify the continuing removal of a child from home necessarily must meet a very high standard. In the final authority, *K and H*, the key paragraph is para [16] in which I described the court's approach thus:

'... at an interim stage the removal of children from their parents is not to be sanctioned unless the child's safety requires interim protection.'

Other significant cases on this issue:

* Cf *Re S (Authorising children's immediate removal)* [2010] EWCA Civ 421, [2010] 2 FLR 873
* *Re F (Care proceedings: interim care order)* [2010] EWCA Civ 826, [2010] 2 FLR 1455

D54   ICO: REMOVAL FROM PARENTS (2)

Re B (Interim care order)

[2010] EWCA Civ 324, [2010] 2 FLR 283 at 290

Court of Appeal

Wall LJ

[16]   In his skeleton argument, Mr Aidan Vine of counsel, on the mother's behalf, advanced two grounds of appeal. Firstly, he submitted that the judge did not apply the correct legal test for approving a care plan for removing children from parental care under an interim care order. Secondly, he argued that the judge approached his decision on the basis that the onus was upon the appellant to show cause why the children should not be placed in foster care.

[17]   In my judgment, neither ground is sustainable, as I think is plain from the extensive citation from the judge's judgment which I have provided. Taking the second ground first, it does not seem to me that, on a fair reading of his judgment, the judge did reverse the burden of proof as the appellant seeks to allege. He rightly found the threshold established. In this respect, the burden of proof was on the local authority, although the point was conceded. The judge rightly then decided that the question was whether it would be 'better for the child to make an order than to make no order' and that he had to consider 'the child's welfare pursuant to the subsection' to which he had already referred. This is a clear reference back to an earlier passage in his judgment in which he had specified, in particular, ss 1(3), 1(5), 31 and 38 of the Children Act 1989, as well as Arts 6 and 8 of the European Convention for the Protection of Human Rights and Fundamental Freedoms 1950 and the United Nations Convention on the Rights of the Child 1989.

[18]   In summary, therefore, the judge was rightly considering a welfare question, and within that welfare question the test was whether or not there was what he described as 'an urgent need to keep the children from their mother for the weeks to which I have referred'. In my judgment, this is not an approach which can be faulted. As the judge noted, the burden of proof was on the local authority to satisfy the court that the threshold criteria were met: whether or not interim care orders were made then became a welfare issue.

[19]   His Honour Judge Cleary was, of course, the judge at first instance in *Re LA (Care: Chronic Neglect)* [2009] EWCA Civ 822, [2010] 1 FLR

80. I note in passing the tribute which Thorpe LJ paid to him in this court in para [5] of his judgment, a tribute which I would seek to echo in relation to the current extempore judgment under appeal in the instant case. In particular, the judge was careful to avoid falling into the trap identified in that case (and in *Re H (A Child) (Interim Care Order)* [2002] EWCA Civ 1932, [2002] 1 FCR 350), namely that the interim order should last until the final hearing and be thus determinative of outcome. In my judgment, moreover, and given the nature of the threshold, the *Re LA* test was plainly met in this case.

[20] In my judgment, therefore, the judge did not apply the wrong test.

[21] Although he does not mention it, we understand that the judge was referred to the decision of this court in *Re B (Care Proceedings: Interim Care Order)* [2009] EWCA Civ 1254, [2010] 1 FLR 1211, which had been handed down on 25 November 2009. In that case, this court approved the test enunciated by the trial judge namely (on the basis that the threshold criteria for an interim order were satisfied): 'whether the continued removal of (the child) from the care of her parents is proportionate to the risk of harm to which she will be exposed if she is allowed to return to her parents care': see para [31]. Had Judge Cleary referred to this passage or applied this test the answer would, in my judgment, once again, have been obvious. Furthermore, as it seems to me, the test approved in *Re B* is one which can be universally applied, and which addresses the judge's observation that 'it is difficult if not impossible to find a rule to which all cases can be compared when faced with these unhappy applications'.

General notes:

The same test, 'whether the continued removal of (the child) from the care of her parents is proportionate to the risk of harm to which she will be exposed if she is allowed to return to her parents care', first set out by HHJ Hamilton, was again endorsed by Wall P in *Re S (A child)* [2010] EWCA Civ 1363 at [8]–[9].

D55 RENEWAL: SCOPE OF HEARING MAY BE LIMITED

Re B (Interim care orders: renewal)

[2001] 2 FLR 1217 at 1222, 1224 and 1226

Family Division

Black J

I entirely accept that the court has a duty to satisfy itself in a judicial manner each time an interim care order application is made that the evidence is sufficient to establish, as s 38(2) of the Children Act 1989 requires, that there are reasonable grounds for believing that the circumstances with respect to the child are as mentioned in s 31(2) and to consider what order, if any, is the appropriate order, bearing in mind the 'no order' principle and the other provisions of s 1.

My initial thought that it might be possible for the local authority to establish when the interim process first began, that s 38(2) of the Children Act 1989 applied and for subsequent courts to rely upon that without further appraisal, confining their consideration when a renewal of the interim care order was sought to whether that remained an appropriate form of order, was not a sound one. As evidence is assembled in preparation for the full care hearing, it is entirely possible that new light is cast upon what were originally thought to be reasonable grounds within s 38(2) of the Children Act 1989. They may be strengthened, but equally they may become weaker so that a subsequent court can no longer say that reasonable grounds exist to believe the circumstances are as mentioned in s 31. For example, a child may be made the subject of an interim care order upon the basis of medical evidence that the child has been subjected to a shaking injury, and further investigations may then reveal that the child, in fact, suffers from an organic disease which has been responsible for its symptoms.

I do not, however, consider that anything in the Children Act 1989 or the European Convention on Human Rights requires that the court, in carrying out its consideration on each interim care order application, must permit a party who opposes the making of an interim care order to call or require to be called what evidence he or she wishes, or to make unlimited submissions. Mr Campbell did not, in fact, pursue his original argument that, to be fair, the hearing must be a full hearing, but rather submitted that all the relevant issues must be considered by the court with a proper degree of involvement from the parties for the hearing to be fair.

In my view, that was a sensible adjustment to his submission, because it is plain that an interim hearing is bound to be circumscribed in its ambit. It is an interim hearing precisely because (and there may be many reasons why this is so) it is too soon to have a full and final hearing. It is, as Cazalet J pointed out in *Hampshire County Council v S* [1993] Fam 158, [1993] 1 FLR 559, a limited hearing required to establish a holding position pending the final hearing. The judge's observations in that case were made with the then President's approval and remain, in my view, as valuable today as they were then. Amongst them is the observation that circumstances prevailing in an interim hearing will almost certainly not permit full evidence to be heard and therefore findings of fact on disputed issues should rarely be made at an interim stage, and that when oral evidence is permitted, cross-examination should be restricted to the issues which are essential at the interim stage so that the interim hearing is not a dress rehearsal of the full hearing.

It is plain that the court has the power to determine its own procedure and to control evidence and submissions. This is accepted on behalf of the appellant and not argued to be a contravention of Art 6 of the European Convention on Human Rights. Directions can be given for the conduct of the proceedings under r 4.14 of the Family Proceedings Rules 1991, and directions given as to the order of speeches and evidence at the hearing under r 4.21 of the Family Proceedings Rules 1991. There are authorities illustrating how the court may, in appropriate cases, limit the scope of the hearing, sometimes rigorously. In *Re B (Minors) (Contact)* [1994] 2 FLR 1, for example, the Court of Appeal held in a contact case that a judge is not obliged to hold a full hearing permitting the parties to call oral evidence and cross-examine any witnesses they choose, but has a broad discretion to conduct the case as is most appropriate for the issues involved and the evidence available. *Devon County Council v S and Others* [1992] 2 FLR 244 illustrates how a judicial duty to investigate may be carried out in different ways, depending on the circumstances of the case. There, the parties were agreed upon the replacement of an interim care order with a full care order, but the justices insisted on hearing considerable oral evidence. On appeal, Thorpe J (as he then was) pointed out that although there was an overriding judicial duty to investigate, the depth of the investigation must reflect the consensus reached between the parties, and lengthy oral evidence was not appropriate.

...

Changes in circumstances will always dictate a review, to a greater or lesser extent, of the whole picture, so that, for example, the separation of a non-abusing parent from an abusing parent will necessitate a reconsideration of whether the children might now return to live with the non-abusing parent. In each case, therefore, the court will have to make decisions tailored to the individual circumstances as to the type and amount of evidence that is appropriate and the scope of submissions and, where there is dispute about this, should give the parties an opportunity to address it on the question. Factors that are likely to be important in the consideration include:

(1) the number, nature and extent of previous hearings and whether the parties were all represented;

(2) the extent to which the simple passage of time necessitates a review of earlier decisions concerning the children;

(3) whether and in what way circumstances have changed since the last fully contested hearing and to what extent this is likely to make a difference to the outcome of the application;

(4) to what extent the evidence that a party wishes to call or the submissions that he wishes to make are material to the issues and likely to affect the outcome of the hearing;

(5) the welfare of the child and the effect of further litigation;

(6) the degree of investigation that the justice of the case requires;

(7) the need to be even-handed in approaching evidence and submissions, so that, for example, a parent is not denied the opportunity to adduce oral evidence on an issue upon which the local authority social worker is permitted to give oral evidence.

Re W (A Minor) (Interim Care Order) [1994] 2 FLR 892, a decision of the Court of Appeal, lends considerable support to this analysis. There was in place in that case an interim supervision order. At what was intended to be a directions hearing only, the local authority applied for an interim care order instead without giving advance notice to the mother and in her absence. The judge refused an adjournment, declined to allow counsel for the mother who was present to cross-examine the social worker or the guardian, and made an interim care order without any oral evidence. Given the format of the hearing and the lack of notice of the changed order sought, the mother's appeal was allowed. In giving the main judgment, Glidewell LJ makes comments which are of wider application than just the facts of the case. He emphasises that an interim hearing is not a trial run of the final hearing and that the responsibility for ensuring that it is not is not merely that of the judge but also the advocates for the parties. He says:

'It is their job to ensure that it is only the matters which are genuinely in issue at the particular hearing which are canvassed, that the evidence is restricted to those issues, and that cross-examination is tightly restricted to what is necessary to deal with those issues justly and fairly.'

He says that as a general proposition some oral evidence and cross-examination should be permitted on an application for an interim order which is of a new kind or is a new order. However, he continues:

'Counsel for the mother submits ... that the same process must follow on each application for a renewal whether the application is for an order in the same terms as the order made previously 4 weeks before or for a different form of order. With respect to him, if the application is for an order in the same terms as that made previously, I am confident that that submission is wrong. If neither party suggests that there has been any relevant change in the circumstances in the intervening time, and neither seeks to make an alteration to the order, it is not necessary to canvass the evidence again, in my judgment. All that is necessary is for the court to be reminded that it had the evidence before it on the last occasion and to be informed that neither party suggests that there is any relevant change of circumstances.'

This is a topic the Lord Justice reverts to again shortly after, at 902C, emphasising that insofar as cross-examination is required on material matters leading to an application for a new form of order, that too:

'is to be restricted to dealing with any change in circumstances. It does not mean canvassing the whole history from the start.'

He concludes by saying that the next hearing in that case would be:

'restricted to [the] change in circumstances, but it is wholly open to the judge at such a hearing to make such a decision as he thinks fit; whether to make an order, and what form to make if he decides to do so. I express no opinion about it. He must do so, of course, having the welfare of the child as the first and paramount consideration in his mind.'

...

Practical considerations do not, of course, outweigh the need to comply with the provisions of the Children Act 1989 and of the European Convention on Human Rights, and may have to give way if they cannot be accommodated within that framework. However, in my judgment it is material here that a conclusion that did not permit matters to be dealt with as District Judge Bradley dealt with them could have undesirable consequences and cause problems for the regime by which interim provision is made for children pending a full hearing of care applications. No doubt in most cases good sense would prevail and further fully contested hearings would only be sought where there was a realistic prospect of the result being different, which in practice would usually mean where there had been a material change of circumstances. However, in those cases where that was not so the following are examples of the sort of problems that, in my judgment, may be caused:

(1)   I agree with the local authority that an inability to have regard to previous decisions in the same case could introduce uncertainty and inconsistency, which may not be helpful to the children.

(2)   It seems to me also that it may cause delay, in the particular case and generally, if parties and the courts were to divert their energies from the preparation for the main hearing to a profusion of hotly contested interim hearings.

(3)   More frequent contests in court may cause ill-feeling and disrupt the development of the working relationships between parents and social workers and others that may be so necessary for the future care of the children concerned in the proceedings.

Accordingly, for all the reasons that I have given, I dismiss the appeal.

Interim or final order

D56 INTERIM OR FINAL ORDER (1)

Re S (Minors) (Care order: implementation of care plan); Re W (Minors) (Care order: adequacy of care plan)

[2002] UKHL 10, [2002] 1 FLR 815 at 836

House of Lords

Lord Nicholls

Interim care orders

[89] I turn to the other 'revisionary application' of the Children Act 1989 adumbrated by the Court of Appeal. This concerns the extended use of interim care orders. The source of the court's power to make an interim care order is s 38 of the Children Act 1989. The power exists when an application for a care order or a supervision order is adjourned (s 38(1)(a)) or the court has given a direction to a local authority under s 37 to undertake an investigation of a child's circumstances (s 38(1)(b)). Section 38 contains tight limits on the period for which an interim care order has effect: 8 weeks initially, thereafter 4 weeks. The circumstances in which an interim care order ceases to have effect include also the disposal of the application for a care order or a supervision order, in both s 38(1)(a) and s 38(1)(b) cases.

[90] From a reading of s 38 as a whole it is abundantly clear that the purpose of an interim care order, so far as presently material, is to enable the court to safeguard the welfare of a child until such time as the court is in a position to decide whether or not it is in the best interests of the child to make a care order. When that time arrives depends on the circumstances of the case and is a matter for the judgment of the trial judge. That is the general, guiding principle. The corollary to this principle is that an interim care order is not intended to be used as a means by which the court may continue to exercise a supervisory role over the local authority in cases where it is in the best interests of a child that a care order should be made.

[91] An interim care order, thus, is a temporary 'holding' measure. Inevitably, time is needed before an application for a care order is ready for decision. Several parties are usually involved: parents, the child's guardian, the local authority, perhaps others. Evidence has to be prepared, parents and other people interviewed, investigations may be required, assessments made, and the local authority must produce its care plan for the child in accordance with the guidance contained in local authority circular LAC(99)29 *Care Plans and Care Proceedings Under the Children Act 1989.* Although the Children Act 1989 itself makes no mention of a care plan, in practice this is a document of key importance. It enables the court and everyone else to know, and consider, the local authority's plans for the future of the child if a care order is made.

[92] When a local authority formulates a care plan in connection with an application for a care order, there are bound to be uncertainties. Even the basic shape of the future life of the child may be far from clear. Over the last 10 years problems have arisen about how far courts should go in attempting to resolve these uncertainties before making a care order and passing responsibility to the local authority. Once a final care order is made, the resolution of the uncertainties will be a matter for the authority, not the court.

[93] In terms of legal principle one type of uncertainty is straightforward. This is the case where the uncertainty needs to be resolved before the court can decide whether it is in the best interests of the child to make a care order at all. In *C v Solihull Metropolitan Borough Council* [1993] 1 FLR 290 the court could not decide whether a care order was in the best interests of a child, there a 'battered baby', without knowing the result of a parental assessment. Ward J made an appropriate interim order. In such a case the court should finally dispose of the matter only when the material facts are as clearly known as can be hoped. Booth J adopted a similar approach, for a similar reason, in *Hounslow London Borough Council v A* [1993] 1 WLR 291, [1993] 1 FLR 702.

[94] More difficult, as a matter of legal principle, are cases where it is obvious that a care order is in the best interests of the child but the immediate way ahead thereafter is unsatisfactorily obscure. These cases exemplify a problem, or a 'tension', inherent in the scheme of the Children Act 1989. What should the judge do when a care order is clearly in the best interests of the child but the judge does not approve of the care plan? This judicial dilemma was described by Balcombe LJ in *Re S and D (Children: Powers of Court)* [1995] 2 FLR 456, 464, perhaps rather too bleakly, as the judge having to choose between 'the lesser of two evils'.

[95] In this context there are sometimes uncertainties whose nature is such that they are suitable for immediate resolution, in whole or in part, by the court in the course of disposing of the care order application. The uncertainty may be of such a character that it can, and should, be resolved so far as possible before the court proceeds to make the care order. Then, a limited period of 'planned and purposeful' delay can readily be justified as the sensible and practical way to deal with an existing problem.

[96] An instance of this occurred in *Re CH (Care or Interim Care Order)* [1998] 1 FLR 402. In that case the mother had pleaded guilty to causing grievous bodily harm to the child. The judge was intensely worried by the sharp divergence of professional view on placement. The local authority cautiously favoured rehabilitation. The child's guardian ad litem believed adoption was the realistic way to promote the child's future welfare. The judge made the care order without hearing any expert evidence on the disputed issue. The local authority would itself obtain expert advice, and then reconsider the question of placement. The Court of Appeal (Kennedy and Thorpe LJJ) held that the fact that a care order was the inevitable outcome should not have deflected the judge from hearing expert evidence on this issue. Even if the issue could not be finally resolved before a care order was made, it was obviously sensible and desirable that, in the circumstances of the case, the local authority should have the benefit of the judge's observations on the point.

[97] Frequently the case is on the other side of this somewhat imprecise line. Frequently the uncertainties involved in a care plan will have to be worked out after a care order has been made and while the plan is being implemented. This was so in the case which is the locus classicus on this subject: *Re J (Minors) (Care: Care Plan)* [1994] 1 FLR 253. There the care plan envisaged placing the children in short-term foster placements for up to a year. Then a final decision would be made on whether to place the children permanently away from the mother. Rehabilitation was not ruled out if the mother showed herself amenable to treatment. Wall J said, at 265A:

> '... there are cases (of which this is one) in which the action which requires to be taken in the interests of children necessarily involves steps into the unknown ... provided the court is satisfied that the local authority is alert to the difficulties which may arise in the execution of the care plan, the function of the court is not to seek to oversee the plan but to entrust its execution to the local authority.'

In that case the uncertain outcome of the treatment was a matter to be worked out after a care order was made, not before. The Court of Appeal decision in *Re L (Sexual Abuse: Standard of Proof)* [1996] 1 FLR 116 was another case of this type: see Butler-Sloss LJ, at 125E–H. So also was the decision of the Court of Appeal in *Re R (Care Proceedings: Adjournment)* [1998] 2 FLR 390.

[98] These are all instances of cases where important issues of uncertainty were known to exist before a care order was made. Quite apart from known uncertainties, an element of future uncertainty is necessarily inherent in the very nature of a care plan. The best laid plans 'gang aft a-gley'. These are matters for decision by the local authority, if and when they arise. A local authority must always respond appropriately to changes, of varying degrees of predictability, which from time to time are bound to occur after a care order has been made and while the care plan is being implemented. No care plan can ever be regarded as set in stone.

[99] Despite all the inevitable uncertainties, when deciding whether to make a care order the court should normally have before it a care plan which is sufficiently firm and particularised for all concerned to have a reasonably clear picture of the likely way ahead for the child for the foreseeable future. The degree of firmness to be expected, as well as the amount of detail in the plan, will vary from case to case depending on how far the local authority can foresee what will be best for the child at that time. This is necessarily so. But making a care order is always a serious interference in the lives of the child and his parents. Although Art 8 contains no explicit procedural requirements, the decision-making process leading to a care order must be fair and such as to afford due respect to the interests safeguarded by Art 8: see *TP and KM v United Kingdom* [2001] 2 FLR 549, para 72. If the parents and the child's guardian are to have a fair and adequate opportunity to make representations to the court on whether a care order should be made, the care plan must be appropriately specific.

[100] Cases vary so widely that it is impossible to be more precise about the test to be applied by a court when deciding whether to continue interim relief rather than proceed to make a care order. It would be foolish to attempt to be more precise. One further general point may be noted. When postponing a decision on whether to make a care order a court will need to have in mind the general statutory principle that any delay in determining issues relating to a child's upbringing is likely to prejudice the child's welfare: s 1(2) of the Children Act 1989.

[101] In the Court of Appeal Thorpe LJ in *Re W and B; Re W (Care Plan)* [2001] EWCA Civ 757, [2001] 2 FLR 582, para [29], expressed the view that in certain circumstances the judge at the trial should have a 'wider discretion' to make an interim care order: 'where the care plan seems inchoate or where the passage of a relatively brief period seems bound to see the fulfilment of some event or process vital to planning and deciding the future'. In an appropriate case, a judge must be free to defer making a care order until he is satisfied that the way ahead 'is no longer obscured by an uncertainty that is neither inevitable nor chronic'.

[102] As I see it, the analysis I have set out above adheres faithfully to the scheme of the Children Act 1989 and conforms to the procedural requirements of Art 8 of the Convention. At the same time it affords trial

judges the degree of flexibility Thorpe LJ is rightly concerned they should have. Whether this represents a small shift in emphasis from the existing case-law may be a moot point. What is more important is that, in the words of Wall J in *Re J (Minors) (Care: Care Plan)* [1994] 1 FLR 253, 262, the court must always maintain a proper balance between the need to satisfy itself about the appropriateness of the care plan and the avoidance of 'over-zealous investigation into matters which are properly within the administrative discretion of the local authority'. This balance is a matter for the good sense of the tribunal, assisted by the advocates appearing before it.

Other significant cases on this issue:

- *Re S and W (Care proceedings)* [2007] EWCA Civ 232, [2007] 2 FLR 275: see D7 – Relationship between court and LA

This case is also included in relation to:

D9   No court intervention once final CO made

D57　INTERIM OR FINAL ORDER (2)

Re G (Interim care order: residential assessment)

[2005] UKHL 68, [2006] 1 FLR 601 at 612, 613 and 620

House of Lords

Lord Clyde and Baroness Hale

LORD CLYDE:

[28] The purpose of the subsection is to enable the court to receive guidance for the making of a decision on the application for a care order. That includes the matters on which it has to be satisfied under s 31(2). The investigation, with regard to which the court may give directions, appears from the statute to be focused on the current state of affairs. That can be seen in the use of the present tense in s 1(3)(e) and (f). It may include an understanding of the present capacity of the parent to overcome any present deficiency. So, to an extent it may look to the future, but only as a matter of a current forecast. What does not seem to be envisaged, is any continuing assessment over a period of months to follow the progress, if any, of the parent in improving his or her capacity to give proper care to the child, or in reducing the risk to the child which led to the interim care order being sought at the outset.

[29] That point is, in my view, supported by the intention of the statute, that the process of examination or assessment should extend only over a relatively short period. The general approach is stated in s 1(2). The life of an interim assessment order under s 38 is only 8 weeks with extensions of only 4 weeks. Under s 32(1) the court must draw up a timetable with a view to disposing of the case without delay. Correspondingly, relatively short periods are envisaged for investigations in s 37(4) and for child assessment orders under s 43(5). It seems from the statute as if the process for obtaining care orders was intended to be rapid and usually to extend over no longer than some 2 or 3 months.

[30] It may be tempting to suppose that the court should remain in control of the future management of the child. But, while the regime introduced by Part IV of the 1989 Act gives the court power to make care orders and supervision orders, it leaves the management of a child who is in care to the local authority. On the grant of a care order, whether interim or final, the local authority not only has a duty under s 33(1) to receive the child into its care, but it also, under s 33(3), assumes parental responsibility for the child. The court may not assume the mantle of responsibility, which by its own order, has been laid upon the shoulders of the local authority. In the present case, the decision whether the course of treatment should be carried out in the Cassel Hospital or in the community, was a matter for the parental responsibility of the local authority.

...

[32] Having received the results of the examination or assessment which has been made under s 38(6), the court has then to decide how to dispose of the application for a care order. There may be occasions where there is a sound justification for prolonging the interim care order. But, I do not read the statutory provisions as envisaging that the process can be prolonged by repeated interim orders, especially if they are granted as matter of administrative procedure, and not of judicial decision. It is for the court to ensure that the application is processed without delay, so that a decision can be reached whether or not the parental responsibility should, as matters stand, remain on the local authority, or whether the continuation of such a position is not necessary for the safety of the child.

BARONESS HALE:

[55] This emphasis upon careful scrutiny of the care plan, formulated in the light of a comprehensive assessment of the child and her family, has inevitably put back the point at which the court is ready to make a final order and thus to relinquish control to the local authority. To return to Lord Nicholls of Birkenhead in *Re S (Minors) (Care Order: Implementation of Care Plan); Re W (Minors) (Care Order: Adequacy of Care Plan)* [2002] UKHL 10, [2002] 2 AC 291, [2002] 1 FLR 815 para [92]:

> 'When a local authority formulates a care plan in connection with an application for a care order, there are bound to be uncertainties. Even the basic shape of the future life of the child may be far from clear. Over the last 10 years problems have arisen about how far courts should go in attempting to resolve these uncertainties before making a care order and passing responsibility to the local authority.'

[56] He went to recount cases falling either side of the line: on the one hand, allowing a limited period of 'planned and purposeful delay' before making the order (see *C v Solihull Metropolitan Borough Council* [1993] 1 FLR 290) and, on the other, where the uncertain outcome of parental treatment was a matter to be worked out after the care order was made, not before (see *Re J (Minors) (Care: Care Plan)* [1994] 1 FLR 253. He concluded at para [99] that:

'Despite all the inevitable uncertainties, when deciding whether to make a care order the court should normally have before it a care plan which is sufficiently firm and particularised for all concerned to have a reasonably clear picture of the likely way ahead for the child for the foreseeable future.'

Further than that, he did not feel able to go.

[57]   In many cases, of course, the child will be the subject of an interim care order made under s 38(1) of the 1989 Act. This does not pre-judge the eventual outcome of the case, as the court has only to be satisfied that there are reasonable grounds for believing that that the threshold criteria for making a full care order are made out (see s 38(2)). Nevertheless, the legal effect while the order is in force, is the same as a full care order (see s 31(11)). This means that the local authority have parental responsibility for the child and can determine the extent to which the parents are able to meet their own responsibility (see s 33(3) and (4)). Thus, the child is fully protected, but the court and the child's guardian remain fully involved in the case. This may contribute to the temptation to remain involved until much of the uncertainty referred to by Lord Nicholls of Birkenhead has been resolved. But that temptation should be resisted if it conflicts with the 'cardinal principle' and the equally important principle that delay in determining their future is bad for children.

Delay

[58]   To my mind, the link between the uncertainty referred to by Lord Nicholls of Birkenhead, and the problem of 'delay' in care proceedings is clear. It is no surprise to find that care proceedings now take far longer than was envisaged when the 1989 Act was passed. As the Lord Chancellor's Department's *Scoping Study on Delay in Children Act Cases* (March 2002) pointed out:

'24.   When the Children Act 1989 was implemented in 1991, it was anticipated that it would take an average of 12 weeks for care cases to be resolved. This has proved over-optimistic and has rarely been realised in practice ... By 1996 care cases were in fact taking 46.1 weeks from the time they started to the time of a final decision.

25.   By the end of 2000, this figure had risen again to an average of 50.3 weeks, 4 times as long as the original projection and almost a year of a child's life. In 2001 the figure has reduced, but is still high at 47.1 weeks.'

[59]   The 1989 Act has several provisions designed to minimise delay and ensure that the case is decided as quickly as possible. Section 1(2) of the 1989 Act requires the court 'to have regard to the general principle that any delay in determining the question is likely to be prejudicial to the

child's welfare'. Section 32 requires a court hearing care proceedings to 'draw up a timetable with a view to disposing of the application without delay' and enables it to give directions for ensuring that the timetable is kept. Section 38 lays down strict time limits for any compulsory intervention in the family, whether by way of an interim care order or an interim supervision order, before the case is finally determined. The initial order can last for up to 8 weeks, and the second order can last for 4 weeks from the end of that 8 weeks, but further orders can only last for 4 weeks at a time (see s 38(4) and (5)). These time limits clearly reflect the expectation that the proceedings would normally last no longer than 12 weeks. The *Review of Child Care Law: report to ministers of an interdepartmental working party* recommended that interim orders should be available both before the threshold criteria were proved and afterwards, if the court required more information before deciding what order, if any, would be the most effective to safeguard the child's welfare. But it assumed that both the adjournment and the interim order should only be for 28 days, as 'normally the presentation of the local authority's plans for the child should enable the court to determine at the time of the main hearing the effectiveness of the order which is contemplated' (para 17.22).

[60] Experience has shown that this was always a forlorn hope. The latest attempt to tackle the problem is the *Protocol for Judicial Case Management in Public Law Children Act Cases* [2003] 2 FLR 719. The President, Lord Chancellor and Secretary of State for Education and Skills begin their foreword thus:

> 'After over a decade of otherwise successful implementation of the Children Act 1989 there remains a large cloud in the sky in the form of delay. Delay in care cases has persisted for too long. The average care case lasts for almost a year. This is a year in which the child is left uncertain as to his or her future, is often moved between several temporary care arrangements, and the family and public agencies are left engaged in protracted and complex legal wranglings.

> The guideline is 40 weeks for the conclusion of care cases. The basis is that a change in the whole approach to case management and a clarification of focus, among all those involved in care cases, is the best way forward.'

Other significant cases on this issue:

- *Re R (Care: plan for adoption: best interest)* [2006] 1 FLR 483
- *Re B (Care order)* [2008] EWCA Civ 131, [2008] 1 FLR 1143

This case is also included in relation to:

D44 Main focus of assessment must be on the child

D45 Therapeutic services must be incidental to gathering necessary information
D49 Section 38(6) funding: House of Lords' dicta

D58 ENSURING NECESSARY EVIDENCE AVAILABLE BEFORE MAKING FINAL ORDER

Re CH (Care or interim care order)

[1998] 1 FLR 402 at 407, 409 and 410

Court of Appeal

Thorpe LJ

In my opinion, the law in this field is now clear. There were a number of first instance decisions which addressed the difficult question of where lies the boundary as between the function of the judge and the function of the local authority in a case where the s 31 criteria are clearly satisfied and a care order is the almost inevitable outcome. The culminating decision at first instance was the decision of Wall J in *Re J (Minors) (Care: Care Plan)* [1994] 1 FLR 253. At 258 he said, having referred to a number of cases on the issue, that he would seek to summarise the principles to be drawn from them. It is enough for this case if I read his third and fourth principles:

'(3)   Before making a care order under s 31 of the 1989 Act, the court must go through a two-stage process. The court must first be satisfied that the threshold criteria of s 31 have been met. Secondly, the court must be satisfied under s 1(5) of the Act that the making of a care order is better for the child than making no order. This involves considering the matters set out in s 1(2) and specifically, the "checklist" set out in s 1(3) of the Act: see s 1(4). When considering the second stage of the process the court takes the child's welfare as its paramount consideration: see s 1 of the Act generally.

(4)   The combination of the factors set out under (1) and (2) above requires the court carefully to scrutinise the care plan prepared by the local authority and to satisfy itself that the care plan is in the child's interests. Thus, if the court is not satisfied the care plan is in the best interests of the child, the court may refuse to make a care order.'

At 261 he said, referring to two earlier cases at first instance:

'Thus in answering the first of the two questions posed at the outset of this judgment it seems to me clear from *C v Solihull Metropolitan Borough Council* [1993] 1 FLR 290 and *Hounslow London Borough*

Council v A [1993] 1 FLR 702 that the court should only pass responsibility over to the local authority by way of final care order when all the facts are as clearly known as can be hoped. Thus, if the court having heard the evidence, is not satisfied by the material aspects of the care plan, the court should decline to make a care order. Local authorities should thus be left in no doubt at all that the care plan will in each case be subject to rigorous scrutiny.'

At 262 he said:

'It will, I hope, be a rare case in which the court's dissatisfaction with the ultimate care plan will be such as to prevent adjudication in a case where the court is satisfied both as to the threshold criteria and that a care order is in the interests of the child. It is very much to be hoped that in a spirit of co-operation and partnership identified by Ward J in [the Solihull case] a local authority will be sensitive to constructive criticism of its care plan from the court based on the evidence which the court has heard, or from the guardian ad litem. By like token the court will be alert to the difficulties faced by local authorities in terms of resources and manpower.

At the end of the day, however, I am in no doubt that it is the court which is charged with the heavy duty of deciding whether or not a care order should be made and that the court will only make final care orders where it is fully satisfied on both stages of the process described in para (3) of the principles which I have set out above.'

Referring to the case before him, he said:

'... the making of interim care orders in cases which are listed as and intended to be the final hearing, and in which the court has heard all the available evidence, needs to be approached with great caution. The court must, in particular, be alert to the danger of using an interim care order as a means of exercising the now defunct supervisory role of the court. The court must also be alert to the danger of diminishing the general principle contained in s 1(2) that "any delay in determining the question is likely to prejudice the welfare of the child".'

I have cited those passages at some length because they are a particularly clear and helpful exposition of this difficult territory. They have been subsequently approved by decisions of this court: *Re T (A Minor) (Care Order: Conditions)* [1994] 2 FLR 423, inferentially in *Re S and D (Children: Powers of Court)* [1995] 2 FLR 456, finally the most recent case *Re L (Sexual Abuse: Standard of Proof)* [1996] 1 FLR 116 in which Butler-Sloss LJ makes plain that the analysis of Wall J is expressly approved and adopted. From her judgment I need read only one sentence (124G–H):

'The point at which the court withdraws from further control over the child and passes the responsibility to the local authority is a matter of the exercise of discretion by the court and will vary with each set of circumstances.'

...

Where the preparation of expert evidence by the parties results in an obvious deficiency and where the judge thereby feels inhibited or handicapped in the performance of the judicial task, then his duty is plain. His duty is to ensure that all necessary evidence is before the court as a prelude to any decision taking. Children Act proceedings are only quasi-adversarial. The inquisitorial role of the judge has been emphasised in a number of authorities commencing with *Re E (A Minor) (Wardship: Court's Duty)* [1984] FLR 457 in the House of Lords. Here, in my judgment, where the judge was so profoundly troubled by the absence of an independent child-centred expert, it was plainly his duty to remedy the deficiency before disposing of the case.

...

In my judgment, the fact that a care order is the inevitable eventual outcome should not deflect the judge from using the litigation process to its maximum effect. There is obviously the prospect that a fuller inquiry might have diminished the distance between the guardian ad litem and the local authority, even if some distance remained. The judge would then have been best placed to express his concerns and his reservations upon the care plan.

The interdisciplinary character of the family justice system emphasises the co-operation that should exist between the court and public authority. It is, from my perception, inconceivable that there should not be reciprocal respect between the court and public authority for their differing functions and differing views. Manifestly, the statutory responsibility post-care order remains solely with the local authority. It is equally manifest that the local authority will pay due regard to the function of the judge in giving judgment upon the care plan after careful appraisal. Manifestly, the local authority will have greater regard for a judgment that is considered and that has embraced all the relevant circumstances and all the necessary expert opinion. I have no doubt that no public authority would wish the judicial appraisal to be preceded by anything less.

Other significant cases on this issue:

- *Re L and H (Residential assessment)* [2007] EWCA Civ 213, [2007] 1 FLR 1370: see D46 – Ensure case fully investigated and all relevant evidence necessary is in place

- *Re M (Care proceedings: best evidence)* [2007] EWCA Civ 589, [2007] 2 FLR 1006: see G56 – No stone must be left unturned?

D59 APPROVAL OF CARE PLAN

Re K (Care proceedings: care plan)

[2007] EWHC 393 (Fam), [2008] 1 FLR 1 at 5 and 11

Family Division

Munby J

[13] The starting point is, of course, the fundamentally important judgment of Wall J in *Re J (Minors) (Care: Care Plan)* [1994] 1 FLR 253, approved by the Court of Appeal in *Re T (A Minor) (Care Order: Conditions)* [1994] 2 FLR 423 and in *Re L (Sexual Abuse: Standard of Proof)* [1996] 1 FLR 116. At 258, Wall J spelt out the obligation of the court:

'... carefully to scrutinise the care plan prepared by the local authority and to satisfy itself that the care plan is in the child's interests.'

He continued:

'... if the court is not satisfied the care plan is in the best interests of the child, the court may refuse to make a care order.'

[14] At 262, Wall J expressed the hope that it would be:

'... a rare case in which the court's dissatisfaction with the ultimate care plan will be such as to prevent adjudication in a case where the court is satisfied both as to the threshold criteria and that a care order is in the interests of the child.'

The same point was made by Nourse LJ in *Re T (A Minor) (Care Order: Conditions)* [1994] 2 FLR 423, at 429:

'... it is the duty of any court hearing an application for a care order carefully to scrutinise the local authority's care plan. If it does not agree with the care plan, it can refuse to make a care order ... The cases in which it is appropriate to take such a course will no doubt be rare.'

That was repeated by Butler-Sloss LJ in *Re L (Sexual Abuse: Standard of Proof)* [1996] 1 FLR 116, at 126.

[15] It is important to appreciate the limit of the court's powers. As I said in *Re L (Care Proceedings: Human Rights Claims)* [2003] EWHC 665 (Fam), [2003] 2 FLR 160, at para [11]:

> 'It is elementary that the only power of the court under Part IV is either to approve or refuse to approve the care plan put forward by the local authority. The court cannot dictate to the local authority what the care plan is to say.'

Nor (see at para [12]) does the High Court have any greater power when exercising its inherent jurisdiction. Thus the court, if it seeks to alter the local authority's care plan, must achieve its objective by persuasion rather than by compulsion.

[16] One technique which, on occasions, can properly be used is to make an interim care order rather than a final care order, inviting the local authority in the meantime to reconsider matters. How far the court can properly go down this road is a matter of some delicacy and difficulty. There are no fixed and immutable rules. It is impossible to define in the abstract or even to identify with any precision in the particular case the point to which the court can properly press matters but beyond which it cannot properly go. The issue is always one for fine judgment, reflecting sensitivity, realism and an appropriate degree of judicial understanding of what can and cannot sensibly be expected of the local authority.

[17] The general principle was explained by Butler-Sloss LJ in a passage in *Re L (Sexual Abuse: Standard of Proof)* [1996] 1 FLR 116, at 124, which she repeated in *Re R (Care Proceedings: Adjournment)* [1998] 2 FLR 390, at 399:

> 'The point at which the court withdraws from further control over the child and passes the responsibility to the local authority is a matter of the exercise of discretion by the court and will vary with each set of circumstances. But at some point, if a care order is made by the court, it must hand over the future arrangements for the child to the local authority. That is not abdication of responsibility by the court; it is acting in accordance with the intention of the legislation. The Children Act provides for many of the most important decisions, including whether to place a child for adoption, to be made by the local authority and therefore there is nothing untoward in the judge leaving the ultimate decision in the hands of the local authority with whom the child is placed.'

She went on to observe in *Re L (Sexual Abuse: Standard of Proof)* [1996] 1 FLR 116, at 125, that:

'An interim care order is to be used for its intended purpose and not to be extended to providing a continuing control over the actions of the local authority.'

Hale LJ made much the same point when she commented in *Re W and B; Re W (Care Plan)* [2001] EWCA Civ 757, [2001] 2 FLR 582, at para [67], that:

'Only in the rare case where the court and the local authority remain at odds over the overall objective of the plan should it be necessary for the court to decline to make the care order and to retain control of the case by means of a series of interim care orders.'

[18] That said, the court is not obliged to retreat at the first rebuff. In an appropriate case the court can properly require the local authority to reconsider its care plan more than once: see for a recent example *Re X; Barnet London Borough Council v Y and X* [2006] 2 FLR 998.

[19] But the court may, nonetheless, find itself faced with a situation where it has to choose the lesser of two evils. As Balcombe LJ said in *Re S and D (Children: Powers of Court)* [1995] 2 FLR 456, at 464, the judge may, despite all his endeavours, be faced with a dilemma:

'... if he makes a care order, the local authority may implement a care plan which he or she may take the view is not in the child or children's best interests. On the other hand, if he makes no order, he may be leaving the child in the care of an irresponsible, and indeed wholly inappropriate parent.'

Balcombe LJ continued:

'It seems to me that, regrettable though it may seem, the only course he may take is to choose what he considers to be the lesser of two evils. If he has no other route open to him ... then that is the unfortunate position he has to face.

... It is an unhappy position, where there is a dispute between all those whose professional duty it is to have the best interests of the children at heart, if they cannot reach agreement. But in those particular circumstances, as I see it, the judge really has no alternative. He has to choose what he believes to be the lesser of two evils. That may be making a care order with the knowledge that the care plan is one which he does not approve, or it may be making no order with the consequences to which I have already adverted.'

[20] Butler-Sloss LJ addressed such a situation in *Re R (Care Proceedings: Adjournment)* [1998] 2 FLR 390, at 398:

'If there had been a realistic alternative to the care plan, the judge was of course entitled to urge the local authority to look carefully at it ... the judge is not a rubber stamp. But if the threshold criteria have been met and there is no realistic alternative to a care order and to the specific plans proposed by the local authority, the court is likely to find itself in the position of being obliged to hand the responsibility for the future decisions about the child to the local authority. In this case ... [t]he child would have to stay in care and in my view there was no alternative to the care plan as the lesser of two evils.'

[21] In practice courts are not very often faced with this dilemma. Wilson J recognised in *Re C (Adoption: Religious Observance)* [2002] 1 FLR 1119, at para [51] that 'a damaging impasse can develop between a court which declines to approve their care plan and the authority which decline to amend it'. But, as he went on to observe:

'The impasse is more theoretical than real: the last reported example is *Re S and D (Children: Powers of Court)* [1995] 2 FLR 456. For good reason, there are often, as in this case, polarised views about the optimum solution for the child: in the end, however, assuming that they feel that the judicial processing of them has worked adequately, the parties will be likely to accept the court's determination and, in particular, the local authority will be likely to amend their proposals for the child so as to accord with it ... In the normal case let there be – in the natural forum of the family court – argument, decision and, sometimes no doubt with hesitation, acceptance: in other words, between all of us a partnership, for the sake of the child.'

A recent example of the process working towards acceptance, albeit reluctant acceptance, by a local authority of the court's view as to the desirable form of care plan can be found in *Re X; Barnet London Borough Council v Y and X* [2006] 2 FLR 998 (see in particular at paras [156], [160] and [162]).

[22] All this, however, is subject to one fundamental qualification which is, as it seems to me, central to the seeming dilemma with which the justices were faced in the present case. It is the point explained by Butler-Sloss LJ in *Re B (Minors) (Termination of Contact: Paramount Consideration)* [1993] Fam 301, [1993] 3 WLR 63, sub nom *Re B (Minors) (Care: Contact: Local Authority's Plans)* [1993] 1 FLR 543 and again in *Re L (Sexual Abuse: Standard of Proof)* [1996] 1 FLR 116.

[23] The starting point is the general principle stated by Butler-Sloss LJ in *Re B (Minors) (Care: Contact: Local Authority's Plans)* [1993] 1 FLR 543 at 548 and 551:

'... once a care order has been made, the court can no longer
monitor the administrative arrangements for the child and has no
say in those arrangements ... After the care order is made, the court
has no continuing role in the future welfare of the child. The local
authority has parental responsibility for the child.'

But this is subject to an important qualification in relation to matters of
contact. As Butler-Sloss LJ expressed it in *Re L (Sexual Abuse: Standard
of Proof)* [1996] 1 FLR 116 at 124, explaining her earlier judgment in
Re B (above):

'The effect of the Children Act is to set aside the former powers of
the court in wardship and to remove from the court any continuing
control over children after the making of a care order unless or until
a further application was made to the court. On the making of a
further application, such as for residence or contact to the child, the
powers of the court and the exercise of discretion under s 1 are
restored for the duration of the application. If the care order
remains in place, other than by control over contact by virtue of the
provisions of s 34, the court has no further part to play in the future
welfare of the child.'

[24] It follows from this that the court, when considering issues of
contact by or to a child in care, is *not* fettered by the care plan, even if the
care plan is one that has previously been considered and approved by the
court. Indeed, in *Re B* the court specifically rejected the local authority's
submissions (see at 548 and 552) that the court 'ought not to make a
contact order if the effect was to undermine or thwart the long-term plans
of the local authority' and that the court 'cannot go behind the long-term
plans of the local authority unless they were acting capriciously or were
otherwise open to scrutiny by way of judicial review'. Butler-Sloss LJ
explained the true principle, at 551:

'The proposals of the local authority, based on their appreciation of
the best interests of the child, must command the greatest respect
and consideration from the court, but Parliament has given to the
court, and not to the local authority, the duty to decide on contact
between the child and those named in s 34(1). Consequently the
court may have the task of requiring the local authority to justify
their long-term plans'

though, she added:

'... to the extent only that those plans exclude contact between
parent and child.'

[25] That is not, of course, to deny the very considerable weight that the local authority's plan may carry because, as Butler-Sloss LJ had just observed:

'... the issue of contact often depends on whether contact would frustrate long-term plans for the child in a substitute home, such as adoption where continuing contact may not be for the long-term welfare of the child. The presumption of contact, which has to be for the benefit of the child, has always to be balanced against the long-term welfare of the child and particularly where he will live in the future. Contact must not be allowed to destabilise or endanger the arrangements for the child and in many cases the plans for the child will be decisive of the contact application.'

[26] Moreover, s 34 of the Children Act 1989 assumes that, at least in the first instance, contact is a matter for the exercise of discretion by the local authority. But the principle is clear. In the final analysis, it is for the court, exercising its powers under s 34, to determine questions of contact, whatever the care plan may or may not have to say on the subject. Furthermore, the role of the court in relation to matters of contact is now enhanced in the light of its duties and powers under ss 26 and 27 of the Adoption and Children Act 2002.

...

[38] The justices seem to have thought that they should not approve the care plan – on one reading of their reasons to have thought that they could not approve the care plan – unless, having scrutinised it, they approved of 'everything in it' (see the passage, quoted at para [6] above, where they said 'We have to scrutinise the care plan and approve of everything in it if we are to make a final care order'). In saying that, and in deciding not to approve the care plan and, accordingly, not to make a care order *because of their concerns about contact*, the justices, I regret to say, fell into plain error. Because the point on which they disagreed with the local authority related only to contact, albeit contact following adoption, the justices were not, as it seems to me, faced with Balcombe LJ's choice of the lesser of two evils. Their statutory powers under s 34 of the Children Act 1989 and ss 26 and 27 of the Adoption and Children Act 2002 provided them with the escape from the dilemma which – erroneously, in my opinion – they thought they were faced with.

[39] What the justices could, and in my judgment should, have done in the circumstances was, as it were, to say:

'Except in relation to contact, we approve the local authority's care plan. In relation to contact we are not prepared to approve the care plan; indeed, we reject it. But that is not a reason why we should refuse to make a care order when all the other circumstances so plainly demand that we do. On the contrary, we must make a care order, though making it explicitly clear that questions of contact will require further consideration by the court and that we are *not* approving the local authority's care plan so far as it relates to contact. K must remain in care. The local authority must share parental responsibility for K with her mother and must now implement its plan for permanency, a plan which, except in relation to contact, we approve.'

[40] The justices could then have gone on to deal with the question of contact, either by making an order then and there, or by giving directions for the future determination of the issue, or by leaving it to the mother (or the children's guardian) to make an appropriate application. In the circumstances, they might have been well advised to adopt the course suggested to me by Miss Lugg, that is to adjourn the placement application (and with it the consideration of contact in accordance with ss 26 and 27 of the Adoption and Children Act 2002) to a hearing after the position of the foster carers had been resolved. The one thing they should *not* have done is the very thing which, unfortunately, they did, that is, to refuse to make a care order because, and only because, of their concerns about contact.

D60   IF FINAL ORDER REFUSED, FOCUSED DIRECTIONS REQUIRED

Somerset County Council v D

[2007] EWCA Civ 722, [2008] 1 FLR 399 at 402, 404 and 404

Court of Appeal

Potter P

[10] On a superficial level, as the judge clearly considered, there are parallels between the facts of the present case and those in a case decided in this court a year ago, namely *Re L (Children) (Care Proceedings: Significant Harm)* [2006] EWCA Civ 1282, [2007] 1 FLR 1068. As in *Re L*, the facts in the present case are not that the parents had actively mistreated any of the children but rather that, by reason of their own personal difficulties and deficits, they had been struggling to provide adequate care for the children ... In other major respects, however, the cases were very different.

...

[16] ... Upon the assumption that, even on the evidence before him (and he had not heard from the parents), it was nonetheless open to the judge in February and March 2007 to decline to make the orders sought by the local authority, and given that his intention was to provide the parents one further opportunity to demonstrate swift improvement, it was plainly incumbent upon him to provide a far more focused and specific framework for the future conduct of the applications than he saw fit to provide. The regrettable position is that not only did he fail to provide that framework on 12 March 2007, but he has since equally failed to do so, in effect dealing with the matter on a 'pillar to post' basis with, even now, no structure or timetable provided for a final decision to be reached ...

...

[18] ... we are clear that, assuming it was properly open to him to take the course that he did, it was essential in the interests of the children that he should have required a specific raft of proposals to be laid before the court, analysed in detail on all sides, and, to the extent that they were approved, made the subject of directions. In particular, he should have laid down a specified timeframe providing for the judge's further substantial review, not at a series of short directions hearings, but at a hearing at which there would be a proper opportunity for consideration of whether, in the light of the sincere but no means confidence building efforts of the parents, investment of yet further time was justified, by reference, of course, to the best interests of the children. In other words, we consider that the judge's disposal fell substantially short of what was necessary by way of ongoing judicial control of the proceedings.

Care or supervision order

D61   CARE OR SUPERVISION ORDER

Re T (Care order)

[2009] EWCA Civ 121, [2009] 2 FLR 574 at 583, 588 and 593

Court of Appeal

Potter P

The law

[27]   As aptly described by Bracewell J in *Re T (A Minor) (Care or Supervision Order)* [1994] 1 FLR 103 at 106H–107B:

> 'The nature of a supervision order is to help and assist the child where the parents have full responsibility for the care and upbringing. It does not involve any statutory level of monitoring and it does not give the local authority parental responsibility. Any conditions attached to a supervision order cannot in themselves be enforced by the court. That was made clear in the case of *Croydon London Borough Council v A (No 3)* [1992] 2 FLR 350; breaches can only be evidence in further proceedings.
>
> The essence of a supervision order is to advise, assist and befriend the child. The directions that may be attached under Sch 3 to the Children Act 1989 are restricted to requiring a responsible person, that is the parent in this case, to take reasonable steps to ensure the child lives at a specified place, presents to a specified person, participates in specified activities and submits to various examinations where appropriate. The limits of such requirements do not, in my judgment begin to address the problems of parents who continue to exercise their parental responsibilities in a way which still merits some criticism.
>
> The contract drawn up between the parents and the local authority cannot be enforced without further court proceedings, whereas a care order places on the local authority a positive duty to ensure the welfare of the child and protect her from inadequate parenting. That is the framework and essence of the Act.'

[28] Remarks to essentially similar effect were made by Waite LJ in *Re V (Care or Supervision Order)* [1996] 1 FLR 776 at 786A–B, emphasising that provisions incorporated into a supervision order are incapable of being enforced directly by any of the ordinary processes by which courts of law enforce obedience to their directions, the only sanction for infringement being a return to court by the supervisor, the ultimate sanction being the making of a care order under which the local authority will begin the necessary powers to enforce its will.

[29] The most detailed analysis of the distinction between the two forms of order is that of His Honour Judge Coningsby QC sitting as a judge of the Family Division in *Re S (J) (A Minor) (Care or Supervision Order)* [1993] 2 FLR 919, referred to in the judgment below. It is not necessary to refer to that analysis of the purposes of this case. I shall, however, refer to a passage directed to the borderline between the appropriateness of a care order on the one hand or a supervision order on the other which may well have influenced the judge in this case. At 957A et seq, His Honour Judge Coningsby stated:

> 'I think there may be cases where one can actually isolate a particular situation where parental responsibility may have to be exercised at a moment's notice by a local authority and is obvious that that is going to be a Care Order case.
>
> However, I do not believe that that is the only approach ... It is not necessary, as I understand the relevant parts of the Children Act, to be able to isolate a likely circumstance for exercising parental responsibility before it becomes right to make a Care Order. I do not believe that the legislation is as restrictive as that. I believe that it is an appropriate approach for the court to look at the case as a whole, to look at the gravity of it, to decide what its view is as to the risk of harm to the child (both physical harm as in this case and also emotional deprivation or failure to thrive because of the situation in the home or of some other situation arising) and to decide whether, in the light of the gravity of the case as a whole, the local authority ought to have imposed upon it the extra duties that I have referred to. If it comes to the conclusion, looking at the case as a whole, that that is so, then it should make a Care Order. Therefore it is not necessary to be able to put one's finger specifically on some aspect of parental responsibility which might need to be exercised by the local authority.'

[30] That was a passage approved and highlighted in *Re B (Care or Supervision Order)* [1996] 2 FLR 693 at 706A per Holman J, who at the same time emphasised that a care order was a more serious order and should only be made if the stronger order were necessary for the protection of the child.

[31] Whilst I would not seek to detract from the substance of the passage I have quoted from the judgment of His Honour Judge Coningsby, I would sound a note of caution. Since the advent of the Human Rights Act 1998 it is necessary also to emphasise and have regard to the issue of proportionality when contemplating the removal of parental responsibility from, or its enforced sharing by, those otherwise entitled to exercise it exclusively.

[32] In this respect, Hale LJ (as she then was) in *Re O (Supervision Order)* [2001] EWCA Civ 16, [2001] 1 FLR 923 at 928–9, rehearsed the differences between a care order and a supervision order in terms of:

(i)   the power under a care order to remove the child without recourse to the court;
(ii)   the sharing of parental responsibility; and
(iii) the potential duration of the orders made, she stated:

'[24] … There are three main points. First, it gives a local authority power to remove the child without recourse even to a family proceedings court in an emergency protection order. The parents' only means of challenging that removal is by an application to discharge the care order, which usually takes some time to be heard, especially if, as in this case, it would have to be transferred to a higher court …

[25]   Secondly, it gives the local authority parental responsibility for the child coupled with the power to control the parents' exercise of that responsibility. Again, the care plan does not suggest that the local authority wished to exercise parental responsibility or control the parent's exercise of it. It expressly stated, for example, "that A's social, moral and academic education will be the responsibility of the parents". Under "Health" it points out that he continues to be in good health and he will need to receive the usual checkups and vaccinations by the health visitor and GP service. This is not indicative of the suggestion that the local authority needs to be in a position to arrange that for him. In any event, it can be done by inserting appropriate requirements in the supervision order.

[26]   The third difference is one of timing. Mr Forbes in particular has argued that it might be difficult to achieve a further order in 3 years' time, but of course that difficulty would only arise if by then the risk of harm had disappeared or almost disappeared, or the need for an order had disappeared or almost disappeared. If that were not the case, the local authority would have to investigate and take any action which was thought appropriate to protect the child.

[27]   … Each case [on the choice between care and supervision orders] is an exercise of discretion on its own particular facts and

earlier case-law may be of limited help in this context. But, in any event, it has to be considered in the light of the Human Rights Act 1998 and Art 8 of the European Convention for the Protection of Human Rights and Fundamental Freedoms 1950 …

[28]   Proportionality … is the key. It will be the duty of everyone to ensure that in those cases where a supervision order is proportionate as a response to the risk presented, a supervision order can be made to work as indeed the framers of the Children Act 1989 always hoped that it would be made to work.'

[33]   In my view, the necessity to consider proportionality means that, in any case where there is a fine balance to be struck as to which order is appropriate, the reasoning behind the order made should be clearly spelt out in the judgment as a matter of detailed analysis rather than overall impression.

[34]   Furthermore, and independently of Human Rights Act 1998 requirements, in an earlier judgment, *Oxfordshire County Council v L (Care or Supervision Order)* [1998] 1 FLR 70, Hale J (as she then was), in allowing an appeal from the Family Proceedings Court, emphasised that cogent and strong reasons are required to force upon a local authority a more draconian order than that for which it has asked. In that case the local authority had applied for supervision orders, whereas the guardian supported the making of a care order. The court had made care orders and the local authority successfully appealed.

[35]   Hale J held, as she reiterated in *Re O*, that where it was agreed that the children should remain living at home, two principal reasons might be advanced for making a care order rather than a supervision order: (i) that the local authority needed the power, not only to remove the children instantly but also to plan for their long-term placement outside the family without a prior judicial sanction. In this connection Parliament intended that the very serious step of removing a child could usually only be done under the sanction of independent judicial authority rather than as a result of administrative decision; (ii) that it was necessary for the local authority to share parental responsibility with the parents; in this connection the fact that considerable help and advice might be necessary over a long period was not itself a reason for making a care order. She went on to make clear that; (iii) it is wrong to impose an order simply to encourage a local authority to perform its statutory duties towards children in need. It would be unfortunate if an order not otherwise justified in the interests of the children were to be justified on the basis that it was necessary to oblige a local authority to fulfil such responsibilities.

…

[44] There appears to be no reported case in which the court has made a care order despite the unanimous agreement of the parties to the making of a supervision order. The authorities directly concerned with the question whether or not, in given circumstances, a care order is to be preferred have all involved adjudication of opposing cases advanced by the parties. Nonetheless, it seems to me clear that, even when that is not so, the power in s 31(5) to make a care order on an application for a supervision order cannot be neutered by an agreement reached between the parties outside the court, particularly where, as here, the proceedings have originated in an application for a care order which has become 'diluted' by the time of the final hearing.

...

[61] On careful consideration, I consider Mr Booth is correct. Read in the light of the decision in *Re O* and the *Oxfordshire County Council* case, the following criticisms of the judgment may justly be made. As already indicated, three reasons were identified in those decisions as justifying the making of a care order even though the children remained living at home. The first was where the local authority needs the power not only to remove the children instantly but also to plan for their long-term placement outside the family without any prior judicial sanction. That was not suggested to be the position here and, on the judge's own assessment, it was not a critical element in his decision. In my view, he was right to take that view. Whatever the misgivings of the family centre at the time of their original assessment, the parents had over the subsequent period of 7 months successfully addressed, to the satisfaction of all the agencies and other professionals involved, matters which the family centre had said were required to be addressed before consideration could be given to returning B to the parents' care. On that basis, the professionals and the judge were all agreed that, contrary to the original assessment, return of B to the care of the parents was the proper course; any residual risk being insufficient to justify non-return to parents whose parenting skills were demonstrably well able to meet B's day-to-day needs to a high standard in a family in which the siblings were being brought up without any cause for concern. So far as ongoing supervision or inspection by the council was concerned, it remained, therefore, to decide what would be a suitable or adequate regime in this respect, whether under the umbrella of a care or supervision order. That regime was the one provided for in the agreement signed by the parents which contained the requirements of the professionals, as supplemented by the judge. Neither they nor he identified anything more as being required by way of practical steps or intervention by the social services. If contrary to the expectation of they experts and the judge, a further 'acute event' were to occur in the future, the council would have available the remedy of an emergency protection order and/or an interim care order should the parents resist the immediate removal of B to care within the extended family.

[62] Turning to the second reason justifying a care order developed by Hale LJ (ie that it was necessary for the local authority to share parental responsibility), as I have already indicated, the judge's decision did not turn upon any aspect of parental responsibility which the parents might be thought unfit to exercise or which might call for intervention on a matter not covered in the parental agreement. Nor did it turn upon any evidence of non co-operation on the part of the parents. It turned upon the length of time that the regime provided for under the agreement might last if it were coupled only with a supervision order, the duration of which might only be one year or (by extension) 3 years (see s 6 of Sch 3 to the 1989 Act), whereas, in the judge's view, if a care order were made, it should not be discharged until B was 5 or started full-time school, whichever was the later (see paras [23] and [52] above).

[63] With the intention of ensuring oversight of B until he was 5 and of school age the judge clearly intended to remove the discretion of the council not to extend the supervision order for 2 years and stated that in his view there should be no application to discharge the care order which he proposed to make before B was 5 years old (some 3 years and 4 months from the date of the judge's order). In my view, having decided that rehabilitation was the proper course and having indicated that the power of the court to remove B without court order was not crucial, by which I take the judge to have meant that it was not the governing factor in his decision, he was wrong to decide the matter on the basis of his own view as to the minimum period over which the protective regime provided for in the parental agreement was likely to be required. That was something which would plainly depend upon the parents' continuing progress. That in turn was a matter which it was appropriate to leave to the council in its final review of the position at the end of the 12-month period of the supervision order. There is no suggestion in this case, nor any reason to suppose that the council was or is other than closely and conscientiously concerned to supervise the safety, care and upbringing of B for as long as may prove necessary, or that it would make other than a careful judgment as to the need to renew the supervision order after 12 months if not satisfied that the parents had fully demonstrated their ability safely to parent B from day to day. No doubt the council will review the matter and consider the question of renewal of the supervision order with great care in the light of the judge's observations and it may well be that it will consider it desirable to extend that order for a period of 2 years thereafter. Indeed, if a supervision order were now substituted for the judge's order, such renewal would take the period of protection achieved several months beyond, rather than short of, B's 5th birthday.

[64] As observed by Hale J in the *Oxfordshire County Council* case, there must in general be cogent and strong reasons to force upon a local authority a more draconian order than that for which it has asked. All the more is that the case when the child's guardian supports the making of a less draconian order as appropriate to the child's needs. In my view, no such strong and cogent reasons were demonstrated in this case. I would, therefore, allow the appeal and vary the care order made by the judge to that of a 12-month supervision order effective from the date of the judgment of this court. The form of the order should record in its preamble the terms of the parental agreement set out in para [17] of this judgment, and the body of the order should include a requirement under s 3 of Sch 3 to the 1989 Act that the parents, as responsible persons, take all reasonable steps to ensure compliance with any direction given by the supervisor under Sch 3.

Application to discharge section 31 order

D62   CHILD AS APPLICANT

Re A (Care: discharge application by child)

[1995] 1 FLR 599 at 599

Family Division

Thorpe J

The short point that is raised by the application this morning is whether in public law proceedings A, a 14-year-old boy, requires leave to issue an application for the discharge of a care order made on 3 February 1994. I accept Miss Trebble's submission that he needs no such leave.

Section 39(1)(b) of the Children Act 1989 provides specifically:

> 'A care order may be discharged by the court on the application of the child himself.'

There is nothing within that section that states or even suggests that the child's right to apply for discharge is subject to some preliminary screening application for leave. There is an obvious distinction between these public law provisions and the private law provisions of s 10 which require a preliminary application for leave by a child who is an intended applicant in private law proceedings. *Practice Direction: Children Act 1989 Applications by Children* [1993] 1 FLR 668, which provides for applications for leave by children to be determined by a judge of the Division, clearly is restricted in its effect to applications brought under s 10 in private law proceedings and does not extend to applications brought in public law proceedings under s 39, which are issued as of right and without prior application for leave.

D63　TEST APPLICABLE

Re S (Discharge of care order)

[1995] 2 FLR 639 at 643 and 645

Court of Appeal

Waite LJ

Section 39 of the Act allows the court to discharge a care order on the application of (inter alios) a parent. Here the jurisdiction is discretionary from the outset (there being no obligation on the parent to satisfy the court that the threshold requirements no longer apply). The issue has to be determined by the court in accordance with s 1 of the Act, which (by s 1(1)) makes the child's welfare the court's paramount consideration, and (by s 1(3) and (4)) makes it mandatory for the court to have particular regard to the child's wishes and needs, the likely effect on him of any change of circumstances, the capability of his parents to meet his needs, the range of powers available to the court and, specifically:

'(3) ...

(e)　any harm which he has suffered or is at risk of suffering; ...'

...

It will be convenient to deal first with Mr Karsten's submission of law – namely that a judge hearing the discharge application would have no jurisdiction to disturb the findings reached by Judge Bowen (as part of his conclusions on the 'threshold requirements' under s 31 of the Children Act 1989) that K had been abused by T and that the mother was aware of the abuse ...

General notes:

As to issue estoppel, see G10 – No strict rule of issue estoppel.

Other significant cases on this issue:

- *Re C (Care: discharge of care order)* [2009] EWCA Civ 955, [2010] 1 FLR 774

CGs / solicitor for the child

D64 ROLE OF CG / SOLICITOR FOR CHILD (1)

R v CAFCASS

[2003] EWHC 235 (Admin), [2003] 1 FLR 953 at 969

Queen's Bench Division

Charles J

[50] The duty of the guardian is to safeguard the interests of the child in the manner prescribed by the rules. In performance of that duty, a guardian (amongst other things) investigates and obtains information, considers the issues in the case from the standpoint of the child, and thus independently from the local authority and the parents. In doing so, the guardian applies s 1(3) and the general principle referred to in s 1(2) of the Children Act 1989, and advises and makes recommendations to the court.

[51] Albeit that it is established by authority that if a court disagrees with the views and recommendation of a guardian it should give reasons for so doing, the guardian is not a decision-maker as to what, if any, order should be made or as to the terms of a care plan.

[52] A guardian will have social work experience that will assist the court in reaching its decision. This assistance and the manner in which a guardian safeguards the interests of the relevant child are provided both in court and, importantly, outside the court by the work done and discussions taken part in by the guardian. Further, this assistance can be useful before the guardian has had an opportunity to investigate the circumstances of the relevant family.

[53] For example, before carrying out his or her own investigations a guardian may be able to provide from an independent social work standpoint, which focuses on the interests of the child, a helpful consideration of: (i) the force of the reasoning of the local authority and thus whether the threshold conditions alleged found the order sought; or (ii) what options are open to the court and what further assessments as to placement in, or outside, the family, contact or other matters should be made and as to their timetabling. But it seems to me to be axiomatic that the weight and usefulness of any advice and recommendation the guardian gives as to the order that should be made in a given case, or as to where a child should live whilst information is gathered to enable a final decision to be made, increases when the guardian has had the opportunity to investigate.

[54] Further, at the time an EPO or an ICO is sought and made, unless the guardian has had earlier dealings with the family, he or she will have no personal knowledge of the events that have led the local authority to seek to remove the child from home (or the earlier removal of the child from home) and, inevitably, only a little time for investigation thereof, even if he or she did not have other urgent commitments.

[55] On the other hand (i) the local authority has to make out the existence of the threshold conditions and the thus the risk of harm, it says, warrants the removal of the child from home based on evidence it has obtained in carrying out its functions, and (ii) the parent or parents of the child will have knowledge of these matters. Thus, it is the parents who are in the best position, with the benefit of publicly funded representation, to address and challenge the grounds put forward by the local authority to give the court jurisdiction to make, and for justifying the making of, the order sought on the basis of the care plan advanced.

[56] Given the need for a guardian to work with the family and the local authority, and the nature of the facts in dispute, it will vary from case to case how appropriate it would be for a guardian to become involved in investigating disputes of primary fact relating to the existence of the threshold conditions. Further, in some cases, the nature and seriousness of the harm suffered and the threshold conditions alleged, together with the lack of any realistic alternative family placement, have the consequence that an interim removal of a child into foster care is the only viable solution.

[57] The guardian is directed to appoint a solicitor (FPR 1991, r 4.11A). The solicitor is to represent the child. The solicitor's role is different from the role of the guardian. In particular, the solicitor does not have the investigatory or social work roles placed on the guardian. In the cases upon which these proceedings are based, CAFCASS took steps to identify a solicitor from the relevant panel (and thus one who had relevant experience in children work) for appointment by the court, and at the relevant hearings the children were represented by such a solicitor. This was not, and as I understood it was not said to be, an act which satisfied or acted as a substitute for compliance with the duty on CAFCASS to make available an officer of the service for appointment as the guardian by the court. Clearly, to my mind, it does not because of the different roles and expertise of the guardian and the solicitor. But in my view, given that it was not making an officer of the service available who would, as the guardian, have appointed a solicitor to represent the children, this was

an appropriate and sensible step for CAFCASS to take and one which promoted the welfare of the children and assisted the court.

[58]   There is an overlap between the roles and expertise of the guardian, the solicitor and indeed the court in examining and testing the strength of the evidence and reasoning that the local authority advances to establish the threshold conditions and the risk of harm to the children. In many ways this is an exercise that a lawyer is trained to do, and is well able to carry out. Further, it does not need the participation of a guardian or a solicitor or a court who have some experience of children cases to know that amongst the relevant issues are the nature and strength of the evidence and reasoning of the local authority, an assessment of the response thereto by the parents and the wider family, an assessment whether there is or may be an alternative family placement, contact and directions as to the future conduct of the case.

D65 ROLE OF CG / SOLICITOR FOR CHILD (2)

Re U (Re-opening of appeal)

[2005] EWCA Civ 52, [2005] 2 FLR 444 at 466

Court of Appeal

Butler-Sloss P

Comments on the role of guardian

...

[98] In the Children Act 1989 the role of the guardian of the child is crucial. A guardian is appointed to represent the child unless the court is satisfied that it is not necessary to do so in order to safeguard the child's interests see s 41(1). The Family Proceedings Rules 1991 (FPR) and the Family Proceedings Courts (Matrimonial Proceedings etc) Rules 1991 set out in detail the statutory requirements of a guardian, usually appointed from the Children and Family Advisory and Support Service (CAFCASS). A guardian is appointed unless the court is satisfied that it is not necessary to do so to safeguard the child's interests. FPR rr 11 and 11A, for example, provide for the powers and duties of a guardian which continue for such time as is specified in the appointment or until terminated by the court, see r 10(9). The independence of the guardian is underlined by the exclusion of anyone who comes within the provisions of r 10(7), such as a person employed by the applicant local authority. This independence on behalf of the child is an essential element in the hearing of a care application. The court is entitled to rely upon and does rely upon the investigations of, and pays close attention to, the recommendations of the guardian who looks at the case from an impartial and objective standpoint. The guardian has a duty to form a view of the application and, where appropriate, to recommend a course honestly believed by the guardian to be in the best interests of the child he/she represents, whether it be to advise the return of the child to the family or to advise the removal of the child permanently from the natural family.

[99] A party is not entitled in a private law dispute to have the court welfare officer removed from the case (now the CAFCASS reporter) on the ground that the report is favourable to the other party. In the same way a party in a public law case is not entitled to attempt to dispense with the guardian or to sideline or marginalise the guardian on the ground that in an earlier part of the case, the guardian's recommendation had been adverse to that party (see, generally, independence of court welfare officer and guardian in *Re S (A Minor) (Guardian ad Litem/Welfare Officer)* [1993] 1 FLR 110). Other than in exceptional circumstances of specific bias or impropriety, the independence of the guardian may not be impugned as a result of the decision of the guardian to support the proposed care plan of the local authority.

[100] In the present case, the guardian at an earlier stage had chaired the experts' meeting which was a normal procedure in a difficult case. There was no good reason to exclude her or her solicitor from the neutral role of chairing the later experts' meeting in which Professor D participated. To do so was to misunderstand and to diminish the role of the guardian. We are surprised that the guardian and the local authority did not demur more strongly at an expensive and unnecessary alternative to the use of the guardian or her solicitor as chairman. The cost of inviting Sir Philip Otton to chair the meeting and to make himself familiar with all the papers added extra cost to the public purse, one which neither the local authority nor the Legal Services Commission should have been asked to bear.

Other significant cases on this issue:

- Cf *Re S and W (Care proceedings)* [2007] EWCA Civ 232, [2007] 2 FLR 275: see D3 – Relationship between local authority and children's guardian

This case is also included in relation to:

H40 Re-opening of final appeal

D66 ROLE OF CG / SOLICITOR FOR CHILD (3)

Re CB and JB (Care proceedings: guidelines)

[1998] 2 FLR 211 at 229

Family Division

Wall J

Question 8: The role of the guardian ad litem and the solicitor instructed by the guardian ad litem

It was a particular decision by the guardian ad litem which, in my judgment, set this case off on the wrong track. That was the decision to instruct Dr PW, an adult forensic psychiatrist, to make a psychiatric assessment of the father in the context of the first, factual limb of a split hearing. However, the responsibility for that decision cannot be laid at the door of the guardian alone. Responsibility for it must be shared by the solicitor for the guardian who should have advised the guardian against it, the other parties who agreed to it, and the court which sanctioned it.

A mistake such as this points up the importance of the relationship between guardians ad litem and the solicitors they instruct. It is very important, in my view, that such a relationship should be intellectually rigorous, as well as professionally compatible. Each must be able to criticise the other: each must be able to curb any excesses or irrelevancies in which the other may be tempted to indulge.

It is essential that solicitor and guardian work in partnership on every aspect of the case, including the definition of issues, the nature of the investigation to be undertaken, the need to instruct experts and the conclusions to be presented to the court in any interim or final report.

Other significant cases on this issue:

- In relation to directions under s 37 of the CA 1989, see *Re CE (Section 37 direction)* [1995] 1 FLR 26 at D41 – Appointment / limited role of children's guardian

This case is also included in relation to:

G35 Psychiatric / psychological evidence unlikely to be relevant

G62 Psychiatric / psychological evidence as to propensity

D67 ONE CG CAN REPRESENT CHILDREN WITH CONFLICTING INTERESTS

Re T and E (Proceedings: conflicting interests)

[1995] 1 FLR 581 at 590

Family Division

Wall J

Since the question of the guardian ad litem's capacity to represent children whose interests conflict has been argued, however, I propose to deal briefly with it. What is the position of a guardian ad litem:

(1) who is appointed to represent more than one child in proceedings; and

(2) who find that the interests of the children he or she is appointed to represent conflict?

Once again, this is not an uncommon situation, and in my judgment there is usually no reason why, as here, the guardian ad litem cannot properly represent all the children involved. The duty of a guardian ad litem appointed in specified proceedings under s 41 is of safeguard the interests of the child or children whom he or she is appointed to represent in the manner prescribed by Family Proceedings Rules, r 4.11. There is nothing in Family Proceedings Rules, r 4.11 which prevents a guardian ad litem representing children whose interests conflict.

Such a situation is, in my judgment, quite different from that in which a child of appropriate age and understanding takes a different view of the case to that of the guardian ad item and wishes to instruct a solicitor direct. In such a situation it is plainly impossible for the guardian ad litem to continue to represent the child: see *Re H (A Minor) (Care Proceedings: Child's Wishes)* [1993] 1 FLR 440 and *Re M (Minors) (Care Proceedings: Child's Wishes)* [1994] 1 FLR 749.

Family Proceedings Rules r 4.11(4), which sets out the matters upon which the guardian ad litem is to advise the court, includes at (e) the following:

'the options available to it in respect of the child and the suitability of each such option including what order should be made in determining the application ...'

In the instant case, the guardian ad litem was able to fulfil that function notwithstanding the conflict of interests between the children. She identified and defined the interests of each child. She then conducted a balancing exercise between the interests of the children and she gave me her view of where the balance fell. She did it in these terms:

'I respectfully suggest that should this honourable court decide that [T's father and his wife] can offer T a good home one of the issues before this honourable court is whether the best interests of T should be sacrificed to the best interests of E. In my view, there is a very clear conflict of interests between T's and E's welfare.

If the girls were to be separated, E will lose everything: her mother, her father, her half-sister. Having contact may mitigate her unhappiness as would to some extent the undivided attention of the adoptive family, should a childless family be found.

Recommendation

I respectfully recommend to this honourable court: that the care order in respect of T be revoked. A residence order in favour of [T's father]. An order freeing E for adoption.'

Whether or not I agree with that conclusion (in the event I did agree with it) it seems to me a proper exercise of the guardian ad litem's duties under r 4.11. In my judgment there is nothing in r 4.11 which prevents a guardian ad litem representing children in public law proceedings where their interests conflict. To have more than one guardian ad litem, as Stuart-White J held in the instant case, is unnecessary and complicates the matter. It is also, in my view, a waste of valuable resources.

This case is also included in relation to:

G59 Experts to be kept up to date / not kept waiting at court

D68   CONFLICT BETWEEN CHILD AND CG

Re A (Contact order)

[2010] EWCA Civ 208, [2010] 2 FLR 577 at 578 and 578

Court of Appeal

Thorpe LJ

[3]   So the application put before the judge was squarely on the basis that the guardian was in conflict with R, for she was not pressing the case as R saw it but the case as she saw it on the balance of the welfare checklist considerations. The application was thus formally put before the court under r 14.12(1)(a) of the Family Proceedings Rules 1991. The circuit judge reviewed the law and the statutory language and correctly directed himself that there should be no tandem arrangement for separate representation of the child unless the child wishes to give instructions which conflict with those of the children's guardian, and is able, in the light of his understanding, to give such instructions. His Honour Judge Grant concluded that although R was a bright and articulate child, he had not the maturity to comprehend and weigh all the complex considerations that s 1 imports and to then arrive at a proportionate, balanced conclusion ...

...

[5]   I am in no doubt at all that the judge was right to rule as he did on this application. There are cases involving children in post-pubertal adolescent rebellion for whom it is very difficult for a guardian to act. Their position, their wishes, their feelings, their opinions so conflict with an objective view of welfare that there has to be a parting of the ways, and our system generously provides for two distinct and equally constituted litigation teams thereafter. That is an extremely expensive solution, and in present days when the family justice system is obliged to seek economy wherever and whenever it can, orders granting separate representation under this rule should, in my opinion, be issued very sparingly.

[6]   This was a perfectly standard situation in which the child's wishes were only an ingredient within the review of the guardian and only one element upon which the guardian had to report to the court. It seems that R expressed feelings that accorded closely with the guardian's professional opinion; namely, that his relationship with his mother should be maintained providing it was safe so to do. The guardian reported that fairly in her report of 6 June, and I can see absolutely nothing to

substantiate the submission of the appellants that the guardian was conflicted and accordingly had to drop out.

D69   CG CANNOT GUARANTEE CONFIDENTIALITY

Re C (Disclosure of information)

[1996] 1 FLR 797 at 799, 800 and 801

Family Division

Johnson J

There was a consensus at the Bar that the following issues arose for decision:

(a)   Is information given by a child to a guardian ever to be regarded as wholly confidential?
(b)   If the court is to be informed, what is the correct procedure?
(c)   What is the test to be applied by the court in the exercise of its discretion to determine which, if any, of the parties are to have access to the confidential information?

As to (a) I accept the joint submission of counsel that it can never be proper for a guardian ad litem to promise a child that information will be withheld from the court. One can of course envisage cases where a troubled child has found in the guardian a friend and confidante to whom the child may wish to divulge information confidentially and which might enable the guardian to provide help which might be desperately needed but which might not be provided if the guardian cannot promise total confidence. However, the guardian ad litem has the limited function of being guardian for the purpose of the proceedings. I accept the joint submission of counsel that it can never be proper for a guardian to promise a child that information disclosed by a child will not be communicated to the court.

...

As to (b), again counsel were agreed in submitting that the importance of the principle involved is such that the question is one which would require transfer of the proceedings to the High Court. There is an important and delicate balancing exercise ...

...

Once notice is given of the application, then each party should in theory be free to make submissions to the court as to whether the information should be withheld. In some cases, even where a party who is potentially affected will not participate in the *Official Solicitor v K* practice, he or she may wish to make representations as to whether or not the court should permit the information to be withheld. However, in many cases (of which the present case is an example) there would seem to be little point in such a party choosing to make representations on the matter because those representations would be made in ignorance of the information or even its subject matter.

Although I was asked to give guidance on the matter it does not seem to me that it is appropriate to go beyond saying that the procedure in each case will be determined by the court in the light of the particular circumstances and demands of the particular case. The procedure to be followed would be such as to enable the court to carry out the balancing exercise referred to by Lord Evershed.

As to (c), I was asked to give guidance as to the test which should be applied in determining whether or not information should be withheld or disclosed. It seems to me, however, that it is unnecessary and indeed inappropriate for me to do so, there being clear guidance in the speeches in the House of Lords in *Official Solicitor v K* (above) and more recently in *Re D (Adoption Report: Confidentiality)* [1995] 2 FLR 687.

Other significant cases on this issue:

- *Re G (Minors) (Welfare report: disclosure)* [1993] 2 FLR 293
- *Re D (Minors) (adoption report: confidentiality)* [1995] 2 FLR 687 at 692
- *Re M (Disclosure)* [1998] 2 FLR 1028

Section 42 access to documents

D70   SECTION 42 NOT TO BE GIVEN RESTRICTIVE MEANING AND NOT TRUMPED BY PII

Re J (Care proceedings: disclosure)

[2003] EWHC 976 (Fam), [2003] 2 FLR 522 at 530, 532, 535 and 536

Family Division

Wall J

The applications for discovery in the instant case

[33] So, why does the case come before me? It comes on an application by the guardian for access to documentation under CA 1989 s 42. It does not, however, come directly to me. There have been other applications for discovery. I need to chart these in some detail in order to demonstrate what, I have to say, seems to me the quite extraordinary misunderstanding of the guardian's role in care proceedings on the part of the local authority resulting in a failure to co-operate with him and to give him the disclosure to which he was plainly entitled.

...

[44] The guardian's principal argument, however, was that the local authority was confusing two concepts: that of PII on the one hand, and that of confidentiality on the other. PII, he submitted, simply did not apply in this case, and such confidentiality which did exist did not override the statutory rights of the guardian under CA 1989 s 42 to access information from the local authority files.

[45] It could not, the guardian submitted, be in the public interest to keep confidential and out of the public domain the fact that a local authority foster carer had been arrested by the police in an ongoing enquiry into child pornography and related child abuse. To the contrary, the public interest was served by making that information available to the court. Furthermore, making the information available did not amount to disclosure, since any such documents remained confidential to the proceedings as laid down by the FPR 1991. The same point met the

objection that disclosure was a breach of the foster parents' right to respect for family life under Art 8 of the European Convention for the Protection of Human Rights and Fundamental Freedoms 1950, which was in any event qualified.

...

The guardian's application under s 42

[60] I have deliberately set out the background to the guardian's application in such detail because, in my judgment, it is manifest that there is simply no answer to it. It is equally apparent, however, that by its defensive – indeed obstructive – attitude the local authority has both greatly increased the costs of the case, and unnecessarily complicated what ought to be very simple care proceedings which, had they been conducted properly, should never have needed to leave the family proceedings court ...

...

[63] If authority for the meaning of the word 'relate' is required, it is to be found in the decision of the Court of Appeal in *Re R (Care Proceedings: Disclosure)*[1] [2000] 3 FCR 721 (*Re R*), upholding the decision of Wilson J to whose careful judgment Dame Elizabeth Butler-Sloss P paid tribute, suggesting that it merited wider dissemination. As it does not appear to have reached the legal department of this local authority, I propose to repeat its main conclusions.

[64] *Re R* concerned what is known as a Part 8 review, that is to say a report prepared by an ACPC for a local authority in the circumstances envisaged by Part 8 of *Working Together under the Children Act 1989: A Guide to Arrangements for Inter-Agency Co-operation for the Protection of Children from Abuse* initially published by the Department of Health and the Department of Education and Science in 1991, since revised, and invariably known as *Working Together*. Paragraph 8.1 provides that:

> 'Whenever a case involves an incident leading to the death of a child, where child abuse is confirmed or suspected, or a child protection issue likely to be of major public concern arises, there should be an individual review by each agency and a composite review by the ACPC.'

[65] The child who had died (AR) was the half-brother of the child (ZR) who was the subject of the care proceedings before Wilson J. The

---

[1]   [2000] 2 FLR 751.

guardian in ZR's proceedings sought disclosure of the Part 8 review in relation to AR. That application was resisted by the ACPC and by the local authority.

[66] In a full and careful judgment, Wilson J decided that: (1) the review was a document held by the local authority; (2) that it was compiled in connection with functions which stand referred to the social services committee under the Local Authority Social Services Act 1970; and (3) that it related to ZR. On the last point, which was not pressed by counsel for the local authority, Wilson J commented:

'If the test had been whether the main focus or primary subject of the document was the child who is the subject of these proceedings, namely ZR (counsel for the guardian) would have been in difficulties. But Parliament has chosen, in my view deliberately chosen, wider words than that. The question is whether the report relates to the child R.'

[67] In the Court of Appeal, counsel for the local authority conceded that she could not challenge Wilson J's interpretation of the statute, and the appeal inevitably failed. The President, giving the leading judgment, said that she could not think of anyone who had a more legitimate interest in the relevant information that might be contained in the review than the guardian.

[68] The ratio decidendi of *Re R* is clear. Section 42 should be given its literal interpretation and should not have read into it a restrictive meaning designed to alter the policy of mutual co-operation between the various welfare and child protection agencies which Parliament has laid down.

[69] In my judgment, *Re R (Care Proceedings: Disclosure)* [2000] 3 FCR 721 applies exactly to the instant case. The report which the guardian wishes to see was prepared by the local authority in response to a complaint by the justices in the proceedings relating to S. It was thus plainly compiled in connection with the local authority's application for a care order relating to S, and equally plainly relates to S. In my judgment, any other analysis is unarguable.

[70] I need, however, to deal with the question that PII somehow trumps s 42. The answer to that seems to me very simple. If the document the guardian wishes to examine and take copies of falls within CA 1989 s 42, PII simply does not arise so far as the guardian's inspection is concerned. In this respect, it seems to me that the argument put forward by the guardian which I have summarised at para [44] and [45] of this judgment is exactly in point, and I accept it.

[71] The point is also addressed by Wilson J and the Court of Appeal in *Re R*. In that case, the guardian argued his case in the alternative. First, he

asserted a right under s 42: alternatively, if that right did not exist, the court should nonetheless order disclosure, notwithstanding that PII would then apply – see *Re R* at 752B–C. It must be remembered that CA 1989 s 42(3) gives the guardian the right to inspect '*regardless of any enactment or rule of law which would otherwise prevent the record in question being admissible in evidence*' (my emphasis). That phrase manifestly embraces PII.

[72] In my judgment, therefore, the cases cited to me by counsel dealing with PII and identified at para [42] of this judgment are irrelevant. The documents with which I am concerned all fall within CA 1989 s 42. The local authority's reliance on PII is misconceived.

[73] I stress, however, that I am dealing only with the rights of the guardian under CA 1989 s 42. What happens to the documents inspected by the guardian thereafter, and who else may be entitled to see them, are quite different questions. In particular, it remains the case, of course, that the documentation in the local authority's possession to which CA 1989 s 42 relates is confidential. Its confidentiality is not abrogated by disclosure to the guardian. Furthermore, the information remains within the ambit of the proceedings, which are themselves confidential. In this context, I think it worthwhile repeating what the President said on this topic in *Re R* at 731–732:

'17.   I think, however, that there is some force in what Miss Macur has said about the use of the Part 8 review. I have no doubt whatever that the guardian ad litem should have the right to read that review, and not the executive summary offered to the media and the parents. The full review should be available to the guardian, as is his right under the interpretation of Wilson J, with which I respectfully agree. How he uses it is another matter. There are areas in the Family Proceedings Rules 1991 which do to some extent limit the way in which information provided to the guardian should be further disseminated.

18.   I can see that the guardian needs the review to see if there is any information relevant to the living child in this case which might help him to give the appropriate advice and provide the appropriate report to the court. That does not mean that the sensitive information needs to be disclosed, and I would have thought that once the guardian ad litem saw the report and saw the relevance of it he would, I am sure, as an experienced guardian (and all guardians are very experienced, being either social workers or probation officers) be very careful as to how he further disseminated any information.

19.   There would be no objection, it would seem to me, if, when the guardian is given the report, there are matters about which the police

or any other agency is particularly concerned (and examples were sought to be given to us by Miss Macur) that the agency could make sure that the guardian knew that the information was particularly sensitive. Guardians are always receiving very sensitive information and dealing with it with the utmost discretion.

20.   It was suggested that there may be guardians who would not be discreet, but that does not affect the principle; it only affects the implementation. If there is any worry about that, it may be that there could be a request to the guardian or indeed a request to the district judge that particular information should not be further disseminated. But to the guardian there can be no doubt that it must be provided, so long as the guardian recognises that any of the information which is not relevant, to the living child should not be passed on, and even relevant information in relation to the living child may need to be dealt with sensitively.

21.   I have gone on about this matter at some length because I recognise that Miss Macur would not be here on behalf of an ACPC (with apparently other ACPCs very concerned) if there was not, in their perception, a problem. At the moment I cannot see a problem, and I hope my observations will go some way to comforting them to the extent that it is appropriate that they should be comforted.'

Other significant cases on this issue:

- As to public interest immunity, see *Re R (Care: disclosure: nature of proceedings)* [2002] 1 FLR 755 at G82 – Public interest immunity
- For an example of circumstances in which the children's guardian's rights under CA 1989, s 42 will not (at least directly) entitle access to a document, see *Nottinghamshire County Council v H* [1995] 1 FLR 115, especially at 121

Emergency protection orders / police protection

D71 EPO: GENERAL CONSIDERATIONS (1)

X Council v B (Emergency protection orders)

[2004] EWHC 2014 (Fam), [2005] 1 FLR 341 at 367

Family Division

Munby J

[57] The matters I have just been considering are so important that it may be convenient if I here summarise the most important points:

(i)   An EPO, summarily removing a child from his parents, is a 'draconian' and 'extremely harsh' measure, requiring 'exceptional justification' and 'extraordinarily compelling reasons'. Such an order should not be made unless the FPC is satisfied that it is both necessary and proportionate and that no other less radical form of order will achieve the essential end of promoting the welfare of the child. Separation is only to be contemplated if immediate separation is essential to secure the child's safety: 'imminent danger' must be 'actually established'.

(ii)   Both the local authority which seeks and the FPC which makes an EPO assume a heavy burden of responsibility. It is important that both the local authority and the FPC approach every application for an EPO with an anxious awareness of the extreme gravity of the relief being sought and a scrupulous regard for the European Convention rights of both the child and the parents.

(iii)   Any order must provide for the least interventionist solution consistent with the preservation of the child's immediate safety.

(iv)   If the real purpose of the local authority's application is to enable it to have the child assessed then consideration should be given to whether that objective cannot equally effectively, and more proportionately, be achieved by an application for, or by the making of, a CAO under s 43 of the Children Act 1989.

(v)   No EPO should be made for any longer than is absolutely necessary to protect the child. Where the EPO is made on an ex parte (without notice) application very careful consideration should be given to the need to ensure that the initial order is made for the shortest possible period commensurate with the preservation of the child's immediate safety.

(vi)   The evidence in support of the application for an EPO must be full, detailed, precise and compelling. Unparticularised generalities will not suffice. The sources of hearsay evidence must be identified. Expressions of opinion must be supported by detailed evidence and properly articulated reasoning.

(vii) Save in wholly exceptional cases, parents must be given adequate prior notice of the date, time and place of any application by a local authority for an EPO. They must also be given proper notice of the evidence the local authority is relying upon.

(viii) Where the application for an EPO is made ex parte the local authority must make out a compelling case for applying without first giving the parents notice. An ex parte application will normally be appropriate only if the case is genuinely one of emergency or other great urgency – and even then it should normally be possible to give some kind of albeit informal notice to the parents – or if there are compelling reasons to believe that the child's welfare will be compromised if the parents are alerted in advance to what is going on.

(ix)   The evidential burden on the local authority is even heavier if the application is made ex parte. Those who seek relief ex parte are under a duty to make the fullest and most candid and frank disclosure of all the relevant circumstances known to them. This duty is not confined to the material facts: it extends to all relevant matters, whether of fact or of law.

(x)   Section 45(7)(b) of the Children Act 1989 permits the FPC to hear oral evidence. But it is important that those who are not present should nonetheless be able to know what oral evidence and other materials have been put before the FPC. It is, therefore, particularly important that the FPC complies meticulously with the mandatory requirements of rr 20, 21(5) and 21(6) of the Family Proceedings Courts (Children Act 1989) Rules 1991. The FPC must 'keep a note of the substance of the oral evidence' and must also record in writing not merely its reasons but also any findings of fact.

(xi)   The mere fact that the FPC is under the obligations imposed by rr 21(5), 21(6) and 21(8), is no reason why the local authority should not immediately, on request, inform the parents of exactly what has gone on in their absence. Parents against whom an EPO is made ex parte are entitled to be given, if they ask, proper information as to what happened at the hearing and to be told, if they ask: (i) exactly what documents, bundles or other evidential materials were lodged with the FPC either before or during the course of the hearing; and (ii) what legal authorities were cited to the FPC. The local authority's legal representatives should respond forthwith to any reasonable request from the parents or their legal representatives either for copies of the materials read by the FPC or for information about what took place at the hearing. It will, therefore, be prudent for those acting for the local authority in such a case to keep a proper note of the proceedings, lest they otherwise find themselves embarrassed by a proper request for information which they are unable to provide.

(xii) Section 44(5)(b) of the Children Act 1989 provides that the local authority may exercise its parental responsibility only in such manner 'as is reasonably required to safeguard or promote the welfare of the child'. Section 44(5)(a) provides that the local authority shall exercise its power of removal under s 44(4)(b)(i) 'only ... in order to safeguard the welfare of the child'. The local authority must apply its mind very carefully to whether removal is essential in order to secure the child's immediate safety. The mere fact that the local authority has obtained an EPO is not of itself enough. The FPC decides whether to make an EPO. But the local authority decides whether to remove. The local authority, even after it has obtained an EPO, is under an obligation to consider less drastic alternatives to emergency removal. Section 44(5) requires a process within the local authority whereby there is a further consideration of the action to be taken after the EPO has been obtained. Though no procedure is specified, it will obviously be prudent for local authorities to have in place procedures to ensure both that the required decision-making actually takes place and that it is appropriately documented.

(xiii) Consistently with the local authority's positive obligation under Art 8 to take appropriate action to reunite parent and child, s 44(10)(a) and s 44(11)(a) impose on the local authority a mandatory obligation to return a child who it has removed under s 44(4)(b)(i) to the parent from whom the child was removed if 'it appears to [the local authority] that it is safe for the child to be returned'. This imposes on the local authority a continuing duty to keep the case under review day by day so as to ensure that parent and child are separated for no longer than is necessary to secure the child's safety. In this, as in other respects, the local authority is under a duty to exercise exceptional diligence.

(xiv) Section 44(13) of the Children Act 1989 requires the local authority, subject only to any direction given by the FPC under s 44(6), to allow a child who is subject to an EPO 'reasonable contact' with his parents. Arrangements for contact must be driven by the needs of the family, not stunted by lack of resources.

General notes:

Note also the subdivision Newborn babies at D10–D13.

This case is also included in relation to:

D4   Intervention must be proportionate

D72 Contact to a child removed under an EPO

D72   EPO: GENERAL CONSIDERATIONS (2)

Re X (Emergency protection orders)

[2006] EWHC 510 (Fam), [2006] 2 FLR 701 at 717

Family Division

McFarlane J

[65]   Many of the matters described by Munby J in *X Council v B* are clearly applicable to the present case. I agree with each and every one of his observations. I regard this list of 14 factors to be 'required reading' for every magistrate and justices' clerk involved in any EPO application. The list should be copied and placed before the court on every occasion that an application is made for an EPO, so that the bench may consider its applicability to the case that is before them. Applicants for an EPO and their legal advisers should consider themselves under a duty to the court to ensure that this list is expressly and in terms drawn to the attention of the bench.

[66]   The only development of the *X Council v B* guidelines that I would offer is in relation to the record of the hearing. It seems to me that the following two steps should be undertaken whenever an application is made without notice for an EPO:

(a)   the hearing ought to be tape recorded. Most magistrates' courts are not wired up for regular recording, but in my view resources ought to be made for the introduction of a small portable tape recorder (or even a dictation recorder). In the absence of such provision then a dedicated note taker, in addition to the clerk, should attend the hearing with the task of compiling a verbatim note;
(b)   paragraph (xi) of the *B Council* guidance limits the requirement to provide information to parents, where the hearing has taken place without notice, to cases where the parents ask for the information. I would go further and say that unless there is very good reason to the contrary, the parents should always be given a full account of the material submitted to the court, the evidence given at the hearing, the submissions made to support the application and the justices reasons whether they ask for this information or not.

This case is also included in relation to:

I20   Case conference records

D73 CONTACT TO A CHILD REMOVED UNDER AN EPO

X Council v B (Emergency protection orders)

[2004] EWHC 2014 (Fam), [2005] 1 FLR 341 at 361

Family Division

Munby J

[49] What does this mean in the context of an EPO? The statutory scheme to be found in ss 43–45 of the Children Act 1989 provides a number of clues. It provides both the local authority and the FPC with a carefully calibrated hierarchy of means by which the state's response to a child's perceived needs can be met. I do not propose to embark upon an exhaustive exegesis but I do wish to draw attention to the following features of the statutory scheme:

(i)   ...
(ii)   ...
(iii)   ...
(iv)   ...
(v)   ...
(vi)   Section 44(13) requires the local authority, subject only to any direction given by the FPC under s 44(6), to allow a child who is subject to an EPO 'reasonable contact' with his parents.

In relation to contact I repeat what I said in *Re M (Care Proceedings: Judicial Review)* [2003] EWHC 850 (Admin), [2003] 2 FLR 171, at [44]:

'If a baby is to be removed from his mother, one would normally expect arrangements to be made by the local authority to facilitate contact on a regular and generous basis. It is a dreadful thing to take a baby away from his mother: dreadful for the mother, dreadful for the father and dreadful for the baby. If the State, in the guise of a local authority, seeks to intervene so drastically in a family's life – and at a time when, ex hypothesi, its case against the parents has not yet even been established – then the very least the State can do is to make generous arrangements for contact. And those arrangements must be driven by the needs of the family, not stunted by lack of resources. Typically, if this is what the parents want, one will be looking to contact most days of the week and for lengthy periods. And local authorities must be sensitive to the wishes of a mother who wants to breast-feed and must make suitable arrangements to enable her to do so – and when I say breast-feed I mean just that, I do not mean merely bottle-feeding expressed breast milk. Nothing less will meet the imperative demands of the European Convention. Contact two or three times a week for a couple of hours a time is simply not enough if parents reasonably want more.'

I draw attention also to what the court said in *Haase v Germany* [2004] 2 FLR 39, at [101]:

'... the removal of the newborn baby from the hospital was an extremely harsh measure. It was a step which was traumatic for the mother and placed her own physical and mental health under strain, and it deprived the newborn baby of close contact with his natural mother and, as pointed out by the applicants, of the advantages of breast-feeding. The removal also deprived the father of being close to his daughter after the birth.'

I emphasise: arrangements for contact must be driven by the needs of the family, not stunted by lack of resources. And I reiterate what the court said in *Haase v Germany*, at para [92]:

'Following any removal into care, a stricter scrutiny is called for in respect of any further limitations by the authorities, for example ... restrictions on parental ... access.'

General notes:

Note also the subdivision Newborn babies at D10–D13.

This case is also included in relation to:

D4   Intervention must be proportionate
D70 EPO: general considerations (1)

D74   RELATIONSHIP BETWEEN EPO AND POLICE PROTECTION

Langley v Liverpool City Council

[2005] EWCA Civ 1173, [2006] 1 FLR 342 at 351, 352, 353 and 354

Court of Appeal

Dyson LJ

The relationship between ss 44 and 46 of the Act

[24]   The first question is whether the judge was right to hold that, once an EPO has been granted and so long as it remains in force, the police cannot exercise the power to remove a child under s 46 even if the statutory criteria for its exercise exist, ie that the constable has reasonable cause to believe that, unless the child is removed, he or she is likely to suffer significant harm.

…

[30]   In my judgment, therefore, there is nothing in the language of the Act which compels the conclusion that s 46 cannot be invoked where an EPO is in force. As Mr Wells points out, it would be most unfortunate if the position were otherwise. Two examples will suffice to demonstrate this. Let us suppose that an EPO is in force, but a constable is unaware of it. He comes across a child who he has reasonable cause to believe would be likely to suffer significant harm if not removed (ie the s 46(1) criteria are satisfied). If the judge is right, the removal of the child, otherwise unimpeachable, is unlawful because, unknown to the officer, an EPO is in force in respect of the child. In my view, the jurisdiction to remove a child under s 46 where an EPO is in force cannot depend on whether the constable is aware of its existence. There is nothing in the Act which suggests that the officer's knowledge is relevant. On the judge's interpretation, the existence of the EPO is fatal: of itself it renders the officer's removal unlawful. If this is right, its implications for the protection of children at risk of significant harm are serious. Since police officers cannot have a comprehensive knowledge of all the EPOs that are in force, they would be at risk of acting unlawfully every time they remove a child under s 46. Such an interpretation would be likely to discourage the police from invoking s 46. In this way, there would be a real danger that one of the important powers provided by Parliament for the protection of children at risk would be emasculated.

[31] In the second example, an EPO has been made in respect of a child on the application of the local authority in Liverpool, and the constable comes across the child in Cornwall. Let us suppose that the officer is aware of the EPO, and he considers that the child is in real danger. He considers that it is necessary to act urgently to remove the child to suitable accommodation in order to protect him or her, and it will take some time to contact the social services of Liverpool City Council to alert them to the need to execute the EPO. It would be most unfortunate if, in such circumstances, the constable were unable to invoke s 46 to protect the child.

[32] The relevant provisions of the Act should be construed so as to further the manifest object of securing the protection of children who are at risk of significant harm. A construction of the Act which prohibits a constable from removing a child under s 46 where he has reasonable cause to believe that the child would otherwise be likely to suffer significant harm would frustrate that object. I would, therefore, reject the judge's interpretation of the Act. The s 46 power to remove a child can be exercised even where an EPO is in force in respect of the child.

[33] The next question is whether, on the assumption that the criteria in s 46(1) are met, there are any limitations on the power of the police to remove a child under s 46 where an EPO is in existence …

…

[36] For the reasons which follow, I would hold that, where a police officer knows that an EPO is in force, he should not exercise the power of removing a child under s 46, unless there are compelling reasons to do so. The statutory scheme shows that Parliament intended that, if practicable, the removal of a child from where he or she is living should be authorised by a court order and effected under s 44 …

…

[40] I would, therefore, hold that: (i) removal of children should usually be effected pursuant to an EPO; and (ii) s 46 should be invoked only where it is not practicable to execute an EPO. In deciding whether it is practicable to execute an EPO, the police must always have regard to the paramount need to protect children from significant harm.

[41] We were shown Home Office Circular 44/2003 on the duties and powers of the police under the Act. This came into force on 9 August 2003. It was not in force at the time of the events with which this appeal is concerned. It does not have any statutory force. Nevertheless, I find what it says about s 46 instructive, viz:

'When to use police protection

14.   Police protection powers should only be used when necessary, the principle being that wherever possible the decision to remove a child from a parent or carer should be made by a court.

15.   All local authorities should have in place arrangements (through their local chief Executive and Clerks to the Justices) whereby out of hours applications for Emergency Protection Orders (EPOs – see paragraphs 49 to 54 below) may be made speedily and without an excess of bureaucracy. Police protection powers should only be used when this is not possible.'

[42]   The circular that was in force in September 2001 was Circular No 54/1991. Paragraph 13 states:

'Section 46 provides for the taking of a child into police protection in cases of emergency when there is no time to apply for an order.'

Both circulars are consistent with my interpretation of the Act.

DIVISION E

ADOPTION

Contents

Generally

Generally

E1   ADVERTISING A CHILD FOR ADOPTION

Re K (Adoption: permission to advertise)

[2007] EWHC 544 (Fam), [2007] 2 FLR 326 at 329 and 334

Family Division

McFarlane J

[9]   The effect of s 97(2) of the 1989 Act must, in my view, prevent a child being identified in an adoption advertisement while proceedings are pending under the 1989 Act and/or the 2002 Act unless the court has dispensed with the requirements of s 97(2) by making an order which permits such advertising to take place (at least where the advert contains reference to the fact that he is subject to pending proceedings).

[10]   The prohibition upon adoption advertising contained in s 123 of the 2002 Act does not apply to adoption agencies, therefore its terms are not relevant to a proposal for advertising that is made by a local authority adoption agency.

[11]   During the currency of an interim care order, there is no jurisdiction for the court to make a specific issue order or prohibited steps order under s 8 of the 1989 Act, which might determine or regulate an issue of parental responsibility between the local authority and the parents (s 91(1) of the 1989 Act). A decision to arrange for a child to be advertised as being available for adoption is an exercise of parental responsibility. Within the context of the legislation, there is no strict requirement upon a local authority to apply to the court for permission to advertise; advertising is simply a step that a local authority is entitled to take in the exercise of its parental responsibility for the child.

...

Principles and guidelines

[36] In the light of that short review of the extant authorities it is possible to identify a number of principles which should apply when a court is asked to consider an application to advertise a child for adoption. The principles can be shortly stated:

(i) Before a child can be advertised by a local authority as being available for adoption, the local authority must be satisfied that the child ought to be placed for adoption.

(ii) When advertising a child as available for adoption, the local authority is acting as an adoption agency under the terms of the 2002 Act. A local authority, therefore, cannot be satisfied that a child ought to be placed for adoption, and therefore the subject of an advertisement, until the child's case has been before the local authority's adoption panel and the panel has made a recommendation as to whether the child should be placed for adoption (Reg 18 of the 2005 Regulations) and, thereafter, the appropriate officer of the authority has decided that the child should be placed for adoption (Reg 19 of the 2005 Regulations and *Re P-B*).

(iii) In determining whether permission should be given to advertise a child for adoption the court is determining a question with respect to the upbringing of the child and one that relates to his adoption and the child's welfare must therefore be the court's paramount consideration (s 1(1)(a) of the 1989 Act; s 1(1) and (2) of the 2002 Act).

(iv) The court and/or the local authority must at all times bear in mind that, in general, any delay in the process is likely to prejudice the child's welfare (s 1(3) of the 2002 Act).

(v) Delay is but one, albeit important, factor in the overall decision. There is also a need for the court to be aware of the duty to act fairly, and be seen to do so, with respect to the other parties in the run up to a full hearing. Family members and the child have rights to a fair trial under Art 6 of the European Convention for the Protection of Human Rights and Fundamental Freedoms 1950 (the Convention) which must be kept in focus.

(vi) Advertising of this nature, particularly if names and a photograph are used, is an incursion upon the child's (and to some extent the family's) Art 8 Convention right to respect for private life. In order to be justified under the Convention, any such advertising must be necessary and proportionate to the needs of the child.

[37] In the light of those principles it is possible to offer the following guidance on this topic. I repeat that the guidance set out below is given following a hearing at which there was no representation or other contribution from BAAF or any other national body concerned with adoption practice. In the future, as case-law develops, I fully anticipate that these guidelines may have to be revisited or fine-tuned to meet the needs of the individual cases:

(i) It is not open to a local authority to place an advertisement advertising a particular child as being available for adoption, or to apply to a court for permission to do so, until the authority has obtained the necessary recommendation from its adoption panel and has decided that the child ought to be placed for adoption in compliance with the 2005 Regulations. A court faced with a premature application made prior to the approved officer deciding in favour of adoption in the light of a recommendation from the adoption panel should refuse permission to advertise.

(ii) Where an application for permission to advertise is made in a case where the court has yet to hold a final hearing in care proceedings and has yet to endorse the local authority's care plan for adoption, the court is unlikely to give permission to advertise for adoption unless the adoption plan is unopposed or there is some exceptional feature of the case that justifies advertising notwithstanding the fact that the court has yet to form its own view on the merits of any adoption care plan (for example where the mother has died or cannot be traced, or the adoption plan is supported by all parties).

(iii) In considering such an application the court is likely to bear in mind the fact that a local authority is at liberty to begin a search for potential adopters by looking at its own list of adopters, accessing any local group or consortium list of adopters, and accessing the National Adoption Register without having to advertise and without having to obtain the court's permission. If an application to advertise is made at this comparatively early stage consideration should also be given to what the advertisement will actually say as to the child's status. Prior to the local authority having legal authority to place the child for adoption (either by consent or by a placement order) any advertisement cannot boldly state that the child is available for adoption.

(iv) Where a final care order has been made and the court has expressly approved the local authority's plan for adoption, but a placement order has not yet been made, it is more likely that the court will look favourably on an application to advertise the child for adoption, without having to look for unusual or exceptional circumstances.

(v) In any case where the court has yet to approve the adoption plan the court is likely to require sight of the precise words that are to be used in the advertisement to describe the child's status at that time.

(vi) An application generally 'to publicise' the child as available for adoption is likely to be seen as too widely drawn. Where the local authority wishes to advertise other than in other specialist adoption publications, the court is likely to require clarity as to the identity or type of other publications that are to be approached. Where publication is proposed in the ordinary national or local media, the organs of which are much less likely to apply the strict criteria described by *Be My Parent*, the court should be shown the precise terms of the full advertisement that is proposed.

(vii) As a matter of common sense, and based upon the submissions made in this case, an advertisement which is anonymous and/or does not contain a photograph of the child, is much less likely to attract a positive response. In most cases the court should consider either granting permission for a full advertisement which identifies the child and carries a photograph, or refusing to give permission at all rather than sanctioning an anonymous advertisement.

E2 TRACING AND GIVING NOTICE TO THE FATHER / WIDER FAMILY

C (A child) v XYZ County Council

[2007] EWCA Civ 1206, [2008] 1 FLR 1294 at 1300 and 1306

Court of Appeal

Arden LJ

The issues for decision

[13] There are two issues for decision. The first issue is whether the 2002 Act imposed a duty on the local authority to make inquiries about long-term care for E with her mother's family and, if those inquiries did not yield a long-term carer for E, with E's father, if identified, and his family. I have already indicated that, in my judgment, there was no such duty unless the interests of the child so require. The second issue is how the court's discretion to give directions about contacting the extended family or father of a child in case of this kind should be exercised.

Issue (1): where a mother places her child from adoption, does s 1 of the 2002 Act impose a duty on the local authority to make inquiries of a child's extended family or father about the possibility of their providing long-term care?

[14] This is a question of statutory interpretation. It is necessary to go back to s 1, which I have set out above. In my judgment, the governing provision is subs (2), because it lays down a 'paramount' or overarching consideration and, not surprisingly, that paramount consideration is the child's welfare. Parliament has added that the reference to welfare is to welfare throughout a child's life and not simply in the short-term future or the child's childhood. All the other provisions of s 1 about decision-making take effect subject to this provision.

[15] The result is that s 1 is child-centred. It is not 'mother-centred'. The emphasis is on the interests of the child and not those of the mother. As the European Court of Human Rights (the Strasbourg court) expressed it in one case, adoption means 'giving a family to a child and not the child to a family' (*Fretté v France (Application No 36515/97)* (2004) 38 EHRR 21, [2003] 2 FLR 9 at [42]). The interests of the child will include the child's interest in retaining its identity, and this is likely to be important to the child in adulthood. But identity is only one factor in the balance that

has to be struck. Section 1 does not privilege the birth family over adoptive parents simply because they are the birth family. This is underscored by s 1(6), which requires the court or adoption agency to consider the whole range of powers available to it in the child's case.

[16] Section 1 then lists a number of matters that the court or adoption agency must have in mind when it makes any decision about adoption. Importantly, those matters include delay (subs (3)). Then subs (4) lists a large number of matters. These are not matters on which the court must necessarily act but it must certainly 'have regard' to them.

[17] There are a number of important points to note about the structure of s 1. The list of matters is not exhaustive. The court is required to have regard to the specified matters 'among others'. It is not therefore an exclusive list. Moreover, s 1 still leaves a great deal to the discretion of the court since it does not prescribe the weight which the court or adoption agency must give to any particular matter. That will depend on what is required to fulfil the paramount consideration. Section 1 stipulates that particular matters are to be taken into account, but does not provide any express machinery for ascertaining those matters. The means of ascertaining those matters is left to the inherent powers of the court or statutory powers of the adoption agency. The legislation is not prescriptive, and it has been left to the exercise of discretion as to whether any means available as a matter of inherent jurisdiction or under statutory powers is actually employed. Finally, with one exception, s 1 does not establish any preference for any particular result or prescribe any particular conclusion. Importantly, as I have said, it does not express a preference for following the wishes of the birth family or placing a child with the child's birth family, though this will often be in the best interests of the child. The one exception is delay. Delay is always to be regarded as in some degree likely to prejudice the child's welfare: see subs (3). Parliament has here made a value judgment about the likely impact of delay and it is not open to the court or the adoption agency to quarrel with that basic value judgment.

[18] In this particular case, subs (4)(c) and (f) are particularly important. They were not in the Adoption Act 1976 and are therefore new. Subsection (4)(c) explicates the extended meaning of the child's welfare, and requires the court to look at the likely effect on the child throughout the child's life of having ceased to be a member of the original family and having become a member of his or her adoptive family. This means that the court will have to take into account the importance to a child of their identity, and accordingly, I will have to deal with this matter when I consider how the discretion should be exercised.

[19] Subsection (4)(f) requires the court to have regard to the relationship 'which the child has' with relatives. Relatives are not confined to legal relationships or close relations (see subs (8)). They would

therefore include de facto relationships. This provision is wide enough to cover relationships that have potential for development in the future. E has no relationship with her father at the present time, other than the blood relationship and the potential social relationship were they ever to be in contact with each other. Their relationship is therefore a matter to be considered under subs (4)(f). Likewise the potential relationship that E has with her grandparents is a matter to be considered under that provision. There is nothing to confine subs (4)(f) to relatives who happen to know of the child's birth.

[20] Subsection (4)(f) requires the court to have regard to the wishes and feelings of a child's relatives and their ability and willingness to provide the child with long-term care. However, that assumes that information is reasonably available about these matters. If the information is not readily available, the court or adoption agency may want to obtain it. But in the light of subs (2) there are only required to do so, if that is required for the purposes of the child's welfare and if they consider it right to take those steps notwithstanding that any delay is likely to prejudice the child's welfare.

[21] It can be seen from this analysis that when a decision requires to be made about the long-term care of the child, whom a mother wishes to be adopted, there is no duty to make inquiries of an absolute kind. There is only a duty to make inquiries, if it is in the interests of the child to make those inquiries. In the present case, the judge considered that in adult life the child would benefit from more information about the child's father. But in the context of the decision-making with which the judge was concerned, I do not consider that that fact could of itself animate indeed the exercise of discretion. The immediate question with which the guardian and local authority were concerned was who would look after the child on a long-term basis. The inquiries had to be focused on that result. That meant looking at the evidence about the prospective carers within the mother's family. It was not enough simply to say that it would be in the child's interests to be placed with her birth family. I will have to consider the evidence on that when I come to consider discretion. Finding out more about the child's background for E's information in the future was secondary to that objective, and it would inevitably lead to delay. In the circumstances, I consider that the judge misdirected himself about what inquiries s 1 required in the instant case.

[22] It is convenient at this point to deal with another argument relevant to the interpretation of s 1. E is a looked-after child, that is a child provided with accommodation by the local authority in exercise of its functions referred to in s 22(1) of the 1989 Act. The guardian points out that before a local authority makes any decision with respect to a child whom they are looking after, they must ascertain the wishes and feelings of persons such as the child's parents: s 22(4) of the 1989 Act. Moreover, under s 23 of the 1989 Act, the local authority must provide

accommodation for a looked after child by placing him with a family, or a relative of his. The guardian submits that the 1989 Act places heavy emphasis on consulting widely within a child's immediate and wider family in order to plan for the child's future. In my judgment, those provisions cannot apply where special provision is made by the 2002 Act. Decisions as to E's long-term care, in circumstances where the mother has given her up for adoption, fall within the 2002 Act. There is no reason to give the care proceedings initiated by the local authority precedence over adoption. The only active proposal for long-term care for E is via adoption. The guardian focuses on the point that there are no proceedings under the 2002 Act, but the reason for that is that the local authority has chosen (incorrectly) to use the 1989 Act instead.

[23]   The guardian accepts that there can be no absolute obligation under s 1 to approach the father or the wider family of the child. But she submits that the circumstances in which this should not occur would be limited to cases such as those where the life of the child would be at risk. The guardian relies on the societal shift towards greater involvement of natural father in the upbringing of children. The guardian accepts that each case must turn on its facts, and that a balancing act has to be conducted in each case. But she rejects the mother's contention that the judge was plainly wrong. She submits that the effect of s 1(4)(c) and (f) is that there is now an *expectation* of disclosure and that the courts should require compelling reasons to prevent it taking place, certainly to a natural father and probably, too, to close members of the wider family. In my judgment, as I have already indicated, the overarching consideration is that of the interests of the child. In many cases disclosure will be in the interests of the child, but it cannot be assumed that it will always be so. Moreover, disclosure has to be directed to an end that furthers the making of the decisions which require to be made. That requirement was not met in the present case.

[24]   The logical consequence of my interpretation of s 1 is that exceptional situations can arise in which relatives, or even a father, of a child remain in ignorance about the child at the time of its adoption. But this result is consistent with other provisions of the 2002 Act. There are situations when the court does not require the consent of the father. For example, the consent of the father without parental responsibility is not required for a placement under ss 19 or 20, and, even if E were to be placed for adoption with her mother's consent but her father later obtained parental responsibility, he would be deemed to have consented to the placing of E for adoption (see above).

[25]   The effect of s 1 as I have held it to be is consistent with the refusal by the court under the Adoption Act 1976 to give notice of adoption proceedings to a father who had had only a fleeting relationship with the child's mother: in *Re H and G (Adoption: Consultation of Unmarried Fathers)* [2001] 1 FLR 646, the President of the Family Division (Dame

Elizabeth Butler-Sloss) ordered that no notice of adoption proceedings needed to be given to a father who had never cohabited with the child's mother. In *Z County Council v R* [2001] 1 FLR 365, a baby, whose mother had refused to disclose the identity of the father, was placed with prospective adopters. The local authority applied for an order freeing the child for adoption. At that stage, the guardian raised the question whether the mother's relatives should be told about the baby's existence and consulted as to whether any of them might wish to offer the child home. The mother opposed this course. Holman J held that there was no reason to doubt the mother's views that the relatives could not care for the baby. Accordingly, he held that it was not in the child's interests to reveal the information. Self-evidently, it would be inappropriate to reveal the existence of a child to a father who was violent, or to relatives who suffered from illnesses which would make it impossible for them to look after the child.

[26] There will be situations in which it is impossible to ascertain who the father is without the mother's co-operation. That situation may not be this case. The recent case of *Re L (Adoption: Contacting Natural Father)* [2007] EWHC 1771 shows that the courts are likely to take the realistic view that, where the only person who knows the father's identity is the mother and she refuses to identify him, there is nothing in practical terms which can usefully be done. Munby J, on an application under the court's inherent jurisdiction, directed in those particular circumstances that, subject to asking the mother once more for the name of the father, no further steps needed to be taken to give a father without parental responsibility notice of intention to place a child for adoption.

...

[39] Accordingly, I conclude that an order directing that information about E should not be disclosed to E's father would not violate his Convention rights under Art 8 because he has no right to be violated. The grandparents have such a right, but non-disclosure to them would not violate their right since ex hypothesi the court would have concluded that E's welfare required that that order be made and they would be able to obtain the information by making their own application under the 1989 Act.

Issue (2): Factors relevant to exercising the discretion in this situation

[40] I propose to start with a few general observations. There will inevitably be a wide variety of cases where there arises the question whether a newborn child should be adopted. Every case has to be determined on its particular facts. The fact that the father or a relative has no right to respect for family life in the particular case does not mean that their position should not be considered: s 1(4)(f) of the 2002 Act applies

irrespective of Art 8 rights. However, the position of a person would command more importance if they were entitled to that right.

[41] I accept the submission of the local authority that the court or adoption agency cannot simply act on what the mother says. It has to examine what she says critically. It is a question of judgment whether what the mother says needs to be checked or corroborated.

[42] The local authority goes on to say that the ordinary rule should be that the near family and father should be identified and informed unless the court is satisfied that such inquiries would be inappropriate. The local authority submits that there is a growing trend towards involving the natural family and the father in such cases. It is no doubt true to say that there are a substantial number of cases where a child who would otherwise be placed for adoption is offered long term care by a member of the family.

[43] I do not consider that this court should require a preference to be given as a matter of policy to the natural family of a child. Section 1 does not impose any such policy. Rather, it requires the interests of the child to be considered. That must mean the child as an individual. In some cases, the birth tie will be very important, especially where the child is of an age to understand what is happening or where there are ethnic or cultural or religious reasons for keeping the child in the birth family. Where a child has never lived with her birth family, and is too young to understand what is going on, that argument must be weaker. In my judgment, in a case such as this, it is (absent any application by any member of the family, which succeeds) overtaken by the need to find the child a permanent home as soon as that can be done.

[44] I now turn to this case.

Other significant cases on this issue:

- *Re C (Adoption) (Disclosure to father)* [2005] EWHC 3385 (Fam), [2006] 2 FLR 589
- *Birmingham City Council v S, R and A* [2006] EWHC 3065 (Fam), [2007] 1 FLR 1223
- *Re L (Adoption: contacting natural father)* [2007] EWHC 1771 (Fam), [2008] 1 FLR 1079
- Cf *Local Authority v M and F; the children by their guardian* [2009] EWHC 3172 (Fam), [2010] 1 FLR 1355: see G25 – Proceedings not to be disclosed to father

E3   ACA 2002, S 19: EFFECT OF CONSENT WHEN CHILD LESS THAN SIX WEEKS OLD

A Local Authority v GC

[2008] EWHC 2555 (Fam), [2009] 1 FLR 299 at 301 and 308

Family Division

Eleanor King J

[13]   The issue for the court to determine is whether the 's 19 consent' to the placement of MM with a view to adoption given by the parents on 22 June is effective in relation to either or both parents despite the fact that it was given before MM was 6 weeks old.

...

[37]   *Conclusion*

(1)   The placement of MM was not an unauthorised placement. Whether she was placed by way of 's 19 consent' or by way of 'written agreement' under reg 35 of the AAR 2005, consent was properly given by MM's mother to her placement for adoption. Such consent can be given when the child is less than 6 weeks old.

(2)   Regardless of whether the consent was merely a 'written agreement' or whether it was capable of being a full 's 19 consent', that consent to placement cannot be relied on as jurisdiction to make an adoption order under the second condition at s 47(4)(b)(i) of the ACA 2002 as MM was not 6 weeks old when her mother consented.

(3)   Both good practice and common sense suggest that 's 19 consents' should only be sought after the child is 6 weeks old as consent given (albeit in writing) prior to that time will not satisfy the second condition in s 47. Failure to delay in obtaining a s 19 consent until after the child is 6 weeks old serves to undermine the objective of 's 19 consent', namely of ensuring speedy, secure, consensual placements of young children outside care proceedings without the uncertainty and delay implicit in an application to dispense with the consent to adoption of either or both parents.

(4)   There remains the issue as to whether:

(i)   consent given by a parent to placement for adoption of a baby before the baby is 6 weeks of age is capable of being a 's 19 consent' with all the accompanying restrictions on a parent's involvement in the life of the child which flow from the giving of such consent; or

(ii)   whether such early consent means the child remains 'accommodated' under s 20 of the Children Act 1989, although placed for adoption.

It is unnecessary for the court to determine this outstanding issue. On the facts of this case all parties are agreed that nothing turns on whether or not the 's 19' restrictions would properly have bitten in MM's case or whether she remained an accommodated child.

[38]   So far as MM is concerned the important matters are that:

(a)   She was placed under a written agreement and therefore her placement with Mr and Mrs X was an authorised placement.

(b)   She was under 6 weeks of age when the consent was signed so prior to an adoption order being made the court must dispense with the consent of each of her parents on the basis that her welfare requires an adoption order to be made.

E4 ACA 2002, S 21: PO SET ASIDE WHERE PANEL PROCESS FLAWED

Re B (Placement order)

[2008] EWCA Civ 835, [2008] 2 FLR 1404 at 1422, 1423, 1427 and 1428

Court of Appeal

Wall LJ

[70] I have reached the conclusion that the recorder was wrong for the simple reason that I do not think that the framework laid down by Parliament can be bypassed or short-circuited. In my judgment, the decision of this court in *Re P-B* accurately states the law. An application for a placement order cannot properly be made by an adoption agency unless the agency decision maker is satisfied that the child in question should be placed for adoption, and Parliament has laid down that the decision maker cannot be so satisfied unless he or she has properly considered the recommendation of the AAP. It must follow, in my judgment, that if the decision of the AAP is flawed in any material respect then the decision maker cannot properly consider the recommendation, and thus cannot be satisfied – in accordance with the process laid down by Parliament – that the child in question should be placed for adoption.

...

[73] What should, in my judgment, have occurred is that the recorder should have adjourned the care proceedings relating to M in order for the adoption agency as a matter of urgency to re-constitute the AAP and for the AAP to reconsider its recommendation in the light of all the information which was available and which should have been before it when it first considered M's case. I am confident that the AAP could have reconvened as a matter of urgency and within a matter of days. Had it done so, the position would have been clarified. In my judgment, the recorder's conclusion that remission would have involved unacceptable delay is untenable.

[74] Equally, I do not think that the recorder was right to consider that the hearing before him had rectified the deficiencies in the process. Of course, the recorder was right to conclude that he had duties and responsibilities under the 1989 Act, and that it was open to him to make care orders on the basis of the care plans placed before him. This, however, misses the point that what the recorder did was to make a specific order – a placement order – under s 22(1) of the 2002 Act in

circumstances in which the due process laid down by Parliament had not been followed. In my judgment, this was not the right course to adopt. The recorder should have adjourned, and any future court, faced with this same dilemma, should also adjourn to enable the AAP to reconsider and for the adoption agency's decision maker also to reconsider.

...

[81] There was, I am pleased to say, substantial agreement at the bar as to the nature of the guidance we should give. First and foremost, of course, the provisions of the 2002 Act and the Regulations must be followed, and not bypassed. More specifically, the guardian suggested the following:

(1) expert reports which have been filed and served in care proceedings and which address the present and future needs of the subject child (including, but not exclusively, dealing with placement issues) should be provided to members of an adoption panel in advance of the relevant meeting and to decision makers for pre-reading;

(2) where such reports are voluminous, as a minimum those sections of the reports setting out the experts' opinion, conclusions and/or recommendations should be provided in advance to the members of the panel and to the decision maker;

(3) a summary of the expert(s)' opinions should only be provided to the panel members and the decision maker in substitution for the reports if:
   (a) the summary is in writing;
   (b) all parties to the care proceedings agree in writing that the summary is fair and accurate and should be provided to the panel and the decision maker in substitution for the reports; and
   (c) copies of the reports are available at the meeting for the members of the panel and the decision maker to consult if desired;

(4) a clear, full and accurate minute of the panel meeting should be made during the meeting with particular attention given to:
   (a) recording the documentation considered by the members of the panel; and
   (b) the questions asked by members of the panel and the answers given by the social worker(s) present; and

(5) the social workers who attend the panel meeting to present the child's case should be invited to approve the record of the note of the questions asked of and answers given by them during the meeting.

[82] To this guidance, which seems to me eminently sensible, I would only add that, in my judgment, it is imperative that the decision to ratify the AAP's decision and to begin the process of applying for a placement order must never be a simple rubber stamp. The circumstances in which the decision is taken should be transparent, and the decision itself minuted. In my judgment, the manner in which the decision was taken in the instant case was unsatisfactory: it was a rubber stamp imposed by the Director of Social Services, who had no real knowledge of the case and who made the decision on the basis of the inaccurate information provided to the Panel. Whilst it may well be that in practice the decision to take proceedings for a placement order will be made by an individual rather than a group, the source and substance of the information given to the decision maker must be clear, and both the decision itself and the reasons for it minuted.

...

[84]   The essence of the guidance, in my judgment, must be that panel members should be made fully and properly aware of all the available material relevant to their decision. It will plainly be a matter of judgment for the local authority medical adviser to the panel in each case to decide whether or not panel members need to read any expert report, or whether or not a summary of it will suffice. There is, however, a clear duty on the local authority which is conducting the care proceedings to ensure both that all relevant material is made available to the Panel, and that the material placed before it is accurate. As important, it seems to me, is the proposition that the decision to proceed to apply for a placement order is properly made, and minuted.

[85]   It will, it seems to me, almost invariably be the case that where the local authority having conduct of the care proceedings is contemplating an application to apply for a placement order in relation to a child: (a) that application is likely to be contested; and (b) the child's future will not have been decided by the court. As was pointed out in the course of argument, a panel's decision is a recommendation and a pre-requisite to the application for a placement order. In these circumstances, the panel will thus almost always have to make its recommendation in the light of the fact that the proceedings are contested, and that the expert evidence before the panel may be neither complete nor that which is ultimately placed before the court. It is for this reason, of course, that the final decision about adoption rests with the court. However, none of this provides any basis for the panel being provided with inaccurate information.

[86]   I would therefore adopt the guidance provided by the guardian, with the additional observations as to the need for transparency in the process of making the application for a placement order.

E5   ACA 2002, S 22: WHEN MUST LA APPLY FOR PO / AAR 2005, REG 19

Re P-B (Placement order)

[2006] EWCA Civ 1016, [2007] 1106 at 1111 and 1114

Court of Appeal

Thorpe and Arden LJJ

THORPE LJ:

[18]   So, in the very shortest summary, the dispute is as to what is meant by the requirement in s 22 that a local authority are to apply for a placement order if they are satisfied that the child ought to be placed for adoption; are the local authority acting under the provisions of Parts III and IV of the 1989 Act, or are the local authority acting as an adoption agency under the terms of the 2002 Act?

[19]   I am in no doubt in my mind that Mr O'Brien is right in his construction. It is in their role as an adoption agency that the local authority must be satisfied, and that process cannot be achieved until there has been complete compliance with the requirements of the 2005 Regulations, namely that the appointed officer has taken the positive decision to endorse the recommendation of the panel.

ARDEN LJ:

[35]   I agree. I would like to add some observations on the first issue, the question of construction arising on s 22(1) of the Adoption and Children Act 2002.

[36]   In the present case the local authority intended to comply with their obligation under reg 19 of the Adoption Agency Regulations 2005. Regulation 19 required them to:

'... take into account the recommendation of the adoption panel in coming to a decision about whether the child should be placed for adoption.'

[37]   I say nothing about the case where the local authority commences proceedings without, for whatever reason, fulfilling or properly fulfilling their statutory obligation under this regulation. Indeed, the position

about that might not come to light for some time and the court might have proceeded to make an order. The resolution of that situation will have to await until it arises. Hopefully it never will. On the point that arises in this case I agree with what Thorpe LJ has said and his analysis.

[38]   There is a separate issue as to what reg 19 means. It clearly imposes a substantive duty to take account of the recommendation of the adoption panel. It is not enough to pay lip service to the recommendation of the adoption panel. On the other hand the duty is only one to take account. Thus it must be open in theory at least for an adoption agency to reach a different view from the recommendation of the adoption panel, but I anticipate that the local authority would have to have strong grounds for doing so.

E6   ACA 2002, S 22: TWIN TRACK PLANNING NOT INCONSISTENT

Re P (Placement orders: parental consent)

[2008] EWCA Civ 535, [2008] 2 FLR 625 at 661

Court of Appeal

Wall LJ

[137]   In our judgment, a local authority can be 'satisfied that the child ought to be placed for adoption' within the meaning of s 22(1)(d) of the 2002 Act even though it recognises the reality that a search for adoptive parents may be unsuccessful and that, if it is, the alternative plan will have to be for long-term fostering. The wording, after all, is 'ought to be' not 'will be'. That being so there can be no objection in principle to dual planning in appropriate cases.

[138]   There can moreover, be compelling pragmatic reasons for adopting dual planning in appropriate cases. In the first place it may shorten the period during which the child has to remain in limbo, a very important consideration particularly if the child is older or has already been in the care system too long. There is, in addition, the important point made by Miss Thirlwall. As experience shows, there are, even now the 2002 Act is in force, many prospective adopters who will come forward only if a placement order has been obtained. The experience of trial judges, as Munby J confirms, is that many local authorities believe, and seemingly with good basis for their belief, that a search for adoptive parents without the benefit of a placement order is a search within an artificially restricted pool. That cannot be for the benefit of the child.

[139]   In our judgment, there is also the important factor that adoption in England and Wales is, as we understand it, no longer largely about the adoption of babies, but about children like D and S who are older, and who have had conscious experience of being parented by their birth mother and father. In the instant case, the effect of that parenting on both S and D has been seriously adverse. Placing a baby for adoption, by comparison, has none of the difficulties associated with the placement of D and S, and Mr Geekie's sequential approach may well be appropriate for such a placement. Given the change which we have identified, however, we are satisfied that the local authority / agency approach to dual planning in the instant case, and in like cases, is permissible as a matter of welfare – see, in particular, ss 1(3), 1(4)(b) to (e) and s 1(6).

Other significant cases on this issue:

* Cf *Re T (Placement order)* [2008] EWCA Civ 248, [2008] 1 FLR
  1721

This case is also included in relation to:

E10 ACA 2002, ss 26 and 27: contact on making PO
E14 ACA 2002, s 52: dispensing with parental consent

E7   ACA 2002, S 24: LEAVE TO APPLY TO REVOKE PO

M v Warwickshire County Council

[2007] EWCA Civ 1084, [2008] 1 FLR 1093 at 1098 and 1104

Court of Appeal

Wilson LJ

[14]   Section 24(5) of the 2002 Act provides that, where an application for the revocation of a placement order has been made and has not been disposed of, the child may not be placed for adoption without the court's leave. Notwithstanding submissions on behalf of the mother to the contrary, the judge held that there was nothing, whether in that subsection or elsewhere, which precluded a placement without leave while an application for *leave* to apply for revocation was pending. I agree with the judge; and in this court the mother does not argue to the contrary. The judge went on to observe, however, that, were an application for leave to have been issued but not to have been disposed of, it would normally be good practice for a local authority either to agree not to place the child until its disposal or at least to agree to give notice, say of 14 days, to the applicant of any proposed placement. In this regard I also agree with him. Given such notice, the applicant might perhaps be able either to take steps to challenge the lawfulness of the decision to place at that juncture or, probably more easily, to seek an expedited hearing of the application for leave, from which might flow, in the fine, developing tradition of collaboration between local authorities and courts, a short further agreed moratorium on placement until the hearing ...

...

[29]   In relation to an application for leave under s 24(3) of the 2002 Act I therefore hold that, on establishment of a change in circumstances, a discretion arises in which the welfare of the child and the prospect of success should both be weighed. My view is that the requisite analysis of the prospect of success will almost always include the requisite analysis of the welfare of the child. For, were there to be a real prospect that an applicant would persuade the court that a child's welfare would best be served by revocation of the placement order, it would surely almost always serve the child's welfare for the applicant to be given leave to seek to do so. Conversely, were there not to be any such real prospect, it is hard to conceive that it would serve the welfare of the child for the application for leave to be granted. But I hesitate to suggest that analysis of welfare will always be satisfactorily subsumed within an analysis of prospect. Take a child who has proved extraordinarily difficult to place; and assume that apparently ideal adopters have at last been found for him but that they demonstrate a wish for him to be placed with them only if such can occur within days of the hearing of the application for leave and, otherwise, a preference to receive another child instead. Might the court not then consider that, although the proposed application for revocation, likely to be heard at a time when, as before, no specific adoptive home was in prospect, had a real prospect of success, nevertheless the child's welfare would not be served by grant of leave? Other, probably better, examples may crop up as exercise of the jurisdiction under s 24(3) develops.

General notes:

The same test has since been applied applications for leave to apply for an adoption order under ACA 2002, s 42(6): *Re A; Coventry County Council v CC and A* [2007] EWCA Civ 1383, [2008] 1 FLR 959 (see E11 – ACA 2002, s 42(6): leave to apply for AO) and to applications for leave to discharge or vary a special guardianship order: *Re G (Special guardianship order)* [2010] EWCA Civ 300, [2010] 2 FLR 696 (see B61 – Application for leave to discharge or vary SGO).

Other significant cases on this issue:

- *NS-H v Kingston upon Hull City Council and MC* [2008] EWCA Civ 493, [2008] 2 FLR 918

E8   ACA 2002, S 24(2): 'PLACED FOR ADOPTION'

Re S (Placement order: revocation)

[2008] EWCA Civ 1333, [2009] 1 FLR 503 at 506

Court of Appeal

Thorpe LJ

[7]   … Section 18(5) required him to focus on a prospective adopter, whilst he chose to focus on a potential adopter … As Mr Stuart Leach has pointed out in his skeleton argument, those two adjectives have distinctly different dictionary meanings. The Oxford English Dictionary describes 'prospective' as an adjective attributive of a person expected or expecting to be something particular in the future; alternatively, as something likely to happen at a future date. 'Potential', by contrast, is defined as an adjective having or showing the capacity to become or develop into something in the future.

[8]   The reality is that L, on and after 14 July 2007, was placed with the carer under the fostering regulations and not under the placement regulations, the adoption regulations. In those circumstances, the local authority had sole parental responsibility for L. Had he been placed under the placement regulations, then parental responsibility would have been shared between the local authority and the carer. As my Lord, Hedley J, has analysed in argument, there are three necessary stages to the statutory placement of a child. The first question that has to be asked by the panel is whether adoption is in the best interests of the child. If the answer to that is in the affirmative, then there is an obligation on the local authority to apply for a placement order. Once the placement order has been granted, it is the responsibility of the panel to consider whether specific individuals – say, Mr and Mrs X – are in principle approved as adopters. If that question is answered in the affirmative, then the third stage for the panel's consideration is whether the child in question is matched to Mr and Mrs X, and therefore to be placed with them.

[9]   As my Lord has observed, the construction of ss 24 and 18 must be considered within that framework, and I fully share his view that a child is not deemed to be placed for the purposes of s 24 until all three stages have been accomplished. Here the only stage accomplished was the first; the current carers had not been approved in principle, nor had L been matched to be placed with them. As the judge himself saw, at the highest the current foster carer had no more than the potential to emerge at a

later stage as a prospective adopter with whom L had not been placed, but whose placement might, under s 18(5)(b), be enlarged from foster to adoptive placement.

Other significant cases on this issue:

- *R(W) v Brent LBC* [2010] EWHC 175 (Admin), [2010] 1 FLR 1914

E9 ACA 2002, S 24(5)

Re F (Placement order)

[2008] EWCA Civ 439, [2008] 2 FLR 550 at 564 and 570

Court of Appeal

Wall LJ

[62] I have set out Mr Cobb's argument in detail, because I have considerable sympathy for it on the facts of this particular case. I am, however, unable to accept it. In my judgment, deeply unattractive as the agency's position is, the judge was right, and, as I have already stated, the appeal has to be dismissed.

[63] In my judgment, Wilson LJ's judgment in the *Warwickshire* case[1] accurately states the law. Section 24 of the 2002 Act is, moreover, in my judgment HRA 1998 compliant. We cannot read in the words Mr Cobb invites us to read in, and no question of a declaration of incompatibility arises. I will endeavour to explain why I take that view.

[64] The first point, it seems to me, is that s 24 has to be read in the context of the overall scheme of the 2002 Act. The 2002 Act reformed the law of adoption. In s 21, it introduced the new concept of the placement order, which is defined in s 21(1) as 'an order made by the court authorising a local authority to place a child for adoption with any prospective adopters who may be chosen by the authority'. The circumstances in which the court is entitled to make a placement order are set out in s 21(2) and (3). Section 21(4) sets out the duration of placement orders.

[65] Section 22 sets out the circumstances in which a local authority is required to apply for a placement order and s 23 sets out the very limited circumstances in which the court is empowered to vary such an order. Section 25 provides that when a placement order is in force, parental responsibility is given to the adoption agency concerned and to any prospective adopters with whom the child is placed. By s 25(4) the adoption agency which has parental responsibility 'may determine that the parental responsibility of any parent or guardian, or of prospective adopters, is to be restricted to the extent specified in the determination'.

[66] Under s 52(1) the court is empowered to dispense with the consent of a parent to the child being placed for adoption, and the effect of the

---

[1] *M v Warwickshire County Council* [2007] EWCA Civ 1084, [2008] 1 FLR 1093.

dispensation is that the parent in question cannot oppose the making of an adoption order without first obtaining the leave of the court (s 47(5)).

[67] This, in my judgment, is the context in which s 24 of the 2002 Act falls to be considered. Mr Cobb accepted, as he had to, that Parliament had the right to limit the class of persons entitled to apply for the revocation of placement orders. He also (rightly in my judgment) accepted that the imposition of the leave filter in s 24(2) was legitimate, and did not constitute a breach of either Convention Arts 6 or 8.

[68] Once it is accepted, as it has to be, that s 24(2) of the 2002 Act is HRA 1998 compliant, it seems to me evident that Parliament has drawn a very clear line between an application for leave to apply for the revocation of a placement order, and the substantive application to revoke. Equally, no criticism was, or could be made of Parliament's insertion of the 'change in circumstances' criterion in s 24(3). Section 24(4) is not here in point.

[69] Against this background, it seems to me to be quite impermissible, either as a canon of construction, or as an exercise under s 3 of HRA 1998 to read the words 'or an application for leave to apply for the revocation of a placement order' into s 24(5). The two are quite distinct, and Parliament, in my judgment, clearly intended that s 24(5) should only apply where a substantive application for the revocation of a placement order had been made – in other words, the applicant had got over the leave hurdle, and was making a substantive application which, consequent upon the grant of leave, would be likely to have been perceived as having a real prospect of success.

[70] In addition, it seems to me that if Parliament had intended to include applications for leave to apply for revocation orders in s 24(5) it would have said so. It has not, and in my judgment, given the plain terms of s 24(2) it is both impermissible and impossible to read s 24(5) as Mr Cobb would have us do.

[71] Equally, in my judgment, s 24(5) is HRA 1998 compliant. The subsection does not deprive a parent in the position of the father in this case of access to the court. What it does is require him to make the application before the child is placed for adoption. This, in my judgment, is consistent with the overall framework of the 2002 Act.

[72] The 2002 Act reformed the law of adoption. It is not, I think, controversial to say that the 2002 Act had four main objectives. The first was to simplify the process. The second was to enable a crucial element of the decision making process to be undertaken at an earlier stage. The third was to shift the emphasis to a concentration on the welfare of the child; and the fourth was to avoid delay. Thus, in the same way that good practice in planning for the future of children within the care system

discourages parents and relatives from putting themselves forward at the last moment to care for a child, the 2002 Act seeks to facilitate the adoption process once the critical stages of care and placement orders – court proceedings in which parents are entitled fully to participate and in which the relevant decisions are taken by a judge – have been passed.

...

What should have happened in the instant case

[97] In my judgment, one of two things should have happened. Firstly, although this is not intended as a criticism, the letter from the father's solicitors on dated 17 January should have contained an additional paragraph along the following lines:

> 'We invite you to give an undertaking that you will take no steps to place (*the child*) with prospective adopters pending the hearing of our client's application. If that undertaking is not received by 10.00 am on 18 January, we shall apply without notice in the first instance to the county court for an order in those terms.'

[98] At the hearing of this appeal, we had some debate about the jurisdiction of the court to grant such an injunction. This is not a subject on which I, like Wilson LJ, whose judgment I have also read in draft, entertain any doubts. I am satisfied that the county court has such jurisdiction and would, moreover, have exercised it as a temporary, holding measure, until both sides could be before the court. The judge would either then have given directions for a swift hearing, or resolved the matter summarily. But even if there had been a summary adjudication against the father, he would have been heard.

[99] What should have happened in the alternative is: (1) that the agency should have replied promptly to the letter of 17 January; and (2) that it should have explained that its plans were at an advanced stage of preparation and, indeed, about to be implemented. It could then itself have applied to the court, on short notice, for leave to place the child for adoption under s 24(5) of the 2002 Act.

[100] Either way, there would have been a hearing on the merits. It might have been very short. Mr Cobb realistically accepted that the judge would have had a very broad discretion to deal with the matter summarily if necessary – see *Re B*[2] to which reference was made earlier in this judgment. If the case had gone against him, the father would have lost. But he would have been heard. The court would have made the decision, and justice would have both been done and been seen to be done.

---

[2]   *Re B (Minors) (Contact)* [1994] 2 FLR 1.

[101]   Local authorities and adoption agencies must understand that it is the court which is in control, and which has been given by Parliament the responsibility for making these decisions. The courts are not a rubber stamp for local authority/agency actions, however, reprehensible.

[102]   In para [14] of his judgment in the *Warwickshire* case, Wilson LJ emphasised the need for good practice to supplement the 2002 Act. I wholeheartedly agree with him. I hope that this judgment makes crystal clear not only what that good practice should be in relation to s 24(5) of the 2002 Act but why good practice is so important. It is for this reason that I propose widespread dissemination of our judgments in this case. Any local authority falling below the standards of good practice, and indulging in the shoddy behaviour demonstrated by the East Sussex County Council in the instant case can expect not only severe judicial displeasure, and applications for judicial review: it is also likely that any repetition of the disgraceful behaviour identified in this case will be visited by orders for costs.

E10 ACA 2002, SS 26 AND 27: CONTACT ON MAKING PO

Re P (Placement orders: parental consent)

[2008] EWCA Civ 535, [2008] 2 FLR 625 at 662

Court of Appeal

Wall LJ

[141] We approach this part of our judgment with caution, as we are conscious that these are early days, and the manner in which adoption agencies apply the terms of the 2002 Act will need to be worked out in practice over time. That such agencies may not fully have grasped the principles behind the 2002 Act is, we think, amply demonstrated by this court's recent decision in *Re F (A Child)* [2008] EWCA Civ 439, sub nom *Re F (Placement Order)* [2008] 2 FLR 550. We therefore offer the following guidance.

[142] Historically, post adoption contact between children and their birth parents has been perceived as highly exceptional. We can, we think, begin our analysis with the decision of the House of Lords in *Re C (A Minor) (Adoption Order: Conditions)* [1989] AC 1, [1988] 2 WLR 474, [1988] 2 FLR 159 (*Re C*), In that case, the child, C, who was 13, had a strong relationship with her brother, M, who was 19. C's mother refused to give her consent to C's adoption on the ground that adoption might harm C's relationship with M. Both the trial judge and this court upheld her refusal to consent, notwithstanding the prospective adopters' acknowledgement of the relationship and their assurance that no impediment would be placed by them on its continuance.

[143] The House of Lords reversed this court's decision, and made an adoption order, attaching to it a condition under s 8(7) of the Children Act 1975 as to contact between C and M. The leading speech was given by Lord Ackner. After an exhaustive review of the authorities prior to 1988, he said the following: – at 17–18, 483 and 167–168 respectively –

'Miss Ryan on behalf of Mrs B conceded that the terms of section 8(7) of the Act of 1975 were unambiguous and on the face of the subsection there was jurisdiction to impose any terms or conditions that the court thought fit. She, however, in essence, repeated the unsuccessful submission made in *In Re V (A Minor) (Adoption: Consent)* [1987] Fam. 57, referred to above, that the subsection only enabled the attachment of such terms and conditions as the court could see would be immediately fulfilled or met and not conditions which involved the intervention or supervision of the court in the future. Thus in her submission the decisions of the Court of Appeal which, expressly or by necessary implication, decided the contrary were wrong.

I cannot agree. It seems to me essential that, in order to safeguard and promote the welfare of the child throughout his childhood, the court should retain the maximum flexibility given to it by the Act and that unnecessary fetters should not be placed upon the exercise of the discretion entrusted to it by Parliament. The cases to which I have referred illustrate circumstances in which it was clearly in the best interests of the child to allow access to a member of the child's natural family. The cases rightly stress that in normal circumstances it is desirable that there should be a complete break, but that each case has to be considered on its own particular facts. No doubt the court will not, except in the most exceptional case, impose terms or conditions as to access to members of the child's natural family to which the adopting parents do not agree. To do so would be to create a potentially frictional situation which would be hardly likely to safeguard or promote the welfare of the child. Where no agreement is forthcoming the court will, with very rare exceptions, have to choose between making an adoption order without terms or conditions as to access, or to refuse to make such an order and seek to safeguard access through some other machinery, such as wardship. To do otherwise would be merely inviting future and almost immediate litigation.'

[144] *Re C* was, of course, decided prior to the passing of the Children Act 1989, and with the 1989 Act came the appreciation that contact orders post adoption could be made under s 8 of that Act, albeit that 'leave' (permission from the court) was required before a birth parent could apply for contact once an adoption order was made. In accordance with *Re C,* however, such orders were perceived to be highly unusual. Two cases decided in 1995 (both called *Re T (Adopted Children: Contact)* [1995] 2 FLR 251 and [1995] 2 FLR 792 respectively) set the tone. In the first, the adopters had agreed to contact once a year. The child's birth mother wanted contact two or three times a year, and sought an order to that effect so that her contact with the child would be secure. The judge made an order for contact once a year. The adopters appealed, and this court set aside the order. Butler-Sloss LJ (as she then was) said [1995] 2 FLR 251 at 256:

'It seems to me that that degree of security that she seeks has to be found in the trust that she must have in these adopters. That is a trust which is undoubtedly held by the local authority and the guardian ad litem, because those experts in this field all believe that at this stage of this child's life it is right for her sake that she should continue to see her mother once a year. They have chosen this family on the basis that they also would recognise it was in the interests of this child that she should continue, certainly for the time being, to see her natural mother. These adopters themselves accept that this is right. This is all in the interests of the child, and, of course, an order under s 8 for contact is made with the welfare of the child of the primary consideration. Nobody is suggesting that if this order is not made then the welfare of this child would not continue to be the primary consideration of these adopters in relation to her continuing contact with her natural mother.'

[145] In the second *Re T* a girl of 20 was given leave to apply for contact on the basis that the adoptive parents of her half-siblings had, without proffering an explanation, resiled from an agreement to provide annual reports on them. Once again, however, it was not envisaged that the applicant would achieve an order for face to face contact. As we read the case, the contact application was perceived as a vehicle to force the adopters to explain why they had not produced the reports.

[146] Since 1995, the value of contact post adoption has been identified in a number of the cases, notably by Ward LJ in *Re G (Adoption: Contact)* [2002] EWCA 761, [2003] 1 FLR 270 and in the dissenting speech of Baroness Hale of Richmond in the Northern Ireland case of *Down Lisburn Health and Social Services Trust v H* [2006] UKHL 36. [2007] 1 FLR 121, both of which, of course, were decided without specific reference to the 2002 Act. However, as we understand it, the position has remained not only that contact orders post adoption are unusual, but, as was said in *Re R (Adoption: Contact)* [2005] EWCA Civ 1128; [2006] 1 FLR 373 at [49], that whilst contact post adoption was 'more common' the jurisprudence was clear, and that 'the imposition on prospective adopters of orders for contact with which they are not in agreement is extremely, and remains extremely unusual'.

[147] All this, in our judgment, now falls to be revisited under ss 26 and 27 of the 2002 Act, given in particular the terms of ss 1(4)(f), 1(6) and (7) and 46(6). In our judgment, the judge in the instant case was plainly right to make a contact order under s 26 of the 2002 Act, and in our judgment the question of contact between D and S, and between the children and their parents, should henceforth be a matter for the court, not for the local authority, or the local authority in agreement with prospective adopters.

[148] We have already expressed both our surprise and dismay that D's contact with her mother was stopped by the local authority unlawfully, and without the authority of an order from the court under s 34(4) of the 1989 Act. The making of the placement orders means, of course, that contact under the 1989 Act is no longer possible, but orders under ss 26 and 27 are not only possible but, in our judgment, necessary.

[149] Furthermore, when the time comes for D and S to be finally placed, it will be the court which will have to make the necessary orders – either for adoption, or for revocation of the placement orders if the children are not to be adopted. At that point, in our judgment, as the facts of this case currently stand, it will be for the court, before making an adoption order, to decide, in accordance with s 46(6) of the 2002 Act, what ongoing contact D and S should have with each other – not for their prospective adopters to do so. The same principle will apply if the children are to be placed in long-term foster care.

[150] The effect of the placement order is substantially to disempower D's and S's parents – see s 25(4) of the 2002 Act. In our judgment, as matters currently stand, the existence of the placement orders should not be an inhibition on the ability of SB in particular to apply to the court to determine questions of contact – and in particular the question of contact between D and S. Indeed, it seems to us highly likely that the placement of the children with adopters or foster carers who are unwilling, in particular, to facilitate contact between D and S would provide a proper basis for leave to be granted to SB under s 24(2) of the 2002 Act (leave to make an application to apply for an order to revoke the placement order) or for leave to apply to oppose the making of an adoption order under s 47(5) of the 2002 Act.

[151] On the facts of this case, there is a universal recognition that the relationship between D and S needs to be preserved. It is on this basis that the local authority/adoption agency is seeking the placement of the children. In our judgment, this means that the question of contact between the two children is not a matter for agreement between the local authority/adoption agency and the adopters: it is a matter which, ultimately, is for the court. It is the court which will have to make adoption orders or orders revoking the placement orders, and in our judgment it is the court which has the responsibility to make orders for contact if they are required in the interests of the two children.

[152] In our judgment, the making of placement orders in the instant case requires additional safeguards for the two children over and above the fact that the court has made contact orders under s 26 of the 2002 Act. We accordingly direct that all further applications in the case, including any application for either child to be adopted, should be listed before the same judge, and that all further applications in the case be reserved to him. Whilst we cannot, of course, fetter the future exercise of his discretion, which he must exercise as he thinks fit on the facts of the case, we are satisfied that he must retain control of the case, and that no final step should be taken in relation to either child without his imprimatur.

[153] We repeat that our reason for taking this view is that the judge's judgment is predicated on the proposition that the relationship between

the two children is of fundamental importance, and that the relationship must be maintained, even if the children are placed in separate adoptive placements, or if one is adopted and the other fostered. In these circumstances it is not, in our judgment, a proper exercise of the judicial powers given to the court under the 2002 Act to leave contact between the children themselves, or between the children and their natural parents to the discretion of the local authority and/or the prospective carers of D and S, be they adoptive parents or foster carers. It is the court which must make the necessary decisions if contact between the siblings is in dispute, or if it is argued that it should cease for any reason.

[154] We do not know if our views on contact on the facts of this particular case presage a more general sea change in post adoption contact overall. It seems to us, however, that the stakes in the present case are sufficiently high to make it appropriate for the court to retain control over the question of the children's welfare throughout their respective lives under ss 1, 26, 27 and 46(6) of the 2002 Act; and, if necessary, to make orders for contact post adoption in accordance with s 26 of the 2002 Act, under s 8 of the 1989 Act. This is what Parliament has enacted. In s 46(6) of the 2002 Act Parliament has specifically directed the court to consider post adoption contact, and in s 26(5) Parliament has specifically envisaged an application for contact being heard at the same time as an adoption order is applied for. All this leads us to the view that the 2002 Act envisages the court exercising its powers to make contact orders post adoption, where such orders are in the interests of the child concerned.

General notes:

Contact in the context of adoption raises the following possibilities for the birth family:

- when a PO is made: see E10 – ACA 2002, ss 26 and 27: contact on making PO;
- when an AO is made: see E12 – ACA 2002, s 46(6): contact on making AO;
- after AO is made: see B39 – CA 1989, s 10(4): birth parent no longer a 'parent' after adoption; B44 – CA 1989, s 10(9): broad assessment / post-adoption contact; and B45 – CA 1989, s 10(9): process when birth family apply after adoption.

This case is also included in relation to:

E6   ACA 2002, s 22: twin track planning not inconsistent
E14   ACA 2002, s 52: dispensing with parental consent

E11   ACA 2002, S 42(6): LEAVE TO APPLY FOR AO

Re A; Coventry County[1] Council v CC and A

[2007] EWCA Civ 1383, [2008] 1 FLR 959 at 964

Court of Appeal

Wilson LJ

[10] The researches of counsel do not reveal any reported decision referable to the grant of leave to apply for an adoption order under s 42(6) of the Act. But counsel were in agreement at the hearing before the judge as to the proper approach to any such application; and the judge accepted and endorsed the approach which they commended to him. Equally, before this court, counsel remain in agreement as to it; and, in turn, I consider that we should accept and endorse it. For, notwithstanding the absence of a decision referable to the grant of leave under s 42(6), there is a recent reported decision of this court referable to the grant of leave to apply for revocation of a placement order under s 24(2) of the Act. It is *M v Warwickshire County Council* [2007] EWCA Civ 1084, [2008] 1 FLR 1093. I would accept and hold that the legal principles relevant to the exercise of the discretion whether to grant leave pursuant to each of the subsections is identical. Thus the welfare of the child is a relevant consideration but, by virtue of s 1(7) of the Act, is not the paramount consideration: see paras [22] and [24] of my judgment in *Re M and L*. Another relevant consideration is whether the proposed application has a real prospect of success: see para [29] of that judgment. Indeed I there observed:

'My view is that the requisite analysis of the prospect of success will almost always include the requisite analysis of the welfare of the child. For, were there to be a real prospect that an applicant would persuade the court that a child's welfare would best be served by [the substantive order sought], it would surely almost always serve the child's welfare for the applicant to be given leave to seek to do so. Conversely, were there not to be any such real prospect, it is hard to conceive that it would serve the welfare of the child for the application for leave to be granted. But I hesitate to suggest that analysis of welfare will always be satisfactorily subsumed within an analysis of prospect.'

---

[1]   The case name should read 'Coventry City Council'.

General notes:

M v Warwickshire County Council [2007] EWCA Civ 1084, [2008] 1 FLR 1093: see E7 – ACA 2002, s 24: leave to apply to revoke PO.

The same test has since been applied to applications for leave to discharge or vary a special guardianship order: *Re G (Special guardianship order)* [2010] EWCA Civ 300, [2010] 2 FLR 696: see B61 – Application for leave to discharge or vary SGO.

Other significant cases on this issue:

- *ASB and KBS v MQS (Secretary of State for the Home Department intervening)* [2009] EWHC 2491 (Fam), [2010] 1 FLR 748

E12   ACA 2002, S 46(6): CONTACT ON MAKING AO

X and Y v A Local Authority (Adoption: procedure)

[2009] EWHC 47 (Fam), [2009] 2 FLR 984 at 995

Family Division

McFarlane J

The appeal against the contact order

[37]   The central point in the appeal, and indeed the point that was effectively conceded in Mr and Mrs X's favour by all parties in their skeleton arguments, was that the process undertaken before and by the justices totally failed to meet the mandatory requirement for the court to consider the wishes and feelings of the adopters on the issue of contact before making any adoption order. ACA 2002, s 46(6) states:

> 'Before making an adoption order, the court must consider whether there should be arrangements for allowing any person contact with the child; and for that purpose the court must consider any existing or proposed arrangements and obtain any views of the parties to the proceedings.'

[38]   The failure to meet the requirements of s 46(6) in this case is both significant and very hard to understand, given the clear statement of those wishes in the social worker's statement and the clear, and correct, advice to the court from the local authority to the effect that Mr and Mrs X required separate representation. Despite that background, the need for Mr and Mrs X to be engaged in the court process on the contact issue seems not to have been within the contemplation of either of the lawyers, the justices' legal adviser or the court itself on 9 January 2009.

[39]   The effect of this failure is compounded by the fact that the court had failed either to appoint a children's guardian or to give reasons why it was not necessary to do so in this case. The result was that the only two parties before the court, namely the father and the local authority, agreed a regime for contact which was not only one to which the adopters would not agree but also, as it turned out, was one about which they were not even informed during telephone communications from the social worker during the day. That result was not only contrary to the clear wording of s 46(6) but was also a breach of the applicants' rights to a fair trial under the European Convention for the Protection of Human Rights and

Fundamental Freedoms 1950 (ECHR), Art 6(1) and, it is agreed, it cannot stand and must be set aside, with the result that a rehearing must now take place.

Failure to follow correct practice and procedure

[40]   Whilst the court's failure to apply ACA 2002, s 46(6) is sufficient to dispose of this appeal, it may nevertheless be helpful for future cases to point out the other errors into which the court was either led or fell:

(a)   The failure to engage the adopters on the issue of contact not only arose from the actions of the local authority and the court on the day of the hearing. The fact that the local authority failed to send a copy of its social work statement to the applicants, so that they could see what was being said about contact (and make observations about it) was a serious omission. It was compounded by the apparent failure of the court to undertake an even handed approach. The court orders of 31 October and 19 December both expressly provide for an adjournment so that the father could consider the social worker's report on contact.

No similar provision was made by the court with respect to the applicants. As the local authority had expressly drawn the court's attention to the need for the applicant's representation, the court's failure to engage the applicants in the process is difficult to understand;

(b)   The reference in the order to granting the father 'leave to apply for contact' was, in so far as it covered his position at that hearing, otiose and bad in law; he did not require the court's leave to make either his application for contact under s 26 (during the currency of the placement order) or for post-adoption contact (see paras [18] and [19] above);

(c)   Including a generally stated grant of 'leave to apply for contact' in this adoption order ran the risk of it being interpreted as the grant of an open-ended facility to the father to apply for contact in the future, after the adoption order has taken effect. Whilst this may not have been the intention of those present in court on 9 January, both the fact that, in law, future leave to apply was all that the father required by way of leave and the wording of the provision in the order, could certainly lead to a future interpretation that he did indeed now have leave to apply for contact;

(d)   The recital in the order to the effect that the father 'may well issue a further application for leave to apply for direct contact' is also unhelpful and, I would suggest (for the reasons given below), bad practice. That recital, coupled with the ambiguously worded 'leave to apply' could be read, by the father at least, as being either an 'amber' or even a 'green' light to come back and seek face-to-face contact at some stage in the not too distant future. That was, I am told, what the adopters read it to mean. Such an application by the father would have been profoundly unwelcome to the adopters and the children and it would come at a time when they ought each to be settling down to a life characterised by a far greater sense of stability and security than had hitherto been the case. The potential for a face-to-face contact application to cut across that stabilising process is, in my view, all too clear.

[41] The reason for suggesting that it is not good practice for a court to leave the potential for a direct contact application pending and unresolved at the stage of making the adoption order is primarily that the approach in law to any post-adoption application by a parent for leave to apply for contact is that adoption orders and any accompanying contact arrangements are intended to be permanent and final with the result that fundamental questions such as contact should not be reopened in the absence of some fundamental change of circumstances (*Re C (A Minor) (Adopted Child: Contact)* [1993] 3 WLR 85, [1993] 2 FLR 431). Against that background it is unsatisfactory both to the parent and to the adopters to leave a known issue concerning post-adoption contact unresolved at the date of the adoption order. The father in the present case may not have been prepared to postpone litigating his claim for direct contact had he clearly understood that he would only be allowed to do so if he could show some fundamental change since the making of the adoption order. Equally, where the adoption order itself contains a recital to the effect that a parent may well apply for leave on a contact issue in due course, the applicants and the children are entitled to feel that the arrangements made by the court lack the essential characteristics of being permanent and final.

[42] In the present case, the better course would have been for the court to have grappled with and determined the issue of any future direct contact (either by a court decision or consent) prior to making the adoption order, on the basis that all parties would then move forward knowing that whatever arrangement was made could only be reopened by an application for leave to apply for a contact order in the event of some fundamental change of circumstances.

General notes:

The judgment also addresses a series of other procedural errors in the conduct of the proceedings. Contact in the context of adoption raises the following possibilities for the birth family:

- when a PO is made: see E10 – ACA 2002, ss 26 and 27: contact on making PO;
- when an AO is made: see E12 – ACA 2002, s 46(6): contact on making AO;
- after AO is made: see B39 – CA 1989, s 10(4): birth parent no longer a 'parent' after adoption; B44 – CA 1989, s 10(9): broad

assessment / post-adoption contact; and B45 – CA 1989, s 10(9): process when birth family apply after adoption.

E13   ACA 2002, S 47(5): LEAVE TO DEFEND ADOPTION PROCEEDINGS

Re P (Adoption: leave provisions)

[2007] EWCA Civ 616, [2007] 2 FLR 1069 at 1073, 1075 and 1081

Court of Appeal

Wall LJ

[15]   The criterion for granting leave is set out in s 47(7) of the 2002 Act, which provides:

> 'The court cannot give leave under subsection ... (5) unless satisfied that there has been a change in circumstances since the placement order was made.'

[16]   However, in approaching the grant or refusal of leave for a parent to defend adoption proceedings under s 47 of the 2002 Act, the question which immediately arises is whether or not the provisions of s 1 of the 2002 Act apply to the application. Section 1(2) provides that where s 1 applies, 'The paramount consideration of the court or adoption agency must be the child's welfare throughout his life'. By s 1(1), s 1 applies 'whenever a court is coming to a decision relating to the adoption of a child'. The question thus becomes: is an application by a parent for leave to defend adoption proceedings 'a decision relating to the adoption of a child?'

[17]   The answer to this question is provided by s 1(7) of the 2002 Act which, it seems to us, is poorly drafted and unnecessarily obscure. We will set it out in full:

> '(7)   In this section, "coming to a decision relating to the adoption of a child", in relation to a court, includes—
>
> (a)   coming to a decision in any proceedings where the orders that might be made by the court include an adoption order (or the revocation of such an order), a placement order (or the revocation of such an order) or an order under section 26 (or the revocation or variation of such an order),
>
> (b)   coming to a decision about granting leave in respect of any action (other than the initiation of proceedings in any court) which may be taken by an adoption agency or individual under

this Act, but does not include coming to a decision about granting leave in any other circumstances.'

[18] The reference to s 26 of the 2002 Act is a reference to an order under s 26(2)(b), which empowers the court to make an order for contact between S and her parents. The parents are indeed making such an application, although it does not impinge on the arguments addressed to us on this appeal.

The meaning of s 1(7) of the 2002 Act

[19] Some time was spent in argument debating the meaning of s 1(7) of the 2002 Act. Having considered the matter carefully, however, we have come to the conclusion that the judicial decision whether or not to give leave to a parent to defend adoption proceedings under s 47(5) of the 2002 Act is 'a decision relating to the adoption of a child' and that, accordingly, it is governed by s 1 of the 2002 Act. We reach that conclusion for the following reasons.

...

[25] In our judgment, therefore, the effect of the final 15 words in s 1(7) of the 2002 Act is that 'coming to a decision relating to the adoption of a child' within s 1(1) and 1(7) of the 2002 Act only applies to decisions under the 2002 Act: it does not include coming to a decision about granting leave in any other circumstances, including, of course, decisions about granting leave in proceedings under the 1989 Act.

A two stage process

[26] In our judgment, analysis of the statutory language in ss 1 and 47 of the 2002 Act leads to the conclusion that an application for leave to defend adoption proceedings under s 47(5) of the 2002 Act involves a two-stage process. First of all, the court has to be satisfied, on the facts of the case, that there has been a change in circumstances within s 47(7). If there has been no change in circumstances, that is the end of the matter, and the application fails. If, however, there has been a change in circumstances within s 47(7) then the door to the exercise of a judicial discretion to permit the parents to defend the adoption proceedings is opened, and the decision whether or not to grant leave is governed by s 1 of the 2002 Act. In other words, 'the paramount consideration of the court must be the child's welfare throughout his life'.

The meaning of 'a change in circumstances'

[27] Before examining in greater detail how the discretion, if it arises, falls to be exercised, it is, we think, necessary to decide what is meant by the phrase 'a change in circumstances since the placement order was made' in s 47(7) of the 2002 Act.

[28] For the father, Miss Platt accepted that not every change in circumstances would suffice to open the door to the exercise of the judicial discretion identified in para [26] above. She accepted that the change in circumstances had to be relevant or material to the question of whether or not leave should be granted. She invited us, however, to decline to put any further gloss on the statute. Parliament, she argued, could have attached an adjective such as 'significant' to the phrase 'change in circumstances', as indeed it had done in s 14D(5) of the 1989 Act in relation to the variation or discharge of a special guardianship order.

[29] Miss Platt submitted that in making a change in circumstances the pre-requisite for the exercise of the discretion under s 47(7) of the 2002 Act, Parliament had chosen not to qualify the change in circumstances in any way. What was required was, simply, 'a change in circumstances'. Miss Platt was, moreover, able to argue that the point was reinforced by the fact that the special guardianship provisions in the 1989 Act referred to in para [28] above were themselves contained within and introduced through the mechanism of the 2002 Act. The word 'significant' which Mr Pressdee invited us to attach to the phrase was simply not there, and had crept in, she argued, only through *Hansard*, to which the judge had been referred, and, at best, represented the relevant ministers' view. This was not, she argued, a satisfactory aid to statutory construction.

[30] We agree with Miss Platt's submissions on this point. We do not think it permissible to put any gloss on the statute, or to read into it words which are not there. The change in circumstances since the placement order was made must, self-evidently and as a matter of statutory construction, relate to the grant of leave. It must equally be of a nature and degree sufficient, on the facts of the particular case, to open the door to the exercise of the judicial discretion to permit the parents to defend the adoption proceedings. In our judgment, however, the phrase 'a change in circumstances' is not ambiguous, and resort to *Hansard* is both unnecessary and inappropriate.

[31] Furthermore, in our judgment, the importation of the word 'significant' puts the test too high. Self-evidently, a change in circumstances can embrace a wide range of different factual situations. Section 47(7) of the 2002 Act does not relate the change to the circumstances of the parents. The only limiting factor is that it must be a change in circumstances 'since the placement order was made'. Against

this background, we do not think that any further definition of the change in circumstances involved is either possible or sensible.

[32] We do, however, take the view that the test should not be set too high, because, as this case demonstrates, parents in the position of S's parents should not be discouraged either from bettering themselves or from seeking to prevent the adoption of their child by the imposition of a test which is unachievable. We therefore take the view that whether or not there has been a relevant change in circumstances must be a matter of fact to be decided by the good sense and sound judgment of the tribunal hearing the application.

The exercise of discretion

[33] Far more important, in our judgment, is the manner in which the experienced judges who are likely to undertake the bulk of these unusual applications exercise their welfare discretion under s 1 of the 2002 Act. We have already considered the terms of s 1(1), (2) and (7). The critical part of the section is, of course, subss (3) and (4). The latter sets out its own checklist of factors to which the court must have regard. These two subsections read as follows:

'(3) The court or adoption agency must at all times bear in mind that, in general, any delay in coming to the decision is likely to prejudice the child's welfare.

(4) The court or adoption agency must have regard to the following matters (among others)—

    (a)   the child's ascertainable wishes and feelings regarding the decision (considered in the light of the child's age and understanding),

    (b)   the child's particular needs,

    (c)   the likely effect on the child (throughout his life) of having ceased to be a member of the original family and become an adopted person,

    (d)   the child's age, sex, background and any of the child's characteristics which the court or agency considers relevant,

    (e)   any harm (within the meaning of which the (1989 Act) which the child has suffered or is at risk of suffering,

    (f)   the relationship which the child has with relatives, and with any other person in relation to whom the court or agency considers the relationship to be relevant, including—

        (i)   the likelihood of any such relationship continuing and the value to the child of its doing so,

       (ii)   the ability and willingness of any of the child's relatives, or of any such person, to provide the child with a secure environment in which the child can develop, and otherwise to meet the child's needs,

(iii) the wishes and feelings of any of the child's relatives, or of any such person, regarding the child.'

[34] Section 1(5) of the 2002 Act is immaterial for present purposes, but s 1(6) reads:

'(6) The court or adoption agency must always consider the whole range of powers available to it in the child's case (whether under this Act or the (1989 Act)); and the court must not make any order under this Act unless it considers that making the order would be better for the child than not doing so.'

[35] Thus, even if the parents are able, on the facts, to identify a change in circumstances sufficient to make it appropriate for the judge to consider whether or not to exercise his discretion to permit the parents to defend the adoption proceedings, the paramount consideration of the court in the actual exercise of the discretion must be the welfare of S throughout her life and, in that context, the court must have regard in particular to the matters set out in s 1(4) of the 2002 Act.

...

Was the hearing fair?

[52] Miss Platt attempted to mount an argument to the effect that the hearing of the application by the parents before the judge for leave to defend the adoption proceedings was unfair because it was not what she described as a full welfare inquiry in which oral evidence was given. We have no hesitation in rejecting that submission for a number of reasons. First, and most obviously, the parents did not seek to give oral evidence, and no notice was given that any of the local authority's witnesses were required for cross-examination. Furthermore, the parents were each separately and ably represented by junior counsel. As the judgment demonstrates, all the arguments properly open to them were fully deployed. In these circumstances, we think it impossible for Miss Platt to argue that the hearing was unfair.

[53] There is, however, a wider point of more general application. The object of the 2002 Act was to simplify the adoption process and to reduce delays in children being placed for adoption and adopted. The instant case had already gone through two substantive hearings, albeit that oral evidence was not called at the placement order hearing. We thus view with great concern the argument that an application for leave under s 47(5) of the 2002 Act requires a full welfare inquiry, with oral evidence and cross-examination.

[54] In our judgment, the fact that a judge is taking the welfare of a child as his paramount consideration does not mean that he must conduct a full welfare hearing with oral evidence and cross-examination in order to reach a conclusion. An experienced judge such as His Honour Judge Corrie is, in our judgment, fully entitled to conclude that such a hearing can fairly be conducted on submissions. Of course, there may be cases in which a particular factual issue requires resolution through oral evidence, but in the instant case oral evidence was plainly unnecessary. Indeed, as para [57] of the judgment demonstrates, the judge effectively decided the case on the basis that even if the parents had established the facts of the material change in circumstances they alleged, the exercise of a welfare-based discretion remained fatal to their application. To reach such a conclusion, a judge who has a detailed knowledge of a case does not, in our judgment, need oral evidence.

Other significant cases on this issue:

- *Re M (Adoption: leave to oppose)* [2010] 1 FLR 238

E14   ACA 2002, S 52: DISPENSING WITH PARENTAL CONSENT

Re P (Placement orders: parental consent)

[2008] EWCA Civ 535, [2008] 2 FLR 625 at 656, 659 and 660

Court of Appeal

Wall LJ

[113]   We welcome the opportunity afforded by this case to revisit s 52(1)(b) of the 2002 Act, and with it, in particular, the phrase 'the welfare of the child requires the consent to be dispensed with'. We propose, accordingly, to address firstly Mr Geekie's question: what is meant by welfare in s 52(1)(b)?

[114]   In our judgment, the answer to this question is self-evident, and is to be found in s 1 of the 2002 Act, which we have set out in full at para [37] of this judgment. Section 1(1) plainly applies when the court is deciding whether or not to dispense with parental consent to a placement order. Such a decision is manifestly 'a decision relating to the adoption of a child'. In these circumstances, s 1(2) of the 2002 Act requires the court (the word is the mandatory 'must') in these circumstances to treat 'the child's welfare throughout his life' as its 'paramount consideration'. 'Paramount consideration' as Lord MacDermott of Belmont classically held in *J v C* [1970] AC 668 [1969] 2 WLR 540, at 711 and 564 respectively, means a consideration which 'rules upon and determines the course to be followed'.

[115]   In this context, in our judgment, 'welfare throughout (the child's) life' plainly means welfare as determined by the court or adoption agency, having regard to the matters set out in s 1(4) of the 2002 Act. Section 1(4) of the 2002 Act provides a checklist far wider than that provided in s 1(3) of the 1989 Act. If and insofar, therefore, as *Re S*[1] gives the impression that the items which have to be taken into account under 'welfare' in s 1 of the 2002 Act are equivalent to the so-called welfare checklist in s 1(3) of the 1989 Act, that impression is, plainly, erroneous. However, even a cursory examination of *Re S* demonstrates, I think, that this is not the case. Since special guardianship orders, which were the focus of the discussion in *Re S*, are made under the 1989 Act, the debate on the appropriateness in any given case of an adoption order as opposed to a

---

[1]   *Re S (Adoption order or special guardianship order)* [2007] EWCA Civ 54, [2007] 1 FLR 819.

special guardianship order required consideration of both s 1(3) of the 1989 Act and s 1(4) of the 2002 Act – see *Re S* at para [48] (i) and (ii):

'[48]   The special nature of the jurisdiction also has implications for the approach of the courts:

(i)   In view of the importance of such cases to the parties and the children concerned, it is incumbent on judges to give full reasons and to explain their decisions with care. Short cuts are to be avoided. It is not of course necessary to go through the welfare checklist line by line, but the parties must be able to follow the judge's reasoning and to satisfy themselves that he or she has duly considered it and has taken every aspect of it relevant to the particular case properly into account.

(ii)   Provided the judge has carefully examined the facts, made appropriate findings in relation to them and applied the welfare checklists contained in s 1(3) of the 1989 Act and s 1 of the 2002 Act, it is unlikely that this court will be able properly to interfere with the exercise of judicial discretion, particularly in a finely balanced case. (We think it no co-incidence that all three of the appeals with which these judgments are concerned fall to be dismissed, although each reaches a different result.)'

[116]   In our judgment, similar considerations apply to applications under s 52(1)(b) of the 2002 Act. The guidance is, we think, simple enough. The judge must, of course, be aware of the importance to the child of the decision being taken. There is, perhaps, no more important or far-reaching decision for a child than to be adopted by strangers. However, the word 'requires' in s 52(1)(b) is a perfectly ordinary English word. Judges approaching the question of dispensation under the section must, it seems to us, ask themselves the question to which s 52(1)(b) of the 2002 gives rise, and answer it by reference to s 1 of the same Act, and in particular by a careful consideration of all the matters identified in s 1(4).

[117]   In summary, therefore, the best guidance, which in our judgment this court can give is to advise judges to apply the statutory language with care to the facts of the particular case. The message is, no doubt, prosaic, but the best guidance, we think, is as simple and as straightforward as that. Moreover, it very much echoes what this court said in *Re S* in relation to special guardianship orders.

[118]   Without wishing to qualify in any way the clarity and simplicity of what we have just said, but in deference to Mr Geekie's careful argument, we think we should add a few words about the Strasbourg jurisprudence to which he referred us.

...

[125] This is the context in which the critical word 'requires' is used in s 52(1)(b). It is a word which was plainly chosen as best conveying, as in our judgment it does, the essence of the Strasbourg jurisprudence. And viewed from that perspective 'requires' does indeed have the connotation of the imperative, what is demanded rather than what is merely optional or reasonable or desirable.

[126] What is also important to appreciate is the statutory context in which the word 'requires' is here being used, for, like all words, it will take its colour from the particular context. Section 52(1) is concerned with adoption – the making of either a placement order or an adoption order – and what therefore has to be shown is that the child's welfare 'requires' *adoption* as opposed to something short of adoption. A child's circumstances may 'require' statutory intervention, perhaps may even 'require' the indefinite or long-term removal of the child from the family and his or her placement with strangers, but that is not to say that the same circumstances will necessarily 'require' that the child be adopted. They may or they may not. The question, at the end of the day, is whether what is 'required' is adoption.

[127] In our judgment, however, this does not mean that there is some enhanced welfare test to be applied in cases of adoption, in contrast to what Mr Geekie called a simple welfare test. The difference, and it is an important, indeed vital, difference, is simply that between s 1 of the 1989 Act and s 1 of the 2002 Act.

[128] In the first place, s 1(2) of the 2002 Act, in contrast to s 1(1) of the 1989 Act, requires a judge considering dispensing with parental consent in accordance with s 52(1)(b) to focus on the child's welfare 'throughout his life.' This emphasises that adoption, unlike other forms of order made under the 1989 Act, is something with lifelong implications. In other words, a judge exercising his powers under s 52(1)(b) has to be satisfied that the child's welfare now, throughout the rest of his childhood, into adulthood and indeed throughout his life, requires that he or she be adopted. Secondly, and reinforcing this point, it is important to bear in mind the more extensive 'welfare checklist' to be found in s 1(4) of the 2002 Act as compared with the 'welfare checklist' in s 1(3) of the 1989 Act; in particular, the provisions of s 1(4)(c) – which specifically directs attention to the consequences for the child 'throughout his life' – and s 1(4)(f). This all feeds into the ultimate question under s 52(1)(b): does the child's welfare *throughout his life* require adoption as opposed to something short of adoption?

...

[131] For completeness, we should add that, as our discussion of the Strasbourg jurisprudence seeks to emphasise, it will not be sufficient simply for a judge to use the words of s 52(1)(b) and s 1(4) of the 2002 Act as a mantra. Equally, the judge is the opposite of a 'rubber stamp'. Self evidently, careful thought must be shown to have gone into the process. The judge must make findings of fact which properly support the need to make placement orders and dispensation of parental agreement to them. In short, the underlying facts, properly analysed, must support the judicial conclusion. If they do not, the placement order may well be called in question.

[132] The need for care, sensitivity and intellectual rigour on the part of judges hearing applications for placement orders is, we think, reinforced by the fact that applications for placement orders will, regularly, be heard and will need to be determined immediately after the court has made a care order in relation to the same child: – see *Re P-B* referred to in para [34] above, and the unreported decision of this court in *Re EN (a child) KN* [2007] EWCA Civ 264 (unreported) 28 March 2007. It is not so long ago that the grant of only a short adjournment between the making of a care order and the application to free a child for adoption (albeit in the context of a litigant acting in person) was held by the European Court of Human Rights to be a breach of the Convention Art 6: – see *P, C and S v United Kingdom* (Application No 56547/00) [2002] 2 FLR 631. Whilst it is highly unlikely that any parents having to face the prospect of immediately sequential care and placement orders will be unrepresented, the likely juxtaposition of the two applications is, in our judgment, an additional reason for the court to examine the cases with particular care.

[133] Equally, where an application for a placement order is sought against the background of a care order with a care plan for adoption, and the application is heard by a judge who has not made the previous care order, the judge considering the application for a placement order will, in particular, need to consider with care the way in which the judge who approved that care plan expressed him or herself in relation to the issue of adoption, the extent to which that judge addressed him or herself in terms not merely to s 1 of the 1989 Act but also to s 1 of the 2002 Act, and the extent to which there has, since the care plan was approved, been any change either in the circumstances or in the assumptions which underlay the care plan and, in particular, which underlay the plan for adoption.

This case is also included in relation to:

E6   ACA 2002, s 22: twin track planning not inconsistent
E10   ACA 2002, ss 26 and 27: contact on making PO

E15   ACA 2002, S 66(1): RECOGNITION OF FOREIGN ADOPTION

D v D (Foreign adoption)

[2008] EWHC 403 (Fam), [2008] 1 FLR 1475 at 1478 and 1482

Family Division

Ryder J

The law

[10]   The adoptions of ND and TD are adoptions under Indian domestic law. They are not 'intercountry adoptions', as that (in UK terms) is the term used for the adoption of a child resident abroad by adopters habitually resident in the UK. As a result of the proliferation of such adoptions the Hague Convention on Protection of Children and Co-operation in respect of Inter-Country Adoption was concluded at The Hague in May 1993. In broad terms, the Hague Convention, which applies in both the UK and India, aims to provide safeguards to ensure that intercountry adoptions take place in the best interests of the child.

[11]   Section 66(1)(c) of the Adoption and Children Act 2002 (the Act) defines 'adoption' as including a 'Convention adoption', which means that Convention adoptions are recognised automatically by operation of law and there does not need to be a repeat adoption domestically. Section 66(1)(d) defines 'adoption' as including an 'overseas adoption', and s 87 allows arrangements to be put in place in England and Wales for the recognition of 'overseas adoptions'. At the present time, in order to qualify as an 'overseas adoption' an adoption has to have been effected in a country specified in the Adoption (Designation of Overseas Adoptions) Order 1973 (SI 1973/19). The designated countries include the USA, all Western European countries and 39 Commonwealth countries, but does not include India, also a Commonwealth country. As with 'Convention adoptions', 'overseas adoptions' are automatically recognised as adoption orders in England and Wales. Pursuant to s 89 an 'overseas adoption' can be impugned by an order of the High Court on the grounds that it is contrary to public policy or that the authority which purported to authorise the adoption was not competent to do so. A 'Convention adoption' can be annulled by the High Court on the grounds that it is contrary to public policy. Apart from these provisions, neither a 'Convention adoption' nor an 'overseas adoption' can be called into questioning any proceedings in England and Wales.

[12] Section 66(1)(e) defines 'adoption' as including an adoption recognised by the law of England and Wales and effected under the law of any other country. This provides for the recognition of a foreign adoption by common law rules where an adoption order is neither a 'Convention adoption' nor an 'overseas adoption'.

[13] Section 1 of the Act provides that in coming to a decision relating to the adoption of a child the paramount consideration of the court must be the child's welfare throughout his life, and sets out the matters which the court must have regard to.

[14] In *Re Valentine's Settlement; Valentine v Valentine* [1965] Ch 831, [1965] 2 WLR 1015, the Court of Appeal considered the question of recognition of an adoption order made in South Africa. Lord Denning said at 841 and 1021 respectively:

'... I start with the proposition stated by James LJ in *Re Goodman's Trusts* [1881–85] All ER Rep 1138 at 1154:

"The family relation is at the foundation of all society, and it would appear almost an axiom that the family relation, once duly constituted by the law of any civilized country, should be respected and acknowledged by every other member of the great community of nations."

That was a legitimation case, but the like principle applies to adoption. But when is the status of adoption duly constituted? Clearly it is so when it is constituted in another country in similar circumstances as we claim for ourselves. Our court should recognise a jurisdiction which mutatis mutandis they claim for themselves; see *Travers v Holley and Holley* [1953] 2 All ER 794 at 800. We claim jurisdiction to make an adoption order when the adopting parents are domiciled in this country and the child is resident here. So also, out of the comity of nations, we should recognise an adoption order made by another country when the adopting parents are domiciled there and the child is resident there.

Apart from international comity, we reach the same result on principle. When a court of any country makes an adoption order for an infant child, it does two things. (i) It destroys the legal relationship theretofore existing between the child and its natural parents, be it legitimate or illegitimate; (ii) it creates the legal relationship of parent and child between the child and its adopting parents, making it their legitimate child. It creates a new status in both, namely the status of parent and child. Now it has long been settled that questions affecting status are determined by the law of the domicil. This new status of parent and child, in order to be recognised everywhere, must be validly created by the law of the domicil of the adopting parent. You do not look at the domicil of the child; for that has no separate domicil of his or her own. The child takes his or her parents' domicil. You look to the parents' domicil only. If you find that a legitimate relationship of parent and child has been validly created by the law of the parents' domicil at the time the relationship is created, then the status so created should be universally recognised throughout the civilized world, provided always that there is nothing contrary to public policy in so recognizing it.'

[15] Collins et al, *Dicey, Morris & Collins on The Conflict of Laws'*, (Sweet and Maxwell Ltd, 14th edn, 2006) deals with recognition of foreign adoptions at para 20-133:

'If the foreign adoption was designed to promote some immoral or mercenary object, like prostitution or financial gain to the adopter, it is improbable that it would be recognised in England. But, apart from exceptional cases like these, it is submitted that the court should be slow to refuse recognition to a foreign adoption on the grounds of public policy merely because the requirements for adoption in the foreign law differ from those of the English law. Here again the distinction between recognizing the status and giving effect to its results is of vital importance. Public policy may sometimes require that a particular result of a foreign adoption should not be given effect to in England; but public policy should only on the rarest occasions be invoked in order to deny recognition to the status itself.'

...

Formulation

[23] Mr and Mrs D applied to adopt (in 2005) in India because they were not eligible to adopt in the UK. It is clear that the process in respect of both the adoptions has been rigorous and directed towards the best interests of ND and TD. These are full adoptions, all links with the birth parents have been severed and the adoptions are irrevocable.

[24] It is in the best interests of ND and TD that they should remain in the care of Mr and Mrs D, that they should be recognised as the adopted children of Mr and Mrs D in this jurisdiction, and that the family should be able to be together in the UK. The post-adoption report in respect of ND indicates that she is flourishing, and it appears that TD is also flourishing. Mr and Mrs D have business interests in India, the UK and the USA and have travelled widely for business purposes. They now wish to settle in the UK, where they have a home as well as substantial business interests, and want to educate the children in the UK. They are asking for recognition of the adoptions in order that there is full and formal recognition of their parental responsibilities for ND and TD and to ensure that TD can comply with the immigration rules for adopted children.

[25] Mr and Mrs D have followed all procedures, both in terms of the adoption and immigration procedures, to the best of their ability. They have done everything in their power to protect and safeguard the best interests of the children. It must now be in the best interests of the children for Mr and Mrs D to have parental responsibility for them and for them to be legally recognised in this country as Mr and Mrs D's adopted children.

[26] There are no public policy considerations which override the best interests of the children or the principle that the court in this country should recognise adoption orders properly made in India under the Hindu Adoption and Maintenance Act 1956.

[27] Mr and Mrs D, ND and TD have an established family life. By recognizing these adoptions, the court is safeguarding the Art 8 rights of ND and TD, as well as those of Mr and Mrs D.

Accordingly, I shall make a declaration that the adoption orders made in respect of ND PD (dob 4 February 2005) and TD PD (dob 29 September 2006) by the Mumbai City Civil Court in India on the 17 October 2005 and the 24 April 2007 respectively are recognised as adoptions in England and Wales within the meaning of s 66(1)(e) and Chapter 4 of the Adoption and Children Act 2002.

E16   ACA 2002, S 67(3)

Re N (Recognition of foreign adoption order)

[2010] 1 FLR 1102 at 1108

Family Division

Bennett J

[33]   I am satisfied that s 67(3) must be interpreted in the light of all of those considerations and must be read down so as to uphold the Art 8 rights of the family and particularly IN in this case.

[34]   Miss Judd has submitted that the correct interpretation of s 67(3)(a) requires the modification of it in the following way: 'If adopted by one of a couple under s 51(2)' – and then Miss Judd submits that the following words should be read into it – 'or its equivalent if the adoption order was made abroad and recognised in England and Wales pursuant to s 66'. I would only slightly modify her submission to this effect: that after the words s 51(2), it is necessary to read into it the following words 'or its equivalent under the foreign law of an adoption order made abroad which is recognised in England and Wales pursuant to s 66'.

[35]   So, in my judgment, I am satisfied for all those reasons that s 67(3), and in particular (b), does not have the effect, if a declaration is made in favour of SN, of depriving HN of parental responsibility for IN jointly with SN.

[36]   Accordingly, I shall declare, being satisfied that the parental responsibility of HN is retained jointly with that of SN, that the adoption order of 13 July 2007 of the Armenian court be recognised by the law of England and Wales.

E17   ACA 2002, SS 84(4) AND 42(7)(A)

Re A (Adoption: removal)

[2009] EWCA Civ 41, [2009] 2 FLR 597 at 618 and 621

Court of Appeal

Wall LJ

[51]   As to the s 84(4) question, the judge pointed out that s 84 was specifically directed to the making of a parental responsibility order in favour of a person or persons living abroad. He identified six reasons why, absent authority, he would not have reached the conclusion that the home referred to in s 84(4) had to be in England and Wales:

(i)   It applies to prospective adopters whose home is abroad and the natural inference would be that the child would, or at least could, for the purposes of s 84(4) have his or her home with them where they lived and where the child would live if adopted.

(ii)   It is essentially a trigger provision to an application followed up by other provisions as to the making of a parental responsibility order with its consequences.

(iii)   Although it has similarities to ss 42(1) and (2) of the 2002 Act those subsections are not referred to in reg 11 of the AFER 2005 and it is only s 42(7) that is so referred to.

(iv)   As a matter of language it does not say where the home has to be, when it easily could have done.

(v)   As Black J explains in *ECC v M* there are conceptual problems concerning what is or is not a home for particular purposes and a construction that enabled this pre-application period to be spent in the actual home of the applicants would avoid these problems. That solution would equate with the domestic situation when the child would have been living with the applicants for an adoption order in their real home. Problems would remain in respect of the observation of the child and the adults abroad, but these could be overcome with inter-country co-operation.

(vi)   The regulations, which inevitably on a free-standing basis have a domestic feel or centre of gravity, are incorporated without express adjustment by Regulations of the AFER 2005 and by the expansion of particular sections to cover orders under s 84 of the 2002 Act by regs 11 and 55 of the AFER 2005. In my view, the Regulations are directory and not mandatory (see for example *Re T (A Minor) (Adoption: Validity of Orders)* [1986] Fam 160, [1986] 2 WLR 538, [1986] 2 FLR 31) and this, coupled with such methods of introduction of domestic regulations in respect of an adoption abroad, and the purposive and sensible approach to be taken to the application of the 2002 Act and the relevant regulations, favours a purposive and sensible approach that should have regard to the point that the relevant adoptive home of the child throughout his or her childhood will be abroad. Such an approach reduces the domestic feel of the regulations and means that they should be interpreted and fulfilled by considering how the decision makers are to be best informed on that basis.

[52]   Finally, in relation to s 42(7) the judge concluded:

'The domestic authorities referred to by Black J, but not McFarlane J, *Re Y* and *Re SL* support the conclusion that for the purposes of s 42(7)(a) the home environment does not have to be in the area of the placing local authority. This supports the view that it does not have to be in this country when the proposed adoption is a foreign adoption. Also, as with s 84(4) (of the 2002 Act), the section, as modified to cover a s 84 order, does not expressly provide that the home environment must be in this country.

I agree with the local authority that for these reasons, and for the reasons given in respect of s 84(4) (of the 2002 Act), the home environment for the purposes of s 42(7)(a) (the 2002 Act) is not confined to one in this country.'

...

Discussion

[59]   Having now carefully reflected on all the arguments addressed to us, I am in no doubt that I prefer the arguments advanced by the local authority. I also respectfully adopt the construction of ss 84(4) and 42(7) formulated by Charles J, together with the reasoning set out at paras [51] and [52] above. In what follows I propose to deal primarily with the points of statutory construction which have weighed most with me ...

Other significant cases on this issue:

* *Re G* [2008] EWCA Civ 105, [2008] 1 FLR 1484, discussed in *Re A* by Wall LJ at [25]–[31]

E18 AO CAN RARELY BE SET ASIDE

Webster v Norfolk County Council and the Children (by their children's guardian)

[2009] EWCA Civ 59, [2009] 1 FLR 1378 at 1407 and 1408

Court of Appeal

Wall LJ

[148] In my judgment, however, the public policy considerations relating to adoption, and the authorities on the point – which are binding on this court – simply make it impossible for this court to set aside the adoption orders even if, as Mr and Mrs Webster argue, they have suffered a serious injustice.

[149] This is a case in which the court has to go back to first principles. Adoption is a statutory process. The law relating to it is very clear. The scope for the exercise of judicial discretion is severely curtailed. Once orders for adoption have been lawfully and properly made, it is only in highly exceptional and very particular circumstances that the court will permit them to be set aside.

[150] We were taken to a number of decisions on the topic. They are nearly all decisions of this court, and thus binding on us. Perhaps the most important is the decision of this court in *Re B (Adoption: Jurisdiction to Set Aside)* [1995] Fam 239, [1995] 3 WLR 40, [1995] 2 FLR 1. In that case ...

...

[152] Swinton Thomas LJ then turned to the application to set aside the adoption order. This is what he said (at 245C, 44–45 and 4–5 respectively):

'In my judgment such an application faces insuperable hurdles. An adoption order has a quite different standing to almost every other order made by a court. It provides the status of the adopted child and of the adoptive parents. The effect of an adoption order is to extinguish any parental responsibility of the natural parents. Once an adoption order has been made, the adoptive parents stand to one another and the child in precisely the same relationship as if they were his legitimate parents, and the child stands in the same relationship to them as to legitimate parents. Once an adoption order has been made the adopted child ceases to be the child of his previous parents and becomes the child for all purposes of the adopters as though he were their legitimate child.

There are certain specific statutory provisions for the revocation of an adoption order. Section 52 of the Adoption Act 1976 provides for the revocation of an adoption or legitimation. Section 53 provides for the annulment of overseas adoptions. Those exceptions provide for specific cases. Unlike certain other jurisdictions, there are no other statutory provisions for revoking a validly made adoption order. Parliament could have so provided if it had wished to do so. Accordingly Mr Levy is compelled to submit that the court has an inherent power to set aside an adoption order made in circumstances such as these where, as he puts it, the order was made under a fundamental mistake of fact.

There are cases where an adoption order has been set aside by reason of what is known as a procedural irregularity: see *Re F (R) (An Infant)* [1970] 1 QB 385, *Re RA (Minors)* (1974) 4 Fam Law 182 and *Re F (Infants) (Adoption Order: Validity)* [1977] Fam 165. Those cases concern a failure to effect proper service of the adoption proceedings on a natural parent or ignorance of the parent of the existence of the adoption proceedings. In each case the application to set aside the order was made reasonably expeditiously. It is fundamental to the making of an adoption order that the natural parent should be informed of the application so that she can give or withhold her consent. If she has no knowledge at all of the application then, obviously, a fundamental injustice is perpetrated. I would prefer myself to regard those cases not as cases where the order has been set aside by reason of a procedural irregularity, although that has certainly occurred, but as cases where natural justice has been denied because the natural parent who may wish to challenge the adoption has never been told that it is going to happen. Whether an adoption order can be set aside by reason of fraud which is unrelated to a natural parent's ignorance of the proceedings was not a subject which was relevant to the present appeal.'

[153] Swinton Thomas LJ then spends some time examining another case (*Re M (Minors) (Adoption)* [1991] 1 FLR 458) (*Re M*), to which I will return) before concluding (at 249B, 48 and 8 respectively):

'There is no case which has been brought to our attention in which it has been held that the court has an inherent power to set aside an adoption order by reason of misapprehension or mistake. To allow considerations such as those put forward in this case to invalidate an otherwise properly made adoption order would, in my view, undermine the whole basis on which adoption orders are made, namely that they are final and for life as regards the adopters, the natural parents, and the child. In my judgment, Mr Holman, who appeared as *amicus curiae*, is right when he submits that it would gravely damage the lifelong commitment of adopters to their adoptive children if there is a possibility of the child, or indeed the parents, subsequently challenging the validity of the order. I am satisfied that there is no inherent power in the courts in circumstances such as arise in this case to set aside an adoption order. Nobody could have other than the greatest sympathy with the applicant but, in my judgment, the circumstances of this case do not provide any ground for setting aside an adoption order which was regularly made. Accordingly, I would dismiss this appeal.'

[154]   Both Simon Brown LJ and Sir Thomas Bingham MR (as they then were) share Swinton Thomas LJ's sympathy with the appellant. I do not, I think, need to cite any passages from Simon Brown LJ's judgment. However, there are two passages from Sir Thomas Bingham's judgment which are, I think, relevant. Firstly, at 251G–H, 50–51 and 10 respectively, he says:

'The act of adoption has always been regarded in this country as possessing a peculiar finality. This is partly because it affects the status of the person adopted, and indeed adoption modifies the most fundamental of human relationships, that of parent and child. It effects a change intended to be permanent and concerning three parties. The first of these are the natural parents of the adopted person, who by adoption divest themselves of all rights and responsibilities in relation to that person. The second party is the adoptive parents, who assume the rights and responsibilities of parents in relation to the adopted person. And the third party is the subject of the adoption, who ceases in law to be the child of his or her natural parents and becomes the child of the adoptive parents.'

[155]   Secondly, at 252E–F, 51 and 11 respectively Sir Thomas Bingham says:

'An adoption order is not immune from any challenge. A party to the proceedings can appeal against the order in the usual way. The authorities show, I am sure correctly, that where there has been a failure of natural justice, and a party with a right to be heard on the application for the adoption order has not been notified of the hearing or has not for some other reason been heard, the court has jurisdiction to set aside the order and so make good the failure of natural justice. I would also have little hesitation in holding that the court could set aside an adoption order which was shown to have been obtained by fraud.

None of these situations pertains here.'

[156] In my judgment, *Re B* places a formidable obstacle in the path of Mr and Mrs Webster. It is, therefore, necessary to look at the cases in which adoption orders have been set aside to see if it is open to a court to set aside the adoption orders relating to A, B and C.

[157] *Re M*, cited at para [153] above, was a case in which an adoption order was set aside. Two girls had been adopted by their mother and stepfather following the former's re-marriage. However, when giving his consent to the adoption, their father had not been told, and did not know, that their mother was suffering from terminal cancer. Following their mother's death, and when their stepfather had difficulty caring for them, they went to live with their father and his new wife. Everyone was agreed that this was in the best interests of the children. The father then appealed against the making of the adoption order, on the ground that his agreement had been given in ignorance of his former wife's condition. This court granted permission to appeal out of time, and set aside the adoption order.

[158] In giving the leading judgment in this court, Glidewell LJ emphasised the highly unusual nature of the case [1991] 1 FLR 458 at 459F–G:

'In my view, this is, as Butler-Sloss, LJ said during the course of argument, a classic case of mistake. It is quite clear that the present appellant was wholly ignorant of his former wife's condition and, had he known of it, he obviously would not have consented to the adoption. That ignorance vitiates his consent and means that it was of no effect. In the absence of that consent it is very doubtful whether the adoption order would have been made. Since it is clearly in the best interest of the children that the adoption order should be set aside, for those reasons, I would extend the time for both these appeals, because formally they are separate appeals, and allow both appeals.

I should say, as a postscript, that this is, if not unique, at the very least a wholly exceptional case. I say that because I do not want the setting aside of this adoption order in these circumstances to be thought of as being some precedent for any related set of facts in some other case. This is, happily, a most unusual case and, in the circumstances and for the reasons I have sought to give, I think it right that the appeals should be allowed.'

[159] In adding her agreement, Butler-Sloss LJ (as she then was) likewise emphasised the unusual features of the case and added that it was 'in no way a precedent for any other adoption case, and these are quite exceptional circumstances' (at 460B).

[160]   The cases to which Swinton Thomas LJ refers in the passage of his judgment in *Re B* which I have cited in para [152] above accurately reflect his summary that adoption orders have been set aside where there has been a procedural irregularity. Thus in *Re F (R) (An Infant)* [1970] 1 QB 385, [1969] 3 WLR 853 this court set aside an adoption order on the application of a mother who had not been served with the adoption proceedings. In *Re RA (Minors)* (1974) 4 Fam Law 182 adoption orders were set aside where they had been obtained by fraud. In *Re F (Infants) (Adoption Order: Validity)* [1977] Fam 165, [1977] 2 WLR 488 this court refused an application for permission to appeal out of time made by adopters who had obtained adoption orders at a time when they were not lawfully married. This court held that the orders were valid on their face, voidable not void, and should stand.

[161]   In my judgment, none of the cases to which I have referred assists Mr and Mrs Webster. To the contrary, they seem to me to reinforce the proposition that adoption orders, validly and regularly obtained, will not be disturbed even if, as in *Re B* they leave the adopted person denied of a proper ethnic identity.

[162]   The most recent case on the subject is the decision of this court *Re K (Adoption and Wardship)* [1997] 2 FLR 221. The case concerned a Bosnian child who had been adopted by an English couple. This court was satisfied that the adoption procedure had been fatally flawed, and that the adoption order should be set aside. Butler-Sloss LJ, who gave the only substantive judgment, conducted a review of the authorities which I have already cited, and concluded (at 228H):

> 'The law seems to me to be clear that there are cases where a fundamental breach of natural justice will require a court to set an adoption order aside.'

[163]   The question, therefore, is whether or not a substantial miscarriage or justice, assuming that this is what has occurred, is or can be sufficient to enable the adoption orders in the present case to be set aside.

DIVISION F

ABDUCTION

Contents

Hague Convention

F1 CONVENTION DESIGNED TO PROTECT INTERESTS OF CHILDREN

Re M (Abduction: Zimbabwe)

[2007] UKHL 55, [2008] 1 FLR 251 at 256

House of Lords

Baroness Hale of Richmond

The Convention and the issues

[11] The Hague Convention on the Civil Aspects of International Child Abduction 1980 (the Convention) is an admirably clear and simple instrument. Its twin objects are set out in Art 1: '(a) to secure the prompt return of children wrongfully removed to or retained in any Contracting State; and (b) to ensure that rights of custody and of access under the law of one Contracting State are effectively respected in the other Contracting States'. However, as the *Explanatory Report on the 1980 Hague Child Abduction Convention* of Professor Elisa Pérez-Vera (HCCH Publications, 1982) (paras 16 and 17) points out, as to rights of custody, the second object is attained only indirectly, through the first.

[12] But it should not be thought that the Convention is principally concerned with the rights of adults. Quite the reverse. The Preamble explains that the contracting states are 'firmly convinced that the interests of children are of paramount importance in matters relating to their custody' and 'desiring to protect children internationally from the harmful effects of their wrongful removal or retention and to establish procedures to ensure their prompt return to the State of their habitual residence, as well as to secure protection for rights of access'. These two paragraphs, as Professor Pérez-Vera explains:

'... reflect quite clearly the philosophy of the Convention in this regard. It can be defined as follows: the struggle against the great increase in international child abductions must always be inspired by the desire to protect children and should be based upon an interpretation of their true interests. Now, the right not to be removed or retained in the name of more or less arguable rights concerning its person is one of the most objective examples of what constitutes the interests of the child.' (para 24)

However:

'The Convention recognises the need for certain exceptions to the general obligations assumed by States to secure the prompt return of children who have been unlawfully removed or retained. For the most part, these exceptions are only concrete illustrations of the overly vague principle whereby the interests of the child are stated to be the guiding criterion in this area.' (para 25)

Hence the Convention is designed to protect the interests of children by securing their prompt return to the country from which they have wrongly been taken, but recognises some limited and precise circumstances when it will not be in their interests to do so.

This case is also included in relation to:

F5   Hearing the child's views
F10   Arts 12 and 13: obligation to return and its exceptions

F2 SUMMARY PROCEDURE / ORAL AND EXPERT EVIDENCE RARE

Re W (Abduction: domestic violence)

[2004] EWCA Civ 1366, [2005] 1 FLR 727 at 733, 737 and 738

Court of Appeal

Thorpe and Wall LJJ

THORPE LJ:

[21] Against that background, I come to consider the judge's anxieties as expressed in the two paragraphs of her judgment that I have already cited. The judge clearly thought that the processes of summary trial that have been repeatedly upheld in the authorities in this jurisdiction risked results that were plainly incompatible with child welfare. She, in my opinion, envisaged or argued the merit of investigations which are manifestly incompatible with the proper approach ordained in English authority. Her statement that a court of first instance ought to be in a position to make findings when an Art 13(b) defence is raised by making directions, at the very least, for appropriate psychological assessments to be made of the parties and the child before sending the child back to a potentially abusive situation is quite unacceptable. The judge's proposal would subvert the essentially summary nature of these special proceedings.

[22] Equally, in the following paragraph, her assessment that, as the authorities stand, there is no realistic chance of an Art 13(b) defence being established without findings of violence or other specific abuse to the child himself is plainly an analysis that is not borne out by the cases. Those of us who have sat in the Family Division trying cases brought under the Hague Convention will have had direct experience of – albeit rare – instances in which an Art 13(b) defence has succeeded without the essential foundation envisaged by the judge. So this is a case which has classically been determined on the written material that each party put before the court. In that classic determination the judge has correctly understood and applied the authorities, and particularly the authority in *Re H (Abduction: Grave Risk)*[1] which I have cited.

[23] As to her concerns, they are perfectly understandable given the responsibility that judges in the Family Division have to bear in these very exceptional cases. The experience and the instinct of the trial judge is

---

[1]   [2003] EWCA Civ 355, [2003] 2 FCR 151, [2003] 2 FLR 141.

always to protect the child and to pursue the welfare of the child. That instinct and experience is sometimes challenged by the international obligation to apply strict boundaries in the determination of an application for summary return. The authorities do restrain the judges from admitting oral evidence except in exceptional cases. The authorities do restrain the judges from making too ready judgments upon written statements that set out conflicting accounts of adult relationships. What the authorities do not do is to inhibit the judge from himself or herself requiring oral evidence in a case where the judge conceives that oral evidence might be determinative. The judge's conduct of the proceedings is not to be restricted by tactical or strategic decisions taken by the parties. However, to warrant oral exploration of written evidence, the judge must be satisfied that there is a realistic possibility that oral evidence will establish an Art 13(b) case that is only embryonic on the written material.

WALL LJ:

[43] To fulfil the court's international obligations under the Hague Convention, judges often have to return children to the country of their habitual residence in circumstances in which, were they hearing proceedings under the Children Act 1989, they would almost certainly investigate the facts in great detail and in all probability grant residence orders to the abducting parent. That, however, is not the function of the court in a Hague Convention case.

[44] In my judgment, it is always of the utmost importance to remember, as Thorpe and Sedley LJJ have indicated, that these are summary proceedings, and that the object of the proceedings, subject to the defences under Art 13, is to ensure that the child or children concerned are returned swiftly to the country of their habitual residence for their futures to be decided in that country where, of course, the relevant welfare investigation will take place.

[45] I entirely agree with what both Thorpe and Sedley LJJ have said about the question of oral evidence and will not seek to repeat it ...

...

[47] ... There may be cases in which a psychiatric report or psychiatric reports on one or both of the parties are necessary, but I entirely agree with Thorpe LJ that the preparation of such reports as a matter of routine would be wholly inconsistent with the summary nature of Hague Convention proceedings and contrary to its intention and spirit which is, as I indicated earlier, designed to ensure the swift return of children to the country of their habitual residence.

F3   USE OF ELECTRONIC TAGGING

Re A (Family proceedings: electronic tagging)

[2009] 2 FLR 891 at 892

Family Divison

Parker J

[4]   The issue before me was whether A should spend substantial periods of time with the mother under an interim order whilst all the many issues in this case are investigated. The father fears that unless safeguards are put in place the mother may remove A again. The mother says that she has no such intention, but accepts that the father has a legitimate concern that needs to be allayed.

[5]   The parties have now agreed that when the child is with the mother, the mother should be subject for the time being to a curfew supported by electronic tagging. On this basis, the parents have agreed that the child will spend substantial periods with each parent in the interim. The availability of tagging arrangements in appropriate cases in family proceedings is apparently not widely known and counsel have asked that I describe them for the assistance of the profession.

[6]   In *Re C (Abduction: Interim Directions: Accommodation by Local Authority)* [2003] EWHC 3065 (Fam), [2004] 1 FLR 653, Singer J said:

'[45]   An innovation in this case was the mother's suggestion that the package of protective measures should include a direction, pursuant to s 5 of the Child Abduction and Custody Act 1985, that she undergo electronic tagging. I take the view that such a direction may be made under that provision if it is necessary "for the purpose of securing the welfare of the child" and/or "to prevent changes in the circumstances relevant to the determination of the application".

[46]   Although in future cases there may be funding issues to be resolved, in principle arrangements for electronic tagging can be made if the court so orders, which I assume it would ordinarily only do with the consent of the individual concerned (or perhaps as a condition, non-compliance with which might bring about alternative safeguards against the perceived risk). I emphasise that such requirements are unlikely to be appropriate save in very few cases.'

At that time there was no specific procedure in place whereby such arrangements might be implemented. Singer J invited the parties to contact the office of the President to assist in making inquiries and arrangements.

[7]   Since that decision, the President's office has devised a procedure whereby electronic tagging can be arranged through the Tagging Team of the National Office for the Management of Offenders (NOMS). Electronic tagging works by monitoring the whereabouts of the person wearing a tag, but only in a specific location. The tag is monitored by a device which needs to be installed in particular premises, that device monitors the tag, and the tagging office is notified if the tagged person is either not in the premises during the relevant times or if the tag is removed.

[8]   The President's office has confirmed that tagging is available in family cases and has provided the following information as to how orders are to be drafted and implemented:

'(1)   An order needs to be made and sealed by 3.30 pm on the day before its implementation.
(2)   A representative will attend the premises to install the device the next day.
(3)   The order must contain the following information:
    (i)   The full name of the person(s) to be tagged.
    (ii)   The full address of the place of curfew.
    (iii) The date and time at which the tagged person agrees to be at home (and any other relevant places) for the installation of the monitoring device.
    (iv)   A schedule of the times at which the court expects the person to be at home (or any other relevant places) so that the service can monitor compliance.
    (v)   The start date of the curfew and, if known, the end date of the curfew, the days on which the curfew operates and the curfew hours each day.
    (vi)   The name and contact details of the relevant officer to whom the service should report to if there is any breach of the above schedule or if the person appears to have removed the tag.'

F4 UNACCEPTABLE DELAY IN DETERMINING PROCEEDINGS

Vigreux v Michel

[2006] EWCA Civ 630, [2006] 2 FLR 1180 at 1193 and 1204

Court of Appeal

Thorpe and Wall LJJ

THORPE LJ:

[40] Furthermore, nowhere did McFarlane J refer to the requirement for maximum expedition or to the extent to which Art 11(3) of Brussels II Revised had been breached. The significance of the Versailles order of 7 December 2005 is heightened by an appreciation of the breach of our Art 11(3) of Brussels II Revised obligations.

[41] What then are the lessons to be learned? Counsel informed us that an application under the Hague Convention used to be designated with a specific prefix to the court number, which assisted preparation and management to ensure compliance with the Hague Convention requirement for expedition. That requirement, which coincidentally is also expressed in Art 11 of Brussels II Revised, is less stringent. Nevertheless it provides:

'The judicial or administrative authorities of Contracting States shall act expeditiously in proceedings for the return of the children.

If the judicial or administrative authority concerned has not reached a decision within six weeks from the date of commencement of the proceedings, the applicant or the Central Authority of the requested State on its own initiative or if asked by the Central Authority of the requesting State, shall have the right to request a statement of the reasons for the delay. If a reply is received by the Central Authority of the requesting State, or to the applicant, as the case may be.'

[42] That requirement led to specific provisions in Part 6 of the Family Proceedings Rules 1991 to introduce abbreviated time limits for the filing of the written cases and to ensure that a Hague application could not be adjourned for more than 21 days. We were informed by the Bar that since the special prefix for Hague Convention cases was removed some 4 years ago there had been some loss in expeditious listing.

[43] The arrival of Brussels II Revised has led to some amendment of the rules but largely in relation to enforcement.

WALL LJ:

The chronology of the English proceedings

[88] Under Art 11(3) of Brussels II Revised, as Thorpe LJ has pointed out, proceedings for the return of a child must be completed in 6 weeks, 'except where exceptional circumstances make this impossible'. No such circumstances apply in the instant case. I therefore strongly endorse Thorpe LJ's observations on the procedural factors which must govern future applications under the Hague Convention and Brussels II Revised. Failure to adhere to the timetables proposed will not only result in the English court being in breach of its international obligations; it will represent an unacceptable abnegation of the court's responsibility properly to address cases of international child abduction – a matter in which, in the past, we have taken legitimate pride.

[89] As a judge of the Family Division for 11 years, I am acutely conscious of the pressures on the judiciary and on those with responsibilities for listing. Article 11(3) of Brussels II Revised, however, does not admit of debate. It simply must be implemented.

F5 HEARING THE CHILD'S VIEWS

Re M (Abduction: Zimbabwe)

[2007] UKHL 55, [2008] 1 FLR 251 at 269

House of Lords

Baroness Hale of Richmond

[57] I would finally comment that, 'exceptional' or not, this is a highly unusual case. Cases under the second paragraph of Art 12 are, in any event, very few and far between. They are the most 'child-centric' of all child abduction cases and very likely to be combined with the child's objections. As pointed out in *Re D*,[1] it is for the court to consider at the outset how best to give effect to the obligation to hear the child's views. We are told that this is now routinely done through the specialist CAFCASS officers at the Royal Courts of Justice. I accept entirely that children must not be given an exaggerated impression of the relevance and importance of their views in child abduction cases. To order separate representation in all cases, even in all child's objections cases, might be to send them the wrong messages. But it would not send the wrong messages in the very small number of cases where settlement is argued under the second paragraph of Art 12. These are the cases in which the separate point of view of the children is particularly important and should not be lost in the competing claims of the adults. If this were to become routine, there would be no additional delay. In all other cases, the question for the directions judge is whether separate representation of the child will add enough to the court's understanding of the issues that arise under the Hague Convention to justify the intrusion, the expense and the delay that may result. I have no difficulty in predicting that in the general run of cases it will not. But I would hesitate to use the word 'exceptional'. The substance is what counts, not the label.

General notes:

Note *W v W (Abduction: joinder as a party)* [2009] EWHC 3288 (Fam), [2010] 1 FLR 1342 (party status of older sibling in Hague Convention proceedings).

---

[1]   *Re D (Abduction: rights of custody)* [2006] UKHL 51, [2007] 1 FLR 961 per Baroness Hale of Richmond at [57]–[62].

Other significant cases on this issue:

- *Re C (Abduction: separate representation of children)* [2008] EWHC 517 (Fam), [2008] 2 FLR 6

This case is also included in relation to:

F1   Convention designed to protect interests of children

F10 Arts 12 and 13: obligation to return and its exceptions

F6   ART 3: 'HABITUALLY RESIDENT'

E v E

[2007] EWHC 276 (Fam), [2007] 1 FLR 1977 at 1983

Family Division

Potter P

Habitual residence

[29]   In dealing with the disputed issue of habitual residence, I start with the following propositions which are not substantially in dispute.

[30]   First, habitual residence is a question of fact to be decided according to all the circumstances of the case. Secondly, where there is a dispute as to whether an established habitual residence has continued to exist or has recently changed, the burden of proof lies on the party who asserts that the change has taken place, the court looking at the evidence as a whole in this respect.

[31]   Thirdly, in this case it is not in dispute that between 1998, when the family moved back to England, and 2 September 2005 when they arrived in Australia, the children, who throughout that time had lived in England, were habitually resident here.

[32]   Fourthly, as a rule, one parent may not unilaterally change a child's habitual residence without the agreement of the other parent, unless quite independent circumstances have arisen pointing to a change. Since it is the mother's case (and there are a number of circumstances which support it) that, when the family arrived in Australia it was, so far as the mother and the children were concerned, not with the intention of living permanently in Australia, but of returning to England (where the mother still had a home to return to and where the children were at school), the burden in this case is upon the father to show that the position was otherwise and that the children became habitually resident in Australia in the course of a very short stay here before returning to England under the terms of the Australian court order where they have since remained.

[33]   Fifthly, in order to establish habitual residence it must be shown that the person concerned was present in the country (i) voluntarily and (ii) for settled purposes and with a settled intention (see *Al Habtoor v Fotheringham* [2001] EWCA Civ 186, [2001] 1 FLR 951; *Re D* (*Abduction: HabitualResidence*) [2005] EWHC 518 (Fam), [2005] 2 FLR 403; *Re M*

(Abduction: Habitual Residence: Relocation) [2004] EWHC 1951 (Fam), [2005] Fam Law 441; (iii) for 'an appreciable period of time' (see *Re J (A Minor) (Abduction: Custody Rights)* [1990] 2 AC 562, sub nom *C v S (A Minor) (Abduction)* [1990] 2 FLR 442. Thus, in *Re B (Child Abduction: Habitual Residence)* [1994] 2 FLR 915 it was held that a short time spent by a mother in another country, with a view to effecting a reconciliation with a father which failed, was insufficient for a settled intention to have been formed as to a change of residence. It is also clear that a stay in a country for the purposes of a holiday only does not mean that a child becomes habitually resident in that country (see: *Re O (A Minor) (Abduction: Habitual Residence)* [1993] 2 FLR 594). On the other hand, in the case of a family move in connection with a husband's temporary employment abroad it has been held that habitual residence was established on the basis that there was an undisputed and settled purpose of both parents to reside for a period of a few months (see *Re R (Abduction: Habitual Residence)* [2003] EWHC 1968 (Fam), [2004] 1 FLR 216).

[34] Sixthly, the fact that: (a) the father, in light of his knowledge that the mother intended returning to England, applied to the Australian Court for a residence order; and (b) the Australian Court made an order in respect of interim arrangements was, and is, not determinative of the question of the habitual residence of the children at that time, because that was neither the basis of the court's jurisdiction nor the purport of its decision. Thus, should I conclude that the children have remained habitually resident in this country despite their brief sojourn in Australia, that conclusion would not be in conflict with any finding made or jurisdiction exercised by the Australian Court. In any event my task is to apply the law of England in deciding the meaning and content of the term 'habitual residence' within the context of this case: see *Re R* (above) at paras [56]–[58].

[35] Seventhly, given that the children returned to England with their mother on 24 October 2005, it is the fact that, at the time of the mother's later alleged wrongful retention of the children in April 2006, they had lived in England for a period of 8 years, interrupted only by a period of 7 weeks residence in Australia, in August/September 2005.

[36] Eighthly, the father's case, as originally advanced in the detailed affidavit of Mr Ranton his solicitor, (who is also qualified as an Australian barrister), has undergone a very significant change. The father's original position therein stated was that, at all times prior to the arrival of the family in Australia, the mother appeared to be happy with the proposal to move there permanently and was 'unshakeable in her view that the move to Australia was the best for the children'; it was only shortly *after* her arrival in Australia that she began to express disquiet about remaining there and to agitate to return to the UK. The ground was thus laid to establish habitual residence in Australia on the basis of a

settled purpose and common intention of both parents to live permanently in Australia, sufficient to establish habitual residence within days of arrival in Australia, and prior to a 'change of heart' by the mother thereafter. In the event, the father has been obliged to retreat from that position in the face of the various matters set out in paras [11]–[15], above, and in particular in the light of the way he put the matter before the Australian Court (see para [17], above).

Other significant cases on this issue:

- *Re A (Abduction: habitual residence)* [2007] EWHC 779 (Fam), [2007] 2 FLR 129
- *Re D (Abduction: inherent jurisdiction)* [2008] EWHC 1246 (Fam), [2009] 1 FLR 1015
- *Re Z (Abduction)* [2008] EWHC 3473 (Fam), [2009] 2 FLR 298
- *Re P-J (Abduction: habitual residence: consent)* [2009] EWCA Civ 588, [2009] 2 FLR 1051

F7 ART 3: 'REMOVAL' AND 'RETENTION'

Re H; Re S (Minors) (abduction: custody rights)

[1991] 2 FLR 262 at 269 and 270

House of Lords

Lord Brandon

The same question arises for decision in both *Re H* and *Re S*. It is what is the meaning in the Convention of the expression 'removal', with its cognate verb removed, on the one hand, and the expression 'retention', with its cognate verb retained, on the other. The question comprises three points which need to be considered separately. The first point is whether removal and retention are both events which occur once and for all on a specific occasion, or whether, while removal is such an event, retention is a state of affairs beginning on a specific occasion, but continuing from day-to-day thereafter. The second point is whether removal and retention are mutually exclusive concepts, so that in any particular situation a child may either be removed or retained, but not both, or whether removal can, and ordinarily will be, followed by continuing retention. The third point is whether removal or retention means removal from, or retention out of, the care of the parent having the custodial rights, or removal from, or retention out of, the jurisdiction of the courts of the child's habitual place of residence.

...

Before addressing the three points in respect of which Mr Munby challenges the view taken by the Court of Appeal, I would make some preliminary observations about the nature and purpose of the Convention. The preamble of the Convention shows that it is aimed at the protection of children *internationally* (my emphasis) from wrongful removal or retention. Article 1(a) shows that the first object of the Convention is to secure the prompt return to the State of their habitual residence (that State being a Contracting State) of children in two categories: (1) children who have been wrongfully removed from the State of their habitual residence to another Contracting State; and (2) children who have been wrongfully retained in a Contracting State other than the State of their habitual residence, instead of being returned to the latter State. The Convention is not concerned with children who have been wrongfully removed or retained within the borders of the State of their habitual residence.

So far as category (1) is concerned, it appears to me that a child only comes within it if it is wrongfully taken out, ie across the frontier, of the State of its habitual residence. Until that happens, although the child may already have been wrongfully removed within the borders of the State of its habitual residence, it will not have been wrongfully removed for the purposes of the Convention. So far as category (2) is concerned, it appears to me that a child can only come within it if it has first been removed rightfully (for example, under a court order or an agreement between its two parents) out of the State of its habitual residence, and subsequently retained wrongfully (for example, contrary to a court order or an agreement between its two parents), instead of being returned to the State of its habitual residence. The wrongful retention of a child in one place in the State of its habitual residence, instead of its being returned to another place within the same State, would not be a wrongful retention for the purposes of the Convention. The typical (but not necessarily the only) case of a child within category (2) is that of a child who is rightfully taken out of the State of its habitual residence to another contracting State for a specified period of staying access with its non-custodial parent, and wrongfully not returned to the State of its habitual residence at the expiry of that period.

In the light of these preliminary observations, I turn to the three points in respect of each of which the view taken by the Court of Appeal has been challenged by Mr Munby. With regard to the first point, whether retention is an event occurring on a specific occasion or a continuing state of affairs, it appears to me that art 12 of the Convention is decisive. I set out that article earlier, but it will be helpful to set it out again now. It provides:

> 'Where a child has been wrongfully removed or retained in terms of article 3 and, at the date of the commencement of the proceedings before the judicial or administrative authority of the contracting state where the child is, a period of less than one year has elapsed from the date of the wrongful removal or retention, the authority concerned shall order the return of the child forthwith.

> The judicial or administrative authority, even where the proceedings have been commenced after the expiration of the period of one year referred to in the preceding paragraph, shall also order the return of the child, unless it is demonstrated that the child is now settled in its new environment ...'

The period of one year referred to in this article is a period measured from the date of the wrongful removal or retention. That appears to me to show clearly that, for the purposes of the Convention, both removal and retention are events occurring on a specific occasion, for otherwise it would be impossible to measure a period of one year from their occurrence. It was submitted by Mr Munby that, in the case of retention, the date from which the period of one year was to be measured was the date of the inception of the retention and that, if art 12 was interpreted in that way, it was not inconsistent with retention being a continuing state of affairs. I find myself unable to accept that submission. To interpret art 12 in that way involves inserting into it words which are not there and, if intended to apply, could readily have been put in. I consider that art 12 leads inevitably to the conclusion that retention, like removal, is an event occurring on a specific occasion.

With regard to the second point, whether removal and retention are mutually exclusive concepts, it appears to me that, once it is accepted that retention is not a continuing state of affairs, but an event occurring on a specific occasion, it necessarily follows that removal and retention are mutually exclusive concepts. For the purposes of the Convention, removal occurs when a child, which has previously been in the State of its habitual residence, is taken away across the frontier of that State; whereas retention occurs where a child, which has previously been for a limited period of time outside the State of its habitual residence, is not returned to that State on the expiry of such limited period. That being so, it seems to me that removal and retention are basically different concepts, so that it is impossible either for them to overlap each other or for either to follow upon the other. This interpretation of the Convention is strongly supported by the fact that, throughout the Convention, removal and retention are linked by the word 'or', rather than by the word 'and', which indicates that each is intended to be a real alternative to the other. It was submitted by Mr Munby that the word 'or', where it links removal and retention, should be construed as meaning 'and/or'. This again involves inserting into the Convention words which are not there, and which could, if intended to apply, readily have been put in. I cannot, therefore, accept that submission.

With regard to the third point, whether removal or retention means removal from, or retention out of, the care of the parent having the custodial rights, or removal from, or retention out of, the jurisdiction of the courts of the State of a child's habitual residence, I am of opinion that the latter meaning is the correct one. I think that follows necessarily from the considerations to which I referred in my preliminary observations about the nature and purpose of the Convention, that the Convention is only concerned with international protection for children from removal or retention, and not with removal or retention within the State of their habitual residence. It was suggested in argument that art 3(b) was difficult to reconcile with the view on the third point, which I have said that I regard as correct. Article 3 (b) specifies the second of two matters required to render a removal or retention wrongful. That second requirement is that at the time of removal or retention, the custody rights of the custodial parent 'were actually exercised, either jointly or alone, or would have been so exercised but for the removal or retention.' It was suggested that, if removal for the purposes of the Convention involved the taking of the child concerned across the frontier of the State of its habitual residence, it might be impossible for the custodial parent to show that the requirement contained in art 3(b) was satisfied. In my view, art 3(b) must be construed widely as meaning that the custodial parent must be maintaining the stance and attitude of such a parent, rather than narrowly as meaning that he or she must be continuing to exercise day-to-day care and control. If the narrow meaning was adopted, it could be said that a custodial parent was not actually exercising his or her custodial rights during a period of lawful staying access with the non-custodial parent. That, as it seems to me, cannot be right. Provided that what I have described as the broader meaning of the requirement contained in art 3(b) is adopted, I do not consider that such requirement is inconsistent with the view on the third point, which I have said that I regard as correct.

Other significant cases on this issue:

- *Re T and J (Abduction: recognition of foreign judgment)* [2006] EWHC 1472 (Fam), [2006] 2 FLR 1290 at [57]
- *RS v KS (Abduction: wrongful retention)* [2009] EWHC 1494 (Fam), [2009] 2 FLR 1231

F8   ART 3: WRONGFUL REMOVAL

Re D (Abduction: rights of custody)

[2006] UKHL 51, [2007] 1 FLR 961 at 971

House of Lords

Baroness Hale

Wrongful removal

[24]   The world would be a simpler place if the Hague Convention had provided that all removal or retention of a child outside the country where he or she is habitually resident without the consent of the other parent or the authority of a court is wrongful. But it does not. The Hague Convention recognises that not all parents have the right to demand the automatic return of children who have been taken away without their consent. It does so by providing that the removal or retention of a child is only wrongful under Art 3 if it is 'in breach of rights of custody attributed to a person, an institution or any other body, either jointly or alone, under the law of the state in which the child was habitually resident immediately before the removal or retention'. These rights may arise 'by operation of law or by reason of a judicial or administrative decision, or by reason of an agreement having legal effect under the law of that state.' In addition, those rights must actually have been being exercised at the time (or would have been had it not been for the wrongful removal). Article 5(a) provides that '"rights of custody" shall include rights relating to the care of the person of the child and, in particular, the right to determine the child's place of residence'.

[25]   The Hague Convention also obliges, in Art 21, the central authorities to assist a 'left behind' parent in realising his or her 'rights of access', not by securing summary return to the home country, but through promoting their peaceful enjoyment, removing obstacles to their exercise, and initiating or assisting the initiation of proceedings to protect them. Article 5(b) provides that '"rights of access" shall include the right to take a child for a limited period of time to a place other than the child's habitual residence'. Thus it was envisaged that the right to have the child to stay away from his home might still amount to 'rights of access' rather than 'rights of custody'. It is quite clear from the Explanatory Report of Professor Elisa Pérez-Vera (April 1981) that the original parties to the Hague Convention drew a deliberate distinction between rights of custody and rights of access and did not intend that mere rights of access should entitle a parent to demand the summary return of the child. As

Professor Pérez-Vera pointed out, such an approach would ultimately lead to 'the substitution of the holders of one type of right by those who held the other' (see para 65).

[26]   Nevertheless it is common ground between all the parties to this case that they are not mutually exclusive concepts. A person may have both rights of access and rights of custody. The question is, do the rights possessed under the law of the home country by the parent who does not have the day to day care of the child amount to rights of custody or do they not? States' laws differ widely in how they look upon parental rights. They may regard the whole bundle of rights and responsibilities which the law attributes to parents as a cake which can be sliced up between the parents: one parent having the custody slice, with the package of rights which that entails, and the other having the access slice, with the different package of rights which that entails. This is by no means an unusual way of looking at the matter. Alternatively, the state may regard the whole bundle of parental rights and responsibilities as inhering, and continuing to inhere, in both parents save to the extent that they are removed or qualified by the necessary effect of a court order or an enforceable agreement between them. The expert evidence in this case demonstrates that there was serious academic debate in Romania about whether the law adopted the first or the second approach. In the event, the Romanian court adopted the former whereas the single joint expert adopted the latter.

[27]   As Professor Pérez-Vera points out, following a long established tradition of the Hague Conference, the Convention does not define the legal concepts used by it. However, Art 5 does make clear the sense in which the concepts of custody and access rights are used, 'since an incorrect interpretation of their meaning would risk compromising the Hague Convention's objects' (see para 83). Custody relates to the care of the child's person rather than his property. It is a narrower concept than that of 'protection of minors' used elsewhere. It may, however, be jointly held. Access includes the right to 'residential access' even across national boundaries.

[28]   In the absence of a supranational body to define and refine these autonomous terms, Member States must strive for consistent practice – not in the content of their domestic laws but in the effect that they give to the particular features of one another's laws. As Lord Browne Wilkinson said in *Re H (Abduction: Acquiescence)* [1998] AC 72, [1997] 1 FLR 872, at 87 and 881 respectively, (albeit in the context of the meaning to be given to 'acquiesced' in Art 13(a) of the Convention):

'An international Convention, expressed in different languages and intended to apply to a wide range of differing legal systems, cannot be construed differently in different jurisdictions. The Convention must have the same meaning and effect under the laws of all contracting states.'

In that case, therefore, English concepts and English law rules about the meaning of acquiescence could have no direct relevance to the interpretation of the Hague Convention. We must be equally prepared to resist projecting the view taken in English law of the rights of parents onto the Hague Convention concepts as they apply to the laws of other member states which may take a different view.

[29] There is no problem when return is requested by the parent with the right to the day-to-day care of the child – or in English terms, the parent with whom it has been determined that the child is to live. The problem is with the characterisation of the other parent's rights. If these amount to joint custody, there is equally no problem. The main debate has been over the effect of what are sometimes referred to as 'travel restrictions' – either a court order prohibiting the removal of the child from the home country or a 'right of veto' giving one parent, who may or may not also have rights of access, the right to insist that the other parent does not remove the child from the home country without his or her consent or a court order.

[30] The internal position in English and Scottish law is clear. Parents who share parental responsibility (that is all married parents and increasing numbers of unmarried parents) each have all the rights and responsibilities of parents. They retain those rights subject only to the practical limitations of any court order and can exercise them independently of one another unless this is inconsistent with a court order. While a residence order is in force, no person may remove the child from the UK without the written consent of each person with parental authority or the leave of a court (s 13(1)(b) of the Children Act 1989). In England, the person with the benefit of the residence order may remove the child for less than one month: s 13(2). Even if there is no residence order, it is a criminal offence for a parent to remove a child from the UK without the consent of each person with parental responsibility or the leave of a court (ss 1 and 6 of the Child Abduction Act 1984; in England with the one month exception for people with the benefit of a residence order).

[31] But the mere fact that English and Scottish parents enjoy such rights of veto does not of itself mean that they enjoy 'rights of custody' within the meaning of the Hague Convention. Hitherto, however, both in England and Scotland, the courts have regarded travel restrictions as giving rise to rights of custody. As long ago as *C v C (Abduction: Rights of Custody)* [1989] 1 WLR 654, [1989] 1 FLR 403, the Court of Appeal held that a court order prohibiting either parent from removing a child from Australia without the other's consent gave the other parent rights of custody under the Hague Convention. Lord Donaldson MR observed,

at 664 and 413 respectively, that the right to determine the child's place of
residence 'may be specific – the right to decide that it shall live at a
particular address or it may be general, eg "within the Commonwealth of
Australia"'. In *Re W (Minors) (Abduction: Father's Rights); Re B (A
Minor) (Abduction: Father's Rights)* [1999] Fam 1, [1998] 2 FLR 146, I
applied the same approach to rights of veto arising by operation of law.
Both cases were relied upon by the Inner House of the Court of Session
in *J, Petitioner* [2005] CSIH 36, 2005 GWD 15–251, where it was held that
the right of veto enjoyed, by virtue of s 2(3) and (6) of the Children
(Scotland) Act 1995, by a parent with the right to contact amounted to
'rights of custody' under the Hague Convention.

[32]   Mr James Turner QC, on behalf of the mother, has questioned
whether a mere right of veto should amount to 'rights of custody'. The
reasoning is simple. If rights of custody 'shall include' the right to
determine the child's place of residence, it is not enough that they include
the right to determine for the time being the country where the child lives
– it must mean the right to determine where the child actually lives. The
Hague Convention envisages a compendium of more than one right.
Furthermore, the purpose of the right to determine the country where the
child lives is simply to facilitate the exercise of the right of access – and
that does not attract the right to demand summary return to the home
country. Indeed, a person possessing a right of veto may have no access
rights at all; whereas a person having access rights may have no veto right.
It would be surprising if a parent who enjoyed a close and continuing
relationship with his child might have no rights of custody whereas a
parent who has not seen his child for years might do so.

[33]   Mr Turner is able to cite other jurisdictions in the common law
world which have taken this view. In 2000, in *Croll v Croll* (2000) 229 F 3d
133, a majority of the US Court of Appeals for the Second Circuit held
that a ne exeat clause in a Hong Kong custody agreement giving custody,
care and control to the mother did not give rights of custody to the father.
That decision was followed in 2002 by the Court of Appeals for the Ninth
Circuit in *Gonzalez v Gutierrez* (2002) 311 F 3d 942; and in 2003 by the
Court of Appeals for the Fourth Circuit in *Fawcett v McRoberts* (2003)
326 F 3d 191(referred to without comment but distinguished in 2006 in
Bader v Kramer (2006) 445 F 3d 346). The majority in *Croll* relied on the
deliberate distinction drawn in the Convention between rights of custody
and rights of access, the lack of international consensus on the issue, and
the published views of Professor AE Anton, chair of the Hague
Conference Commission which had drafted the Hague Convention at
(1981) 30 ICLQ 537, at 546.

[34]   The majority in *Croll* were able to point to two decisions in the
Supreme Court of Canada to demonstrate a lack of international
consensus. In *Thomson v Thomson* [1994] 3 SCR 551, the court had held
that removal in breach of a ne exeat clause in an interim custody order

was in breach of rights of custody held by the court, in order to preserve its jurisdiction to make a final determination, but expressed the view that such a clause in a final order would not give the other parent rights of custody. In *DS v VW and JS and Rodrigue Blais* [1996] 2 SCR 108, *Thomson* was relied upon a fortiori where any prohibition upon removal had been implicit in the custody order made in the United States.

[35] However, in 2004 the United States Court of Appeals for the Eleventh Circuit in *Furnes v Reeves* (2004) 362 F 3d 702 rejected the reasoning of the majority in *Croll* in preference for the dissenting views of Sotomayor CJ. They pointed out that to order return of the child did not convert the other parent's rights of access into rights of custody, because there was no obligation to return the child to that other parent. The object was to maintain the status quo and the jurisdiction of the home country over any disputes. The observations in both Canadian cases were obiter. Apart from them, known opinion elsewhere in the common law world was united. Thus the full court of the Family Court of Australia, in *JR v MR* (unreported) 22 May 1991, had followed the English decision in *C v C*, as did Lindenmayer J at first instance in *Director General, Department of Families, Youth and Community Care v Hobbs* [1999] FamCA 2059. The Constitutional Court of South Africa had reached the same result in *Sonderup v Tondelli* (2001) (1) SA 1171 (CC). The Israeli High Court, in *Foxman v Foxman* (5271/92) in 1992 had also held that rights of custody should include cases where parental consent is required to remove the child from the country of residence. To these might have been added New Zealand, which has gone further still and held that rights of access can in themselves amount to 'rights of custody': *G v B* [1995] NZFLR 49; *D v C* [1999] NZFLR 97; see also *Hunter v Murrow (Abduction: Rights of Custody)* [2005] EWCA Civ 976, [2005] 2 FLR 1119 (para [42], below).

[36] I acknowledge the force of Mr Turner's argument, especially when viewed against the original paradigm case of abduction by a non-custodial parent from the custodial primary carer. It is also the case that some parents who possess a right of veto have in fact very limited contact – if any – with their children, so that to force a child to return to the home country simply for the sake of obtaining permission to leave which will almost certainly be granted seems heavy handed. But the circumstances of families are infinitely various. It is an object of the Hague Convention to enable such decisions to be taken in the courts of the home country where those circumstances can (in most cases) better be investigated and evaluated. It is not for the courts of the requested state to start making value judgments about the merits of the case, save to the very limited extent that the Hague Convention permits this. As far as the Hague Convention is concerned, a person either has rights of custody or he does not – the quality of his relationship with the child is not in point. It would, at the very least, be an odd result if a Hague Convention designed to secure the summary return of children wrongfully removed from their home countries were not to result in the return of children

whose removal had clearly been in breach of the laws, court orders or enforceable agreements in the home country.

[37]   Therefore, in common with the understanding of the English and Scottish courts hitherto, and with what appears to be the majority of the common law world, I would hold that a right of veto does amount to 'rights of custody' within the meaning of Art 5(a). I see no good reason to distinguish the court's right of veto, which was recognised as 'rights of custody' by this House in *Re H (A Minor) (Abduction: Rights of Custody)* [2000] 2 AC 291, [2000] 1 FLR 374, from a parental right of veto, whether the latter arises by court order, agreement or operation of law.

[38]   I would not, however, go so far as to say that a parent's potential right of veto could amount to 'rights of custody'. In other words, if all that the other parent has is the right to go to court and ask for an order about some aspect of the child's upbringing, including relocation abroad, this should not amount to 'rights of custody'. To hold otherwise would be to remove the distinction between 'rights of custody' and 'rights of access' altogether. It would be also inconsistent with the decision of this House in *Re J (A Minor) (Abduction: Custody Rights)* [1990] 2 AC 562 sub nom *C v S (A Minor) (Abduction)* [1990] 2 FLR 442. There an unmarried father had no parental rights or responsibility unless and until a court gave him some; but he did, of course, have the right to go to court to seek such an order. This was held not to amount to 'rights of custody' within the meaning of Art 5(a). Nor could a subsequent order grant him such rights if by then the child's habitual residence had been changed.

General notes:

For further analysis of the alternative approach to rights of custody taken in the US courts in *Croll v Croll*, see also the speech of Lord Hope at [11]–[19]. Note also the more cautious approach of Lord Carswell at [74] who expressly reserved his position on the issue.

This case is also included in relation to:

F13   Art 15: effect of determination by requesting state
F14   Art 20: human rights arguments
F15   Art 21 and rights of access: addressing the real issue

F9   ARTS 3 AND 5: 'RIGHTS OF CUSTODY'

Kennedy v Kennedy

[2009] EWCA Civ 986, [2010] 1 FLR 782 at 785 and 788

Court of Appeal

Thorpe LJ

[9]   We have before us the skeleton argument of Mr Scott-Manderson in the court below, and in paras 12 and 13, equally paras 42–48 inclusive, Mr Scott-Manderson emphasised that the court's approach to the determination of whether or not a parent exercised rights of custody is a two-stage process. The first stage involves an investigation of the law of the State of habitual residence immediately prior to removal, and the second and ultimately decisive stage involves a consideration of what Mr Scott-Manderson labelled the supranational concept. Despite that submitted approach the issue was decided by the President solely on an evaluation of the father's rights of custody according to the domestic law of Spain. Mr Scott-Manderson explains that the President's judgment must be understood in the context of the manner in which the trial before him proceeded. All the emphasis was upon the resolution of the dispute between the two experts. All the emphasis was upon the President's determination of the law of Spain. Despite the extent to which Mr Scott-Manderson had emphasised that the ultimate question had to be decided according to the autonomous law of the Hague Convention, the President did not include within his judgment any reference to that ultimate stage or express any opinion on what were the father's rights of custody, not according to the law of Spain, but according to the autonomous law of the Hague Convention.

[10]   That Mr Scott-Manderson was correct in his presentation in the court below simply cannot be in doubt. There is a clear line of authority in this jurisdiction to the effect that the ultimate determining factor must be the international law of the Hague Convention. That was clearly established in this court in the case of *Hunter v Murrow (Abduction: Rights of Custody)* [2005] EWCA Civ 976, [2005] 2 FLR 1119 at 1119. In the course of his judgment Dyson LJ said at para [47]:

'[47]   The next question is whether those rights are properly to be characterised as "rights of custody" within the meaning of Articles 3 and 5(b) of the Convention. I shall refer to this as "the Convention question". This is a matter of international law and depends on the application of the autonomous meaning of the phrase "rights of custody". Where, as in the present case, an application is made in the courts of England and Wales, the autonomous meaning is determined in accordance with English law as the law of the court whose jurisdiction has been invoked under the Convention. But as Lord Browne-Wilkinson said in *Re H (Abduction: Acquiescence)* [1998] AC 72 at page 87F, the Convention cannot be construed differently in different jurisdictions: it must have the same meaning and effect under the laws of all Contracting States. In *R v Secretary of State for the Home Department, ex p Adan* [2001] 2 AC 477 at page 517 when referring to the meaning of the Geneva Convention relating to the Status of Refugees, Lord Steyn said:

> "In practice it is left to national courts, faced with material disagreement on an issue of interpretation, to resolve it. But in so doing it must search, untrammelled by notions of its national legal culture, for the true autonomous and international meaning of the treaty. And there can only be one true meaning.'"

...

[20] In a sense the value of the President's judgment below is that it concludes the issues at the first stage. He was not asked to continue to determine the ultimate question. However, it is perfectly apparent to me that the father has rights of custody under the international and autonomous law of the Hague Convention. As was pointed out by Baragwanath J at para [175] in the New Zealand authority to which I have referred:

> 'Increasingly and in different jurisdictions the relationship of the unmarried father with an abducted child is classified in domestic law as a right of custody rather than merely of access, and consideration is needed as to whether a change in construction of the Convention should follow.'

To like effect in para [176]:

> 'These factors evidence a fundamental change in attitudes to the relationship between child and father where the parents are unmarried. They enhance the importance to the child of the father and the status of the father's role in relation to the child.'

[21] Plainly the international and autonomous law of the Hague Convention has moved significantly since the decisions of Munby J in the year 2003.[1] In our jurisdiction this shift is marked by the arrival of the Adoption and Children Act 2002, which from 1 December 2003 accorded to the unmarried father automatic parental responsibility if registered on

---

[1]   *Re JB (Child Abduction) (rights of custody: Spain)* [2003] EWHC 2130 (Fam), [2004] 1 FLR 796.

the birth certificate as the father. It seems to me that in the world of 2008, when this removal occurred, this jurisdiction, and most others searching for the extent of the father's rights under the autonomous law, would hold that they constituted rights of custody within the meaning of Arts 3 and 5.

Other significant cases on this issue:

- *Re F (Abduction: rights of custody)* [2008] EWHC 272 (Fam), [2008] 2 FLR 1239 (no acquiescence, children's objections)
- *A v B (Abduction: declaration)* [2008] EWHC 1514 (Fam), [2009] 1 FLR 1253

F10 ARTS 12 AND 13: OBLIGATION TO RETURN AND ITS EXCEPTIONS

Re M (Abduction: Zimbabwe)

[2007] UKHL 55, [2008] 1 FLR 251 at 257, 262 and 265

House of Lords

Baroness Hale of Richmond

The Convention and the issues

...

[13]   The basic obligation to return the child is spelled out in Art 12:

'Where a child has been wrongfully removed or retained in terms of Article 3 and, at the date of the commencement of the proceedings before the judicial or administrative authority of the Contracting State where the child is, a period of less than one year has elapsed from the date of the wrongful removal or retention, the authority concerned shall order the return of the child forthwith.

The judicial or administrative authority, even where the proceedings have been commenced after the expiration of the period of one year referred to in the preceding paragraph, shall also order the return of the child, unless it is demonstrated that the child is now settled in its new environment.'

As Professor Pérez-Vera points out, Art 12 and Art 18 are complementary, despite their different character (para 106). Article 18 reads:

'The provisions of this Chapter do not limit the power of a judicial or administrative authority to order the return of the child at any time.'

[14]   Thus one of the exceptions to the duty of return is contained within Art 12 itself. If the proceedings are begun within a year of the removal, there is a duty to return 'forthwith'. Even if they are begun more than a year later, there is still a duty to return, but not 'forthwith', unless the child is now settled in its new environment. These proceedings were begun more than 2 years after the children had been removed. Notwithstanding the precarious immigration position, the trial judge found that 'overall and on fine balance' the children were now settled in their new environment. Hence there is no duty under Art 12 to return them.

[15]   This gives rise to the two most important issues in the case: (1) once the children are settled, is there a discretion nevertheless to return them under the Convention or must their return be sought and ordered under some other jurisdiction; and (2) if there is such a discretion, on what principles should it be exercised and how far, if at all, do they differ from the principles which would apply to the court's power to return them under some other jurisdiction?

[16]   Three further exceptions are spelled out in Art 13:

'Notwithstanding the provisions of the previous Article, the judicial or administrative authority of the requested State is not bound to order the return of the child if the person, institution or other body which opposes its return establishes that—

(a)   the person, institution or other body having the care of the person of the child was not actually exercising the custody rights at the time of removal or retention, or had consented to or subsequently acquiesced in the removal or retention; or

(b)   there is a grave risk that his or her return would expose the child to physical or psychological harm or otherwise place the child in an intolerable situation.
The judicial or administrative authority may also refuse to order the return of the child if it finds that the child objects to being returned and has attained an age and degree of maturity at which it is appropriate to take account of its views.'

...

[29]   In theory at least, therefore, there are three solutions: (1) once any ground of opposition has been made out, so that there is no duty to return the child, the court must consider whether to use other powers, outside the Convention, to return the child; or (2) the Art 13 and 20 grounds, being permissive only, contain within them a discretion nevertheless to return the child, but the Art 12 ground, not being so limited, does not; or (3) all of the grounds contain within them a discretion to return nonetheless.

[30]   Despite its attractive simplicity and the distinction of its source, solution (1) can be rejected. A discretion not to return is imported into the words of Art 13 itself. The passage cited from Professor Pérez-Vera is taken, as already seen, from her discussion of Arts 12 and 18; when discussing Arts 13 and 20, she states:

'In general, it is appropriate to emphasise that the exceptions in these two articles do not apply automatically, in that they do not invariably result in the child's retention; nevertheless, the very nature of these exceptions gives judges a discretion – and does not impose upon them a duty – to refuse to return a child in certain circumstances.' (para 113)

Thus Art 13 clearly envisages that the discretion may result in a decision to return within the Convention procedures. Those procedures, involving as they do the central authorities of each contracting state and, in this country at least, favourable legal aid for the claimants, are different from those of the ordinary law. The same applies to Art 20.

[31] The choice between solutions (2) and (3) is much more difficult. As judges at all levels have acknowledged, there is much to be said for either view. However, I have reached the conclusion, not without considerable hesitation, that Art 12 does envisage that a settled child might nevertheless be returned within the Convention procedures. The words 'shall ... unless' leave the matter open. It would be consistent with all the other exceptions to the rule of return. It would avoid the separate and perhaps unfunded need for proceedings in the unusual event that summary return would be appropriate in a settlement case. It recognises the flexibility in the concept of settlement, which may arise in a wide variety of circumstances and to very different degrees. It acknowledges that late application may be the result of active concealment of where the child has gone. It leaves the court with all options open. Furthermore, the difference between the two solutions is by no means as great as is sometimes assumed. This depends upon the scope of the discretion to be exercised both within and without the Convention procedures.

Discretion under the ordinary law and under the Convention

[32] The difference between the two was summed up thus by Thorpe LJ in *Cannon v Cannon*, at para [38]:

'For the exercise of a discretion under the Hague Convention requires the court to have due regard to the overriding objectives of the Convention whilst acknowledging the importance of the child's welfare (particularly in a case where the court has found settlement), whereas the consideration of the welfare of the child is paramount if the discretion is exercised in the context of our domestic law.'

There has been a tendency in some quarters to take each of these approaches further than they should properly be taken, thus exaggerating the differences between them.

...

[38] In my view, each of the extreme positions outlined above is incorrect. In the recent rather oddly entitled case of *Re J (A Child) (Custody Rights: Jurisdiction)* [2005] UKHL 40, [2006] 1 AC 80, [2005] 2 FLR 802 this House made clear the approach to be adopted in wrongful removal or retention cases falling outside the Hague Convention. The child's welfare is indeed the paramount consideration. But the court does have the power to order the immediate return of the child to a foreign jurisdiction without conducting a full investigation of the merits. As Ormrod LJ put it in *Re R (Minors) (Wardship: Jurisdiction)* (1981) 2 FLR 416, at 425:

> '"Kidnapping", like other kinds of unilateral action in relation to children, is to be strongly discouraged, but the discouragement must take the form of a swift, realistic and unsentimental assessment of the best interests of the child, leading, in proper cases, to the prompt return of the child to his or her own country, but not the sacrifice of the child's welfare to some other principle of law.'

[39] Thus there is always a choice to be made between summary return and a further investigation. There is also a choice to be made as to the depth into which the judge will go in investigating the merits of the case before making that choice. One size does not fit all. The judge may well find it convenient to start from the proposition that it is likely to be better for a child to return to his home country for any disputes about his future to be decided there. A case against his doing so has to be made. But the weight to be given to that factor and to all the other relevant factors, some of which are canvassed in *Re J*, will vary enormously from case to case. No doubt, for example, in cases involving Hague Convention countries the differences in the legal systems and principles of law of the two countries will be much less significant than they might be in cases which fall outside the Convention altogether.

[40] On the other hand, I have no doubt at all that it is wrong to import any test of exceptionality into the exercise of discretion under the Hague Convention. The circumstances in which return may be refused are themselves exceptions to the general rule. That in itself is sufficient exceptionality. It is neither necessary nor desirable to import an additional gloss into the Convention.

[41] But there remains a distinction between the exercise of discretion under the Hague Convention and the exercise of discretion in wrongful removal or retention cases falling outside the Convention. In non-Convention cases the child's welfare may well be better served by a prompt return to the country from which she was wrongly removed; but that will be because of the particular circumstances of her case, understood in the light of the general understanding of the harm which wrongful removal can do, summed up in the well-known words of Buckley LJ in *Re L (Minors) (Wardship: Jurisdiction)* [1974] 1 WLR 250, at 264:

> 'To take a child from his native land, to remove him to another country where, maybe, his native tongue is not spoken, to divorce him from the social customs and contacts to which he has been accustomed, to interrupt his education ... are all acts ... which are likely to be psychologically disturbing to the child, particularly at a time when his family life is also disrupted.'

[42] In Convention cases, however, there are general policy considerations which may be weighed against the interests of the child in the individual case. These policy considerations include, not only the swift return of abducted children, but also comity between the contracting states and respect for one another's judicial processes. Furthermore, the Convention is there, not only to secure the prompt return of abducted children, but also to deter abduction in the first place. The message should go out to potential abductors that there are no safe havens among the contracting states.

[43] My Lords, in cases where a discretion arises from the terms of the Convention itself, it seems to me that the discretion is at large. The court is entitled to take into account the various aspects of the Convention policy, alongside the circumstances which gave the court a discretion in the first place and the wider considerations of the child's rights and welfare. I would, therefore, respectfully agree with Thorpe LJ in the passage quoted in para [32] above, save for the word 'overriding' if it suggests that the Convention objectives should always be given more weight than the other considerations. Sometimes they should and sometimes they should not.

[44] That, it seems to me, is the furthest one should go in seeking to put a gloss on the simple terms of the Convention. As is clear from the earlier discussion, the Convention was the product of prolonged discussions in which some careful balances were struck and fine distinctions drawn. The underlying purpose is to protect the interests of children by securing the swift return of those who have been wrongfully removed or retained. The Convention itself has defined when a child must be returned and when she need not be. Thereafter the weight to be given to Convention considerations and to the interests of the child will vary enormously. The extent to which it will be appropriate to investigate those welfare considerations will also vary. But the further away one gets from the speedy return envisaged by the Convention, the less weighty those general Convention considerations must be.

[45] By way of illustration only, as this House pointed out in *Re D (Abduction: Rights of Custody)* [2006] UKHL 51; [2007] 1 AC 619, [2007]

1 FLR 961, para [55], 'it is inconceivable that a court which reached the conclusion that there was a grave risk that the child's return would expose him to physical or psychological harm or otherwise place him in an intolerable situation would nevertheless return him to face that fate.' It was not the policy of the Convention that children should be put at serious risk of harm or placed in intolerable situations. In consent or acquiescence cases, on the other hand, general considerations of comity and confidence, particular considerations relating to the speed of legal proceedings and approach to relocation in the home country, and individual considerations relating to the particular child might point to a speedy return so that her future can be decided in her home country.

[46]　In child's objections cases, the range of considerations may be even wider than those in the other exceptions. The exception itself is brought into play when only two conditions are met: first, that the child herself objects to being returned and secondly, that she has attained an age and degree of maturity at which it is appropriate to take account of her views. These days, and especially in the light of Art 12 of the United Nations Convention on the Rights of the Child 1989, courts increasingly consider it appropriate to take account of a child's views. Taking account does not mean that those views are always determinative or even presumptively so. Once the discretion comes into play, the court may have to consider the nature and strength of the child's objections, the extent to which they are 'authentically her own' or the product of the influence of the abducting parent, the extent to which they coincide or are at odds with other considerations which are relevant to her welfare, as well as the general Convention considerations referred to earlier. The older the child, the greater the weight that her objections are likely to carry. But that is far from saying that the child's objections should only prevail in the most exceptional circumstances.

[47]　In settlement cases, it must be borne in mind that the major objective of the Convention cannot be achieved. These are no longer 'hot pursuit' cases. By definition, for whatever reason, the pursuit did not begin until long after the trail had gone cold. The object of securing a swift return to the country of origin cannot be met. It cannot any longer be assumed that that country is the better forum for the resolution of the parental dispute. So the policy of the Convention would not necessarily point towards a return in such cases, quite apart from the comparative strength of the countervailing factors, which may well, as here, include the child's objections as well as her integration in her new community.

[48]　All this is merely to illustrate that the policy of the Convention does not yield identical results in all cases, and has to be weighed together with the circumstances which produced the exception and such pointers as there are towards the welfare of the particular child. The Convention itself contains a simple, sensible and carefully thought out balance between various considerations, all aimed at serving the interests of

children by deterring and where appropriate remedying international child abduction. Further elaboration with additional tests and checklists is not required.

General notes:

It is suggested that any authorities on Arts 12 and 13 that pre-date this decision need to be treated with care: see further the analysis of Baroness Hale in this case at [33]–[37].

Subsequent cases on this issue:

- *BT v JRT (Abduction: conditional acquiescence and consent)* [2008] EWHC 1169 (Fam), [2008] 2 FLR 972 (consent)
- *Re F (Abduction: rights of custody)* [2008] EWHC 272 (Fam), [2008] 2 FLR 1239 (no acquiescence, children's objections)
- *F v M (Abduction: grave risk of harm)* [2008] EWHC 1467 (Fam), [2008] 2 FLR 1263 (no grave risk / intolerable situation)
- *F v M and N (Abduction: acquiescence: settlement)* [2008] EWHC 1525 (Fam), [2008] 2 FLR 1270 (child settled, no acquiescence)
- *M v M (Abduction: settlement)* [2008] EWHC 2049 (Fam), [2008] 2 FLR 1884 (children not settled, children did not object)
- *Re S (Abduction: children's representation)* [2008] EWHC 1798 (Fam), [2008] 2 FLR 1918 (children's objections)
- *Re G (Abduction)* [2008] EWHC 2558 (Fam), 2009] 1 FLR 760 (child did not object)
- *M v T (Abduction)* [2008] EWHC 1383 (Fam), [2009] 1 FLR 1309 (no consent / acquiescence, no grave risk / intolerable situation, children did not object)
- *Re Z (Abduction)* [2008] EWHC 3473 (Fam), [2009] 2 FLR 298
- *Re E (Abduction: intolerable situation)* [2008] EWHC 2122 (Fam), [2009] 2 FLR 485 (grave risk / intolerable situation)
- *Re P-J (Abduction: habitual residence: consent)* [2009] EWCA Civ 588, [2009] 2 FLR 1051 (no consent)
- *RS v KS (Abduction: wrongful retention)* [2009] EWHC 1494 (Fam), [2009] 2 FLR 1231 (intolerable situation)
- *Re H (Abduction)* [2009] EWHC 1735 (Fam), [2009] 2 FLR 1513 (grave risk of harm)
- *C v H (Abduction: consent)* [2009] EWHC 2660 (Fam), [2010] 1 FLR 225 (no consent)
- *De L v H* [2009] EWHC 3074 (Fam), [2010] 1 FLR 1229 (no acquiescence)

This case is also included in relation to:

F1   Convention designed to protect interests of children
F5   Hearing the child's views

F11　ART 13: ACQUIESCENCE

Re H (Abduction: acquiescence)

[1997] 1 FLR 872 at 884

House of Lords

Lord Browne-Wilkinson

Summary

To bring these strands together, in my view the applicable principles are as follows:

(1)　For the purposes of Art 13 of the Convention, the question whether the wronged parent has 'acquiesced' in the removal or retention of the child depends upon his actual state of mind. As Neill LJ said in *Re S (Minors)* 'the court is primarily concerned, not with the question of the other parent's perception of the applicant's conduct, but with the question whether the applicant acquiesced in fact'.

(2)　The subjective intention of the wronged parent is a question of fact for the trial judge to determine in all the circumstances of the case, the burden of proof being on the abducting parent.

(3)　The trial judge, in reaching his decision on that question of fact, will no doubt be inclined to attach more weight to the contemporaneous words and actions of the wronged parent than to his bare assertions in evidence of his intention. But that is a question of the weight to be attached to evidence and is not a question of law.

(4)　There is only one exception. Where the words or actions of the wronged parent clearly and unequivocally show and have led the other parent to believe that the wronged parent is not asserting or going to assert his right to the summary return of the child and are inconsistent with such return, justice requires that the wronged parent be held to have acquiesced.

Other significant cases on this issue:

- *D v S (Abduction: acquiescence)* [2008] EWHC 363 (Fam), [2008] 2 FLR 293
- *B-G v B-G (Abduction: acquiescence)* [2008] EWHC 688 (Fam), [2008] 2 FLR 965
- *BT v JRT (Abduction: conditional acquiescence and consent)* [2008] EWHC 1169 (Fam), [2008] 2 FLR 972 (consent)

F12   ART 13: CHILD'S OBJECTIONS

Re W (Abduction: child's objections)

[2010] EWCA Civ 520, [2010] 2 FLR 1165 at 1169 and 1170

Court of Appeal

Wilson LJ

[16] The father's first ground of appeal related to the age of G. At the time of the judge's decision she was aged six years and one month and, when interviewed by the Cafcass officer, she was a fortnight short of her sixth birthday. Mr Devereux argued that the defence based on a child's objections could not, or should not, apply to so young a child. He conceded that in *Re R (Child Abduction: Acquiescence)* [1995] 1 FLR 716 this court, by a majority, took into account the objections of two boys of whom the younger was only a month older than G. But he submitted that to take into account the objections of a child so young was very rare; that in the reported jurisprudence of England and Wales there was no example of it in relation to a child quite as young as G; that in the discretionary exercise the objections of the boys in *Re R* were ultimately overridden; and lastly that the notion that a child aged six could fall within the defence based on a child's objections was outside the contemplation of those who signed the Hague Convention in 1980.

[17] Mr Devereux's last submission seems to have been well founded. The defence was originally devised as an escape route for mature adolescents only slightly younger than the age of 16 at which, under Art 4, the Convention ceases to apply: Beaumont and McEleavy, The Hague Convention on International Child Abduction (Oxford University Press, 1999) at 178 and 191. But over the last thirty years the need to take decisions about much younger children not necessarily in accordance with their wishes but at any rate in the light of their wishes has taken hold: see Art 12 of the United Nations Convention on the Rights of the Child 1989 and note, for EU states, the subtle shift of emphasis given to Art 13 of the Hague Convention by Art 11(2) of Council Regulation (EC) No 2201/2003 (Brussels II Revised). Fortunately Art 13 was drawn in terms sufficiently flexible to accommodate this development in international thinking; and, although her comment was obiter, I am clear that, in context, the observation of Baroness Hale of Richmond in *Re D (Abduction: Rights of Custody)* [2006] UKHL 51, [2007] 1 AC 619, [2006] 3 WLR 989, [2007] 1 FLR 961, at [59], that 'children should be heard far more frequently in Hague Convention cases than has been the practice hitherto' related to the defence of a child's objections.

[18] I therefore concluded that in any full appeal Mr Devereux would not be able to persuade us that the age of G by itself foreclosed the possibility that she had objections to returning to Ireland of which account should be taken under Art 13. There is however a concern, which I share, that the lowering of the age at which a child's objections may be taken into account might gradually erode the high level of achievement of the Convention's objective, namely – in the vast majority of cases – to secure a swift restoration of children to the states from which they have been abducted. Such is a consideration of policy which should always carry significant weight in exercise of the discretion whether to refuse to order the return of an objecting child, but particularly so if that child is young; and Black J was right expressly to refer to it. A considerable safeguard against such erosion is to be found in the well-recognised expectation that in the discretionary exercise the objections of an older child will deserve greater weight than those of a younger child: *Re R*, cited above, per Balcombe LJ at 731A.

...

[22] Earlier confusion in our jurisprudence about the meaning of the phrase 'to take account' in Art 13 (exemplified, for example, in *Re T (Abduction: Child's Objections to Return)* [2000] 2 FLR 192 at 204B–D) has in my view now been eliminated. The phrase means no more than what it says so, albeit bounded of course by considerations of age and degree of maturity, it represents a fairly low threshold requirement. In particular it does not follow that the court should 'take account' of a child's objections only if they are so solidly based that they are likely to be determinative of the discretionary exercise which is to follow: see *Re D* above per Baroness Hale of Richmond, at [57], and *Re J and K (Abduction: Objections of Child)* [2004] EWHC 1985 (Fam), [2005] 1 FLR 273, at [31].

F13   ART 15: DETERMINATION BY REQUESTING STATE

Re D (Abduction: rights of custody)

[2006] UKHL 51, [2007] 1 FLR 961 at 975

House of Lords

Baroness Hale

Article 15

[39]   Article 3 makes it quite clear that, however wrongful the removal might be in the eyes of the English or Scottish laws of parental responsibility, what matters is whether it is 'in breach of rights of custody attributed to a person ... under the law of the state in which the child was habitually resident immediately before ...'. Plainly, therefore, the first question is 'what rights does that person have under the law of the home country'? The second question is, 'are those rights 'rights of custody' within the meaning of the Convention'? What is the court in a requested state to do if uncertain of the answers? Article 15 contemplates that it may seek a determination from the authorities of the requesting state:

> 'The judicial or administrative authorities of a contracting state may, prior to the making of an order for the return of the child, request that the applicant obtain from the authorities of the state of the habitual residence of the child a decision or other determination that the removal or retention was wrongful within the meaning of Article 3 of the Convention, where such decision or determination may be obtained in that state. The central authorities of the contracting states shall so far as practicable assist applicants to obtain such a decision or determination.'

The last sentence indicates that this is something other than the assertion or certificate of the central authority (cf the certificate as to the law of the requesting state which, under Art 8, sometimes accompanies a request from one central authority to another). It is a determination by the authorities having the power within the requesting state to make authoritative decisions relating to rights over children (see Professor Pérez-Vera, op cit, at para 86). The reference to 'administrative authorities' caters for those states in which some decisions about children are entrusted to bodies which are more administrative than judicial in character (see ibid, para 44).

[40] In this case, being unable to decide between the competing experts, the judge requested the father to obtain an Art 15 decision. The mother challenged the jurisdiction of the Romanian Court of First Instance which concluded that it did not have jurisdiction. The father appealed. The Court of (First) Appeal held that the first instance court had been wrong to refuse jurisdiction but that the father's rights did not amount to rights of custody for the purposes of Art 3 of the Hague Convention. The father launched a further appeal. In a fully reasoned judgment, the final Court of Appeal in Bucharest upheld the first appeal court's decision. It held that the equality of rights enjoyed by parents before their divorce is subject to exceptions. On divorce, the court is obliged to award custody to one or the other. The parent with custody shall exercise parental rights and fulfil parental duties. The parent without custody keeps his right to have personal contact with the child and to watch over his upbringing, education and professional training. The effect of divorce is to divide the bundle of rights between the parents. The agreement of the non-custodial parent is only required to certain specified measures – adoption and the loss or re-acquisition of Romanian citizenship. Otherwise, the divorced non-custodial parent does not have a right of veto of measures taken by the custodial parent relating to the child's person. His right to 'watch over' is not a right to direct. Law 272/2004, which came into effect on 1 January 2005, requiring both parents to give their consent to the removal of a child from Romania, was not retrospective in its effect. Not surprisingly, therefore, the Bucharest Court of Appeal concluded that the removal of the child in December 2002 had not been wrongful. (It is perhaps worth noting that, according to a note provided by the Romanian Ministry of Justice, the Romanian central authority had originally taken the same view of the father's rights as eventually did the Bucharest court and declined to transmit the father's request. It only did so after the father had launched proceedings here.)

[41] How then should the courts of the requested state respond to such a determination? Most certainly not as they did in this case. Having received a determination, binding between the parties, in the final court of the requesting state, the English High Court proceeded in effect to allow the father to challenge that ruling by adducing fresh expert evidence. The fact that the expert was jointly instructed does not cure the vice. This was a question on which there were known to be two views. The vice is that he was asked at all; and furthermore that he was asked to answer questions about the rights which the father enjoyed under Romanian law. The fact that a first instance court in Romania had reached a different conclusion in another case shortly before this decision (the *Rada* case) is not a sufficient reason for an English court to query the decision of the final Court of Appeal in Romania in the instant case. The ultimate result was that the English trial judge took a different view from the view taken in Romania. She ordered the return of the child to a country whose courts had authoritatively ruled that the mother was within her rights to remove the child to live in this country.

[42] How could this have happened? On 28 July 2005, the Court of Appeal handed down its decision in *Hunter v Murrow (Abduction: Rights of Custody)* [2005] EWCA Civ 976, [2005] 2 FLR 1119. The English court had made an Art 15 request to the New Zealand court concerning a child whose unmarried parents had separated before he was born and had never lived together, although father and child had had considerable contact by informal agreement with the mother. It appears that the father had neither parental responsibility nor rights of veto. Nevertheless, the New Zealand court held that the access which the father had enjoyed by virtue of the agreement with the mother amounted to 'rights of custody' for the purpose of the Hague Convention. As the researches of counsel demonstrated, this takes the concept of 'rights of custody' further than it has been taken in other common law jurisdictions.

[43] The Court of Appeal declined to accept that ruling. But their reasoning is important. They did not challenge the ruling as to the content of the father's rights in New Zealand law. They merely challenged the characterisation of those rights as rights of custody for Convention purposes. This was on the basis, long established in the English application of the Convention, that rights of custody are to be distinguished from mere rights of access: see, most recently, *Re V-B (Abduction: Custody Rights)* [1999] 2 FLR 192 and *Re P (Abduction Consent)* [2004] EWCA Civ 971, [2005] Fam 293, [2004] 2 FLR 1057. *Hunter v Murrow* afforded no warrant at all for allowing the father to challenge the Romanian court's decision as to the content of his rights under Romanian law. Save in exceptional circumstances, for example where the ruling has been obtained by fraud or in breach of the rules of natural justice, it must be conclusive as to the parties' rights under the law of the requesting state.

[44] Indeed, Art 15 might be thought to go further. The foreign court is asked to rule on whether the removal is wrongful in Convention terms. The Court of Appeal relied upon the decision of this House in *Re J* (para [38], above), the authority cited by Lowe, Everall and Nicholls, *International Movement of Children* (Family Law, 2004), para 15.9, in support of their proposition that 'a declaration made under Art 15 can be no more than persuasive, and cannot bind the parties or the authorities of the requested state, who will accept as much or as little of the judgment as they choose.' But *Re J* was not an Art 15 case. It is one thing to fail to give effect to a foreign custody order which is not binding upon the courts of this country. It is another thing to fail to give effect to a ruling, which the courts of this country have themselves requested, as to the content and effect of foreign law. Given, however, that the Hague Convention terms have an autonomous meaning, it is possible to contemplate the possibility that the foreign court's characterisation of the effect of its domestic law in Hague Convention terms is mistaken. We are here concerned, not with domestic law, but with the effect given domestically to autonomous terms in an international treaty which are meant to be applied consistently by all member states. We, just as much as they, are bound by Lord Steyn's injunction, in the context of the United Nations Convention Relating to the Status of Refugees 1951 and Protocol of 1967, in *R v Secretary of State for the Home Department ex parte Adan; R v Same ex parte Subaskaran; R v Same ex parte Aitseguer* [2001] 2 AC 477, [2001] INLR 44, at 517 and 56 respectively:

> 'In practice it is left to national courts, faced with a material disagreement on an issue of interpretation, to resolve it. But in doing so it must search, untrammelled by notions of its national legal culture, for the true autonomous and international meaning of the treaty. And there can only be one true meaning.'

The foreign court is much better placed than the English to understand the true meaning and effect of its own laws in Convention terms. Only if its characterisation of the parent's rights is clearly out of line with the international understanding of the Convention's terms, as may well have been the case in *Hunter v Murrow*, should the court in the requested state decline to follow it.

[45] While ultimately, therefore, the decision is one for the courts of the requested state, those courts must attach considerable weight to the authoritative decision of the requesting state on both issues. I do not share the view of the Court of Appeal that Art 15 would be more useful were it directed solely to ascertaining rights under the domestic law of the requesting state. It could with advantage draw a clearer distinction between the two issues. The reasons for rejecting a determination of the first issue will be different from the reasons for rejecting a determination on the second. But we still have something to learn from the requesting state's characterisation of the position.

[46] Perhaps one day, the problem will disappear. All member states will accord equal parental responsibility to all parents, with universal rights of veto, and all will regard these as rights of custody. There is a general trend towards shared parental authority – and even shared parenting – after separation and divorce, but it is not universal. It is not so very long ago that the law of this country was very different. Particularly when a country first accedes to the Hague Convention, it may be useful in cases of doubt to obtain an authoritative ruling on the content and effect of their law. It is in their interests, and those of the applicant, that this be obtained as quickly as possible. It is sad that it took so long in this case, but the Romanian authorities must be mystified indeed that the English courts have ordered the return to Romania of a child whose removal the Romanian final court of appeal has authoritatively and irrevocably determined was not wrongful.

General notes:

See also the speech of Lord Brown at [77]–[84].

Other significant cases on this issue:

- *Re T (Abduction: rights of custody)* [2008] EWHC 809 (Fam), [2008] 2 FLR 1794

This case is also included in relation to:

F8   Art 3: wrongful removal
F14 Art 20: human rights arguments
F15 Art 21 and rights of access: addressing the real issue

F14   ART 20: HUMAN RIGHTS ARGUMENTS

Re D (Abduction: rights of custody)

[2006] UKHL 51, [2007] 1 FLR 961 at 983

House of Lords

Baroness Hale

Human rights

[63]   Two human rights issues have been canvassed before us. First are the Art 8 of the European Convention for the Protection of Human Rights and Fundamental Freedoms 1950 (the European Convention) rights of all the parties to this case to respect for their family life. Second is the Art 6 right of the mother to a fair trial of the issue between her and the father. On the one hand, the plaintiff in a Hague Convention case has the benefit of automatic legal aid, without merits or means test, enhanced by the services of the specialist practitioners to whom these cases are referred by the central authority. On the other hand, the defendant is only entitled to legal aid on the usual means and merits tests, and may well not find his or her way to a specialist solicitor in the early days when crucial decisions have to be taken and affidavits filed. This, it is argued, it not the 'equality of arms' which is inherent in the concept of a fair trial.

[64]   In this case, however, the mother has been adequately represented throughout. It is by no means clear that had counsel been available when the case took a wrong turn on 1 August 2005 the outcome would have been any different. Nor is this the case in which to explore whether the outcome either way would represent a disproportionate interference in the right to respect for the family lives of either of these parents with their child.

[65]   Such arguments are not, however, always irrelevant in Hague Convention cases. Article 20 of the Hague Convention reserves the right of Member States to refuse to return a child if 'this would not be permitted by the fundamental principles of the requested state relating to the protection of human rights and fundamental freedoms'. Article 20 is not incorporated into the Child Abduction and Custody Act 1985. At that stage, there was no human rights instrument incorporated into UK domestic law. The Human Rights Act 1998 (the 1998 Act) has now given the rights set out in the European Convention legal effect in this country. By virtue of s 6 of the 1998 Act, it is unlawful for the court, as a public authority, to act in a way which is incompatible with a person's European

Convention rights. In this way, the court is bound to give effect to the European Convention rights in Hague Convention cases just as in any other. Article 20 of the Hague Convention has been given domestic effect by a different route.

Other significant cases on this issue:

*   *Re J (Child returned abroad: Convention rights)* [2005] UKHL 40, [2005] 2 FLR 802 per Baroness Hale at [42]–[45]

This case is also included in relation to:

F8   Art 3: wrongful removal
F13   Art 15: determination by requesting state
F15   Art 21 and rights of access: addressing the real issue

F15   ART 21 AND RIGHTS OF ACCESS: ADDRESSING THE REAL ISSUE

Re D (Abduction: rights of custody)

[2006] UKHL 51, [2007] 1 FLR 961 at 984

House of Lords

Baroness Hale

Rights of access

[66]   In many Hague Convention cases, the 'left behind' parent is seeking, not the day-to-day care of the child, but to keep the same sort of relationship which he or she enjoyed with the child before the abduction. Sometimes this could never be done unless the child returns to live permanently in the home country. Not all countries are as sanguine about allowing the primary carer to relocate to another country as we have been. Sometimes, however, sensible arrangements could be made to translate the contact which was enjoyed in the home country into contact across international borders. Now that travel within Europe is so accessible and inexpensive, and so many other means of communication at long distance exist, this should be a real possibility in many cases. It is thought that many Hague Convention cases could be settled on this basis were the machinery available to do so. Such settlements would be much more likely if the parties have not become entrenched in their hostility as a result of the Hague Convention proceedings.

[67]   At the moment, however, the claim for return under the Hague Convention proceeds in its summary and (usually) speedy way. Any application for a residence, care or supervision order under the Children Act 1989 (or their equivalents elsewhere in the UK) has to await the determination of the Hague proceedings: see s 9 of the Child Abduction and Custody Act 1985. Under Art 16 of the Hague Convention, the court cannot decide upon the merits of rights of custody until it has been determined that the child is not to be returned under the Convention. But this does not apply to contact and rights of access. I notice that in *Hunter v Murrow*[1] (para [42], above), at para [31], Thorpe LJ canvassed the possibility of revisiting the decisions in *Re G (A Minor) (Enforcement of Access Abroad)* [1993] Fam 216, [1993] 1 FLR 669 and *Re T and Others (Minors) (Hague Convention: Access)* [1993] 2 FLR 617 in the light of

---

[1]   *Hunter v Murrow (Abduction: Rights of Custody)* [2005] EWCA Civ 976, [2005] 2 FLR 1119.

more recent international jurisprudence. It would not be beyond the wit of man to devise a procedure whereby the facilitation of rights of access in this country under Art 21 were in contemplation at the same time as the return of the child under Art 12.

This case is also included in relation to:

F8   Art 3: wrongful removal
F13 Art 15: determination by requesting state
F14 Art 20: human rights arguments

Brussels II Revised

F16   BRUSSELS II REVISED: ARTS 11 AND 42

Re A (Custody decision after Maltese non-return order)

[2006] EWHC 3397 (Fam), [2007] 1 FLR 1923 at 1925, 1926, 1946 and 1948

Family Division

Singer J

[5]   The application before me is maybe the first of its kind in England and Wales, but I cannot be absolutely certain of that. It is an application which has only been possible since the regulation to which I will refer to as BIIR came into force. The full title of that instrument is Council Regulation (EC) Number 2201/2003 of 27 November 2003 Concerning Jurisdiction and the Recognition and Enforcement of Judgments in Matrimonial Matters and the Matters of Parental Responsibility, repealing Council Regulation (EC) No 1347/2000 (Brussels II Revised). It will therefore be readily apparent why I refer to it as BIIR.

[6]   Amongst its many provisions, BIIR complements or supplements the Hague Convention on Child Abduction incorporated into English law in the Child Custody and Abduction Act 1985 by grafting some specific provisions onto the Hague Convention in cases which involve a removal or retention as between two Member States of the European Union, as long as one of them is not Denmark.

[7]   The relevant Article for present purposes is Art 11 of BIIR. Where a court refuses to return a child pursuant to Art 13 of the Hague Convention, then the home court (in this case England) must be notified of that fact and sent the relevant documents very swiftly. It is then open to either parent within 3 months to move the home court 'so that the court can examine the question of custody of the child'. Article 11 goes on to make it clear that, notwithstanding the fact that the requested court (Malta in this case) declined to order the return of the child under the Hague Convention, the judgment of this court under these provisions, having examined the question of custody, can reach a conclusion which does indeed require the return of the child to England, as well as dealing

with other matters concerning his custody. In that event and subject to the issue of a certificate under Art 42 of BIIR, the order of the English court is immediately enforceable without more ado and without reinvestigation of the merits within the jurisdiction of the requested court, Malta. The relevant provisions, which I have summarised and referred to only as far as is necessary for present purposes, are contained in Arts 11(6), (7) and (8) and 42 of BIIR.

...

[9] I should at this point refer to Art 42 to a somewhat greater extent. Article 42 is the Article of BIIR which is within the section of that regulation dealing with the enforceability of certain judgments, including judgments which require the return of a child. Art 42 says this in para (1):

> 'The return of a child ... entailed by an enforceable judgment given in a Member State shall be recognised and enforceable in another Member State without the need for a declaration of enforceability and without any possibility of opposing its recognition if the judgment has been certified in the Member State of origin in accordance with paragraph 2.'

[10] The certificate referred to can only be issued by the judge of origin, that is to say me, if I make an order to that effect, according to Art 42(2) of BIIR, and only if:

> '(a) the child was given an opportunity to be heard, unless a hearing was considered inappropriate having regard to his or her age or degree of maturity;
> (b) the parties were given an opportunity to be heard; and
> (c) the court has taken into account in issuing its judgment the reasons for and evidence underlying the order issued pursuant to Article 13 of the 1980 Hague Convention.
>
> In the event that the court or any other authority takes measures to ensure the protection of the child after its return to the State of habitual residence, the certificate shall contain details of such measures.'

[11] Before I leave Art 42 of BIIR I should mention that an additional provision of Art 42(1) is to this effect:

> 'Even if national law does not provide for enforceability by operation of law, notwithstanding any appeal, of a judgment requiring the return of the child mentioned in Article 11(b)(8), the court of origin may declare the judgment enforceable.'

In other words, if I make an order entailing S's return to this jurisdiction, and if I issue a certificate as envisaged by Art 42, then, notwithstanding the absence of any provision of English law expressly to that effect, I can answer question 10 in the certificate whether the judgment is enforceable in the Member State of origin by saying, yes, if I direct, as in such circumstances I would, that the judgment and order be immediately enforceable whether or not any application for permission to appeal is made or granted.

...

[108] Therefore, I do not feel able to place any reliance on what are said to be the child's wishes not to return to England, quite apart from the fact that they are only a consideration which, in my view, would not have added significantly to what, in my view, is said to be an Art 13(b) case, which no longer, on the evidence I have read and heard, stands up. I have already commented on the fact that, as I read the order, Magistrate Coppini was not finding that the additional defence of the child's objections under Art 13(a) was established.

[109] BIIR contains a passage in Art 11(4), which I will read it in its entirety:

> 'A court cannot refuse to return a child on the basis of article 13(b) of the 1980 Hague Convention if it is established that adequate arrangements have been made to secure the protection of the child after his or her return.'

This strengthens the obligation to return by limiting the Art 13(b) defence even more than, certainly in English law, it has been constrained by, in effect, requiring the court to consider whether adequate arrangements have been made to secure the protection of the child after his or her return. This, of course, presumes that such a need is perceived in what would be an Art 13(b) situation.

[110] Again, I am not being in any sense critical, but the fact is, apart from the request made at the magistrate's direction between the central authorities that led, so far as I can tell, to no information being forthcoming (partly no doubt because the nature of the risk was not apparent at that stage) there was no information before the court in Malta as to what, if anything, could have been done to protect S after return to England. The magistrate refers to it in the passage I have read where, having referred to the child's own views, he says:

> 'As yet, no proof has been provided to the satisfaction of this court that adequate arrangements have been made to secure the protection of the child after his return.'

...

[116] So what I propose to do is to say that, having examined the question of custody of S, I order that he remain living with his mother (as previously ordered by the Buxton magistrates in 2002) and with that purpose, he be returned to the jurisdiction of England and Wales by the father and/or as directed in any enforcement proceedings in Malta which may be necessary to achieve that end.

[117] The court of its own motion orders that S is henceforth until further order during his minority a ward of this court. I shall direct that the mother should be the plaintiff in the wardship proceedings. The father shall be the first defendant. S, by his guardian, Teresa Julian, represented as before by CAFCASS Legal, should be the second defendant. I shall make an order that the wardship proceedings be restored for directions, including directions as to future contact with the father, before Singer J if available no sooner than five days after S's return to this jurisdiction and no later than 21 days after that return, on application by the mother and/or the guardian. I will also direct, as provided for in Art 42(1) of BIIR, that this judgment is enforceable forthwith, notwithstanding any appeal.

[118] I shall prepare the certificate and draw to the associate's attention that, under r 7.51 of the Family Proceedings Rules 1991, the court must serve the certificate on all the parties and on the central authority of England and Wales. I would like to see the order in draft before it is finalised. An expedited transcript will be prepared at public expense.

F17   BRUSSELS II REVISED: ARTS 11 AND 19

Re RD (Child Abduction) (Brussels II Revised: Arts 11(7) and 19)

[2009] 1 FLR 586 at 590 and 600

Family Division

Singer J

The scope of Art 11(7) of BIIR

[17] The first question which falls for decision in this case is whether F's application under Art 11(7) of BIIR is competent.

[18] BIIR came into force on 1 March 2005 and is binding on all EU Member States with the exception of Denmark. It is subject therefore to that exception that I use the term Member State in this judgment. Article 11 of BIIR has the effect of 'complementing' or 'supplementing' practice and procedure in Hague abduction cases between Member States. Paragraphs (2) to (5) of Art 11 relate to the Hague proceedings themselves, conducted in the courts of the Member State to which the child has been removed or where the child is retained (the Receiving State). The relevant paragraphs for present purposes are 11(6), (7) and (8) which grafted on a wholly new jurisdictional opportunity for the unsuccessful party to the Hague litigation in the Receiving State to re-litigate the question of return to the child's Home State in the courts of the Home State ...

[19] It is, in my judgment, beyond argument that the document transmission requirements imposed by Art 11(6) on the Receiving State, and the notification and submission invitation requirements on the court or Central Authority of the Home State contained in Art 11(7), only arise where 'a court has issued an order on non-return pursuant to Art 13 of the 1980 Hague Convention': the express opening words of Art 11(6).

[20] Only where the child's non-return is pursuant to Art 13 of the Hague Convention, therefore, is the Home Court competent 'to examine the question of custody of the child' as envisaged by Art 11(7). And it is only such a welfare-based inquiry which can lead to a 'judgment which requires the return of the child issued by a court having jurisdiction under this Regulation' which Art 11(8) renders summarily enforceable under the provisions of s 4 (and especially Arts 40(1)(b) and 42, and the certificate to be issued in the Annex IV standard form).

[21] The preliminary Recital 18 to BIIR refers forward to the Art 11(6) and (7) requirements as obligations which arise 'where a court has decided not to return a child on the basis of Art 13 of the 1980 Hague Convention'. The June 2005 updated version of the Practice Guide reflects the same position at para 3 of s VII which (in its relevant parts) reads:

'Having regard to the strict conditions set out in article 13 of the 1980 Hague Convention and article 11(2) to (5) of the Regulation, the courts are likely to decide that the child shall return in the vast majority of cases.

However, in those exceptional cases where a court nevertheless decides that a child shall not return pursuant to article 13 of the 1980 Hague Convention, the Regulation foresees a special procedure in article 11(6) and (7).'

[22] My conclusion is therefore that F in this case is not entitled to apply under Art 11(7) of BIIR. In the event no party in this (or in the parallel case) argued to the contrary at the final hearings.

...

Summary of conclusions

[67] To summarise therefore, the following are the conclusions which I have reached and which I regard as determinative of the central question whether there is any jurisdictional basis upon which F can pursue a welfare-based inquiry to determine where RD resides and what contact arrangements should apply.

- As Art 13 of the Hague Convention was not the basis for the Portuguese non-return order, BIIR Arts 11(6) to (8) do not apply. F's October 2007 application expressly and solely based on these provisions must therefore fail.
- There is no jurisdiction to 'save' that process by amendment to seek relief under specific provisions of the Children Act and/or the inherent jurisdiction. If, contrary to that conclusion, a discretion to permit amendment is available to F then I would decline to permit amendment.
- In any event, any such reconstituted application would have to be stayed if not indeed dismissed pursuant to requirements imposed upon the English court by BIIR Art 19(2) and (3). The English court must defer to the apparent determination of the Portuguese court to proceed with M's Oporto parental responsibility application with which it was first seised, unless and until it emerges that the Portuguese court concludes that it has no jurisdiction.

- The same considerations require the application of BIIR Art 19 to F's January 2008 Children Act application.
- Accordingly I propose to strike out the Art 11(6) application, and to stay the Children Act proceedings.

F18   BRUSSELS II REVISED: ART 11(7)

M v T (Abduction: Brussels II Revised, Art 11(7))

[2010] EWHC 1479 (Fam), [2010] 2 FLR 1685 at 1690 and 1692

Family Division

Charles J

[16]   So I pause to ask, what is the legal approach to be taken to an application under Art 11(7)? I ask that question because plainly it informs the general approach that should be taken to such cases. As to that, I gratefully adopt and apply the reasoning and conclusions of Singer J in a case called *Re A; HA v MB (Brussels II Revised: Art 11(7) Application)* [2007] EWHC 2016 (Fam), [2008] 1 FLR 289. The most relevant part of the judgment is from para [66] onwards. In particular I highlight paras [83], [87] and [91] which state:

> '[83]   The scheme is cogent and comprehensive. The courts of the Member State away from which a child has been unlawfully removed or retained continue to have jurisdiction until the Article 10 conditions are met. Thus the ability of parents (and any institution or body having rights of custody) to seise the home court notwithstanding that the child has in fact acquired habitual residence in another Member State continues (absent acquiescence) for a minimum period of one year after the holder of rights of custody "has or should have had knowledge of the whereabouts of the child", and the child is settled in the new environment. At what point, if at all, the parents' ability to seise the home court comes to an end depends upon the attainment of one of the conditions in sub-paragraphs (i) to (iv), which follow a logical progression.
>
> …
>
> [87]   Clearly F has not acquiesced in A's removal or retention. The general situation described the first part of Article 10(b) is, in my judgment, established. None of the additional conditions set out in Article 10(b)(i) to (iii) which would bring to an end England's retention of jurisdiction has been satisfied. As for paragraph (b)(iv), "a judgment on custody that does not entail the return of the child" has not yet been issued by the English court. It is of course the result for which M contends.
>
> [88]   It follows that until such an order is issued F remained and remains able to seise the English court under the general

jurisdictional rule set out in Article 8, as read subject to Article 10. F in October 2006 launched the applications under the Children Act which I have described. Lodging and serving those applications with the court satisfied the requirements of English domestic law and of Article 16(1)(a), so that the English court became validly seised.

...

[91] It follows that I agree with the first two sentences of a new paragraph which has been added to the June 2005 version of the Practice Guide. It is contained within Section VII, The Rules on Child Abduction, and reads:

"4. The court of origin is competent to deal with the substance of the case in its entirety

Articles 11(7) and 42

The court of origin which takes a decision in the context of Article 11(7) is competent to deal with the substance of the case in its entirety. Its jurisdiction is therefore not limited to deciding on the question of the child, but may also decide for example on access rights. *The judge should, in principle, be in the position that he or she would have been in if the abducting parent had not abducted the child* but instead had seised the court of origin to modify a previous decision on custody or to ask for authorisation to change the habitual residence of the child. It could be that the person requesting return of the child did not have the residence of the child before the abduction or even that that person is willing to accept a change in the habitual residence of the child in the other Member State provided that his or her visiting rights are modified accordingly.

The words which I have italicised should be understood, in my view, as though they read "the judge should, in principle, be in the position to exercise the jurisdiction that he or she would have been in if the abducting parent had not abducted the child ..."'

I also note that at the end of the judgment Singer J, in an annex, sets out a table of 'Outgoing EU/Hague applications refused by court abroad' which shows an increasing number, but not significant numbers given the number of cases that are heard under the Hague Convention in this country.

[17] What I take from Singer J's conclusions is that from his table and the points I have already made, there are likely to be growing numbers of cases under Art 11(7). As to the jurisdiction and role of the court, it seems

to me: first, that what the court is not doing is carrying out an appeal process in respect of a decision of a foreign court or anything akin to that. Secondly, it seems to me that the court is not itself applying Art 13 or a Hague jurisdiction as such. Rather, it seems to me, that what the court is doing is exercising the jurisdiction it always held under Art 10 which is a welfare jurisdiction and, therefore, it is a welfare approach that has to be applied. Within that approach applying English law, there is the ability of the court to order a summary return of a child to another jurisdiction. So it seems to me that the court in exercising its welfare jurisdiction has the power to make a summary order under Art 11(7) in an appropriate case (see by analogy to the decision of the House of Lords in *Re J (A Child: Custody Rights Jurisdiction)* [2005] UKHL 40, [2006] 1 AC 80, [2005] 3 WLR 14 sub nom *J (Child Returned Abroad: Convention Rights)* [2005] 2 FLR 802). In particular, I would draw attention to para [26] of the speech of Baroness Hale of Richmond in *Re J* which identifies that summary orders are within the jurisdiction of the court and from para [29] onwards where she deals with the factors to be taken into account by the court in making the choice as to whether or not to order a summary return or to embark upon a welfare inquiry.

[18] Necessarily, a summary return does not involve a full welfare inquiry or anything approaching it, albeit it that it is applying a welfare test. In the present context it would, however, inevitably involve an effective rejection or an effective refusal not to follow the decision of the foreign court not to return the child under Art 13, but that is inherent in Art 11(7) itself. It seems to me that cases could well arise for a variety of reasons in which this court may feel it appropriate to exercise its jurisdiction under Art 11(7) on a summary basis albeit applying a welfare test. There may, for example, be differences if the refusing court acted under Art 13a rather than 13b. In that context Art 11(4) may have some relevance.

...

[20] So it seems to me, given the existence of the power and jurisdiction to make a summary order and having regard to the history of this case and the lessons that could be learned from it, that as soon as possible after an application under Art 11(7) is issued, there should be directions from the court in which the court should expressly consider the approach that is to be taken to the case, namely: is the case to be determined on a summary basis and/or is there to be a welfare inquiry and, if so, what is to be the extent of that welfare inquiry and, therefore, what directions need to be made in that context? Also importantly, at that first directions hearing or as soon as possible thereafter, the issue whether or not the child should be joined and, if so, the representation of the child, should be determined.

[21]   Generally it, therefore, seems to me – and in this as I understand it I was supported by those who were representing Cafcass Legal and its High Court team – that they should be notified as soon as such an application is made and at the first directions hearing the court should consider whether or not the child should be joined and/or whether Cafcass Legal or its High Court team should be invited to make representations to the court concerning the approach that the court should take in the given case. Further, if child is joined and Cafcass are to take an active part, it is clearly of importance that at the first directions hearing and thereafter directions are given to them as to the role that they are expected to perform. Initially that role could be arguing on behalf of a child that a summary process should not or should be adopted. If the court decides there should not be a summary process and their role would be to assist the court in determining the nature and extent of the welfare inquiry, and in carrying it out.

[22]   Additionally, and at an early stage, it seems to me that there is a need to consider issues relating to interim contact. That was done in this case but the issue, as I see it, needs to be considered both as to whether interim contact should take place and whether or not it should take place within this jurisdiction. Following on from the decision of Singer J (which I have referred to and in particular, paras [95] onwards) if an order for contact was made in this jurisdiction that would not amount to an order for return. That founded my decision in January to order interim contact in this country in March. There were practical advantages to that in the sense that the mother's attendance in the UK for those directions was covered by her public funding as is normal albeit the contact was not. I record that that contact has been of considerable assistance to the court, and as I understand it also to the guardian, and it seems to me to the parties in determining their positions in this case.

[23]   The other thing, of course, that needs to be closely looked at is the timetable for a final determination of the Art 11(7) case. It seems to me that that has to be done by reference to and to reflect the urgency reflected by Art 11 itself, remembering the inevitable fact that what the court is dealing with is a child who was habitually resident here and who, as a result of a wrongful removal or a retention is in another country.

Other significant cases on this issue:

- *Re F (Abduction: refusal to return)* [2009] EWCA Civ 416, [2009] 2 FLR 1023
- *Re H (Jurisdiction)* [2009] EWHC 2280 (Fam), [2010] 1 FLR 598

Non-Hague Convention

F19 WELFARE PRINCIPLE APPLIES

Re J (Child returned abroad: Convention rights)

[2005] UKHL 40, [2005] 2 FLR 802 at 807, 808 and 809

House of Lords

Baroness Hale

The issue of principle

[14]   The issue, therefore, is how, if at all, it is relevant that the laws and procedures in the country to which the child is to be returned are very different from those which would apply if the child's future were to be decided here. Competing views have been expressed in the Court of Appeal. One view is encapsulated in the judgment of Ward LJ in the case of *Re JA (Child Abduction: Non-Convention Country)* [1998] 1 FLR 231, the other in the judgment of Thorpe LJ in the case of *Osman v Elasha* [2000] Fam 62, [1999] 2 FLR 642.

…

[17]   Both judgments were based on what their authors saw as a consistent line of previous authority, on the one hand expecting that the foreign system of law would be broadly comparable to our own and, on the other hand, assuming that it will be in the child's best interests to return to his home country even if its system of family law is very different from our own. As this is the first time that the issue has come before this House, it seems right to remind ourselves of first principles.

The principles

[18]   Three points can be readily agreed. First, since 1925, any court which is determining any question with respect to the upbringing of a child has had a statutory duty to regard the welfare of the child as its paramount consideration. Before that, the principle that the welfare of the individual child might outweigh any other considerations had been developed by the Chancery judges in the exercise of their inherent jurisdiction over children. The statutory duty was first laid down by s 1 of

the Guardianship of Infants Act 1925 and later consolidated in s 1 of the Guardianship of Minors Act 1971. It applied to 'any proceedings in any court' and the court was expressly instructed to disregard whether from any other point of view the claim of the father was superior to that of the mother or vice versa. That proposition was regarded as too obvious to require repetition when the welfare principle was re-enacted in s 1(1) of the Children Act 1989. It applies in any proceedings where the court has jurisdiction to determine a question concerning a child's upbringing, whether on an application for an order under the Children Act 1989 itself, as in this case, or in the inherent jurisdiction of the High Court.

...

[20]   Secondly, however, the application of the welfare principle may be specifically excluded by statute; one example is the Child Abduction and Custody Act 1985, passed to give effect in domestic law to two international treaties, the Hague Convention and the European Convention on the Recognition and Enforcement of Decisions Concerning Custody of Children and on the Restoration of Custody of Children 1980. Both treaties were motivated by the belief that it is in the best interests of children for disputes about their future to be decided in their home countries, and that one parent should not be able to take a child from one country to another, either in the hope of obtaining a tactical advantage in the dispute or to avoid the effects of an order made in the home country. Instead of deciding the dispute itself, therefore, the country to which the child was taken agreed that with very few exceptions it would either send the child back or enforce the order made in the home country. This necessarily meant that the receiving country might, on occasion, have to do something which was not in the best interests of the individual child involved. The States which became parties to these treaties accepted this disadvantage to some individual children for the sake of the greater advantage to children in general. Parents would be deterred from moving their children across borders without consent. States which sent other countries' children back could expect that other States would send their own children back in return. The obligations were mutual and reciprocal.

[21]   The Convention is widely regarded as a great success, particularly in combating the paradigm case which its authors had in mind: the child who was living with one parent but snatched or spirited away by the other. Currently the Convention is in force between the UK and the Contracting States listed in Sch 2 to the Child Abduction and Custody (Parties to Convention) Order 1986, as amended. The two most recent entrants are Brazil and Lithuania. In at least three Contracting States, Turkey, Turkmenistan and Uzbekistan, the predominant religion practised by their populations is Islam.Obviously, the cultures and legal systems of the Contracting States will differ widely from one another. All are prepared to accept these differences for the sake of the reciprocal benefits which

membership can bring. But one group of states is conspicuous by its absence. These are States which adopt some form of Shariah law.

[22] There is no warrant, either in statute or authority, for the principles of the Hague Convention to be extended to countries which are not parties to it. Section 1(1) of the Children Act 1989, like s 1 of the Guardianship of Infants Act 1925 before it, is of general application. This is so even in a case where a friendly foreign State has made orders about the child's future. This was explained by Morton J in *Re B's Settlement; B v B* [1940] Ch 54, at 63–64:

> 'I desire to say quite plainly that in my view this Court is bound in every case, without exception, to treat the welfare of its ward as being the first and paramount consideration, whatever orders may have been made by the Courts of any other country.'

[23] Despite some critical initial comment by authors on private international law, that view has now become orthodox. It was expressly approved by the Judicial Committee of the Privy Council in *McKee v McKee* [1951] AC 352, which emphasised that there was a choice open to the trial judge:

> 'It is possible that a case might arise in which it appeared to a court, before which the question of custody of an infant came, that it was in the best interests of that infant that it should not look beyond the circumstances in which its jurisdiction was invoked and for that reason give effect to the foreign judgment without further inquiry. It is, however, the negation of the proposition ... that the infant's welfare is the paramount consideration, to say that where the learned trial judge has in his discretion thought fit not to take the drastic course above indicated, but to examine all the circumstances and form an independent judgment, his decision ought for that reason to be overruled. Once it is conceded that the court of Ontario had jurisdiction to entertain the question of custody and that it need not blindly follow on order made by a foreign court, the consequence cannot be escaped that it must form an independent judgment on the question, although in doing so it will give proper weight to the foreign judgment. What is the proper weight will depend on the circumstances of each case.'

[24] This House, in the leading case of *J and Another v C and Others* [1970] AC 668, (1969) FLR Rep 360, regarded it as clearly decided by *Re B's Settlement; B v B* and *McKee v McKee* that the existence of a foreign order would not oust the jurisdiction or preclude the operation of the welfare principle. This applies a fortiori where the foreign court would have had jurisdiction to make an order but has not done so, so that no question of comity arises: see Lord Guest at 700G–701B, Lord MacDermott at 714F–G, and Lord Upjohn at 720C–E.

[25] Hence, in all non-Convention cases, the courts have consistently held that they must act in accordance with the welfare of the individual child. If they do decide to return the child, that is because it is in his best interests to do so, not because the welfare principle has been superseded by some other consideration. This was so, even in those cases decided around the time that the Hague Convention was being implemented here, where it was held that the courts should take account of its philosophy: see, for example, *G v G (Minors) (Abduction)* [1991] 2 FLR 506. The Court of Appeal, in *Re P (A Minor) (Child Abduction: Non-Convention Country)* [1997] Fam 45, [1997] 1 FLR 780, has held that the Hague Convention concepts are not to be applied in a non-Convention case. Hence, the first two propositions set out by Hughes J in this case were entirely correct: the child's welfare is paramount and the specialist rules and concepts of the Hague Convention are not to be applied by analogy in a non-Convention case.

[26] Thirdly, however, the court does have power, in accordance with the welfare principle, to order the immediate return of a child to a foreign jurisdiction without conducting a full investigation of the merits. In a series of cases during the 1960s, these came to be known as 'kidnapping' cases. The principles were summed up by Buckley LJ in *Re L (Minors) (Wardship: Jurisdiction)* [1974] 1 WLR 250, at 264, rightly described by Ward LJ in *Re P (A Minor) (Child Abduction: Non-Convention Country)* and *Re JA (Child Abduction: Non-Convention Country)* as the locus classicus:

'To take a child from his native land, to remove him to another country where, maybe, his native tongue is not spoken, to divorce him from the social customs and contacts to which he has been accustomed, to interrupt his education in his native land and subject him to a foreign system of education, are all acts (offered here as examples and of course not as a complete catalogue of possible relevant factors) which are likely to be psychologically disturbing to the child, particularly at a time when his family life is also disrupted. If such a case is promptly brought to the attention of a court in this country, the judge may feel that it is in the best interests of the infant that these disturbing factors should be eliminated from his life as speedily as possible. A full investigation of the merits of the case in an English court may be incompatible with achieving this. The judge may well be persuaded that it would be better for the child that those merits should be investigated in a court in his native country.'

[27] He went on to emphasise that in doing so the court was not punishing the parent for her conduct, but applying the cardinal rule. The same point was made by Ormrod LJ in *Re R (Minors) (Wardship: Jurisdiction)* (1981) 2 FLR 416, at 425: the 'so-called kidnapping' of the child, or the order of a foreign court, were relevant considerations:

'but the weight to be given to either of them must be measured in terms of the interests of the child, not in terms of penalising the "kidnapper", or of comity, or any other abstraction. "Kidnapping", like other kinds of unilateral action in relation to children, is to be strongly discouraged, but the discouragement must take the form of a *swift, realistic and unsentimental assessment of the best interests of the child, leading, in proper cases, to the prompt return of the child to his or her own country*, but *not* the sacrifice of the child's welfare to some other principle of law.' (first emphasis mine)

[28] It is plain, therefore, that there is always a choice to be made. Summary return should not be the automatic reaction to any and every unauthorised taking or keeping a child from his home country. On the other hand, summary return may very well be in the best interests of the individual child.

Other significant cases on this issue:

- *Re H (Abduction: non-Convention application)* [2006] EWHC 199 (Fam), [2006] 2 FLR 314.
- *E v E* [2007] EWHC 276 (Fam), [2007] 1 FLR 1977.

This case is also included in relation to:

A9 Culture and welfare
F20 No 'strong presumption' in favour of return
F21 Other relevant factors
H39 Limits on appeal court's authority

F20   NO 'STRONG PRESUMPTION' IN FAVOUR OF RETURN

Re J (Child returned abroad: Convention rights)

[2005] UKHL 40, [2005] 2 FLR 802 at 812

House of Lords

Baroness Hale

Making the choice

[29]   How then is the trial judge to set about making that choice? His focus has to be on the individual child in the particular circumstances of the case. The policy considerations which have led this country to enter into international treaties for the good of children in general are irrelevant. A fortiori, the hope that countries which have not yet become parties to such treaties might be encouraged to do so in future is irrelevant. There may be good reasons why those countries are unable to join the club. They may well believe that it would be contrary to the fundamental principles of their laws to accept the reciprocity entailed. As my noble and learned friend Lord Hoffmann pointed out in the course of the argument, they may have no incentive to join if their children are returned to them without their having to return other children to a system which is so completely different from their own. This is all pure speculation and has nothing to do with the welfare of the little boy whose future has to be decided in this case.

[30]   Nevertheless, it was urged upon us by Mr Setright QC, for the father, that there should be 'a strong presumption' that it is 'highly likely' to be in the best interests of a child subject to unauthorised removal or retention to be returned to his country of habitual residence so that any issues which remain can be decided in the courts there. He argued that this would not mean the application of the Hague Convention principles by analogy, but the results in most cases would be the same.

[31]   That approach is open to a number of objections. It would come so close to applying the Hague Convention principles by analogy that it would be indistinguishable from it in practice. It relies upon the Hague Convention concepts of 'habitual residence', 'unauthorised removal', and 'retention'; it then gives no indication of the sort of circumstances in which this 'strong presumption' might be rebutted; but at times Mr Setright appeared to be arguing for the same sort of serious risk to the child which might qualify as a defence under Art 13(b) of the Convention.

All of these concepts have their difficulties, even in Convention cases. For example, different approaches have been taken in different countries to the interpretation of the vital concept of habitual residence. By no means everyone shares our view, which is based on the exercise of parental authority: see R Schuz, *Habitual residence of children under the Hague Child Abduction Convention – theory and practice* [2001] 13 CFLQ 1. There is no warrant for introducing similar technicalities into the 'swift, realistic and unsentimental assessment of the best interests of the child' in non-Convention cases. Nor is such a presumption capable of taking into account the huge variety of circumstances in which these cases can arise, many of them very far removed from the public perception of kidnapping or abduction.

[32] The most one can say, in my view, is that the judge may find it convenient to start from the proposition that it is likely to be better for a child to return to his home country for any disputes about his future to be decided there. A case against his doing so has to be made. But the weight to be given to that proposition will vary enormously from case to case. What may be best for him in the long run may be different from what will be best for him in the short run. It should not be assumed, in this or any other case, that allowing a child to remain here while his future is decided here inevitably means that he will remain here for ever.

This case is also included in relation to:

A9 Culture and welfare
F19 Welfare principle applies
F21 Other relevant factors
H39 Limits on appeal court's authority

F21   OTHER RELEVANT FACTORS

Re J (Child returned abroad: Convention rights)

[2005] UKHL 40, [2005] 2 FLR 802 at 813

House of Lords

Baroness Hale

[33]   One important variable, as indicated in *Re L (Minors) (Wardship: Jurisdiction)* [1974] 1 WLR 250, is the degree of connection of the child with each country. This is not to apply what has become the technical concept of habitual residence, but to ask in a common sense way with which country the child has the closer connection. What is his 'home' country? Factors such as his nationality, where he has lived for most of his life, his first language, his race or ethnicity, his religion, his culture, and his education so far will all come into this.

[34]   Another closely related factor will be the length of time he has spent in each country. Uprooting a child from one environment and bringing him to a completely unfamiliar one, especially if this has been done clandestinely, may well not be in his best interests. A child may be deeply unhappy about being recruited to one side in a parental battle. But if he is already familiar with this country, has been here for some time without objection, it may be less disruptive for him to remain a little while longer while his medium and longer term future is decided than it would be to return.

[35]   This brings me to the question of different legal conceptions of welfare …

[37]   Like everything else, the extent to which it is relevant that the legal system of the other country is different from our own depends upon the facts of the particular case. It would be wrong to say that the future of every child who is within the jurisdiction of our courts should be decided according to a conception of child welfare which exactly corresponds to that which is current here. In a world which values difference, one culture is not inevitably to be preferred to another. Indeed, we do not have any fixed concept of what will be in the best interests of the individual child. Once upon a time it was assumed that all very young children should be cared for by their mothers, but that older boys might well be better off with their fathers. Nowadays we know that some fathers are very well able to provide everyday care for even their very young children and are quite prepared to prioritise their children's needs over the demands of their own careers. Once upon a time it was assumed that mothers who had

committed the matrimonial offence of adultery were only fit to care for their children if the father agreed to this. Nowadays we recognise that a mother's misconduct is no more relevant than a father's: the question is always the impact it will have on the child's upbringing and well-being. Once upon a time it may have been assumed that there was only one way of bringing up children. Nowadays we know that there are many routes to a healthy and well-adjusted adulthood. We are not so arrogant as to think that we know best.

[38]   Hence our law does not start from any a priori assumptions about what is best for any individual child. It looks at the child and weighs a number of factors in the balance, now set out in the well-known 'check-list' in s 1(3) of the Children Act 1989; these include his own wishes and feelings, his physical, emotional and educational needs and the relative capacities of the adults around him to met those needs, the effect of change, his own characteristics and background, including his ethnicity, culture and religion, and any harm he has suffered or risks suffering in the future. There is nothing in those principles which prevents a court from giving great weight to the culture in which a child has been brought up when deciding how and where he will fare best in the future. Our own society is a multi-cultural one. But looking at it from the child's point of view, as we all try to do, it may sometimes be necessary to resolve or diffuse a clash between the differing cultures within his own family.

[39]   In a case where the choice lies between deciding the question here or deciding it in a foreign country, differences between the legal systems cannot be irrelevant. But their relevance will depend upon the facts of the individual case. If there is a genuine issue between the parents as to whether it is in the best interests of the child to live in this country or elsewhere, it must be relevant whether that issue is capable of being tried in the courts of the country to which he is to be returned. If those courts have no choice but to do as the father wishes, so that the mother cannot ask them to decide, with an open mind, whether the child will be better off living here or there, then our courts must ask themselves whether it will be in the interests of the child to enable that dispute to be heard. The absence of a relocation jurisdiction must do more than give the judge pause for thought (as Hughes J put it in this case); it may be a decisive factor. On the other hand, if it appears that the mother would not be able to make a good case for relocation, that factor might not be decisive. There are also bound to be many cases where the connection of the child and all the family with the other country is so strong that any difference between the legal systems here and there should carry little weight.

[40]   The effect of the decision upon the child's primary carer must also be relevant, although again not decisive. A child who is cared for by nannies or sent away to boarding school may move between households, and indeed countries, much more readily than a child who has always looked to one parent for his everyday needs, for warmth, for food, clean

clothing, getting to school, help with homework and the like. The courts are understandably reluctant to allow a primary carer to profit from her own wrongdoing by refusing to return with her child if the child is ordered to return. It will often be entirely reasonable to expect that a mother who took the risk of uprooting the child will return with him once it is ordered that he should go home. But it will sometimes be necessary to consider whether it is indeed reasonable to expect her to return, the sincerity of her declared refusal to do so, and what is to happen to the children if she does not.

[41] These considerations should not stand in the way of a swift and unsentimental decision to return the child to his home country, even if that home country is very different from our own. But they may result in a decision that immediate return would not be appropriate, because the child's interests will be better served by allowing the dispute to be fought and decided here. Our concept of child welfare is quite capable of taking cultural and religious factors into account in deciding how a child should be brought up. It also gives great weight to the child's need for a meaningful relationship with both his parents. It does not follow, therefore, that a Saudi Muslim boy who is mainly cared for by nannies and nursery schools will be better off living with his mother and maternal grandparents in multi-cultural London than with his father or some other female relative in his home country.

This case is also included in relation to:

A9   Culture and welfare
F19 Welfare principle applies
F20 No 'strong presumption' in favour of return
H39 Limits on appeal court's authority

DIVISION G

CASE MANAGEMENT

Contents

Other witnesses

Disclosure within proceedings

Disclosure beyond proceedings / media attendance

Children Act 1989, s 91(14)

Other witnesses

G66 Leave to cross-examine own witness

G66 Acceptance of child to give part evidence

G67 Parents etc compellable to give evidence

G68 If parents etc refuse: inferences appropriate

G69 If parents etc refuse: inferences inappropriate

G70 CA 1989 s 98: self-incrimination made in such proceedings

G71 CA 1989 s 98: disclosure of evidence to the police

G72 CA 1989 s 98: no absolute protection

G73 Immunity from suit

Disclosure within proceedings

G74 Statement of general principles (1)

G75 Statement of general principles (2)

G76 Privilege during key terms

G77 Legal advice: privilege itself

G78 Litigation privilege: does not arise in non-adversarial proceedings

G79 Litigation privilege: arises in adversarial proceedings

G80 Legal professional privilege not overridden by a general duty of disclosure

G81 Effect of legal professional privilege

G82 Public interest immunity

G83 Privileged discussions for conciliation

G84 ECHR Art 8 as a basis for non-disclosure

G85 Secure: either c) documents

Disclosure beyond proceedings/media attendance

G86 Access: publicity and disclosure (?) (CA 1989 proceedings)

G87 Media attendance

G88 AJA 1960 s 12(1)

G89 AJA 1960 s 12(2)

G90 Process where publication of name/etc is to be restrained

Children Act 1989 s 91(14)

G91 Main guidance

G92 Additional guidance (?)

G93 Additional guidance (?) including application for permission to apply

ECtHR: Art 6

G1   OPPORTUNITY TO COMMENT / PUBLIC HEARING / PUBLIC PRONOUNCEMENT

Moser v Austria

(Application number 12643/02) [2007] 1 FLR 702 at 715, 716, 717 and 718

European Court of Human Rights

[80]   The first applicant raised further complaints under Art 6 of the Convention which, so far as relevant, reads as follows:

> In the determination of his civil rights and obligations ..., '1 everyone is entitled to a fair and public hearing ... Judgment shall be pronounced publicly but the press and public may be excluded from all or part of the trial in the interests of morals, public order or national security in a democratic society, where the interests of juveniles or the protection of the private life of the parties so require, or to the extent strictly necessary in the opinion of the court in special circumstances where publicity would prejudice the interests of justice.'

A: The lack of opportunity to comment on the reports relied on by the Juvenile Court

....

[85]   Having regard to the difference between the purpose pursued by the respective safeguards afforded by Art 6(1) and Art 8 (see, *McMichael v United Kingdom* (1995) 20 EHRR 205, at para 91), the court considers it necessary in the present case to examine the first applicant's complaint also under Art 6(1) and, more precisely under the principle of equality of arms, since the Youth Welfare Office was the party opposing the first applicant in the proceedings.

[86]   The principle of equality of arms – one of the elements of the broader concept of a fair trial – requires that each party should be afforded a reasonable opportunity to present his or her case under

conditions that do not place him or her at a substantial disadvantage
vis-à-vis his or her opponent (see, among many other authorities, *Dombo
Beheer BV v The Netherlands* (1993) 18 EHRR 213, at para 33). Each part
must be given the opportunity to have knowledge of and to comment on
the observations filed or evidence adduced by the other party (see, for
instance, *Ruiz-Mateos v Spain* (1993) 16 EHRR 505, at para 63;
Nideröst-Huber v Switzerland (1998) 25 EHRR 709, at para 24;
Buchberger, cited above, at para 50).

[87]   It is not disputed that the courts relied on reports by the Youth
Welfare Office and the Juvenile Court Assistance Office and that the first
applicant had not been given the opportunity to comment on them. The
court is not convinced by the Government's argument that the applicant
had access to the file throughout the proceedings. It was not for the
applicant, who was moreover unrepresented in the first instance
proceedings, to inspect the case-file in order to become aware of any
reports filed by the opposite party, but for the courts to inform her and to
provide her with an opportunity to comment thereon.

[88]   Having further regard to the considerations under Art 8, the court
finds that there has been a violation of Art 6(1) in that the proceedings
breached the principle of equality of arms.

B: The lack of a public hearing

...

[91]   According to the court's case-law, the right to a public hearing
under Art 6 entails an entitlement to an 'oral hearing' unless there are
exceptional circumstances that justify dispensing with such a hearing (see,
for instance, *Stallinger and Kuso v Austria* (1997) 26 EHRR 81, at para 51,
and *Jacobsson (Allan) v Sweden (No 2)* (19 February 1998) *Reports of
Judgments and Decisions* 1998 – I, at para 46).

[92]   In the present case, there were no such circumstances. Neither did
the proceedings concern highly technical issues or purely legal questions
(see, as regards these criteria, *Schuler-Zgraggen v Switzerland* (1995)
21 EHRR 404, at para 58, and *Varela Assalino v Portugal* (unreported)
25 April 2002). Thus, the first applicant was entitled to a hearing. The
court does not share the Government's view that the first applicant's
questioning on 2 August 2000 qualified as a hearing for the purpose of
Art 6(1). It observes that the first applicant had appeared before the
Juvenile Court of her own motion. Moreover, it follows from the Juvenile
Court's decision of 3 December 2000 that she gave some factual
information on her situation. However, there is no indication that this
'hearing' of the first applicant encompassed all factual and legal aspects
of the case. The appellate court did not hold a hearing either.

[93] In any case, it remains to be examined whether the first applicant was entitled to a public hearing. The court reiterates that the public character of proceedings protects litigants against the administration of justice in secret with no public scrutiny; it is also one of the means whereby confidence in the courts can be maintained. By rendering the administration of justice visible, publicity contributes to the achievement of the aim of Art 6(1), a fair hearing, the guarantee of which is one of the foundations of a democratic society (see *B and P v United Kingdom*, cited above, para [36] with a reference to *Sutter v Switzerland* (1984) 6 EHRR 272, at para 26).

[94] However, the requirement to hold a public hearing is subject to exceptions. This is apparent from the text of Art 6(1) itself, which contains the provision that 'the press and public may be excluded from all or part of the trial ... where the interests of juveniles or the private life of the parties so require, or to the extent strictly necessary in the opinion of the court in special circumstances where publicity would prejudice the interests of justice'. Moreover, it is established in the court's case-law that, even in a criminal law context where there is a high expectation of publicity, it may on occasion be necessary under Art 6 to limit the open and public nature of proceedings in order, for example, to protect the safety or privacy of witnesses or to promote the free exchange of information and opinion in the pursuit of justice (*B and P v United Kingdom*, cited above, para 37 with further references).

[95] In *B and P v United Kingdom* (cited above, para 39) the court found that it was inconsistent with Art 6(1) for a state to designate an entire class of cases as an exception to the general rule of public hearings where considered necessary in the interests of morals, public order or national security or where required by the interests of juveniles or the protection of the private life of the parties. It noted, moreover, that the child residence proceedings which were at stake, were prime examples of proceedings where the exclusion of the press and public may be justified in order to protect the privacy of the child and parties and to avoid prejudicing the interests of justice.

[96] The court considers that there are a number of elements which distinguish the present case from *B and P v United Kingdom*. In that case, the court attached weight to the fact that the courts had a discretion under the Children Act 1989 to hold proceedings in public if merited by the special features of the case and a judge was obliged to consider whether or not to exercise his or her discretion in this respect if requested by one of the parties. The court noted that in both cases the domestic courts had given reasons for their refusal to hear the case in public and that their decision was moreover subject to appeal (ibid, para 40). The court notes that the Austrian Non-Contentious Proceedings Act now in force gives the judge a discretion to hold family-law and guardianship proceedings in public and contains criteria for the exercise of such discretion. However, no such safeguards were provided for in the Non-Contentious Proceedings Act 1854. It is, therefore, not decisive that the applicant did not request a public hearing, since domestic law did not provide for such a possibility (see *Osinger v Austria* (unreported) 24 March 2005, para 49, and *Diennet v France* (1996) 21 EHRR 554, para 31) and the courts' practice was to hold hearings in camera.

[97]   Moreover, the case of *B and P v United Kingdom* concerned the parents' dispute over a child's residence, thus, a dispute between family members, ie individual parties. The present case concerns the transfer of custody of the first applicant's son to a public institution, namely the Youth Welfare Office, thus opposing an individual to the State. The court considers that in this sphere, the reasons for excluding a case from public scrutiny must be subject to careful examination. This was not the position in the present case, since the law was silent on the issue and the courts simply followed a long-established practice to hold hearings in camera without considering the special features of the case.

[98]   Having regard to these considerations, the court finds that lack of a public hearing was in breach of Art 6(1) of the Convention.

C: The lack of any public pronouncement of the decisions

...

[101]   The court has applied the requirement of the public pronouncement of judgments with some degree of flexibility. Thus, it has held that despite the wording which would seem to suggest that reading out in open court is required, other means of rendering a judgment public may be compatible with Art 6(1). As a general rule, the form of publicity to be given to the judgment under domestic law must be assessed in the light of the special features of the proceedings in question and by reference to the object and purpose of Art 6(1). In making this assessment, account must be taken of the entirety of the proceedings (see, *B and P v United Kingdom*, previously cited, para [45]; *Pretto v Italy* (1983) 6 EHRR 182, at paras 25–27; and *Axen v Germany* (1983) 5 EHRR 195, at paras 30–32).

[102]   It is not disputed that none of the courts' decisions was pronounced publicly. Therefore, it remains to be examined whether publicity was sufficiently ensured by other means. In the case of *B and P v United Kingdom* (cited above, paras [46]–[48]), the court found that alternative means of giving the public access to the courts' decisions, similar to those referred to by the Government in the present case, were sufficient. In doing so, it relied on the fact that the courts were entitled to hold proceedings in camera. In the case of *Sutter v Switzerland* (cited above, paras 33–34) to which the Government referred, the court found that the publicity requirement was satisfied by the fact that anyone who established an interest could consult or obtain a copy of the full text of

the Military Court of Cassation, together with the fact that that court's most important judgments were published in an official collection. However, in that case a public hearing had been held by the lower instance and the court had regard to the particular nature of the issues dealt with by the military Court of Cassation.

[103] The court finds that in the present case, in which dispensing with a public hearing was not justified in the circumstances, the above means of rendering the decisions public, namely giving persons who establish a legal interest in the case access to the file and publishing decisions of special interest, mostly of the appellate courts or the Supreme Court, did not suffice to comply with the requirements of Art 6(1).

[104] Consequently there has been a violation of Art 6 on account of the failure to pronounce the courts' decisions publicly.

This case is also included in relation to:

D1 Consider alternatives to removal / inherent procedural rights

G2   LEGAL ASSISTANCE

P, C and S v United Kingdom

[2002] 2 FLR 631 at 648 and 649

European Court of Human Rights

B.   The court's assessment

1.   GENERAL PRINCIPLES

[88]   There is no automatic right under the Convention for legal aid or legal representation to be available for an applicant who is involved in proceedings which determine his or her civil rights. Nonetheless Art 6 may be engaged under two inter-related aspects.

[89]   First, Art 6(1) of the Convention embodies the right of access to a court for the determination of civil rights and obligations (see *Golder v UK* (1979–80) 1 EHRR 524, at para 36). Failure to provide an applicant with the assistance of a lawyer may breach this provision, where such assistance is indispensable for effective access to court, either because legal representation is rendered compulsory as is the case in certain Contracting States for various types of litigation, or by reason of the complexity of the procedure or the type of case (see *Airey v Ireland* (1979–80) 1 EHRR 305, at paras 26–28, where the applicant was unable to obtain the assistance of a lawyer in judicial separation proceedings). Factors identified as relevant in the *Airey* case in determining whether the applicant would be able to present her case properly and satisfactorily without the assistance of a lawyer included the complexity of the procedure, the necessity to address complicated points of law or to establish facts, involving expert evidence and the examination of witnesses, and the fact that the subject-matter of the marital dispute entailed an emotional involvement that was scarcely compatible with the degree of objectivity required by advocacy in court. In such circumstances, the court found it unrealistic to suppose that the applicant could effectively conduct her own case, despite the assistance afforded by the judge to parties acting in person.

[90]   It may be noted that the right of access to court is not absolute and may be subject to legitimate restrictions. Where an individual's access is limited either by operation of law or in fact, the restriction will not be incompatible with Art 6 where the limitation did not impair the very essence of the right and where it pursued a legitimate aim, and there was a reasonable relationship of proportionality between the means employed and the aim sought to be achieved (*Ashingdane v UK* (1985) 7 EHRR 528,

at para 57). Thus, though the pursuit of proceedings as a litigant in person may on occasion not be an easy matter, the limited public funds available for civil actions renders a procedure of selection a necessary feature of the system of administration of justice, and the manner in which it functions in particular cases may be shown not to have been arbitrary or disproportionate, or to have impinged on the essence of the right of access to court (see the judgment *Del Sol v France* (unreported), of 26 February 2002, *Ivison v UK* (unreported) 16 April 2002). It may be the case that other factors concerning the administration of justice (eg the necessity for expedition or the rights of other individuals) could also play a limiting role as regards the provision of assistance in a particular case, though such restriction would also have to satisfy the tests set out above.

[91] Secondly, the key principle governing the application of Art 6 is fairness. In cases where an applicant appears in court notwithstanding lack of assistance of a lawyer and manages to conduct his or her case in the teeth of all the difficulties, the question may nonetheless arise as to whether this procedure was fair (see, for example, *McVicar v UK* (unreported) 7 May 2002, paras 50–51 (to be published in EHRR)). There is the importance of ensuring the appearance of the fair administration of justice and a party in civil proceedings must be able to participate effectively, inter alia, by being able to put forward the matters in support of his or her claims. Here, as in other aspects of Art 6, the seriousness of what is at stake for the applicant will be of relevance to assessing the adequacy and fairness of the procedures.

2. APPLICATION IN THE PRESENT CASE

...

[94] The court has paid careful attention to the reasons given by the trial judge in this case, whose long judgment received merited praise in the Court of Appeal for the thoroughness of his analysis and who had first-hand experience of the events and participants. It also notes that the Court of Appeal considered that the proceedings had been fair, an opinion shared by counsel for the guardian ad litem, who represented S.

[95] Nonetheless, P was required as a parent to represent herself in proceedings which as, the Court of Appeal observed, were of exceptional complexity, extending over the course of 20 days in which the documentation was voluminous and which required a review of highly complex expert evidence relating to the applicant's fitness to parent their daughter. Her alleged disposition to harm her own children, along with her personality traits, were at the heart of the case, as well as her relationship with her husband. The complexity of the case, along with the importance of what was at stake and the highly emotive nature of the subject matter, lead this court to conclude that the principles of effective access to court and fairness required that P receive the assistance of a

lawyer. Even if P was acquainted with the vast documentation in the case, the court is not persuaded that she should have been expected to take up the burden of conducting her own case. It notes that at one point in the proceedings, which were conducted at the same time as she was coping with the distress of the removal of S at birth, P broke down in the court room and the judge, counsel for the guardian ad litem and a social worker, had to encourage her to continue (see para [61] above).

[96]   The court notes that the judge himself commented that if P had been represented by a lawyer her case would have been conducted differently. Though he went on in his judgment to give the opinion that this would not have affected the outcome of the proceedings, this element is not decisive as regards the fairness of the proceedings. Otherwise, a requirement to show actual prejudice from a lack of legal representation would deprive the guarantees of Art 6 of their substance (*Artico v Italy* (1981) 3 EHRR 1, at para 35). Similarly, while the judge considered that the case would turn on the cross-examination of P, where a lawyer would only have been able to give limited assistance, that assistance would nonetheless have furnished P with some safeguards and support.

[97]   While it is also true that P and C were aware that the freeing application was likely to follow the care application within a short time, this does not mean however that they were in an adequate position to cope with the hearing when it occurred. This hearing also raised difficult points of law and emotive issues, in particular since the issuing of the care order, and the rejection of the applicants' claims to have S returned home, must have had a significant and distressing impact on the parents.

[98]   Nor is the court convinced that the importance of proceeding with expedition, which attaches generally to childcare cases, necessitated the draconian action of proceeding to a full and complex hearing, followed within one week by the freeing for adoption application, both without legal assistance being provided to the applicants. Though it was doubtless desirable for S's future to be settled as soon as possible, the court considers that the imposition of one year from birth as the deadline appears a somewhat inflexible and blanket approach, applied without particular consideration of the facts of this individual case. S was, according to the care plan, to be placed for adoption and it was not envisaged that there would be any difficulty in finding a suitable adoptive family (eight couples were already identified by 2 February 1999). Yet though S was freed for adoption by the court on 15 March 1999, she was not in fact placed with a family until 2 September 1999, a gap of over 5 months for which no explanation has been given, while the adoption order which finalised matters on a legal basis was not issued until 27 March 2000, more than one year later. Her placement was therefore not achieved by her first birthday in May in any event. It is not possible to speculate at this time as to how long the adjournment would have lasted had it been granted in order to allow the applicant P to have

representation at the care proceedings, or for both parent applicants to be represented at the freeing for adoption proceedings. It would have been entirely possible for the judge to place strict time limits on any lawyers instructed, and for instructions to be given for re-listing the matter with due regard to priorities. As the applicants have pointed out, S was herself in a successful foster placement and unaffected by the ongoing proceedings. The court does not find that the possibility of some months' delay in reaching a final conclusion in those proceedings was so prejudicial to her interests as to justify what the trial judge himself regarded as a procedure which gave an appearance of 'railroading' her parents.

[99] Recognising that the courts in this matter were endeavouring in good faith to strike a balance between the interests of the parents and the welfare of S, the court is nevertheless of the opinion that the procedures adopted not only gave the appearance of unfairness but prevented the applicants from putting forward their case in a proper and effective manner on the issues which were important to them. For example, the court notes that the judge's decision to free S for adoption gave no explanation of why direct contact was not to be continued or why an open adoption with continued direct contact was not possible, matters which the applicants apparently did not realise could, or should, have been raised at that stage. The assistance afforded to P by the counsel for other parties' and the latitude granted by the judge to P in presenting her case was no substitute, in a case such as the present, for competent representation by a lawyer instructed to protect the applicants' rights.

[100] The court concludes that the assistance of a lawyer during the hearing of these two applications which had such crucial consequences for the applicants' relationship with their daughter was an indispensable requirement. Consequently, the parents did not have fair and effective access to court as required by Art 6(1) of the Convention. There has, therefore, been a breach of this provision as regards the applicant parents, P and C.

Other significant cases on this issue:

- Cf *Re B (Care order: adjournment of fact-finding hearing)* [2009] EWCA Civ 1243, [2010] 2 FLR 1445

This case is also included in relation to:

D2   Removal of child (at birth) and permanent separation

ECtHR: Art 8 – inherent procedural rights

G3 SUFFICIENT INVOLVEMENT: GENERAL STATEMENT

TP and KM v United Kingdom

(Case 28945/95) [2001] 2 FLR 549 at 569

European Court of Human Rights

[72] The Court further recalls that whilst Art 8 contains no explicit procedural requirements, the decision-making process involved in measures of interference must be fair and such as to afford due respect to the interests safeguarded by Art 8:

'[W]hat has to be determined is whether, having regard to the particular circumstances of the case and notably the serious nature of the decisions to be taken, the parents have been involved in the decision-making process, seen as a whole, to a degree sufficient to provide them with the requisite protection of their interests. If they have not, there will have been a failure to respect their family life and the interference resulting from the decision will not be capable of being regarded as "necessary" within the meaning of Article 8.' (see *W v United Kingdom* (1988) 10 EHRR 29, 50).

[73] It has previously found that the failure to disclose relevant documents to parents during the procedures instituted by the authorities in placing and maintaining a child in care meant that the decision-making process determining the custody and access arrangements did not afford the requisite protection of the parents' interests as safeguarded by Art 8 (see *McMichael v United Kingdom* (1995) 20 EHRR 205, 241).

Other significant cases on this issue:

* *Venema v The Netherlands* (Application No 35731/97) [2003] 1 FLR 552
* *Haase v Germany* (Application No 11057/02) [2004] 2 FLR 39

G4 SUFFICIENT INVOLVEMENT: INFORMATION AND OPPORTUNITY TO PUT CASE

Kosmopoulou v Greece

(Case 60457/00) [2004] 1 FLR 800 at 809

European Court of Human Rights

[49] As regards the applicant's interests, the court notes that the national courts made two orders (on 27 August and 23 September 1997) provisionally suspending her visiting rights, without hearing representations from her. The visiting rights were suspended shortly after they had been granted by the court of first instance, namely at a moment that was particularly crucial if the 9½-year-old child was to be reunited with her mother and establish regular contact with her. The court further notes that the report prepared by the psychiatric department of the Athens Children's Hospital on 25 June 1998 was released to the applicant only on 22 February 2002, that is approximately 3½ years later. The court reiterates in this respect that it is of paramount importance for parents always to be placed in a position enabling them to put forward all arguments in favour of obtaining contact with the child and to have access to all relevant information which was at the disposal of the domestic courts (*Sahin v Germany; Sommerfield v Germany; Hoffmann v Germany* (2003) 36 EHRR 33, [2002] 1 FLR 119, para 71). The court further notes that none of the three psychologists who drafted the medical report of 26 June 1997 examined the applicant in order to reach their conclusions. It follows that in the present case the applicant was not involved in the decision-making process to a degree sufficient to provide her with the requisite protection of her interests (*Hoppe v Germany* [2003] 1 FLR 384, para [52]). Thus, she did not enjoy the appropriate procedural guarantees which would have enabled her to challenge effectively the suspension of her visiting rights.

[50] Having regard to the foregoing and to the respondent State's margin of appreciation, the court is not satisfied that the procedural approach adopted by the domestic courts was reasonable in all the circumstances or provided them with sufficient material to reach a reasoned decision on the question of access to the applicant's daughter. There has, therefore, been a violation of Art 8 of the Convention.

Other significant cases on this issue:

- *Jucius and Juciuviene v Lithuania* (Application No 14414/03) [2009] 1 FLR 403
- *Dolhamre v Sweden* (Application No 67/04) [2010] 2 FLR 912

G5   SUFFICIENT INVOLVEMENT: EVIDENTIAL BASIS

Sahin v Germany, Sommerfeld v Germany

(Cases 30943/96 and 31871/96) [2003] 2 FLR 671 at 684

European Court of Human Rights (Grand Chamber)

3.   The court's assessment

[64]   In determining whether the refusal of access was 'necessary in a democratic society', the court has to consider whether, in the light of the case as a whole, the reasons adduced to justify this measure were relevant and sufficient for the purposes of Art 8(2) of the Convention. Undoubtedly, consideration of what lies in the best interest of the child is of crucial importance in every case of this kind. Moreover, it must be borne in mind that the national authorities have the benefit of direct contact with all the persons concerned. It follows from these considerations that the court's task is not to substitute itself for the domestic authorities in the exercise of their responsibilities regarding custody and access issues, but rather to review, in the light of the Convention, the decisions taken by those authorities in the exercise of their power of appreciation (see *Hokkanen v Finland* (1995) 19 EHRR 139, [1996] 1 FLR 289, at para 55, and *Kutzner v Germany*, at paras 65–66, see also the UN Convention, paras [39]–[41] above).

[65]   The margin of appreciation to be accorded to the competent national authorities will vary in accordance with the nature of the issues and the importance of the interests at stake. Thus, the court has recognised that the authorities enjoy a wide margin of appreciation, in particular when deciding on custody. However, a stricter scrutiny is called for as regards any further limitations, such as restrictions placed by those authorities on parental rights of access, and as regards any legal safeguards designed to secure the effective protection of the right of parents and children to respect for their family life. Such further limitations entail the danger that the family relations between a young child and one or both parents would be effectively curtailed (see *Elsholz v Germany* (2002) 34 EHRR 58, [2000] 2 FLR 486, at para 49; and *Kutzner v Germany*, at para 67).

[66]   Article 8 requires that the domestic authorities should strike a fair balance between the interests of the child and those of the parents and that, in the balancing process, particular importance should be attached to the best interests of the child, which, depending on their nature and

seriousness, may override those of the parents. In particular, a parent cannot be entitled under Art 8 of the Convention to have such measures taken as would harm the child's health and development (see *Elsholz v Germany* (2002) 34 EHRR 58, [2000] 2 FLR 486, at para 50; *TP and KM v United Kingdom* (2002) 34 EHRR 2, [2001] 2 FLR 549, at para 71; *Ignaccolo-Zenide v Romania* (2001) 31 EHRR 7, at para 94; and *Nuutinen v Finland* (2002) 34 EHRR 15, at para 128).

[67] In the present case, the competent German courts adduced relevant reasons to justify their decisions refusing access, namely the serious tensions between the parents which were communicated to the child and the risk that visits would affect her and interfere with her undisturbed development in the residual family provided by the mother (see paras [16] and [26] above). At that time, an attempt at family therapy, which had been part of an agreement between the parents, had failed. In those circumstances the decisions can be taken to have been made in the interest of the child (see *Buscemi v Italy* (unreported) 16 September 1999, at para 55). On this point, the Grand Chamber shares the view of the chamber (see para 43 of the chamber's judgment).

[68] The court considers that it cannot satisfactorily assess whether those reasons were 'sufficient' for the purposes of Art 8(2) without at the same time determining whether the decision-making process, seen as a whole, provided the applicant with the requisite protection of his interests (see *W v United Kingdom* (1988) 10 EHRR 29, at para 64; *Elsholz v Germany*, at para 52; and *TP and KM v United Kingdom*, at para 72).

[69] The chamber concluded that the national authorities had overstepped their margin of appreciation, thereby violating the applicant's rights under Art 8 of the Convention. In its judgment, the chamber referred to the evidence before the district court and the regional court and continued:

'46. The court notes that at no stage of the proceedings had the child been heard in court. The regional court sought clarification from the expert on whether questioning the child, aged about 5 at the relevant time, at a hearing in court would be a psychological strain for her. The expert explained that she had not directly asked the child about her father. In her view, the risk in hearing the child in court on her relationship with her father and any direct questioning in this respect was that, in this conflict, the child might have the impression that her statements were decisive. The regional court, regarding the expert's opinion as reliable, refrained from hearing the child, finding that such questioning would have amounted to a psychological strain.

47. In the court's opinion, the German courts' failure to hear the child reveals an insufficient involvement of the applicant in the

access proceedings. It is essential that the competent courts give careful consideration to what lies in the best interests of the child after having had direct contact with the child. The regional court should not have been satisfied with the expert's vague statements about the risks inherent in questioning the child without even contemplating the possibility to take special arrangements in view of the child's young age.

48.   In this context, the court attaches importance to the fact that the expert indicated that she herself had not asked the child about her father. Correct and complete information on the child's relationship to the applicant as the parent seeking access to the child is an indispensable prerequisite for establishing a child's true wishes and thereby striking a fair balance between the interests at stake.'

[70] The Grand Chamber, for its part, observes that whether the decision-making process sufficiently protected a parent's interests depends on the particular circumstances of each case.

[71]   In the proceedings before the district court and the regional court, the applicant was placed in a position enabling him to put forward all arguments in favour of obtaining a visiting arrangement and he also had access to all relevant information which was relied on by the courts (see, mutatis mutandis, *TP and KM v United Kingdom* (2002) 34 EHRR 2, [2001] 2 FLR 549, at paras 78–83; and *P, C and S v United Kingdom* (2002) 35 EHRR 31, [2002] 2 FLR 631, at paras 136–138).

[72]   The evidential basis for the district court's decision included the parents' submissions, the statements of several nurses on the child's development following the parents' separation and a statement of the youth office (see para [15] above). The regional court additionally ordered a psychological expert opinion on the question whether contact with the applicant was in the child's interest, but, upon the expert's advice, decided against hearing the child in court (see paras [18], [22]–[23] above). The expert delivered her opinion after having met the applicant, the child and the child's mother on several occasions (see para [21] above).

[73]   As regards the issue of hearing the child in court, the court observes that as a general rule it is for the national courts to assess the evidence before them, including the means to ascertain the relevant facts (see *Vidal v Belgium* (22 April 1992), Series A, No 235-B 17, at para 33). It would be going too far to say that domestic courts are always required to hear a child in court on the issue of access to a parent not having custody, but this issue depends on the specific circumstances of each case, having due regard to the age and maturity of the child concerned.

[74]   In this connection the court notes that the child was about 3 years and 10 months old when the appeal proceedings started, and 5 years and

2 months at the time of the regional court's decision. The expert reached her conclusion namely that a right of access without prior contact to overcome the conflicts between the parents was not in the child's interests, after several meetings with the child, her mother and the applicant father. Consulted on the question of hearing the child in court, she plausibly explained that the very process of questioning entailed a risk for the child. Such a risk could not be avoided by special arrangements in court.

[75] Considering the methods applied by the expert when meeting the child and her cautious approach in analysing the child's attitude towards her parents, the court is of the opinion that the regional court did not overstep its margin of appreciation when relying on her findings, even in the absence of direct questions on the child's relationship to the applicant.

[76] In this context, the court notes that, in the course of the proceedings before the regional court, the applicant unsuccessfully challenged the expert for bias and criticised her scientific approach. The applicant pursued these arguments in the present proceedings, but the court has no cause to doubt the professional competence of the expert or the manner in which she conducted her interviews with all concerned.

[77] Having regard to the foregoing and to the respondent State's margin of appreciation, the court is satisfied that the German courts' procedural approach was reasonable in the circumstances and provided sufficient material to reach a reasoned decision on the question of access in the particular case. The court can therefore accept that the procedural requirements implicit in Art 8 of the Convention were complied with.

[78] Accordingly, there has been no violation of Art 8 of the Convention in the present case.

General notes:

This decision marked the conclusion of a series of cases which saw the rise and fall of a challenge to the German system of dealing with private law disputes. The series began with *Elsholz v Germany* (Case 25735/94) [2000] 2 FLR 486) reached its high point with the decision of the Chamber of the ECtHR in *Sahin v Germany, Sommerfeld v Germany, Hoffmann v Germany* (Cases 30943/96, 31871/96, 34045/96) [2002] 1 FLR 119, and saw the start of a retreat in *Hoppe v Germany* (Case 28422/95). The retreat was completed in this decision of the Grand Chamber of the ECtHR.

ECJ: jurisdiction

G6 JURISDICTION UNDER BRUSSELS II REVISED

Re A (Area of freedom, security and justice)

(Case 523/07) [2009] 2 FLR 1 at 6, 7, 9, 11 and 12

European Court of Justice

[20] Taking the view that the interpretation of the regulation was necessary for it to resolve the dispute before it, the Korkein hallinto-oikeus decided to stay the proceedings and to refer the following questions to the court for a preliminary ruling:

'1.(a) Does … [the] Regulation … apply to the enforcement, such as in the present case, of a public-law decision made in connection with child protection, as a single decision, concerning the immediate taking into care of a child and his or her placement outside the home, in its entirety,

(b) or, having regard to the provision in Article 1(2)(d) of the regulation, only to the part of the decision relating to the placement outside the home?

2. How is the concept of habitual residence in Article 8(1) of the regulation, like the associated Article 13(1), to be interpreted in Community law, bearing in mind in particular the situation in which a child has a permanent residence in one Member State but is staying in another Member State, carrying on a peripatetic life there?

3.(a) If it is considered that the child's habitual residence is not in the latter Member State, on what conditions may an urgent measure (taking into care) nevertheless be taken in that Member State on the basis of Article 20(1) of the regulation?

(b) Is a protective measure within the meaning of Article 20(1) of the regulation solely a measure which can be taken under national law, and are the provisions of national law concerning that measure binding when the article is applied?

(c) Must the case, after the taking of the protective measure, be transferred of the court's own motion to the court of the Member State with jurisdiction?

4.   If the court of a Member State has no jurisdiction at all, must it dismiss the case as inadmissible or transfer it to the court of the other Member State?'

...

[29]   Therefore, the answer to the first question is that Art 1(1) of the regulation must be interpreted as meaning that a decision ordering that a child be immediately taken into care and placed outside his original home is covered by the term 'civil matters', for the purposes of that provision, where that decision was adopted in the context of public law rules relating to child protection.

...

[44]   Therefore, the answer to the second question is that the concept of 'habitual residence' under Art 8(1) of the regulation must be interpreted as meaning that it corresponds to the place which reflects some degree of integration by the child in a social and family environment. To that end, in particular the duration, regularity, conditions and reasons for the stay on the territory of a Member State and the family's move to that State, the child's nationality, the place and conditions of attendance at school, linguistic knowledge and the family and social relationships of the child in that State must be taken into consideration. It is for the national court to establish the habitual residence of the child, taking account of all the circumstances specific to each individual case.

...

[65]   In light of the foregoing considerations, the answer to the third question is that a protective measure, such as the taking into care of children, may be decided by a national court under Art 20 of the regulation if the following conditions are satisfied:

* the measure must be urgent;
* it must be taken in respect of persons in the member state concerned; and
* it must be provisional.

[66]   The taking of the measure and its binding nature are determined in accordance with national law. After the protective measure has been taken, the national court is not required to transfer the case to the court of another Member State having jurisdiction. However, insofar as the protection of the best interests of the child so requires, the national court which has taken provisional or protective measures must inform, directly or through the central authority designated under Art 53 of the regulation, the court of another Member State having jurisdiction.

...

[72] Therefore, the answer to the fourth question is that, where the court of a Member State does not have jurisdiction at all, it must declare of its own motion that it has no jurisdiction, but is not required to transfer the case to another court. However, insofar as the protection of the best interests of the child so requires, the national court which has declared of its own motion that it has no jurisdiction must inform, directly or through the central authority designated under Art 53 of the regulation, the court of another Member State having jurisdiction.

Other significant cases on this issue:

* *E v E* [2007] EWHC 276 (Fam), [2007] 1 FLR 1977 (thorough analysis of 'habitual analysis')
* *Re Rinau* C-195-08 PPU, [2008] 2 FLR 1495 (particularly about Brussels II Revised, Art 42)
* *Re S (Habitual residence)* [2009] EWCA Civ 1021, [2010] 1 FLR 1146

General principles

G7 RECUSAL

Re F (Contact)

[2007] EWHC 2543 (Fam), [2008] 1 FLR 1163 at 1184

Family Division

Sumner J

[179]   I turn to the law. I make it clear that all such applications have to be considered seriously even if they are, as here, in part wild and extravagant. I remind myself of a passage from the judgment of Burton J in *Ansar v Lloyds TSB Bank plc* [2006] EWCA Civ 1462, [2006] ICR 1565 approved by the Court of Appeal where he said, para [19]:

> 'The nature of the allegations may, on occasion, be decisive although it does not follow that even if an allegation of wholly outrageous conduct, such as the taking of a bribe, were made, that would necessarily qualify as a ground for recusal, if it was manifestly fanciful or unfounded.'

[180]   The Court of Appeal accepted Burton J's summary of the law set out in 11 paragraphs. I have also been referred to the judgment of the Court of Appeal in *Howell and Others v Lees-Millais and Others* [2007] EWCA Civ 720, [2007] All ER (D) 64 (Jul). For the purposes of this application I set out the following principles:

(i)   Justice must be seen to be done but that does not mean that judges should too readily accept suggestions of appearance of bias thereby encouraging parties to believe that they might thereby obtain someone more likely to favour their case.

(ii)   The fact that a judge had commented adversely on a party or witness or found them to be unreliable would not found an objection unless there were further grounds.

(iii)   A real danger of bias might well be thought to arise—

    (a)   if there was personal friendship or animosity between a judge and any member of the public involved in the case,

    (b)   if the judge was too closely acquainted with such a person,

(c)   if the judge had rejected the evidence of such a person or expressed views in such extreme or unbalanced terms such as to throw doubts on their ability to approach the person or the issue with an open mind,

(d)   or for those or other reasons cause doubt in the ability of the judge to ignore extraneous matters or prejudices and bring an objective judgment to bear.

(iv)   A judge should resist the temptation to recuse himself simply because it would be more comfortable to do so as for instance when the litigant appears to have lost confidence in the judge.

(v)   The test remains, having considered all the circumstances bearing on the suggestion that the judge could be biased, whether those circumstances would lead a fair minded and informed observer adopting a balanced approach to conclude that there was a real possibility that the tribunal was biased.

[181]   Such applications are not uncommon in the Family Division from litigants in person. That is understandable given the highly emotional aspect of many of the cases, the tense atmosphere, and the antipathy that often exists between the parties. That is added to by the merits of judicial continuity. It may lead to the same judge giving a series of judgments between the same parties, often with one of them being unsuccessful on a number or all occasions.

[182]   Those factors which are not comprehensive may give rise to an appearance that the judge is too involved, or that the prospect of favouring the party who has not so far been successful becomes improbable. There is an added factor. The sheer number of decisions taken by a particular judge, or the length of time over which they have presided in relation to particular parties, may make it prudent for a fresh approach to be preferred. This is particularly so when it might assist the losing party more readily to understand the situation and thereby increase the prospects of some agreement between the parties.

G8   SPECTRUM OF PROCEDURE

Re B (Minors) (contact)

[1994] 2 FLR 1 at 5

Court of Appeal

Butler-Sloss LJ

Mr Bennett argued that in any case not falling within the limited category defined in the *Cheshire County Council*[1] decision, a judge is obliged to hold a full hearing, permitting the parties to call oral evidence and cross-examine any witness they may choose. In my view a judge in family cases has a much broader discretion both under the Children Act 1989 and previously to conduct the case as is most appropriate for the issues involved and the evidence available (see the judgment of Sir Stephen Brown P in *W v Ealing London Borough Council*[2] (above)). There is a spectrum of procedure for family cases from the ex parte application on minimal evidence to the full and detailed investigations on oral evidence which may be prolonged. Where on that spectrum a judge decides a particular application should be placed is a matter for his discretion. Applications for residence orders or for committal to the care of a local authority or revocation of a care order are likely to be decided on full oral evidence, but not invariably. Such is not the case on contact applications which may be and are heard sometimes with and sometimes without oral evidence or with a limited amount of oral evidence.

I agree with counsel that there is sufficient information before this court upon which we can form a view whether these applications should be heard by a judge on oral evidence or whether in the exercise of the discretion of this court, they can properly be determined upon the written evidence and submissions of counsel. The considerations which should weigh with the court include:

(1)   whether there is sufficient evidence upon which to make the relevant decision;

(2)   whether the proposed evidence (which should be available at least in outline) which the applicant for a full trial wishes to adduce is likely to affect the outcome of the proceedings;

---

[1]   *Cheshire County Council v M* [1993] 1 FLR 463, which is explained and distinguished in the present case by Butler-Sloss LJ earlier in her judgment.

[2]   [1993] 2 FLR 788.

(3)   whether the opportunity of cross-examine the witnesses for the local authority, in particular in this case the expert witnesses, is likely to affect the outcome of the proceedings;

(4)   the welfare of the child and the effect of further litigation – whether the delay in itself will be so detrimental to the child's well-being that exceptionally there should not be a full hearing. This may be because of the urgent need to place the child, or as is alleged in this case, the emotional stress suffered by both children, and particularly D;

(5)   the prospects of success of the applicant or a full trial;

(6)   does the justice of the case require a full investigation with oral evidence?

Other significant cases on this issue:

- *W v Ealing London Borough Council* [1993] 2 FLR 788 at 794
- *Re C (Contact: conduct of hearing)* [2006] EWCA Civ 144, [2006] 2 FLR 289

G9 RULES OF EVIDENCE RELAXED

Re U (Serious injury: standard of proof) Re B

[2004] EWCA Civ 567, [2004] 2 FLR 263 at 270 and 272

Court of Appeal

Butler-Sloss P

[13] ... The strict rules of evidence applicable in a criminal trial which is adversarial in nature is to be contrasted with the partly inquisitorial approach of the court dealing with children cases in which the rules of evidence are considerably relaxed ...

...

[22] In family proceedings the procedures and the rules of evidence are different from criminal trials. In the first place the material available to the court is likely to be much more extensive than would be admitted in a criminal trial. In the second place the standard of proof to be applied before reaching a conclusion adverse to the parent or carer is, as we have set out above, also different. Given a similar background to that in *R v Cannings* a judge would be required to ask himself which of two possible explanations, human agency or unascertained natural cause, is the more probable. If persuaded by clear and cogent evidence that it was more likely to be the former the court is entitled to reach a conclusion adverse to the parent or carer.

This case is also included in relation to:

H18 Application of R v Cannings

G10   NO STRICT RULE OF ISSUE ESTOPPEL

Re B (Children Act proceedings) (issue estoppel)

[1997] 1 FLR 285 at 286, 293 and 295

Family Division

Hale J

In August 1996 the proceedings relating to G and D were transferred to the High Court for the determination by a judge of the Family Division of the preliminary issue as to whether in these proceedings the father is bound by the finding of sexual abuse in the proceedings relating to the other children.

The question is one of great practical importance in the work of the family jurisdiction. This case happens to involve a finding of sexual abuse, but in principle this is no different from a finding of physical abuse, or indeed any other finding of fact which is relevant to a person's suitability to care for children. Again, this case happens to involve a positive finding against the father, but in principle the same should apply in relation to negative findings, unless a different burden of proof was applied.

There are many reasons why it is just and convenient for findings of fact to be made in proceedings concerning the children against whom the abuse is alleged to have taken place and when events are fresh in everyone's minds: see, for example, the guidance given by Wall J in *Re G (A Minor) (Care Proceedings)* [1994] 2 FLR 69. It then frequently arises that findings made in one set of proceedings are relevant, even crucial, in another. At one end of the spectrum, exactly the same parties are involved: findings are made in care proceedings when a care order is made, and will be relevant in later proceedings to discharge the care order. Then come cases involving the same child but different parties: the most obvious example is an adoption application relating to a child in care; but another example would be care proceedings relating to a child after a finding of sexual abuse had been made in private law proceedings between his parents; or vice versa, where private law proceedings follow care proceedings. Then come cases involving different children; in these the adult parties may be identical, if they are children of the same two parents; but it is perhaps more likely that they will not be entirely identical, as different parents may be involved. In some of these, the applicant local authority, who may loosely be termed the accuser, and the respondent parent, who may loosely be termed the accused, are the same, as happens to be the situation here. In others, a completely different local authority may be involved.

...

This takes us back to first principles. According to Diplock LJ in *Mills v Cooper* [1967] 2 QB 459, 468, 'issue estoppel' is not a rule of evidence, but 'a particular application of the general rule of public policy that there should be finality in litigation'. This is the main rationale behind the doctrine, although it is also important that no one should be bothered with the same action twice. But as Diplock LJ had earlier pointed out in *Thoday v Thoday* [1964] P 181, 197:

'"Estoppel" merely means that, under the rules of the adversary system of procedure upon which the common law of England is based, a party is not allowed, in certain circumstances, to prove in litigation particular facts or matters which, if proved, would assist him to succeed as plaintiff or defendant in an action. If the court is required to exercise an inquisitorial function and may inquire into facts which the parties do not choose to prove, or would under the rules of the adversary system be prevented from proving, this is a function to which the common law concept of estoppel is alien. It may well be a rational rule to apply in the exercise of such an inquisitorial function to say that if a court having jurisdiction to do so has once inquired into the truth of a particular allegation of fact and reached a decision thereon, another court of co-ordinate jurisdiction in the exercise of its own discretion should not re-embark on the same inquiry, but should accept the decision of the first court. But this is a different concept from estoppel as hitherto known in English law. It will be interesting to watch its development in future cases ...'

A different approach was developed in the divorce jurisdiction because of the inquisitorial elements which it contained. The inquisitorial element is even more apparent in children's cases. Numerous citations can be made from the law reports in support of that proposition, but in this case we need look no further than the case of *B v Derbyshire County Council* [1992] 1 FLR 538. Previous care proceedings in relation to this same child had been dismissed 20 months earlier; justices held that the doctrine of res judicata prevented them hearing evidence adduced in the previous proceedings, and in the absence of any fresh evidence, dismissed the current case. Allowing the appeal, Sir Stephen Brown P said this, at 545F:

'... I find it very difficult to conceive of any situation or circumstance in which the ... doctrine of res judicata could be applicable, but it is impossible to consider every hypothetical set of circumstances which might come before a court. However, in the context of care proceedings, it is most unlikely ever to be applicable.'

Later on, at 546A, he commented:

'What has happened in this case is symptomatic of the adversarial approach, where technical points are taken in order to secure a particular result. What will become more apparent from 14 October 1991 [when the Children Act 1989 came into force] is that what the court is concerned with is the whole welfare of the child and that its task is to investigate, in an inquisitorial manner if necessary, the interests of the child.'

But if the courts' inquisitorial function means that the strict doctrine of issue estoppel can rarely, if ever, apply in children's cases, this does not mean that the court is bound to allow the parties to call evidence on each and every issue which may be relevant in the proceedings. Several authorities attest to the existence of a discretion in the court as to how the hearing should be conducted ...

...

It seems to me that the weight of Court of Appeal authority is against the existence of any strict rule of issue estoppel which is binding upon any of the parties in children's cases. At the same time, the court undoubtedly has a discretion as to how the inquiry before it is to be conducted. This means that it may on occasions decline to allow a full hearing of the evidence on certain matters even if the strict rules of issue estoppel would not cover them. Although some might consider this approach to be a typical example of the lack of rigour which some critics discern in the family jurisdiction, it seems to me to encompass both the flexibility which is essential in children's cases and the increased control exercised by the court rather than the parties which is already a feature of the court's more inquisitorial role in children's cases (and beginning to gain ground in other litigation as shown in the Woolf Report on *Access to Justice*).

Hence, if the applicant in one set of proceedings wishes to rely on findings made in previous proceedings in order to prove a case, the court will have to consider how this should be done. Frequently, although such findings are not necessarily accepted by the party concerned, that party will accept that a challenge to them in later proceedings will be futile. The court may then simply rely upon the findings made earlier. Sometimes, the party concerned or some other party will wish to challenge them. In such an event, it seems to me, the court may wish to be made aware, not only of the findings themselves, but also of the evidence upon which they were based. It is then for the court to decide whether or not to allow any issue of fact to be tried afresh. There are no doubt many factors to be borne in mind, among them the following:

(1) The court will wish to balance the underlying considerations of public policy:

  (a) that there is a public interest in an end to litigation – the resources of the courts and everyone involved in these proceedings are already severely stretched and should not be employed in deciding the same matter twice unless there is good reason to do so;

(b)   that any delay in determining the outcome of the case is likely to be prejudicial to the welfare of the individual child; but

(c)   that the welfare of any child is unlikely to be served by relying upon determinations of fact which turn out to have been erroneous; and

(d)   the court's discretion, like the rules of issue estoppel, as pointed out by Lord Upjohn in *Carl Zeiss Stiftung v Rayner & Keeler Ltd (No 2)* [1967] 1 AC 853, 947, 'must be applied so as to work justice and not injustice'.

(2)   The court may well wish to consider the importance of the previous findings in the context of the current proceedings. If they are so important that they are bound to affect the outcome one way or another, the court may be more willing to consider a rehearing than if they are of lesser or peripheral significance.

(3)   Above all, the court is bound to want to consider whether there is any reason to think that a rehearing of the issue will result in any different finding from that in the earlier trial. By this I mean something more than the mere fact that different judges might on occasions reach different conclusions upon the same evidence. No doubt we would all be reluctant to allow a matter to be relitigated on that basis alone. The court will want to know:

(a)   whether the previous findings were the result of a full hearing in which the person concerned took part and the evidence was tested in the usual way;

(b)   if so, whether there is any ground upon which the accuracy of the previous finding could have been attacked at the time, and why therefore there was no appeal at the time; and

(c)   whether there is any new evidence or information casting doubt upon the accuracy of the original findings.

It follows that the answer to the question posed is 'not necessarily'. The local authority will obviously wish to assert that the father has sexually abused two other children. It will be for the trial judge to decide how this is to be proved. He will no doubt wish to consider whether there appears to be some real reason to cast doubt upon the earlier findings.

Other significant cases on this and related issues:

- *Ladd v Marshall* (1954) FLR Rep 422
- *Re B (Split hearings: jurisdiction)* [2000] 1 FLR 334 per Butler-Sloss P
- *Re D (Child: threshold criteria)* [2001] 1 FLR 274
- *Re M and MC (Care: issues of fact: drawing of orders)* [2002] EWCA Civ 499, [2003] 1 FLR 461
- *Re S-B (Children)* [2009] UKSC 17, [2010] 1 FLR 1161 at [46]

- *Re W (Care proceedings)* [2008] EWHC 1188 (Fam), [2010] 1 FLR 1176
- *Re I (Care proceedings: fact-finding hearing)* [2010] EWCA Civ 319, [2010] 2 FLR 1462

G11   SEPARATE JR / HR PROCEEDINGS GENERALLY TO BE AVOIDED

Re S and W (Care proceedings)

[2007] EWCA Civ 232, [2007] 2 FLR 275 at 296

Court of Appeal

Wall LJ

[89] We direct that the case should be heard by a judge with authorisation to sit in the Administrative Court because the guardian made clear her determination to seek judicial review of the decision of the fostering panel and, if necessary, the local authority's decisions; (1) to change the care plan in relation to CO; (2) not to implement the care plans in relation to CH and L; and (3) its refusal properly to reconsider when invited to do so by the judge. We were pleased that Mrs Gosling was able to agree that permission to apply for judicial review would not be disputed by the local authority, and that there was an arguable case for it. This will undoubtedly speed up the process.

[90] We have already made the point that it would be wholly undesirable to have separate proceedings under Part IV of the 1989 Act running concurrently with proceedings for judicial review in relation to what is essentially the same subject matter. There is abundant authority this is a course against which this court has set its face: – see, in particular, *Re V (Care Proceedings: Human Rights Claims)* [2004] EWCA Civ 54, [2004] 1 WLR 1433, [2004] 1 FLR 944; its sequel *Re V (Care: Pre-birth Actions)* [2004] EWCA Civ 1575, [2005] 1 FLR 627 and *Re J (Care: Assessment: Fair Trial)* [2006] EWCA Civ 545, [2007] 1 FLR 77 – see, in particular, the judgment of Wilson LJ, at para [30].

[91] This court's view remains very firmly that whilst care proceedings are pending, any issue under the European Convention for the Protection of Human Rights and Fundamental Freedoms 1950 (the Convention) which arises falls to be dealt with in the care proceedings, not in separate proceedings under the Human Rights Act 1998 (HRA 1998). The same applies where judicial review is concerned. Thus it is, for example, misconceived for a guardian or parent to seek judicially to review a care plan in proceedings separate from the pending care proceedings themselves. Any consideration of the care plan and its appropriateness can and should normally be dealt with within the care proceedings.

[92] The highly unusual circumstances of this case may make it appropriate for the guardian to consider seeking judicial review of the decision-making processes of both the local authority and the fostering panel. If that is the case, it must be done either within the care proceedings or in proceedings for judicial review which are consolidated with the care proceedings and heard at the same time by the same judge.

[93] Finally, we revert to *Re S; Re W*.[1] That case, of course, concerned possible remedies available to parents *after* final care orders had been made, and the court which had made them no longer had any role under Part IV of the 1989 Act. The case is nonetheless helpful, however, because it demonstrates that where an action under HRA 1998, (or, in our judgment, proceedings for judicial review) are available to parents (or, in the instant case, the children's guardian) the actions of the local authority can be controlled by the remedies available to the court under HRA 1998 and judicial review. Thus an unlawful decision of a local authority can be quashed: – see the decision of Holman J in *Re M (Care: Challenging Decisions by Local Authority)* [2001] 2 FLR 1300, approved by Lord Nicholls of Birkenhead in para [46] of his speech in *Re S; Re W*. Lord Nicholls of Birkenhead reverts to the point in para [62] of his speech, where he says:

> '[62] Thus, if a local authority fails to discharge itsparental responsibilities properly, and in consequence the rights of the parents under art 8 are violated, the parents may, as a longstop, bring proceedings against the authority under s 7. I have already drawn attention to a case where this has happened. I say "as a longstop", because other remedies, both of an administrative nature and by way of court proceedings, may also be available in the particular case. For instance, Bedfordshire council has an independent visitor, a children's complaints officer and a children's rights officer. Sometimes court proceedings by way of judicial review of a decision of a local authority may be the appropriate way to proceed. In a suitable case an application for discharge of the care order is available. One would not expect proceedings to be launched under s 7 until any other appropriate remedial routes have first been explored.'

[94] Although Lord Nicholls of Birkenhead is discussing possible actions after the making of a final care order, his words seem to us equally apposite to pending care proceedings. The circumstances in which applications for judicial review will be appropriate in pending proceedings will, we think, be highly unusual, and we remain of the view that in the overwhelming majority of cases, Convention considerations will fall to be dealt with under Part IV of the 1989 Act without recourse to an action under HRA 1998 or proceedings for judicial review. However, on the

---

[1]   [2002] UKHL 10, [2002] 1 FLR 815. See D9 – No court intervention once final care order made; and D56 – Interim or final order (1).

particular facts of this case, where the care proceedings are to be reheard, and the local authority's decision-making process is a key issue, we take the view that judicial review proceedings are not only appropriate but may be necessary in order to protect the children from removal from their present foster carers without the court's approval pending the final determination.

[95]   We retain the hope that the local authority, after further reflection, will agree that the only proper way forward is to leave the children in their current placement under interim orders, and for the court to give directions for the filing of appropriate independent professional evidence designed to promote the best interests of all three children. This is not, of course, to say that the local authority is not entitled to form a view about the children's future and put it before the judge: of course it is. What is impermissible, in our judgment, is the local authority's apparent belief that it can ignore the court's views, and change its care plans for the children at will and without reference to the guardian or the court.

Other significant cases on this issue:

- *X Council v B (Emergency protection orders)* [2004] EWHC 2014 (Fam), [2005] 1 FLR 341 at 356

This case is also included in relation to:

D7   Relationship between court and LA
D8   Relationship between LA and CG

G12   APPLICATION AND PROPER NOTICE

Re K (Procedure: Family Proceedings Rules)

[2004] EWCA Civ 1827, [2005] 1 FLR 764 at 765 and 767

Court of Appeal

Thorpe LJ

[4]   There was a continuing investigation by the local authority, and on 24 November the social worker and team leader visited the mother at home and informed her that they would be suggesting to the court that the children should be transferred from her care to that of the father. The matter was the subject of a case conference on the following day, but, bizarrely, there was no mention at the case conference of the local authority's current thinking.

[5]   On that day the father's solicitors dispatched a letter, which it is accepted was received by the mother on the following day. The material paragraphs read as follows:

> 'As you are no doubt aware, over the past weeks and months N has been intensely concerned about the welfare of the children and about his lack of contact with them. The situation seems to him not to have improved and he is now intending to make an application to the court next Friday for interim residence of the children. Although we have not yet had the court order the hearing will take place next Friday at the High Court and you should be there for 10.30 am.
>
> He wishes to give you advance notice of this and to give you the opportunity of agreeing to a change of residence for the children on a temporary basis, while mental health and other issues are investigated. If you do so agree, kindly let us know as soon as possible so that we can make plans with the assistance of the guardian and with social services.'

[6]   On 29 November the local authority filed an addendum to its s 7 report in which it conveyed to the court its opinion that the father's application for an interim residence order deserved serious consideration. It seems, bizarrely, that the local authority denied the mother sight of that addendum and she did not receive it until 1 December, probably a day after it was made available to the father.

[7]   When the parties assembled on 3 December the mother was handed a statement from the father in support of his application. She also had to

digest, as did all other parties, a short report from the guardian, in which she said [she would support the father's application for an interim residence order] ...

...

[12] ... It is evident – I would even say self-evident – that the procedure adopted between 25 November and 3 December is simply incapable of justification or support. Quite apart from the standards that are required of this jurisdiction by the European Convention for the Protection of Human Rights and Fundamental Freedoms 1950 (the European Convention), and in particular Arts 6 and 8, this procedure would not have begun to satisfy the basic standard of fairness that has always been required by the family justice system in this jurisdiction.

[13] A solicitor's letter, which purports to give notice to a litigant in person that a contact review was being elevated into a hearing at which she risks losing the care of her children, is simply not good enough. There are Family Proceedings Rules 1991, and one of their primary purposes is to avoid procedural unfairness. If people disregard the provisions of the Family Proceedings Rules then they risk procedural unfairness. There was no formal application issued. The father's statements in support were not properly served upon the mother. She had no opportunity of responding. The chronology that I have already recited demonstrates in itself the injustice of the hearing below, and it needs no further explanation from me as to why it is not compliant with the European Convention or in accordance with the fundamental standards of justice that are so important in cases involving the care of children and in cases in which one of the litigants acts in person.

[14] It would suffice to allow this appeal simply on the basis of procedural unfairness. But I am equally persuaded that this order cannot be justified on the ground that there were legitimate professional concerns (expressed not only by the local authority but also by the guardian) and, therefore, plainly this was a decision within the wide ambit of the judge's discretion taken for the protection of children.

[15] Of course I accept that in any case where children are at immediate risk of harm the court has a power and a responsibility to intervene to protect them. But this present case was just nowhere near that point of intervention ...

G13   CAPACITY / ROLE OF OFFICIAL SOLICITOR

RP v Nottingham City Council and the Official Solicitor (Mental capacity of parent)

[2008] EWCA Civ 462, [2008] 2 FLR 1516 at 1529, 1549, 1558, 1560 and 1561

Court of Appeal

Wall LJ

[47]   There is, however, a further point which needs to be understood and emphasised. Both the relevant rules of court and the leading case of *Masterman-Lister*[1] make it clear that once either counsel or SC had formed the view that RP might not be able to give them proper instructions, and might be a person under a disability, it was their professional duty to have the question resolved as quickly as possible. This point will become more apparent when I consider the case of *Masterman-Lister* later in this judgment (see in particular paras [111]–[127], below). For present purposes, it is sufficient to state that in my judgment it would have been a serious breach of her professional and ethical code were SC to have continued to take instructions from a person whom she had reason to believe did not have the capacity to instruct her. She was, accordingly, duty bound to seek a professional opinion on RP's capacity to do so.

...

[134]   In compliance with my judgment handed down on 30 January 2008, the Official Solicitor placed before this court a great deal of material relating to his position both in the instant case and generally. As this judgment is already very long, I do not propose to attempt a summary of that material. In my judgment, however, this is material which is important and which should be in the public domain. Accordingly, what I have done is to prepare an edited version of the Official Solicitor's statement prepared for this court, which I have attached to this judgment as a supplement. This document also exhibits the advice which the Official Solicitor had sought and obtained from leading counsel on his role as litigation friend for parents under the Adoption and Children Act 2002 (the 2002 Act); it also deals with the merits of RP's case from the Official Solicitor's perspective.

---

[1]   *Masterman-Lister v Brutton & Co; Masterman-Lister v Jewell* [2002] EWCA Civ 1889 and [2003] EWCA Civ 70.

...

[169]   There is no doubt of the impact on care proceedings of the allegation that the parents of the children concerned suffer from learning difficulties or other disabilities. In the instant case, the local authority properly raises the question and seeks guidance on it. It puts the dilemma facing local authorities in the following way:

'The local authority does however welcome the guidance of the Court as to whether further or other steps should in the future be taken to ensure the spirit of the [Mental Capacity Act 2005] and the [European] Convention rights of the parent are properly respected during the course of care proceedings in which there is an issue as to that parent's capacity. In particular:

(1)   Should further or other safeguards be put in place to ensure that a parent is properly informed and insofar as possible understands the appointment and role of the Official Solicitor and if so what is the responsibility of the local authority?

(2)   Does the local authority have obligations to ensure the regular review of a parent's litigation capacity during the course of care proceedings at times when significant decisions are required to be made by that parent? If so, how is the local authority to achieve this without placing undue pressure upon the parent or intruding upon a proper solicitor-client relationship?

(3)   Pursuant to the Public Law Outline (PLO) guide to Case Management in Public Law Proceedings (2008) the local authority is required, pre the issue of public law proceedings, to commission any specialist assessments needed following an initial social work assessment. At this stage, the provision of independent legal advice for the parent is limited. Is it appropriate for the local authority to invite an expert to consider the issue of litigation capacity at this stage?'

...

[174]   All this to my mind indicates strongly not only that the question of adult capacity to give instructions needs to be addressed at the earliest opportunity, but that the local authority will be expected, in the pre-proceedings phase of the case, to be on the alert for the possibility that a parent in particular may be a protected person and may not have the capacity to give instructions in the proceedings.

[175]   It is, I think, inevitable that in its pre-proceedings work with a child's family, the local authority will gain information about the capacity of the child's parents. The critical question is what it does with that information, particularly in a case where the social workers form the view that the parent in question may have learning difficulties.

[176] At this point, in many cases, the local authority will be working with the child's parents in an attempt to keep the family together. In my judgment, the practical answer in these circumstances is likely to be that the parent in question should be referred to the local authority's adult learning disability team (or its equivalent) for help and advice. If that team thinks that further investigations are required, it can undertake them: it should, moreover, have the necessary contacts and resources to commission a report so that as soon as the pre-proceedings letter is written, and proceedings are issued, the legal advisers for the parent can be in a position, with public funding, to address the question of a litigation friend. It is, I think, important that judgments on capacity are not made by the social workers from the child protection team.

[177] As to the first question, a litigation friend, whether the Official Solicitor or otherwise, cannot become involved unless and until proceedings are issued. Once proceedings are issued, the question of the parent's representation becomes and remains a matter for the parent's legal advisers. Prior to the institution of proceedings, the issue is a different one, and the local authority should feel free to offer whatever advice is appropriate, although, as I have already said, it seems to me that any advice given to the parent in question should come from the local authority's adult learning disability team.

[178] The question of ensuring that a parent during proceedings is properly informed and understands the role of the litigation friend – and, in particular the role of the Official Solicitor – must be a matter for that parent's legal team, and for the Official Solicitor himself. During care proceedings, the likelihood is that the local authority (certainly in the shape of the child protection team) and the parent are likely to be in adversarial positions, and the child protection team would, I think, have a clear conflict of interest were it to seek to ensure that the parent in question fully understood the role of his or her litigation friend.

[179] As to the second question, the answer is, I think, 'no' except in those unusual cases where a parent becomes incapacitated and a social worker from the adult learning disabilities team becomes involved in order to support the parent.

[180] I fully recognise that this is an area in which local authorities are in a difficult position, as they frequently stand in an adversarial position vis-a-vis parents, yet at the same time they have a duty to those parents to attempt, wherever possible to ensure that they can remain united with their children. On the facts thrown up by the instant case, I am satisfied that the local authority did its duty by facilitating and by not obstructing the instruction of HJ. More than this I do not think it was required to do, and even doing so much has brought upon it the unwarranted accusation of having somehow prevented RP from presenting her case by paying a biased expert to advise that RP was not competent to give instructions.

[181] Once proceedings have been issued, therefore, local authorities must play the case as neutrally as possible. In the pre-proceedings phase, however, the local authority, in my view, is given the task by the PLO of acquiring information which is to be made available when proceedings are issued. In the pre-proceedings phase local authorities should feel free to do whatever is necessary in social work terms to assist parents who may become protected parties. My view, however, is that this is best achieved by members of the adult learning disabilities team who do not have responsibility for the children concerned.

...

[183] On 1 October 2007 (after the making of the orders against which RP has appealed) the Mental Capacity Act 2005 came into effect. The Act, with its accompanying Code of Practice, statutorily defined capacity in a way that closely reflects the principles articulated in *Masterman-Lister*. The current law is summarised at paras 46–53 of the Official Solicitor's statement, which is annexed to this judgment. That statement also contains a model form of certificate as to capacity to conduct proceedings, which usefully sets out the criteria that should be addressed by anyone giving an opinion on capacity.

Other significant cases on this issue:

* *Re M (Assessment: Official Solicitor)* [2009] EWCA Civ 315, [2009] 2 FLR 950 (judge should be slow to refuse Official Solicitor's request for medical assessment)
* *Re W (Care proceedings)* [2008] EWHC 1188 (Fam), [2010] 1 FLR 1176

G14   MCKENZIE FRIENDS

In the matter of the children of Mr O'Connell, Mr Whelan and Mr Watson

[2005] EWCA Civ 759, [2005] 2 FLR 967 at 971 and 1000

Court of Appeal

Wall LJ

Introduction

[7] It is, furthermore, plain to us that, in family proceedings, both the concept of the *McKenzie* friend itself, and the role he or she can properly play in the proceedings have themselves undergone a process of evolution and change since the term *McKenzie* friend was first used in 1970 following the appeal to this court in the defended divorce case of *McKenzie v McKenzie* [1971] P 33. It is also apparent to us that judicial dicta in some of the early, pre-Children Act cases dealing with *McKenzie* friends do not always seem apt a generation or so later.

...

Discussion

...

[127] The court must plainly retain control over its own procedure. We use slightly different language in our summary in para [128] below, but the underlying principles being applied are, in our view, the same.

[128] Thus, dealing first with the manner in which applications for the appointment of a *McKenzie* friend should be treated, we have already made it clear that we accept in their entirety the submissions made to us by Mr Spon-Smith. In particular, we highlight the following points:

(1)   The purpose of allowing a litigant in person the assistance of a *McKenzie* friend is to further the interests of justice by achieving a level playing field and ensuring a fair hearing. We endorse the proposition that the presumption in favour of allowing a litigant in person the assistance of a *McKenzie* friend is very strong, and that such a request should only be refused for compelling reasons.

Furthermore, should a judge identify such reasons, (s)he must explain them carefully and fully to both the litigant in person and the would-be *McKenzie* friend.

(2) Where a litigant in person wishes to have the assistance of a *McKenzie* friend in private family law proceedings relating to children, the sooner that intention is made known to the court and the sooner the court's agreement for the use of the particular *McKenzie* friend is obtained, the better. In the same way that judicial continuity is important, the *McKenzie* friend, if she/he is to be involved, will be most useful to the litigant in person and to the court if she/he is in a position to advise the litigant throughout.

(3) We do not think it good practice to exclude the proposed *McKenzie* friend from the courtroom or chambers whilst the application by the litigant in person for her/his assistance is being made. The litigant who needs the assistance of a *McKenzie* friend is likely to need the assistance of such a friend to make the application for her/his appointment in the first place. In any event, it seems to us helpful for the proposed *McKenzie* friend to be present so that any concerns about him can be ventilated in her/his presence, and so that the judge can satisfy herself/himself that the *McKenzie* friend fully understands her/his role (and in particular the fact that disclosure of confidential court documents is made to her/him for the purposes of the proceedings only – as to which see paras [132]–[138] below) and that the *McKenzie* friend will abide by the court's procedural rules.

(4) In this context it will always be helpful for the court if the proposed *McKenzie* friend can produce either a short curriculum vitae or a statement about herself/himself, confirming that she/he has no personal interest in the case, and that she/he understands both the role of the *McKenzie* friend and the court's rules as to confidentiality.

(5) We have already stated that any litigant in person who seeks the assistance of a *McKenzie* friend should be allowed that assistance unless there are compelling reasons for refusing it. The following, of themselves, do not, in our judgment, constitute compelling reasons:

(1) that the litigant in person appears to the judge to be of sufficient intelligence to be able to conduct the case on his own without the assistance of a *McKenzie* friend;

(2) the fact that the litigant appears to the judge to have a sufficient mastery of the facts of the case and of the documentation to enable him to conduct the case on his own without the assistance of a *McKenzie* friend;

(3) the fact that the hearing at which the litigant in person seeks the assistance of a *McKenzie* friend is a directions appointment, or a case management appointment;

(4) (subject to what we say below) the fact that the proceedings are confidential and that the court papers contain sensitive information relating to the family's affairs.

[129] We do, of course, understand the point made to us by both Mr Duncan Watson and Ms Gill that a parent who is in conflict with his or her former partner or spouse may well be wary of allowing a stranger who is not legally qualified into a private hearing in order to assist his or her estranged partner in relation to the dispute between them. But we think there are several powerful factors which properly outweigh a reliance on any such reluctance. The first is the compelling Art 6 argument. In each of the cases before us, the party opposing the litigant in person was legally represented by solicitors and counsel. Even if the litigant in person is unrepresented from choice, the Art 6 argument for allowing him a *McKenzie* friend remains powerful.

[130] Secondly, the proceedings remain confidential. The presence of the *McKenzie* friend does not affect the confidentiality of the proceedings. Thirdly, as Mr Spon-Smith pointed out, participation in court proceedings involves a discussion of personal matters in front of a variety of strangers, albeit that they have an official function of some kind or another ...

[131] Finally, and this is the point to which we now turn, the court can, in our view, ensure that the confidentiality of the proceedings is protected against unauthorised wider disclosure of information.

General notes:

The involvement of McKenzie Friends is now the subject of the Practice Guidance: McKenzie Friends (Civil and Family Courts) (July 2010) [2010] 2 FLR 962. Rights of audience / to conduct litigation (as opposed to assistance) are now regulated under the Legal Services Act 2007, Part III Reserved Legal Activities.

Other significant cases on this issue:

- *Re N (McKenzie Friend: rights of audience)* [2008] EWHC 2042 (Fam), [2008] 2 FLR 1899
- *Re J (Residential assessment: rights of audience)* [2009] EWCA Civ 1210, [2010] 1 FLR 1290

G15   JUDICIAL TREATMENT OF LITIGANTS IN PERSON

Re R (Residence order)

[2009] EWCA Civ 445, [2010] 1 FLR 509 at 514

Court of Appeal

Ward LJ

[14]   The judge asked questions which are recorded on four pages of the transcript compared with nearly 15 pages taken to record the cross-examination of the father. Those questions began in this way:

'Judge Hooper: Mr R, the way I propose to proceed with this, as is my usual – not, of course, invariable practice (no practice should be invariable in cases about the welfare of children) is to first of all [ask] [mother] some questions myself based on what I understand to be the issues arising, so as to relieve you of the burden of having to put questions directly to her. However, when I have finished I shall invite you to tell me whether there are any other matters that you wish to challenge her on, the point being that I may say, well, since I don't have to decide everything that parents in cases like this are likely to want to raise, it may not actually be necessary to investigate such a matter as you may have, quite understandably, in mind.'

[15]   Having asked his questions, the judge then said:

'Very well. We have reached the stage, Mr R, where I say two things. First of all, please bear in mind that I don't have to decide everything that has been mentioned or explored today at the hearing, only what I decide is necessary on your application for residence of L. That excludes more than it includes as we all know, because it depends on issues to do with his welfare. Given that the only purpose of cross-examination is to undermine the other side's case or to advance your own is there anything else you would want me to put to [mother] in support of your case as to L's welfare.

Mr R: No, there isn't, no.'

Mrs Seddon proceeded to re-examine her client.

[16]   As more and more parties are forced to appear in person, so judges are frequently required delicately to maintain a level balance to the playing field. Give the litigant in person no help and he will complain: take too active a role and the other side complains. There is no easy way out of that dilemma. It must be left to the individual good sense of the judge to decide how and when to intervene, the circumstances varying infinitely. Here I am totally satisfied that the judge preserved his neutrality. He was helpful but not hostile. The questions were asked courteously and invariably couched in the language of leading evidence-in-chief rather than of cross-examination, wholly consistent with the non-adversarial atmosphere judges strive to achieve in family proceedings. If ever a point came when the judge was acting both 'as father's advocate' and as judge in demanding answers to his own questions, it came at this point:

> 'Q: Well, let's just take it in stages. L remained at Mr and Mrs R's house after the evening discussion that you have discussed.
>
> A: Yes.
>
> Q: Do you agree or disagree that the outcome of the discussion was that L should remain permanently with Mr and Mrs R?
>
> A: On their side, but not on mine.
>
> Q: Miss H, may I beg you to try to answer the question. Do you agree or disagree that the outcome of the discussion was that L should remain permanently at their house.
>
> A: Disagree.
>
> Q: Disagree. That's very helpful. Thank you very much. I'm just going to note that, you see, so that I can get that down. "Disagree outcome was L should remain". What do you say the outcome of the discussion was?
>
> A: There wasn't really any outcome ...'

I do not see in that exchange any sign of the judge putting pressure, still less undue pressure, on the mother. The question needed to be answered. The judge pressed for the answer in a thoroughly courteous and neutral way. There is not the slightest chance that a fair-minded and informed observer, sitting in the back of His Honour Judge Hooper's court, would have concluded, having considered the judge's conduct of that examination, that there was any possibility that the judge was biased. In my judgment, there is no substance at all in the complaint that this was an unfair hearing and I reject that ground of appeal.

This case is also included in relation to:

A5 Wishes of the child
H17 Rejecting Cafcass recommendation

G16   NEED FOR INFORMATION ABOUT PARALLEL PROCEEDINGS

Re M and N (Parallel family and immigration proceedings)

[2008] EWHC 2281 (Fam), [2008] 2 FLR 2030 at 2038

Family Division

Munby J

[36]   In summary, in cases where a parent in family proceedings is also involved in some other relevant matter – for example, an asylum or immigration dispute with the Home Office, criminal proceedings or a criminal investigation, a housing dispute, etc – then:

(i)   Practitioners acting for the parent in the family proceedings have an ongoing duty to remain au courant with what is going on elsewhere even if the other matter is being handled by other professionals.

(ii)   The parents, as part of their ongoing obligation to be frank and open with the court, are under a duty to instruct those advising them in any other relevant matter to keep their family solicitors informed of what is going on. And it is the duty of those advising them in the other matter, having received such authority, to keep the family solicitors informed accordingly.

(iii)   Practitioners involved in family proceedings have a duty to take adequate steps before each hearing to find out, from the solicitors or other professional advisers acting for their client in any other relevant matter, what has been going on, where the other matters have got to and, in cases where some formal decision is anticipated, when that decision is likely to be given.

(iv)   With a view to minimising the room for uncertainty or misunderstanding, it is preferable to obtain copies of the correspondence and other documents on the other solicitors' files rather than attempting to find out what is going on by means of questions and answers in correspondence which may, through lack of understanding, miss the point or be misunderstood.

(v)   If the practitioners acting for the parent in the family proceedings are finding it difficult to obtain the relevant information from the solicitors or other professional advisers acting for their client in the other matter, then prompt consideration needs to be given – and at the earliest possible stage – to approaching the court with a view to inviting the court either to make a peremptory order that the other advisers deliver a complete copy of their file to the solicitors acting

in the family proceedings or to make an order pursuant to the
Protocol. Such applications should not be left to the next directions
or other hearing which has already been fixed if waiting until then
may generate inappropriate delay.

(vi) Where the outcome in the family proceedings is dependent upon or
likely to be affected by the decision of some third party,
consideration should be given – at the earliest possible stage in the
proceedings – as to whether and if so how that third party decision
maker should be brought into some appropriate form of direct
engagement with the family proceedings.

G17　GUIDELINES FOR DNA TESTING

Re F (Children) (DNA Evidence)

[2007] EWHC 3235 (Fam), [2008] 1 FLR 348 at 361

Family Divison

Anthony Hayden QC sitting as a deputy High Court Judge

[32]　As Dr Haizel put it,

> 'getting the question correct has an impact on the interpretation of
> tests results. This is reflected in the results of our validation work
> using cases where the outcome is known. The validation work
> demonstrated (in this case) that simply selecting the likelihood ratio
> of the highest value where the wrong hypothesis has been applied
> and the most likely relationship between the individuals are not
> therefore represented, resulted in an incorrect interpretation of the
> tests.'

I emphasise that the consequences for this family and these children of
this breakdown of understanding could have been potentially very
serious. For that reason and in the hope of being of assistance in the
future, I have tried below to distil some of the points that have arisen
throughout the course of this case in the hope that similar problems may
be averted in the future:

(i)　Any order for DNA testing made by the Family Courts should be
made pursuant to the Family Law Act 1969.

(ii)　The order should specify that it is being made pursuant to the
1969 Act and either the company who is to undertake the testing
should be named or the order should direct that the company
identified to undertake the testing is selected in accordance with the
1969 Act, from the Ministry of Justice's accredited list. Only
accredited companies may be instructed.

(iii)　The taking of samples from children should only be undertaken
pursuant to the express order of the court. If a need arises for
further samples to be taken, that should be arranged only with the
approval of the court. If all the parties agree on the need for further
samples to be taken, the application may be made in writing to the
judge who has conduct of the matter. These requirements should be
communicated to the identified DNA company in the letter of
instruction.

(iv) Save in cases where the issue is solely confined to paternity testing, where the identified company may have its own standardised application form, all requests for DNA testing should be by letter of instruction.

(v) The letter of instruction should emphasise that the responsibilities on DNA experts are identical to those of any expert reporting in a family case and that their overriding obligation is to the court. Further, if any test carried out in pursuance of their instruction casts any doubt on, or appears relevant to the hypothesis set by their instructions, they should regard themselves as being under a duty to draw that to the attention of the court and the parties.

(vi) Any letter of instruction to a DNA company should set out in clear terms precisely what relationships are to be analysed and, where the information is available, the belief of the parties as to the extent of their relatedness. (In recent decades British society has become much more culturally diverse. Some cultures have different attitudes to consanguine relationships, others include children within the family for a variety of reasons (usually highly laudable) who may have remote or indeed no genetic connection to the adults. In these cases, separate statements from the parties setting out the family history and dynamics is likely to be helpful.)

(vii) The letter of instruction should always make clear that if there appears to the DNA expert to be any lack of clarity or ambiguity in their written instructions, or if they require further guidance, they should revert to the solicitor instructing them. The solicitor should keep a note or memorandum of any such request.

(viii) The reports prepared for the court by the DNA experts should bear in mind that they are addressing lay people. The report should strive to interpret their analysis in clear language. Whilst it will usually be necessary to recite the tests undertaken and the likely ratios derived from them, care should be given to explain those results within the context of their identified conclusions.

(ix) Particular care should be taken in the use of phrases such as 'this result provides good evidence'. That is a relative term (and was here overtaken by stronger contrary evidence). Such expressions should always be set within the parameters of current DNA knowledge and should identify in plain terms the limitations as to the reliability of any test carried out. A 'likelihood ratio' by definition is a concept which has uncertainty inherent within it. The extent of uncertainty will vary from test to test and the author of the report must identify and explain those parameters (eg it is not always possible to demonstrate a half-sibling relationship by DNA testing, even where it is given that a biological relationship exists).

(x) In this case, Orchid Cellmark conducted all the tests undertaken by Anglia DNA but also some further additional tests. Though it is not a feature of the evidence here, I would also add that where any particular test and subsequent ratio of likelihood is regarded as in any way controversial within the mainstream of DNA expertise, the use of the test and the reasons for its use should be signalled to the court within the report.

Other significant cases on this issue:

- *Re L (Paternity testing)* [2010] EWCA Civ 1239, [2010] 2 FLR 188 (putative father refusing to undergo testing: whether to order testing of sibling)

G18 USE OF VIDEO EVIDENCE

B v B (Court bundles: video evidence)

[1994] 1 FLR 323 at 326

Family Division

Wall J

[15] Where videos of interviews with children form part of the evidence in the case there should either be a directions appointment at which their use is discussed and directions about their use given; alternatively the parties' respective solicitors should attempt to agree about the manner in which they are to be used. Thus:

(a) Where there is to be a challenge to the technique used or debate as to the interpretation of what the child or interviewer has said, transcripts should be obtained and placed in a separate bundle.
(b) If the judge is to be asked to view the videos in private before the trial begins:
    (i)   the agreement of all the parties to this course should be obtained;
    (ii) the parties should endeavour to agree those parts of the interviews which the judge should look at;
    (iii) a transcript should be provided to the judge.
(c) Where it is intended that the video should be played in court in addition or as an alternative to a private viewing by the judge, early arrangements should be made for the provision of the relevant equipment, agreement reached on the parts of the interviews which are to be played and transcripts provided.

G19 EVERYTHING SHOULD BE DONE IN COURT AND ON RECORD

Re Z (Unsupervised contact: allegations of domestic violence)

[2009] EWCA Civ 430, [2009] 2 FLR 877 at 884

Court of Appeal

Wall LJ

[18] … I need to be very careful at this point because we do not have a transcript of the hearing, nor do we have a transcript of the judgment which the judge ultimately gave. It does appear, however, that at the outset counsel went to see the judge to obtain from him an indication of the nature of his views in relation to the allegations made by the mother.

[19] I do not wish to say more about this than is strictly necessary but, in my judgment, the days for such private consultations between the judge and counsel are long over. I simply do not see how such discussions can properly survive the Human Rights Act 1998 and, equally, I do not think it right or appropriate – even if, as is undoubtedly the case, counsel obtained instructions to go and see the judge – that they should have done so. In my judgment, in cases involving children everything should be done in court and should be on the record. There should not be private discussions between the judge and counsel, particularly, as in this case, it appears that the judge gave an indication, although he went on to hear the case, that the allegations made by the mother did not, in his mind, amount to very much.

This case is also included in relation to:

B28 No short-cut in fact-finding process

Particular case management issues arising from public law cases

G20   PROCEDURAL UNFAIRNESS IN CARE PROCEEDINGS (1)

Re G (Care: challenge to local authority's decision)

[2003] 2 FLR 42 at 49

Family Division

Munby J

The law

[28] The principle of audi alterem partem, that no man or woman is to be condemned unheard, is one of the oldest rules of our administrative law. Well nigh four centuries ago it is to be found in *Boswel's Case* (1606) 6 Co Rep 48b and *Bagg's Case* (1615) 11 Co Rep 93b, where Seneca's Medea (lines 199–200) is prayed in aid. It was what we would now think of as an Art 8 case, for King Cleon of Corinth has ordered Medea to leave the country. She asks for permission to plead her case, only to be told by King Cleon that it is always right to obey the orders of a king. She replies: Qui statuit aliquid parte inaudita altera, aequum licet statuerit, haud aequus fuit (He who decides something without hearing the other side, even if he makes a fair decision, has not himself been fair).

[29] In *R v Chancellor, Masters and Scholars of the University of Cambridge (Dr Bentley's Case)* (1723) 1 Str 557, at 567, Fortescue J founded the principle on the Biblical account (Genesis, chap 3, vv 9–13) of the expulsion of Adam and Eve from the Garden of Eden: 'even God himself did not pass sentence upon Adam before he was called upon to make his defence' – though as Oliver J once had occasion to observe (*Midland Bank Trust Co Ltd and Another v Green and Another (No 3)* [1979] Ch 496 at 512B) the common law has in relation to this famous incident been a trifle selective in its application of the Biblical doctrine. Be that as it may, secular man at the threshold of the third millennium looks not to the sacred texts of a revealed religion but rather to Art 6 and, in the present context, more particularly to Art 8 of the European Convention. But the fundamental principle is the same: parents are not to be condemned unheard when the State, in the guise of a local authority, seeks to take their children away from them.

[30] These are matters which I considered at some length in *Re L (Care: Assessment: Fair Trial)* [2002] EWHC 1379 (Fam), [2002] 2 FLR 730. I need not repeat what I there said. For present purposes the important point, and one which local authorities must appreciate, though too often it seems they do not, is that Art 8 affords parents who are involved in care proceedings not merely substantive protection against any inappropriate interference with their private and family life by public authorities but also significant procedural safeguards. As the court said in *McMichael v United Kingdom* (1995) 20 EHRR 205 at para 87:

> 'Whilst Art 8 contains no explicit procedural requirements, the decision-making process leading to measures of interference must be fair and such as to afford due respect to the interests safeguarded by Art 8.'

[31] The fundamental rule was articulated by the court as long ago as 1988 in *W v United Kingdom* (1988) 10 EHRR 29 at paras 63–64:

> 'The decision-making process must therefore ... be such as to secure that [the parents'] views and interests are made known to and duly taken into account by the local authority and that they are able to exercise in due time any remedies available to them ... what therefore has to be determined is whether, having regard to the particular circumstances of the case and notably the serious nature of the decisions to be taken, the parents have been involved in the decision-making process, seen as a whole, to a degree sufficient to provide them with the requisite protection of their interests. If they have not, there will have been a failure to respect their family life and the interference resulting from the decision will not be capable of being regarded as "necessary" within the meaning of Art 8.'

[32] Moreover, and as I pointed out in *Re L (Care: Assessment: Fair Trial)* [2002] EWHC 1379 (Fam), [2002] 2 FLR 730, at para [105]:

> 'Art 8 imposes positive obligations of disclosure on a local authority.'

[33] The local authority is under a duty to make full and frank disclosure of all key documents in its possession or available to it, including, in particular, attendance notes of meetings and conversations and minutes of case conferences, core group meetings and similar meetings. I recognise that this imposes a heavy burden on local authorities, but there are, as I pointed out in *Re L* at paras [140]–[151], good reasons why that should be so.

[34] So procedural fairness is something mandated not merely by Art 6 but also by Art 8. To an extent – and whilst the care proceedings themselves are on foot – Arts 6 and 8 march side by side. As I pointed out in *Re L* at paras [87] and [113]:

> '... unfairness in the trial process may involve a violation not merely of a parent's rights under Art 6(1) but also of his or her rights under Art 8 ...
>
> Unfairness at *any* stage of the litigation process may involve breaches not merely of Art 8 but also of Art 6.' (original emphasis)

[35] But in relation to the procedural requirements imposed by Art 8, it is also important for local authorities to appreciate, as I said in *Re L* at para [88], that:

> 'the protection afforded ... by Art 8 ... is *not* confined to unfairness in the *trial* process ... Art 8 guarantees fairness in the decision-making process at *all* stages of child protection.' (original emphasis)

[36] So Art 8 requires that parents are properly involved in the decision-making process not merely before the care proceedings are launched, and during the period when the care proceedings are on foot (the issue which I was concerned with in *Re L*), but also – and this is what is important for present purposes – after the care proceedings have come to an end and whilst the local authority is implementing the care order (the issue which Holman J was concerned with in *Re M (Care: Challenging Decisions by Local Authority)* [2001] 2 FLR 1300 and the President in *C v Bury Metropolitan Borough Council* [2002] EWHC 1438 (Fam), [2002] 2 FLR 868).

[37] I make no apology for repeating here what I said in *Re L (Care: Assessment: Fair Trial)* [2002] EWHC 1379 (Fam), [2002] 2 FLR 730 at paras [149] and [151], because what has happened in the present case suggests that the full implications of Art 8 are still not properly understood. Having referred at some length to the important observations of Charles J in *Re R (Care: Disclosure: Nature of Proceedings)* [2002] 1 FLR 755, I continued:

> 'Too often in public law proceedings both the level of disclosure and the extent of a parent's involvement in the crucial phases of the out of court decision-making processes fall short not just of the well-established requirements of domestic law ... but also of the standards which are now demanded by Arts 6 and 8 of the Convention. The present case is in many ways an all too characteristic example of an all too frequent phenomenon. Not the least important of the many important messages which, as it seems

to me, we all need to absorb from what Charles J has so clearly told us in *Re R* is the need for change in the prevailing culture – a culture of reluctant and all too often inadequate disclosure.

...

The State, in the form of the local authority, assumes a heavy burden when it seeks to take a child into care. Part of that burden is the need, in the interests not merely of the parent but also of the child, for a transparent and transparently fair procedure at all stages of the process – by which I mean the process both in and out of court. If the watchword of the Family Division is indeed *openness* – and it is and must be – then documents must be made openly available and crucial meetings at which a family's future is being decided must be conducted openly and with the parents, if they wish, either present or represented. Otherwise there is unacceptable scope for unfairness and injustice, not just to the parents but also to the children.' (original emphasis)

[38] There is one further matter to which I drew attention in *Re L* (see paras [153]–[155]) and which requires emphasis. Social workers should at all times keep clear, accurate, full and balanced notes of all relevant conversations and meetings between themselves and/or with parents, other family members and others involved with the family. And where important meetings are held there should be a written agenda circulated in advance to all concerned. Clear, accurate, full and balanced minutes of the meeting (identifying in particular what information has been given to the meeting and by whom) should be taken by someone nominated for that task before the meeting begins. And, as soon as possible after the meeting, the minutes should be agreed by those present as being an accurate record of the meeting and then be immediately disclosed to all parties.

[39] Every local authority involved in child protection is a 'public authority' within the meaning of s 6 of the Human Rights Act 1998. Accordingly, s 6(1) of the Human Rights Act 1998, when read in conjunction with ss 1(1) and 6(6), makes it 'unlawful' for a local authority whilst engaged in child protection to act (or fail to act) in a way which is incompatible with Art 8. In accordance with s 7(1)(a), any parent who claims that a local authority has acted, or proposes to act, in a way which is made unlawful by s 6(1) can bring freestanding proceedings against the authority seeking relief under s 8 of the Human Rights Act 1998. So, as I pointed out in *Re L (Care: Assessment: Fair Trial)* at para [91], even if there are no care or other proceedings on foot, a parent who claims to have been the victim of unfair decision-making by a local authority has a remedy founded on breach of Art 8 which can be vindicated either in proceedings for judicial review and/or by a freestanding application under the Human Rights Act 1998.

[40] These principles quite plainly apply to the kind of situation with which I am here concerned. The leading case, as the parents correctly submitted to Singer J on 16 December 2002, is Holman J's decision in *Re M (Care: Challenging Decisions by Local Authority)*. My brother's judgment is perfectly clear. In *Re L*, I sought to emphasise its significance. But the present case would suggest that its true significance has still not been appreciated by local authorities and those who advise them. Let me try again.

[41] In *Re M* a full care order had been made on 10 November 2000. The care plan dated 23 October 2000 which had been approved by the court contemplated rehabilitation of the child to the mother or, if that failed, and subject to assessment, to the father. At a meeting on 23 April 2001 – after the care proceedings had come to an end – the local authority decided fundamentally to change the care plan, abandoning all plans for rehabilitation with either parent and approving contingent plans for adoption. The parents were not invited to that meeting and, as Holman J found (at 1310F), would not have been permitted to attend if they had sought to do so. Holman J held that the local authority had acted unlawfully on 23 April 2001 because, as he put it (at 1311A):

'in the particular circumstances of this case, the decision-making process seen as a whole did not involve the parents to a degree sufficient to provide them with the requisite protection of their interests, and ... it was objectively (but unwittingly) unfair.'

[42] Quashing the local authority's decision, he added (1311G, 1313C):

'the meeting on 23 April proved to be the decisive meeting in the decision-making process, and neither parent had any opportunity to address it, or to clarify any factual issues with the persons participating at the meeting.

...

I have heard nothing at all to satisfy me that there was any necessity to deny each parent an opportunity to attend at, and address, this critical meeting.'

[43] The fact that a local authority has parental responsibility for children pursuant to s 33(3)(a) of the Children Act 1989 does not entitle it to take decisions about those children without reference to, or over the heads of, the children's parents. A local authority, even if clothed with the authority of a care order, is not entitled to make significant changes in the care plan, or to change the arrangements under which the children are living, let alone to remove the children from home if they are living with their parents, without properly involving the parents in the decision-making process and without giving the parents a proper opportunity to make their case before a decision is made. After all, the fact that the local authority also has parental responsibility does not deprive the parents of their parental responsibility.

[44] A local authority can lawfully exercise parental responsibility for a child only in a manner consistent with the substantive and procedural requirements of Art 8. There is nothing in s 33(3)(b) of the Children Act 1989 that entitles a local authority to act in breach of Art 8. On the contrary, s 6(1) of the Human Rights Act 1998 requires a local authority to exercise its powers under both s 33(3)(a) and s 33(3)(b) of the Children Act 1989 in a manner consistent with both the substantive and the procedural requirements of Art 8.

[45] In a case such as this, a local authority, before it can properly arrive at a decision to remove children from their parents, must tell the parents (preferably in writing) precisely what it is proposing to do. It must spell out (again in writing) the reasons why it is proposing to do so. It must spell out precisely (in writing) the factual matters it is relying on. It must give the parents a proper opportunity to answer (either orally and/or in writing as the parents wish) the allegations being made against them. And it must give the parents a proper opportunity (orally and/or in writing as they wish) to make representations as to why the local authority should not take the threatened steps. In short, the local authority must involve the parents properly in the decision-making process. In particular, the parents (together with their representatives if they wish to be assisted) should normally be given the opportunity to attend at, and address, any critical meeting at which crucial decisions are to be made.

[46] The local authority's counsel, as I have said, sought to argue before Singer J on 16 December 2002 that the court was being asked to interfere inappropriately with the local authority's statutory powers under the care order. Support for that submission was sought to be derived from what Lord Nicholls of Birkenhead said in *Re S (Minors) (Care Order: Implementation of Care Plan); Re W (Minors) (Care Order: Adequacy of Care Plan)* [2002] UKHL 10, [2002] 2 AC 291, [2002] 1 FLR 815. The submission, with all respect to counsel, was completely misconceived.

[47] I accept, of course, as Lord Nicholls of Birkenhead put it (see *Re S (Minors) (Care Order: Implementation of Care Plan); Re W (Minors) (Care Order: Adequacy of Care Plan)* at paras [23]–[28] and [42]), that it is a cardinal principle of the Children Act 1989 that, after a final care order has been made, the court is not empowered to intervene in the way the local authority discharges its parental responsibility under the care order and that the court retains no supervisory role in monitoring the authority's discharge of its responsibilities. But it is vital to appreciate that what Lord Nicholls of Birkenhead was there referring to – and the only thing he was referring to – was the power of the court – the Family Division – when exercising its jurisdiction under the Children Act 1989 or in wardship.

[48] Lord Nicholls of Birkenhead was not disputing the power of the court – the Family Division or the Administrative Court – to intervene when exercising its powers of judicial review or when exercising its jurisdiction under the Human Rights Act 1998. He expressly acknowledged (see para [24]) that the High Court's judicial review jurisdiction – the jurisdiction exercised by the Administrative Court – remains available (see also in this connection what I said in *Re F; F v Lambeth London Borough Council* [2002] 1 FLR 217 at paras [45]–[47] and [51] and *A v A Health Authority and Others; Re J and Linked Applications* [2002] EWHC 18 (Fam/Admin), [2002] Fam 213, sub nom *A (A Patient) v A Health Authority; Re J; R (S) v Secretary of State for the Home Department* [2002] 1 FLR 845 at paras [47]–[56]). Lord Nicholls of Birkenhead recognised (see paras [54]–[57]) the continuing obligation of a local authority to comply with Art 8 after a care order has been made and acknowledged (see paras [61]–[63], [72] and [81]) that breaches of Art 8 could be remedied by an application brought under ss 7 and 8 of the Human Rights Act 1998. Indeed, he expressly approved Holman J's decision in *Re M (Care: Challenging Decisions by Local Authority)* [2001] 2 FLR 1300 describing Holman J (para [46]) as 'proceeding squarely within the extended jurisdiction conferred by ss 7 and 8' of the Human Rights Act 1998 and as having 'applied the provisions of the Human Rights Act 1998 in the manner Parliament intended, there in respect of a breach of Art 8'. Moreover, and as the parents' solicitor pointed out to Singer J on 16 December 2002, Lord Nicholls of Birkenhead stated (at para [79]) that the decision 'whether rehabilitation is still a realistic possibility', and that was the very question raised in the present case:

> '... attract[s] a high degree of judicial control. It must be doubtful whether judicial review will always meet this standard, even if the review is conducted with the heightened scrutiny discussed in *R (Daly) v Secretary of State for the Home Department* [2001] UKHL 26, [2001] 2 AC 532.'

[49] Quite plainly, in my judgment, Lord Nicholls of Birkenhead was accepting that parents who find themselves in the kind of position in which the parents in *Re M* and the parents in the present case found themselves, have an effective remedy available to them in the Family Division under the Human Rights Act 1998. Lord Mackay of Clashfern took precisely the same view (see para [109]).

[50] This, as it seems to me, is a classic example of the kind of case where, whatever may have been the position previously, the Human Rights Act 1998 gives parents treated as badly as the parents in this case

appear to have been treated by Authority X, effective remedies for the
breach by a local authority of either the substantive or the procedural
requirements of Art 8.

[51] I should add that my analysis of *Re M* and *Re S (Minors) (Care
Order: Implementation of Care Plan); Re W (Minors) (Care Order:
Adequacy of Care Plan)* [2002] UKHL 10, [2002] 2 AC 291, [2002] 1 FLR
815 accords entirely, so far as I can see, with the analysis of the President
in *C v Bury Metropolitan Borough Council* at paras [41]–[57], an analysis
with the whole of which I respectfully agree. I draw attention to what the
President said at para [56]:

> 'The approach of the court to a challenge to the procedures followed
> and the care plan adopted by the local authority which is being
> criticised has to be broader and more investigative than prior to the
> implementation of the Human Rights Act 1998 and the court must
> apply the requirements of Art 8(2) of the Convention. As Holman J
> said in *Re M* at 1313 there is a heavy responsibility and wide
> discretion placed on the court in considering, after the event, the
> lawfulness of a local authority decision-making process.'

G21   PROCEDURAL UNFAIRNESS IN CARE PROCEEDINGS (2)

Re J (Care: assessment: fair trial)

[2006] EWCA Civ 545, [2007] 1 FLR 77 at 86

Court of Appeal

Wilson LJ

[25] All that said, however, I consider that there were two features of the manner in which the local authority reached and communicated their care plan which fell short of proper standards of fairness and transparency in a local authority's conduct of care proceedings:

(a) Prior to their decision, whenever it was reached, that their care plan should be for C's immediate adoption, the local authority should in some way have invited the mother to comment upon the concerns which, provisionally, were inclining them in that direction ...

(b) When, at the third stage of the meeting on 10 August 2005, the local authority communicated their decision to the mother, they did not make clear, as full transparency required, that this was a decision on their part to which neither Ms Scott Doe nor the guardian had expressly assented ...

[26] It is, however, one thing for me, following application of (let me confess) little more than my instinct for fairness and transparency, to criticise the local authority in the above two respects; it would be quite another for me to conclude that there was any infringement by the local authority of the mother's human rights. On the contrary I am convinced that there was no such infringement of her rights, whether under Art 6 or under Art 8 of the Convention. Neither of the suggested departures from good practice was sufficiently substantial to infect the fairness of the proceedings ... When, however, complaints about the local authority's conduct were articulated, albeit not with the limited focus which I would favour, they became the subject of intensive debate in the proceedings, disproportionate to their significance.

[27] In *Re V (Care: Pre-Birth Actions)* [2004] EWCA Civ 1575, [2005] 1 FLR 627 this court considered a local authority's appeal against an order at the conclusion of care proceedings that they should pay each parent damages in the sum of £100 for having infringed their rights under Art 6 of the Convention ... Following the birth such proceedings were duly issued and, prior to making the award of damages, the trial judge

had made a care order referable to the baby. The basis of the judge's conclusion that the local authority had infringed the rights of the parents under Art 6 of the Convention was that, prior to the birth, they should more clearly have explained their concerns to the parents and indicated the manner in which they might seek to allay them. In setting aside the award of damages, this court held that there had been no infringement of the parents' human rights first because the matters which were the subject of complaint had pre-dated both the child's birth and thus, of course, the initiation of proceedings and, second, because, upon any review of them as a whole, the proceedings could not be categorised as unfair.

[28]   In *Re V*, Thorpe LJ said, at para [4]:

'It seems to me almost self-evident that the order which [counsel for the local authority] challenges is unprincipled, but we have heard full submissions from him to enable us to deliver a judgment to discourage repetition of such an outcome in other cases. We have also heard from [counsel] for the guardian, who warns us that as a consequence in part of the case of *Re L*[1] ... long trials of alleged breaches of Arts 6 and 8 [of the Convention] rights are beginning to encumber local authority applications for care orders, with consequential delay and expense that ultimately proves wasted.'

He concluded at para [24] 'by suggesting that trial judges should be extremely cautious in reading too much into para [154] of the judgment of Munby J'.

[29]   In *Re V*, Wall LJ said, at para [29]:

'The mischief identified by the case ... lies in the fact that the judge has isolated a sentence in the judgment of a judge of the Family Division dealing with issues of good practice, and has elevated an alleged failure by the local authority to comply with the practice identified in that sentence into a breach of the parents' Art 6 [of the Convention] rights ...'

He added at para [33] that judges who hear care proceedings:

'... should be acute to identify and weed out barren arguments under the Human Rights Act 1998 and the Convention which do not relate either to the identification of the threshold criteria under s 31 of the [Children] Act, or the ultimate welfare disposal of issues in the case.'

[30]   ... I believe that, had *Re V* been brought to his attention, the judge would have kept a tighter rein upon the forceful attempts on behalf of the mother to divert the focus of the hearing towards the local authority's alleged failures to observe the precepts commended in *Re L*; would more

---

[1]   *Re L (Care: assessment: fair trial)* [2002] EWHC 1379 (Fam), [2002] 2 FLR 730.

clearly have appreciated the distinction between non-compliance with those precepts and infringement of human rights; and would not have granted permission to appeal. It is true that the appeal gives to this court the opportunity, from the foot of a different factual situation from that in *Re V*, to give further guidance as to the proper management of allegations of non-compliance with the precepts commended in *Re L*. In particular it gives us the opportunity to stress that, although any actual infringement of parental human rights in the course of care proceedings, far from being brushed under the carpet, must in court be rooted out and exposed, the precepts must not be used as a bandwagon, to be drawn across the tracks of the case and to de-rail the proceedings from their prompt travel towards the necessary conclusions referable to, and in the interests of, the child. No doubt it is a difficult balance for trial judges to strike; but we here will support those who deal robustly with suggestions of such minor non-compliance with the precepts commended by Munby J as could never sensibly be translated into an infringement of human rights ...

Other significant cases on this issue:

- *Re C (Breach of human rights: damages)* [2007] EWCA Civ 2, [2007] 1 FLR 1957

G22   PREPARATION AND DISCLOSURE: DUTIES OF LA

Re R (Care: disclosure: nature of proceedings)

[2002] 1 FLR 755 at 772, 773, 773, 773 and 775

Family Division

Charles J

Preparation of evidence and disclosure

It was rightly accepted that all parties are under a duty to make full and frank disclosure. Initially, this places a heavy burden on a local authority when presenting their case (see, for example, para 4 of the *Practice Direction: Case Management* (31 January 1995) [1995] 1 FLR 456). As that *Practice Direction* provides, it is also their duty and that of their legal advisers to confine issues and evidence to what is reasonably considered necessary for the proper presentation of the case. A proper presentation is, naturally, one that is fair and that has proper regard to Art 6 of the Convention.

...

In such a case, the local authority are effectively seeking to prove criminal offences to the civil standard. In my judgment, the difference in procedures that exists between the criminal courts and the family courts (e g *Practice Direction: Case Management* (31 January 1995) [1995] 1 FLR 456, the making of the case in family courts in statements without a charge or indictment, the hearing being in private in the family courts and the wider obligations relating to disclosure on respondents and their experts in family cases) does not lead to or found an argument that requirements of fairness in respect of the identification of the allegations made and the evidence, both oral and documentary, to be relied on to prove them by the person advancing those allegations, namely the local authority, is substantially different to that of a prosecuting authority.

...

Although this was not the case here, in my view too, often the allegations have to be looked for in, and extracted from, the body of lengthy statements put in by social workers which seek to recount the story thus far and therefore they have to be sought in various places set out in a narrative form by the local authority.

A separate identification of the allegations that the local authority seek to establish and thus the facts they seek to prove to establish, (i) the existence of the threshold criteria and, (ii) the reasons why the care plan proposed best promotes the welfare of the relevant child, would, in my view, helpfully focus thinking on the issues in the proceedings and thus, for example, the need to identify the evidence, both oral and documentary, on which the local authority rely (see again para 1 of *Best Practice Guide* (June 1997)).

...

Important parts of the preparation of statements and thus the evidence that the local authority are to rely on are: (a) a proper understanding of the relevant legal principles, the issues in the case and the procedures of the court (see again *Best Practice Guide* (June 1997), in particular paras 1–5 thereof) and, with that background:

'...

(b) a proper examination of the background material and thus the relevant files;
(c) a proper discussion with the relevant witnesses to ensure, so far as possible, that their statements contain a full and proper account of the relevant matters, which include the central matters seen or heard by that witness, the sources of hearsay being recorded by that witness, and the relevant background to and the circumstances in which the matters set out took place; and
(d) a proper consideration of what further information or material should be obtained.'

By reason of their respective training and experience, all of the above are basic issues for a litigation lawyer, but not necessarily for a social worker (see again *Practice Direction: Case Management* (31 January 1995) [1995] 1 FLR 456 and in particular paras 1 and 4 thereof, which make it clear that duties are imposed on the parties' legal advisers).

If this work is done properly, it would also mean or lead to the following:

(a) experts being instructed on a properly informed basis;
(b) statements exhibiting appropriate background material; and
(c) additional appropriate discovery.

...

All the above duties of all the parties continue with appropriate modifications throughout the preparation of the case and thus to the time when a consideration of the reports of experts falls to be carried out.

In relation to disclosure, there seems to be a general reluctance of many involved in family proceedings to disclose documents. In part, this is justifiably based on the nature of the procedure which, like judicial review, is based on statements and the obligation of the public body involved and other parties to make full disclosure. This leads to the discouragement by the courts of fishing expeditions for discovery or applications for discovery that can be described as Micawberism (see, again, paras 2 and 4 of the *Practice Direction: Case Management* (31 January 1995) [1995] 1 FLR 456).

However, it seems to me that, additionally, this reluctance is also often incorrectly based on views relating to confidentiality and an assertion that records of the local authority are subject to public interest immunity. Both of these are large subjects and this judgment is not an appropriate place to address them in any detail. However, in my view, issues relating to confidentiality and public interest immunity in the context of Children Act proceedings are regularly misunderstood and asserted as a reason why disclosure has not been made, or for refusing a request for disclosure made of a local authority, a guardian ad litem and experts in connection with proceedings under the Children Act 1989.

In my judgment, the first thing that needs to be remembered is that when disclosure in respect of proceedings under the Children Act 1989 falls to be considered, the first question, as it is in other proceedings, is whether the material passes the relevant threshold test for disclosure. This test has had a number of formulations, but one regularly used in relation to it is and remains whether disclosure is necessary for the fair disposal of the proceedings; see the old RSC Ord 24, r 13 and now CPR 31.17, which in its first part reflects the definition of standard disclosure in CPR 31.6, which is in the following terms:

'Standard disclosure requires a party to disclose only—

(a) the documents on which he relies; and
(b) the documents which—
   (i) adversely affect his own case;
   (ii) adversely affect another party's case; or
   (iii) support another party's case; and
(c) the documents which he is required to disclose by a relevant practice direction.'

Also, it now needs to be remembered that issues of disclosure engage Convention rights in family proceedings, particularly Arts 6 and 8.

Other significant cases on this issue:

- *Brent London Borough Council v N (foster carers) and P (by her guardian)* [2005] EWHC 1676 (Fam), [2006] 1 FLR 310

- *Re K (Order delay)* [2007] EWHC 2090 (Fam), [2008] 1 FLR 572 (local authority should have done more when police failed to disclose information)

This case is also included in relation to:

D5   Reunification not an overriding factor
G23   Preparation and disclosure: mirror duties of respondents
G24   Disclosure of relevant notes
G41   Court / parties / experts bound by findings made / not made
G45   Use of experts: general guidance
G51   Responsibilities on receipt of report
G75   Statement of general principles (2)
G82   Public interest immunity
H29   Costs: illustration in public law

G23 PREPARATION AND DISCLOSURE: MIRROR DUTIES OF RESPONDENTS

Re R (Care: disclosure: nature of proceedings)

[2002] 1 FLR 755 at 774 and 787

Family Division

Charles J

Preparation of evidence and disclosure

…

It is not only the applicant local authority and their advisers who have duties in respect of the preparation of cases and the instruction of experts: all the respondents also have such duties.

The guardian has access to the local authority's files. However, in my view, this access does not mean that the other respondents should treat, or regard, the guardian as a bloodhound or a detective or otherwise rely on the guardian to take primary responsibility to check that there has been full and proper preparation of evidence, disclosure and instructions to experts. In my view, that is not the role of the guardian and, in any event, other respondents will be likely to have different interests to the minors represented by the guardian. That was certainly the case here.

It follows, in my judgment, that all respondents and their advisers:

(a)   have mirror duties and responsibilities to those I have set out relating to the local authority in respect of their evidence;

(b)   should check the decisions made as to the experts to be instructed and the terms of those instructions and thus the input they want to have into those terms;

(c)   should consider whether it appears that the local authority have performed their duties in preparing the case and as to disclosure;

(d)   should consider what further information or material should be obtained; and

(e)   should pursue issues as to disclosure at interlocutory hearings if they have not been agreed.

All the above duties of all the parties continue with appropriate modifications throughout the preparation of the case and thus to the time when a consideration of the reports of experts falls to be carried out.

...

That leads on to the duty of respondents and their advisers to give a full
account of their case and position and thus to provide third party
confirmation where it is available. Their duty to give a full account means
that they should not adopt a stance of: 'You prove it'. A full account of
what the respondents accept and what they deny should be given as soon
as possible. This will help to identify and confine the issues.

Further, the respondents and their advisers should consider whether they
wish further documents or information to be provided by the local
authority, the guardian, an expert or another respondent.

This case is also included in relation to:

D5   Reunification not an overriding factor
G22 Preparation and disclosure: duties of LA
G24 Disclosure of relevant notes
G41 Court / parties / experts bound by findings made / not made
G45 Use of experts: general guidance
G51 Responsibilities on receipt of report
G75 Statement of general principles (2)
G82 Public interest immunity
H29 Costs: illustration in public law

G24   DISCLOSURE OF RELEVANT NOTES

Re R (Care: disclosure: nature of proceedings)

[2002] 1 FLR 755 at 778

Family Division

Charles J

Further, generally I make the point that, in my judgment, both local authorities and guardians ad litem should be more willing than they seem to be at present to exhibit their notes of relevant conversations and incidents that are relied on as evidence for findings at the threshold or welfare stage of proceedings, rather than to embark on what is a time-consuming and difficult exercise of preparing summaries of those notes.

In this context, the practice of the Official Solicitor of exhibiting attendance records was referred to by leading counsel for the father and I agree that:

(a)   it would have been beneficial if this practice had been adopted in this case by both the local authority and the guardian;

(b)   it is likely to be beneficial in many cases if this practice were to be so adopted.

This does not mean that the relevant social worker and the guardian do not give a summary or point to the most important parts of the notes, but has the result that the parties and the court can more readily see the context in which certain statements were made or events took place.

In this case, in advancing the case on sexual abuse the local authority relied on allegations made to and events in the presence of (i) the foster-mother and a lady who helped her and was herself a foster-mother, (ii) social workers, (iii) a doctor who examined the boys and (iv) the guardian, but only some of the relevant contemporaneous notes were disclosed. This caused serious problems and should not have happened.

To my mind, all the notes of the foster-carers were relevant because they gave a contemporaneous record of the circumstances in which the allegations relied on were made and which led up to the making of those allegations. Notes recording and containing references to the allegations were of most relevance, but, in my judgment, notes of other matters were relevant to give an indication of the matters noted more generally and the approach of the two foster-carers to note-taking.

Further, those further notes were likely to be relevant to the allegations of neglect. The failure to either (i) gather together all the notes of the foster-carers (ii) or to go through the history and background with them, led to the experts being instructed and this case being opened on an incorrect basis as to when the first allegations of sexual abuse were made.

Additionally, the guardian, in correspondence through her solicitors, resisted a request that she should disclose her contemporaneous notes of meetings relating to passages in her report that were relied on as allegations of sexual abuse made by the boys ...

When the issue of disclosure of the guardian's notes was raised during the hearing, after some initial reluctance, her counsel, in my judgment correctly, accepted that the notes were relevant and should be disclosed and, as he said, when you analysed the position it became clear why that was the case. In short, they were contemporaneous notes of conversations with, amongst others, the boys concerning the sexual abuse alleged and more general behaviour and conduct of the boys. They therefore contained a contemporaneous record of highly relevant exchanges.

Other significant cases on this issue:

- Cf *Re L (Children) (Care proceedings: significant harm)* [2006] EWCA Civ 1282, [2007] 1 FLR 1068: see G53 – Disclosure of documents on which reliance is placed

This case is also included in relation to:

D5   Reunification not an overriding factor
G22 Preparation and disclosure: duties of LA
G23 Preparation and disclosure: mirror duties of respondents
G41 Court / parties / experts bound by findings made / not made
G45 Use of experts: general guidance
G51 Responsibilities on receipt of report
G75 Statement of general principles (2)
G82 Public interest immunity
H29 Costs: illustration in public law

G25 PROCEEDINGS NOT TO BE DISCLOSED TO FATHER

Local Authority v M and F; the Children by their Guardian

[2009] EWHC 3172 (Fam), [2010] 1 FLR 1355 at 1359

Family Division

Hedley J

The jurisdiction of the court

[18] As I have indicated, it is common ground that the court has the jurisdiction to make the order sought. It is to be found in r 4.7(5)(b) of the Family Proceedings Rules 1991 (the FPR). It is unsurprisingly a power that has been rarely exercised in relation to a parent whose whereabouts is known. Even where it has been exercised, the father concerned did not have parental responsibility but was nevertheless heard on the application. The case of *Re AB (Care Proceedings: Service on Husband Ignorant of Child's Existence)* [2003] EWCA Civ 1842, [2004] 1 FLR 527 appears to be the only occasion on which this provision has been considered by the Court of Appeal and did involve a party with parental responsibility. That case, although requiring disclosure, does acknowledge the jurisdiction of the court. It is said that if the order were made here it would represent a new step in two respects: first, discharging a party with parental responsibility; and, secondly, doing so without hearing counsel on his behalf.

[19] I think the second aspect is probably inevitable in this case. Counsel so instructed would have to act without any reference to the father himself or else the whole exercise would be self-defeating. In any event, the advocate to the court has clearly set out the issues that require to be addressed. The second issue does not, therefore, trouble me as otherwise it might have done. It seems to me that the first should initially be considered within Ms Fatima's framework.

Advocate to the court's framework

[20] This starts as it should, with a consideration of Art 6 and the essential context of fairness. Any proceedings under Part IV of the 1989 Act are grave matters for any family. To deprive a parent with parental responsibility of any involvement in those proceedings is self-evidently a

grave step. Indeed even to restrict their involvement by a partial
withholding of disclosure is a grave step. At the same time the right of
access to the court is not an absolute one and not every limitation or even
exclusion is unlawful. As the European Court said in *Ashingdane v United
Kingdom* (Application No 8225/78) (1985) 7 EHRR 528 at para 57:

'... the limitations applied must not restrict or reduce the access left
to the individual in such a way or to such an extent that the very
essence of the right is impaired [and] a limitation will not be
compatible with Article 6(1) if it does not pursue a legitimate aim
and if there is not a reasonable relationship of proportionality
between the means employed and the aim sought to be achieved.'

That statement of principle is, of course, of the utmost value and has
been often applied since. It finds expression in English law in the
judgment of Dame Elizabeth Butler-Sloss P in the case of *Re H and G
(Adoption: Consultation of Unmarried Fathers)* [2001] 1 FLR 646 where at
para [43] she says this:

'This raises the difficult question of the impact of the rights of other
parties under Art 8, and the welfare principles, on the right to a fair
trial. There must, however, in principle, be some qualification of the
right of a party to be heard in proceedings. This would be likely to
arise under two separate categories, namely, a policy decision of the
court, in the exercise of its right to run its own proceedings within
the requirements that there should be a fair trial, and, secondly, the
practicalities of service on a potential litigant or his attendance at
the hearing. There will be cases where notice to a father would create
a significant physical risk to the mother, to children in the family, or
to other people concerned in the case (see for instance *Re X (Care:
Notice of Proceedings)* [1996] 1 FLR 186). That might result in the
court balancing the fairness to the father of notice, against the real
risks of the consequences of such *notice*.'

[21] Thus it is submitted (correctly in my view) that the requirements of
Art 6 will be highly fact specific and vary from case to case. On the other
hand it is essential never to lose sight of the fact that any incursion into
what would normally be regarded as an Art 6 right is a serious matter and
the more so where the nature of the proceedings is in itself very serious.

[22] As is apparent, no judgment can be reached without a proper
analysis of the impact of Art 8. It is equally apparent in the context of
this case that the Art 8 rights of both parents and also their children are
fully engaged. Moreover, respect for Art 8 rights may also of itself have
procedural implications, as the European Court pointed out in *W v
United Kingdom* (Application No 9749/82) (1987) 10 EHRR 29. It follows
that the court must be aware of the implications for the parties of both
sets of rights.

The rights of the parties in this case

[23] Article 8(1) of course provides a qualified right, that qualification appearing in Art 8(2). The consideration of these matters involves the court in having in mind the whole breadth of the evidence available. The children have a right to family life. That involves a relationship with both parents. It also involves a right not to be pawns in a battle of violent intensity (or indeed intense violence) between those two parents but to an upbringing in reasonable calm and safety within, if possible, a parental home. The mother has a right both to have a relationship with her children and to bring them up and a right to do so without threat of violence or other harm from the other parent. The father has a right to a relationship with his children though his right to bring them up is rendered nugatory by his current indeterminate sentence of imprisonment.

[24] All parties have Art 6 rights too. The father's have been set out. The mother has the right to participate without the proceedings in themselves being the means of endangering life and limb. The children too have a right to have their future determined in proceedings to which both parents have contributed but through which they themselves (or a potential carer) are not thereby endangered.

[25] The vital question is whether all these rights can be accommodated. If they cannot the court must determine which rights are to predominate and how that is to be accomplished. By the same token the court must consider how, if some rights are to be compromised or even superseded, that is to be affected by the least interference in any such rights.

The balance to be struck in this case

[26] The starting points are two-fold: first, that the father should be entitled to participate in this case; and secondly that the children and mother should not be put at risk of serious harm by the conduct of the proceedings. In considering the first the court should start with full participation then consider partial participation, effected in this case by the disclosure of redacted documents and then, only as a device of last resort, his exclusion from the proceedings. In considering the second, the court must be alert both to the risk and to the magnitude of the consequences should the risk eventuate, and must also consider whether and to what extent that risk can be managed by the court's control of its own processes.

[27] As to the question of risk and consequences, I have already set out my view. In my judgment, the father, although incarcerated, represents a real and substantial risk to the children and their mother. I am also satisfied that through his contacts outside prison he will pursue the mother and, if he finds her, seek vengeance upon her; nor will he scruple

to ensure that the children are not affected. I have concluded that only his exclusion from the proceedings will realistically achieve that end; although the extensive redaction of documents is possible, there are so many documents which would have to pass through so many hands that the risk of accidental disclosure of a crucial piece of information would be very high.

[28] On the other hand to do that would be to take the unprecedented step of excluding a father with parental responsibility, whose whereabouts are not unknown, from any knowledge of, let alone participation in, care proceedings involving his children. Clearly the countervailing features must be overwhelming to justify such a course.

Conclusion

[29] There are two further factors that influence my decision in this case. First, the father has shown no interest in making any contact with his children. He has always had and retains the right to apply for contact under Part II of the 1989 Act. So far as he is concerned his children are presently living with their mother without any contact to him and that is indeed exactly what the position in fact is. Moreover as things stand, the local authority would not have it otherwise. Secondly, the order to discharge him must be kept under review; were he actually to seek contact or were the local authority to seek to remove the children from the care of the mother, the matter would have to be reconsidered and the balance re-addressed. I should add that I am wholly unpersuaded at present that discharging the father and directing that the fact of the proceedings are not disclosed to him will significantly inhibit the local authority in the assessment they are actually undertaking.

[30] In all the circumstances of this case I have concluded that I should discharge the father as a party to these proceedings. When the actual unfairness of that to him in this case is weighed against the risk of disclosure, leading the father to the whereabouts of the mother and children and the consequence of any such discovery, I have no doubt as to where the balance lies at the moment …

Other significant cases on this issue:

- *Re C (Care: consultation with parents: not in child's best interests)* [2005] EWHC 3390 (Fam), [2006] 2 FLR 787
- Cf *Re C (A child) v X, Y and Z County Council* [2007] EWCA Civ 1206, [2008] 1 FLR 1294: see E2 – Tracing and giving notice to father / wider family

G26 TWIN-TRACK AND CONCURRENT PLANNING

Re D and K (Care plan: twin-track-planning)

[1999] 2 FLR 872 at 873 and 873

Family Division

Bracewell J

In the current case the local authority recognised that the care plan presented an option of rehabilitation to the natural family or permanency outside the family and this was plain from October 1998 when care proceedings were commenced in respect of the newborn child K and the care plan in respect of D was under review.

However, the option of an adoptive placement which eventually formed the basis of the care plan for both children was not even addressed until May 1999, some 4 weeks only before the final hearing in the High Court. In consequence throughout the hearing, the local authority have been able only to speculate as to the time-scale of placement and the availability of adoptive parents suitable for children with complex needs and with an urgent requirement for permanency.

Twin track planning

...

In such cases it should be made abundantly clear to the natural family at the earliest date that the local authority are considering two options: namely rehabilitation within a strictly time-limited framework, or adoption outside the family and that inquiries are proceeding on a twin track so that the court can be presented with well-researched options in order to prevent delay. Such a course requires an approach from a local authority which breaks the mould of sequential planning.

Local authorities traditionally have exhausted the possibility of rehabilitation to parents or extended family before even beginning to address the possibility of permanency outside the family. I recognise that there can be tension between on the one hand giving every opportunity for assessment of the parents and extended family, which may involve many and varied inquiries, and on the other hand seeking to prevent delay for the children by planning for permanence. However, provided the local authority make it clear to the parents and family that twin track planning in no way pre-empts outcome, then the process can only be in the interests of the child. For too long there has been a culture in which adoption has been regarded as the equivalent of failure and therefore a procedure to be considered only as a last resort when all else has been tried and has not succeeded. Such sequential planning often promotes delay with serious consequences for the welfare of the child.

Whenever care proceedings are commenced the court should be proactive at an early directions hearing by inquiring of the local authority whether twin track planning is suitable for that case and if so giving appropriate directions. As part of their overall role, designated care judges should liaise with their director or assistant director of social services with responsibility for children, with the chairman of adoption, and fostering panels, with panel managers of guardians ad litem, and with other concerned persons in order to ensure that within that area there is a general co-operation and understanding of the principles in order to provide facilities for twin track planning to be undertaken in suitable cases.

It is now well researched that children deprived of permanent parenting grow up with unmet psychological needs and far too many children have to wait too long before permanent families are found for them when they cannot return to their natural families. The longer the delay, the more difficult it is to place children who often become progressively more disturbed in limbo, thereby rendering the task of identifying suitable adoptive families a lengthy and uncertain process. The older the child, the greater is the risk of breakdown in an adoptive placement. It is therefore incumbent on local authorities and guardians to seek to prevent these delays by identifying clearly the options available for the court by twin track planning as opposed to sequential planning.

Concurrent planning

Local authorities should consider in each case whether it is suitable for 'concurrent planning' within the meaning of the scheme developed by the Lutheran social services in the USA, the state of Washington and now widespread throughout the states of the USA over a period of 20 years' experience. It is defined as: 'The process of working towards family reunification, while at the same time establishing an alternative permanent plan'. The aim is to reduce the number of moves a child experiences in care, and to reduce temporary placements. The project involves the recruitment of foster-parents who are carefully selected and trained and who are willing to foster children on the basis that they will work with the natural family towards rehabilitation within a strictly timed framework but, in the event of rehabilitation being ruled out, wish to adopt the children. Contact between carers and birth children is encouraged and there is openness between the parties, about the primary aim of rehabilitation with the alternative secondary plan of permanent placement. Placement stability is a top priority.

G27 INTERFACE BETWEEN CARE AND CRIMINAL PROCEEDINGS

Re W (Care order: sexual abuse)

[2009] EWCA Civ 644, [2009] 2 FLR 1106 at 1117 and 1120

Court of Appeal

Wall LJ

[39] ... There is an almost embarrassing volume of authority on the interrelationship between criminal and care proceedings. But what is clear beyond peradventure is that it is for the family court: (1) to be aware at all stages of what is happening in the criminal proceedings; and (2) to be the proactive co-ordinator of the proceedings, to ensure that each is heard timeously and with as little prejudice as possible to the competing interests involved.

[40] I confess to a strong sense of déjà vu when I read my first instance decision in *Re A and B (Minors) (No 2)* [1995] 1 FLR 351, one of the authorities cited to us by counsel. The use of the word 'minors' betrays its antiquity. It was a private law case in which a father sought contact but was also the subject of a botched child sexual abuse allegation which grossly delayed the contact proceedings and acted to the detriment of the children. This I analysed, no doubt at tedious length, in *Re A and B (Minors) (No 1) (Investigation of Alleged Abuse)* only reported at [1995] 3 FCR 389. Having investigated the allegations of abuse, I made a contact order. I then examined what had gone wrong. I see that I said that the proper agency to co-ordinate the civil and criminal strands of a case was the court, and I added: – [1995] 1 FLR 351 at 354:

'A principal message of this judgment is that in private law cases where sexual abuse is alleged and a local authority are involved in a concurrent but independent investigation of the allegations it is essential:

(1)   that there is coordination of the private law litigation and the local authority's investigation; and
(2)   that the principal coordinating agency for the proper disposal of the issues in the case is the court.

However, if the court is to be the coordinating agency, it is vital that proper procedures are in place to ensure that the case is heard expeditiously. Above all, however, as I said in *Re G (Children's*

Cases: Instruction of Experts) (above), the court needs to take a proactive role in procedural issues.

In this case the father's application for contact was issued on 15 May 1992. He was unable to obtain even an interim hearing until 14 December 1992 following an appeal to the judge from the refusal of a district judge to list his application for interim contact. It was shocking that the father should have been reduced to appealing out of time so as to obtain a result which could and should have been achieved very much earlier. Further, the matter was not finally heard and decided until 12 April 1994. Such a delay was wholly unacceptable. Directions appointments must be regarded as of critical importance. Although traditionally dealt with by district judges they should be dealt with by a judge and preferably by the judge who was to try the case. The lack of planning in this case had resulted in directions as to essential expert evidence not being given for nearly 10 months after the father had commenced his application for contact. Further, where, as in this case, there were private law proceedings and sexual abuse was alleged and a local authority was involved in a concurrent but independent investigation it was essential that the court acted as the principal coordinating agency. There should be tightly drawn orders for directions, an effective use of s 7 of the 1989 Act (welfare reports and reports from the local authority), and efficient use of the court structure to ensure both the appropriate level and earliest possible hearing date for the trial.'

[41] I was not, of course, saying anything new in *Re A and B (No 2)*. Indeed, two of the leading cases on the interface between care and criminal proceedings pre-date the 1989 Act: – see *R v Exeter Juvenile Court ex parte H and HR v Waltham Forest Juvenile Court ex parte B* [1988] 2 FLR 214 and *R v B County Council ex parte P* [1991] 1 WLR 221, [1991] 1 FLR 470. If that were not clear enough, the judgment of Butler-Sloss LJ (as she then was) giving the leading judgment in this court in *Re TB (care proceedings: criminal trial)* [1995] 2 FLR 801 makes it clear beyond peradventure that the starting point is that the existence of criminal proceedings is not a reason to adjourn the care proceedings.

[42] Matters have, however, moved on since 1995, and speaking for myself, I find it deeply dispiriting that some 17 years after the implementation of the Children Act 1989, no notice appears to have been taken in this case of the more recent decision of the criminal division of this court in *R v L* [2006] EWCA Crim 1902, [2006] 1 WLR 3092, [2007] 1 FLR 462 (*R v SL*) in which the then President of the Queen's Bench Division, Sir Igor Judge (now, of course, the Lord Chief Justice) chaired a constitution which included the President of the Family Division, and which heard an appeal from a criminal conviction for (inter alia) the manslaughter of a child following the hearing of care proceedings in which Hedley J had held that he could not determine which of the child's

two parents had inflicted on him the injuries which caused his death. Dealing with the question of practice, Sir Igor said:

'72.   Until relatively recently, the problems addressed in this case were most unlikely to have arisen. It was once thought that where the facts of an individual case might give rise to a criminal prosecution, the prosecution should be concluded before any care or equivalent proceedings took place. This no doubt reflected a former rule of law that civil proceedings could not be pursued until the conclusion of criminal proceedings. However, since the advent of the Children Act 1989, with its emphasis on the paramountcy of the welfare of any child the subject of care proceedings, and the consequent need for expedition in the disposal of such proceedings, the position has changed. The current practice is summarised in the judgment of Butler-Sloss LJ, in *Re TB (Care Proceedings; Criminal Trial)* [1995] 2 FLR 801.

One starts with the fact that the criminal proceedings of themselves are not a reason to adjourn the care proceedings. There must be some detriment to the children in the broadest terms for not bringing on the care proceedings because delay is detrimental generally to the children. I think that we do have to hold the line that in the majority of cases, unless there are circumstances which warrant taking a different course, that the care proceedings should come on, even if they are to be heard before the criminal proceedings. That is in line with the President's ruling and it is a ruling which this court ought respectfully to follow.

Nothing in this judgment should be taken to suggest or imply that any alteration in the practice of the Family Division is called for.

73.   We emphasise however, that because procedural and evidential difficulties can arise when there are in existence parallel care proceedings in respect of a child and criminal proceedings against a person connected with that child in respect of a serious offence against the child (or any person connected with the child), it is essential that there should be close liaison between the local Social Services Authority conducting the care proceedings and the Crown Prosecution Service. Wherever possible, linked criminal and care directions hearings should take place as the cases progress. Since November 1993 there has been in operation in the Greater London area a Practice Statement issued by the Presiding Judges and the Family Division Liaison Judge for London with the approval of the Senior Presiding Judge, which sets out a scheme for the purposes of identifying cases where difficulties are likely to arise and provides for linked direction hearings to take place in the Crown Court to which the criminal case has been committed before one of a number of judges nominated for the purposes of the scheme.

74.   The main object of the scheme is to timetable both the criminal and the care proceedings, to decide which should be heard first, and to ensure that each is heard without avoidable delay. This includes determining whether the care proceedings should be heard in the High Court or the County Court. It provides for close liaison between the judge and the listing officers in the Crown Court, and the Principal Registry at the Royal Courts of Justice. The further object is to determine so far as possible the procedural and evidential issues in one case which impinge upon the other. These include disclosure of evidence as between the two sets of proceedings; requests for third-party disclosure in the criminal proceedings and any issues of public interest immunity arising there from; and any requests for leave to interview children in care for the purpose of the criminal proceedings. The statement also provides that, where directions in linked care and criminal proceedings are not complied with, the case must immediately be restored for hearing before the directions judge. A similar scheme is at present being developed for the use in the Manchester area.

75.   *When this case came before Hedley J, it had not been the subject of such coordination or directions and we are told that it was not until a very late stage that the Crown Prosecution Service were aware of the state of the care proceedings and the evidence available within them. That is a most undesirable state of affairs, which we hope will be avoided in future as schemes, such as the London scheme to which we have referred and which we endorse and encourage, are instituted nationwide.* (Emphasis supplied)

[43]   None of this appears to have happened in the instant case. In my judgment, there can be no excuse for either the profession or the judiciary not knowing about or following what is – or should be – a well-established protocol particularly when, as here (and I am conscious that I am repeating myself but the point is of great importance) the care centre and the Crown Court sit in the same building and there are many judges who have what have become known in the profession as both care and serious sex crime 'tickets' – that is to say that they are authorised by the Lord Chancellor and the President of the Family Division to hear both criminal trials involving rape and public law care proceedings.

....

[45]   In my judgment, where there are concurrent care and criminal proceedings, it is essential that each is kept fully informed of the other, and that the judge having the conduct of the care proceedings exercises his or her case management functions not only with a full knowledge of the state of play in the criminal proceedings, but with a view to ensuring that each is heard at an appropriate time.

General notes:

Note also *Re M (Care: disclosure to police)* [2008] 2 FLR 390: see G48 – Special care required by experts involved in both family and criminal proceedings.

Other significant cases on this issue:

• *Re L (Care proceedings: risk assessment)* [2009] EWCA Civ 1008, [2010] 1 FLR 790 (in which it was decided that the criminal trial should take place before the civil trial).

Representation of child

G28 APPLICATION BY CHILD TO DEFEND PROCEEDINGS WITHOUT GAL

Re N (Contact: minor seeking leave to defend and removal of guardian)

[2003] 1 FLR 652 at 653, 655 and 659

Family Division

Coleridge J

See B40 – CA 1989, s 10(8): application for leave by child

G29 FPR 1991, R 9.2A: SEPARATE REPRESENTATION

Mabon v Mabon

[2005] EWCA Civ 634, [2005] 2 FLR 1011 at 1016, 1019, 1019 and 1020

Court of Appeal

Thorpe and Wall LJJ

THORPE LJ:

[23] There are a number of factors which pointed strongly towards the grant of separate representation in the present case. The applicants were at the date of judgment aged respectively 17, 15, and 13. What remained was a disposal hearing. As Mr Everall eloquently put it, without separate representation how were they to know what their parents were contending for: were there cross-applications for residence, what were the contact applications? It was simply unthinkable to exclude young men from knowledge of and participation in legal proceedings that affected them so fundamentally. They had been seen by an experienced family practitioner who had no doubts as to the sufficiency of their understanding: hardly surprising given that they are educated, articulate and reasonably mature for their respective ages.

[24] In my judgment, it is unnecessary to search through the judgment below to assemble a list of factors that were insufficiently weighed and a list of factors that were impermissibly weighed. I am in no doubt that the judge was plainly wrong. That conclusion is fortified by the subsequent report from Dr Gay, which was of course not available to the judge. Dr Gay had had the opportunity of assessing the three eldest boys both collectively and individually. The flavour of his assessment is encapsulated in the following citation:

> 'What is clear is that all three boys are very able. They are quick in terms of being articulate and perceptive. Andrew is perhaps the more (sic) articulate of the three boys; being the middle of the three he tends to be the spokesman, whilst Craig is the more (sic) quiet and thoughtful of the three.'

[25] Insofar as I have been critical of the judge's conclusion, I would like to express my regard for the care that he gave to his judgment and to his equally careful search for the right outcome. In our system, we have traditionally adopted the tandem model for the representation of children

who are parties to family proceedings, whether public or private. First, the court appoints a guardian ad litem, who will almost invariably have a social work qualification and very wide experience of family proceedings. He then instructs a specialist family solicitor who, in turn, usually instructs a specialist family barrister. This is a 'Rolls Royce' model and is the envy of many other jurisdictions. However, its overall approach is essentially paternalistic. The guardian's first priority is to advocate the welfare of the child he represents. His second priority is to put before the court the child's wishes and feelings. Those priorities can in some cases conflict. In extreme cases the conflict is unmanageable. That reality is recognised by the terms of r 9.2A. The direction set by r 9.2A(6) is a mandatory grant of the application provided that the court considers 'that the minor concerned has sufficient understanding to participate as a party in the proceedings concerned'. Thus the focus is upon the sufficiency of the child's understanding in the context of the remaining proceedings.

[26] In my judgment, the rule is sufficiently widely framed to meet our obligations to comply with both Art 12 of the UN Convention and Art 8 of the European Convention, providing that judges correctly focus on the sufficiency of the child's understanding and, in measuring that sufficiency, reflect the extent to which, in the twenty-first century, there is a keener appreciation of the autonomy of the child and the child's consequential right to participate in decision-making processes that fundamentally affect his family life.

[27] Mr McFarlane, in his skeleton argument, suggested that the decision of Coleridge J in *Re N (Contact: Minor Seeking Leave to Defend and Removal of Guardian)* [2003] 1 FLR 652 was an unduly cautious and, therefore, regressive assessment of the sufficiency of the child's understanding. That may be because Mr McFarlane had successfully persuaded the judge to focus upon issues such as the ramification of proceedings and the risk of significant emotional harm from direct involvement. Mr Everall did not seek to pursue that criticism, accepting that Coleridge J had reached a legitimate conclusion, having regard to the fact that the child was only 11 and that the judge had properly regarded the context of those proceedings.

[28] The guidance given by this court in *Re S (A Minor) (Independent Representation)* [1993] Fam 263, [1993] 2 FLR 437 on the construction of r 9.2A is now 12 years old. Much has happened in that time. Although the UK had ratified the UN Convention some 15 months earlier, it did not have much impact initially and it is hardly surprising that it was not mentioned by this court on 26 February 1993. Although the tandem model has many strengths and virtues, at its heart lies the conflict between advancing the welfare of the child and upholding the child's freedom of expression and participation. Unless we in this jurisdiction are to fall out of step with similar societies as they safeguard Art 12 rights, we must, in

the case of articulate teenagers, accept that the right to freedom of expression and participation outweighs the paternalistic judgment of welfare.

[29]   In testing the sufficiency of a child's understanding, I would not say that welfare has no place. If direct participation would pose an obvious risk of harm to the child, arising out of the nature of the continuing proceedings and, if the child is incapable of comprehending that risk, then the judge is entitled to find that sufficient understanding has not been demonstrated. But judges have to be equally alive to the risk of emotional harm that might arise from denying the child knowledge of and participation in the continuing proceedings.

...

[32]   In conclusion, this case provides a timely opportunity to recognise the growing acknowledgement of the autonomy and consequential rights of children, both nationally and internationally. The FPR are sufficiently robustly drawn to accommodate that shift. In individual cases, trial judges must equally acknowledge the shift when they make a proportionate judgment of the sufficiency of the child's understanding.

WALL LJ:

[36]   I have had the opportunity of reading Thorpe LJ's judgment in draft. I entirely agree with it, and like him, I would allow this appeal. I add a short judgment of my own in order to reflect the on-going debate within the family justice system about the manner in which the voice of the child is best heard and heeded in family proceedings. In this context, I would like, in particular, to associate myself with the views expressed by Thorpe LJ in paras [28], [29] and [32] of his judgment.

...

[42]   The judge's reluctance to remove the guardian in the instant case is summarised in the paragraph from his judgment set out by Thorpe LJ in para [18] of his, and I respectfully agree with the criticisms of his approach identified by counsel in their skeleton arguments and analysed by Thorpe LJ in para [23] of his judgment. The judge, it seems to me, was motivated by two particular considerations. The first was his laudable desire to protect the three children from the effects of the litigation. The second was his belief that the children were not, in reality, expressing their own views, but those of their father. In those circumstances, the strength and validity of their views were, in the judge's eyes, substantially, if not entirely, devalued, and could be advanced by the guardian.

[43]   My difficulty with that approach is that the judge seems to me, with all respect to him, to have perceived the case from the perspective of the

adults. From the boys' perspective, it was simply impossible for the guardian to advance their views or represent them in the proceedings. He would, no doubt, faithfully report to the judge what the boys were saying, but the case he would be advancing to the judge on their behalf would be (or was likely to be) directly opposed to what the boys were actually saying.

[44] In these circumstances, I do not agree with the judge that the only advantage from independent representation was 'perhaps the more articulate and elegant expression of what I already know'. That analysis overlooks, in my judgment, the need for the boys, on the facts of this particular case, to emerge from the proceedings (whatever the result) with the knowledge that their position had been independently represented and their perspective fully advanced to the judge.

[45] In these circumstances I regard *Re N (Contact: Minor Seeking Leave to Defend and Removal of Guardian)* [2003] 1 FLR 652 as a careful exercise of judicial discretion by Coleridge J to the facts of a particular, and highly complex, case. I do not find it of any assistance in determining this appeal.

Other significant cases on this issue:

- *W v W (Abduction: joinder as a party)* [2009] EWHC 3288 (Fam), [2010] 1 FLR 1342 (party status of older sibling in Hague Convention proceedings)

Without notice applications

G30 WITHOUT NOTICE APPLICATIONS: GENERAL PRINCIPLES (1)

Re S (ex parte orders)

[2001] 1 FLR 308 at 320

Family Division

Munby J

I can therefore summarise the relevant legal principles and the practice which in my judgment should be followed in the Family Division on applications for ex parte injunctions as follows:

(1) The circumstances in which ex parte relief is obtained in the Family Division vary very widely. What follows is not intended to be treated as a set of inflexible rules. In this area of practice, particularly in the Family Division, there can be no rigid rules. Circumstances alter cases and, in the final analysis, every case must be considered on its own facts.

(2) That said, generally speaking the following practice should be adopted both in ancillary relief cases and in cases relating to children, including cases where injunctive relief is sought against third parties or the world at large.

(3) This is subject to the need to recognise that in cases involving a child the court may have to act swiftly and decisively in order to safeguard the child's welfare.

(4) Those who seek relief ex parte are under a duty to make the fullest and most candid and frank disclosure of all the relevant circumstances known to them. This duty is not confined to the material facts: it extends to all relevant matters, whether of fact or of law. The principle is as applicable in the Family Division as elsewhere. Those who fail in this duty, and those who misrepresent matters to the court, expose themselves to the very real risk of being denied interlocutory relief whether or not they have a good arguable case or even a strong prima facie case.

(5) It is an elementary principle of natural justice that a judge cannot be shown evidence or other persuasive material in an ex parte application on the basis that it is not at a later stage to be revealed to

the respondent. The respondent must have an opportunity to see the material which was deployed against him at the ex parte hearing and an opportunity, if he wishes to apply for the discharge or variation of the injunction either on the return day or earlier, to submit evidence in answer and, in any event, to make submissions about the applicant's evidence.

(6)   It follows that those who obtain ex parte injunctive relief are under an obligation to bring to the attention of the respondent, and at the earliest practicable opportunity, the evidential and other persuasive materials on the basis of which the ex parte injunction was granted.

(7)   Accordingly, generally speaking it is appropriate when granting ex parte injunctive relief in the Family Division for the court to require the applicant (and, where appropriate, the applicant's solicitors) to give the following undertakings:

(a)   where proceedings have not yet been issued, to issue and serve on the respondent either by some specified time or as soon as practicable proceedings either in the form of the draft produced to the court or otherwise as may be appropriate;

(b)   where the application has been made otherwise than on sworn evidence, to cause to be sworn, filed and served on the respondent as soon as practicable an affidavit or affidavits substantially in the terms of the draft affidavit(s) produced to the court or, as the case may be, confirming the substance of what was said to the court by the applicant's counsel or solicitors; and

(c)   subject to (a) and (b) above, to serve on the respondent as soon as practicable (i) the proceedings, (ii) a sealed copy of the order, (iii) copies of the affidavit(s) and exhibit(s) containing the evidence relied on by the applicant and (iv) notice of the return date including details of the application to be made on the return date.

(8)   A person who has given an undertaking to the court is under a plain and unqualified obligation to comply to the letter with his undertaking. Where the undertaking is to do something by a specified time, then time is of the essence. A person who finds himself unable to comply timeously with his undertaking should either (i) apply for an extension of time before the time for compliance has expired or (ii) pass the task to someone who has available the time in which to do it.

(9)   Whether or not express undertakings to this effect have been given, but subject to any order to the contrary, an applicant who obtains ex parte injunctive relief is under an obligation to the court, and the solicitor acting for the applicant is under an obligation both to the court and to his lay client, to carry out the various steps referred to in (7) above.

(10) Any ex parte order containing injunctions should set out on its face either by way of recital or in a schedule, a list of all affidavits, witness statements and other evidential materials read by the judge.

The applicant's legal representatives should whenever possible liaise with the associate with a view to ensuring that the order as drawn contains this information. On receipt of the order from the court the applicant's legal representatives should satisfy themselves that the order as drawn correctly sets out the relevant information and, if it does not, take urgent steps to have the order amended under the slip rule.

(11) Persons injuncted ex parte are entitled to be given, if they ask, proper information as to what happened at the hearing and to be told, if they ask, (i) exactly what documents, bundles or other evidential materials were lodged with the court either before or during the course of the hearing and (ii) what legal authorities were cited to the judge.

(12) The applicant's legal representatives should respond forthwith to any reasonable request from the respondent or his legal representatives either for copies of the materials read by the judge or for information about what took place at the hearing.

(13) Given this, it would be prudent for those acting for the applicant in such a case to keep a proper note of the proceedings, lest they otherwise find themselves embarrassed by a proper request for information which they are unable to provide.

G31　WITHOUT NOTICE APPLICATIONS: GENERAL PRINCIPLES (2)

Re S (ex parte orders)

[2007] 1 FLR 1600 at 1608

Family Division

Charles J

[37]　There is a natural temptation for applicants to seek, and courts to grant, relief to protect vulnerable persons whether they are children or vulnerable adults. In my view this can lead (and experience as the applications judge confirms that it does lead) to practitioners making without notice applications which are not necessary or appropriate, or which are not properly supported by appropriate evidence. Also there is in my view a general practice of asking the court to grant without notice orders over a fairly extended period with express permission to apply to vary or discharge on an inappropriately long period of notice (often 48 hours). It seems to me that on occasions this practice pays insufficient regard to the interests of both the persons in respect of whom and against whom the orders are made, and that therefore on every occasion without notice relief is sought and granted the choice of the return date and the provisions as to permission to apply should be addressed with care by both the applicants and the court. Factors in that consideration will be an estimation of the effect on the person against whom the order is made of service of the order and how that is to be carried out.

[38]　Inevitably on a without notice application the court hears from only the applicant. Good practice, fairness and indeed common sense demand that on any such application the applicant should provide the court with:

(i)　a balanced, fair and particularised account of the events leading up to the application and thus of the matters upon which it is based. In many cases this should include a brief account of what the applicant thinks the respondent's case is, or is likely to be;

(ii)　where available and appropriate, independent evidence;

(iii)　a clear and particularised explanation of the reasons why the application is made without notice and the reasons why the permission to apply to vary or discharge the injunction granted should be on notice (rather than immediately or forthwith as in the standard collection and location orders) and why the return date should not be within a short period of time. As to that I accept and acknowledge that a reference to notice being given if practicable, or for a short period of notice (say 2 working hours or just 2 hours if a weekend or holiday period is imminent), may often provide an appropriate balance to avoid a sequence of effectively without notice applications, and that in some cases a longer period of notice may be appropriate; and

(iv) in many cases an account of the steps the applicant proposes concerning service, the giving of an explanation of the order and the implementation of an order. This is likely to be of particular importance in cases such as this one where emotional issues are involved and family members of a person who lacks capacity are the subject of the injunctions and orders. In such cases, as here, information as to those intentions is likely to inform issues as to the need for, and the proportionality of, the relief sought and granted.

[39] As to point (ii), I pause to mention that, in my view, it is surprising and disappointing how many times a without notice application for relief is made in the Family Division based only on largely unparticularised assertions by one side of serious allegations without any third party material to support them, or more generally the basis for the relief sought. I appreciate that in many instances there is a very real urgency and there will not be third party evidence of allegations of abusive behaviour that are readily available but in others there will be. A classic example, which occurs regularly, is that an applicant who seeks a return of children to his or her care fails to provide any third party evidence (e g from a school, a GP or records in their possession) to confirm that he or she is indeed the primary carer of the relevant children.

[40] Guidance has often been given on the information to be provided and the procedure to be followed in seeking without notice relief (see at first instance *Re S (Ex Parte Orders)* [2001] 1 WLR 211, [2001] 1 FLR 308, *W v H (Ex Parte Injunctions)* [2001] 1 All ER 300 (by analogy *X Council v B (Emergency Protection Orders)* [2004] EWHC 2015 (Fam), [2005] 1 FLR 341 and *Re X (Emergency Protection Orders)* [2006] EWHC 510 (Fam), [2006] 2 FLR 701) and in the Court of Appeal *Moat Housing Group South Ltd v Harris* [2005] EWCA Civ 287, [2006] QB 606, [2005] 2 FLR 551 in particular at paras [63]–[69], and see also the notes to Part 25 of the Civil Procedure Rules 1998 (CPR) *Practice Note (Official Solicitor, CAFCASS and the National Assembly for Wales: Urgent and Out of Hours Cases in the Family Division of the High Court)* [2006] 2 FLR 354).

[41] Naturally I endorse that guidance and do not seek to add to it save to emphasise the points made above and to record my own observations that practitioners: (a) too regularly do not follow and implement that guidance; and (b) by such failure show an insufficient appreciation of the exceptional nature of without notice relief and the impact it has (or potentially has) on the rights, life and emotions of the persons against whom it is granted.

[42] As to this I acknowledge that the courts must take part of the blame for such failures by granting relief without notice in cases when: (a) the guidance has not been followed; and (b) the impact on the person against whom the relief is granted could be considerable.

[43] I add that additionally there is a need: (a) to comply strictly with undertakings given at the time the order is made; and (b) to keep full and proper records of what is put before the court and said to the court. This should include a record of the times of the hearing so that a transcript can be more easily obtained. The availability of a transcript does not, however, reduce the duty of those applying for without notice relief to keep a full record of what the court was shown and was told.

General notes:

For an example of an appropriate without notice application see *Re D (Unborn baby)* [2009] EWHC 446 (Fam), [2009] 2 FLR 313 at D10 – Removal at birth, without notice, in exceptional circumstances.

Other significant cases on this issue:

- *C v C (Without notice orders)* [2005] EWHC 2741 (Fam), [2006] 1 FLR 936

Fact-finding (split) hearings

G32 PURPOSE OF SPLIT HEARINGS

Re B (Children) (Sexual abuse: standard of proof)

[2008] UKHL 35, [2008] 2 FLR 141 at 164

House of Lords

Baroness Hale

[74]   Care proceedings are not a two-stage process. The court does have two questions to ask. Has the threshold been crossed? If so, what will be best for the child? But there are many cases in which a court has two or more questions to ask in the course of a single hearing. The same factual issues are often relevant to each question. Or some factual disputes may be relevant to the threshold while others are relevant to the welfare checklist: it may be clear, for example, that a child has suffered an injury while in the care of the mother, but whether the father or stepfather has a drink problem and has been beating the mother up is extremely relevant to the long-term welfare of the child.

[75]   The purpose of splitting the hearing is not to split the two questions which the court must answer. It is to separate out those factual issues which are capable of swift resolution so that the welfare professionals have a firm foundation of fact upon which to base their assessments of family relationships and parenting ability: see *Re S (Care Proceedings: Split Hearing)* [1996] 2 FLR 773. A fact-finding hearing is merely one of the case management possibilities contemplated by the new Public Law Outline. It is not a necessary pre-condition for the core professional assessment, which the Public Law Outline now expects should normally be done before the proceedings even begin (Judiciary of England and Wales and Ministry of Justice, *The Public Law Outline, Guide to Case Management in Public Law Proceedings*, President's Practice Direction, April 2008, para 9.2, pre-proceedings checklist and Flowchart). There is no point in splitting the issues if the facts cannot be determined relatively quickly, still less if it is unlikely to result in clear cut findings to help the professionals in their work.

[76]   But the finding of those facts is merely part of the whole process of trying the case. It is not a separate exercise. And once it is done the case is part heard. The trial should not resume before a different judge, any more

than any other part heard case should do so. In the particular context of care proceedings, where the character and personalities of the parties are important components in any decision, it makes no sense at all for one judge to spend days listening to them give evidence on one issue and for another judge to send more days listening to them give evidence on another. This is not only a wasteful duplication of effort. Much useful information is likely to fall between the gaps. How can a judge who has not heard the parents give their evidence about how the child's injuries occurred begin to assess the risk of letting them care for the child again? The experts may make their assessments, but in the end it is for the judge to make the decision on all the evidence before him. How can he properly do that when he has heard only half of it?

General notes:

Attention is particularly drawn to:

(1) the Practice Direction: Residence and Contact Orders: Domestic Violence and Harm issued in January 2009 [2009] 2 FLR 1400 (which is to be applied: see, for example, *Re Z (unsupervised contact: allegations of domestic violence)* [2009] 2 FLR 877 at [27]–[28], and cf *Re R (family proceedings: no case to answer)* [2008] EWCA Civ 1619, [2009] 2 FLR 83; and

(2) the President's Guidance in relation to Split Hearings [2010] 2 FLR 1897.

Other significant cases on this issue:

• See *Re G and B (fact-finding hearing)* [2009] EWCA Civ 10, [2009] 1 FLR 1145 (there were exceptions to the general rule that the same judge should hear both parts of a split hearing)

This case is also included in relation to:

H3 Standard of proof
H12 Inherent probabilities may be relevant

G33 PURPOSE / PROS AND CONS

Re Y and K (Split hearing: evidence)

[2003] EWCA Civ 669, [2003] 2 FLR 273 at 276 and 282

Court of Appeal

Thorpe and Hale LJJ

THORPE LJ:

[8] I turn then to Mr Stonor's submissions. He essentially presents them in three distinct compartments. First, he criticises the judge generally for, as he would characterise it, treating the split hearing inquiry as something akin to a criminal process in which the prosecution were held to have failed to make a prima facie case. His second and more specific criticism of the judge is in his assessment and rejection of the expert medical evidence. His third criticism is of the judge's rejection of the evidence as to T's several complaints.

[9] I take those three in turn. Both counsel have referred us to *Re B (Minors) (Contact)* [1994] 2 FLR 1, and particularly to the judgment of Butler-Sloss LJ in which she gave guidance as to the procedure to be adopted in Children Act proceedings. There is no doubt at all that the guidance that she there offered applies to split trials as well as to any other sort of hearing. But it is equally clear that Butler-Sloss LJ did not have split trials in mind when she offered her broad guide. All that *Re B (Minors) (Contact)* establishes is the breadth of the spectrum of permissible procedures and the generous extent of the judge's discretion in deciding how to proceed in individual cases.

[10] But the purpose of a preliminary hearing is to determine what has happened historically and to provide a firm foundation to all parties to prepare their cases for the disposal hearing, the purpose of which is to determine the child's future. The local authority has to base its plans for the future on the crucial judicial findings of fact and equally upon the judge's assessment of adult credibility and reliability. Often there will be hot disputes of fact between the adults in the case. Often there will be hot denials from an adult who is charged with abuse. Local authorities are not in a position to make an assessment of where the truth lies. It is up to judges to perform that task. Here it is said the judge's task is half done. For example, we know what he thought of the mother's sister as a witness of fact, and we know also what he made of her motivation; but we have no assessment of the father's evidence or of his responsibility.

HALE LJ:

[28] An application for a care or supervision order under s 31 of the Children Act 1989 is a single application encompassing: first, the finding of the necessary facts; secondly, applying judgment as to whether the court is satisfied that the threshold criteria in s 31(2) of the Children Act 1989 are made out; and thirdly, the exercise of discretion as to what will be in the best interests of the child.

[29] The issues can be taken in stages. The advantages of doing so are that it can nip unwarranted intervention in the bud, or, on the other hand, that further assessments can be conducted on a firm foundation of fact: see *Re S (Care Proceedings: Split Hearing)* [1996] 2 FLR 773. But split hearings do have their disadvantages. The main one, amply demonstrated in this case, is delay. There can also be problems in ensuring that the same judge hears all parts of what is a part-heard case.

[30] Another more subtle disadvantage is that it can produce an impression that the fact-finding exercise is akin to that of a criminal trial. In a criminal trial, of course, the defendant is a competent witness in his own defence, but he is not compellable. Care proceedings, however, are civil proceedings in every respect; and indeed they are designed to be an objective inquiry into the condition and future of the child: see for example, *Re L (A Minor) (Police Investigation: Privilege)* [1997] AC 16, sub nom *Re L (Police Investigation: Privilege)* [1996] 1 FLR 731.

Other significant cases on this issue:

- *North Yorkshire County Council v SA* [2003] EWCA Civ 839, [2003] 2 FLR 849 per Butler-Sloss P at [37]

This case is also included in relation to:

G67 Parents etc compellable to give evidence

G34   IMPORTANCE OF IDENTIFYING PRECISELY THE PURPOSE OF FACT-FINDING HEARING

Re A (Children: split hearing)

[2006] EWCA Civ 714, [2007] 1 FLR 905 at 914

Court of Appeal

Wall LJ

[33]   The second point of importance is that where the court is contemplating a split hearing in a case involving children it is in my view essential that the issues to be resolved in the first limb of the hearing are clearly defined and that the consequences of any such findings are fully understood by the parties. Thus if the court is dealing with a single-issue case in which the facts found will determine the threshold criteria under s 31(2) of the 1989 Act, the directions which are given by the court and which set up the first limb of that hearing must: (1) identify precisely the purpose of the hearing, namely to decide whether or not the threshold criteria are established; and (2) identify with as much precision as possible the facts upon which the local authority relies and which it asserts will, if proved, establish the criteria.

[34]   Alternatively, if the purpose of the first limb, as here, is not to decide whether or not the threshold criteria are satisfied, but to resolve an issue of fact which will affect the manner in which subsequent assessments of the parties are to be made, the issues which the court is being asked to resolve once again and the facts which it is being invited to find must, in my judgment, be clearly spelled out. In either case, this is best done by an order of the court which sets up the first limb of the hearing, and that order should identify clearly the issues which are to be addressed.

[35]   Equally, it seems to me that once the first limb of the hearing has been completed, and the judge has delivered judgment, it would usually be sensible for there to be a short discussion in court between counsel and the judge to clarify the consequences of any findings which the judge has made. In a genuinely single issue case, for example where a serious injury or an allegation of sexual abuse is the only factor which would enable the threshold to be crossed, a finding that the allegations have not been established to the requisite standard will mean that the threshold had not been established and the proceedings would have to be dismissed.

[36] If on the other hand the allegations are proved and the threshold criteria are established, the court must move on to assessment. Thus where the purpose of the first limb of a split hearing is not to determine threshold criteria but to give the opportunity of findings of fact to be made which will inform the consequential assessment of the parties and the conduct of the case, it is, in my view, essential when the judge has made or declined to make relevant findings, that the state of the case consequential on the judge's judgment on the first limb is clearly understood by everybody and preferably recorded in an order of the court.

Other significant cases on this issue:

- *Re O and N (care: preliminary hearing)* [2002] EWCA Civ 1271, [2002] 2 FLR 1167 per Ward LJ at [15]–[16]
- *North Yorkshire County Council v SA* [2003] EWCA Civ 839, [2003] 2 FLR 849 per Butler-Sloss P at [37]
- *CL v East Riding Yorkshire Council, MB and BL* [2006] EWCA Civ 49, [2006] 2 FLR 24 per Wall LJ at [19]

G35 PSYCHIATRIC / PSYCHOLOGICAL EVIDENCE UNLIKELY TO BE RELEVANT

Re CB and JB (Care proceedings: guidelines)

[1998] 2 FLR 211 at 217

Family Division

Wall J

Question 1

(a) Why did the split hearing for which the district judge gave directions, for which he laid down a sensible and realistic timetable and for which the case was pre-eminently suited, not take place?

(b) When a split hearing is ordered in relation to an issue of fact which goes to the threshold criteria under s 31 of the Children Act 1989, is it normally sensible to permit a psychiatric or psychological assessment of the parties to be undertaken at the first stage? Equally, should evidence of propensity or character be admitted at the first stage, or, indeed, at all?

The answers to both parts of this question are interrelated. The short answer to the first part of the question is that both the parties and the court allowed themselves to be diverted away from the simple issue of fact into addressing issues which were irrelevant to it. In particular, the guardian ad litem sought to introduce into the factual inquiry a psychiatric assessment of the father. This led inexorably to the introduction of a psychological assessment of the mother, evidence from psychologists as to propensity and then, quite inappropriately to a sterile and irrelevant argument about psychiatric and psychological methodology. The result was inordinate delay and the abandonment of the split hearing – that is up until the commencement of the final hearing before me when the one issue in the case reasserted itself.

The lessons to be learned from this part of the case are, in my judgment, the following:

(i) Where the court (as here) decides that a factual issue or factual issues in a case are critical to the establishment of the threshold criteria under s 31 of the Children Act 1989, and that the case is thus suitable for a split hearing, both the parties and the court should at all times maintain their focus on the factual issue or issues and not allow themselves to be diverted from them without very good reason.

(ii)   The essence of a split hearing is the clear identification of the issue to be tried first. The parties and the court must concentrate their energies upon assembling the evidence which will enable that issue to be tried. Tight directions must be given and the case timetabled to ensure that the factual issue is heard speedily.

(iii)   It is essential in a split hearing not only that all the parties should keep their eye firmly on the ball, but that the timetable laid down by the court is strictly adhered to.

(iv)   Evidence which is relevant to the assessment of the parents or other family members if and when the threshold criteria are established should not be permitted unless for some reason it is of direct relevance to the factual issue being tried. It is the essence of a split hearing that assessments of the parties and their capacity to parent their children need to be carried out on the basis of the facts found by the court. Ex hypothesi that can only be done after the court has decided both that the threshold criteria have been satisfied and the factual basis upon which they have been satisfied.

(v)   Evidence of propensity or a psychiatric or psychological assessment of one of the parties is unlikely to be of any assistance in resolving a purely factual issue. There will in any event be before the court evidence from the local authority and the parents relating to the history of the case and the backgrounds of each of the parents. A psychologist or psychiatrist instructed to undertake an assessment of a parent for the first stage of a split hearing is unlikely to have a complete knowledge of the facts.

(vi)   Furthermore, such a witness may, as here, express opinions as to propensity or as to responsibility for a child's injuries which are both prejudicial and wrong. The assessment of adult credibility as to the responsibility for a child's injuries (often the critical factual issue) remains the function of the judge. In my judgment, therefore, a psychiatric or psychological assessment of the parties should not be permitted at the first stage of a split trial unless the particular facts of the case demonstrate that such evidence is or is likely to be directly relevant to the factual issue to be tried.

(vii)   Expert evidence as to the assessment of risk once the threshold criteria have been established is, of course, another matter. But the essence of such an assessment is that the psychiatrist or psychologist makes his or her assessment on the basis of facts found by the court and parental reaction to them.

(viii) It may be appropriate when timetabling a split hearing, to put in place a timetable for the second stage of the hearing which will take place if the threshold criteria are established. It may well be sensible to give a party leave prior to the hearing of the first stage to show the papers to the psychiatrist or psychologist if and when the threshold criteria are established, in order to save time and enable the party in question to pencil in appointments and establish a timetable for such an assessment. But the purpose of any such direction is simply to ensure that time is not wasted and that the parties do not have to wait until findings are made by the court before putting in place the structure which will enable the second stage of the hearing to take place as quickly as possible: it is not to facilitate inappropriate psychiatric or psychological evidence being given at the first stage.

(ix) Clearly, the local authority social workers will have been working with and observing the child's parents and family members from the moment the child is received into its care. Nothing in what I have said above is designed to inhibit the local authority from putting in at the first stage factual evidence relating to the history of the case and the background of the parties, or relevant evidence of observation. Such evidence is usually necessary for a proper understanding of the case. Equally, the local authority will, as the case progresses, be carrying out a continuous assessment of the parents and their behaviour. However, there can be no full assessment of the parents by the local authority in a split hearing case until the court has made its primary findings of fact and the basis upon which the threshold criteria have been established is known through findings of fact made by the court.

In the instant case, the adult forensic psychiatrist instructed by the guardian ad litem, Dr PW, expressed views about the propensity of the father to injure children which, in my judgment, he should not have made and which were not borne out by the evidence. RH, a consultant clinical psychologist, expressed an opinion as to propensity which wrongly exculpated the mother. In addition to this misleading and unhelpful evidence, the effect of the respective reports was, as I have already indicated, to provoke serial applications for further psychological and psychiatric opinions, with the consequences I have already described.

This case is also included in relation to:

D66 Role of CG / solicitor for child (3)
G62 Psychiatric/psychological evidence as to propensity

G36   CONCESSIONS: IS FACT-FINDING PROCESS NECESSARY

A County Council v DP, RS, BS (by the children's guardian)

[2005] EWHC 1593 Fam, [2005] 2 FLR 1031 at 1034, 1037 and 1040

Family Division

McFarlane J

(1)   Lawfulness – the submissions

[8]   Mr Tolson's primary submission is that, as there is no effective application for a public law order, any investigation of whether the Children Act 1989 s 31 threshold is crossed would be unlawful.

…

(2)   Lawfulness – analysis

[16]   I favour the argument of Mr Tolson's opponents, summarised above, to the effect that until the court has determined the facts as best it can, and evaluated whether or not the threshold is passed, it is not appropriate to say that there will in fact be no public law order. All that can be said at the present stage is that no party is positively seeking such an order. That is insufficient to render otherwise 'lawful' proceedings 'unlawful' insofar as they may consider various findings of fact.

[17]   Once properly constituted care proceedings have been commenced within the statutory context of Part IV of the Children Act, they remain lawfully established unless and until they are either concluded or withdrawn. The question of whether or not a particular fact finding exercise is conducted within those proceedings is a question for the court's discretion and is not a matter that will, of itself, be 'unlawful'.

[18]   Mr Tolson's submissions, possibly anticipating the above conclusion, go further. He submits that, if (which is not the case here) all the parties to a case apply to have the proceedings withdrawn, then the court has no option but to grant their request and cannot keep the case alive contrary to the common will. The implication of his submission is that, given the positions of the other parties in this case, they should be applying to withdraw the s 31 application and that if that application were made it would have to be granted. The result thus reached would deprive the court of its jurisdiction to conduct the fact finding hearing.

[19] The fall-back submission set out at para [18] (above) fails, in my view, for two reasons:

(i) the local authority is not in fact applying to withdraw the application for the reasons summarised by Mr Vater. Those are, in my judgment, legitimate and sound considerations;

(ii) I do not accept the submission that a court is bound to allow the withdrawal of proceedings where all of the parties agree that that should occur. Family Proceedings Rules 1991, r 4.5(4) expressly provides that a precondition of withdrawal is that 'the court thinks fit'. There is thus a judicial discretion and it does not, therefore, follow as night follows day that the court's jurisdiction to continue with the proceedings would end simply because the parties all agree that the proceedings should be withdrawn.

The withdrawal provisions (and indeed the guardian system in public law itself) came into existence as a result of childcare tragedies in the 1970s and 1980s. The court's role in such matters is not to be that of a neutered 'rubber stamp' for the parties' requests.

[20] In view of my conclusion that these are and remain lawfully constituted proceedings under Part IV of the Children Act, it is not necessary for me to consider whether there is alternative jurisdiction within private law proceedings arising in part from the need to consider 'harm' within the context of the welfare checklist (s 1(3)) or under the inherent jurisdiction. In view of the time available for the preparation of this judgment, I will not, therefore, consider the merits of those submissions.

(3) Exercise of discretion

[21] If it is lawful for the court to conduct a fact finding exercise despite the fact that at this stage no party is seeking a public law order, it is common ground that the court has a discretion whether, on the individual facts of each case, it is right and necessary to do so.

[22] The relevant case-law is to be found in the following decisions:

- *Re G (A Minor) (Care Proceedings)* [1994] 3 WLR 1211, [1994] 2 FLR 69 (Wall J)
- *Stockport Metropolitan Borough Council v D* [1995] 1 FLR 873 (Thorpe J)
- *Re B (Agreed Findings of Fact)* [1998] 2 FLR 968 (Butler-Sloss and Thorpe LJJ)

- *Re M (Threshold Criteria: Parental Concessions)* [1999] 2 FLR 728 (Butler-Sloss LJ and Wall J)
- *Re D (Child: Threshold Criteria)* [2001] 1 FLR 274 (Schiemann, Thorpe and Mummery LJJ)

[23] It is not necessary to read substantial parts of this case-law into this judgment. Indeed I note that, in a former life, I was myself rightly discouraged in *Re M (Threshold Criteria: Parental Concessions)* from taking the Court of Appeal through the authorities because the law on this point is not in any particular doubt (see 731B).

[24] The authorities make it plain that, amongst other factors, the following are likely to be relevant and need to be borne in mind before deciding whether or not to conduct a particular fact finding exercise:

(a) the interests of the child (which are relevant but not paramount);
(b) the time that the investigation will take;
(c) the likely cost to public funds;
(d) the evidential result;
(e) the necessity or otherwise of the investigation;
(f) the relevance of the potential result of the investigation to the future care plans for the child;
(g) the impact of any fact finding process upon the other parties;
(h) the prospects of a fair trial on the issue;
(i) the justice of the case.

[25] The court is well familiar with the concept of 'necessity', arising as it does from Art 8 of the European Convention and, indeed, from the pre-Human Rights Act 1998 case-law to which I have been referred. It is rightly at the core of Mr Tolson's submissions in this case and, without overtly labouring the issue by including substantial descriptive text in this judgment, it is at the forefront of my consideration of the point. Amongst the pertinent questions are: is there a pressing need for such a hearing? Is the proposed fact finding hearing solely, as Mr Tolson puts it, 'to seek findings against the father on criminal matters for their own sake'? Is the process, which will be costly and time consuming, with potentially serious consequences for the father if it goes against him, proportionate to any identified need?

...

[29] Dealing shortly with some of the arguments that have been raised, I would make the following observations:

(i) it is not possible for me to hold at this stage, without further investigation, that the experts' meeting process was procedurally flawed so as to be unfair. Any European Convention, Art 6, unfairness is, in any event, to be judged in relation to the proceedings as a whole and not solely one element of them. Now is, therefore, not the stage at which this argument can come into play or be given any substantial weight;

(ii)   the gulf between the father's position and the central allegations is indeed wide. I note that in all of the reported cases, the parents had made significant concessions on threshold and/or the factual substrata. That is not the case here;

(iii)   if there is a real potential for these facts to be litigated in the future then they should be litigated now and not some years hence. The father has made it plain to the guardian that his eventual aim is unsupervised contact, to include staying contact. Mr Tolson says that this is in the long term, when either B is seen to be too old to be at risk of this form of abuse and/or is asking for more contact;

(iv)   the public interest in the identification of the perpetrators of child abuse and the public interest in children knowing the truth about past abuse are important factors (see *Re K (Non-Accidental Injuries: Perpetrator: New Evidence)* [2004] EWCA Civ 1181, [2005] 1 FLR 285).

[30]   In addition I am struck by what, with respect to him, I may call the intellectual dishonesty of the father's position. His stance on the factual dispute (which is, in effect, to accept no culpable behaviour) is completely incompatible with his acceptance of limited, long-term, supervised contact. This, as is candidly admitted, is a 'pragmatic' position to avoid the feared consequences of the proposed investigation. It is a tactical position. It is not child-focused and has no internal logic. The apparent unanimity of view about the final orders hides the reality of a very substantial and important factual dispute between the father and the other parties.

[31]   Drawing all of these matters together, I have come to the clear view that a full hearing of the factual evidence in relation to the fracture of B's arm and his respiratory collapse is necessary, justified and proportionate. Such a hearing is in B's best interests. In particular, I regard it as almost inevitable that there will be a request for more open contact by the father in the future. I see his current tactical position as being temporary and opportunistic. There is a pressing need for these facts to be considered and findings, if possible, to be made one way or the other on the evidence.

G37   DISPENSING WITH FACT-FINDING HEARING

Re F-H (Dispensing with fact-finding hearing)

[2008] EWCA Civ 1249, [2009] 1 FLR 349 at 358, 359 and 362

Court of Appeal

Wilson LJ

[26] There is no doubt that in family proceedings the court has a discretion whether to hear evidence in relation to disputed matters of fact with a view to determining them. In *A County Council v DP and Others* [2005] EWHC 1593, [2005] 2 FLR 1031, McFarlane J, at para [24], helpfully identified, by reference to previous authorities, nine matters which the court should bear in mind before deciding whether to conduct a particular fact-finding exercise. I have no doubt that, notwithstanding that in the present case a decision had been made in the exercise of such a discretion to arrange for the disputed facts, in relation in particular to the allegations against A, to be determined at the hearing fixed to begin on 7 April 2008, Her Honour Judge Hughes also even at that stage retained a discretion to decline to conduct it. Nevertheless in my view additional considerations fall to be weighed by a judge who is considering, at the outset of a prearranged fact-finding hearing, whether in effect to abort it. That judge should weigh, with appropriate respect, the previous decision that the exercise should be undertaken and should ask whether any fresh circumstances, or at least any circumstances freshly discovered, should lead her or him to depart from the chosen forensic course. Equally she or he should weigh the costs already incurred in the assembly of the case on all sides and the degree to which a refusal at that stage to conduct the hearing would waste them. Furthermore she or he should weigh any special features such as, in the present case, the facts that a girl then aged 16 had been shown the court room, that she had participated in discussions with the guardian as to the way in which she would prefer to give evidence and that she was thus expecting that she would imminently be giving oral evidence in some way or another, although the judge should not on the other hand ignore the girl's likely apprehension at that prospect. What needs, however, to be avoided at all costs is a sudden decision to abort the hearing in circumstances in which, later, the findings not then made might after all be considered to be necessary. So a judge in the position of Her Honour Judge Hughes on 8 April should in my view act most cautiously before putting the forensic programme into reverse.

...

[28] It was surely irrelevant for the judge to consider, as her second reason, that the threshold to the making of a care order under s 31 of the Act could be crossed by reference to many matters other than those, even if established, in relation to sexual abuse on the part of A. The fact that certain material need not be considered before a conclusion is reached that the court has *power* to make a care order in no way supports a conclusion that it does not need to be considered before deciding whether the *optimum outcome* for the children is to make such an order. An allied, but quite different, situation arises when a judge who surveys the whole case reasonably considers that, by reference to agreed matters of historical fact, the chance of the court's approval of a child's return to his parents is so remote as to render it unnecessary for it to embark upon an attempt to resolve other, disputed matters relating to their care of him; in such circumstances one would not expect a fact-finding hearing to have been arranged in the first place but, if arranged, it might be a valid exercise of a judge's discretion to decide at the outset of the fact-finding hearing not to conduct it after all. But such a situation was far from that which obtained in the present case: here, as the judge knew, three children, all of an age at which their views would be of great importance, were pressing to return to the care of the mother in circumstances in which, at the hearing before Her Honour Judge Cox only 2 months previously, even the children's guardian had, albeit unsuccessfully, supported the mother's bid to secure their immediate return without further forensic inquiry. So in the present case there was a very live issue as to whether the children should be returned to the mother, with the result that their safety from sexual abuse in the event of return, not just from abuse on the part of A who, as the judge observed, might well be able to be prevented from coming into contact with them, was a matter of crucial importance. The judge's observation at the start of her expression of her fourth reason, namely that neither A nor indeed B was in any event to be part of the mother's future household, was therefore of scant relevance.

[29] Of course I share the judge's distaste at the prospect that B would give oral evidence against her brother and, to a lesser extent, that the younger children would give evidence, albeit only through their ABE interviews already conducted, against their half-brother. The judge's point about the added prejudice to any resumption of relations between them and A following such evidence may also have been valid – so far as it went.

[30] The judge was also entitled, in her fifth reason, to refer to the criminal proceedings which might be brought against A and, if so, which would probably require B then to give oral evidence against him in that forum. I do not, however, accept that the possibility, as it then was, of criminal proceedings against A was a matter which should have helped to dissuade the judge from conducting the fact-finding hearing. At the end of this judgment, in the light of the fact that we have been told that A has indeed now been charged with committing offences against B and the younger children and that his trial is fixed to take place on 8 December 2008, I will return to the difficulties which that impending trial now presents. It is obvious, however, that, in the light of the different standard of proof, the result of criminal proceedings may not obviate the need for an analogous inquiry in family proceedings. Were A to be convicted in the criminal proceedings, then, assuming reasonable specificity of the basis of his conviction, there would probably be no need for further inquiry in the family proceedings as opposed, of course, to a most important assessment of the consequences of the jury's verdict in terms of the needs of the abused children and of the capacity of the mother to serve them. Equally, however, the local authority may learn that an acquittal in criminal proceedings has followed so comprehensive an implosion of the prosecution case that it would be highly unlikely that the allegations could be established even to the satisfaction of the family court on the balance of probabilities. But in my experience there is a common, median outcome of such criminal proceedings in which, although the defendant has been acquitted, the evidence against him, as presented to the jury, was nevertheless considered by the relevant professionals to have carried a cogency reasonably likely to attract its acceptance on the balance of probabilities; in such circumstances the need for an inquiry in the family proceedings will remain and, if it has been lengthily delayed until the criminal proceedings have been determined, such may prove to have been highly unfortunate.

[31] No doubt, as she indicated in part of her third reason, the judge's task of determining the facts in relation to the allegations against A would have been difficult. It seems clear that her decision, probably unopposed, would have been that, albeit by video-link, B should indeed give oral evidence to her. The evidence of the three younger children, however, would have been confined to their ABE interviews. The other witnesses giving oral evidence would have been A, the mother and the child and adolescent psychiatrist to whom I have referred. But the difficulty of the exercise should not have contributed to its abandonment. As part of her fifth reason the judge stated that it was 'not the role of this court' to carry out the exercise. Two days later she echoed her remark by observing, with only the most superficial validity, that the judge was not the jury. But in *Re B (Children) (Care Proceedings: Standard of Proof) (CAFCASS Intervening)* [2008] UKHL 35, [2008] 3 WLR 1, [2008] 2 FLR 141 Baroness Hale of Richmond recently said, in an analogous context, at para [59]: 'I do not underestimate the difficulty of deciding where the truth lies but that is what the courts are for'.

[32] In the course of articulation of her first reason the judge pointed out that 'therapists', and I believe that by that word she intended to include Vista which was about to embark on the risk assessment, could view the videotaped interviews for themselves 'and reach their own conclusions and may take the case on a worst scenario basis if they feel it appropriate to do so'. Again in explaining her third reason the judge

referred to the possibility that the mother could develop protective skills 'assuming the worst case scenario'. In my view it was wrong for the judge to consider it preferable that the 'therapists' should reach their own conclusions. The responsibility for choosing the optimum future programme for the children lies with the court; and it is a necessary incident to the discharge of its responsibility that it should decide what the relevant facts are so that it can make the wisest choice. Furthermore the proposition that therapists, assessors and other professionals should work 'on a worst scenario basis' seems to me, on analysis, entirely misconceived. I have no doubt that, by her reference to a worst scenario basis, the judge was referring to the hypothesis that A *had* sexually abused the children rather than to a hypothesis – bad enough – that for example the mother had encouraged E and to a lesser extent D to make false allegations of sexual abuse. But for the courts and other professionals to work on the basis that any or all of these four children *had* been sexually abused in circumstances in which (if it be the case) they *had not* been sexually abused, had falsely alleged that they had been sexually abused and had been encouraged by their mother to make that false allegation, would be shockingly inappropriate. Nowhere in her judgment did the judge grapple with the fact that, although it was said that the mother believed the allegations of the children, the local authority did not believe the allegations of E and maintained that, in grave dereliction of her maternal responsibilities, the mother had encouraged E to concoct his false allegation, had encouraged D falsely to embellish her allegation and, conversely, had at one stage put pressure on B to retract her true allegation. How can it be said that the court did not need to determine the validity of these grave criticisms of the mother prior to reaching any decision to return the younger children to her?

[33] In care proceedings the courts determine facts, whether at a bespoke fact-finding hearing or otherwise, in order to provide terra firma upon which the courts and the professionals called upon to advise them can all operate. They need not just *firm* ground but, for obvious reasons, the *same* ground upon which to operate. The judge considered, in my view mistakenly, that it was sufficient that the mother believed that the allegations of all four children were true. The judge did not even hear the mother give oral evidence before concluding, as the first reason for her decision, that it sufficed that the mother believed them; she merely accepted from the position statement filed on her behalf that the mother believed the allegations. Even if the mother did genuinely believe the allegations, I have said enough to indicate that such was an entirely insufficient foundation for the future work of the court and its professional witnesses in the proceedings. In the event, however, as I have indicated at para [23] above, the mother admitted to the experts at Vista only 8 days after the judge's determination that she did not know whether she believed the allegations against A. By proceeding primarily by reference to the mother's perceived belief in the truth of the allegations, the judge had laid the foundations for future work in the case not in

concrete but in sand; and, only 8 days later, the mother's admission to the professionals had washed the sand away.

[34] In the course of his submissions this afternoon Mr Verdan has taken us in some detail through three or four interim reports by Vista with a view to seeking to persuade us that, for its part, Vista sees no real need for the veracity of the allegations against A to be determined by the court prior to the compilation of its final report. My first reaction to that suggestion has been to remind myself that, in the last analysis, what matters is not what Vista considers that it needs but what the court considers that it, the court, needs in order that it can properly discharge its responsibilities to these children ...

[35] My conclusion is that, insofar as it is possible to do so, facts need to be found as to whether the four children were sexually abused by A and that the judge's order, drafted in arresting terms to the effect that the local authority be precluded from making the allegations, should be set aside. In relation to the two subsidiary issues which on 10 April the judge also refused to determine, I consider that on balance she was acting within the ambit of her discretion in concluding that an inquiry into whether the mother had subjected the children to more frequent changes of home than were necessary was, even if it resulted in a finding to that effect, so unlikely to prove significant at the outcome stage that she would decline to conduct it. In that, however, the father of the younger children has been putting himself forward as a carer for the children, I consider that there was no good reason for declining to rule upon the local authority's allegations against him that he failed to take reasonable steps to save his children from continuing to suffer in the mother's home. No doubt that issue would not, on its own, deserve a bespoke fact-finding hearing but might rather be determined at the outcome stage were his candidacy for their care to appear live.

G38 DEPARTURE FROM SCHEDULE OF FINDINGS SOUGHT

Re G and B (Fact-finding hearing)

[2009] EWCA Civ 10, [2009] 1 FLR 1145 at 1149 and 1150

Court of Appeal

Wall LJ

[16] All that said, however, the following propositions seem to me to be equally valid. Where, as here, the local authority had prepared its schedule of proposed findings with some care, and where the fact-finding hearing had itself been the subject of a directions appointment at which the parents had agreed not to apply for various witnesses to attend for cross-examination, it requires very good reasons, in my judgment, for the judge to depart from the schedule of proposed findings. Furthermore, if the judge is, as it were, to go *'off piste'*, and to make findings of fact which are not sought by the local authority or not contained in its schedule, then he or she must be astute to ensure: (a) that any additional or different findings made are securely founded in the evidence; and (b) that the fairness of the fact-finding process is not compromised.

[17] It is, of course, axiomatic that judges are entitled to disagree with an expert witness. But this proposition also has an equally obvious corollary. There must be material upon which the judge in question can safely found his or her disagreement, and he or she must fully explain the reasons for rejecting the expert's evidence: – see, for example, *Re M (Residence)* [2002] EWCA Civ 1052, [2002] 2 FLR 1059 at para [57], per Thorpe LJ.

[18] In the instant case, I think it a great pity that the judge went down the 'unlawful killing' road. It was not a road signposted by the schedule of findings prepared by the local authority. It was in no sense necessary for the satisfaction of the threshold criteria. In addition, and more significantly, it was not supported by the medical and pathological evidence.

[19] In my judgment, this appeal succeeds first and foremost on the second of the two 'core' grounds. However, once the judge had embarked on unlawful killing, and indicated that in her view it was 'probable', she was, in my judgment, plainly wrong to refuse the father an adjournment, however, time-consuming and inconvenient the delay may have been. It is,

with respect to the judge, not enough for her to say, as she did in para [17] of her judgment, that 'it was always apparent that the court intended to investigate the cause of AB's death'.

[20] The major point, however, in my judgment, is that the evidence, taken as a whole, did not warrant a judicial finding that AB was unlawfully killed by one or both of his parents, even taking into account the fact that the judge was entitled to make an adverse assessment of the parents' (and in particular the father's) credibility.

...

[23] I am very conscious of the fact that in paras [74] to [76] of her speech in *Re B (Children) (Care Proceedings: Standard of Proof) (CAFCASS Intervening)* [2008] UKHL 35, [2008] 3 WLR 1 sub nom *B (Care Proceedings: Standard of Proof), Re* [2008] 2 FLR 141, Baroness Hale of Richmond gave forceful expression to the proposition that the same judge should hear the fact-finding and the welfare aspects of a care case, where there had been what has become known as a 'split hearing' ...

[24] I entirely and respectfully agree with Baroness Hale of Richmond that in the ordinary case where there is a split hearing then, as a matter of good practice, the same judge should take both limbs. Indeed, that is already the rule: – see *Re G (Care Proceedings: Split Trials)* [2001] 1 FLR 872. However there will, inevitably, be exceptions. What, for example, if the judge dies or is taken seriously ill after he or she had heard the first limb? In my judgment, it is unlikely to be proportionate, or in the interests of the child or children concerned or in conformity with the overriding objective for the court to start again from scratch.

[25] Similar considerations, it seems to me, also apply where a litigant has legitimately lost confidence in the judge, or where there is an appearance of bias.

Other significant cases on this issue:

- *Re G (Residence: restrictions on further applications)* [2008] EWCA Civ 1468, [2009] 1 FLR 894 (s 91(14) order and residence order set aside: judge should have adjourned to allow father, a litigant in person, to consider his position)
- Cf *Re W-P (Fact-finding hearing)* [2009] EWCA Civ 216, [2009] 2 FLR 200 (case remitted for rehearing for a variety of reasons including judge not putting own hypothesis to experts)
- *Re M (Children)* [2009] EWCA Civ 1216, [2010] 1 FLR 1089 (if refuse adjournment for reasons of delay, must establish what the likely delay would be)

- Cf *Re B (care order: adjournment of fact finding hearing)* [2009] EWCA Civ 1243, [2010] 2 FLR 1445 (necessary to grant a very late application to adjourn)

G39   ROLE OF CG / SOLICITOR FOR CHILD AT FACT-FINDING

Lancashire County Council v R

[2008] EWHC 2959 (Fam), [2010] 1 FLR 387 at 393

Family Division

Ryder J

The child's guardian

[30]   Mrs A-G has not given opinion evidence during this hearing. She has very properly instructed her counsel to ask searching and often illuminating questions both as to the lay and medical evidence and makes no submissions on the facts in issue.

Other significant cases on this issue:

- *B v B (Child abuse: contact)* [1994] 2 FLR 713 at 732

G40 RECORDING THE FINDINGS / LATER EVIDENCE

Re M and MC (Care: issues of fact: drawing of orders)

[2002] EWCA Civ 499, [2003] 1 FLR 461 at 462

Court of Appeal

Thorpe LJ

[6] The order drawn to reflect that judgment is in many ways deficient. Nowhere can the reader glean what was the outcome of the day's trial. It is, in my opinion, important to observe the formalities. Where a court has directed the determination of specific issues then the judgment of the court performing the task should first address those issues in turn, and specifically, so that it is evident that there has been a complete and thorough performance of the operation. Then those findings should be set out in the order drawn to record the outcome of the day's proceedings. The order can then go on to make such further directions as are appropriate, such as the direction recited in this order to the effect that the first, second, third and fourth respondents must file statements detailing their respective positions in reaction to judgment by a certain date.

G41 COURT / PARTIES / EXPERTS BOUND BY FINDINGS MADE / NOT MADE

Re R (Care: disclosure: nature of proceedings)

[2002] 1 FLR 755 at 765 and 767

Family Division

Charles J

The approach at the welfare or disposal stage, having regard to the decision not to pursue the allegations of sexual abuse

...

Here, the decision of the local authority not to pursue the serious allegations of sexual abuse and the decisions of the guardian and TR to join in and accept that approach has the consequence that any such problem does not arise, because no finding of sexual abuse has been or can be made at this stage ...

Subject to the possibility of arguments based on, for example, abuse of process, the decision of the local authority not to pursue the allegations of sexual abuse does not preclude them from pursuing such allegations in the future. However, in my judgment, both the court and the local authority have to approach this case on the basis of the present position and, thus, that the allegations of sexual abuse have not been pursued.

Re M and R (Child Abuse: Evidence) [1996] 2 FLR 195 confirms that the decision of the local authority not to pursue the allegations of sexual abuse means that if the threshold criteria are satisfied on a different basis (ie neglect and emotional harm) then, at the welfare or disposal stage, the court cannot assess risk on the basis either (a) that there was sexual abuse or, and importantly, (b) on the basis of a suspicion that there was or might have been sexual abuse, as alleged by the younger boys. A similar but not identical situation would have arisen if the allegations of sexual abuse had been pursued and the court had been unable to make findings that there had been sexual abuse, or who the perpetrators were, to the requisite standard of proof.

...

In my judgment, the existence of these proceedings and the decision therein not to pursue the allegations means that the position is now different from that which existed during the period that the allegations were pursued during the currency of the proceedings because:

(a)   the allegations have been put before a court but have not been proved for the purposes of either s 31 or s 1 of the Children Act 1989, or otherwise;

(b)   it follows that the court and the local authority are not authorised, pursuant to statute, to interfere in the lives of the relevant individuals by reason of any public law orders made in these proceedings on the basis that the sexual abuse alleged by the three younger boys, or some of those acts of sexual abuse, have taken place;

(c)   further, at the welfare or disposal stage of these proceedings and thus in recommending and approving care plans, the local authority and the court should not, in my judgment, assess risk for the purposes of s 1 and thus (i) what public law order should be made, and (ii) the terms of the care plan on the basis that allegations of sexual abuse and future risk based thereon have been established.

Additionally, in my judgment, having regard to the circumstances that now exist, unless and until the local authority either:

(1)   pursue further proceedings to seek to establish to the civil standard that the sexual abuse alleged by the three younger boys has occurred; or

(2)   a significant change in circumstances occurs

it would be wrong for the local authority:

(a)   to advance care plans; and

(b)   thereafter, if public law orders are made, to proceed in their dealings with the family on the basis:

   (i)   that the fact that the local authority have not proceeded with and are not seeking to establish the allegations of sexual abuse made by the younger boys makes no real difference because, for example, the local authority believe those allegations or some of them to be true or believe that the younger boys have been sexually abused; or

   (ii)   as they have done during the period that the interim care orders were in place (and thus on the basis set out in s 38(2) of the Children Act 1989) that the local authority had reasonable grounds for believing that those allegations of sexual abuse would be established.

First, in my judgment, any existing belief of the local authority concerning the allegations of sexual abuse has to be re-assessed and re-evaluated at all levels of the local authority in the light of the evidence and the issues that have arisen in this case. In my judgment, it is incumbent on the officers at all relevant levels of this local authority to urgently and thoroughly review the position of the local authority having regard to the existing position. In other words, existing mindsets have to be re-visited and, where appropriate, altered.

Secondly, if after such re-evaluation the local authority or some of its officers still hold the belief that the allegations or some of them are true, none the less, in my judgment, unless and until the local authority decide to seek to establish the allegations of sexual abuse to the civil standard or there is a significant change in circumstances, the local authority in the performance of their statutory duties cannot properly deal with any of the family and, in particular, with the father and C on the basis that the local authority believe that either (i) the younger boys have been sexually abused or (ii) there has been any sexual relationship or activity between the father and C.

In my judgment, unless and until the local authority decide to seek to establish the allegations of sexual abuse to the civil standard or there is a significant change in circumstances, the local authority have to proceed on the basis that part of the relevant background is that those allegations have not and will not be proved and established to that standard and, therefore, as part of the threshold pursuant to which, or as part of the basis upon which, the local authority is entitled to interfere in the lives of this family.

Other significant cases on this issue:

- *Re N (Sexual abuse allegations: professionals not abiding by findings of fact)* [2005] 2 FLR 340 at [18]
- *D v B and Others (Flawed sexual abuse enquiry)* [2006] EWHC 2987 (Fam), [2007] 1 FLR 1295 at e g [15(ix)]
- Cf *Re S-B (Children)* [2009] UKSC 17, [2010] 1 FLR 1161: see H4 – Decisions must be made on facts found not suspicions

This case is also included in relation to:

D5   Reunification not an overriding factor
G22 Preparation and disclosure: duties of LA
G23 Preparation and disclosure: mirror duties of respondents
G24 Disclosure of relevant notes
G45 Use of experts: general guidance
G51 Responsibilities on receipt of report
G75 Statement of general principle (2)
G82 Public interest immunity
H29 Costs: illustration in public law

G42 DANGER OF PREJUDGING WELFARE STAGE: PUBLIC LAW

Re L (Care proceedings: risk assessment)

[2009] EWCA Civ 1008, [2010] 1 FLR 790 at 797, 802 and 803

Court of Appeal

Wall LJ

[20] Having gone on to consider the failure to seek medical assistance, and the position of the grandparents on both sides, the judge concluded her judgment with the following paragraph:

'[52] It has been suggested that there is sufficient evidence upon which the court could make a finding that there has been a global family failure to protect R. It follows from what is set out above that such a finding would indeed be appropriate.'

[21] Had the judge's judgment ended at this point, it would, in my view, have been fireproof. Most unfortunately, however, she went on to say:

'and in the light of that and the rest of my judgment, (the local authority) are invited to draw up a timetable to bring these proceedings to a conclusion with the minimum of delay for R.'

[22] In my judgment, these words are capable of only one meaning, and that is the meaning given to them by the mother and those advising her: it is that the judge has decided the rest of the case. To put the matter another way, the judge's view plainly was as follows: the fact that there has been a 'global family failure' to protect the child and the fact that she could not rule out the mother as perpetrator meant that R must be the subject of a care order, and adopted outside the family.

[23] In my judgment, the citation from the judge's judgment set out in para [21] above is a non sequitur and a serious error on the part of the judge. That she meant what the words appear to say is plain from subsequent events. On 27 February 2009, the judge directed the local authority to file and serve its final care plan and placement order application by 30 April 2009. The same guardian was appointed in the placement order proceedings, which were to be consolidated with the care proceedings. Furthermore, when on 17 June 2009 the judge became aware that the criminal trial of the mother and the father was due to take place in September 2009, she made an order of her own motion, of which we

only have a draft, in which she listed the final hearing of the care proceedings for 1–4 September, that is to say prior to the criminal trial.

[24] It is, unfortunately, impossible to reach any other conclusion than that the judge had prejudged the outcome of the care proceedings. It is, unfortunately, equally impossible to come to any other conclusion than that her assessment of that outcome plainly influenced the decision which is in fact the subject matter of the appeal.

...

[39] In my judgment, Mr Belben's submissions are to be preferred on the facts of this particular case. Despite the skill and moderation with which the contrary was argued by Mr Miller, I am in no doubt at all that the judge's decision to refuse the mother an independent assessment was, on the facts of this case, plainly wrong.

...

[45] In my judgment, therefore, the judge's refusal to order the assessment sought by the mother was plainly wrong. It is not only unfair to the mother on the facts of the case, but the judge has fallen into the trap of prejudging the case at the finding of fact stage, and imposing her premature assessment of the outcome of the care proceedings without giving the mother an opportunity to present her case fully to the court.

General notes:

The facts found stood but the welfare hearing was remitted to be heard by another judge.

Other significant cases on this issue:

- Cf *Re E (Contact)* [2009] EWCA Civ 1238, [2010] 1 FLR 1738: see B30 – Danger of prejudging welfare stage: private law

G43   APPEAL LIES AFTER FIRST STAGE

Re B (Split hearing: jurisdiction)

[2000] 1 FLR 334 at 336 and 343

Court of Appeal

Butler-Sloss P and Schiemann LJ

BUTLER-SLOSS P:

In accordance with some earlier decisions of the High Court, the case was decided suitable to be a split trial; first, as to the issues which are raised by the judge in his judgment and, secondly, as a result of his findings, what the disposal should be in relation to the child.

The problem for this court was that the judge gave a careful, reasoned judgment. He did not make any actual declarations and he did not make any specific order. The question that has arisen in the court was, what was the jurisdiction of this court to deal with this matter? Having considered this problem with some care, bearing in mind that it is not the function of this court to deal with findings rather than with orders or judgments as the High Court requires, or with determinations such as s 77 of the County Court Act requires, we have considered very carefully the appropriate way in which we should deal with this case.

If, as I have come to the conclusion, it is necessary to find that the judge was wrong, for this court to sit back and say that it is not appropriate for us to intervene at this stage at the conclusion of these preliminary issues being dealt with, but to allow the case to continue for another 3 days and then for there to be an appeal by one or more of the parties (which would by then be 7½ days' hearing), and then for the Court of Appeal to say that the judge went wrong in his judgment given on 1 September 1999, would be to fly in the face of common sense and an approach to the disposal of litigation which would be totally contrary to Lord Woolf's proposals in the new civil procedure approach which permeates through civil litigation, and certainly within the Family Division.

I am satisfied for my part that the way in which this case was presented to the court was by way of a hearing of a preliminary issue. The preliminary issue was that of causation. The decision, which was very much dependent upon the medical evidence, was crucial to the final decision of the court as to where this child should live and with whom. The determination of the preliminary issues was crucial to the disposal of the care proceedings. Without it it would be impossible for the local authority and guardian to put forward the appropriate proposals to the judge, or indeed for the mother and grandparents to be able to meet those proposals. I can see why, in this particular case, there was a split hearing. Whether such a hearing presents other difficulties is another matter.

Mr Ames, representing the grandparents who had not had an opportunity to argue this below, in his excellent submissions to us, has cited the obvious example of a preliminary issue, an issue such as a defence in limitation or in civil personal injury cases of liability. But preliminary issues are not limited to such obvious examples. There are other examples which we have canvassed with counsel during argument upon which findings are made which are of enormous importance, although not necessarily entirely determinative of the second part of the hearing. But such issues which are determined as a preliminary part of the case, which are crucial to the final determination, can be treated, if appropriate, as a determination for the purpose of allowing the Court of Appeal to hear it without waiting for the second part of the hearing. In this case, in the unusual circumstances which prevail, I am satisfied that this court does have jurisdiction to deal with the issues which were determined by the judge and that those are issues determined in accordance with s 77 of the County Court Act.

Having granted permission to appeal …

SCHIEMANN LJ:

This is a case where the parties wished the judge to determine a number of issues prior to going on to hear the rest of the case at a later date. The judge did so and gave a full judgment on the points which he had been asked to determine. He then adjourned the proceedings. For reasons I can well understand, he did not, and was not asked to, incorporate his determinations in a formal order. If those determinations had been so incorporated in a formal order, there would have been a right of appeal quite clearly under s 72 of the County Courts Act.

I do not consider that the absence of this formal step deprives the court of jurisdiction to consider the appeal. To hold otherwise would merely mean that the parties, of necessity, would have to take various formal steps and then come back to the court, or alternatively, to leave them to conclude a further estimated 3 days of hearing and then come back to court in order to argue precisely the same points that have been argued in the case.

Experts

G44 ROLE AND RESPONSIBILITIES OF EXPERT WITNESSES

Meadow v General Medical Council (Her Majesty's Attorney-General intervening)

[2006] EWCA Civ 1390, [2007] 1 FLR 1398 at 1409 and 1472

Court of Appeal

Clarke MR, Thorpe LJ

CLARKE MR:

The role and responsibilities of the expert witness

[21] In para [20] of his judgment the judge quoted what are now well-known principles identified by Cresswell J in *National Justice Compania Naviera SA v Prudential Assurance Co Ltd ('The Ikarian Reefer')* [1993] 2 Lloyd's Rep 68, at 81–82. Those principles were approved by Otton LJ in *Stanton v Callaghan* and are now accepted and understood throughout what may be called the expert witness community. Cresswell J put them thus:

> 'The duties and responsibilities of expert witnesses in civil cases include the following:
>
> 1. Expert evidence presented to the court should be, and should be seen to be, the independent product of the expert uninfluenced as to form or content by the exigencies of litigation (*Whitehouse v Jordan* [1981] 1 WLR 246, 256, per Lord Wilberforce).
>
> 2. An expert witness should provide independent assistance to the court by way of objective unbiased opinion in relation to matters within his expertise (see *Polivitte Ltd v Commercial Union Assurance Co plc* [1987] 1 Lloyd's Rep 379, 386, per Garland J and *Re R (A Minor) (Expert's Evidence)* [1991] 1 FLR 291, per Cazalet J). An expert witness in the High Court should never assume the role of an advocate.
>
> 3. An expert witness should state the facts or assumptions upon

which his opinion is based. He should not omit to consider material facts which could detract from his concluded opinion (*In Re R*).

4.   An expert witness should make it clear when a particular question or issue falls outside his expertise.

5.   If an expert's opinion is not properly researched because he considers that insufficient data is available, then this must be stated with an indication that the opinion is no more than a provisional one (*In Re R*). In cases where an expert witness who has prepared a report could not assert that the report contained the truth, the whole truth and nothing but the truth without some qualification, that qualification should be stated in the report (*Derby & Co Ltd v Weldon* The Times, 9 November 1990, per Staughton LJ).

6.   If, after exchange of reports, an expert witness changes his view on a material matter having read the other side's expert's report or for any other reason, such change of view should be communicated (through legal representatives) to the other side without delay and when appropriate to the court.

7.   Where expert evidence refers to photographs, plans, calculations, analyses, measurements, survey reports or other similar documents, these must be provided to the opposite party at the same time as the exchange of reports (see 15.5 of the *Guide to Commercial Court Practice*).'

The judge added at the end of that quotation that in addition to those considerations, the expert witness will know that he must give evidence honestly and in good faith and must not deliberately mislead the court. He will not expect to receive protection if he is dishonest or malicious or deliberately misleading.

THORPE LJ:

[250]   The courts have defined the standards expected of expert witnesses, classically in the judgment of Cresswell J in *The Ikarian Reefer* [1993] 2 Lloyd's Rep 68. We were told that the standards which he set for experts in civil cases apply equally at criminal trials. Identical standards apply to witnesses in family proceedings: see *Re R (A Minor) (Expert's Evidence)* [1991] 1 FLR 291, per Cazalet J and *Vernon v Bosley (No 1)* [1997] 1 All ER 577, at 612.

This case is also included in relation to:

G64   Exposure of expert witness to disciplinary proceedings

G45 USE OF EXPERTS: GENERAL GUIDANCE

Re R (Care: disclosure: nature of proceedings)

[2002] 1 FLR 755 at 795

Family Division

Charles J

Lessons to be learned

These appear above and included amongst them are the following:

(a) All involved should consider with care the instructions to be given to an expert.

(b) The expert should check that he or she can carry out and is carrying out those instructions and should confirm this.

(c) All involved should consider and review the report of an expert when it is received and, where relevant, raise points with the expert and other parties relating to the performance of the expert's instructions, his or her reasoning, the factual basis of his or her views and the relevance of his or her views to the proceedings.

(d) All involved in giving joint instruction should take a full part at all stages and thus attend meetings with the relevant experts, or at least comment in respect of them.

(e) If an expert is not jointly instructed, those who do not join in the instructions should none the less (i) consider how that expert should be instructed and (ii) his or her report, and raise points on both as soon as is practicable.

(f) If, as here, an expert has videoed interviews that fact should be disclosed and the desirability of the expert reviewing the video before completing his or her report and of the parties, if they wish to do so, viewing the videos at an early stage should be considered.

Other significant cases on this issue:

- *Re CB and JB (Care proceedings: guidelines)* [1998] 2 FLR 211

This case is also included in relation to:

D5 Reunification not an overriding factor
G22 Preparation and disclosure: duties of LA

G23 Preparation and disclosure: mirror duties of respondents
G24 Disclosure of relevant notes
G41 Court / parties / experts bound by findings made / not made
G51 Responsibilities on receipt of report
G75 Statement of general principles (2)
G82 Public interest immunity
H29 Costs: illustration in public law

G46 FURTHER GUIDANCE ON USE OF EXPERTS / EXPERTS' RESPONSIBILITIES

Oldham Metropolitan Borough Council v GW and PW

[2007] EWHC 136 (Fam), [2007] 2 FLR 597 at 618

Family Division

Ryder J

[90] Nothing in what follows should be taken to detract from the strong body of guidance given in previous decisions of the Court of Appeal and this court relating to experts. In that regard, it is perhaps wise to emphasise the principles set out by Cresswell J in *National Justice Compania Naviera SA v Prudential Assurance Co Ltd ('The Ikarian Reefer')* [1993] 2 Lloyd's Rep 68, at 81, Cazalet J in *Re R (a Minor) (Experts' Evidence) (Note)* [1991] 1 FLR 291 and the summary of relevant case-law that can be found in *A County Council v K, D and L*, per Charles J (above).[1]

[91] In addition to the guidance formulated by the Court of Appeal in this case, I have also recommended that:

(i) Local authorities should always write a letter of instruction when asking a potential witness for a report or an opinion, whether that request is within proceedings or pre-proceedings, e g when commissioning specialist assessment materials, reports from a treating expert or other evidential materials, and the letter of instruction should conform to the principles set out by the Family Justice Council at www.family-justice-council.org.uk and the Chief Medical Officer at Annex B para [21] of 'Bearing Good Witness' (2006) 30 October and Charles J in *A County Council v K, D and L* (above) at para [89].

(ii) When requesting and collating existing materials, all parties should be vigilant to record requests of third parties for disclosure and their responses, so that the spectre of partial disclosure, which tends only to prove a case rather than give full and frank information, can be dispelled. Furthermore, great care must be exercised when placing reliance on materials that have not been produced either as 'original medical (or other professional) records' or in response to an

---

[1]   [2005] EWHC 144 (Fam), [2005] 1 FLR 851.

instruction from a party as these materials may contain an assumption as to the standard of proof, the admissibility or otherwise of hearsay evidence and other important procedural and substantive questions that relate to the differing purposes of other inquiries (eg criminal or disciplinary proceedings).

(iii) Once instructed, experts in their advice to the court should conform to the best practice of their clinical training and, in particular, should describe their own professional risk assessment process and/or the process of differential diagnosis that has been undertaken, highlighting factual assumptions, deductions therefrom and unusual features of the case. They should set out contradictory or inconsistent features. They should identify the range of opinion on the question to be answered, giving reasons for the opinion they hold. They should highlight whether a proposition is a hypothesis (in particular a controversial hypothesis) or an opinion deduced in accordance with peer reviewed and tested technique, research and experience accepted as a consensus in the scientific community. They should highlight and analyse within the range of opinion an 'unknown cause', whether that be on the facts of the case (eg there is too little information to form a scientific opinion) or whether by reason of limited experience, lack of research, peer review or support in the field of skill and expertise that they profess. The use of a balance sheet approach to the factors that support or undermine an opinion can be of great assistance.

(iv) An expert should be asked at the earliest stage and, in any event, should volunteer an opinion whether another expert is required to bring a skill or expertise not possessed by those already involved or in the rare case a second opinion to a key issue that has been identified by the court and, if possible, what the question is that should be asked of that expert. In any event, far greater heed should be paid to advice from experts as to the questions that they are able to answer and that might be relevant to the court's determination.

(v) The 'Code of Guidance for Expert Witnesses in Family Proceedings' at Appendix C to the Protocol (above) should be amended to incorporate the recommendations made above.

G47 TREATING / FORENSIC EXPERTS

O-M, GM (and KM) v The Local Authority, LO and EM

[2009] EWCA Civ 1405, [2010] 2 FLR 58 at 69

Court of Appeal

Wall LJ

[44] In the first place, as Wall LJ explained in the *Oldham* case[1] ([2006] 1 FLR 543, 552 at para [46]:

> 'Whilst there is a clear distinction to be drawn between the functions of treating clinicians and expert witnesses, I agree with Miss Singleton (counsel for the local authority) that the fact that Dr A had had some clinical involvement by reason of his initial review of the MRI scan did not, of itself, affect his capacity to act as an expert witness, I also agree with Miss Singleton that a blanket approach which precludes treating clinicians from becoming jointly instructed witnesses in respect of children they have in fact treated runs the risk of the court being deprived of expertise and excellence in those cases where children have been fortunate enough to have encountered clinically one of the diminishing number of doctors who are also ready willing and able to participate in the forensic process. At the same time, however, the fact that an important opinion is being expressed by an expert who had had clinical involvement seem to me to provide an additional argument for a second opinion, if one is called for by the parents.'

[45] Secondly, we think it important to recall the context in which Thorpe LJ dealt with the distinction between the clinician and the court appointed expert. In *Re B*,[2] the psychiatrist whose report was before the judge was the doctor treating the child for sexual abuse which that doctor believed had occurred: she was engaged in a therapeutic relationship with the child: her position was thus wholly incompatible with the issue before the court, which was whether or not the child had been sexually abused. Clearly, a clinician treating a child for sexual abuse which the clinician believes has occurred is incapable of giving an objective opinion about whether or not the child has been abused. It was in this context that Thorpe LJ stated:

---

1   *W v Oldham MBC* [2005] EWCA Civ 1247.
2   *Re B (Sexual abuse: expert's report)* [2000] 1 FLR 871.

'It ought to be elementary for any professional working in the family justice system that the role of the expert to treat is not to be muddled with the role of the expert to report. If the mother's solicitors wished to meet the application of 15 August 1999 by asserting that F had been sexually abused on one or both of the unsupervised contacts in October 1998, it was surely incumbent upon them to put before the judge the outcome of the investigative interviews, and probably conducted in accordance with the *Memorandum of Good Practice on Video-Recorded Interviews with Child Witnesses for Criminal Proceedings* (Home Office, 1992) (the *Memorandum of Good Practice*), probably conducted by an experienced police officer and an experienced social worker jointly. The failure to adduce that evidence in response to the application of 15 August seems to me to be curious.

Secondly, the mother's solicitors should have seen that it was quite impossible for Dr Bazeley-White to make any forensic contribution to the pending litigation. It was an error of judgment on their part to have instructed her to report. The letter that they wrote seeking a report ignores all guidance, which has been bountifully supplied by experienced judges of the Family Division, as to the importance of ensuring that any instructions for a forensic report are impartial and, wherever possible, are joint and agreed with the other side. A unilateral appeal to an expert for a partial report is something which should have disappeared from the litigation scene many years ago.

I do not criticise Dr Bazeley-White for conducting an interview with F that immediately introduced anatomically correct dolls and then proceeded to a string of leading questions. Obviously, those characteristics are in clear breach of the guidelines that have been available to consultants, at least since the publication of the *Report of the Inquiry into Child Abuse in Cleveland 1987* (1988) (Cm 412) (the *Cleveland Report*). But her function was therapeutic and it may be that in her professional judgment that is what the child's therapy required. Where I criticise Dr Bazeley-White was in ever accepting instructions to prepare a forensic report. She should have had the experience and the judgment to perceive that she was disqualified from making any forensic contribution by the nature of her medical reference and by the nature of the work that she had done in response to that reference.

The judge's discretionary conclusion that the deficiencies in Dr Bazeley-White's contribution could be remedied by some sort of fresh start on joint instructions is simply unrealistic. He should have perceived that flaws as profound as this are simply incapable of rectification. His order was plainly wrong and must be set aside.'

Other significant cases on this issue:

- *Oxfordshire County Council v DP, RS and BS* [2005] EWHC 2156 (Fam), [2008] 2 FLR 1708

G48 SPECIAL CARE REQUIRED BY EXPERTS INVOLVED IN BOTH FAMILY AND CRIMINAL PROCEEDINGS

Re M (Care: disclosure to the police)

[2008] 2 FLR 390 at 394 and 402

Family Division

Baron J

[14] I understand that increasingly, the same experts are being used in both family and criminal proceedings. I expect, as a matter of practicality, this may be a necessity. But to my mind, it is undesirable unless very clear guidelines are set out by the relevant medical colleges, so that doctors do not cross any impermissible line. Evidence which is made available to an expert in one context, cannot be allowed to slip out in another. Experts wearing two hats, therefore have to be clear about the boundaries and limits of their role. As a counsel of perfection, it would be preferable if different professionals were used, but in the real world, that may not be possible. Accordingly, I urge that such guidelines as are necessary, are made on an urgent basis.

...

[30] I wish to point out that that extemporary judgment was delivered in the context of concern that had been raised by the mother's legal team, about the disclosure by the local authority to the police of a report from an adult psychiatrist called Professor Mortimer, who had been commissioned to provide a viability assessment as to the mother's future capabilities as a mother for N. That disclosure should not, in my view, have been made without my express permission. In fact, the police immediately interviewed Professor Mortimer, and there were concerns about her future role in any criminal proceedings, based upon the disclosure which had been made without my express permission, or without the considered consent of all parties. I offered all the opportunity to argue the point in detail before me, but in the event the police decided that they would not seek to rely upon the Mortimer report. In my view, disclosure of such material, if it is contemplated within criminal proceedings, should be done only after the court has expressly considered the matter and given its permission, if appropriate. If all parties consent, then I expect in reality the judge will make the order, but proper consideration has to be given to the precise contents of each document.

This means that in every case, the legal advisers of alleged perpetrators must be very watchful, in case the disclosure might prejudice their client within the criminal context.

G49 MATERIAL THAT SHOULD AND SHOULD NOT BE SENT TO EXPERT

Re S (Expert evidence)

[2008] EWCA Civ 365, [2008] 2 FLR 1163 at 1166 and 1166

Court of Appeal

Thorpe LJ

[8] It seems to me that it can be said powerfully that if in accordance with Charles J's conclusion at para (c), allegations that have not been pursued or proved by the local authority at the disposal stage of proceedings are not to be considered by the court in assessing risks and in considering what public law orders should be made, then logically that material should not be considered by the jointly instructed expert; logically, because, most evidently, it would be irrelevant for the expert to consider and opine upon something irrelevant to the judge's task at disposal ...

...

[10] ... I would fully support all that Charles J said in *Re R (Care: Disclosure: Nature of Proceedings)*[1] and I am clear that his words are by logical extension to be applied to the preparation of material conveyed to experts.

[11] Secondly, I would say that, in instructing experts, nothing relevant must be excluded but, equally, material that is unnecessary (because irrelevant) must be rigorously excluded. Experts should be spared files of documents which are peripheral or of little relevance to their essential task. The cost of the expert's involvement is simply unnecessarily inflated by overburdening the expert with papers that are not significant to the expert's defined task.

[12] Thirdly, I would say that it is important that local authorities should abstain from introducing into proceedings, and sending to experts, material which will inevitably be perceived – perhaps reasonably perceived by the adult who is being assessed – as being unfair; unfair in the sense that it is purely prejudicial. This is a case, again familiar, in which the parents are said to have a bad record of co-operation with professionals. The incapacity to co-operate with professionals is often a powerful consideration in the conclusion that a care order is necessary. It may

---

[1]   [2002] 1 FLR 755.

almost be the single consideration and, accordingly, where there is already a history of fractious relationships, untrusting relationships between the family and the professionals, it is important that their capacity to improve co-operation is not unnecessarily prejudiced by a litigation presentation that is regarded by the family as a blow below the belt.

G50 EXPERT MUST REVIEW INSTRUCTIONS GIVEN AND RAISE ANY PROBLEMS

Re K (Contact: mother's anxiety)

[1999] 2 FLR 703 at 705

Family Division

Wall J

As I made clear to Ms C, and repeat for the purposes of this judgment, it is of course sensible for any expert instructed in child proceedings to be given a brief by the court; but the expert must always review the brief and if the expert comes to the view that he/she simply cannot fulfil the obligations imposed on him/her under the order without direct access to the child or the parties, the expert should always raise that matter with those instructing him/her and, if necessary, with the court. I am reasonably confident that had an application been made to the court for Ms C to see D it would have been granted, as indeed it was on a later occasion.

G51 RESPONSIBILITIES ON RECEIPT OF REPORT

Re R (Care: disclosure: nature of proceedings)

[2002] 1 FLR 755 at 779

Family Division

Charles J

Experts' reports

There are a number of authorities relating to the instruction and role of experts. Save to a very limited extent, I do not propose to add to them. First, I have already made the point that all parties owe duties in respect of the identification and instruction of experts. Secondly, and also relevant here, is the point that once a report from an expert is received it should be considered by all the parties and their legal advisers to check:

(a)   that the expert has reported in accordance with his or her instructions;
(b)   whether that party wishes to put any further points to that expert, which would include points on his or her reasoning and also points as to what facts or matters the expert has considered and whether he or she agrees that other facts or matters are relevant and would make a difference; and
(c)   the role that the expert should play at the hearing and thus whether and if so when, and as to what, the expert should give oral evidence.

This case is also included in relation to:

D5   Reunification not an overriding factor
G22   Preparation and disclosure: duties of LA
G23   Preparation and disclosure: mirror duties of respondents
G24   Disclosure of relevant notes
G41   Court / parties / experts bound by findings made / not made
G45   Use of experts: general guidance
G75   Statement of general principles (2)
G82   Public interest immunity
H29   Costs: illustration in public law

G52   ECHR, ART 6: EXPERT 'LIKELY TO HAVE A PREPONDERANT INFLUENCE'

Re L (Care: assessment: fair trial)

[2002] EWHC 1379 (Fam), [2002] 2 FLR 730 at 759 and 761

Family Division

Munby J

[107]   But *Mantovanelli v France* (1997) 24 EHRR 370 illustrates an important aspect of fairness for the purposes of Art 6 which has, as it seems to me, significant if thus far wholly unrecognised implications for procedure in family cases.

...

[113]   I derive from *Mantovanelli* two principles of particular importance for present purposes:

(i)   First, that the fair trial guaranteed by Art 6 is not confined to the 'purely judicial' part of the proceedings. Unfairness at *any* stage of the litigation process may involve breaches not merely of Art 8 but also of Art 6. This is potentially very important bearing in mind that, as I explained in *Re B (Disclosure to Other Parties)* [2001] 2 FLR 1017, at [56], [64], [67], whereas rights under Art 8 are inherently qualified and can be – and often have to be – balanced against other rights, including other rights under Art 8, a parent's right to a fair trial under Art 6 is absolute. It cannot be qualified by reference to, or balanced against, the child's or anyone else's rights under Art 8. The right to a fair trial under Art 6 cannot be compromised or watered down by reference to Art 8.

(ii)   Secondly, that where a jointly instructed or other sole expert's report, though not binding on the court is 'likely to have a preponderant influence on the assessment of the facts by [the] court' there may be a breach of Art 6 if a litigant is denied the opportunity – *before* the expert produces his report – (a) to examine and comment on the documents being considered by the expert and (b) to cross-examine witnesses interviewed by the expert and on whose evidence the report is based – in short to participate effectively in the process by which the report is produced.

[114]   In *Mantovanelli* itself the court held that the earlier defects in the procedure were not cured by the litigants' ability to make 'submissions to the [trial] court on the content and findings of the report after receiving it' because that did not afford them 'a real opportunity to comment effectively on it'. A fortiori, and perhaps hardly surprisingly, in *Buchberger v Austria* (unreported) 20 December 2001 the court held (paras 43–45, 51) that there had been breaches of both Art 6 and Art 8 where, in what we would call public law proceedings, reliance was placed on a report of the youth welfare office which was never seen by the applicant mother. It made no difference (para 48) that the report related to a meeting with the applicant herself and that accordingly it could be said that she knew the facts mentioned in the report.

General notes:

Although in *Re V (Care: pre-birth actions)* [2004] EWCA Civ 1575, [2005] 1 FLR 627 the Court of Appeal warned that trial judges should be extremely cautious in reading too much into para [154] of this judgment, which it said was merely intended to draw attention to certain principles of practice that deserved emphasis, no such caution was entered in respect of the extract of the judgment reproduced here.

G53 DISCLOSURE OF DOCUMENTS ON WHICH RELIANCE PLACED

Re L (Children) (Care proceedings: significant harm)

[2006] EWCA Civ 1282, [2007] 1 FLR 1068 at 1075 and 1088

Court of Appeal

Wilson and Wall LJJ

WILSON LJ:

[21] *Second*, the letter of instruction to Mrs Westmacott was along conventional, yet crucial, lines. By it she was reminded that the welfare of the children was paramount; with it were enclosed the documents filed in the proceedings; and in it she was invited to interview the parents and the children. The letter continued:

> 'It is understood that you will not deal independently with any one party without reference to the others and it is essential that there are no informal unrecorded discussions with any of the professionals ... involved in the case. If documents are exchanged with one party, please copy them to all others.'

[22] But there was a wholesale departure on the part of Mrs Westmacott from this last instruction. I feel sure that she departed from it with the utmost bona fides, in the interests (as she saw it) of the children. Instead she acted rather like a guardian in the compilation of a report for the disposal stage of a hearing. So Mrs Westmacott went to the children's school; studied their special educational needs files and interviewed their teachers; and from one or both of such sources extracted information which seems to have proved highly influential in the development of her opinion. The lawyers for the parents have not seen those files nor any note of those interviews. Furthermore, when Mrs Westmacott attended the offices of the local authority, she spoke to the social workers and requested to read their voluminous files referable to the family; and the local authority, so Miss Campbell (their counsel) tells us, acceded to her request without demur. Yet the lawyers for the parents have never seen these files. Thus arises a vast question, never considered by the judge: to what extent was the crucial evidence of Mrs Westmacott that the children were suffering, and were likely to suffer, significant harm informed by material to which the parents were afforded no access?

WALL LJ:

[66] For the local authority, Miss Campbell's vigorous defence of Mrs Westmacott only partly assuaged my concerns. I find it difficult, I have to say, to disentangle the knots caused by poor case preparation, an apparently unheralded threshold hearing and the fact that Mrs Westmacott had written her report for a final hearing. There is, for example, no reason in principle why an expert should not have access to local authority files, if he or she is to express an opinion and takes the view that an examination of those files is necessary to enable him or her to express that opinion. But the concomitant is obvious. The court and the parties, particularly in this case the parents, must have access to the same material. Nothing an expert does should be secret, or not open to examination by the other parties. How else are they to test the expert's methodology and the soundness of his or her conclusions? Equally, I find it unacceptable that Mrs Westmacott was not prepared to show the documents to counsel when asked to do so in cross examination.

[67] However, Mrs Westmacott's report is dated 2 February 2006. She gave evidence to the judge on 1 June 2006. On the face of it there was ample time for the father's advisers to seek directions for the disclosure of the documentation on which she relied. Furthermore, Mrs Westmacott herself made it clear that had she been investigating the question of significant harm for threshold she would have done other work.

[68] In my judgment, Mrs Westmacott's evidence may have a value when applied to a final hearing. Whether or not it does will be a matter for the judge who takes that hearing. Its value in relation to a threshold, however, and dispute over threshold, is, in my view, compromised. It was not appropriate for the judge to place such reliance on it in this context and in my judgment the fact that he did so is sufficient to vitiate his conclusion.

Other significant cases on this issue:

* Cf *Re R (Care: disclosure: nature of proceedings)* [2002] 1 FLR 755 at G24 – Disclosure of relevant notes

This case is also included in relation to:

D18 Dangers of social engineering

G54 OBTAINING A SECOND EXPERT'S OPINION (1)

W v Oldham Metropolitan Borough Council

[2005] EWCA Civ 1247, [2006] 1 FLR 543 at 546 and 549

Court of Appeal

Wall LJ

[10] I can state my conclusion at once, because I accept a submission made in their supplementary submission by Mr Hayden QC, Mr Karl Rowley and Mr Bansa Singh Hayer acting in this court on behalf of both parents. In the course of their argument about the provision of expert evidence in family proceedings they say:

'In many cases (probably the majority) a clear picture will emerge from a constellation of factors (eg paediatric, radiological, parental history, medical records) which will cumulatively point the court towards certain conclusions. Though those conclusions may be resisted by parents, it would be both unrealistic and unnecessary to permit parents to obtain "mirror reports" in every discipline. In a certain number of cases, however, eg non-accidental head injury (NAHI), or pathologically "unascertained" infant death, certain evidence may become pivotal and by its very nature not easily receptive to a challenge in the absence of any other expert opinion. In our submission, in those cases, the court should be slow to decline an application for a second expert. Strict case management (in accordance with the protocol) should also permit such evidence to be identified within a reasonable timescale.'

...

Authorities

[35] We were provided with a bundle of authorities by the parties. In my judgment, the only decision which is directly on the point is the decision of this court in *Daniels v Walker (Practice Note)* [2000] 1 WLR 1382. This decision must, in my judgment, be viewed with a modicum of caution from a family perspective, since experts in family proceedings (particularly in the field of paediatric neuroradiology) are a precious and scarce resource, whereas in civil proceedings experts in less arcane fields are not only more numerous, but also more willing to undertake forensic work.

[36]   With that important proviso, the question for this court in *Daniels v Walker* was what approach judges should adopt when a single expert, who has been jointly instructed, makes a report and one side or other is unhappy with the report. The context was an injury suffered by the claimant some 10 years previously when he was 6 or 7 years old and had been struck by a car. His injuries were very serious. There was a very substantial report by a jointly instructed occupational therapist, about which the defendant's solicitors were unhappy. However, the claimant's solicitors refused to make their client and his family available to be interviewed by an expert nominated by the defendant's solicitors. The defendant applied to the judge, who refused him permission to call any further expert evidence on the point, but allowed him to put written questions to the expert. The defendant appealed to this court, which allowed his appeal. Giving the leading judgment, the Master of the Rolls, Lord Woolf (as he then was), neatly encapsulated the point in the following two paragraphs:

'27 ... Where a party sensibly agrees to a joint report and the report is obtained as a result of joint instructions in the manner which I have indicated, the fact that a party has agreed to adopt that course does not prevent that party being allowed facilities to obtain a report from another expert, or, if appropriate, to rely on the evidence of another expert.

28 In a substantial case such as this, the correct approach is to regard the instruction of an expert jointly as the first step in obtaining expert evidence on a particular issue. It is to be hoped that in the majority of cases it will not only be the first step but the last step. If, having obtained a joint expert's report, a party, for reasons which are not fanciful, wishes to obtain further information before making a decision as to whether or not there is a particular part (or indeed the whole) of the expert's report which he or she may wish to challenge, then they should, subject to the discretion of the court, be permitted to obtain that evidence.'

[37]   In my judgment, these two paragraphs, with the proviso I have identified, apply to the instant case. It is to be noted that both Lord Woolf MR and Latham LJ in *Daniels v Walker* rejected an analysis based on the Convention, Art 6. It is, of course, the case that the Human Rights Act 1998 had not been enacted when *Daniels v Walker* was decided on 3 May 2000. However, Lord Woolf MR remarked:

'Article 6 could not possibly have anything to add to the issue on this appeal. The provisions of the CPR, to which I have referred, make it clear that the obligation on the court is to deal with cases justly. If, having agreed to a joint expert's report a party subsequently wishes to call evidence, and it would be unjust having regard to the overriding objective of the CPR not to allow that party to call evidence, they must be allowed to call it.'

[38]   It is in the light of these observations that I am content, speaking for myself, to rely on the overriding objective in the CPR, and not to consider the case in Convention Art 6 terms.

[39]   The proviso which I have identified finds appropriate expression, in my judgment, in the submission made by counsel for the parents, which I have recorded in para [10] of this judgment. They rightly recognise that it would be both unrealistic and unnecessary for the court to permit parents to obtain a second opinion in every discipline. Such a second opinion, accordingly, should in my judgment normally only be permitted where the question to be addressed by the chosen expert goes to an issue of critical importance for the judge's decision in the case. For the reasons I have already given, the instruction of experts in family cases needs to be stringently controlled by the court, but in the circumstances described by Messrs Hayden, Rowley and Hayer in the extract I have cited, they are, in my judgment, right to submit that the court should be slow to decline an application for a second expert.

[40]   It is, I think, also important to remember that a second opinion does not necessarily mean additional litigation and substantial additional litigation costs. If the second opinion confirms the first, my experience is that the issues in the case addressed by the two experts are likely to be radically reduced, if not eliminated. However, as is self-evident, any medical consensus must be a true medical consensus – that is with each medical discipline making its proper contribution. The medical consensus in the hearing before Her Honour Judge Newton was only a consensus because all the other doctors, including the neurologists and neuroradiologists, deferred to Dr A.

Two further points

[41]   I wish to add two further points. The first is that time-tabling in care cases is not only a statutory duty (see Children Act 1989, s 32), but forms an essential part of the *Protocol for Judicial Case Management in Public Law Children Act Cases* (June 2003) [2003] 2 FLR 719 (the Protocol). As counsel for the parents point out, the Protocol is sufficiently flexible to accommodate the obtaining of a second opinion in appropriate cases, but plainly, the likely need for a second opinion requires to be recognised and acted upon at as early a stage of the proceedings as possible. As the chronology of the instant case demonstrates, had a report from Dr B been ordered on 22 February 2005, the judge's timetable for the hearing on 5 April 2005 could have been sustained. By 22 March 2005, obtaining a report from Dr B would have meant an adjournment of the 5 April 2005 fixture, and an adjournment on the first day of the hearing would have meant substantial further delay.

[42] The second point is more general. Cases in the family justice system involving the deaths of, or serious injuries to, children are heard by experienced, specially selected and qualified judges. One of the reasons, in my judgment, why the family justice system has not been the subject of the criticism to which the criminal justice system has recently been exposed, is that family judges rarely decide cases on the evidence of a single expert.

[43] Following the decision of the criminal division of this court in *R v Cannings* [2004] EWCA Crim 1, [2004] 1 All ER 725 and the government's announcement that a number of decisions made in the criminal and the family courts would be referred to the two divisions of this court, only two family cases have in fact reached this court. They are reported as *Re U (Serious Injury: Standard of Proof); Re B* [2004] EWCA 567, [2004] 2 FLR 263. In both cases the challenge failed. The judgment of the court was given by the President, Dame Elizabeth Butler-Sloss P. In para [26] she pointed out that in a family case involving the death or the non-accidental injury to a child:

'... the judge invariably surveys a wide canvass, including a detailed history of the parents' lives, their relationship and their interaction with professionals. There will be many contributions to this context, family members, neighbours, health records, as well as the observation of professionals such as social workers, health visitors and children's guardian.'

[44] Thus, in a child case involving complex and serious injuries, the expert evidence has to be carefully analysed, fitted into a factual matrix and measured against assessments of witness credibility. To achieve justice for parents and for children, medical evidence given in court is tested fully by the advocates, and family judges subject it to rigorous analysis. In this context, where complex medical issues arise, the need for a second opinion on any critical medical issue in the case is, in my experience, rendered all the more important. Furthermore, its provision and analysis by the judge may well render the final judicial decision more secure.

This case is also included in relation to:

H32 Appeal against case management decisions (1)

G55   OBTAINING A SECOND EXPERT'S OPINION (2)

Re S; WSP v Hull City Council

[2006] EWCA Civ 981, [2007] 1 FLR 90 at 94, 95 and 96

Court of Appeal

Wilson LJ

[13]   It seems that the impetus behind the application by the parents for permission to instruct experts independently of the instruction of other experts by the local authority and by the guardian was the decision of this court in *W v Oldham Metropolitan Borough Council* [2005] EWCA Civ 1247, [2006] 1 FLR 543. In that in his judgment the judge described the parties as in two camps which held diametrically opposed views about the effect of that decision, it seems clear that it was this perceived disagreement which led to his unusual permission to appeal against his case management decisions.

...

[15]   In giving the only substantive judgment in the *Oldham* case Wall LJ explained that the judge had been wrong to deny the father the opportunity to collect a second opinion from a paediatric neuroradiologist in advance of the hearing. He said:

'[31]   It was, in my view, clear from the date of Dr A's first report ... that the evidence of the MRI scan was critical to the medical conclusion that K had suffered NAHI. It was equally clear that the other doctors, including the neuroradiologists, deferred to Dr A. Thus, the case turned pivotally on Dr A. But Dr A was the only medical witness properly capable of assessing the MRI scan, and the medical consensus on which the judge relied depended on Dr A's analysis of the MRI scan being correct.

[32]   In such circumstances, I am quite clear, speaking for myself, that parents in the position of this mother and father are entitled to a second opinion.'

In my view the judgment of Wall LJ in the *Oldham* case represents, first, a reaffirmation of the desperate importance, not only for the child but also for the parents, that these particularly difficult fact-finding exercises should yield the correct conclusion; and, secondly, a statement that the family justice system should guard against the danger that its specialist judges may too readily assume that an expert report which accords with their preconceptions about established medical wisdom cannot effectively be challenged.

[16] That said, however, I believe that there was a significant misunderstanding before the judge, perhaps in both camps, of the reach of the decision in the *Oldham* case. It was – and is – submitted on behalf both of the local authority and of the guardian that the decision largely turned upon the fact that Dr A had had a minor degree of clinical involvement in the baby's case. I disagree. At para [46] Wall LJ specifically dismissed the suggestion that his degree of involvement disabled him from acting as an expert witness and described it as only an additional argument in favour of a second opinion. But the major misunderstanding, in my view, lies in the submissions on behalf of the parents. I am convinced that this court did not intend to suggest that, at the outset of a court's arrangements for the assembly of expert evidence, it should favour the instruction of two or more experts in the same discipline additional, indeed, to such experts already destined to give evidence because of their clinical involvement in the child's case. Wall LJ refers on more than one occasion to 'a second opinion'; and indeed, in that it was even prior to the issue of proceedings that Dr A had articulated his crucial opinion, the question in that case was whether a second, subsequent opinion should be collected from within the same sphere of expertise. Furthermore the decision stresses that justification for a second opinion lies only in circumstances in which the first opinion is 'pivotal'; and, until the first set of expert reports is to hand, it cannot be discerned whether any one of them, or, if so, which one of them, is the pivot around which the others turn.

...

[18] In my view the *Oldham* case is no authority whatever for the extravagant submissions made to the judge on behalf of the parents and now made to us by Mr Collier QC on behalf of the father. Quite apart from the attendant public expense, what was the logical argument in favour of contributions from two consultant neuroradiologists; from two consultant ophthalmologists; and from two consultant neurosurgeons? What was objectionable in the subscription of all parties to a carefully crafted letter of instruction to one top expert in each discipline, whose duty of total impartiality the joint instruction could only confirm? How could it be said at that stage before the judge that there was an expert whose evidence was not only adverse to the parents but pivotal and so justified a second opinion?

[19] The only argument which runs in any way counter to the conclusion that the judge was correct – and at the very least entitled – to favour the joint instruction of single experts is the risk of delay in the event that it was only at a later stage that, in the light in particular of the *Oldham* case, the court were to favour the taking of a second opinion. In his courageous submissions to us this morning Mr Collier has stressed this point ... In para [12] of his judgment the judge said:

'It may be that the opinions of these single joint experts will be accepted and if so the case will likely be speedily resolved. If they are not then the court would likely be asked at that time for permission to instruct another expert or tier of experts, and the observations of the Court of Appeal in *Oldham* would be of advantage to a dissatisfied parent.'

I take that passage as being an acknowledgement on the part of the judge, which I would endorse, that it may be that at the review on 16 June, in the light of the reports then to hand, the father and mother will be in a position to press for, and indeed perhaps to obtain, permission to collect a second expert opinion in one or more disciplines. Although it may be possible for any such second opinion or opinions to be collected between 16 June and 19 July, or at least between 16 June and 7 August, in time for the fact-finding hearing to proceed as fixed, there is no denying that a direction for such further evidence might jeopardise the holding of the fact-finding hearing on those dates. Such a risk Mr Kirk QC on behalf of the local authority recognises. The tail, however, would be wagging the dog were the court, in this case or routinely, to favour what would otherwise be the premature collection of expert evidence in order not to jeopardise a hearing in the event that it were later to prove appropriate for it to be collected.

Other significant cases on this issue:

- *Norfolk County Council v Webster and Others* [2006] EWHC 2898 (Fam), [2007] 2 FLR 415
- *Re J* [2008] 1 FLR 1501 (application for shadow expert refused)
- *Re SK (Local authority: expert evidence)* [2007] EWHC 3289 (Fam), [2008] 2 FLR 707
- *Leeds City Council v YX and ZX (Assessment of sexual abuse)* [2008] EWHC 802 (Fam), [2008] 2 FLR 869 (the second expert's independence compromised by various factors including that she was the pupil of the expert who had provided the original report)

G56 NO STONE MUST BE LEFT UNTURNED?

Re M (Care proceedings: best evidence)

[2007] EWCA Civ 589, [2007] 2 FLR 1006 at 1006, 1007 and 1008

Court of Appeal

Thorpe LJ

[1] This is a familiar enough case, in which a very young baby is found on x-ray examination in the paediatric department of a local hospital to have fractures: in this instance, a rare fracture of the ulna and a commonplace tibial fracture. As is so often the case, the parents are distraught and have no seeming explanation, nor can they seemingly recall any expression of the extreme pain that a child inevitably experiences at the moment of fracture. So, there is a deep mystery and medical experts are introduced to try and resolve the vitally important issue of causation.

...

[3] On 30 March Miss Wiley, who has presented the mother's case vigorously throughout, reintroduces the possibility of a very rare condition, osteogenesis imperfecta, which might incline the bones of the child to break abnormally easily. She had cross-examined two of the experts, Dr Lloyd and Dr Chapman, in that territory and on 30 March she applied successfully to Her Honour Judge Coates for leave for Professor Patton, a leading expert on genetics and on osteogenesis imperfecta, to carry out an examination and consultation when it seems that he was fortuitously in the area.

[4] The examination duly took place and he reported in these terms:

'I did not find evidence of a family history of osteogenesis imperfecta from my interview with M's parents nor did I find any additional clinical signs of osteogenesis imperfecta on examination. In addition Dr Chapman states there was no radiological evidence for any underlying condition that would predispose to fractures. On the basis of this I believe a diagnosis of osteogenesis imperfecta is extremely unlikely in M.'

[5] However, he did go on to add, in a passage that the judge was later to criticise:

'While the probability of a positive result here is very small, I believe
it is advisable to carry out genetic testing as the level of proof must
be as high as possible and having raised the possibility of testing in
the cross-examination it would be wrong to dismiss testing on
grounds of costs or inconvenience alone.'

[6] So, it is not surprising, with that encouragement, that on 30 April
2007 the judge had an application from Miss Wiley for permission to refer
the case to Professor Bishop, who would, from a sample of M's blood,
carry out a test which now can be completed in 6 to 8 weeks and now
costs some £5,000. Apparently the test used to take much longer and cost
much more.

[7] The judge made the well-founded point that Dr Patton had exceeded
his brief in giving his own view as to the forensic justification for a test.
She then referred to the arguments of the parties. Miss Wiley essentially
submitted that a decision of such grave consequence should not be taken
without the best available evidence. The local authority opposed the
application, the guardian ultimately came round to oppose and the judge
concluded by saying:

'In forming my view I must look at the case as widely as possible and
the very strenuous efforts of the mother to get osteogenesis
imperfecta to the forefront of everybody's mind by considering this
case. There is no justification for putting the child through the test
given the conclusions by Dr Patton before he goes on to give an
opinion about what is best left to the court.'

...

[10] Miss Wiley has complained that the judge in her appropriately brief
judgment did not do full justice to the argument that she had advanced.
She says that she advanced below the argument that she presents to this
court in her grounds of appeal. However, it seems to me that her first
ground of appeal is essentially the submission that the judge recorded,
namely, that the very best evidence was essentially required for the
determination of such an important issue.

[11] Her second ground of appeal was to the effect that where parents
deny abuse it is unreasonable for the court to refuse to allow the test. That
proposition was obviously unsustainable and was revised to the
submission that, in the circumstances of this particular case, the judge
unreasonably refused the test. Then it is said that the judge erred in
substituting her view for that of Professor Patton and Dr Lloyd, and that
the judge finally erred in relying on the absence of aftermath or pain as
one of her reasons to depart from Professor Patton's recommendation.

[12] I will deal with these grounds comprehensively, since all of them, in the end, amount to a challenge to the exercise of judicial discretion. It does seem to me very important to draw a clear boundary between a medical decision as to what was clinically required in order to inform the future treatment of the child and a forensic decision as to what was necessary to ensure the proper determination of the issue in the causation hearing. Clearly, the medical decision is for the doctors and, equally clearly, the forensic decision is a case management decision for the judge.

[13] In the present case, the doctors were not expressing a medical opinion on clinical grounds and, insofar as they ventured an opinion on what was forensically required, they were trespassing onto judicial territory. The discretion of the judge in taking case management decisions is particularly generous. The judge here clearly decided that enough was enough, and enough had been achieved in Professor Patton's considered view that in this particular child osteogenesis imperfecta was extremely unlikely. The judge clearly placed considerable emphasis on the fact that the expensive blood test which was urged upon her had been demonstrated to establish osteogenesis imperfecta in cases where there were no other clinical signs in only one percent of three hundred cases researched. The judge also attached weight to the fact that testing for osteogenesis imperfecta is only 90% accurate.

[14] So this seems to me not only a permissible decision but a wise decision. There has to be a point at which the garnering of evidence is sufficiently full and thorough to enable the court to arrive at a conclusion, even on the elevated balance of probabilities standard of proof. It seems to me that Miss Wiley's argument comes close to saying that no stone must be left unturned. I do not accept that. The value to be derived from submitting this child to what is an invasive investigation was too small to justify the considerable cost both in cash and in time. I have no hesitation at all in upholding the judge's conclusion.

Other significant cases on this issue:

- *Re CH (Care or interim care order)* [1998] 1 FLR 402: see D58 – Ensuring necessary evidence available before making final order
- *Re L and H (Residential assessment)* [2007] EWCA Civ 213, [2007] 1 FLR 1370: see D46 – Ensure case fully investigated and all relevant evidence necessary is in place

G57 INSTRUCTION OF OVERSEAS EXPERT

Re M (Adoption: leave to oppose)

[2010] 1 FLR 238 at 254

Family Division

HHJ Newton sitting as a High Court Judge

[64] Apart from the fact that it would be impertinent of me to consider doing so, I have no desire whatsoever to discourage the instruction of foreign experts in appropriate cases. They clearly have a valuable role to play in many of the more challenging cases within the family justice system.

[65] But there may be a special need for caution where an overseas expert is instructed. The expert concerned is unlikely to be known to practitioners and judges. He may have no familiarity with the high standards of neutrality imposed in family cases in the UK. The level of monitoring by his professional body may be different. He may be accepted as a forensic practitioner in foreign courts, yet be remote by many years from clinical practice. He may not be required to undertake continuing professional development to UK standards. He may be instructed because he is willing to advance a highly controversial proposition, which no UK expert would be prepared to advance.

[66] Whilst the Practice Direction: Experts in Family Proceedings Relating to Children, [2009] 2 FLR 1383 is silent on the instruction of overseas experts, many, if not all, of the difficulties highlighted in this case may be obviated in future by strict compliance with that practice direction.

[67] In terms of additional procedural safeguards, I suggest that there should be early consideration of any proposal to instruct an overseas expert at the case management conference. The party seeking permission should explain in writing:

(a) what special expertise is possessed by the overseas expert, by reference to a full curriculum vitae;
(b) particularly where public funds are involved, as they usually will be, why a UK based expert is not to be instructed;
(c) precisely what steps have been taken to locate an appropriately qualified UK based expert;

(d)   that the proposed overseas expert has confirmed a familiarity with the practice direction and a willingness to comply with its requirements.

[68]   If the court is minded to grant leave to instruct an overseas expert, careful consideration will then need to be given to the practicalities of experts' meetings and court attendance if required, and finally the cost implications.

General notes:

The judgment also contains a salutary warning to solicitors against the back door instruction of experts.

G58 EXPERTS' MEETING

Oxfordshire County Council v DP, RS and BS

[2005] EWHC 2156 (Fam), [2008] 2 FLR 1708 at 1725

Family Division

McFarlane J

[96] The experts' meeting held in August 2004 has been a matter of comment and controversy in this case. It was planned at an advocates' meeting on the 16 August. There was agreement between the advocates that the local authority should invite the treating clinicians to the meeting. There is a dispute before me as to the agreement, if any, as to the role of the treating clinicians at the meeting. Junior counsel for the father recalls that the role was to be limited to providing factual information and clarification of the notes in order to assist the instructed experts. The local authority and child's teams recall no such restriction and anticipated that the clinicians would be treated as full experts who would give an opinion. The short written note of the advocates' meeting does not shed light on the issue.

[97] It was also agreed that any party could submit questions to be put to the experts. In the event, only the local authority and the guardian submitted questions. Copies of these questions were not supplied to the parents' lawyers until well after the event. On the other hand, for some reason, the father's legal team do not seem to have turned their minds at all to the submission of questions.

[98] The treating clinicians, namely Drs TA, Kaye P, T and D, were invited to attend the 26 August experts' meeting. Other than the invitation to attend, they were not provided with any letter of instruction or guidance upon the role that they were expected to undertake. There seems to have been no attempt to comply with the Appendix to the Protocol on Case Management regarding experts insofar as the treating clinicians were concerned.

[99] The local authority sent 'a copy of the medical/expert evidence which has been filed with the Court to date' to Dr P and Dr T by letter dated 24 August (so that it will have been received the day of, or the day before, the meeting). Dr TA told me that, as a treating clinician, he was surprised to have been invited to the experts' meeting. He had been sent the parents' statements, may have seen the notes of the case conference of 8 April, but had not seen the reports of the other experts. He told me that he had only read the other experts' reports on the morning of his

appearance at this hearing. Dr D does not appear to have been sent any documentation, but in the event was unable to attend the meeting.

[100] The meeting was conducted by Mr Trueman, the child's solicitor. It was tape recorded; however the tape has subsequently been scrubbed and was not transcribed. A note was taken by a member of Mr Trueman's firm, but she had no knowledge of the case and her note may not be a verbatim record.

[101] After the meeting, Mr Trueman prepared a draft heads of agreement document, which, after some amendment, each of the six attendees signed and approved in its entirety.

[102] A recital of the bald history of the involvement of the treating clinicians in this process will reveal to all with a knowledge of childcare proceedings a number of significant flaws, namely:

(a)   Leave of the court was required for the disclosure of any of the documents in the case to these doctors, none of whom fell into the category of 'an expert whose instruction by a party has been authorised by the court' (FPR 1991, r 4.23(1)(f)): no such leave had been sought or given by the court;

(b)   Dr TA had not seen the reports of any of the other experts;

(c)   If the treating clinicians were to see some of the documentation in the case, why was it limited to the medical reports? Why were not the statements of the parents and Mrs H and the ambulance team disclosed?

(d)   There was no clarity as to the role of the clinicians at the meeting – were they simply there to clarify matters, or to give a concluded 'expert' view;

(e)   No guidance was given to the clinicians as to what was expected of them;

(f)   If, as it transpired was the case, the clinicians were to be treated as experts within the court process, no attempt was made to comply with the Protocol, or to instruct these witnesses in the duties of an expert in court proceedings, (for example Dr P had never attended an experts' meeting before and considered the purpose was to reach a consensus);

(g)   If they were to be treated as experts in the case, why were they not required to produce a concluded expert's report prior to the meeting, or, in any event, after it, explaining their opinion.

[103] Nothing in what I have said thus far should be taken as indicating that the treating clinicians will not of course possess expertise and great experience in their specialist field. For example, I have already paid tribute to the contribution Dr TA was able to make to the court's understanding of this area of medicine. To that extent they are 'experts.' There is however a difference between the position of a treating clinician and that of an expert who has been instructed to provide an overview opinion for the purposes of court proceedings.

[104] The current practice and procedure regarding the instruction of expert witnesses has been developed and honed by countless decisions and guidance over the past 15 years. There is a detailed section of the Protocol dealing with it. The expert owes particular duties and responsibilities to the court, which must be spelled out in the letter of instruction and recited in his or her report. The letter of instruction itself properly receives very careful input from all parties during its draft stages. Finally, and of importance, the expert process is very much under the control of the court.

[105] For the future, it is my view that there may well be cases where treating clinicians will provide a useful source of information for the instructed experts at an experts' meeting. If invited to such a meeting, the ground rules for their attendance must be clearly established between the parties and, importantly, sanctioned by the court in advance. The clinician must be clearly instructed that his or her role is to provide information and to clarify parts of the history that may be unclear, but is not to take part, alongside the instructed experts, in providing an overview opinion or conclusion.

[106] Where it is proposed to seek an overview opinion from one of the doctors who has treated a child, then that proposal must be expressly raised with the other parties and with the court. If permission is given to instruct one of the treating clinicians as an expert, then that instruction and all that flows from it must be conducted in accordance with the rules, the Protocol and established practice in exactly the same manner as it would be for an 'expert' who is brought into the case and who has not treated the child.

[107] here will be cases, maybe many cases, where it is not only appropriate but highly desirable for one or more of the treating clinicians to be instructed to provide an opinion for the court process. All that I am attempting to spell out in this judgment is that, if that is to happen, it must be done properly and with the court's knowledge and permission.

[108] Finally on this point, nothing I have said is intended to inhibit the treating clinicians from expressing an opinion as to the causation of any particular symptoms. Such an expression of opinion or diagnosis is an essential part of evaluating the treatment and care needs of the patient when in their care. It will often also properly be required by social services, police and other authorities in deciding what if any action needs to be taken to protect a child or prosecute an offender. It is, as I have attempted to describe, a different role and process from providing a

comprehensive opinion for the court based on a considered view of all of the available material in the build up to a court hearing.

[109] Before leaving the question of the experts' meeting, it must in any event be borne in mind that what is said at an experts' meeting is not strictly evidence in the case. Experience shows that the manner in which experts express themselves at such meetings is less guarded than when they are writing reports for the court or giving oral evidence. The meeting and the dialogue are an important event in the preparation for the hearing, but any record of the meeting does not have evidential status. Mr Tolson submitted that the experts' meeting in this case resulted in 'trial by expert.' That might be a sound submission if the result of the meeting were treated by the courts as having a verdict-like status, but it does not have that status or anything approaching it. The trial of these issues has taken place in this court. The evidence upon which any judicial conclusion is based will be the written and oral evidence that has been submitted and thoroughly tested by the forensic process rather than any note of an experts' meeting, the purpose of which is limited to clarifying issues and flagging up areas of agreement or dispute.

G59   EXPERTS TO BE KEPT UP TO DATE / NOT KEPT WAITING AT COURT

Re T and E (Proceedings: conflicting interests)

[1995] 1 FLR 581 at 592, 593, 594, 594 and 595

Family Division

Wall J

Further points of practice relating to expert evidence in children's cases

The case has also thrown up two points of practice which are in my judgment of importance. They both relate to expert evidence and the manner in which that evidence is provided to the court.

(1)   KEEPING THE EXPERT UP TO DATE

...

As counsel for the local authority frankly accepted, this sequence of events was unsatisfactory and a matter of some embarrassment to him and to his instructing solicitor. I therefore repeat what I said in Re M, with two riders:

(1)   It is the duty of the solicitors who instruct an expert witness to ensure that the witness is kept up to date with developments in the case relevant to his or her opinion. Any such developments should not only be communicated to, but wherever possible discussed with the expert involved as far as in advance of the trial as is possible.

(2)   It is the duty of the advocate calling an expert witness to satisfy him or herself:
   (a)   that the witness has seen any relevant fresh material which has come into existence since the expert's report was written and is aware of any fresh developments in the case; and
   (b)   that the expert's opinion either remains the same despite, or has changed as a consequence of, reading the additional material or learning of the new developments.

(3)   It is unacceptable for any expert witness in a child case whose evidence goes either to the disposal of the case or to issues canvassed by the guardian ad litem in his or her report to give evidence without having read the guardian ad litem's report.

(2) TIMETABLING EXPERT WITNESSES

It is, I regret to say, my experience that the profession sometimes (I am not suggesting that this occurred here) treats the convenience of expert witnesses with a casualness which is unconducive to any concept of mutual co-operation and which is likely to reinforce the reluctance which many expert witnesses have about giving evidence in court. The legal profession simply must realise that expert witnesses are busy people with many professional commitments, and that giving evidence in court is both time-consuming and takes the expert away from other important professional commitments.

Not only, therefore, should experts not be kept waiting when they come to court (judges usually ensure that this does not occur by interposing the expert witness where necessary) but more importantly, the time set aside for their evidence should be carefully calculated so that the expert witness is not required to return on another occasion to complete his or her evidence.

...

In my judgment, however, simply to arrange for the expert to attend and for the parties to have a fair estimate of how long he or she is likely to be in the witness-box is no longer good enough. In my view, the time may now have come to be much more stringent in the timetabling of expert evidence ...

In *Vernon v Bosley* (1994) *The Times*, August 5, Sedley J held that the court had both the power and the duty in a proper case to achieve finality in its proceedings by placing a firm and realistic limit on the examination, cross-examination and re-examination of the expert witnesses to be called before it. He thus laid down a timetable for the duration of the evidence of a number of expert witnesses. He made it clear that the limits were not cast in bronze; they might not even be reached, and if they were reached in circumstances in which it was apparent that fairness required them to be extended, the court would retain the power to extend them. But such extensions, he said, would only be granted where something unforeseen made it necessary to do so.

...

Having done so, I can see no good reason, if proper professional discipline is imposed, why the approach of Sedley J in *Vernon v Bosley* should not be applied to expert evidence in children cases. Thus, if in any case the directions proposed by Cazalet J in *Re C* (above) were in place, I can see no reason why part of that process should not be a direction that the expert in question attend for a period of x hours, on a given date, and that the time for examination, cross-examination and re-examination be defined.

The issue here is not the advocate's freedom to exercise a professional discretion to conduct a case without unwarranted judicial interference. It is about professional and intellectual discipline. It is also about the duty of the court to be proactive in children cases in defining relevant issues and limiting evidence to those issues. The reluctance of the court in a child case to exclude relevant evidence is not a licence to disobey the rules either of procedure or of evidence.

Other significant cases on this issue:

- *Re G (Care proceedings: split trials)* [2001] 1 FLR 872 at 876
- *Re T (Abuse: standard of proof)* [2004] EWCA Civ 558, [2004] 2 FLR 838 at [35]–[37] (relevant photographs not seen by all the experts before writing their reports)

This case is also included in relation to:

D67 One CG can represent children with conflicting interests

G60   COST OF EXPERT ASSESSMENTS

Calderdale Metropolitan Borough Council v S and the Legal Services Commission

[2004] EWHC 2529 (Fam), [2005] 1 FLR 751 at 758, 761 and 763

Family Division

Bodey J

[34]   I suggested in argument that the problem may be likened to the elephant: easy to recognise, but difficult to define. It is relatively easy to recognise intuitively from experience (a) the sort of report which ought to be at the expense of the local authority; and relatively easy to distinguish it from (b) the sort of jointly commissioned specialist forensic overview, undertaken usually with access to all the case papers, which leads to a substantial and definitive assessment conventionally expected to be funded by all the parties (except those unaffected by it) in whatever proportions may be just (see below). However it is much less easy to identify the defining distinction, or to produce a formula as to how precisely that distinction is or should be drawn. Nor does there appear to be any statutory or regulatory guidance on the point.

[35]   In these circumstances, unless or until some such guidance is produced other than by the court, then, in my judgment, the best that can be done as regards the sort of jointly commissioned reports under discussion is to identify and suggest the following non-exhaustive considerations:

(a)   The court has to exercise its discretion to apportion the relevant costs fairly and reasonably, bearing in mind all the circumstances of the particular case.

(b)   In exercising its discretion, the court will have regard to the reasonableness of how the local authority has conducted the information-gathering process and with what degree of competence and 'thoroughness' (ie how much work and effort has it invested already and to what effect?).

(c)   This reference to the competence and 'thoroughness' (or otherwise) of the local authority's basic preparatory work is a relevant factor because there may be cases where a local authority has done quite little preparation or else has prepared rather poorly. The court will use its experience and 'feel' to be alert for this. If, for example, a local authority proposes the instruction of an independent social worker consultant (which for good practical reasons is agreed to be done on a joint-instruction basis) where the work would normally have been expected to be undertaken by the local authority as part of its core preparation, then the local authority will certainly or almost certainly be ordered to pay 100% of the costs involved.

(d)　The court will have regard to the extent to which the report in question goes *merely* to satisfying the so-called 'threshold' for state intervention, as distinct from helping the court to decide more generally what overall 'disposal' would best serve the interests of the child's welfare.

(e)　A further consideration is the type of expert concerned and the nature of his or her involvement with the family and/or of his or her role in the case. 'Treating' experts and others who have had a 'hands on' role with the family already are more likely to have to be paid for, if they charge a fee, by the local authority. Conversely, the fees of a purely forensic expert brought in specifically to make a full overview report to the court within the context of his or her discipline are much more likely to be ordered to be shared in principle between the parties.

(f)　One reason that the costs of a jointly commissioned report ordered by the court will generally speaking be ordered to be shared in some way (as to which see below) is that each party has an interest in having confidence in the integrity of the forensic process. If, however, a party genuinely opposes a report being jointly commissioned, or disputes the need for a report at all, then, provided this opposition is mounted for substantive reasons and not merely cosmetically or tactically, the court may take this factor into account in deciding how to exercise its discretion.

(g)　The fact that a party is publicly funded is not a reason for taking a different decision about costs from that which would otherwise have been taken. It would be wrong to pin a costs responsibility on the LSC which would not otherwise have been ordered against the publicly funded individual concerned (s 22 of the Access to Justice Act 1999).

[36]　Nothing in the above is intended to imply that there should usually be an argument before the court about who should pay for jointly commissioned assessments and reports. To the contrary, such questions should wheresoever possible be resolved by agreement in a collaborative way, having regard to the guidance which may appear in reported authorities and to the particular circumstances of the case in question. It goes without saying that any issues as to funding should be resolved one way or the other before rather than after the definitive joint instructions are delivered to the expert.

[37]　Turning to the instant case, any reading of the joint instructions to Miss Clarke and of her report make it immediately clear which side of the line it falls: namely on the side where the costs of the report ought in some way to be shared (see (d) below). This is because:

(a)   it is self-evidently a report designed primarily to assist the court as
       to the so-called welfare or 'disposal' part of the case: (what changes
       need to be made by the mother and the father respectively and what
       are the chances of their being able to make them within a timescale
       relevant to the twins?). The above summary of the problems faced
       by the mother demonstrates that the local authority had a perfectly
       sound case on 'the threshold' *without* Miss Clarke's report, albeit
       that its case turned out to be strengthened by the report;
(b)   it was a report agreed by all parties to be necessary and was dealt
       with in the context of ongoing legal proceedings;
(c)   each party had an interest in such a report being made available to
       the court and each had the potential of benefit from it, even though
       it turned out not to assist the mother or the father;
(d)   the local authority had already worked conscientiously and
       effectively in organising comprehensive assessment reports of a less
       specialist type (see above): there was clearly no question here of the
       local authority attempting to duck its responsibility to present a
       proper case for the court and/or of its trying to get a sharing of
       costs which it should have borne alone;
(e)   there would have been potential problems under Art 6 of the
       European Convention for the Protection of Human Rights and
       Fundamental Freedoms 1950 if the local authority had tried to go
       ahead with such a comprehensive psychological report on a
       unilateral instruction at its own expense. There is much force in the
       local authority's point that parents need to know that reports which
       may prove to have 'a preponderant influence' (per Munby J at
       para [113](ii) of *Re L (Care: Assessment: Fair Trial)* [2002] EWHC
       1379 (Fam), [2002] 2 FLR 730) are not being prepared at the sole
       expense of the local authority – in which event they may feel that the
       local authority calls the tune;
(f)   there would be doubtful saving of expense to the LSC's budget if
       reports like this, having been obtained at the sole expense of the
       local authority, were to give rise to subsequent applications by
       dissatisfied parents for second opinions, effectively at the expense of
       the LSC.

[38]   Accordingly I reject the LSC's cross-appeal that the local authority
should be ordered to pay 100% of the costs of Miss Clarke's report. I am
satisfied that in principle some sharing of the expense of it is fair and
reasonable and I now deal with the approach to such sharing.

(iv)   The local authority's appeal

[39]   This court can only interfere with the decision of the family
proceedings court to order a 50/50 apportionment of the relevant costs if
satisfied that the decision was plainly wrong. The stated reasons of the
family proceedings court were threefold: 'The Local Authority is under a
duty to safeguard children within their area. The Local Authority is the

Applicant in this case. The Local Authority supports the other parties in the need to appoint an expert to assist the Court'.

[40] Miss Hamilton criticises those reasons as being irrelevant to the real issue and/or as failing to explain why any of those three propositions should have led to a 50/50 outcome.

[41] It is trite to say that the reasons of a family proceedings court should not be subjected to undue criticism or scrutiny on appeal: one reason for this is that the justices have to give their reasons immediately and often without opportunity for preparation or reflection.

[42] That said, I am satisfied here that Miss Hamilton succeeds in her criticisms, in that there is nothing in the reasons which significantly addresses or seeks to resolve the real issue between the parties. In such circumstances the family proceedings court's decision can be characterised as 'plainly wrong', if only for lack of adequate reasons.

...

[48] Mr Reddish submits strongly that the court should follow the LSC's published guidance, partly (a) because of its provenance, coming as it does from the senior legal adviser in the policy and legal department of the LSC and partly (b) as a result of its having been widely consulted upon, including for example with the Association of Lawyers for Children, the National Association of Guardians, the circuit and district judges, the justices' clerks and the Local Government Association.

I accept the first of these propositions and acknowledge the propriety of the LSC's attempt to protect public funds by giving guidance to practitioners. I am dubious about the second point, since the evidence before me seems clearly to show that, whilst the organisations and individuals just mentioned were indeed consulted, the Association of Directors of Social Services was not, and was merely 'provided with' the guidance for information. Nothing particularly turns on this, as the LSC is not bound to consult; but I mention it to rebut the implicit suggestion in the LSC's case that local authorities have in some way been parties to guidance on which, through Calderdale Metropolitan Borough Council, they are now seeking to renege, by asking the court to dissent from it.

[49] Miss Hamilton submits not only that the LSC's published guidance is 'special pleading' designed solely to reduce its own exposure, but also that it is unbalanced and fails to take any account of the financial impact of the 'moiety' approach on local authorities.

[50] She further submits that such an approach has no jurisdictional basis, since the court makes orders against *parties* not against funds. She supports this submission by reference to the Family Proceedings Court (Children Act 1989) Rules 1991, r 22, to the effect that:

> '... the court may, at any time during the proceedings in that court, make an order that a party pay the whole or any part of the costs of any other party ...'

and to CPR r 44.3(1) that:

> '... the court has a discretion as to whether costs are payable by one party to another.'

[51] I find Miss Hamilton's submissions persuasive. Whilst there may be some superficial attraction in a pragmatic 50/50 apportionment of public money, such an approach is out of step with the rationale and conventional use of costs orders and is, in my judgment, inappropriate. Take, for example, this very case. The positions of three parties have been informed by Miss Clarke's report: the mother, the father and the children's guardian, each publicly funded. I am not persuaded that the local authority's budget should pay 50% of the expense, when it constitutes only 25% of the parties benefiting.

The fact that the LSC's budget would have to pay the other 75% is unfortunate for the LSC; but it is in the last analysis merely a product of the fact that, by statute, rule and regulation, it has been put in the position of having to fund and protect the interests of three parties to these proceedings.

...

[55] For the above reasons I allow the local authority's appeal from the order of the family proceedings court and replace it with an order following Standard Variable Direction EC4 (which will result in the local authority paying 25% and the LSC paying 3 x 25% of the costs in question) namely that: *The reasonable costs of the assessment and report by Lorraine Clarke dated 10 February 2004 be apportioned equally between parties, including the local authority, and the publicly funded parties' shares be a proper expense on their respective public funding certificates.*

General notes:

Where the assessment is to carried out under CA 1989, s 38(6), see Division D 'Section 38(6) assessments: funding' (D49–D50).

G61　TRUTHFULNESS: THE ULTIMATE ISSUE

Re M and R (Child abuse: evidence)

[1996] 2 FLR 195 at 205, 205, 207, 208, 209 and 211

Court of Appeal

Butler-Sloss LJ

(3)　Expert evidence

Many if not all family law cases involving children feature expert opinion evidence. Recently the proper limits of such evidence have been the subject of a number of decisions. A conflict exists between obiter dicta of this court in *Re S and B (Minors) (Child Abuse: Evidence)* [1990] 2 FLR 489 (since followed – also obiter – by two other Court of Appeal decisions) and the Civil Evidence Act 1972 – which was not cited to the court in any of those three decisions. This conflict has been and is the source of much unnecessary forensic activity, and should be resolved. The point in question was taken in this appeal, though not persisted in. We think it right to express our views on this point in an attempt to resolve the conflict.

...

In cases involving suspected child abuse, the expert evidence may relate to the presence and interpretation of physical signs. But it may also relate to the more problematic area of the presence and interpretation of mental, behavioural and emotional signs. That evidence often necessarily includes if not a conclusion, at least strong pointers as to the witness's view of the likely veracity of the child (ie credibility): indeed, his diagnosis and the action taken by the local authority may depend on the conclusion reached. The evidence also frequently includes a conclusion as to whether or not the child has been abused. At one time it was thought that an expert witness could not give evidence of his opinion on an issue in the case, especially not when it was the ultimate issue, determinative of the case ...

The Law Reform Committee was asked to consider this question ... That committee recommended (17th Report, Cmnd 4489 (1970)):

...

That recommendation led directly to the Civil Evidence Act 1972. Relevant for our purposes is s 3:

> 'Admissibility of expert opinion and certain expressions of non-expert opinion
>
> (1)   Subject to any rules of court made in pursuance of Part I of the Civil Evidence Act 1968 or this Act, where a person is called as a witness in any civil proceedings, his opinion on any relevant matter on which he is qualified to give expert evidence shall be admissible in evidence.
>
> (2)   It is hereby declared that where a person is called as a witness in any civil proceedings, a statement of opinion by him on any relevant matter on which he is not qualified to give expert evidence, if made as a way of conveying relevant facts personally perceived by him, is admissible as evidence of what he perceived.
>
> (3)   In this section "relevant matter" includes an issue in the proceedings in question.'

So it is right to say (as the textbooks do) that the ultimate issue rule has been abandoned (unmourned by the ghost of Wigmore and the editor of *Cross and Tapper on Evidence* – see (Butterworths, 8th edn, 1995), p 552).

...

Against that background it is not surprising that family law judges have received (without it would seem objection, demur, embarrassment, or prejudice) expert opinion evidence, including evidence as to the accuracy or truthfulness of child complainants. Johnson J in *Note: Re B (Child Sexual Abuse: Standard of Proof)* [1995] 1 FLR 904 lists a few out of many possible examples where experienced family judges have admitted such evidence without question ...

But this practice was challenged by obiter dicta of this court in *Re S and B (Minors)* (above) ...

The majority of the court (Glidewell and Stocker LJJ) found that Miss Tranter, as an expert, could express her opinion on A's psychiatric state and her propensity to fantasise, and could support those opinions by her opinion that A's account was apparently credible, but:

> 'What ... was not admissible was any direct expression of opinion that A was telling the truth, and not telling malicious lies. The boundary between the two expressions of views is fine, but it does seem to me that [her] evidence crossed that line ...' (*Re S and B (Minors) (Child Abuse: Evidence)* [1990] 2 FLR 489, 498E–F.)

But as the trial judge recognised that ultimately the question of credibility was for him, it was clear that he did not rely on her expression of opinion, and so the appeal failed.

...

Two further decisions of the Court of Appeal have followed that authority: *Re FS (Child Abuse: Evidence)* [1996] 2 FLR 158 (with dicta as to 'usurping the function of the judge'), and *Re N (Child Abuse: Evidence)* [1996] 2 FLR 214. Unfortunately, in neither of these cases was the court referred to the Civil Evidence Act 1972, and we do not believe that those courts would have expressed themselves in the terms they did had they been aware of that Act. Accordingly we regard those obiter remarks also as having been made per incuriam.

...

So the passing of the Act should not operate to force the court to, in Wigmore's words, 'waste its time in listening to superfluous and cumbersome testimony' provided that the judge never loses sight of the central truths: namely that the ultimate decision is for him, and that all questions of relevance and weight are for him. If the expert's opinion is clearly irrelevant, he will say so. But if arguably relevant but in his view ultimately unhelpful, he can generally prevent its reception by indicating that the expert's answer to the question would carry little weight with him. The modern view is to regulate such matters by way of weight, rather than admissibility.

But when the judge is of the opinion that the witness's expertise is still required to assist him to answer the ultimate questions (including, where appropriate, credibility) then the judge can safely and gratefully rely on such evidence, while never losing sight of the fact that the final decision is for him.

G62   PSYCHIATRIC / PSYCHOLOGICAL EVIDENCE AS TO PROPENSITY

Re CB and JB (Care proceedings: guidelines)

[1998] 2 FLR 211 at 219

Family Division

Wall J

Question 2

Is it an appropriate application of the principles laid down in *Re M and R (Child Abuse: Evidence)* [1996] 2 FLR 195 for expert psychiatric or psychological evidence to be adduced as to the propensity of a parent to injure a child or as to the likelihood of a parent having done so?

In my judgment, the short answer to this question is usually 'no', and almost certainly 'no', where, as indicated in answer to question 1 above, the court is dealing with an issue of fact in a split hearing upon which the threshold criteria depend. 'Never' is a difficult word to say in the Family Division, but I do not believe it was the intention of the Court of Appeal in *Re M and R (Child Abuse: Evidence)* (above) that evidence as to adult credibility or propensity to commit acts of physical abuse should be routinely given by psychologists or psychiatrists and be routinely admissible as probative of the factual issue as to whether or not a particular parent perpetrated a particular act of abuse.

In *Re M and R (Child Abuse: Evidence)* the Court of Appeal, commenting on my rejection in another case of the argument that previous decisions of the Court of Appeal on the point were per incuriam because of the terms of s 3(3) of the Civil Evidence Act 1972, said this (at 210H):

'But while Wall J was wrong in his construction of s 3, we have no reason to believe that he was wrong in holding the doctor's evidence on the credibility of two women giving evidence of abuse of them when they were children dealt with an issue that did not require her expertise. The evidence was inadmissible because irrelevant, not because it went to the ultimate issue in the case.'

I accordingly agree with a submission made by the father at an interlocutory stage of the case in the following terms:

'Although *Re M and R (Child Abuse: Evidence)* [1996] 2 FLR 195 establishes that expert evidence may be admissible, *if relevant*, in respect of the ultimate issue, it is submitted that the underlying rationale for the use of expert evidence should be kept firmly in focus – viz to assist the court in drawing inferences and conclusions where the tribunal of fact does not possess the necessary expertise to carry out that task ...

[RH's evidence] ... is in essence evidence of credibility. It is submitted that it is inadmissible not because it goes to one of the ultimate issues in the case (viz did the mother inflict one or other of the injuries) but because it is irrelevant and unnecessary.

It is irrelevant and unnecessary because the court has the expertise, experience and knowledge to assess credibility.'

In this case, I ruled most of the psychiatric and psychological evidence irrelevant and thus inadmissible on this basis. The evidence I admitted as to the propensity of the mother to perpetrate the abuse on CB (or, more accurately, to the effect that she had not shaken CB) was, as I have stated, flawed and, as I found, plainly wrong.

Other significant cases on this issue:

* *A County Council v K, D and L* [2005] EWHC 144 (Fam), [2005] 1 FLR 851 at [29]
* *Re C (Care proceedings: sexual abuse)* [2008] EWCA Civ 1331, [2009] 2 FLR 46
* *Lancashire County Council v R* [2008] EWHC 2959 (Fam), [2010] 1 FLR 387 at {58]–[60]

This case is also included in relation to:

D66 Role of CG / solicitor for child (3)
G35 Psychiatric / psychological evidence unlikely to be relevant

G63 LITTLE RELIANCE TO BE PLACED ON PSYCHOMETRIC TESTS

Re S (Care: parenting skills: personality tests)

[2004] EWCA Civ 1029, [2005] 2 FLR 658 at 676, 689 and 680

Court of Appeal

Ward, Arden and Scott Baker LJJ

WARD LJ:

[55] It seems to me that Ms Ballam's concerns, shared by the judge, arose out of Mr Hunt's adverse conclusions about the mother's veracity. Those conclusions also need to be analysed.

[56] The following points can be made about them:

(i)   His impression of a lack of candour came solely from the Lie-Scale results. He said:

'The lack of candour was signalled only by those two scores, the two scores on those two questionnaires, and that raised a sort of little red flag. "Bing! Could be a problem here".

Q: But in itself, then, its value is fairly restricted is it not?
A: Well I don't – different psychologists may give you a different answer to that – I don't personally believe very much in resting key interpretations on just one source of information. I don't believe in questionnaires to the extent that "Ah-ha, this reading is above … 'a certain value', … therefore it must be the case" I mean I would also try and modify my opinion of personality questionnaires with my impression of the individual as a person, what we would call "clinical impressions".

(ii) He went on, however, to acknowledge that he had not detected any sign or signal of a lack of candour in his long interview with her and his questioning of her.

(iii) Moreover he was saying:

'But in a sense what I am saying is, regrettably I can't draw much inference from the questionnaire. The questionnaires in a sense are telling us very little.

Q: I see.

A: Because the technical problem of the validity scales not being within normal limits. So it's almost like saying "Well, the questionnaires are sort of, in a sense meaningless".

Q: I am sorry the questionnaires ...?

A: Are almost meaningless. In this case. But you know, that was not my main conclusion of (the mother) as a person ...

Q: Yes.

A: That she is untruthful, no.'

(iv) Finally,

'I think the Lie-Scale is not a perfect test of honesty, by any means.

Q: Yes.

A: I think it's a thumb measure, meant to be a safeguard to the examiner doing the test interpretations, rather than "Is this person truthful, is this person deceitful".

Q: And again, that brings me to the point that it is with caution that we can rely on the results of these Lie-Scale tests?

A: I would say so yea. Considerable caution. Not to be interpreted too much at face value: "Ah-ha, he scores 8, therefore he lies".

Q: Are you saying they are indicative rather than diagnostic?

A: Your Honour, that's very nicely put indeed. Yes. A sort of suggestion of possible problem areas, but not – not diagnostic. I do not know of any paper and pencil test which is diagnostic of truthfulness. I doubt that there is one.'

[57] Upon analysis that evidence amounts to this: very little reliance should be placed upon these personality tests. In fact, I would go so far as to say they are more likely to obfuscate the judicial process than assist it. Judges are there to decide questions of credibility. They do so day in and day out. They do not need personality tests to assist them in that task. Judges are probably far better off without them.

[58] Thus I conclude that His Honour Judge Nigel Fricker QC placed undue weight upon observations in a report so largely recanted in the oral evidence. Of course there is, as the guardian recognised, a need for some caution in considering the answers of a parent whose back is to the wall because his or her children are at risk of being removed from him or her. No judge looks at the evidence through rose-tinted spectacles but no judge needs a personality test to warn him or her of the dangers.

ARDEN LJ:

[66] I agree with both judgments, and specifically associate myself with the observations made by Ward and Scott Baker LJJ about the use of the evidence from the psychometric tests (referred to below as personality

tests) in this case and about the delays in the institution and prosecution of criminal proceedings against AD's parents.

[67] In my judgment, the principal issue for the judge was the mother's parenting skills. If the judge was (exceptionally) minded to rely on the results of the personality tests, he had first to assess their validity, both generally and for the purpose of this case. The qualifications to the test results properly made by Mr Hunt in his evidence, to my mind, demonstrate that personality testing of this kind cannot be used to resolve issues such as parenting skills unless they are validated by other evidence.

SCOTT BAKER LJ:

[71] I wish to add emphasis of my own on two points. First, I do not think the court was assisted by the reports of Mr Hunt in this case. In particular I do not feel that psychometric testing ordinarily has any place in cases of this kind. It is for the judge to evaluate the facts and assess questions of credibility. He sees the witnesses give evidence and has an overview of the whole picture of the case. It is important that expert witnesses or purported experts should not trespass into his field of responsibility.

Other significant cases on this issue:

* *Re L (Children) (Care proceedings: significant harm)* [2006] EWCA Civ 1282, [2007] 1 FLR 1068 at [25] and [69]

G64 EXPOSURE OF EXPERT TO DISCIPLINARY PROCEEDINGS

Meadow v General Medical Council (Her Majesty's Attorney-General intervening)

[2006] EWCA Civ 1390, [2007] 1 FLR 1398 at 1403, 1416, 1419, 1421 and 1431

Court of Appeal

Clarke MR

Part I: Immunity from FTP proceedings

INTRODUCTION

[5] This part of the appeal arises out of a point taken by the judge and not by or on behalf of Professor Meadow, either before the FPP[1] or in the grounds of appeal to the High Court. It is common ground that at common law a witness, whether he is giving evidence of fact or opinion, and whether or not he is an expert witness, has immunity from civil suit in respect of evidence which he gives in court. It is also common ground that the immunity extends to any statement the witness makes for the purpose of giving evidence. Where it exists the witness has immunity even in a case where he gave his evidence dishonestly or in bad faith. The judge recognised in para [10] of his judgment that before this case the immunity had not been extended to prevent the bringing of FTP proceedings.[2]

...

Should the immunity be extended to FTP proceedings?

[44] This involves considering whether there should be a wholesale (or blanket) extension and, if not, whether there should be a partial extension and, if so, what.

Wholesale extension?

...

---

[1]   Fitness to Practice Panel: see [2].

[2]   Defined as 'disciplinary, regulatory or fitness to practice proceedings' at [3].

[49] In short, it would be wrong in principle for the court to cut across or impliedly to limit the powers of an FPP by extending the immunity from civil suit to FTP proceedings. In *X (Minors) v Bedfordshire County Council* [1995] 2 AC 633, [1995] 2 FLR 276 the House of Lords was considering whether a local authority owed a duty of care in discharging a statutory function. Lord Browne-Wilkinson said at 739 and 290 respectively that the question whether there was such a common law duty and, if so, its ambit, must be profoundly influenced by the relevant statutory framework and added:

> '... a common law duty of care cannot be imposed on a statutory duty if the observance of such common law duty of care would be inconsistent with, or have a tendency to discourage, the due performance by the local authority of its statutory duties.'

So here, the extension of the immunity would be inconsistent with the duty of the FPP to investigate and determine the FTP proceedings against the expert.

Partial extension?

[50] I would also answer this question in the negative, for essentially the same reasons ...

...

[66] I should add that in reaching these conclusions I have not overlooked the problems adverted to by the judge and emphasised by Thorpe LJ in his judgment. He has set out there some of the history of recent events in the particular field with which this case is concerned. It is to be hoped that a solution to the particular problems identified can be found by discussion between those directly concerned, and that, if appropriate, changes can be made, including changes to the relevant rules governing the GMC. In particular, it does seem to me that it should be possible to devise a scheme which reduces to an absolute minimum the risk of expert witnesses being vexed by unmeritorious complaints to regulatory bodies like the GMC.

[67] However, for the reasons that I have given, it seems to me that the solution to particular problems in particular professions must be reached by discussion and, if appropriate, rule change, not by what to my mind would be an unprincipled extension of the common law immunity from civil suit. Ms Davies was right not to challenge the jurisdiction of the GMC, either before the FPP or before the judge. For these reasons I would allow this part of the appeal and hold that the FPP had jurisdiction to entertain the allegations against Professor Meadow.

Part II: Serious professional misconduct

[68]   This part of my judgment should be read after and in the light of
the judgments of Auld and Thorpe LJJ, which I have read in draft. They
have set out the facts in considerable detail and it would serve no useful
purpose for me to do the same. They have concluded that the judge was
correct to allow the appeal from the decision of the FPP that Professor
Meadow was guilty of serious professional misconduct. It follows that the
GMC's appeal on this question will be dismissed. I have reached a
different conclusion from the other two members of the court and thus
find myself in a minority. In these circumstances I do not think that it is
appropriate for me to do any more than shortly to express the reasons for
my conclusion that Professor Meadow was guilty of serious professional
misconduct.

[69]   As to the relevant test, I agree with the approach adopted by
Auld LJ in paras [117]–[127], below. I turn to the facts ...

...

[96]   For these reasons I would have allowed the appeal. Since this is a
minority view, the question of sanction does not arise. However, it is right
to observe that the GMC did not seek to uphold the sanction of erasure
from the register. It was in my opinion correct not to do so. In all the
circumstances of the case, erasure was not appropriate. Indeed, given the
professor's experiences since the trial, the mitigating factors referred to by
Auld LJ, his long and distinguished service to the public and his age a
finding of serious professional misconduct would be enough.

Other significant cases on this issue:

•   *Southall v General Medical Council* [2010] EWCA Civ 407, [2010]
      2 FLR 1550

This case is also included in relation to:

G44 Role and responsibilities of expert witnesses

Other witnesses

G65   LEAVE TO CROSS-EXAMINE OWN WITNESS

Re P (Witness summons)

[1997] 2 FLR 447 at 453

Court of Appeal

Wilson J

In parenthesis I would advert to one other point which exercised the court in that case. It was that, were a witness summons to have been issued against the girl, the stepfather would, in any event, have been able only to examine her in chief and that this would probably have been unproductive and unsatisfactory. In the 6 years since that case was decided the 1989 Act has come into force and the sui generis semi-inquisitorial nature of proceedings thereunder has increasingly become accepted. In my experience, where fairness requires that an advocate should be able to cross-examine rather than suffer the handicap of examination-in-chief, the court will itself occasionally call the witness so that cross-examination can take place. Had it been appropriate for N to be ordered to come to court in this case, that course might have been followed.

G66   ATTENDANCE OF CHILD TO GIVE ORAL EVIDENCE

Re W (Children) (Abuse: oral evidence)

[2010] UKSC 12, [2010] 1 FLR 1485 at 1493

Supreme Court

Baroness Hale

Conclusions in principle

[22] However tempting it may be to leave the issue until it has received the expert scrutiny of a multidisciplinary committee, we are satisfied that we cannot do so. The existing law erects a presumption against a child giving evidence which requires to be rebutted by anyone seeking to put questions to the child. That cannot be reconciled with the approach of the European Court of Human Rights, which always aims to strike a fair balance between competing European Convention rights. Article 6 requires that the proceedings overall be fair and this normally entails an opportunity to challenge the evidence presented by the other side. But even in criminal proceedings account must be taken of the Art 8 rights of the perceived victim: see *SN v Sweden* (Application No 34209/96) (2002) 39 EHRR 304. Striking that balance in care proceedings may well mean that the child should not be called to give evidence in the great majority of cases, but that is a result and not a presumption or even a starting point.

[23] The object of the proceedings is to achieve a fair trial in the determination of the rights of all the people involved. Children are harmed if they are taken away from their families for no good reason. Children are harmed if they are left in abusive families. This means that the court must admit all the evidence which bears upon the relevant questions: whether the threshold criteria justifying State intervention have been proved; if they have, what action if any will be in the best interests of the child? The court cannot ignore relevant evidence just because other evidence might have been better. It will have to do the best it can on what it has.

[24] When the court is considering whether a particular child should be called as a witness, the court will have to weigh two considerations: the advantages that that will bring to the determination of the truth and the damage it may do to the welfare of this or any other child. A fair trial is a trial which is fair in the light of the issues which have to be decided. Mr Geekie accepts that the welfare of the child is also a relevant consideration, albeit not the paramount consideration in this respect. He is right to do so, because the object of the proceedings is to promote the welfare of this and other children. The hearing cannot be fair to them unless their interests are given great weight.

[25] In weighing the advantages that calling the child to give evidence may bring to the fair and accurate determination of the case, the court will have to look at several factors. One will be the issues it has to decide in order properly to determine the case. Sometimes it may be possible to decide the case without making findings on particular allegations. Another will be the quality of the evidence it already has. Sometimes there may be enough evidence to make the findings needed whether or not the child is cross-examined. Sometimes there will be nothing useful to be gained from the child's oral evidence. The case is built upon a web of behaviour, drawings, stray remarks, injuries and the like, and not upon concrete allegations voiced by the child. The quality of any ABE interview will also be an important factor, as will be the nature of any challenge which the party may wish to make. The court is unlikely to be helped by generalised accusations of lying, or by a fishing expedition in which the child is taken slowly through the story yet again in the hope that something will turn up, or by a cross-examination which is designed to intimidate the child and pave the way for accusations of inconsistency in a future criminal trial. On the other hand, focused questions which put forward a different explanation for certain events may help the court to do justice between the parties. Also relevant will be the age and maturity of the child and the length of time since the events in question, for these will have a bearing on whether an account now can be as reliable as a near-contemporaneous account, especially if given in a well-conducted ABE interview.

[26] The age and maturity of the child, along with the length of time since the events in question, will also be relevant to the second part of the inquiry, which is the risk of harm to the child. Further specific factors may be the support which the child has from family or other sources, or the lack of it, the child's own wishes and feelings about giving evidence, and the views of the child's guardian and, where appropriate, those with parental responsibility. We endorse the view that an unwilling child should rarely, if ever, be obliged to give evidence. The risk of further delay to the proceedings is also a factor: there is a general principle that delay in determining any question about a child's upbringing is likely to prejudice his welfare: see the Children Act 1989, s 1(2). There may also be specific risks of harm to this particular child. Where there are parallel criminal proceedings, the likelihood of the child having to give evidence twice may increase the risk of harm. The parent may be seeking to put his child through this ordeal in order to strengthen his hand in the criminal proceedings rather than to enable the family court to get at the truth. On the other hand, as the family court has to give less weight to the evidence of a child because she has not been called, then that may be damaging

too. However, the court is entitled to have regard to the general evidence of the harm which giving evidence may do to children, as well as to any features which are particular to this child and this case. That risk of harm is an ever-present feature to which, on the present evidence, the court must give great weight. The risk, and, therefore, the weight, may vary from case to case, but the court must always take it into account and does not need expert evidence in order to do so.

[27]   But on both sides of the equation, the court must factor in what steps can be taken to improve the quality of the child's evidence and at the same time to decrease the risk of harm to the child. These two aims are not in opposition to one another. The whole premise of Achieving Best Evidence and the special measures in criminal cases is that this will improve rather than diminish the quality of the evidence to the court. It does not assume that the most reliable account of any incident is one made from recollection months or years later in the stressful conditions of a courtroom. Nor does it assume that an 'Old Bailey style' cross-examination is the best way of testing that evidence. It may be the best way of casting doubt upon it in the eyes of a jury but that is another matter. A family court would have to be astute both to protect the child from the harmful and destructive effects of questioning and also to evaluate the answers in the light of the child's stage of development.

[28]   The family court will have to be realistic in evaluating how effective it can be in maximising the advantage while minimising the harm. There are things that the court can do but they are not things that it is used to doing at present. It is not limited by the usual courtroom procedures or to applying the special measures by analogy. The important thing is that the questions which challenge the child's account are fairly put to the child so that she can answer them, not that counsel should be able to question her directly. One possibility is an early videoed cross-examination as proposed by Pigot. Another is cross-examination via video-link. But another is putting the required questions to her through an intermediary. This could be the court itself, as would be common in continental Europe and used to be much more common than it is now in the courts of this country.

[29]   In principle, the approach in private family proceedings between parents should be the same as the approach in care proceedings. However, there are specific risks to which the court must be alive. Allegations of abuse are not being made by a neutral and expert local authority which has nothing to gain by making them, but by a parent who is seeking to gain an advantage in the battle against the other parent. This does not mean that they are false but it does increase the risk of misinterpretation, exaggeration or downright fabrication. On the other hand, the child will not routinely have the protection and support of a Cafcass guardian. There are also many more litigants in person in private proceedings. So if

the court does reach the conclusion that justice cannot be done unless the child gives evidence, it will have to take very careful precautions to ensure that the child is not harmed by this.

[30] It will be seen that these considerations are simply an amplification of those outlined by Smith LJ in the *Medway* case,[1] at para [45], but without the starting point, at para [44]. The essential test is whether justice can be done to all the parties without further questioning of the child. Our prediction is that, if the court is called upon to do it, the consequence of the balancing exercise will usually be that the additional benefits to the court's task in calling the child do not outweigh the additional harm that it will do to the child. A wise parent with his child's interests truly at heart will understand that too. But rarity should be a consequence of the exercise rather than a threshold test (as in *Huang v Secretary of State for the Home Department; Kashmiri v Secretary of State for the Home Department* [2007] UKHL 11, [2007] 2 AC 167, [2007] 2 WLR 581, [2007] 1 FLR 2021, para [20]).

[31] Finally, we would endorse the suggestion made by Miss Branigan QC for the child's guardian, that the issue should be addressed at the case management conference in care proceedings or the earliest directions hearing in private law proceedings. It should not be left to the party to raise. This is not, however, an invitation to elaborate consideration of what will usually be a non-issue.

Other significant cases on this issue:

* *Re J (child giving evidence)* [2010] EWHC 962 (Fam), [2010] 2 FLR 1080

---

[1] *LM (by her guardian) v Medway Council, RM and YM* [2007] EWCA Civ 9, [2007] 1 FLR 1698.

G67   PARENTS ETC COMPELLABLE TO GIVE EVIDENCE

Re Y and K (Children) (Care Proceedings: Split Hearing)

[2003] EWCA Civ 669, [2003] 2 FLR 273 at 281 and 282

Court of Appeal

Thorpe and Hale LJJ

THORPE LJ:

[27]   Before concluding judgment, I would like to express my gratitude to Hale LJ who has pointed out that an ill-considered remark of mine in a judgment in yet another case of *Re B (Non-Accidental Injury)* [2002] EWCA Civ 752, [2002] 2 FLR 1133 led Mr Stonor in the court below to concede that he was not entitled to insist on either parent giving evidence. The point was not directly raised in *Re B (Non-Accidental Injury)* and was certainly not argued, and the observation on my part, to the effect that parents at split hearings were perfectly free to give evidence or not as they saw fit, was unguarded. Hale LJ has, during the course of argument, demonstrated the falsity of that proposition and I would only say in advance that I entirely agree with all her criticisms and with the conclusion that she is to reach on that point.

HALE LJ:

[31]   Even in civil proceedings it used to be (a very long time ago) that the parties were not competent witnesses. But that was abrogated in civil proceedings by s 2 of the Evidence Act 1851. The general principle is that all competent witnesses are also compellable witnesses. This is set out in *Phipson on Evidence* (Sweet and Maxwell, 15th edn, 2000) at paras 8–15:

> 'All witnesses competent to give evidence are in general compellable to do so. Refusal to be sworn when compellable, or, after being sworn refusal to answer an admissible question, is a contempt of court.'

There are some exceptions, but none of those listed in *Phipson* apply, although there remains a residual discretion in the court to refuse to compel a compellable witness if to do so would be a fishing exercise, speculation or oppression. This will rarely be the case in care proceedings where the parents' explanations of what has happened to their child are usually an important factor in understanding the case.

[32] What reason then is there to think anything to the contrary? Generally, of course, a witness in civil proceedings may refuse to answer a particular question on the ground that the answer may incriminate him. But this privilege against self-incrimination is expressly dealt with by the Children Act 1989, s 98(1):

'In any proceedings in which a court is hearing an application for an order under Part IV or V, no person shall be excused from—

(a) giving evidence on any matter; or

(b) answering any question put to him in the course of his giving evidence,

on the ground that doing so might incriminate him or his spouse of an offence.'

The counter-balance to this abrogation of the privilege against self-incrimination is that the answers cannot be used in criminal proceedings: see s 98(2). This caters for the problem encountered *Saunders v United Kingdom* (1996) 23 EHRR 313. The only other indication to the contrary were the dicta of Thorpe LJ in *Re B (Non-Accidental Injury)* [2002] EWCA Civ 752, [2002] 2 FLR 1133, at para [7]. But it is clear, as he has confirmed today, that that was a 'by-the-way' remark, not addressed to any issue in that particular case, for it was not argued before the court and there was no reference to s 98 which would of course have clarified matters.

[33] I note that the Law Commission in the recent informal consultation paper of the Criminal Law Team on *Successfully Prosecuting Cases of Non-accidental Death or Serious Injury of Children*, published 19 December 2002, stated in para 3.19:

'In addition it seems likely that a judge hearing civil proceedings can compel a person to explain the circumstances in which a child has been injured.'

Then, after a reference to *Re B (Minors) (Contact)* [1994] 2 FLR 1 in para 3.20, they go on in para 3.21 to quote the contrary decision of Elizabeth Lawson QC in *Re M (Care Proceedings: Disclosure: Human Rights)* [2001] 2 FLR 1316, in which she had in fact compelled a mother to give evidence in the case.

[34] We are glad, therefore, to have the opportunity today of clarifying the situation. Parents can be compelled to give evidence in care proceedings; they have no right to refuse to do so; they cannot even refuse to answer questions which might incriminate them. The position is no different in a split hearing from that in any other hearing in care proceedings. If the parents themselves do not wish to give evidence on their own behalf there is, of course, no property in a witness. They can nevertheless be called by another party if it is thought fit to do so, and the most appropriate person normally to do so would be the guardian acting on behalf of the child.

[35] Having said all this, it is of course a completely separate question from whether it is appropriate to halt the inquiry before it has been completed. For all the reasons given by Thorpe LJ, I agree that this was a completely inappropriate case in which to do that and I am glad to record that had the case proceeded further it was the intention of both parents to give evidence before the court, and it has not been sought to be argued on their behalf today that they could not have been compelled to do so.

This case is also included in relation to:

G33 Purpose / pros and cons

G68   IF PARENTS ETC REFUSE: INFERENCES APPROPRIATE

Re O (Care proceedings: evidence)

[2004] 1 FLR 161 at 163

Family Division

Johnson J

The mother's failure to give evidence

[12]   In giving judgment he said:

> 'The mother has filed two statements but has not been prepared to support them by sworn oral evidence. Nor has she been prepared to be challenged by being asked questions in court. Therefore, insofar as those statements consists of denials or exculpatory explanations, I attach no weight to them.'

[13]   This decision, simply to attach no weight to the mother's statements, was in my view wrong. The judge could, and in my view should, have gone further. As a general rule, and clearly every case will depend in its own particular facts, where a parent declines to answer questions or, as here, give evidence, the court ought usually to draw the inference that the allegations are true.

[14]   In cases concerning children there is, in my judgment, no room for the 'no comment' interview found in criminal cases ...

[15]   Although I recognise that care proceedings can understandably be perceived as adversarial by parents who are at risk of losing their children, the objective is not to punish the parent but to seek to achieve what is best for the children.

[16]   In the present case the district judge went on to consider a number of considerations supporting or discrediting what L had said and eventually concluded that what she had said was true. However, in my view, unless there was some sensible reason to the contrary, the mother's failure to give evidence should have been determinative of the allegations.

G69   IF PARENTS ETC REFUSE: INFERENCES INAPPROPRIATE

Re U (Care proceedings: criminal conviction: refusal to give evidence)

[2006] EWHC 372 Fam, [2006] 2 FLR 690 at 696 and 698

Family Division

Holman J

[22] The judgment of Hale LJ in *Re Y and K (Children) (Care Proceedings: Split Hearing)* [2003] EWCA Civ 669, [2003] 2 FLR 273, at 282 and 283, with which Thorpe LJ expressly agreed, is technically obiter. It is obiter because the decision of the Court of Appeal in that case was that the judge had been wrong to stop the case, and the issue of the compellability of the parents did not necessarily arise for decision by the Court of Appeal (see the opening sentence of para [35] of the judgment of Hale LJ). However, the judgment of Hale LJ is obviously one of very great weight and authority and, in my view, convincingly demonstrates and establishes that parents in care proceedings such as these are compellable witnesses and that 'they cannot even refuse to answer questions which might incriminate them'.

[23] It follows, in my view, and was indeed expressly accepted by Miss Cover on his behalf, that the failure of the father to file a statement and his refusal to give oral evidence or to answer any questions, has placed him since April 2005, and continues to place him, in contempt of court. There are few sanctions available to me. I cannot effectively imprison him, for he is already serving a life sentence. I cannot fine him, for most probably he has little, if any, means. I consider, by application of the approach in *Hadkinson v Hadkinson* [1952] P 285, (1952) FLR Rep 287 that I have a wide discretion to refuse to permit him to take any active role at all in these proceedings until the contempt is removed. I accordingly also have a discretion to limit or restrict the role he may play. But the very thing I want him to do is to take a full and active role, including the giving of evidence ...

[24] Different considerations may apply to cross-examination of the mother. As those present know, my initial reaction was (as it remains) that it was very unfair to the mother personally to have to be cross-examined, in fact for a second time, on behalf of the father if he himself would not give evidence and permit cross-examination of himself on her behalf. In the criminal trial the sole issue was the guilt of the father and the question: did he kill S? There could be the innuendo, without any direct allegation, that it was the mother who had killed S. But this hearing is concerned with a different question, namely: who killed S? Realistically, and as indeed turned out, any cross-examination on behalf of the father to the effect that he had not done so, effectively involved the proposition that it was she who had done so. It is, in my view, grossly unfair that the mother should have to face that allegation, which in effect she has at this hearing, without having the opportunity to cross-examine the person making it.

[25] However, it later seemed to me that I must allow the cross-examination, despite the unfairness, for three reasons. First, I felt that the mother, although greatly upset by the burden of giving evidence, could nevertheless cope with such cross-examination, as indeed she did. Secondly, the nature of these proceedings is essentially inquisitorial and concerned ultimately with the welfare of living children. Thirdly, having regard to the observation of Lopes LJ in the Court of Appeal in *Allen v Allen* [1894] P 248 at 253–255, the evidence of the mother could not found a finding against the father unless his advocate had had the opportunity to cross-examine her. Giving the reserved judgment of the court, Lopes LJ said, at 254:

'... No evidence given by one party affecting another party in the same litigation can be made admissible against that other party, unless there is a right to cross-examine ...'

The proposition is stated in *Halsbury's Laws of England* (Butterworths, 4th edn reissue, 2002) vol 17(1), at para 1023, and *Allen* is cited as the leading authority for it.

[26] In the event, Miss Ball QC on behalf of the mother, and acting upon the instructions of the mother herself, withdrew her earlier opposition to the mother being cross-examined on behalf of the father although he was still in contempt. The result has been that this hearing has proceeded with the full and exactly the same involvement of and on behalf of the father as if he had not been in contempt, save that he has continued to deny me the benefit of his own evidence.

Advice of Mr G

[27] Mr G has had no opportunity to explain or justify his position, and so I must be circumspect in what I say. I found his advice surprising in a number of respects, which perhaps reveals the huge cultural gulf which may still exist between those whose practice is predominantly in criminal courts and those who endeavour to make reliable decisions about the future of vulnerable children. He formulated the issue as whether it would 'help' the father's appeal if he gave evidence. In my view, the relevant question, if any, is whether it would hinder that appeal ...

[28] In my view, the whole tenor of the advice is indeed highly tactical and includes the tactic of hoping the mother might 'change her story'. I have every expectation that there will be a later application for all the evidence given by the mother in this hearing to be transcribed, and probably some or all of that given by the experts – in particular, Mr Richards – for it all to be picked over to try to identify discrepancies for use at the appeal and, indeed, any subsequent retrial. Meantime, the father has not said a further word. I regard that outcome as cunning, manipulative and very unfair to the position of the mother. I would have been marginally more sympathetic to the advice and to the position taken by the father if he had not given any evidence at all at his criminal trial, but had consistently and for all purposes asserted a right against self-incrimination. I note, further, that Mr G's advice was that the father should not be 'involved in' these proceedings, viz this hearing, if he can avoid it. But the father did not heed that part of the advice; rather, he has been present throughout and involved to the hilt, save only for the refusal to give evidence.

...

Adverse inferences

[30] Against this background Miss Ball QC has urged me to draw adverse inferences from the father's refusal to give evidence, and has relied in particular on the authority of the House of Lords in *TC Coombs & Co (A Firm) v IRC* [1991] 2 AC 283, and the passage in the headnote under per curiam (1). That seems to me to do no more than describe and illustrate the very broad discretion of a court to draw adverse inferences, which must be exercised in a very fact-specific context. The obiter comment of Johnson J in *Re O (Care Proceedings: Evidence)* [2003] EWHC 2001 (Fam), [2004] 1 FLR 161, at 163, para [13], is again very fact-specific.

[31] I am not prepared, in the circumstances of this case, to draw any adverse inference against the father that because he has contumaciously refused to give evidence or before this court to answer the allegations, it justifies an inference that the allegations are true. I think it would be unfair to him to do so in the light of the advice he has actually received from Mr G. I have said that I found the advice surprising in a number of respects, but it is still the advice that the father has received from his criminal barrister in whom he has confidence. So I make crystal-clear that I do not draw any adverse inference against the father whatsoever.

Other significant cases on this issue:

- *Re B (Non-accidental injury)* [2002] EWCA Civ 752, [2002] 2 FLR 1133 at [26]: see H21 – Expert not categorical

G70   CA 1989, S 98: 'STATEMENT OR ADMISSION MADE IN SUCH PROCEEDINGS'

Cleveland County Council v F

[1995] 1 FLR 797 at 799 and 803

Family Division

Hale J

The mother now seeks two directions:

'(1)   that any statement whether oral or written made by or on behalf of [the mother] to a party herein or to their representative or the guardian ad litem in this case be confidential and not be disclosed to anyone other than a party to this case or to this court; and

(2)   that the [police] do disclose to the court their full file relating to their investigation into the death of M including the Home Office pathologist's report and that copies be made available to all parties.'

The first of these directions raises a novel point which as far as anyone involved in this case is aware has not previously been decided. The mother has not yet made any statement either to the social workers or to the guardian ad litem. She recognises the importance of doing so for the sake of her children. But she is nervous of the consequences, not only for herself, but also for the father. The father supports the mother in her application and if it is granted in relation to her he seeks a similar direction for himself. How far is it open to the court to provide in advance that any statement they may make will be confidential to these proceedings?

It is important to recognise at the outset that any such statement is unlikely to be admissible in any subsequent criminal proceedings. Section 98 of the Children Act 1989 provides as follows:

'(1)   In any proceedings in which a court is hearing an application for an order under Part IV or V, no person shall be excused from –

(a)   giving evidence on any matter; or

(b)   answering any question put to him in the course of his giving evidence, on the ground that doing so might incriminate himself or his spouse of an offence.

(2)   A statement or admission made in such proceedings shall not be admissible in evidence against the person making it or his spouse in proceedings for an offence other than perjury.'

This is modelled on similar provisions in s 33(2) of the Family Law Act 1986 and s 48(2) of the Children Act itself. They reflect the view that it is more important to encourage witnesses in child protection proceedings to be frank than it is either to preserve the citizen's privilege against self-incrimination or to secure admissible evidence for use in a prosecution.

All parties in the present case have urged me to place a wide construction upon the words 'a statement or admission made in such proceedings'. This clearly covers anything a person says in the witness-box and anything a person says in his or her own statement filed in the proceedings. In the very recent case of *Oxfordshire County Council v P* [1995] 1 FLR 552, Ward J held that the privilege extends to an oral admission made by a mother to the guardian ad litem, who was appointed by the court and under a duty to investigate for the court. I respectfully agree. But I would also hold that it extends to oral statements made to social workers who are charged with carrying out the local authority's duties of investigation in a child protection case, at least once the proceedings have begun, as is the case here.

It follows that anything which the mother says to the guardian ad litem or a social worker investigating this case cannot be used in evidence against her in any criminal proceedings, and similarly any statement made by the father cannot be used against him. The guardian ad litem in the *Oxfordshire* case was quite wrong to make a witness statement attesting to the mother's admissions for use in the prosecution of the mother. Those admissions were not admissible and in my view the care court would not have been able to render them so. This affords the parents considerable protection and, it is to be hoped, a considerable incentive to co-operate with the investigation and assessment in the interests of the older children.

But the mother and father are not married to one another, so that the privilege afforded by s 98 does not prevent what the mother says being used in proceedings against the father and vice versa. This is perhaps the main reason why the mother seeks the additional protection of this court. But it should also be borne in mind that hearsay evidence of a statement made outside court by one person making accusations against another is not admissible in criminal proceedings against that other person. So it is, to say the least, unlikely that anything said by either parent to a social worker or to the guardian ad litem could possibly form part of the evidence in any prosecution of either of them.

That may be the practical answer in this case. But it is also strongly argued on the mother's behalf that she is far more likely to speak freely if she knows in advance that what she says cannot be revealed to anyone else, in particular the police, and that this will be in her children's best interests, in enabling the court to reach the right decisions about their future. But does the court have any power to give such an assurance?

...

In this case, however, the parents have not yet spoken, and so on such evidence yet exists, although it is inconceivable that the evidence of either a social worker or the guardian would not contain an account of anything relevant said to them by either parent. It would clearly be going far too far to say that the leave of the court has to be obtained before any information which is obtained for the purpose of child care proceedings can be disclosed to others. The normal child protection procedures would become impossible to operate if that were so.

But does the court have any power to direct that such putative statements should remain confidential? This must be possible in a proper case. The court would undoubtedly have had power to do so in the exercise of its inherent jurisdiction and has now been given considerable control over the conduct of the investigation in child care cases generally. However, it is conceded on behalf of the mother that any direction I might give today could not bind, although it may perhaps influence, future judges in the exercise of their discretion on any subsequent application for the disclosure of evidence. It will therefore be impossible to give the mother or the father any absolute guarantee.

Hence it is argued on behalf of both the local authority and the guardian that I should make no direction at all. The parents will be adequately protected by the prohibition in s 98(2) and the general law against anything they say being used in any criminal proceedings against them. This should be sufficient to encourage them both to speak freely to the guardian and the social workers.

What then are we arguing about? The guardian, and no doubt the social workers, would wish to be in a position to inform the other members of the case conference, including the police, if anything relevant is said. This would not be for their direct use, but as a pointer to them in conducting their own investigations. It seems to me that there can be no possible objection to this. The guardian would, however, wish to go one step further and convey to others the broad effect of what has been said. This seems to me to fall within the practice commended by Ward J in the *Oxfordshire* case, where he said (at p 562):

'I would hope, therefore, that a practice can quickly be developed permitting the free exchange of information between the social services and the police but on a basis that:

(i)   The information is treated by the police as confidential information.

(ii) Accordingly, it may be used by the police to shape the nature and range of inquiries they undertake in the investigation of the alleged criminal offences. They may be permitted to use the information for that investigation but they are not permitted to use it as evidence in any criminal proceedings that may follow.

(iii) If they wish to use as evidence information arising from and in the care proceedings, then they must seek the leave of the court as in wardship cases.'

This seems to me to strike exactly the right balance in a situation such as this. The only qualification which I would venture to place upon what the judge is reported to have said is that this court cannot give leave to the police to use as evidence information obtained in care proceedings if for other reasons that information is inadmissible. For the reasons I have already given, anything incriminating which either parent might say against him or herself or the other is unlikely to be admissible in those criminal proceedings.

I was initially attracted by the argument put forward on behalf of the mother, because of the high value we all place upon seeking to achieve the right result for these children, which I would be prepared to put above the other interests involved. But this is not the perhaps more usual case in which knowing what has happened to the particular child is vital to deciding upon that child's future. And, for the reasons I have already given, under the general law, the parents should be able to talk freely without the fear that this will be used against them. Once they have understood that, any direction as to confidentiality, limited as it must be, and with the risk that it must carry of impeding the proper exercise of the functions of others, cannot make a great deal of difference to what they decide to do. I therefore decline to make the first direction sought.

General notes:

The wide construction of 'statement or admission made in such proceedings' was doubted by Butler-Sloss LJ in *Re G (Social worker: disclosure)* [1996] 1 FLR 276 at 284.

G71   CA 1989, S 98: DISCLOSURE OF EVIDENCE TO THE POLICE

Re EC (Disclosure of material)

[1996] 2 FLR 725 at 732

Court of Appeal

Swinton Thomas LJ

Prior to the hearing of the care proceedings, there were five members of SC's family who fell under suspicion of having caused her injuries. Each of them gave evidence. Before they gave evidence, the judge gave them this warning:

> 'Before you give evidence I have to tell you, as I will tell the others who give evidence, that anything you say from the witness-box cannot be used in any criminal trial against you which relates to the death of SC.'

Where relevant the judge added the words 'or your wife' and 'or your husband'. That statement by the judge was somewhat wider than the words of s 98 envisage.

The judge did not tell any witness that the evidence given by that witness would remain confidential. The proceedings themselves are confidential but subject to the power of the judge, in appropriate circumstances, to order disclosure. Nothing in s 98 detracts from that power. Section 98(2) gives protection only against statements being admissible in evidence in criminal proceedings except for an offence of perjury. Accordingly, the judge could not give any guarantee for all time as to confidentiality, even had he wished to do so because the law makes no provision which would enable him to do so. It may well be that in fairness to persons giving evidence in these circumstances judges may wish to point this out to a witness to whom the warning is given and, almost certainly, a legal adviser should do so.

I have no doubt that the judge was right to hold that he had a discretion to order disclosure of this material. Nor is it fettered in the manner suggested by Miss Parker, although there may well be factors which apply to s 98(2) material which would militate against disclosure in the exercise of the judge's discretion.

Miss Parker submitted that the phraseology of s 98, namely 'A statement shall not be admissible in evidence against the person making it ... in proceedings for an offence other than perjury', covers a police investigation into a suspected offence. In my judgment, the use of the words 'proceedings' and 'evidence' clearly indicates that the section encompasses court proceedings and evidence given in those proceedings and not a police inquiry into the commission of an offence.

In the light of the authorities, the following are among the matters which a judge will consider when deciding whether to order disclosure. It is impossible to place them in any order of importance, because the importance of each of the various factors will inevitably vary very much from case to case:

(1) The welfare and interests of the child or children concerned in the care proceedings. If the child is likely to be adversely affected by the order in any serious way, this will be a very important factor.

(2) The welfare and interests of other children generally.

(3) The maintenance of confidentiality in children cases.

(4) The importance of encouraging frankness in children's cases. All parties to this appeal agree that this is a very important factor and is likely to be of particular importance in a case to which s 98(2) applies. The underlying purpose of s 98 is to encourage people to tell the truth in cases concerning children, and the incentive is that any admission will not be admissible in evidence in a criminal trial. Consequently, it is important in this case. However, the added incentive of guaranteed confidentiality is not given by the words of the section and cannot be given.

(5) The public interest in the administration of justice. Barriers should not be erected between one branch of the judicature and another because this may be inimical to the overall interests of justice.

(6) The public interest in the prosecution of serious crime and the punishment of offenders, including the public interest in convicting those who have been guilty of violent or sexual offences against children. There is a strong public interest in making available material to the police which is relevant to a criminal trial. In many cases, this is likely to be a very important factor.

(7) The gravity of the alleged offence and the relevance of the evidence to it. If the evidence has little or no bearing on the investigation or the trial, this will militate against a disclosure order.

(8) The desirability of co-operation between various agencies concerned with the welfare of children, including the social services departments, the police service, medical practitioners, health visitors, schools, etc. This is particularly important in cases concerning children.

(9) In a case to which s 98(2) applies, the terms of the section itself, namely, that the witness was not excused from answering incriminating questions, and that any statement of admission would

not be admissible against him in criminal proceedings. Fairness to the person who has incriminated himself and any others affected by the incriminating statement and any danger of oppression would also be relevant considerations.

(10) Any other material disclosure which has already taken place.

I have, then, to apply those general considerations to the present case ...

General notes:

Note also *Chief Constable of Greater Manchester v KI and KW (by their children's guardian, Cafcass Legal) and NP* [2007] EWHC 1837 (Fam), [2008] 1 FLR 504: see I6 – Inherent jurisdiction: police wishing to interview children.

Other significant cases on this issue:

There is a long series of cases involving issues of disclosure to the police including:

- *A Local Authority v D (Chief Constable of Thames Valley Police intervening)* [2006] EWHC 1465 (Fam), [2006] 2 FLR 1053
- *Re X Children* [2007] EWHC 1719 (Fam), [2008] 1 FLR 589
- *Re M (Care disclosure to police)* [2008] 2 FLR 390
- *Re X (Disclosure for purposes of criminal proceedings)* [2008] EWHC 242 (Fam), [2008] 2 FLR 944
- *Northumberland County Council v Z, Y, X (By her children's guardian) and the Government of the Republic of Kenya* [2009] EWHC 498 (Fam), [2009] 2 FLR 696
- *Re P (Care proceedings: disclosure)* [2008] EWHC 2197 (Fam), [2009] 2 FLR 1039
- *Re H (Care proceedings: disclosure)* [2009] EWCA Civ 704, [2009] 2 FLR 1531

G72 CA 1989, S 98: NO ABSOLUTE PROTECTION

Re L (Care: confidentiality)

[1999] 1 FLR 165 at 166 and 168

Family Division

Johnson J

The five surviving children were placed with foster-parents when the parents were charged with murder in June 1997. The criminal trial is expected to begin in June 1999 although of course there is the possibility of postponement, appeal and retrial. Accordingly, it was undoubtedly in the interests of the children that decisions about their future should be made in the care proceedings in advance of the criminal trial. However, it is this that has given rise to the problem. On behalf of each of the parents leading counsel have submitted that it is unfair for the parents to be expected to give evidence in these care proceedings because to do so might prejudice their position in the criminal process. Until now the understanding amongst those concerned with care proceedings has I believe been that parents may speak frankly in these proceedings without risk of prejudice. In the words of Mr Allen Levy QC, appearing here on behalf of the guardian, Parliament had intended, and thought it had provided, that care proceedings should be 'ring fenced'. The submission on behalf of the parents is that whatever may have been the objective, Parliament has failed to achieve complete protection for parents in this situation.

Section 98(2) of the Children Act 1989 provides that:

'A statement or admission made in such proceedings shall not be admissible in evidence against the person making it or his spouse in proceedings for an offence other than perjury.'

Coupled with the provisions of s 12 of the Administration of Justice Act 1960 that statutory provision may have seemed to afford adequate protection. However, the submission is that s 98 does not preclude a parent being cross-examined as to such statements or admissions.

...

My conclusion is that s 98(2) does not afford a protection to the parents in this case which can be described as absolute. It would seem that the ring fence envisaged by Mr Levy may have significant gaps and I had thought that it would be possible and appropriate to seek to plug those gaps by way of injunctions. In *Cleveland County Council v F* [1995] 1 FLR 797, 803 Hale J posed the question:

'... does the court have any power to direct that such ... statements should remain confidential? This must be possible in a proper case. The court would undoubtedly have had power to do so in the exercise of its inherent jurisdiction and has now been given considerable control over the conduct of the investigation in child care cases generally. However, it is conceded on behalf of the mother that any direction that I might give today could not bind, although it may perhaps influence, future judges in the exercise of their discretion on any subsequent application for the disclosure of evidence. It will therefore be impossible to give the mother or the father any absolute guarantee.'

Later, at 804D Hale J referred to any direction as to confidentiality as 'limited as it must be'.

It would clearly be wrong for a judge hearing care proceedings to make any order that might be thought to trespass on the jurisdiction of the judge conducting the criminal trial. Initially, I had thought that it would be possible to achieve absolute protection for the parents by making an injunction the effect of which would be to preclude any party or person present at the hearing of the care proceedings from divulging anything said whether in writing or orally by the parents except for the purpose of arriving at decisions about the future upbringing of the children. The risks relied upon on behalf of the father were of cross-examination by the Crown, on behalf of the mother of cross-examination by counsel for the father. On reflection it seems to me that no injunction, however skilfully drafted, could afford absolute protection because of the possibility of variation in its terms, particularly if there were a significant change in circumstances or if a co-defendant were able to show that there was a substantial risk of injustice without modification of the prohibition. Indeed such an injunction, and possibly s 98(2) itself, might fall foul of Art 6 of the European Convention on Human Rights.

The result has been that, on advice, neither parent has given evidence before me. Whether the reason was the risk of prejudice in the criminal proceedings or simply a desire to avoid having to give evidence in these proceedings or a combination of both, is a matter of speculation. This decision is to be regretted because one would hope that all parents would feel able to and would be willing to speak frankly in care proceedings. In the present case the practical consequences will be more limited than in other cases. For example in a case, unlike the present, where a care order was resisted and the only basis of the application was the alleged killing of a child, then the consequence would be serious indeed.

Two observations seem to me to be appropriate. The first is that this problem arises only if the care proceedings are heard before the final criminal trial. I hope that the submissions made in the present case will not be used as a basis for seeking postponement of care proceedings until the conclusion of related criminal proceedings. The second observation is that the submissions on behalf of these parents seems to me to be lacking in any substantial merit. If the parents give evidence and tell the truth in both proceedings then there is no risk to them at all. To this suggestion counsel's response was that even truthful witnesses can make statements that show signs of inconsistency. That suggestion does not seem to me to do justice to the criminal process. If for one reason or another, perhaps nervousness, perhaps mental limitation, a parent gave evidence at the second trial which was in some respects inconsistent with evidence previously given, one would hope and expect that the trial judge, counsel and the jury would be able to make proper allowance. There is a risk but not it seems to me to a bona fide honest witness. For the dishonest witness the difficulty of course remains. As I said in the course of argument, I have myself experience of a care case in which a parent conceded responsibility for a death albeit contesting the matter vigorously at his subsequent murder trial.

In the present case I will have to consider in due course what inference I should draw from the failure of the parents to give evidence.

I need now to consider a further application made on behalf of the police for the disclosure of some documents in the care proceedings not previously disclosed and for leave to obtain a transcript of the evidence in these care proceedings ...

G73   IMMUNITY FROM SUIT

Meadow v General Medical Council (Her Majesty's Attorney-General intervening)

[2006] EWCA Civ 1390, [2007] 1 FLR 1398 at 1405

Court of Appeal

Clarke MR

See G64 – Exposure of expert witness to disciplinary proceedings

Other significant cases on this issue:

- *Hinds v Liverpool County Court* [2008] EWHC 665 (QB), [2008] 2 FLR 63 at [40]–[41] (Cafcass employees who carry out their duties in good faith but carelessly should not owe a duty of care)

Disclosure within proceedings

G74 STATEMENT OF GENERAL PRINCIPLES (1)

Re D (Minors) (adoption report: confidentiality)

[1995] 2 FLR 687 at 689, 694, 699 and 700

House of Lords

Lord Mustill

My Lords, it is a first principle of fairness that each party to a judicial process shall have an opportunity to answer by evidence and argument any adverse material which the tribunal may take into account when forming its opinion. This principle is lame if the party does not know the substance of what is said against him (or her), for what he does not know he cannot answer. The requirement of openness is particularly important in proceedings for adoption, not only because it may lead to the deprivation of parental rights, in the self-centred meaning of that word, but because a successful application to adopt brings about a total rupture of the mutual relationship of responsibility and dependency which is the essence of the parental bond. The unique character of the relationship which the parent will lose, and the generally irreversible nature of the loss, make it specially important that in simple fairness to the parent he or she is aware of anything which may tend to bring it about. There is more to it than this, however, since fairness to a parent is a reflection of fairness to the child. The erasure of the bond with the natural parent and the creation of an entirely new set of responsibilities and dependencies shared with the adopters is an event of critical importance in the life of the child, whose paramount welfare demands that such a momentous step is taken only after a process which is as fair and thorough as can be devised.

Pulling in the other direction is an impulse towards the confidentiality of sensitive personal information. There are two distinct although often cumulative reasons why this impulse is a feature of proceedings for adoption. First, in a process where the judge is dependent to a great extent on second-hand knowledge of the circumstances it is in the interests of all those who are potentially affected by his decision that the information furnished to him shall be as full and candid as possible; and candour is promoted if those who investigate and report their findings and opinions can do so with a degree of confidence that the dispute will not be exacerbated, and hence the welfare of the child imperilled, by the disclosure of material which may arouse resentment. Secondly, where the child has made allegations or expressed wishes to the author of the report, there may be circumstances where full disclosure may put at risk the welfare of the child: including, in this term, its physical and psychological security. For these and other reasons adoption has traditionally been regarded as unique, or nearly so, in the degree of confidentiality maintained, and the practical reasons for making sure that disclosure does not create unnecessary risk have been given statutory reinforcement by s 1 of the Children Act 1989, with its insistence that, in determining questions with respect to its upbringing, the welfare of the child shall be the court's paramount consideration.

...

For my part I have no hesitation in saying that a strong presumption in favour of disclosing to a party any material relating to him or her is the point at which the judge should start. It is true, as frequently emphasised, that the requirements of natural justice are not invariable, and that circumstances must alter cases. Nevertheless the opportunity to know about and respond to adverse materials is at the heart of a fair hearing. Adoption is an unusual process, but it calls for fairness as much as any other, and indeed with special intensity, for the reasons already given. Rule 53(2) strongly reinforces this opinion since it is a formal recognition that the confidential nature of the adoption process must not be carried to extremes.

Equally, however, there must be some limit to the duty of disclosure, as r 53(2) itself makes clear. No formula can be stated which will answer every case, the more so since the factors which may exceptionally speak against disclosure may be quite different from those involved in the present case, and other interests may be at risk besides those of the child. Plainly, where it is suggested that disclosure may harm the child the court will take the matter very seriously, but it should look closely at both the degree of likelihood that harm will occur, and the gravity of the harm if it does in fact occur. To say that harm must be certain would in my opinion pitch the test too high, since future events cannot be predicted with complete confidence, but a powerful combination of likelihood and seriousness of harm will be required before the requirements for a fair trial can be overridden.

To this proposition I would add two riders. First, I do not think it helpful to approach the decision by reference to burden of proof. This conception is apposite for the assessment of evidence on a disputed question of fact, but here the facts material to the exercise of the discretion under r 53(2) are all known; what is in issue is whether there is sufficient in them to justify the exceptional exercise of the discretion to withhold disclosure.

Secondly, I feel no doubt that in cases of real uncertainty the court may legitimately take into account the significance to the application for adoption of freeing the information which it is sought to withhold. If the material is unlikely to carry great weight in the decision the pressure to reveal it, so that it can be answered, is correspondingly less. But this requires caution, however logical it may be, for in the atmosphere of rancour and suspicion which may pervade a contested adoption an assurance from the court that the material is innocuous may not be the same as seeing for oneself.

I now turn to see how this conclusion sits with the decided cases.

...

Next, I must refer to certain decisions of the European Commission and Court of Human Rights, and of the Committee of Ministers, namely *Hendriks v Netherlands* (1982) 5 EHHR 223, *W v United Kingdom* (1987) 10 EHRR 29, and the case of *McMichael (Case of) v United Kingdom* (51/1993/446/525), 24 February 1995. On the view which I have formed of the English law there is no need to engage the important general question which would have arisen if the conclusions impelled by the English legislation and decided cases had differed in important respects from the jurisprudence of the European tribunals. The language of the European Convention on Human Rights naturally causes the discussion to be couched in terms of rights, whilst I would prefer a different vocabulary, but in substance the principles to be derived from that jurisprudence are entirely consistent with those which I propose. In particular, the conflation in *McMichael* of the remedies under Arts 6 and 8 of the Convention shows that full disclosure will usually advance the interests both of a fair trial and of the parties to the parental relationship. On the other hand, there is nothing in these decisions to suggest that disclosure can never be properly withheld if the interests of the child so demand; and it is significant that in *McMichael*, a case where the reports were kept from the parents as a matter of general practice in Scotland, the court expressly referred in para 88 of its judgment to the fact that no special reasons for withholding them had been advanced.

...

At the close of thoughtful submissions to which the House is much indebted, counsel together invited your Lordships to state the principles in terms to which courts might in future have recourse with the need to analyse an ever-increasing number of judgments, not all of them easy to reconcile. In response, I tender the following propositions, with which I understand all of your Lordships are in accord.

It is a fundamental principle of fairness that a party is entitled to the disclosure of all materials which may be taken into account by the court when reaching a decision adverse to that party. This principle applies with particular force to proceedings designed to lead to an order for adoption, since the consequences of such an order are so lasting and far-reaching.

When deciding whether to direct that notwithstanding r 53(2) of the Adoption Rules 1984 a party referred to in a confidential report supplied by an adoption agency, a local authority, a reporting officer or a guardian ad litem shall not be entitled to inspect the part of the report which refers to him or her, the court should first consider whether disclosure of the material would involve a real possibility of significant harm to the child.

If it would, the court should next consider whether the overall interests of the child would benefit from non-disclosure, weighing on the one hand the interest of the child in having the material properly tested, and on the other both the magnitude of the risk that harm will occur and the gravity of the harm if it does occur.

If the court is satisfied that the interests of the child point towards non-disclosure, the next and final step is for the court to weigh that consideration, and its strength in the circumstances of the case, against the interest of the parent or other party in having an opportunity to see and respond to the material. In the latter regard the court should take into account the importance of the material to the issues in the case.

Non-disclosure should be the exception and not the rule. The court should be rigorous in its examination of the risk and gravity of the feared harm to the child, and should order non-disclosure only when the case for doing so is compelling.

G75 STATEMENT OF GENERAL PRINCIPLES (2)

Re R (Care: disclosure: nature of proceedings)

[2002] 1 FLR 755 at 775

Family Division

Charles J

It has been established by high authority in this country that, generally, confidentiality is not a valid reason for non-disclosure of material that passes the relevant threshold test for disclosure (see, for example, *Science Research Council v Nassé; Leyland Cars (BL Cars Ltd) v Vyas* [1980] AC 1028, 1067A and *D v National Society for the Prevention of Cruelty to Children* [1978] AC 171, 230C–D. In both passages, in the relevant speeches in the House of Lords *Alfred Crompton Amusement Machines Ltd v Customs and Excise Commissioners (No 2)* [1974] AC 405 is cited and the most often cited passage therein is at 433H, where Lord Cross says that confidentiality is not a separate head of privilege but it may be a very material consideration to bear in mind when privilege is claimed on the ground of public interest, and see further *Wallace Smith Trust Co Ltd (In Liquidation) v Deloitte Haskins & Sells (A Firm) and Another* [1997] 1 WLR 257 in particular at 273F–274B).

It follows from that that something over and above or in addition to the simple assertion of confidentiality is needed to lead to a conclusion that disclosure of material that passes the relevant threshold test for disclosure can be refused in proceedings.

In proceedings concerning children, significant harm to a child has been taken into account in the consideration of the competing interests involved when determining whether disclosure of relevant material known to the court but not to one of the parties can be refused (see, for example, *Re D (Minors) (Adoption Reports: Confidentiality)* [1996] AC 593, sub nom *Re D (Adoption Reports: Confidentiality)* [1995] 2 FLR 687, where, however, it is made clear that non-disclosure will be the exception and should only occur when the case for it is compelling).

In a recent case, *Re B (Disclosure to Other Parties)* [2001] 2 FLR 1017, Munby J carried out a very helpful review of authorities and in particular those relating to the Convention. He concluded that the Art 8 rights of any person, if they are sufficiently engaged, could found an order that relevant material should not be disclosed. Thus, he concludes that there is room for a balancing of competing interests under Arts 6 and 8 and a conclusion based thereon that some relevant material should not be disclosed in proceedings.

To my mind, this is an interesting development which arguably is not on all fours with the general approach previously adopted in the English courts that confidentiality was not a ground for refusing disclosure of relevant material (see again, for example, *Alfred Crompton Amusement Machines Ltd v Customs and Excise Commissioners (No 2)* [1974] AC 405).

I comment that to my mind issues discussed in *Re B (Disclosure to Other Parties)* [2001] 2 FLR 1017 also relate to interesting points as to the basis on which disclosure of material relating to children by, for example, the media can be enjoined and, in particular, whether an injunction can be based on Art 8 and/or the public interest in promoting the welfare of children, rather than simply on duties of confidence. These issues are well outside the ambit of this judgment, but the decisions made in respect of them in other cases may have an impact on disclosure for the purposes of proceedings under the Children Act 1989 and, indeed, other proceedings whether held in private or in public.

Importantly, as was done by the House of Lords in *Re D (Minors) (Adoption Reports: Confidentiality)* [1996] AC 593, sub nom *Re D (Adoption: Reports: Confidentiality)* [1995] 2 FLR 687, at the end of his judgment in *Re B (Disclosure to Other Parties)* [2001] 2 FLR 1017, Munby J emphasised the point that it is only if the case for non-disclosure is convincingly and compellingly demonstrated that an order for non-disclosure will be made and in most cases the needs of a fair trial will demand that there be no restrictions on disclosure even if the case for restrictions is made out, the restrictions must go no further than is strictly necessary.

I respectfully agree with that.

Other significant cases on this issue:

- *Re C (Children: disclosure)* [2010] EWCA Civ 239, [2010] 2 FLR 22 (order upheld requiring parent to disclose to guardian ad litem correspondence with MP)

This case is also included in relation to:

D5 Reunification not an overriding factor
G22 Preparation and disclosure: duties of LA
G23 Preparation and disclosure: mirror duties of respondents
G24 Disclosure of relevant notes

G76   PRIVILEGE: DEFINING KEY TERMS

S County Council v B

[2000] 2 FLR 161 at 167

Family Division

Charles J

As can be seen from, for example, the notes to the Rules of the Supreme Court, Ord 24 and the speech of Lord Nicholls (who was in the minority) in *Re L (A Minor) (Police Investigation: Privilege)* [1997] AC 16, 33C–F, sub nom *Re L (Police Investigation: Privilege)* [1996] 1 FLR 731, 744G–745A:

(1)   Legal professional privilege is often classified under two sub-headings, namely: legal advice privilege and litigation privilege.

(2)   In that classification, legal advice privilege is a term used to describe material that is privileged whether or not litigation is in existence or pending. Originally it was confined to advice or communication between solicitor and client concerning litigation, but from an early stage it was extended to cover non-litigious business (see the *Derby Magistrates* case [1996] 1 AC 487, 505B–E, [1996] 1 FLR 513, 524G–525B. As that citation shows, it was pointed out that it was not easy to discover why a like privilege has been refused to others and I would add that in the modern age it is not easy to see why the logic, purpose and public interest underlying the privilege when litigation is not contemplated supports the privilege in respect of communications with a lawyer but not, for example, communications with an accountant on the same subject matter.

(3)   In that classification, litigation privilege covers two areas, namely: (a) communications between a solicitor (or a lawyer) and *third parties* which come into existence after litigation is contemplated, or commenced, and made with a view either to obtaining or giving advice in relation to it, or of obtaining or collecting evidence to be used in it, or obtaining information which may lead to the obtaining of such evidence (see *Anderson v Bank of British Columbia* (1876) 2 Ch D 644, 650, and (b) communications between the client (or a non-lawyer) and third parties, the dominant purpose of which is to obtain legal advice, or to conduct or aid in the conduct of litigation in reasonable prospect (see, for example, *Waugh v British Railways Board* [1980] AC 521).

As appears from the above classification, litigation privilege covers communications with third parties for two purposes, namely (i) obtaining legal advice in respect of litigation, and (ii) to conduct or aid in the conduct of litigation by, for example, obtaining evidence.

This case is also included in relation to:

G79 Litigation privilege arises in adversarial proceedings
G80 Legal professional privilege not overridden by general duty of disclosure
G81 Effect of legal professional privilege

G77   LEGAL ADVICE PRIVILEGE ARISES

R v Derby Magistrates' Court ex parte B

[1996] 1 FLR 513 at 515, 521, 527 and 528

House of Lords

Lord Taylor

My Lords, these consolidated appeals raised important questions concerning legal professional privilege and the scope of s 97 of the Magistrates' Courts Act 1980. The appellant challenged by way of judicial review the issue by the stipendiary magistrate for Derby of summonses pursuant to s 97 requiring him and his former solicitor to produce certain documents in the course of committal proceedings against the appellant's stepfather. The Divisional Court refused the application but certified points of law of general public importance.

...

In *Balabel v Air India* [1988] Ch 317, the basic principle justifying legal professional privilege was again said to be that a client should be able to obtain legal advice in confidence.

The principle which runs through all these cases, and the many other cases which were cited, is that a man must be able to consult his lawyer in confidence, since otherwise he might hold back half the truth. The client must be sure that what he tells his lawyer in confidence will never be revealed without his consent. Legal professional privilege is thus much more than an ordinary rule of evidence, limited in its application to the facts of a particular case. It is a fundamental condition on which the administration of justice as a whole rests.

...

In the course of his judgment in the Divisional Court, McCowan LJ indicated that he not only felt bound by *R v Ataou*, but he also agreed with it. He continued:

> 'These further points were made by Mr Francis. He says that if a man charged with a criminal offence cannot go to a solicitor in the certainty that such matters as he places before him will be kept private for all time, he may be reluctant to be candid with his solicitors. Surely, however, it ought to be an incentive to him to tell the truth to his solicitors, which surely cannot be a bad thing.

Mr Francis went on to suggest that his client's reputation would be damaged if the disclosures were to go to suggest that he was the murderer. For my part, I would be able to bear with equanimity that damage to his reputation. In the interests of justice and of the respondent, it would be a good thing that that reputation should be so damaged.'

One can have much sympathy with McCowan LJ's approach, especially in relation to the unusual facts of this case. But it is not for the sake of the appellant alone that the privilege must be upheld. It is in the wider interests of all those hereafter who might otherwise be deterred from telling the whole truth to their solicitors. For this reason I am of the opinion that no exception should be allowed to the absolute nature of legal professional privilege, once established. It follows that *R v Barton* and *R v Ataou* were wrongly decided, and ought to be overruled. I therefore considered these appeals should be allowed on both grounds and the case remitted to the High Court, with a direction that the decisions of the stipendiary magistrate dated 21 June and 8 August 1994 be quashed.

Other significant cases on this issue:

• *A Local Authority v B* [2008] EWHC 1017 (Fam), [2009] 1 FLR 289 (the presence of a social worker as appropriate adult did not remove legal advice privilege that would otherwise have attached to a vulnerable juvenile's conversation with a solicitor at a police station)

G78 LITIGATION PRIVILEGE DOES NOT ARISE IN NON-ADVERSARIAL PROCEEDINGS

Re L (Police investigation: privilege)

[1996] 1 FLR 731 at 735 and 736

House of Lords

Lord Jauncey

Miss Kushner submitted that Dr France's report was the subject of legal professional privilege, that such privilege was absolute (*R v Derby Magistrates' Court ex parte B* [1996] 1 FLR 513) and that it could be overridden neither in the public interest nor in furtherance of the paramountcy of the child's interests. The *Oxfordshire*[1] case was wrongly decided.

...

It is clear from the reasoning of the Lord Chief Justice and of the other members of the committee that the reference to legal professional privilege was in the context of the relationship between solicitor and client. Indeed there was no occasion to consider whether and in what other circumstances absolute legal professional privilege might apply. Notwithstanding this Miss Kushner maintained that the absolute nature of the privilege attaching to the solicitor/client relationship extended equally to all other forms of legal professional privilege.

My Lords, I reject this contention. There is, as Mr Harris QC for the respondents, the city council and the police authority, pointed out, a clear distinction between the privilege attaching to communications between solicitor and client and that attaching to reports by third parties prepared on the instructions of a client for the purpose of litigation. In the former case the privilege attaches to all communications whether related to litigation or not but in the latter case it attaches only to documents or other written communications prepared with a view to litigation (*Waugh v British Railways Board* [1980] AC 521, 533B, 537G and 544B). There is this further distinction that whereas a solicitor could not without his client's consent be compelled to express an opinion on the factual or legal merits of the case a third party who has provided a report to a client can be subpoenaed to give evidence by the other side and cannot decline to

---

[1] *Oxfordshire County Council v M and Another* [1994] Fam 151, [1994] 2 WLR 393, [1994] 1 FLR 175, [1994] 2 All ER 269, CA.

answer questions as to his factual findings and opinion thereon. There is no property in the opinion of an expert witness (*Harmony Shipping Co SA v Saudi Europe Line Ltd* [1979] 1 WLR 1380, Lord Denning MR at 1386G).

Litigation privilege, as it has been called, is an essential component of adversarial procedure. In *Worrall v Reich* [1955] 1 QB 296 it was held that one party to a litigation could not be compelled to produce to the other party a medical report obtained for the purposes of the action. This case was followed in *Re Saxton, deceased, Johnson and Another v Saxton and Another* [1962] 1 WLR 968 in relation to the report of a handwriting expert where Lord Denning MR at 972 said:

> 'In short, it is one of our motions of a fair trial that, except by agreement, you are not entitled to see the proofs of the other side's witnesses.'

In *Causton v Mann Egerton (Johnsons) Ltd* [1974] 1 WLR 162 which concerned the disclosure of medical reports in a personal injury action, Roskill LJ at 170 said:

> 'I am clearly of the view that this court has no power to order production of privileged documents... so long as we have an adversary system, a party is entitled not to produce documents which are properly protected by privilege if it is not to his advantage to produce them, and even though their production might assist his adversary ...'

Finally in *Waugh v British Railways Board* [1980] AC 521 Lord Simon of Glaisdale at 536A said:

> 'This system of adversary forensic procedure with legal professional advice and representation demands that communications between lawyer and client should be confidential, since the lawyer is for the purpose of litigation merely the client's alter ego. So too material which is to go into the lawyer's (ie the client's) brief or file for litigation. This is the basis for the privilege against disclosure of material collected by or on behalf of a client for the use of his lawyer in pending or anticipated litigation ...'

Lord Denning, Roskill LJ and Lord Simon all emphasised the important part which litigation privilege plays in a fair trial under the adversarial system. This raises the question of whether proceedings under Part IV of the Act are essentially adversarial in their nature. If they are, litigation privilege must continue to play its normal part. If they are not, different considerations may apply.

In *Official Solicitor v K* [1965] AC 201, which concerned disclosure of a guardian ad litem's report in wardship proceedings, Lord Evershed at 218E pointed out that the purpose of the judicial inquiry was to make a decision about the future upbringing of the infant whereby the infant was in a special position distinct from that of other parties. Lord Devlin at 240A quoted with approval the following dictum of the trial judge, Ungoed-Thomas J:

> 'The jurisdiction regarding wards of court which is now exercised by the Chancery Division is an ancient jurisdiction deriving from the prerogative of the Crown as parens patriae. It is not based on the rights of parents, and its primary concern is not to ensure their rights but to ensure the welfare of the children.'

He later stated at 241A:

> 'Where the judge is not sitting purely, or even primarily, as an arbiter but is charged with the paramount duty of protecting the interests of one outside the conflict, a rule that is designed for just arbitrament cannot in all circumstances prevail.'

Lord Scarman in *Re E (A Minor) (Wardship: Court's Duty)* [1984] FLR 457 pointed out at 488F–G that a court in wardship proceedings was not exercising an adversarial jurisdiction and that:

> 'Its duty is not limited to the dispute between the parties: on the contrary, its duty is to act in the way best suited, in its judgment, to serve the true interest and welfare of the ward. In exercising wardship jurisdiction, the court is a true family court. Its paramount concern is the welfare of its ward. It will, therefore, sometimes be the duty of the court to look beyond the submissions of the parties in its endeavour to do what it judges to be necessary.'

Since the judgment in *Official Solicitor v K* there have been numerous pronouncements by judges of the Family Division stressing that proceedings in wardship are non-adversarial. It is not necessary to refer to these and I simply refer back to the passages which I have already quoted from the judgment of Sir Stephen Brown in the *Oxfordshire* case. In these passages the President was, as I understand him, equating the position in Children Act proceedings to wardship proceedings. The above dictum would appear to provide firm support for the proposition that proceedings under Part IV of the Act are, like wardship proceedings, essentially non-adversarial in their nature.

However, Miss Kushner argued that such statutory proceedings were not to be equiparated to wardship proceedings. This submission goes too far. It is, of course, true that once a care order under Part IV of the Act has been made it is the local authority and not the court which has the direct responsibility for the child, but until such an order has been made the role of the court under the Act does not differ significantly from its role in wardship proceedings. In reaching a decision in either case the primary consideration was and is the welfare of the child.

I agree with the President that care proceedings are essentially non-adversarial. Having reached that conclusion and also that litigation privilege is essentially a creature of adversarial proceedings it follows that the matter is at large for this House to determine what if any role it has to play in care proceedings.

Before Dr France could report it was necessary to obtain the leave of the district judge under r 4.23 to disclose to him the court papers. His report appears to have been based entirely on the hospital case notes and there is no suggestion that he had any communication with the appellant. Accordingly all the material to which he had access was material which was already available to the other parties. To that extent the position is similar to that in *Re Saxton*. However, in these proceedings which are primarily non-adversarial and investigative as opposed to adversarial the notion of a fair trial between opposing parties assumes far less importance. In the latter case the judge must decide the case in favour of one or other party upon such evidence as they choose to adduce however much he might wish for further evidence on any point. In the former case the judge is concerned to make a decision which is in the best interest of the child in question and may make orders which are sought by no party to the proceedings (ss 10(1)(b), 31(5), 34(5) of the Act). Furthermore the court has wide powers under r 4.11(9), (10) of the rules to require the guardian ad litem to obtain expert reports and other assistance. Thus the court is seeking to reach a decision which will be in the best interests of someone who is not a direct party and is granted investigative powers to achieve that end. In these circumstances I consider that care proceedings under Part IV of the Act are so far removed from normal actions that litigation privilege has no place in relation to reports obtained by a party thereto which could not have been prepared without the leave of the court to disclose documents already filed or to examine the child. In reaching this conclusion I attach considerable importance to the following dictum of Sir Stephen Brown P in the *Oxfordshire* case at 161F and 184H respectively:

'If a party, having obtained the leave of the court, where to be able to conceal, or withhold from the court, matters which were of importance and were relevant to the future of the child, there would be a risk that the welfare of the child would not be promoted as the Children Act requires.'

I would add that if litigation privilege were to apply to Dr France's report it could have the effect of subordinating the welfare of the child to the interests of the appellant in preserving its confidentiality. This would appear to frustrate the primary object of the Act.

I differ from the President with his great experience of proceedings under the Act only in as much as he concluded that in the foregoing circumstances the court had power to *override* the privilege. The *Oxfordshire* case was, however, argued on the assumption that the privilege existed but could be overridden. This case was also argued on the same assumption in the Court of Appeal, but the Master of the Rolls expressed doubt as to whether the assumption was rightly made. His doubts were in my view well founded. The better view is that litigation privilege never arose in the first place rather than that the court has power to override it. It is excluded by necessary implication from the terms and overall purpose of the Act. This does not of course affect privilege arising between solicitor and client.

The form of the order in the *Oxfordshire* case has been used on many occasions by judges in the Family Division. It is a sensible and competent order and I see no grounds for interfering with a practice which experienced judges have found to work well.

General notes:

The litigation finally concluded in the ECtHR: see *L v United Kingdom (Disclosure of expert report)* (Case 34222/96) [2000] 2 FLR 322.

Some doubt has been cast on the reasoning in this case by the decision of the House of Lords in *Three Rivers District Council v Governor and Company of the Bank of England (No 6)* [2004] UKHL 48, most particularly by Lord Rodger at [53].

G79   LITIGATION PRIVILEGE ARISES IN ADVERSARIAL PROCEEDINGS

S County Council v B

[2000] 2 FLR 161 at 163 and 180

Family Division

Charles J

This case concerns triplets, one girl and two boys all born on 8 November 1997. Their names are N, A and A.

Their guardian ad litem has made an application, which is supported by the local authority and the mother of the three children that the father be ordered to disclose in these proceedings (a) the identity of, and (b) copies of, the reports and notes of the medical experts the father is proposing to instruct in connection with the preparation and presentation of his defence to criminal proceedings. The criminal proceedings have been brought against him under s 18 of the Offences against the Person Act 1861 in respect of injuries suffered by N. It is this application that is the subject of this judgment.

...

The passage in the speech of Lord Jauncey[1] that was relied on particularly by counsel for the guardian ad litem to support his alternative submissions that either legal professional privilege cannot be claimed by the father in respect of the material the guardian ad litem seeks, or that the father does not have an absolute right to refuse to produce such material is at 24G–25C and 736D–G respectively, and is in the following terms:

'It is clear from the reasoning of the Lord Chief Justice and of the other members of the committee that the reference to legal professional privilege was in the context of the relationship between solicitor and client. Indeed, there was no occasion to consider whether and in what other circumstances absolute legal professional privilege might apply. Notwithstanding this, Miss Kushner maintained that the absolute nature of the privilege attaching to the solicitor–client relationship extended equally to all other forms of legal professional privilege.

---

[1]   *Re L (A Minor) (Police Investigation: Privilege)* [1996] 1 FLR 731, HL. See G78 – Litigation privilege does not arise in non-adversarial proceedings.

My Lords, I reject this contention. There is, as Mr Harris for the city council and the police authority, pointed out, a clear distinction between the privilege attaching to communications between solicitor and client and that attaching to reports by third parties prepared on the instructions of a client for the purposes of litigation. In the former case the privilege attaches to all communications whether related to litigation or not, but in the latter case it attaches only to documents or other written communications prepared with a view to litigation: *Waugh v British Railways Board* [1980] AC 521, 533B, 537G and 544B. There is this further distinction that whereas a solicitor could not without his client's consent be compelled to express an opinion on the factual or legal merits of the case, a third party who has provided a report to a client can be subpoenaed to give evidence by the other side and cannot decline to answer questions as to his factual findings and opinion thereon. There is no property in the opinion of an expert witness: *Harmony Shipping Co SA v Saudi Europe Line Ltd; Same v Orri (Trading as Saudi Europe Line); Same v Davis and Another* [1979] 1 WLR 1380, 1386G, per Lord Denning MR.'

I accept that if this extract is read in isolation it provides support for the arguments advanced by counsel on behalf of the guardian ad litem, and for the contention that my conclusions as to the effect of the *Derby Magistrates*[2] case, and more generally as to legal professional privilege, are wrong. However, in my judgment it should not be read in isolation and when it is read in context, and indeed when it is further analysed on its own, it does not lead to the conclusion that the arguments advanced on behalf of the guardian ad litem in this case are correct.

In my judgment, when read in context this passage is simply an introduction to, and does not form part of, the essential reasoning of the majority in the speech of Lord Jauncey. This is because:

(i)   it is part of the passage which leads to the posing of the vital question at 25H and 737E respectively, namely: 'This raises the question of whether proceedings under Part IV of the Act are essentially adversarial';

(ii)   it is at odds with the next two sentences at 25H and 737E respectively, namely: 'If they are, litigation privilege must continue to play its normal part. If they are not different considerations may apply', and

(iii) it is thus not part of the essential reasoning that it is the nature of care proceedings (ie that they are essentially non-adversarial) that means that the role litigation privilege has to play in care proceedings is at large for the House in *Re L* (26H and 738F

---

[2]   *R v Derby Magistrates' Court ex parte B* [1996] 1 FLR 513, HL. See G77 – Legal advice privilege arises.

respectively) and the conclusion that the court in care proceedings does not *override* litigation privilege but that it *never arose* in the first place (27G–H and 739D–E).

In my judgment, it follows that in context the passage relied on by counsel for the guardian ad litem is not part of the ratio and further, or alternatively, it should be read as referring to the establishment and existence of the privilege rather than to its effect once established.

Further and importantly:

(a)   in my judgment the majority in *Re L* are concerned with, and are only dealing with, the establishment and thus the existence of litigation privilege in care proceedings and if they had been dealing with material that was the subject of litigation privilege by reference to other proceedings (i) they would have done so expressly, and (ii) in particular they would have explained how the Children Act 1989 and the essentially non-adversarial nature of proceedings under it could affect rights established elsewhere. It is one thing to conclude that the Children Act 1989 and the nature of proceedings under it has the result that a privilege does not arise in such proceedings and quite another to say that they remove, or affect, rights based on the public interest and which come into existence in, or in respect of, other proceedings, and

(b)   if the majority were considering the issue whether litigation privilege in contrast to solicitor and client privilege gives rise to a qualified rather than an absolute right, again they would have done so expressly and the sentences at 25H and 737E respectively (quoted in para (ii) above) indicate that they were not considering this question.

Further, if the passage relied on by counsel for the guardian ad litem is considered in isolation in my judgment it does not lead to the wide-reaching alternative results he seeks to establish. My reasons for this conclusion are:

(a)   the passage makes no reference to the aspect of litigation privilege concerned with communications between lawyers and third parties, and indeed it expressly refers to reports of third parties prepared on the instructions of the *client*;

(b)   the cited passages from *Waugh v British Railways Board* all refer to the establishment of the dominant purpose test and not to the other aspects of litigation privilege, and

(c)   the reference to subpoenaing a third party who has provided a report correctly limits what he can be compelled to answer to his factual findings and opinions, and as shown by *Harmony Shipping Co SA v Saudi Europe Line Ltd; Same v Orri (Trading as Saudi Europe Line); Same v Davis and Another* [1979] 1 WLR 1380,

1385 D–E a third party cannot be compelled to give evidence of matters covered by legal professional privilege (and I return to this point later when dealing with the question whether the father should be ordered to disclose the identity of the experts he instructs solely for the purposes of the criminal proceedings).

In my judgment these points show that the majority in *Re L*, were not dealing with the points advanced by counsel for the guardian ad litem in this case, which as the questions I have set out earlier and numbered (A) and (B) show have several aspects.

In my judgment, for the reasons set out above, the decision in *Re L*:

(1) is not authority which founds the alternative propositions advanced by counsel for the guardian ad litem in this case, namely either (a) that the father cannot in these proceedings assert legal professional privilege in respect of his communications (direct or indirect) with the medical experts he instructs in connection with the criminal proceedings or in respect of their reports, or (b) that he only has a qualified right to assert that such material should not be disclosed in these proceedings;

(2) does not alter my conclusions based on the *Derby Magistrates* case and earlier authority that when, and from the time that, it comes into existence litigation privilege in respect of material such as that under consideration in this case confers an absolute right on the litigant or potential litigant. (This conclusion is naturally subject to the qualification raised in the *Derby Magistrates* case that such a right may cease to exist if the litigant no longer had any interest in continuing to assert the privilege.)

This case is also included in relation to:

G76 Privilege: defining key terms
G80 Legal professional privilege not overridden by general duty of disclosure
G81 Effect of legal professional privilege

G80 LEGAL PROFESSIONAL PRIVILEGE NOT OVERRIDDEN BY A GENERAL DUTY OF DISCLOSURE

S County Council v B

[2000] 2 FLR 161 at 183

Family Division

Charles J

The duty of disclosure in cases concerning the welfare of children

In my judgment it was correctly common ground that in proceedings in the Family Division concerning the welfare of children there is a high duty of full and frank disclosure of all matters within the knowledge, custody power or control of parties which are material to welfare whether those matters are favourable to, or adverse to, their own particular case (see *Oxfordshire County Council v P* [1995] Fam 161, 166E, [1995] 1 FLR 552, 557A). That case concerned disclosure by a guardian ad litem of information given to her in the preparation of her report to a duty social worker who in turn informed the police. It was therefore not concerned with information that was subject, or potentially subject, to legal professional privilege. Additionally, I comment in respect of this case that there is now later authority relating to disclosure of material to the police.

As to the accepted existence, of this duty, I was also referred to *Essex County Council v R* [1994] Fam 167, [1993] 2 FLR 826 in particular at 168–9 and 828–829 respectively, *Re DH (A Minor) (Child Abuse)* [1994] 1 FLR 679 in particular 704B. All these cases were referred to in the speeches in *Re L*.[1] In particular, Lord Jauncey refers to them at [1997] AC 16, 28C–H, [1996] 1 FLR 731, 739G–740E, under the heading 'Voluntary disclosure' where he cites some of the passages from them that I was referred to and expressly states that in view of his conclusion on legal professional privilege he does not find it necessary to come to a decision on the point asserted that there was a duty to make voluntary disclosure of all matters likely to be material to the welfare of a child, and thus of the report in question in *Re L*.

The question, however, arises in this case whether the accepted existence of this duty of disclosure overrides a right of a party to Children Act

---

[1] *Re L (A Minor) (Police Investigation: Privilege)* [1996] 1 FLR 731, HL. See G78 – Litigation privilege does not arise in non-adversarial proceedings.

proceedings where the welfare of the child is the court's paramount consideration to claim legal professional privilege which arises in, or in connection with, other proceedings. In my judgment, the existence of this duty does not do so. My reasons for this conclusion are:

(a)   It is accepted in the *Derby Magistrates*[2] case that legal professional privilege can be removed, excluded, overridden or qualified by statute (see [1996] 1 AC 487, 507G–H, [1996] 1 FLR 513, 527D–F). As is shown by the cases relating to the privilege against self-incrimination (see, for example, *Re London United Invest-ments plc* [1992] Ch 578, 594G–599G and *Bishopsgate Investment Management (In Provisional Liquidation) v Maxwell; Cooper v Maxwell; Mirror Group Newspapers plc v Maxwell* [1993] Ch 1, 18G–20H, 39C and 56A–G) the removal etc of a right or privilege (i) has to be done by statute, and (ii) can be achieved by express words or necessary implication. If it is not done expressly the implication must be clear because, for example, if the common-law right, or privilege, was not removed etc, the statute would be prevented from achieving its obvious purpose. The duty of disclosure in cases concerning children is not one imposed by statute and it arises in cases concerning children that are not based on statute, as well as those that are. Of itself therefore the duty cannot remove, exclude, override or qualify legal professional privilege and the common-law rights it confers once it has been established.

(b)   In cases under the Children Act 1989 it can be said that the duty is based on the statute, but as I have explained in my judgment the House of Lords in *Re L* do not decide that the effect of the Children Act 1989 is to override or qualify legal professional privilege. Rather, they decide that legal professional privilege did not arise in respect of the report under consideration in that case.

(c)   The House of Lords in *Re L* recognise and confirm that some material relevant to the welfare of the child who is the subject of proceedings where his welfare is the court's paramount considera-tion is subject to legal professional privilege and does not have to be volunteered in the proceedings, namely communications between a party and his or her lawyer (see [1997] AC 16, 24H–25A and 27H, [1996] 1 FLR 731, 736E–G and 739E).

(d)   Point (c) is subject to the duties of advisers not to mislead but it is a recognition and confirmation that the important public interest in promoting the welfare of children, the statutory duty imposed by s 1 of the Children Act 1989 and what Lord Jauncey describes as the primary object of the Act ([1997] AC 16, 27F, [1996] 1 FLR 731, 739D) do not lead to the conclusion (i) that legal professional privilege does not arise or have a part to play in cases under the Children Act 1989, or (ii) that legal professional privilege andthe

---

[2]   *R v Derby Magistrates' Court ex parte B* [1996] 1 FLR 513, HL. See G77 – Legal advice privilege arises.

public interest on which it is based is always subordinated to the public interest in promoting the welfare of children.

(e) This recognition and confirmation shows (i) that legal professional privilege has a place in proceedings under the Children Act 1989,(ii) that there are public interests that are strong enough to compete with and override the public interest in promoting the welfare of children that underlies the Children Act 1989 and the wardship jurisdiction, and thus proceedings where on all, or some, of the issues that arise the paramount concern of the court is the welfare of a child, and (iii) that the duty of disclosure in cases relating to children under the Children Act 1989 which is based on the nature of those proceedings and the purposes of the Children Act 1989 does not override or qualify legal professional privilege or the rights it confers when it has been established.

(f) In my judgment it should be remembered when issues based on public interest arise in cases concerning children that all issues in respect of such proceedings are not governed by the paramountcy principle, for example (i) the exercise of the power under s 38(6) to order an assessment and thereby obtain further evidence (see *Re C (A Minor) (Interim Care Order: Residential Assessment)* [1997] AC 489, sub nom *Re C (Interim Care Order: Residential Assessment)* [1997] 1 FLR 1 and *Re M (Residential Assessment Directions)* [1998] 2 FLR 371), and (ii) in my view the establishment of the threshold criteria and thus the jurisdiction of the court to go on to the 'welfare or disposal' stage in care proceedings (see *Re M (A Minor) (Care Order: Threshold Conditions)* [1994] 2 AC 424, [1994] 2 FLR 577 and *Southwark London Borough Council v B* [1998] 2 FLR 1095). These examples show that in respect of some issues relating to admission of evidence and jurisdiction the paramountcy principle does not apply and therefore does not apply to the issue whether legal professional privilege arises, or can be overridden, when such issues are considered by the court.

(g) More generally as to point (f) in proceedings relating to children the interests of adults, and in particular their parents, are affected. It follows that there is a need to be fair to them and the fact that in deciding what order should be made in respect of a child the court applies the paramountcy principle does not mean that in determining how the proceedings should be conducted fairly and thus, for example, whether legal professional privilege arises or can be overridden that principle should also apply. As to this it is to be noted that (i) *Re C (A Minor) (Interim Care Order: Residential Assessment)* [1997] AC 489, sub nom *Re C (Interim Care Order: Residential Assessment)* [1997] 1 FLR 1 and *Re M (Residential Assessment Directions)* [1998] 2 FLR 371 show that the court determines what best promotes the welfare of the child in a given case on the basis of the admissible and available evidence, but in determining what that evidence should be its paramount concern is not the welfare of the child, and (ii) in the *Derby Magistrates* case the House of Lords recognise and confirm that in establishing legal professional privilege the courts have been concerned with identifying how the overall public interest in doing justice is best served and the identification of a condition on which the administration of justice as a whole rests (see Lord Taylor at [1996] 1 AC 487, 507D, [1996] 1 FLR 513, 527B).

(h) Although I confess that it is not clear to me what developments in practice the majority in *Re L* had in mind when leaving open the argument based on voluntary disclosure (at [1997] AC 16, 28H, [1996] 1 FLR 731, 740E), in my judgment by doing so they did not have in mind or leave open (i) an argument that the duty to disclose might override legal professional privilege in respect of communications between solicitor and client, or (ii) legal professional privilege that has arisen outside proceedings under the Children Act 1989. In my judgment this follows from their rejection of the conclusion in the *Oxfordshire* case [1994] Fam 151, 161, [1994] 1 FLR 175, 185 that the court had power to override the privilege and their express statement that: 'This does not of course affect privilege arising between solicitor and client' (see 27F–H and 739E–F). As I understand it the reference to 'this' is the conclusion that litigation privilege never arose in the first place.

(i) In *Oxfordshire County Council v P* [1995] Fam 161, 166B, [1995] 1 FLR 552, 557F Ward J links the duty of disclosure in cases concerning children to that relating to ancillary relief, which in turn is linked to, or is similar to, the duty or obligation to give discovery in other civil proceedings. That last duty, or obligation, is subject to an exception in respect of material covered by legal professional privilege and in my judgment there is no necessary implication that either of the other two duties should override or qualify legal professional privilege once it has been established.

This case is also included in relation to:

G76 Privilege: defining key terms
G79 Litigation privilege arises in adversarial proceedings
G81 Effect of legal professional privilege

G81 EFFECT OF LEGAL PROFESSIONAL PRIVILEGE

S County Council v B

[2000] 2 FLR 161 at 186 and 188

Family Division

Charles J

Overall conclusion on legal professional privilege

In my judgment, for the reasons I have given:

(1)   the father can claim legal professional privilege in respect of his (direct or indirect) communications with, and the reports of, the medical experts he instructs solely for the purposes of the criminal proceedings, and

(2)   on that basis (and thus so long as he has not waived the privilege) the father has an absolute right to refuse to disclose such communications and reports in these care proceedings.

Disclosure of the names of the experts instructed by the father in the criminal proceedings

At an early stage of these proceedings it appeared that this was the relief sought against the father. Later it was put as an alternative. The only purpose for seeking and making such an order would be to enable the guardian ad litem and other parties to these care proceedings to approach such experts and seek evidence from them either voluntarily or pursuant to a subpoena.

The purpose of making such an order would therefore be to obtain from those witnesses the material that I have concluded is covered by legal professional privilege and which the father has an absolute right to refuse to disclose.

It was argued that such an order could and should be made because there is 'no property in a witness' and reliance was placed on the passage in the speech of Lord Jauncey in *Re L* [1997] AC 16, 25B, [1996] 1 FLR 731, 736G where he refers to *Harmony Shipping Co SA v Saudi Europe Line Ltd; Same v Orri (Trading as Saudi Europe Line); Same v Davis and Another* [1979] 1 WLR 1380, 1386G.

In my judgment a witness or potential witness should not volunteer material that is covered by legal professional privilege and should not be compelled by the court to provide such material unless of course the witness has the consent of the person who has the benefit of the privilege. In my judgment this flows from the nature of legal professional privilege and the rights it gives, namely that the privilege is the client's privilege and it gives him an absolute right to refuse disclosure.

...

In my judgment it follows that the father can refuse to, and should not be ordered to, disclose the names of the experts he instructs for the purposes of the criminal proceedings.

This does not mean that the father has any 'property in those experts' and in this case there is no need to consider potentially difficult questions relating to what the position would be if one party approached an expert who had already given a report or advice covered by litigation privilege to another party on the basis that he was content that the expert should not disclose any of that material and should only give his expert view on material that is known to both parties. This is because as I have explained earlier:

(a) this is not the position of the guardian ad litem and does not reflect the reason why the order for disclosure is being sought in these care proceedings, and

(b) in these care proceedings it is unlikely that leave would be given to admit such additional expert evidence.

This case is also included in relation to:

G76 Privilege: defining key terms
G79 Litigation privilege arises in adversarial proceedings
G80 Legal professional privilege not overridden by general duty of disclosure

G82   PUBLIC INTEREST IMMUNITY

Re R (Care: disclosure: nature of proceedings)

[2002] 1 FLR 755 at 776 and 777

Family Division

Charles J

Importantly, as was done by the House of Lords in *Re D (Minors) (Adoption Reports: Confidentiality)* [1996] AC 593, sub nom *Re D (Adoption: Reports: Confidentiality)* [1995] 2 FLR 687, at the end of his judgment in *Re B (Disclosure to Other Parties)* [2001] 2 FLR 1017, Munby J emphasised the point that it is only if the case for non-disclosure is convincingly and compellingly demonstrated that an order for non-disclosure will be made and in most cases the needs of a fair trial will demand that there be no restrictions on disclosure even if the case for restrictions is made out, the restrictions must go no further than is strictly necessary.

I respectfully agree with that. Further, in my judgment, this approach underlay and underlies the correct approach to public interest immunity.

Public interest immunity is a descriptive term for a basis for refusing disclosure of relevant material at a trial. It is based on a public interest that is strong enough to compete with, and sometimes prevail over, the public interest in there being a fair trial and, consequently to that end, disclosure of all material that passes the relevant threshold test for disclosure. Thus, it gives rise to the need to consider competing public interests.

Since *R v Chief Constable of West Midlands Police ex parte Wiley; R v Chief Constable of Nottinghamshire Police ex parte Sunderland* [1995] 1 AC 274, there has been a considerable review of the law, practice and approach relating to public interest immunity, which included statements to both Houses of Parliament, which were adopted by the Labour Government that followed.

...

That review and decisions of the court in other areas are relevant to the question whether public interest immunity attaches to material in the hands of a local authority. In my judgment, the result of that review and those authorities is that:

(a) any case on public interest immunity that precedes *R v Chief Constable of West Midlands Police ex parte Wiley; R v Chief Constable of Nottinghamshire Police ex parte Sunderland* [1995] 1 AC 275 or post-dates it but does not include a careful consideration of that case and the developments in the law and practice relating to public interest immunity that followed should be regarded with caution and carefully reconsidered. For example, in my judgment, that applies to the decision of the Court of Appeal in *Re M (A Minor: Disclosure of Material)* [1990] 2 FLR 36;

(b) general statements that one sees in textbooks and hears that social work records are covered by public interest immunity, which is a widely stated class claim, should now be consigned to history;

(c) anyone advancing a claim to public interest immunity in respect of material held by a local authority should take advice and set out with particularity the harm that it is alleged will be caused to the public interest, for example the proper conduct of the duties of a local authority in respect of the protection of children, if material which passes the threshold test for disclosure is disclosed with or without appropriate redaction in the relevant proceedings; and

(d) before embarking on a claim to public interest immunity or another basis for opposing disclosure consideration should be given to the question whether the material passed the threshold test for disclosure and if so why.

Generally, I make the point that, as Munby J emphasised in *Re B (Disclosure to Other Parties)* [2001] 2 FLR 1017, in respect of claims for non-disclosure based on Art 8 a compelling case for non-disclosure based on public interest immunity needs to be made out and any non-disclosure must go no further than is strictly necessary, having regard to the competing public interests.

Other significant cases on this issue:

• *Re J (Care proceedings: disclosure)* [2003] EWHC 976 (Fam), [2003] 2 FLR 522: see D69 – Section 42 not to be given restrictive meaning and not trumped by PII

This case is also included in relation to:

D5   Reunification not an overriding factor
G22   Preparation and disclosure: duties of LA
G23   Preparation and disclosure: mirror duties of respondents
G24   Disclosure of relevant notes
G41   Court / parties / experts bound by findings made / not made
G45   Use of experts: general guidance
G51   Responsibilities on receipt of report
G75   Statement of general principles (2)

H29 Costs: illustration in public law

G83   PRIVILEGED DISCUSSIONS FOR CONCILIATION

Re D (Minors) (conciliation: privilege)

[1993] 1 FLR 932 at 935 and 937

Court of Appeal

Bingham MR

See A15 – Statements made in conciliation generally not admissible

G84   ECHR, ART 8 AS A BASIS FOR NON-DISCLOSURE

Re B (Disclosure to other parties)

[2001] 2 FLR 1017 at 1019, 1020, 1022, 1023, 1038 and 1039

Family Division

Munby J

[1] This is the fourth occasion in recent months when I have had to consider the implications of Art 8 of the European Convention for the Protection of Human Rights and Fundamental Freedoms 1950 in the context of disputes as to the disclosure of documents filed or generated forensically in the course of proceedings in the Family Division or in county courts exercising family jurisdiction.

[2] In February 2001, I had to consider whether the Art 8 rights of a proven perpetrator of sexual abuse justified withholding from the victims of his abuse the court's findings against him: *Re X (Disclosure of Information)* [2001] 2 FLR 440. In May 2001, I had to consider whether the Art 8 rights of a general practitioner's patients would be breached by the communication to a regulatory authority of medical records and other confidential information about them held on the court file: *A Health Authority v X (Discovery: Medical Conduct)* [2001] 2 FLR 673. In June 2001, I had to consider whether the publication by a disgruntled litigant of the details of proceedings under Part IV of the Family Law Act 1996 heard in chambers infringed her opponent's rights under, inter alia, Art 8: *Clibbery v Allan* [2001] 2 FLR 819. Now in July 2001 I have to consider whether one of the parties to litigation can set up her Art 8 rights as a ground for resisting the disclosure to another litigant of documents which would otherwise be in the trial bundle.

…

[6] This dispute has raised the important question of the extent to which, if at all, the decision of the House of Lords in *Re D (Minors) (Adoption Reports: Confidentiality)* [1996] AC 593, sub nom *Re D (Adoption Reports: Confidentiality)* [1995] 2 FLR 687 requires to be re-visited in the light of the Human Rights Act 1998, in particular having regard to Art 8. On this issue I have had the benefit of detailed arguments from Miss Sarah Phillimore of counsel on behalf of the mother, Mr David Williams of counsel on behalf of W, Miss Rachael Young of counsel on behalf of R, Mr Gary Crawley of counsel on behalf of the

children's guardian ad litem and Miss Marianna Hildyard of counsel on behalf of the local authority. I am grateful to each of them for their very great assistance. As will appear in due course they have helpfully directed my attention to a substantial volume of Convention case-law.

...

[13]   The mother concluded by saying:

'Neither my children nor myself feel that our privacy is invaded if [G] or [W] have access to the documents in the care proceedings. However the situation regarding [R] is completely different. He has not been involved with my family for many years, and when he was involved it was as a violent and frightening man. He has no need for any information relating to myself, [K, S or B] and only a very limited need for information regarding [H]. I therefore request that this court acknowledge and protect my family's right to privacy.'

[14]   That, if I may say so, is a powerful and moving plea which I find wholly understandable in human terms. Lawyers and others who spend their professional lives dabbling in the stuff of other people's misery may not always appreciate as much as they should the embarrassment and worse – sometimes, understandably, the shame, humiliation and anger – that someone in the mother's position must feel as strangers pick over and dissect the most intimate aspects of private and family life. Recognition of that reality of course underlies the restrictions which the Family Division traditionally imposes on the public dissemination of information relating to proceedings in chambers, more particularly when those proceedings concern children. That is not an issue with which I am here concerned. But the situation with which I am concerned can equally give rise to a powerful feeling that, as the mother says here, her family's right to privacy is being invaded, as she would have it for no legitimate or appropriate purpose, in a manner which she says, and I accept, makes her feel sickened and disgusted. I do not dwell on these matters in any way to criticise or condemn the mother. Far from it. Her feelings are entirely human and natural. Understandably she wishes to protect her family and her children.

...

[16]   R for his part says that fairness demands that he sees documents without which, he says, he cannot have a fair trial. He is entirely content that in the documents which are supplied to him there should be removed or obliterated all references to the current addresses of the children and the other parties and all identifying references to any of the children's schools. Subject to that, he claims to be entitled to see all the documents in just the same way as each of the other parties to the proceedings.

...

[62]   So, say Miss Phillimore and Mr Williams, R's right to see the documents is not itself absolute. A limited qualification of his right is acceptable if reasonably directed towards a clear and proper objective – in the present case, the legitimate aim being the protection of the Art 8 rights of the children *and the mother* – and if representing no greater qualification of R's rights than the situation calls for. That, they say, is to be assessed by reference to the usual Convention criteria of proportionality between the means employed and the aim sought to be achieved. They assert that, even if he is not supplied with the documents to which they take objection, R's right to a fair trial will not be compromised and there will be no breach of his rights under Art 6.

[63]   So far as concerns the general point of principle I agree with Miss Phillimore and Mr Williams.

[64]   In the first place, although R is entitled under Art 6 to a fair trial, and although his right to a fair trial is absolute and cannot be qualified by either the mother's or the children's or, indeed, anyone else's rights under Art 8, that does *not* mean that he necessarily has an absolute and unqualified right to see all the documents. This seems to me to follow quite clearly from the Court's decisions in *Doorson v The Netherlands* (1996) 22 EHRR 330 and *Campbell and Fell v United Kingdom* (1984) 7 EHRR 165 (as from the Commission's earlier decision in *Hendriks v The Netherlands* (1983) 5 EHRR 223) and from what the Privy Council said in *Brown v Stott (Procurator Fiscal, Dunfermline) and Another* [2001] 2 WLR 817. On this aspect of the matter I see nothing in subsequent Convention jurisprudence to cast any doubt on what the House of Lords said in *Re D (Minors) (Adoption Reports: Confidentiality)* [1996] AC 593, sub nom *Re D (Adoption Reports: Confidentiality)* [1995] 2 FLR 687.

...

[66]   Secondly, however, I am satisfied that there is no longer, if there ever was, any warrant for saying that the only interests capable of denying a litigant access to the documents in a proper case are the interests of the *child(ren)* involved in the litigation. If the interests of a child are capable in a proper case of having this effect then so in principle, it seems to me, must the interests of anyone else who is involved, whether as victim, party or witness, and who can demonstrate that their Art 8 rights are sufficiently engaged. Whatever may have been the position in domestic law prior to the coming into force of the Human Rights Act 1998 and at the time when the House of Lords decided *Re D (Minors) (Adoption Reports: Confidentiality)* [1996] AC 593, sub nom *Re D (Adoption Reports: Confidentiality)* [1995] 2 FLR 687 s 6(1) and 6(3)(a) of the Act forbid me, as a public authority, to act in a way which is incompatible with a Convention right. The Act accordingly, in my judgment, requires me to have regard in this context to the Art 8 rights of the mother and W as well as of the children. Section 2(1) of the Act requires me to 'take into account' any judgment of the European Court of Human Rights which is 'relevant to the proceedings' with which I am concerned. The Court's decisions in *Doorson v The Netherlands* (1996) 22 EHRR 330, *Z v Finland* (1998) 25 EHRR 371 and *Campbell and Fell v United Kingdom* (1984) 7 EHRR 165, in particular, and the Privy Council's analysis in *Brown v Stott (Procurator Fiscal, Dunfermline) and Another* [2001] 2 WLR 817 make it impossible in my judgment to confine the exception recognised by Lord Mustill in *Re D (Minors) (Adoption Reports: Confidentiality)* [1996] AC 593, sub nom *Re D (Adoption Reports: Confidentiality)* [1995] 2 FLR 687 to cases where there is reason to fear harm to the *child(ren)*. There can be cases, in my judgment, where a litigant's right to see the documents may have to give way not merely in the interests of the child(ren) involved but also, or alternatively, to the Art 8 rights of one or more of the adults involved, whether as victim, party or witness. If and insofar as the House of Lords decided the contrary in *Re D* (and it is not at all certain that it did), then to that extent its decision, in my judgment, can no longer stand in the light of the Human Rights Act 1998. In my judgment, *Re D* can no longer stand as authority for the proposition that only the child(ren)'s interests can be taken into account.

[67] Applying the Convention case-law to which I have already referred the position can be summarised for present purposes as follows:

(1)   R is entitled under Art 6 to a fair trial. So also, of course, are the mother, the children, W and G. The parties' rights to a fair trial are absolute. Their rights to a fair trial cannot be qualified by the mother's or the children's or anyone else's rights under Art 8.

(2)   R's right to a fair trial means that he (like all the other parties) is entitled to be involved in the decision-making process, seen as a whole, to a degree sufficient to provide him with the requisite protection of his interests. He must be able to participate in such a way as will enable him not only to influence the outcome of the proceedings but also to assess his prospects of thereafter making an appeal to any relevant appellate court. He must have a reasonable opportunity to present his case – including his evidence – under conditions that do not place him at a substantial disadvantage vis-à-vis his opponents. He must have a reasonable opportunity to have knowledge of and comment on the observations filed or evidence adduced by the other parties.

(3)   Prima facie this means that R is entitled to disclosure of *all* materials which may be taken into account by the court when reaching a decision adverse to him. If he is a party to the proceedings he is prima facie entitled to see *all* the documents that are available to the other parties.

(4)   Nevertheless the decision-making process, although it must be fair to R (and to all the other parties), must also, so far as is compatible

with that overriding requirement, be such as to afford due respect to the interests of the children, the other parties and the witnesses safeguarded by Art 8.

(5)   So, a limited qualification of R's right to see the documents may be acceptable if it is reasonably directed towards a clear and proper objective – in other words, if directed to the pursuit of the legitimate aim of respecting some other person's rights under Art 8 – and if it represents no greater a qualification of R's rights than the situation calls for. There may accordingly be circumstances in which, balancing a party's prima facie Art 6 right to see all the relevant documents and the Art 8 rights of others, the balance *can* compatibly with the Convention be struck in such a way as to permit the withholding from a party of some at least of the documents. The balance is to be struck in a way which is fair and which achieves a reasonable relationship of proportionality between the means employed and the aim sought to be achieved, having regard to the nature and seriousness of the interests at stake and the gravity of the interference with the various rights involved.

(6)   Bearing in mind the importance of the rights guaranteed by Art 6, and the fact that, as Sedley LJ pointed out in *Douglas, Zeta-Jones, Northern and Shell plc v Hello! Ltd* [2001] 1 FLR 982, para 141, Art 8 guarantees only 'respect' for and not inviolability of private and family life, any restriction of a party's right to see the documents in the case must, as it seems to me, be limited to what the situation imperatively demands. Non-disclosure can be justified only when the case for doing so is, to use Lord Mustill's word, 'compelling' or where it is, to use the Court's words in *Campbell and Fell v United Kingdom* (1984) 7 EHRR 165, 'strictly necessary'.

(7)   Moreover, to adopt Lord Mustill's word, the court must be 'rigorous' in its examination of the risk and gravity of the feared harm to the child or other person whose Art 8 rights are said to be engaged.

(8)   Finally, any difficulties caused to a litigant by a limitation on his right to see all the documents must be sufficiently counterbalanced by proedures designed to ensure, in accordance with the principles in (2) above, that he receives a fair trial.

(9)   At the end of the day the court must be satisfied that whatever procedures are adopted, and whatever limitations on a litigant's access to documents may be imposed, everyone involved in the proceedings receives a fair trial.

[68]   Before leaving questions of principle there is one final matter that must not be forgotten. It is encapsulated in Lord Mustill's reference to 'the interest of the child in having the material properly tested'. As I have already observed, it is not only the individual litigant's right to a fair trial which may point in the direction of disclosure of the documents to him. The interests of the other litigants may well point in the same direction, for the children and other parties also have a right to a fair trial and, as

part of their right to a fair trial, the right to have the forensic materials properly tested. It may well be that only if there is disclosure to *all* concerned can the children and other parties to the proceedings be confident that the materials have been properly tested. So it may often be that disclosure of the documents to the individual litigant is not merely for his benefit but also for the benefit of the others and the children in particular.

Other significant cases on this issue:

- *Re X (Adoption: confidential procedure)* [2002] EWCA Civ 828, [2002] 2 FLR 476 at [14]–[16]
- *Re A (a child) (care proceedings: non-disclosure)* [2009] EWCA Civ 1057, [2010] 2 FLR 1757

G85 SECURE EDITING OF DOCUMENTS

Re R (Secure editing of documents)

[2007] 2 FLR 759 at 760 and 762

Family Division

Peter Jackson QC sitting as a deputy High Court judge

[1] Great efforts are made to protect the anonymity of adopters in confidential adoption proceedings. In the relatively few cases of other kinds that call for the same approach – of which this case and *Re F (A Child) (Indirect Contact Through Third Party)* [2006] EWCA Civ 1426, [2007] 1 FLR 1015 are examples – there is every reason why the same care should be taken.

[2] The court has overall control of the litigation process and has a clear responsibility to take all necessary measures to ensure that confidential information is not given out as a side-effect of legal proceedings.

[3] Disturbingly, this is exactly what happened in this case, which came before me recently. The father was applying for contact to his three young children. For good reason the mother's new married name and current address were not to be disclosed. Despite this, the father was sent the information in inefficiently edited documents. This is not the first case in which such a thing has happened. I will describe what occurred and suggest how it could be avoided in future.

...

[17] Overall, the careless distribution of documents gathered for the purposes of litigation has amounted to a gross breach of the mother's right to respect for her private and family life.

[18] In order to avoid repetition of instances of this kind, I have brought the circumstances of this case to the attention of the President of the Family Division, who has approved the following statement by way of future guidance.

[19] Wherever sensitive confidential information is to be protected, the following procedure should apply:

(1) The court should identify that a case falls into this category and make a clear statement that special restrictions will apply.

(2)   A direction should be given that information of a clearly specified kind *shall not* be contained in any document filed, gathered or circulated in the proceedings. It is insufficient to *allow* the information to be withheld.

(3)   In considering whether to order documentary disclosure, the court should bear in mind the risk that confidential information may inadvertently be compromised, and avoid making unnecessarily wide orders. It is notoriously burdensome to edit large amounts of documentation accurately and mistakes are easily made.

(4)   The chain of possession should be spelled out. The documents should in the first instance be gathered by one appropriately selected party and only released once they have been carefully checked.

(5)   Responsibility for the process should be given to one or more named individuals. The guardian's solicitor, where there is one, may be the obvious candidate. The solicitor for the party who wishes to withhold the information might well be given the opportunity to check the edited documents before they go to the party from whom the information is to be withheld. A timetable can be imposed to avoid delay.

(6)   There should always be a second editor where there is a significant volume of material to be edited, or where the potential consequences of inadvertent disclosure are serious.

(7)   The editing/checking process should be carried out by someone who knows the details of the case and the importance of the task. It is not an administrative task that can be delegated. Where appropriate the person(s) carrying out the task should be identified by name ('AB') rather than by title ('the mother's solicitor').

(8)   The editor(s) should know exactly what they are trying to protect. It is obviously not sufficient to say 'the mother's name and address' if the editor does not know what they are.

(9)   The procedure should be tailored to the circumstances of the case.

Disclosure beyond proceedings / media attendance

G86 ACCESS, PUBLICITY AND DISCLOSURE IN CA 1989 PROCEEDINGS

Clayton v Clayton

[2006] EWCA Civ 878, [2007] 1 FLR 11 at 19, 27, 35, 35, 36 and 47

Court of Appeal

Potter P, Wall LJ

POTTER P:

Legal restraints upon access, publicity, and disclosure in Children Act proceedings

[23] Although this appeal is concerned with questions of publicity relating to Children Act proceedings, rather than access by the public to the proceedings themselves, it is helpful to set out the overall legal framework in relation to restrictions on access, publicity, and disclosure in Children Act proceedings. Such restrictions constitute an exception to the general principle that justice is administered in open court, laid down in the seminal decision of *Scott v Scott* [1913] AC 417, (1913) FLR Rep 657.

Access

[24] So far as access is concerned, the position is, in broad terms, that set out by Dame Elizabeth Butler-Sloss P in *Clibbery v Allan* [2002] EWCA Civ 45, [2002] Fam 261, [2002] 1 FLR 565 in which she summarised the effect of the current procedures in family proceedings as an exception to the general rule as follows:

'[43] ... With the exception of wardship and certain declarations in medical cases heard in the High Court, the jurisdiction of the High Court Family Division and of the county courts with family jurisdiction, whether public or private, remains based on statute and regulated by the statutory framework. The hearing of cases is divided into those which are heard in open court and those heard in chambers. The way in which those cases are heard are regulated by rules and not by custom. In all cases, except adoption which has its separate Adoption Rules 1984, the 1991 Rules [the Family Proceedings Rules 1991] direct the court and the parties to the procedure to be adopted and the way in which each case is to be heard.'

[25] Rule 4.16(7) of the Family Proceedings Rules 1991 provides that:

'(7) Unless the court otherwise directs, a hearing of, or directions appointment in, proceedings to which this Part [Part IV] applies shall be in chambers.'

[26] The effect of r 4.16(7) is thus to secure privacy for proceedings under the Children Act 1989 (the 1989 Act) unless the court orders that the matter be heard in open court rather than chambers. Such orders are rare.

[27] The position was clearly summarised by Butler-Sloss LJ in *Re PB (Hearings in Open Court)* [1996] 2 FLR 765, at 769B–D:

'Despite the arguments advanced by Dr P, it is abundantly clear that the courts are bound by r 4.16(7) to hear child cases generally in private. That was obviously the intention of the Rules Committee and it follows the long-established practice in the hearing of child cases. Subrule (7) allows for all or part of the case to be heard in public. In the light of the long-established practice it is unlikely that the judges will, other than rarely, hear the evidence relating to the welfare of the child in public. The judgment is in a somewhat different position. It may be that the practice of giving judgment in private is partly due to the parties not asking for it to be heard in public and partly because in the county court, where the vast majority of children cases are heard, it is less likely that there will be issues of public interest. Where issues of public interest do arise it would seem entirely appropriate to give judgment in open court providing, where desirable in the interests of the child, appropriate directions are given to avoid identification. If the case raises issues of principle or law, the judgments are increasingly provided to the law reporters and are published in the large number of law reports which report family cases. But the majority of cases are of no interest to anyone beyond the parties and their families.'

[28] The position is different in the Court of Appeal. As stated by Butler-Sloss LJ in *Re PB*, at 768F–G:

'Appeals in the Court of Appeal are almost invariably heard in public but oral evidence is almost never given and the appeal is conducted on the documents written and oral argument. The documents placed before the Court of Appeal include a transcript or agreed note of the judgment of the court appealed and frequently some or all of the transcript of the proceedings. It is the practice for the Court of Appeal to give a direction for non-identification of the child in child appeals, exercising the High Court's inherent jurisdiction to protect the child.'

But see the further observations of Thorpe LJ in *Pelling v Bruce-Williams (Secretary of State for Constitutional Affairs Intervening)* [2004] EWCA Civ 845, [2004] Fam 155, [2004] 2 FLR 823, as quoted below at para [41].

[29] The judgment of the Court of Appeal in *Re PB* was considered by the European Court of Human Rights in *B v United Kingdom*; *P v United Kingdom* (2002) 34 EHRR 529; [2001] 2 FLR 261 in which the European Court of Human Rights held that the provisions of r 4.16(7) were compliant with the European Convention for the Protection of Human Rights and Fundamental Freedoms 1950 (the European Convention). It stated, at paras [39] and [40]:

'[39] The applicants submit that the presumption in favour of a private hearing in cases under the Children Act 1989 should be reversed. However, while the Court agrees that Art 6(1) states a general rule that civil proceedings, inter alia, should take place in public, it does not find it inconsistent with this provision for a State to designate an entire class of case as an exception to the general rule where considered necessary for the interests of morals, public order or national security or where required by the interests of juveniles or the protection of the private life of the parties (see *Campbell and Fell v United Kingdom* (1984) 7 EHRR 165, Paras 86–87), although the need for such a measure should always be subject to the Court's control (see, for example, *Riepan v Austria* (Case 35115/97) (unreported) 14 November 2000). The English procedural law can therefore be seen as a specific reflection of the general exceptions provided for by Art 6(1).

[40] Furthermore, the English Tribunals have a discretion to [40] hold Children Act 1989 proceedings in public if merited by the special features of the case, and the judge must consider whether or not to exercise his or her discretion in this respect if requested by one of the parties.'

Publicity and disclosure

[30] So far as publicity and disclosure are concerned s 12(1) of the Administration of Justice Act 1960 (the 1960 Act) as substituted by s 108(5) of, and Sch 13 para 14.2, of the 1989 Act treats children's cases as an exception to the general rule relating to the publication of court proceedings. Section 12 provides that:

'(1) The publication of information relating to proceedings before any court sitting in private shall not in itself be contempt of court except in the following cases, that is to say—

(a) where the proceedings—
   (i) relate to exercise of the inherent jurisdiction of the High Court in respect of minors;
   (ii) are brought under the Children Act 1989, or
   (iii) otherwise relate wholly or mainly to the maintenance or upbringing of a minor ...

(2) Without prejudice to the foregoing subsection, the publication of the text or summary of the whole or part of an order made by a court sitting in private shall not in itself be contempt of court except where the court (having power to do so) expressly prohibits publication.

(3) ...

(4) Nothing in this section shall be construed as implying with any publication is punishable as contempt of court which would not be so punishable apart from the section *and in particular where the publication is not so punishable by reason of being authorised by rules of court.'*

[31] The words I have italicised in subs (4) are those of an amendment made by s 62 of the Children Act 2004 (the 2004 Act). The meaning of the word 'publication' in s 12(1) is effectively the same as that in the law of defamation, so that the statutory restrictions apply to most forms of communication to individuals or wider dissemination through the media.

[32] The recently published Family Proceedings (Amendment No 4) Rules 2005 which came into force on 31 October 2005 have introduced into Part X of the FPR a new r 10.20A which provides for limited exceptions to the blanket rule against disclosure. It reads as follows:

'**10.20A Communication of information relating to proceedings**

(1) This rule applies to proceedings held in private to which these Rules apply where the proceedings—

(a) relate to the exercise of the inherent jurisdiction of the High Court with respect to minors;
(b) are brought under the Act of 1989; or

(c)   otherwise relate wholly or mainly to the maintenance or upbringing of a minor.

(2)   For the purposes of the law relating to contempt of court, information relating to the proceedings (whether or not contained in a document filed with the court) may be communicated—

(a)   where the court gives permission;
(b)   subject to any direction of the court, in accordance with paragraphs (3) or (4) of this rule; or
(c)   where the communication is to—
    (i)   a party,
    (ii)   the legal representative of the party,
    (iii)   a professional legal adviser,
    (iv)   an officer of the service or a Welsh Family Proceedings Officer,
    (v)   the Welfare Officer,
    (vi)   the Legal Services Commission,
    (vii)   an expert whose instruction by a party has been authorised by the court, or
    (viii) a professional acting in furtherance of the protection of children.

(3)   A person specified in the first column of the following table may communicate to a person listed in the second column such information as is specified in the third column for the purpose or purposes specified in the fourth column.'

[33]   The table referred to is headed 'Communication of information without permission of the court'. It permits the following pertinent disclosures to be made by a party to, among other persons:

(i)   a lay adviser or McKenzie Friend any information relating to the proceedings;
(ii)   the party's spouse, cohabitant or close family member for the purpose of confidential discussions enabling the party to receive support from his spouse or close family member;
(iii)   a health care professional or body providing counselling services for children or families to enable the party or any child of the party to obtain health care/counselling; the Children's Commissioner or Children's Commissioner for Wales;
(iv)   a mediator;
(v)   a person conducting an approved research project;
(vi)   a personal body responsible for investigating or determining complaints in relation to legal representatives or professional advisers;

(vii) an elected representative or peer to enable them to give advice, investigate any complaint or raise any question of policy or procedure;

(viii) the General Medical Council (GMC) for the purposes of making a complaint to the GMC;

(ix) a police officer for the purposes of a criminal investigation;

(x) and a member of the Crown Prosecution Service (CPS), to enable the CPS to discharge its functions under any enactment.

[34] The table also provides that the recipient of the information from the party under its provisions may only communicate that information further for the purposes for which he or she received it or for professional development or training '*providing that any communication does not, or is not likely to, identify any person involved in the proceedings without that person's consent*' (emphasis added).

[35] While s 12 of the 1960 Act is comprehensive in relation to the matters which (with the exceptions mentioned) may be not be publicly disclosed, it does not extend to the naming of the child who is the subject of the proceedings. A useful practical guide to the ambit of s 12 of the 1960 Act appears in the form of a working list set out by Munby J in his judgment in *Re B (A Child) (Disclosure)* [2004] EWHC 411 (Fam), [2004] 2 FLR 142 at para [82](v)–(vii); see also para [64]–[65].

Section 97 of the Children Act 1989

[36] Section 97 of the 1989 Act, as amended by s 72 of the Access to Justice Act 1999 and s 62(1) of the 2004 Act provides as follows:

'97 Privacy for children involved in certain proceedings

(1) Rules made under Section 144 of the Magistrates' Courts Act 1980 may make provision for a magistrates' court to sit in private in proceedings in which any powers under this Act or the Adoption and Children Act 2002 may be exercised by the court with respect to any child.

(2) No person shall publish to the public at large or any section of the public any material which is intended, or likely, to identify—

(a) Any child as being involved in proceedings before the High Court, a county court or a magistrates' court in which any power under this Act or the Adoption and Children Act 2002 may be exercised by the court with respect to that or any other child; or

(b) An address or school as being that of a child being involved in any such proceedings.

(3) In any proceedings for an offence under this section it shall be a defence for the accused person to prove that he did not know, and had no reason to suspect, the published material was intended, or likely, to identify the child.

(4) The court or the Lord Chancellor may, if satisfied that the welfare of the child requires it, by order dispense with the requirements of subsection (2) to such extent as may be specified in the order.

(5) For the purposes of this section
"publish" includes—
(a) include in a programme service (within the meaning of the Broadcasting Act 1990); or caused to be published; and
"material" includes any picture or representation.

(6) Any person who contravenes this section shall be guilty of an offence and liable, on summary conviction, to a fine not exceeding level 4 on the standard scale.'

[37] There has been no detailed judicial consideration of s 97 of the 1989 Act, though it has been referred to in passing in *Kelly v British Broadcasting Corporation* [2001] Fam 59, [2001] 1 FLR 197, at 78F and 221 respectively, and *Her Majesty's Attorney-General v Pelling* [2005] EWHC 414 (Admin), [2006] 1 FLR 93 at para [28]. It was also briefly mentioned in the form in which the section was originally enacted in the 1989 Act (ie as relating only to proceedings in the magistrates' court) in *Re PB* at 768G–H. Referring to the question of privacy for proceedings in the magistrates' courts, Butler-Sloss LJ said:

'In the magistrates' courts the procedure has varied in the past according to whether the cases before 1991 were public or private law cases. Family proceedings now heard in the magistrates' courts are bound by s 97 of the Children Act 1989 amending s 69 of the Magistrates' Courts Act 1980 and by r 16(7) of the Family Proceedings Courts (Children Act 1989) Rules 1991. In general the public is not admitted to family proceedings in the magistrates' court, but the press often are admitted.'

[38] The Court of Appeal has recently had occasion to consider s 97 in a limited respect in *Pelling v Bruce-Williams (Secretary of State for Constitutional Affairs Intervening)* [2004] EWCA Civ 845, [2004] Fam 155, [2004] 2 FLR 823, at para [16], where, giving the judgment of the court, Thorpe LJ stated at para [53] that s 97(2) of the 1989 Act did not extend to appellate proceedings in the Court of Appeal.

[39] The ambit of s 97 of the 1989 Act is the subject of detailed submissions by the appellant in this case and I shall turn to them shortly hereafter.

Section 39 of the Children and Young Persons Act 1933

[40] For the purposes of completeness, I refer to s 39 of the Children and Young Persons Act 1933 (the 1933 Act) which provides:

'(1)   In relation to any proceedings in any court ... the court may direct that—

(a)   No newspaper report of the proceedings shall reveal the name, address, or school, or include any particulars calculated to lead to the identification, of any child or young person concerned in the proceedings, either as being the person by or against or in respect of whom proceedings are taken, or being a witness therein;

(b)   No picture shall be published in any newspaper as being or including a picture of any child or young person so concerned in the proceedings as aforesaid;

except in so far (if at all) as may be permitted by the direction of the court.'

[41] So far as the hearing of appeals is concerned, in *Pelling v Bruce-Williams* (see above) the appellant took objection to a notice to the public regarding reporting restrictions posted outside the court. The Court of Appeal held that the court had jurisdiction to impose such restrictions under the inherent jurisdiction of the court in relation to children, and under s 39 of the 1933 Act, at the court's discretion. Having so stated at para [54], Thorpe LJ went on:

'But it is not so evident that either the inherent or statutory jurisdiction justifies the imposition of an automatic restriction without the exercise of a specific discretion in the individual case. Indeed in his subsequent written submission, Mr Cobb suggests that for the future the court should, both at the outset and the conclusion of each appeal concerning children, exercise its specific discretion either to impose or refuse prohibition on the identification of the parties to the appeal. It would, therefore, seem to us to be desirable for the Master of the Rolls and the President to review the standard practice of this court to reflect developments since the decision pronounced in *Re R (Minor) (Court of Appeal: Order against Identification)* [1999] 2 FLR 145 in 1998. This reconsideration should perhaps extend to applications to permission to appeal listed for oral hearing. In relation to such hearings, Mr Cobb submits that the need for caution is all the greater given that:

(a)   permission to appeal is ordinarily sought in the first instance court where statutory protections;

(b)   applications for permission to the Court of Appeal are ordinarily considered by a single Lord Justice on paper which would have the protection of confidentiality under CPR r 52.3(3)–(4)

(c)   oral hearings for permission are often listed without notice at which the respondent is not present to argue against publicity.'

[42]   Having earlier emphasised at para [50] that questions relating to the publicity to be accorded to Children Act proceedings are essentially policy questions, Thorpe LJ stated, at para [55]:

'Policy questions do have to be addressed against this background: in reality, although the Family Proceedings Rules 1991 confer on the judge in any case the discretion to lift the veil of privacy, there is such a strong inherited convention of privacy that the judicial mind is almost never directed to the discretion and, in rare cases where an application is made, a fair exercise may be prejudiced by the tradition or an unconscious preference for the atmosphere created by a hearing in chambers. Judges need to be aware of this and to be prepared to consider another course where appropriate.'

[43]   It is right to note that the review called for by Thorpe LJ in para [54] of his judgment has not yet taken place. However, there is at the time of this judgment a governmental review in progress which is examining the whole question of openness (or 'greater transparency' as it is often called) in relation to proceedings involving children for the purpose of issuing a consultation paper with a view to making decisions on the matters of policy involved.

...

Discussion

SECTION 97 OF THE 1989 ACT

[48]   Mr Brian Jubb, who has appeared as advocate to the court instructed by CAFCASS Legal, supports the position of the appellant that, whereas the prohibition on publication contained in s 97 of the 1989 Act prevents identification of children involved in Children Act proceedings while the proceedings continue, such prohibition ends when the proceedings are concluded. My initial reaction to his position was one of surprise because, as I understand it, the family courts have proceeded hitherto upon the assumption that the statutory prohibition outlasted the existence of the proceedings, so that any identification of a child as *having been* involved in Children Act proceedings which have ended would

equally amount to a breach of s 97. However, having heard the arguments, I consider that Mr Jubb was right to adopt the position that he did.

[49] First, the language of subs (2) which prohibits publication of any material 'intended, or likely, to identify ... any child *as being involved* in any proceedings before the High Court,' (emphasis added) is on the face of it language which relates to proceedings which are current. Its form is explicable as a provision designed to prevent harassment of children while the proceedings continue. Secondly, subs (2) is a penal provision (see subs (6)) and as such falls to be construed restrictively.

[50] Thirdly, the prohibition in s 97(2) constitutes a specific restriction on the media's right of free expression under Art 10 of the European Convention. In this respect, s 3(1) of the 1998 Act requires that:

> 'So far as it is possible to do so, primary legislation and subordinate
> legislation must be read and given effect in a way that is compatible
> with the [European] Convention rights.'

[51] It is plainly open to be argued in relation to s 97 that, headed as it is 'Privacy for Children Involved in Certain Proceedings', the focus should be on Art 8 considerations and thus a European Convention compatible construction should lead to an interpretation in accordance with previous judicial assumption that the wording, though inapt, should be read as extending to prevent publication of any material likely to identify the child as *having been* involved in the proceedings once complete. However, given the existence of s 12 of the 1960 Act which is apt to prevent publication or reporting of the substance of, or the evidence or issues in, the proceedings (save insofar as permitted by the court or as revealed in any judgment delivered in open court), I do not think that, as a generality, it is right to assume that identification of a child as having been involved in proceedings will involve harm to his or her welfare interests or failure to respect the child's family or private life.

[52] There is a further point which arises under the European Convention jurisprudence, and it is this. The terms of Art 10(2), which provides that the exercise of that freedom proclaimed in Art 10(1) may be subject to such restrictions or penalties as are prescribed by law, give rise to a requirement of legal certainty, not least as to the length or period of the prohibition. I have already expressed the view that, on a straightforward reading, the words themselves are to be read as limited to the duration of the proceedings; but, even if this were not so, the terms of s 3 of the 1998 Act require that the legislation be so construed.

[53] That does not of course mean that the provisions of s 12 of the 1960 Act are diluted or otherwise affected. So that while, following an end to the proceedings, the prohibition on identification under s 97 will cease to have effect, the limitation upon reporting information relating to the proceedings themselves under s 12 of the 1960 Act will remain.

[54]   Nor does it mean that, in the course of Children Act proceedings conducted within the High Court, the judge may not, in the welfare interest of the child and in order to protect his or her privacy under Art 8, make an injunction or order which prohibits the identification of the child not simply to the extent set out in s 97(2) of the 1989 Act, but for a period beyond the end of the proceedings (eg until the age of 18). However, in deciding to make a long-term injunction aimed at restricting the reporting and publication of proceedings involving children, the court is obliged in the face of challenge to conduct a balancing exercise between the Art 8 rights of the child and the Art 10 rights of the parent asserting such right, and/ or, where press or media interest is involved, the Art 10 right to report and discuss the circumstances surrounding, as well as the issues arising out of, a case of public interest. In the instant appeal, of course, the focus is not upon the past, ie in relation to the original kidnapping and recovery of C, all of which received high publicity at the time and are expressly exempted from the purview of the injunction, but upon future public discussion of the Children Act proceedings.

[55]   In relation to the exercise of the inherent jurisdiction of the High Court to make orders for the protection of children, the law has developed and been clarified in recent years, in particular by the House of Lords decision in *Re S (A Child) (Identification: Restrictions on Publication)* [2004] UKHL 47, [2005] 1 AC 593, [2005] 1 FLR 591 in which Lord Steyn gave the leading judgment, with which the rest of their Lordships expressed agreement. In that case, Lord Steyn shortly referred to a plethora of previous authority upon the nature and extent of the inherent jurisdiction of the High Court to make orders restricting the discussion and reporting of cases concerning children (see para [22] of his judgment). Lord Steyn made clear that, so far as the existence and scope of the jurisdiction was concerned, such authorities no longer require to be considered, because the foundation of the jurisdiction to restrain publicity in such cases is now derived from rights under the European Convention. At the same time, Lord Steyn also made clear that the authorities referred to might remain of some interest in regard to the ultimate balancing exercise to be carried out as between the competing European Convention rights.

[56]   This approach has the beneficial effect that, with the substitution of the European Convention for the inherent jurisdiction of the High Court as the source of the power to grant anti-publicity injunctions in such cases, it is clear that the power to grant such an injunction on welfare grounds in Children Act proceedings now applies equally to proceedings in the county court as in the High Court, whatever the precise ambit of s 97 of the 1989 Act.

[57] In *Re S*, the conflict was between the child's Art 8 rights to privacy on the one hand and the Art 10 rights of the media to report *criminal* proceedings on the other. As stated by Lord Steyn at para [17] neither Article 8 or 10 as such has precedence over the other and, where the values under the two Articles are in conflict, an intense focus on the comparative importance of the specific rights being claimed in the individual cases is necessary. The justification for interfering with or restricting each right must be taken into account and, finally, the proportionality test must be applied to each.

[58] In *A Local Authority v W, L, W, T & R; (By the Children's Guardian)* [2005] EWHC 1564 (Fam), [2006] 1 FLR 1, I summarised the effects of the judgment in *Re S* in this way:

'There is express approval of the methodology in *Campbell v MGN Ltd* in which it was made clear that each Article propounds a fundamental right which there is a pressing social need to protect. Equally, each Article qualifies the right it propounds so far as it may be lawful, necessary, and proportionate to do so in order to accommodate the other. The exercise to be performed is one of parallel analysis in which the starting point is presumptive parity, in that neither Article has precedence over or trumps the other. The exercise of parallel analysis requires the court to examine the justification for interfering with each right and the issue of proportionality is to be considered in respect of each. It is not a mechanical exercise to be decided on the basis of rival generalities. An intense focus on the comparative importance of the specific rights being claimed in the individual cases is necessary before the ultimate balancing test in the terms of proportionality is carried out.'

[59] Both *Re S* and *A Local Authority v W* were concerned with orders made contra mundum, the effect of which would be to prevent the media exercising their right otherwise uninhibited by statute, fully to report and comment upon criminal proceedings in order to protect a child who was *not* a party, victim or witness in those proceedings. In such an extreme case, both authorities make clear that the grant of any such injunction would and should be rare indeed. However, neither decision was concerned with an order directed to a parent in Children Act proceedings in order to prevent public discussion by the parent of arrangements made, proposed, or ordered in relation to his child, when such discussion would be harmful to the welfare of that child. In such a case, as it seems to me, the observation of Lord Steyn that earlier case-law on the inherent jurisdiction of the High Court may be relevant in regard to the balancing exercise to be carried out under the European Convention provisions applies, because the injunction is sought and granted as part of the court's consideration of a question regarding the upbringing of the child concerned: see s 1(1) of the 1989 Act. In such a case, the child's welfare, which of course includes respect for his or her privacy free from damaging publicity, is the court's paramount consideration see *Re Z (A Minor) (Identification: Restrictions on Publication)* [1997] Fam 1, [1996] 1 FLR 191, per Ward LJ, at 23C–E, 23H–24A, 28B–D and 29D–E, and per Sir Thomas Bingham MR, at 33B–D. Nonetheless, it does not exclude the necessity for the court to consider: (a) the right of the child under Art 8 of the European Convention to privacy, both in relation to the proceedings and the confidentiality of his or her personal data; (b) the right of the parent under Art 10 to tell his or her story to the world; and (c) in the case of an application by media interests, their wish to publish or broadcast the story and/or to comment on the issues involved.

[60] Before leaving the topic of the proper construction of s 97 of the 1989 Act, I should add that I am conscious that the arguments for the restrictive reading which I consider to be appropriate may also be applicable to the broadly similar wording of s 39 of the 1933 Act (see para [40], above) which is of course a provision applying to *any* proceedings in *any* court and is in wide use in the criminal courts in respect of child victims and witnesses. I do not so hold, as the matter does not arise directly in this appeal and has not been argued before us. Quite apart from any differences in wording, there is in relation to criminal trials no similar restraint upon reporting the detail of the trial to that embodied in s 12(1) of the 1960 Act. Thus the effect of permitting a newspaper to report the identity of a child or young person in a case embodying lurid detail as to which there is no restraint on reporting, may have a far more devastating effect on the Art 8 rights of the child concerned. And, even if the imperative of restrictive construction applies to s 39 of the 1933 Act, judges in criminal proceedings will enjoy a power deriving from the child's European Convention rights to make orders similar to those made hitherto, provided that the court has considered the question with care in the course of undertaking the requisite balancing exercise between the effect upon the Art 8 rights of the child concerned and the Art 10 rights of the media: see *Re S*, at paras [23] and [26]–[27].

...

CONCLUSION

[75] I would allow the appeal and discharge the injunction. In its place I would make a prohibited steps order pursuant to s 8 and s 10(1)(b) of the 1989 Act restraining the father until further order from revisiting Portugal with C (he has the rest of Europe in which to take her on holiday if he so wishes) and further restraining him from involving C in any way with the publication of any information relating to his abduction of her. I would add that in my judgment, the father would be wise not to write about it, but ultimately that is a matter for him. That, after all, is what freedom of speech is about. If the father thinks that an exculpatory

account to the world of his discreditable behaviour in abducting C will serve any purpose, he must be free to write it. What he is not free to do is to involve C in that process.

...

[77] The practical consequence which flows from this judgment is that henceforth it will be appropriate for every tribunal, when making what it believes to be a final order in proceedings under the 1989 Act, to consider whether or not there is an outstanding welfare issue which needs to be addressed by a continuing order for anonymity. This will, I think, be a useful discipline for parties, judges and family practitioners alike. If there is no outstanding welfare issue, then it is likely that the penal consequences of s 97 of the 1989 Act will cease to have any effect, and the parties will be able to put into the public domain any matter relating to themselves and their children which they wish to publish, *provided* that the publication does not offend against s 12 of the 1960 Act.

[78] Our judgments in this case are likely to have an impact, and must not be misunderstood. The fact that the provisions of s 97(2) of the 1989 Act cease to operate after the conclusion of the proceedings does not mean that parents are free at that point to draw their children into an ongoing public debate about their welfare or other wider issues. The court, after the conclusion of the proceedings, retains its welfare jurisdiction and will be able to intervene where a child's welfare is put at risk by inappropriate parental identification for publicity purposes. Quite where the line is to be drawn between s 1 of the 1989 Act and Arts 8 and 10 of the European Convention in this context remains to be seen, although I venture to think that in practice most parents will recognise it. But let those parents who do not, be in no doubt that the court's powers under the ss 1 and 8 of the 1989 Act remain, as do its powers to grant injunctions.

[79] So far as this father is concerned, he would do well to reflect on his conduct. His incapacity to recognise the dangerous folly of his abduction of his daughter may in some measure be due to the mother's willingness to co-operate in his wishes to obtain a shared residence order in respect of C. The statement which she put in, however, demonstrated a more jaundiced (and possibly more realistic) view of the father. She appears to have accepted shared residence with reluctance, recognising that the welfare of her child in that respect was a separate matter from the question whether (as the mother plainly believed and believes) the father's concerns to publicise his daughter's identity are focused on his own interests and the interests of fathers generally rather than upon those of C. C's own interests are plainly best promoted by leaving the past behind and avoiding, rather than receiving, publicity in connection with family proceedings. It appears to be the father's intention to publicise the fact that he was involved in proceedings in relation to his own daughter, C,

which ended in the shared parenting agreement publicised by Hedley J in his judgment and that the child is happy and stable as a result. By reason of s 12 of the 1960 Act he will not be at liberty to re-canvass the issues explored in the Children Act proceedings and, on that basis, I am not prepared to infer that the nature of any such publication will be damaging to C. Nor do I consider it necessary to refer the matter back to the judge for consideration of that issue. However, if the father continues to fail to recognise his former parental shortcomings and persists in his attempts to involve C in his attempts at self-exculpation, I fear that further proceedings will ensue. I hope that he will take heed of that warning.

WALL LJ:

[81] I entirely agree with the President's judgment, which I have had the advantage of reading in draft. I also agree with the result which he proposes ...

...

Health warning

[114] I should, however, make it clear that in giving the appellant (and other parents in his position) liberty to identify themselves and their children in post proceedings communications of the kind identified in para [106], above, the court is emphatically not authorising a free for all in which the rights of children cease to be respected. The court retains its powers (to which I allude in more detail later in this judgment) post proceedings to intervene to protect the paramount best interests of children if parental conduct crosses the line which divides legitimate parental freedom of expression on the one hand, and children's welfare and respect for their Art 8 rights on the other.

[115] I anticipate that it may take some time for the full implications of our decision in this case to bed down. No doubt the courts may need, on future occasions, to examine individual instances to see whether the line identified in para [114] above has been crossed. It is for this reason, among others, that I wholeheartedly endorse what the President says in paras [77]–[79] of his judgment. In particular, the discipline of considering, at the end of what is anticipated as being the 'final' hearing in any proceedings under the 1989 Act needs to take into account: (1) whether there is going to be any need for continuing anonymity; (2) whether the children concerned are likely to be identified in the future for any particular purpose; and (3) if so what activities would be appropriate. This discipline will, I think, focus parental minds on the future best interests of their children and ensure that questions of future identification, insofar as they can be, are sensibly addressed.

[116] There is, moreover, a second, non-legal point. In the post proceedings period, parents would also be wise to reflect that, certainly in my experience, the relationship between themselves and their children is rarely enhanced by parents talking about their children in public or identifying them as the unwilling participants in family disputes. Children are entitled to their privacy, and even if the law now allows parents, after the conclusion of proceedings, to engage sensibly in activities such as those identified in para [106] of this judgment, and to identify their children in the process, they would, in my judgment, be wise to think several times before doing so. It is not perhaps well enough understood that one of the primary purposes of hearing children's cases in private is to protect the privacy to which children are entitled. Parents who breach that privacy may well pay a price in terms of their relationships with their children.

General notes:

Only the length of the extract included has led to the exclusion of larger parts of Wall LJ's judgment, with its analysis of s 97 of the CA 1989 (beginning at [92]) and of s 12 of the AJA 1960 (beginning at [118]).

Other significant cases on this issue:

- *A Local Authority v D (Chief Constable of Thames Valley Police intervening)*; *Re D* [2006] EWHC 1465 (Fam), [2006] 2 FLR 1053
- *Moser v Austria* (Application No 12643/02) [2007] 1 FLR 702: see I11 – Opportunity to comment/public hearing/public pronouncement (for an ECtHR perspective)
- *Re Webster; Norfolk County Council v Webster and Others* [2006] EWHC 2733 (Fam), [2007] 1 FLR 1146 at [65]–[78] (access to hearings by eg the media), [48]–[52] and [57]–[64] (reporting of hearings: the statutory restrictions), and [53]–[56] and [79]–[80] (reporting of hearings: judicial discretion and the balancing exercise)
- *A Local Authority v K* [2007] EWHC 1250 (Fam), [2007] 2 FLR 914 (local authority seeking to disclose to mother's employer findings made in care proceedings)
- *Re X (Children)* [2007] EWHC 1719 (Fam), [2008] 1 FLR 589 (CPS seeking permission to use documents in criminal investigation)
- *Re R (Identification: restriction on publication)* [2007] EWHC 2742 (Fam), [2008] 1 FLR 1252
- *Re LM (Reporting restrictions: coroner's inquest)* [2007] EWHC 1902 (Fam), [2008] 1 FLR 1360
- *D v Buckinghamshire County Council* [2008] EWCA Civ 1372, [2009] 1 FLR 881 (disclosure to Department for Children, Schools and Families)

- *Medway Council v G and Others* [2008] EWHC 1681 (Fam), [2008] 2 FLR 1687
- *Z County Council v TS, DS, ES and A* [2008] EWHC 1773 (Fam), [2008] 2 FLR 1800
- *Northumberland County Council v Z, Y, X (by her children's guardian) and the Government and Republic of Kenya* [2009] EWHC 498 (Fam), [2009] 2 FLR 696
- *Re Stedman* [2009] EWHC 935 (Fam), [2009] 2 FLR 852
- *Re N (Family proceedings: disclosure)* [2009] EWHC 1663 (Fam), [2009] 2 FLR 1152 (party wishing to make complaint about expert)
- *Re S-C (Contempt)* [2010] EWCA Civ 21, [2010] 1 FLR 1478
- *Re B, C and D (By the children's guardian)* [2010] EWHC 262 (Fam), [2010] 1 FLR 1708

G87   MEDIA ATTENDANCE

Re Child X (Residence and contact: rights of media attendance: FPR Rule 10/28(4))

[2009] EWHC 1728 (Fam), [2009] 2 FLR 1467 at 1481, 1484, 1486 and 1494

Family Division

Potter P

[34]   These matters provide the immediate background to the change introduced by r 10.28, which confers upon the media in the form of 'duly accredited representatives of news gathering and reporting organisations' an effective right to be present at private hearings of children proceedings, subject to a direction of the court that they may not attend the proceedings, or part of the proceedings, on grounds set out in r 10.28(4)(a) and (b). However, what the rules do not do is to effect any substantial change in the right of the press, once having been admitted to the proceedings with the opportunity to observe them in progress, thereafter to report the detail of such proceedings to the public (who have no such right to be present).

[35]   What goes on in the proceedings remains subject to the terms of s 12(1) of the AJA, the effect of which is to forbid disclosure of the details of proceedings concerning children, save to the limited extent set out by Munby J in 'a working list' in his judgment in *Re B (A Child) (Disclosure)* [2004] EWHC 411 (Fam), [2004] 2 FLR 142, accompanied by the threat of proceedings for contempt of court in respect of organs of the media who transgress its terms.

[36]   While the provisions of s 12 of the AJA are not apt to prevent disclosure of the name of the parties or the identity of any child the subject of the proceedings, that is achieved by s 97(2) of the 1989 Act (as amended by s 72 of the Access to Justice Act 1999 and s 62(1) of the Children Act 2004) which provides that:

'No person shall publish to the public at large or any section of the public any material which is intended, or is likely, to identify—

(a)   Any child as being involved in proceedings before the High Court, a County Court or a Magistrate's Court in which any power under this Act or the Adoption and Children Act 2002 may be exercised by the Court in respect of that or any other child or

(b) An address or school as being that of the child being involved in any such proceedings.'

[37] Further, s 39(1) of the Children and Young Persons Act 1933 provides that:

'In relation to any proceedings in any Court ... the Court may direct that—

(a) No newspaper report of the proceedings shall reveal the name, address, or school, or include any particulars calculated to lead to the identification, of any child or young person concerned in proceedings, either as being the person by or against or in respect of whom proceedings are taken, or being a witness therein;

(b) no picture shall be published in any newspapers being or including a picture of any child or young person so concerned in the proceedings as aforesaid;

(c) except in so far (if at all) as may be permitted by the direction of the Court.'

[38] The net result of all this is that, while the press are entitled to report on the nature of the dispute in the proceedings, and to identify the issues in the case and the identity of the participating witnesses (save those whose published identity would reveal the identity of the child in the case), they are not entitled to set out the content of the evidence or the details of matters investigated by the court. Thus the position has been created that, whereas the media are now enabled to exercise a role of 'watchdog' on the part of the public at large and to observe family justice at work for the purpose of informed comment upon its workings and the behaviour of its judges, they are unable to report in their newspapers or programmes the identity of the parties or the details of the evidence which are likely to catch the eye and engage the interest of the average reader or viewer.

...

[45] Put in terms of the European Convention, the position seems to me to be as follows. The restrictions, ie the grounds for exclusion under r 10.28(4) are in broad terms Art 6 compliant. Paragraph (a)(i) is within the legitimate aim of protecting the interests of juveniles and grounds (a)(ii), (iii) and (b) are legitimised under the heading of 'special circumstances where publicity would prejudice the interests of justice'. It is to be noted in passing that nothing is included in the rule to provide for exclusion of the press where the Art 8 interests of the parties (as opposed

to those of the child) so require. However, one can envisage a situation
where a ground for exclusion, at least for part of the proceedings, might
be required to protect the Art 8 interests of the parties which could
properly justify exclusion of the media under ground (b) to prevent the
press from hearing and/or reporting allegations of an outrageous or
intimate nature before the court's decision as to whether or not they were
established. This might well constitute a serious and irredeemable
invasion of the privacy and/or family life of an adult party if the press
were not excluded.

[46] The task faced by the court in deciding whether or not to exclude
the press in the welfare or privacy interests of a party or third party is to
conduct the balancing exercise and process of parallel analysis first
considered by the House of Lords in *Campbell v MGN Ltd* [2004] UKHL
22, [2004] 2 AC 457, [2004] 2 WLR 1232, [2004] UKHRR 648 and further
elaborated in *Re S (Identification: Restrictions on Publication)* [2004]
UKHL 47, [2005] 1 AC 593, [2004] 3 WLR 1129, [2005] 1 FLR 591 in
respect of the interplay between Arts 8 and 10 of the European
Convention. At para [17], Lord Steyn observed that four propositions
emerged clearly from the decision in *Campbell*:

'First, neither Article has as such precedence over the other.
Secondly, where the values under the two articles are in conflict, an
intense focus on the comparative importance of the specific rights
being claimed in the individual case is necessary. Thirdly, the
justifications for interfering with or restricting each right must be
taken into account. Finally, the proportionality test must be applied
to each. For convenience I will call this the ultimate balancing test.'

[47] The structure of Arts 8 and 10 are both the same; accordingly, the
same considerations apply to the rights protected by each and to the
grounds for restricting those rights. In relation to the interference with
either right it is necessary to consider whether the interference complained
of corresponds to a pressing social need, whether it is proportionate to
the legitimate aim pursued, and whether the reasons given by the national
authority to justify it are relevant and sufficient. All cases are, to an
extent, fact specific and, in relation to press freedom, the question to be
asked is that articulated by Lord Hoffman in the *Campbell* case at
para [56]:

'When press freedom comes into conflict with another interest
protected by the law, the question is whether there is sufficient public
interest in *that particular publication* to justify curtailment of the
conflicting rights.' (Emphasis added)

In that respect, the positive obligations which are imposed on the State
under Art 8 are to respect, and therefore, to protect the interests of private
and family life which embrace the right of autonomy, dignity, respect,

self-esteem, the right to control the dissemination of private and confidential information and to establish and develop relationships with other people. In relation to the question of confidentiality, as Lord Phillips CJ stated in *HRH The Prince of Wales v Associated Newspapers Ltd* [2006] EWCA Civ 1776; [2007] 3 WLR 222 at para [68]:

> 'The test to be applied in considering whether it is necessary to restrict freedom of expression in order to prevent the disclosure of information received in confidence is not simply whether the information is a matter for public interest but whether, in all the circumstances, it is in the public interest that the duty of confidence should be breached. The Court will need to consider whether, having regard to the nature of the information and all the relevant circumstances, it is legitimate for the owner of the information to seek to keep it confidential or whether it is in the public interest that the information should be made public.'

[48] While the task for the court to perform in relation to r 10.28(4) is to apply the same process as the House of Lords in *Re S*, the outcome in terms of the hegemony accorded to the Art 10 rights of the press over the Art 8 rights of the child is by no means necessarily the same. In *Re S*, the court was concerned with an application to restrain the right of the press freely to report criminal proceedings and, in particular, to report the identity of the adult defendant in those proceedings in order to protect the identity and privacy of the defendant's child who was not involved in the proceedings in any way. The dispositive feature in the decision of the House of Lords was: (a) the emphasis it placed upon the importance of the public and media interest in enjoying the uninhibited right both to attend and report on all criminal proceedings; (b) the fact that the child who was sought to be protected was not the subject of or involved in the proceedings in any way; (c) the fact that the provisions of s 39 of the Children and Young Persons Act 1933 directed to the question of child protection in relation to criminal proceedings limited the court's powers to any child or young person concerned in the proceedings as a party or a witness; thus, the right not to be identified which the child was asserting was contemplated but not recognised by domestic legislation. None of those considerations applies to the issues in this case. Whilst the principle of open justice is important in civil proceedings concerning children, the need for the protection of children from publicity in the course of proceedings which concern them, was long ago recognised at common law in *Scott v Scott*, and is provided for in the statutory provisions as to identification to which I have referred at paras [29]–[31] above.

...

The application to exclude

[51] By way of general observation it is important to make the following matters clear. First, private law family cases concerning the children of celebrities are no different in principle from those involving the children of anyone else. An application by a celebrity who happens also to be a parent who is unable to agree with a former spouse or partner over the appropriate arrangements for their child(ren) is not governed by any principle or assumption more favourable to the privacy of the celebrity than that applied to any other parent caught up in the court process. In this respect, and in very different circumstances concerning the publication of the identity of a barrister who had been convicted of criminal offences, (*C v Crown Prosecution Service* [2008] EWHC 854 (Admin), (2008) *The Times* 20 February), Thomas LJ rejected the submission that, in conducting the *Re S* balancing exercise there involved the Court should have regard to the public profile of the appellant:

> '[34] That is because it is fundamental that all persons are equal before the law of England and Wales, as embodied in our common law, our legislation and the Conventions to which this party (*sic*) has subscribed.
>
> [35] No person in this country can enjoy a different status because he holds a public position. It is important to stress that.'

[52] However, in considering whether or not to exclude the press under r 10.28(4)(a)(i), the focus is upon the interests of the child and not the parents. It is almost axiomatic that the press interest in and surrounding the case will be more intense in the case of children of celebrities; and the need for protection of the child from intrusion or publicity, and the danger of leakage of information to the public will similarly be the more intense.

[53] Second, r 10.28 provides that, in order to exclude the press on any of the grounds stated, the court must be satisfied that it is *necessary* to do so. That is wording which picks up and reflects the provisions of the European Convention relevant to the balancing act which the court has to perform as set out in Arts 6(1), 8(2) and 10(2) of the European Convention. We are here concerned with a restriction on the freedom of expression of the media under Art 10(1), (namely the right to receive and impart information and ideas without interference) for the purpose of the protection of the rights of the child to respect for her private and family life.

[54] So far as necessity is concerned, as stated in *R v Shayler* [2002] UKHL 11, [2003] 1 AC 247, [2002] 2 WLR 754, [2002] UKHRR 603, per Lord Bingham of Cornhill at para [23]:

'"Necessary" has been strongly interpreted; it is not synonymous with "indispensable", neither has it the flexibility of such expressions as "admissible", "ordinary", "useful", "reasonable" or "desirable": *Handiside v United Kingdom* (1976) 1 EHRR 734, 754 para 48. One must consider whether the interference complained of corresponds to a pressing social need, whether it is proportionate to the legitimate aim pursued and whether the reasons given by the national authority to justify it are relevant and sufficient under Art 10(2): *The Sunday Times v United Kingdom* (1979) 2 EHRR 245, 277–278 para 62.'

[55] Third, since the ECHR has already held FPR r 4.16(7) to be European Convention-compliant in a form which effectively excluded the press from admission, the introduction of a provision which gives the media the clear prima facie right to be present during the proceedings, subject only to exclusion on limited grounds is plainly European Convention-compliant from the point of view of the media's Art 10 rights. In the light of the wording of r 10.28(4) and the European Convention jurisprudence, the question of necessity in respect of the derogations from those rights must be approached on the basis set out by Lord Bingham of Cornhill above, in the context of the particular facts of the case, and with an eye to the question whether any information received in confidence is involved and therefore at risk by reason of press attendance, as to which see the observations of Lord Phillips CJ quoted at para [47] above.

[56] Fourth, so far as the practice direction of 20 April 2009 is concerned, its reference to the exercise of the court's *discretion* to exclude media representatives from all or part of the proceedings is, strictly speaking, not accurate. In *Financial Times Ltd v Interbrew SA* [2002] EWCA Civ 274, [2002] 2 Lloyd's Rep 229 at para [58] Sedley LJ made clear that where the court has a duty to apply a test of necessity in relation to a series of questions as to legitimacy and proportionality, the duty of the court is to proceed through the balancing exercise, making a value judgment as to the conflicts which arise, rather than to regard the matter simply as an exercise of discretion as between two equally legitimate courses. Thus references to the court's discretion in para [3.1] and in the heading to para [5] in the practice direction dated 20 April 2009 are a misnomer. Nonetheless, the balancing act involved in the weighing of the conflicting but interlocking rights and restraints embodied in Art 10 and Art 8 of the European Convention are highly fact-sensitive from case to case. Thus, in performing the necessary balancing act, and in particular the ultimate test of proportionality, it is the judge dealing with the case who is the person best placed to make the necessary decision.

[57] Fifth, the burden of satisfying the court of the grounds set out in r 10.28(4) is upon the party or parties who seek exclusion, or the court itself in a case where it takes steps of its own motion, to exclude the press. This will be an easier burden to satisfy in the case of temporary exclusion

in the course of the proceedings, in order to meet concerns arising from the evidence of the particular witness or witnesses.

[58] Sixth, in deciding whether or not the grounds advanced for exclusion are sufficient to override the presumptive right of the press to be present and in particular whether or not an order for total exclusion is proportionate, it will be relevant to have regard to the nature and sensitivities of the evidence and the degree to which the watchdog function of the media may be engaged, or whether its apparent interests lie in observing, and reporting on matters relating to the child which may well be the object of interest, in the sense of curiosity, on the part of the public but which are confidential and private and do not themselves involve matters of public interest properly so called. However, while this may be a relevant consideration, it in no sense creates or places any burden of proof or justification upon the media. The burden lies upon the applicant to demonstrate that the matter cannot be appropriately dealt with by allowing the press to attend, subject as they are to the statutory safeguards in respect of identity and under the provisions of s 12 of the 1960 Act.

...

[87] In the light of the media interest to be anticipated in cases involving the children of 'celebrities', whether national or local, I do not consider the provisions of para [6.4] to be an adequate provision to protect the interests of the press and I am of the view that it requires to be reconsidered. Meanwhile, although the practice direction does not expressly so provide, I consider that it is incumbent upon an applicant who wishes to exclude the media from a substantive hearing ab initio to raise the matter with the court prior to the hearing for consideration of the need to notify the media in advance of the proposed application and that, if this is done, the court should require the applicant to notify the media via the CopyDirect service in accordance with the procedure provided for in the Cafcass practice note. The court should at the same time make directions for the hearing of the application whether by way of special appointment or consideration at the outset of the next substantive hearing. It is, of course, not necessary for the matter to be dealt with by a High Court judge and it should, wherever possible, be dealt with by the trial judge. In the light of the view I have expressed, I consider that para [6.4] of the practice direction of 20 April 2009 should be read as if there were added at the end of the final sentence in that paragraph the words 'and should do so by means of the Press Association CopyDirect service, following the procedure set out in the Official Solicitor/Cafcass practice note dated 18 March 2005'.

G88   AJA 1960, S 12 (1)

Re B (A child) (disclosure)

[2004] EWHC 411 Fam, [2004] 2 FLR 142 at 171

Family Division

Munby J

The law: s 12 – summary

[81] Since it is apparent that there is still widespread misunderstanding as to the precise ambit of s 12 it may be helpful if I attempt to summarise the learning. In doing so I wish to emphasise that what follows is not to be treated as if it were a statutory formulation – it is not – nor as a substitute for applying the words of s 12 itself. Moreover, any attempt to summarise an extensive and subtle jurisprudence will inevitably suffer from the inherent difficulties and defects of the exercise. There is no substitute for a careful study of the reported cases. That said, I hope that what follows may provide some practical assistance to those, unfamiliar with all the nuances of the jurisprudence, who may lack the time or opportunity to study the case-law.

[82] For present purposes the relevant principles can, I think, be summarised as follows:

(i)   Section 12(1)(a) of the Administration of Justice Act 1960 has the effect of prohibiting the publication of:

> 'information relating to proceedings before any court sitting in private … where the proceedings (i) relate to the exercise of the inherent jurisdiction of the High Court with respect to minors; (ii) are brought under the Children Act 1989; or (iii) otherwise relate wholly or mainly to the … upbringing of a minor.'

(ii)   Subject only to proof of knowledge that the proceedings in question are of the type referred to in s 12(1)(a), the publication of such information is a contempt of court.

(iii) There is a 'publication' for this purpose whenever the law of defamation would treat there as being a publication. This means that most forms of dissemination, whether oral or written, will constitute a publication. The only exception is where there is a communication of information by someone to a professional, each acting in furtherance of the protection of children.

(iv) Specifically, there is a 'publication' for this purpose whether the dissemination of information or documents is to a journalist or to a Member of Parliament, a Minister of the Crown, a Law Officer, the Director of Public Prosecutions, the Crown Prosecution Service, the police (except when exercising child protection functions), the GMC, or any other public body or public official. The Minister of State for Children is not a child protection professional. Disclosure to the Minister of State cannot, therefore, be justified on the footing of the exception to the general principle.

(v) Section 12 does not of itself prohibit the publication of:

    (a) the fact, if it be the case, that a child is a ward of court and is the subject of wardship proceedings or that a child is the subject of residence or other proceedings under the Children Act 1989 or of proceedings relating wholly or mainly to his maintenance or upbringing;

    (b) the name, address or photograph of such a child;

    (c) the name, address or photograph of the parties (or, if the child is a party, the other parties) to such proceedings;

    (d) the date, time or place of a past or future hearing of such proceedings;

    (e) the nature of the dispute in such proceedings;

    (f) anything which has been seen or heard by a person conducting himself lawfully in the public corridor or other public precincts outside the court in which the hearing in private is taking place;

    (g) the name, address or photograph of the witnesses who have given evidence in such proceedings;

    (h) the party on whose behalf such a witness has given evidence; and

    (i) the text or summary of the whole or part of any order made in such proceedings.

(vi) Section 12 prohibits the publication of:

    (a) accounts of what has gone on in front of the judge sitting in private;

    (b) documents such as affidavits, witness statements, reports, position statements, skeleton arguments or other documents filed in the proceedings, transcripts or notes of the evidence or submissions, and transcripts or notes of the judgment (this list is not necessarily exhaustive);

    (c) extracts or quotations from such documents;

    (d) summaries of such documents.

These prohibitions apply whether or not the information or the document being published has been anonymised.

(vii) (By way of example of how the principles in (v) and (vi) inter-relate) in a case such as the present case s 12 does not of itself prohibit the publication of:

(a)   the issues in the case as being whether the mother suffered from Munchausen's Syndrome by Proxy and whether she had killed (or attempted to kill) her child(ren) by, for instance, smothering or poisoning;

(b)   the identity of the various medical experts who have given evidence in relation to those issues; and

(c)   which of the parties each expert has given evidence for or against.

(viii) Irrespective of the ambit of s 12 of the Administration of Justice Act 1960, s 97(2) of the Children Act 1989 makes it a criminal offence to:

> 'publish any material which is intended, or likely, to identify ... any child as being involved in any proceedings before [a family court] in which any power under [the 1989] Act may be exercised by the court with respect to that or any other child.'

(ix)   This is all subject to any specific injunction or other order that a court of competent jurisdiction may have made in any particular case.

General notes:

This decision predates – indeed precipitated – changes in both the primary and secondary legislation but the continuing usefulness of this extract was expressly stated in eg *A Local Authority v D (Chief Constable of Thames Valley Police intervening); Re D* [2006] EWHC 1465 (Fam), [2006] 2 FLR 1053 at [61], and in *Clayton v Clayton* [2006] EWCA Civ 878, [2007] 1 FLR 11 at [35]: see G86 – Access, publicity and disclosure in CA 1989 proceedings.

G89   AJA 1960, S 12 (2)

A v Ward

[2010] EWHC 16 (Fam), [2010] 1 FLR 1497 at 1529

Family Division

Munby J

[112] Where, then, is the line to be drawn? The key is provided, of course, by the statutory principle, reproducing the common law principle to be found in *Re Martindale*, that what is protected, what cannot be published without committing a contempt of court, is 'information relating to [the] proceedings'. And from the various authorities I have been referred to one can, I think, draw the following further conclusions about what is and what is not included within the statutory prohibition:

(i)   'Information relating to [the] proceedings' includes:
    (a)   documents prepared for the purpose of the proceedings; and
    (b)   information, even if not reduced to writing, which has emerged during the course of information gathering for the purpose of proceedings already on foot.
(ii)   In contrast, 'information relating to [the] proceedings' does *not* include:
    (a)   documents (or the information contained in documents) not prepared for the purpose of the proceedings, even if the documents are lodged with the court or referred to in or annexed to a witness statement or report; or
    (b)   information (even if contained in documents falling within para (i)(a)) which does not fall within para (i)(b);

unless the document or information is published in such a way as to link it with the proceedings so that it can sensibly be said that what is published is 'information relating to [the] proceedings'.

[113]   Put shortly, it is not a breach of s 12 to publish a fact about a child, even if that fact is contained in documents filed in the proceedings, if what is published makes no reference to the proceedings at all. After all, as Lord Denning MR said in *Re F*, it is not a contempt to publish information about the child, only to publish 'information relating to the proceedings in court'. Or, as Scarman LJ put it, 'what is protected from publication is the proceedings of the court'.

[114]   In other words one has to distinguish between, on the one hand, the mere publication of a fact (fact X) and, on the other hand, the publication of fact X in the context of an account of the proceedings, or the publication of the fact (fact Y) that fact X was referred to in the proceedings or in documents filed in the proceedings. The publication of fact X may not be a breach of s 12; the publication of fact Y will be a breach of s 12 even if the publication of fact X alone is not.

[115]   It follows that there is much material contained in the trial bundles which Her Honour Judge Plumstead had before her – much information and many documents – the publication of which will *not* involve any contempt of court under s 12 *unless* (and I wish to emphasise the point) the information or documents are published as part of or in the context of an account of the care proceedings or in such a way as to link them with the care proceedings – in which case there will, as I have explained, be a contempt under s 12.

Other significant cases on this issue

* *A v Payne and Williams; A v G and N* [2009] EWHC 736 (Fam), [2009] 2 FLR 463 (although solicitor and guardian had committed a contempt of court in disclosing reports there had been no ill motive: neither was replaced in the case)

G90 PROCESS WHERE JUDGMENT IN CHAMBERS IS TO BE RELEASED

British Broadcasting Corporation v Cafcass Legal and Others

[2007] EWHC 616 (Fam), [2007] 2 FLR 765 at 778

Family Division

Munby J

[44] Now on one view, if the question arises (whether of the court's own motion or on application made) as to whether a judgment delivered in chambers is to be released (either in anonymised or, indeed, in non-anonymised form), the only principled approach is that:

(i) the court must first give everyone referred to in the judgment an opportunity of considering, before the judgment is released even in anonymised form, whether or not to apply for an order protecting their anonymity – that was, in substance, done in the present case;

(ii) if anyone wishes to make such an application it must be made in compliance with the requirements of s 12 of the Human Rights Act 1998 and the *President's Practice Direction (Applications for Reporting Restriction Orders)* 18 March 2005, [2005] 2 FLR 120 and the *Practice Note (Official Solicitor: Deputy Director of Legal Services: CAFCASS: Applications for Reporting Restriction Orders)* [2005] 2 FLR 111 – that, as I have already observed, was not done in this case; and

(iii) the court should not release the judgment (even in anonymised form) until *after* it has adjudicated on any application for anonymity.

[45] I say the only principled approach, because it can be said with some force that no other approach properly gives effect to the court's twin obligations: first, its obligation properly to consider the Convention rights of those seeking to protect their anonymity and, at the same time, secondly, its obligation properly to consider the Convention rights of those who would be adversely affected by an anonymity order and, in particular, its obligation to comply with s 12(2) of the Human Rights Act 1998.

[46] As against that, it can be said with some force that a rigorous compliance with this principled approach may have the disadvantages: (i) of condemning those involved to an unnecessarily complex procedure in every case, when (it may be said) in many (or even, perhaps, in most) cases where an anonymised judgment is published there will either be no one seeking in fact to 'name names' or no one with an interest in preventing the 'naming of names'; and (ii) of reducing the number of judgments which are in fact released for publication.

[47] I have rehearsed these points in some detail because the present case, in light of the way it has come before the court and has been argued (see below), has focused attention on problems which have hitherto not been subjected to as much scrutiny as the complexity of the issues – both the issues of principle and the issues of practicality – might be thought to warrant. (I might add that the point which Mr Busuttil has very properly and helpfully raised in this case was not raised before me in the *Webster* litigation, where it was accepted that if an injunction to protect anonymity was even arguably appropriate – as I held it was – it was appropriate for me to 'hold the ring' by granting an interim injunction until after final judgment in the care proceedings, leaving it to the media, and indeed anyone else who objected, to apply to discharge it: see *Re Webster; Norfolk County Council v Webster and Others* [2006] EWHC 2733 (Fam), [2007] 1 FLR 1146, at [116]–[119], *Norfolk County Council v Webster and Others (No 2)* [2006] EWHC 2898 (Fam), [2007] 2 FLR 415, at [59], [62]–[64], and para 4 of the order set out in para [71] of the latter judgment.)

[48] But these, again, are not issues which I can resolve today within the confines of this directions hearing. And they are, moreover, as can be seen, issues of some complexity on which the parties may wish to adduce more detailed arguments than those which have been prepared for the purposes of this hearing ...

[49] Since the hearing, and indeed since I prepared this judgment, Ryder J has given judgment in *Oldham Metropolitan Borough Council v GW & PW* [2007] EWHC 136 (Fam), [2007] 2 FLR 597. He dealt with this point at para [103], when he observed that:

'In the "ordinary" circumstance I would have been constrained not to release this judgment until after there had been an adjudication on anonymity, involving service of a restraint application upon the media in accordance with the President's *Practice Direction* ... and the *Practice Note* ... and so as to comply with section 12(2) of the Human Rights Act 1998. However, fortuitously, in this case and at an earlier stage of the proceedings those steps were take and a *contra mundum* order was made.'

I am inclined to agree; indeed, I have some difficulty in seeing any answer to Ryder J's analysis.

Other significant cases on this issue:

- *Re B; X Council v B (No 2)* [2008] EWHC 270 (Fam), [2008] 1 FLR 1460

Children Act 1989, s 91(14)

G91   MAIN GUIDELINES

Re P (Section 91(14) guidelines) (residence and religious heritage)

[1999] 2 FLR 573 at 589 and 592

Court of Appeal

Butler-Sloss LJ

The statutory power to restrict applications by parents was introduced by the Children Act 1989 from 14 October 1991, although similar orders had previously been made under the inherent jurisdiction of the court.

...

There is no guidance in the section as to the circumstances in which the restriction may be imposed in a Children Act application. Such an omission, is, no doubt, intentional and designed to give the court a wide discretion. Contrast the language of s 42 of the Supreme Court Act 1981 which requires the Attorney-General to show that the litigant has habitually and without reasonable ground instituted vexatious proceedings before the court can impose any restriction. From the cases which I have cited above, it can be seen that the most likely reason for granting a restriction requiring leave to make an application is where the applicant has already made repeated and unreasonable applications with no hope of success. In those cases the applicant must have crossed the line between a reasonable application and one which is both unreasonable and has become or is becoming oppressive. The operation of the section is not however limited to oppressive or semi-vexatious applications. Orders have been made pre-emptively to apply to cases where the conduct of the applicant has not yet reached that level or there is no criticism of the applicant's conduct but none the less there are circumstances where, in the best interests of the child, it is necessary to prevent unmeritorious inter partes applications. It is always a balancing exercise between the welfare of the child and the right of unrestricted access of the litigant to the court.

A number of guidelines may be drawn from the cases to which I have referred above, and I am also indebted to Wall J for the helpful summary of propositions set out in part III of his judgment. It is, however, important to remember that these are only guidelines intended to assist and not to replace the wording of the section.

Guidelines

(1) Section 91(14) should be read in conjunction with s 1(1) which makes the welfare of the child the paramount consideration.

(2) The power to restrict applications to the court is discretionary and in the exercise of its discretion the court must weigh in the balance all the relevant circumstances.

(3) An important consideration is that to impose a restriction is a statutory intrusion into the right of a party to bring proceedings before the court and to be heard in matters affecting his/her child.

(4) The power is therefore to be used with great care and sparingly, the exception and not the rule.

(5) It is generally to be seen as an useful weapon of last resort in cases of repeated and unreasonable applications.

(6) In suitable circumstances (and on clear evidence), a court may impose the leave restriction in cases where the welfare of the child requires it, although there is no past history of making unreasonable applications.

(7) In cases under para (6) above, the court will need to be satisfied first that the facts go beyond the commonly encountered need for a time to settle to a regime ordered by the court and the all too common situation where there is animosity between the adults in dispute or between the local authority and the family and secondly that there is a serious risk that, without the imposition of the restriction, the child or the primary carers will be subject to unacceptable strain.

(8) A court may impose the restriction on making applications in the absence of a request from any of the parties, subject, of course, to the rules of natural justice such as an opportunity for the parties to be heard on the point.

(9) A restriction may be imposed with or without limitation of time.

(10) The degree of restriction should be proportionate to the harm it is intended to avoid. Therefore the court imposing the restriction should carefully consider the extent of the restriction to be imposed and specify, where appropriate, the type of application to be restrained and the duration of the order.

(11) It would be undesirable in other than the most exceptional cases to make the order ex parte.

An absolute prohibition on making any application to the court would not in my view be an order under s 91(14), which presupposes an (ex parte) application to the court. An order imposing an absolute prohibition would have to be made under the inherent jurisdiction of the court: see *Re R (Residence: Contact: Restricting Applications)* [1998] 1 FLR 749, per Wilson J at 760.

Other significant cases on this issue:

- *Re P (Children Act 1989, ss 22 and 26: local authority compliance)* [2000] 2 FLR 910
- *Re C (Prohibition on further applications)* [2002] EWCA Civ 292, [2002] 1 FLR 1136
- *Re B (Section 91(14) order: duration)* [2003] EWCA Civ 1966, [2004] 1 FLR 871
- *Re C-J (Section 91(14) order)* [2006] EWHC 1491 (Fam), [2006] 2 FLR 1213

G92   ADDITIONAL GUIDELINES (1)

Re C (Litigant in person: section 91(14) order)

[2009] EWCA Civ 674, [2009] 2 FLR 1461 at 1464

Court of Appeal

Wall LJ

[13] ... I would like to take this opportunity to set out what, in my judgment, should happen procedurally when the court is minded to make an order under s 91(14) of the Children Act 1989

(1)   Ideally, such an application should be made in writing on notice in the normal way. The court can then, having heard all relevant submissions, make an order one way or the other.

(2)   There will, however, be cases in which the question of a s 91(14) order arises either during or at the end of a hearing. It may arise on the application of one of the parties, or on the court's own initiative. One or more of the parties before the court may be unrepresented.

(3)   In the circumstances identified in para (2), the court may make an order under s 91(14). It is, however, of the utmost importance that the party or parties or other persons affected by the order, particularly if they are in person:

     (a)   understand that such an application is being made, or that consideration is being given to making a s 91(14) order;

     (b)   understand the meaning and effect of such an order; and

     (c)   have a proper opportunity to make submissions to the court in answer to the application or to the suggestion that a s 91(14) order be made.

(4)   Where the parties (and in particular the person affected by the s 91(14) order) are represented, it may be possible for the court to deal with the matter in argument without a formal application, although if the representative for the party affected seeks a short adjournment to take instructions, such an application should normally be granted. If there is a substantive objection to the s 91(14) order, then the court should require the application to be made formally on notice in the normal way.

(5)   Where the party affected by a proposed s 91(14) order is in person it is particularly important that he or she:

     (a)   understands the effect of such an order; and

     (b)   is given a proper opportunity to respond to it. This may mean adjourning the application for it to be made in writing and on notice.

(6) Where the parties are both or all in person, there is a powerful obligation on any court minded to make a s 91(14) order to explain to them the course the court is minded to take. This will involve the court telling the parties in ordinary language what a s 91(14) order is; and what effect it has, together with the duration of the order which the court has in mind to impose. Above all, unrepresented parties must be given the opportunity to make any submissions they wish about the making of such an order, and if there is a substantive objection on which a litigant wishes to seek legal advice the court should either normally not make an order; alternatively it can make an order and give the recipient permission to apply to set it aside within a specified time.

(7) None of this guidance is designed to address the merits of s 91(14) orders, which as my Lord has indicated are exceptional, and in relation to which there is now a substantial jurisprudence.

G93 ADDITIONAL GUIDELINES (2) INCLUDING APPLICATION FOR PERMISSION TO APPLY

Re S (Permission to seek relief)

[2006] EWCA Civ 1190, [2007] 1 FLR 482 at 500 and 501

Court of Appeal

Wall LJ

Discussion

[72] As stated in paras [2]–[5] of this judgment, above, these two applications have thrown up a number of issues. They can, we think, be summarised as follows:

(1) Is it permissible to attach conditions to a s 91(14) order?
(2) What is the correct approach both for the court and for a person subject to a s 91(14) order when an application for permission to apply is made?
(3) In what circumstances is it appropriate to make a s 91(14) order expressed to be without limit of time or to last until the sixteenth birthday of a relevant child.
(4) Is it necessary for notice to be given to the other party—
    (a) when an application for an order under s 91(14) is to be made?
    (b) when an application for permission to apply is being made?
(5) How do these considerations apply to the applications currently before this court?

(1) THE ATTACHMENT OF CONDITIONS

[73] For the reasons given by Mr Hepher set out in paras [63]–[65] of this judgment, we are of the clear view that it is not permissible to attach conditions to a s 91(14) order beyond stating how long it is to last, and identifying the type of relief to which it applies. This conclusion seems to us to flow from the wording of s 91(14) itself, and from the fact that the power to impose conditions expressly given by s 11(7) of the Act is restricted to s 8 orders.

[74] There are, however, other considerations which both lend strong support to the same conclusion, and also impinge on the other questions which we have posed. The first, of course, is that whilst s 91(14) does not

impose an absolute prohibition on applications to the court, it is, nonetheless a fetter imposed by Parliament on parties' rights of access to the court in relation to their children. It plainly creates a judicial discretion as to the circumstances in which it falls to be used, but in our judgment must otherwise be applied as enacted, and without the accretion of any judicial interpretative gloss. Had Parliament intended s 91(14) to create the power to impose conditions when making an order under it, Parliament, we think, would have said so.

...

[77] In summary, therefore, whilst it is permitted by the Act, and may well be appropriate for the court to impose a particular course of treatment on a party as a condition of making a contact order under s 8 of the Act, it is in our judgment impermissible to impose conditions on a s 91(14) order, and in particular impermissible to require that a party undergo treatment as a pre-condition of making an application for permission to apply.

(2) THE CORRECT APPROACH TO AN APPLICATION FOR PERMISSION TO APPLY

[78] In relation to the judicial approach to applications for permission to apply, we should say, by way of preliminary observation, that we see no inconsistency between Thorpe LJ's test in *Re A (Application for Leave)* [1998] 1 FLR 1 set out at para [53], above: ('Does this application demonstrate that there is any need for renewed judicial investigation?') and Butler-Sloss LJ's test in *Re P (Section 91(14) Guidelines) (Residence and Religious Heritage)* [1999] 2 FLR 573 set out at para [54], above: ('the applicant must persuade the judge that he has an arguable case with some chance of success'). In our judgment the two complement each other. A judge will not, we think, see a need for renewed judicial investigation into an application which he does not think sets out an arguable case. In the first application, His Honour Judge Murdoch adopted the *Re A* approach, albeit with a cross reference to *Re P*. This seems to us perfectly sensible.

[79] It is self-evident that a party who is the subject of an order under s 91(14) of the Act which has been made because of particular conduct by that party must have addressed that conduct if his application for permission to apply is to warrant a renewed judicial investigation or to present an arguable case. Thus, to take an obvious example, a man who has been made the subject of a s 91(14) order following findings of fact by the court of both persistent domestic violence to his former partner and his children and a fixed and delusional belief that his children are the victims of parental alienation syndrome, is unlikely to succeed in an application for permission to apply for contact or residence if he makes it without any acceptance of the court's previous findings.

[80] This is, of course, quite different from parties being told that they cannot make an application because they have not fulfilled identified conditions imposed in the s 91(14) order. The need to address the court's findings and the reasons for the imposition of the s 91(14) order are matters of evidence which go to the success or failure of the application for permission to apply: the imposition of conditions on a s 91(14) order is an impermissible bar to an application for permission to apply being made at all.

[81] It may well be, however, that the court is unable properly to address an application for permission to apply because it does not have sufficient information to enable it to make a decision. It may also be that the only means whereby the necessary information can be obtained is to give the applicant for permission the opportunity to obtain it by means of allowing access to the court papers by an appropriate expert. Thus if, for example, there is a question mark over an applicant's mental heath, or some other aspect of his personality which affects his suitability to have contact with his children, it may well be that the application cannot properly be resolved without a report from an expert who had been given access to the court papers.

[82] This, of course, was the application made by CE post judgment. We will discuss that particular application when we give our decision in relation to his application. What is plain, however, is that an applicant for permission to apply must not put the cart before the horse. If, in order properly to mount an application for permission to apply, an applicant requires access by an expert to the court papers in order to report on the applicant's current state of mind and the appropriateness of the application, the proper course, it seems to us, is to make the application for permission to apply, but to invite the court, before adjudicating upon it, to give directions for all the relevant evidence to be obtained. If, as we think will sometimes be the case, this requires a report on the applicant's current state of mind by reference to the court papers, the court should, in appropriate cases, adjourn the application, and not decide it until the report is available. Had that course been adopted in CE's case at the outset, it is possible that the judge, as he himself recognised, might well have acceded to it.

[83] Where an application for permission to apply is being contemplated, therefore, careful thought needs to be given to the evidence which is required for its proper presentation. If that presentation requires a preliminary report, the court should be invited to order it prior to, and as a necessary ingredient of, its ultimate adjudication.

The circumstances in which a s 91(14) order should be made either
without restriction of time or until a relevant child attains the age of 16

[84] It is clear from *Re P (A Minor) (Residence Order: Child's Welfare)*
*[*2000] Fam 15, [1999] 3 WLR 1164, sub nom *Re P (Section 91(14)*
Guidelines) (Residence and Religious Heritage) [1999] 2 FLR 573 that a
s 91(14) order can properly be made without limit of time or for the
period over which the court, absent exceptional circumstances, has
jurisdiction to make orders in relation to children under s 8 of the Act.
This is normally the age of 16 – see s 9(6) although there is special
provision for a residence order made in favour of third parties: see s 12(5)
of the Act, neither of which we need to set out.

[85] In our judgment, however, orders made without limit of time, and
orders expressed to last until a child is 16 should be the exception rather
than the rule, and where they are made, the reasons for making them
should be fully and carefully set out.

[86] We take this view for a number of reasons. We do not seek in any
way to say that there are not cases in which such orders are necessary to
further the welfare of the children concerned. This court has as much
experience as any of obsessional parents who continue to damage their
children by relentless litigation in circumstances where the children's
welfare is wholly subordinate to the continuing power battle between
them, or where one parent behaves in a manner which makes future
contact between him or her and the children impossible to contemplate as
being in the children's interests. Such cases are, however, the tiny minority,
and in the majority the function of the court, in our judgment, is not to
give up, or to give the appearance that it is permanently shutting the door
of the court in the litigant's face. This is, of course, particularly the case
where contact should be taking place, but is being frustrated by the
behaviour of the resident parent, as, for example, in *Re B (Section 91(14)*
Order: Duration) [2003] EWCA Civ 1966, [2004] 1 FLR 871.

[87] The principal thrust of the extensive jurisprudence in this court on
the subject of parental contact is that it is, generally speaking, in the
interests of children to maintain a relationship with their absent parent
unless there are compelling circumstances which render it contrary to
their welfare to do so. This, not infrequently, involves the court in
imaginative initiatives designed to preserve relationships between absent
parents and their children. The provisions of the Children and Adoption
Act 2004, when implemented, should broaden the powers of the court to
engage non-forensic interventions to the same end.

[88] There is currently no power to compel absent parents to have
contact with their children, and the statistics relating to the numbers of
absent parents who give up and abandon the attempt to have any
relationship with their children are alarming. The clear thrust of the Act,

and the approach of the courts to the relationship between the absent parent and the child has been to foster it wherever possible, provided always that such contact is safe for the child: – see, in particular, the decision of this court in *Re L.*[1]

[89]   Thus, in each case in which s 91(14) of the Act is invoked, it behoves the court to consider carefully what mischief the section is designed to address, and in particular whether or not it is going to be possible, at the end of a defined period, to re-investigate the question, and to attempt the restoration of the relationship between absent parent and child.

[90]   Section 91(14) of the Act has been described as both draconian and flexible. Both descriptions are apt. Its use, however, has to be carefully controlled by the court as part of its over-arching strategy, which is to preserve and foster relationships wherever possible. An order which is indeterminate, or which is expressed to last until the sixteenth birthday of the relevant child is, in effect, an acknowledgement by the court that nothing more can be done. As we have already made clear, cases in which the court reaches the end of the road do exist, and there are cases in which it is essential for the welfare of the children and the physical health and sanity of the resident parent that an indefinite halt is called to litigation. But if the court has indeed reached that stage, it needs to spell out its reasons clearly, so that the parents – and in particularly the parent who is the subject of the s 91(14) order knows precisely where he or she stands, and precisely what issues he or she had to address if an application for permission to apply is going to be possible.

Notice to the other party

[91]   We are in complete agreement with those authorities which make it clear that before a s 91(14) order is made, the person affected by it should have a proper opportunity to consider it and be heard on it. In practice, however, the need for an order under s 91(14) may only become apparent during the course of a hearing, or otherwise at relatively short notice. Where this happens, the court must ensure, if need be by a short adjournment, that the person on the receiving end, particularly if he or she is a litigant in person, has had a full opportunity to consider the making of such an order, and to voice objections to it.

[92]   We think a greater degree of flexibility is permissible where the question is whether or not a resident parent needs to be served in the first instance with an application for permission to apply. We think there is much sense, in certain sensitive circumstances, for the court to direct, in the first instance, that the application be not served on the other party until such time as the court has had the opportunity to consider it and to decide whether it is necessary for the other side to be served.

---

[1]   [2000] 2 FLR 334.

[93] An obvious example is a case in which the stress of previous litigation has destabilised the family, and in which the fragile capacity of the resident parent may well be adversely affected by the service of an application for permission to apply, particularly if that application is unmeritorious or unlikely to succeed. Plainly, if the court takes the view that there is sufficient merit in the application to make it appropriate for the other party to be served, and that an inter partes hearing is appropriate, that is another matter.

[94] We would therefore respectfully urge caution before following to the letter the passage from Hale J's judgment in *Re N (Section 91(14) Order)* [1996] 1 FLR 356 which we have set out at para [47] of this judgment, and the statement by Thorpe LJ in *Re A (Application for Leave)* [1998] 1 FLR 1 that an application for permission to apply should be determined inter partes (at 3E–F). It is, in our view, open to a judge when making a s 91(14) order to direct that any application for permission to apply during its operation shall not, in the first instance, be served on the respondent to it, but should be considered by the judge on paper. The judge will then decide whether or not an inter partes hearing is required.

[95] We do not, however, think that an applicant for permission to apply should be denied an oral hearing if that is what he or she seeks. Whilst a judge may properly, therefore, direct that the application will, in the first instance, be considered by him or her on the papers, we take the view that if the litigant is dissatisfied with a paper refusal, he or she should be afforded an oral hearing, however, unmeritorious the application may prove to be.

Other significant cases on this issue:

- *Stringer* v *Stringer* [2006] EWCA Civ 1617, [2007] 1 FLR 1532 at [9]–[10]
- *Re J (A child) (Restrictions on applications)* [2007] EWCA Civ 906, [2008] 1 FLR 369 (s 91(14) order could properly be made without limit and would cease to have effect when child reached eighteenth birthday)
- *Re C (Contact order: variation)* [2008] EWCA Civ 1389, [2009] 1 FLR 869 (s 91(14) order overturned and case remitted for rehearing)
- *Re G (Residence: restrictions on further applications)* [2008] EWCA Civ 1468, [2009] 1 FLR 894 (s 91(14) order and residence order set aside)
- *Re N (Section 91(14))* [2009] EWHC 3055 (Fam), [2010] 1 FLR 1110 (order against both parents for 4 years)
- *Re A (Contact: section 91(14))* [2009] EWCA Civ 1548, [2010] 2 FLR 151 (order made on an inappropriately summary basis)

- *Re G (Restricting contact)* [2010] EWCA Civ 470, [2010] 2 FLR 692 (indirect contact should have been allowed and s 91(14) order for 5 years was too long)

DIVISION H

JUDGMENT, COSTS AND APPEALS

Contents

Appeals

Judgment: general

H1   ROLE OF JUDGE AT FIRST INSTANCE

Independent News Ltd v A (by the Official Solicitor)

[2009] EWHC 2858 (Fam), [2010] 1 FLR 916 at 925

Hedley J

[22]   I have been the beneficiary of much learning in reading and hearing the submissions of counsel. I have been invited to consider the history of the jurisdictions which preceded the 2005 Act. I have had the principles of *Scott v Scott* traced through up to the present time. I have been escorted through the Strasbourg jurisprudence in respect of privacy and have had the advantage of a thorough review of the relevant statutory provisions.

[23]   Yet I must bear in mind the proper role of the first instance judge as more than once recently depicted by the Court of Appeal. My task is to find the facts and to identify the issues. It is then to set out the law that I propose to apply and then to reason through the conclusion based on that application. Faithfulness to that role necessarily precludes an exhaustive review or critique of the learning deployed before me and it should not be thought that because not every case nor every point is deployed in this judgment, that I have ignored or overlooked it. I must content myself with the more modest task assigned me by the Court of Appeal and thereby risk a charge of want of respect for the learning deployed.

General notes:

The actual decision was overturned by the Court of Appeal.

H2   BURDEN OF PROOF

Re H and R (Child sexual abuse: standard of proof)

[1996] 1 FLR 80 at 95

House of Lords

Lord Nicholls of Birkenhead

The burden of proof

The power of the court to make a care or supervision order only arises if the court is 'satisfied' that the criteria stated in s 31(2) exist. The expression 'if the court is satisfied', here and elsewhere in the Act, envisages that the court must be judicially satisfied on proper material. There is also inherent in the expression an indication of the need for the subject matter to be affirmatively proved. If the court is left in a state of indecision the matter has not been established to the level, or standard, needed for the court to be 'satisfied'. Thus in s 31(2), in order for the threshold to be crossed, the conditions set out in paras (a) and (b) must be affirmatively established to the satisfaction of the court.

The legal burden of establishing the existence of these conditions rests on the applicant for a care order. The general principle is that he who asserts must prove. Generally, although there are exceptions, a plaintiff or applicant must establish the existence of all the preconditions and other facts entitling him to the order he seeks. There is nothing in the language or context of s 31(2) to suggest that the normal principle should not apply to the threshold conditions.

This case is also included in relation to:

D17 CA 1989, s 31(2): 'Likely to suffer significant harm'

H3   STANDARD OF PROOF

Re B (Children) (Sexual abuse: standard of proof)

[2008] UKHL 35, [2008] 2 FLR 141 at 148, 162 and 164

House of Lords

Lord Hoffman and Baroness Hale

LORD HOFFMAN:

[13] My Lords, I would invite your Lordships fully to approve these observations. I think that the time has come to say, once and for all, that there is only one civil standard of proof and that is proof that the fact in issue more probably occurred than not. I do not intend to disapprove any of the cases in what I have called the first category, but I agree with the observation of Lord Steyn in *McCann*'s case [2003] 1 AC 787, [2002] 3 WLR 1313, [2002] UKHRR 1286 (at 812, 1329 and 1303 respectively) that clarity would be greatly enhanced if the courts said simply that although the proceedings were civil, the nature of the particular issue involved made it appropriate to apply the criminal standard.

[14] Finally, I should say something about the notion of inherent probabilities. Lord Nicholls of Birkenhead said, in the passage I have already quoted, that:

'the court will have in mind as a factor, *to whatever extent is appropriate in the particular case*, that the more serious the allegation the less likely it is that the event occurred and, hence, the stronger should be the evidence before the court concludes that the allegation is established on the balance of probability.'

[15] I wish to lay some stress upon the words I have italicised. Lord Nicholls of Birkenhead was not laying down any rule of law. There is only one rule of law, namely that the occurrence of the fact in issue must be proved to have been more probable than not. Common sense, not law, requires that in deciding this question, regard should be had, to whatever extent appropriate, to inherent probabilities. If a child alleges sexual abuse by a parent, it is common sense to start with the assumption that most parents do not abuse their children. But this assumption may be swiftly dispelled by other compelling evidence of the relationship between parent and child or parent and other children. It would be absurd to suggest that the tribunal must in all cases assume that serious conduct is unlikely to have occurred. In many cases, the other evidence will show that

it was all too likely. If, for example, it is clear that a child was assaulted by one or other of two people, it would make no sense to start one's reasoning by saying that assaulting children is a serious matter and therefore neither of them is likely to have done so. The fact is that one of them did and the question for the tribunal is simply whether it is more probable that one rather than the other was the perpetrator.

BARONESS HALE:

[64] My Lords, Lord Lloyd of Berwick's prediction proved only too correct. Lord Nicholls of Birkenhead's nuanced explanation left room for the nostrum, 'the more serious the allegation, the more cogent the evidence needed to prove it', to take hold and be repeated time and time again in fact-finding hearings in care proceedings (see, for example, the argument of counsel for the local authority in *Re U (A Child) (Department for Education and Skills Intervening); Re B (A Child) (Department for Education and Skills Intervening)* [2004] EWCA Civ 567, [2005] Fam 134, at 137. It is time for us to loosen its grip and give it its quietus.

...

[70] My Lords, for that reason I would go further and announce loud and clear that the standard of proof in finding the facts necessary to establish the threshold under s 31(2) or the welfare considerations in s 1 of the 1989 Act is the simple balance of probabilities, neither more nor less. Neither the seriousness of the allegation nor the seriousness of the consequences should make any difference to the standard of proof to be applied in determining the facts. The inherent probabilities are simply something to be taken into account, where relevant, in deciding where the truth lies.

[71] As to the seriousness of the consequences, they are serious either way. A child may find her relationship with her family seriously disrupted; or she may find herself still at risk of suffering serious harm. A parent may find his relationship with his child seriously disrupted; or he may find himself still at liberty to maltreat this or other children in the future.

[72] As to the seriousness of the allegation, there is no logical or necessary connection between seriousness and probability. Some seriously harmful behaviour, such as murder, is sufficiently rare to be inherently improbable in most circumstances. Even then there are circumstances, such as a body with its throat cut and no weapon to hand, where it is not at all improbable. Other seriously harmful behaviour, such as alcohol or drug abuse, is regrettably all too common and not at all improbable. Nor are serious allegations made in a vacuum. Consider the famous example of the animal seen in Regent's Park. If it is seen outside the zoo on a stretch of greensward regularly used for walking dogs, then of course it is

more likely to be a dog than a lion. If it is seen in the zoo next to the lions' enclosure when the door is open, then it may well be more likely to be a lion than a dog.

[73] In the context of care proceedings, this point applies with particular force to the identification of the perpetrator. It may be unlikely that any person looking after a baby would take him by the wrist and swing him against the wall, causing multiple fractures and other injuries. But once the evidence is clear that that is indeed what has happened to the child, it ceases to be improbable. Someone looking after the child at the relevant time must have done it. The inherent improbability of the event has no relevance to deciding who that was. The simple balance of probabilities test should be applied.

Other significant cases on this issue:

- *R (D) v Life Sentences Review Commission* [2008] UKHL 33, [2009] 1 FLR 700
- *Re S-B (Children)* [2009] UKSC 17, [2010] 1 FLR 1161 at [10]–[14]

This case is also included in relation to:

G32 Purpose of split hearings
H12 Inherent probabilities may be relevant

H4 DECISIONS MUST BE ON FACTS FOUND NOT SUSPICIONS

Re S-B (Children)

[2009] UKSC 17, [2010] 1 FLR 1161 at 1164 and 1166

Supreme Court

Baroness Hale

[8] The leading case on the interpretation of these conditions is the decision of the House of Lords in *Re H (Minors) (Sexual Abuse: Standard of Proof)* [1996] AC 563, [1996] 2 WLR 8, [1996] 1 FLR 80. Three propositions were established which have not been questioned since. First, it is not enough that the court suspects that a child may have suffered significant harm or that there was a real possibility that he did. If the case is based on actual harm, the court must be satisfied on the balance of probabilities that the child was actually harmed. Second, if the case is based on the likelihood of future harm, the court must be satisfied on the balance of probabilities that the facts upon which that prediction was based did actually happen. It is not enough that they may have done so or that there was a real possibility that they did. Third, however, if the case is based on the likelihood of future harm, the court does not have to be satisfied that such harm is more likely than not to happen. It is enough that there is:

> 'a real possibility, a possibility that cannot sensibly be ignored having regard to the nature and gravity of the feared harm in the particular case' (per Lord Nicholls of Birkenhead, at 585F, 23 and 95 respectively).

[9] Thus the law has drawn a clear distinction between probability as it applies to past facts and probability as it applies to future predictions. Past facts must be proved to have happened on the balance of probabilities, that is, that it is more likely than not that they did happen. Predictions about future facts need only be based upon a degree of likelihood that they will happen which is sufficient to justify preventive action. This will depend upon the nature and gravity of the harm: a lesser degree of likelihood that the child will be killed will justify immediate preventive action than the degree of likelihood that the child will not be sent to school.

...

[15] In *Re B*, the House also declined an invitation to overrule the decision of the Court of Appeal in *Re M and R (Minors) (Sexual Abuse: Expert Evidence)* [1996] 2 FLR 195. This was concerned with the stage after the court is satisfied that the threshold has been crossed. The court has then to decide what order, if any, to make. The welfare of the child is the paramount consideration: 1989 Act, s 1(1). In deciding whether or not to make a care or supervision order, the court must have regard in particular to the so-called 'checklist' of factors: 1989 Act, s 1(3), (4). These include '(e) any harm which he has suffered or is at risk of suffering'.

[16] In *Re M and R*, the Court of Appeal determined that s 1(3)(e) should be interpreted in the same way as s 31(2)(a). The court must reach a decision based on facts, not on suspicion or doubts. Butler-Sloss LJ said this:

'[Counsel's] point was that if there is a real possibility of harm in the past, then it must follow (if nothing is done) that there is a risk of harm in the future. To our minds, however, this proposition contains a non sequitur. The fact that there might have been harm in the past does not establish the risk of harm in the future. The very highest it can be put is that what might possibly have happened in the past means that there may possibly be a risk of the same thing happening in the future. Section 1(3)(e), however, does not deal with what might possibly have happened or what future risk there may possibly be. It speaks in terms of what has happened or what is at risk of happening. Thus, what the court must do (when the matter is in issue) is to decide whether the evidence establishes harm or the risk of harm.'

[17] In agreeing with this approach in *Re B*, at para [56], Baroness Hale of Richmond commented that in such a case:

'as indicated by Butler-Sloss LJ ..., the "risk" is not an actual risk to the child but a risk that the judge has got it wrong. We are all fallible human beings, very capable of getting things wrong. But until it has been shown that we have, it has not been shown that the child is in fact at any risk at all.'

Re M and R was also approved by Lord Nicholls of Birkenhead in *Re O and N; Re B* [2003] UKHL 18, [2004] 1 AC 523, [2003] 1 FLR 1169, a case to which we shall return.

Other significant cases on this issue:

- Cf *Re R (Care: disclosure: nature of proceedings)* [2002] 1 FLR 755: see G41 – Court / parties / experts bound by findings made / not made

This case is also included in relation to:

H24 Identifying perpetrators: standard of proof
H25 Identifying perpetrators: the pool of possible perpetrators
H26 Identifying perpetrators: caution where cannot identify
H27 Identifying perpetrators: the risk the judge has got it wrong

H5   ASSEMBLING THE JIGSAW

Re A (Non-accidental injury: medical evidence)

[2001] 2 FLR 657 at 659

Family Division

Bracewell J

[70] It is undoubtedly true that the frontiers of medical science are constantly being pushed back and that the state of knowledge is increasing all the time. That is why I find that when presented with a speculative theory based on an unlikely hypothetical base an expert will rarely discount it and will in effect never say never. Fanciful speculation is not an appropriate method of inquiry. What is needed and what the experts have done in this case is to piece together all the available information and look at the differential diagnosis. Many of the experts in this case specialise within a particular and very narrow field and by reason of being experts of referral at centres of excellence they acquire special knowledge and skill. However, concentration on a very narrow area of expertise can sometimes render it difficult for the expert to see the whole picture. In this regard I find that the pathologists are at a disadvantage when compared with the clinicians.

[71] The judge has the duty of sifting the evidence from the experts, who form their assessments within their particular area of expertise, and the judge has to decide the case by reference to the various issues. Although the medical evidence is of very great importance it is not the only evidence in the case. Explanations given by carers and the credibility of those involved with the child concerned are of great significance. All the evidence, both medical and non-medical has to be considered in assessing whether the pieces of the jigsaw form a clear, convincing picture of what happened.

Other significant cases on this issue:

- *Re T (Abuse: standard of proof)* [2004] EWCA Civ 558, [2004] 2 FLR 838 at [33]
- *Leeds City Council v YX and ZX* [2008] EWHC 802 (Fam), [2008] 2 FLR 869

H6   FINDINGS MAY BE SELECTIVE

Re F (Shared residence order)

[2003] 2 FLR 397 at 403

Court of Appeal

Thorpe LJ

[19]   ... One of the functions of the judge is of course to make express findings. Another function of the judge is to be selective and to make findings that are relevant and necessary for the disposal of the issue. It is not incumbent on the judge to elaborate or extend judgments by making findings on every area or every issue, and it is open to a judge to confine him or herself to those matters which he or she selects as significant and necessary.

H7 EXTENT OF REASONING (1)

Re T (Contact: alienation: permission to appeal)

[2002] EWCA Civ 1736, [2003] 1 FLR 531 at 545

Court of Appeal

Arden LJ

[37]   Miss Parker drew the court's attention to *English v Emery Reimbold & Strick Ltd; DJ and C Withers (Farms) Ltd v Ambic Equipment Ltd, Verrechia (trading as Freightmaster Commercials) v Commissioner of Police of the Metropolis* [2002] EWCA Civ 605, [2002] 1 WLR 2409. In that case, this court considered the requirement for a judgment to give reasons. The principles laid down in that case as to the need to give reasons apply, at least as a minimum, in these care proceedings, and accordingly, I set out the relevant passages in full. This court held:

'17.   As to the adequacy of reasons, as has been said many times, this depends on the nature of the case: see for example *Flannery and Another v Halifax Estate Agencies Ltd* [2000] 1 WLR 377 at 382. In *Eagil Trust Co Ltd v Pigott-Brown* [1985] 3 All ER 119, Griffiths LJ stated that there was no duty on a judge, in giving his reasons, to deal with every argument presented by counsel in support of his case:

"When dealing with an application in chambers to strike out for want of prosecution, a judge should give his reasons in sufficient detail to show the Court of Appeal the principles on which he has acted, and the reasons which led him to his decision. They need not be elaborate. I cannot stress too strongly that there is no duty on a judge in giving his reasons to deal with every argument presented by counsel in support of his case. It is sufficient if what he says shows the parties, and if need be the Court of Appeal the basis on which he acted ... (see Sachs LJ in *Knight v Clifton* [1971] 2 All ER 378 at 392–393, [1971] Ch 700 at 721)."

18.   In our judgment, these observations of Griffiths LJ apply to judgments of all descriptions. But when considering the extent to which reasons should be given it is necessary to have regard to the practical requirements of our appellate system. A judge cannot be said to have done his duty if it is only after permission to appeal has been given and the appeal has run its course that the court is able to conclude that the reasons for the decision are sufficiently apparent to

enable the appeal court to uphold the judgment. An appeal is an expensive step in the judicial process and one that makes an exacting claim on judicial resources. For these reasons permission to appeal is now a nearly universal prerequisite to bringing an appeal. Permission to appeal will not normally be given unless the applicant can make out an arguable case that the judge was wrong. If the judgment does not make it clear why the judge has reached his decision, it may well be impossible within the summary procedure of an application for permission to appeal to form any view as to whether the judge was right or wrong. In that event permission to appeal may be given simply because justice requires that the decision be subjected to the full scrutiny of an appeal.

19.   It follows that, if the appellate process is to work satisfactorily, the judgment must enable the appellate court to understand why the judge reached his decision. This does not mean that every factor which weighed with the judge in his appraisal of the evidence has to be identified and explained. But the issues the resolution of which were vital to the judge's conclusion should be identified and the manner in which he resolved them explained. It is not possible to provide a template for this process. It need not involve a lengthy judgment. It does require the judge to identify and record those matters which were critical to his decision. If the critical issue was one of fact, it may be enough to say that one witness was preferred to another because the one manifestly had a clearer recollection of the material facts or the other gave answers which demonstrated that his recollection could not be relied upon.

20.   The first two appeals with which we are concerned involved conflicts of expert evidence. In *Flannery and Another v Halifax Estate Agencies Ltd* Henry LJ quoted from the judgment of Bingham LJ in *Eckersley v Binnie* (1987) 18 Con LR 1 at 77–78 in which he said that "a coherent reasoned opinion expressed by a suitably qualified expert should be the subject of a coherent reasoned rebuttal". This does not mean that the judgment should contain a passage which suggests that the judge has applied the same, or even a superior, degree of expertise to that displayed by the witness. He should simply provide an explanation as to why he has accepted the evidence of one expert and rejected that of another. It may be that the evidence of one or the other accorded more satisfactorily with facts found by the judge. It may be that the explanation of one was more inherently credible than that of the other. It may simply be that one was better qualified, or manifestly more objective, than the other. Whatever the explanation may be, it should be apparent from the judgment.

21.   When giving reasons a judge will often need to refer to a piece of evidence or to a submission which he has accepted or rejected.

Provided that the reference is clear, it may be unnecessary to detail, or even summarise, the evidence or submission in question. The essential requirement is that the terms of the judgment should enable the parties and any appellate tribunal readily to analyse the reasoning that was essential to the judge's decision.'

[38]   Thus, where *English v Emery Reimbold & Strick Ltd; DJ and C Withers (Farms) Ltd v Ambic Equipment Ltd, Verrechia (trading as Freightmaster Commercials) v Commissioner of Police of the Metropolis* applies, perfection is not required of the judge. The test is pragmatic, and depends on the nature of the case. But the bottom line is that the essential findings and reasoning must be clear. It is on the basis of *English v Emery Reimbold & Strick Ltd; DJ and C Withers (Farms) Ltd v Ambic Equipment Ltd, Verrechia (trading as Freightmaster Commercials) v Commissioner of Police of the Metropolis* that I reached the conclusion expressed in the last paragraph of this judgment with respect to the principal issue relied on by the father, namely alienation by the mother. This is not a case where there is any additional obligation due to the fact that these are care proceedings.

This case is also included in relation to:

H34 Responsibilities of advocates at first instance

H8 EXTENT OF REASONING (2)

Re G (Care proceedings: placement for adoption)

[2005] EWCA Civ 896, [2006] 1 FLR 47 at 53

Court of Appeal

Ward LJ

The judgment

[17] The real issue for us is to consider whether this judgment, as it stands, meets the 'essential test' identified by Thorpe LJ in *Re B (Appeal: Lack of Reasons)* [2003] EWCA Civ 881, [2003] 2 FLR 1035 at [11], namely:

> 'does the judgment sufficiently explain what the judge has found and what he has concluded as well as the process of reasoning by which he has arrived at his findings, and then his conclusions?'

The disappointed party is entitled to know why he has lost.

Other significant cases on this issue:

- *Re F (Contact: lack of reasons)* [2006] EWCA Civ 792, [2007] 1 FLR 65

H9 ECHR, ART 8: SUFFICIENT INVOLVEMENT – REASONS MUST BE SUFFICIENT

Elsholz v Germany

(Case 25735/94) [2000] 2 FLR 486 at 498

European Court of Human Rights

[52] The Court does not doubt that these reasons were relevant. However, it must be determined whether, having regard to the particular circumstances of the case and notably the importance of the decisions to be taken, the applicant has been involved in the decision-making process, seen as a whole, to a degree sufficient to provide him with the requisite protection of his interests (*W v United Kingdom* (1987) 10 EHRR 29, 50, para 64). It recalls that in the present case the District Court considered it unnecessary to obtain an expert opinion on the ground that the facts had been clearly and completely established for the purposes of art 1711 of the Civil Code (see para [16] above). In this connection, the District Court referred to the strained relations between the parents and in particular to the mother's objections to the applicant which she imparted to the child. The Court considers that the reasons given by the District Court are insufficient to explain why, in the particular circumstances of the case, expert advice was not considered necessary, as recommended by the Erkrath Youth Office. Moreover, taking into account the importance of the subject-matter, namely, the relations between a father and his child, the Regional Court should not have been satisfied, in the circumstances, by relying on the file and the written appeal submissions without having at its disposal psychological expert evidence in order to evaluate the child's statements. The Court notes in this context that the applicant, in his appeal, challenged the findings of the District Court and requested that an expert opinion be prepared to explore the true wishes of his child and to solve the question of access accordingly, and that the Regional Court had full power to review all issues relating to the request for access.

[53] The combination of the refusal to order an independent psychological report and the absence of a hearing before the Regional Court reveals, in the Court's opinion, an insufficient involvement of the applicant in the decision-making process. The Court thus concludes that the national authorities overstepped their margin of appreciation, thereby violating the applicant's rights under Art 8 of the Convention.

H10 EXPRESS REFERENCE TO ECHR?

D MCG v Neath Port Talbot County Borough Council

[2010] EWCA Civ 821, [2010] 2 FLR 1827 at 1834

Court of Appeal

Wilson LJ

[22] We should add in this regard that the judge did not make express reference to the rights of the mother and of the girls to respect for their family life under Art 8 of the European Convention for the Protection of Human Rights and Fundamental Freedoms 1950. By her grounds, the mother has complained that the rights of all four of them were infringed; and in this regard Miss Campbell has brought to our attention the recent decision of this court, by judgments handed down after the date of the judge's judgment, in *EH v A London Borough Council* [2010] EWCA Civ 344, [2010] 2 FLR 661. She has shown us the arresting statement of Baron J, who gave the leading judgment, at [64], namely that:

> 'In a case where the care plan leads to adoption the full expression of the terms of Article 8 must be explicit in judgment ...'

It is clear that Wall LJ, as he then was, agreed, at [98], with that apparent instruction of Baron J, albeit that, in giving a short final judgment, Smith LJ did not specifically associate herself with it. It goes without saying that, in making placement orders, a judge must not infringe rights under Art 8 and that in some cases the safest means of avoiding infringement may be for him expressly to consider the rights and the circumstances in which interference with them is permissible. We are also extremely conscious of the desirability that this court should speak with one voice, even beyond the realms in which the doctrine of binding precedent so dictates. That said, it is, of course, unusual for a judge to be required to include any particular set of words in his judgment. The more usual approach is to assume, unless he has demonstrated to the contrary, that the judge knew how to perform his functions and what matters to take into account: *Piglowska v Piglowski* [1999] 1 WLR 1360, [1999] 2 FLR 763, at 1372G and 784 respectively, per Lord Hoffmann. Perhaps when the next appeal against a placement order arrives before us upon the basis of a complaint that there was no *express* reference to Art 8, we will have to consider whether, when considered in context, the instruction of this court in *EH* is as absolutist as it at first appears.

General notes:

Cf *Re G (Children)* [2006] UKHL 43, [2006] 2 FLR 629: see A4 – Importance of using welfare checklist.

The Court of Appeal also commented at [19]:

'It would however be very helpful to this court if, at the outset of a judgment in a care case, the judge were to introduce all the parties and to explain their different proposals for the future of the children; and then, before turning to the history (and later of course to analysis of the issues), if he were briefly to summarise the current circumstances of the children and of each of the adult protagonists. It is also obviously far preferable if the evidence in relation to particular areas of the case can be collected together rather than that, as this judge was constrained to do, he should, apparently from his notebook, work through – without much comment as to what he accepted and what he did not accept – the evidence given by each witness in the order in which he had received it.'

Other significant cases on this issue:

- *Re H (Contact order)* [2002] 1 FLR 22 at 37 (Wall J)
- Cf *Re G (Children)* [2006] UKHL 43, [2006] 2 FLR 629: see A4 – Importance of using welfare checklist

H11 JUDGMENT OFTEN AS IMPORTANT AS THE ORDER

L v London Borough of Bromley

[1998] 1 FLR 709 at 718

Family Division

Wilson J

But that is far from being the end of the case. This appeal is, for me at least, an object lesson to the effect that in family matters the judgment articulated by the judge is, or in this case the reasons written by the magistrates are often quite as important as the actual orders themselves. In my view the local authority had to bring these appeals because of a shortcoming in the magistrates' reasons which was gravely prejudicial to the authority's planning of the future of one of these three children. I refer to A.

I have considerable sympathy with the magistrates in this case, as in all others where it is my duty to survey their reasons. I find it difficult enough to craft a judgment on my own in my own time. The magistrates are cast with the duty of drafting reasons, as it were in committee, and are often compelled for practical reasons, if for no other, to draft them in circumstances of considerable haste, often late in the day. It is clear to me that the magistrates in Bromley took a great deal of trouble in the production of these reasons.

Other significant cases on this issue:

- *Re S-B (Children)* [2009] UKSC 17, [2010] 1 FLR 1161: see H26 – Identifying perpetrators: caution where cannot identify

This case is also included in relation to:

D30 Contact at the discretion of the LA
D34 Orders / comments affecting contact after prospective adoption

Judgment: lay evidence

H12 INHERENT PROBABILITIES MAY BE RELEVANT

Re S-B (Children)

[2009] UKSC 17, [2010] 1 FLR 1161 at 1165

Supreme Court

Baroness Hale

[10] The House of Lords was invited to revisit the standard of proof of past facts in *Re B (Care Proceedings: Standard of Proof)* [2008] UKHL 35, [2009] 1 AC 11, [2008] 3 WLR 1, [2008] 2 FLR 141, where the judge had been unable to decide whether the alleged abuse had taken place. The suggestion that it would be sufficient if there were a 'real possibility' that the child had been abused was unanimously rejected. The House also reaffirmed that the standard of proof of past facts was the simple balance of probabilities, no more and no less.

[11] The problem had arisen, as Lord Hoffmann explained, because of dicta which suggested that the standard of proof might vary with the gravity of the misconduct alleged or even the seriousness of the consequences for the person concerned (para [5]). He pointed out that the cases in which such statements were made fell into three categories. In the first were cases which the law classed as civil but in which the criminal standard was appropriate. Into this category came sex offender orders and anti-social behaviour orders: see *B v Chief Constable of the Avon and Somerset Constabulary* [2001] 1 WLR 340 and *R (McCann and Others) v Crown Court at Manchester; Clingham v Kensington and Chelsea Royal London Borough Council* [2002] UKHL 39, [2002] 3 WLR 1313, [2002] UKHRR 1286. In the second were cases which were not about the standard of proof at all, but about the quality of evidence. If an event is inherently improbable, it may take better evidence to persuade the judge that it has happened than would be required if the event were a commonplace. This was what Lord Nicholls of Birkenhead was discussing in *Re H (Minors) (Sexual Abuse: Standard of Proof)* [1996] AC 563, [1996] 2 WLR 8, [1996] 1 FLR 80 above, at 586, 23 and 95 respectively. Yet, despite the care that Lord Nicholls had taken to explain that having regard to the inherent probabilities did not mean that the standard of proof was higher, others had referred to a 'heightened standard of proof' where the allegations were serious. In the third category, therefore, were cases in which the judges were simply confused about whether they were talking about the standard of proof or the role of inherent probabilities in deciding whether it had been discharged. Apart from cases in the first category, therefore, 'the time has come to say, once and for all, that there is only one civil standard of proof and that is proof that that the fact in issue more probably occurred than not' (para [13]).

[12] This did, of course, leave a role for inherent probabilities in considering whether it was more likely than not that an event had taken place. But, as Lord Hoffmann went on to point out at para [15], there was no necessary connection between seriousness and inherent probability:

'It would be absurd to suggest that the tribunal must in all cases assume that serious conduct is unlikely to have occurred. In many cases, the other evidence will show that it was all too likely. If, for example, it is clear that a child was assaulted by one or other of two people, it would make no sense to start one's reasoning by saying that assaulting children is a serious matter and therefore neither of them is likely to have done so. The fact is that one of them did and the question for the tribunal is simply whether it is more probable that one rather than the other was the perpetrator.'

Baroness Hale of Richmond made the same point, at para [73]:

'It may be unlikely that any person looking after a baby would take him by the wrist and swing him against the wall, causing multiple fractures and other injuries. But once the evidence is clear that that is indeed what has happened to the child, it ceases to be improbable. Someone looking after the child at the relevant time must have done it. The inherent improbability of the event has no relevance to deciding who that was. The simple balance of probabilities test should be applied.'

Other significant cases on this issue:

- *Leeds City Council v YX and ZX* [2008] EWHC 802 (Fam), [2008] 2 FLR 869 (inherent probabilities expressly referred to in refusing to make sexual abuse finding)
- *Re M (Fact-finding hearing: burden of proof)* [2008] EWCA Civ 1261, [2009] 1 FLR 1177

This case is also included in relation to:

G32 Purpose of split hearings
H3   Standard of proof

H13   ASSESSING HEARSAY EVIDENCE

Re W (Minors) (Wardship: evidence)

[1990] 1 FLR 203 at 214, 218 and 227

Court of Appeal

Butler-Sloss and Neill LJJ

BUTLER-SLOSS LJ:

In wardship, therefore, the rules as to the reception of statements made by children to others, whether doctors, police officers, social workers, welfare officers, foster-mothers, teachers or others, may be relaxed and the information may be received by the judge. He has a duty to look at it and consider what weight, if any, he should give to it. The weight which he places upon the information is a matter for the exercise of his discretion. He may totally disregard it. He may wish to rely upon some or all of it. Unless uncontroversial it must be regarded with great caution. In considering the extent to which, if at all, a judge would rely on the statements of a child made to others, the age of the child, the context in which the statement was made, the surrounding circumstances, previous behaviour of the child, opportunities for the child to have knowledge from other sources, any knowledge, as in this case, of a child's predisposition to tell untruths or to fantasise, are among the relevant considerations.

...

The reliability of the person relating what the child said is of vital importance. Mrs F is an entirely respectable person, a responsible and experienced foster-mother of many years, and was clearly doing her best to give an accurate account.

NEILL LJ:

In my judgment, the correct approach to the matter is to recognise that in wardship proceedings, which are of a special kind and which involve to some extent the exercise by the court of a parental or administrative jurisdiction, hearsay evidence is admissible as a matter of law, but that this evidence and the use to which it is put has to be handled with the greatest care and in such a way that, unless the interests of the child make it necessary, the rules of natural justice and the rights of the parents are fully and properly observed.

General notes:

Although this decision is specifically in wardship proceedings, such evidence will be admissible in other proceedings by virtue of s 1 of the Civil Evidence Act 1995 and/or s 96 of the Children Act 1989 and the Children (Admissibility of Hearsay Evidence) Order 1993. The guidance about assessing the weight to be given to the evidence remains useful, although note also the statutory factors set out in s 4 of the Civil Evidence Act 1995.

Other significant cases on this issue:

- *D v B and Others (Flawed sexual abuse inquiry)* [2006] EWHC 2987, [2007] 1 FLR 1295 at [15(xiv)]

H14 LUCAS AND TURNBULL SELF-DIRECTIONS

EH v Greenwich LBC, AA and A (Children)

[2010] EWCA Civ 344, [2010] 2 FLR 661 at 673, 680 and 681

Court of Appeal

Baron J, Wall LJ

BARON J:

[49] Despite those submissions, I consider that the judge was entitled to come to the clear conclusion after hearing the evidence that the mother had lied about the sighting in the street particularly in the light of his findings about her reliability in November. On that occasion she had most assuredly lied.

[50] However, once he had made that finding, the judge should have gone on to consider: (i) why the mother might have lied; and (ii) whether the whole of the evidence was capable of proving a continuing relationship about which she had lied consistently over time.

[51] If the judge had undertaken that analysis, he would have realised that the only credible evidence was to the effect that the mother had been with the father on one occasion in a crowded shopping street. Whilst her denial might have demonstrated that she could never be trusted to work honestly with professionals for the benefit of the children, there could have been another/other explanation(s) and he should have considered them.

[52] The facts in this case could tend to suggest a plausible alternative. Moreover this mother did not have a good relationship with the local authority and so she had never been given proper guidance or help to deal with her separation from the father.

WALL LJ:

[80] I propose to identify only a few of the traps. They relate largely to identification evidence. The first concerns the *Turnbull* direction. In this regard, what he judge said was:

'If I were directing a jury in a criminal case, I would give them a *Turnbull* direction, warning them that they must be careful on such uncorroborated evidence of identification. As against that, the standard of proof in this case is different from that in a criminal case. I do not have to be sure. I have to decide on the balance of probability.'

[81] With great respect to the judge, this will not do. The judge *is* the jury for this purpose, and in my judgment, it is imperative that where judges in care proceedings are dealing with highly controversial identification evidence, it is imperative that they give *themselves* a *Turnbull* direction. This is not a tiresome mantra which a judge must recite in order to tick a box for this court: judges need to remind *themselves* of the dangers of identification evidence.

...

[87] In my judgment, this approach is, once again, impermissible. If what the judge was actually saying was that the fact that the mother was lying to him led him to these conclusions: (a) he should have said so in terms; and (b) he should have given himself what has become known as a *Lucas* direction. Once again, this is not a tedious mantra designed to make the life of the circuit bench more difficult than it is already: it is a formula designed to make the decision-maker stop and think carefully about the decisions being made. There is no evidence in the judgment that the judge even considered a *Lucas* direction in any shape or form.

General notes:

Cf per Charles J in *A County Council v K, D and L* [2005] EWHC 144 (Fam), [2005] 1 FLR 851 at 857:

'[28] Further, in my view, in determining the facts, a court should have regard to the guidance given in *R v Lucas (Ruth)* [1981] QB 720 and *R v Middleton* [2000] TLR 293. As appears therefrom, a conclusion that a person is lying or telling the truth about point A does not mean that he is lying or telling the truth about point B. Also I accept that there can be many reasons why a person might not tell the truth to a court concerned with the future upbringing of a child. Further, I of course recognise that witnesses can believe that their evidence contains a correct account of relevant events, but be mistaken because, for example, they misinterpreted the relevant events at the time or because they have over time convinced themselves of the account they now give.'

Judgment: expert evidence

H15 THE EXPERT ADVISES, BUT THE JUDGE DECIDES

Re B (Care: expert witness)

[1996] 1 FLR 667 at 669

Court of Appeal

Ward LJ

I reject Mr Horrocks' submission that this case raises important issues of principle in child care cases as to the court's treatment of expert evidence. A similar submission, albeit in a wholly different context, met with a very sharp rebuff from Lord President Cooper who declared in *Davie v Magistrates of Edinburgh* 1953 SC 34, 40:

> '... the parties have invoked the decision of a judicial tribunal and not an oracular pronouncement by an expert.'

In a sense the position in children's cases is a fortiori because s 1 of the Children Act 1989 imposes a duty on the court to be satisfied as to, and to give paramount consideration to, the child's welfare, which emphasises the need for the court to exercise its independent judgment of the material facts. Whilst, therefore, I agree with the Lord President's conclusions, I would not wish to adopt quite such a stringent tone. Nothing in this judgment should be thought to undermine, or to undervalue, that great success of the Children Act which has been very firmly to establish the tangible benefits of an interdisciplinary approach to this work. The court invariably needs and invariably depends upon the help it receives from experts in this field. The court has no expertise of its own, other than legal expertise.

Another success of the Children Act has been the training, including and especially the training in related disciplines, which all judges receive. By their special allocation to this work, they acquire a body of knowledge which, strictly speaking, cannot be substituted for the evidence received, but which can be deployed to spot any weakness in the expert evidence. That is the judicial task. The expert advises, but the judge decides. The judge decides on the evidence. If there is nothing before the court, no facts or no circumstances shown to the court which throw doubt on the expert evidence, then, if that is all with which the court is left, the court must accept it. There is, however, no rule that the judge suspends judicial belief simply because the evidence is given by an expert.

Other significant cases on this issue:

* *Re F (Sterilisation: mental patient)* [1989] 2 FLR 376 at 442
* *Re B (Non-accidental injury)* [2002] EWCA Civ 752, [2002] 2 FLR 1133: see H21 – Expert not categorical

This case is also included in relation to:

H19 Has the expert approached the matter with an open mind

H16 JUDGE MUST GIVE REASONS IF REJECTS EXPERT EVIDENCE

Re B (Split hearing: jurisdiction)

[2000] 1 FLR 334 at 339 and 340

Court of Appeal

Butler-Sloss P, Otton LJ

BUTLER-SLOSS P:

The failure to challenge the medical evidence by other evidence which was logically probative, the failure of the judge to analyse the evidence of the radiologist's reasoning he could not fault, leads me to the conclusion that he has, unfortunately, on this occasion fallen into error. This is a very experienced judge for whom everyone would have the greatest possible respect. But the judge does have an obligation to give reasons why he should set aside the medical evidence, which was strong, in favour of his view that, because the grandmother and the other witnesses were clearly not lying, the medical evidence could not stand. He did not, for instance, deal at all with the explanation given by Dr Hall as to why, on the evidence of early healing, the injury had to be at least 7 days old.

OTTON LJ:

The circumstances when judges of the High Court can reject the evidence of a body of medical opinion are rare. This situation was considered by the House of Lords in *Bolitho (Deceased) v City and Hackney Health Authority* [1998] AC 232, when revisiting the well-known test of *Bolam v Friern Hospital Management Committee* [1957] 1 WLR 582. Although an action for damages for personal injury arising out of alleged medical negligence, certain observations are of relevance in this case. Lord Browne-Wilkinson, giving the sole speech, with which the other members of the committee agreed, said at 243:

> 'In the vast majority of cases the fact that distinguished experts in the field are of a particular opinion will demonstrate the reasonableness of that opinion ... But if, in a rare case, it can be demonstrated that the professional opinion is not capable of withstanding logical analysis, the judge is entitled to hold that the body of opinion is not reasonable or responsible.

I emphasise that in my view it will very seldom be right for a judge to reach the conclusion that views genuinely held by a competent medical expert are unreasonable ... It is only where a judge can be satisfied that the body of expert opinion cannot be logically supported at all that such opinion will not provide the benchmark by reference to which the defendant's conduct falls to be assessed.'

Save for the evidence of the grandmother, there was nothing to suggest that the evidence of the experts was not logically supportable.

This is not one of the rare cases where it was demonstrated that professional opinion was not capable of withstanding logical analysis. Accordingly, in my view, the judge was not entitled to reject the uncontradicted medical findings and opinion and to conclude that this opinion was either unreasonable or irresponsible.

If a judge is minded to take that course, he is under a duty to give reasons for doing so. In *Flannery and Another v Halifax Estate Agencies Ltd (Trading as Colleys Professional Services)* [2000] 1 WLR 377, the Court of Appeal gave guidance on the general duty of a professional judge to give reasons for his decision, particularly in relation to expert evidence. Henry LJ said (at pp 381G–382B):

'We make the following general comments on the duty to give reasons.

(1) The duty is a function of due process, and therefore of justice. Its rationale has two principal aspects. The first is that fairness surely requires that the parties especially the losing party should be left in no doubt why they have won or lost. This is especially so since without reasons the losing party will not know (as was said in *Ex parte Dave*) whether the court has misdirected itself, and thus whether he may have an available appeal on the substance of the case. The second is that a requirement to give reasons concentrates the mind; if it is fulfilled, the resulting decision is much more likely to be soundly based on the evidence than if it is not.

(2) The first of these aspects implies that want of reasons may be a good self-standing ground of appeal. Where because no reasons are given it is impossible to tell whether the judge has gone wrong on the law or the facts, the losing party would be altogether deprived of his chance of an appeal unless the court entertains an appeal based on the lack of reasons itself.

(3) The extent of the duty, or rather the reach of what is required to fulfil it, depends on the subject matter. Where there is a straightforward factual dispute whose resolution depends simply on which witness is telling the truth about events which he claims to recall, it is likely to be enough for the judge

(having, no doubt, summarised the evidence) to indicate simply that he believes X rather than Y; indeed there may be nothing else to say. But where the dispute involves something in the nature of an intellectual exchange, with reasons and analysis advanced on either side, the judge must enter into the issues canvassed before him and explain why he prefers one case over the other. This is likely to apply particularly in litigation where as here there is disputed expert evidence; but it is not necessarily limited to such cases.'

In this case, the judge, who is a most experienced and much respected judge, acknowledged that he could not accept the reasoning of the doctors, yet did not give any reasons as to why he felt compelled to reject their evidence.

Other significant cases on this issue:

- *Re M-W (Care proceedings: expert evidence)* [2010] EWCA Civ 12, [2010] 2 FLR 46

H17　REJECTING CAFCASS RECOMMENDATION

Re R (Residence order)

[2009] EWCA Civ 445, [2010] 1 FLR 509 at 532 and 538

Court of Appeal

Rix and Moore-Bick LJ

RIX LJ:

[59] Similarly, I consider that the judge has erred in rejecting Dr Cochrane's conclusions without hearing Dr Cochrane for himself. It is widely recognised in the authorities that this should not happen if it can be avoided. Thus in *Re CB (Access: Attendance of Court Welfare Officer)* [1995] 1 FLR 622 at 629 (CA), Purchas LJ said:

> 'In cases where there are clear-cut recommendations and warnings such as those present in the second report, as indeed there were in the first report, in my judgment, it is wrong for a judge to proceed to form conclusions directly contrary to such recommendations without availing himself of the opportunity of receiving further assistance from the court welfare officer in the form of evidence. It is open to the judge to adjourn the case and demand the presence of the court welfare officer. The court welfare officer may vary his opinion in the light of the evidence or in the light of points put to him by the judge or, alternatively, he may hold his opinions. Whichever event occurs, the judge, having availed himself of the opportunity of receiving the further evidence, may then make his decision applying his own discretion. But to apply his discretion without availing himself of that opportunity is, in my judgment, a defective exercise of discretion.'

[60] In *Re C (Section 8 Order: Court Welfare Officer)* [1995] 1 FLR 617, the judge upheld the status quo (residence with the mother) in accordance with (and not contrary to) the slight preference of the court welfare officer, but the complaint of the father was that he should not have done so without adjourning to permit the officer to attend. However, the judge had been able to see the teenage boy in question to obtain his own views. This court dismissed the appeal, upholding the judge's exercise of discretion not to adjourn. Hale J said that where a report was without any firm recommendation in any particular direction, it was unnecessary to adjourn and it would have been open to the judge to conduct his own

evaluation of the relevant considerations and to weigh them slightly differently, even in favour of the father, without the presence of the court officer. She added (at 620):

'Thus the case of *Re CB* cannot be a hard-and-fast rule of law. Procedural straitjackets in cases of this kind would be most undesirable, especially in the light of the balancing act which is required by the paramount consideration of the child's welfare and the provisions as to delay in s 1(2). Many factors will have to be taken into account in the exercise of the court's discretion. These will include how much further assistance the court welfare officer can give, and the extent to which it would be safe and proper to depart from any recommendations made.'

[61] In *Re W (Residence)* [1999] 2 FLR 390, this court allowed an appeal from a judge who had departed from the court welfare officer's recommendation as to residence. The officer had been present on that occasion, but the judge had failed to reason his disagreement with her report. Thorpe LJ said (at 394–395):

'In relation to the role of the court welfare officer, it cannot be too strongly emphasised that in private law proceedings the court welfare service is the principal support service available to the judge in the determination of these difficult cases. It is of the utmost importance that there should be free co-operation between the skilled investigator, with the primary task of assessing not only the factual situations but also attachments, and the judge with the ultimate responsibility of making the decision. Judges are hugely dependent upon the contribution that can be made by the welfare officer, who has the opportunity to visit the home and to see the grown-ups and the children in much less artificial circumstances than the judge can ever do. It is for that very good practical reason that authority has established clearly, since at least the decision of this court in *W v W (A Minor: Custody Appeal)* [1988] 2 FLR 505, 513, that judges are not entitled to depart from the recommendation of an experienced court welfare officer without at least reasoning that departure. The more recent decision of this court in *Re A (Children: 1959 UN Declaration)* [1998] 1 FLR 354 emphasises the importance of the judge testing any misgivings that he may have developed from the written report with the court welfare officer in the witness box. This judge had the opportunity to voice such misgivings as he had developed during the welfare officer's oral evidence and he did not do so.'

[62] In the present case, I have sympathy for the difficult position that the judge was put in by reason of the absence of the Cafcass officer. Ward LJ considers that the mother's successful opposition, on the basis of the undesirability of delay, to the father's application for an adjournment

for him to obtain legal representation, justified the judge's decision to proceed in the absence of the Cafcass officer, despite his disagreement with her as to the proper outcome. In my judgment, however, the adjournment argument proceeded on a different basis, and did not depend on the absence of the Cafcass officer. In any event, the judge, in my judgment, failed to articulate the basis of his disagreement with the report. He discounted the views of the child and ignored the recommendation of the report. He did not argue his disagreement with Dr Cochrane in outcome: he simply referred to Dr Cochrane's recommendation and passed on. His reason must have been that the child had settled. That, however, was just another way of saying that the wishes of the child (who had made the best he could of his situation) and the recommendation of the reporter were to be put aside. The judge did not explain why the 7 months' sojourn with the father was to be preferred to the lifetime's upbringing by the mother, especially where that upbringing had been acknowledged as successful. I do not consider that the judge properly addressed these matters, which he was required to do, all the more so in the absence of Dr Cochrane.

[63] I would respectfully agree entirely with what Hale J said in *Re C*, that the absence of the court welfare officer cannot be allowed to put the court into a procedural straitjacket. That, however, was a case where the judge confirmed the officer's recommendation, where the court had been able to hear the child, and where the real issue on appeal had been the entirely procedural question whether the judge could properly form his own view, in the absence of the officer, when an adjournment to permit the officer's attendance had been considered and refused. The issue did not concern the judge's own reasoning. In the present case, however, the judge had not heard (and did not listen to) the child, he had not rejected an adjournment to permit the attendance of the Cafcass officer, he ignored her recommendation, and the reason advanced (by implication) for doing so is unsatisfying.

MOORE-BICK LJ:

[77] Finally, there is Dr Cochrane's recommendation itself. As I have already said, the judge did not discuss it or the grounds on which it was based in any detail and having said that he proposed to examine its underlying rationale, he failed to explain the grounds on which he disagreed with her conclusion. Mr Hepher submitted that it is not right for a judge to depart from the recommendation made by the Cafcass officer without first hearing from the officer in person and that if necessary the proceedings should be adjourned to enable the officer to attend. He based that submission on the observations of Purchas LJ in *Re CB (Access: Attendance of Court Welfare Officer)* [1995] 1 FLR 622 and of Thorpe LJ in *Re W (Residence)* [1999] 2 FLR 390, at 395 to which Ward LJ and Rix LJ have referred.

[78] I agree with Ward LJ that there can be no hard and fast rule in a matter of this kind, especially in a case where the attendance of the Cafcass officer will require an adjournment when many other factors, not least delay, will have to be taken into account. That was recognised by Hale J in *Re C (Section 8 Order: Court Welfare Officer)*. That case was very different from the present, however, since the judge did not decline to follow the welfare officer's recommendation and the only question was whether he should have granted an adjournment to enable the welfare officer to attend. Since the report was essentially neutral I do not find it surprising that the court affirmed the judge's right to make his own evaluation on the basis of the material before him. I am not sure that the result would have been the same if there had been a clear recommendation from which the judge had been minded to depart.

[79] Ultimately, as Hale J, pointed out, what really matters is how much further assistance the Cafcass officer can be expected to give and the extent to which it would be safe or proper to depart from any recommendation without first obtaining his or her response. In general, however, I think that unless there are strong reasons to do otherwise judges should follow the guidance of Thorpe LJ in *Re A (Children: 1959 UN Declaration)* [1998] 1 FLR 354 and, if minded to depart from the recommendation of an experienced Cafcass officer, should test any misgivings that they may have with the officer in the witness box before reaching a final decision. In this case the judge cannot be accused of not giving reasons for departing from the recommendation in the Cafcass report, but he does not appear to have considered whether he should test his misgivings with Dr Cochrane. It is true that at the outset of the hearing he had refused an application by the father for an adjournment to enable him to obtain legal representation, in part on the grounds that it would delay the outcome of the proceedings. It is also true that the application was opposed by the mother on those grounds. However, it is unlikely that at that stage the judge had formed any clear view about the likely outcome of the case, so there is no reason to think that one of the factors he had already taken into account when considering an adjournment was the opportunity it might afford of enabling Dr Cochrane to attend. Had he considered the question again at the close of the parties' submissions, I do not think that he could properly have concluded in a finely balanced case of this kind that her attendance was unlikely to be of any significant assistance.

[80] Like Rix LJ, I am left with the clear impression that the judge was overwhelmingly influenced by the fact that L had settled with his father and that that factor led him to brush aside without giving them proper consideration other factors which tended to point in favour of returning him to his mother. The fact that L had settled well and was happy at his new school was undoubtedly a matter of considerable importance, but Dr Cochrane was well aware of the situation and in the light of the other matters to which she refers it had not led her to recommend that he should remain with his father. That fact alone, therefore, could not justify disregarding the other factors to which I have referred, nor can it justify a failure to hear from Dr Cochrane before rejecting her recommendation.

General notes:

Note that Ward LJ would have upheld the judge's decision.

This case is also included in relation to:

A5   Wishes of the child
G15   Judicial treatment of litigants in person

H18 APPLICATION OF R V CANNINGS

Re U (Serious injury: standard of proof); Re B

[2004] EWCA Civ 567, [2004] 2 FLR 263 at 272

Court of Appeal

Butler-Sloss P

[23] In the brief summary of the submissions set out above there is a broad measure of agreement as to some of the considerations emphasised by the judgment in *R v Cannings*[1] that are of direct application in care proceedings. We adopt the following:

(i) The cause of an injury or an episode that cannot be explained scientifically remains equivocal.

(ii) Recurrence is not in itself probative.

(iii) Particular caution is necessary in any case where the medical experts disagree, one opinion declining to exclude a reasonable possibility of natural cause.

(iv) The court must always be on guard against the over-dogmatic expert, the expert whose reputation or amour propre is at stake, or the expert who has developed a scientific prejudice.

(v) The judge in care proceedings must never forget that today's medical certainty may be discarded by the next generation of experts or that scientific research will throw light into corners that are at present dark.

Other significant cases on this issue:

- *Re X (non-accidental injury: expert evidence)* [2001] 2 FLR 90 (an example of 'the expert who has developed a scientific prejudice' in relation to so-called temporary brittle bone disease)
- *A Local Authority v S* [2009] EWHC 2115 (Fam), [2010] 1 FLR 1560

This case is also included in relation to:

G9 Rules of evidence relaxed

---

[1] [2004] EWCA Crim 1, [2004] 1 All ER 725.

H19 HAS THE EXPERT APPROACHED THE MATTER WITH AN OPEN MIND

Re B (Care: expert witness)

[1996] 1 FLR 667 at 670

Court of Appeal

Ward LJ

That being the question, Mr Horrocks faces the inevitable difficulty of persuading this court to interfere with the balancing exercise which is a matter for the judge who has seen and heard the witnesses. It is not for this court to interfere unless the judge was plainly wrong. He was clearly mindful of the doctor's impressive qualifications and her considerable and wide experience, both in child paediatrics, in child assessment and in psychotherapy. The clear implication is that he acknowledged that this level of expertise compelled the court to give added weight to her evidence which was accordingly entitled to command the court's respect. That notwithstanding, he found her evidence to be flawed. He made these findings:

> '[The doctor] at an early stage in her report, took up a scathing and, I consider, merciless stance which she adopted throughout that report and continued in her oral evidence.'

And:

> '[The doctor's] whole approach throughout the assessment was that K remained at great risk from both parents. She clearly did not conceive the possibility that one parent might be blameless. I am satisfied that, despite her qualifications, she has allowed in this instance her feelings about the mother to affect her thinking and her judgment.'

Referring to the contact visit observed by the doctor, the judge said:

> 'There is not a single phrase in it supportive of the mother. I find that very surprising. Having myself observed the mother over 4 days, and having heard her give evidence, I am frankly astonished that the doctor cannot find it possible to say anything positive about this mother.'

Those are damaging findings against this expert. They cannot possibly be challenged as incorrect in this court. The judge went on to find that, as the mother had told him (and he believed the mother), she found the doctor frightening and powerful and he, having seen her seeking to dominate both evidence-in-chief and cross-examination, understood the mother's feelings about the doctor.

The mother gave evidence, which he accepted, that she had come to the conclusion, however belatedly, that the father was responsible for the injuries. She did not disclose those feelings to the doctor, because of the unsympathetic approach she felt she was receiving from the doctor. The judge found as a fact that the mother and father had separated immediately after the first assessment and that the doctor had been shown to be wrong in her view of the couple's relationship. I should add, as did the judge, that the guardian had taken a contrary view of that aspect of the matter at that time, and he praised the guardian for being more perceptive. He finally said:

> 'Judging by the way she gave her evidence, [the doctor] has a formidable personality. She has been dogmatic in her assertions in this case. Indeed she herself has said that in this case she was being dogmatic. Most troubling of all was the total denigration by her of the evidence of others and, in particular, [Mrs A], whom she sought to ridicule.
>
> I regretfully conclude that there is hostility by [the doctor] to the mother, which must largely have derived from a belief that the mother was an abuser, or was covering up deliberately for the father. That I find not to be so. [The doctor] therefore started her assessment on a false premise and she has allowed that false premise to dominate her thinking.
>
> Of course I must consider her evidence in conjunction with other evidence in this case supportive of her views, and notably that of the guardian, but in the end I must myself assess the witness. [The doctor] did not impress me as a witness in whom I could have proper confidence ...'

This case is also included in relation to:

H15 The expert advises, but the judge decides

H20 IS THE EXPERT'S FACTUAL BASIS SOUND

Re W (Care: threshold criteria)

[2007] EWCA Civ 102, [2007] 2 FLR 98 at 112

Court of Appeal

Wall LJ

[46] We find it both regrettable and surprising that JS was not prepared to assist the judge by commenting on what Miss R had observed. The basic function of an expert witness is to advise the court on matters which are within the expertise of the witness and outwith the expertise of the judge. The judge has to make findings of fact, and to draw inferences from the facts found. The task of experts is to assist judges in that process, not by telling them what the facts are or should be, but by giving them the benefit of expert opinion on questions within the area of the experts' expertise. This is, we think, elementary. JS's refusal to comment on Miss R's observations (whether they were accurate or inaccurate) has, we think two consequences. It not only put the judge in an extremely difficult position by depriving him of important expert evidence on a critical part of the case (the differences between KW's behaviour in the foster home and during contact with her mother): it also strikes us as a sufficient derogation from the basic duty owed by an expert witness to the court to cast doubt on the objectivity and soundness of JS's evidence.

[47] In para [95] of the judgment, a paragraph on which Mr Keehan relies, the judge goes on to say:

> 'She (JS) agreed that whilst she described mother's behaviour as sometimes disinhibited, for example, aggressive outbursts to doctors, no such behaviour had been observed by contact to supervisors (sic). Her good behaviour at final contact was attributed by JS to the mother being aware that it was a final contact and the session being regulated. It did not happen out of the blue. This could not correlate to the mother's day to day behaviour when she was under stress.'

[48] Whilst we see the force of the point JS is making, we think Mr Keehan entitled to pray this paragraph in aid in his overall critique of JS's evidence.

[49] The matters listed in paras [44]–[48] above are not isolated examples. We give two further instances recorded by the judge. In

para [68], having reviewed a number of authorities cited to him as relevant to para 7 of the revised threshold criteria document, he turned to JS's report and evidence:

> '... I say at the outset that I found her a somewhat dogmatic witness who under cross-examination by Mr Keehan seemed, for reasons which are not clear, defensive. She is a lady of experience and qualifications and I am surprised that she gave me the impression of someone who was disturbed to be questioned so closely, particularly when the questioning concerned a case of such complexity and such sensitivity. Having said that I find no reason to doubt her findings but nevertheless looked for other evidence to confirm if her arguments were substantiated by other evidence.'

[50] The qualification in the final sentence of this paragraph is, in our judgment, highly unusual when made in relation to an expert witness as opposed to a witness of fact. Furthermore, and with all respect to the judge, we think it led him into error, since it was plain that the reports of JS carried considerable weight with other witnesses, including the local authority and the guardian. It will already have been observed that para 7 of the revised threshold criteria document was based exclusively on JS's report of 21 December 2005 The judge also records in para [119] of his judgment that 'the guardian placed reliance on JS's report in evidence'.

[51] We therefore take the view that in looking to other evidence to confirm whether or not JS's evidence was substantiated by that other evidence, the judge placed himself in the position of arguing in a circle, and that this led him to accept JS's evidence without subjecting it to a sufficiently critical analysis.

H21 EXPERT NOT CATEGORICAL

Re B (Non-accidental injury)

[2002] EWCA Civ 752, [2002] 2 FLR 1133 at 1139

Court of Appeal

Thorpe LJ

[25] It seems that on that very carefully stated and carefully balanced appraisal the judge would have been failing in his primary protective function if he were to have acceded to some submission that because the doctor had not been prepared to say in medical language that there was a confident diagnosis therefore there was no evidence of risk of harm. The elevation of a medical opinion to the status of a confident medical diagnosis is very much a matter of art and bounded by medical conventions that are fully recognised and, indeed, negotiated at a professional level. What this doctor was saying was that the child's condition was entirely consistent with non-accidental injury and that there was no other more probable explanation. The case, in my view, is as straightforward as that. Although Mr Storey sought to say this is some dangerous invasion of the right of parents to presumptions of innocence and to safeguards from adverse findings absent the strongest and clearest of evidence, those submissions, in my opinion, are not realistic in the facts and circumstances of this particular case.

[26] The parents had their opportunity to make their contribution to the judicial investigation; they chose not to do so beyond submitting statements. It seems to me that although the judge, rightly, drew no inferences from that, there were inevitably risks of consequences for them in having stood aside.

H22 JUDGE MUST ASSESS AGAINST TOTALITY OF THE EVIDENCE

A County Council v K, D and L

[2005] EWHC 144 (Fam), [2005] 1 FLR 851 at 861 and 869

Family Division

Charles J

[41] The point that medical expert evidence is but one part of the evidence available to the court at the fact-finding stage of the case is supported and demonstrated by *Re U; Re B* at paras [25], [26] and [27], where the President said:

'[25] Contrast [with the position in *Cannings*] the role of the judge conducting the trial of a preliminary issue in care proceedings. The trial is necessary not to establish adult guilt, nor to provide an adult with the opportunity to clear his name. The trial of a preliminary issue is the first, but essential, stage in a complex process of child protection through the medium of judicial proceedings.

[26] It is for the purpose of satisfying that threshold that the local authority seeks to prove specific facts against the parent or parents. Only if it succeeds in that task can its application for a care or supervision order proceed. Thus the preliminary issue of fact constitutes the gateway to a judicial discretion as to what steps should be taken to protect the child and to promote his welfare. In those circumstances we must robustly reject Mr Cobb's submission that the local authority should refrain from proceedings or discontinue proceedings in any case where there is a substantial disagreement amongst the medical experts. *For the judge invariably surveys a wide canvas, including a detailed history of the parents' lives, their relationship and their interaction with professionals. There will be many contributions to this context, family members, neighbours, health records, as well as the observation of professionals such as social workers, health visitors and children's guardian.*

[27] In the end the judge must make clear findings on the issues of fact before the court, resting on the evidence led by the parties and such additional evidence as the judge may had required in the exercise of his quasi-inquisitorial function. All this is the prelude to a further and fuller investigation of a range of choices in search of the protection and welfare of children. A positive finding against a

parent or both parents does not in itself preclude the possibility of rehabilitation. All depends on the facts and circumstances of the individual case.' (emphasis added)

...

Upshot

[63]　I am, therefore, able to reach a conclusion as to cause of death and injury that is different to, or does not accord with, the conclusion reached by the medical experts as to what they consider is more likely than not to be the cause having regard to the existence of an alternative or alternatives which they regard as reasonable (as opposed to fanciful or simply theoretical) possibilities. In doing so I do not have to reject the reasoning of the medical experts, rather I can accept it but on the basis of the totality of the evidence, my findings thereon and reasoning reach a different overall conclusion.

Other significant cases on this issue:

*   *A County Council v A Mother, a Father and X, Y and Z (by their guardian)* [2005] EWHC 31 (Fam), [2005] 2 FLR 129 at [44]
*   *Re W (Care: threshold criteria)* [2007] EWCA Civ 102, [2007] 2 FLR 98 at [57]

H23 ASSESSING EXPERT EVIDENCE: SUMMARY

A County Council v A Mother, a Father and X, Y and Z (by their guardian)

[2005] EWHC 31 (Fam), [2005] 2 FLR 129 at 144

Family Division

Ryder J

[46] I am well aware of the cautions that have been repeatedly expressed about the court declining to follow un-contradicted expert evidence or preferring lay evidence in the face of cogent medical analysis. I have not forgotten those cautions (see, for example, *Re B (Non Accidental Injury: Compelling Medical Evidence)* [2002] EWCA Civ 902, [2002] 2 FLR 599), but I have at the same time adopted the wise dicta of Stuart-Smith LJ in *Loveday v Renton* [1990] 1 Med LR 117 at 125:

> 'In reaching my decision a number of processes have to be undertaken. The mere expression of opinion or belief by a witness, however eminent, that the vaccine can or cannot cause brain damage, does not suffice. The court has to evaluate the witness and soundness of his opinion. Most importantly this involves an examination of the reasons given for his opinions and the extent to which they are supported by the evidence. The judge also has to decide what weight to attach to a witness's opinion by examining the internal consistency and logic of his evidence; his precision and accuracy of thought as demonstrated by his answers; how he responds to searching and informed cross-examination and in particular the extent to which a witness faces up to and accepts the logic and proposition put in cross-examination or is prepared to concede points that are seen to be correct; the extent to which a witness has conceived an opinion and is reluctant to re-examine it in light of later evidence, or demonstrates a flexibility of mind which may involve changing or modifying opinions previously held; whether or not a witness is biased or lacks independence.'

Other significant cases on this issue:

- *Re W (Care: threshold criteria)* [2007] EWCA Civ 102, [2007] 2 FLR 98

This case is also included in relation to:

I17   No substitute for factual analysis and risk assessment

Identifying perpetrators

H24 IDENTIFYING PERPETRATORS: STANDARD OF PROOF

Re S-B (Children)

[2009] UKSC 17, [2010] 1 FLR 1161 at 1171

Supreme Court

Baroness Hale

[34] The first question listed in the statement of facts and issues is whether it is now settled law that the test to be applied to the identification of perpetrators is the balance of probabilities. The parties are agreed that it is and they are right. It is correct, as the Court of Appeal observed, Re B[1] was not directly concerned with the identification of perpetrators but with whether the child had been harmed. However, the observations of Lord Hoffmann and Baroness Hale of Richmond, quoted at para [12] above, make it clear that the same approach is to be applied to the identification of perpetrators as to any other factual issue in the case. This issue shows quite clearly that there is no necessary connection between the seriousness of an allegation and the improbability that it has taken place. The test is the balance of probabilities, nothing more and nothing less.

[35] Of course, it may be difficult for the judge to decide, even on the balance of probabilities, who has caused the harm to the child. There is no obligation to do so. As we have already seen, unlike a finding of harm, it is not a necessary ingredient of the threshold criteria. As Wall LJ put it in Re D (Care Proceedings: Preliminary Hearing) [2009] EWCA Civ 472, [2009] 2 FLR 668, at para [12], judges should not strain to identify the perpetrator as a result of the decision in Re B:

> 'If an individual perpetrator can be properly identified on the balance of probabilities, then ... it is the judge's duty to identify him or her. But the judge should not start from the premise that it will only be in an exceptional case that it will not be possible to make such an identification.'

---

[1]   Re B (Children) (Sexual abuse: standard of proof) [2008] UKHL 35, [2008] 2 FLR 141.

[36] There are particular benefits in making such a finding in this context, especially where there is a split hearing. Miss Frances Judd QC, on behalf of the children's guardian in this case, has stressed that the guardian would rather have a finding on the balance of probabilities than no finding at all. There are many reasons for this. The main reason is that it will promote clarity in identifying the future risks to the child and the strategies necessary to protect him from them. For example, a different care plan may be indicated if there is a risk that the parent in question will ill-treat or abuse the child from the plan that may be indicated if there is a risk that she will be vulnerable to relationships with men who may ill-treat or abuse the child.

[37] Another important reason is that it will enable the professionals to work with the parent and other members of the family on the basis of the judge's findings. As the Court of Appeal said in *Re K (Non-Accidental Injuries: Perpetrator: New Evidence)* [2004] EWCA Civ 1181, [2005] 1 FLR 285, at para [55]:

> 'It is paradigmatic of such cases that the perpetrator denies responsibility and that those close to or emotionally engaged with the perpetrator likewise deny any knowledge of how the injuries occurred. Any process, which encourages or facilitates frankness, is, accordingly, in our view, to be welcomed in principle.'

Often, it is not only the parents, but the grandparents and other members of the family, who may be the best resource to protect the child in the future but who are understandably reluctant to accept that someone close to them could be responsible for injuring a child. Once that fact is brought home to them by a clear finding based upon the evidence, they may be able to work with the professionals to keep the child within the family.

[38] *Re K* also suggested, at para [56], that there would be long-term benefits for the child, whatever the outcome of the proceedings:

> '... we are also of the view that it is in the public interest that children have the right, as they grow into adulthood, to know the truth about who injured them when they were children, and why. Children who are removed from their parents as a result of non-accidental injuries have in due course to come to terms with the fact that one or both of their parents injured them. This is a heavy burden for any child to bear. In principle, children need to know the truth if the truth can be ascertained.'

This case is also included in relation to:

H25   IDENTIFYING PERPETRATORS: THE POOL OF POSSIBLE PERPETRATORS

Re S-B (Children)

[2009] UKSC 17, [2010] 1 FLR 1161 at 1173

Supreme Court

Baroness Hale

[39]   The second and third questions in the statement of facts and issues ask whether judges should refrain from seeking to identify perpetrators at all if they are unable to do so on the civil standard and whether they should now be discouraged from expressing a view on the comparative likelihood as between possible perpetrators. These appear to be linked but they are distinct.

[40]   As to the second, if the judge cannot identify a perpetrator or perpetrators, it is still important to identify the pool of possible perpetrators. Sometimes this will be necessary in order to fulfil the 'attributability' criterion. If the harm has been caused by someone outside the home or family, for example at school or in hospital or by a stranger, then it is not attributable to the parental care unless it would have been reasonable to expect a parent to have prevented it. Sometimes it will desirable for the same reasons as those given above. It will help to identify the real risks to the child and the steps needed to protect him. It will help the professionals in working with the family. And it will be of value to the child in the long run.

[41]   In *North Yorkshire County Council v SA* [2003] EWCA Civ 839, [2003] 2 FLR 849, the child had suffered non-accidental injury on two occasions. Four people had looked after the child during the relevant time for the more recent injury and a large number of people might have been responsible for the older injury. The Court of Appeal held that the judge had been wrong to apply a 'no possibility' test when identifying the pool of possible perpetrators. This was far too wide. Dame Elizabeth Butler-Sloss P, at para [26], preferred a test of a 'likelihood or real possibility'.

[42]   Miss Susan Grocott QC, for the local authority, has suggested that this is where confusion has crept in, because in *Re H* this test was adopted in relation to the prediction of the likelihood of future harm for the purpose of the threshold criteria. It was not intended as a test for identification of possible perpetrators.

[43] That may be so, but there are real advantages in adopting this approach. The cases are littered with references to a 'finding of exculpation' or to 'ruling out' a particular person as responsible for the harm suffered. This is, as the President indicated, to set the bar far too high. It suggests that parents and other carers are expected to prove their innocence beyond reasonable doubt. If the evidence is not such as to establish responsibility on the balance of probabilities it should nevertheless be such as to establish whether there is a real possibility that a particular person was involved. When looking at how best to protect the child and provide for his future, the judge will have to consider the strength of that possibility as part of the overall circumstances of the case.

This case is also included in relation to:

H4   Decisions must be on facts found not suspicions
H24   Identifying perpetrators: standard of proof
H26   Identifying perpetrators: caution where cannot identify
H27   Identifying perpetrators: the risk the judge has got it wrong

H26   IDENTIFYING PERPETRATORS: CAUTION WHERE CANNOT IDENTIFY

Re S-B (Children)

[2009] UKSC 17, [2010] 1 FLR 1161 at 1173 and 1174

Supreme Court

Baroness Hale

[39]   The second and third questions in the statement of facts and issues ask whether judges should refrain from seeking to identify perpetrators at all if they are unable to do so on the civil standard and whether they should now be discouraged from expressing a view on the comparative likelihood as between possible perpetrators. These appear to be linked but they are distinct.

...

[44]   As to the third question, times have changed since *Re O*.[1] Barring unforeseen accidents, the same judge will preside over both parts of the hearing. While it is helpful to have a finding as to who caused the injuries if such a finding can be made, the guardian's view is that it is positively unhelpful to have the sort of indication of percentages that the judge was invited to give in this case. Lord Thorpe J suggested ([2009] EWCA Civ 1048) at para [17], that judges should be cautious about amplifying a judgment in which they have been unable to identify a perpetrator: 'better to leave it thus'. We agree.

Other significant cases on this issue

* *Re M (Fact-finding hearing: burden of proof)* [2008] EWCA Civ 1261, [2009] 1 FLR 1177 (cannot find that X was the perpetrator but Y was a possible perpetrator)

This case is also included in relation to:

H4   Decisions must be on facts found not suspicions
H24   Identifying perpetrators: standard of proof
H25   Identifying perpetrators: the pool of possible perpetrators
H27   Identifying perpetrators: the risk the judge has got it wrong

---

[1]   *Re O and N; Re B* [2003] UKHL 18, [2003] 1 FLR 1169.

H27 IDENTIFYING PERPETRATORS: THE RISK THE JUDGE HAS GOT IT WRONG

Re S-B (Children)

[2009] UKSC 17, [2010] 1 FLR 1161 at 1174

Supreme Court

Baroness Hale

[45] If the judge can identify a perpetrator on the balance of probabilities, what is to be done about the risk that he may be wrong and that someone else was in fact responsible? We are indeed all fallible human beings. We can make mistakes, however hard we try to pay careful attention to the quality of the evidence before us and reach findings which are rationally based upon it.

[46] However, once the court has identified a perpetrator, the risk is not a proven risk to the child but a risk that the judge has got it wrong. Logically and sensibly, although the judge cannot discount that risk while continuing to hear the case, he cannot use it to conclude that there is a proven risk to the child. But, all the evidence (if accepted by the judge) relating to all the risk factors that the judge has identified remains relevant in deciding what will be best for the child. And he must remain alive to the possibility of mistake and be prepared to think again if evidence emerges which casts new light on the evidence which led to the earlier findings. It is now well settled that a judge in care proceedings is entitled to revisit an earlier identification of the perpetrator if fresh evidence warrants this (and this court saw an example of this in the recent case of *Re I (A Child) (Contact Application: Jurisdiction), Re* [2009] UKSC 10, [2010] 1 FLR 361). The guardian also submits that the professionals will find it easier to work with this approach.

[47] It is important not to exaggerate the extent of the problem. It only really arises in split hearings, which were not originally envisaged when the Children Act 1989 was passed. In a single hearing the judge will know what findings of fact have to be made to support his conclusions both as to the threshold and as to the future welfare of the child. Moreover, cases rarely come as neatly packaged as this one does. In most cases, the injuries are such that, even if one parent was not responsible for causing them, she was undoubtedly responsible for failing to protect the child from the person who did cause them. In many cases, there are other risks to the child besides the risk of physical injury. The evidence which is relevant to identifying the perpetrator will also be relevant to identifying the other

risks to the child and to assessing what will be best for him in the future. But clearly the steps needed to protect against some risks will be different from the steps needed to protect against others. And the overall calculus of what will be best for the child in the future will be affected by the nature and extent of the identified risks. There are many, many factors bearing upon the child's best interests and the identification of risks is only one of them.

This case is also included in relation to:

H4 Decisions must be on facts found not suspicions
H24 Identifying perpetrators: standard of proof
H25 Identifying perpetrators: the pool of possible perpetrators
H26 Identifying perpetrators: caution where cannot identify

Costs

H28 COSTS: PRINCIPLES IN PRIVATE LAW CASES

Re T (Order for costs)

[2005] EWCA Civ 311, [2005] 2 FLR 681 at 690 and 694

Court of Appeal

Wall LJ

The principles relating to costs in family proceedings relating to children

[36] The principles, which fall to be applied, are not, we think, in dispute. The judge summarised them succinctly in the following way:

'2.1 The CPR apply. Under normal circumstances, according to r 44.3(2) (a), the general rule is that costs should follow the event, although the court can make a different order (r 44.3(2)(b)).

2.2 However, this general rule does not apply to family proceedings (Family Proceedings (Miscellaneous Amendments) Rules 1999).

2.3 It is suggested that even in family proceedings, the general rule is probably the starting point but can more easily be displaced (*Gojkovic v Gojkovic (No 2)* [1992] Fam 40).

2.4 In cases involving children in particular, costs awarded against one parent or another are exceptional since the court is anxious to avoid the situation where a parent may feel "punished" by the other parent which will reduce co-operation between them. This will only impinge ultimately on the welfare of the child or the children concerned (*London Borough of Sutton v Davis (Costs) (No 2)* [1994] 2 FLR 569; *Re M (Local Authority's Costs)* [1995] 1 FLR 533).

2.5 The conduct of the parties is in reality the major consideration when deciding whether or not an exceptional order for costs should be made. It should only be made if the penalised party has been unreasonable in his or her conduct. Moreover the 'unreasonableness' must relate to the conduct of the litigation rather than the welfare of the child (*R v R (Costs: Child Case)* [1997] 2 FLR 95).

2.6 One has to be very careful in this distinction when, as in the case of (the mother), the apparent unreasonableness is as a result of the personality of the relevant party. In such circumstances, there is often an overlap of that party's conduct of the litigation and the conduct relating to the welfare of the child.

2.7 At the beginning of my involvement (the father) was applying for contact in relation to A as well as J. His welfare has also been a concern from time to time throughout. However, the costs in dispute have been incurred in relation to J's welfare alone.'

...

Discussion and analysis

[46] Despite the extensive citation of authority, we think the principles governing the award of costs in children's cases are well established and more than adequately summarised by the judge in the extract from her judgment, which we have set out at para [36] above.

General notes:

For costs on appeal see *EM v SW* [2009] EWCA Civ 311, applied by Sumner J in *Re S (Leave to remove: costs)* [2010] 1 FLR 834, in which Sumner J also considered the law on costs on a rehearing.

Other significant cases on this issue:

- *EC-L v DM (Child abduction: costs)* [2005] EWHC 588 (Fam), [2005] 2 FLR 772
- *Re B (Indemnity costs)* [2007] EWCA Civ 921, [2008] 1 FLR 205
- *Re C (Costs: enforcement of foreign contact order)* [2007] EWHC 1993 (Fam), [2008] 1 FLR 619
- *Re F (Family proceedings: costs)* [2008] EWCA Civ 938, [2008] 2 FLR 1662
- *Re N (A child)* [2009] EWHC 2096 (Fam), [2010] 1 FLR 454
- *Re J (Costs of fact-finding hearing)* [2009] EWCA Civ 1350, [2010] 1 FLR 1893

This case is also included in relation to:

B20 Costs orders

H29 COSTS: ILLUSTRATION IN PUBLIC LAW

Re R (Care: disclosure: nature of proceedings)

[2002] 1 FLR 755 at 797

Family Division

Charles J

I would accept the submissions made as to the likelihood that if the allegations of sexual abuse had never been made leading counsel would not have been involved. One of the problems not mentioned in submissions which seems to me to arise is that if in fact full and earlier discovery had been made it does not necessarily follow that allegations of sexual abuse would not have been made in this case: the case may have taken on different aspects. But the underlying reality at this stage is that allegations of sexual abuse have been abandoned and, to my mind, as I said in my judgment, the primary responsibility for that abandonment and therefore the waste of time lies with the local authority. Albeit that as I said in my judgment, others, it seems to me, notwithstanding what has been submitted to me, had some duties and some responsibilities in this respect.

I am not attracted by an approach as advocated at the Bar of trying to strip out involvement of leading counsel or strip out involvement as to days.

I have had regard to the fact that the issue arises between two sets of public funding, admittedly from different budgets. But it seems to me that I should reflect what I regard as the primary duty and thus the primary failing in an order for costs.

I think the correct approach is to take a robust and round approach to this without seeking to attribute and apportion in any particular way. In taking that approach, I have regard to the fact that leading counsel perhaps would not have been involved in this case on behalf of any of the respondents, although I think that leading counsel might none the less have been involved on behalf of the local authority.

It is a rough and ready approach. I have toyed with the idea of making an order relating to days of the hearing, apart from the opening day, and saying that it should be X number of days that are paid. I have changed from that to think that I should order a percentage of the costs of each of the first four respondents which covers additional preparation time and the involvement of leading counsel.

It seems to me that the correct order for me to make in all the circumstances is that the local authority should pay 25% of the costs of the first, second and third respondents and should pay 15% of the costs of the fourth respondent, which reflects the difference in representation.

The guardian, in my judgment very properly, makes no application for costs.

I would also express the view, which can be conveyed, for what it is worth, to the Legal Services Commission that this is an issue between publicly funded bodies. They may, as a matter of discretion, wish to take that into account in deciding whether or not they enforce this order having regard to the circumstances of the case and the way in which legal aid is granted in family proceedings.

This case is also included in relation to:

D5 Reunification not an overriding factor
G22 Preparation and disclosure: duties of LA
G23 Preparation and disclosure: mirror duties of respondents
G24 Disclosure of relevant notes
G41 Court / parties / experts bound by findings made / not made
G45 Use of experts: general guidance
G51 Responsibilities on receipt of report
G75 Statement of general principle (2)
G82 Public interest immunity

Appeals

H30   APPEAL FROM FPC: ACHIEVING A STAY

Re J (A minor) (residence)

[1994] 1 FLR at 369 at 374

Family Division

Singer J

There then ensued an extremely unfortunate series of events which I am satisfied in the result has not done particular harm, although it must have been very upsetting to the mother, and indeed her advisers, who were sent from pillar to post trying to get a stay. I have not heard full argument about the matter. I may, therefore, be wrong when I say that there appears to be, in the rules governing procedure in the magistrates' court on applications under the Children Act, no provision expressly permitting them to grant a stay. It is, of course, true that, when they make, for instance, an order which has the effect of transferring residence from one party to the other, they can say that this should happen today, next week, next month or next year; and I have no doubt that there are cases where they come back into court, announce their decision and the disappointed parent then says, 'Well, you have not yet said when the transfer is to take place; we would like to consider an appeal; would you defer the handover for a period to enable legal aid applications to be made if necessary and an appeal lodged, and then an application for a continuation of the stay can be made to a High Court judge?'

I can see how, in practical terms, the magistrates might agree to that and that would be a proper exercise, in my view, of their discretion under s 11(7) because they would not have made an order before that point specifying when the handover was to take place. But in this case the parties had left court on 4 June 1993. The appeal had been lodged and I cannot at the moment see any jurisdictional basis upon which the magistrates – who at this point were functus because they had discharged their obligations – could have directed a stay in the absence, as I currently understand it, of any express provision giving them that power. It is disappointing to hear that those responsible for listing in Manchester took the view that there was no jurisdiction in the High Court to grant a stay unless and until an application had been made to the court below, which resulted in the inevitable ping-pong situation of the magistrates saying they have not got jurisdiction and the High Court saying that it has not got jurisdiction, all of which took up quite a deal of time until the mother, worn down through attrition, decided simply to concentrate on getting the case heard, as it has been today.

It is my not fully considered view that, where magistrates make an order (whether or not they defer its operation) which it is intended to appeal (whether or not a notice of appeal had been lodged at that point) there should be no difficulty in securing a relatively immediate and, if necessary, informal hearing before a High Court judge, preferably sitting in the locality, or a liaison judge if he is available, or any High Court judge sitting in London, to deal, simply as a holding operation, with what may otherwise cause great difficulties if not done in time, namely the stay of the operation of a magistrates' order pending an appeal, and indeed any other directions that are necessary. I would think it extremely unfortunate if those responsible for getting cases before judges at an appropriate level in any part of the country made it difficult to apply for a stay.

General notes:

Attention is drawn to CA 1989, s 40, Orders pending appeals in cases about care or supervision orders; as to which, see *Re M (A minor) (Appeal: interim order)* [1994] 1 FLR 54.

H31   URGENT APPEALS TO COURT OF APPEAL

Re S (Child proceedings: urgent appeals)

[2007] EWCA Civ 958, [2007] 2 FLR 1044 at 1047

Court of Appeal

Wall LJ

[8]   As I indicated earlier, it seems to me that this case raises a number of unsatisfactory features, and I wish simply to deal with one of them so that the profession is given information about what can and cannot occur. As I indicated earlier, the order was made on a Friday. The appellant's notice, which was filed on 3 July, seeks a stay of the judge's order; but the judge's order had, of course, been implemented, and there was no application to this court for a stay, save for the request in the appellant's notice. I regard that as highly unsatisfactory, given that the father's case was that the child should never have been removed.

[9]   What could have happened – I forebear to say *should* have happened – what could have happened is as follows: the judge could have been asked for a stay. If he refused it, he could have been asked to delay implementation or enforcement of the order for a sufficient period of time to allow the appellant to approach this court. As I say, 22 June was a Friday. The judge could have been asked, for example, to delay the implementation of the order until close of business on 25 June, and if he refused to delay it, and if he insisted on the order being implemented on 22 June, counsel for the father could have made immediate contact with this court by telephone, and could have asked for an urgent stay until an on-notice hearing, which would have taken place on 25 June or shortly afterwards.

[10]   Had that occurred, it is highly likely that this court would have listed the application for permission to appeal as a matter of urgency, with the appeal to follow if permission was granted. Whether it gave permission or refused it, this court is also likely to have given robust case management directions, designed to ensure that the substantive proceedings were heard swiftly. This case has plainly drifted on the ground in a wholly unsatisfactory manner, and, in my view, it is quite unacceptable for there to be a final hearing date as long away as 18 February 2008, in proceedings which have been going on for the best part of, if not more than, a year. I repeat, therefore, and re-emphasise, the practice in this court in relation to urgent applications related to children.

In office hours, a potential appellant who wishes to apply for an immediate stay should contact the Court of Appeal office at the Royal Courts of Justice on the conventional telephone number, 0207 947 6000; out of hours, such an appellant should contact the security offices of the Royal Courts of Justice, 0207 947 6260. In either event, the appellant will be able to speak to a Deputy Master who, in turn, will speak to a Lord Justice. Provided the latter is satisfied that the matter is appropriately urgent, and a short stay is called for, he or she will either grant a stay, or arrange for the matter to be listed at short notice for a short oral hearing, on notice to the other parties, within the time frame permitted by the judge at first instance. If the court is then satisfied either that permission to appeal should be granted or that the application for permission should be listed urgently, with appeal to follow if permission is granted, it will give such a direction. In children's cases or other cases of urgency, this court can move very swiftly indeed. Thus, had that procedure been followed in the instant case, it is highly unlikely that the child would have been separated from his father without a short on-notice oral hearing for a stay in this court. The child would have been permitted to continue to reside with his father pending the hearing of the application for a stay, or if a stay had been granted, up until the application for permission to appeal, or, in the instant case, as permission to appeal was granted, until the hearing of the appeal itself.

[11] As I have already stated, this court is also likely to have made a direction for an urgent listing and fixed a date for that hearing. It must be emphasised that these facilities are designed to cater for urgent cases and must not be abused. When a potential applicant is legally represented, it will always be appropriate for that legal representative to make the approach to this court, but clearly the profession needs to understand that the emergency facilities are always available to deal with urgent child cases and can be speedily accessed by the profession by telephone where necessary. If it is objected that such an application in such a case would not be covered by public funding, I am in no doubt at all that this court would accept an undertaking from the parties' legal advisers to file the appellant's notice once public funding had been obtained. Plainly, an application will need to be made urgently for the certificate to be extended, and in the scenario I have envisaged, it is highly likely that this court would also encourage the Legal Services Commission to consider an application for funding as a matter of the greatest urgency.

[12] I propose to invite the President to make available to the designated family judges both paras [26] and [27] of Wilson LJ's judgment in *Re A (A Child)* [2007] EWCA Civ 899 which covers the same ground, and this extract from my judgment dealing with the same point, so that they can be widely disseminated within the judiciary hearing family cases, and made available both to the Family Law Bar Association and Resolution, to ensure that the message given in those two cases is clearly known to its members.

H32   APPEAL AGAINST CASE MANAGEMENT DECISIONS (1)

W v Oldham Metropolitan Borough Council

[2005] EWCA Civ 1247, [2006] 1 FLR 543 at 549

Court of Appeal

Wall LJ

[33] I am equally conscious that this court does not encourage interlocutory appeals against case management decisions made by experienced judges. I understand also the funding difficulties in mounting such appeals. However, if a second opinion on a critical medical issue is thought to be necessary, it is essential that if, as is likely, the judge has refused permission to appeal, an application for permission to appeal is made to this court swiftly and at the earliest opportunity. Any such application should be marked as urgent. Such applications in children's cases, properly marked as urgent, are placed quickly before a specialist Lord Justice, and if perceived to have merit, will be listed for hearing within days. Self-evidently, the more time goes by, the more difficult any such application is to mount.

[34] This judgment is not an encouragement to a disappointed party to challenge pre-final hearing case management decisions, but such decisions do, sometimes, throw up points of fundamental importance. That is the case here. In such circumstances, a party should not hesitate to seek permission to appeal. Such an application, as I have already stated, will be dealt with swiftly in this court. In the instant case, the parents could also make the point that the original application had not been opposed either by the local authority or the guardian.

This case is also included in relation to:

G54 Obtaining a second expert's opinion

H33 APPEAL AGAINST CASE MANAGEMENT DECISIONS (2)

Re P and P (Care proceedings: appointment of experts)

[2009] EWCA Civ 610, [2009] 2 FLR 1370 at 1374

Court of Appeal

Wall LJ

[16] The moral of this case is that the capacity of this court to act swiftly is not limited to cases which require a stay. If there is a particular reason for expedition, or if an advocate wishes to engage this court as a matter of urgency, he or she should either speak to a Deputy Master on the telephone, or ask to be put through to a Lord Justice with family experience. In cases of lesser urgency, but which still require expedition, the advocate should invite the office to place the papers before such a Lord Justice as a matter of urgency. The Lord Justice concerned will then, in consultation with the listing office and with colleagues, be able to give directions designed to resolve the application swiftly. We re-emphasise that the system is not to be abused. The issue must be one which requires urgent attention.

[17] It is, furthermore, self-evident that case management decisions by the High Court and the circuit bench are not to be challenged on a whim, or because one party simply happens to disagree with them. They are discretionary decisions in which the allocated judge enjoys a very wide discretion to deal with the case within the confines of the overriding objective and taking into account the best interests of the child. There must be a point of substance which requires an urgent challenge and speedy resolution. In the overwhelming majority of cases, no such point will arise. Where it does, however, speed is of the essence. Delay, as the 1989 Act makes clear, is usually contrary to the interests of children, as well as being the enemy of justice in most child cases.

H34 RESPONSIBILITIES OF ADVOCATES AT FIRST INSTANCE

Re T (Contact: alienation: permission to appeal)

[2002] EWCA Civ 1736, [2003] 1 FLR 531 at 537 and 545

Court of Appeal

Thorpe and Arden LJJ

THORPE LJ:

[13] However, it seems to me that, as a matter of practice, when a judgment is handed down by a judge of the Family Division in this building, the aggrieved party should consider in advance of the hand-down fixture whether or not an application for permission is to be made and if the decision is to apply, then the application should be made at the hand-down. The judge thereby has an opportunity to give on the requisite form his or her reasons for rejecting the application, the statement of which may be of some value to this court if the permission application is subsequently renewed.

ARDEN LJ:

[39] In the same case,[1] this court also considered whether it was appropriate for a judge to be invited to amplify his reasons.

> *'Amplification of reasons*
>
> 22. In *Flannery and Another v Halifax Estate Agencies Ltd* at 383 the court made two suggestions with a view to preventing unnecessary appeals on the ground of the absence of reasons. It suggested that one remedy open to the appeal court would be to remit the matter to the trial judge with an invitation or requirement to give reasons. In *Flannery and Another v Halifax Estate Agencies Ltd* this was not considered appropriate because more than 1 year had passed since the hearing. The delay between hearing and appeal will normally be too long to make a remission to the trial judge for further reasons a desirable course. The same is not true of the position shortly after judgment has been given.

---

[1]   *English v Emery Reimbold & Strick Ltd; DJ and C Withers (Farms) Ltd v Ambic Equipment Ltd, Verrechia (trading as Freightmaster Commercials) v Commissioner of Police of the Metropolis* [2002] EWCA Civ 605, [2002] 1 WLR 2409.

23. The other suggestion made by the court in *Flannery and Another v Halifax Estate Agencies Ltd* was that the respondent to an application for permission to appeal on the ground of lack of reasons should consider inviting the judge to give his reasons, and his explanation as to why they were not set out in the judgment, in an affidavit for use at the leave hearing if leave be granted.

24. We are not greatly attracted by the suggestion that a judge who has given inadequate reasons should be invited to have a second bite at the cherry. But we are much less attracted at the prospect of expensive appellate proceedings on the ground of lack of reasons. Where the judge who has heard the evidence has based a rational decision on it, the successful party will suffer an injustice if that decision is appealed, let alone set aside, simply because the judge has not included in his judgment adequate reasons for his decision. The appellate court will not be in as good a position to substitute its decision, should it decide that this course is viable, while an appeal followed by a re-hearing will involve a hideous waste of costs.

25. Accordingly, we recommend the following course. If an application for permission to appeal on the ground of lack of reasons is made to the trial judge, the judge should consider whether his judgment is defective for lack of reasons, adjourning for that purpose should he find this necessary. If he concludes that it is, he should set out to remedy the defect by the provision of additional reasons refusing permission to appeal on the basis that he has adopted that course. If he concludes that he has given adequate reasons, he will no doubt refuse permission to appeal. If an application for permission to appeal on the ground of lack of reasons is made to the appellate court and it appears to the appellate court that the application is well founded, it should consider adjourning the application and remitting the case to the trial judge with an invitation to provide additional reasons for his decision or, where appropriate, his reasons for a specific finding or findings. Where the appellate court is in doubt as to whether the reasons are adequate, it may be appropriate to direct that the application be adjourned to an oral hearing, on notice to the respondent.

The approach of the appellate court

26. Where permission is granted to appeal on the grounds that the judgment does not contain adequate reasons, the appellate court should first review the judgment, in the context of the material evidence and submissions at the trial, in order to determine whether, when all of these are considered, it is apparent why the judge reached the decision that he did. If satisfied that the reason is apparent and that it is a valid basis for the judgment, the appeal will be dismissed. This was the approach adopted by this court, in the light of *Flannery*

and Another v Halifax Estate Agencies Ltd in *Ludlow v National Power plc* (unreported) 17 November 2000. If despite this exercise the reason for the decision is not apparent, then the appeal court will have to decide whether itself to proceed to a rehearing, or to direct a new trial.'

[40] *English v Emery Reimbold & Strick Ltd; DJ and C Withers (Farms) Ltd v Ambic Equipment Ltd, Verrechia (trading as Freightmaster Commercials) v Commissioner of Police of the Metropolis* was not of course a decision in care proceedings in the Family Division, which unlike normal civil litigation have a quasi-inquisitorial nature (see the judgment of Wilson J in *Re L (Minors) (Care Proceedings: Solicitors)* [2001] 1 WLR 100). However, I do not see why the principle that a judge might be invited to amplify his reasons if they are not clear should not equally apply in such proceedings too ...

[41] In a complex case, it might well be prudent, and certainly not out of place, for the judge, having handed down or delivered judgment, to ask the advocates whether there are any matters which he has not covered. Even if he does not do this, an advocate ought immediately, as a matter of courtesy at least, to draw the judge's attention to any material omission of which he is then aware or then believes exists. It is well established that it is open to a judge to amend his judgment, if he thinks fit, at any time up to the drawing of the order. In many cases, the advocate ought to raise the matter with the judge in pursuance of his duty to assist the court to achieve the overriding objective (Civil Procedure Rules 1998, r 1.3, which does not as such apply to these proceedings); and in some cases, it may follow from the advocate's duty not to mislead the court that he should raise the matter rather than allow the order to be drawn. It would be unsatisfactory to use an omission by a judge to deal with a point in a judgment as grounds for an application for appeal if the matter has not been brought to the judge's attention when there was a ready opportunity so to do. Unnecessary costs and delay may result. I should make it clear that there are general observations for assistance in future cases, and that I make no criticisms of counsel in this case.

General notes:

Cf *Egan v Motor Services (Bath)* [2007] EWCA Civ 1002, [2008] 1 FLR 1346 (when judge circulates draft judgment it is only exceptionally appropriate to ask for any point of substance to be reconsidered).

Other significant cases on this issue:

- *Re M (Fact-finding hearing: burden of proof)* [2008] EWCA Civ 1261, [2009] 1 FLR 1177

This case is also included in relation to:

H7   Extent of reasoning (1)

H35　AVOIDING OVER-REPRESENTATION

Birmingham City Council v H (No 3)

[1994] 1 FLR 224 at 225

House of Lords

Lord Keith

It is desirable that something should be said about the level of separate representation of parties, all at public expense, which was a feature of this appeal. The appellant, R, proceeding through his guardian ad litem, was represented by solicitors and by senior and junior counsel funded by the Legal Aid Board, and rightly so. Birmingham City Council, which supported the appeal, was similarly represented, at the expense of the Birmingham community charge or council tax payers.

Separate solicitors and also senior and junior counsel appeared for each of the mother, the father and the guardian ad litem to the mother. These three had lodged a joint written case. The mother and the father were funded by the Legal Aid Board, and the mother's guardian ad litem by Birmingham City Council. There was no significant difference between the arguments for those who supported the appeal or between the arguments for those who resisted it.

In the circumstances there must be a serious question whether the degree of separate representation was necessary, or in any event whether the employment of so many senior counsel was justified. It is to be hoped that in future cases where a similar question may arise serious consideration will be given by solicitors and counsel to the practicability and desirability where appropriate of securing joint representation with a view to minimising the burden on public funds.

Other significant cases on this issue:

* *Re S and D (Children: powers of court)* [1995] 2 FLR 456

H36 PERMISSION TO APPEAL

Re W (Permission to appeal)

[2007] EWCA Civ 786, [2008] 1 FLR 406 at 412

Court of Appeal

Wall LJ

[20] GW, therefore, and others in his position must understand that our function in the present case is very limited indeed. Our task is to review the decision made by McFarlane J on 7 March 2007. We have to put to ourselves the proposition set out in the second sentence of para [16] above. That question itself can be broken down to the following:

(1) Did the judge arguably make any error of law in reaching his conclusion?

(2) Was there, arguably, insufficient material on which the judge could properly make the findings of fact and the assessments of the witness which he did make?

(3) Is it arguable that the order he made was not properly open to him in the exercise of his judicial discretion?

(4) Is there, arguably, any error in the exercise of that discretion which enables us to say that his order was, arguably, plainly wrong?

[21] It is only if the answer to any one of these questions is 'yes' that we can give GW permission to appeal. We are thus considering only the first of the four points identified by GW as set out in para [14] above. We stress that this is not a matter of choice. The Court of Appeal, as GW himself points out in the papers presented to us, is a court created by Parliament, and governed by Act of Parliament, currently the Supreme Court Act 1981. Under that Act and the CPR, the *only* points we have jurisdiction to consider are whether or not GW should be granted permission to appeal against McFarlane J's order of 7 March 2007, and whether, in so doing, he should be permitted to adduce fresh evidence.

H37   G V G: INTERFERING WITH JUDICIAL DISCRETION: 'PLAINLY WRONG'

G v G (Minors: custody appeal)

[1985] FLR 894 at 896

House of Lords

Lord Fraser of Tullybelton

From that decision the mother appealed to the Court of Appeal ([1985] FLR 70). Sir John Arnold P gave the first judgment and, before dealing fully with the facts of the case, he referred generally to the method of trying appeals in cases concerning the custody of children. After referring to some recent reported cases on the subject, the President said, at p 72:

> 'Those cases exhibit some degree of homogeneity, of course; but they also seem, at first sight, to exhibit a degree of semantic dichotomy. It is a discernible thread running through, I think, every one of those cases and the cases cited in them, that it is not decisive of an appeal in this court from the decision of the court below, exercising the particular discretionary jurisdiction of deciding the custody of children (but also, I think, any discretionary jurisdiction), that the result of the exercise of discretion would, or might, have been different if the members of the court of Appeal had themselves been exercising the discretion. There has to be more than that before the discretionary decision can be overturned. The question, if there be one, is: How much more?'

He stated his conclusion in the following passage, at p 73:

> 'I believe that there is a way of reconciling these cases. I believe that if the court comes to the conclusion, when examining the decision at first instance, that there is so blatant an error in the conclusion that it could only have been reached if the judge below had erred in his method of decision – sometimes called the balancing exercise – then the court is at liberty to interfere; but that, if the observation of the appellate court extends no further than that the decision in terms of the result of the balancing exercise was one with which they might, or do, disagree as a matter of result, then that by itself is not enough, and that falls short of the conclusion, which is essential, that the judge has erred in his method. I cannot think of any case in which this particular issue had to be faced, in which that method of determination is not intellectually satisfactory, logically supportable

or consistent with the result of any of the cases in the appellate courts; and I shall approach this case on the footing that what this court should seek to do is to answer the question whether the court discerns a wrongness in the result of so striking a character as to make it a legitimate conclusion that there must have been an error of method – apart, of course, from a disclosed inclusion of irrelevant or exclusion of relevant matters.'

Miss Platt, who appeared for the mother both in the Court of Appeal and before your Lordships, criticized that statement of principle. I hope that I shall not misrepresent her contention if I summarize it as follows. It falls into two parts. The first is that when an appellate court is exercising its jurisdiction in cases concerned with children, in which the welfare of the children has been declared by Parliament to be the first and paramount consideration –see the Guardianship of Minors Act 1971 – special rules apply. Secondly, it was said that in such cases the only proper way in which an appellate court can assess whether the judge of first instance has exercised his jurisdiction correctly is to carry out the same balancing exercise between the various factors in favour of and against each party as the judge at first instance has done, and if it reaches a different conclusion from his as to what is in the best interests of the child, it must allow the appeal.

The argument which I have thus crudely summarized was of course expanded and elaborated, and was very persuasively presented, but I am of opinion that it is unsound. I entirely reject the contention that appeals in custody cases, or in other cases concerning the welfare of children, are subject to special rules of their own. The jurisdiction in such cases is one of great difficulty, as every judge who has had to exercise it must be aware. The main reason is that in most of these cases there is no right answer. All practicable answers are to some extent unsatisfactory and therefore to some extent wrong, and the best that can be done is to find an answer that is reasonably satisfactory. It is comparatively seldom that the Court of Appeal, even if it would itself have preferred a different answer, can say that the judge's decision was wrong, and unless it can say so, it will leave his decision undisturbed. The limited role of the Court of Appeal in such cases was explained by Cumming-Bruce LJ in *Clarke-Hunt v Newcombe* (1983) 4 FLR 482, where he said, at p 486:

'There was not really a right solution; there were two alternative wrong solutions. The problem of the judge was to appreciate the factors pointing in each direction and to decide which of the two bad solutions was the least dangerous, having regard to the long-term interests of the children, and so he decided the matter. Whether I would have decided it the same way if I had been in the position of the trial judge I do not know. I might have taken the same course as the judge and I might not, but I was never in that situation. I am sitting in the Court of Appeal deciding a quite different question:

has it been shown that the judge to whom Parliament has confided the exercise of discretion, plainly got the wrong answer? I emphasize the word "Plainly". In spite of the efforts of [counsel] the answer to that question clearly must be that the judge has not been shown plainly to have got it wrong.'

That passage, with which I respectfully agree, seems to me exactly in line with the conclusion of Sir John Arnold P in the present case, which I have already quoted. The reason for the limited role of the Court of Appeal in custody cases is not that appeals in such cases are subject to any special rules, but that there are often two or more possible decisions, any one of which might reasonably be thought to be the best, and any one of which therefore a judge may make without being held to be wrong. In such cases, therefore, the judge has a discretion and they are cases to which the observations of Asquith LJ, as he then was, in *Bellenden (Formerly Satterthwaite) v Satterthwaite* [1948] 1 All ER 343 apply. My attention was called to that case by my noble and learned friend Lord Bridge of Harwich, after the hearing in this appeal. That was an appeal against an order for maintenance payable to a divorced wife. Asquith LJ said, at p 345:

'It is, of course, not enough for the wife to establish that this court might, or would, have made a different order. We are here concerned with a judicial discretion, and it is of the essence of such a discretion that on the same evidence two different minds might reach widely different decisions without either being appealable. It is only where the decision exceeds the generous ambit within which reasonable disagreement is possible, and is, in fact, plainly wrong, that an appellate body is entitled to interfere.'

I would only add that, in cases dealing with the custody of children, the desirability of putting an end to litigation, which applies to all classes of case, is particularly strong because the longer legal proceedings last, the more are the children, whose welfare is at stake, likely to be disturbed by the uncertainty.

Nevertheless, there will be some cases in which the Court of Appeal decides that the judge of first instance has come to the wrong conclusion. In such cases it is the duty of the Court of Appeal to substitute its own decision for that of the judge. The circumstances in which the Court of Appeal should substitute its own decision have been described in a number of reported cases to some of which our attention was drawn. We were told by counsel that practitioners are finding difficulty in ascertaining the correct principles to apply because of the various ways in which judges have expressed themselves in these cases. I do not think it would be useful for me to go through the cases and to analyse the various expressions used by different judges and attempt to reconcile them exactly. Certainly it would not be useful to inquire whether different shades of meaning are intended to be conveyed by words such as 'blatant error' used by the President in the present case, and words such as 'clearly wrong', 'plainly wrong', or simply 'wrong' used by other judges in other cases. All these various expressions were used in order to emphasize the point that the appellate court should only interfere when they consider that the judge of first instance has not merely preferred an imperfect solution which is different from an alternative imperfect solution which the Court of Appeal might or would have adopted, but has exceeded the generous ambit within which a reasonable disagreement is possible. The principle was stated in this House by my noble and learned friend Lord Scarman in *B v W (Wardship: Appeal)* [1979] 1 WLR 1041, where, after mentioning the course open to the Court of Appeal if it was minded to reverse or vary a custody order, he said at p 1055F:

> 'But at the end of the day the court may not intervene unless it is satisfied either that the judge exercised his discretion upon a wrong principle or that, the judge's decision being so plainly wrong, he must have exercised his discretion wrongly.'

The same principle was expressed in other words, and at slightly greater length, in the Court of Appeal (Stamp, Browne and Bridge LJJ) in *Re F (A Minor) (Wardship: Appeal)* [1976] Fam. 238, where the majority (Browne and Bridge LJJ) held that the court had jurisdiction to reverse or vary a decision concerning a child made by a judge in the exercise of his discretion, if they considered that he had given insufficient weight or too much weight to certain factors. Browne LJ said at p 257E:

> 'Apart from the effect of seeing and hearing witnesses, I cannot see why the general principle applicable to the exercise of the discretion in respect of infants should be any different from the general principle applicable to any other form of discretion.'

Bridge LJ, as my noble and learned friend then was, agreed with Browne LJ and I quote a passage from his speech where, after stating that his view was different from that of the judge, he went on to say at p 266:

> 'Can this conclusion prevail or is there some rule of law which bars it? The judge was exercising a discretion. He saw and heard the witnesses. It is impossible to say that he considered any irrelevant matter, left out of account any relevant matter, erred in law, or applied any wrong principle. On the view I take, his error was in the balancing exercise. He either gave too little weight to the factors favourable, or too much weight to the factors adverse to the father's claim that he should retain care and control of the child.
>
> The general principle is clear. If this were a discretion not depending on the judge having seen and heard the witnesses, an error in the balancing exercise, if I may adopt that phrase for short, would entitle

the appellate court to reverse his decision [authorities cited]. The reason for a practical limitation on the scope of that principle where the discretion exercised depends on seeing and hearing witnesses is obvious. The appellate court cannot interfere if it lacks the essential material on which the balancing exercise depended. But the importance of seeing and hearing witnesses may vary very greatly according to the circumstances of individual cases. If in any discretion case concerning children the appellate court can clearly detect that a conclusion, which is neither dependent on nor justified by the trial judge's advantage in seeing and hearing witnesses, is vitiated by an error in the balancing exercise, I should be very reluctant to hold that it is powerless to interfere.'

The decision in *Re F (A Minor) (Wardship: Appeal)* [1976] Fam 238 is also important because the majority rejected, rightly in my view, the dissenting opinion of Stamp LJ at p 254, who would have limited the right of the Court of Appeal to interfere with the judge's decision in custody cases to cases 'where it concludes that the course followed by the judge is one that no reasonable judge having taken into account all the relevant circumstances could have adopted'. That is the test which the court applies in deciding whether it is entitled to exercise judicial control over the decision of an administrative body, see the well-known case of *Associated Provincial Picture Houses Ltd v Wednesbury Corporation* [1948] 1 KB 223. It is not the appropriate test for deciding whether the Court of Appeal is entitled to interfere with the decision made by a judge in the exercise of his discretion.

H38   FINELY BALANCED CASES

Re N (Residence: hopeless appeals)

[1995] 2 FLR 230 at 235 and 236

Court of Appeal

Butler-Sloss and Ward LJJ

BUTLER-SLOSS LJ:

In such a finely balanced case, where the judge had to balance the possibility of sexual abuse in the future against the actuality of emotional abuse in the present and the future, he chose to go down one path rather than the other and it is absolutely impossible, in my judgment, for this court to interfere.

There is nothing in the judgment that shows that the judge was wrong in principle; that he failed to take into account what he should have taken into account, or that he did not take into account what he should have taken into account. Standing back in this difficult and disturbing case I, for one, could not say that he was plainly wrong ...

WARD LJ:

It may be an irony that the more finely balanced the decision, and the more acutely the judge has agonised over his decision, the less prospect there is of that decision being successfully appealed. The understandable reaction of the disappointed party is that the judge has got it wrong; therein lies the fallacy. That fallacy was exposed by the House of Lords in *G v G (Minors: Custody Appeal)* [1985] FLR 894. The fallacy is this: in a case involving the welfare of a child there is often no right answer. There cannot be an absolute of right where the choice is between two solutions, each of which is imperfect. That state of affairs does, therefore, confront the profession with the necessity, I would say duty, of making a dispassionate analysis of the judgment, to identify whether there is any prospect at all of persuading the Court of Appeal that the factual substratum of the judgment can be attacked, bearing in mind how difficult it is successfully to sustain such an attack; and if not, whether the balance, so finely held, can ever be said to be plainly wrong.

H39   LIMITS ON APPEAL COURT'S AUTHORITY

Re J (Child returned abroad: Convention rights)

[2005] UKHL 40, [2005] 2 FLR 802 at 805 and 806

House of Lords

Baroness Hale

[4] The issue of principle in this case is the proper approach to applications for the summary return of children to countries which are not parties to the Hague Convention on the Civil Aspects of International Child Abduction 1980 (the Hague Convention). But it is also another example of intervention by the Court of Appeal in the exercise of discretion by a trial judge despite the fact that he had, in the view of the appeal court, properly directed himself on the law. I believe that the Court of Appeal was wrong on both points.

....

Should the Court of Appeal have intervened?

[10] The Court of Appeal appears to have intervened on the basis, first, that the judge's conclusion on the risk was not justified by the evidence and, secondly, that he had given it too much weight in his overall conclusion. Yet the assessment of the risk depended entirely on the judge's evaluation of the father's present intentions and likely future behaviour and its impact upon the child. There was objective evidence of the risk in the fact that the father had made the allegations in writing and then withdrawn them when he saw that they were damaging, rather than helping, his case. Whether he might do so again depended crucially on the judge's evaluation of his oral evidence. The judge was the only person who could do this. He concluded that, while the father was sincere in his current intention not to raise such allegations again, there was a serious risk that if disputes arose in future, as they might easily do, he would resurrect them. These were findings of credibility and primary fact with which, for all the reasons explained by Lord Hoffmann in *Piglowska v Piglowski* [1999] 1 WLR 1360, [1999] 2 FLR 763, at 1372–1373 and 784 respectively, an appeal court is not entitled to interfere.

[11] Furthermore, once the judge has made such a finding, it becomes a factor to be weighed in the balance in the exercise of his discretion. To say that it should not have tipped the balance in a case such as this, which the judge regarded as a difficult one, is tantamount to saying that it should not have been taken into account at all or that the other considerations were so strongly in favour of return that it should not have been allowed to outweigh them. But even the brief account of the facts given above shows that this was not a case in which all other considerations pointed only one way. The age of the child, the length of time he had lived here and the substantial connection of both mother and child with this country were all relevant.

[12] If there is indeed a discretion in which various factors are relevant, the evaluation and balancing of those factors is also a matter for the trial judge. Only if his decision is so plainly wrong that he must have given far too much weight to a particular factor is the appellate court entitled to interfere: see *G v G* [1985] 1 WLR 647, [1985] FLR 894. Too ready an interference by the appellate court, particularly if it always seems to be in the direction of one result rather than the other, risks robbing the trial judge of the discretion entrusted to him by the law. In short, if trial judges are led to believe that, even if they direct themselves impeccably on the law, make findings of fact which are open to them on the evidence, and are careful, as this judge undoubtedly was, in their evaluation and weighing of the relevant factors, their decisions are liable to be overturned unless they reach a particular conclusion, they will come to believe that they do not in fact have any choice or discretion in the matter. On that ground alone, and even assuming that the principles applied by the judge were indeed correct, I would allow this appeal.

Other significant cases on this issue:

*   *Vigreux v Michel* [2006] EWCA Civ 630, [2006] 2 FLR 1180 per Wall LJ at [51]–[53]

This case is also included in relation to:

A9   Culture and welfare
F19   Welfare principle applies
F20   No 'strong presumption' in favour of return
F21   Other relevant factors

H40 RE-OPENING OF FINAL APPEAL

Re U (Re-opening of appeal)

[2005] EWCA Civ 52, [2005] 2 FLR 444 at 446, 447 and 449

Court of Appeal

Butler-Sloss P

The application of the principles of Taylor v Lawrence

[4] CPR r 52.17 is headed 'Reopening of final appeals'. Rule 52.17(1) provides:

> 'The Court of Appeal or the High Court will not reopen a final determination of any appeal unless—
>
> (a) it is necessary to do so in order to avoid real injustice;
> (b) the circumstances are exceptional and make it appropriate to reopen the appeal; and
> (c) there is no alternative effective remedy.'

[5] By para (2) 'appeal' includes an application for permission to appeal. There is no doubt that this rule is specifically intended to reflect the reasoning in the judgment of this court in *Taylor v Lawrence*. While this authority is very well known in the legal profession, it seems to us especially important to explain its effect in the context of our decision in this case. There is a pressing public interest, which has to be understood, in confining the circumstances in which the court will reopen an appeal that has already been finally determined to cases of the most exceptional kind; and this is so across all areas of the law, including family law. Accordingly we make no apology for addressing the authority of *Taylor v Lawrence* in some detail.

[6] In that case judgment had been given against the defendants in a county court action. They appealed in part on the ground of an appearance of bias by the judge. It emerged that the judge and his wife had engaged the claimants' solicitors to amend their wills the night before judgment was given in the action. The appeal was dismissed in January 2001. Later, the defendants learnt that the judge had not paid for the services provided by the solicitors during the trial. The defendants applied for permission to reopen their appeal. The application was heard and determined by a constitution of five judges of this court (Lord Woolf CJ, Lord Phillips of Worth Matravers MR, Ward, Brooke and Chadwick LJJ). As is made clear in the judgment of the court delivered by the Lord Woolf CJ, a court of five was exceptionally constituted in order to resolve the important issue of jurisdiction that arose in the case, namely whether there is any power at all to reopen an appeal which has been finally determined.

...

[8] As the court pointed out at 540, the availability of a claim to set aside a judgment obtained by fraud does not mean there are no other situations where serious injustice may occur if there is no power to reopen an appeal. And so the court proceeded to consider, and ultimately to accept (though in guarded terms), the submission by counsel for the defendants to the effect that the Court of Appeal indeed possessed the jurisdiction to reopen previously concluded decisions of its own.

...

Discussion

[16] It is clear that whenever the residual jurisdiction established by the judgment in *Taylor v Lawrence* is sought to be invoked, the court must be satisfied that the case falls within the exceptional category there described before it will accede to the application and reopen the case. One may without levity ask the question, how exceptional is exceptional? The language used by the court (and in CPR r 52.17(1)) is necessarily general: apart from the descriptive phrase 'exceptional circumstances', the requirements are that the probability of a significant (CPR – 'real') injustice must be clearly established, and that there be no effective alternative remedy.

[17] It seems to us to be of the first importance to distinguish the kind of case in which the residual jurisdiction might properly be invoked from one where all that is said is that there exists fresh evidence which could have a substantial effect on the outcome of the case. The principles upon which this court, on a first appeal brought in the ordinary way, will admit new evidence and decide the case in light of it (or remit the matter for a fresh trial) are well known. They are encapsulated in the decision in *Ladd v Marshall* [1954] 1 WLR 1489, (1954) FLR Rep 422 (which is referred to in *Taylor v Lawrence*) with some little modification since the CPR came into force into which it is unnecessary to go. There are essentially three requirements: (a) the evidence could not have been obtained with reasonable diligence for use at the trial; (b) the evidence would probably have had an important (though not necessarily decisive) influence on the result of the case; (c) the evidence must be credible (though it need not be incontrovertible).

[18] These requirements are of an altogether different and less demanding order from what must be shown to invoke the residual jurisdiction to reopen a concluded appeal. The *Ladd v Marshall* rules may promote the admission of fresh evidence where there is no more than a possibility that an injustice, in the shape of a factually erroneous result at the trial, has been perpetrated. The possibility, it is true, must be more than merely fanciful. But the *Taylor v Lawrence* jurisdiction can, in our judgment, only be properly invoked where it is demonstrated that the integrity of the earlier litigation process, whether at trial or at the first appeal, has been critically undermined. We think this language appropriate because the jurisdiction is by no means solely concerned with the case where the earlier process has or may have produced a wrong result (which must be the whole scope of a fresh evidence case), but rather, at least primarily, with special circumstances where the process itself has been corrupted. The instances variously discussed in *Taylor v Lawrence* or in other learning there cited are instructive. Fraud (where relied on to reopen a concluded appeal rather than found a fresh cause of action – *Wood v Gahlings*); bias; the eccentric case where the judge had read the wrong papers; the vice in all these cases is not, or not necessarily, that the decision was factually incorrect but that it was arrived at by a corrupted process. Such instances are so far from the norm that they will inevitably be exceptional. And it is the corruption of justice that as a matter of policy is most likely to validate an exceptional recourse; a recourse which relegates the high importance of finality in litigation to second place.

[19] By contrast a fresh evidence case may disclose nothing to suggest that the process of justice has been corrupted. It may just be that fresh evidence, not previously available or at least not reasonably obtainable for use at the trial, has come along which had it been admitted at trial might have had a significant impact on the result. Such instances are, broadly, the stuff of first-time-round appeals based on new evidence. They are, categorically, not the proper subject matter of *Taylor v Lawrence* applications. The principle of finality yields so as to allow a first appeal on *Ladd v Marshall* grounds. But it will prevail so as to disallow a second appeal – a *Taylor v Lawrence* application – on such grounds.

[20] Even so, is there no case in which fresh evidence might justify a *Taylor v Lawrence* application in the absence of some other factor which has corrupted the litigation process? Since, as the court's judgment shows, the ultimate rationale of *Taylor v Lawrence* is the correction of injustice, it would surely be wrong to answer with an absolute negative. The examples we have mentioned – bias, and the others – cannot be said to constitute the only proper instances for the jurisdiction's application. Nothing in the reasoning justifies so straitjacketed an approach. Indeed, it does not justify a brightline rule by which, for any application to reopen an appeal to succeed, it must be shown that the litigation process has been corrupted, as we have put it. In our view the case where the process has been corrupted is the paradigm case: not necessarily the only case.

[21] However if the discovery of fresh evidence is ever to justify reopening a concluded appeal, the case must at least have this in common with the instances of corrupted process: the injustice that would be perpetrated if the appeal is not reopened must be so grave as to overbear the pressing claims of finality in litigation – especially pressing where what is contemplated is a second appeal. Finality is itself a function of justice, and one of great importance. Here the observations of Lord Wilberforce in *The Ampthill Peerage* [1977] AC 547, set out in *Taylor v Lawrence*, particularly repay attention. Now, it is to be noted that the strictures to be found in the *Ladd v Marshall* principles, not least the requirement that the fresh evidence proffered could not have been obtained with reasonable diligence for use at the trial, are justified by the demands of finality; and *Ladd v Marshall* applies to a first appeal. To entertain a second appeal on fresh evidence grounds, greater strictures are required. It follows that, as we have already indicated, *Ladd v Marshall* grounds will in principle not suffice to justify a second appeal.

[22] What will? In our judgment it must at least be shown, not merely that the fresh evidence demonstrates a real possibility that an erroneous result was arrived at in the earlier proceedings (first instance or appellate), but that there exists a powerful probability that such a result has in fact been perpetrated. That, in our view, is a necessary but by no means a sufficient condition for a successful application under CPR r 52.17(1). It is to be remembered that apart from the requirement of no alternative remedy, '[t]he effect of reopening the appeal on others and the extent to which the complaining party is the author of his own misfortune will also be important considerations' (*Taylor v Lawrence*, at 547). Earlier we stated that the *Taylor v Lawrence* jurisdiction can only be properly invoked where it is demonstrated that the integrity of the earlier litigation process, whether at trial or at the first appeal, has been critically undermined. That test will generally be met where the process has been corrupted. It may be met where it is shown that a wrong result was earlier arrived at. It will not be met where it is shown only that a wrong result may have been arrived at.

Other significant cases on this issue:

- Cf *K v K (Abduction) (No 2)* [2009] EWHC 3378 (Fam), [2010] 1 FLR 1310 (application to reconsider / reverse judgment in Hague Convention case after judgment given but before order perfected)

This case is also included in relation to:

D65 Role of CG / solicitor for child (2)

DIVISION I

MISCELLANEOUS

Contents

Social services

Human rights: miscellaneous domestic authorities

I1 MEANING OF 'FAMILY LIFE'

Singh v Entry Clearance Officer, New Delhi

[2004] EWCA Civ 1075, [2005] 1 FLR 308 at 328

Court of Appeal

Munby J

[58] Before turning to the central issue there are certain preliminary observations I wish to make. The first point is perhaps obvious but needs to be borne in mind. If one takes what until recently was the traditional or conventional form of family it can be seen that there are, in principle, four key relationships. First, there is the relationship between husband and wife. Secondly, there is the relationship between parent and child. Thirdly, there is the relationship between siblings. And, fourthly, there are relationships within the wider family: for example, the relationships between grandparent and grandchild, between nephew and uncle and between cousins. Each of these relationships can in principle give rise to family life within the meaning of Art 8: see, for example, *Abdulaziz, Cabales and Balkandali v United Kingdom* (1985) 7 EHRR 471, at para 62 (family life includes 'the relationship that arises from a lawful and genuine marriage'), *Berrehab v The Netherlands* (1989) 11 EHRR 322, at para 21 ('a child born of such a union [a lawful and genuine marriage] is ipso jure part of that relationship; hence from the moment of the child's birth and by the very fact of it, there exists between him and his parents a bond amounting to "family life", even if the parents are not then living together'), *Marckx v Belgium* (1979–80) 2 EHRR 330, at para 45 ('"family life", within the meaning of Art 8, includes at least the ties between near relatives, for instance, those between grandparents and grandchildren') and *Boyle v United Kingdom* (1995) 19 EHRR 179 (nephew and uncle).

[59] It is also clear that 'family life' is not confined to relationships based on marriage or blood, nor indeed is family life confined to formal relationships recognised in law. Thus family life is not confined to married couples. A de facto relationship outside marriage can give rise to family life (*Abdulaziz, Cabales and Balkandali v United Kingdom* (1985) 7 EHRR 471, at para 63), even if the parties do not live together (*Kroon and Others* *v The Netherlands* (1995) 19 EHRR 263, at para 30), and even if the couple consists of a woman and a female-to-male transsexual (*X, Y and Z v United Kingdom* (1997) 24 EHRR 143, [1997] 2 FLR 892, at para 37). So there can be family life between father and child even where the parents are not married: *Keegan v Ireland* (1994) 18 EHRR 342, at para 44. Likewise there can be family life between a parent and a child even where there is no biological relationship: *X, Y and Z v United Kingdom* (1997) 24 EHRR 143, [1997] 2 FLR 892, at para 37 (family life existed as between the female-to-male transsexual partner of a woman and the child she had conceived by artificial insemination by an anonymous donor). A formal adoption creates family life between the adoptive parents and the child: *X v Belgium and The Netherlands* (1975) D&R 75, *X v France* (1982) 31 D&R 241, *Pini et al v Romania* (unreported) 22 June 2004. Family life can exist between foster-parent and foster-child: *Gaskin v United Kingdom* (1990) 12 EHRR 36, [1990] 1 FLR 167.

[60] Now the Strasbourg court has never sought to define what is meant by family life, nor has it even sought to identify any minimum requirements that must be shown if family life is to be held to exist. That is hardly surprising. After all, the considerations that bear upon the question of whether there is family life as between two childless cohabiting adults (perhaps of the same sex) are not the same as those that bear upon the question of whether there is family life as between (say) an uncle and his nephew. And the considerations that bear upon the question of whether there is family life as between a father and his child may differ markedly depending on whether he was married to the mother, whether he has any blood relationship with the child, or whether, for example, his relationship is founded on adoption (perhaps recognised, perhaps not) or on a fostering arrangement.

[61] I have referred to the traditional or conventional form of family. That takes me on to my second point. Quite apart from the fact that the form the family has until recently tended to take in Protestant northern Europe differs in certain respects from what would until recently have been familiar in Catholic Mediterranean Europe, we need to remember, as Professor Lawrence Stone's great works have taught us, that what we currently view as the traditional or conventional form of family is itself a comparatively modern development. Moreover, and perhaps more to the point, we have to recognise that there have been very profound changes in family life in recent decades.

[62] These changes have been driven by four major developments. First, there have been enormous changes in the social and religious life of our country. The fact is that we live in a secular and pluralistic society. But we also live in a multi-cultural community of many faiths. One of the paradoxes of our lives is that we live in a society which is at one and the same time becoming both increasingly secular but also increasingly diverse in religious affiliation. Our society includes men and women from

every corner of the globe and of every creed and colour under the sun. Secondly, there has been an increasing lack of interest in – in some instances a conscious rejection of – marriage as an institution. As Dr Stephen Cretney has noted in his book *Family Law in the Twentieth Century: A History* (Oxford University Press, 2003), at p 33, although there is no lack of interest in family life (or at least in intimate relationships), the figures demonstrate a striking decline in marriage. Thirdly, there has been a sea-change in society's attitudes towards same-sex unions. Within my professional lifetime we have moved from treating such relationships as perversions to be stamped out by the more or less enthusiastic enforcement of a repressive criminal law to a ready acknowledgment that they are entitled not merely to respect but also, in principle, to equal protection under the law: see *Ghaidan v Godin-Mendoza* [2004] UKHL 30, [2004] 3 WLR 113, [2004] 2 FLR 600, especially the speech of Baroness Hale of Richmond. Fourthly, there have been enormous advances in medical, and in particular reproductive, science so that reproduction is no longer confined to 'natural' methods. Many children today are born as a result of 'high-tech' in vitro fertilisation methods almost inconceivable even a few years ago.

[63] The result of all this is that in our multi-cultural and pluralistic society the family takes many forms. Indeed, in contemporary Britain the family takes an almost infinite variety of forms. Many marry according to the rites of non-Christian faiths. There may be one, two, three or even more generations living together under the same roof. Some people choose to live on their own. People live together as couples, married or not, and with partners who may not always be of the opposite sex. Children live in households where their parents may be married or unmarried. They may be the children of polygamous marriages. They may be brought up by a single parent. Their parents may or may not be their natural parents. Their siblings may be only half-siblings or step-siblings. Some children are brought up by two parents of the same sex. Some children are conceived by artificial donor insemination. Some are the result of surrogacy arrangements. The fact is that many adults and children, whether through choice or circumstance, live in families more or less removed from what until comparatively recently would have been recognised as the typical nuclear family. As Baroness Hale of Richmond observed in *Ghaidan v Godin-Mendoza* [2004] UKHL 30, [2004] 3 WLR 113, [2004] 2 FLR 600 at [141]:

'if [a] couple are bringing up children together, it is unlikely to matter whether or not they are the biological children of both parties. Both married and unmarried couples, both homosexual and heterosexual, may bring up children together. One or both may have children from another relationship: this is not at all uncommon in lesbian relationships and the court may grant them a shared residence order so that they may share parental responsibility. A lesbian couple may have children by donor insemination who are brought up as the children of them both: it is not uncommon for each of them to bear a child in this way. A gay or lesbian couple may foster other people's children.'

[64] Many of these changes have given rise to profound misgivings in some quarters. We live in a society which, on many social, ethical and religious topics, no longer either thinks or speaks with one voice. These are topics on which men and woman of different faiths or no faith at all hold starkly differing views. All of those views are entitled to the greatest respect but it is not for a judge to choose between them. The days are past when the business of the judges was the enforcement of morals or religious belief. The Court of King's Bench, or its modern incarnation the Administrative Court, is no longer *custos morum* of the people. And a judge, although it may be that on occasions he can legitimately exercise the functions of an aedile, is no censor.

[65] The law, as it seems to me, must adapt itself to these realities, not least in its approach to the proper ambit of Art 8. Mr Garnham rightly accepted that the European Convention is a living instrument which must be interpreted in the light of present-day conditions: see *Selmouni v France* (2000) 29 EHRR 403, at para 101. This is, I think, particularly important in the context of family law. *X, Y and Z v United Kingdom* (1997) 24 EHRR 143, [1997] 2 FLR 892 is a striking example of the approach of the Strasbourg court to the modern view of what a family is. That, it will be recalled, was the case of a woman (Y) living together with a female-to-male transsexual (X) and having a child (Z) by donor insemination. Holding that family life existed both between X and Y and also between X and Z, the court said at paras 36–37:

'The court recalls that the notion of "family life" in Art 8 is not confined solely to families based on marriage and may encompass other de facto relationships. When deciding whether a relationship can be said to amount to "family life", a number of factors may be relevant, including whether the couple live together, the length of their relationship and whether they have demonstrated their commitment to each other by having children together or by any other means.

In the present case, the court notes that X is a transsexual who has undergone gender reassignment surgery. He has lived with Y, to all appearances as her male partner, since 1979. The couple applied jointly for, and were granted, treatment by AID to allow Y to have a child. X was involved throughout that process and has acted as Z's "father" in every respect since the birth. In these circumstances, the court considers that de facto family ties link the three applicants. It follows that Art 8 is applicable.'

[66] In principle I can see no reason why any of the various relationships I have just been describing – why any of the various forms of the family I have just been considering – should be disentitled to the protection of Art 8. On the face of it, in my judgment, all are examples or manifestations of 'family life' within the meaning of Art 8.

[67] I have referred to the increasing religious diversity of our society. This takes me on to my third point. We live, or strive to live, in a tolerant society increasingly alive to the need to guard against the tyranny which majority opinion may impose on those who, for whatever reason, comprise a weak or voiceless minority. Equality under the law, human rights and the protection of minorities have to be more than what Brennan J in the High Court of Australia once memorably described as 'the incantations of legal rhetoric'. Although historically this country is part of the Christian west, and although it has an established church which is Christian, we sit as secular judges serving a multi-cultural community of many faiths in which all of us can now take pride. We are sworn to do justice 'to all manner of people'. Religion – whatever the particular believer's faith – is no doubt something to be encouraged but it is not the business of government or of the secular courts, though the courts will, of course, pay every respect and give great weight to a family's religious principles. Article 9 of the European Convention, after all, demands no less. So the starting point of the law is a tolerant indulgence to cultural and religious diversity and an essentially agnostic view of religious beliefs. A secular judge must be wary of straying across the well-recognised divide between church and state. It is not for a judge to weigh one religion against another. The court recognises no religious distinctions and generally speaking passes no judgment on religious beliefs or on the tenets, doctrines or rules of any particular section of society. All are entitled to equal respect, whether in times of peace or, as at present, amidst the clash of arms. In this context I can do no better than to repeat what Scarman LJ (as he then was) said in *Re T (Minors) (Custody: Religious Upbringing)* (1981) 2 FLR 239 in a long passage at 244–245 which, beginning with the words 'We live in a tolerant society', is too long to quote but demands reading in full.

[68] Within limits the law – our family law – will tolerate things which society as a whole may find undesirable. Where precisely those limits are to be drawn is often a matter of controversy. There is no 'bright-line' test that the law can set. The infinite variety of the human condition precludes arbitrary definition. As *Alhaji Mohamed v Knott* [1969] 1 QB 1 shows, our law is prepared to recognise as valid a potentially polygamous marriage entered into by a girl who in our eyes would be underage. That was a case of a 26-year-old Nigerian Muslim man who entered into a potentially polygamous marriage in Nigeria with a Nigerian girl aged 13; both were domiciled in Nigeria and the marriage was valid according to Nigerian law. Our law also, of course, recognises arranged marriages. But forced marriages, whatever the social or cultural imperatives that may be said to justify what remains a distressingly widespread practice, are rightly considered to be as much beyond the pale as such barbarous practices as female genital mutilation and so-called 'honour killings'.

[69] This leads on to the point made by Mr Blake when he appropriately drew our attention to Thorpe LJ's important observations in *Re E (Abduction: Non-Convention Country)* [1999] 2 FLR 642. The legal context there was very different – whether the English court should order the peremptory return of an abducted Muslim child to the Sudan – but Thorpe LJ's comments are of much wider significance. At 647 he said:

'The welfare principle as paramount has been the cornerstone of the family justice system in this jurisdiction for many years. We regard it as a touchstone in measuring the quality of other family justice systems. Article 3 of the United Nations Convention on the Rights of the Child 1989 requires no less. But what constitutes the welfare of the child must be subject to the cultural background and expectations of the jurisdiction striving to achieve it. It does not seem to me possible to regard it as an absolute standard.'

He continued by calling on 'States to respect a variety of concepts of child welfare derived from differing cultures and traditions' and said that 'A recognition of this reality must inform judicial policy'. And at 649 he drew attention to:

'the importance of according to each State liberty to determine the family justice system and principles that it deems appropriate to protect the child and to serve his best interests. There is an obvious threat to comity if a State whose system derives from Judaeo-Christian foundations condemns a system derived from an Islamic foundation when that system is conceived by its originators and operators to promote and protect the interests of children within that society and according to its traditions and values.'

[70] I respectfully agree. Pill LJ said much the same at 651:

'I have no difficulty in accepting the judge's conclusion that the application of Muslim law to this Muslim family is appropriate and acceptable. It is submitted on behalf of the mother that the welfare of children, paramount in English law, must take priority over notions of international comity and respect for foreign courts in non-Convention States. In my judgment the two are not inevitably in conflict. These are Sudanese children. Their welfare may well be served by a decision in accordance with Sudanese law which may be taken to reflect the norms and values of the Sudanese society in which they live.'

[71] All of these considerations have, in my judgment, to inform our understanding of what is meant in contemporary Britain by the 'family life' referred to in Art 8.

[72] But such is the diversity of forms that the family takes in contemporary society that it is impossible to define, or even to describe at anything less than almost encyclopaedic length, what is meant by 'family life' for the purposes of Art 8. The Strasbourg court, as I have said, has never sought to define what is meant by family life. More importantly for present purposes, and this is a point that requires emphasis, the Strasbourg court has never sought to identify any minimum requirements that must be shown if family life is to be held to exist. That is because there are none. In my judgment there is no single factor whose existence is crucial to the existence of family life, either in the abstract or even in the context of any particular type of family relationship. It may be useful for present purposes, however, to focus attention on one particular aspect of the Art 8 jurisprudence.

[73] The Strasbourg case-law recognises that in some instances family life arises ipso jure. That is so in the case of a lawful and genuine marriage, both in respect of the relationship between husband and wife and also (see the passage in *Berrehab v The Netherlands* at para [21] that I quoted in para [58] above) the relationship between the parents and their children. The same principle applies in relation to the children of de facto unions. As the court said in *Lebbink v The Netherlands* [2004] 2 FLR 463, at [35]:

> 'The court recalls that the notion of "family life" under Art 8 of the Convention is not confined to marriage-based relationships and may encompass other de facto "family" ties where the parties are living together out of wedlock. A child born out of such a relationship is ipso jure part of that "family" unit from the moment and by the very fact of its birth. Thus there exists between the child and the parents a relationship amounting to family life.'

[74] Where there is no family life ipso jure then one has to look to all the circumstances. In many cases cohabitation will be a relevant consideration and in certain contexts it may be more or less important. But it can never be determinative. As the Commission said in *Boyle v United Kingdom* (1995) 19 EHRR 179 at para 15:

> 'cohabitation is ... not a prerequisite for the maintenance of family ties which are to fall within the scope of the concept of "family life". Cohabitation is a factor amongst many others, albeit often an important one, to be taken into account when considering the existence or otherwise of family ties.'

[75] Take the question of whether there is family life as between the partners in a de facto relationship outside marriage. As the court observed in *Lebbink v The Netherlands* [2004] 2 FLR 463 at [36]:

> 'Although, as a rule, cohabitation may be a requirement for such a relationship, exceptionally other factors may also serve to demonstrate that a relationship has sufficient constancy to create de facto "family ties".'

An illuminating example of such a case is *Kroon and Others v The Netherlands* (1995) 19 EHRR 263, where the court held that the relationship between a man and a woman amounted to family life because, even though they chose neither to marry nor to live together, they had a stable relationship which had produced four children.

[76] Plainly in the context of non-marital relationships between adults the question of cohabitation is likely to loom large, though even in that context, as *Kroon and Others v The Netherlands* shows, cohabitation is not determinative. But in the very nature of things cohabitation is likely to play a much less significant role, for example, in assessing whether there is family life as between grandparent and grandchild or between uncle and nephew: grandparents and uncles, after all, however active a role they play in the lives of their grandchildren, nephews and nieces, tend not to live under the same roof with them.

[77] Family life arises ipso jure as between father and child where the child was conceived either in wedlock (*Berrehab v The Netherlands* (1989) 11 EHRR 322, at para 21) or during the course of a stable relationship between unmarried parents (*Keegan v Ireland* (1994) 18 EHRR 342, at para 44, *Kroon and Others v The Netherlands*, at para 30, *Lebbink v The Netherlands*, at para [35]). However, sometimes the relationship between the child's unmarried parents will be so exiguous that there will be no ipso jure family life as between the natural father and his child. But family life may nonetheless be shown to exist. As the court said in *Nylund v Finland* (Application No 27110/95) (unreported) 29 June 1999 at p 14:

> 'the court considers that Art 8 cannot be interpreted as only protecting "family life" which has already been established but, where the circumstances warrant it, must extend to the potential relationship which may develop between a natural father and a child born out of wedlock. Relevant factors in this regard include the nature of the relationship between the natural parents and the demonstrable interest in and commitment by the natural father to the child both before and after the birth.'

The court made the same point in *Lebbink v The Netherlands*, at para [36]:

'The existence or non-existence of "family life" for the purposes of Art 8 is essentially a question of fact depending upon the real existence in practice of close personal ties. Where it concerns a potential relationship which could develop between a child born out of wedlock and its natural father, relevant factors include the nature of the relationship between the natural parents and the demonstrable interest in and commitment by the father to the child both before and after its birth.'

[78] In *Nylund v Finland* (Application No 27110/95) (unreported) 29 June 1999 the father's claim to family life failed. In *Lebbink v The Netherlands* [2004] 2 FLR 463 it succeeded, even though, as the court noted, the father had not sought to recognise his daughter, Amber, and had never formed a 'family unit' with Amber and her mother as they had never cohabited. The court explained why at paras [37]–[40]:

'... Consequently, the question arises whether there are other factors demonstrating that the applicant's relationship with Amber has sufficient constancy and substance to create de facto "family ties". The court does not agree with the applicant that a mere biological kinship, without any further legal or factual elements indicating the existence of a close personal relationship, should be regarded as sufficient to attract the protection of Art 8.

However, in the instant case the court notes that Amber was born out of a genuine relationship between the applicant and Ms B that lasted for about 3 years and that, until this institution was abolished when Amber was about 7 months old, the applicant was Amber's auxiliary guardian. It observes that the applicant's relation with Ms B ended in August 1996 when Amber was about 16 months old.

The court further notes that, although the applicant never cohabited with Ms B and Amber, he had been present when Amber was born, that – as from Amber's birth until August 1996 when his relation with Amber's mother ended – he visited Ms B and Amber at unspecified regular intervals, that he changed Amber's nappy a few times and baby-sat her once or twice, and that he had several contacts with Ms B about Amber's impaired hearing.

In these circumstances the court concludes that, when the applicant's relationship with Ms B ended, there existed – in addition to biological kinship – certain ties between the applicant and Amber which were sufficient to attract the protection of Art 8 of the Convention.'

[79] I agree with Dyson LJ that what he calls the core principle is to be found in *Lebbink v The Netherlands* at para [36]:

'The existence or non-existence of "family life" for the purposes of Art 8 is essentially a question of fact depending upon the real existence in practice of close personal ties.'

Typically the question will be, as the court put it in the same case at para [37], whether there is 'a close personal relationship', a relationship which 'has sufficient constancy and substance to create de facto "family ties"'.

[80]   In the case of the parent–child relationship a central issue will often be what the court both in *Nylund v Finland* (Application No 27110/95) (unreported) 29 June 1999 and again in *Lebbink v The Netherlands* [2004] 2 FLR 463 referred to as the parent's 'demonstrable interest in and commitment to the child'. A parent's cohabitation or lack of cohabitation with the child will often be significant – sometimes highly significant – but as *Lebbink v The Netherlands* demonstrates, it cannot be decisive. As long ago as 1988 it had been made clear in *Berrehab v The Netherlands* (1989) 11 EHRR 322, at para 21, that:

'The court ... does not see cohabitation as a sine qua non of family life between parents and minor children.'

General notes:

Although the leading judgment in this case was delivered by Dyson LJ it is this broad review of the meaning of 'family life' by Munby J that is of particular significance to family law practitioners.

I2 MARGIN OF APPRECIATION

Evans v Amicus Healthcare Ltd (Secretary of State for Health intervening)

[2004] EWCA Civ 727, [2004] 2 FLR 766 at 785

Court of Appeal

Thorpe LJ

[62] We have set out earlier in this judgment what we recognise as the policy of the 1990 Act. Mr Coppel, whose argument is adopted by the Authority and by Mr Johnston, makes it his principal submission that the adoption of such a policy is 'clearly within the area where the state will be accorded a broad discretion'. 'The state authorities', he submits, 'are entitled to be accorded a broad margin of discretion in deciding where the balance should be struck'.

[63] We consider propositions of this breadth to be a wrong starting point. The margin of appreciation (a solecism originating in the literal rendering in the English text of the decision in *Handyside v United Kingdom* (1976) 1 EHRR 737 of the French phrase 'marge d'appréciation', meaning margin of appraisal or judgment) is a tool by which the Strasbourg court gauges the relationship of a State's act to the European Convention. It has no direct relevance to the process by which a court adjudicates, within a State, on the compatibility of a measure adopted by the executive or the legislature, for it is only at the end of that process that the State's act crystallises. This is why Lord Hope of Craighead in *R v Director of Public Prosecutions ex parte Kebilene and Others* [2000] AC 326, [2000] UKHRR 176, at 381 and 197 respectively, took such care to distinguish the Strasbourg approach from what he characterised domestically as the discretionary area of judgment. Discretion implies a choice between two or more legitimate (and, therefore, proportionate) courses, and where Parliament has made such a choice the courts have no power of intervention under the Human Rights Act 1998. To invoke a supposed 'margin of discretion' by contrast is to collapse two distinct concepts into a single nebulous one.

[64] What is, therefore, critical in deciding whether the point of intervention has been reached is the legitimacy, in European Convention terms, of the choice that Parliament has made. As Lord Nicholls of Birkenhead said in *Wilson v First County Trust Ltd (No 2)* [2003] UKHL 40, [2004] 1 AC 816 at [70]:

'Assessment of the advantages and disadvantages of the various legislative alternatives is primarily a matter for Parliament. The possible existence of alternative solutions does not in itself render the contested legislation unjustified ... The court will reach a different conclusion from the legislature only when it is apparent that the legislature has attached insufficient importance to a person's Convention right ... The more the legislation concerns matters of broad social policy, the less ready will be a court to intervene.'

[65] The last of these propositions is not gratuitous or free-standing. It follows logically from the preceding propositions, for this reason: while legislation modifying individuals' private law liabilities can be expected not to infringe their European Convention rights without clear justification, legislation directed to the implementation and management of social policy may well have to infringe some individuals' European Convention rights in the interests of consistency. But the test is the same in both cases: could a less drastic means have been used to achieve the chosen end without infringing the primary right of the claimant?

Inherent jurisdiction / wardship

I3 JURISDICTION AND CA 1989, S 100(2)

E v London Borough of X

[2005] EWHC 2811, [2006] 1 FLR 730 at 736

Family Division

Potter P

Jurisdiction

[27] The object of the intervention of the court in respect of the care or welfare of child, whether by way of wardship proceedings or when exercising its inherent jurisdiction outside wardship, has always been to promote the welfare of the child; see *A v Liverpool City Council and Another* [1982] AC 363, (1981) 2 FLR 222 per Lord Wilberforce at 371 and 224 respectively. Although the limits of the inherent jurisdiction have never been defined in this respect, the court has nonetheless recognised that it will not exercise its powers in respect of children so as to interfere with powers granted to a person or institution such as a local authority unless the statute granting such powers expressly so permits: see *Re W (A Minor) (Wardship: Jurisdiction)* [1985] AC 791, [1985] FLR 879 per Lord Scarman at 797 and 882 respectively:

> 'The High Court cannot exercise its powers, however wide they may be, so as to intervene on the merits in an area of concern entrusted by Parliament to another public authority. It matters not that the chosen public authority is one that acts administratively whereas the court, if seized of the same matter, would act judicially. If Parliament in an area of concern defined by Statute (the area in this case being the care of children in need or trouble) prefers power to be exercised administratively instead of judicially, so be it. The courts must be careful in that area to avoid assuming a supervisory role or reviewing power over the merits of decisions taken administratively by the selected public authority.'

See also *Re Z (A Minor) (Identification: Restrictions on Publication)* [1997] Fam 1, [1996] 1 FLR 191 at 23B and 207 respectively.

[28]   In this context, it is specifically provided by s 100(2) of the Children Act 1989 that:

'No court shall exercise the High Court's inherent jurisdiction with respect to children—

(a)   so as to require a child to be placed in the care, or put under the supervision, of a local authority;

(b)   so as to require a child to be accommodated by or on behalf of a local authority;

(c)   so as to make a child who is the subject of a care order a ward of court; or

(d)   for the purpose of conferring on any local authority power to determine any question that has arisen, which may arise, in connection with any aspect of parental responsibility for a child.'

[29]   The question therefore arises whether to proceed with the hearing would be a breach of that statutory provision or of the wider principle articulated by Lord Scarman so that I should decline to perform the exercise previously ordered by Bracewell J in respect of which the local authority did not seek to appeal.

[30]   The position which has been reached in these proceedings so far as the local authority is concerned is that it does not propose, nor is it sought by or on behalf of E, that this court should exercise its inherent jurisdiction for any of the purposes set out in s 100(2) of the 1989 Act; nor does the local authority seek to make any application for the court to exercise its inherent jurisdiction to make any order in respect of E: see s 100(3). Thus, for the court to proceed to determine the age of E pursuant to the order of Bracewell J would not involve any breach of s 100 of the 1989 Act. Nor has Miss Craig so submitted.

[31]   Nor, if the court were to proceed to do so, would it be exercising an appellate or supervisory function in respect of the local authority's age assessment. That assessment was conducted under a non-statutory internal procedure of the local authority carried out in accordance with the guidance given by Stanley Burnton J in *B v London Borough of Merton* [2003] EWHC 1689 (Admin), [2003] 2 FLR 888. I am being asked on E's behalf to conduct an inquiry by way of original (and not appellate or review) jurisdiction for the purposes of the court in the exercise of its wardship function on the basis of the evidence now available to it, a good deal of which was not available to the local authority. To do so will not in itself interfere with the exercise of the statutory powers of the local authority, in relation to which there are no provisions governing age assessment. While the local authority is at liberty, and, indeed, no doubt obliged, to withhold care services it would otherwise supply to a person if it is satisfied that party is not a child, the statute does not prescribe what method of assessment should be adopted for that purpose. It does not seem to me that, if the question of the age of a putative child becomes an issue in wardship proceedings, a decision of the court to adjudicate upon that issue for the purposes both of establishing or confirming its protective jurisdiction and furthering the welfare of the child, the court should decline to deal with it simply because a local authority has conducted an earlier age assessment on the basis of more limited evidence and for a more limited statutory purpose.

[32] Having said that, however, if the court is satisfied that wardship proceedings are being misused, in the sense that they are being carried on solely for the purpose of obtaining a decision or order which by-passes or interferes with a process of age assessment by a local authority, then it would be inappropriate for the court to exercise its wardship jurisdiction for that purpose. While the 1989 Act does not expressly so provide, it is inherent in its structure and content that a local authority, in any case where doubts are raised in respect of the age of a putative child in need of care and protection, should make an age assessment and, according to its results, decide whether to take measures in respect of the 'child' under the provisions of the 1989 Act. It is thus an area in which, in the words of Lord Scarman, the court must be careful to avoid assuming a supervisory role or reviewing power over the merits of the local authority's decision.

[33] Is the position here such that those observations apply? In the special circumstances of this case, I do not think it is. There is no suggestion that the proceedings were inappropriately commenced (see para [23] above). The question of doubt as to E's age only arose in the mind of the local authority *in the course* of these proceedings in the unusual circumstances described. When it did arise, Singer J rightly directed the authority to conduct an age assessment before the matter was further considered. When the matter returned for further consideration before Bracewell J, I am told that Miss Craig aired the submissions which she has made before me. However, Bracewell J was not prepared to treat the age assessment as dispositive of the question of E's age for the wider purpose of the wardship proceedings in which the court is required to consider the position of the subject child on a broad welfare basis. In that respect the position of E at that time was that her fate would be entirely at large on termination of the foster placement in which she was currently placed but from which she was about to be ejected. She would effectively be parentless and the local authority would have washed its hands of her. That being so, Bracewell J no doubt considered that in relation to: (a) the need to determine the jurisdiction of the court in wardship; and (b) general welfare concerns in respect of E in her limbo of uncertainty as to her age, it was appropriate to make a judicial determination of E's age, having afforded her a sufficient opportunity to gather evidence in that respect.

[34]   The court having so ordered, if objection was to be taken to the judicial determination of E's age in the wardship proceedings, the proper course was to have appealed the order of Bracewell J. Instead, on the basis that the order was effective and thereafter unchallenged, E's advisers were encouraged to proceed to obtain further evidence for the purpose of the hearing on the basis that thereafter the matter would be appropriately dealt with in the wardship proceedings, the date for any proceedings for judicial review being due to expire well before the date fixed for the hearing of the issue.

[35]   In these circumstances, I see no reason to decline to deal with the issue in accordance with the order of Bracewell J. Indeed, it would be unjust to E to do so. For the reasons I have set out, it is neither the intention nor the effect of my determination to constitute an appeal or review of the age assessment. Although in the ensuing paragraphs of my judgment, I refer in some detail to the content of the age assessment, that is because, at the request of the local authority I have received it in evidence in the inquiry before me, the nature of which is more inquisitorial than adversarial for the purpose of establishing E's age. In that respect, at the outset of the hearing I made it clear to the local authority, who were content, that I would treat the views and conclusions stated in the age assessment as being the bona fide views and conclusions of Miss N and Miss M on the basis of the interviews conducted by them and the evidence before them as referred to in the assessment, without the necessity to hear their oral evidence to that effect. That being so, I have felt it appropriate to explain carefully the reasons why, in the event, I differ from their conclusions.

I4 WARDSHIP CANNOT INTERFERE WITH PROPER EXERCISE OF PUBLIC LAW POWERS

S v S

[2008] EWHC 2288 (Fam), [2009] 1 FLR 241 at 245

Family Division

Munby J

[14] The wardship jurisdiction is theoretically without limit, but it is well recognised by long-standing authority at the very highest level that whatever may be its theoretical ambit the jurisdiction is subject (in accordance with well-known principle) to certain fundamental limitations on its proper exercise. One such limitation (and the one that is applicable in these circumstances) is that wardship may not be used in such a way as to – and it is as a matter of law ineffective to – prevent the exercise of statutory powers conferred by Parliament, whether upon a court or upon a Minister, whether upon a judicial body or upon an administrative body, as part of a statutory scheme which, upon its proper construction, is intended by Parliament to be exclusive and thereby, by implication, to oust the jurisdiction of the court.

[15] I am not going to take up time rehearsing the well-known authorities. It suffices to identify the two leading cases which deal with the matter as one of general principle: first the well-known statement of Lord Scarman in *Re W (A Minor) (Wardship: Jurisdiction)* [1985] AC 791, [1985] 2 WLR 892, [1985] FLR 879, at 797, 986 and 882 respectively and secondly the equally well-known statement of principle by Ward LJ in *Re Z (A Minor) (Identification: Restrictions on Publication)* [1997] Fam 1, [1996] 2 WLR 88, [1996] 1 FLR 191, at 23, 104–105 and 207–208 respectively. As Ward LJ points out in that case, the principle has many applications: one being that the wardship judge cannot interfere with the proper exercise by a local authority of its statutory functions under the care legislation and another (being the relevant one for present purposes) that the wardship judge cannot in the exercise of that jurisdiction interfere with the exercise by the Secretary of State for the Home Department of her powers in relation to matters of immigration and asylum.

[16] In relation to that particular subject matter, which is the subject matter with which I am concerned today, the classic authority is the judgment of Russell LJ in *Re Mohamed Arif (An Infant); Nirbai Singh (An Infant)* [1968] Ch 643, [1968] 2 WLR 1290, [1968] 2 All ER 145. The working out of these principles in the context of asylum and immigration, and specifically the working out of these principles in the analysis and explanation of the proper relationship between the Secretary of State, the Administrative Court and the Family Division is to be found in the judgment of Hoffmann LJ (as he then was) in *R v Secretary of State to the Home Department (ex parte T)* [1995] 1 FLR 293, [1994] Imm AR 368, and more recently in my own judgment in *Re A (Care Proceedings: Asylum Seekers)* [2003] EWHC 1086 (Fam), [2003] 2 FLR 921.

[17] Having identified the relevant authorities I do not take up time analysing them further. The simple fact of the matter is that the Family Division of the High Court of Justice cannot, even in the exercise of its inherent jurisdiction, make orders which in any way impinge upon or prevent the exercise by the Secretary of State of powers lawfully conferred upon her in the context of immigration and asylum. Indeed, in strict law the mere fact that the child is a ward of court does not, as Hoffmann LJ explained in *Ex parte T*, prevent the removal of that child from the jurisdiction if done by the Secretary of State in pursuance of her statutory powers. In practice, of course, the pendency of wardship proceedings usually persuades the Secretary of State to stay her hand, and therefore in practice – as we are all too well aware – the pendency of wardship proceedings tends to operate de facto as a brake upon the exercise by the Secretary of State of the powers which she would otherwise wish to exercise. As the authorities make clear it is important in these circumstances that the Family Division exercises its wardship powers with great care and circumspection and that it avoids its process being used for some impermissible purpose or in a way which impermissibly impacts upon the proper exercise by the Secretary of State of her powers.

[18] That is one important principle in play in this situation. The other principle, which is the other aspect of the same fundamental principle, is that if it is sought to challenge the exercise by the Secretary of State of her statutory powers then the proper and, indeed, the only proper forum for such challenge is the Administrative Court in an application by way of judicial review and/or pursuant to the Human Rights Act 1998. It is fundamental that challenges to the exercise by public officials or public tribunals of statutory powers are matters of public law to be dealt with in the Administrative Court, which deals with matters of public law, and not to be dealt with in the Family Division, which exists, in the sense in which the phrase is used by administrative lawyers, to deal with private law cases and not public law cases.

General notes:

Wardship / the inherent jurisdiction continue to be used in certain abduction situations: see eg:

- *Re F (Abduction: removal outside the jurisdiction)* [2008] EWCA Civ 842, [2008] 2 FLR 1649
- *B v D (Abduction: inherent jurisdiction)* [2008] EWHC 1246 (Fam), [2009] 1 FLR 1015
- *Re S (Wardship: peremptory return)* [2010] EWCA Civ 465, [2010] 2 FLR 1960 (local authority using wardship to secure the return of child to England from Spain)
- *ES v AJ* [2010] EWHC 1113 (Fam), [2010] 2 FLR 1257 (mother seeking order for father to return children to England from Cameroons)
- *Re T (Wardship: review of police protection decision) (No 1)* [2010] 1 FLR 1017; *Re T (Wardship: review of police protection decision) (No 2)* [2008] EWHC 196 (Fam), [2010] 1 FLR 1026; *Re T (Wardship: impact of police intelligence)* [2009] EWHC 2440 (Fam), [2010] 1 FLR 1048 (a series of cases involving the recovery of a child from India and police resisting disclosure of information)

Other significant cases on this issue:

- Cf *Re L (Care order: immigration powers to remove)* [2007] EWHC 158 (Fam), [2007] 2 FLR 789 on the construction of Children Act 1989, s 33(7)
- For an example of public law challenge in such matters, see eg *EM (Lebanon) v Secretary of State for the Home Department* [2008] UKHL 64, [2008] 2 FLR 2067

I5   MEDICAL TREATMENT

Re K (Medical treatment: declaration)

[2006] EWHC 1007 (Fam), [2006] 2 FLR 883 at 885, 888, 893 and 894

Family Division

Potter P

[1]   On 6 April 2006, on the application of a teaching hospital NHS Trust (the Trust), I made a declaration to enable the medical staff of the Trust to remove from the abdomen of a baby in their care a tube necessary to maintain her nutrition, and to move to a regime of palliative care in order to allow her to die peacefully over a short period of time. I indicated that I would give my reasons later. They are now set out below. Since making my declaration K has in fact died. However, I state my reasons as at the time of the application.

...

[13]   That position has now been reached and the application before me seeks a declaration in the following terms; which for convenience I have slightly rephrased:

'1. K, as a child, lacks capacity to make decisions about medical treatment to be delivered to herself for her physical healthcare.

2. Having regard to K's best interests, and in the opinion of the Consultant and Health Care Team treating K at the applicant Trust:

(i)   It should lawful for the applicant Trust, having regard to the fact that the responsible Paediatric Medical Consultants have reached a decision that K's medical condition and prognosis are such that it should lawful, to discontinue parenteral nutrition;

(ii)   it is lawful that the infusion of fluids should cease;

(iii)   K should continue to receive full non-life prolonging palliative care, offering relief of any distress with analgesic and anxiolytic medication and should be allowed to die in comfort and dignity.'

...

[37]   In the course of Dr N's evidence, he referred to the publication by the Royal College of Paediatrics and Child Health: *Withholding or*

Withdrawing Life Sustaining Treatment in Children: *A Framework for Practice* (General Medical Council, 2nd edn, 2004). This publication is a guide to treating consultants on the ethics of withholding or withdrawing life support in cases of this kind. It is not authoritative as to the law. However its purpose is to provide a framework on which to construct a reasoned and compassionate approach to withholding or withdrawing treatment from patients and it is stated in the foreword to the 1st edition to be 'framed within the existing law and upholding the rights of the child' ...

...

[42] This is a comparatively unusual case to come before the court in the sense that the declaration sought is non-contentious, all parties concerned being in agreement with the views of the medical professionals involved that life-prolonging treatment should cease. Indeed, I was told in the course of argument that, had the necessity for parental consent simply rested with the father and mother in this case, the matter would not have come to court, the medical professionals being satisfied that their ethical and legal obligations would not be breached by the action now proposed. However, the case is now before the court for decision, and the court is not tied to or bound by the clinical assessment of what is in K's interests. The court must reach its own conclusion on the basis of a broad spectrum of considerations after careful consideration of the evidence before it: see *Re T (A Minor) (Wardship: Medical Treatment)* [1997] 1 WLR 242, [1997] 1 FLR 502, at 250 and 509 respectively, per Butler-Sloss LJ; *Airedale NHS Trust v Bland* [1993] AC 789 at 834; *R (Burke) v General Medical Council* [2004] EWHC 1879 (Admin), [2005] QB 424, [2004] 2 FLR 1121 per Munby J at paras [93]–[95].

[43] As stated by Thorpe LJ in *Re S (Adult Patient: Sterilisation)* [2001] Fam 15, [2000] 2 FLR 389, at 30E and 403 respectively:

'In deciding what is best for the disabled patient the judge must have regard to the patient's welfare as the paramount consideration. That embraces issues far wider than the medical. Indeed it would be undesirable and probably impossible to set bounds to what is relevant to a welfare determination.'

[44] Dame Elizabeth Butler-Sloss P made clear in the same case at 28 that the principle of the 'best interests' of the patient as applied by the court extends beyond the considerations governing the propriety and advisability of medical treatment developed in *Bolam v Friern Hospital Management Committee* [1957] 1 WLR 582 and:

'The judicial decision will incorporate broader ethical, social, moral and welfare considerations.'

As stated by Hedley J in *Portsmouth NHS Trust v Wyatt* [2004] EWHC 2247 (Fam), [2005] 1 FLR 21, at para [23]:

> 'Best interests must be given a generous interpretation. As Dame Elizabeth Butler-Sloss P said in *Re A (Male Sterilisation)* [2000] 1 FLR 549 at 555:
>
>> "... best interests encompasses medical, emotional and all other welfare issues ... The infinite variety of the human condition never ceases to surprise and it is that fact that defeats any attempt to be more precise in the definition of best interest".'

[45] In *Re A (Male Sterilisation)* [2000] 1 FLR 549, at 560, Thorpe LJ commended the 'balance sheet' method of assessment when considering the best interests of the patient. He stated that the court:

> 'should draw up a balance sheet ... of actual benefit ... [and] any counterbalancing disbenefits ... an obvious instance ... would be the apprehension, the risk, and the discomfort inherent in the operation. Then the judge should enter ... the potential gains and losses in each instance making some estimate of the extent of the possibility of the gain or loss might accrue ...[in order to] be better placed to strike a balance between the sum of the certain and possible gains against the sum of the certain and possible losses. Obviously, only if the account is in relatively significant credit will the judge conclude that the application is likely to advance the best interests [of the person lacking capacity].'

[46] In *Re L (Medical Treatment: Benefit)* [2004] EWHC 2713 (Fam), [2005] 1 FLR 491, Dame Elizabeth Butler-Sloss P summed up the balancing process in words of particularly helpful application in this case. She said, at paras [12]–[13]:

> 'The task therefore is for me to weigh up that which is sometimes called the "benefits and dis-benefits" but which I would prefer to call the advantages of giving or not giving potential treatments, and to balance them in order to decide the best interests of L with regard to his future treatment. I should like to refer to a passage in the judgment of Lord Donaldson in *Re J (A Minor) (Wardship: Medical Treatment)* [1991] Fam 33, [1991] 1 FLR 366 at 47 and 375 respectively:
>
>> "There is without doubt a very strong presumption in the favour of a course of action which will prolong life, but ... it is not irrebuttable ... [A]ccount has to be taken of the pain and suffering and quality of life which the child will experience if life is prolonged. Account is also to be taken of the pain and

suffering involved in the proposed treatment itself ... We know that the instinct and desire for survival is very strong. We all believe in and assert the sanctity of human life ... [E]ven very severely handicapped people find a quality of life rewarding which to be un-handicapped may seem manifestly intolerable. People have an amazing adaptability. But in the end there are cases in which the answer must be that it is not in the interests of the child to subject it to treatment which would cause increased suffering and produce no commensurate benefit, giving the fullest possible weight to the child's and mankind's, desire to survive".'

[47] The reference to that which is 'intolerable' has received echoes in subsequent cases involving the withdrawal or withholding of life-sustaining treatment. However, in para [12] of her judgment in *Re L*, last quoted, Dame Elizabeth Butler-Sloss P put the matter thus:

'There is a strong presumption in favour of preserving life, but not where treatment would be futile, and there is no obligation on the medical profession to give treatment which would be futile. I agree with Hedley J [in *Wyatt*] that the court should be focusing on best interests rather than the concept of intolerability, although the latter may be encompassed within the former.'

Further, in *Wyatt v Portsmouth NHS Trust* [2005] EWCA Civ 1181, [2005] 1 WLR 3995, [2006] 1 FLR 554, having reviewed the authorities and set out the 'intellectual milestones' for the judge in a case of this kind, Wall LJ said at paras [90]–[91]:

'We urge caution in the application to children of factors relevant to the treatment of adults, although some general statements of principle plainly apply to both. We repeat that *R (Burke) v General Medical Council (Official Solicitor intervening)* [2005] QB 424 concern the prospective withdrawal of A & H, competent adult patient. It was not concerned with what was meant by best interests in the context of the treatment of an incompetent child. At best, therefore, Munby J's identification of "intolerability" as the touchstone of best interests is obiter ...

We do not, however, dismiss "intolerability" as a factor all together. As we have already stated, we agree with Hedley J that whilst "intolerable to the child" should not be seen either as a gloss on or a supplementary guide to best interests, it is, as he said, a valuable guide in the search for best interests in his kind of case.'

[48] In this case, it is quite clear that if TPN is withdrawn it will result in K's death shortly thereafter. It is her life support. It is therefore vital to bear in mind that English law places a very heavy burden on those who

are advocating a course which would lead inevitably to the cessation of a human life. In doing so, however, I take particular guidance from those passages in the judgments of Lord Donaldson of Lymington MR and Balcombe LJ in *Re J (A Minor) (Wardship: Medical Treatment)* [1991] Fam 33, [1991] 1 FLR 366, at 47 and 52, 375 and 380 respectively, highlighted by the Court of Appeal in *Wyatt v Portsmouth NHS Trust* at paras [71] and [74]. The first has already been set out at para [46], above. The second reads as follows:

> 'I would deprecate any attempt by this court to lay down.. an all-embracing test since the circumstances of these tragic cases are so infinitely various. I do not know of any demand by the judges who have to deal with these cases at first instance for this court to assist them by laying down any test beyond that which is already the law: that the interests of the ward are the first and paramount consideration, subject to the gloss on that test which I suggest, that in determining where those interests lie the court adopts the standpoint of the reasonable and responsible parent who has his or her child's best interest at heart.'

[49] Given that K is presently stable and that the withdrawal of TPN will inevitably lead to death within a comparatively short time, Miss Laura Davidson for the Trust has rightly drawn to my attention two recent decisions concerning the withdrawal of treatment in cases where the patient's condition was not imminently life-threatening providing that life-sustaining treatment continued, but where withdrawal of that treatment would cause death because the patients were incapable of surviving without it. In both, the court refused to sanction immediate withdrawal.

[50] In *W Healthcare NHS Trust v KH* [2004] EWCA Civ 1324, [2005] 1 WLR 834 the court was concerned not with a baby but with an adult who lacked capacity and had severe multiple sclerosis and a poor quality of life. She lived in a care home and had been fed by way of a percutaneous-gastronomy tube (PEG) for 5 years. She was admitted to hospital after her PEG fell out. Her family resisted a declaration sought by the Trust that it was in her best interests to re-insert it, because they believed that she would have wished to be allowed to die with dignity. The consequence of not granting the declaration would have been that KH would have died slowly of thirst and starvation, although her suffering would have been alleviated by drugs. As is made clear in para [27] of the judgment of Brooke LJ, the judge came to the conclusion that in KH's present state he could not say that life-prolonging treatment would provide no benefit and he found that death by, in effect, starvation would be even less dignified than the death that she would face in due course if kept artificially alive for more weeks, months or possibly years. In a short judgment, having reviewed the authorities, Brooke LJ stated at para [29]:

'The judge, having rightly put on one side the question of whether there was a legally binding advance directive, looked, on the one hand, at the consequences of withdrawing nutrition and the effect this would have and, on the other hand, at the continuance of a life in which there is some feeling of pain, some sensation and some slight ability to answer questions. He came to the conclusion that it was in the best interests of the patient to accede to the unanimous wish of those who are responsible for her treatment.

As I have said, the Official Solicitor supports this application. These cases are always agonisingly difficult ... but judges have to apply the law as they find it. English law, as it stands at present, places a very heavy burden on those who are advocating a course which would lead inevitably to a cessation of a human life. In my judgment, it impossible for this court to interfere with the judge's judgment.'

[51] It is persistently stated in the authorities that all cases of this kind are highly fact sensitive: see for instance per Wall LJ in *Wyatt v Portsmouth NHS Trust* at para [114]. There are a number of crucial distinctions between the facts of this case and those in the case of *KH*. In that case, it was the unanimous view of those concerned with the treatment of KH that the PEG should be re-inserted. Here the reverse is the case and the views of the medical advisers that nutrition should cease are endorsed by the parents and the local authority. In the case of KH she was a sentient adult. In this case, baby K is sentient, in the sense that she has some (uncertain) appreciation of what goes on around her, but her feelings and capacity to appreciate pleasure, pain or the sheer sensation of 'being alive' are those of a child with a developmental age of 3 months. She is a young and a significantly underdeveloped baby who has no power of speech and has no apparent purposeful movement.

[52] In the case of KH, although unable to swallow and incontinent, there was no evidence of regular and continuing discomfort distress as there is in K's case, as the result of her profound feeding problems, her cycle of repeated vomiting, and the invasive and prolonged use of TPN as a substitute for her nutritional needs. She can experience no form of pleasure or well-being to be derived from ordinary ingestion of milk or food.

[53] The more recent case of *An NHS Trust v MB (A Child Represented by CAFCASS as Guardian Ad Litem)* [2006] EWHC 507 (Fam), [2006] 2 FLR 319 affords a much closer parallel to K's case. MB suffered from spinal muscular atrophy, a severe form of degenerative and progressive neurological genetic condition. He was aged 10 months and had been unable to breathe without artificial ventilation for 8 months. He could not swallow properly and had been fed by way of gastrostomy tube for 4 months. He also suffered from epileptic fits. The doctors responsible for his care wished to withdraw his endo-tracheal tube with the inevitable consequence that he would die within a few minutes because he would be unable to breathe. The application was however opposed by his parents on the grounds that, as the persons who knew him best and were constantly attendant upon him, they were convinced that he felt and could display pleasure and recognised his parents, brother and sister and that he could see, hear and take in certain television and DVD programmes and music on CDs which were played to him. They accepted that a number of the procedures to which he was submitted caused him discomfort and pain but thought that the doctor's evidence to that effect was exaggerated. The judge considered the evidence and the benefits and burdens to MB drawn up in a 'balance sheet' by the guardian.

[54]   The judge addressed those benefits and burdens on the basis that MB was a child of 18 months who, despite his condition, had the size and development of the child of that age and that he had normal, age-appropriate cognition and power of thought as well as normal, age-appropriate capacity for moods and emotions, including the capacity to feel pleasure from the stimuli he received. He could both hear and see. The judge was satisfied that he could and did still feel touch and that, just as there were some touches which were painful and he did not like, there were others, particularly the stroking and handling of his parents and siblings, which he liked and which the judge assumed gave him a sense of pleasure.

[55]   The judge accepted the evidence of the parents that MB was attentive to TV, DVDs, CDs, stories and speech and that they gave pleasure to him. He also derived pleasure from his relationship with his parents and siblings, which pleasure was not short-lived or occasional but available to him as a constant part of his life for long periods of everyday. Although he had the absence of pleasures normally associated with childhood such as crawling, exploring, taking first steps, and playing with other children, he was left with a core of pleasure, in particular that derived from his relationship with his parents and family. Despite a long list of dis-benefits and burdens, including a number of periodical procedures which caused pain, and despite the fact that it was clear that MB was going to die within about a year (though possibly he might live longer or die sooner), the judge held at para [102]:

'I do not consider that from one day to the next all the routine discomfort, distress and pain that the doctors describe (but not the ones that I have now excluded) outweigh those benefits so that I can say that it is in his best interests that those benefits and life itself could immediately end. On the contrary, I positively consider that his life still does have benefits, and it is his life, which we should enable to continue, subject to excluding the treatment I have identified.'

[56] I am grateful for the reference to that case. However, I do not consider that it precludes a different decision in the case of K. The factual differences readily appear from para [106] of the judgment where the judge stated:

'I wish to stress that this is a very fact specific decision taken in the actual circumstances as they are for this child and today. These circumstances include, critically, the facts that he already has been and is on ventilation and has already survived the age of 18 months; he is assumed not to be brain-damaged; he is in a close relationship with a family that have spent and are able to spend very considerable time with him; and does already have an accumulation of experiences and the cognition to gain pleasure from them.'

[57] In this case K is less than 6 months old and has a developmental age of only 3 months. She has no accumulation of experiences and cognition comparable with that of MB. She is not, and with her short expectation of life is never likely to be, in a position to derive pleasure from DVDs or CDs and the only indication of real feelings of pleasure in her limited developmental state is enjoyment of a bath. On the evidence before me there is no realistic sense in which one can assign to her the simple pleasure of being alive or having other than a life dominated by regular pain, distress and discomfort and unrelieved by the pleasures of eating. Her muscular function is already severely diminished and any pleasure which might otherwise develop through increased activity and stimulation of the senses is denied to her. She has no prospect of relief from this pitiful existence before an end which is regarded as virtually certain by the age of one year and likely to be appreciably less. If her line is not removed she will continue to suffer pain and distress from the invasive treatment which she already experiences and the prospect is of the likely necessity for removal of her line in the near future which will merely add to her distress. If she were to have the necessary further surgical operation to replace the line, she would require mechanical ventilation which is also invasive and painful. There would be no improvement in her condition or improvement in her expectation of life. In these circumstances, I have no doubt that it would not only be a mercy, but it is in her best interests, to cease to provide TPN while she is still clinically stable, so that she may die in peace and over a comparatively short space of time, relieved by the palliative treatment contemplated, which will cause her neither pain nor discomfort and will enable her to live out her short life in relative peace in the close care of her parents who love her.

[58] For those reasons I am content to grant declarations in the terms set out by me in para [13] of this judgment.

I6 INHERENT JURISDICTION: POLICE WISHING TO INTERVIEW CHILDREN

Chief Constable of Greater Manchester v KI and KW (by their children's guardian, Cafcass Legal) and NP

[2007] EWHC 1837 (Fam), [2008] 1 FLR 504 at 508

Family Division

Ryder J

[12] In *Re M (Care: Leave to Interview Child)* [1995] 1 FLR 825 Hale J, as she then was, was asked to give permission for the interview of two boys in relation to their father's defence to a charge of rape against his partner's daughters. The interview was proposed by the father's solicitor, who intended to conduct the interview himself and at the time the children were in the interim care of a local authority. The court identified the following propositions, among others:

(i) At 826: It is 'beyond question' that the court is entitled to require its consent before anyone interviews a ward of court: *Re R and Others (Minors) (Wardship: Criminal Proceedings)* [1991] Fam 56, [1991] 2 WLR 912, [1991] 2 FLR 95 at 98.

(ii) At 827: Until the child is old enough to decide for himself, a parent undoubtedly has some control over whom he may see and who may see him.

(iii) At 827: The court's control over interviewing its wards also suggests (though not conclusively) that there is some parental responsibility here.

(iv) At 827: There is binding authority that consent to an interview of a child is a matter which can be dealt with by way of a specific issue order which is defined in s 8(1) of the Act as 'an order giving directions for the purpose of determining a specific question which has arisen, or which may arise, in connection with any aspect of parental responsibility for a child' and accordingly it follows that consent to an interview is an aspect of parental responsibility: *Re F (Specific Issue: Child Interview)* [1995] 1 FLR 819.

(v) At 828: Parents do not have unlimited powers, even over matters which may be aspects of their responsibility. They cannot exercise their powers in such a way as to infringe the rights of others. If they do so, the court must provide a remedy.

(vi) At 828: The court itself has accepted that there are limits to its powers to protect wards of court where these conflict with the rights and powers of others. Thus, for example, the court has no power to prohibit a child being called to give evidence in a criminal trial and there are limits upon its powers to control interviews such as this.

(vii) At 828: The court has to weigh any potential harm to the child against the interests of justice. These are at least as strong where the defence wishes to interview potential witnesses as they are where the prosecution wishes to do so. The child's welfare cannot be the sole or overriding consideration.

(viii) At 828: Even if this is a matter in which parents have some responsibility it does not follow that it is a matter of the child's 'upbringing' in which by virtue of s 1(1) of the 1989 Act the welfare of the child is paramount.

[13]   Lest it be thought that *Re M* might be regarded as persuasive, if not conclusive, of the issues before this court (having regard to the authorities therein cited and relied upon), Hale J went on to record that in *Re F* (above) Waite LJ had been prepared to assume that the general welfare provisions of s 1 of the 1989 Act applied to the case, but went on to observe at 823 that:

'I think it right to record that I am not aware of any authority in which the precise limits of a "question with respect to the upbringing of a child" for the purposes of section 1(1)(a) have been defined. It may be that in some other case, another day, it will be necessary to consider precisely the ambit of such a question.'

This court is asked on behalf of the mother to examine that question in circumstances where (as distinct from the position before Hale J in *Re M*) the essential question of permission is not agreed.

[14]   In *Re F* (above) a father's defence solicitors wished to interview twin boys aged 11 to discover how much, if anything, either of them saw of an incident or its aftermath whereby the father was charged with assault occasioning actual bodily harm and indecent assault against their mother and affray. The mother refused to give her consent for the boys to be interviewed. A specific issue order was granted which was upheld on appeal.

[15]   In *Re K (Minors) (Wardship: Criminal Proceedings)* [1988] Fam 1, [1987] 3 WLR 1233, [1988] 1 FLR 435, Waterhouse J, in the course of holding that it would be a constitutional impropriety for the wardship court to intervene in the statutory process governing the conduct of a criminal trial and in matters within the jurisdiction of the Crown Court so as to grant or refuse leave for minors to be called as witnesses at a criminal trial, went on to observe at 11E:

'In many cases, the wardship court is likely to be involved at an early stage because leave will have been sought for the police to interview a ward. In such circumstances it is inevitable that the court will have to perform a balancing exercise, weighing the potential damage to the child against the public interest, as a responsible parent would do. In reaching a decision, the best interests of a child may not be the first and paramount consideration ...'

Although the proposition appears not to have been in issue between the parties, the conclusion as to the test to be applied is the same as that of Hale J in *Re M*.

[16] In *Re R* (above) a father charged with serious sexual offences against his three oldest daughters applied for permission to interview one of his sons who had been made a ward of court, with a view to calling him as a defence witness at the trial. Having considered the ratio of *Re K* and in approving the same, Lord Donaldson MR said at 65H:

'This principle we would state in the following terms. Children, whether wards of court or not, are citizens owing duties to society as a whole (including other children), which are appropriate to their years and understanding. Those duties are defined both by the common law and by statute. In the context of the conduct of criminal proceedings in court, the definition and enforcement of these duties have been entrusted by law exclusively to the court in which the proceedings are being conducted and it is not for the wardship court, whatever the theoretical scope of its jurisdiction, to use that jurisdiction to interfere with the performance by the criminal courts of their lawful duties.'

[17] The settled basis of the decisions in each of these cases, whether express or implied, is that the grant or refusal of consent to the interview of a child is an aspect of parental responsibility that can be controlled by the court, in its modern jurisdiction by the use of a specific issue order, but in any event in the inherent jurisdiction and that the test to be applied by the court is a balance of rights and interests within which the child's welfare is not the paramount consideration. The basis for the latter proposition appears to be that a reasonable parent would weigh their child's interests against the public interest and that parents, no more so than the wardship court in the exercise of its prerogative parens patriae jurisdiction, cannot rely exclusively on the child's interests where to do so would interfere with the rights of others, ie where rights may conflict.

[18] The historic origin of the distinct tests was analysed in *Re Z (A Minor) (Identification: Restrictions on Publication)* [1997] Fam 1, [1996] 2 WLR 88, [1996] 1 FLR 191. In this well-known case, extensive media attention led to the child being protected by injunctive relief and the child's mother then sought to relax that protection believing that a television broadcast would benefit her daughter. In the course of an extensive review of the authorities at 30D Ward LJ held that:

'The disclosure by a parent of confidential information relating to the child is an exercise of parental responsibility. As already set out it can be restrained by a prohibited steps order. If the court is considering whether or not steps should be taken by a parent in meeting his parental responsibility for a child, then, beyond question, the court is determining a question with respect to the upbringing of a child. Welfare becomes the paramount consideration.'

[19] The elegant submissions of Mr James Munby QC, as he then was, are reflected with approval in the judgment of Ward LJ. It was submitted that there are two aspects to the *exercise* of the inherent jurisdiction: namely, the custodial jurisdiction which seeks to protect the welfare of the child, and the ancillary jurisdiction which exists to protect the integrity of the court's own proceedings in the interests of the administration of justice. It is only in the custodial jurisdiction that upbringing is directly in issue, ie the welfare of a child is being protected and the child's best interests prevail, whereas in the ancillary jurisdiction where the child's interests are or may be in conflict with a third party, the court must conduct a balancing exercise.

[20] Ward LJ dealt with the relevant legal analysis at 19F to 23A and in summary at 23B to 24C. In determining whether an aspect of parental responsibility that was susceptible of control by the court under s 8 of the 1989 Act or in the inherent jurisdiction was also a question of upbringing, ie within the custodial rather than the ancillary jurisdiction of the court, after setting out examples of both species of decision at 28B to 29D, Ward LJ came to the following conclusion:

'In my judgment a question of upbringing is determined whenever the central issue before the court is one which relates to how the child is being reared.'

It was in this context that the court decided that a parental decision to disclose a child's confidential information was, on the facts of the case, both an aspect of parental responsibility and a question related to the upbringing of the child.

[21] It cannot be said that the decision in *Re Z* provides authority for the proposition that all aspects of parental responsibility are also questions relating to the upbringing of the child. The decision of that court was informed by the concept that there were distinct tests and that a choice had to be made. On the facts of *Re Z*, the duty of confidence owed to the child was held to be absolute, whereas the parent's right to decide what is in the child's best interests was not absolute and could be overridden. The decision was said to involve no conflict with any third party rights, rather the issue focused exclusively on the care of the child and the decision which her mother had made.

[22] Mr Hayden also drew the court's attention to *Re J (A Minor) (Wardship)* [1984] FLR 535 per Wood J and the authorities therein relied upon. Save that, in common with those cases that have been cited above, there is a recognition in the judgment of Wood J that there has to be a proper balance between the protection of a ward and the rights of others, I do not think this takes the argument any further.

[23] I return, then, to the key issue, which is whether the decision to interview a child is exclusively a question within upbringing or whether there are competing interests to balance. No one doubts that consent to an interview is an aspect of parental responsibility, nor that there are serious welfare considerations, but is such a question exclusively a matter concerning the rearing of a child or is it a question where the undoubted issue of that child's welfare interacts with the rights and interests of others?

[24] In my judgment, there can be few clearer examples of the interdependence of rights than the role of the citizen in the criminal process of the state, no matter that that citizen is a child. The administration of criminal justice and the rights of others are clearly engaged and may well be in conflict with a simple welfare analysis.

[25] It is undoubtedly helpful and, in my judgment, necessary to re-cast the question having regard to the enactment of the Human Rights Act 1998. Although, by reason of the urgency of this application, which has had to be interposed in a part-heard list, I have heard no submissions on the point, it is necessary, in my judgment, to cross check the court's conclusion on the decided authorities with a modern interpretation of the rights engaged. If there are rights engaged other than the European Convention for the Protection of Human Rights and Fundamental Freedoms 1950, Art 8 rights of the child then, by analogy with the decision of the House of Lords in *Re S (Identification: Restrictions on Publication)* [2004] UKHL 47, [2005] 1 AC 593, [2005] 1 FLR 591, it would be necessary to conduct a balancing exercise between the competing rights, considering the proportionality of the potential interference with each right independently. That would support and, arguably, would be determinative of the test to be applied.

[26] That the children's Art 8 rights are engaged is clear. Article 8 embraces the right to maintain one's privacy or to waive that privacy and share what would otherwise be private with others (see Munby J in *Re Roddy (A Child) (Identification: Restriction on Publication)* [2003] EWHC 2927 (Fam), [2004] 2 FLR 949, at para [36]). Furthermore, the Art 8 rights of the children, their brother and mother are all engaged in the context of the family life that exists between them and which is now compromised.

[27]   The Art 6 rights of the defendant, their brother and the prosecution as respects the right to a fair trial are engaged and there is a clear interdependency between their brother's Art 6 rights and both his and the girls' Art 8 rights in so far as there is a risk that the he may be wrongly convicted and thereby wrongly deprived with his sisters of the family life which they would otherwise enjoy. Even as this judgment is written, the uncertainty over the interviews and the lack of knowledge as to what the girls may say has caused delay to the arraignment and a renewed bail application. It should also be noted that the Art 6 rights that are engaged are absolute and arguably take priority over the Art 8 rights against which they fall to be balanced.

[28]   I do not pretend to have described an exhaustive list of the rights that are engaged. I do not doubt that it would have been necessary to do so and that the proportionality of the interference with each of them would have had to be considered and balanced were the outcome of this application to have been in any doubt. However, for reasons that I shall shortly describe, I am of the clear view that the welfare balance comes down firmly in favour of the interview of the children by the Chief Constable and, accordingly, the balance of rights on the facts of this case points in one direction only, namely, in favour of the application. Nevertheless, in my judgment, the cross-check with an analysis of rights confirms me in the view that there are multiple rights in play and that the appropriate test must be a balance of the same rather than a discrete welfare inquiry.

General notes:

For disclosure to the police, see *Re EC (Disclosure of material)* [1996] 2 FLR 725 at G71 – CA 1989, s 98: disclosure of evidence to police.

Determining / telling of paternity

I7 GENERALLY BEST FOR TRUTH TO BE KNOWN

Re H and A (Paternity: blood tests)

[2002] EWCA Civ 383, [2002] 1 FLR 1145 at 1146 and 1153

Court of Appeal

Thorpe LJ

[1] Mr B appeals, with the permission of this court, His Honour Judge Elystan Morgan's refusal of his application for an order that blood samples be taken from the respondent's twins to whose paternity he lays claim. The application took advantage of the amendment of s 21 of the Family Law Reform Act 1969 achieved with effect from 1 April 2001 by the Child Support, Pensions and Social Security Act 2000. The effect of the amendment was to introduce into s 21(3) an additional clause (b) so that the subsection provides:

> '(3) A blood sample may be taken from a person under the ageof sixteen years, not being such a person as is referred to in sub-section (4) of this section—
>
> (a) if the person who has the care and control of him consents; or
>
> (b) where that person does not consent, if the court considers that it would be in his best interests for the sample to be taken.'

[2] This small but significant amendment effectively reversed the effect of the decision of Wall J in *Re O; Re J (Children) (Blood Tests: Constraint)* [2000] Fam 139, [2000] 1 FLR 418.

...

[28] In addition to my misgivings as to whether the necessary balancing exercise was correctly performed, I doubt whether the judge gave sufficient weight to the importance of certainty. Over 30 years ago in his speech in *S (An Infant, by her Guardian ad Litem the Official Solicitor to*

the Supreme Court) v S; W v Official Solicitor (Acting as Guardian ad Litem for a Male Infant Named PHW) [1972] AC 24, (1970) FLR Rep 619, Lord Hodson said:

'The only disadvantage to the child which is put forward as an argument against the use of a blood test, not for therapeutic purposes but to ascertain paternity, is that the child is exposed to the risk that he may lose the protection of the presumption of legitimacy.

Without seeking to depreciate the value of this presumption it is, I think, fair to say that whatever may have been the position in the past the general attitude towards illegitimacy has changed and the legal incidents of being born a bastard are now almost non-existent. I need not dilate upon this, for I recognise that it is impossible to say that there is no stigma of bastardy even though it be no more than the indirect stigma of the imputation of unchastity to the mother of the child so described. On the other hand, it is difficult to conceive of cases where, assuming illegitimacy in fact, it is to the advantage of the child that this legal status of legitimacy should be preserved only perhaps to be displaced by firm evidence of illegitimacy decided later in his or her life from a blood test.

The interests of justice in the abstract are best served by the ascertainment of the truth and their must be few cases where the interests of children can be shown to be best served by the suppression of truth. Scientific evidence of blood groups has been available since the early part of this century and the progress of serology has been so rapid that in many cases certainty or near certainty can be reached in the ascertainment of paternity. Why should the risk be taken of a judicial decision being made which is factually wrong and may later be demonstrated to be wrong?'

[29] Those principles have been consistently applied in subsequent cases, including *Re H (A Minor) (Blood Tests: Parental Rights)* [1997] Fam 89, [1996] 2 FLR 65 and *Re T (Paternity: Ordering Blood Tests)* [2001] 2 FLR 1190. The judge sought to distinguish those two authorities in his concluding paragraph, which I have cited above. It draws the distinction that in those two cases there were serious doubts as to the husband's procreative capacities. I do not consider that that factual distinction begins to displace the points of principle to be drawn from the cases: first, that the interests of justice are best served by the ascertainment of the truth and secondly, that the court should be furnished with the best available science and not confined to such unsatisfactory alternatives as presumptions and inferences. It seems to me obvious that all that Lord Hodson expressed in the passage that I have cited applies with even greater force and logic in a later era. First, there have been huge scientific advances with the arrival of DNA testing. Scientists no longer require blood, thus removing what for some is the unbearable process of its extraction. Of even greater importance is the abandonment of the legal concept of legitimacy achieved by the Family Law Reform Act 1987.

[30] The judge made it plain that in the absence of scientific evidence then the issue was to be decided on the application of 'a very important, well established principle ... that is, the presumption of the legitimacy of children born during the currency of the marriage'. He went on to refer to the case of *Serio v Serio* (1983) 4 FLR 756. Twenty years on I question the relevance of the presumption or the justification for its application. In the nineteenth century, when science had nothing to offer and illegitimacy was a social stigma as well as a depriver of rights, the presumption was a necessary tool, the use of which required no justification. That common law presumption, only rebuttable by proof beyond reasonable doubt, was modified by s 26 of the Family Law Reform Act 1969 by enabling the presumption to be rebutted on the balance of probabilities. But as science has hastened on and as more and more children are born out of marriage it seems to me that the paternity of any child is to be established by science and not by legal presumption or inference. Were the judge's order to stand in the present case the consequence would be a long and acrimonious trial of the paternity issue when, in the absence of the only decisive evidence, each side would resort to evidence of marginal or doubtful worth in the determination to prevail. Such a development would be wasteful of both legal costs and judicial time.

[31] As I have said my profoundest misgiving stems from the judge's confidant conclusion that to grant the application would be to destroy the twins' family. However I do not consider that the evidence available to this court permits that very serious consequence to be dismissed as fanciful or even sufficiently unlikely as to be excluded as a factor to be brought into the balance. I conclude that the appeal must be allowed but that the application must be remitted for re-trial. That is not so dire an outcome for the parties as usual since it offers the opportunity to transfer not only the remitted application but all outstanding applications to the Family Division for trial by a judge of the Division. It seems to me important that he should at the earliest opportunity take control of the proceedings establishing clear directions and boundaries by orders and directions designed to bring these proceedings to a close as swiftly and economically as possible. It is in my judgment essential that he should have within the range of orders available to his discretion an order under s 21(3)(b) of the Family Law Reform Act 1969. I would also invite CAFCASS Legal to arrange for the separate representation of the twins in the continuing proceedings.

General notes:

For the process of obtaining DNA testing, see *Re F (Children) (DNA Evidence)* [2007] EWHC 3235 (Fam), [2008] 1 FLR 348: see G17 – Guidelines for DNA testing.

Other significant cases on this issue:

* *Lambeth London Borough Council v S, C, V and J (by his guardian)* [2006] EWHC 326 (Fam), [2007] 1 FLR 152
* *Re J (Paternity: welfare of child)* [2006] EWHC 2837 (Fam), [2007] 1 FLR 1064
* *Re D (Paternity)* [2006] EWHC 3545 (Fam), [2007] 2 FLR 26
* *M v W (Declaration of parentage)* [2006] EWHC 2341 (Fam), [2007] 2 FLR 270
* *Re F (Paternity: jurisdiction)* [2007] EWCA Civ 873, [2008] 1 FLR 225
* *Jevremovic v Serbia*, application 3150/05, [2008] 1 FLR 550
* *Re L (Identity of birth father)* [2008] EWCA Civ 1388, [2009] 1 FLR 1152

I8   JURISDICTION TO ORDER MOTHER TO TELL CHILD OF PATERNITY

Re F (Paternity: jurisdiction)

[2007] EWCA Civ 873, [2008] 1 FLR 225 at 226, 228 and 229

Court of Appeal

Thorpe LJ

[3]   The proceedings came before His Honour Judge Meston QC for the first time on 18 January 2007. He had clearly prepared most conscientiously for that hearing and at the outset drew counsel's attention to two reported cases. The first is the case of *J v C and Another* [2006] EWCA Civ 551, [2007] Fam 1, sub nom *J v C (Void Marriage: Status of Children)* [2006] 2 FLR 1098. The second case is also, by chance, reported under the initials *J v C*. It is the decision of Sumner J at first instance and is reported at *Re J (Paternity: Welfare of Child)* [2006] EWHC 2837 (Fam), [2007] 1 FLR 1064, sub nom *J v C* [2006] All ER (D) 147 (Nov). The relevance of these two cases is that in the first at para [41] of Wall LJ's leading judgment, doubt is cast on the justiciability of orders under s 8 of the Children Act 1989 to require a parent to disclose to a child the truth of his or her parentage. That perhaps influenced Sumner J to say in para [12] of his judgment, given in November 2006, that he was presuming that he had the jurisdiction to make such an order but concluded on the merits that he should not exercise it.

...

[8]   It seems to me absolutely clear, and even Miss Butler, in the course of her submissions, conceded that a specific question as to whether or not a child should be told the truth of his or her parentage is a question which has arisen or which may arise in connection with an aspect of parental responsibility for a child ...

...

[14]   ... It is perfectly obvious to me that in the course of its protective function the family justice system has since time immemorial taken difficult decisions to promote the welfare of children. In the context of history of origins sometimes the discretionary outcome is that children should be protected from knowledge; sometimes the discretionary outcome has been that the children should be told the truth. That the court's responsibility to take those decisions in the event of adult dispute

has never, in my experience, been in doubt or in question. I do not think that Wall LJ intended to put them in doubt or question.

[15]   I say that because he and I both sat as members of a constitution on 28 November 2006 that decided the appeal of *Re C (Contact: Moratorium: Change of Gender)* [2006] EWCA Civ 1765, [2007] 1 FLR 1642. In that case we allowed an appeal from a decision of Coleridge J, which imposed a 2-year moratorium on any progress in a biological father's campaign to ensure that children should be informed of the truth of their paternity and that consequently he should have contact. The only basis on which we allowed the appeal was that the two issues before Coleridge J had been conflated and nobody had invited him to separate out the issue of whether the children should be told, from the issue as to whether the father should have contact.

[16]   Accordingly, intervening as we did, we approved and directed the immediate commencement of work by the National Youth Advocacy Service to impart the crucial information and to assist the children in adjustment to it. So, if Wall LJ had any reservations, which I doubt he did, in May 2006 he certainly had none by late November.

[17]   I only finally mention one aspect of Miss Butler's presentation; namely, the question of enforceability. She says that since plainly any such order would not be enforceable then it follows that there is no jurisdiction to make it or a submission to like effect. It seems to me that any argument in relation to the enforceability of a s 8 order, that a parent tell the child the truth about paternity, is completely theoretical and, to that extent, unreal. In almost all these cases where children have been brought up to a certainty, which is for their own protection to be destroyed by the imparting of a different truth, it is likely that mental health professionals will need to be involved to help the children through the process and indeed the whole family, including the parents. In a case such as *J v C* where Mrs C was open to receiving advice from an expert and following that advice, then enforceability does not arise.

[18]   Assuming a parent who, out of obstinacy or emotional disturbance, was challenging the judicial discretionary decision by a threat to ignore the order, it is manifest that such a parent only magnifies the difficulty and with it the need for professional intervention. So, in a case such as that it would be quite pointless to order the reluctant parent to do the job. Such a parent is the worst possible person to carry out the delicate task and in reality the court would meet the challenge by simply putting in place alternative mechanisms for the imparting of the sensitive information.

Contraceptive advice

I9 CONTRACEPTIVE ADVICE WITHOUT PARENTAL KNOWLEDGE / CONSENT

Gillick v West Norfolk and Wisbech Area Health Authority and Another

[1986] 1 FLR 224 at 239

House of Lords

Lord Fraser

See A14 – Parental authority dwindles

Other significant cases on this issue:

- *R (Axon) v The Secretary of State for Health and the Family Planning Association* [2006] EWHC 37 (Admin), [2006] 2 FLR 206

Parental alienation

I10   PARENTAL ALIENATION EXISTS BUT IS NOT A SYNDROME

Re O (Contact: withdrawal of application)

[2003] EWHC 3031 (Fam), [2004] 1 FLR 1258 at 1277

Family Division

Wall J

Parental alienation

[91]   Parental alienation is a well-recognised phenomenon. In the recent case of *Re M (Intractable Contact Dispute: Interim Care Orders)* [2003] EWHC 1024 (Fam), [2003] 2 FLR 636, a mother had persuaded her children, quite falsely, that their father had physically and sexually abused them, and that their paternal grandparents were also a danger to them. She refused to allow their father to have any contact with them, and disobeyed court orders for contact. I found that her conduct was causing the children significant harm, and invited the local authority to take care proceedings, the outcome of which was the removal of the children from their mother, and residence orders in favour of their father. That, in my judgment, was a clear case of parental alienation.

[92]   I agree with Dr Claire Sturge and Dr Danya Glaser in their report for the Court of Appeal in the seminal case of *In Re L (A Child) (Contact: Domestic Violence); In Re V (A Child); In Re M (A Child); In Re H (Children)* [2001] Fam 260, [2000] 2 FLR 334 and published at [2000] Fam Law 615 (*Contact and Domestic Violence – the Experts' Court Report*), that the term 'parental alienation syndrome' is a misnomer. As Sturge and Glaser put it at 622:

> 'We do not consider it to be a helpful concept and consider that the sort of problems that the title of this disorder is trying to address is better thought of as implacable hostility. The essential and important difference is that the Parental Alienation Syndrome assumes a cause (seen as misguided or malign on the part of the resident parent) which leads to a prescribed intervention whereas the concept (which no one claims to be a "syndrome") is simply a

statement aimed at the understanding of particular situations but for which a range of explanations is possible and for which there is no single and prescribed solution, this depending on the nature and individuality of each case.'

[93] However one looks at it, however, the instant case is not one of parental alienation by O's mother against his father. All the professional opinions in the case, including, of course, those of the two circuit judges who saw and heard the mother in the witness box, negative parental alienation. To suggest otherwise is, I regret to say, part and parcel of the father's attempt to absolve himself of responsibility.

Other significant cases on this issue:

• *Re D (intractable contact dispute)* [2004] EWHC 727 (Fam), [2004] 1 FLR 1226 at [12]

This case is also included in relation to:

B12 General points (1)

I11 NO GENDER BIAS IN FAMILY JUSTICE SYSTEM

Re Bradford, Re O'Connell

[2006] EWCA Civ 1199, [2007] 1 FLR 530 at 561 and 561

Court of Appeal

Wall J

Some general observations

[93] Amongst the advantages of transparency, it seems to me, is the opportunity to dispel the myth that there is a gender bias against fathers within the family justice system, and that the bias operates, in particular, improperly to deny non-residential fathers contact with their children. I do not doubt that there are cases in which contact between non-residential fathers and their children is not ordered when the principal reason for the breakdown of contact is the attitude of the children's mother. But in my experience, it is far more common for contact to break down due to the behaviour of the non-residential father.

[94] These two cases are, in my judgment, clear examples of the latter category. The findings of the trial judge in both cases are that the reason these children are not having contact their fathers is exclusively due to the father's own behaviour. It is idle for either Mr Bradford or Mr O'Connell to blame either the system or the children's mothers. The judicial findings in both cases are clear. These are not cases of parental alienation syndrome on the part of the residential parent, and Mr O'Connell deceives himself if he persists in believing that his children's attitude towards him is the responsibility of his former wife and her husband.

...

[96] The position of the family courts is clear. I attempted to summarise it in *Re O (Contact: Withdrawal of Application)* [2003] EWHC 3031 (Fam), [2004] 1 FLR 1258. In that case, I made a number of general observations in that case, some of which are, it seems to me, applicable to both of the current applications. At 1260 I said:

'*The critical role of both parents in the lives of their children post separation—*

(3) The courts recognise the critical importance of the role of both

parents in the lives of their children. The courts are not anti-father and pro-mother or vice-versa. The court's task, imposed by Parliament in s 1 of the Children Act 1989 in every case is to treat the welfare of the child or children concerned as paramount, and to safeguard and promote the welfare of every child to the best of its ability.

Terminating non-resident parents' contact with their children is a matter of last resort—

(4)   Unless there are cogent reasons against it, the children of separated parents are entitled to know and have the love and society of both their parents. In particular, the courts recognise the vital importance of the role of non-resident fathers in the lives of their children, and only make orders terminating contact when there is no alternative.

Parental alienation

(5)   The father asserts that this is a case in which the mother has deliberately alienated O from him. It is not. The principal reason that that O is hostile to contact with his father is because of his father's behaviour, and not because his mother has influenced O against his father. Unfortunately, the father is quite unable to understand or accept this. The father's reliance in this case on the so called 'parental alienation syndrome' is misplaced.

Blaming the system

(6)   ...

Parental responsibility for the failure of contact

(7)   Parents must, however, take their share of responsibility for the state of affairs they have created. Blaming the system, as the father does in this case, is no answer. He must shoulder his share of the responsibility for the state of affairs he has helped to bring about. All the evidence is that he has proved incapable of doing so.'

[97]   I stand by everything I said in that case. I repeat that the press, and some parents' pressure groups need to understand that the reasons fathers in particular fail sometimes to remain in contact with their children is not due to gender bias in the system, but to their own conduct. These two cases give me the opportunity to repeat a message which is inadequately heard, and even if it is not heeded, the judgment is in the public domain. Neither of these cases can even remotely be described as 'secret justice',

and I have deliberately taken the unusual step of reserving judgment in the two applications so that, in considering the two cases in detail, I could re-examine my own practice thoroughly.

Neglect

I12 BUMPING ALONG THE BOTTOM

Re E (Care proceedings: social work practice)

[2000] 2 FLR 254 at 256

Family Division

Bracewell J

In my experience in cases of neglect, abuse and failure to thrive it is quite common to find that children have been left to deteriorate in inadequate homes year upon year with no effective action. Intervention which may be described as sticking plaster does not address the fundamental issues and social workers often appear unwilling to make crucial decisions in favour of intervention and they tolerate wholly inappropriate parenting, even when faced with serious evidence of concern and lack of parental co-operation with professionals, so that the children drift, become more damaged and vulnerable. Repeated referrals failed to trigger protective action in this case. Professor Olive Stephenson, professor emeritus of social work studies at the University of Nottingham, addressed this issue in an article 'Child and Family Social Work' (1996) vol 1, p 16. In a paragraph headed appropriately 'Bumping along the bottom', she said this:

> 'It is evident from present research and other work undertaken by the author that in long-term cases of neglect social workers have got used to certain families bumping along the bottom or nearly falling off the edge. As time goes on there may seem less reason for taking action when children have survived thus far. Magistrates will ask, "So what has changed?" The effect is to tolerate the status quo until an incident necessitates a proper assessment of the contemporary family situation. The incident may be of physical and sexual abuse. In some neglectful families it may be that sexual abuse is by an outsider and reflects a lack of parental observation or control. Another kind of incident may be a change of worker who sees the family with fresh eyes and is alarmed. This evidence tends to confirm that there may be a dulled response to certain well known families who are not providing good enough care.'

A measured approach to dealing with these sort of cases was set out in the Orange Book, the guide for social workers undertaking a comprehensive assessment at pp 7–8:

'Social workers often have lengthy involvements with chronically neglecting families but find it difficult to make judgments about the standards of parental care and the effect these have on the child's safety and development. Neglecting families can drift for years beyond the boundaries of acceptable parenting without a systematic assessment being made of the situation. The neglected child requires the same structured and rigorous approach to assessment and treatment as any other abused child. An involvement of paediatric and health visitor colleagues is just as critical in order to clarify the effect that neglect is having on the child's physical and emotional development. It is particularly difficult to identify emotional abuse in its own right, that is when it is not a component of some other form of abuse. It requires an ability to recognise symptoms of emotional disturbance and to connect them to particular patterns of behaviour. Probably more than any other category of abuse, however, this area is fraught with value judgment and subjective opinion. Although research and knowledge give little guidance, practitioners must be alert to the needs of the severely and persistently rejected, isolated or cowering child, or in contrast the intensely over protected and smothered child. When emotional abuse is recognised the same vigorous steps need to be taken to investigate, protect, assess and treat these children, using a structured and systematic approach and calling on specialist paediatric, psychiatric and psychological skills where appropriate.

Timely intervention reduces the chance of a child being emotionally damaged in an abusing or neglectful home. Leaving a child in a dysfunctional home can result in such permanent disturbance that when the child is finally removed he or she is unable to make relationships, form healthy attachments, or cope with substitute carers.'

The present case is an example of a pattern of abusive parenting ranging through the children in turn with history repeating itself over a 20-year period.

This case is also included in relation to:

I18   Social work practice

Non-accidental head injury

I13 THE TRIAD / GEDDES II AND III

R v Harris, Rock, Cherry and Faulder

[2005] EWCA Civ Crim 1980, [2008] 2 FLR 412 at 425, 427, 430 and 433

Court of Appeal

Gage LJ

The triad and the unified hypothesis

[56] At the heart of these appeals, as they were advanced in the notices of appeal and the appellants' skeleton arguments, was a challenge to the accepted hypothesis concerning 'shaken baby syndrome' (SBS); or, as we believe it should be more properly called, non-accidental head injury (NAHI). The accepted hypothesis depends on findings of a triad of intracranial injuries consisting of encephalopathy (defined as disease of the brain affecting the brain's function); subdural haemorrhages (SDH); and retinal haemorrhages (RH). For many years the coincidence of these injuries in infants (babies aged between 1 month and 2 years) has been considered to be the hallmark of NAHI. Not all three of the triad of injuries are necessary for NAHI to be diagnosed, but most doctors who gave evidence to us in support of the triad stated that no diagnosis of pure SBS (as contrasted with impact injuries or impact and shaking) could be made without both encephalopathy and subdural haemorrhages. Professor Carol Jenny, a paediatrician and consultant neuro-trauma specialist called by the Crown, went further and said that she would be very cautious about diagnosing SBS in the absence of retinal haemorrhages. In addition, the Crown points to two further factors of circumstantial evidence, namely that the injuries are invariably inflicted by a sole carer in the absence of any witness; and that they are followed by an inadequate history, incompatible with the severity of the injuries.

[57] Between 2000 and 2004 a team of distinguished doctors led by Dr Jennian Geddes, a neuropathologist with a speciality in work with children, produced three papers setting out the results of their research into the triad. In the third paper, 'Geddes III', the team put forward a new hypothesis, 'the unified hypothesis', which challenged the supposed

infallibility of the triad. It was called the unified hypothesis because it relied on the proposal that there was one unified cause of the three intracranial injuries constituting the triad; that cause was not necessarily trauma. It is important to note that the new hypothesis did not seek to show that the triad was inconsistent with NAHI. It did, however, seek to show that it was not diagnostic.

[58] When Geddes III was published it was, and still is, very controversial. It is not overstating the position to say that this paper generated a fierce debate in the medical profession, both nationally and internationally. In the course of the hearing of these appeals we have heard evidence from a number of very distinguished medical experts with a range of different specialities most of whom had in witness statements expressed views on one side or other of the debate. However, early on in the hearing it became apparent that substantial parts of the basis of the unified hypothesis could no longer stand. Dr Geddes, at the beginning of her cross-examination, accepted that the unified hypothesis was never advanced with a view to being proved in court. She said that it was meant to stimulate debate. Further, she accepted that the hypothesis might not be quite correct; or as she put it:

'I think we might not have the theory quite right. I think possibly the emphasis on hypoxia – no, I think possibly we are looking more at raised pressure being the critical event.'

And later in her evidence:

'Q Dr Geddes, cases up and down the country are taking place where Geddes III is cited by the defence time and time again as the reason why the established theory is wrong.

A That I am very sorry about. It is not fact; it is hypothesis but, as I have already said, so is the traditional explanation. ... I would be very unhappy to think that cases were being thrown out on the basis that my theory was fact. We asked the editor if we could have "Hypothesis Paper" put at the top and he did not, but we do use the word "hypothesis" throughout.'

[59] Despite these frank admissions the triad and Geddes III have been a focus of much of the medical issues in these appeals. We propose to set out the salient features of each in a little more detail. We do so not only as a backdrop to these appeals but in an effort to inform those involved in future trials as to the current accepted state of medical science, as we understand it from the evidence before us, on some of the very difficult issues which are raised in criminal and civil trials involving allegations of NAHI.

...

The triad

[63]   As already stated, when the three elements of the triad coincide for
some years conventional medical opinion has been that this is diagnostic
of NAHI. Typically the brain is found to be encephalopathic; bleeding is
found in the subdural space between the dura and the arachnoid subdural
haemmorhages; and there are retinal haemorrhages. There may also be
other pathological signs such as subarachnoid bleeding and injuries at the
craniocervical junction. Further, there may be injuries to nerve tissue
(axonal injuries) and external signs of broken bones, bruising and other
obvious injuries such as extradural oedema (bruising). Determining these
findings requires medical experts from a number of different disciplines
interpreting often very small signs within the complex structures of an
infant's brain and surrounding tissue.

[64]   The mechanism for these injuries is said to be the shaking of the
infant, with or without impact on a solid surface, which moves the brain
within the skull damaging the brain and shearing the bridging veins
between the dura and the arachnoid. The shaking may also cause retinal
haemorrhages. In the sense that the explanation for the triad is said to be
caused by shaking and/or impact it also is a unified hypothesis, albeit that
each element is said to be caused individually by trauma.

[65]   The triad of injuries becomes central to a diagnosis of NAHI when
there are no other signs or symptoms of trauma such as bruises or
fractures.

The unified hypothesis ('Geddes III')

[66]   Dr Geddes and her colleagues, following research into almost 50
paediatric cases without head injury, proposed that the same triad of
injuries could be caused by severe hypoxia (lack of oxygen in the tissues)
which in turn led to brain swelling. The hypothesis was that brain swelling
combined with raised intracranial pressure (ICP) could cause both
subdural haemorrhages and retinal haemmorhages. Thus, it was argued
that any incidents of apnoea (cessation of breathing) could set in motion
a cascade of events which could cause the same injuries as seen in the
triad. It will be appreciated that there are many events which could
accidentally cause an episode of apnoea.

[67]   In Geddes III the unfied hypothesis was summarised as follows:

'Our observations in the present series indicate that, in the immature
brain, hypoxia both alone and in combination with infection is
sufficient to activate the pathophysiological cascade which
culminates in altered vascular permeability and extravasation of
blood within and under the dura. In the presence of brain swelling
and raised intracranial pressure, vascular fragility and bleeding

would be exacerbated by additional hemodynamic forces such as venous hypertension, and the effects of both sustained systemic arterial hypertension and episodic surges in blood pressure.'

Thus, it was suggested that all the injuries constituting the triad could be attributed to a cause other than NAHI. We understand that this paper has been much cited in both criminal and civil trials since its publication.

[68] The criticism of Geddes III is that it is not hypoxia and/or brain swelling which causes subdural haemorrhages and retinal haemorrhages but trauma. As an example of why the hypothesis is not correct Dr Jaspan, giving evidence in the appeal of Rock, demonstrated that CT scans taken of Heidi's brain showed that there was little or no brain swelling at a time when subdural haemorrhages and retinal haemorrhages were shown to be present. As a result of critical papers published in the medical journals, as we have already stated, Dr Geddes when cross-examined frankly admitted that the unified hypothesis could no longer credibly be put forward. In cross-examination she accepted that she could no longer support the hypothesis that brain swelling was the cause of subdural haemorrhages and retinal haemmorhages. She did, however, state that she believed that raised intracranial pressure (ICP) might prove to be an independent cause of both lesions. When asked by Mr Horwell if she had published a paper on this hypothesis she said that she had not and that her research was still incomplete. It was clear from subsequent questions in cross-examination that this work was still in its early stages and that many questions remain, as yet, unresolved.

[69] In our judgment, it follows that the unified hypothesis can no longer be regarded as a credible or alternative cause of the triad of injuries. This conclusion, however, is not determinative of the four appeals before us. There are many other medical issues involved in cases of alleged NAHI. Further, there remains a body of medical opinion which does not accept that the triad is an infallible tool for diagnosis. This body of opinion, whilst recognising that the triad is consistent with NAHI, cautions against its use as a certain diagnosis in the absence of other evidence. These four appeals raise different medical issues and do not necessarily fail because the unified hypothesis has not been validated. But it does mean that the triad, itself a hypothesis, has not been undermined in the way envisaged by the authors of Geddes III.

[70] Mr Horwell, in his final submissions invited the court to find that the triad was proved as a fact and not just a hypothesis. On the evidence before us we do not think it possible for us to do so. Whilst a strong pointer to NAHI on its own we do not think it possible to find that it must automatically and necessarily lead to a diagnosis of NAHI. All the circumstances, including the clinical picture, must be taken into account. In any event, on general issues of this nature, where there is a genuine difference between two reputable medical opinions, in our judgment, the

Court of Criminal Appeal will not usually be the appropriate forum for these issues to be resolved. The focus of this court will be (as ours has been) to decide the safety of the conviction bearing in mind the test in fresh evidence appeals which we set out below. That is not to say that such differences cannot be resolved at trial. At trial, when such issues arise, it will be for the jury (in a criminal trial) and the judge (in a civil trial) to resolve them as issues of fact on all the available evidence in the case (see *R v Kai-Whitewind* [2005] EWCA Crim 1092, [2006] Crim LR 349).

...

Degree of force

[76] This leads on to a very important issue which arises in these appeals and will no doubt arise in many cases where the triad of injuries is present. It is the question of how much force is necessary to cause those injuries. There is a measure of common ground between the doctors on this issue. Generally it is agreed that there is no scientific method of correlating the amount of force used and the severity of the damage caused. To state the obvious, it is not possible to carry out experiments on living children. Further, experience shows that the human frame reacts differently in different infants to the same degree of force. However the medical opinion on this issue appears to be divided into those who maintain that severe injuries can confidently be ascribed to a traumatic cause, for example (but not only) Dr Rorke-Adams, a very experienced paediatric neuropathologist, and those who maintain that very little force may cause very serious injuries, for example Dr John Plunkett, a distinguished anatomical, clinical and forensic pathologist.

[77] It is quite impossible for this court to make any finding on this issue beyond referring to some general propositions with which both counsel agreed. First, common sense suggests that the more severe the injuries the more probable they will have been caused by greater force than mere 'rough handling'. We note that the most recent *Update from the Ophthalmology Child Abuse Working Party; Royal College of Ophthalmologists* (2004) concludes:

> 'It is highly unlikely that the forces required to produce retinal haemorrhage in a child less than 2 years of age would be generated by a reasonable person during the course of (even rough) play or an attempt to arouse a sleeping or apparently unconscious child.'

[78] Secondly, as Mr Peter Richards, a very experienced neurosurgeon with a speciality in paediatrics, pointed out, if rough handling of an infant or something less than rough handling, commonly caused the sort of injuries which resulted in death, the hospitals would be full of such cases. In our view, this points to the fact that cases of serious injuries

caused by very minor force such as might occur in normal handling or rough handling of an infant, are likely to be rare or even extremely rare.

[79] But, thirdly, as Dr Plunkett demonstrated by his research and in particular by reference to an amateur video of a child falling from a 3 foot high railing, described as part of a play tree-house, which resulted in catastrophic injuries, there will be cases where a small degree of force or a minor fall will cause very severe injuries. We shall have more to say about Dr Plunkett's research later in this judgment, but at this stage we repeat that the evidence suggests that cases where this occurs are likely to be very rare.

[80] Fourthly, although the younger the infant or child, the more vulnerable it is likely to be, it is not possible to conclude that age is necessarily a factor in deciding whether injuries are caused by strong force or a minimal degree of force or impact. The balance of the evidence is that, although an infant's skull is more pliable than that of an older child, the internal organs and vessels are as robust as those of an older child. The vulnerability of an infant arises from the fact that its head is generally larger in proportion to its body than in an older child and its neck muscles are weaker and not as well developed as in older children, hence the significance of injuries at the site of the craniocervical junction.

...

Retinal haemorrhages

[97] Retinal haemorrhage is the third limb of the triad. It will be recalled that Professor Carol Jenny told us that, in her view, in a case of pure shaking extreme caution should be exercised before a diagnosis of NAHI is made in the absence of retinal haemmorhage. We see the force of this evidence. In cases of injuries alleged to have been caused by an impact or impacts, the evidence suggests that it is not a prerequisite for retinal haemorrhages to be found. Again, we understand the logic of this proposition.

[98] It is agreed between the expert ophthalmologists and ophthalmic surgeons that a rapid rise in intracranial pressure can cause retinal haemorrhages although the amount and type of pressure required to cause such haemorrhages is a matter of debate. The appellants' expert ophthalmic surgeon, Dr Gillian Adams, said that retinal haemorrhages could be caused by a spike or surge of venous pressure. Mr Peter Richards said that in his experience of carrying out brain surgery, artificially induced very high venous pressure did not cause retinal haemorrhages.

[99] Some of the ophthalmic experts stated that retinal haemorrhages caused by shaking or impact demonstrate entirely different characteristics

from retinal haemorrhages arising from other causes. Others said that no distinction can be made between retinal haemorrhages arising from different causes.

[100] Again, in the context of these appeals, we make no findings in respect of these differences of opinion. In future cases before a criminal or civil court, the type and extent of retinal haemorrhage and its place in the constellations of symptoms will be a matter for the court to evaluate in each individual case. We bear them in mind when reaching our conclusions in these four appeals. We also bear in mind Mr Horwell's submission that the real question in these appeals is how much force is necessary to cause not just one element of the triad, but all three.

Other significant cases on this issue:

- *A Local Authority v S* [2009] EWHC 2115 (Fam), [2010] 1 FLR 1560
- *R v Henderson; Butler; Oyediran* [2010] EWCA Crim 1269, [2011] 1 FLR 407

Sexual abuse

I14 FAILURE TO FOLLOW ABE GUIDELINES

Re B (Allegation of sexual abuse: child's evidence)

[2006] EWCA Civ 773, [2006] 2 FLR 1071 at 1080

Court of Appeal

Hughes LJ

[40] There was no question of this evidence being inadmissible for failure to comply with the ABE guidelines, and that has not been suggested in argument for either parent. In a family case evidence of this kind falls to be assessed, however unsatisfactory its origin. To hold otherwise would be to invest the guidelines with the status of the law of evidence and it would invite the question: which failures have the consequence of inadmissibility? Clearly some failures to follow the guidelines will reduce, but by no means eliminate, the value of the evidence. Some may be purely technical and have no impact at all on value. Others may reduce the value almost to vanishing point.

[41] The question for us in this case is whether the judge was compelled to the conclusion that he must disregard this evidence altogether. Mr Anelay submits that the failures here were so wholesale that that must be the consequence, on the basis that otherwise there is no point in having the guidelines.

[42] With that submission I do not agree. The purpose of the ABE guidelines is not disciplinary; it is to present the court and for that matter the parents with the most reliable evidence which can be obtained. In every case the judge cannot avoid the task of weighing up the evidence, warts and all, and deciding whether or not it has any value or none. Everything will depend on the facts of the case. The exercise has perhaps something in common with the one which judges are used to carrying out when confronted with hearsay evidence, often in a family case third or fourth-hand hearsay.

[43] On the other hand, I agree with Mr Anelay that the fact that one is in a family case sailing under the comforting colours of child protection is

not a reason to afford to unsatisfactory evidence a weight greater than it can properly bear. That is in nobody's interests, least of all the child's.

[44]   It is clear to me that the judge was fully aware of the deficiencies of this evidence. They had been very extensively canvassed in front of him. He expressed himself in understated terms, but he reminded himself of the ABE guidelines and in particular those relating to an initial contact interview. As he reminded himself explicitly, the guidelines were not followed. He held that this was in effect an interview without the proper safeguards of video recording. He said that the failure to record the questions had made the task of evaluating the child's statement a difficult one.

[45]   That was the right approach. The judge then analysed what S had said over two of three pages of his judgment. In my view, he was entitled to reach his overall conclusion that S had been abused and by her father, by the combination of this evidence with the evidence which was independent of it; that is to say, the independent evidence that she had been abused by someone, the evidence that her friend K had been abused also, and that K had attributed it to father, and the evidence of their joint sexualised play. What was said in interview was consistent with that evidence. It was not likely that S, having been abused by someone at the age of 5, should have been abused by someone other than the father who abused her friend K, but should nevertheless say that it was him.

Other significant cases on this issue:

*   *Re D (Child Abuse: interviews)* [1998] 2 FLR 10

I15 RCPCH GUIDANCE ETC

Leeds City Council v YX and ZX

[2008] EWHC 802 (Fam), [2008] 2 FLR 869 at 890, 892, 894 and 897

Family Division

Holman J

The Royal College of Paediatrics and Child Health New Guidance

[102] A final development in the medical material in this case is the imminent publication of a new document by the Royal College of Paediatrics and Child Health, 'The physical signs of child sexual abuse, an evidence based review and guidance for best practice'. This is currently dated March 2008 and, I understand, will be published on 2 April 2008. I am very grateful indeed to the Royal College for generously and freely making an advance copy available for use in this case and for study and consideration by all the experts in this case.

[103] As I understand it, this is a fundamentally new document. It does not so much revise as replace the previous guidelines published by the Royal College of Physicians, most recently revised in 1997. The new document is long, detailed and, in places, highly technical. At the risk of over-simplification, I understood from all the paediatricians who gave oral evidence that the new document is more conservative and cautious as to the reliability of physical signs as evidence of abuse. It has, as I understand it, led Drs Hobbs and Crawford, in particular, to be more cautious about some of the views they express in the present case.

[104] At paragraph 1.2 in the 'Introduction' the document refers to the metaphor of a jigsaw puzzle. As the reference in the footnote indicates, this metaphor was apparently first coined in 1990 by Dr Hobbs himself, and another author, Dr JM Wynne, and Dr Hobbs has used the jigsaw metaphor in the present case. The report says,

> 'Recognition that a child has been sexually abused has been likened to completing a jigsaw whereby the individual pieces of information need to be put together before the full picture can emerge. This metaphor is particularly apt when it comes to interpreting the significance of a single physical sign of sexual abuse, which is just one part of the diagnostic jigsaw.'

[105] Whilst the purpose of the metaphor is to stress, as the document goes on to make plain, the importance of considering 'all physical findings together with other important clinical information including the history, child's behaviour, demeanour and statements made by the child', I myself feel that the metaphor (like many analogies or metaphors) can be misleading. It tends to presuppose that all the pieces can be fitted together, and that there is a 'full picture' to be made. By presupposing that each piece of information does fit somewhere in the picture, it may ascribe some weight or significance to each piece of information and obscure the important point that 0 plus 0 plus 0 still equals 0. If the jigsaw metaphor is helpful at all, then, in my view, it is important to think of a pile of jigsaw pieces in which pieces from more than one jigsaw have been muddled up. There may be pieces which, on examination, do not fit the jigsaw under construction at all, but which require to be discarded or placed on one side.

[106] Professor Heger, on the other hand, strongly suggests the mathematical approach that 0 plus 0 plus 0 still equals 0. Whilst that may be mathematically true, it is, in my view, dangerous and equally mistaken to adopt so mathematical an approach. Professor Heger said during her oral evidence, 'To me if one finding does not support a diagnosis, I credit that finding as zero.' I cannot and do not accept that at all. In a case like this, individual pieces of information cannot be viewed in isolation. To say that a given piece of information standing alone is not probative of anything, does not necessarily mean that it has a value of zero. Each piece of information does need to be weighed and assessed in the context of all the other pieces of information.

...

[114] The overall 'Evidence Statement' of the Royal College at page 97 of the new document states in relation to reflex anal dilatation and anal laxity as follows:

'Reflex anal dilatation has been described in children who allege anal abuse and sexual abuse. It has been described in a higher proportion of children who allege anal abuse than in those who allege sexual abuse. There is a paucity of data on the prevalence of reflex anal dilatation in children selected for non-abuse. However, in one study of children selected for non-abuse, it was noted in 5%. The use of the term 'anal gaping' by some authors may reflect what others describe as reflex anal dilatation or anal laxity.

There is insufficient evidence to determine the significance of laxity or reduced anal tone in relation to sexual abuse. It has been described in sexually abused children, but there are no studies of anal laxity in children selected for non-abuse.'

...

[124] There are not, and cannot be, reliable statistics or data about the true prevalence of sexual abuse by parents, for reasons described in paras 1.11 and 1.12 of the new Royal College document. But there is no data in that document, or of which I am aware, to undermine the proposition that a majority of parents in our society do not sexually abuse their children. The starting point must be that it is improbable that a parent of otherwise good character would sexually abuse, or has sexually abused, his or her child in the sort of deliberately penetrative way under consideration in this case. (Less serious forms of touching such as kissing or stroking the external genital area are not what is under consideration. If there has been abuse at all, it must clearly have involved deliberate penetration by a finger, penis or object of the vagina and/or the anus.)

[125] In my view, the degree of inherent improbability tends to be heightened by the facts and chronology of this case. As I have already described, from late November 2005 and, in particular, from 21 March 2006, both these parents were well aware that they and A were under intense and continuing scrutiny, and that there would inevitably be further follow up medical examinations. They would have known that there was a high risk of any sexual abuse being exposed.

[126] I must, and do, give weight also to the fact that A has never given the least indication of abuse, and has always denied it when asked. She has denied it to her mother, to her headteacher, Mrs C, to social workers and to her guardian. Two different social workers, Miss Ali and Miss Ellwood, in different periods of time (May 2006 and January/February 2007) have done specialised work designed to enable her to disclose or hint at abuse, or, at any rate, to reveal or indicate any underlying fears or insecurity. She revealed and indicated nothing. On the contrary, she gave every indication of being a happy and well integrated member of a happy and well functioning family.

[127] I fully accept the view and observation of Dr Hobbs that the pressures on a child *not*, I emphasise the word 'not', to disclose abuse may be very great. The child may well understand that the effect would be to break up the family and even cause a parent to be imprisoned. But I agree also with a comment by Professor Heger that, 'We walk a very dangerous line if we only believe children when they disclose abuse, but not when they deny abuse'.

...

[142] I have been invited to make some more general observations or give any appropriate guidance for future cases. For instance, there was some discussion during the evidence about the problem of a lack of scale when magnification is used on a colposcope. I consider, however, that I do not have a sufficient evidential base to enable or entitle me safely to make general guideline observations. The new document of the Royal College of Paediatrics and Child Health will be published imminently. It is a considered document, and the product of very great work and consultation amongst many experts. For a period, that document should be enabled to permeate and influence the approach rather than the observations of a single judge after hearing limited evidence which has been very specifically focused on the facts of this case.

[143] I wish only to stress, as that document does at paragraphs 1.2 and 1.13, the very great importance of including in any assessment every aspect of a case. Very important indeed is the account of the child, considered, of course, in an age appropriate way. An express denial is no less an account than is a positive account of abuse. It is also, in my opinion, very important to take fully into account the account and demeanour of the parents, and an assessment of the family circumstances and general quality of the parenting. The medical assessment of physical signs of sexual abuse has a considerably subjective element, and unless there is clearly diagnostic evidence of abuse (eg the presence of semen or a foreign body internally) purely medical assessments and opinions should not be allowed to predominate. Even 20 years after the Cleveland Inquiry, I wonder whether its lessons have fully been learned.

I16 WHAT WE HAVE LEARNED: A SHORT SUMMARY

Re G (Adoption: ordinary residence)

[2002] EWHC 2447 (Fam), [2003] 2 FLR 944 at 959

Family Division

Wall J

Furthermore, we have, over the last 10 years – and this is what makes this case so unusual in my experience because one can look back 10 years – learned a great deal about allegations of sexual abuse and the manner in which they should be investigated. We have learned to be particularly cautious of allegations which emerge in the context of marital breakdown where one of the parties suffers from mental ill-health; where the allegations resemble marital sexual complaints which one party makes against the other in the course of the proceedings. We have also learned the very subtle processes whereby suggestible children adopt their parents' belief systems without coming anywhere near them being coached. We have learned more and more about the correct way of interviewing children – for how long, what sort of questions, the inappropriateness of the child's carer being present and so on, and we have learned the real dangers of involving anatomical dolls in the process.

Other significant cases on this issue:

- *KS v GS (a minor: sexual abuse)* [1992] 2 FLR 361 (misuse of anatomically correct dolls)
- *Re M (Sexual abuse allegations)* [1999] 2 FLR 92 (interviewing techniques including the misuse of leading questions / coaxing)

Induced / fabricated illness

I17 NO SUBSTITUTE FOR FACTUAL ANALYSIS AND RISK ASSESSMENT

A County Council v A Mother, a Father and X, Y and Z (by their guardian)

[2005] EWHC 31 (Fam), [2005] 2 FLR 129 at 161 and 164

Family Division

Ryder J

[154] Joint working is not simply talking to those professionals with whom one agrees. It involves talking to representatives of all points of view on the record. Sometimes that will require a strategic decision as to whether the need for the provision of services for a child is more important than the preservation of the integrity of criminal evidence pending a criminal trial or indeed the very pursuit of that trial. Decisions of that kind and the management and strategic discussion of issues of that nature are described in the central government guidance: *Complex Child Abuse Investigations: Inter-Agency Issues* which is issued under s 7 of the Local Authority Social Services Act 1970 and is binding on local authorities.

[155] I acknowledge that an individual case involving one mother and her child or children would not normally be regarded as complex but its factual content may be just as complex and allegedly systemic as any circumstance of multiple institutional abuse and its ramifications for both nuclear and extended families may be just as serious. In this case there should have been formal inter-disciplinary strategy and planning or management meetings and such meetings as there were should have been more honest in their acknowledgement and appraisal of different professional perspectives. The overviews of the case should not have been left to LS and Detective Constable LM: they should have been in the hands of more senior colleagues and a inter-disciplinary strategic system.

[156] Strategic discussions at all levels in this case could have isolated the more reliable elements of the histories that were available and would have helped to provide a more informed information base for diagnosis. They may even have been able to prevent the crisis that eventually unfolded.

[157] There are very real issues that this case has highlighted arising out of the circumstance when a local authority that has not had the strategic shared control of the investigations but is forced on costs grounds to adopt the witness statements of the many police witnesses as their primary case. The social work analysis is almost completely disempowered and the context that becomes known from the taking of evidence is lost.

[158] The police investigation was insufficiently objective to be a proper medium for this court's purposes: it reflects the adversarial nature of the criminal process not the essentially inquisitorial nature of this process. The ramifications of the problem I am identifying are significant. I do not propose to do more than identify the problem and urge inter-disciplinary discussion of it to lead to informed recommendation in due course.

...

[175] The terms 'Munchausen's Syndrome by Proxy' and 'Factitious (and Induced) Illness (by Proxy)' are child protection labels that are merely descriptions of a range of behaviours, not a paediatric, psychiatric or psychological disease that is identifiable. The terms do not relate to an organised or universally recognised body of knowledge or experience that has identified a medical disease (ie an illness or condition) and there are no internationally accepted medical criteria for the use of either label.

[176] In reality, the use of the label is intended to connote that in the individual case there are materials susceptible of analysis by paediatricians and of findings of fact by a court concerning fabrication, exaggeration, minimisation or omission in the reporting of symptoms and evidence of harm by act, omission or suggestion (induction). Where such facts exist the context and assessments can provide an insight into the degree of risk that a child may face and the court is likely to be assisted as to that aspect by psychiatric and/or psychological expert evidence.

[177] All of the above ought to be self-evident and has in any event been the established teaching of leading paediatricians, psychiatrists and psychologists for some while. That is not to minimise the nature and extent of professional debate about this issue which remains significant, nor to minimise the extreme nature of the risk that is identified in a small number of cases.

[178] In these circumstances, evidence as to the existence of MSBP or FII in any individual case is as likely to be evidence of mere propensity which would be inadmissible at the fact-finding stage (see *Re CB and JB (Care Proceedings: Guidelines)* [1998] 2 FLR 211). For my part, I would consign the label MSBP to the history books and however useful FII may apparently be to the child protection practitioner I would caution against its use other than as a factual description of a series of incidents or behaviours that should then be accurately set out (and even then only in the hands of the paediatrician or psychiatrist/psychologist). I cannot emphasise too strongly that my conclusion cannot be used as a reason to re-open the many cases where facts have been found against a carer and the label MSBP or FII has been attached to that carer's behaviour. What I seek to caution against is the use of the label as a substitute for factual analysis and risk assessment.

Other significant cases on this issue:

- *P, C and S v United Kingdom* [2002] 2 FLR 631 especially at [131]–[133]: see D2 – Removal of child (at birth) and permanent separation
- *Re B (Threshold criteria: fabricated illness)* [2002] EWHC 20 (Fam), [2004] 2 FLR 200
- *Re X* [2006] 2 FLR 701 especially at [67]–[69] and [82]

This case is also included in relation to:

H23 Assessing expert evidence: summary

Social services

I18 SOCIAL WORK PRACTICE

Re E (Care proceedings: social work practice)

[2000] 2 FLR 254 at 257

Family Division

Bracewell J

I pose the question, 'Why in this case has there been such a waste of precious and scarce resources used over the years to no avail and without recognition that there is a striking similarity in respect of the history of each child?'. There are, in my judgment, some clear answers from which lessons can and should be learnt and applied to future similar cases.

(1) Every social work file should have as the top document a running chronology of significant events which is kept up to date as events unfold. It was only when Mrs G went through the jumbled mass of documentation that the pattern of abuse was so apparent as to demand immediate although belated action. Social work personnel change over the years. Families may cross local authority boundaries, files become bulky. But if, as a matter of routine and good practice, the local authority maintain and regularly update an on-going chronology highlighting key points in the continuation records, then it will be relatively straightforward to identify serious and deep rooted problems rather than the circumstances triggering the instant referral.

(2) Lack of co-operation by parents is never a reason to close a file or remove a child from a protection register. On the contrary, it is a reason to investigate in greater depth.

(3) Referrals by professionals such as health visitors and teachers should be given great weight and investigated thoroughly. They are at the front line and are a potential source of valuable information.

(4) Line managers and those with power of decision-making should never make a judgment to take no action without having full knowledge of the file and consulting with those professionals who know the family.

(5) Children who are part of a sibling group should not be considered in isolation but should be considered in the context of family history. In cases in which previous children have been brought to the

attention of social services, the details of their cases should be considered in assessing what went wrong historically and whether appropriate change has been effected. History has a habit of repeating itself in a recognisable pattern, as in this case.

(6)   Working or attempting to work with families must be time-limited, so that an effective timetable is laid down within which changes need to be achieved. In the absence of clearly laid down objectives and achievements within an identified time-scale, cases tend to drift and children can become vulnerable and damaged without the problems being effectively addressed.

Had these matters been looked at and followed in the current case, effective intervention would, in my judgment, have occurred many years ago to protect these children from the years of dysfunctional parenting which has left them so damaged and vulnerable. I hope that the lessons to be learnt from this case will assist local authorities up and down the country in dealing with other similar cases.

This case is also included in relation to:

I19 PARENTS' REPRESENTATIVES' ATTENDANCE AT CASE CONFERENCES

R v Cornwall County Council ex p LH

[2000] 1 FLR 236 at 236, 243 and 245

Queen's Bench Division

Scott Baker J

Cornwall County Council, the respondent, does not as a matter of policy permit the attendance of a solicitor to represent a parent at a child protection conference. Nor, as a matter of policy, does it permit a parent who has attended such a conference to be provided with a copy of the minutes. The applicant seeks judicial review of decisions in respect of a child protection conference held on 22 January 1999 to consider the welfare of her children (i) not to allow the presence of her solicitor, and (ii) not to provide her with a copy of the minutes. It is said that other local authorities take a different view. The present situation has for some time been a matter of concern to solicitors practising family law in Cornwall.

...

Having considered all the documents in this case and the history of this matter it seems to me clear that the respondent has decided as a matter of policy that solicitors will not be permitted to attend case conferences on behalf of parents for any purpose other than reading out a prepared statement. Whilst I can well see the need to prevent the conference from becoming unnecessarily confrontational there are many helpful contributions a solicitor may make as is apparent from the Law Society's June 1997 memorandum.

The respondent has not, per Sedley LJ in *Rixon*,[1] articulated any good reason for departing from the guidance in *Working Together*. It is true that para 6.18 refers to legal representation as such not being appropriate. But at the same time it clearly envisages the presence of a lawyer. The difficulty into which the respondent's policy has placed it is illustrated by its position that someone who is a solicitor cannot be regarded as a friend for the purposes of accompanying a parent at a case conference. Why should a mother not be accompanied by her brother just because he happens to be a solicitor practising in family law?

---

[1] *R v London Borough of Islington ex parte Rixon* [1997] ELR 66, per Sedley J at 71A–D. See I21 – Application of LASSA 1970, s 7.

In my judgment a blanket ban on solicitors of the kind operated by the respondent is contrary to the statutory guidance and is unlawful. Other authorities operate a different policy and seem to manage it perfectly successfully. In my judgment the solution is simple. The chair of the conference has a discretion as to who should be permitted to attend the conferences and for what purpose. Such a discretion should be exercised without the present background prohibition. Indeed it seems to me that in general solicitors ought to be allowed to attend and participate unless and until it is felt they will undermine the purpose of the conference by, for example, making it unnecessarily confrontational. I should have thought any experienced chair would be well able to assess the situation. As para 6.18 points out, it is incumbent on the chair to clarify the role of (the solicitor).

Turning to the minutes, the respondent initially sought to advance an argument based on public interest immunity. However, this was, in my view, rightly abandoned ...

The respondent's attitude seems to me to presuppose that the parent or solicitor will not act responsibly with the minutes. In my view that presumption is misplaced. It can reasonably be assumed that most who are furnished with minutes will behave responsibly. Were there reasons in a particular case to suppose that minutes would be misused it would be open to the chair of the conference to withhold them for specific reasons.

...

Conclusion

Although a good deal of water has now passed under the bridge in the present case and any order of this court may be of little practical benefit to the applicant, the case raises points that are of some general concern. In these circumstances I propose to grant declarations that the respondent acted unlawfully in the present case in failing to allow the applicant's solicitors to continue to attend the case conference and failing to provide a copy of the minutes to the applicant or her solicitor. In my judgment the respondent's practice in not, as a matter of course, allowing a parent to have a solicitor at a case conference was unlawful as was its refusal as a matter of course to permit those present to have a copy of the minutes. I will of course hear any argument as to the precise form of the declarations.

This case is also included in relation to:

I21   Application of LASSA 1970, s 7

I20   CASE CONFERENCE RECORDS

Re X (Emergency protection orders)

[2006] EWHC 510 (Fam); [2006] 2 FLR 701 at 709

Family Division

McFarlane J

[29] In line with the guidance, and in accordance with fairness, good practice and, if proceedings take place, the need for the court to have an accurate record of what is said in all parts of a case conference, I consider the following to be basic requirements in this regard:

(a)   if the circumstances are sufficient to justify the exclusion of the parents from part of a case conference (such circumstances are described in the paragraphs of guidance referred to above), or the parents are otherwise absent, a full minute should nevertheless be taken of everything that is said during the conference;

(b)   if it is considered necessary to treat part of what is minuted as confidential from the parents, that part of the minutes should be disclosed for approval to the professionals who attended the conference, but that part of the draft/approved minutes should be maintained separately from the body of the minutes which are sent to the parents;

(c)   the non-confidential section of the minutes should expressly record at the appropriate stage that confidential information was disclosed or discussed;

(d)   the need for continued confidentiality with respect to confidential sections of the minutes should be kept under review by the conference chair, with confidentiality only being maintained if it continues to be necessary.

This case is also included in relation to:

D71   EPO: general considerations (2)

I21   APPLICATION OF LASSA 1970, S 7

R v Cornwall County Council ex p LH

[2000] 1 FLR 236 at 238

Queen's Bench Division

Scott Baker J

Section 7 of the Local Authorities Social Services Act 1970 provides that:

'(1)   Local authorities shall, in the exercise of their social services functions, including the exercise of any discretion conferred by any relevant enactment, act under the general guidelines of the Secretary of State.'

Section 7A makes similar provision for local authorities to exercise social services functions in accordance with directions given by the Secretary of State.

In *R v London Borough of Islington ex parte Rixon* [1997] ELR 66 Sedley J said at 71A–D:

'What is the meaning and effect of the obligation to "act under the general guidelines of the Secretary of State?" Clearly guidance is less than direction, and the word "general" emphasises the non-prescriptive nature of what is envisaged. Mr McCarthy, for the local authority, submits that such guidance is no more than one of the many factors to which the local authority is to have regard. Miss Richards submits that in order to give effect to the words "shall … act", a local authority must follow such guidance unless it has and can articulate a good reason for departing from it. In my judgment Parliament in enacting s 7(1) did not intend local authorities to whom ministerial guidance was given to be free, having considered it, to take it or leave it. Such a construction would put this kind of guidance on a par with the many forms of non-statutory guidance issued by departments of state. While guidance and direction are semantically and legally different things and while "guidance does not compel any particular decision" (*Laker Airways Ltd v Department of Trade* [1977] QB 643, at p 714 per Roskill LJ), especially when prefaced by the word "general", in my view Parliament by s 7(1) has required local authorities to follow the path charted by the Secretary of State's guidance with liberty to deviate from it where the local authority judges on admissible grounds that there is a good reason to do so, but without freedom to take a substantially different course.'

At 73 he pointed out that a failure to comply with the statutory policy guidance is unlawful and can be corrected by means of judicial review.

I adopt these observations of Sedley J, as he then was, as a correct statement of law.

This case is also included in relation to:

I19   Parents' representatives' attendance at case conferences

INDEX

References are to paragraph numbers.